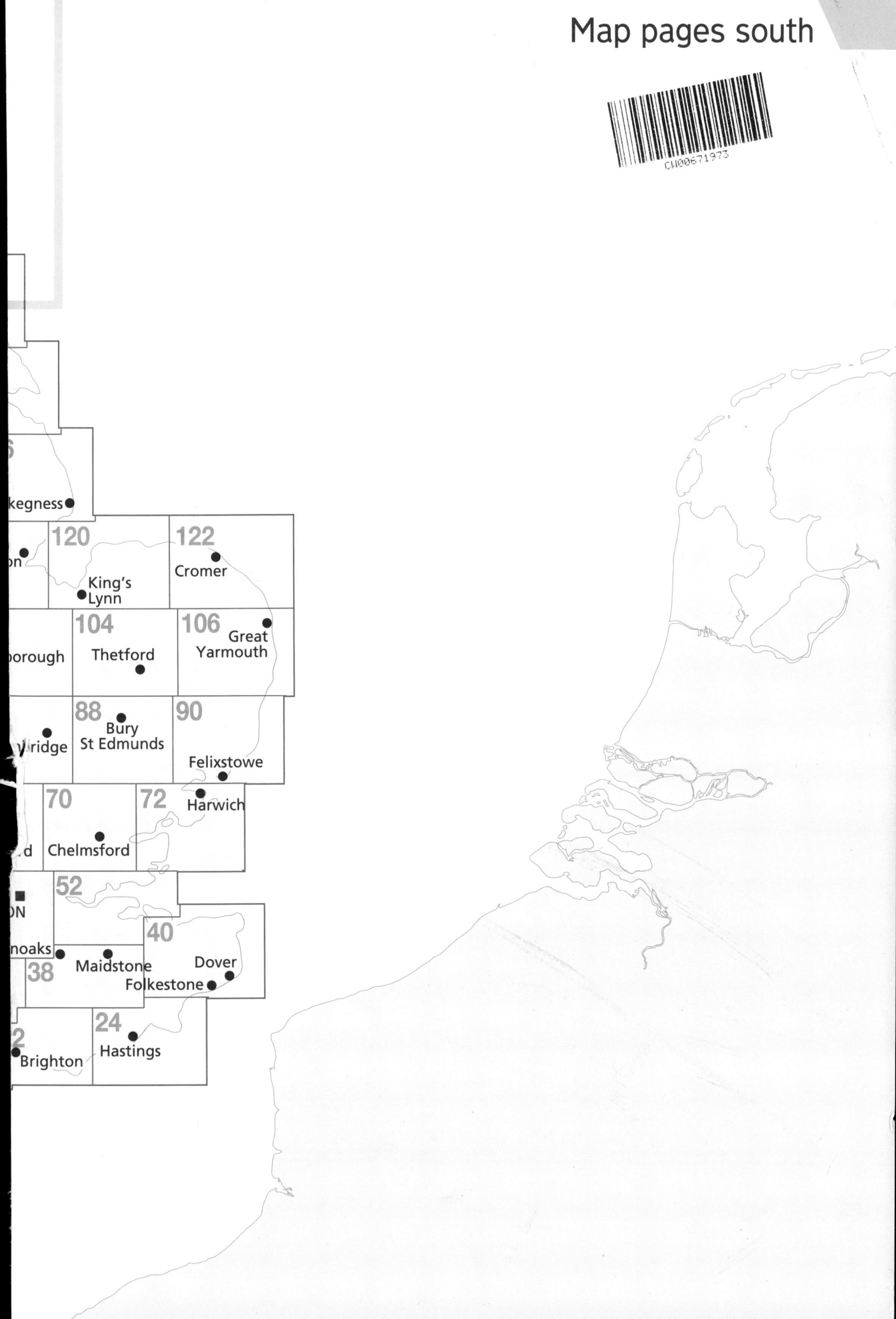

CW00671973

AA

2024
Easy Read
BRITAIN

Scale 1:148,000
or 2.34 miles to 1 inch

23rd edition July 2023 © AA Media Limited 2023
Original edition printed 2000.

All cartography in this atlas edited, designed and produced
by the Mapping Services Department of AA Media Limited
(A05842).

This atlas contains Ordnance Survey data © Crown copyright
and database right 2023. Contains public sector information
licensed under the Open Government Licence v3.0

Published by AA Media Limited, whose registered office is
Grove House, Lutyens Close, Basingstoke, Hampshire
RG24 8AG, UK. Registered number 06112600.

ISBN: 978 0 7495 8336 1

A CIP catalogue record for this book is available from
The British Library.

Disclaimer: The contents of this atlas are believed to be
correct at the time of the latest revision, it will not contain
any subsequent amended, new or temporary information
including diversions and traffic control or enforcement systems.
The publishers cannot be held responsible or liable for any
loss or damage occasioned to any person acting or refraining
from action as a result of any use or reliance on material in this
atlas, nor for any errors, omissions or changes in such material.
This does not affect your statutory rights.

The publishers would welcome information to correct
any errors or omissions and to keep this atlas up to date.
Please write to the Atlas Editor, AA Media Limited, Grove House,
Lutyens Close, Basingstoke, Hampshire RG24 8AG, UK.
E-mail: *roadatlasfeedback@aamediagroup.co.uk*

Acknowledgements: AA Media Limited would like to thank the
following for information used in the creation of this atlas:
Cadw, English Heritage, Forestry Commission, Historic Scotland,
National Trust and National Trust for Scotland, RSPB, The Wildlife
Trust, Scottish Natural Heritage, Natural England, The Countryside
Council for Wales. Award winning beaches from 'Blue Flag' and
'Keep Scotland Beautiful' (summer 2022 data):
for latest information visit *www.blueflag.org* and
www.keepscotlandbeautiful.org
Printed by Oriental Press, Dubai

* The UK's most up-to-date atlases based on a comparison of 2023
UK Road Atlases available on the market in November 2022.

Contents

Map pages south	inside front cover
Route planner	*II–VII*
Atlas symbols	*VIII–1*
Road maps 1:148,000 scale	2–283
Channel Islands 1:100,000 scale	9
Isle of Man 1:200,000 scale	154
Isles of Scilly 1:148,000 scale	10
Orkney Islands 1:450,000 scale	275
Shetland Islands 1:450,000 scale	281
Western Isles 1:480,000 scale	282–283
Restricted junctions	284–285
Index to place names	286–368
County, administrative area map	286–287
Place name index	288–368
Map pages north	inside back cover

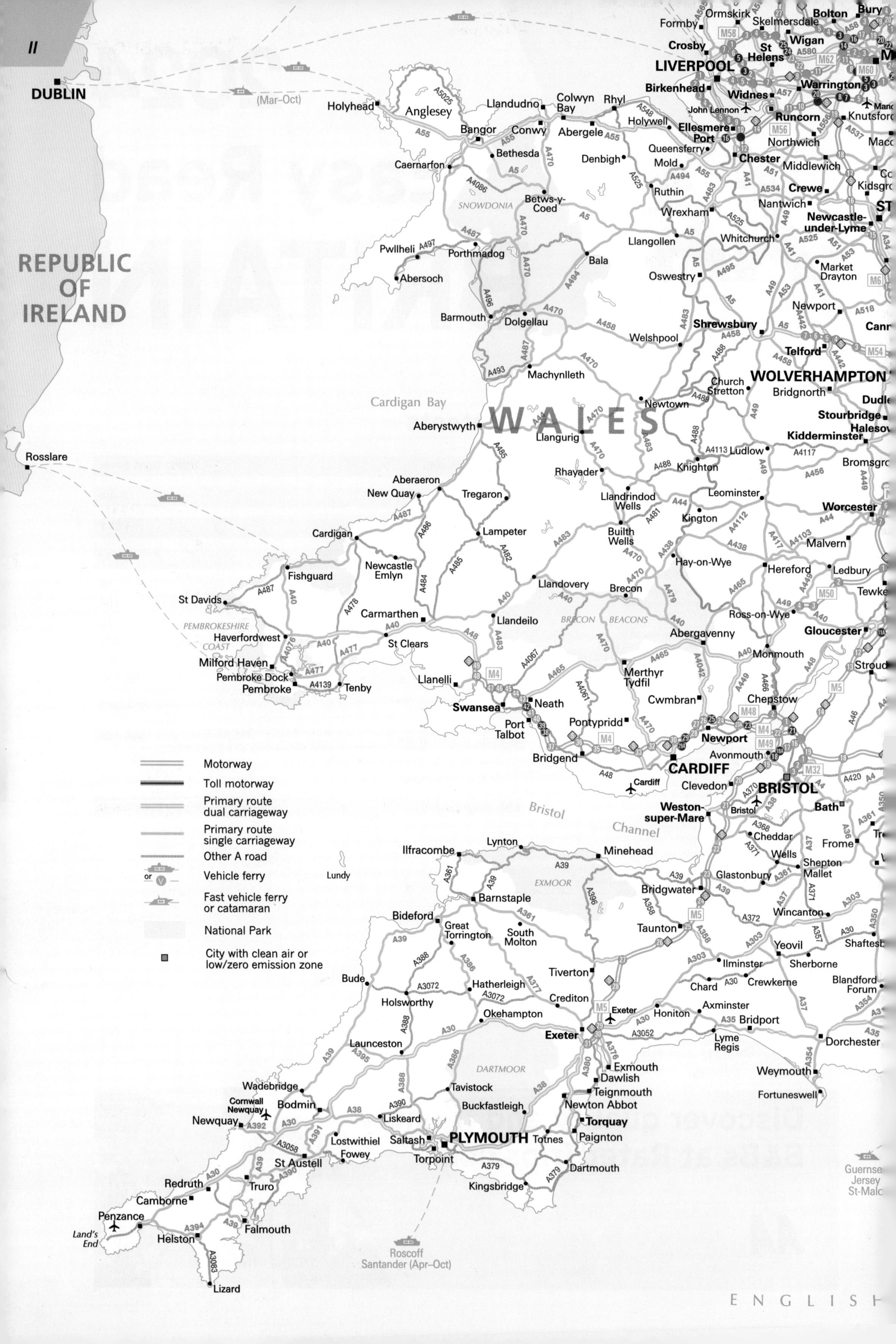

DUBLIN
(Mar–Oct)
REPUBLIC OF IRELAND
Rosslare
Holyhead
Anglesey
Llandudno
Colwyn Bay
Rhyl
Bangor
Conwy
Abergele
Bethesda
Caernarfon
SNOWDONIA
Betws-y-Coed
Denbigh
Holywell
Queensferry
Mold
Ruthin
Wrexham
Llangollen
Pwllheli
Porthmadog
Abersoch
Bala
Barmouth
Dolgellau
Machynlleth
Welshpool
Newtown
Cardigan Bay
Aberystwyth
WALES
Llangurig
Rhayader
Aberaeron
New Quay
Tregaron
Llandrindod Wells
Builth Wells
Lampeter
Cardigan
Newcastle Emlyn
Fishguard
St Davids
PEMBROKESHIRE COAST
Haverfordwest
Milford Haven
Pembroke Dock
Pembroke
Tenby
Carmarthen
St Clears
Llandeilo
Llandovery
Brecon
BRECON BEACONS
Llanelli
Swansea
Neath
Port Talbot
Bridgend
Pontypridd
Merthyr Tydfil
Cwmbran
Abergavenny
Monmouth
Chepstow
Newport
CARDIFF
Cardiff
Hay-on-Wye
Kington
Knighton
Ludlow
Leominster
Hereford
Ross-on-Wye
Ormskirk
Formby
Skelmersdale
Bolton
Bury
Wigan
Crosby
St Helens
LIVERPOOL
Birkenhead
Widnes
Warrington
John Lennon
Runcorn
Knutsford
Ellesmere Port
Northwich
Chester
Middlewich
Crewe
Nantwich
Newcastle-under-Lyme
Whitchurch
Market Drayton
Oswestry
Shrewsbury
Newport
Telford
Church Stretton
WOLVERHAMPTON
Bridgnorth
Stourbridge
Kidderminster
Bromsgrove
Worcester
Malvern
Ledbury
Gloucester
Stroud
Avonmouth
Clevedon
BRISTOL
Bristol
Bath
Weston-super-Mare
Cheddar
Wells
Frome
Shepton Mallet
Glastonbury
Bristol Channel
Lynton
Ilfracombe
Minehead
Lundy
EXMOOR
Barnstaple
Bridgwater
Bideford
Great Torrington
South Molton
Taunton
Wincanton
Yeovil
Shaftesbury
Sherborne
Ilminster
Chard
Crewkerne
Blandford Forum
Bude
Holsworthy
Hatherleigh
Tiverton
Crediton
Okehampton
Exeter
Honiton
Axminster
Bridport
Lyme Regis
Dorchester
Weymouth
Fortuneswell
Launceston
DARTMOOR
Exmouth
Dawlish
Teignmouth
Newton Abbot
Torquay
Paignton
Totnes
Dartmouth
Kingsbridge
Tavistock
Buckfastleigh
Wadebridge
Bodmin
Cornwall Newquay
Newquay
Liskeard
Lostwithiel
Fowey
Saltash
PLYMOUTH
Torpoint
St Austell
Truro
Redruth
Camborne
Penzance
Land's End
Helston
Falmouth
Lizard
Roscoff
Santander (Apr–Oct)
Guernsey
Jersey
St-Malo
ENGLISH
Motorway
Toll motorway
Primary route dual carriageway
Primary route single carriageway
Other A road
Vehicle ferry
Fast vehicle ferry or catamaran
National Park
City with clean air or low/zero emission zone

ENGLAND
Barnsley
Doncaster
Doncaster Sheffield
Rotherham
SHEFFIELD
Bawtry
Thorne
Scunthorpe
Humberside
Grimsby
Cleethorpes
Brigg
Rotterdam (Europoort)
Market Rasen
Gainsborough
Louth
Mablethorpe
Retford
Worksop
Chesterfield
Lincoln
Horncastle
Skegness
Buxton
Bakewell
Mansfield
Matlock
Alfreton
Newark-on-Trent
Sleaford
Ashbourne
Ilkeston
Boston
The Wash
Sheringham
Cromer
Hunstanton
DERBY
NOTTINGHAM
Grantham
Long Eaton
East Midlands
North Walsham
Aylsham
Fakenham
Burton upon Trent
Loughborough
Melton Mowbray
Spalding
King's Lynn
Bourne
Dereham
Norwich
Caister-on-Sea
THE BROADS
Great Yarmouth
Lichfield
Tamworth
Oakham
Stamford
LEICESTER
Wisbech
Swaffham
Wigston
Peterborough
Downham Market
March
Nuneaton
Hinckley
Market Harborough
Attleborough
Bungay
Beccles
Lowestoft
Corby
Chatteris
COVENTRY
Rugby
Kettering
Ely
Thetford
Diss
Southwold
Huntingdon
Royal Leamington Spa
Warwick
Daventry
Northampton
St Neots
Bury St Edmunds
Newmarket
Cambridge
Stowmarket
Aldeburgh
Stratford-upon-Avon
Towcester
Bedford
Woodbridge
Ipswich
Banbury
Brackley
Milton Keynes
Haverhill
Sudbury
Royston
Felixstowe
Hook of Holland
Chipping Norton
Leighton Buzzard
Baldock
Halstead
Harwich
Stevenage
Stansted
Braintree
Luton
Bicester
Dunstable
Bishop's Stortford
Colchester
Witney
Aylesbury
Hertford
Clacton-on-Sea
Burford
Oxford
Thame
St Albans
Hatfield
Harlow
Chelmsford
Witham
Maldon
Faringdon
Abingdon-on-Thames
High Wycombe
Watford
Burnham-on-Crouch
Wantage
Beaconsfield
Brentwood
Southend
Southend-on-Sea
Maidenhead
Slough
LONDON
City
Basildon
Canvey Island
Tilbury
Sheerness
Reading
Windsor
Bracknell
Heathrow
Richmond
Dartford
Gravesend
Rochester
Chatham
Margate
Marlborough
Newbury
Staines-upon-Thames
Croydon
Swanley
Ramsgate
Sandwich
Woking
Sevenoaks
Canterbury
Deal
Basingstoke
Leatherhead
Redhill
Maidstone
Farnham
Guildford
Dorking
Reigate
Tonbridge
Andover
East Grinstead
Royal Tunbridge Wells
Ashford
Channel Tunnel Terminal
Dover
Alton
Gatwick
Crawley
Folkestone
Hythe
Dunkirk
Calais
Winchester
Horsham
Tenterden
Crowborough
Billingshurst
Petersfield
Romsey
Eastleigh
Southampton
Midhurst
SOUTH DOWNS
Uckfield
Heathfield
Rye
New Romney
Strait of Dover
Channel Tunnel
Calais / Coquelles Terminal
SOUTHAMPTON
Arundel
Shoreham-by-Sea
Lewes
Hastings
Bexhill-on-Sea
NEW FOREST
Ringwood
Chichester
Worthing
Brighton
Lymington
Gosport
Portsmouth
Bognor Regis
Newhaven
Eastbourne
Christchurch
Cowes
Ryde
Newport
Sandown
Freshwater
Shanklin
Isle of Wight
Guernsey
Jersey
St-Malo
Caen (Ouistreham)
Cherbourg
Bilbao (Apr–Oct)
Santander
0 10 20 30 miles
0 10 20 30 40 kilometres
CHANNEL
FRANCE
Dieppe

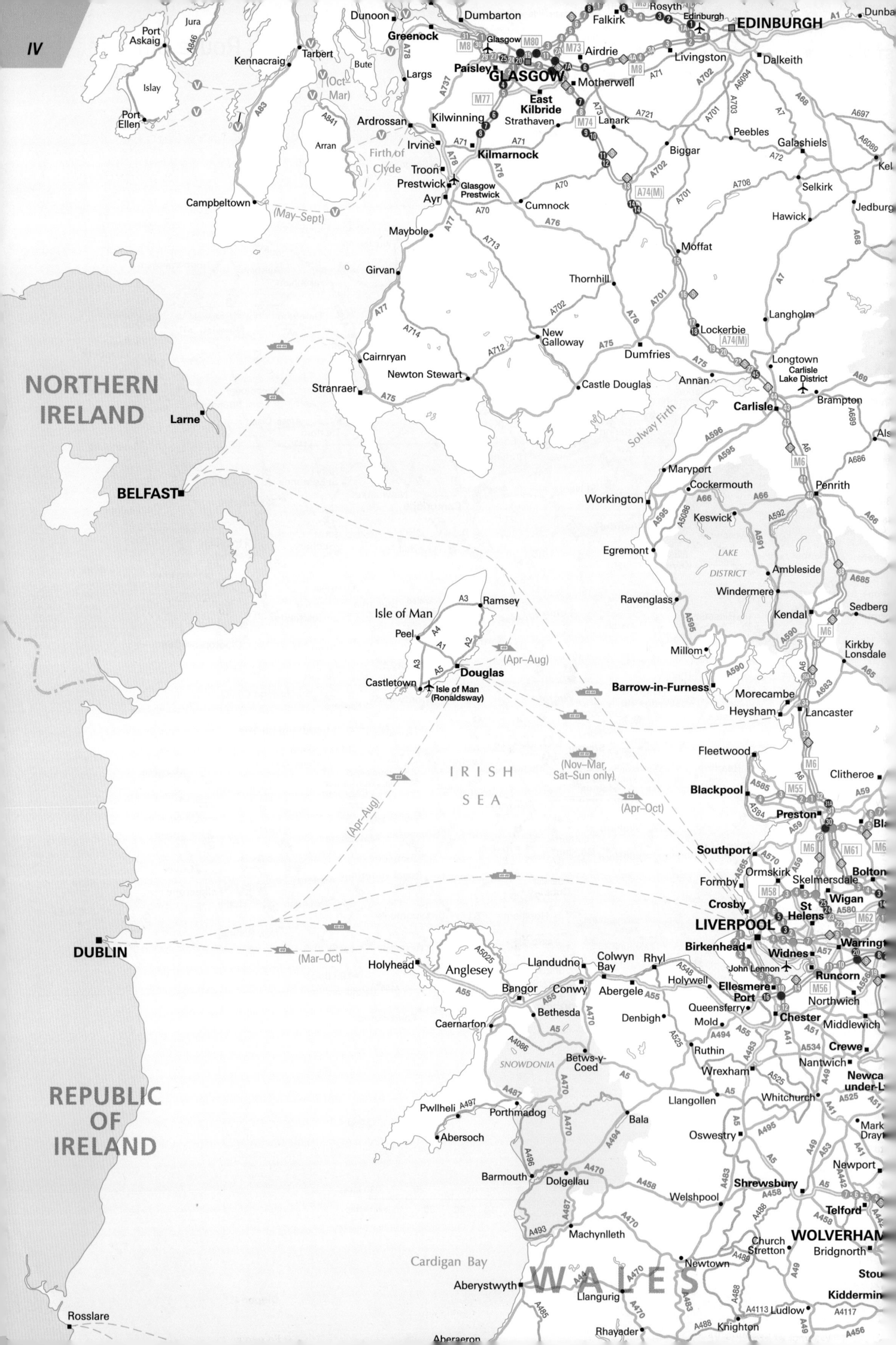

EMERGENCY DIVERSION ROUTES

In an emergency it may be necessary to close a section of motorway or other main road to traffic, so a temporary sign may advise drivers to follow a diversion route. To help drivers navigate the route, black symbols on yellow patches may be permanently displayed on existing direction signs, including motorway signs. Symbols may also be used on separate signs with yellow backgrounds.

Motorway
Toll motorway
Primary route dual carriageway
Primary route single carriageway
Other A road
or ∇ Vehicle ferry
Fast vehicle ferry or catamaran
National Park
City with clean air or low/zero emission zone

0   10   20   30 miles
0 10 20 30 40 kilometres

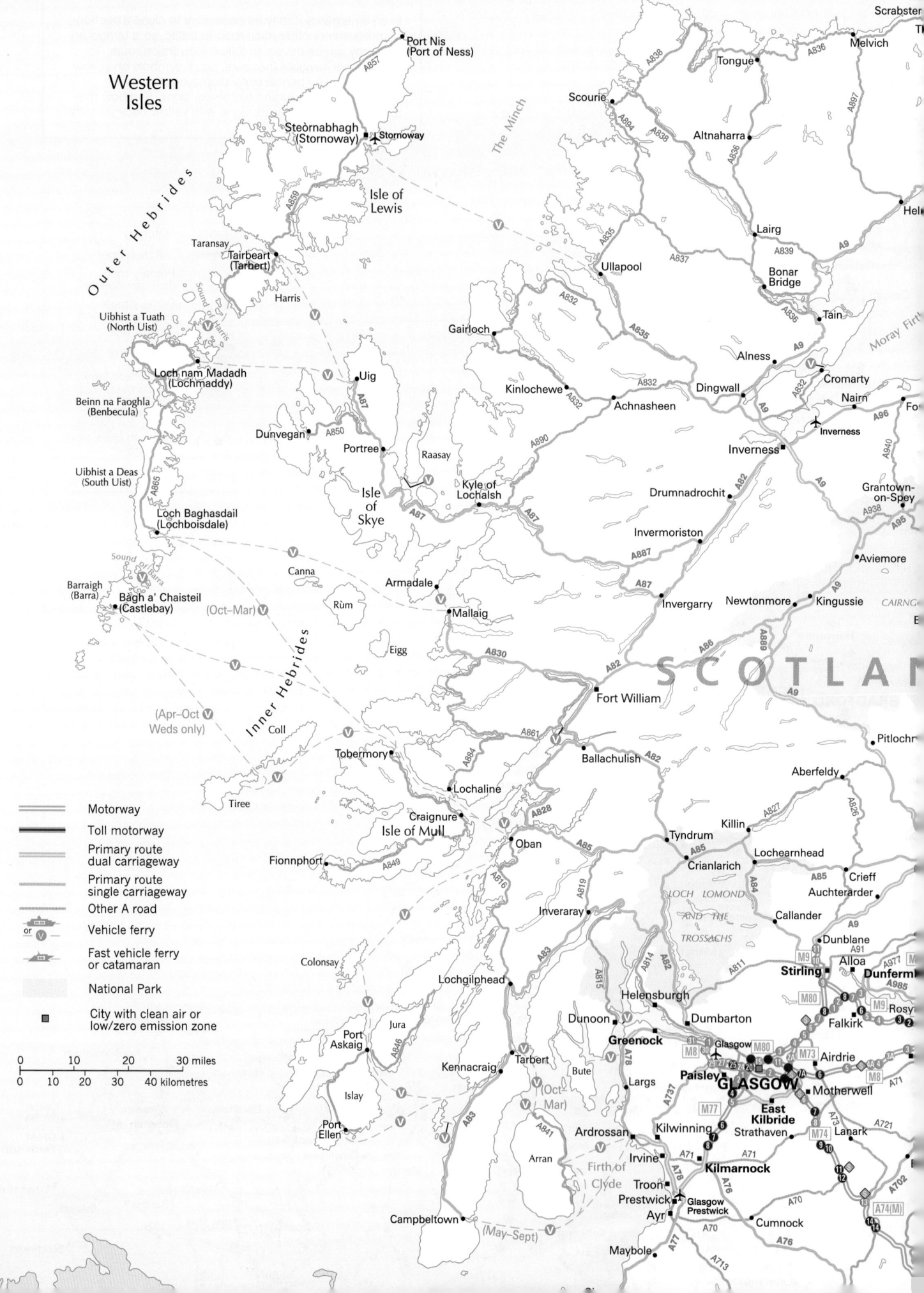

Western
Isles

Port Nis
(Port of Ness)

Steòrnabhagh
(Stornoway)
Stornoway

Isle of
Lewis

Taransay
Tairbeart
(Tarbert)

Harris

Uibhist a Tuath
(North Uist)

Loch nam Madadh
(Lochmaddy)

Beinn na Faoghla
(Benbecula)

Uig

Dunvegan

Portree

Raasay

Uibhist a Deas
(South Uist)

Loch Baghasdail
(Lochboisdale)

Isle
of
Skye

Kyle of
Lochalsh

Barraigh
(Barra)

Bàgh a' Chaisteil
(Castlebay)

(Oct–Mar)

Canna

Rùm

Armadale

Mallaig

Eigg

Scrabster

Melvich

Tongue

Scourie

Altnaharra

A836

A838

A838

A894

A897

The Minch

Lairg

Bonar
Bridge

A836

A835

A839

A9

Hel

Ullapool

A837

Gairloch

Kinlochewe

Achnasheen

A832

A832

A890

Tain

Moray Firth

Alness

Dingwall

Cromarty

Nairn

A96

Fo

Inverness

Inverness

Drumnadrochit

Invermoriston

A82

A9

A940

Grantown-
on-Spey

A938

A95

Aviemore

Invergarry

A887

A87

A86

Newtonmore

Kingussie

A9

CAIRNG

SCOTLAN

Fort William

A830

A82

A861

A9

Pitlochr

Inner Hebrides

Coll

Tobermory

Lochaline

Ballachulish

A82

Aberfeldy

A826

Tiree

Craignure

Isle of Mull

Oban

A828

A849

A816

A85

A85

Killin

Tyndrum

A85

Crianlarich

Lochearnhead

A84

Crieff

Auchterarder

Fionnphort

LOCH LOMOND

AND THE

TROSSACHS

Callander

A9

Dunblane

A91

Inveraray

A819

A83

A811

M9

Stirling

Alloa

Dunferml

A985

Colonsay

Jura

Port
Askaig

Lochgilphead

Helensburgh

A814

A82

A815

Dunoon

Dumbarton

Rosy

Falkirk

M80

M9

8

A971

Greenock

Glasgow

M80

Airdrie

M73

M8

Paisley

GLASGOW

Motherwell

A73

Tarbert

Bute

Largs

A737

A78

Kennacraig

(Oct–
Mar)

East
Kilbride

Kilwinning

M77

M74

Lanark

Strathaven

A721

Islay

Ardrossan

Irvine

A78

A71

Kilmarnock

A76

Port
Ellen

A83

Arran

Troon
Prestwick

A77

A713

Campbeltown

(May–Sept)

Firth of
Clyde

Glasgow
Prestwick

Ayr

Cumnock

A70

A76

Maybole

A841

A77

A70

A702

A74(M)

Motorway

Toll motorway

Primary route
dual carriageway

Primary route
single carriageway

Other A road

or   V   Vehicle ferry

Fast vehicle ferry
or catamaran

National Park

City with clean air or
low/zero emission zone

0   10   20   30 miles
0 10 20 30 40 kilometres

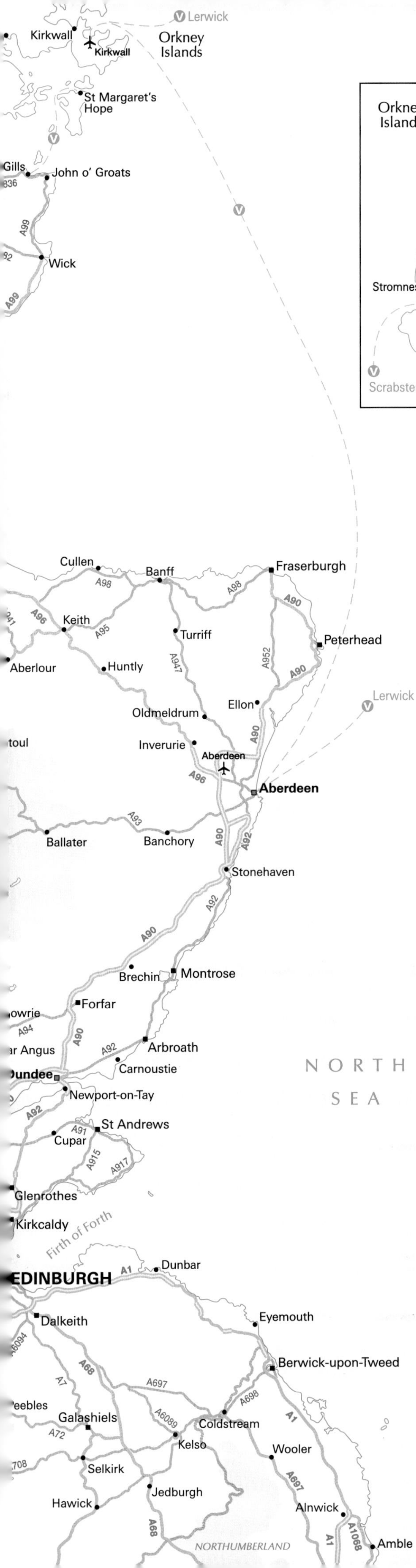

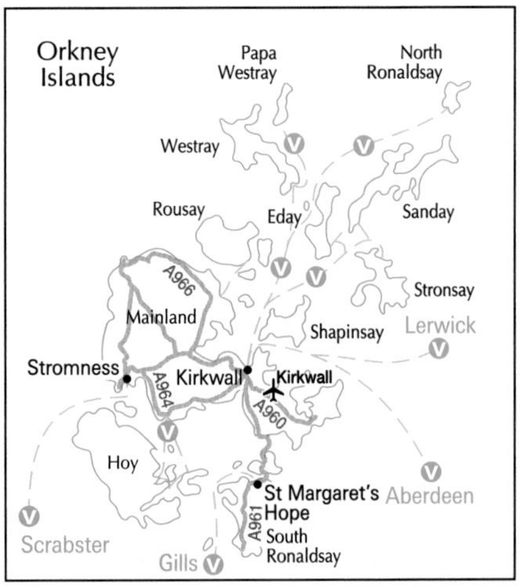

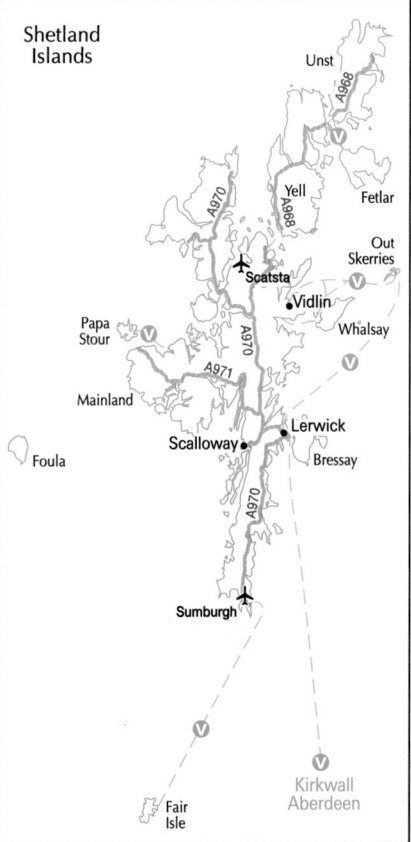

Kirkwall
Orkney Islands
Kirkwall
Lerwick
St Margaret's Hope
Gills
John o' Groats
Wick

Orkney Islands
Papa Westray
North Ronaldsay
Westray
Rousay
Eday
Sanday
Mainland
Stronsay
Shapinsay
Lerwick
Stromness
Kirkwall
Kirkwall
Hoy
St Margaret's Hope
Aberdeen
Scrabster
South Ronaldsay
Gills

Shetland Islands
Unst
Yell
Fetlar
Scatsta
Out Skerries
Vidlin
Whalsay
Papa Stour
Mainland
Foula
Scalloway
Lerwick
Bressay
Sumburgh
Fair Isle
Kirkwall
Aberdeen

Cullen
Banff
Fraserburgh
Keith
Turriff
Peterhead
Aberlour
Huntly
Ellon
Oldmeldrum
Lerwick
Inverurie
Aberdeen
Aberdeen
Ballater
Banchory
Stonehaven

NORTH SEA

Brechin
Montrose
Forfar
Arbroath
Carnoustie
Dundee
Newport-on-Tay
St Andrews
Cupar
Glenrothes
Kirkcaldy

Firth of Forth

EDINBURGH
Dunbar
Dalkeith
Eyemouth
Berwick-upon-Tweed
Peebles
Galashiels
Coldstream
Kelso
Wooler
Selkirk
Jedburgh
Hawick
Alnwick
Amble
NORTHUMBERLAND

FERRY OPERATORS

Hebrides and west coast Scotland
calmac.co.uk
skyeferry.co.uk
western-ferries.co.uk

Orkney and Shetland
northlinkferries.co.uk
pentlandferries.co.uk
orkneyferries.co.uk
shetland.gov.uk/ferries

Isle of Man
steam-packet.com

Ireland
irishferries.com
poferries.com
stenaline.co.uk

North Sea (Scandinavia and Benelux)
dfdsseaways.co.uk
poferries.com

Isle of Wight
wightlink.co.uk
redfunnel.co.uk

Channel Islands
condorferries.co.uk

France and Belgium
brittany-ferries.co.uk
condorferries.co.uk
eurotunnel.com
dfdsseaways.co.uk
poferries.com

Northern Spain
brittany-ferries.co.uk

Atlas symbols

Motoring information

M4	Motorway with number
Toll / T4	Toll motorway with toll station
6	Motorway junction with and without number
5	Restricted motorway junctions
Fleet / S R / Todhills	Motorway service area, rest area
	Motorway and junction under construction
A3	Primary route single/dual carriageway
11	Primary route junction with and without number
3	Restricted primary route junctions
S	Primary route service area
BATH	Primary route destination
A1123	Other A road single/dual carriageway
B2070	B road single/dual carriageway
	Minor road more than 4 metres wide, less than 4 metres wide
	Roundabout
	Interchange/junction
	Narrow primary/other A/B road with passing places (Scotland)
	Road under construction
	Road tunnel
	City with clean air zone, low/zero emission zone

Toll	Road toll
	Steep gradient (arrows point downhill)
5	Distance in miles between symbols
or V–V	Vehicle ferry (all year, seasonal)
	Fast vehicle ferry or catamaran
or P–P	Passenger ferry (all year, seasonal)
	Railway line, in tunnel
	Railway station, tram stop, level crossing
	Preserved or tourist railway
✈ H	Airport (major/minor), heliport
F	International freight terminal
H	24-hour Accident & Emergency hospital
C	Crematorium
P+R	Park and Ride (at least 6 days per week)
	City, town, village or other built-up area
628 ▲	Height in metres
637 / Lecht Summit	Mountain pass
	Snow gates (on main routes)
	National boundary
	County or administrative boundary

Touring information

To avoid disappointment, check opening times before visiting

Scenic route		Zoological or wildlife collection		County cricket ground	
Tourist Information Centre		Bird collection, aquarium		Rugby Union national stadium	
Tourist Information Centre (seasonal)		RSPB site		International athletics stadium	
Visitor or heritage centre		National Nature Reserve (England, Scotland, Wales)		Horse racing	
Picnic site		Local nature reserve		Show jumping/equestrian circuit	
Caravan site (AA inspected)		Wildlife Trust reserve		Motor-racing circuit	
Camping site (AA inspected)		Forest drive		Air show venue	
Caravan & camping site (AA inspected)		National trail		Ski slope (natural)	
Abbey, cathedral or priory		Viewpoint		Ski slope (artificial)	
Ruined abbey, cathedral or priory		Waterfall		National Trust site	
Castle		Hill-fort		National Trust for Scotland site	
Historic house or building		Roman antiquity		English Heritage site	
Museum or art gallery		Prehistoric monument		Historic Scotland site	
Industrial interest		Battle site with year		Cadw (Welsh heritage) site	
Aqueduct or viaduct		Preserved or tourist railway		Other place of interest	
Garden, Arboretum		Cave or cavern		Boxed symbols indicate attractions within urban area	
Vineyard		Windmill		World Heritage Site (UNESCO)	
Brewery or distillery		Monument or memorial		National Park and National Scenic Area (Scotland)	
Country park		Beach (award winning)		Forest Park	
Showground		Lighthouse		Sandy beach	
Theme park		Golf course		Heritage coast	
Farm or animal centre		Football stadium		Major shopping centre	

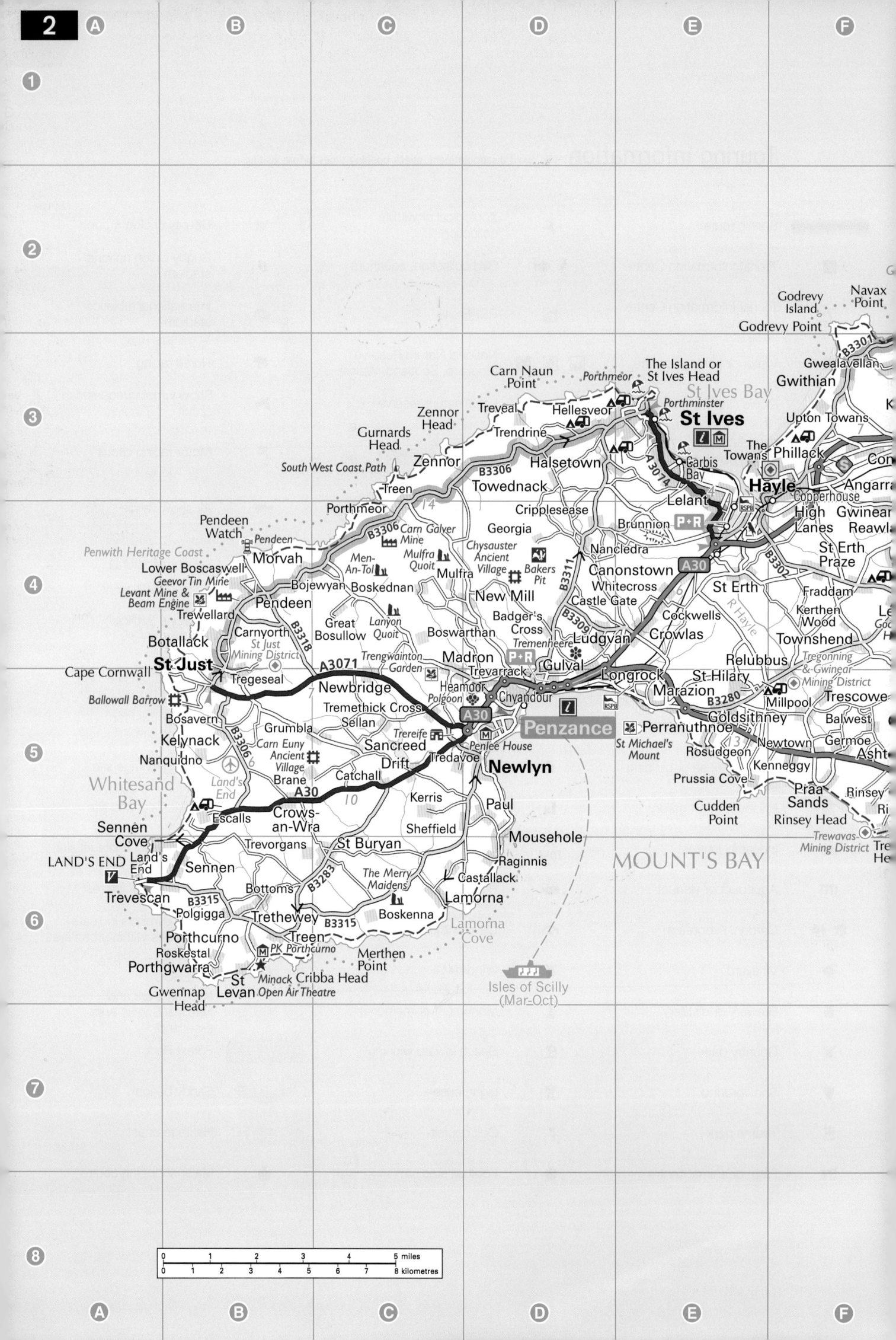

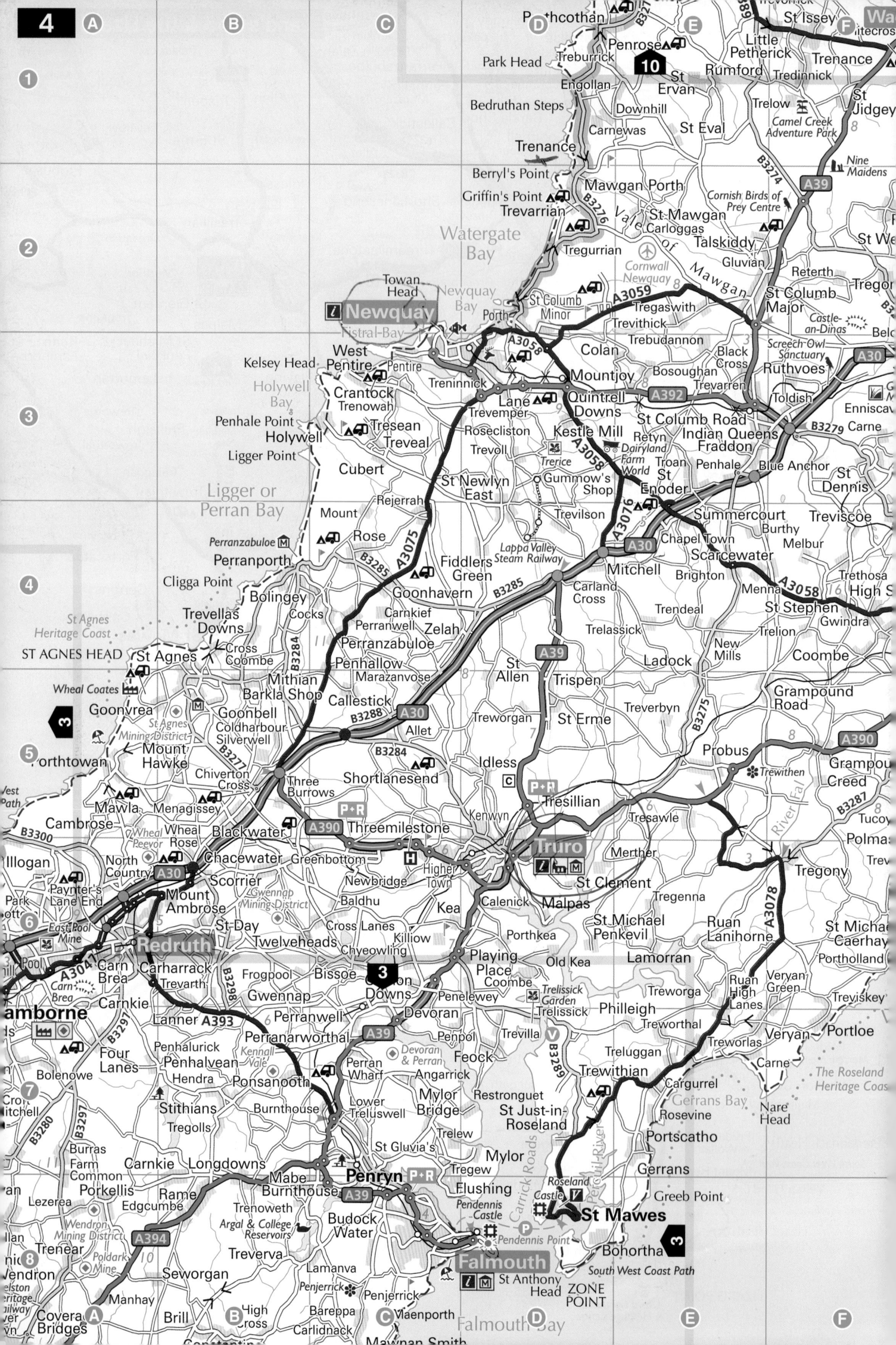

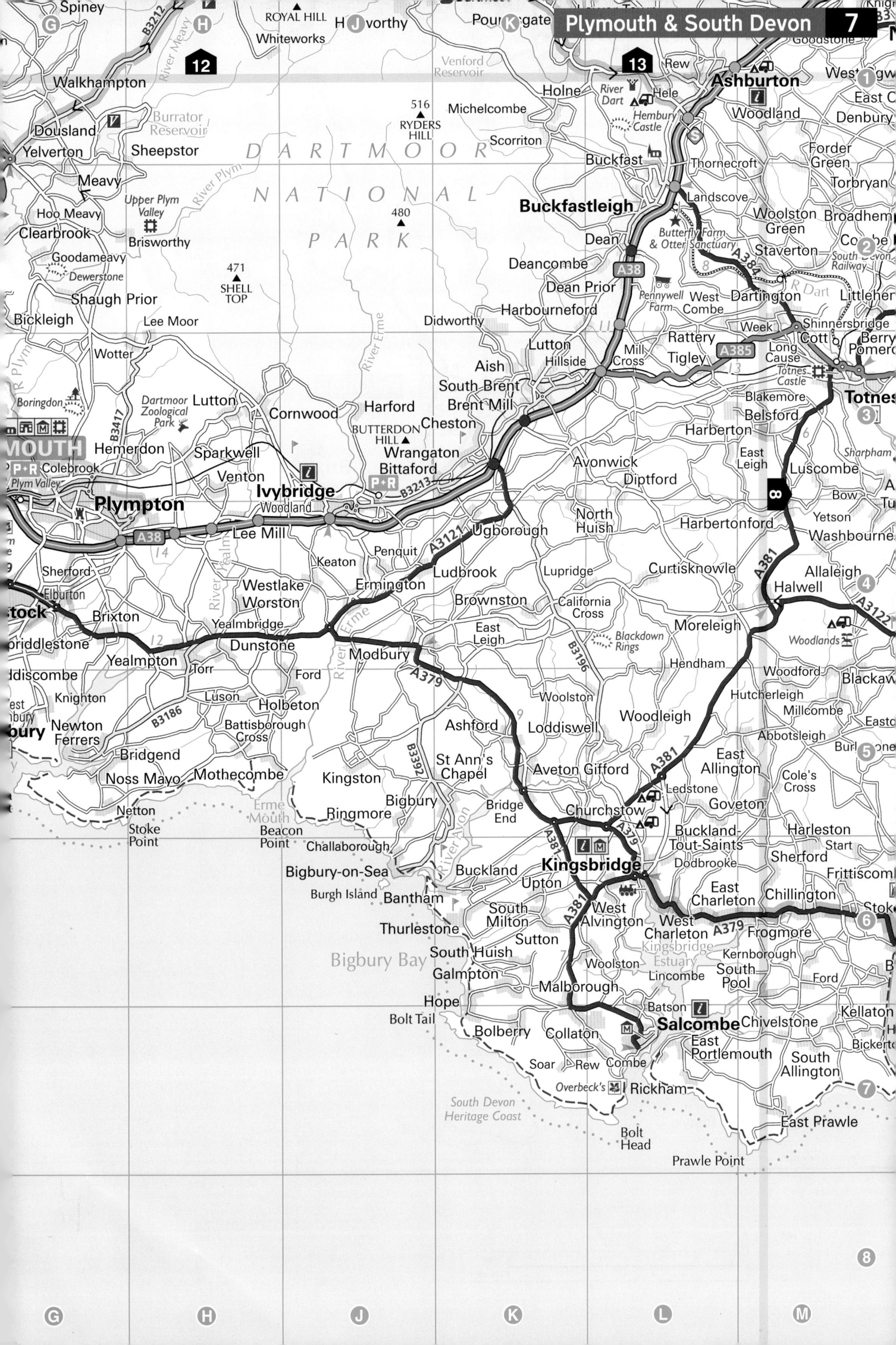

Spiney

ROYAL HILL

H J vorthy

Whiteworks

Pour gate K

Goodstone

West gw 1

B3212

H

12

Venford Reservoir

Holne

River Dart

Rew

13

East C

Ashburton

Walkhampton

S

Woodland

Denbury

Dousland

Burrator Reservoir

V

Sheepstor

Michelcombe

516 RYDERS HILL

Scorriton

Hembury Castle

Hele

Thornecroft

Forder Green

Torbryan

Yelverton

Meavy

River Plym

Buckfast

Buckfastleigh

Landscove

Woolston Green

Broadhem

DARTMOOR

Butterfly Farm & Otter Sanctuary

Combe 2

Hoo Meavy

Clearbrook

Upper Plym Valley

480

Dean

A38

West Combe

Pennywell Farm

A384

Staverton

South Devon Railway

Goodameavy

Brisworthy

NATIONAL

Deancombe

Dartington

R Dart

Littleher

Dewerstone

471 SHELL TOP

Dean Prior

Week

Long Cause

Cott

Berry Pomero

Bickleigh

Shaugh Prior

PARK

River Erme

Harbourneford

Didworthy

Lutton

Mill Cross

Rattery

Tigley

A385

Totnes Castle

Shinnersbridge

Lee Moor

Wotter

Aish

Hillside

13

Totnes

MOUTH

Boringdon

Dartmoor Zoological Park

Lutton

Cornwood

Harford

South Brent

Brent Mill

Avonwick

Blakemore

Belsford

3

P+R

Colebrook

Hemerdon

Sparkwell

BUTTERDON HILL

Cheston

Diptford

Harberton

East Leigh

Luscombe

Sharpham

Plym Valley

Venton

i

Wrangaton Bittaford

P+R

B3213

Ugborough

North Huish

Harbertonford

Bow

8

Yetson

Plympton

A38

Woodland

Lee Mill

Penquit

A3121

Ludbrook

Lupridge

Curtisknowle

Moreleigh

A381

Washbourne

Allaleigh

Halwell

4

A3122

14

Keaton

Ermington

Brownston

California Cross

Blackdown Rings

Woodlands

Sherford

Westlake

Worston

East Leigh

Hendham

Woodford

Blackaw

Brixton

Yealmbridge

B3196

Hutcherleigh

Millcombe

Abbotsleigh

5

tock

riddlestone

12

Dunstone

River Erme

Modbury

A379

Woolston

Woodleigh

Easto one

bury

Yealmpton

Torr

Ford

Ashford

Loddiswell

East Allington

Cole's Cross

Burl

Newton Ferrers

Luson

Holbeton

B3186

Knighton

Battisborough Cross

B3392

St Ann's Chapel

Aveton Gifford

A381

Ledstone

Goveton

Harleston

Bridgend

Mothecombe

Kingston

Bigbury

Bridge End

Churchstow

A379

Buckland-Tout-Saints

Dodbrooke

Start

Sherford

Noss Mayo

Netton

Erme Mouth

Ringmore

Beacon Point

River Avon

Buckland

Kingsbridge

i M

East Charleton

Chillington

Frittiscom

Stoke Point

Challaborough

i M

Upton

West Alvington

West Charleton

A379

Frogmore

6

Stok

Bigbury-on-Sea

Burgh Island

Bantham

South Milton

Sutton

A381

Kingsbridge Estuary

Kernborough

Ford

Thurlestone

South Huish

Woolston

Lincombe

South Pool

B

Bigbury Bay

Galmpton

Malborough

Hope

Batson

i

East Portlemouth

Kellaton

Bolt Tail

Bolberry

Collaton

M

Salcombe

Chivelstone

Bickert

South Allington

Soar

Rew

Combe

7

Overbeck's

Rickham

East Prawle

South Devon Heritage Coast

Bolt Head

Prawle Point

8

G   H   J   K   L   M

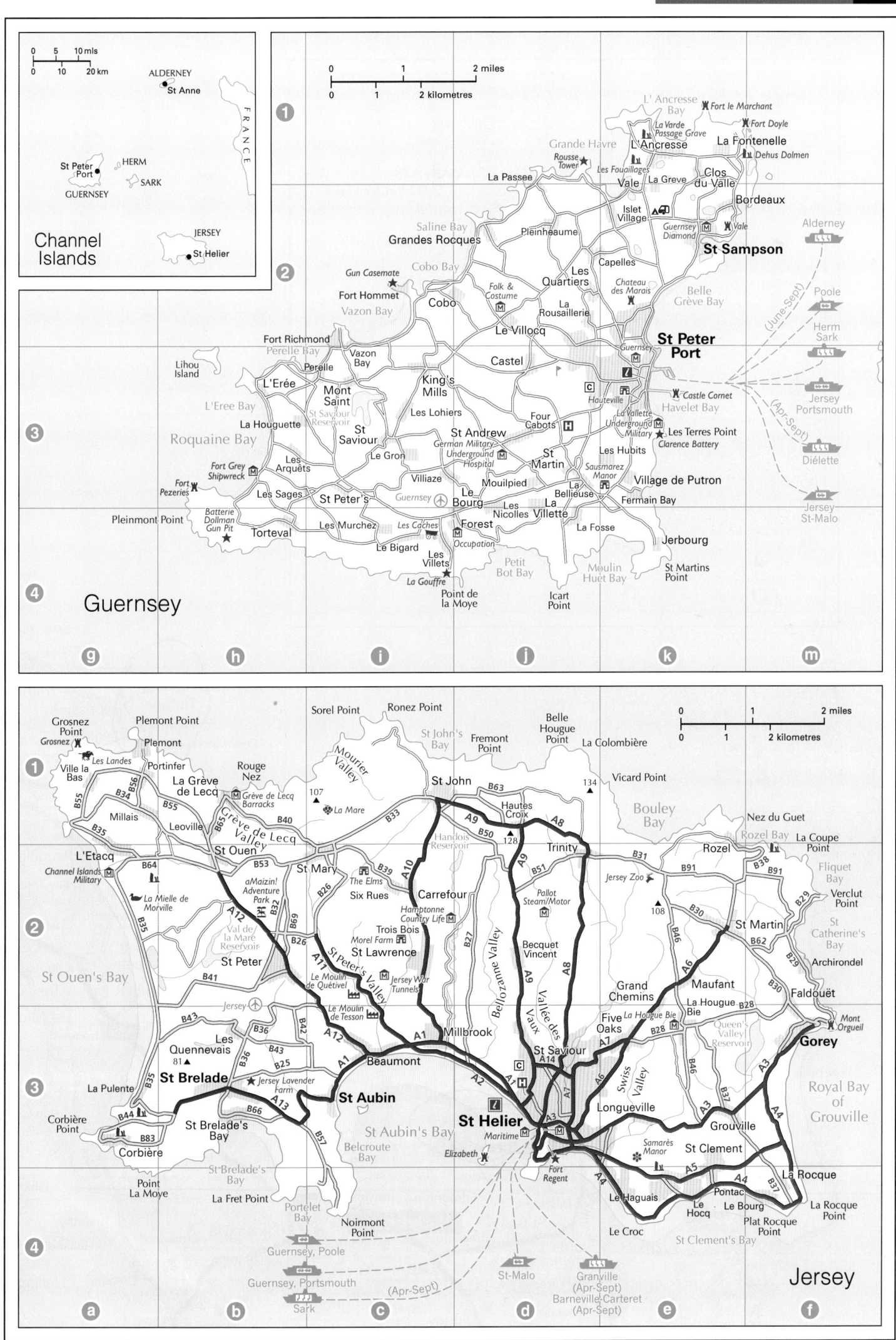

Channel Islands

0 5 10 mls
0 10 20 km

ALDERNEY
• St Anne

FRANCE

St Peter Port • HERM
GUERNSEY   SARK

JERSEY
• St Helier

Guernsey

0   1   2 miles
0 1 2 kilometres

L' Ancresse Bay
• Fort le Marchant
Fort Doyle
La Varde Passage Grave
Dehus Dolmen
Grande Havre
Rousse Tower
Les Fouaillages
L'Ancresse
La Fontenelle
La Greve
Clos du Valle
Bordeaux
Vale
Guernsey Diamond
Islet Village
St Sampson
Belle Grève Bay
La Passee
Saline Bay
Grandes Rocques
Pleinheaume
Les Quartiers
Capelles
Chateau des Marais
La Rousaillerie
Gun Casemate
Fort Hommet
Cobo Bay
Vazon Bay
Cobo
Folk & Costume
Le Villocq
St Peter Port
Guernsey
Castle Cornet
Havelet Bay
Fort Richmond
Perelle Bay
Vazon Bay
Perelle
Castel
Hauteville
La Vallette Underground Military
Les Terres Point
Clarence Battery
Lihou Island
L'Erée
Mont Saint
King's Mills
Four Cabots
Les Hubits
L'Eree Bay
La Houguette
St Saviour Reservoir
St Saviour
Les Lohiers
St Andrew
German Military Underground Hospital
St Martin
Sausmarez Manor
La Bellieuse
Village de Putron
Roquaine Bay
Les Arquêts
Le Gron
Villiaze
Mouilpied
Le Bourg
Les Nicolles
La Villette
Fermain Bay
Fort Grey Shipwreck
Les Sages
St Peter's
Les Murchez
Les Caches
Forest
La Fosse
Fort Pezeries
Batterie Dollman Gun Pit
Torteval
Le Bigard
Occupation
Petit Bot Bay
St Martins Point
Jerbourg
Pleinmont Point
Les Villets
La Gouffre
Point de la Moye
Moulin Huet Bay
Icart Point

Alderney
Poole (June-Sept)
Herm Sark
Jersey Portsmouth (Apr-Sept)
Diélette
Jersey St-Malo

g h i j k m
1 2 3 4

Jersey

0   1   2 miles
0 1 2 kilometres

Grosnez Point
Grosnez
Sorel Point
Ronez Point
St John's Bay
Fremont Point
Belle Hougue Point
La Colombière
Bouley Bay
Nez du Guet
Plemont Point
Plemont
Mourier Valley
Vicard Point
Ville la Bas
Les Landes
Portinfer
Rouge Nez
St John
Hautes Croix
Rozel Bay
La Coupe Point
La Grève de Lecq
La Mare
Trinity
Rozel
Fliquet Bay
Millais
Leoville
Grève de Lecq Barracks
Grève de Lecq Valley
St Ouen
Handois Reservoir
Jersey Zoo
St Martin
Verclut Point
L'Etacq
Channel Islands Military
St Mary
aMaizin! Adventure Park
The Elms
Carrefour
Pallot Steam/Motor
St Catherine's Bay
La Mielle de Morville
Val de la Mare Reservoir
Six Rues
Hamptonne Country Life
Morel Farm
Trois Bois
St Lawrence
Becquet Vincent
Grand Chemins
Maufant
Archirondel
Faldouët
St Peter
St Peter's Valley
Le Moulin de Quétivel
Jersey War Tunnels
Bellozanne Valley
Vallée des Vaux
La Hougue Bie
Queen's Valley Reservoir
Mont Orgueil
St Ouen's Bay
Le Moulin de Tesson
Millbrook
Five Oaks
Gorey
Les Quennevais
Beaumont
St Saviour
Swiss Valley
Longueville
Royal Bay of Grouville
St Brelade
Jersey Lavender Farm
St Aubin
St Helier
Grouville
La Pulente
St Aubin's Bay
Maritime
St Clement
La Rocque
Corbière Point
St Brelade's Bay
Belcroute Bay
Elizabeth
Samarès Manor
Pontac
La Rocque Point
Corbière
St-Brelade's Bay
Fort Regent
Le Haguais
Le Bourg
Plat Rocque Point
Point La Moye
La Fret Point
Portelet Bay
Noirmont Point
Le Croc
Le Hocq
St Clement's Bay

Guernsey, Poole
Guernsey, Portsmouth
Sark (Apr-Sept)
St-Malo
Granville (Apr-Sept)
Barneville-Carteret (Apr-Sept)

a b c d e f
1 2 3 4

Isles of Scilly

White Island

St Helen's

King Charles's Castle

Lower Town

ST MARTIN'S

38 49 St Martin's Head

Old Grimsby

Cromwell's Castle

BRYHER 42

Old Blockhouse

Higher Town

The Town

New Grimsby

Isles of Scilly Heritage Coast

Great Ganilly

Tresco Abbey

TRESCO

Eastern Isles

Crow Bar *Crow Sound*

Samson

Innisidgen Tombs

Bant's Carn Burial

A3110

ST MARY'S

North West Passage

Harry's Walls

Higher & Lower Moors

Hugh Town

Deep Point

Garrison Walls

Porth Hellick Down Tomb

Isles of Scilly (St Mary's)

Old Town

Peninnis Head

Penzance (Mar-Oct)

Broad Sound

St Mary's Sound

Middle Town

Annet

Gugh

St Agnes

ST AGNES

Smith Sound

Horse Point

Western Rocks

0		1		2 miles
0	1		2 kilometres	

a b c d

Witchcraft & Magic

Pentire Point - Widemouth Heritage Coast

Boscastle

Trevalga

Castle

Trethevey

TINTAGEL HEAD

Tintagel **Bossiney**

Old Post Office Tregatta

Penhallic Point

Trewarmett

Treknow

Trebarwith

Penpethy

Treligga

Rockhead

Delabole

Pengelly

South West Coast Path

Trevi

Valley Truckle

Port Isaac Bay

Westdowns

Lanteglos

Rumps Point

Kellan Head

Varley Head

Trewetha

St Teath

Helstone

Port Quin Bay

Trewalder

Treveigha

Pentire Point

Port Quin

Port Isaac

Knightsmill

Treburgett

Michae

New Polzeath

Bee Centre

Plain Street

Trelights

Pendoggett

A39

Hayle Bay

Treharrock

Trenewth

Stepper Point

Polzeath

St Endellion

Trelill

Trequite

Trevose Head Heritage Coast

Gunver Head

Hawker's Cove

Trebetherick

Tregellist

St Tudy

TREVOSE HEAD

Mother Ivey's Bay

Crugmeer

Trevanger Pityme

St Minver

Tredrizzick

Lank

Prideaux Place

Went

Dinas Head

Harlyn Bay

Trewethern

St Kew

Trevose

Trevone Treator

Rock

Tredrizzick

Hendra

Penp

Constantine Bay

Harlyn

Lobster

Splatt

Stoptide

St Kew Highway

Windmill

Padstow

Chapel Amble

Constantine Bay

Dinas

Bodieve

St Mabyn

Blisland

Treyarnon

Towan

St Merryn

Tregonce

Tregunna

Trehemborne

Shop

Trevorrick

Trevanson

Edmonton

Tredethy

Porthcothan

St Issey

Wadebridge

Egloshayle

Croanford

Hellandbridge

Penrose

Treburrick

Whitecross

Royal Cornwall

St Breock

Treneague

Sladesbridge

Pencarrow House

Burlawn

Colquite

Helland

Park Head

St Ervan

4

Little Petherick

Trenance

Rumford

Tredinnick

Hay

St Breock Downs Monolith

5

Lane End

Washaway

Bedruthan Steps

Engollan

Trelow

St Jidgey

Polbrock

Car

Dunmere

Trenan

Downhill

Nine

Brocton

0		1		2		3		4		5 miles	
0	1	2	3	4	5	6	7		8 kilometres		

A B C D E F

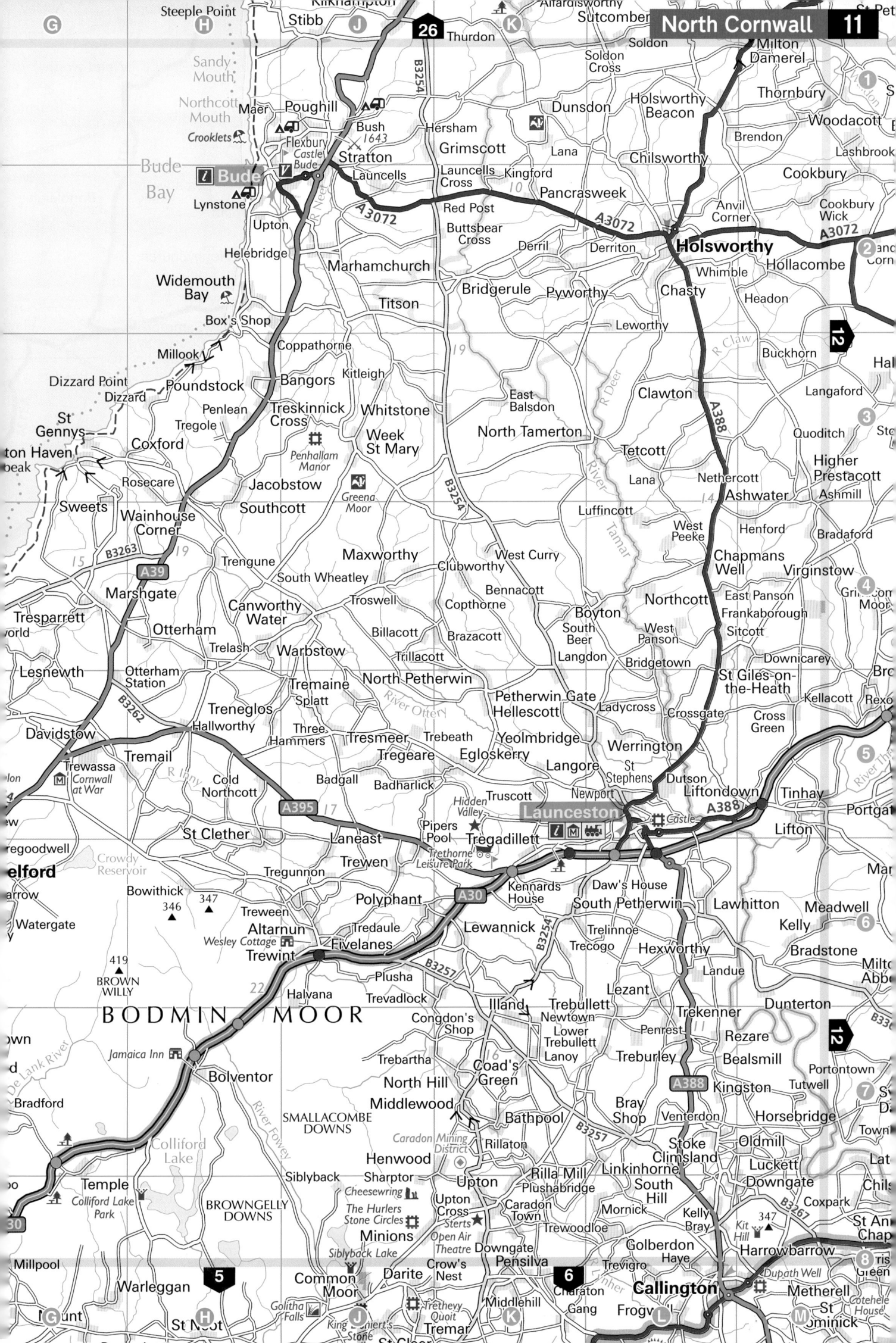

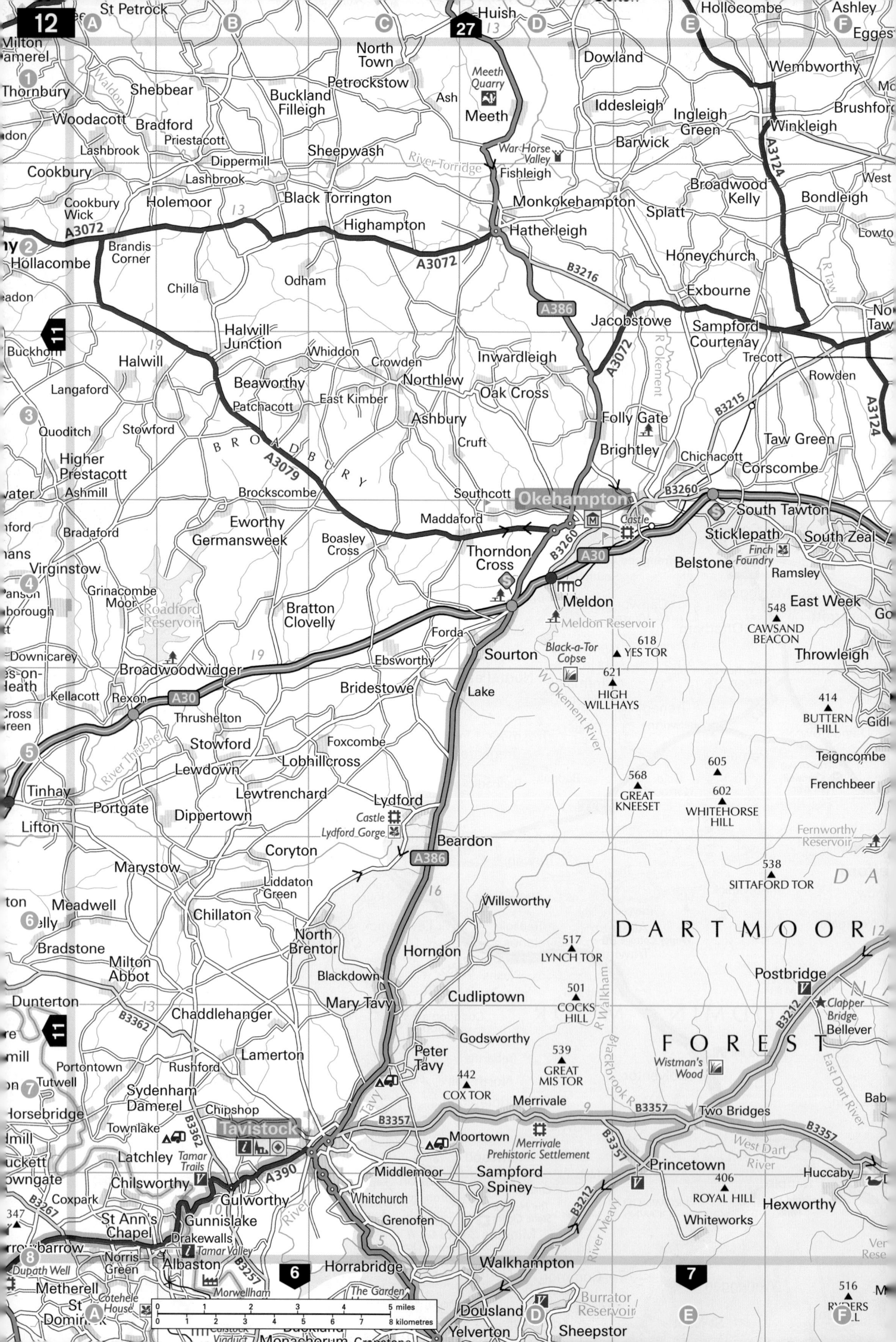

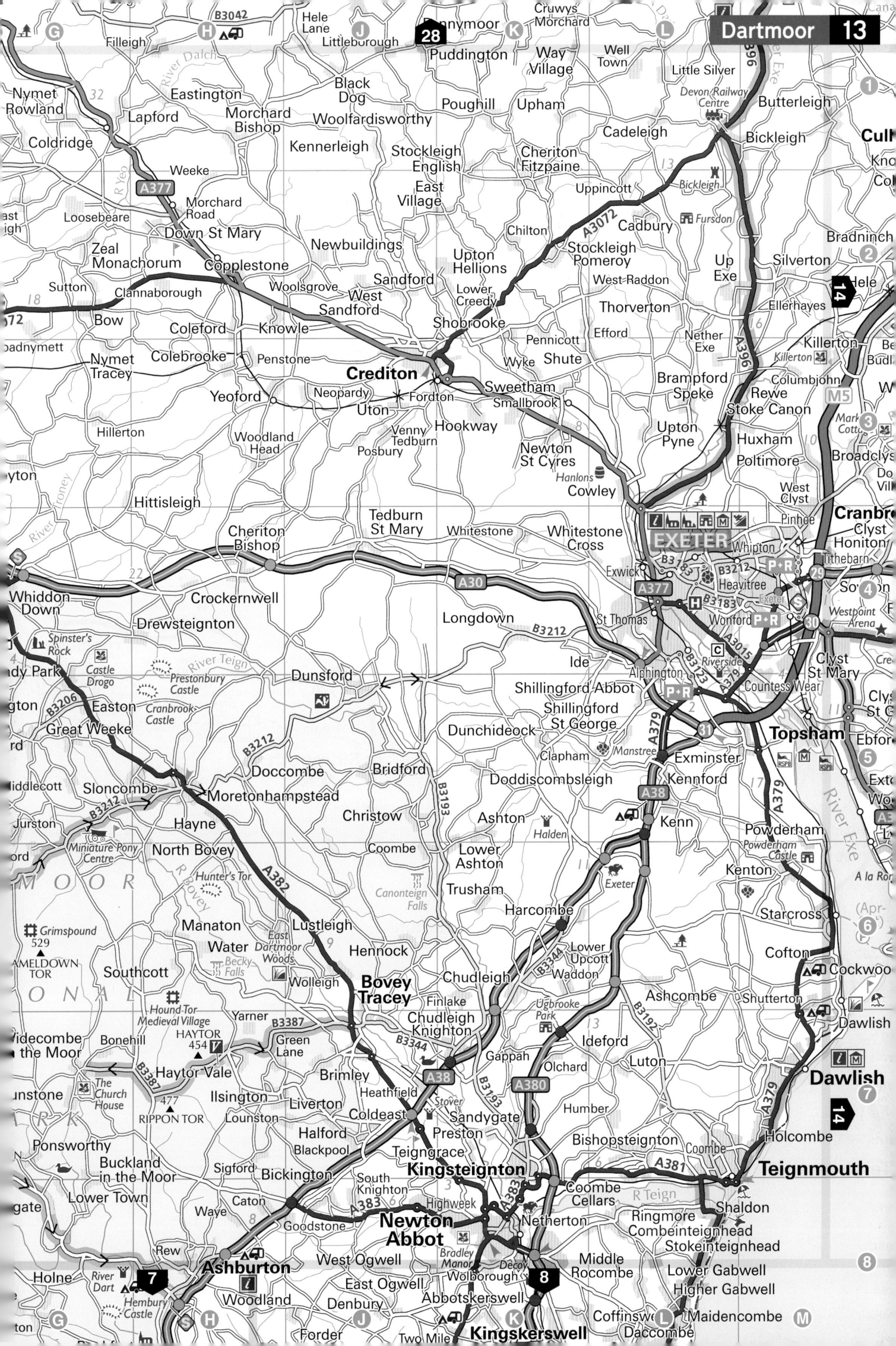

LYME BAY

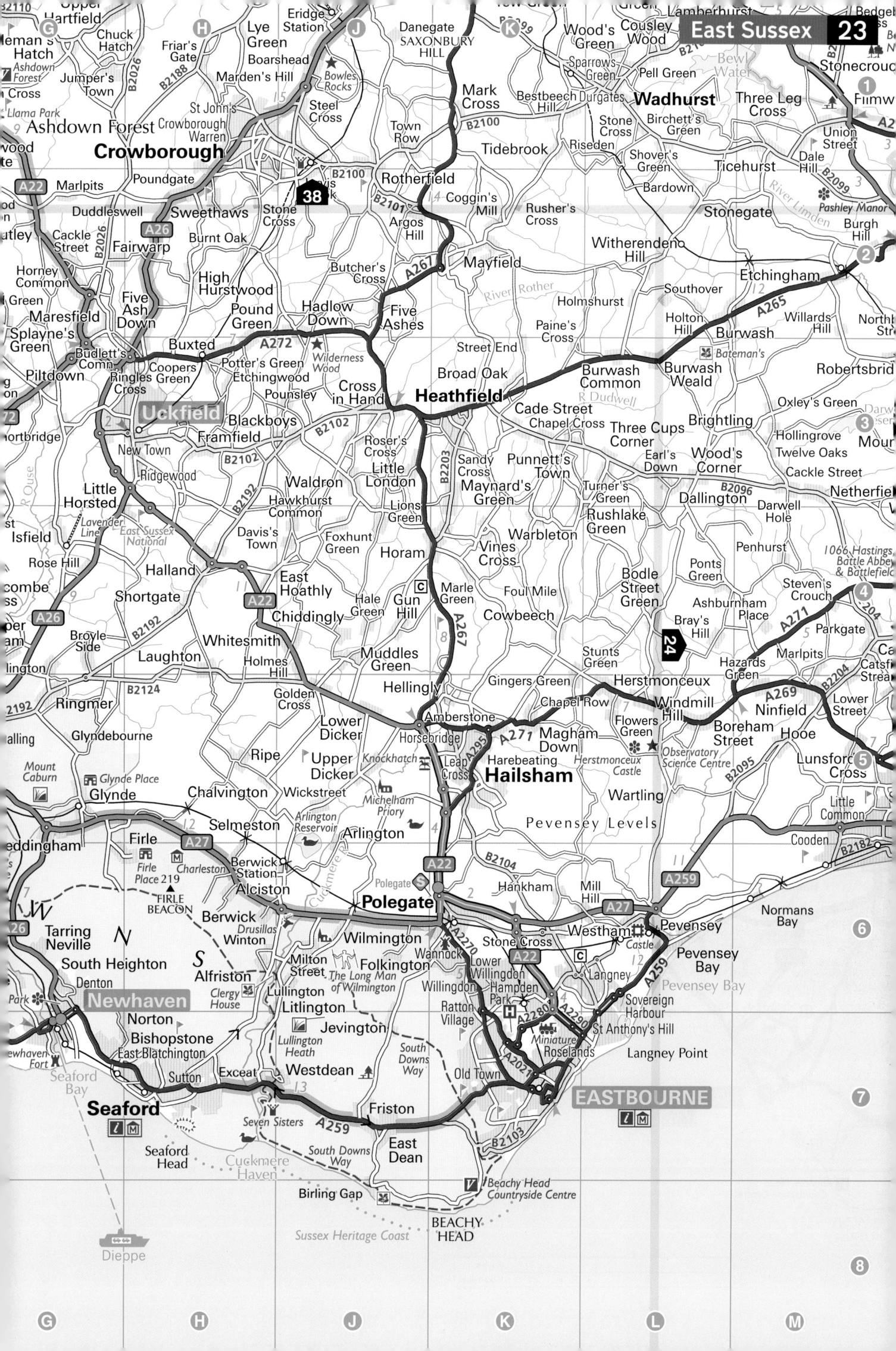

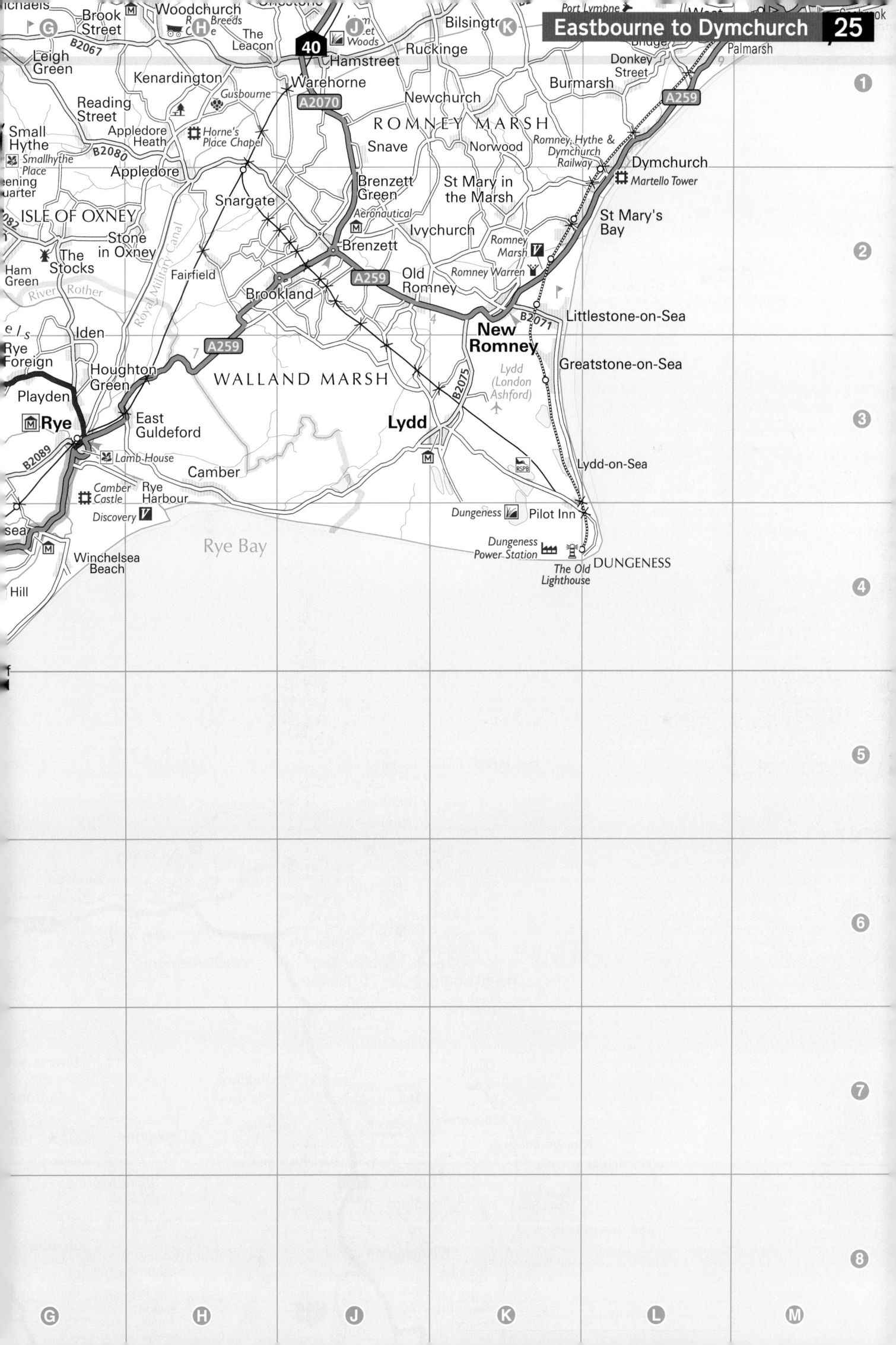

A B C D E F

1
2
3
4
5
6
7
8

North West Point

Lundy Heritage Coast

LUNDY

142

Marine Reserve

Shutter Point

Surf Point

Bideford (Apr-Oct)
Ilfracombe (Apr-Oct)

BARNSTAPLE

OR

BIDEFORD BA

HARTLAND POINT

Shipload Bay

Titchberry

Damehole Point

Hartland Abbey & Gardens

Brownsham

Stoke

B3248

Velly

Clovelly

Hart Heritag

Hartland Quay

Hartland

Higher Clovelly

Buck's Mills

Speke's Mill Mouth

4

B3237

Milford

Docton Mill

Philham

Milky Way

Buck's Cross

A39

Elmscott

Edistone

Woolfardisworthy

Cranford

Pa

Hardisworthy

Tosberry

Parkh
Ash

South Hole

Welcombe

Ashmanswo

Mead

Darracott

Meddon

East
Putford

Gooseham
Mill

Woolley

Gooseham

Eastcott

East
Youlstone

Dinworthy

Gnome Reserve

W
Put

Morwenstow

West Youlstone

Colscott

Higher Sharpnose Point

A39

Bradworthy

South West Coast Path

Shop

Woodford

Kimworthy

Sutcombe

Lower Sharpnose Point

Tamar Lakes

Steeple Point

Kilkhampton

Alfardisworthy

Sutcombemill

Stibb

Thurdon

Soldon

Soldon
Cross

River

0   1   2   3   4   5 miles
0 1 2 3 4 5 6 7 8 kilometres

A

D 11 E F

B3254

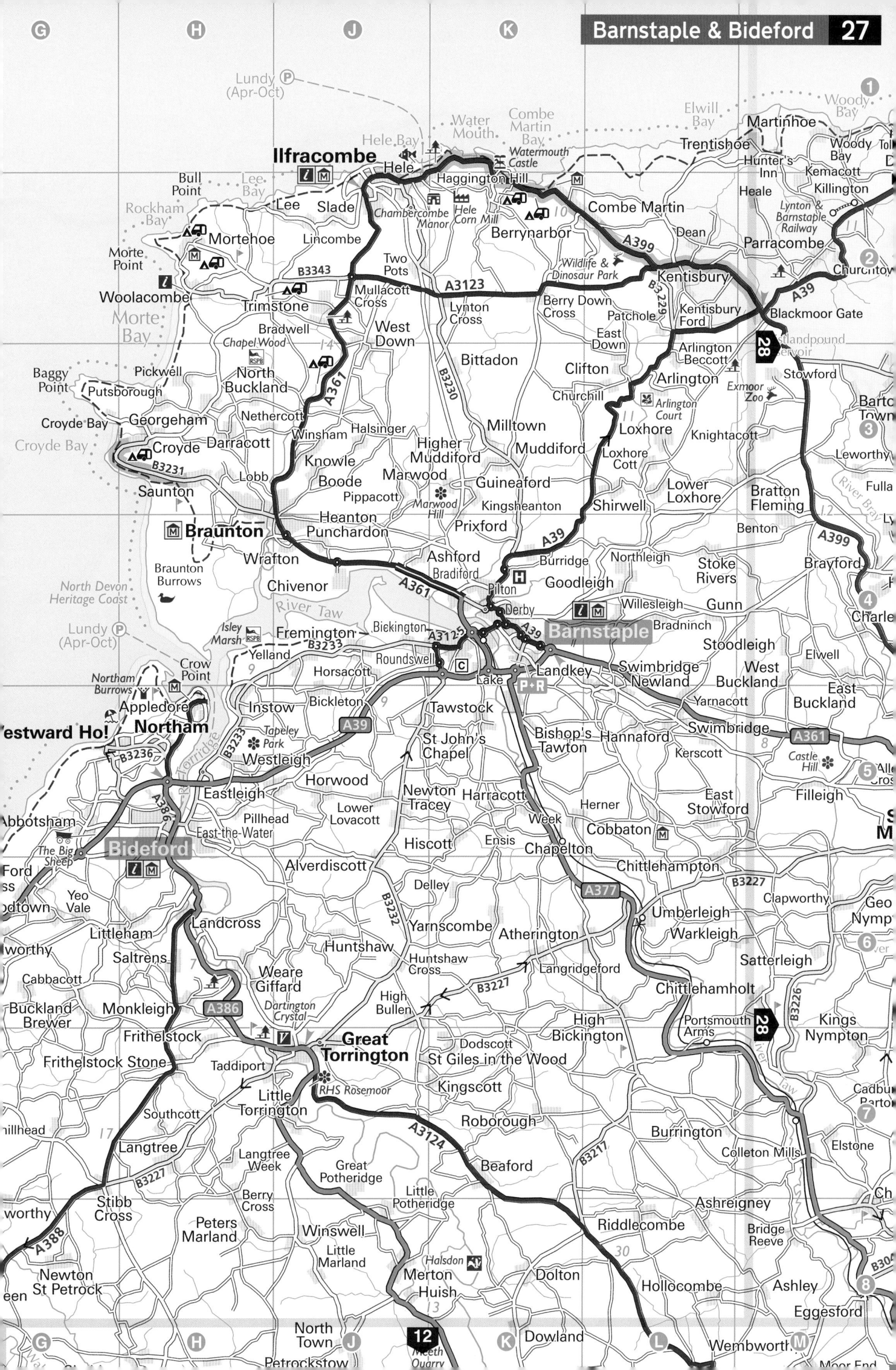

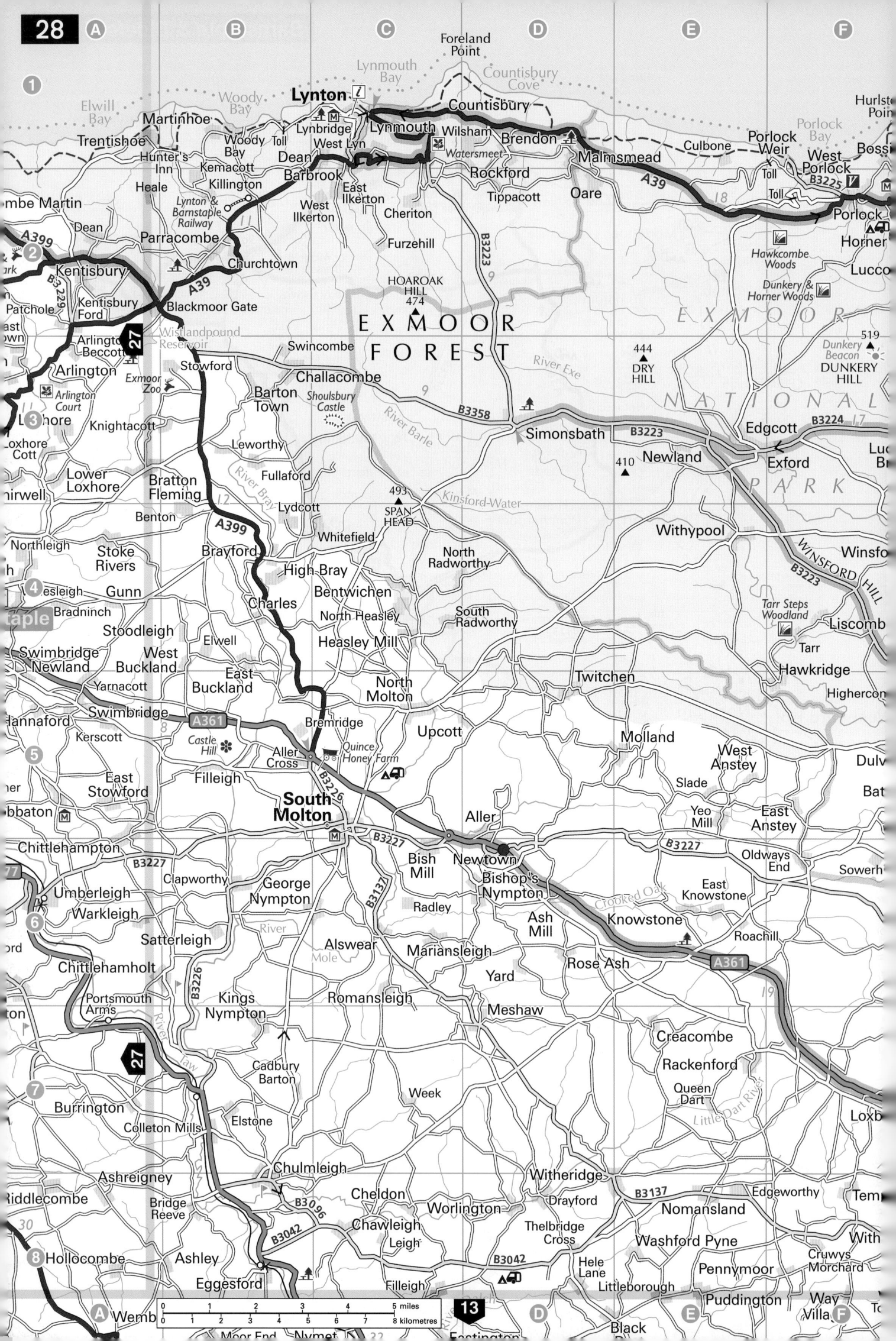

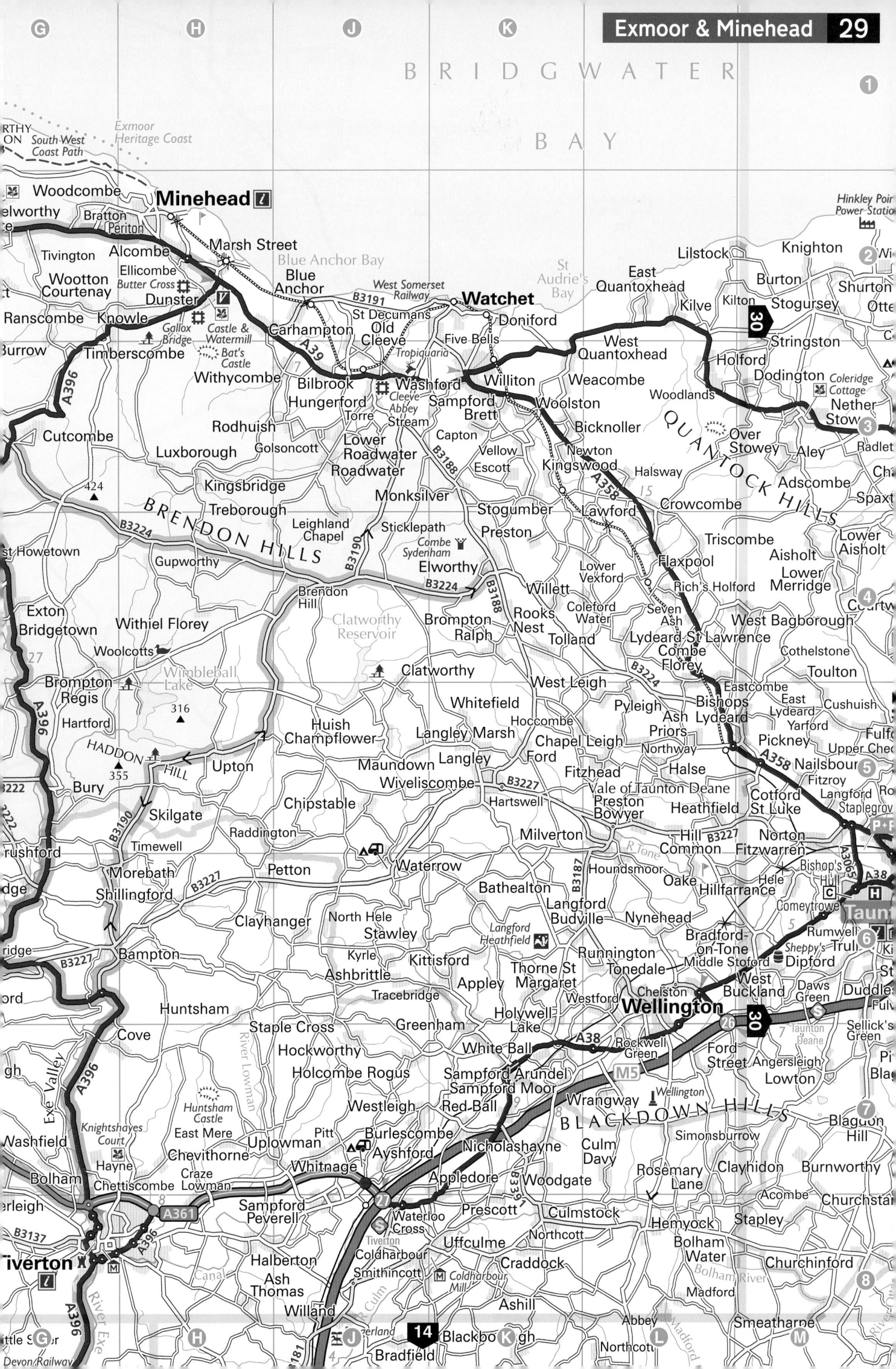

B R I D G W A T E R

B A Y

G H J K

Woodcombe
Exmoor Heritage Coast
South West Coast Path
Minehead *i*
Bratton Periton
Alcombe
Marsh Street
Blue Anchor Bay
Blue Anchor
West Somerset Railway
Watchet
St Audrie's Bay
Lilstock
Knighton
Burton
Shurton
East Quantoxhead
Kilve
Kilton
Stogursey
Otte
elworthy
Tivington
Ellicombe
Butter Cross
Dunster
Wootton Courtenay
B3191
St Decumans
Doniford
West Quantoxhead
Holford
Stringston
Dodington
Nether Stow
Coleridge Cottage
Hinkley Poir Power Statio
Ranscombe
Knowle
Gallox Bridge
Castle & Watermill
Carhampton
Old Cleeve
Five Bells
Williton
Weacombe
Woodlands
Burrow
Timberscombe
Bat's Castle
Withycombe
Bilbrook
Washford
Sampford Brett
Woolston
Bicknoller
Newton
Kingswood
Halsway
QUANTOCK HILLS
Over Stowey
Aley
Radlet
A396
Cutcombe
Hungerford
Torre
Cleeve Abbey Stream
Capton
Yellow
Escott
Halse
Crowcombe
Adscombe
Spaxt
Rodhuish
Lower Roadwater
Roadwater
B3188
Lawford
Triscombe
Aisholt
Lower Aisholt
424
Luxborough
Golsoncott
Monksilver
Stogumber
Preston
Lower Vexford
Flaxpool
Lower Merridge
Lower
Kingsbridge
Treborough
Leighland Chapel
Sticklepath
Combe Sydenham
Elworthy
B3224
Willett
Rich's Holford
Seven Ash
West Bagborough
Cothelstone
Courtw
B3224
BRENDON HILLS
B3190
Gupworthy
Brendon Hill
B3224
Rooks Nest
Coleford Water
Lydeard St Lawrence
Combe Florey
Toulton
st Howetown
Clatworthy Reservoir
Brompton Ralph
Tolland
Eastcombe
Bishops Lydeard
East Lydeard
Yarford
Cushuish
Fulf
Exton
Bridgetown
Withiel Florey
Woolcotts
Clatworthy
West Leigh
Whitefield
Hoccombe
Chapel Leigh
Ash Priors
Northway
Pyleigh
Pickney
A358
Upper Chec
Nailsbour
Fitzroy
Langford
Staplegrov
Brompton Regis
Wimbleball Lake
316
Huish Champflower
Langley Marsh
Langley
Ford
Fitzhead
Halse
Cotford St Luke
A358
Hartford
A396
HADDON HILL
355
Upton
Maundown
Wiveliscombe
B3227
Hartswell
Vale of Taunton Deane
Preston Bowyer
Heathfield
P+R
Bury
Skilgate
Chipstable
Milverton
Hill
B3227
Norton Fitzwarren
A303
A38
B3222
Timewell
Raddington
Waterrow
Houndsmoor
Oake
Hillfarrance
Bishop's Hill
H
A3065
rushford
Morebath
Shillingford
B3227
Petton
Bathealton
Langford Budville
Nynehead
Hele
Comeytrowe
Taun
dge
Clayhanger
North Hele
Stawley
Langford Heathfield
Bradford-on-Tone
Middle Stoford
Sheppy's
Dipford
Rumwell
Trul
B3227
Bampton
Kyrle
Kittisford
Thorne St Margaret
Appley
Runnington
Tonedale
West Buckland
Daws Green
Duddle
ridge
Ashbrittle
Tracebridge
Westford
Chelston
S
Fulv
Sellick's Green
Huntsham
Staple Cross
Greenham
Holywell Lake
Wellington
A38
26
30
Taunton Deane
Cove
Hockworthy
White Ball
Rockwell Green
Ford Street
Angersleigh
Lowton
Pi
Bla
A396
Exe Valley
Huntsham Castle
Holcombe Rogus
Westleigh
Red Ball
M5
Wrangway
Wellington
BLACKDOWN HILLS
Simonsburrow
Blagdon Hill
Knightshayes Court
East Mere
Uplowman
Pitt
Whitnage
Ayshford
Sampford Arundel
Sampford Moor
Appledore
Nicholashayne
Culm Davy
Woodgate
Rosemary Lane
Clayhidon
Burnworthy
Acombe
Churchstan
Bolham
Hayne
Chettiscombe
Craze Lowman
A361
Sampford Peverell
Burlescombe
Prescott
Culmstock
Hemyock
Stapley
erleigh
Tiverton *i*
M
A396
Canal
River Exe
Coldharbour
Tiverton
Uffculme
Craddock
Bolham Water
Bolham River
Churchinford
B3137
ittle S
Devon Railway
A396
B3181
River Culm
Halberton
Ash Thomas
Willand
Smithincott
Coldharbour Mill
Waterloo Cross
Northcott
Ashill
Abbey
Madford
Smeatharp
G H J K L M
14
Bradfield
Blackbo ugh
Northcott
8

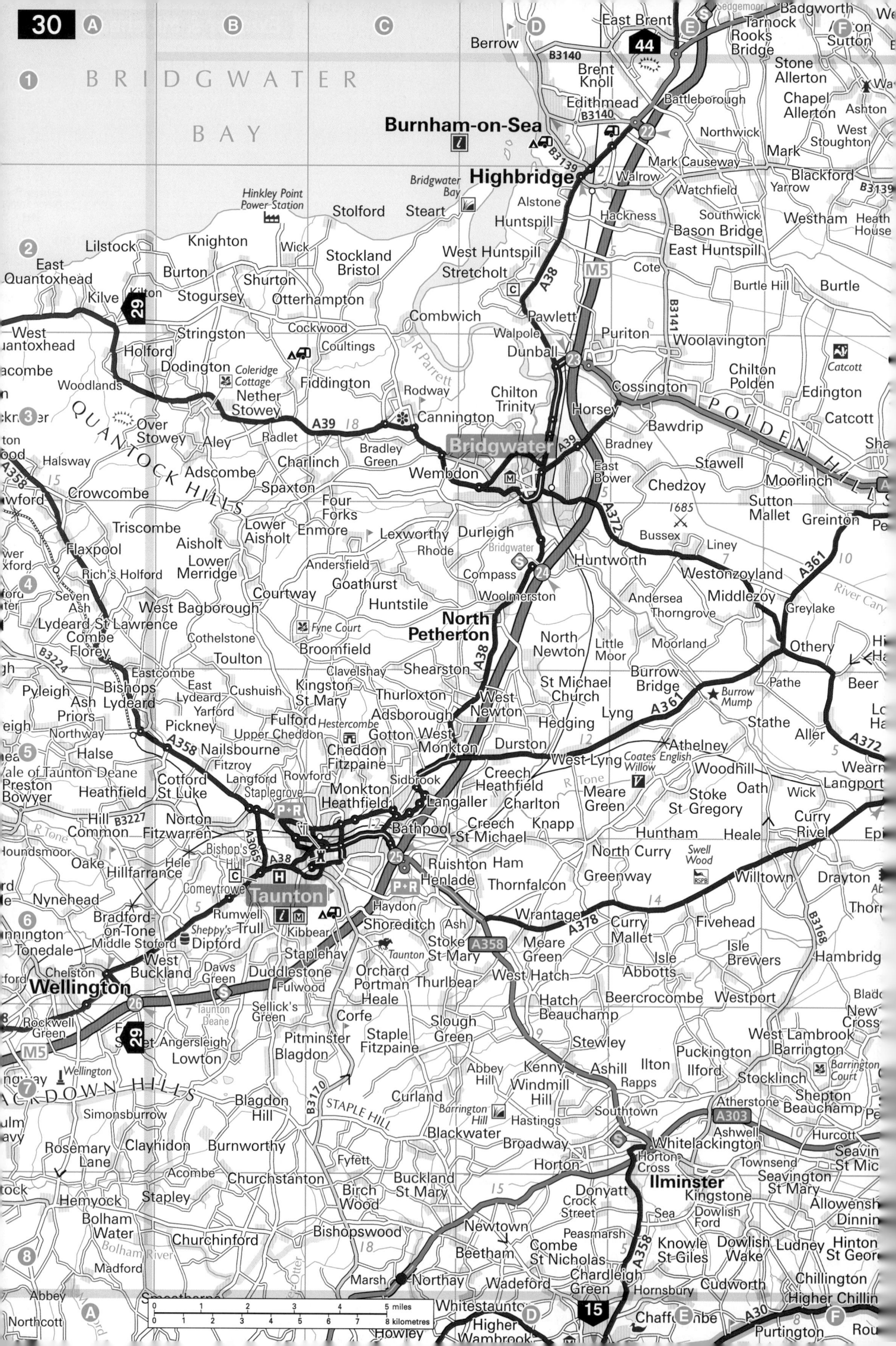

Draycott • Priddy • East Water • Emborough • Stratton-on-the-Fosse • Newbury • Upper Vobster • Mells

Rodney Stoke • Old Ditch • Green Ore • Gurney Slade • Downside • Holcombe • Highbury • Vobster • Coleford • Whatley

Cocklake • Rodney Stoke • Westbury-sub-Mendip • Ebbor Gorge • Binegar • Nettlebridge • Ham • Little Elm

Wedmore • Latcham • Theale • Wookey Hole • West Horrington • Ashwick • Oakhill • Stoke St Michael • East End • Downhead • Chantry • Castle

Bagley • Panborough • Henton • Lower Milton • South Horrington • East Horrington • Nunney Catch

Westhay Moor • Worth • Coxley Wick • Wells • Dulcote • Dinder • Darshill • Shepton Mallet • Dean • Leighton • Cloford • Trudoxhill

Meare • Stileway • Lower Godney • Upper Godney • Polsham • Worminster • Croscombe • West Compton • Doulting • Cranmore • East Cranmore • Wanstrow

Westhay • Godney • North Town • North Wootton • Pilton • Charlton • East Somerset Railway • Chesterblade • Higher Alham • West Town

Meare Fish House • Northload Bridge • Brindham • Westholme • East Compton • Royal Bath & West • Prestleigh • Stoney Stratton • Batcombe • Upton Noble

Glastonbury • Glastonbury Tor • Havyatt • West Pennard • Pylle • Evercreech • Westcombe • Milton Clevedon • North Brewham

Walton • Clarks Village • Asney • Edgarley • Woodland Street • West Bradley • East Pennard • Hembridge • Lamyatt • West End • South Brewham

Street • Butleigh Wootton • West Town • Coxbridge • Tilham Street • Parbrook • Huxham Green • Wraxall • Ditcheat • Bruton • King Alfred Tower

Overleigh • Baltonsborough • Gosling Street • Ham Street • Stone • Alhampton • Wyke Champflower • Ansford • Cole • Redlynch • Stoney Stoke • Hardway

Compton Dundon • Butleigh • Southwood • Four Foot • Hornblotton Green • Clanville • Pitcombe • Shepton Montague • Charlton Musgrove

Dundon • Silver Street • West Lydford • East Lydford • Alford • Castle Cary • Bratton Seymour • Wincanton • Bayford

Somerton • Littleton • Kingweston • Keinton Mandeville • Lydford on Fosse • Lovington • Wheathill • Galhampton • Yarlington • Winsanton

Pitney • Charlton Mackrell • Babcary • Foddington • North Barrow • Brookhampton • Woolston • Lattiford

Midney • Charlton Adam • South Barrow • North Cadbury • Blackford • Holton • Maperton • North Cheriton • South Cheriton

Upton • South Hill • Catsgore • Kingsdon • Lytes Cary Manor • Downhead • Sparkford • Little Weston • Compton Pauncefoot • Horsington

Knole • Little Load • Podimore • West Camel • Queen Camel • South Cadbury • Charlton Horethorne • Abbas Combe

Long Load • Northover • Ilchester • RNAS Yeovilton • Bridgehampton • Wales Camel • Sutton Montis • Marston Magna • Charlton Horethorne • Templecombe

Milton • Witcombe • Ash • Draycott • Yeovilton • Chilton Cantelo • Limington • Corton Denham • Stowell • Milborne Wick • Yenston

Treasurer's House • Tintinhull Garden • Chilthorne Domer • Ashington • West Mudford • Rimpton • Adber • Sandford Orcas • Henstridge Ash • Henstridge

Hurst • Stoke sub Hamdon • Montacute • Tintinhull • Mudford Sock • Mudford • Milborne Port • Henstridge

Norton sub Hamdon • Ham Hill • Montacute House • Odcombe • Preston Plucknett • Yeovil Marsh • Up Mudford • Trent • Oborne • Purse Caundle

Wigborough • Little Norton • Chiselborough • West Coker • Brympton • Barwick • Over Compton • Nether Compton • Stallen • Goathill • Sherborne Old Castle • Stalbridge Weston

West Chinnock • East Chinnock • Burton • Bradford Abbas • Sherborne • North Wootton • Haydon • Alweston • Stourton Caundle

Middle Chinnock • Hardington Moor • East Coker • Stoford • Thornford • Sherborne Castle & Gardens • Folke • Bishop's Caundle

Haselbury Plucknett • Hardington Mandeville • Pendomer • Sutton Bingham • Beer Hackett • Lillington • Longburton • Crouch Hill • Holwell

Crewkerne • North Perrott • Haselbury Marsh • Closworth • Ryme Intrinseca • Yetminster • Knighton • Boys Hill • Sandhills • Packers • King's Hazelbury

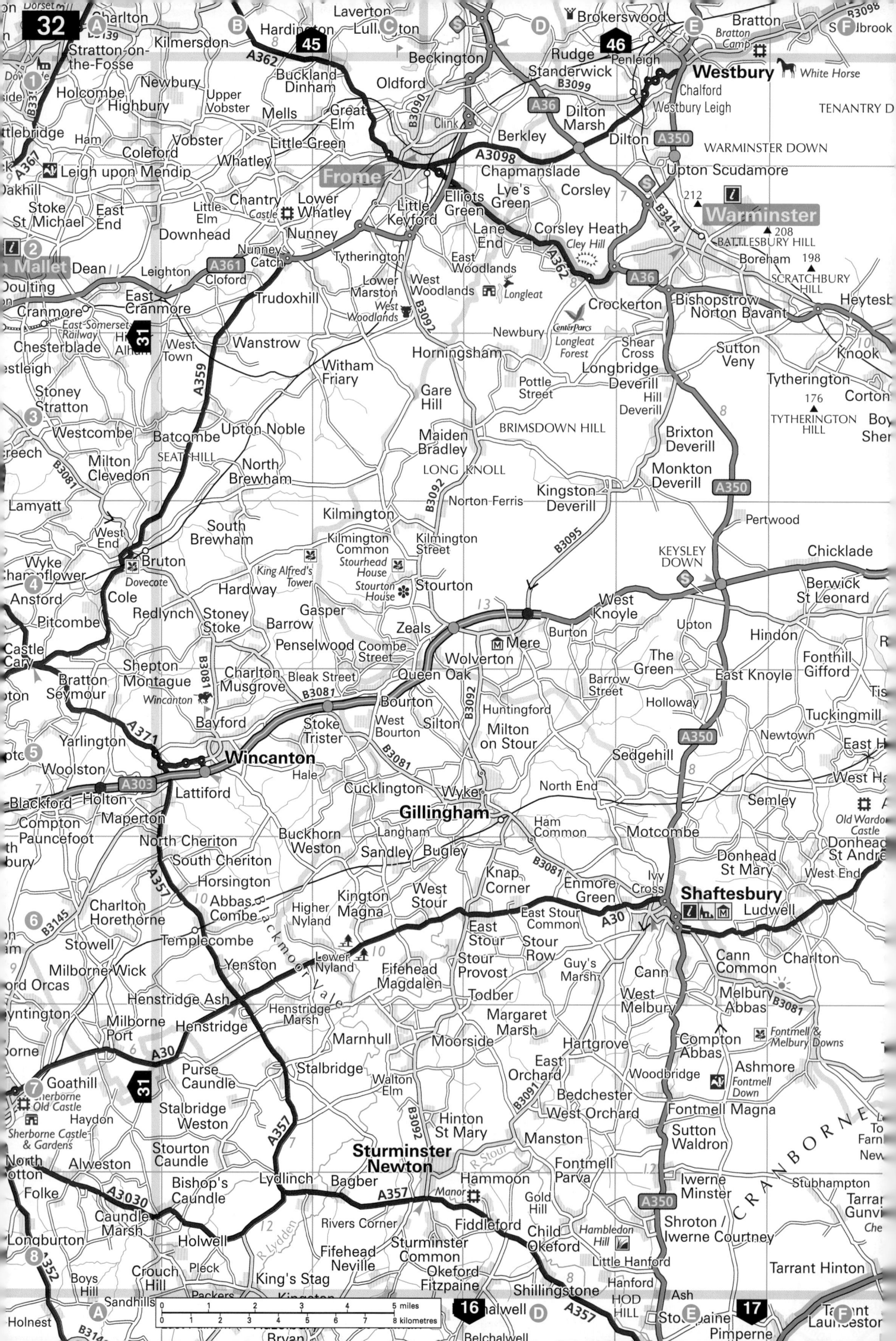

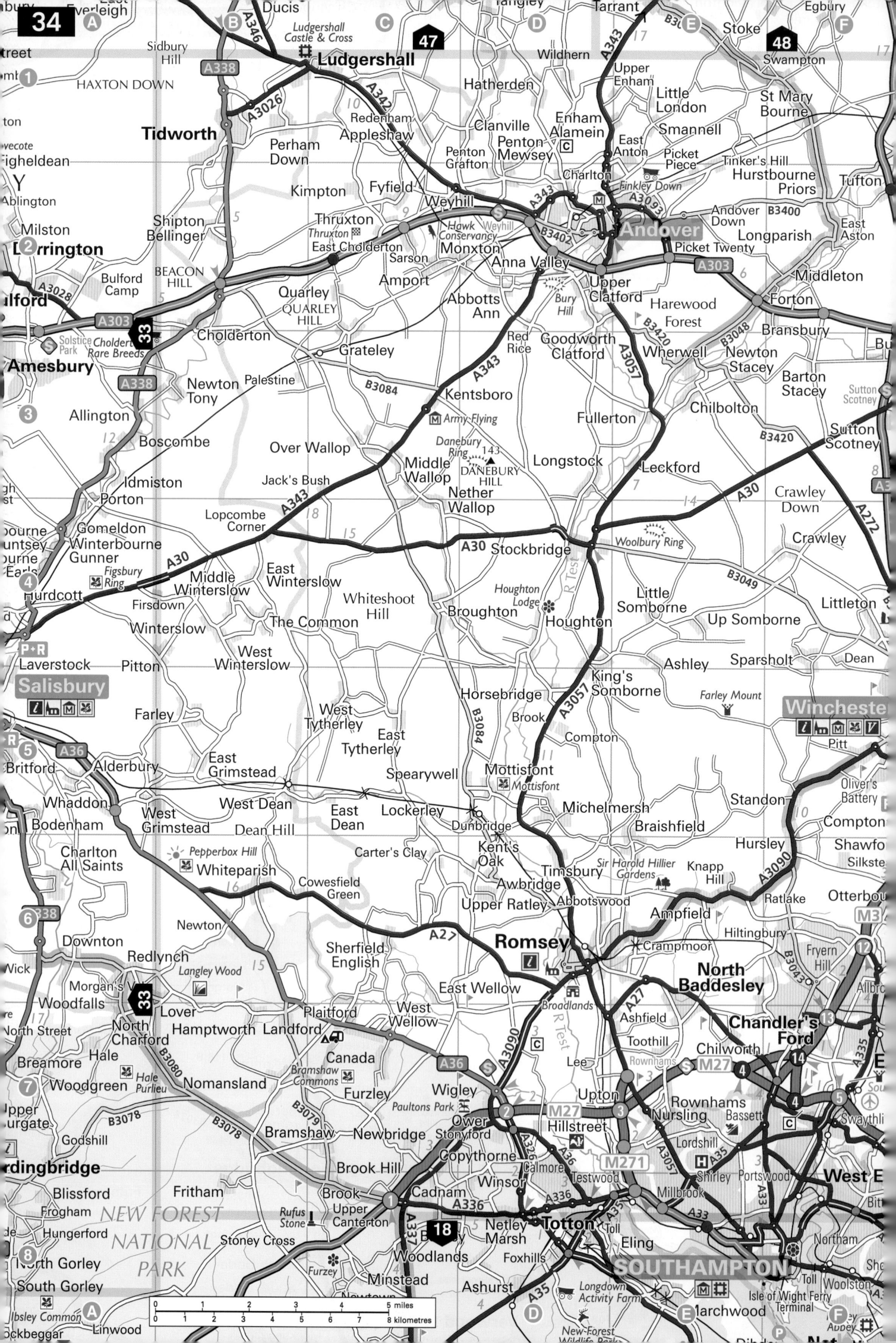

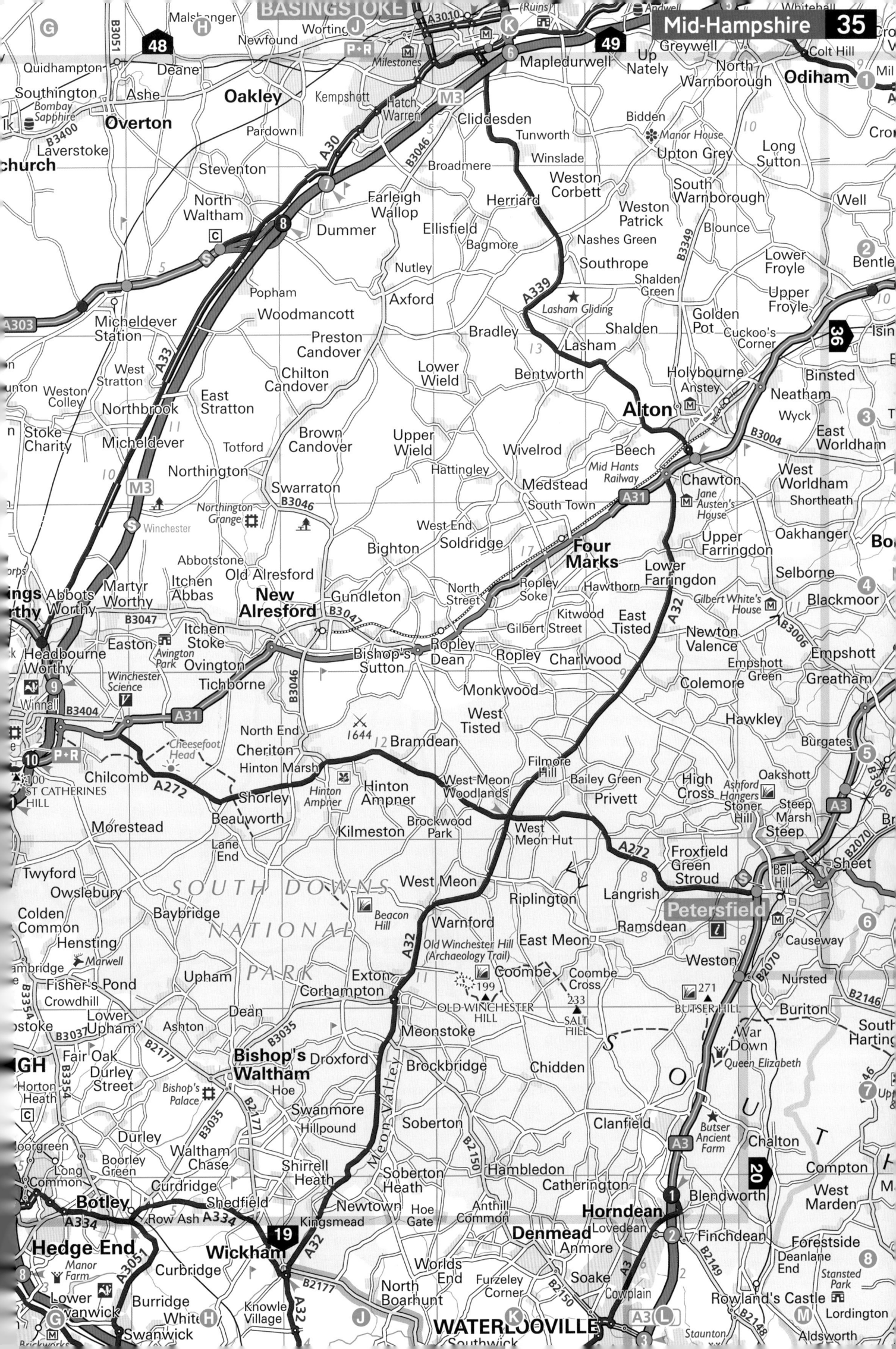

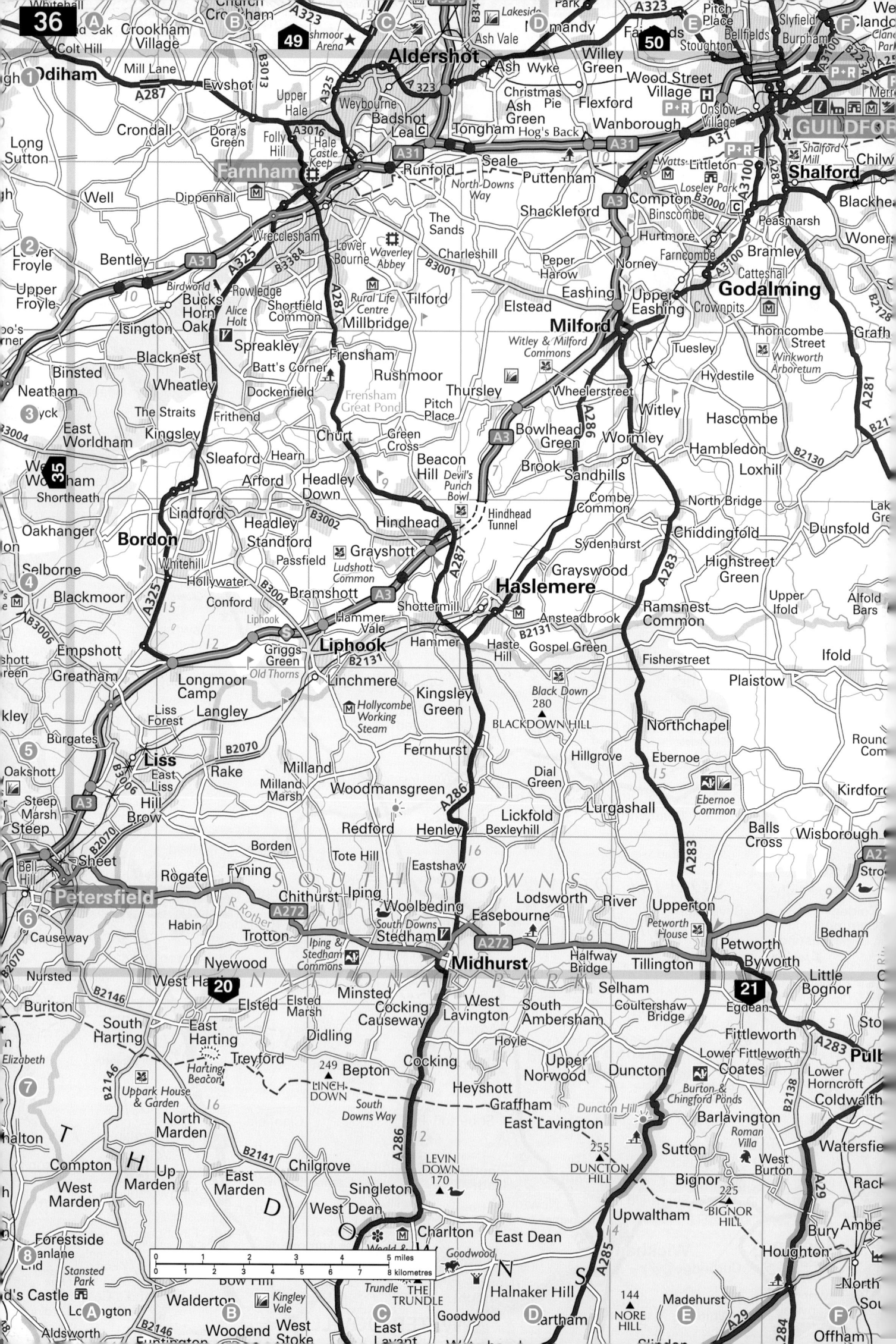

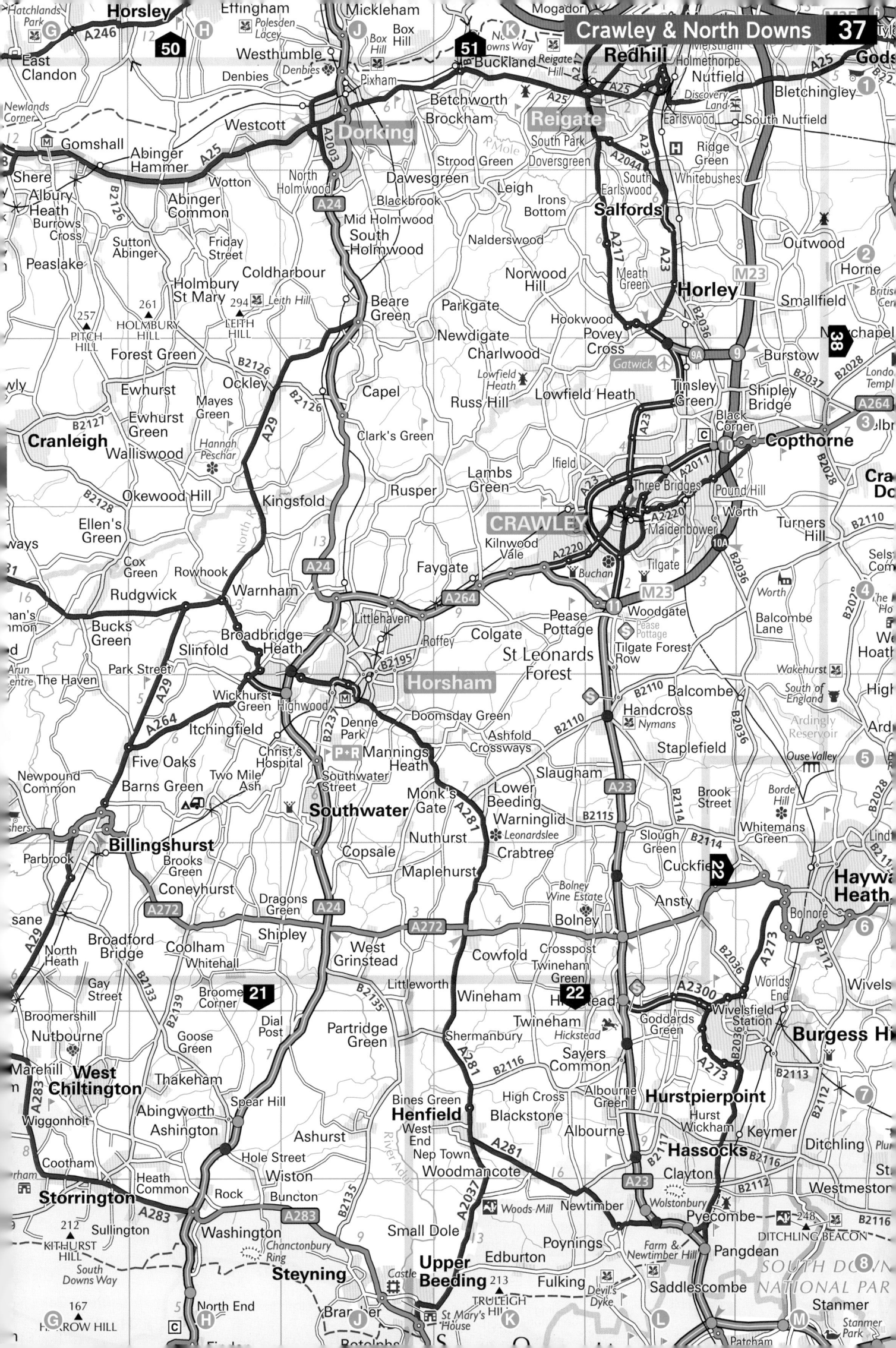

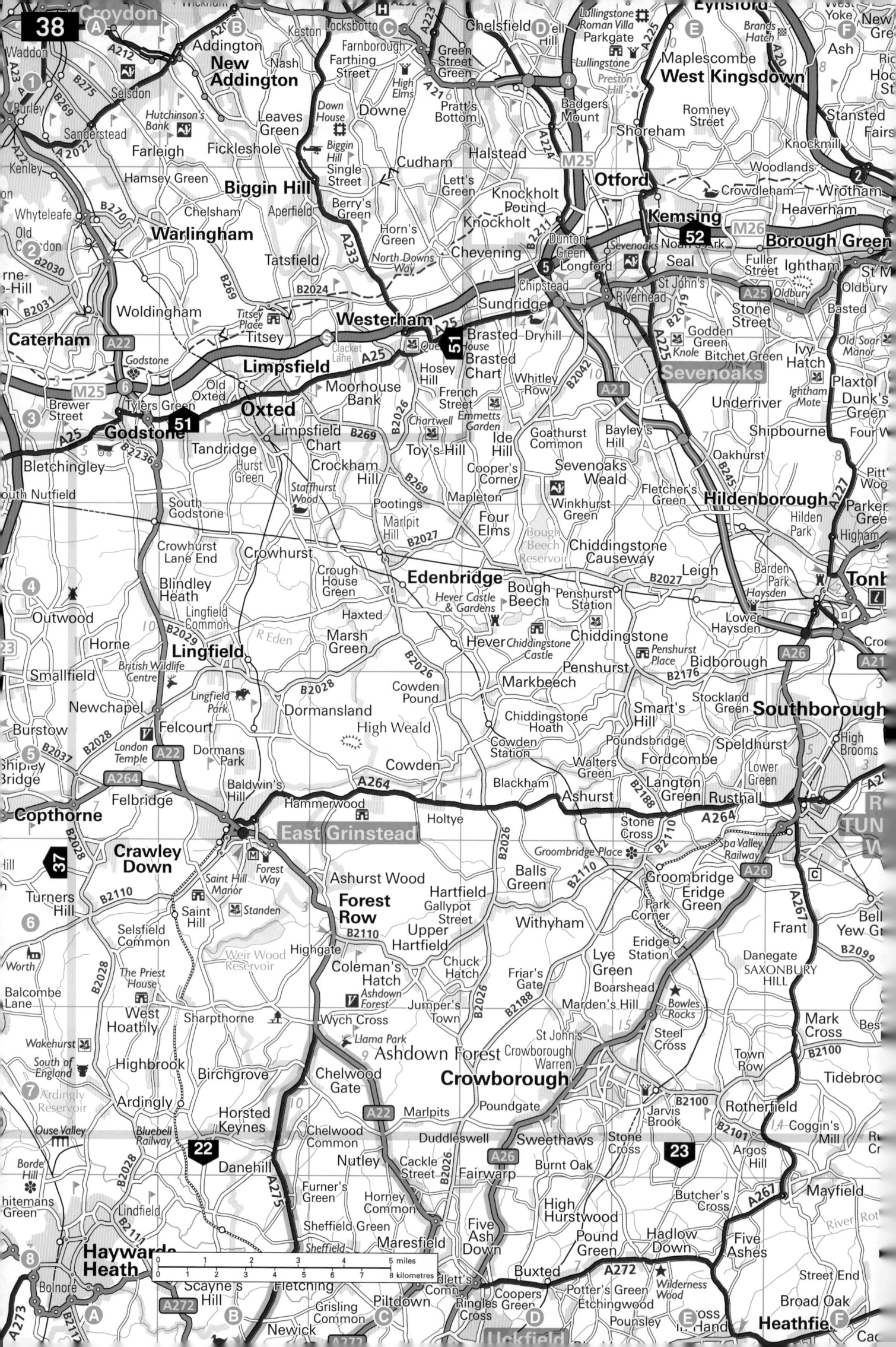

Sitting...

Snodland · West Malling · Ditton · Aylesford · **MAIDSTONE** · Bearsted · Thurnham · Hollingbourne · Harrietsham · Lenham

West Peckham · Coxheath · Boughton Monchelsea · Sutton Valence · Ulcombe · Grafty Green · Boughton Malherbe · Egerton

Paddock Wood · Marden · Staplehurst · Headcorn · Smarden · Biddenden

Brenchley · Horsmonden · Goudhurst · Cranbrook · Sissinghurst · Tenterden · St Michaels

Lamberhurst · Kilndown · Hartley · Benenden · Rolvenden · Small Hythe

Wadhurst · Flimwell · Hawkhurst · Sandhurst · Newenden · Wittersham · ISLE OF OXNEY

Ticehurst · Hurst Green · Bodiam · Northiam · Beckley · Peasmarsh

Burwash · Etchingham · Robertsbridge · Salehurst · Staplecross · Clayhill · Horns Cross

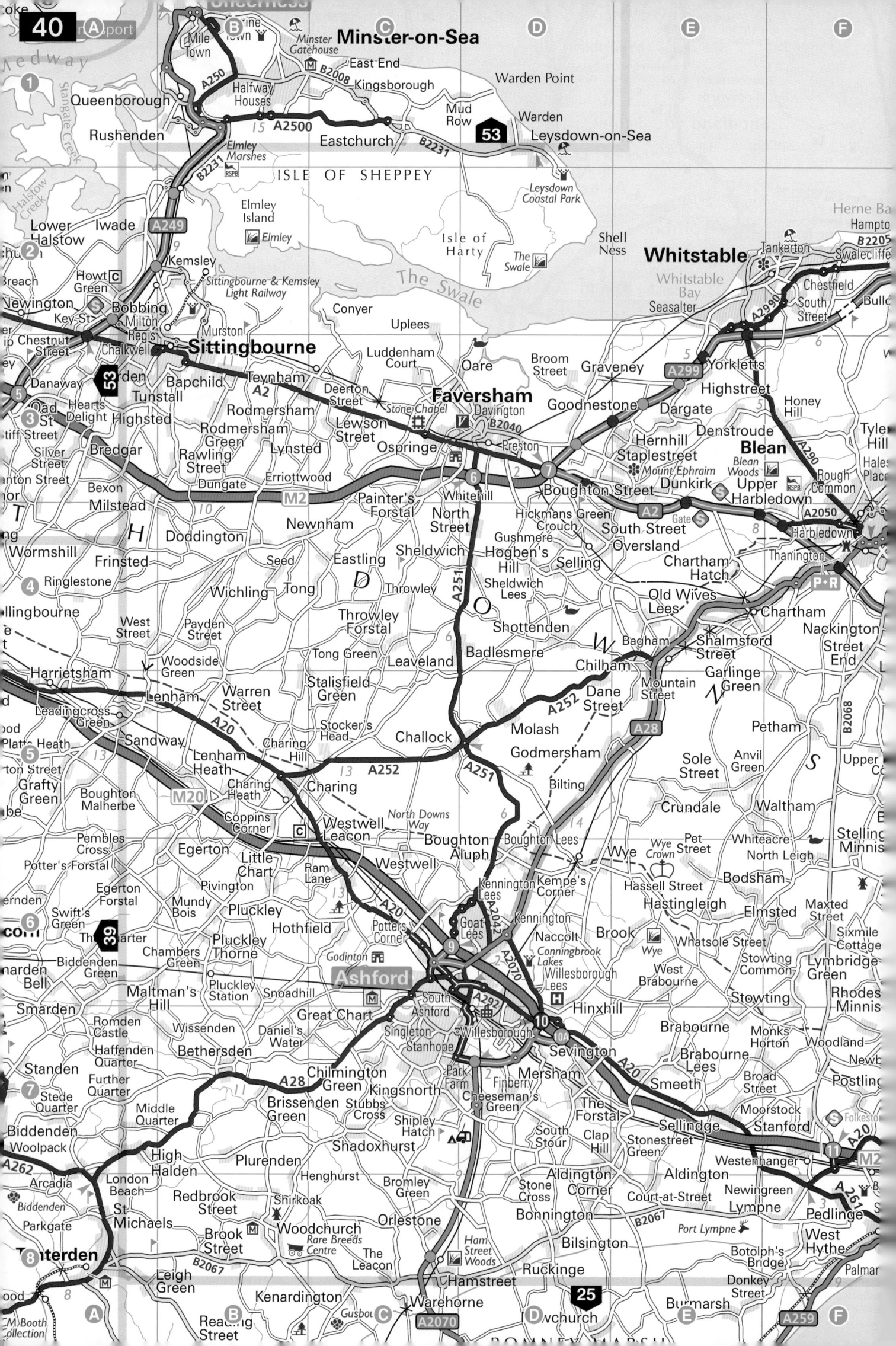

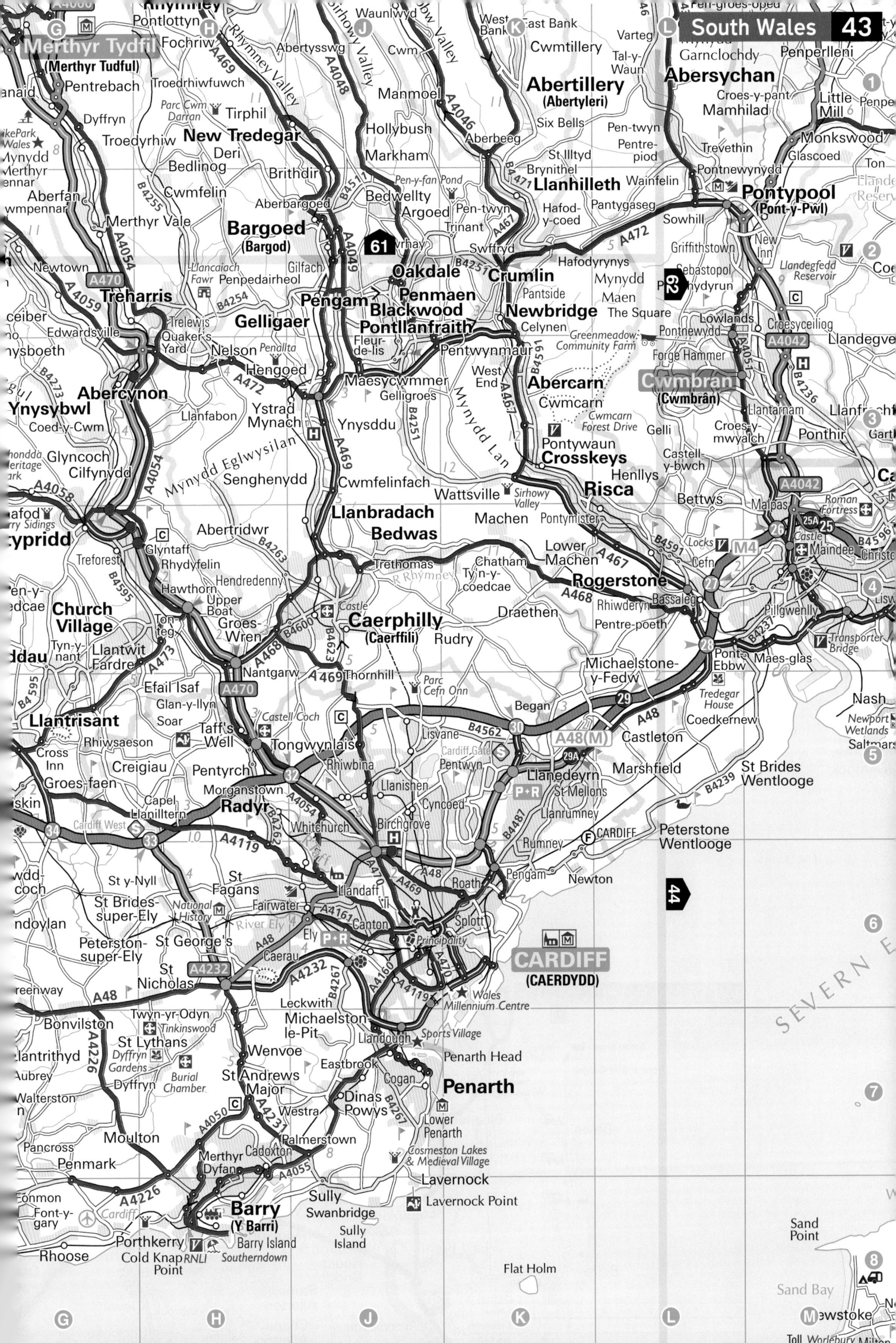

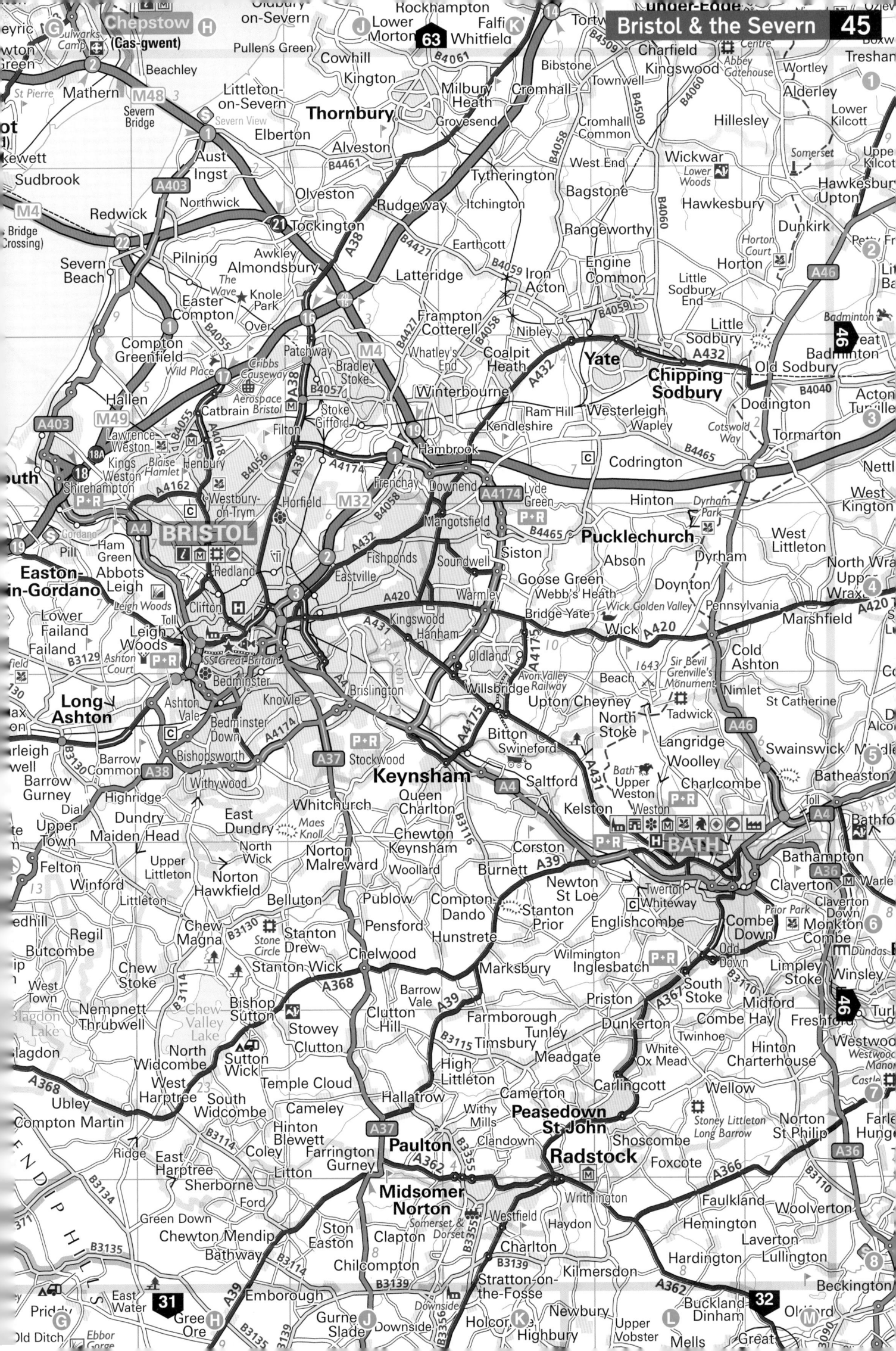

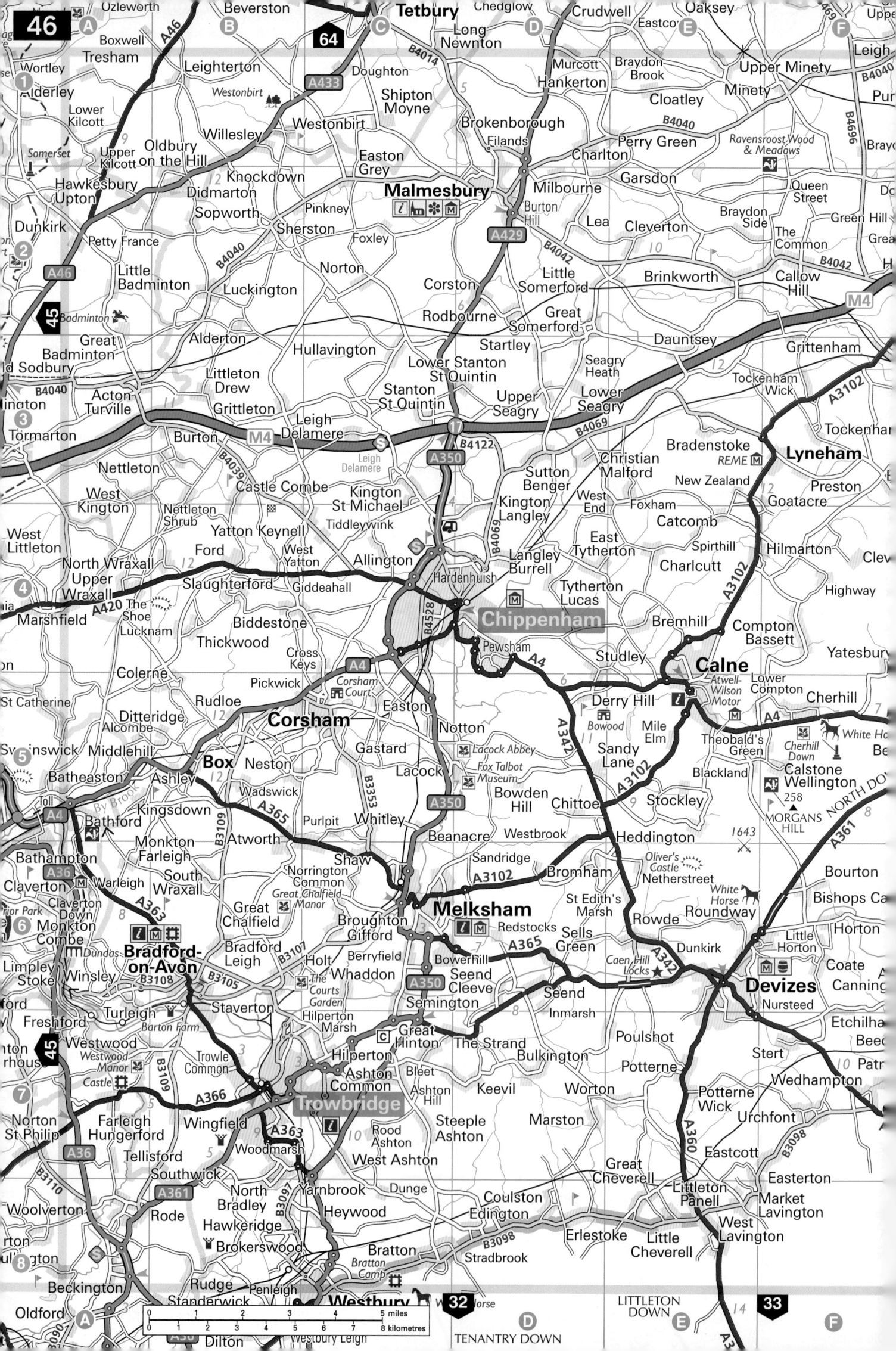

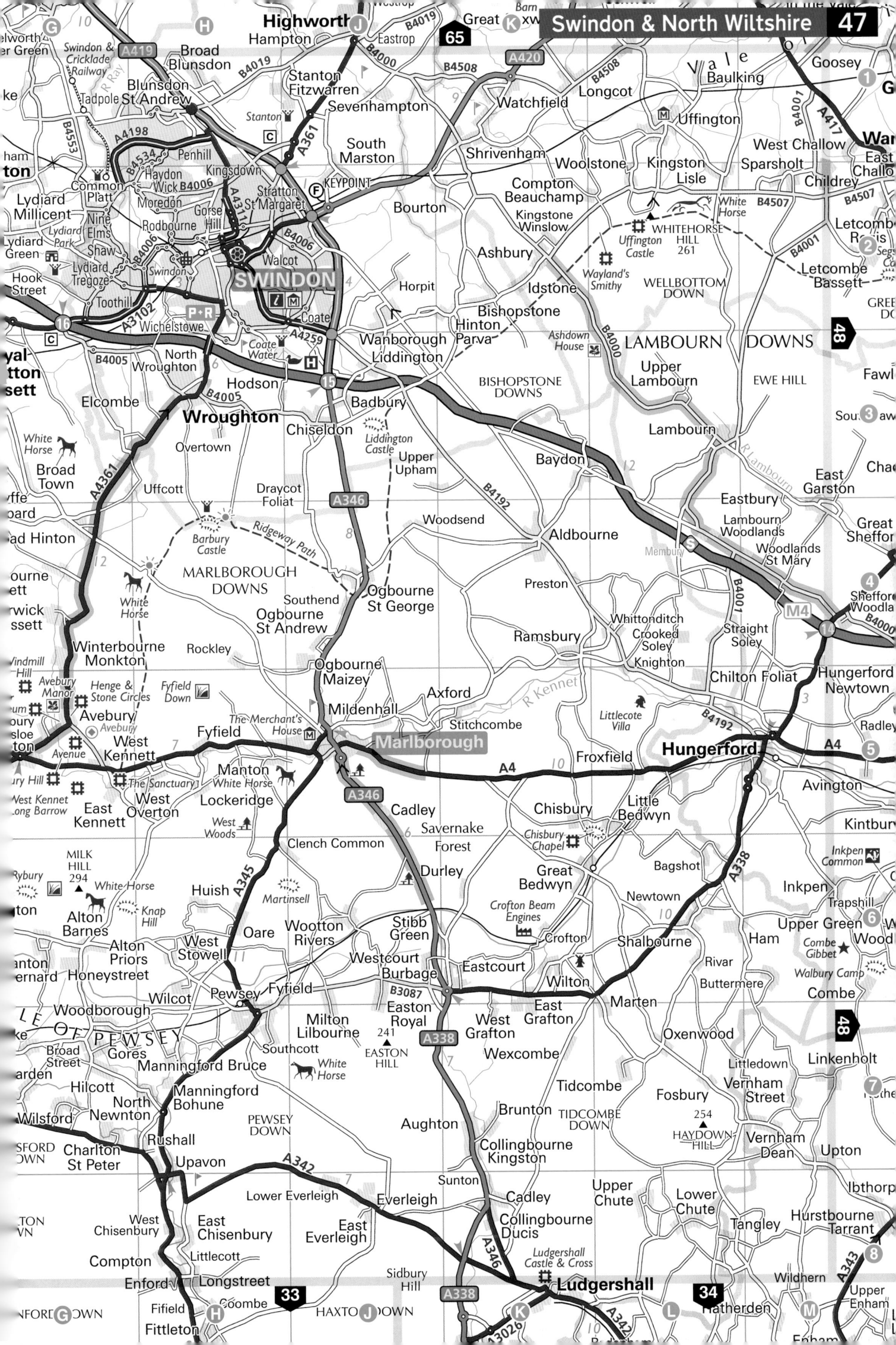

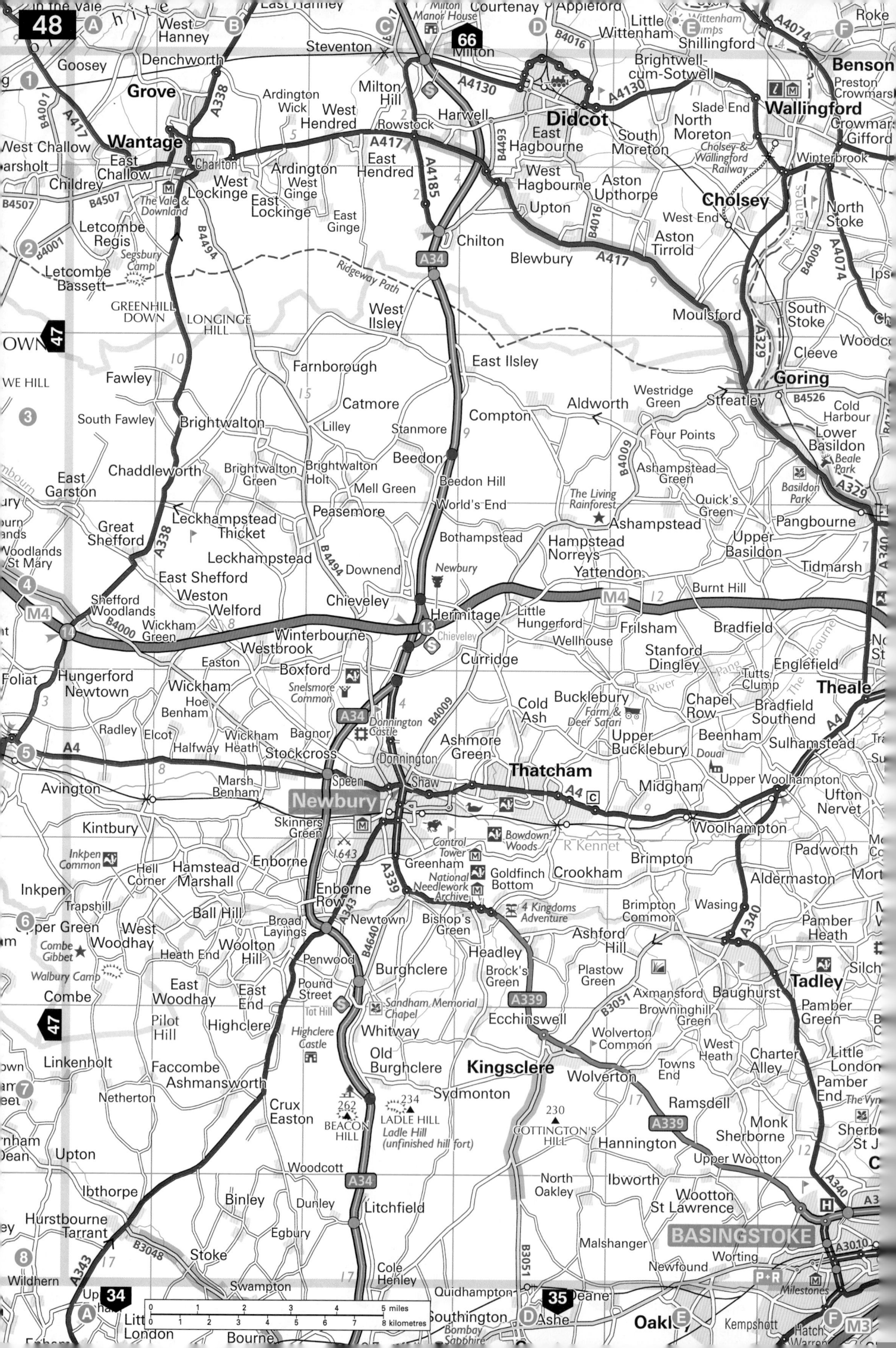

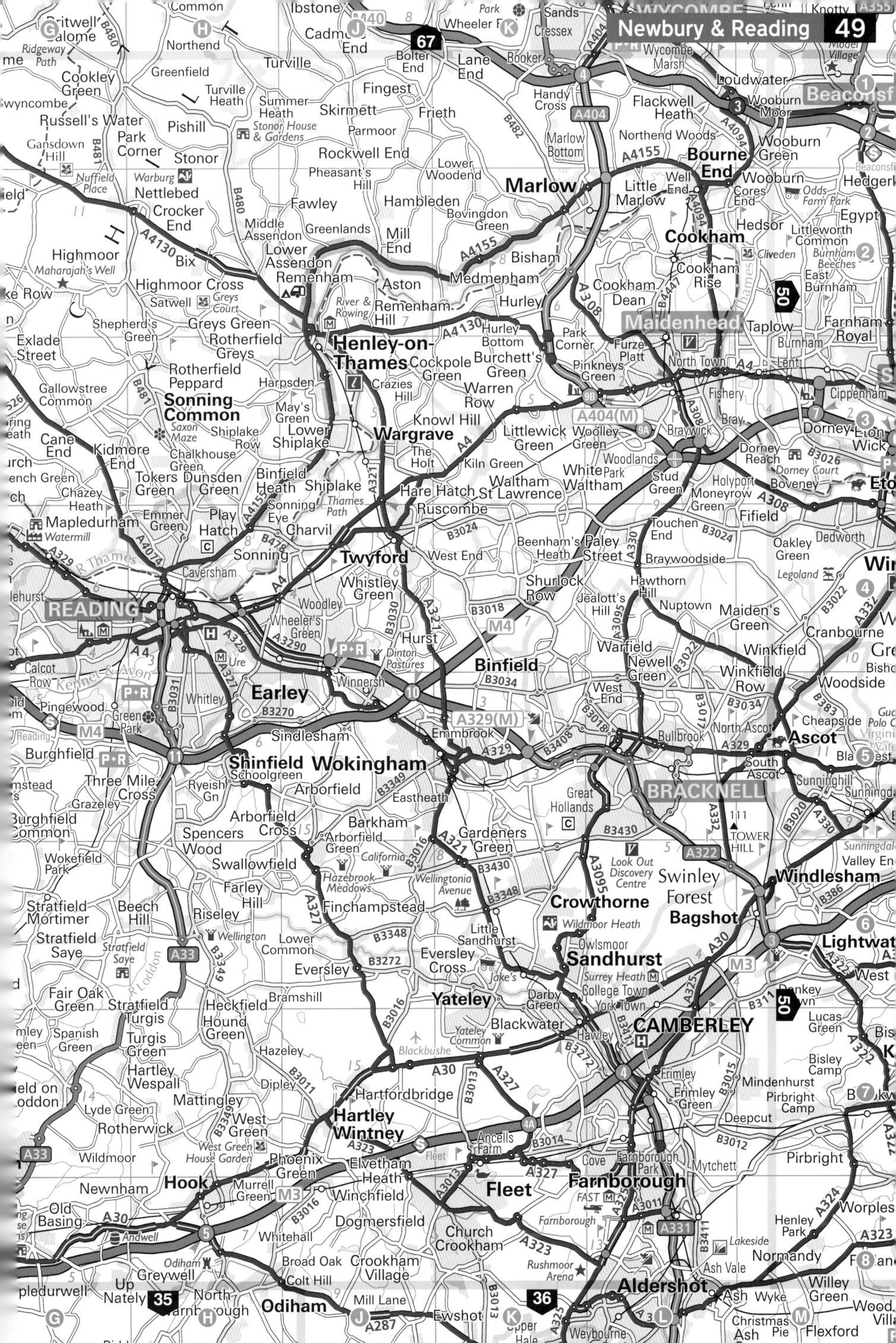

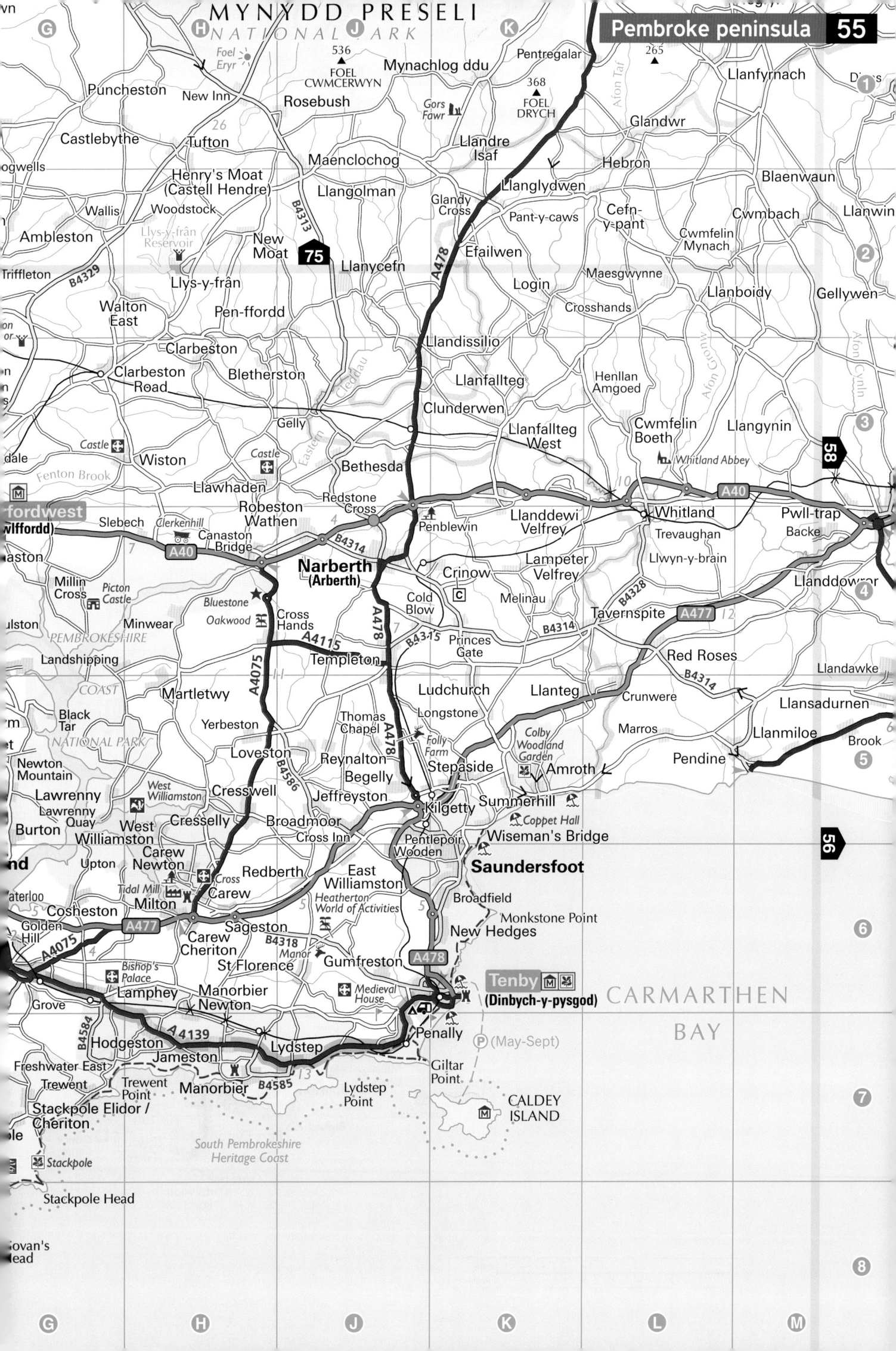

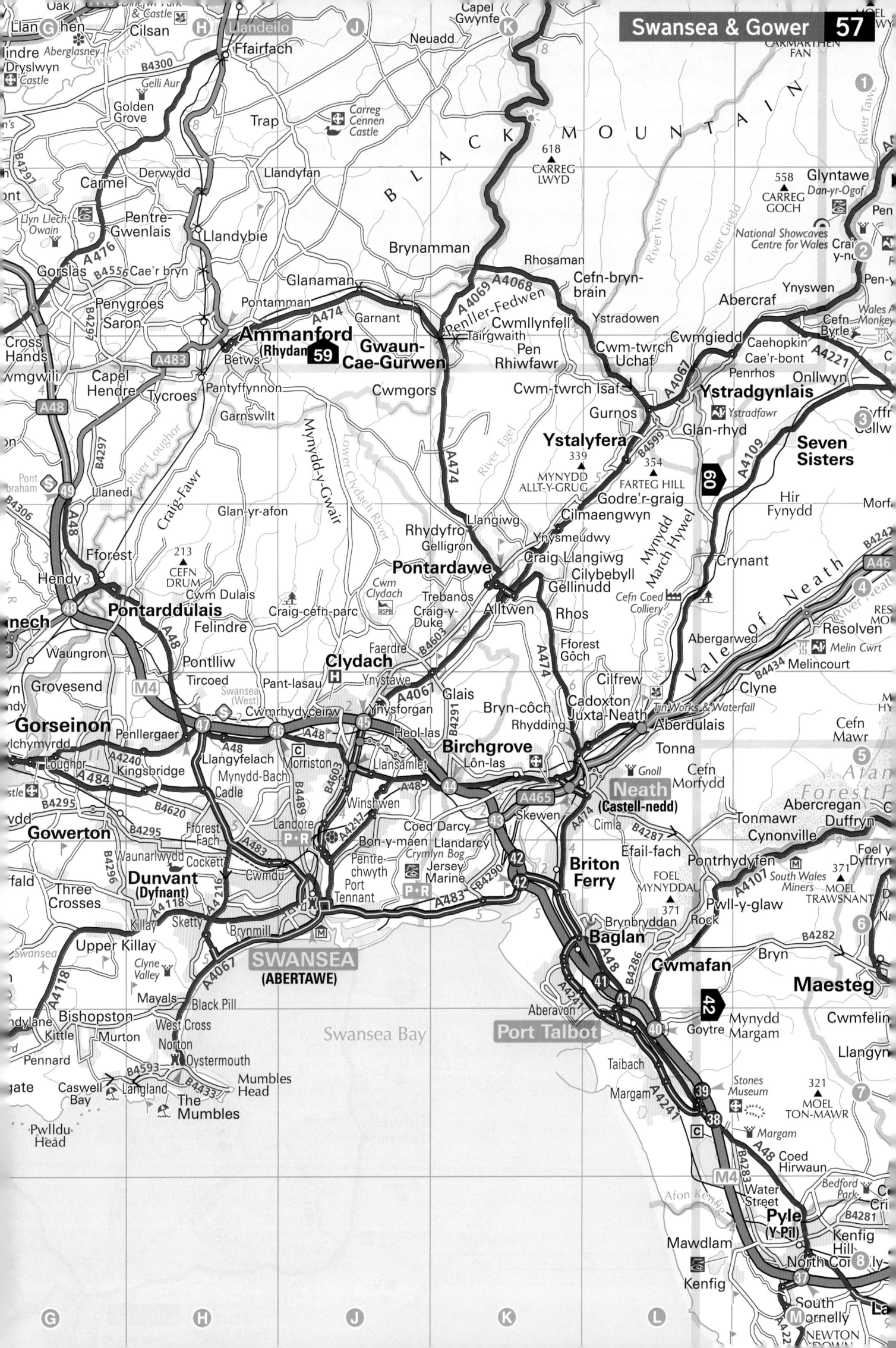

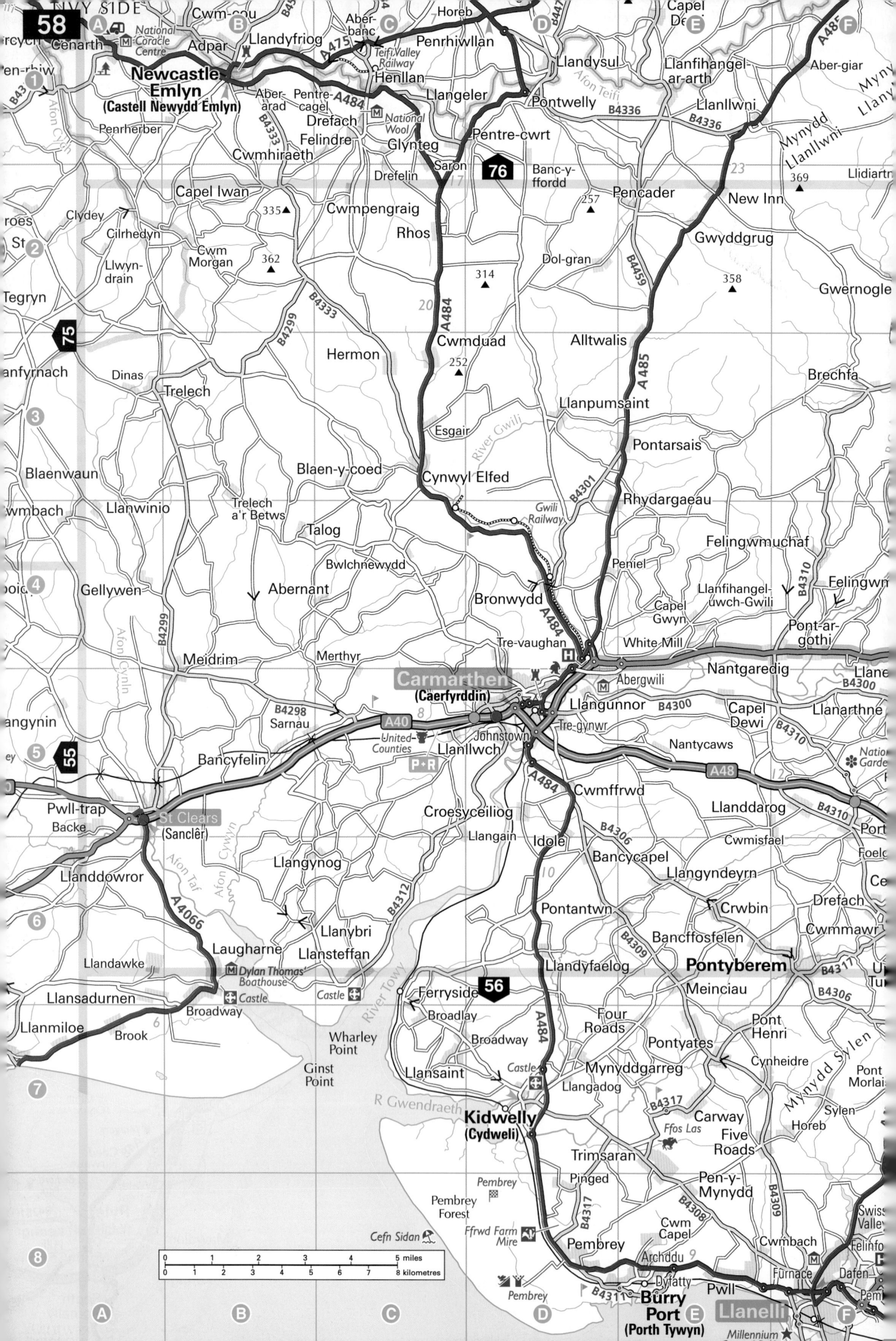

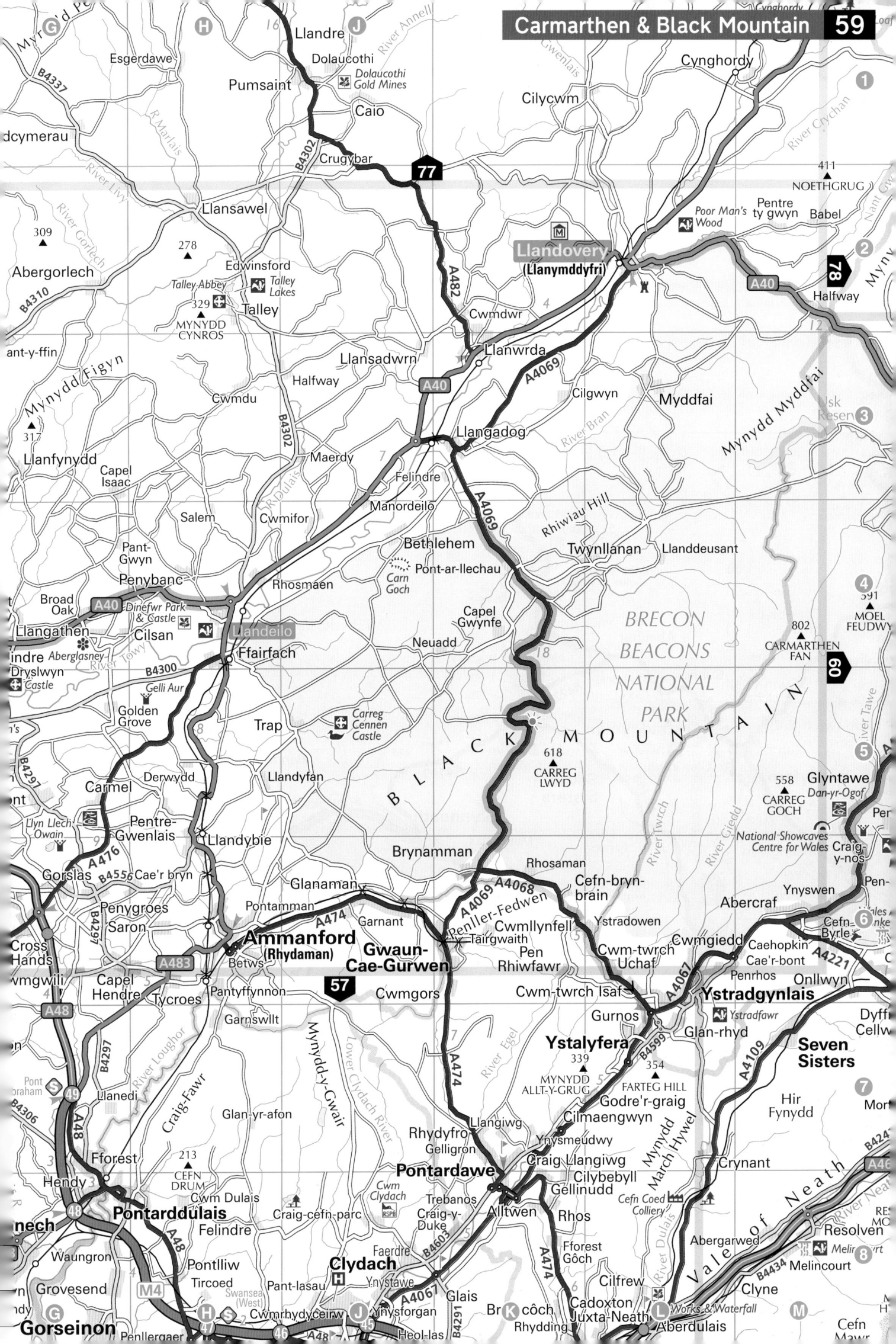

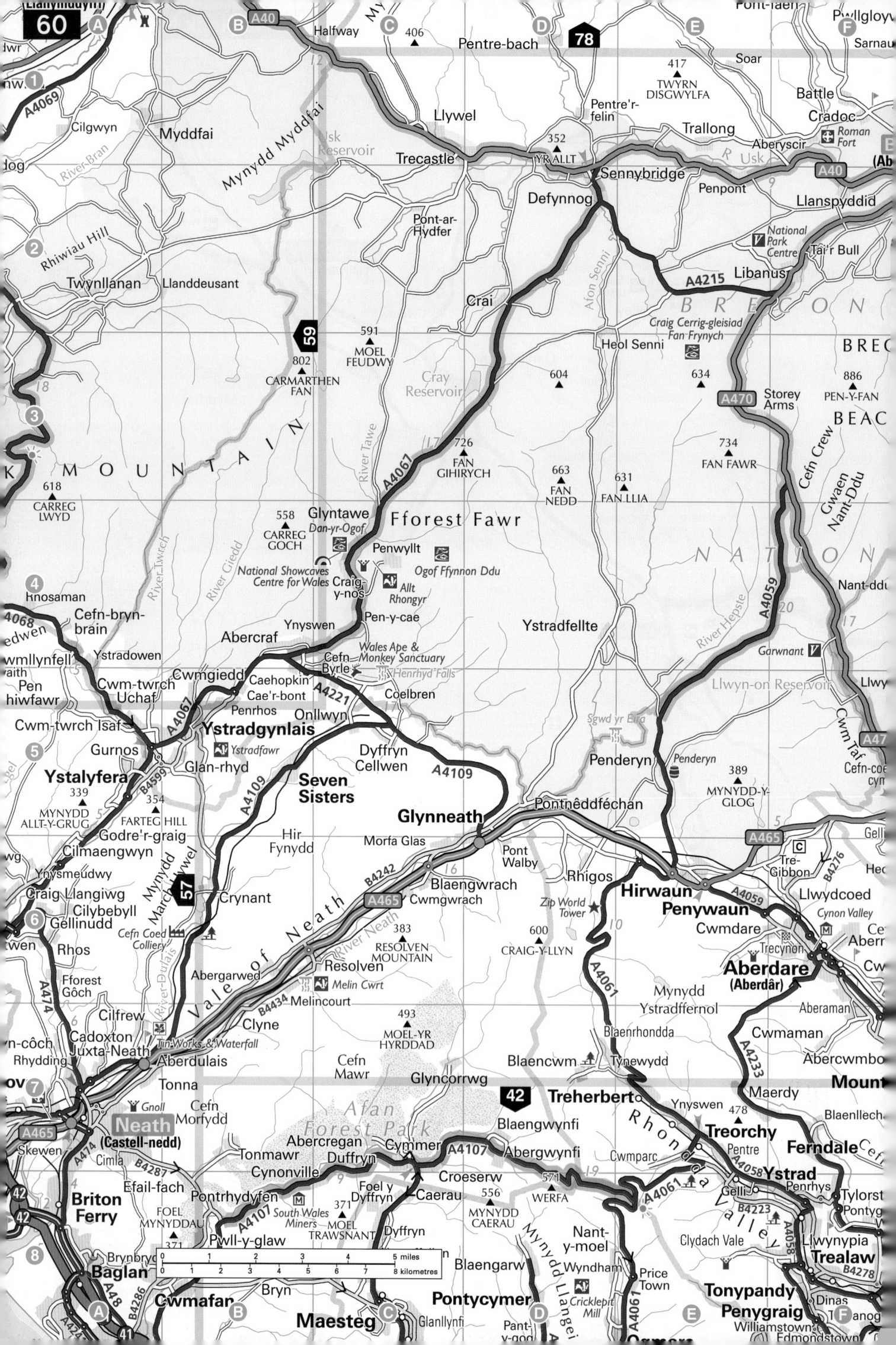

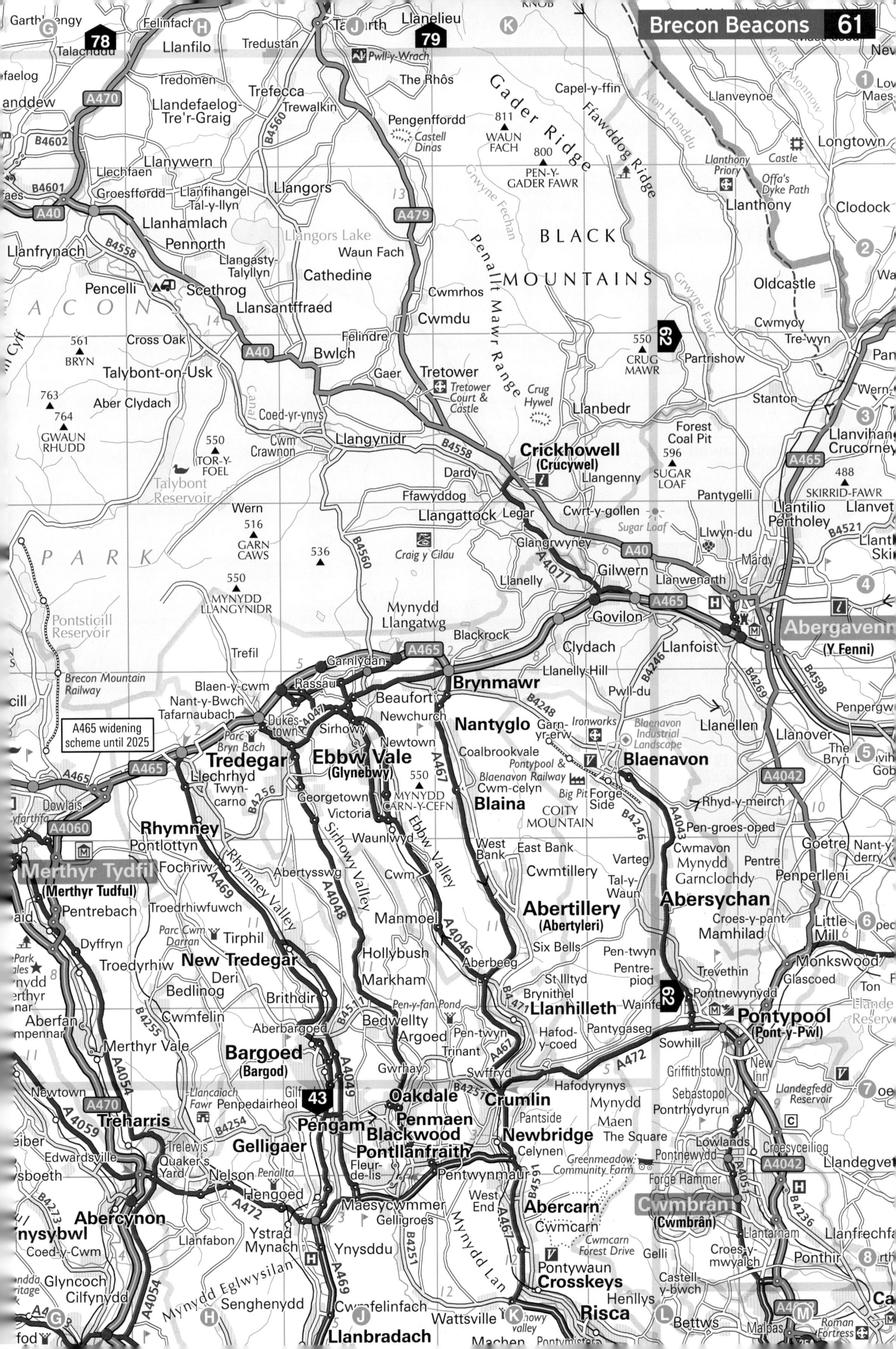

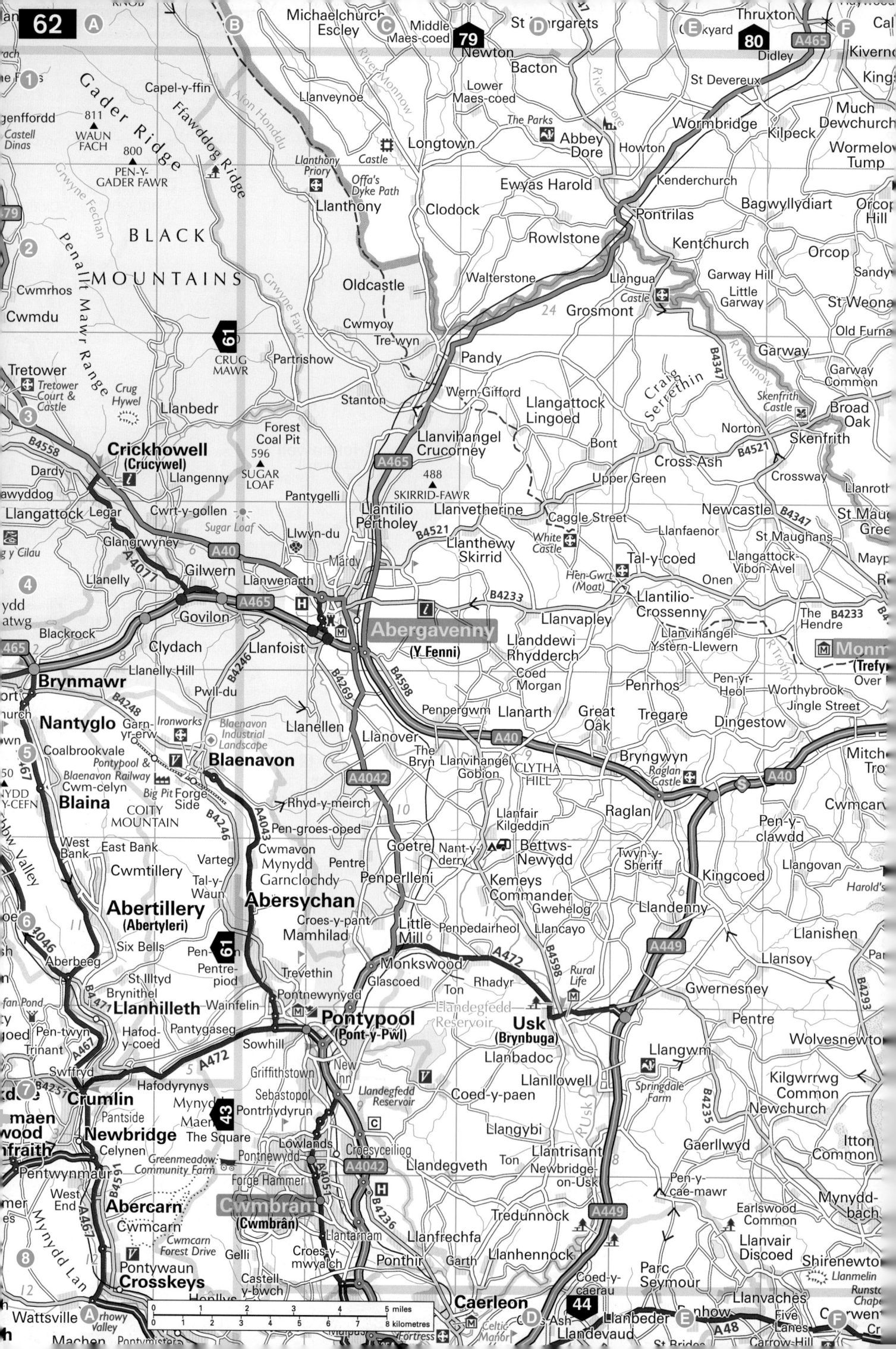

Aconbury
Newtown
Fownhope
Lower Buckenhill
Peartree Green
Sollers Hope
80
Hellens
Donnington
Tillers Green
Bromsberrow Heath
Kings
Pendock

Little Dewchurch
Ballingham
Brockhampton
Carey
Stocking
How Caple
Westons Cider
Much Marcle
Lyne Down
Dymock
St Mary's Church
Kempley
Playley Green
Lowbands
Elde

Little Birch
Much Birch
Pen-allt
Fawley Chapel
Perrystone Hill
Kempley Green
Poolhill
Redmarley D'Abitot
Staunton
Snig's End
Corse

A49
Hoarwithy
Llandinabo
King's Caple
Foy
Hole-in-the-Wall
Crow Hill
A449
Upton Bishop
Four Oaks
Shaw Common
Three Choirs
Brand Green
Upleadon
A42

Harewood End
Strangford
Brampton Abbotts
Phocle Green
4
Upton Crews
3
Gorsley
B4221
Newent
Blackwellsend Green
A4208
Hartpury

Netherton
Baysham
Rudhall
Linton
Gorsley Common
Kilcot
Malswick
Kent's Green
64

St Owen's Cross
etire
Upper Grove Common
Bridstow
S
Linton Hill
Aston Crews
Little Gorsley
Clifford's Mesne
Highleadon
Rudford
Maisemor

michaelchurch
A49
Peterstow
Ross-on-Wye
Weston under Penyard
Lea
Aston Ingham
B4216
Taynton
Tibberton
B4215
Highnam

B4521
Wilson
Wilton
Ashfield
Tudorville
Ryeford
Bromsash
B4222
Glasshouse
Dursley Cross
May Hill
Huntley
Bulley
RSPB
3

Three Ashes
Glewstone
A40
Hom Green
Coughton
Pontshill
East Dean
Boxbush
Glasshouse Hill
Longhope
Birdwood
A40
Churcham
GLOUC

cloudy
Llangarron
Pencraig
A4137
Goodrich Castle
Walford
Howle Hill
Hope Mansell
Mitcheldean
Little London
Blaisdon
Oakle Street
19
Hemps
Minsterwort

angrove
Marstow
Goodrich
Kerne Bridge
Crooked End
Drybrook
A4136
Abenhall
Plump Hill
Northwood Green
Elmore Back
Elmore

Welsh
ewton
Whitchurch
Old Forge
Wye Valley
B4234
Ruardean
Welsh Bicknor
Harrow Hill
Nailbridge
Flaxley
Chaxhill
Westbury-on-Severn
Farleys End
Quedgeley

Crocker's Ash
Great Doward
Symonds Yat (East)
Symonds Yat
Lower Lydbrook
Ruardean Hill
Brierley
Broadmoor
Popes Hill
Elton
Bollow
Longney
4

Dixton
Little Doward
Symonds Yat (West)
Doward
English Bicknor
Worrall Hill
Upper Lydbrook
Cinderford
Littledean
Stantway
Boxbush
Rodley
Hardwicke
Epney
B4008

Castle
The Kymin
Staunton
Christchurch
Hillersland
Berry Hill
Edge End
Sculpture Trail
Mile End
B4226
Ruspidge
A4151
Westbury Court Garden
Broadoak
Milton End
Upper Framilode
12

Wyesham
Monmouthshire
B4228
B4028
Broadwell
Beechenhurst Lodge
Forest
of
Dean
Upper Soudley
Newnham on Severn
Arlingham
Fretherne
Saul
Moreton Valence
5

enallt
Redbrook
Whitecliff
Coleford
Newland
Milkwall
New Fancy
Ruddle
Dean Heritage Centre
Lower Soudley
Brain's Green
Northington
Whitminster
B4071
Westend
Nupend
Naste

Pen-twyn
e-eagle
Perrygrove Railway
Highbury Wood
Puzzlewood
Sling
RSPB
Parkend
Yorkley
Blakeney
Awre
Frampton-on-Severn
Claypits
13
Stonehouse

Narth
hills
Clearwell
Marsh Lane
Ellwood
Stowe
Whitecroft
Nibley
Etloe
Slimbridge Wetland Centre
Shepherds Patch
Alkerton
Eastington
Cambridge
Middle Street
6

Whitebrook
Maryland
St Briavels Castle
B4231
Bream
B4234
Allaston
Dean Forest Railway
Purton
Slimbridge
Moorend
Frocester
Coaley
Tithe Barn
Leonard Stanley

Llandogo
Coldharbour
Hewelsfield
St Briavels
Lydney
Sharpness
Hinton
Halmore
Gossington
Lower Cam
Far Green
Nympsfield

Broadstone
Catbrook
Aylburton
Alvington
Smallbrook
Newtown
Wanswell
A38
Coaley
Nymp
Uley Long

Tintern
Tintern Abbey
Woolaston Common
Park Hill
Netherend
Hook Street
B4066
Breadstone
Berkeley Heath
The Quarry
Ashmead Green
Uley
64

Chapel Hill
A466
Offa's Dyke Path
Wye Valley
High Woolaston
Woolaston
River Severn
Berkeley
Dr Jenner's
Berkeley Road
Stinchcombe
B4058
B4066
7

Wye Valley
A48
Boughspring Lancaut
Stroat
Bevington
Woodford Stone
Ham
Newport
B4060
North Nibley
Dursley
Pitt Court
Millend
Woodmancote
A4135

Lancaut
Woodcroft
Tidenham
Wibdon
National Diving Centre
Shepperdine
Nupdown
Lower Stone
Michaelwood
S
Bournstream
Coombe
Lasbo

Castle
Tutshill
Sedbury
Oldbury-on-Severn
Hill
Oldbury Naite
Falfield
Whitfield
M5
Wotton-under-Edge
Newark Park
Ozle

Chepstow
(Cas-gwent)
Bulwarks Camp
2
Mathern
M48
Beachley
H
Littleton-on-Severn
Rockhampton
Lower Morton
Cowhill
Tortworth
B4509
Charfield
Kingswood
Abbey Gatehouse
Heritage Centre
Wortley
Alderley
Lower

St Pierre
45
B4061
Milbury Heath
romhall
Townwell
B4060
Treshar

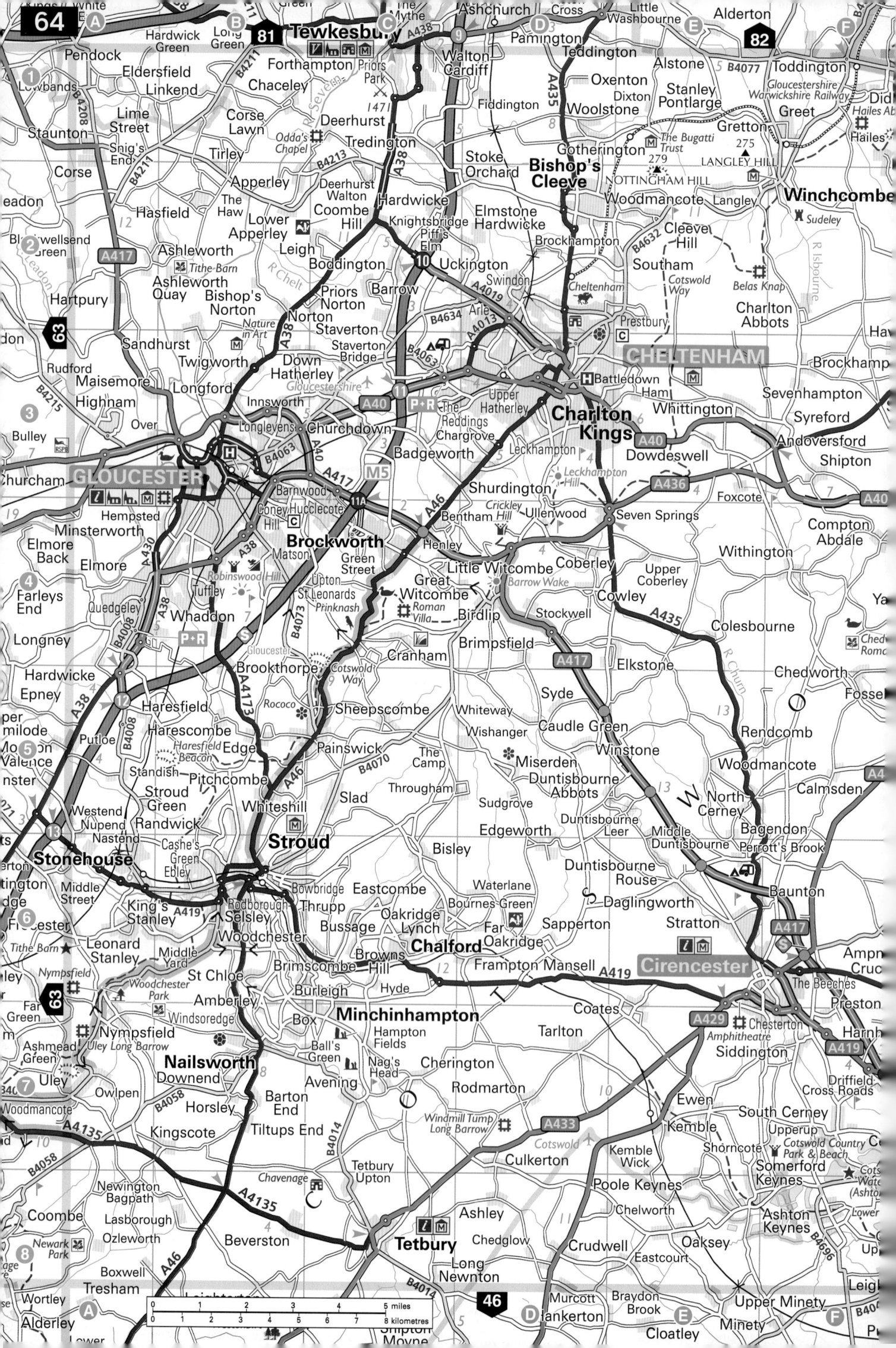

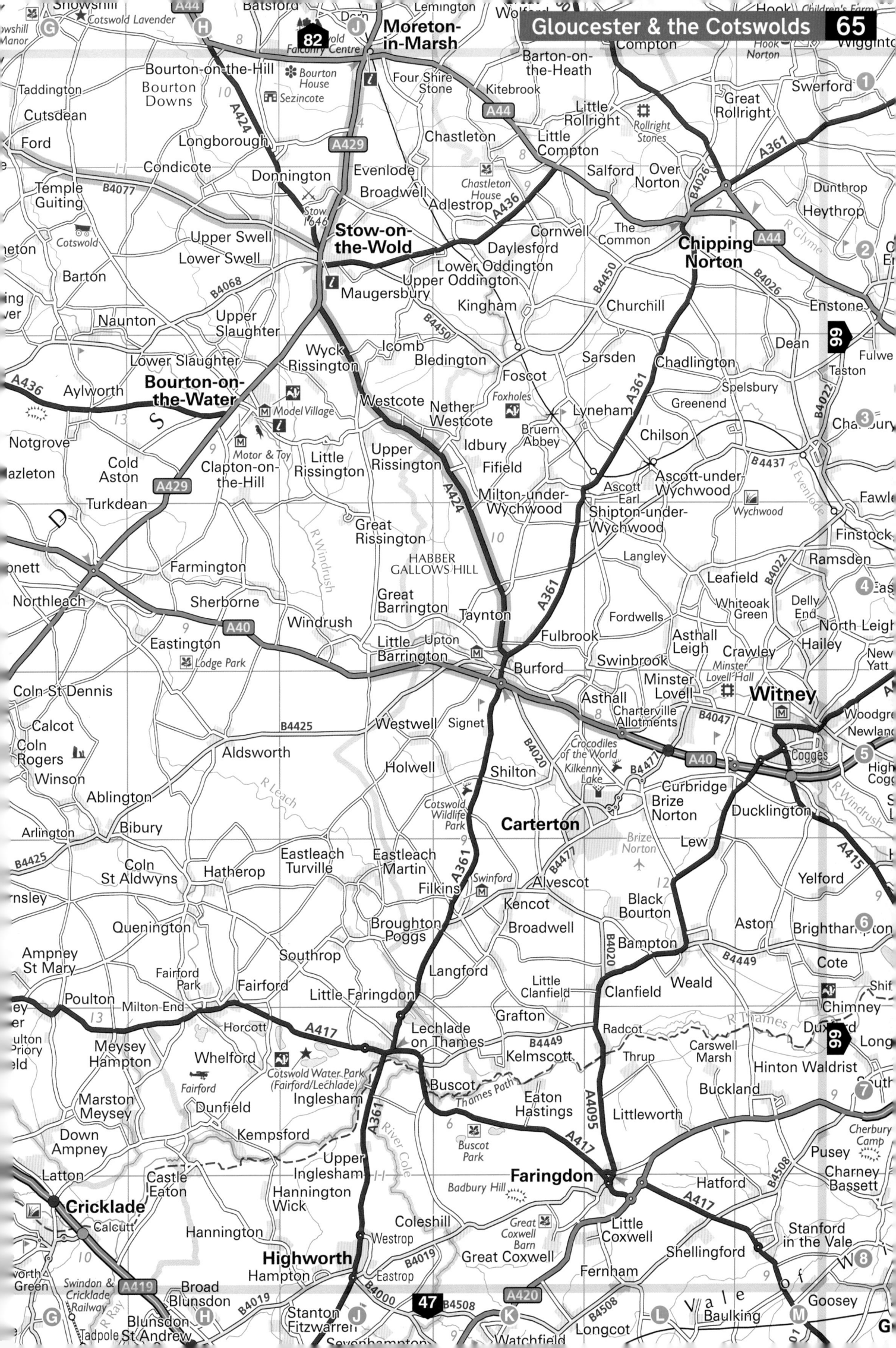

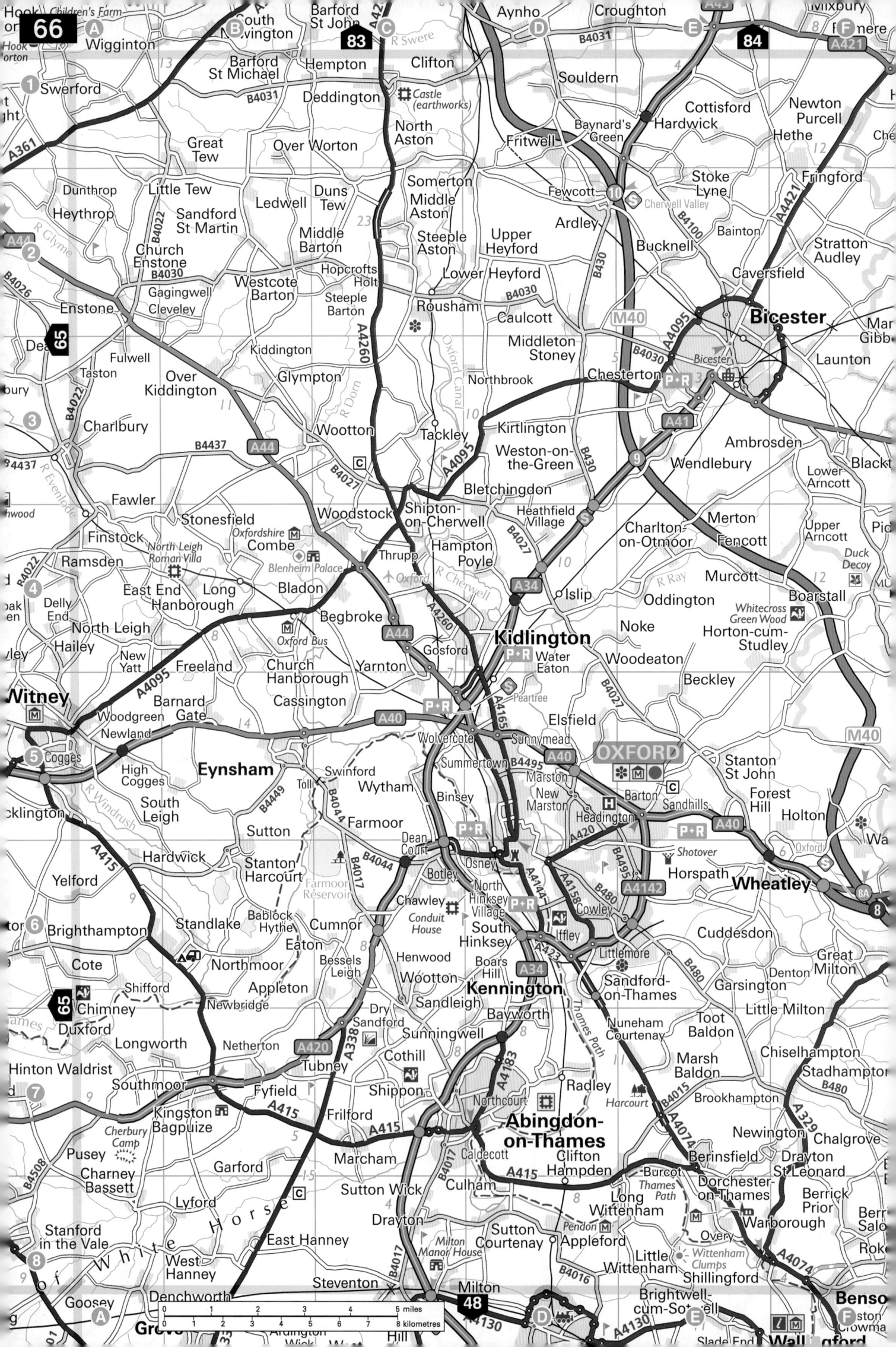

G
H
1
84
J
13
K
Bletchley
B403A

Thornborough
Nash
Waddesdon
Brickhill
Fro

Gawcott
Singleborough
Great Horwood
Thrift Farm
Newton Longville
Little Brickhill
Great Brickhill
Potsgrove
1

Padbury
Adstock
B4033
Little Horwood
Stoke Hammond
A5

Preston Bissett
Hillesden
Addington
Winslow
Mursley
Drayton Parslow
Linslade
Stockgrove
King's Wood
A5
2
A4

Steeple Claydon
Shipton
Swanbourne
Hollingdon
Soulbury
Leighton Buzzard
Leighton Buzzard Railway

Twyford
Middle Claydon
East Claydon
Granborough
Stewkley
Hoggeston
Linslade
Hockl
Clipstone

on
Claydon House
B4032
Dunton
Wing
Littleworth
Ascott
Grove
Stanbridg
B440

ndon
Calvert
Botolph Claydon
North Marston
Cublington
Burcott
Ledburn
Little Billington
Billingt
Eat
Gre

Edgcott
Finemere Wood
Oving
Whitchurch
Aston Abbotts
Nup End
Crafton
Wingrave
Horton
Slapton
3

A41
Grendon Underwood
QUAINTON HILL 186
Pitchcott
Hardwick
Weedon
Rowsham
Hulcott
Long Marston
Wilstone
Cheddington
Ivinghoe
Northall
B489

Kingswood
Quainton
Woodham
Buckinghamshire Railway Centre
Berryfields
Bierton
Burcott
Puttenham
Astrope
Marsworth
Windmi
4
Ast

Ludgershall
Westcott
Waddesdon
C
Watermead
Kingsbrook
Broughton
Wilstone Green
Tringford
Bulbourne
A41

Rushbeds Wood
Wotton Underwood
Waddesdon Manor
Upper Winchendon
Aylesbury
Buckland
Drayton Beauchamp
Tring Wharf
New Mill
Tring
B4635

Dorton
Upper Pollicott
Ashendon
Nether Winchendon
Stone
Lower Hartwell
H
Bedgrove
Aston Clinton
Weston Turville
Wilstone Green
Wigginton

Chilton
Lower Pollicott
Cuddington
Upton Dinton
Southcourt
Stoke Mandeville
Bucks Goat Centre
Halton
Dancersend
Hastoe
Wiggint
5

Chearsley
Long Crendon Courthouse
Westlington
A418
Sedrup
Bishopstone
North Lee
B4009
Worlds End
Wendover Woods
Ridgeway Path
Wigginton Bottom
Berkh

easington
Long Crendon
Haddenham
Ford
Marsh
Kimble Wick
Nash Lee Chiltern
A413
St Leonards
Wendover
Buckland Common
Cholesbury

ghall
Lower End
Tiggywinkles Wildlife Hospital
Aston Sandford
Little Kimble
Butler's Cross
Kingsash
Lee Clump
Hawl

rd
Shabbington
Thame
Church End
A4129
Owlswick
Meadle
Ellesborough
Great Kimble
Dunsmore
The Lee
Hunts Green
Lee Common
Bellingd

ck
A418
Rycote
Rycote Chapel
Kingsey
Ilmer
Askett
Pulpit Hill
Little Hampden
Ballinger Common
Chartri
6

ington
A329
Moreton
Towersey
Longwick
Monks Risborough
Whiteleaf
Cross (hill carving)
A413
Potter Row

ilton Common
B4012
Skittle Green
Pitch Green
Princes Risborough
Great Hampden
Prestwood
South Heath
Chesham
B485

A40
Emmington
Henton
Horsenden
Saunderton
Loosley Row
Great Missenden
Hyde Heath

Tetsworth
Sydenham
B4445
B4009
Bledlow
Chinnor & Princes Risborough Railway
Lacey Green
Bryant's Bottom
Roald Dahl
68

seley
Chalford
Kingston Stert
Chinnor
LODGE HILL 209
Rout's Green
Speen
Heath End
Little Kingshill
Little Missenden
Amershar

atchford
Postcombe
Oakley
Crowell
A4010
Saunderton
Walter's Ash
Great Kingshill
Cryers Hill
Amersham Old Town
7

toke
Adwell
Kingston Blount
Radnage
Bennett End
Bledlow Ridge
Bradenham
Hughenden Valley
Holmer Green
C

nage
Wheatfield
Aston Rowant
6
The City
West Wycombe
Naphill
Widmer End
Penn Street
A404

ton
South Weston
Lewknor
2
Beacon's Bottom
Hell-Fire
Hughenden Manor
Hazlemere
Tylers Green
Winchmore Hill
A355

Pyrton
Shirburn
5
Stokenchurch
A40
Horsley's Green
West Wycombe Park
Downley
HIGH WYCOMBE
Penn
Knotty Green
8

Cuxham
Watlington
B4009
Ibstone
Piddington
Sands
Cressex
P+R
Forty Green
Bekonscot Model Village

rightwell operton
Christmas Common
B482
Cadmore End
Wheeler End
Booker
Wycombe Marsh
A40
Loudwater
Wooburn

Britwell Salome
Northend
M40
8
Lane End
Bolter End
A404
B474

ne
Ridgeway Path
B480
G
Cookley Green
H
urville Heath
Greenfield
49
J
Fingest
Summer
Turvil
Bolter End
K
Handy Cross
L
Flackwell
M
Beaconsf

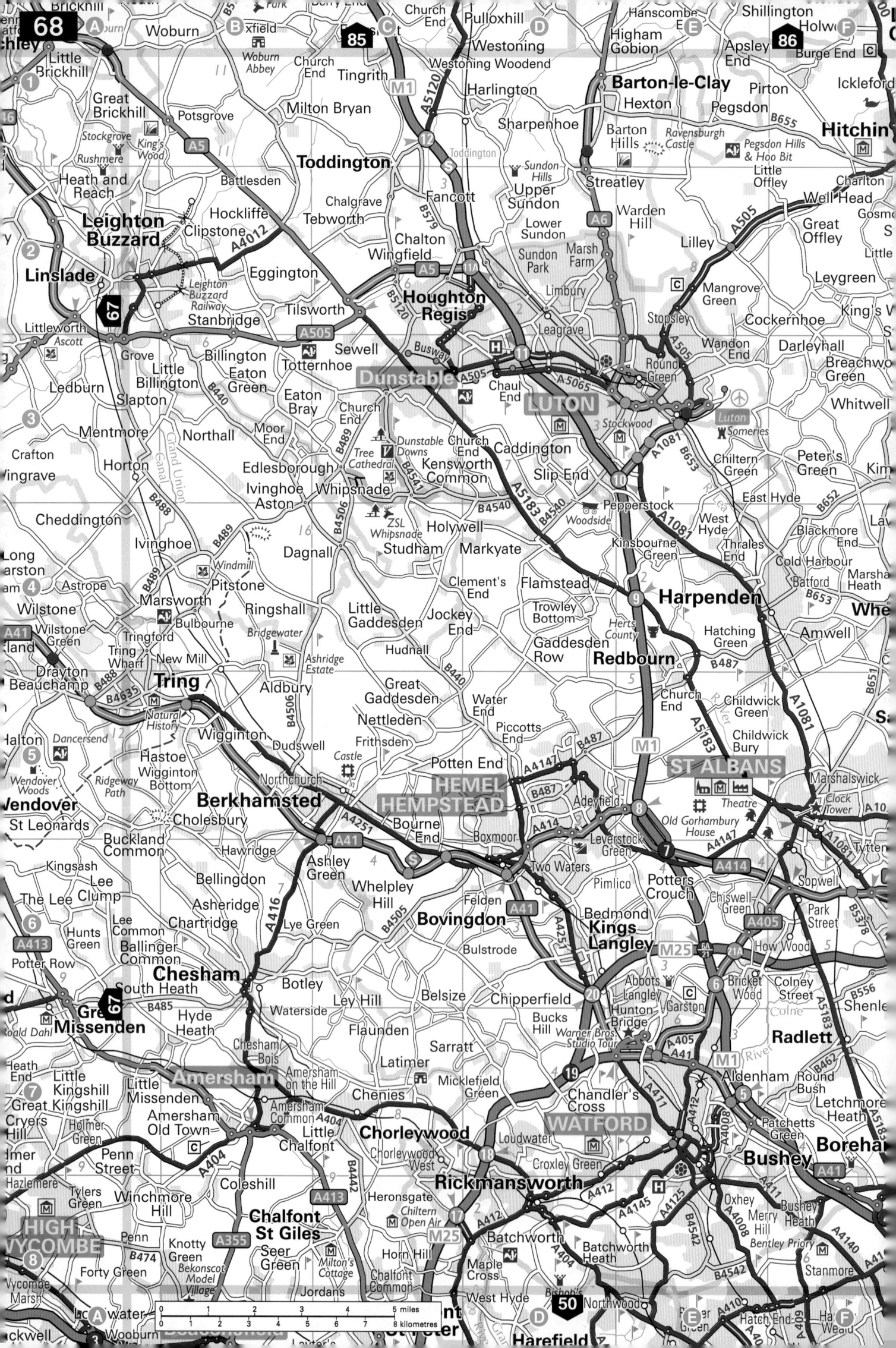

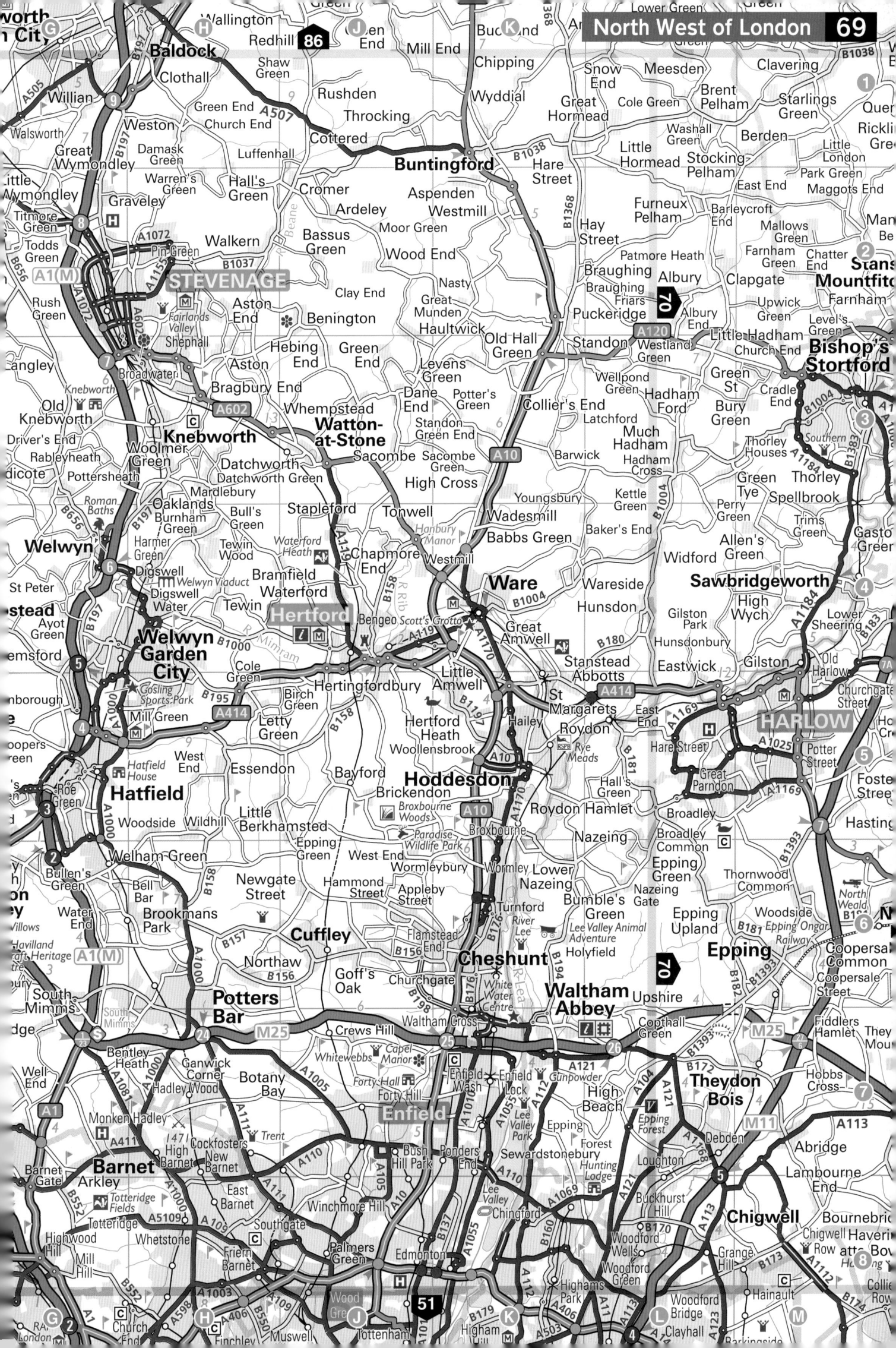

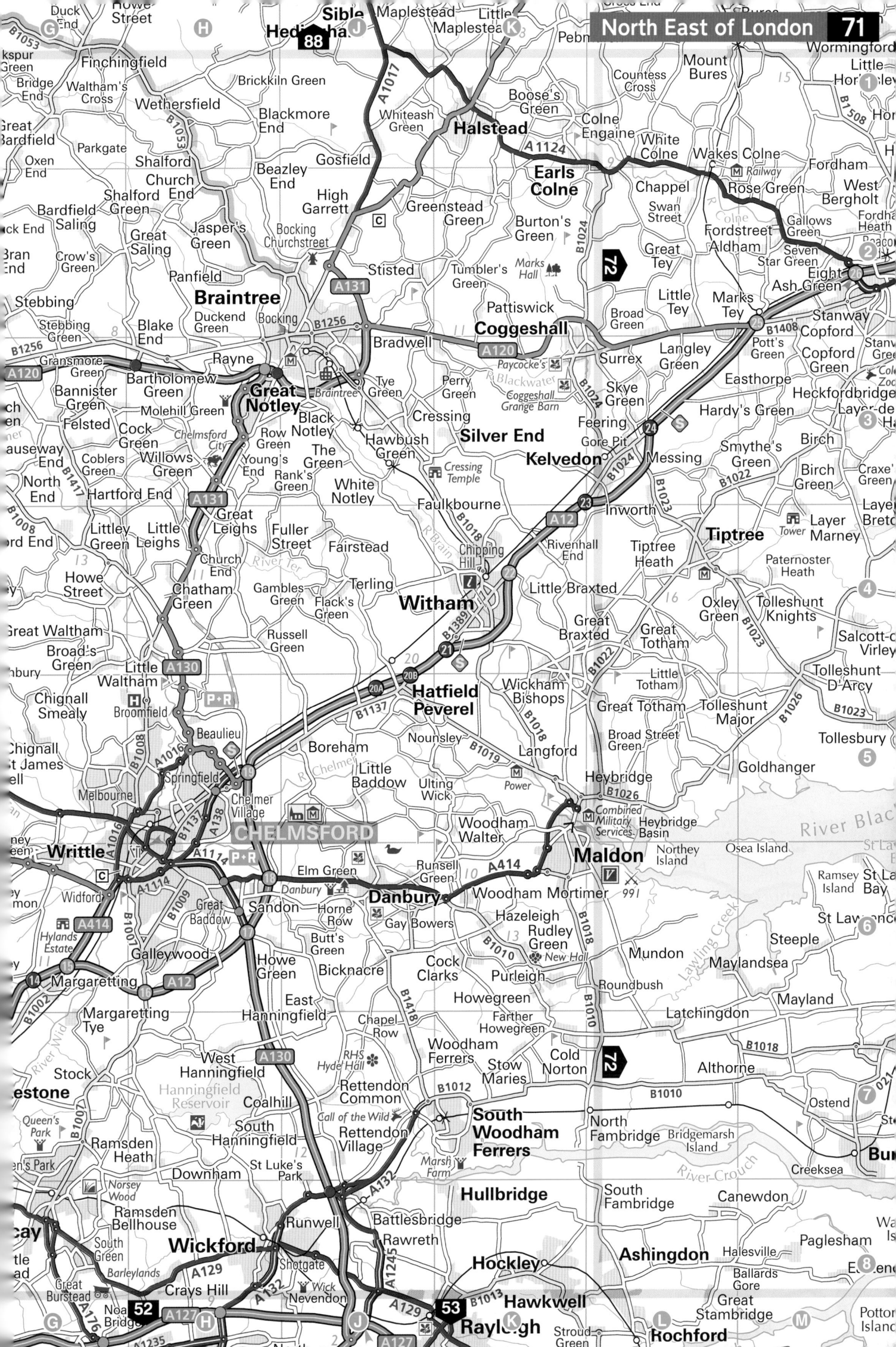

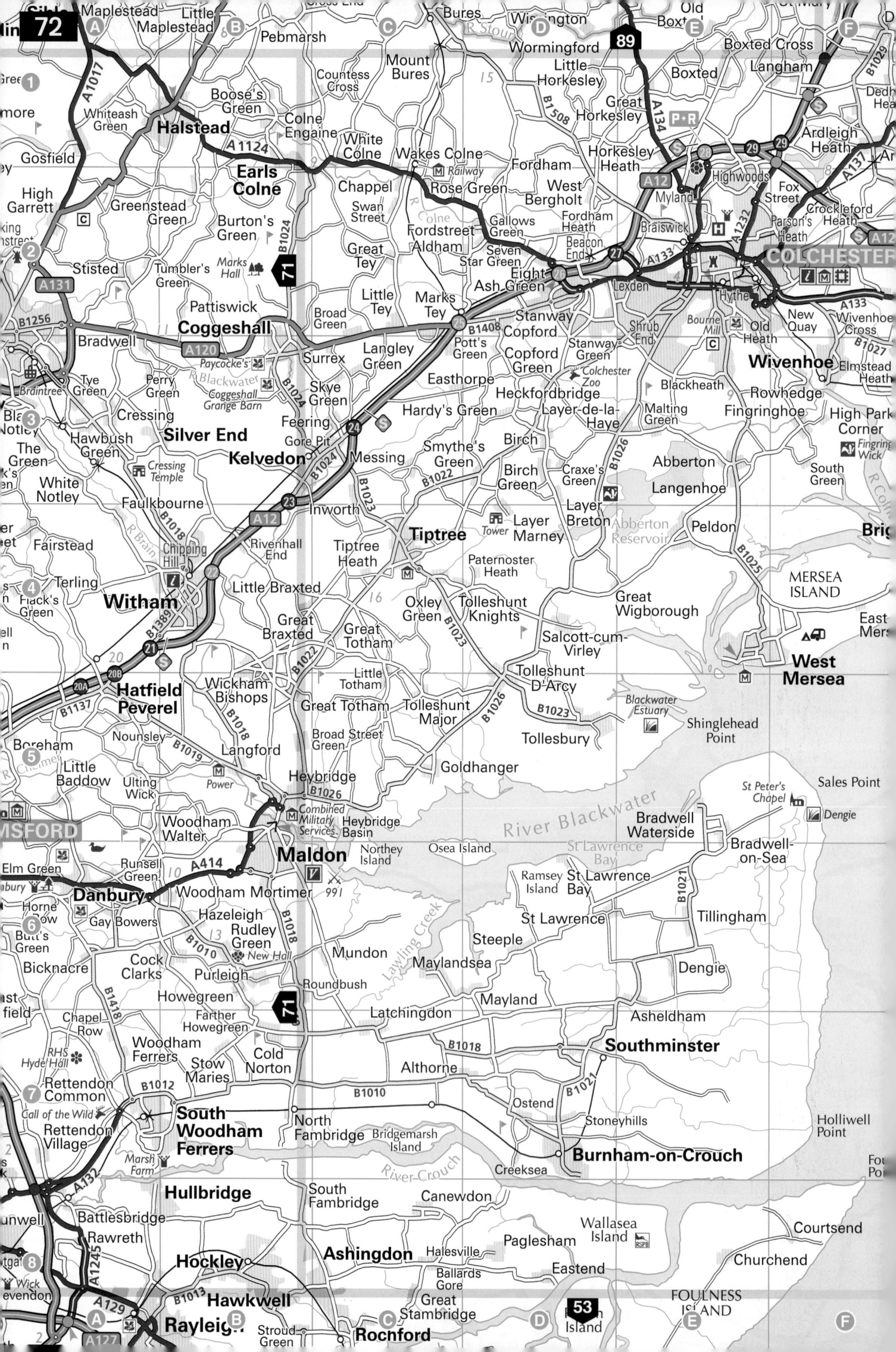

Brantham

ford M⃝ Cattawade
dge Cottage⃝ G⃝
ngtree

H⃝ Holbrook B⃝ J⃝ **90**

Gate

International
Ferry
Terminal

K⃝P⃝ *The Redoubt* ★

Felixstowe⃝ 62⃝ A154

Mistley Towers

River Stour

Wrabness

Parkeston Quay

Bath Side P⃝

M⃝ *Landguard Fort*

⊞ Mistley

New Mistley

Mistley
Heath

Bradfield

Bradfield Heath

B1352

Ramsey

Stour
Estuary

Parkeston

Upper
Dovercourt

Harwich
Harbour

Dovercourt

P⃝

Landguard
Point

Horsleycross
Street

Wix

A120

Little
Oakley

Harwich

M⃝

B1035

Horsley
Cross

19

Wix
Green

Great
Oakley

Tendring
Heath

Stones
Green

Pennyhole
Bay

Great
Bromley

Little
Bentley

Tendring Green

17

Hook of Holland

ad

A133

ating
een

Hare Green

B1414

Goose
Green

B1035

Beaumont

Horsey
Island

▣ *Hamford Water*

Frating
ad Row

Tendring

C⃝

Thorpe
Green

B1033

Thorpe-
le-Soken

Kirby-
le-Soken

*The Naze
& Tower* V⃝ The Naze

Great
Bentley

S⃝

Weeley

B1033

16

B1441

Weeley
Heath

Kirby Cross

B1034

**Walton-on-
the-Naze**

Aingers
Green

A133

B1414

Cook's
Green

Frinton-on-Sea

Thorrington

Little Clacton

B1442

Great
Holland

B1032

Samson's
Corner

Great
Clacton

▲ Holland Haven

Hurst
Green

B1027

St Osyth

Rush
Green

B1032

Holland-
on-Sea

ea

Jaywick

Colne
Point ▣

Point Clear

CLACTON-ON-SEA

ℹ⃝

Colne Point

①
②
③
④
⑤
⑥
⑦
⑧

G⃝   H⃝   J⃝   K⃝   L⃝   M⃝

G   H   J   K

1

2

76

3

4

5

6

7

8

Ceredigion
Heritage Coast

Cardigan
Island
Mwnt Beach
Parcllyn
Aberporth
Cardigan Island
Coastal Farm
Y Ferwig
Blaenannerch
Gwbert on Sea
Penparc
Tremain
Blaenport
Poppit
Sands
Abbey &
Coach House
Pembrokeshire
Coast Path
St Dogmaels
Cardigan
(Aberteifi)
Beula
Bridgend
Llangoedmor
B4570
St Dogmaels Moylgrove
Heritage Coast
Ceibwr
Bay
Welsh
Wildlife Centre
Llechryd
Ponthirw
Pen-y-
bryn
Llandygwydd
Moylegrove
Monington
Teifi
Marshes
Castle
TIVY SIDE
Trwyn y bwa
Glanrhyd
Llantood
Cilgerran
Afon Teifi
Nat
Abercych
Cenarth
Cora
DINAS
Gethsemane
Bridell
Pen-rhiw
Cent
as Head
HEAD
Newport
Bay
Berry Hill
Nevern
B4582
Pontgarreg
Pengelli
Forest
A487
Rhoshill
B4332
New
E
(Castell M
Bryn-
Henllan
Felindre
Farchog
19
Newchapel
Penrherbe
Parrog
Newport
Eglwyswrw
Boncath
Dinas Cross
Castell
Henllys
B4332
Mynydd
Melyn
Carreg
Coetan
Pontygynon
Llanfair-
Nant-Gwyn
Blaenffos
aun)
311
Pentre
Ifan
Whitechurch
Bwlch-y-groes
Clydey
Llanychaer
MYNYDD
CAREGOG
Crosswell
Pontyglasier
Cilrhedyn
Penlan
Uchaf
Star
Cwm
Gwaun
Brynberian
21
PEMBROKESHIRE COAST
Crymych
Llwyn-
drain
Pontfaen
Tafarn-
y-bwlch
Foel Drygarn
Tegryn
B4329
MYNYDD PRESELI
Hermon
Foel
Eryr
NATIONAL PARK
536
265
58
Puncheston
FOEL
CWMCERWYN
Mynachlog ddu
Pentregalar
Llanfyrnach
Dinas
New Inn
368
Rosebush
Gors
Fawr
FOEL
DRYCH
Glandwr
Castlebythe
26
Tufton
Llandre
Isaf
Hebron
Blaenwaun
gwells
Maenclochog
Henry's Moat
(Castell Hendre)
Llanglydwen
Cefn-
y-pant
Cwmbach
Llanwin
Wallis
Woodstock
Llangolman
B4313
Glandy
Cross
Pant-y-caws
Cwmfelin
Mynach
Ambleston
Llys-y-frân
Reservoir
New
Moat
Efailwen
Maesgwynne
Llanboidy
Gellywen
riffleton
B4329
Llanycefn
55
Login
rd Gest
Walton
East
Pen-ffordd
Crosshands
Clarbeston
Llandissilio
Llanfallteg
Henllan
Amgoed
Clarbeston
Road
Bletherston
Clunderwen
Llanfallteg
West
Llangynin
Castle
Gelly
Cwmfelin
Boeth
Whitland Abbey
ale
Wiston
Castle
Bethesda
A40
Fenton Brook
Llawhaden
Redstone
10
M-trap
ffordd)
Slebech
Clerkenhill
Robeston
Wathen
Penblewin
Llanddewi
Velfrey
hitland
Trevaughan
Backe
Canaston

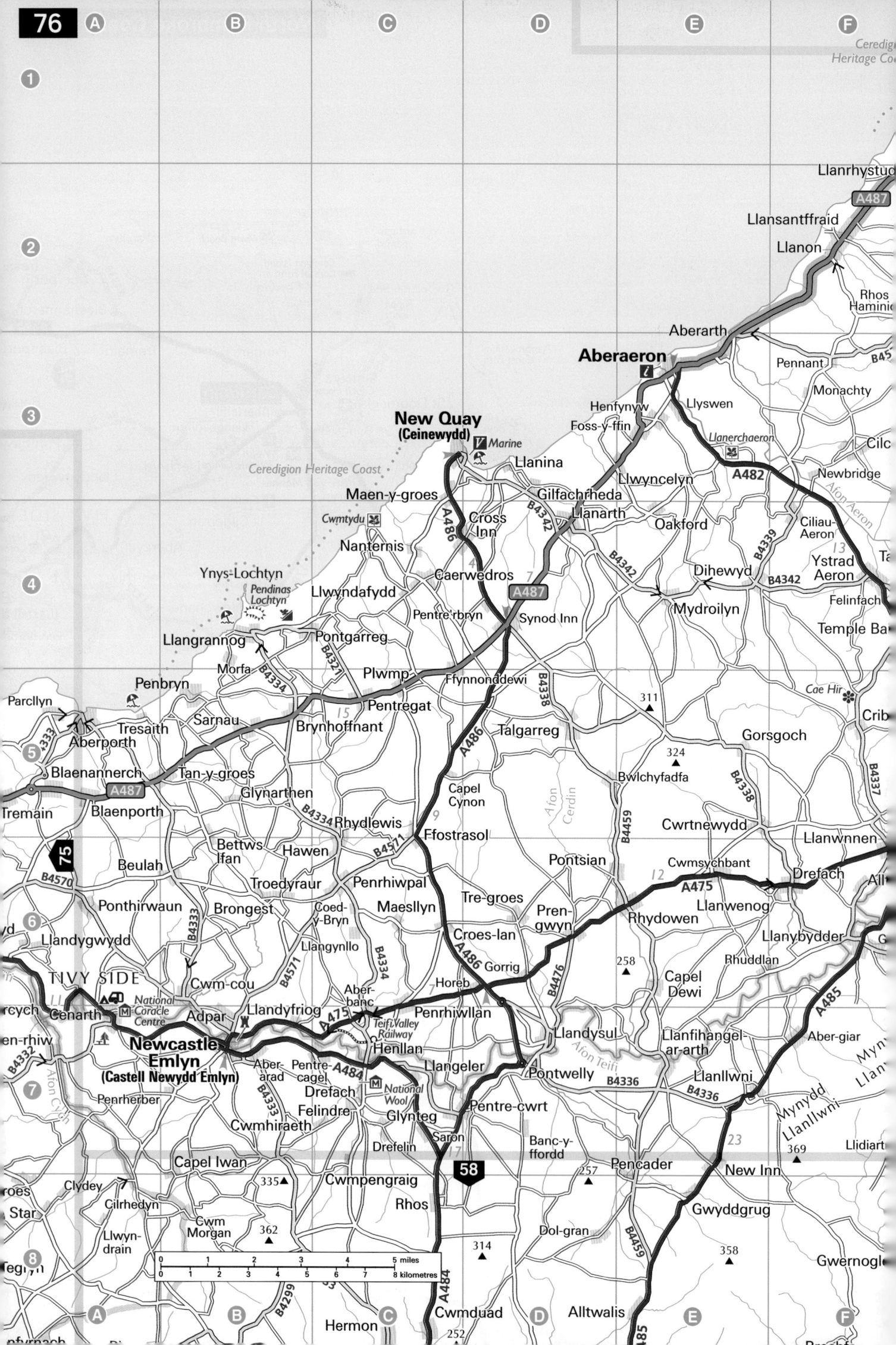

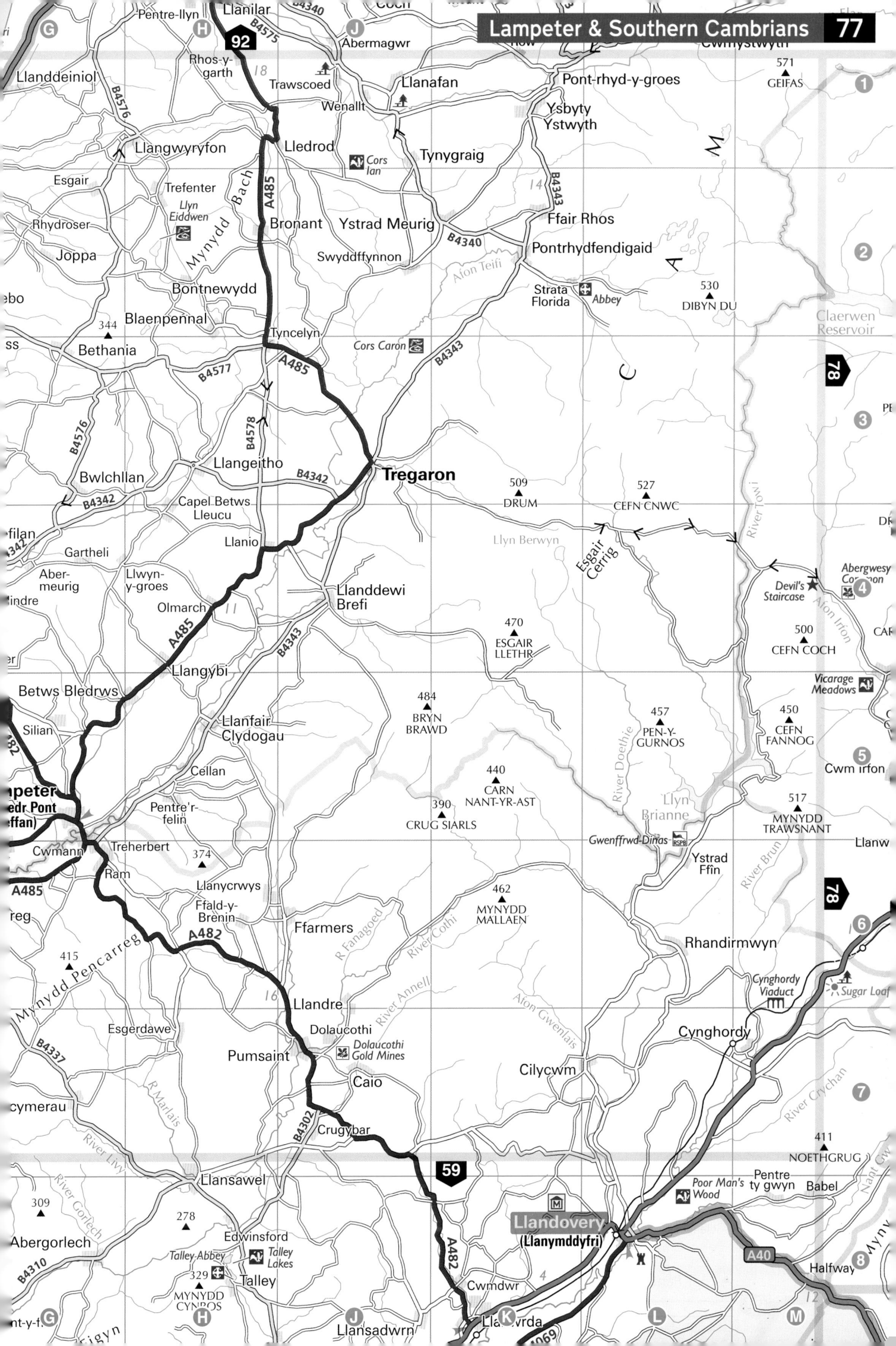

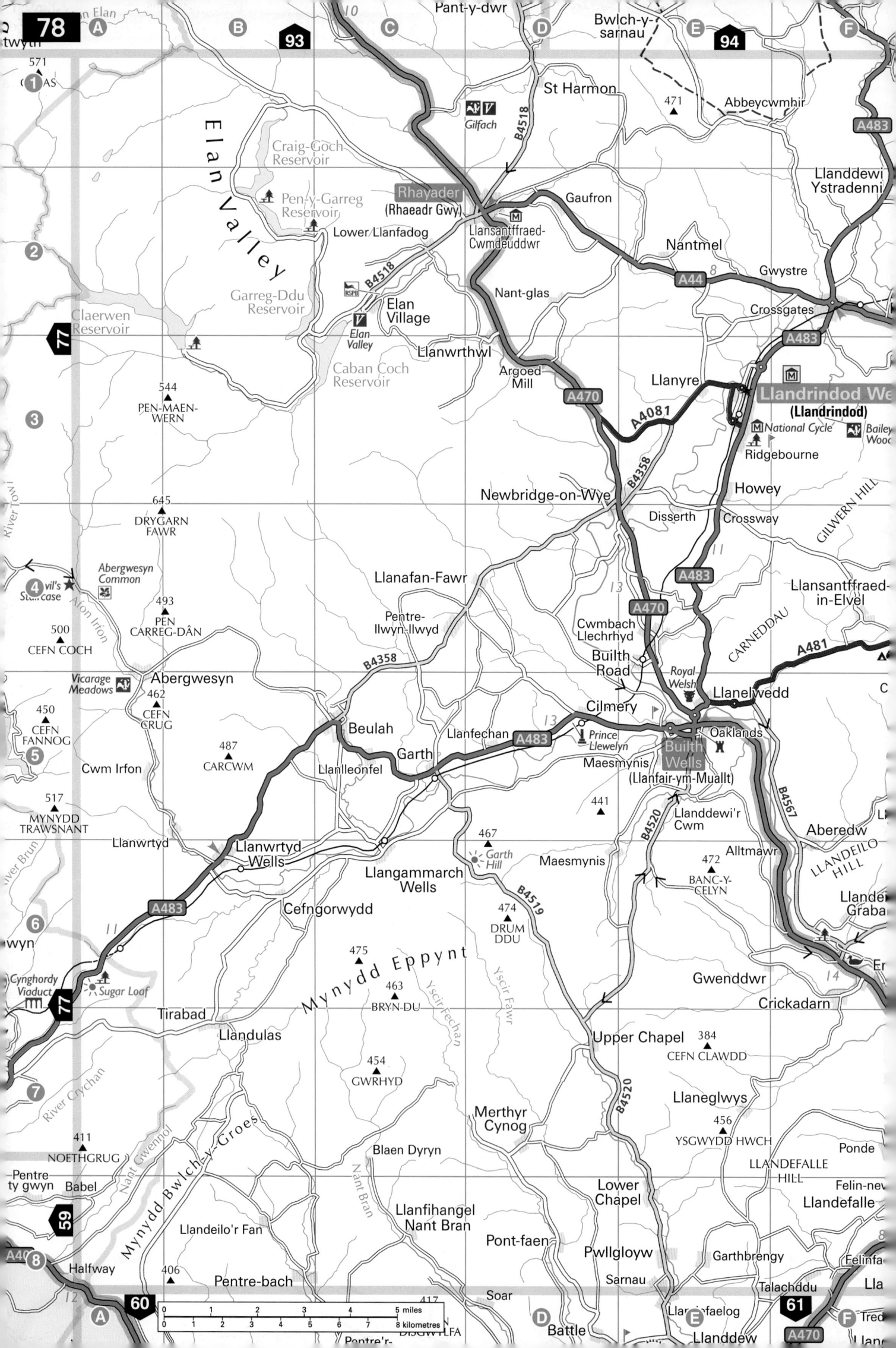

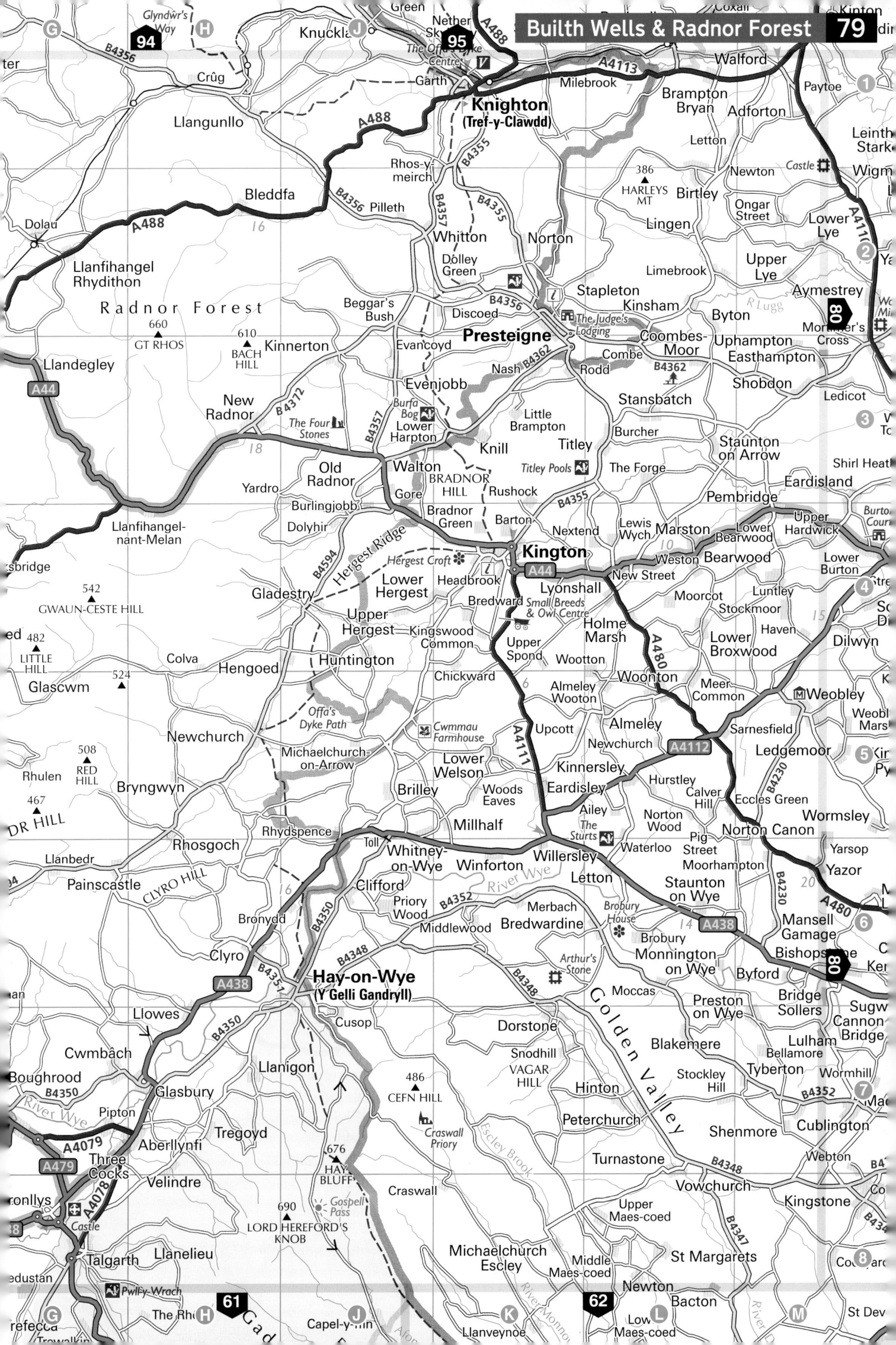

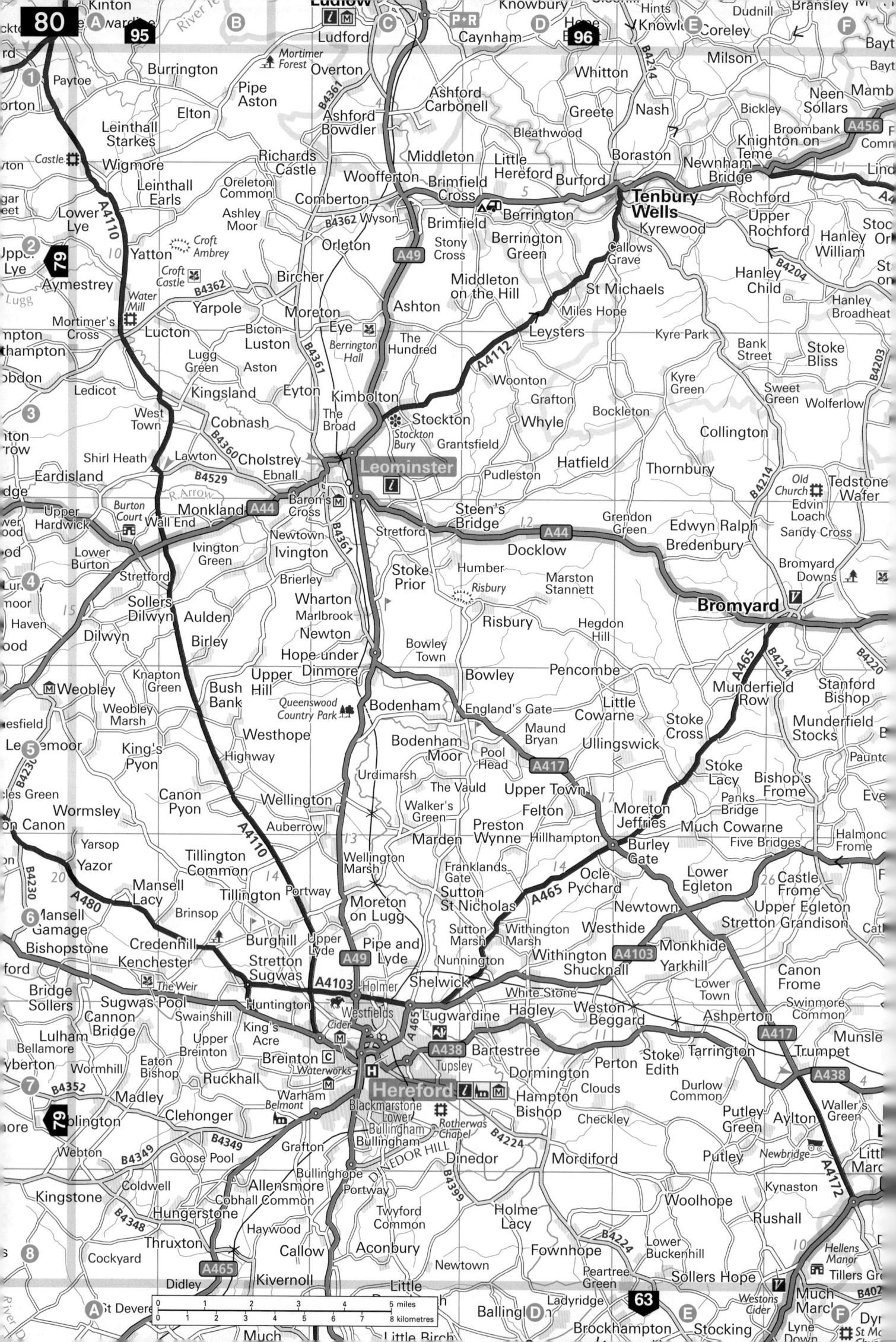

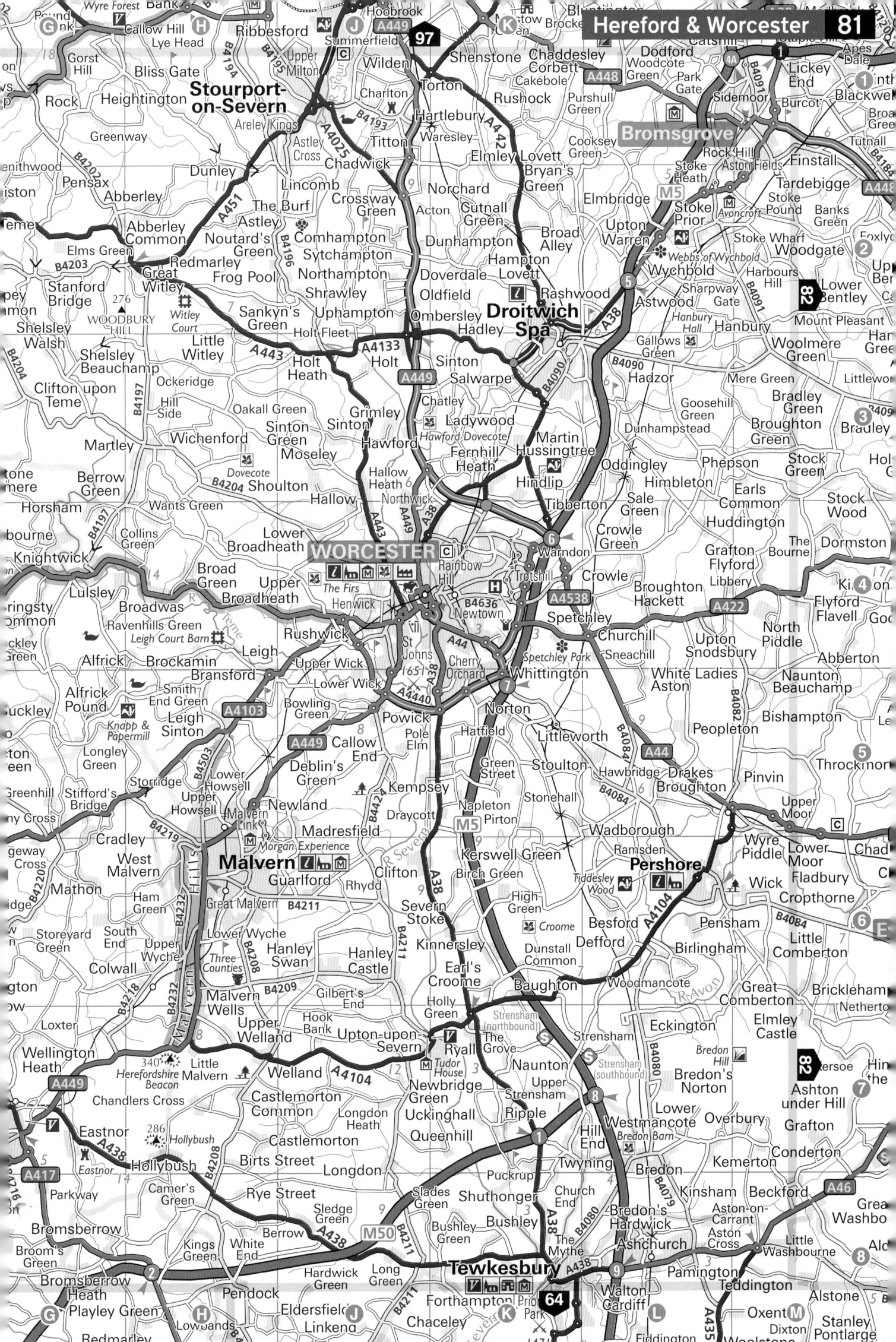

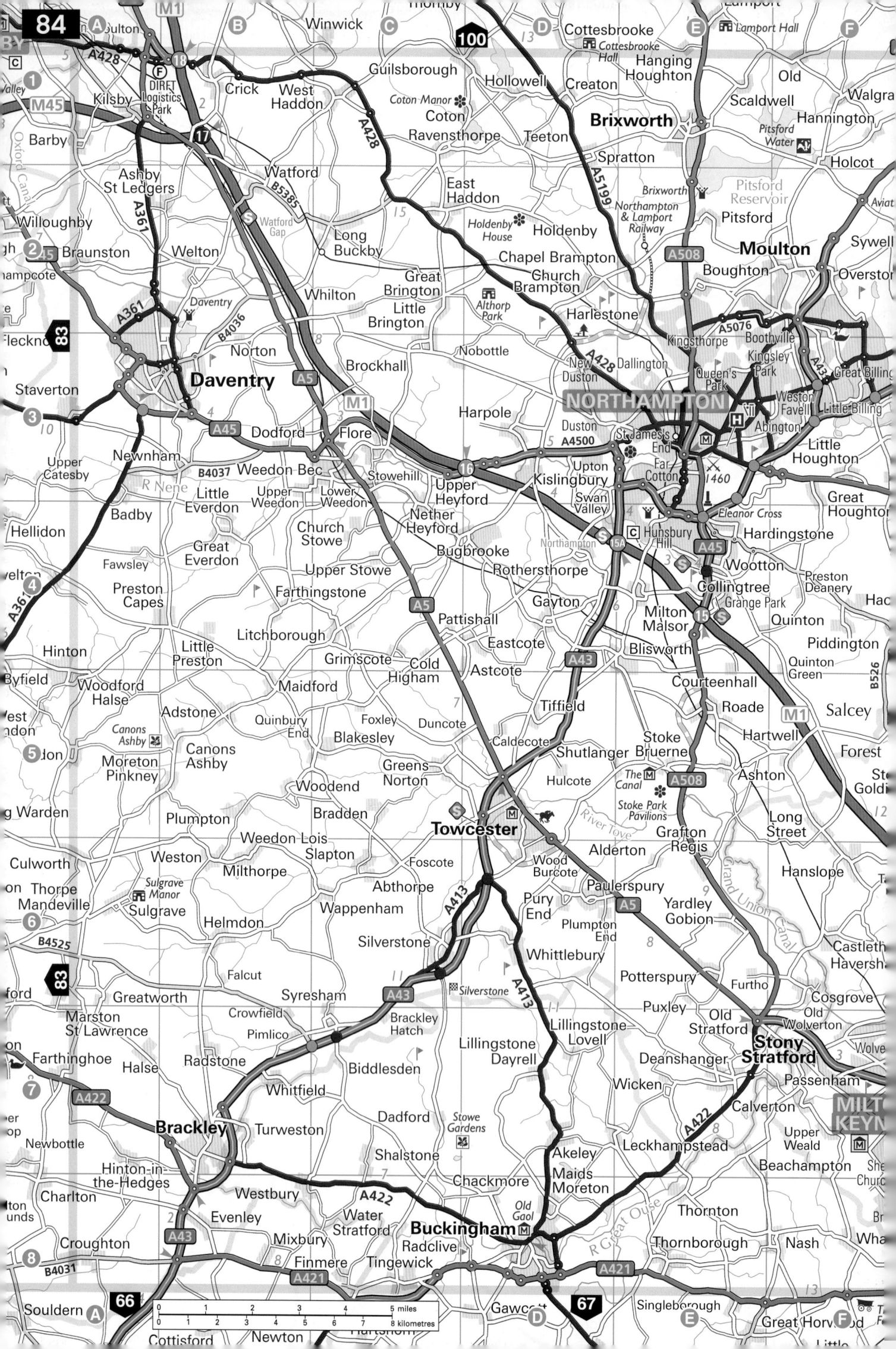

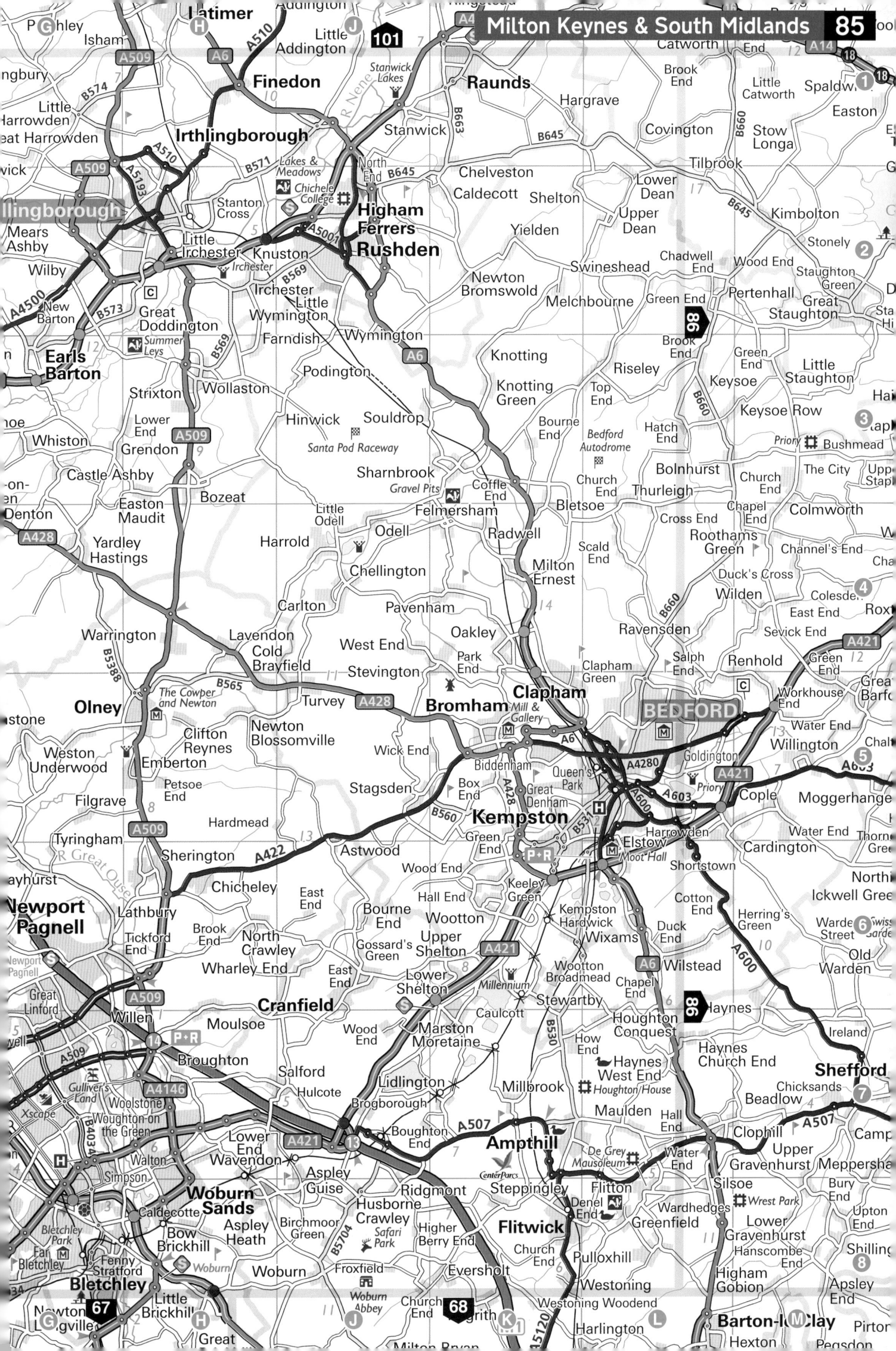

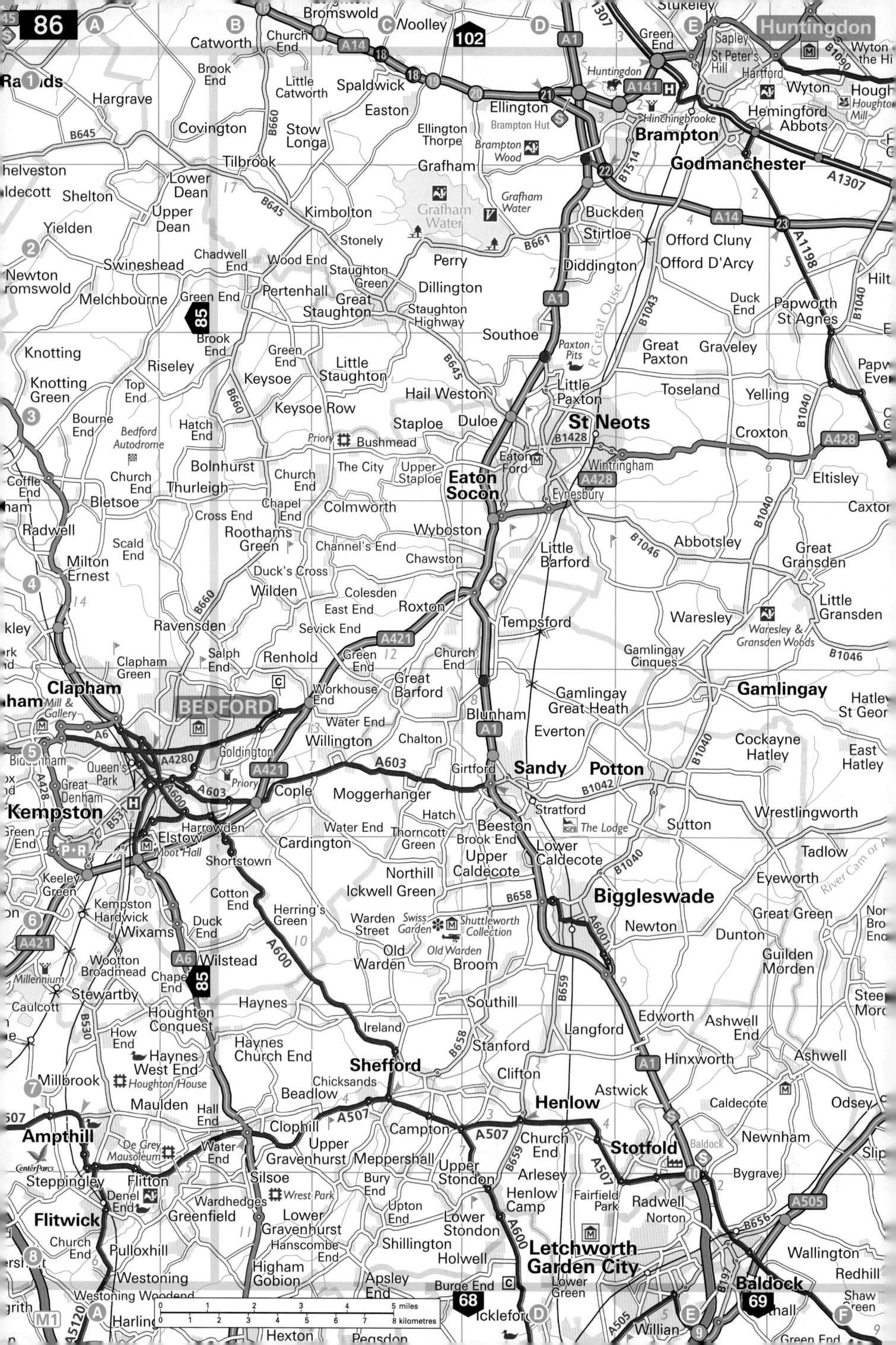

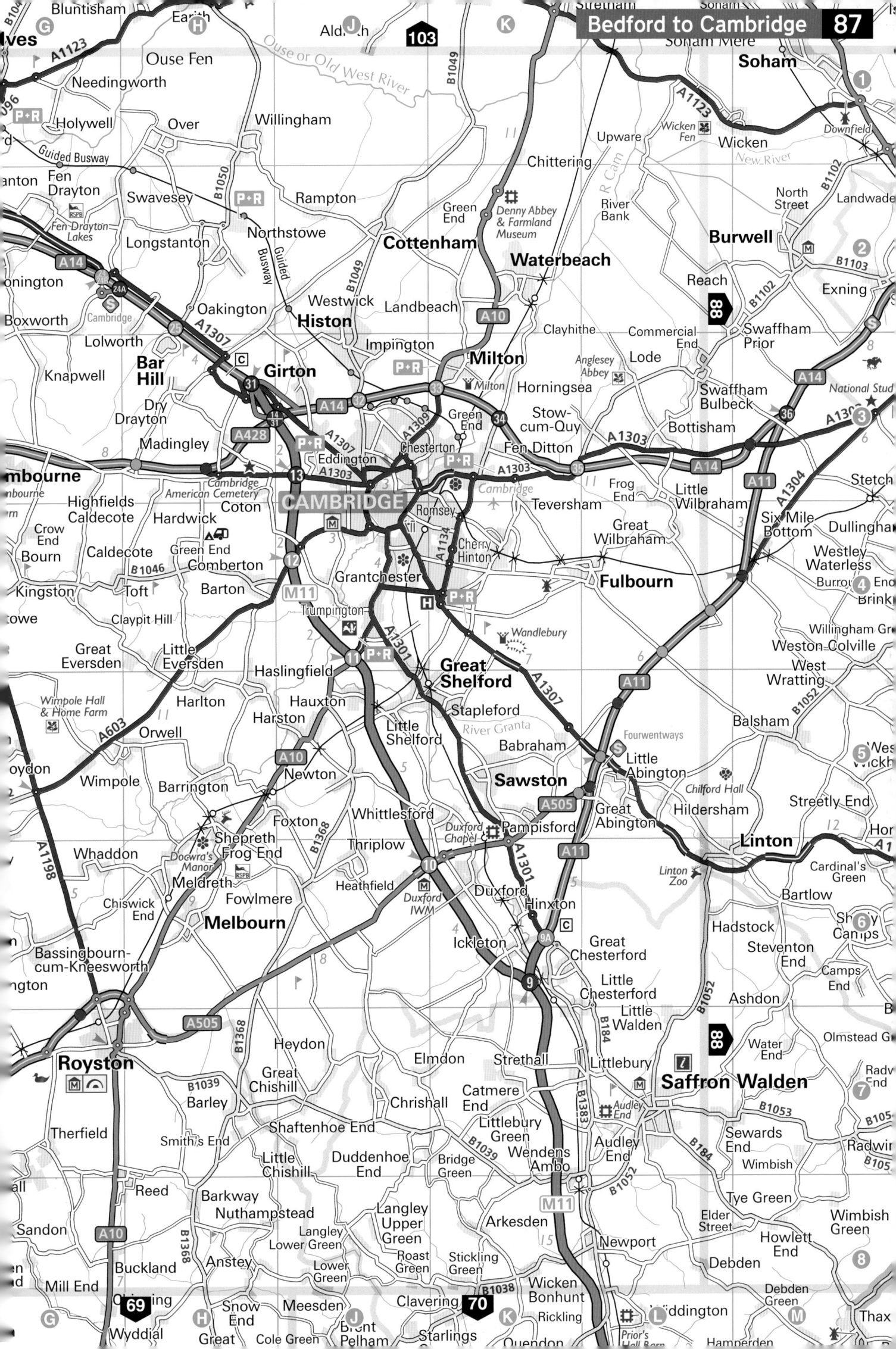

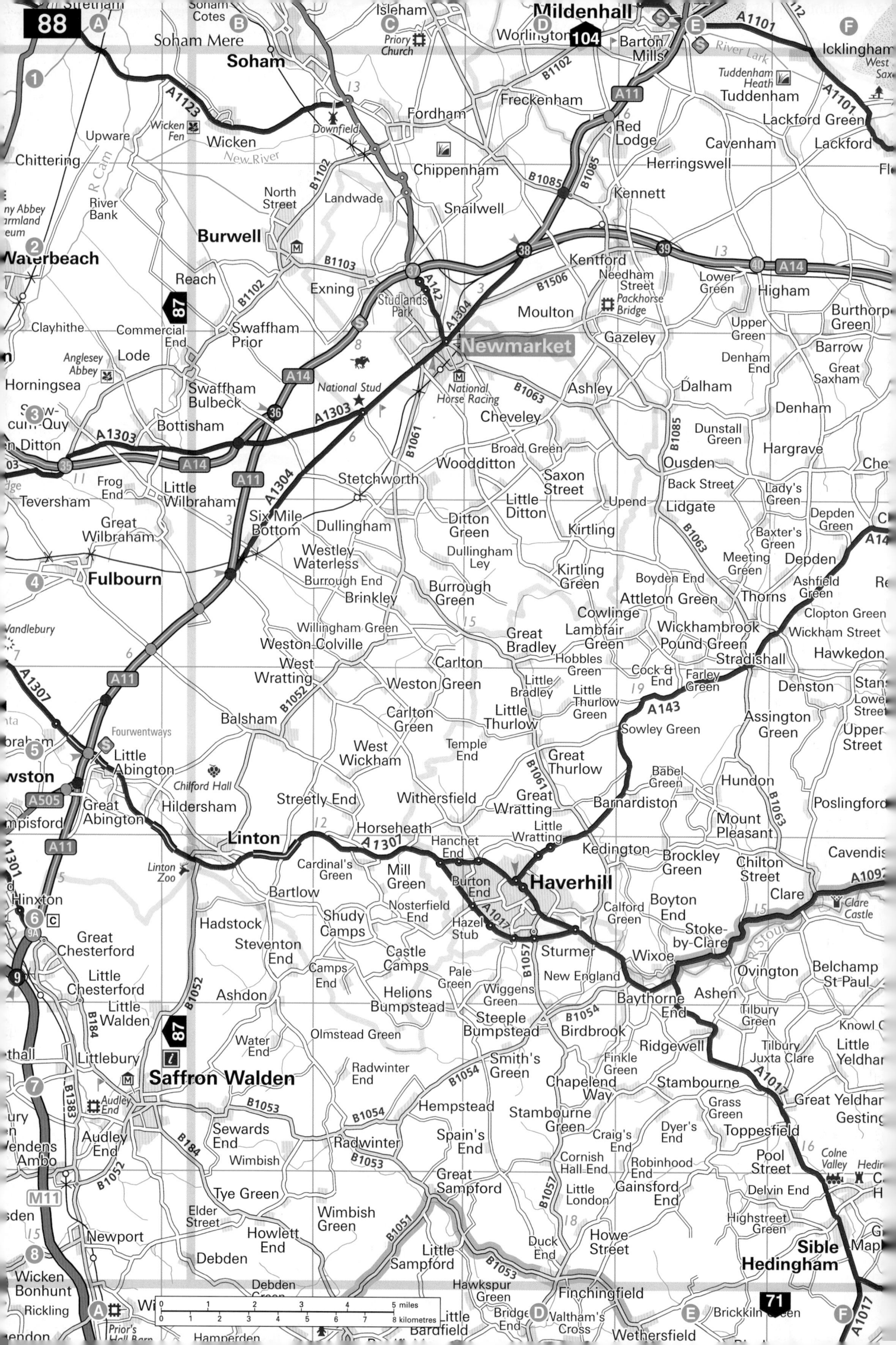

G H J 105 K

Bardwell
Ixworth Thorpe
Stanton Wattisfield
Troston Bangrove Upthorpe Walsham le Willows Allwood Green Mill Street Thornham Parva
Ampton Great Livermere Wyken Cranmer Green Gislingham Thornham Magna
Brockley Ingham West Street Crowland Finningham Wickham Street
Culford Timworth Ixworth Langham Badwell Ash Westhorpe Wickham Skeith
Fornham St Genevieve Timworth Green Conyer's Green Hunston Long Thurlow Wyverstone Street Wickham Green
Saints Fornham St Martin Upper Town Grimstone End Stowlangtoft Badwell Green Wyverstone Cotton Brockford Street
Marham Park Cattishall Great Barton Pakenham Stanton Street Great Ashfield Bacton
Moreton Hall Battlies Green Thurston Thurston Planche Norton Little Green Hunston Green Earl's Green Bacton Green Cow Green Ford's Green Canhams Green Mendlesham
Bury St Edmunds Blackthorpe Beyton Green Beyton Tostock Norton Elmswell Base Green Haughley Green Brown Street Mendlesham Green
Horringer Newton Park Kingshall Street Woolpit Broadgrass Gn Wetherden Gipping Middlewood Green
Rushbrooke Hessett Haughley Dagworth Old Newton Saxham Street Stonham
High Green Nowton Rougham Drinkstone Woolpit Green Borley Green Harleston Stowupland Forward Green Earl Stonham
Pinford End Sicklesmere Bradfield St George Drinkstone Green Clopton Green Onehouse Stowmarket Creeting St Peter
Hawstead Little Welnetham Maypole Green Rattlesden Buxhall Fen Street Buxhall Food Combs Ford Creeting St Mary
Hawstead Green Great Welnetham Bradfield St Clare Gedding Poystreet Green Mill Green Great Finborough Combs Needham Market
Mickley Green Bradfield Combust Bush Green Bradfield Woods Felsham Hightown Green Battisford Tye Moats Tye Needham Lake Baylham House Rare Breeds
Melon Green Hoggards Green Oldhall Green Cross Green Great Green Brettenham Battisford Barking
Stanningfield Windsor Green Cockfield Thorpe Green Cooks Green Cross Green Charles Tye Ringshall Barking Tye Lower Street
Harrow Green Lawshall Lawshall Green Thorpe Morieux Hitcham Causeway Bird Street Wattisham Ringshall Stocks Baylham Upper Street
Cross Green Audley End Shimpling Street Preston St Mary Hitcham Street Hitcham Nedging Tye Great Bricett Offton Great Blakenham
Giffords Hall Shimpling Alpheton Guildhall Kettlebaston Greenstreet Green Naughton Somersham Little Blakenham
Boxted Bridge Street Lavenham Little Hall Brent Eleigh Bildeston Nedging Ash Street Flowton
Stanstead Kentwell Hall & Gardens Swingleton Green Monks Eleigh Chelsworth Semer Whatfield Elmsett Bramford
Glemsford Melford Hall Milden Lindsey Tye Aldham Sproughton
Long Melford Acton Little Waldingfield Rose Green Lindsey Stone Street Wolves Wood Burstall
Foxearth Liston Newman's Green Great Waldingfield St James's Chapel Kersey Tye Kersey Hadleigh Heath Hadleigh Duke Street Hintlesham
Borley Chilton Mill Green Wicker Street Green Kersey Coram Street Hadleigh Heath Chattisham
Sudbury Cornard Tye Edwardstone Groton Horners Green Bower House Tye Layham Coles Green Copdock
Ballingdon Great Cornard Newton Boxford Calais Street Whitestreet Green Polstead Heath Upper Layham Little Wenham
Bulmer Middleton Little Cornard Hagmore Green Stone Street Polstead Raydon Great Wenham Capel St Mary
Bulmer Tye Great Henny Assington Rose Green Leavenheath Stoke-by-Nayland Shelley Lower Raydon Holton St Mary Bentley
Wickham St Paul Henny Street Workhouse Green Honey Tye Nayland Thorington Street Stratford St Mary Higham Dedham East End
Alphamstone Lamarsh Dorking Tye Old Boxted Boxted Cross Langham Flatford Mill & Bridge Cottage Manningtree
Cross End Bures Wissington Wormingford Little Horkesley Great Mistley
Pebmarsh Mount Bures

Boose's Green
Countess Cross
72 J K L M

A B C D E F

1

2

3

4

5

6

7

8

Stanton · Wattisfield · andle Street · Mellis · Yaxley · Dennam · Stradbroke
Upthorpe · Walsham le Willows · Allwood Green · Mill Street · Thornham Parva · Eye · Braiseworth · Redlingfield Green · Horham · Wootten Green · Coal Street
Wyken · Cranmer Green · Thornham Magna · Stoke Ash · Standwell Green · Occold · Redlingfield · Athelington · Stanway Green
West Street · Langham · Crowland · Finningham · Wickham Street · Wickham Green · Thorndon · Dublin · Southolt · Fingal Street · Worling
Badwell Ash · Four Ashes · Badwell Green · Westhorpe · Wickham Skeith · Rishangles · Hestley Green · Bedingfield · Bedfield · Co
Hunston · Long Thurlow · Wyverstone Street · Wyverstone · Cotton · Brockford Street · Brockford Green · Bedingfield Green · Wetheringsett · Kenton · Monk Soham · Bedfield Little Gre
Stowlangtoft · Great Ashfield · Earl's Green · Cow Green · Mendlesham · Park Green · Aspall · Blacksmith's Green · Wetherup Street · Debenham · Post Mill
Stanton street · Hunston Green · Bacton · Ford's Green · Canhams Green · Mendlesham Green · Middlewood Green · Mickfield · Winston · Fen Street · Ashfield cum Thorpe · Earl Soham
Norton Little Green · Norton · Elmswell · Base Green · Haughley Green · Ward Green · Gipping · Old Newton · Winston Green · Winton · Cretingham
Woolpit · Broadgrass Gn · Wetherden · Haughley · Dagworth · Saxham Street · Little Stonham · Mill Green · Framsden · Monewden
Woolpit Green · Borley Green · Harleston · Stowupland · Forward Green · Creeting St Peter · Stonham Aspal · Mid Suffolk · Suffolk Owl Sanctuary · Pettaugh · Charsfield
Clopton Green · Onehouse · Stowmarket · Earl Stonham · Crowfield Green · Helmingham Hall · Crowfield · Helmingham · Gosbeck · Otley · Otley Green
Rattlesden · Buxhall Fen Street · Buxhall · Great Finborough · Combs Ford · Combs · Creeting St Mary · Ashbocking · Clopton Corner · Clopton
Poystreet Green · Mill Green · Moats Tye · Battisford · Needham Market · Needham Lake · Coddenham · Hemingstone · Swilland · Burgh
Hightown Green · Brettenham · Battisford Tye · Charles Tye · Ringshall · Barking · Baylham House Rare Breeds · Bells Cross · Barham · Grundisburgh
Cooks Green · Cross Green · Bird Street · Barking Tye · Lower Street · Henley · Witnesham · Boot Street · Great Bealings
Hitcham Causeway · Hitcham Street · Hitcham · Wattisham · Ringshall Stocks · Baylham · Upper Street · Claydon · Culpho
Bildeston · Nedging Tye · Great Bricett · Greenstreet Green · Offton · Great Blakenham · Akenham · Tuddenham St Martin · Playford · Little Bealings
Monks Eleigh Green · Chelsworth · Semer · Nedging Ash Street · Naughton · Somersham · Little Blakenham · Whitton · Westerfield · Rushmere St Andrew · P+R
Lindsey Tye · Whatfield · Flowton · Bramford · Castle Hill · IPSWICH · Kesgrave
Rose Green · Lindsey · St James's Chapel · Stone Street · Aldham · Wolves Wood RSPB · Elmsett · Sproughton · Burstall · Chantry · Gainsborough · Suffolk
Wicker Street Green · Kersey Tye · Kersey · Coram Street · Hadleigh · Duke Street · Hintlesham · Washbrook · P+R
Horners Green · Calais Street · Kersey Upland · Hadleigh Heath · Chattisham · Coles Green · Copdock · Belstead · Wherstead · Orwell Bridge · Nacton
Bower House Tye · Layham · Upper Layham · Little Wenham · Jimmy's Farm & Wildlife Park · Orwell · Levington
Polstead Heath · Great Wenham · Freston · Woolverstone
Stone Street · Whitestreet Green · Raydon · Shelley · Capel St Mary · Bentley · Tattingstone White Horse · Tattingstone · Pin Mill
Nayland · Thorington Street · Polstead · Lower Raydon · Holton St Mary · Holbrook · Chelmondiston · River Orwell
Stoke-by-Nayland · Higham · East Bergholt · East End · Upper Street · Stutton · Lower Holbrook · Erwarton · Shotley
Old Boxted · Stratford St Mary · Dedham · Brantham · Alton Water · Harkstead
Boxted Cross · Langham · Flatford Mill & Bridge Cottage · Cattawade · Mistley Towers · Holbrook Bay
Boxted · Dedham Heath · Manningtree · Mistley · New Mistley · Wrabness · Stour Estuary · Parkeston Quay · Parkeston · International Ferry Terminal
Great · rawford · Bradfield · Upper · Churc

A14 · A1308 · A140 · A1120 · A1078 · A1071 · A12 · A137 · A1214 · A1156 · A1067 · A1156

B1113 · B1088 · B1115 · B1078 · B1070 · B1068 · B1087 · B1029 · B1080 · B1456 · B1077 · B1079 · B1117 · B1118

106 · 89 · 73

Huntingfield · Walpole · B1117 · J · T...ngton · **107** · K · B1387 · G · H

Laxfield · Heveningham · Ubbeston Green · Pouy Street · High Street · A144 · A12 · B1125 · Dunwich Forest · Suffolk Coast · 1

...dish Street · ...dish · Owl's Green · Goddard's Corner · Peasenhall · Sibton · Yoxford · Darsham · Westleton Heath · Dunwich · Grey Friars

Capon's Green · A1120 · Badingham · Middleton · Westleton · Minsmere · RSPB · Dunwich Heath

Dennington · Bruisyard · Bruisyard Street · B1120 · B1122 · Middleton Moor · North Green · Theberton · Eastbridge · 2

...tead · ...d · Shawsgate · Castle · Cransford · Brabling Green · A12 · Carlton Meres · Rendham · Kelsale · East Green · Poplar Street · Leiston Abbey

North Green · B1119 · Great Glemham · Benhall Street · Benhall Green · Swefling · **Saxmundham** · Sternfield · Carlton · Knodishall · Coldfair Green · Power Station · Sizewell

Mill Green · B1116 · Parham · ...leburgh · Stratford St Andrew · B1119 · B1121 · **Leiston** · Aldringham · 3

Easton · Hacheston · Silverlace Green · Friday Street · Farnham · Snape · Friston · Knodishall Common · B1353 · Thorpe Ness · B1122 · Thorpeness

Marlesford · Little Glemham · Gromford · Snape Street · Snape Maltings · North Warren · RSPB

Lower Hacheston · Blaxhall · B1069 · Snape · RSPB · Iken

Wickham Market · Campsea Ash · Tunstall · Tunstall Forest · High Street · **Aldeburgh** · Aldeburgh Bay · 4

Pettistree · A1152 · Rendlesham · B1078 · River Alde

Upper Ufford · Ufford · Lower Ufford · Friday Street · 10 · B1438 · Eyke · Chillesford · Sudbourne · B1084 · 5

Melton · Bromeswell · B1084 · 12 · Butley · Butley High Corner · Castle · Orford

Woodbridge · Rendlesham Forest · Capel Green · Capel St Andrew · Orford Ness · Orford Ness

Sutton Hoo · B1083 · Sutton Heath · Orfordness-Havergate · RSPB

Woodbridge Tide Mill · Sutton · Boyton · River Ore

...am · Waldringfield · Shottisham · Hollesley · North Weir Point · Suffolk Heritage Coast · 6

...am · B1083 · Hollesley Bay

Newbourne · Hemley · Ramsholt · Shingle Street

Kirton · River Deben · Alderton · Bawdsey · 7

Falkenham

Trimley St Mary · 59 · Felixstowe Ferry · 8

Walton · Old Felixstowe · 60

61

Felixstowe · 62 · A154 · P · M

G · Landguard Fort · H · J · K · L · M · Landguard Point · ...ich ...bour

| 0 | 1 | 2 | 3 | 4 | 5 miles |
| 0 | 1 2 3 4 | 5 6 7 | 8 kilometres |

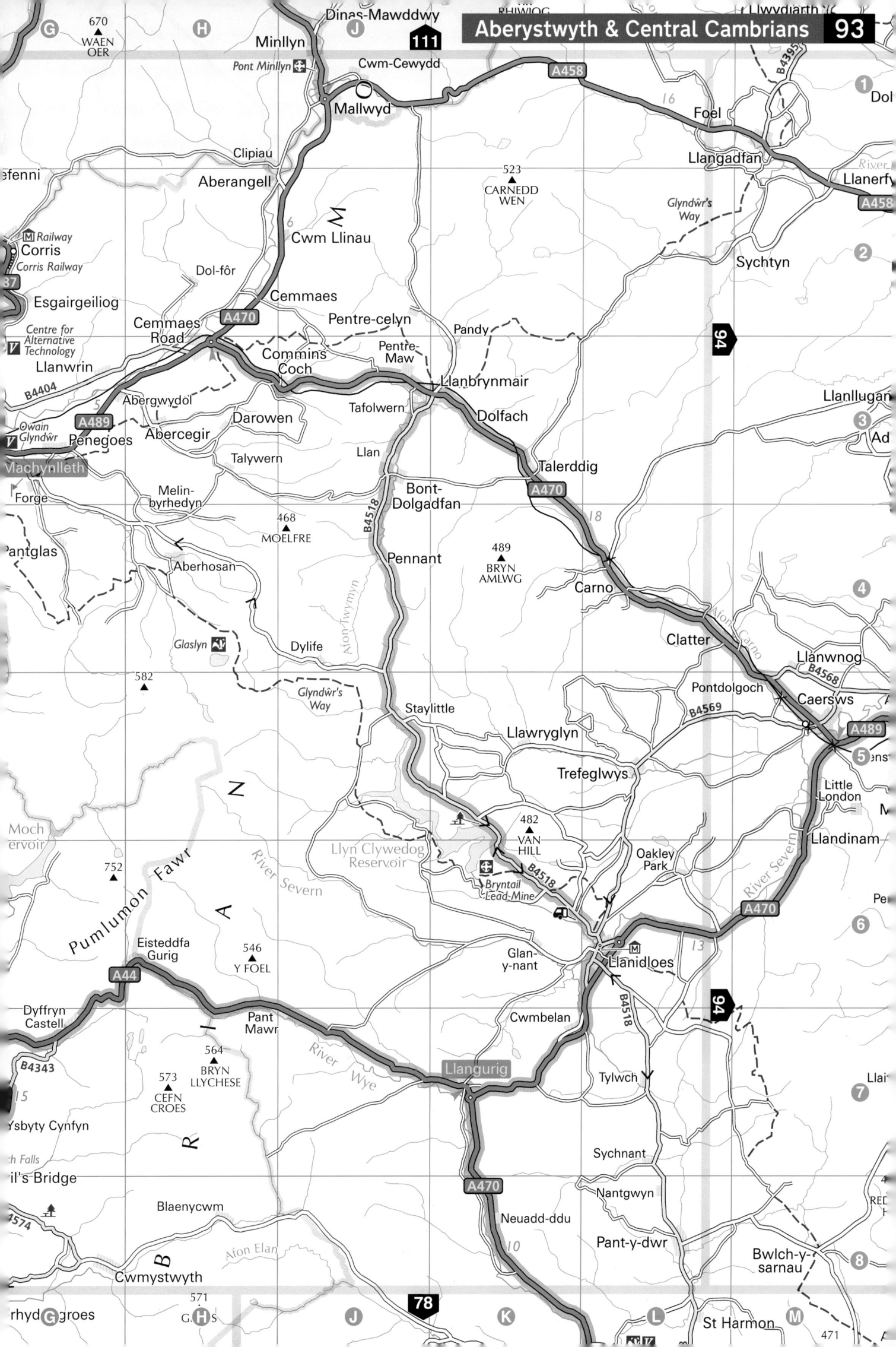

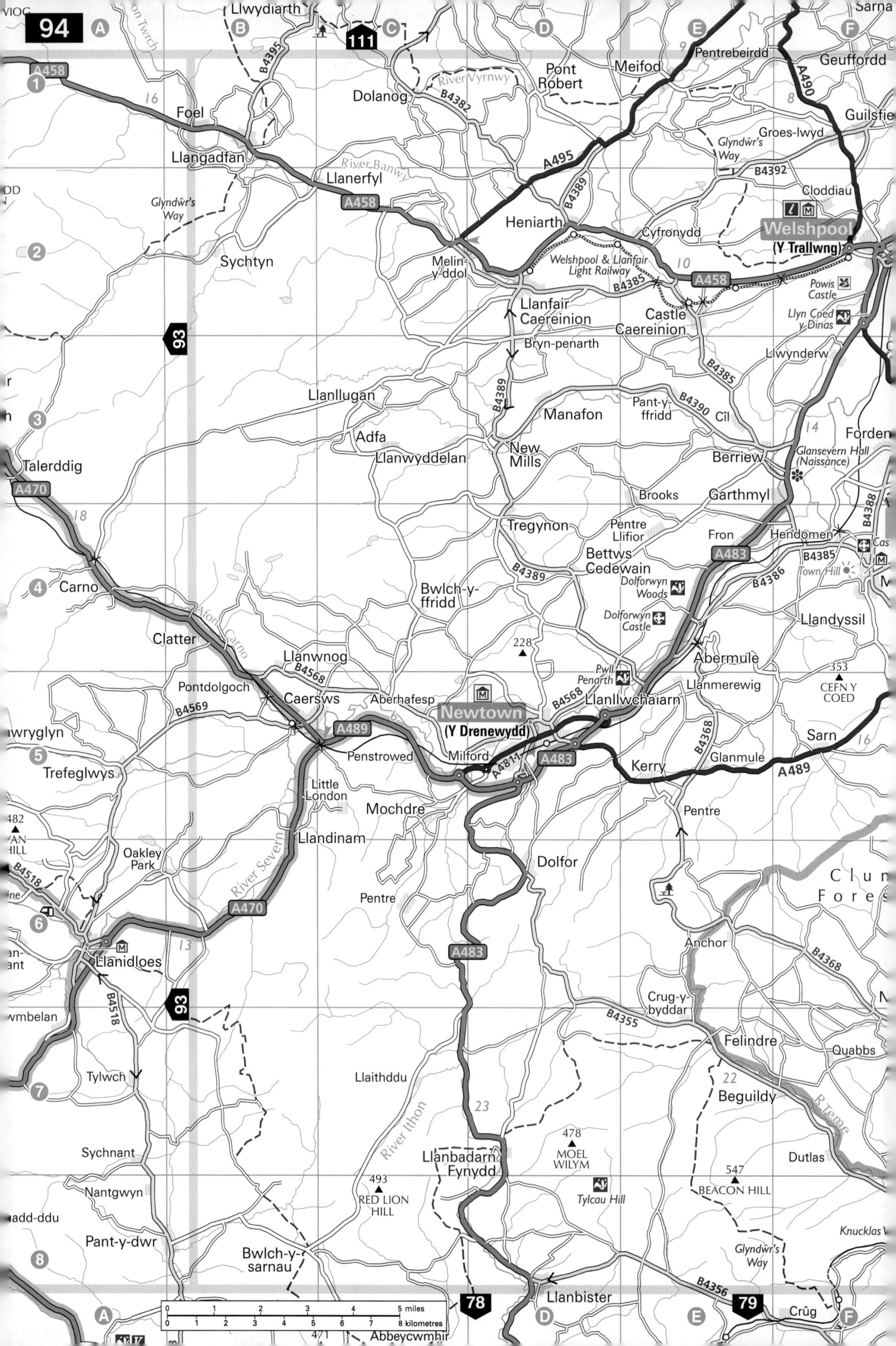

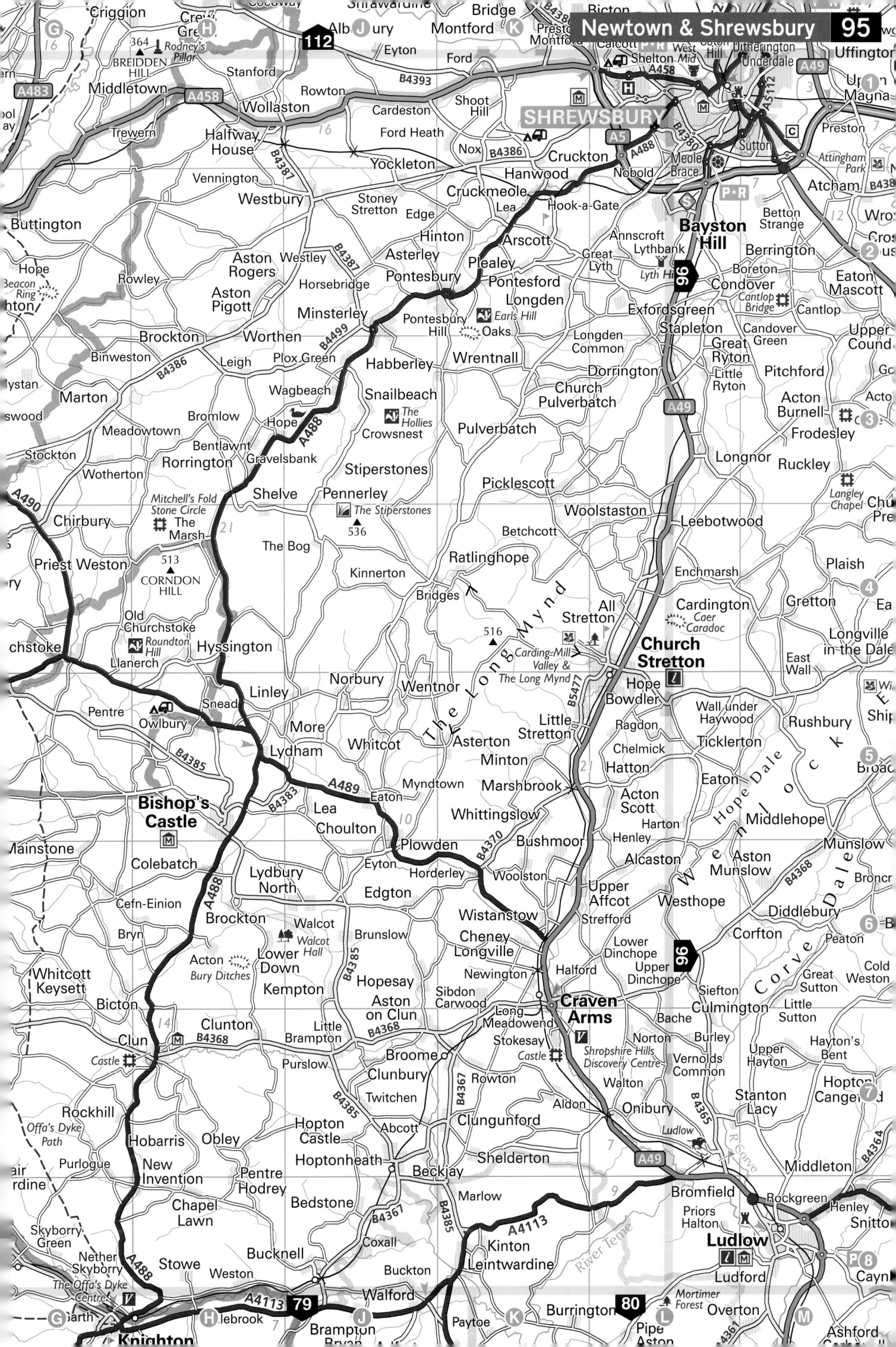

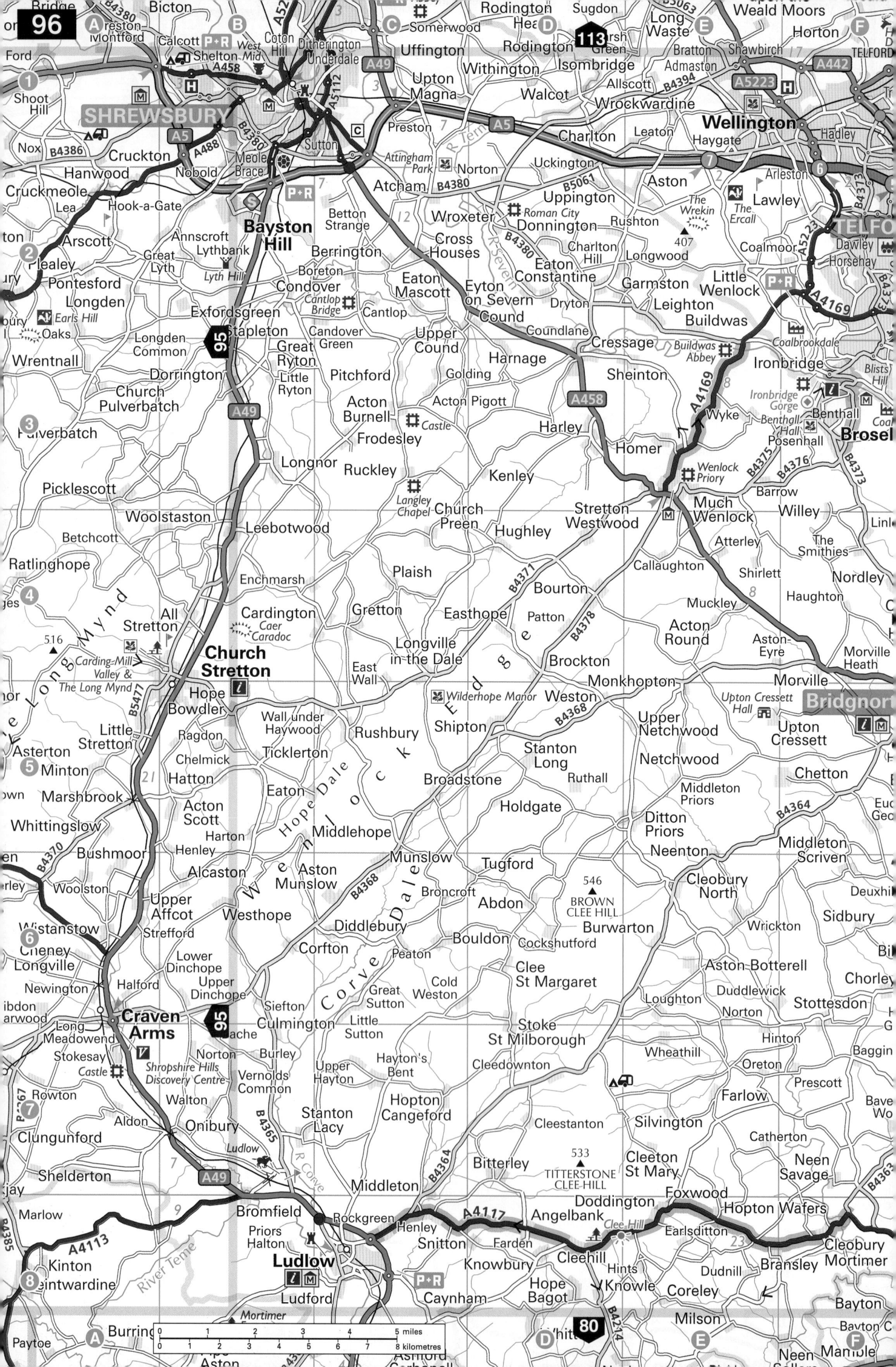

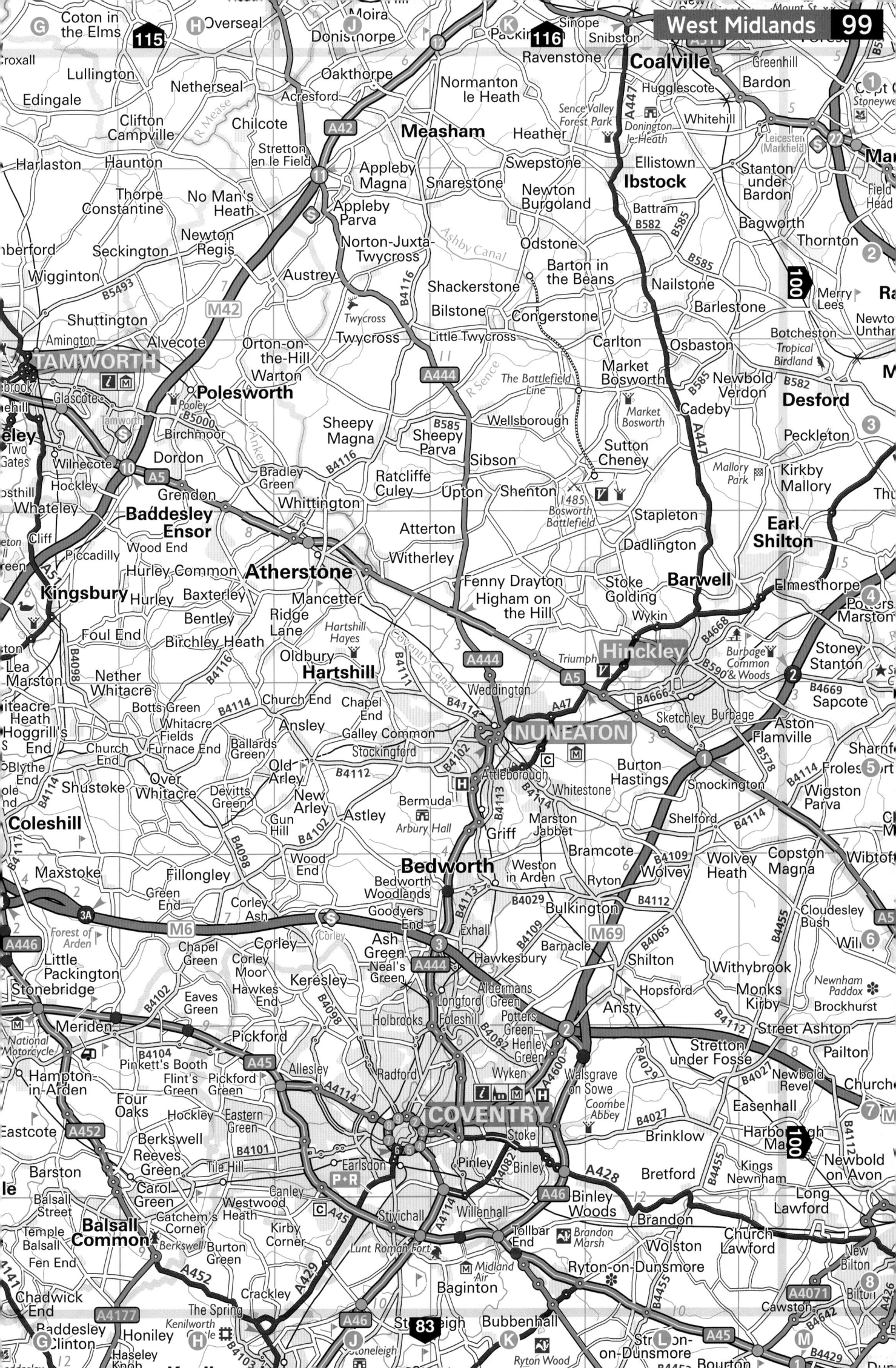

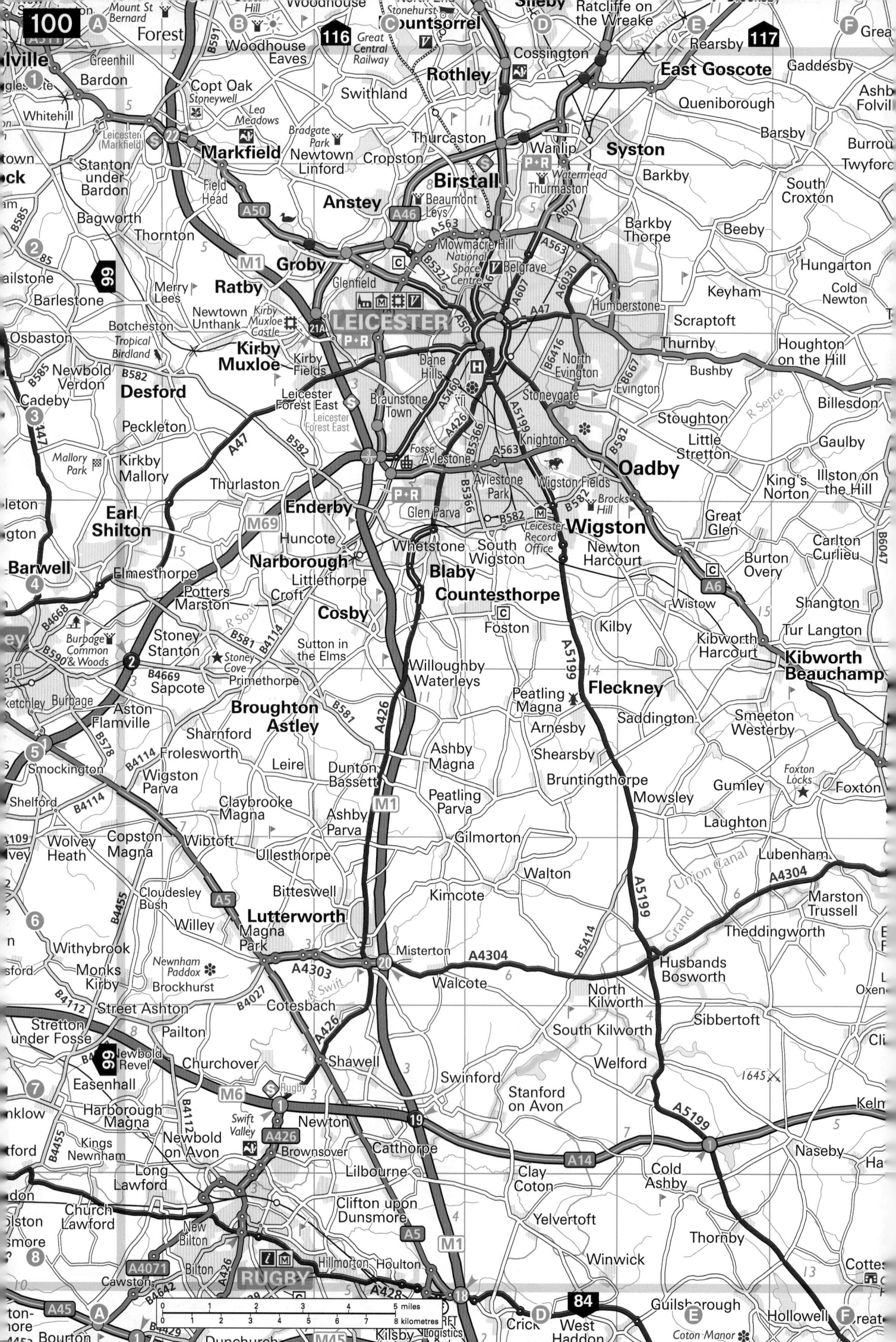

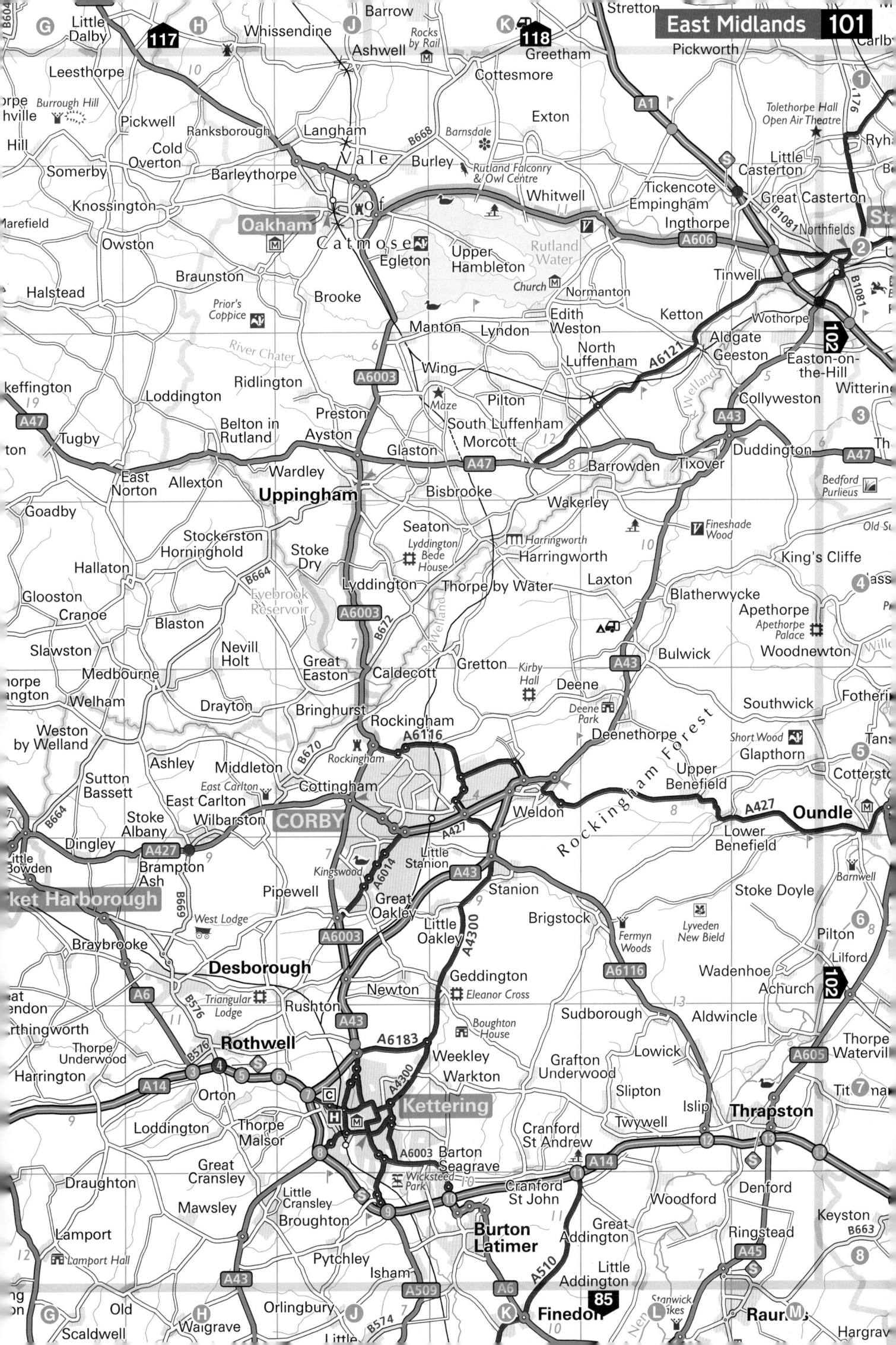

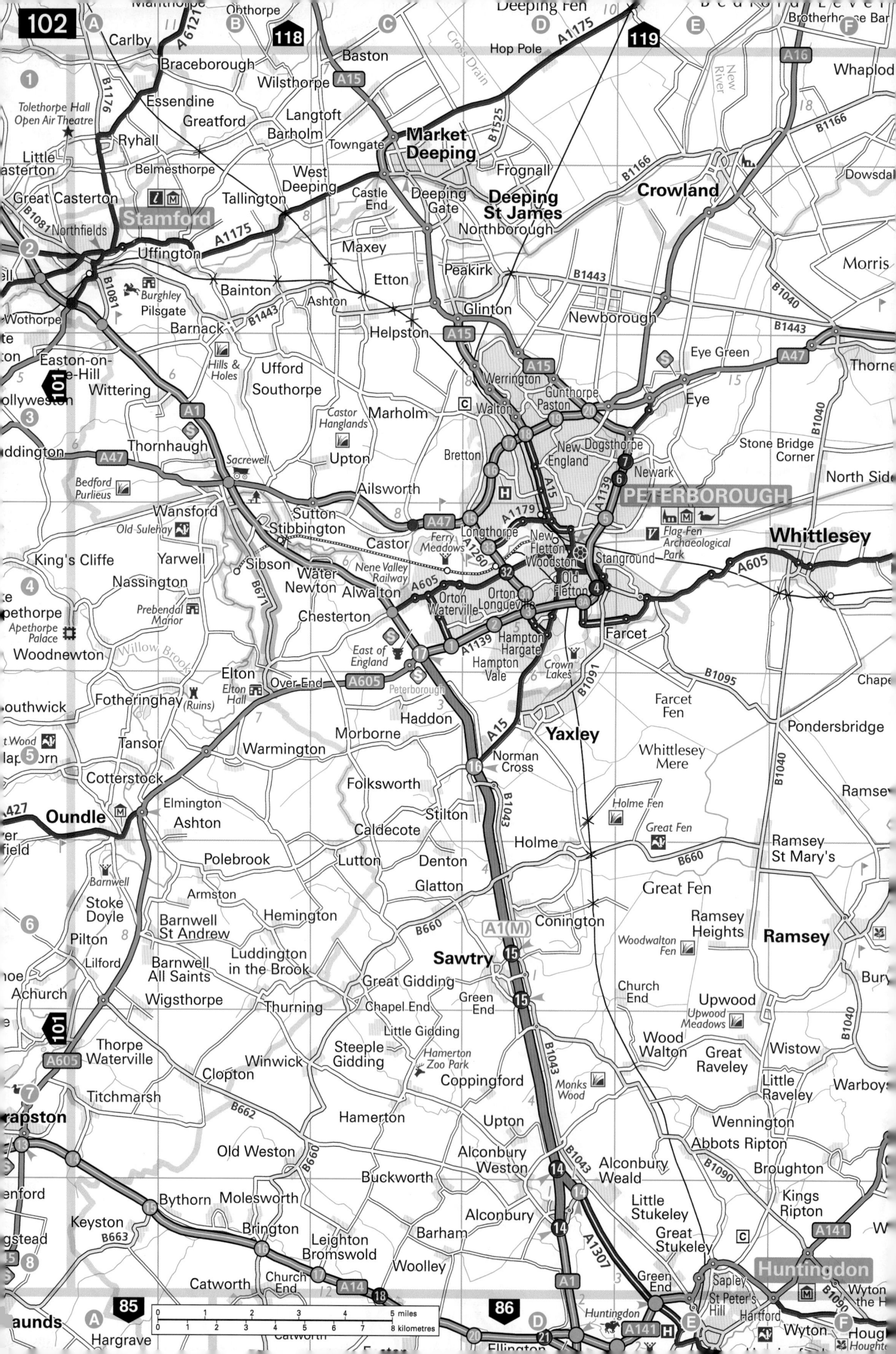

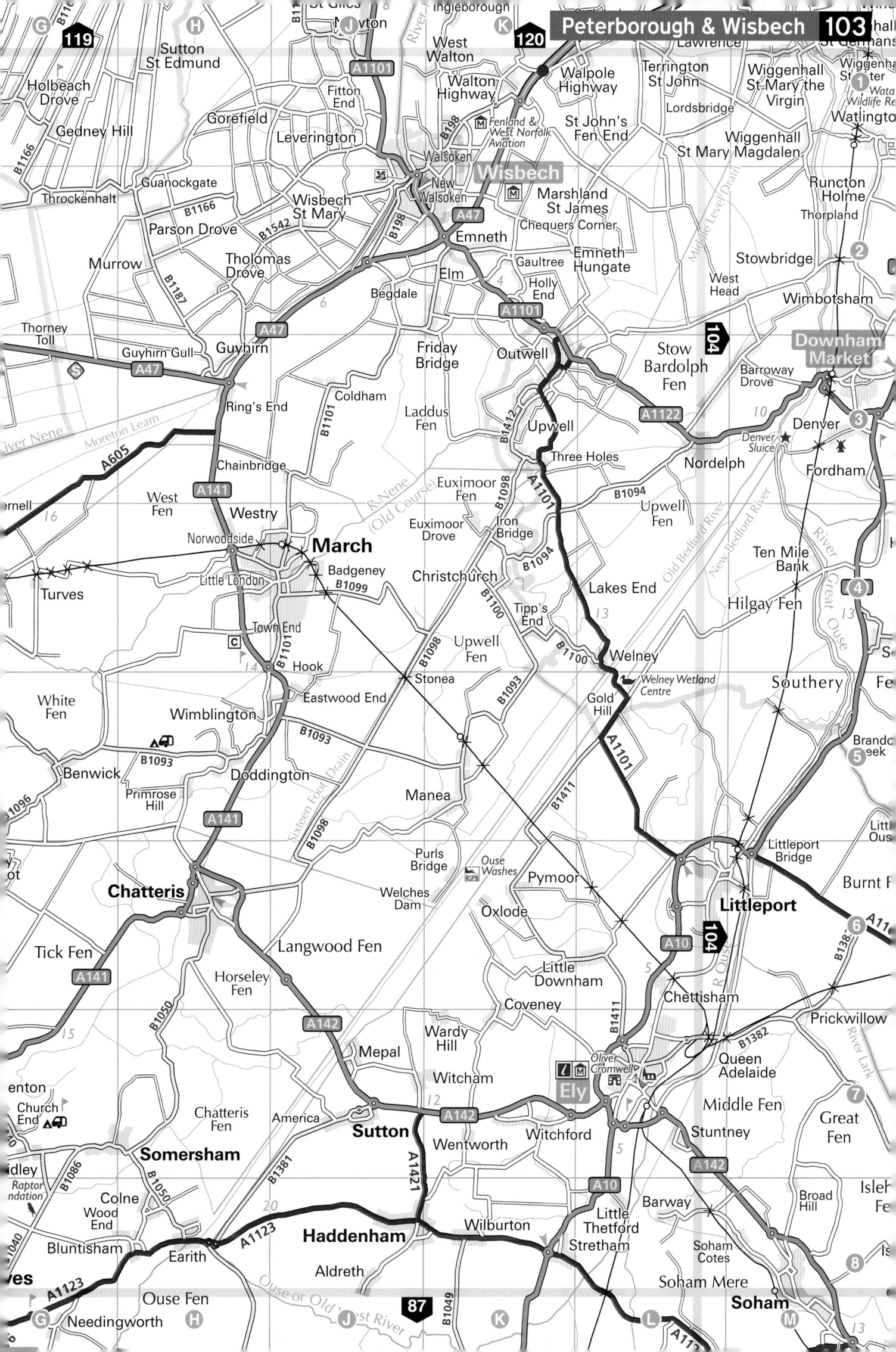

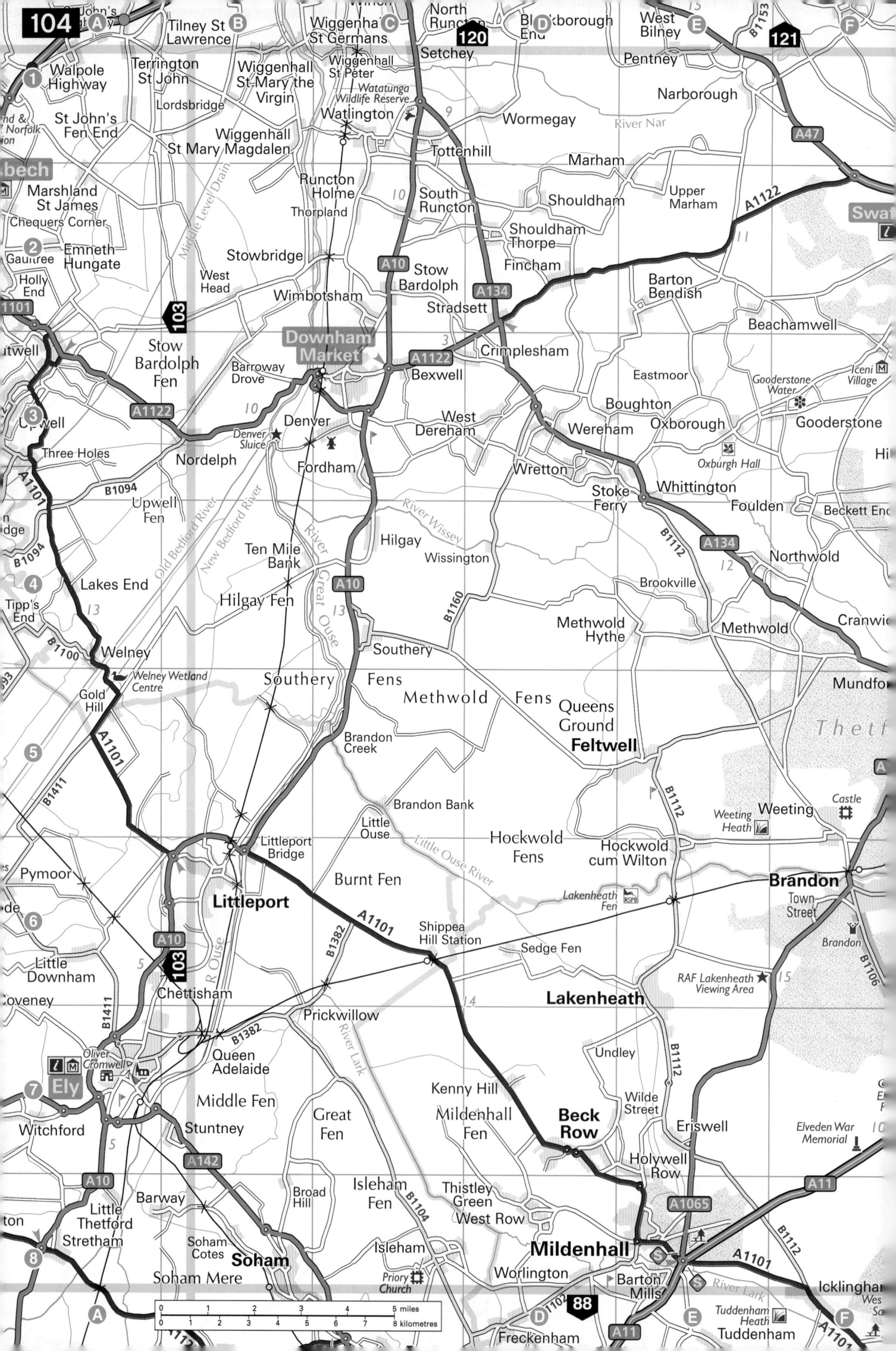

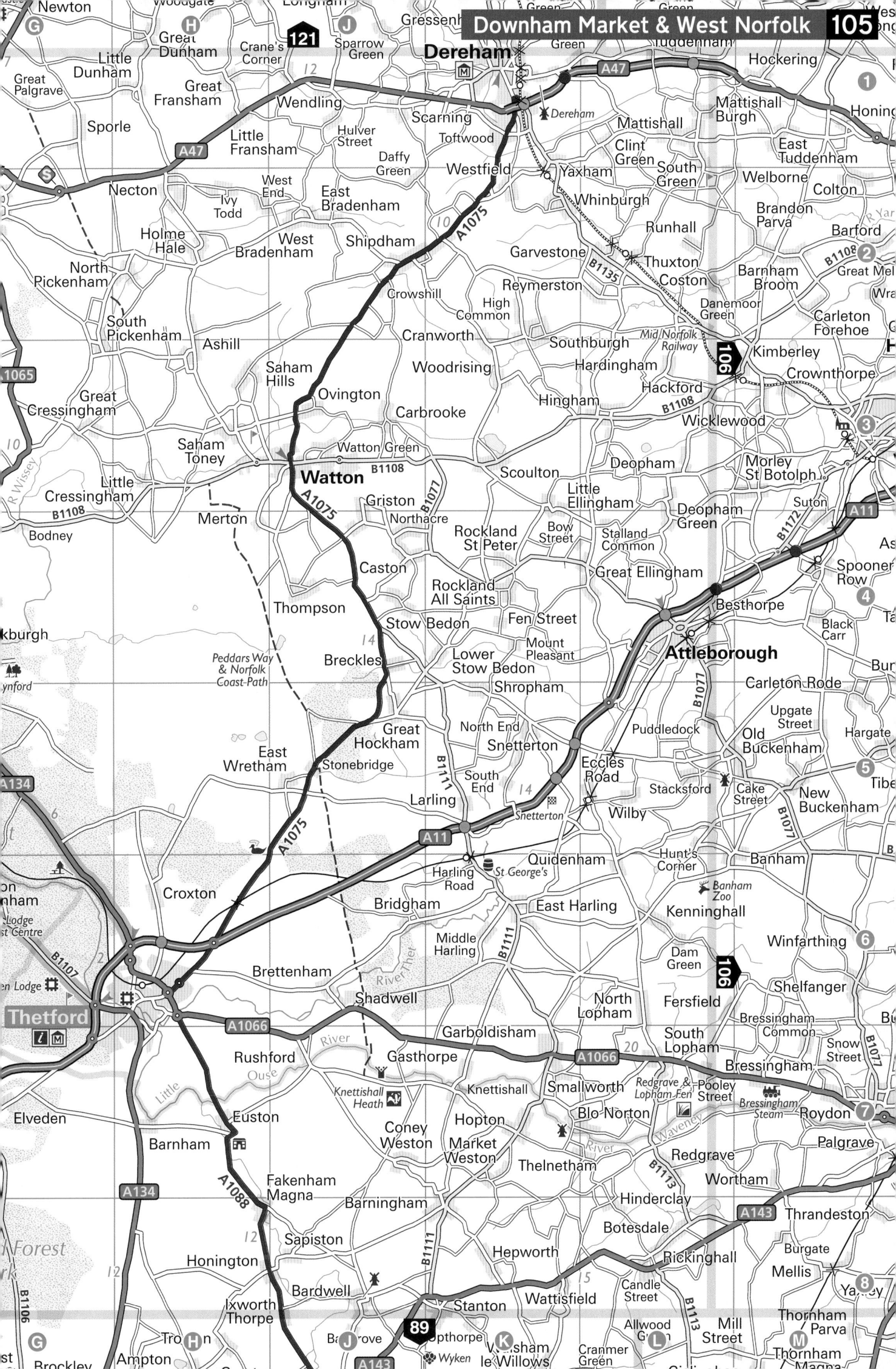

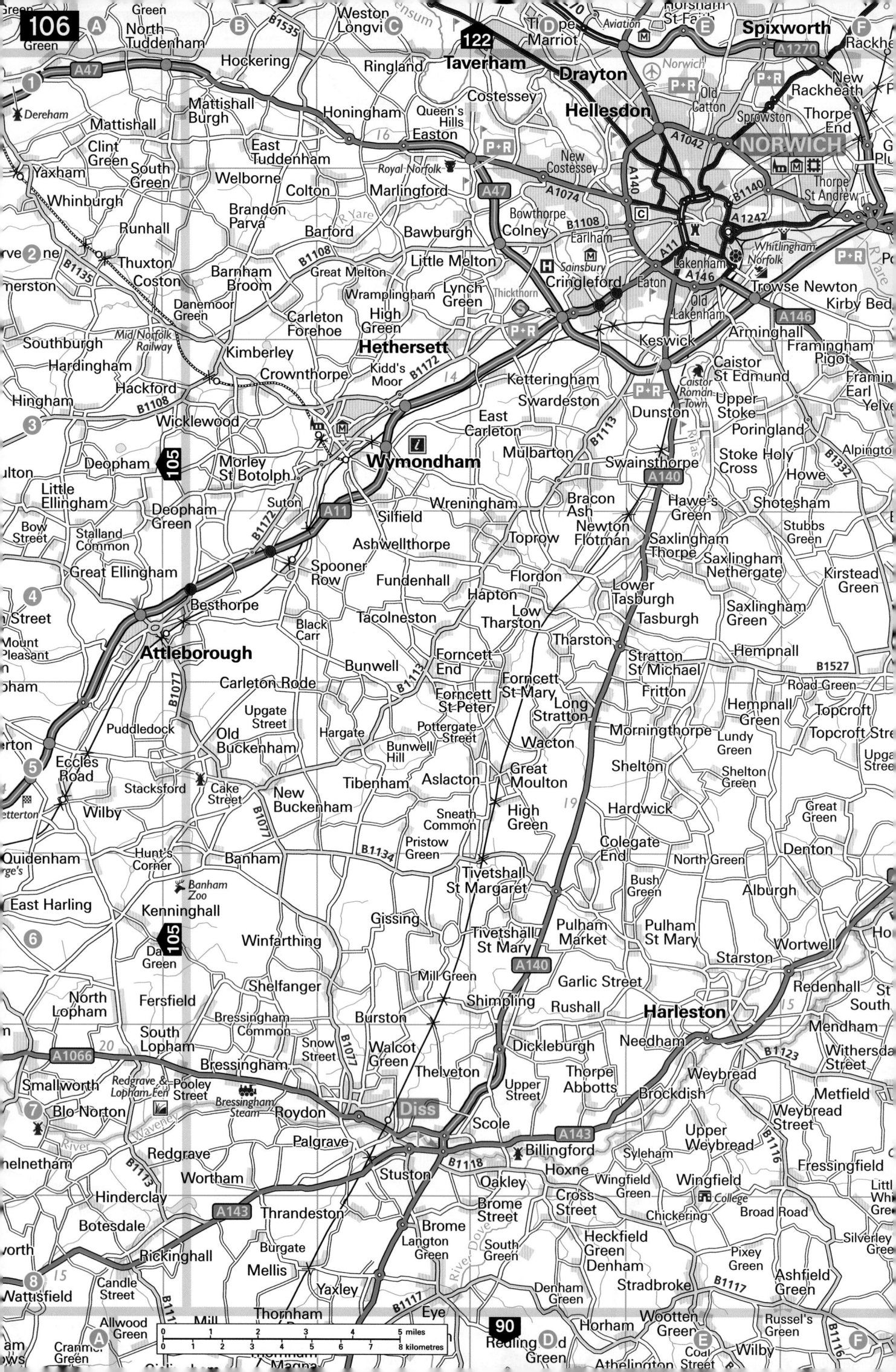

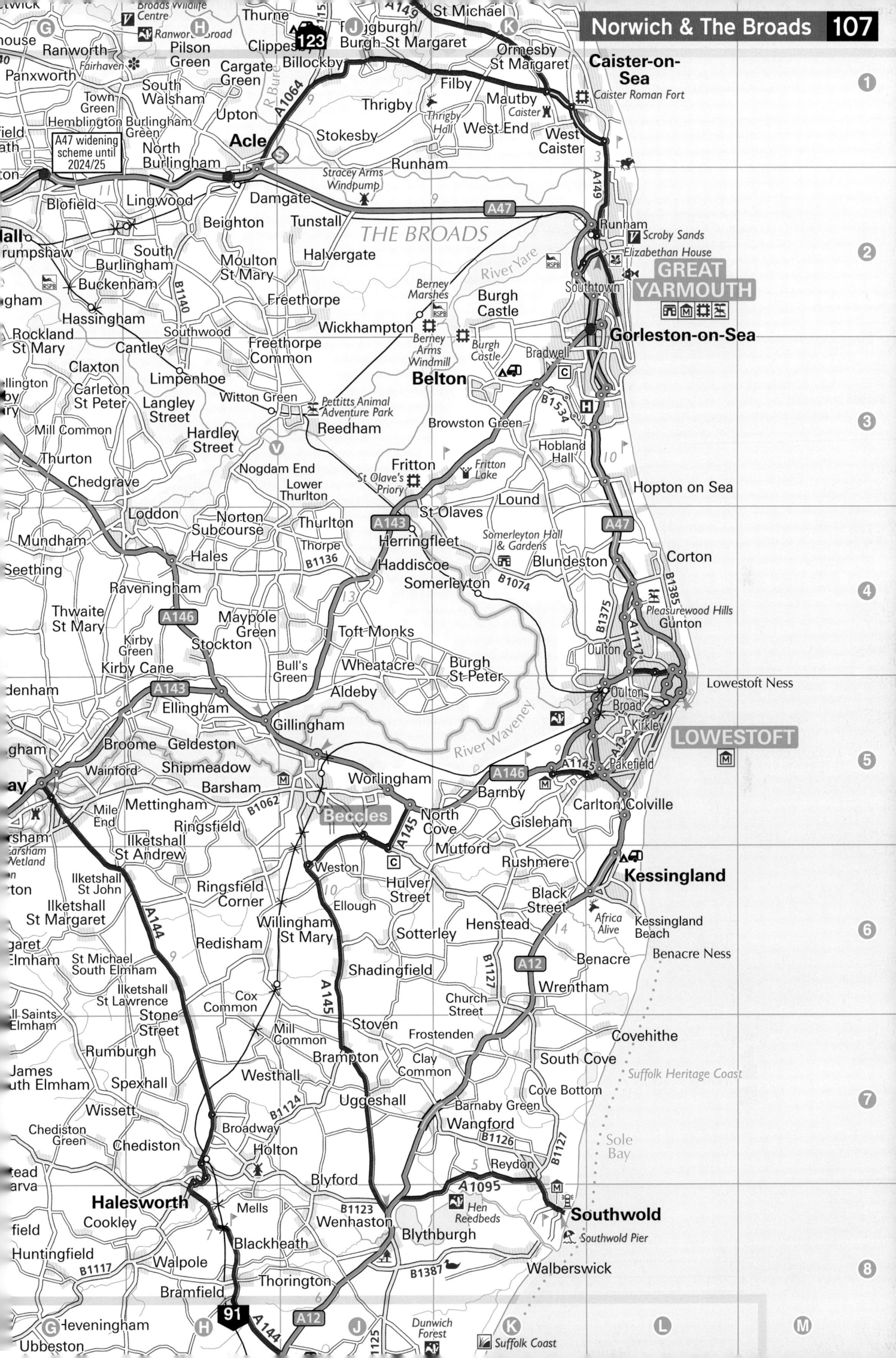

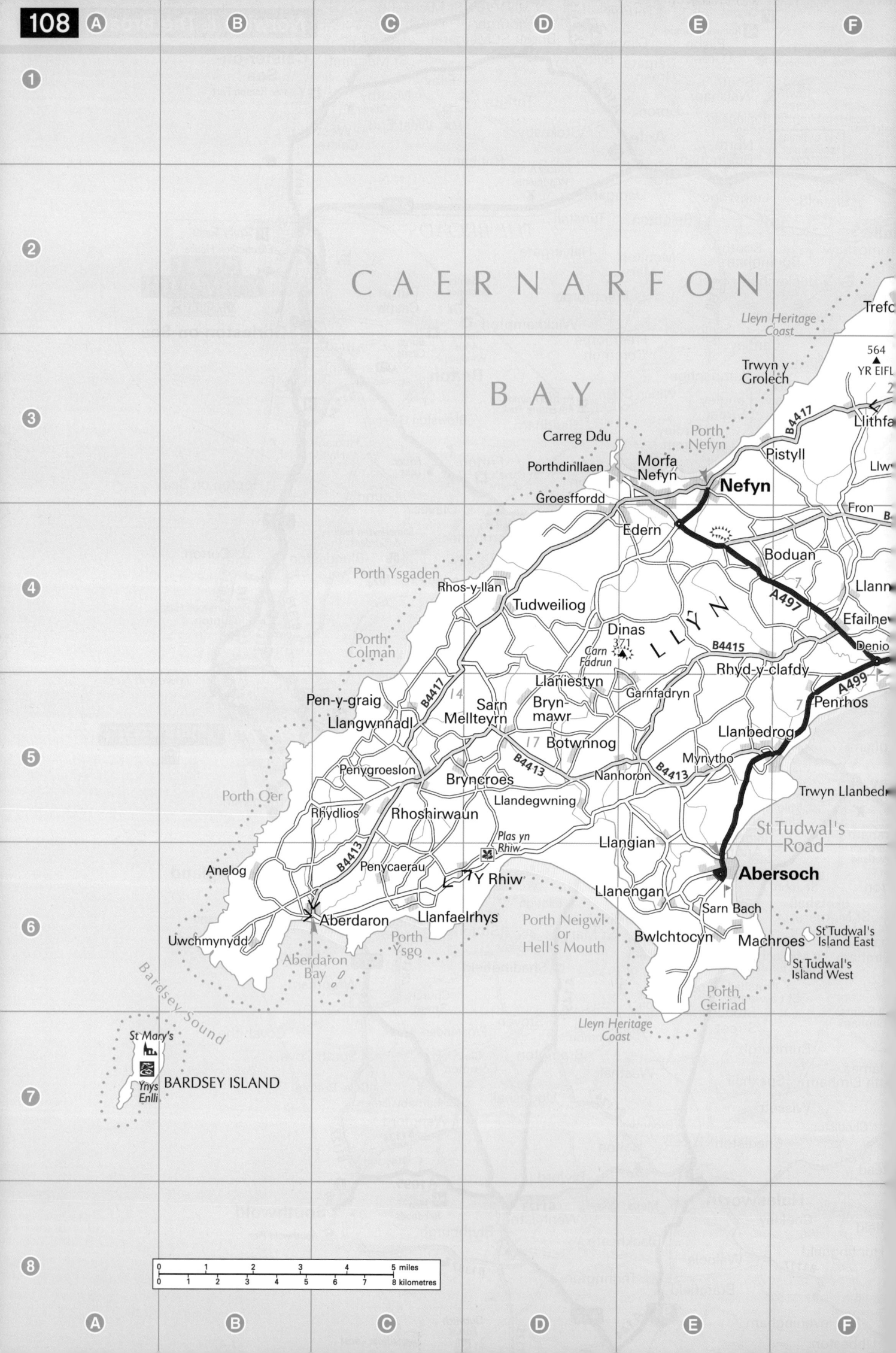

CAERNARFON

BAY

Lleyn Heritage
Coast

Trefc

564
▲ YR EIFL

B4417

Llithfa

Trwyn y
Grolech

Pistyll

Porth
Nefyn

Carreg Ddu

Llw

Porthdinllaen

Morfa
Nefyn

Nefyn

Groesffordd

Fron

Edern

B

Boduan

Porth Ysgaden

Rhos-y-llan

Tudweiliog

A497

7

Llann

Llŷn

Efailne

Dinas

371

B4415

Carn
Fadrun

Denio

Porth
Colman

Rhyd-y-clafdy

Llaniestyn

Pen-y-graig

14

B4417

Sarn
Mellteyrn

Bryn-
mawr

Garnfadryn

7

A499

Penrhos

Langwnnadl

Llanbedrog

Botwnnog

17

Mynytho

Penygroeslon

B4413

Nanhoron

B4413

Trwyn Llanbed

Porth Oer

Bryncroes

Llandegwning

St Tudwal's
Road

Rhydlios

Rhoshirwaun

Plas yn
Rhiw

Llangian

Abersoch

Anelog

B4413

Penycaerau

Y Rhiw

Llanengan

Sarn Bach

St Tudwal's
Island East

Aberdaron

Llanfaelrhys

Porth Neigwl
or
Hell's Mouth

Bwlchtocyn

Machroes

Uwchmynydd

Porth
Ysgo

Aberdaron
Bay

St Tudwal's
Island West

Porth
Geiriad

Lleyn Heritage
Coast

Bardsey Sound

St Mary's

Ynys
Enlli

BARDSEY ISLAND

0   1   2   3   4   5 miles
0 1 2 3 4 5 6 7 8 kilometres

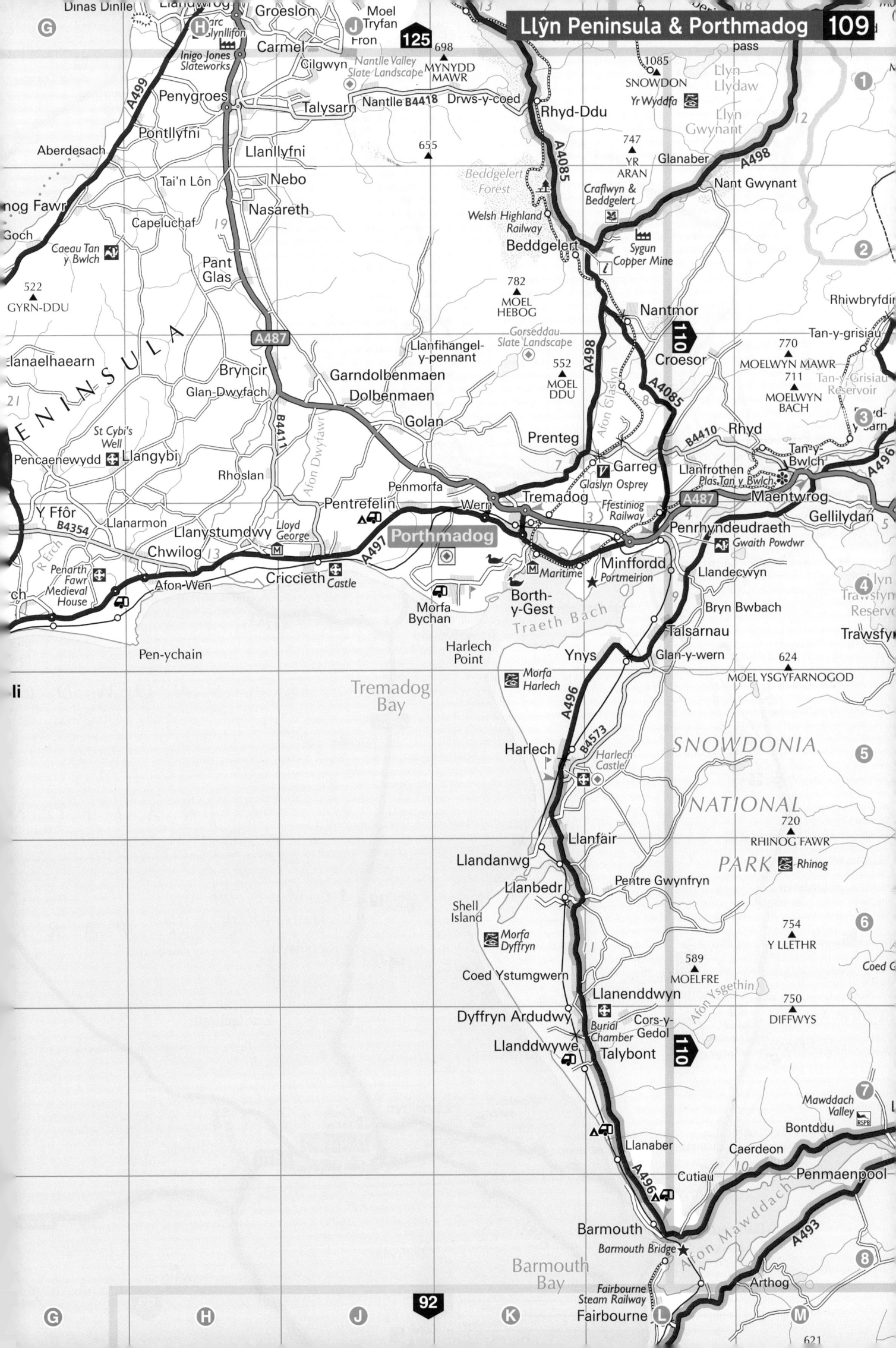

G **H** **J**

Dinas Dinlle
Llandwrog
Groeslon
Moel Tryfan
Fron
Carmel
Parc Glynllifon
Inigo Jones Slateworks
Cilgwyn
Nantlle Valley Slate Landscape
MYNYDD MAWR 698
125
Penygroes
Talysarn Nantlle B4418 Drws-y-coed
Rhyd-Ddu
Pontllyfni
Llanllyfni
655
A4085
SNOWDON 1085
Yr Wyddfa
Llyn Llydaw
1
Aberdesach
Tai'n Lôn
Nebo
747 YR ARAN
Glanaber
Llyn Gwynant
A498
Nasareth
Nant Gwynant
2
nog Fawr
Goch
Capeluchaf
Beddgelert Forest
Welsh Highland Railway
Craflwyn & Beddgelert
522 GYRN-DDU
Pant Glas
Beddgelert
Sygun Copper Mine
Rhiwbryfdir
A487
782 MOEL HEBOG
Nantmor
Tan-y-grisiau
PENINSULA
Bryncir
Llanfihangel-y-pennant
Gorseddau Slate Landscape
110
Croesor
770
MOELWYN MAWR
21
Glan-Dwyfach
Garndolbenmaen
552 MOEL DDU
A498
A4085
711
MOELWYN BACH
Tan-y-Grisiau Reservoir
St Cybi's Well
Dolbenmaen
8
B4410
Rhyd
3
Pencaenewydd
Llangybi
Golan
Prenteg
7
Garreg
Llanfrothen
Plas Tan y Bwlch
Tan-y-Bwlch
A496
Y Ffôr
Rhoslan
Penmorfa
Glaslyn Osprey
A487
Maentwrog
B4354
Llanarmon
Pentrefelin
Wern
Tremadog
Ffestiniog Railway
4
Penrhyndeudraeth
Gellilydan
Llanystumdwy
Lloyd George
Porthmadog
3
Gwaith Powdwr
Chwilog 13
Criccieth Castle
Maritime
Minffordd
Llandecwyn
R Erch
Afon-Wen
Morfa Bychan
Borth-y-Gest
Portmeirion
Bryn Bwbach
4
Penarth Fawr Medieval House
Traeth Bach
9
Trawsfyn Reserv
Pen-ychain
Harlech Point
Ynys
Glan-y-wern
624
MOEL YSGYFARNOGOD
Trawsfy
Tremadog Bay
Morfa Harlech
Talsarnau
A496
li
SNOWDONIA
5
Harlech
B4573
Harlech Castle
NATIONAL
720
RHINOG FAWR
Rhinog
PARK
Llanfair
Llandanwg
Pentre Gwynfryn
Llanbedr
754 Y LLETHR
6
Shell Island
Morfa Dyffryn
589 MOELFRE
11
Coed Ystumgwern
Llanenddwyn
Afon Ysgethin
750 DIFFWYS
Dyffryn Ardudwy
Burial Chamber
Cors-y-Gedol
110
Llanddwywe
Talybont
Mawddach Valley
7
Llanaber
A496
Cutiau
Penmaenpool
Caerdeon
10
Bontddu
Afon Mawddach
A493
Barmouth
Barmouth Bridge
8
Barmouth Bay
Fairbourne Steam Railway
92
Fairbourne
621

G **H** **J** **K** **L** **M**

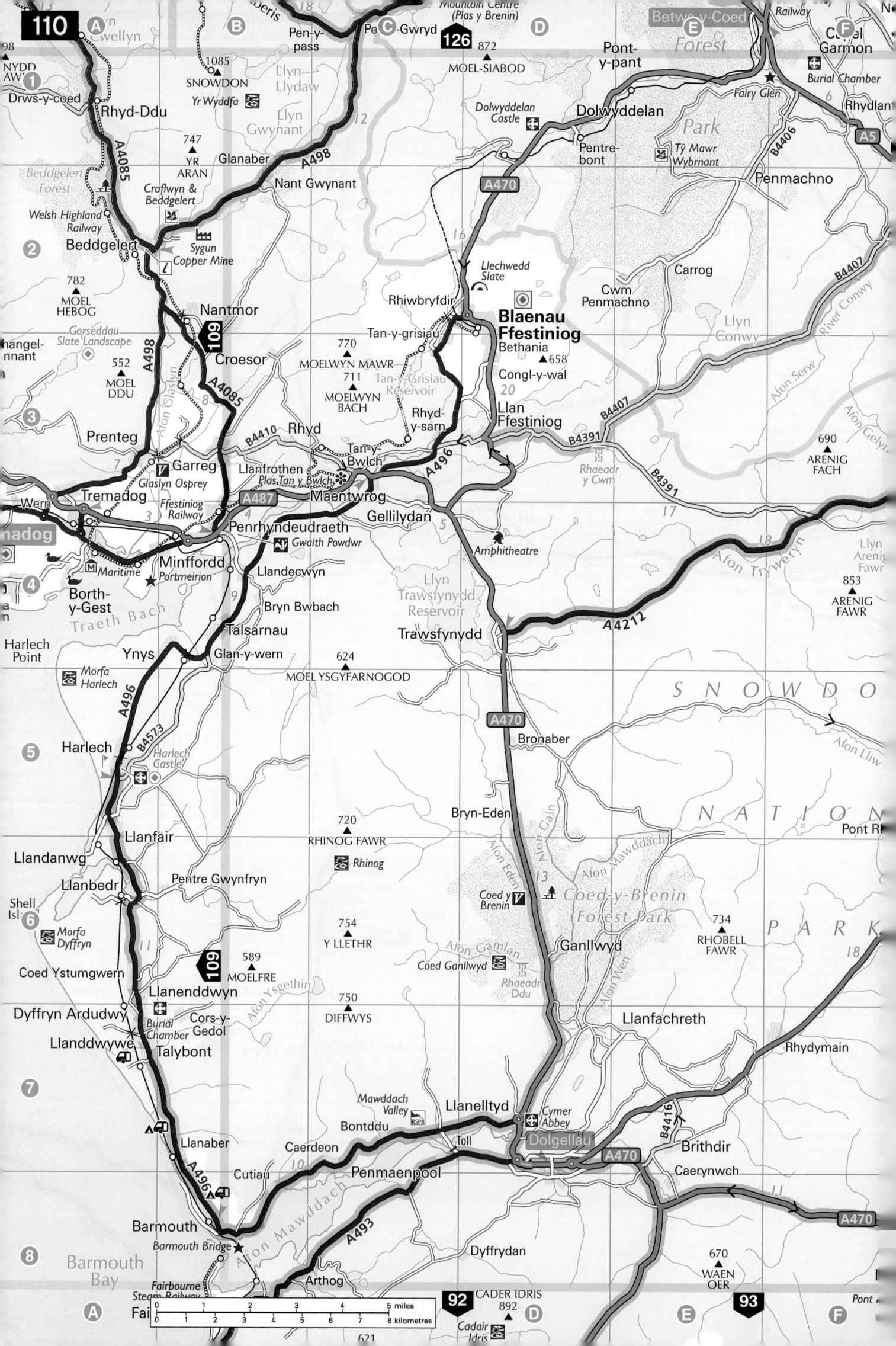

G
Mynydd
Hiraet
H
127
J
V Llyn Brenig
K
L
Efe
B5105
Snowdonia 111

Llyn Alwen
Reservoir
Clocaenog
Pwll-glâs
A525
Graigf
Graig Clw

Rhydlydan
Alwen Reservoir
B5105
Clawdd-newydd
R Clwyd
R Alyn
1
Hentre

Cefn-brith
Pentre-llyn-cymmer
Clocaenog Forest
Churchyard Cross
Bryn Saith Marchog
Derwen
Pandy'r Capel
Llanelidan
B5429

Glasfryn
B4501
Llanfihangel Glyn Myfyr
Melin-y-wîg
A494
Gwyddelwern
B5436

RNEDD Y-FILAST 669
B5105
Cerrigydrudion
Ty-nant
Dinmael
Betws Gwerfil Goch
A5104
Afon Morwynion
Llan silic Mountai Mo
B5437

fan
B4501
Llangwm
Maerdy
Rug Chapel
A494
Corwen
Carrog
Llangollen Railway
631

S
611
FOEL GOCH
A5
Druid
Rug
Bonwm
A5
Llidiart-y-parc
Glyndyfrdw
Glyndyfrdw

Ciltalgarth
Glan-yr-afon
Glan-yr-afon
A494
Llangar Old Parish Church
Cynwyd
MOEL FFERNA
Moel Fferna 631

Celyn
Afon Trywer
Fron-goch
Sarnau
Bethel
R Dee
B4401

The National te Water Centre
Cefn-ddwysarn
B4402
Llandderfel
Llandrillo
Berwyn
R Ceiriog
4

lidiardau
Rhiwlas
B4401
B4401
Crogen
Cadwst
784 CADER BRONWEN

N
Rhyd-uchaf
Bala
Llanfor
Pale
Pennant
827 CADER BERWYN
Llanarmon Dyffryn Ceiriog
5

Byd Mary Jones World V
B4391
Rhos-y-gwaliau
Y Berwyn (Berwyn Ridge section)
Llanga

Llanycil
A
Parc
Bala Lake Railway
B4403
Llyn Tegid
Llangower
Llanuwchllyn
Pandy

534
Llanrhaeadr-ym-Mochnant
6

T
626 MOEL-Y-GEIFR
Ty-nant
Pennant-Melangell
Pencraig
Cefn Coch
B4396
B4580

Y Berwyn (Lake Vyrnwy section)
Llangynog
Penybontfawr
B4396
Pen-y-Garnedd
Pedairffordd
Rhos-y-brith
112

U
Z
Lake Vyrnwy
B4393
Hirnant
Bethel
B4391
7

lanymawddwy
Llanwddyn
V RSPB
Abertridwr
B4393
Tycrwyn
Llanfyllin
A490

Llanerch
544 TIR RHIWIOG
Ddol-Cownwy
Fachwen
Llanfihangel-yng-Ngwynfa
8

inas-Mawddwy
Afon Twrch
Llwydiarth
B4395

Cwm-Cewydd
93
A458
H
J
K
94
L
River Vyrnwy
Pont Robert
M
Meifod

Dolanog
B4382

Mallwyd

Chowley
Barbridge
Peckforton
H
G Harthill
Clutton 129 oxton
Higher
Hurwardsley
H
Peckfort
J
130
Radmore
Green
K
Rease
Heath
Crewe
Green
A530
Gresty
Green
1
Barton
Barnhill
Bulkeley
Ridley Green
Brindley
Burland
A51
A534
Wistaston
Willaston
Shavington
Fuller's Moor
Watermill
Brown Knowl
Gallantry Bank
Croxton Green
Faddiley
B5341
Acton
Dorfold Hall
Stoneley Green
Nantwich
A500
Hough
Weston
Stretton
A41
Bickerton
8
Gradeley Green
Butt Green
Haymoor Green
stletown
Duckington
Cholmondeley Castle
A49
Chorley
Ravensmoor
Stapeley
Chorlton
Wybunbury
Balter Hea
Edge Green
Tilston
Hampton Green
Hetherson Green
BeWilderwood
Bickley Moss
Wrenbury
Hack Green
Secret Bunker
Hatherton
Buddle
Horton Green
Hampton Heath
A530
Sound
Broomhill Green
Hankelow
A529
B5071
Hunsterson
A51
Walgherton
Blakenhall
Shocklach
Ebnal
Bickley
Norbury Common
Pinsley Green
Aston
Newhall
Audlem
Bridgemere
2
Checkley
Chorlton Lane
No Man's Heath
Norbury
Marbury
Marley Green
Dodd's Green
Royal's Green
Lightwood Green
Buerton
Kinsey Heath
114
Checkl Green
ington Heath
Malpas
Bradley
Bell o' th' Hill
Wirswall
Hollyhurst
Burleydam
Coxbank
A525
Woo
Upper Threapwood
Oldcastle Heath
Higher Wych
Grindley Brook
Whitchurch
A525
Broughall
Wilkesley
Adderley
Dorrington
Knighton
Bearstone
3
Tallarn Green
Eglwys Cross
The Chequer
Redbrook
Catteralslane
Ash Magna
Ightfield
Calverhall
A529
Norton in Hales
Muckle
4
an's
Bronington
A495
Alkington
Ash Parva
Betton
B5026
anmer
Arowry
Tilstock
Prees Heath
Longslow
Sandylane
A53
Fenn's, Whixall & Bettisfield Mosses
Platt Lane
Steel Heath
Prees Higher Heath
Moreton Say
Longford
Almington
1459
Hookg
Blore
hampton
Canal
Welsh End
Hollinwood
B5476
A49
A41
Sandford
Bletchley
Ternhill
Market Drayton
A529
The Fouralls
Chipnall
5
Bettisfield
Whixall
Coton
Prees
Darliston
Fauls
Lostford
Sutton
Woodseaves
Cheswardine
Lipley
Balmer Heath
Northwood
Quina Brook
Prees Lower Heath
Marchamley Wood
Wollerton
Stoke Heath
Wistanswick
Lockleywood
Great Soud
Lyneal
Paddolgreen
Prees Green
Heathcote
Millgreen
Goldstone
Little Soudley
Wolverley
Newtown
Ryebank
Lowe
B5065
Hawkstone
Marchamley
Hodnet
Stoke upon Tern
Hungryhatton
6
Ellen
Brownheath
Loppington
Weston-under-Redcastle
Wixhill
Hodnet Hall
High Hatton
Ollerton
Peplow
Hinstock
Sambrook
Eyton
Wem
Commonwood
Aston
Barkers Green
Lee Brockhurst
Moston
Bury Walls
Booley
Child's Ercall
Stanford Bridge
Howle
A41
114
Pickst
Noneley
Tilley
Preston Brockhurst
Besford
Stanton upon Hine Heath
Ellerdine Heath
Eaton upon Tern
Myddle
Alderton
Clive
Grinshill
Castle
Moreton Corbet
Moretonmill
A442
Great Bolas
Chetwynd
Eyton
Newton on the Hill
Yorton Heath
A49
Shawbury
Edgebolton
Cold Hatton
R Meese
Meeson
Edgmond Ma
7
church
Harmer Hill
Old Woods
Rowton
Cold Hatton Heath
Cherrington
Tibberton
Edgmond
B5067
Merrington
Preston Gubbals
Hadnall
Little Wytheford
Great Wytheford
Walton
Moortown
Waters Upton
B5062
Longford
Church Aston
Valford Heath
Bomere Heath
Astley
Bings Heath
B5063
Crudgington
Kynnersley
Leaton
Fitz
Albrighton
1403
Poynton Green
Poynton
High Ercall
Cotwall
Tern
Eyton upon the Weald Moors
Preston upon the Weald Moors
A518
8
Rosehill
A5124
S
Haughton
A5223
L
Sleapford
TELGORD
Donnington
Bicton
Harlescott
Battlefield
Haughmond Abbey
Roden
Sugdon
Longdon upon Tern
Hoo & Dinosaur
F
Lilyhur
Calcott
West Mid
Coton Hill
Ditherington
Underdale
A49
Uffington
Upton Magna
96
Roden Heath
Somerwood
Rodington
Marsh Long Waste
Bratton
Shawbirch
A442
Granville
M
Trench
Lord
Shelton
G
H
A458
A512
J
Withingto
Walcot
Wrockwardine
Allsatt
B4394
Admaston
A5223
Donnington
Lilyhut

G 131 H J K 132 Wirksworth

Onecote • Butterton • Wetton • Alstonefield • Alsop en le Dale • Longcliffe
Morridge Side • Grindon • Hope • Milldale • Parwich • Brassington • Little Bolel
Ford • Stanshope • Tissington • Ballidon • National Stone • Whatsta
A523 • Back o' th' Brook • Ilam • Carsington • Warmbrook • Alder
Waterfall • R Manifold • Dove Dale • Bradbourne • Hopton • Gorseybank
Peak Wildlife Park • Ilam Park • Carsington Water • Upper Town • Millers Green • Ashleyhay
Winkhill • Calton • Thorpe • Fenny Bentley • Hognaston • Kirk Ireton • B5023
Waterhouses • Blore • Kniveton • Blackwall • Idridgehay
Ipstones • Cauldon • 15 • Rowfield • Biggin • Ireton Wood • Ecclesbourne Valley Railway
Foxt • Cauldon Lowe • A52 • Swinscoe • Mapleton • A515 • Atlow • Hulland Ward • Hillclifflane • Turnditch • Cowen Lane
B5053 • A52 • Ashbourne • Hulland • Shottle
Froghall • Upper Cotton • Near Cotton • Stanton • Mayfield • Clifton • A517 • Bradley • Cross o' th' hands • Hazel
Whiston • Cotton Dell • Ramshorn • Middle Mayfield • Osmaston • Mugginton Lane End
Kingsley Holt • Whiston Eaves • Farley • Wootton • Church Mayfield • Wyaston • A52 • Mugginton • Western Underwood
Oakamoor • Alton • Ellastone • Snelston • Darley Moor • Shirley • Commonside • Brailsford
Threapwood Head • B5032 • Upper Ellastone • Lower Ellastone • Hales Green • Rodsley • Ednaston • Brailsford Green • Kedleston
Threapwood • Norbury • B5033 • Yeaveley • Hollington • Over Burrows • Kirk Langley
Bradley in the Moors • Denstone • Roston • Great Cubley • Alkmonton • Thurvaston • Longlane • Langley Green • Kedleston Hall
Greatgate • B5030 • Croxden • Rocester • Little Cubley • Longford • Bupton • Lees Green • Lees • Langley Common • Mackw
Hollington • Abbey • Marston Montgomery • Waldley • Potter Somersal • Boylestone • Cropper • Radbourne • Mickleover
Lower Tean • Combridge • Crakemarsh • Somersal Herbert • Harehill • Lane Ends • Trusley • B5020
Checkley • Beamhurst • Stramshall • Spath • Doveridge • Oaks Green • Sapperton • Sutton on the Hill • Dalbury • A516
Fole • A522 • Upper Nobut • 6 • A50 • Church Broughton • Burnaston
Lower Leigh • Withington • Redfern's Cottage • Uttoxeter • Foston • Burnheath • Etwall • Find
Godstone • Painleyhill • Highwood • Sudbury Hall • Sudbury • Hatton • Hilton • A50
Field • Bramshall • Blounts Green • Birch Cross • Marchington • Scropton • Coton in the Clay • Marston on Dove • Egginton • S
Kingstone • Loxley Green • Netherland Green • Moreton • Tutbury • Rolleston on Dove • A38 • Willingt
A518 • The Blythe • Scounslow Green • Gorsty Hill • B5017 • Fauld • Alder Moor • Craythorne • Parson's Hill • B5008
Heatley • Marchington Woodlands • Draycott in the Clay • Hanbury • Woodend • Stretton • A511 • Newton Solney
Drointon • Dapple Heath • Newborough • Anslow • Beam Hill • Horninglow • Burton upon Trent • Bretby
Newton • Abbots Bromley • A515 • Anslow Gate • Anslow Lees • Stapenhill • Stanhope • Bretby
Blithfield Reservoir • B5234 • FA National Football Centre • Callingwood • National Forest • Winshill • Newhall
Admaston • Stockwell Heath • Newchurch • Rangemore • Branston • A444 • Church Gresley • Castle Gresley
Haywood • Mill Green • Hoar Cross • Tatenhill • Branston Water Park • Walton-on-Trent • Coton Park • Mount Pleasant
Colwich • Bishton • Colton • Woodmill • Dunstall • A514 • Stanton • Cauldwell • Linton
Mavesyn Ridware • Hamstall Ridware • Hadley End • Olive Green • Barton-under-Needwood • Rosliston • Linton Heath • Overseal
Slitting Mill • Blithbury • Hill Ridware • Morrey • Yoxall • Weaverslake • Woodhouses • Efflinch • Conkers
Upper Longdon • Brereton • Nethertown • Trent Valley • Barton Green • Wychnor • Coton in the Elms • Donis
Rugeley • Brereton Hill • Armitage • A513 • King's Bromley • Orgreave • Overley • A38 • Lullington • Netherseal • Acresford
Longdon • Handsacre • B5014 • Rileyhill • National Memorial • Croxall • Edingale

G 98 H J K L 99 M

A51 • A515 • Stonywell • Elmhurst • Alrewas • Fradley
Cannock Wood • Castle Ring • Longdon Green

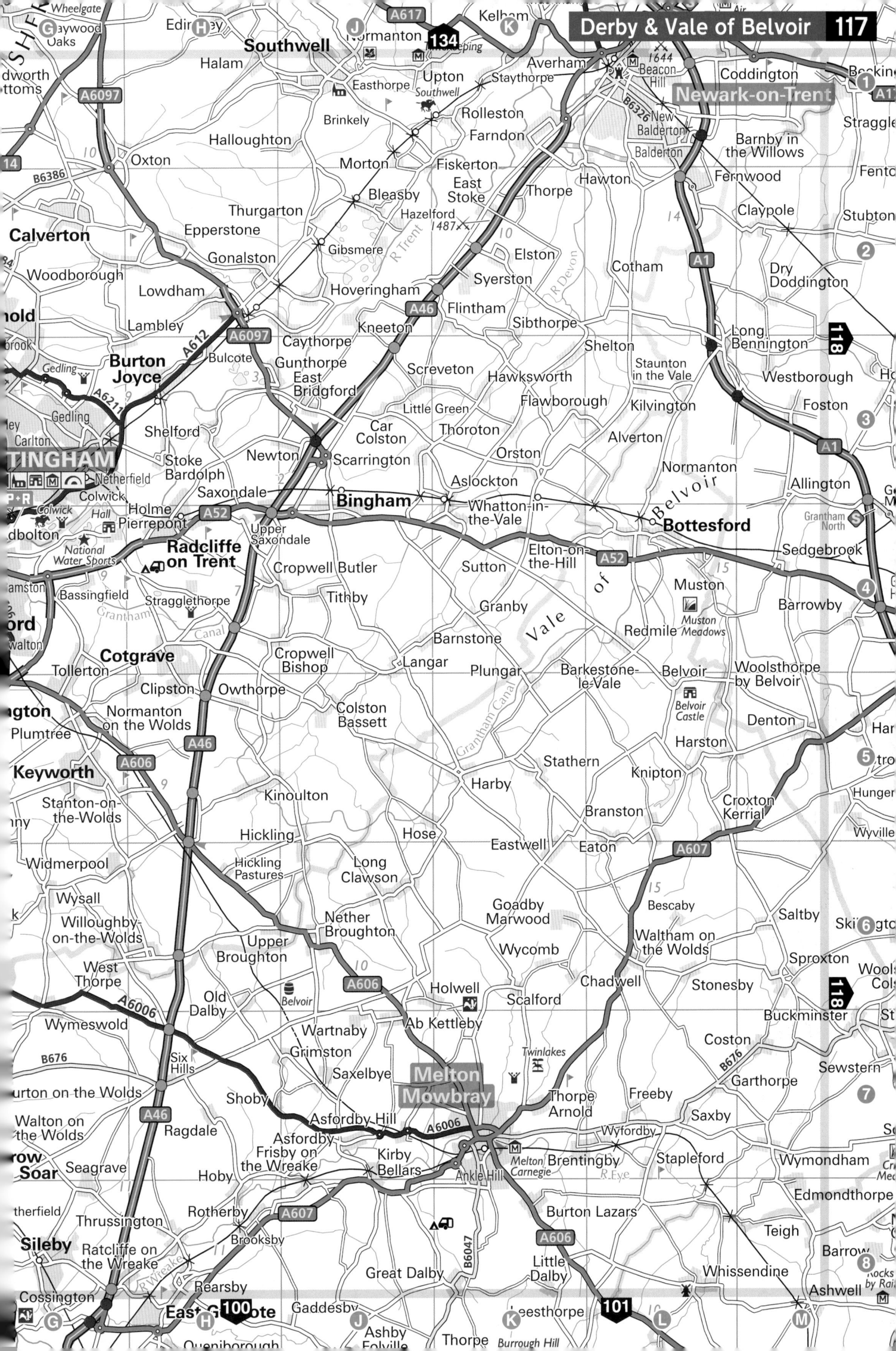

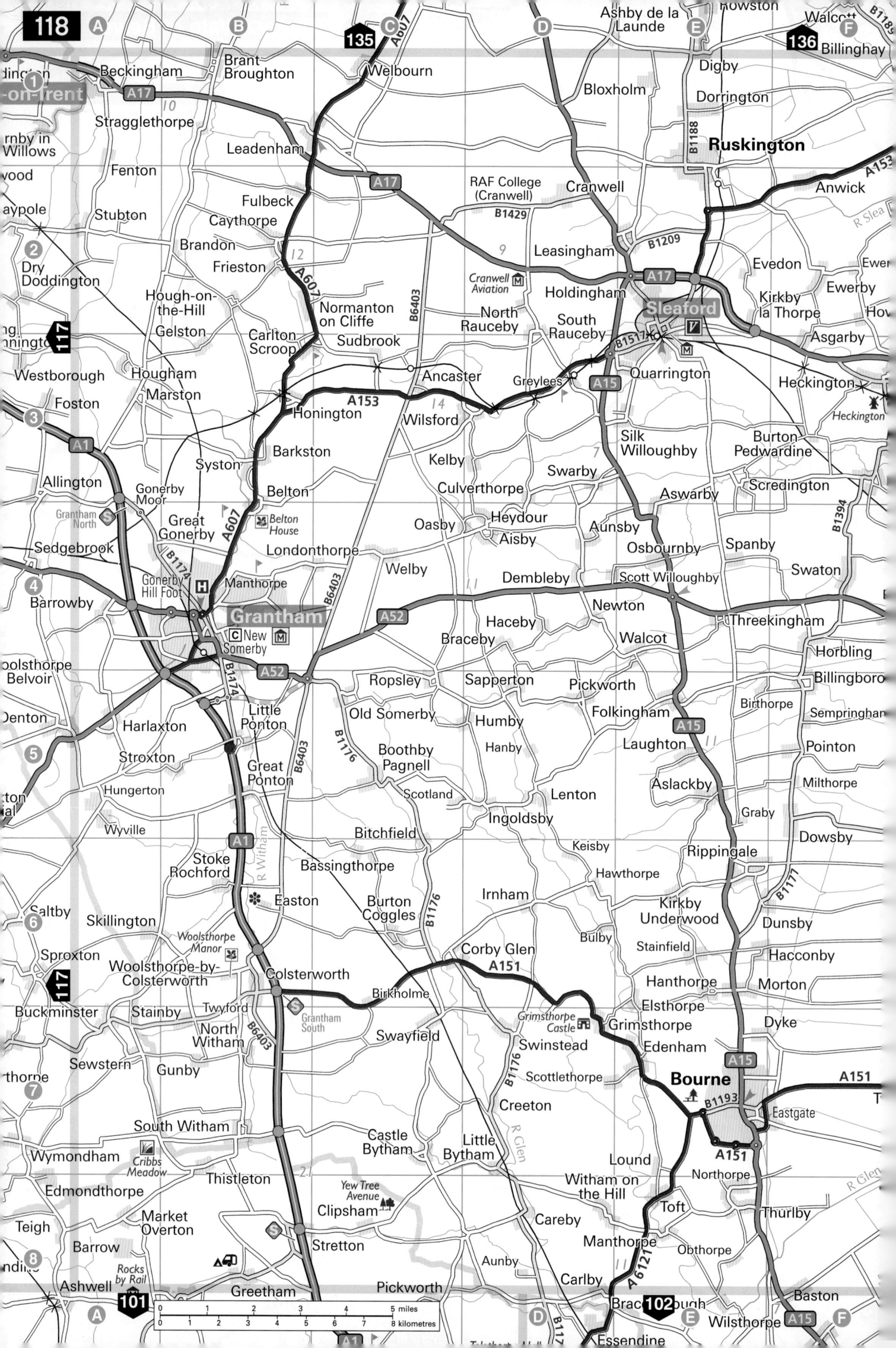

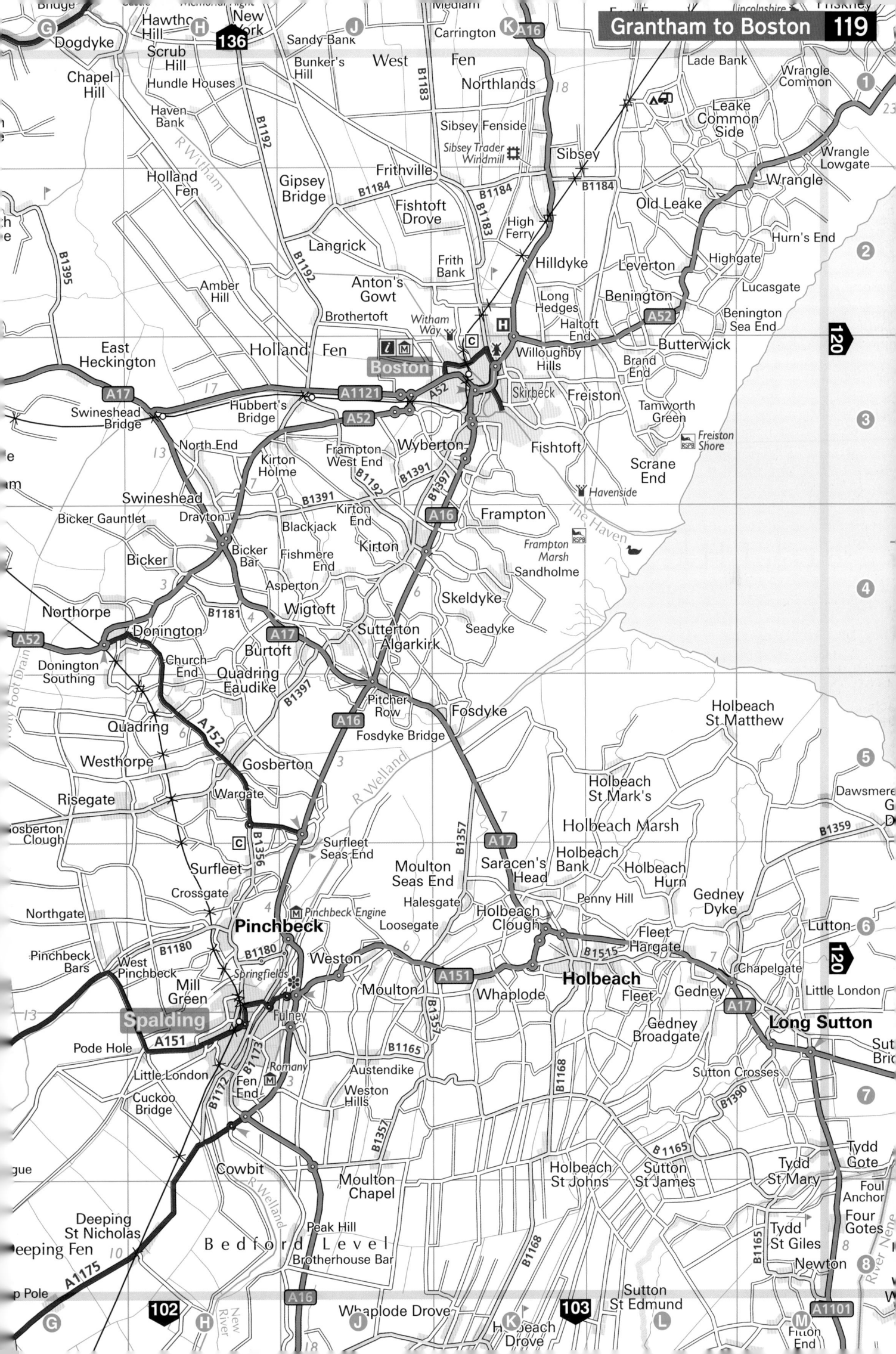

Friskney
Friskney Eaudike

137

olnshire

Wrangle
ommon
1

23

Wrangle
Lowgate
Wrangle

Hurn's End
2

ucasgate

gton
End

119

3

THE · WASH

Holme
Dunes
Holme n
the Sea

Old
Hunstanton

Hunstanton

Ringstead

A149

Norfolk
Lavender

Heacham

4

Sedgeford

Snettisham
Snettisham Park
Southgate

RSPB Snettisham
Ingoldisthorpe
Shern

B1440
12

ach
thew
5

Dawsmere

Gedney
Drove End

B1359

Dersingham
Doddshill

Dersingham Bog
Wolferton
Sandringh

West
Newton

B1440

Babingley River

6 Lutton

119

Castle
Rising

A149

B1439

hapelgate
Little London

North
Wootton

Castle

A148

Congham
Roydon

Long Sutton

Sutton
Bridge

Wingland

South Wootton

A1078

A148

Roydon
Common

Pott
Row

osses
7

Walpole
Cross Keys

Little
London

West
Lynn

Gaywood

A149

4

H

Bawsey

B1145

Gayton

11

A17

Clenchwarton

South
Lynn

A148

King's Lynn

Fairstead

C

Leziate

Ashwick

Tydd
St Mary

Tydd
Gote

Walpole
St Andrew

Hay Green

Tilney
All Saints

A47

i

M

Fair Green

East
Winch

Foul
Anchor
Four
Gotes

Walpole
St Peter

Tilney High End

12

Saddlebow

A10

A47

Middleton

B1165

Tydd
St Giles
8 Newton

Ingleborough

St John's
Highway

Tilney St
Lawrence

West
Winch

North
Runcton

Blackborough
End

Wes
Biln

River Nene

8

West
Walton

A1101

Fitton
End

Highway

Wiggenhall
St Mary the
Virgin

Wiggenhall
St Peter

Setchey

Pentne

Wiggenhall
St Germans

Watatunga
Wildlife Reserve

ordsbridge

0 1 2 3 4 5 miles
0 1 2 3 4 5 6 7 8 kilometres

R Great Ouse

The Wash

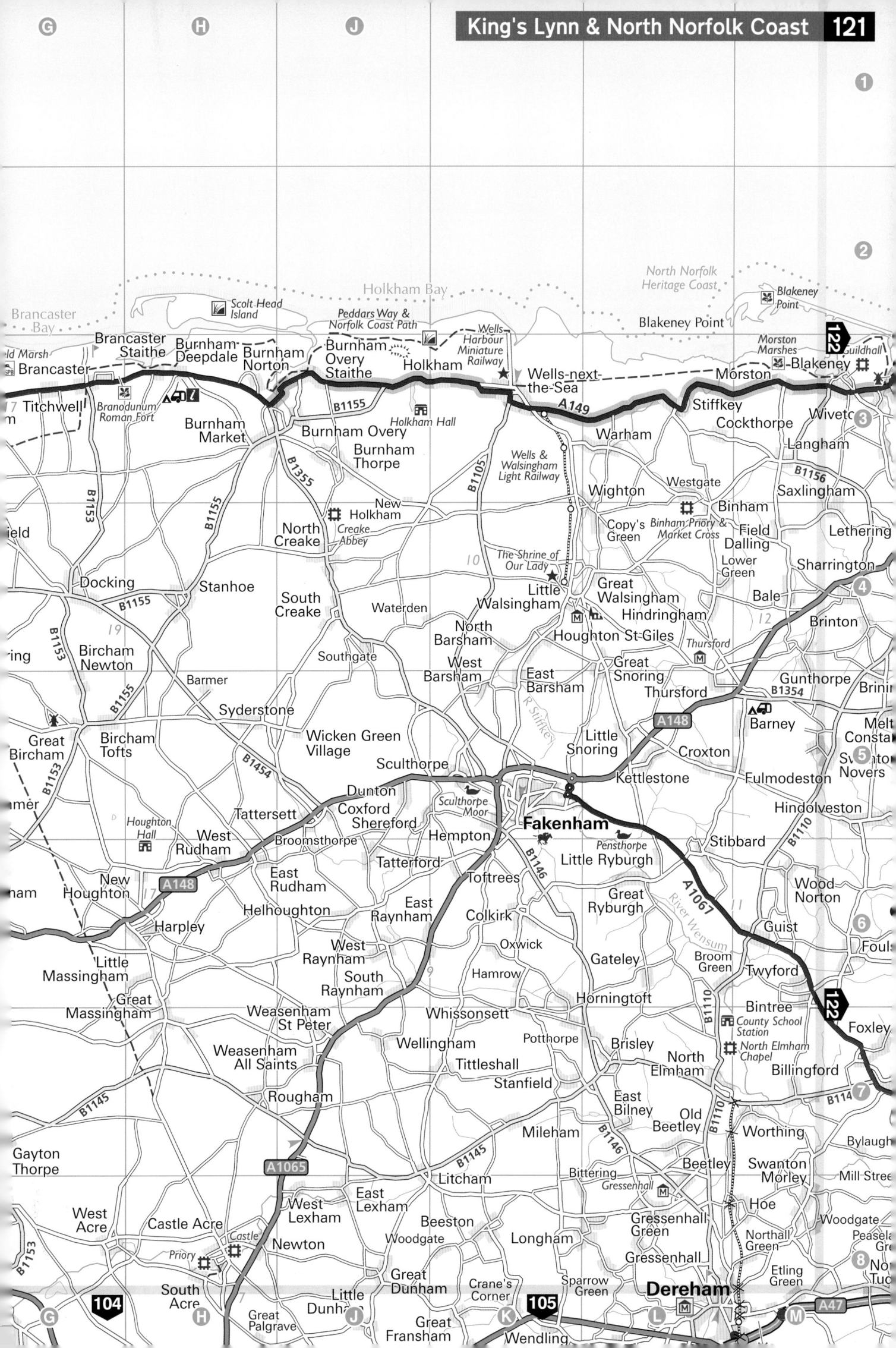

G   H   J

1

2

North Norfolk
Heritage Coast

Holkham Bay

Scolt Head
Island

Peddars Way &
Norfolk Coast Path

Wells
Harbour
Miniature
Railway

Blakeney
Point

Blakeney Point

Brancaster
Bay

Brancaster
Staithe

Burnham
Deepdale

Burnham
Norton

Burnham
Overy
Staithe

Burnham
Overy

Holkham

Wells-next-
the-Sea

Morston
Marshes

Guildhall

122

Blakeney

Old Marsh

Brancaster

Titchwell

Branodunum
Roman Fort

Burnham
Market

Holkham Hall

A149

Warham

Morston

Stiffkey
Cockthorpe

Wiveton

Langham

B1155

Burnham
Thorpe

Wells &
Walsingham
Light Railway

Wighton

Westgate

Saxlingham

Docking

B1155

New
Holkham

Creake
Abbey

Copy's
Green

Binham Priory &
Market Cross

Binham

Field
Dalling

Lethering

B1153

North
Creake

The Shrine of
Our Lady

Lower
Green

Sharrington

Stanhoe

South
Creake

Waterden

Little
Walsingham

Great
Walsingham

Hindringham

Bale

4

Bircham
Newton

B1153

Southgate

North
Barsham

Houghton St Giles

Thursford

Brinton

12

Gunthorpe

Barmer

West
Barsham

East
Barsham

Great
Snoring

Thursford

B1354

Brini

Great
Bircham

Syderstone

R Stiffkey

Little
Snoring

A148

Barney

Melt
Consta

B1153

Bircham
Tofts

Wicken Green
Village

Croxton

Fulmodeston

Sv
Novers

5

B1454

Sculthorpe

Kettlestone

Hindolveston

Houghton
Hall

Dunton

Sculthorpe
Moor

Fakenham

Penthorpe

Stibbard

B1110

Tattersett

Coxford
Shereford

Hempton

Little Ryburgh

B1146

West
Rudham

Broomsthorpe

Tatterford

Toftrees

Great
Ryburgh

A1067

Wood
Norton

New
Houghton

A148

17

East
Rudham

East
Raynham

Colkirk

Great
Ryburgh

River Wensum

11

Guist

6

Harpley

Helhoughton

Oxwick

Gateley

Broom
Green

Twyford

122

Little
Massingham

West
Raynham

Hamrow

Horningtoft

Bintree

Foul

Great
Massingham

South
Raynham

Whissonsett

Wellingham

Potthorpe

Brisley

County School
Station

Foxley

Weasenham
St Peter

Tittleshall

North
Elmham

North Elmham
Chapel

Billingford

Weasenham
All Saints

Stanfield

East
Bilney

Old
Beetley

B1110

B114

7

Rougham

Mileham

B1146

Worthing

Bylaugh

B1145

Litcham

Beetley

Swanton
Morley

Mill Stree

Gayton
Thorpe

A1065

East
Lexham

Bittering

Gressenhall

Hoe

Woodgate

West
Acre

Castle Acre

West
Lexham

Beeston

Woodgate

Longham

Gressenhall
Green

Northall
Green

Peasela

B1153

Priory

Castle

Newton

Great
Dunham

Gressenhall

Etling
Green

No
Tud

8

104

South
Acre

Little
Dunha

Crane's
Corner

Sparrow
Green

Dereham

A47

G   H   J   K   105   L   M

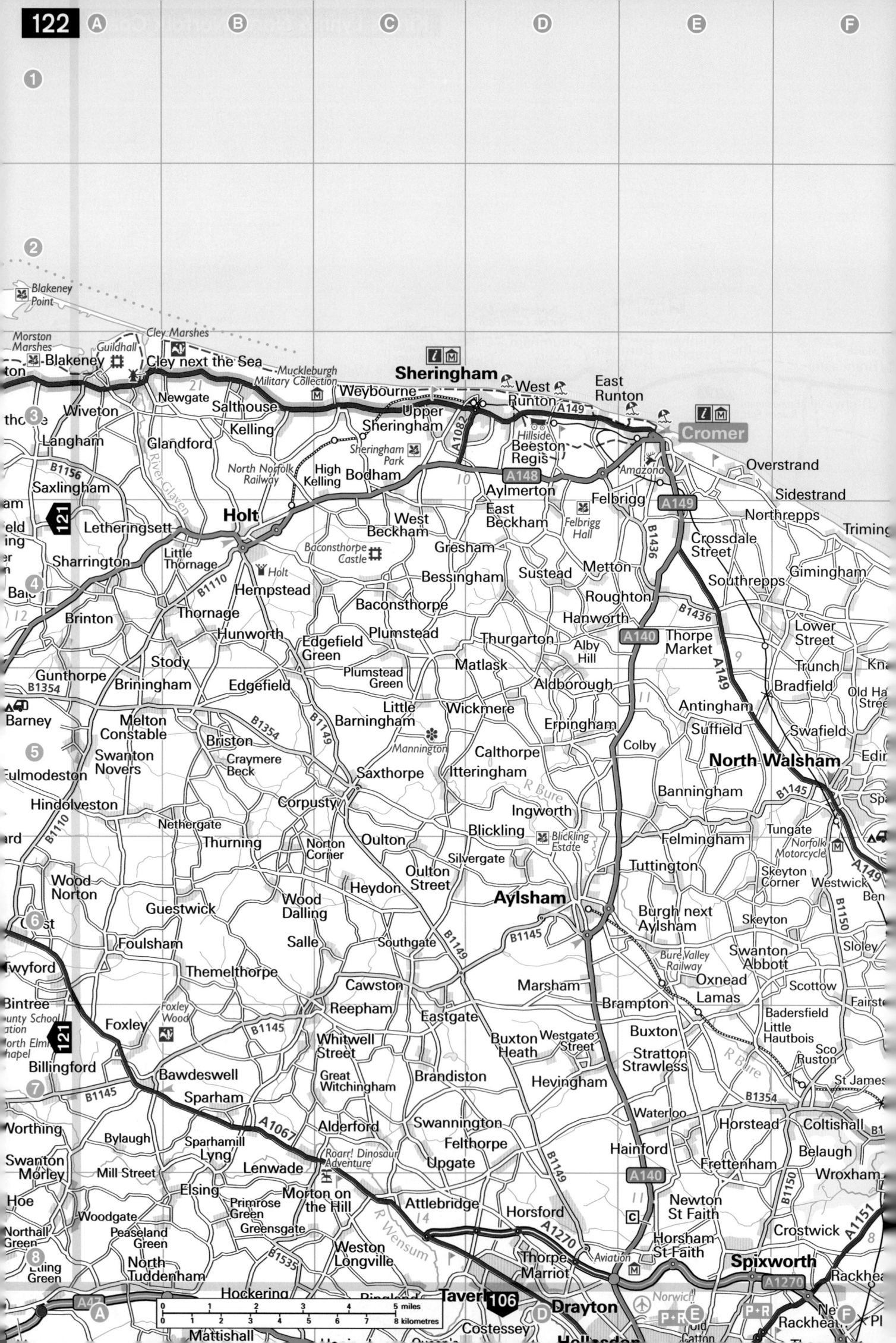

G H J K

1
2
3
4
5
6
7
8

Mundesley
w Mill
Paston
B1159
Bacton
horpe
Walcott
Pollard
Street
Witton
Ridlington
Ridlington
Street
Happisburgh
Crostwight
Happisburgh
Common
Whimpwell Green
Eccles on Sea
Hempstead
ng
gate
East
Ruston
Lessingham
Ingham
Corner
Sea Palling
ad
Ingham
Waxham
Dilham
Stalham
Calthorpe
Street
burgh
The
Broads
Low
Street
Stalham
Green
Hickling
Horsey Corner
Sutton
Fen
RSPB
Sutton
Hickling Green
Horsey
Barton
Turf
Hill Common
Horsey Windpump
Pennygate
Wood
Street
Hickling
Heath
Hickling
Broad
gate
Neatishead
Barton
Broad
Catfield
Catfield
Common
Martham
Broad
West
Somerton
East
Somerton
Irstead
Sharp
Green
Potter
Heigham
hreehammer
Common
Ludham
Martham
Winterton-on-Sea
oveton
RAF Radar
BeWILDerwood
A1062
Johnson
Street
Bastwick
Cess
Hemsby
Hole
per
eet
Horning
Upper Street
Repps
R.Thurne
Hemsby
Newport
Ormesby
Broad
wick
Bure
Marshes
Rollesby
A149
Ormesby
St Michael
Scratby
Broads Wildlife
Centre
Thurne
B1152
Fleggburgh/
Burgh St Margaret
Ormesby
St Margaret
California
Ranworth
Ranworth Broad
Pilson
Green
Clippesby
Billockby
107
Caister-on-
Sea
Panx
orth
Fairhaven
Cargate
Green
Filby
Caister Roman Fort
Town
South
Walsham
Thrigby
Mautby
M
1064
9

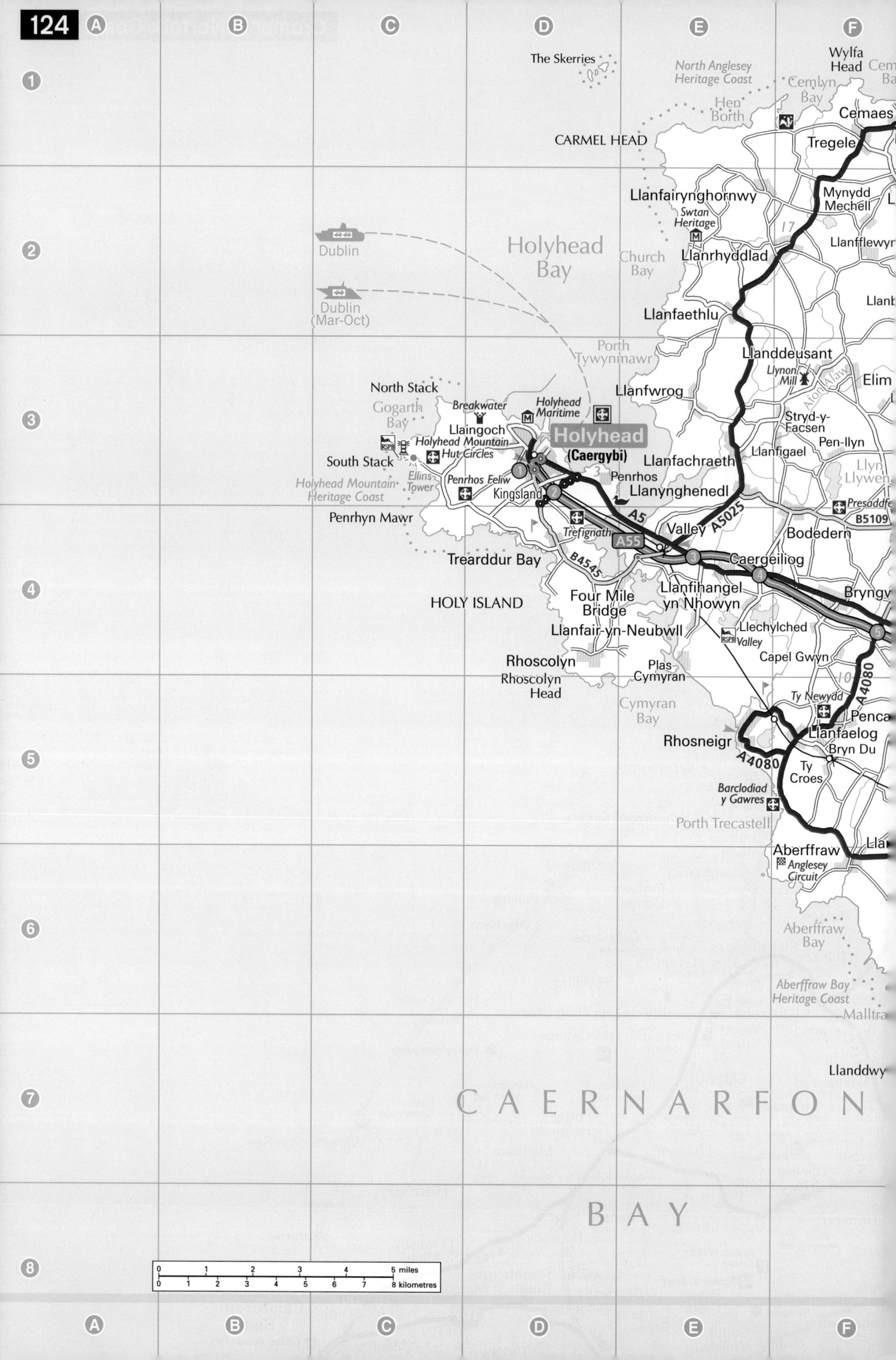

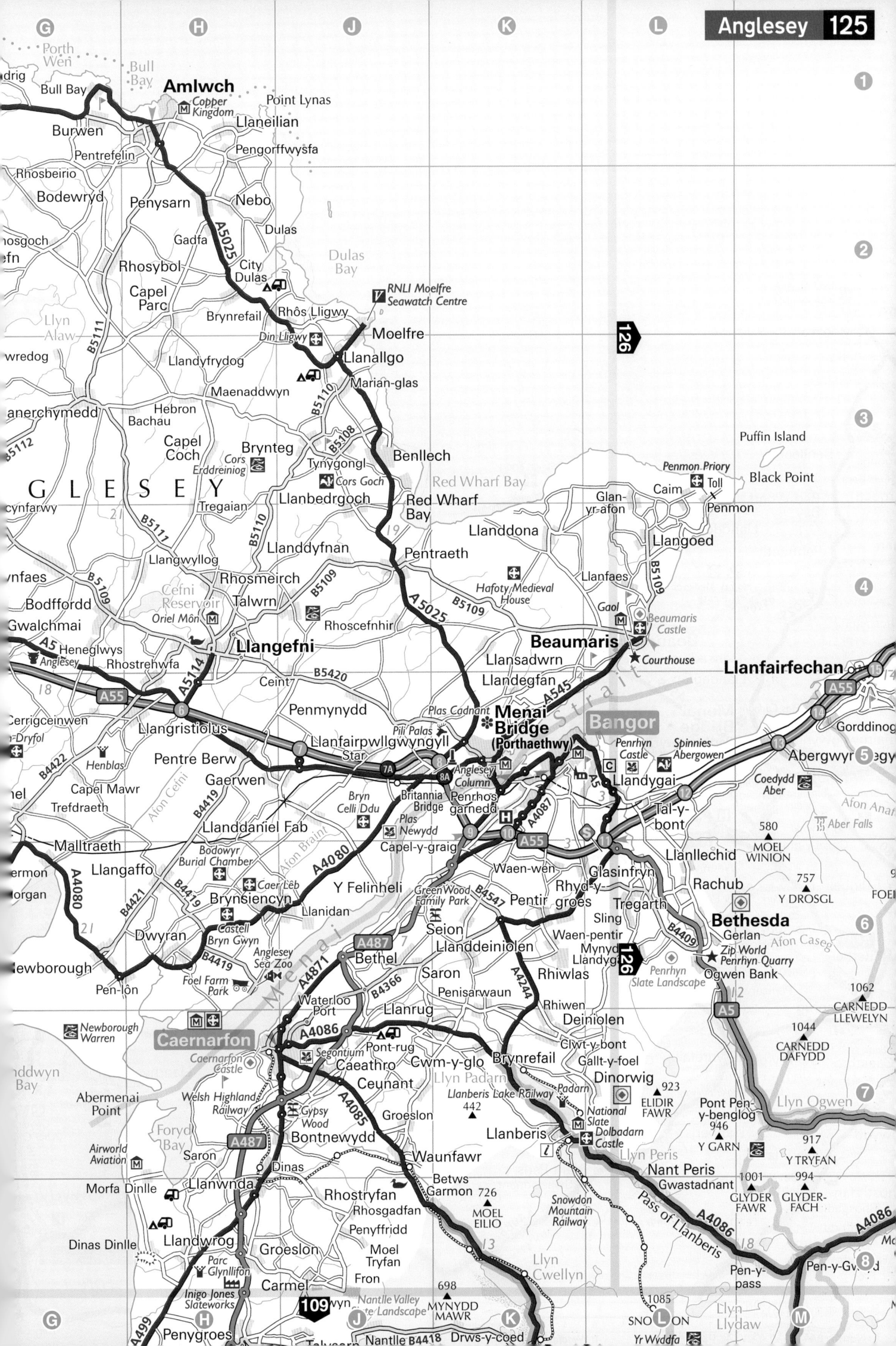

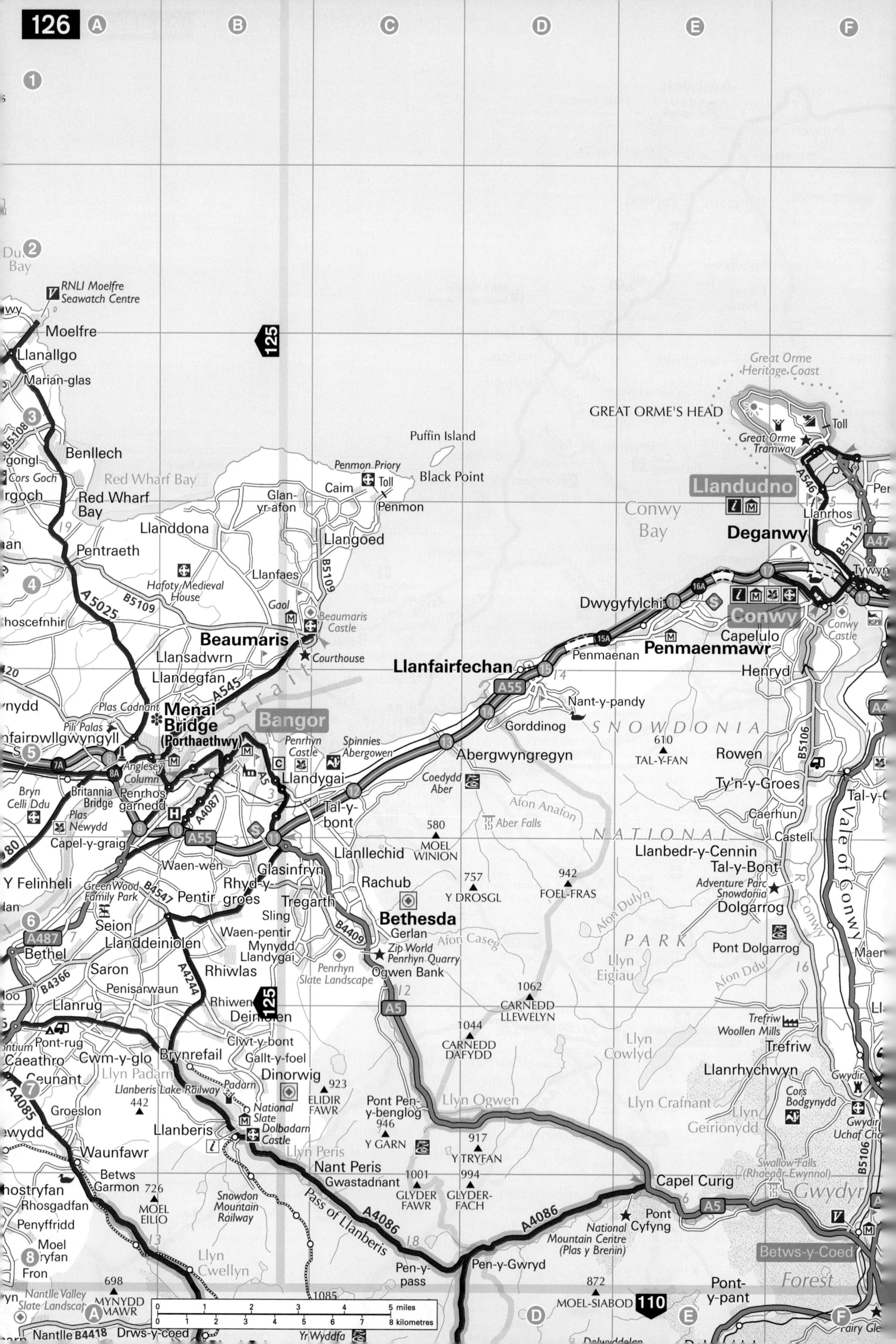

A   B   C   D   E   F

1

2

Du...
Bay

RNLI Moelfre
Seawatch Centre

Moelfre

Llanallgo

Marian-glas

3

Benllech

B5108

Cors Goch

rgoch

Red Wharf Bay

Red Wharf
Bay

Llanddona

Pentraeth

Glan-
yr-afon

Caim

Puffin Island

Penmon Priory   Toll

Black Point

Penmon

GREAT ORME'S HEAD

Great Orme
Heritage Coast

Great Orme
Tramway   Toll

Per

4

an

hoscefnhir

A5025

B5109

Llangoed

Llanfaes

Hafoty Medieval
House

Gaol

Beaumaris
Castle

Llandudno

Conwy
Bay

A546

Llanrhos

Deganwy

B5115   A47

Tywyn

20

Beaumaris

Llansadwrn

Llandegfan

A545

Courthouse

Dwygyfylchi

16A

16

Penmaenan

15A

Conwy

Conwy
Castle

RSPB

18

nydd

Plas Cadnant

Pili Palas

Menai
Bridge
(Porthaethwy)

Bangor

Penrhyn
Castle

Spinnies
Abergowen

Llandygai

Llanfairfechan

A55

14

Gorddinog

Nant-y-pandy

Abergwyngregyn

15

Penmaenmawr

610

TAL-Y-FAN

Rowen

Henryd

B5106

SNOWDONIA

Ty'n-y-Groes

fairpwllgwyngyll

S

5

7A

Anglesey
Column

8A

Bryn
Celli Ddu

Plas
Newydd

Penrhos
garnedd

Britannia
Bridge

H

A4087

A55

Coedydd
Aber

Afon Anafon

Aber Falls

Tal-y-
bont

12

13

580

MOEL
WINION

Caerhun

Castell

Llanbedr-y-Cennin

Tal-y-Bont

NATIONAL

80

Capel-y-graig

9

Waen-wen

Glasinfryn

Rhyd-y-
groes

Pentir

Llanllechid

Rachub

Tregarth

757

Y DROSGL

Gerlan

942

FOEL-FRAS

Afon Dulyn

Adventure Parc
Snowdonia

Dolgarrog

Y Felinheli

GreenWood
Family Park

B4547

Waen-pentir

Bethesda

B4409

Afon Caseg

Mynydd
Llandygai

Zip World
Penrhyn Quarry

PARK

Llyn
Eigiau

Pont Dolgarrog

Maen

6

A487

Bethel

B4366

Saron

Penisarwaun

A4244

Rhiwlas

Penrhyn
Slate Landscape

Ogwen Bank

Afon Ddu

16

Trefriw
Woollen Mills

Llanddeiniolen

Rhiwen

Deiniolen

Clwt-y-bont

Gallt-y-foel

1062

CARNEDD
LLEWELYN

Llyn
Cowlyd

Trefriw

7

Caeathro

Ceunant

Llanrug

Brynrefail

Llyn Padarn

A4085

Groeslon

442

Llanberis Lake Railway

Padarn

Dinorwig

923

ELIDIR
FAWR

Cors
Bodgynydd

Llanrhychwyn

Gwydir
Uchag Cho

Waunfawr

Pont-rug

Cwm-y-glo

National
Slate

Dolbadarn
Castle

A5

1044

CARNEDD
DAFYDD

Pont Pen-
y-benglog

946

Y GARN

Llyn Ogwen

Llyn Crafnant

Llyn
Geirionydd

Swallow Falls
(Rhaeadr-Ewynnol)

Gwydyr

hostryfan

Rhosgadfan

Penyffridd

Moel
ryfan

Fron

Betws
Garmon

726

MOEL
EILIO

Snowdon
Mountain
Railway

Nant Peris

Gwastadnant

Llyn Peris

917

Y TRYFAN

1001

994

GLYDER
FAWR

GLYDER-
FACH

Capel Curig

A5

6

National
Mountain Centre
(Plas y Brenin)

Betws-y-Coed

8

698

MYNYDD
MAWR

Llyn
Cwellyn

Pass of Llanberis

A4086

18

Pen-y-
pass

Pen-y-Gwryd

872

MOEL-SIABOD

110

Pont-
y-pant

Forest

Nantlle Valley
Slate Landscape

Nantlle

B4418

Drws-y-coed

1085

Yr Wyddfa

Pont
Cyfyng

Fairy Gle

A   B   C   D   E   F

0   1   2   3   4   5 miles
0 1 2 3 4 5 6 7 8 kilometres

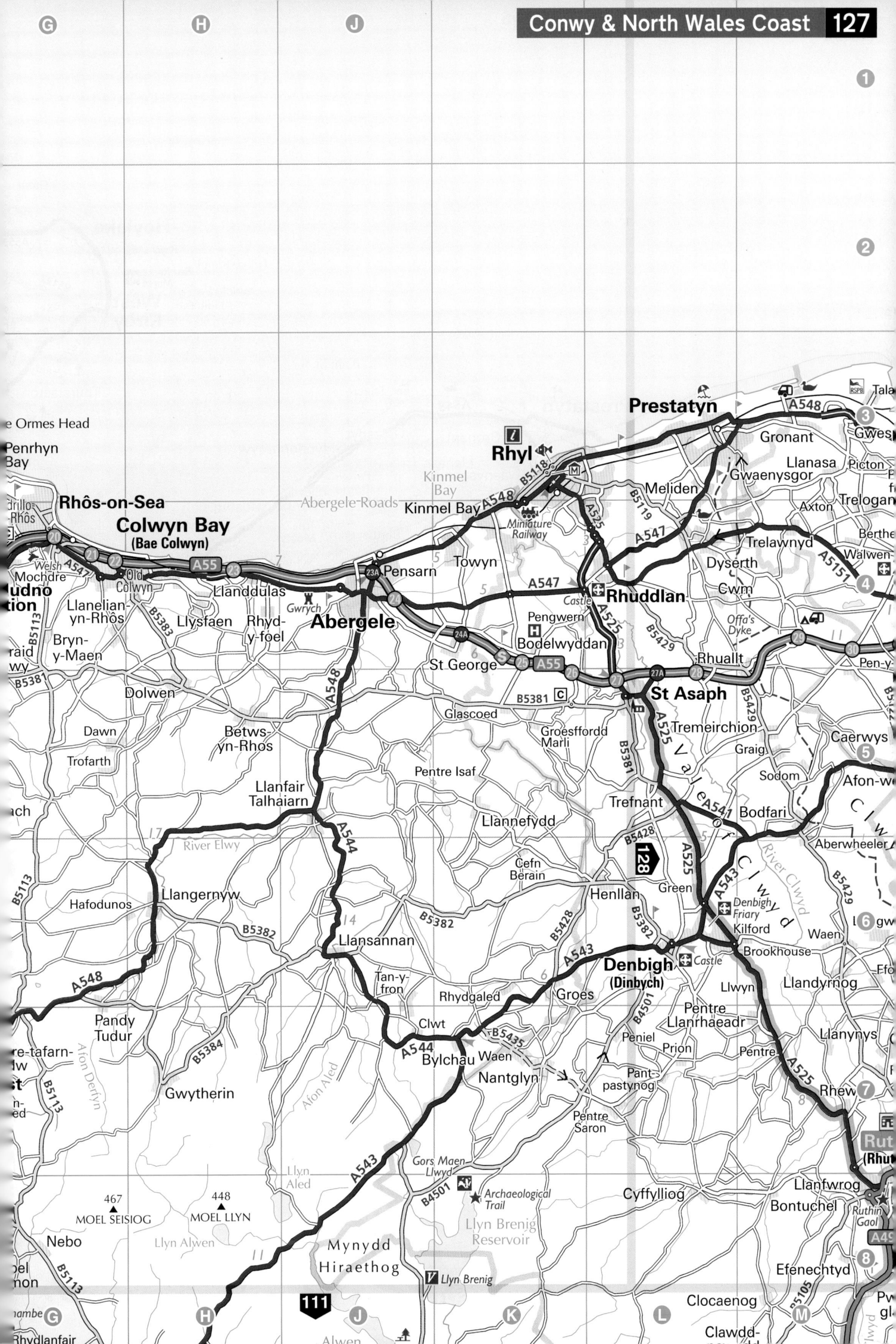

G · H · J

1
2
3
4
5
6
7
8

e Ormes Head

Penrhyn
Bay

Rhôs-on-Sea

Colwyn Bay
(Bae Colwyn)

Prestatyn

Rhyl

Kinmel
Bay

Abergele-Roads

Kinmel Bay

Gronant

Llanasa

Gwaenysgor

Meliden

Picton

Trelogan

Berthe

Walwen

A5151

Towyn

A548

Miniature
Railway

Pensarn

Llanddulas

Gwrych

Old
Colwyn

A55

A547

A548

Llandno
tion

Llanelian-
yn-Rhôs

Bryn-
y-Maen

B5383

Llysfaen

Rhyd-
y-foel

Abergele

A547

Pengwern

Bodelwyddan

Rhuddlan

Dyserth

Cwm

Offa's
Dyke

Rhuallt

A525

A55

St George

St Asaph

B5381

Tremeirchion

Graig

Sodom

Caerwys

Afon-w

Dolwen

Betws-
yn-Rhos

Pentre Isaf

Glascoed

Groesffordd
Marli

A525

Trefnant

Bodfari

Aberwheeler

Dawn

Trofarth

Llanfair
Talhaiarn

Llannefydd

B5428

Cefn
Berain

A544

River Elwy

Llangernyw

A543

Denbigh
Friary

Kilford

Brookhouse

Waen

Hafodunos

B5382

A548

B5382

Llansannan

Henllan

Green

A525

Denbigh
(Dinbych)

Castle

Llwyn

Llandyrnog

Llanynys

Pandy
Tudur

B5384

Tan-y-
fron

Rhydgaled

Clwt

A544

Bylchau

Groes

B5435

Waen

Nantglyn

Peniel

Prion

Pentre
Llanrhaeadr

Pentre

A525

Rhew

Gwytherin

A543

Pant-
pastynog

Pentre
Saron

Rut

(Rhu

MOEL SEISIOG
467

MOEL LLYN
448

Llyn
Aled

Gors Maen
Llwyd

Archaeological
Trail

Cyfylliog

Llanfwrog

Bontuchel

Ruthin
Gaol

Nebo

Llyn Alwen

B4501

Llyn Brenig
Reservoir

Mynydd
Hiraethog

Llyn Brenig

Clocaenog

Efenechtyd

B5113

G · H · J · K · L · M

111

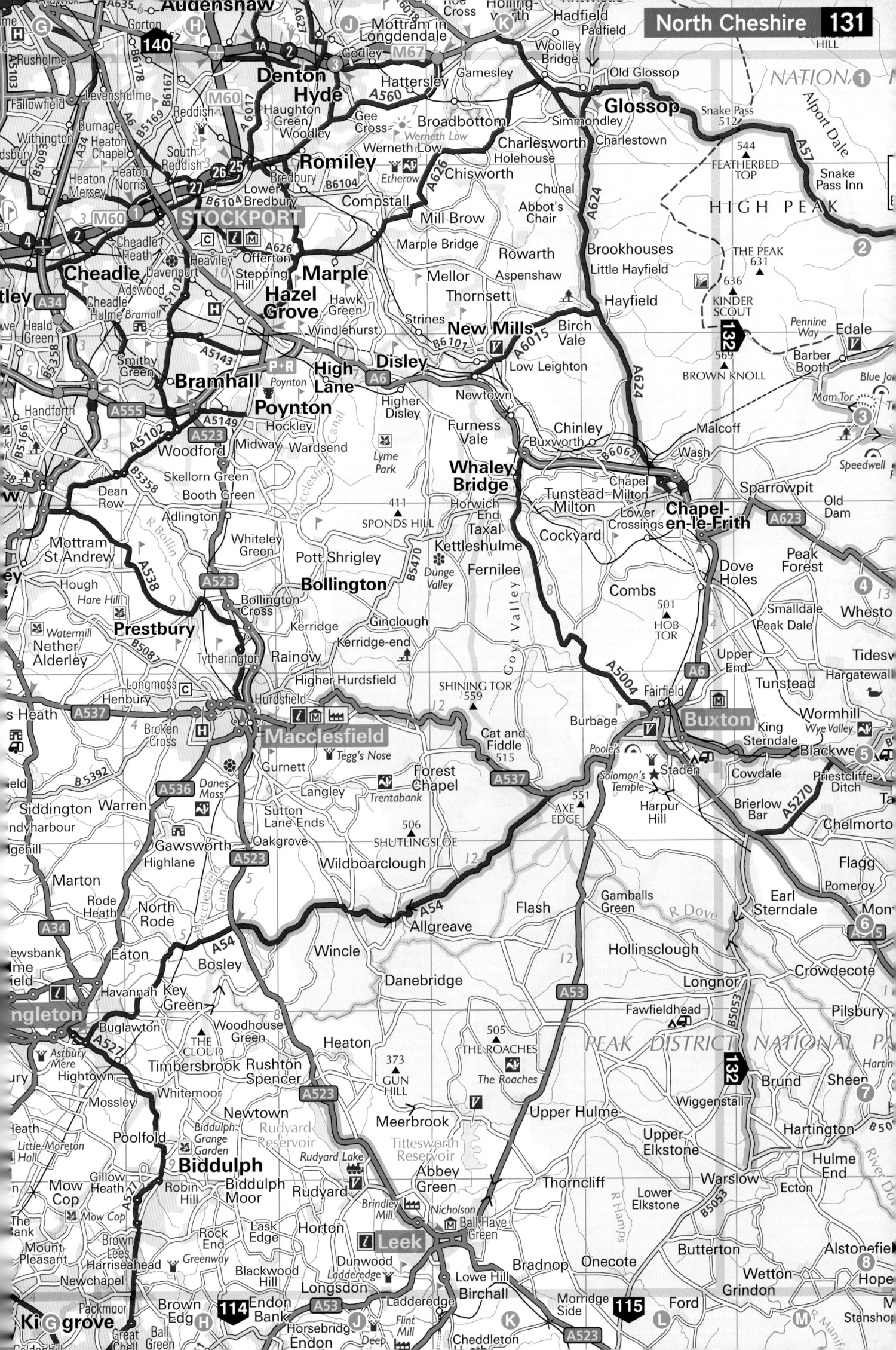

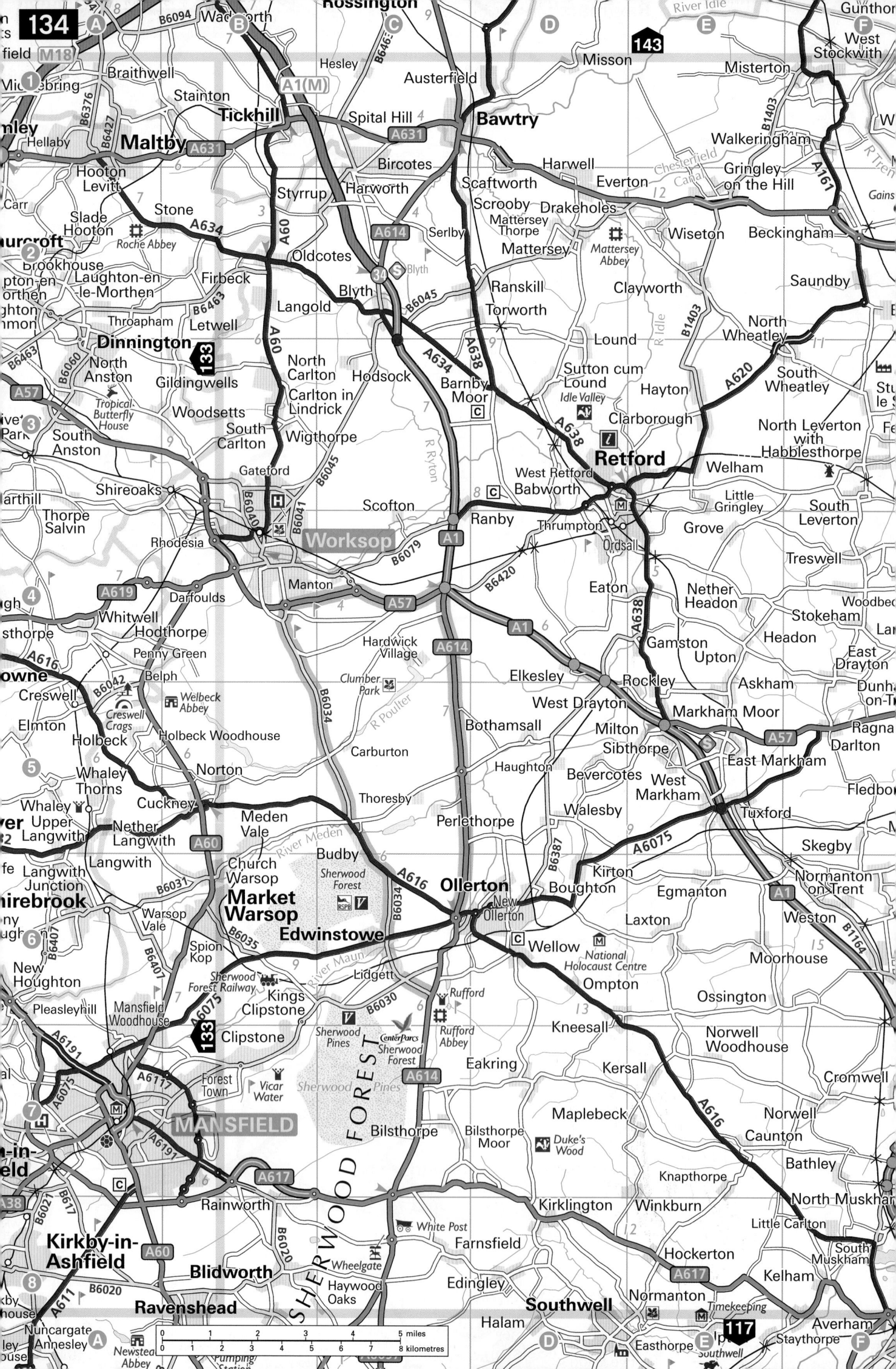

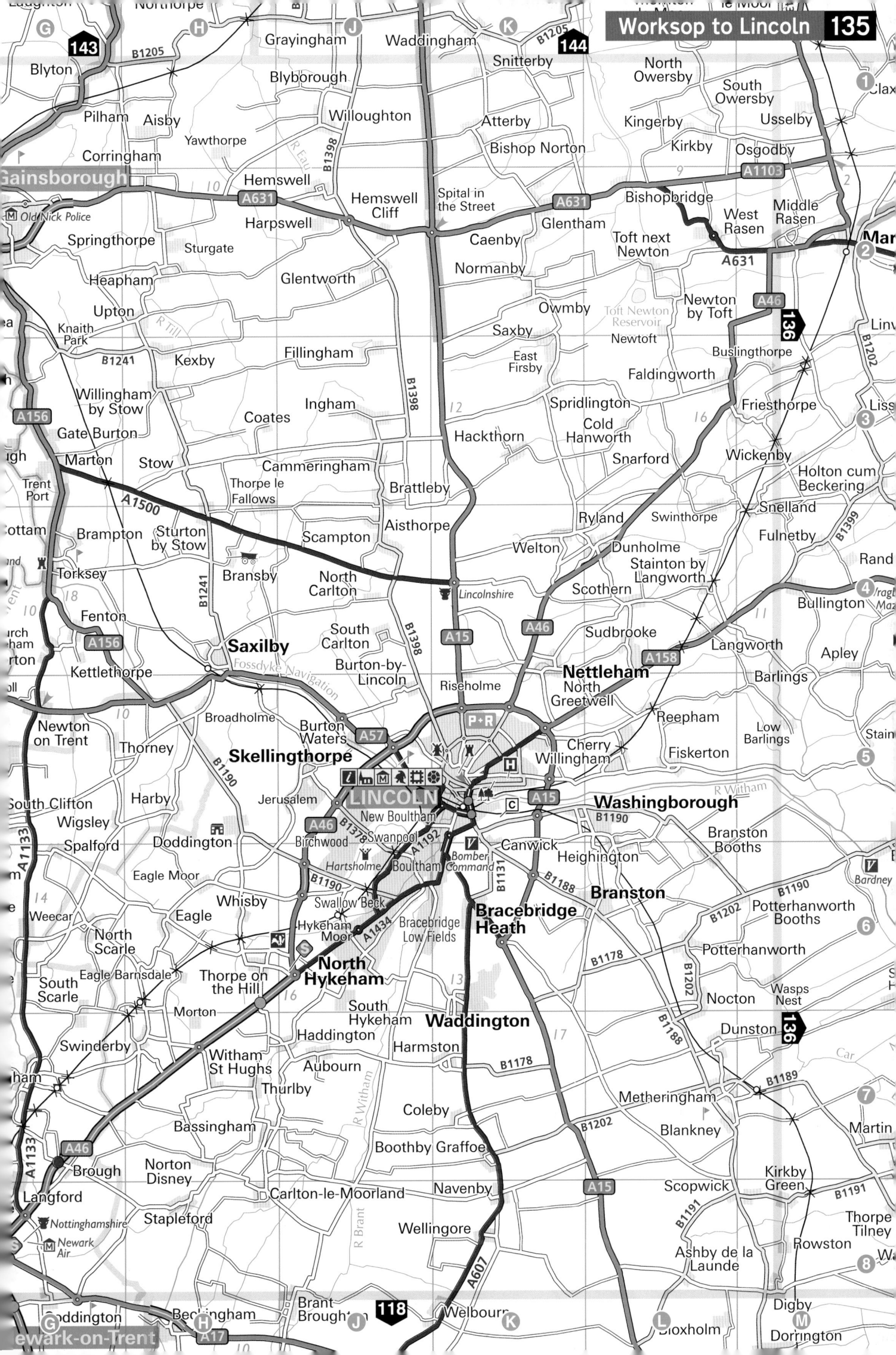

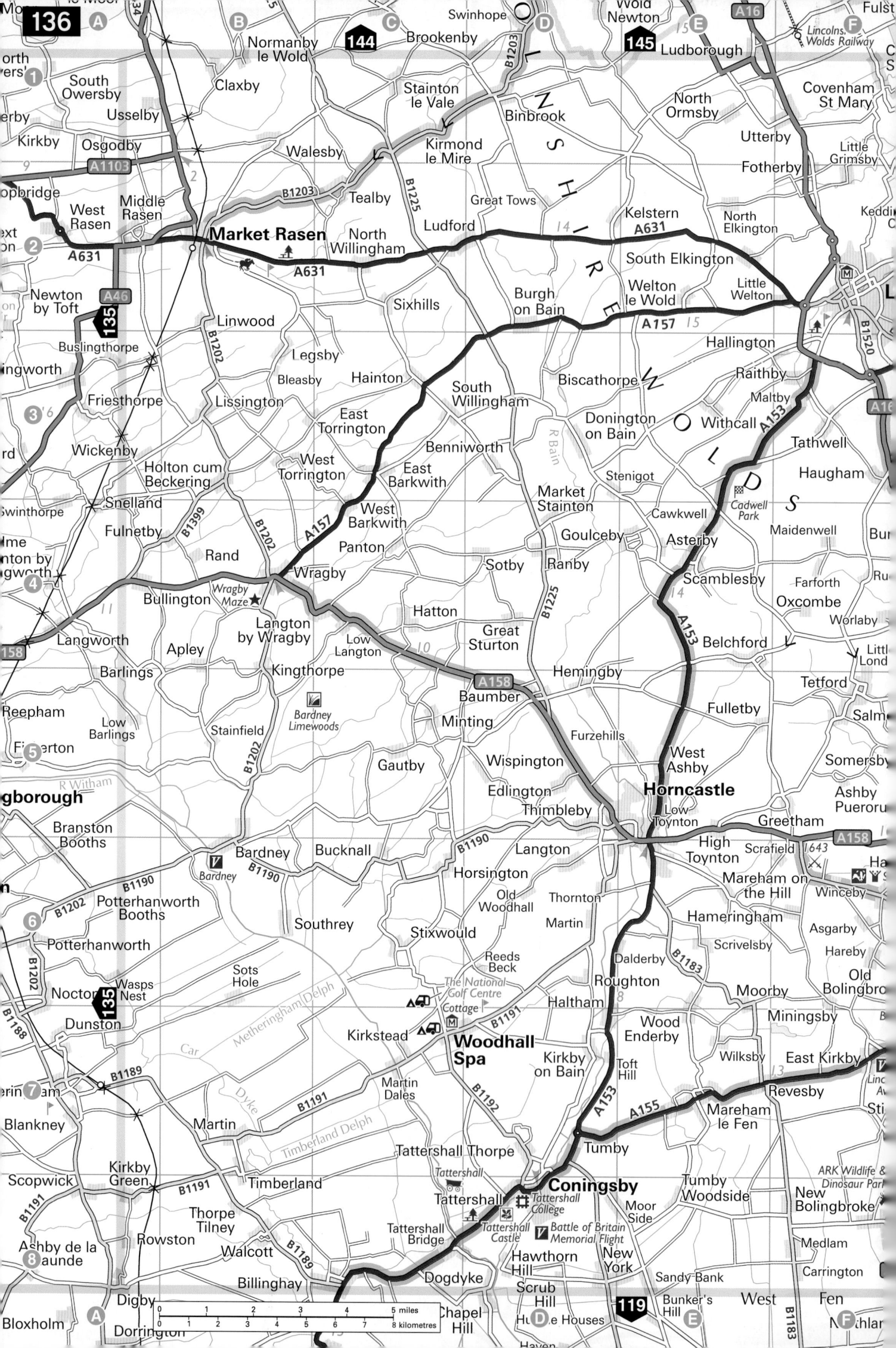

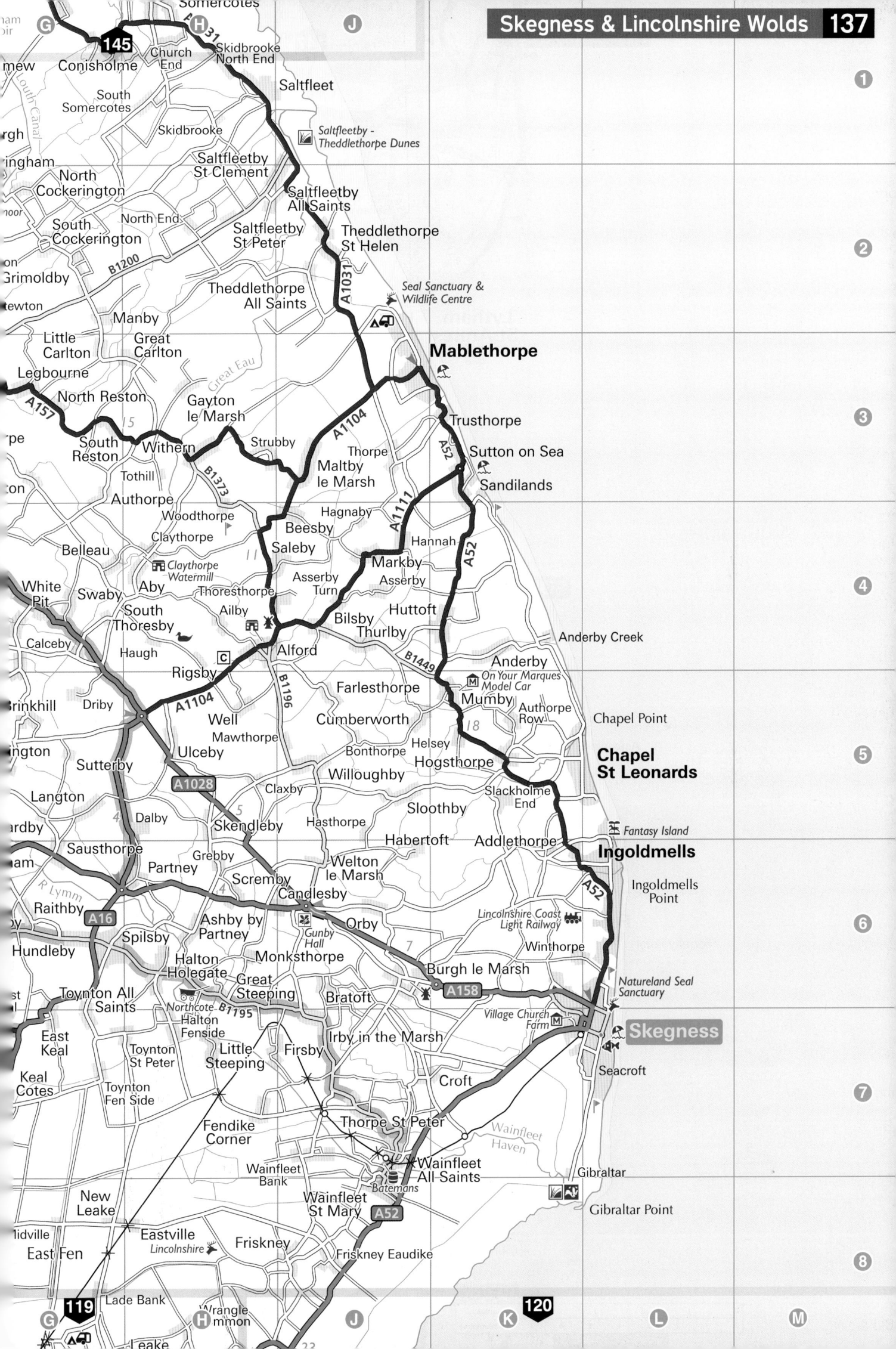

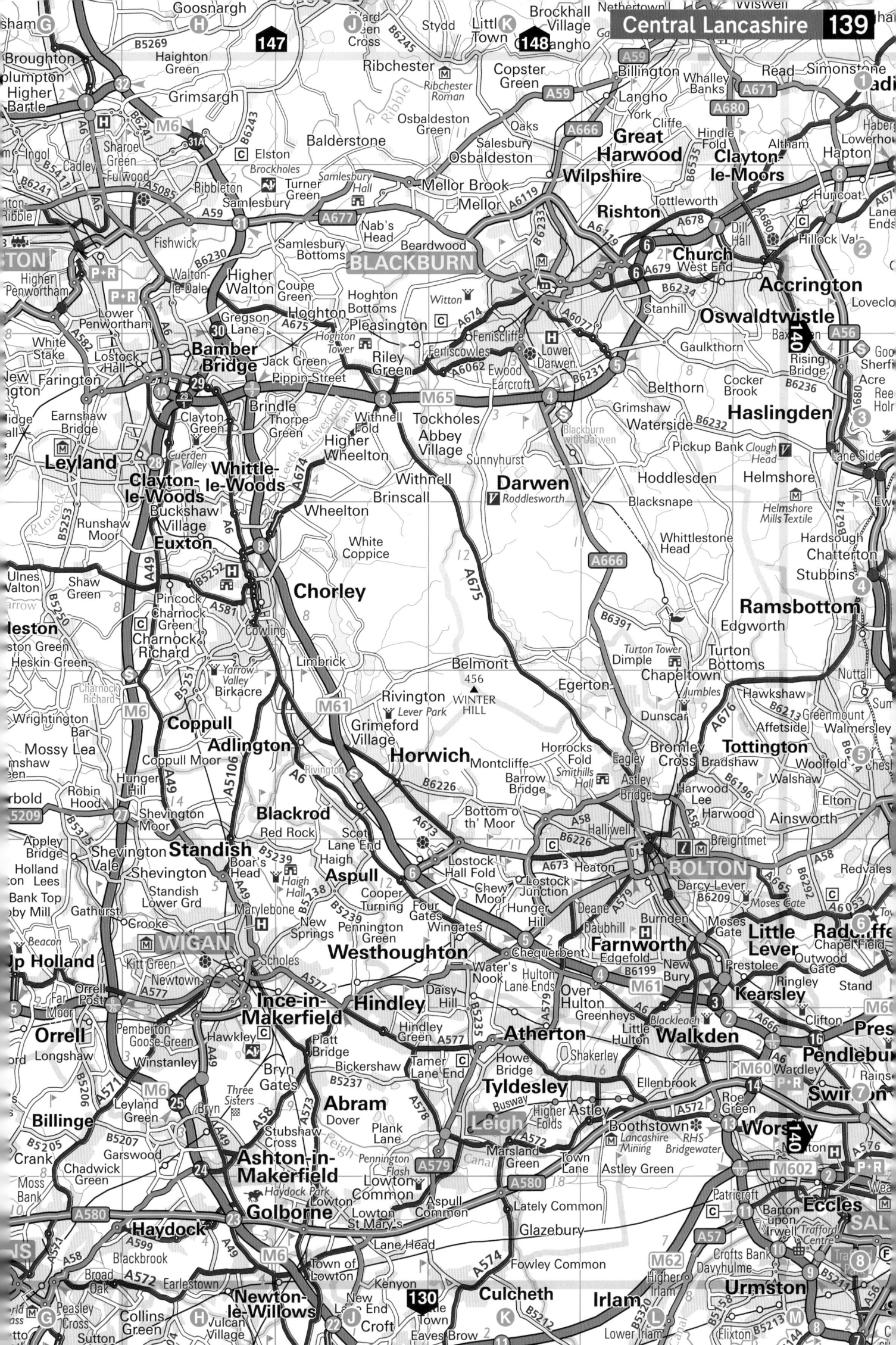

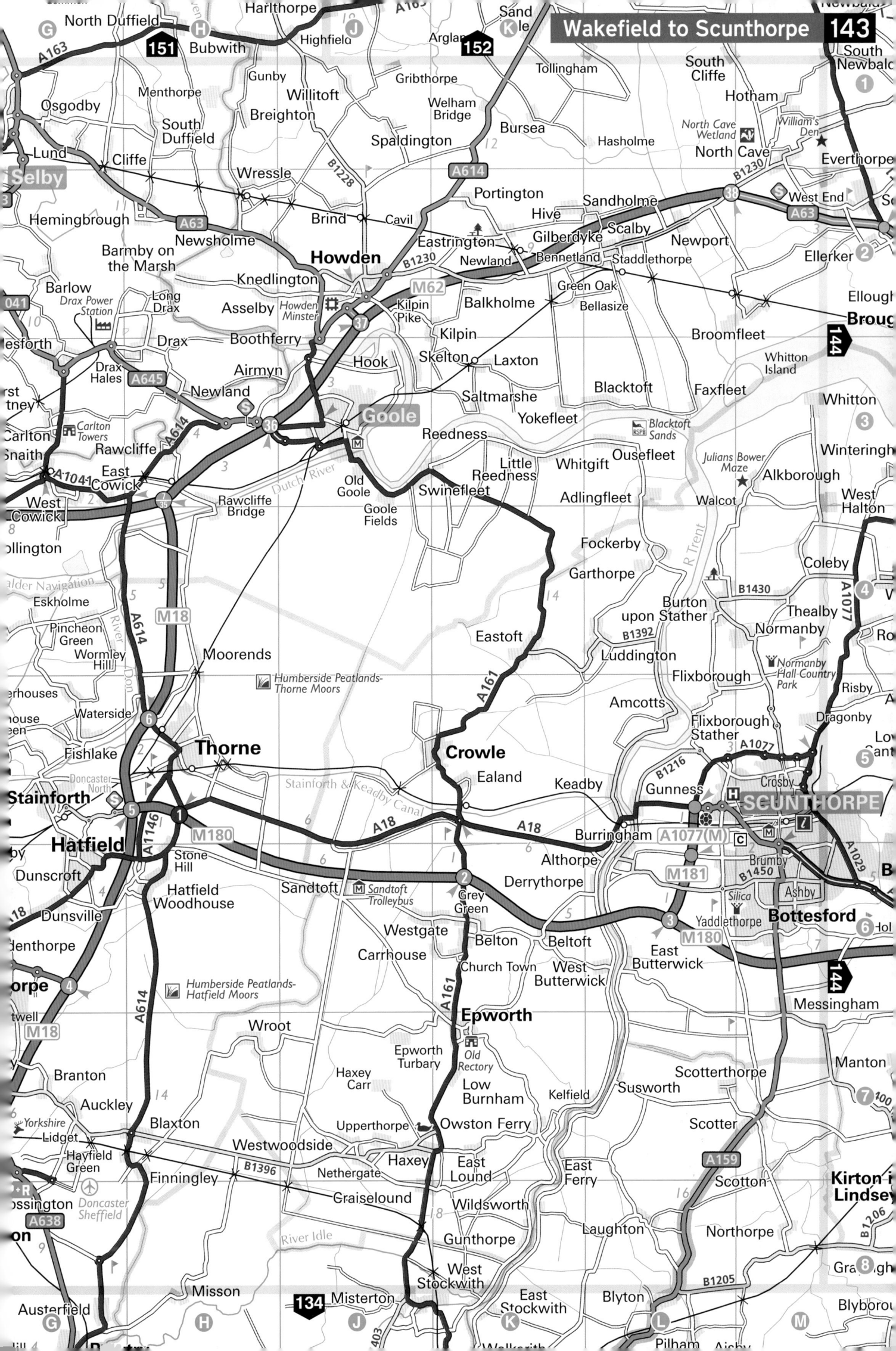

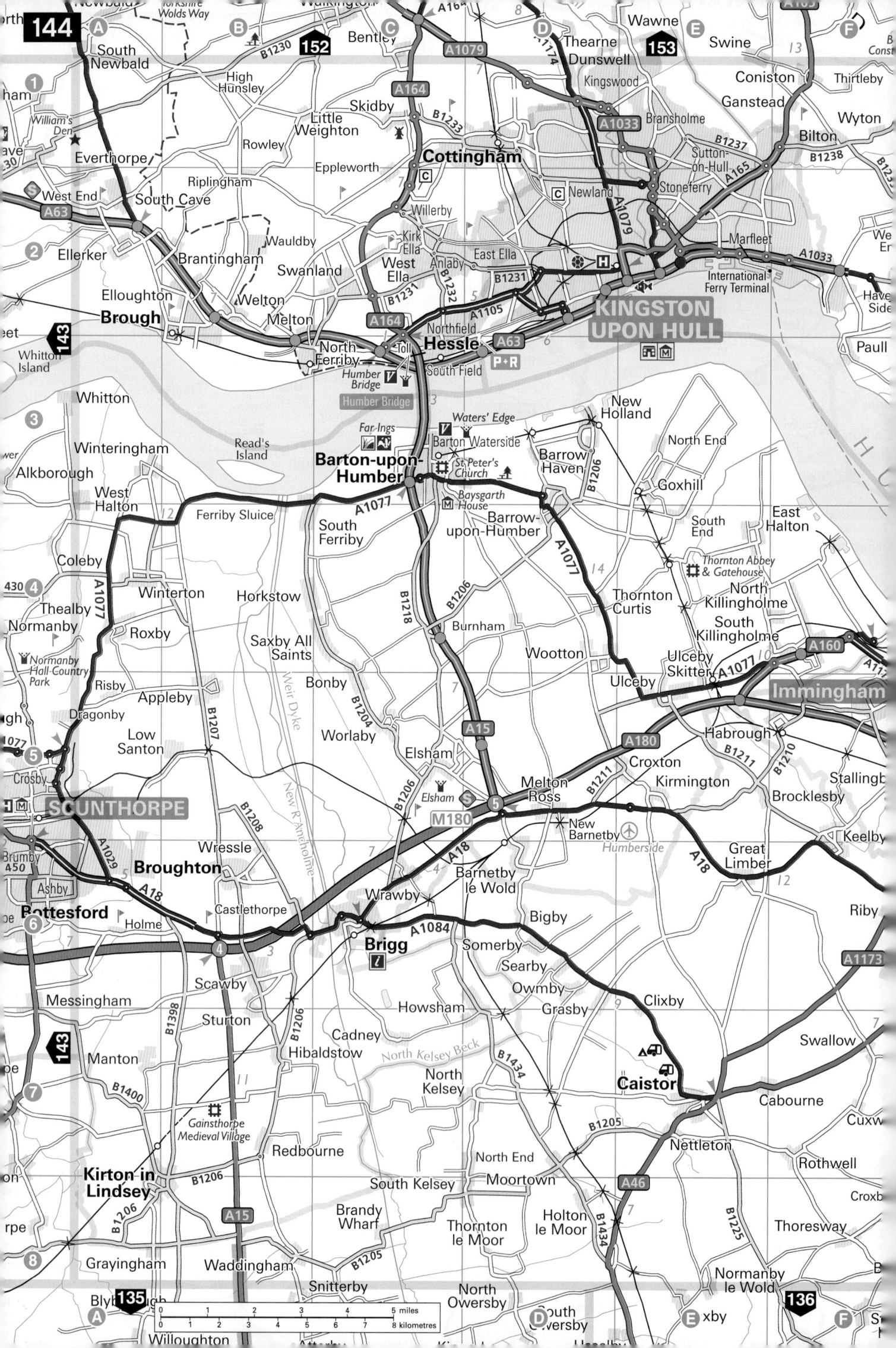

G   H   J

1

B1238 B1242 Newton
`153` Garton
Flinton   Grimston
Humbleton Fitling   Hilston
atley
Owstwick
Elstronwick Danthorpe North
End   Tunstall
n End Burton Roos   Waxholme
on Pidsea
B1362 West Rimswell B1242   Owthorne
Thorngumbald Halsham End East End B1362 *Lighthouse* **Withernsea**
Ryehill Keyingham A1033 Hollym
A1033 Ottringham Winestead Holmpton
A1033 Holmpton
Patrington Out
Newton
Patrington *RAF*
Haven Welwick *Holmpton*
Bunker
Sunk Weeton B1445 Easington
Island Skeffling
South End

2

3

4

Spurn
Heritage
Coast
Kilnsea
Spurn Point

5

ESTUARY

GRIMSBY

SPURN HEAD

A180
A1210 West Marsh
Great A1136 **Cleethorpes**
Coates Little
esby Coates A180
Nunsthorpe A46 Thrunscoe
A46 A16 *Cleethorpes* *Cleethorpes Coast*
H C A1098 *Light Railway*
Bradley Scartho Rotterdam (Europoort)
Laceby B1203 **Humberston**
y upon Waltham A16 B1219
mber **New Waltham**
Barnoldby Holton A1031 *Tetney*
le Beck *Waltham* le Clay *Marshes* RSPB
Beelsby Brigsley North
A18 Ashby cum End Tetney
Hatcliffe Fenby Waithe Tetney
Lock
West Grainsby North
Ravendale North Cotes
East Thoresby Marshchapel
Ravendale West Eskham
ope Wold QB1201 End 29 *Donna*
B1203 Newton A16 Churchthorpe Grainthorpe *Nook*
Fulstow North
Covenham Somercotes
Lincolnshire *Reservoir* A1031
Wolds Railway Covenham Conisholme Church
`136` St Bartholomew End Skidbrooke
G H J ham K South L North End
North St Mary Somercotes Saltfle M
Ormsby

6

7

8

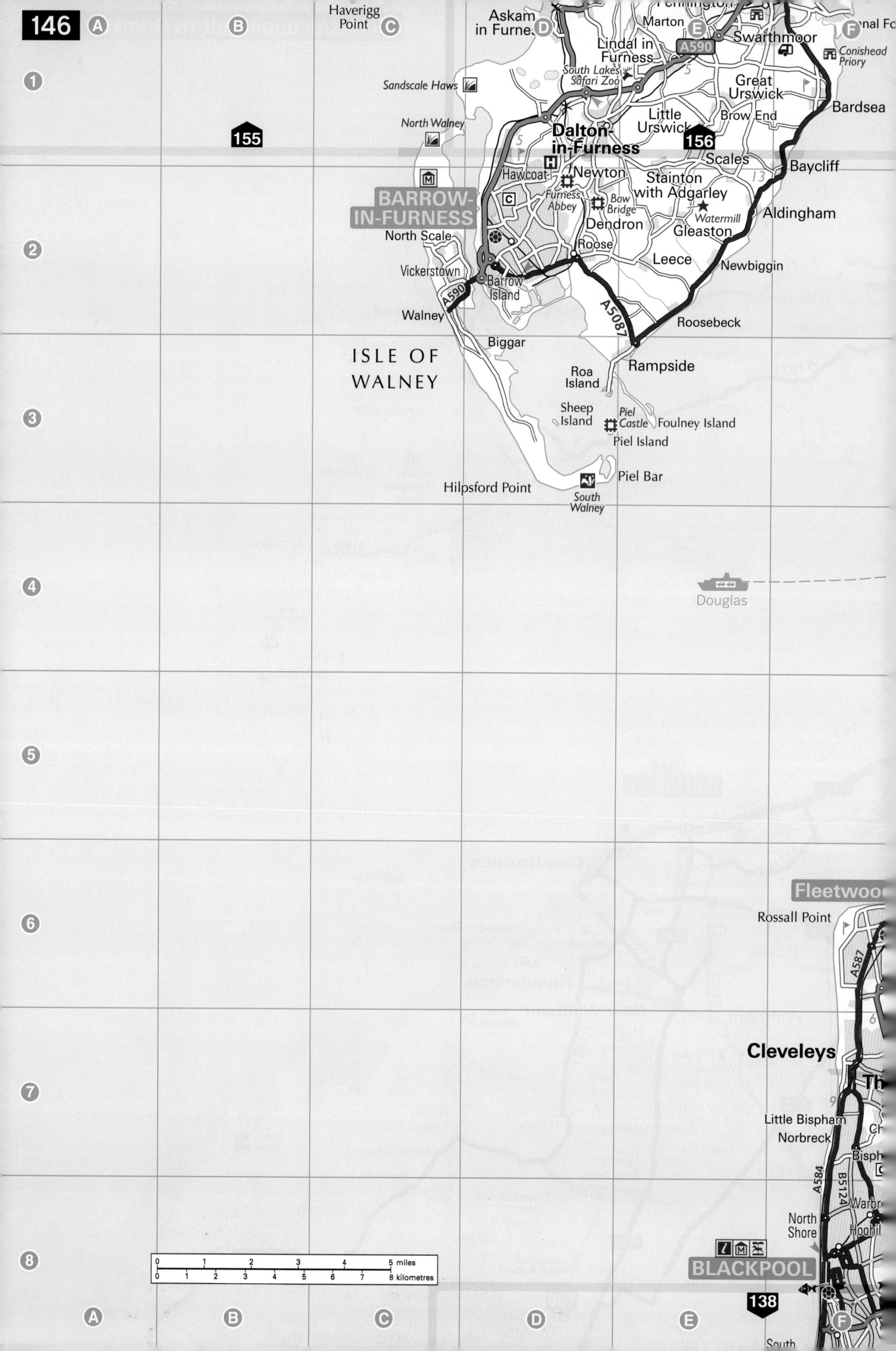

A   B   Haverigg Point C   Askam in Furne... D   Marton   E   Swarthmoor   F

1

Sandscale Haws

North Walney

155

Pennington   Conishead Priory

Lindal in Furness   A590

South Lakes Safari Zoo   Great Urswick   Little Urswick   Brow End   Bardsea

Dalton-in-Furness

156   Scales   Baycliff

BARROW-IN-FURNESS

Hawcoat   Newton   Stainton with Adgarley   Aldingham

H   Furness Abbey   Bow Bridge   Watermill   Gleaston

C   Dendron   Roose

2

North Scale

Vickerstown   Roose   Leece   Newbiggin

Barrow Island   A5087

Walney   Roosebeck

Biggar   Rampside

ISLE OF WALNEY

Roa Island

Sheep Island   Piel Castle   Foulney Island

3   Piel Island

Hilpsford Point   Piel Bar

South Walney

4   Douglas

5

Fleetwoo

6   Rossall Point   A587

Cleveleys

7   Th

Little Bispham   Ch

Norbreck   Bisph

A584   B524

North Shore   Warbr   Hoohil

8   BLACKPOOL

0   1   2   3   4   5 miles
0   1   2   3   4   5   6   7   8 kilometres

138   F

A   B   C   D   E   South

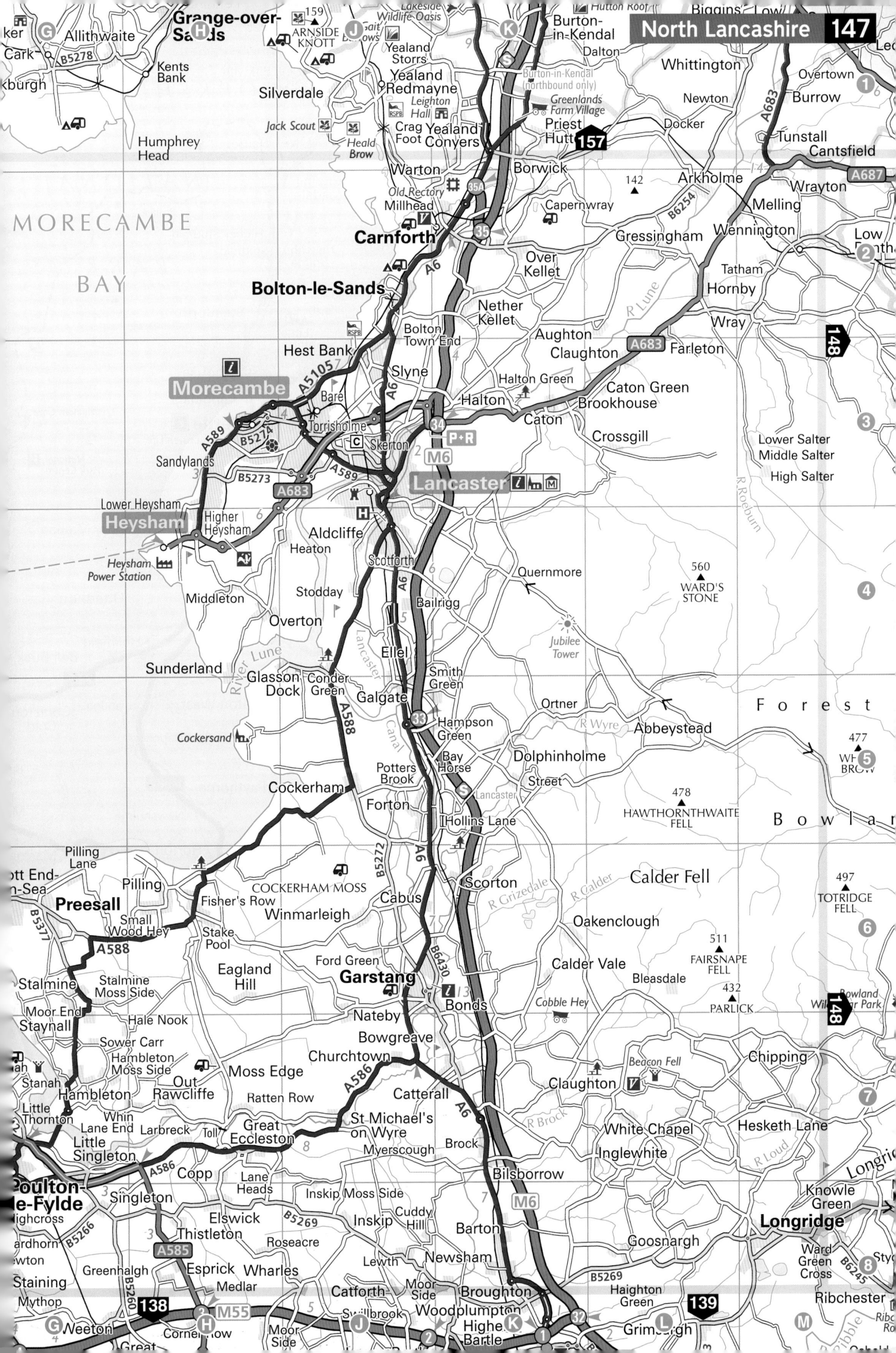

MORECAMBE BAY

Grange-over-Sands
Allithwaite
Kents Bank
ARNSIDE KNOTT
Silverdale
Humphrey Head
Jack Scout
Heald Brow
Yealand Storrs
Yealand Redmayne
Leighton Hall
RSPB
Crag Foot
Yealand Conyers
Warton
Old Rectory
Millhead
Carnforth
Bolton-le-Sands
Hest Bank
RSPB
Bolton Town End
Slyne
Bare
Morecambe
Torrisholme
Skerton
Lancaster
Sandylands
Heysham
Lower Heysham
Higher Heysham
Heysham Power Station
Middleton
Aldcliffe
Heaton
Scotforth
Stodday
Overton
River Lune
Sunderland
Glasson Dock
Conder Green
Galgate
Ellel
Cockersand
Cockerham
Potters Brook
Forton
Hollins Lane
Pilling Lane
Pilling
Fisher's Row
COCKERHAM MOSS
Winmarleigh
Cabus
Scorton
Preesall
Small Wood Hey
Stake Pool
Eagland Hill
Ford Green
Garstang
Stalmine
Stalmine Moss Side
Hale Nook
Nateby
Bowgreave
Churchtown
Moor End
Staynall
Sower Carr
Hambleton Moss Side
Moss Edge
Catterall
St Michael's on Wyre
Myerscough
Brock
Bilsborrow
Hambleton
Little Thornton
Whin Lane End
Larbreck
Toll
Great Eccleston
Ratten Row
Little Singleton
Poulton-le-Fylde
Highcross
Copp
Lane Heads
Singleton
Inskip Moss Side
Inskip
Cuddy Hill
Barton
Newsham
Elswick
Thistleton
Roseacre
Lewth
Moor Side
Broughton
Woodplumpton
Higher Bartle
Staining
Mythop
Greenhalgh
Medlar
Catforth
Swillbrook
Corner Row
Great
Neeton

Whittington
Overtown
Burrow
Newton
Docker
Tunstall
Cantsfield
Arkholme
Wrayton
Melling
Gressingham
Wennington
Capernwray
Tatham
Hornby
Over Kellet
Wray
Nether Kellet
Aughton
Claughton
Farleton
Caton Green
Brookhouse
Halton Green
Halton
Caton
Crossgill
Lower Salter
Middle Salter
High Salter
Quernmore
WARD'S STONE
Jubilee Tower
Ortner
Abbeystead
FOREST
Bailrigg
Smith Green
Hampson Green
Bay Horse
Dolphinholme
Street
HAWTHORNTHWAITE FELL
Bowland
Calder Fell
TOTRIDGE FELL
Oakenclough
Calder Vale
FAIRSNAPE FELL
Bleasdale
PARLICK
Cobble Hey
Chipping
Claughton
Beacon Fell
White Chapel
Inglewhite
Hesketh Lane
Knowle Green
Longridge
Goosnargh
Haighton Green
Grimsargh
Ribchester
Ward Green Cross

Burton-in-Kendal
Biggins
Dalton
Priest Hutt
Greenlands Farm Village
Burton-in-Kendal (northbound only)
Lakeside Wildlife Oasis
Hutton Roof

Kirkby
B5278
Cark
Flookburgh
Winder

A683
A687
A6254
A683
A6
A5105
A589
B5274
B5273
A683
A588
B5272
A6
B6430
A586
A585
B5269
B5266
B5260
A588
B5377
M6
M55

142
159
560
477
478
511
432
497

157
138
139
147
148

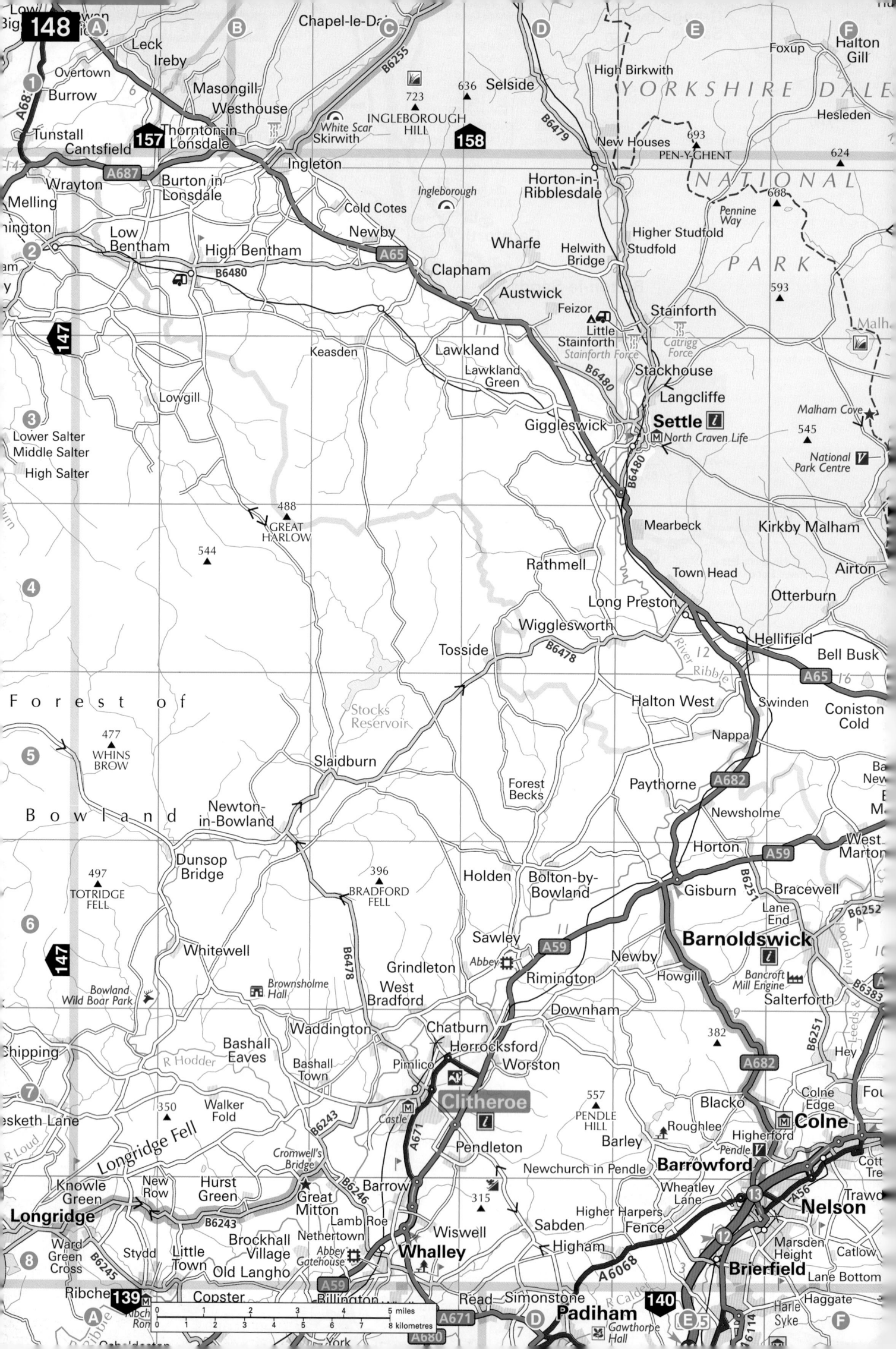

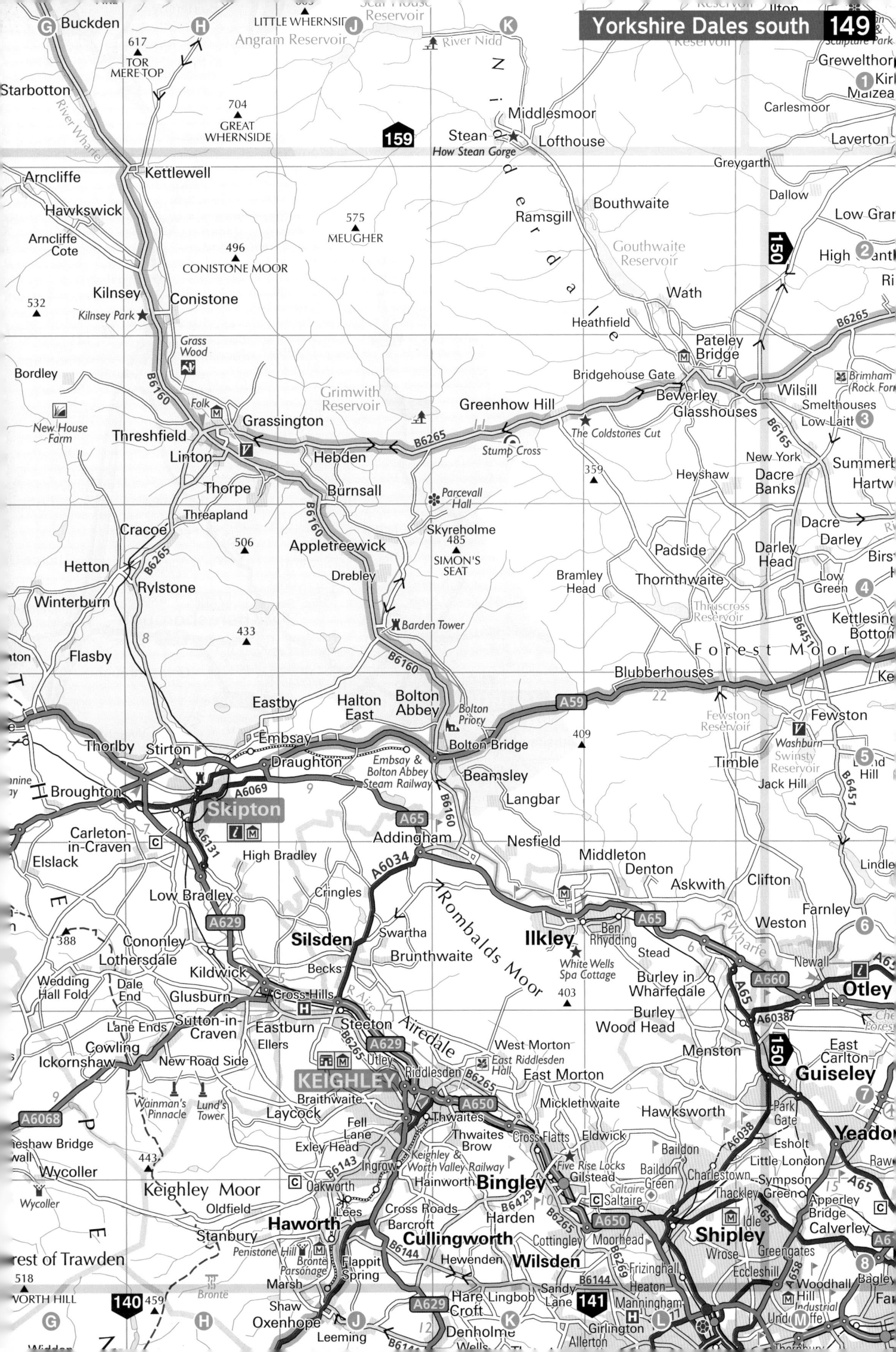

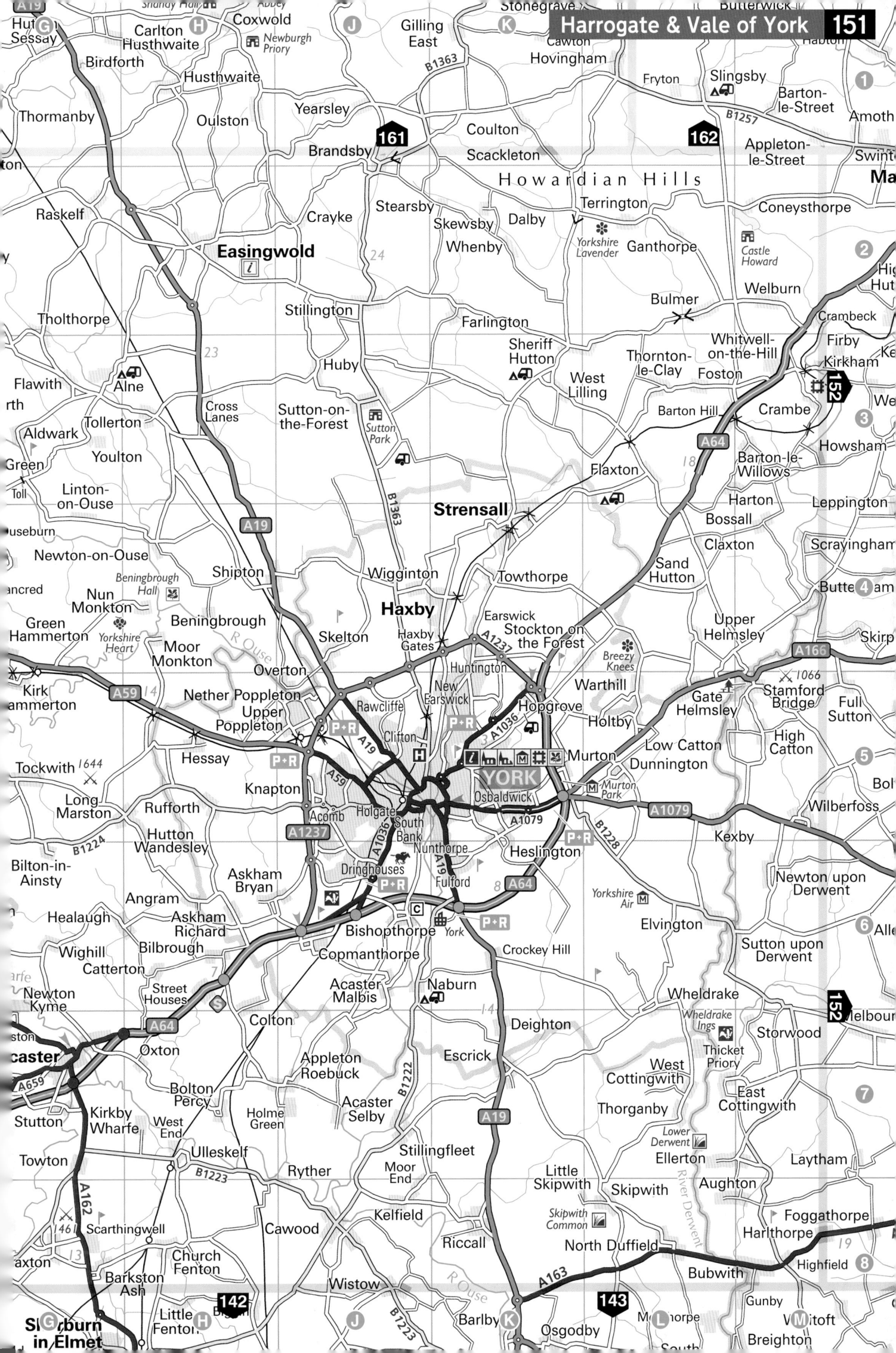

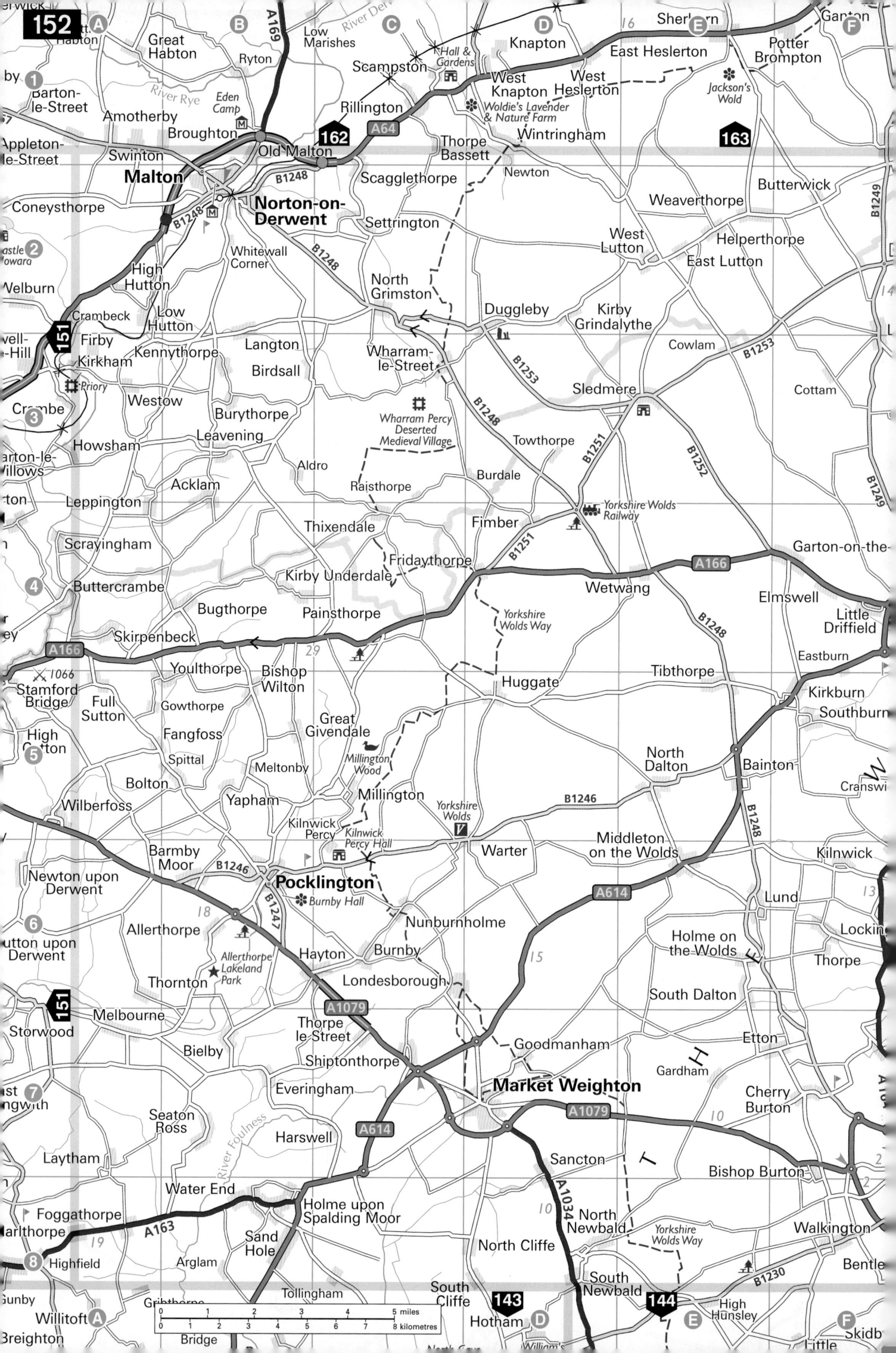

Flamborough Head
Heritage Coast

G Hunmanby **H** Reighton **J**

Fordon
Speeton
B1229
Wold Newton
Burton Fleming
163
A165
Grindale
11
Buckton
Bempton
B1229
Bempton Cliffs RSPB
Thornwick Bay
North Landing
Flamborough Cliffs
Selwicks Bay
Flamborough
FLAMBOROUGH HEAD
Marton
B1255
B1259
B1253
Rudston Monolith
Boynton
Sewerby
Hall & Gardens
Bessingby
B1423
Bondville Model Village
Carnaby
Hilderthorpe
Bridlington
BRIDLINGTON BAY

Haisthorpe
Thornholme
World of Rock
Kilham
Burton Agnes
Bridlington Animal
12
S
A1165

Harpham
A614
Lowthorpe
Little Kelk
Fraisthorpe
Nafferton
D
L
Gransmoor
Great Kelk
Lissett
Barmston
Gembling
15
B1242
16
Ulrome
Foston on the Wolds
Upton
Skipsea Castle
Skipsea
Wansford
B1249
Beeford
Skipsea Brough
Skerne
Brigham
North Frodingham
A165
Rotsea
Dunnington
Atwick
Hempholme
Bewholme
B1242
Nunkeeling
Honeysuckle Farm
Tophill Low
Burshill
Brandesburton
A1035
Hornsea
Seaton
Hornsea Mere
Hornsea Freeport
Aike
Foss Hill
6
Sigglesthorne
Wassand Hall & Gardens
Rolston
Leven
Catwick
Goxhill
Arram
Little Catwick
Rise
Mappleton
Eske
7
Long Riston
B1243
Great Hatfield
Mappleton Sands
A1035
Routh
Little Hatfield
B1242
ey
Tickton
Hull Bridge
Arnold
H
North End
Great Cowden
Meaux
New Ellerby
Withernwick
Weel
Skirlaugh
Marton
West Newton
Mount Pleasant
Woodmansey
O
Aldbrough
A1174
R Hull
Wawne
A165
Old Ellerby
East Newton
8
L
B1238
B1242
Garton
Thearne
Dunswell
D
Swine
Burton Constable Hall
Flinton
Grimston
144
Kingswood
Coniston
Thirtleby
145
Humbleton
Hilston
Bransholme
Ganstead
Wyton
Sproatley
Ellington

1

2

3

4

5

6

7

8

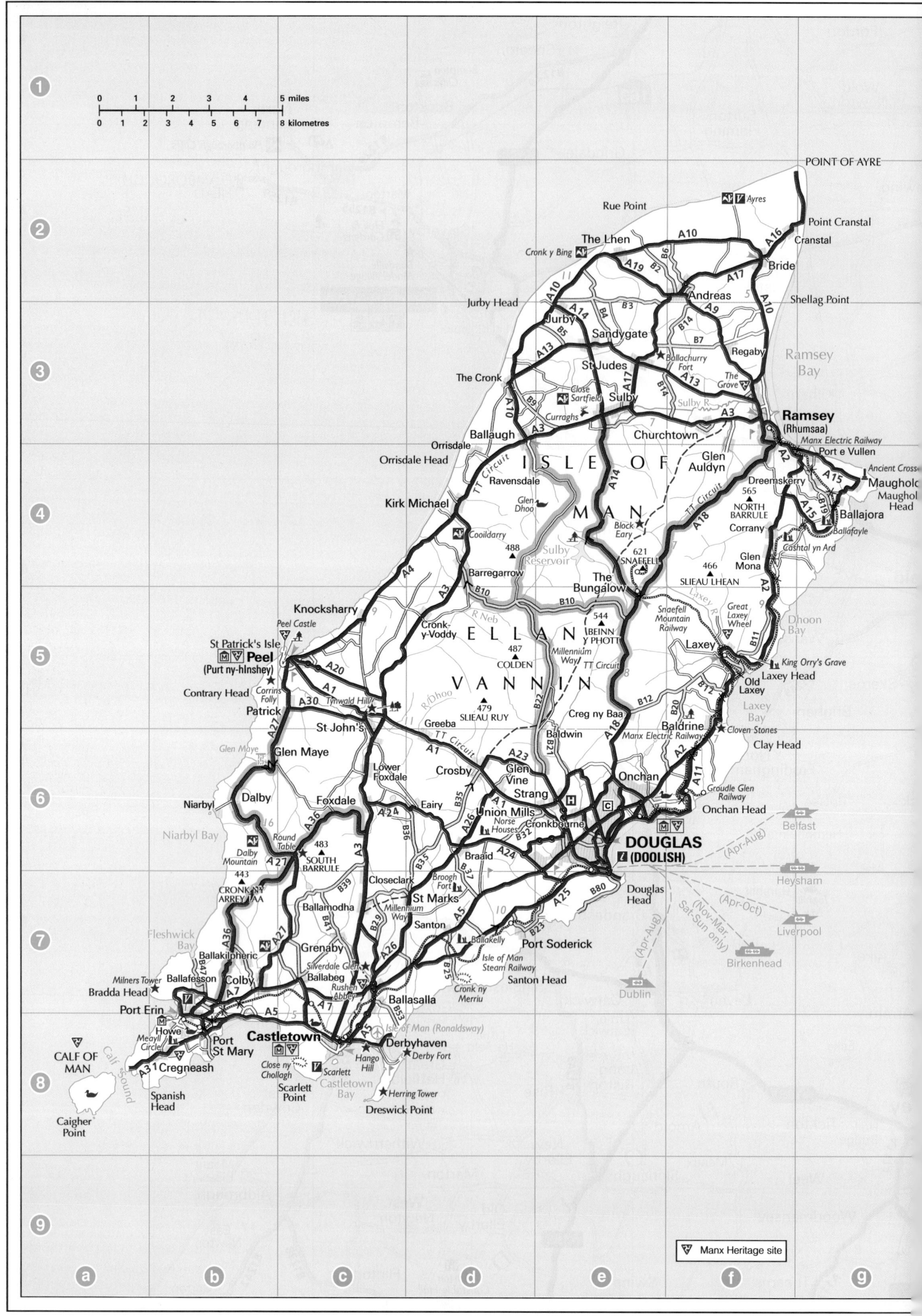

POINT OF AYRE

Rue Point

Ayres

Point Cranstal

The Lhen

Cranstal

Cronk y Bing

A10

Bride

A19

B6

B2

A16

Jurby Head

A10

A14

Andreas

A17

Shellag Point

Jurby

B4

B3

A9

B5

Sandygate

Regaby

B14

Ramsey Bay

The Cronk

A13

St Judes

Ballachurry Fort

B7

Ballaugh

A17

Sulby

B14

Ramsey (Rhumsaa)

Orrisdale

A3

Churchtown

Sulby R.

A3

Manx Electric Railway

Orrisdale Head

ISLE OF

Close Sartfield

Curraghs

7

Port e Vullen

Ravensdale

MAN

Glen Auldyn

A2

A15

Kirk Michael

Glen Dhoo

A14

Dreemskerry

Ancient Cross

Maughold

Cooildarry

488

Block Eary

565

A18

NORTH BARRULE

A15

Ballajora

Maughold Head

Barregarrow

B10

621 SNAEFELL

Corrany

Ballafayle

Cashtal yn Ard

Knocksharry

Peel Castle

B10

The Bungalow

466 SLIEAU LHEAN

Glen Mona

St Patrick's Isle

Cronk-y-Voddy

544 BEINN-Y-PHOTT

Snaefell Mountain Railway

Great Laxey Wheel

Dhoon Bay

Peel (Purt ny-hInshey)

ELLAN

A20

487 COLDEN

Millennium Way

TT Circuit

Laxey

King Orry's Grave

Contrary Head

Corrins Folly

A30

Tynwald Hill

R.Dhoo

479 SLIEAU RUY

VANNIN

B22

B11

Laxey Head

Patrick

A27

A1

Creg ny Baa

B20

B12

Old Laxey

St John's

Greeba

A18

B12

Laxey Bay

Glen Maye

Baldwin

Manx Electric Railway

Clay Head

Glen Maye

A1

TT Circuit

A23

Glen Vine

A2

Cloven Stones

Niarbyl

Dalby

Lower Foxdale

Crosby

Strang

Onchan

A11

Groudle Glen Railway

Niarbyl Bay

Round Table

Foxdale

Eairy

B35

A1

Union Mills

Cronkbourne

Onchan Head

Dalby Mountain

483 SOUTH BARRULE

A36

A24

Norse Houses

B32

H

C

Belfast

443 CRONK NY ARREY LAA

A3

B36

Braaid

A24

DOUGLAS (DOOLISH)

(Apr-Aug)

B29

Closeclark

B35

Brough Fort

A25

Heysham

Ballamodha

Millennium Way

St Marks

A5

B80

Douglas Head

Liverpool

Fleshwick Bay

A36

B41

Santon

B23

(Apr-Oct)

Grenaby

A27

Ballabeg

Ballakelly

Isle of Man Steam Railway

(Nov-Mar, Sat-Sun only)

Birkenhead

Ballakilpheric

Silverdale Glen

B26

Port Soderick

Milners Tower

Ballafesson

Colby

A7

Rushen Abbey

Ballasalla

B25

Cronk ny Merriu

Santon Head

(Apr-Aug)

Bradda Head

A7

Ballabeg

B53

Port Erin

A5

A7

Dublin

Howe

Meayll Circle

Castletown

Derbyhaven

Derby Fort

A3

Cregneash

Port St Mary

Close ny Chollagh

Scarlett

Hango Hill

Isle of Man (Ronaldsway)

CALF OF MAN

Spanish Head

Scarlett Point

Castletown Bay

Herring Tower

Dreswick Point

Caigher Point

Manx Heritage site

St Bees
Egremont
Lowes
Court
Wilton
164
Thornhill
Carleton
Haile
Coulderton
Middletown
Blackbeck
Nethertown
Beckermet
Calder Bridge
Braystones
Ponsonby
Sellafield
Station
Cross
Calder
Wellington
B5344
Gosforth
Santon
Santon Bridge
Seascale
Hallsenna Moor
Drigg
Holmrook
Eskdale
Green
Beckfoot
Saltcoats
Ravenglass
Roman Bath
House
Muncaster Castle,
Hawk & Owl Centre
A595
Newbiggin
Broad Oak
Waberthwaite
Corney
Loganbeck
Beckfoot
Hycemoor
Selker Bay
Bootle
Swinside
Stone Circle
Hyton
Annaside
Gutterby Spa
Whitbeck
The Green
Whicham
Silecroft
Kirksanton
A5093
Millom
Steel Green
Borwick
Rails
Hodbarrow
Haverigg
Haverigg
Point
Askam
in Furness
Sandscale Haws
North Walney
146
**BARROW-
IN-FURNESS**
North Scale
Vickerstown

LAKE D
K
HAYCOCK
L
KIRK
FELL
GREAT GA
PILLAR
899
1
Wasdale
Head
692
SEATALLAN
978
964 SCAFE
SCAFELL PIKE
2
Nether
Wasdale
West Water
Burnmoor
Tarn
R Irt
River Mite
156
Boot
Hardknott
Fort
Hard
Pa
3
River Esk
Ravenglass
& Eskdale
Railway
Devoke
Water
LAKE DISTRICT
Hall
Dunnerdale
NATIONAL
573
WHITFELL
Ulph
4
PARK
Broughton
Mills
Lower
Hawthwaite
Duddon
Bridge
Bro
5
Lady
Hall
Foxfiel
600
BLACK
COMBE
Hallthwaites
Arnaby
Bridge End
The Hill
Sand Side
Soutergate
6
156
Dalt
in-F
Hawcoat
Furness
Abbey
7
8

652
HARTER
FELL
3

Worm Gill
River Bleng
River Ehen

G   H   J   K   L

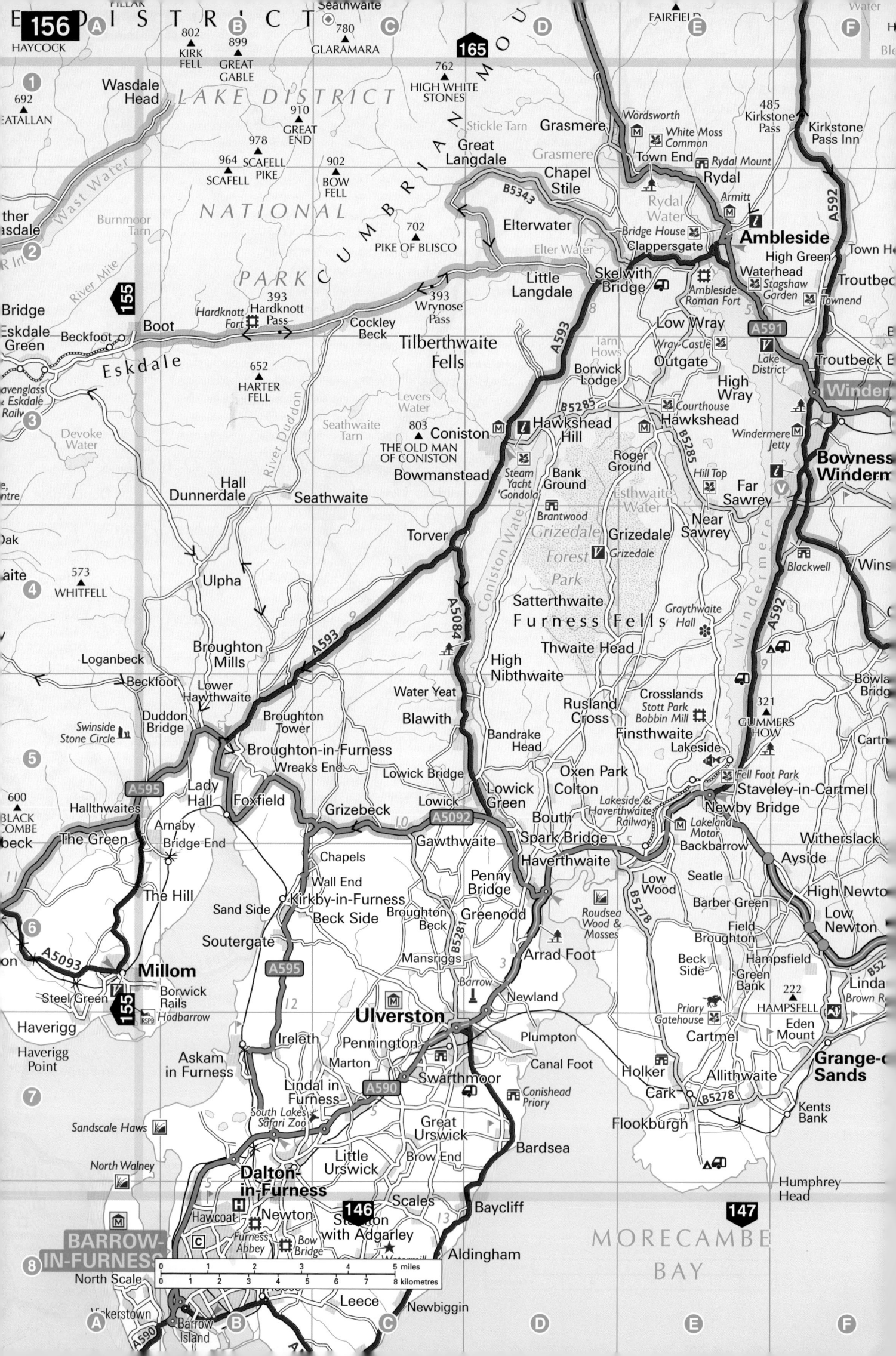

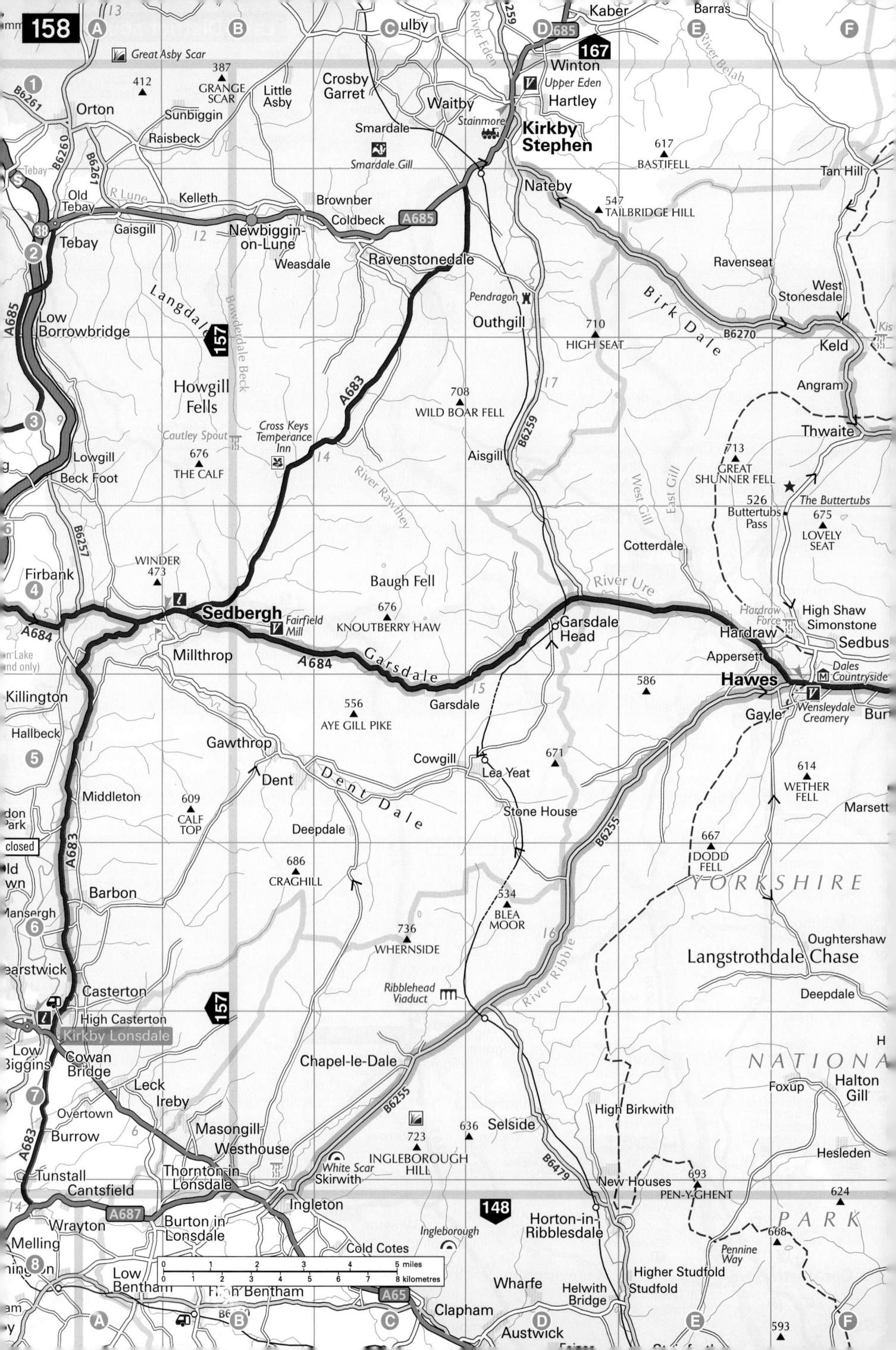

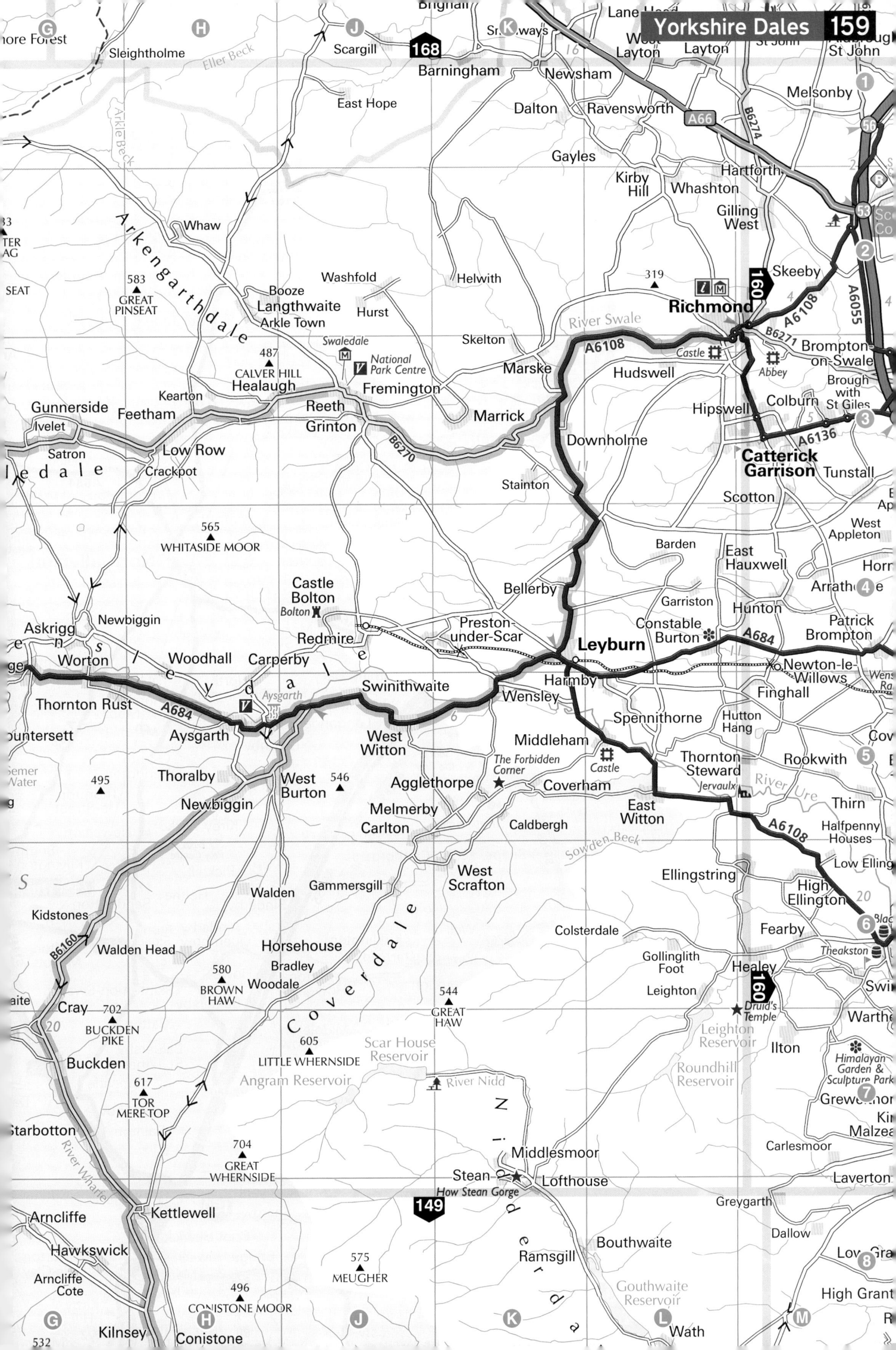

G H J 168 K ways
St.
1
Brignall
Lane Head
Scargill
West
Layton
Layton
St John
Melsonby
ore Forest
Sleightholme
Eller Beck
Barningham
Newsham
56
Dalton
Ravensworth
A66
B6274
R
Whaw
Gayles
Hartforth
53
Kirby
Hill Whashton
Gilling
West
Skeeby
319
Richmond
TER
AG
583
GREAT
PINSEAT
Booze
Langthwaite
Arkle Town
Washfold
Hurst
Helwith
River Swale
A6108
160
A6108
B6271
Brompton-
on-Swale
B6108
A6055
SEAT
Swaledale
National
Park Centre
Skelton
Castle
Abbey
Brough
with
St Giles
487
CALVER HILL
Healaugh
Fremington
Marske
Hudswell
Colburn
3
Gunnerside
Feetham
Reeth
Grinton
Marrick
Marske
Hipswell
A6136
Ivelet
B6270
Downholme
Catterick
Garrison
Tunstall
Satron
Low Row
Crackpot
Stainton
Scotton
West
Ap
ledale
West
Appleton
565
WHITASIDE MOOR
Barden
East
Hauxwell
Horn
Castle
Bolton
Bolton
Bellerby
Garriston
Hunton
Arrath e
4
Askrigg
Newbiggin
Redmire
Preston-
under-Scar
Constable
Burton
A684
Patrick
Brompton
Worton
Woodhall
Carperby
Leyburn
Harmby
Newton-le-
Willows
Wens
Ra
Thornton Rust
A684
Aysgarth
Swinithwaite
Wensley
Finghall
ountersett
West
Witton
Middleham
Spennithorne
Hutton
Hang
Cov
emer
Water
495
Thoralby
West
Burton
546
Agglethorpe
The Forbidden
Corner
Castle
Thornton
Steward
Jervaulx
Rookwith
5
Newbiggin
Melmerby
Carlton
Coverham
East
Witton
River Ure
Thirn
West
Scrafton
Caldbergh
Sowden Beck
A6108
Halfpenny
Houses
Kidstones
B6160
Walden
Gammersgill
Ellingstring
High
Ellington
Low Elling
20
Walden Head
Colsterdale
Fearby
6
Bla
702
BUCKDEN
PIKE
Cray
Horsehouse
Bradley
Woodale
580
BROWN
HAW
Coverdale
605
LITTLE WHERNSIDE
Scar House
Reservoir
Gollinglith
Foot
Leighton
Healey
Theakston
Druid's
Temple
160
Swi
aite
20
Buckden
617
TOR
MERE TOP
Angram Reservoir
544
GREAT
HAW
River Nidd
Leighton
Reservoir
Roundhill
Reservoir
Ilton
Himalayan
Garden &
Sculpture Park
7
Starbotton
704
GREAT
WHERNSIDE
Middlesmoor
Stean
How Stean Gorge
Lofthouse
Carlesmoor
Laverton
Arncliffe
Kettlewell
149
Greygarth
Low Gra
8
Hawkswick
Ramsgill
Bouthwaite
Dallow
Arncliffe
Cote
575
MEUGHER
Gouthwaite
Reservoir
High Grant
532
Kilnsey
G 496
CONISTONE MOOR
H Conistone J K Wath L M

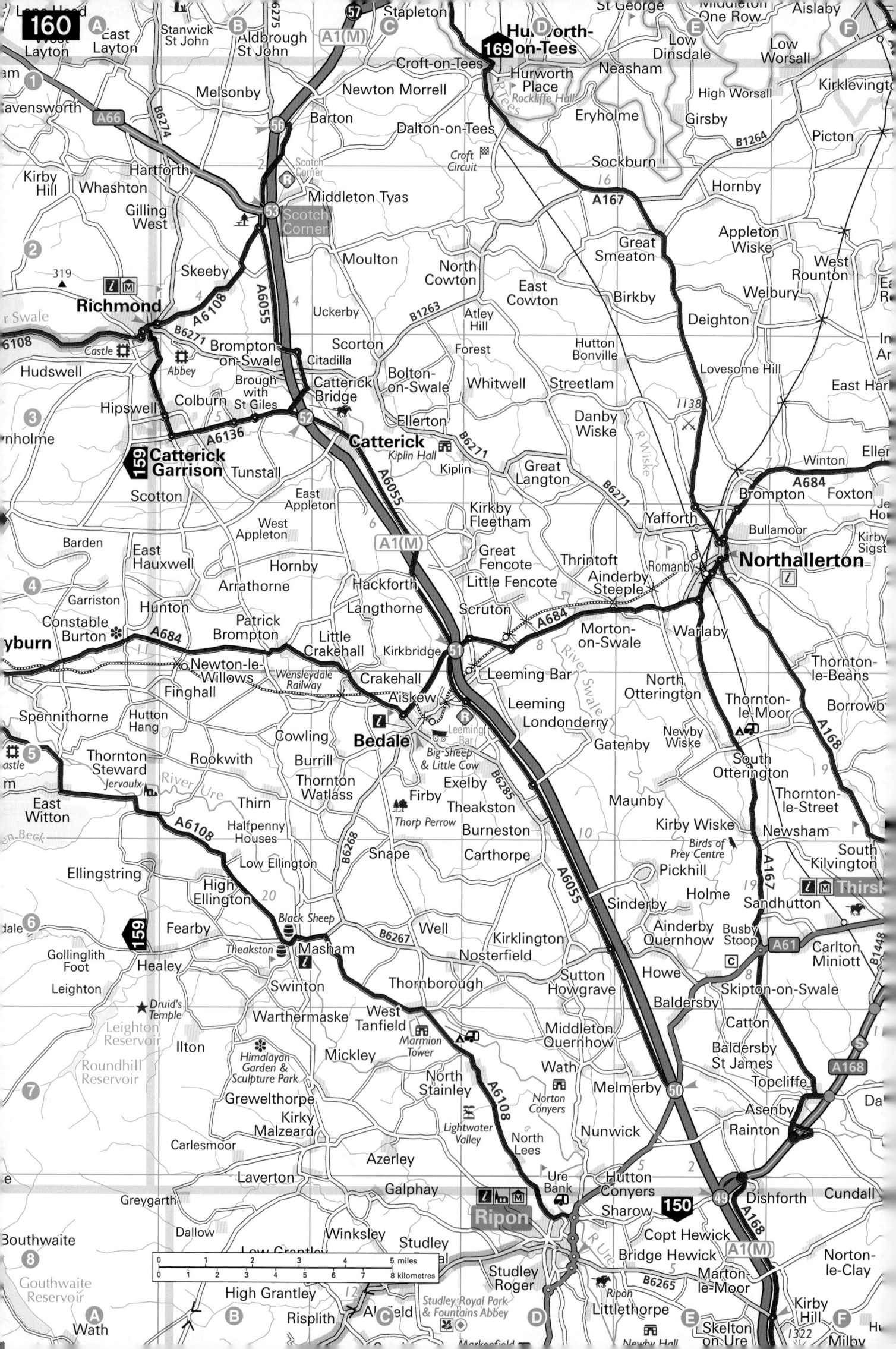

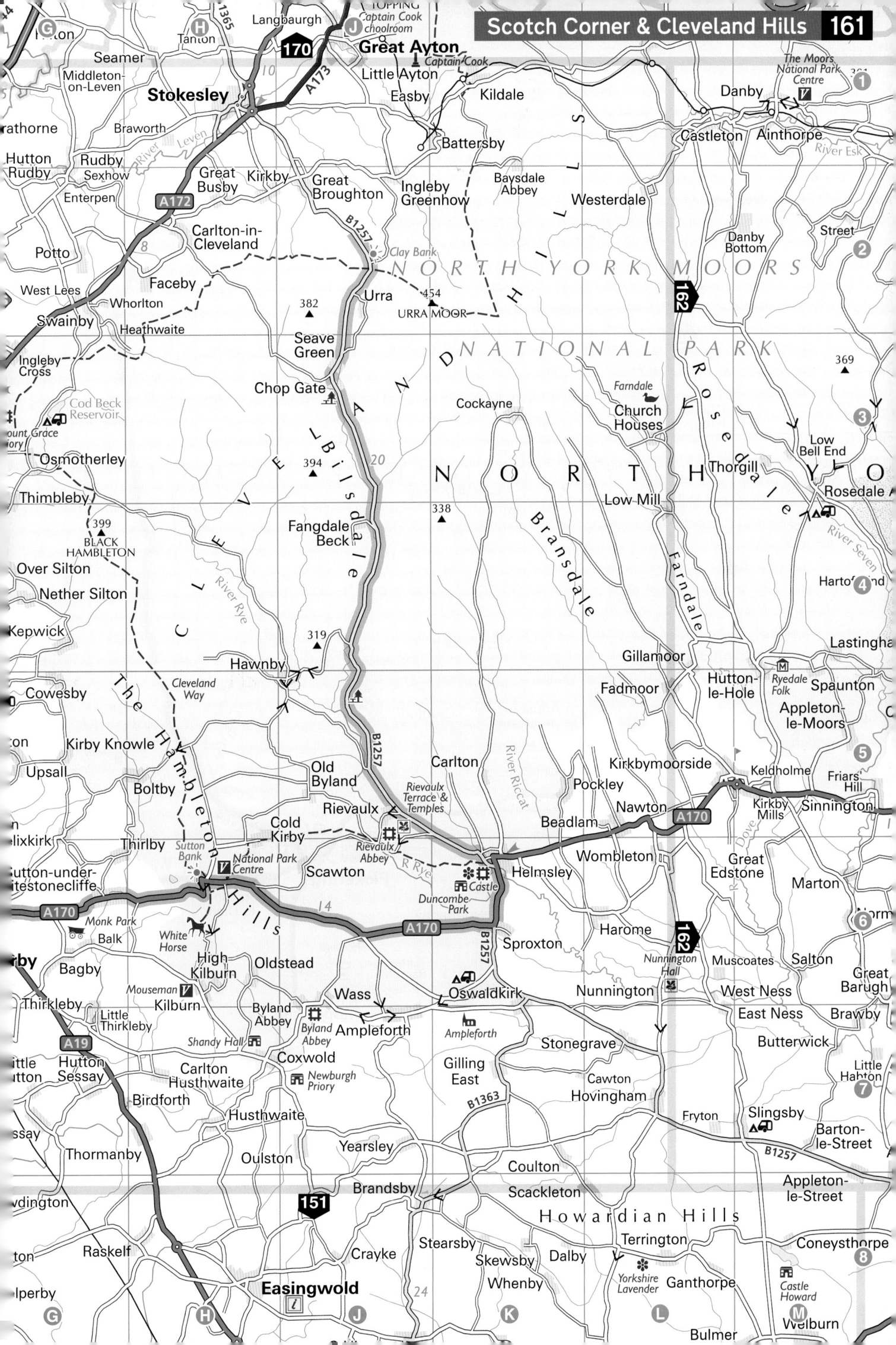

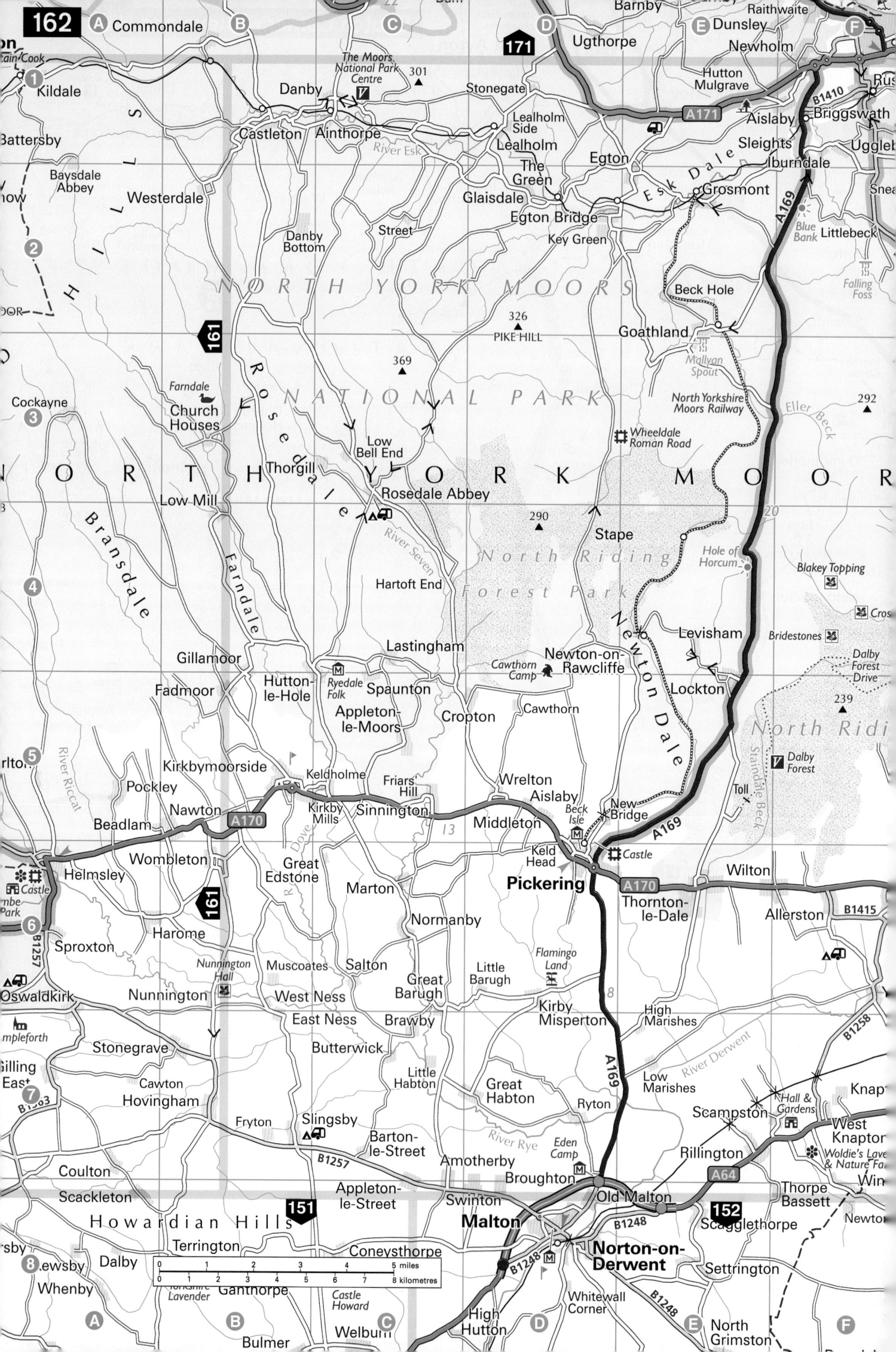

G H J

1

2

3

4

5

6

7

8

sby

Sgwick
Bay

insacre

High Hawsker

 sker

Raw

Fylingthorpe

71

Ness Point or
North Cheek

Robin Hood's Bay

Old Coastguard

Robin
Hood's Bay

Old Peak or
South Cheek

Ravenscar

20

Staintondale

Hayburn
Wyke

Harwood
Dale

Cloughton
Newlands

Cloughton
Wyke

Cloughton

Cromer Point

A165

Burniston

Cleveland Way

kley

Broxa

Silpho

Suffield

Scalby

Newby

North Bay Railway

angdale
End

Hackness

A171

Castle

rest Park

Wrench
Green

Everley

Scarborough

Falsgrave

awdon

Bee Dale

Ruston

nainton

Brompton-
by-Sawdon

Forge Valley
Wood

West
Ayton

East
Ayton

Betton

A170

C

River Derwent

Sea Cut

H

Oliver's Mount

P+R

A165

P+R

Osgodby

Cayton Bay

Eastfield

The
Wyke

Hutton
Buscel

Irton

Seamer

Crossgates

B1261

High
Killerby

Fair Collection

Wykeham

Cayton

Lebberston

Gristhorpe

Filey Brigg

A1039

Filey

e

C

a

s

B1261

A64

R Hertford

Folkton

Bird Garden
& Animal Park

Muston

Filey Bay

Willerby

A1039

West
Flotmanby

16

Sherburn

Ganton

Staxton

Flixton

7

Hunmanby

Flamborough Head
Heritage Coast

ast Heslerton

Potter
Brompton

Jackson's
Wold

Fordon

Reighton

Speeton

Butterwick

Foxholes

Wold
Newton

153

Burton
Fleming

Bempton
Cliffs

RSPB

Weaverthorpe

B1249

Grindale

A165

Buckton

Bempton

B1229

ton

Helperthorpe

West
ton

East Lutton

C

Thwing

Octon

14

Marton

B1255

Sewerby

Hall &
Garden

Bondville

G H J K L M

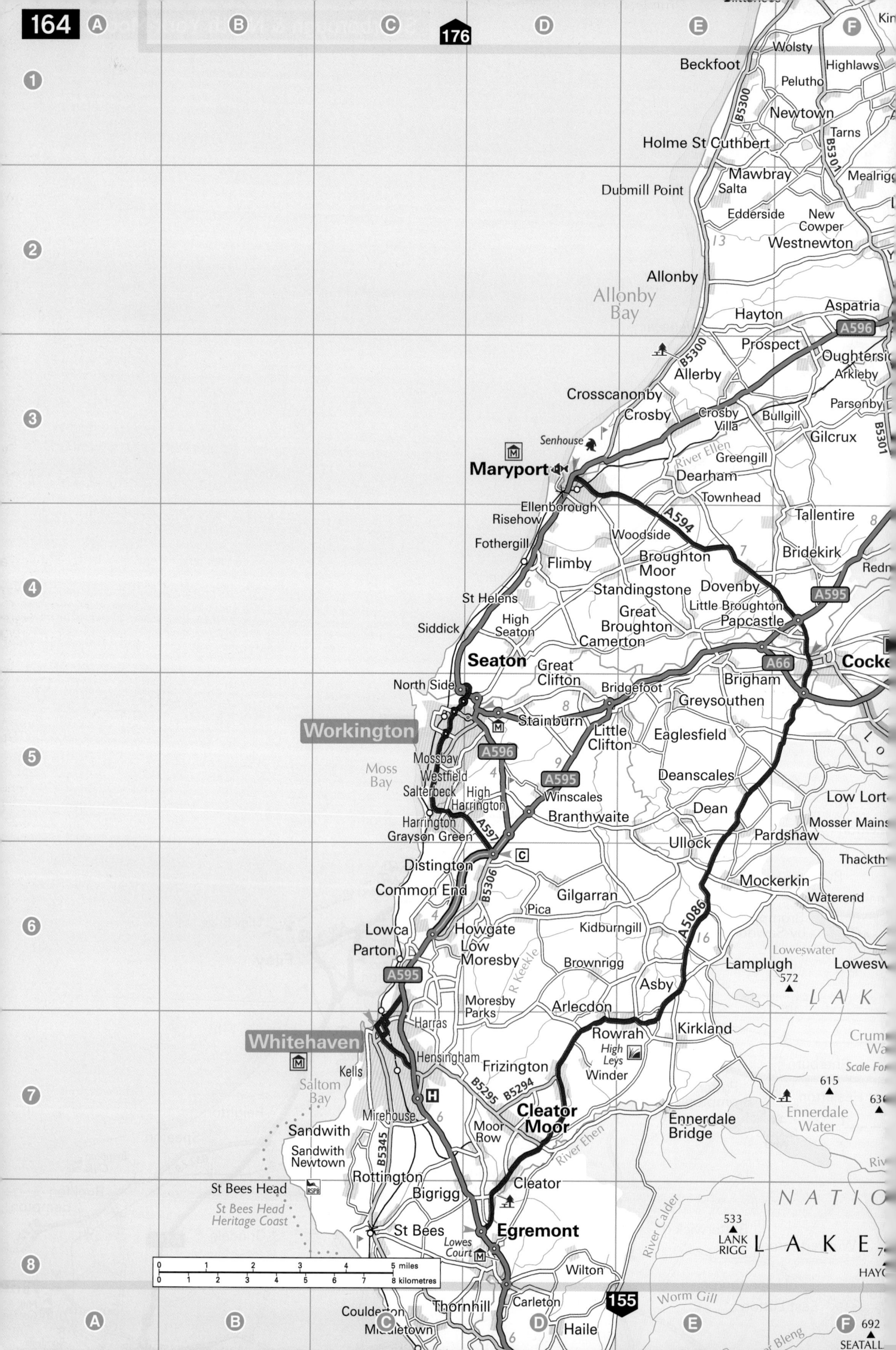

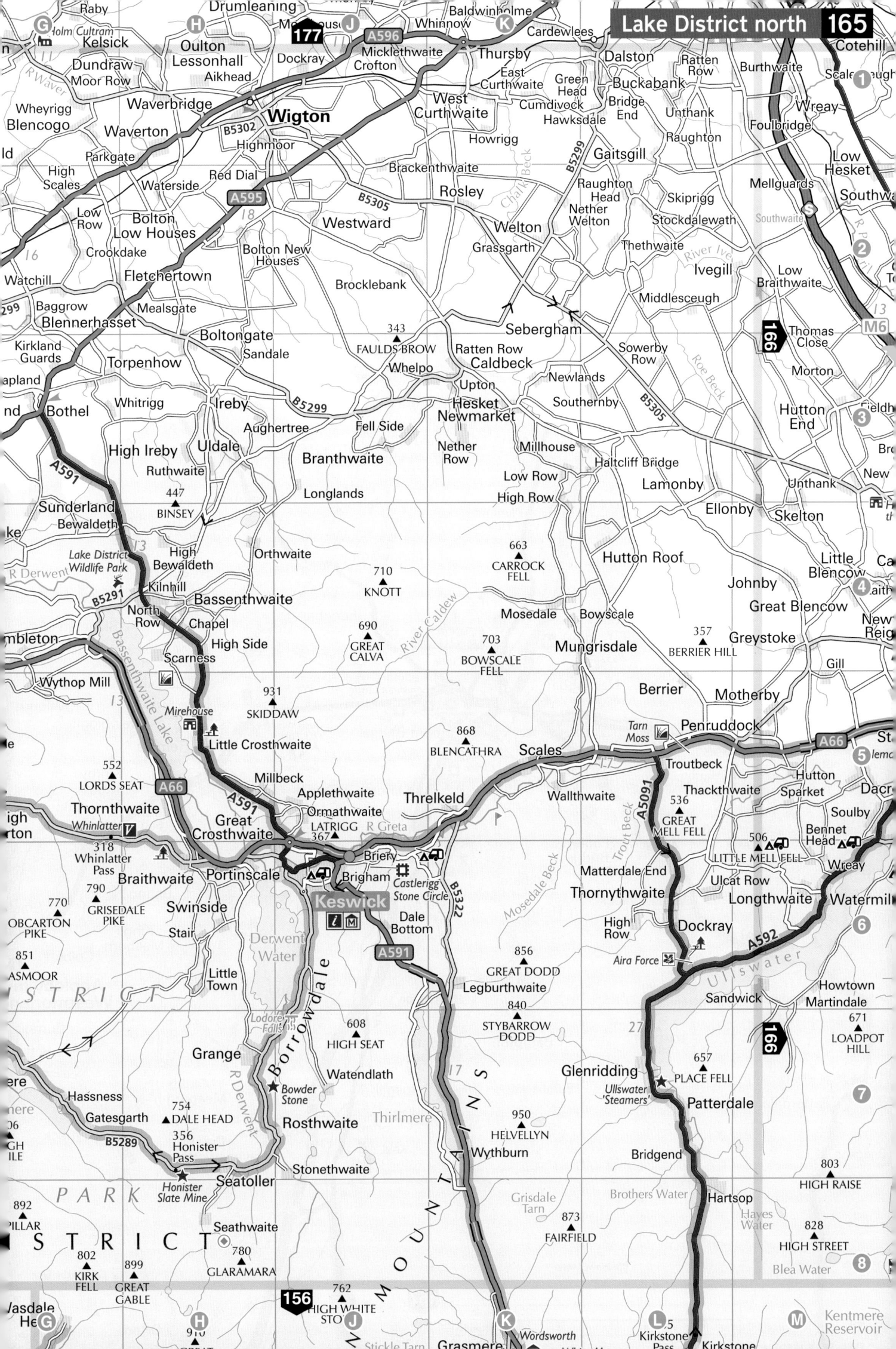

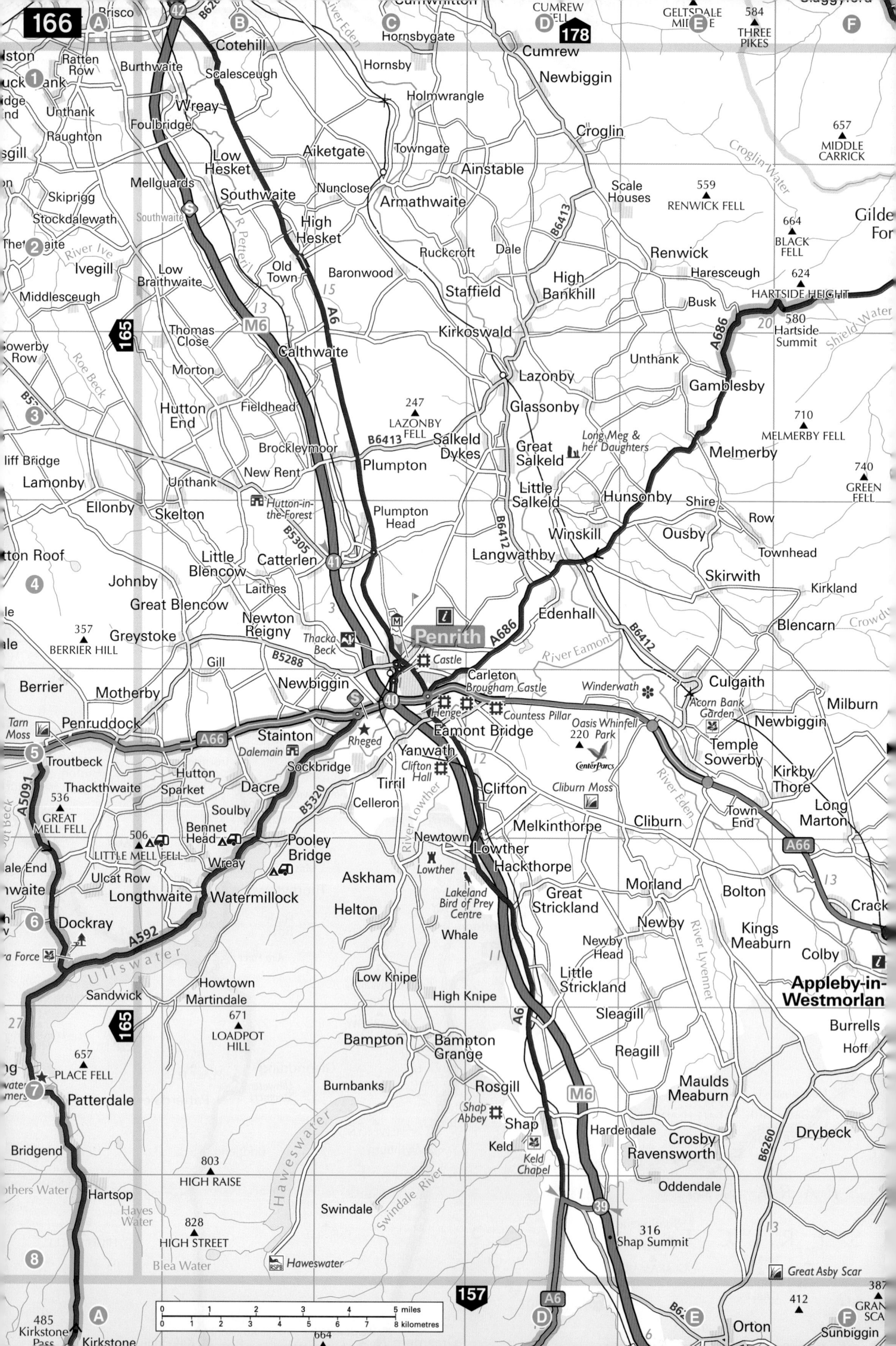

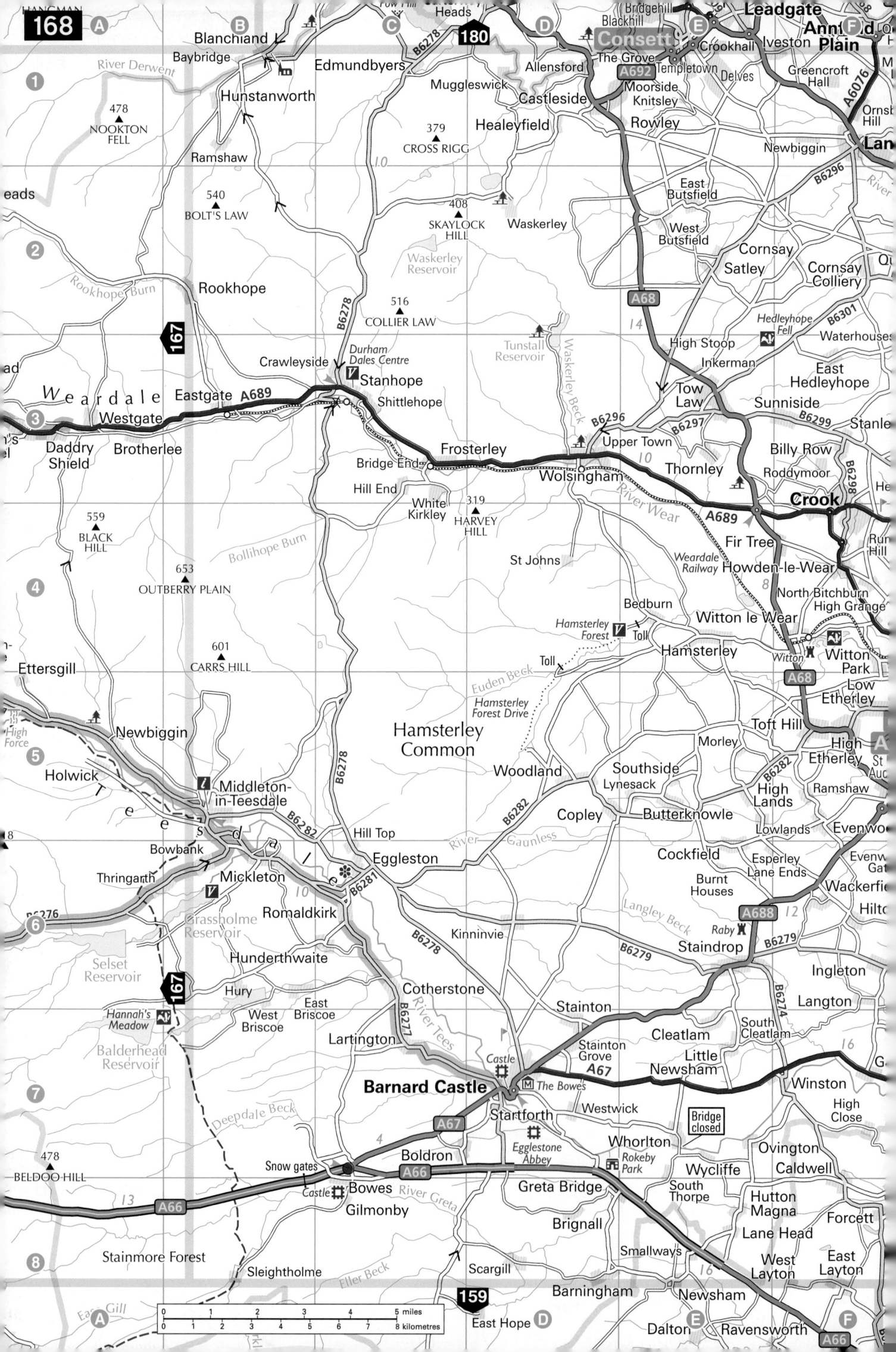

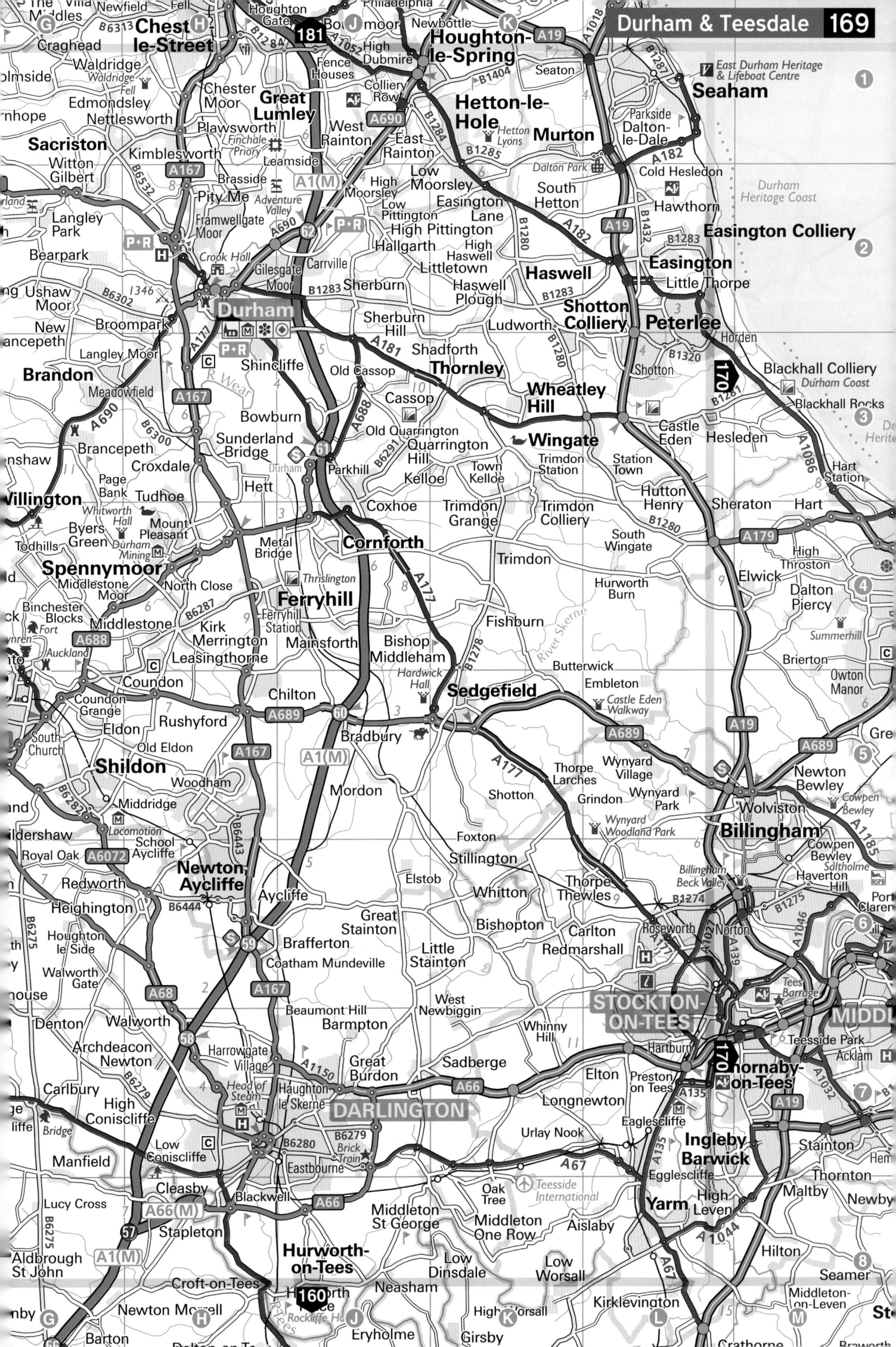

G · H · J

1
2
3
4
5
6
7
8

Hummersea Scar

on
Skinningrove
Ironstone
Mining
Loftus
lin
w
Upton
Boulby
Staithes
Captain Cook &
Staithes
Dalehouse
Easington
Port Mulgrave
Liverton
Mines
n
pe
Hinderwell
North Yorkshire and
Cleveland Heritage Coast
Roxby
Newton
Mulgrave
Runswick
Bay
on
Handale
Runswick
Kettleness
Goldsborough
Borrowby
B1366
Overdale
Wyke
sholm
Scaling
B1266
Ellerby
A174
Lythe
Gerrick
Sandsend
Wyke
Mickleby
Sandsend
i M
Scaling
Dam
West
Barnby
East
Barnby
Raithwaite
Whitby
22
Dunsley
Ugthorpe
Newholm
Abbey
Saltwick
Bay
The Moors
National Park
Centre
162
Hutton
Mulgrave
Ruswarp
301
Stonegate
Aislaby
410
Sneaton
High Hawsker
G · H · J · K · L · M
Lealholm
A171
Briggswath

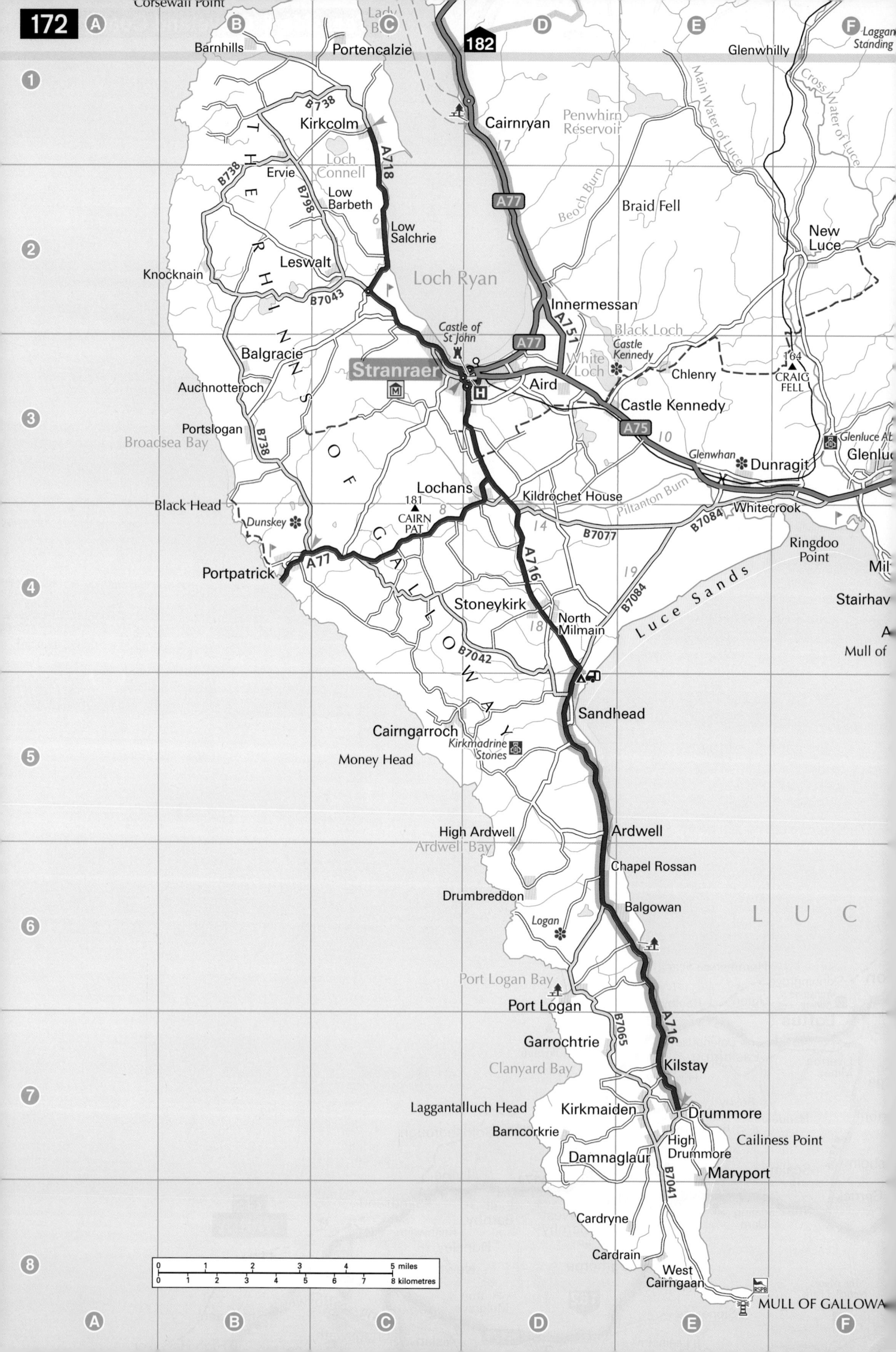

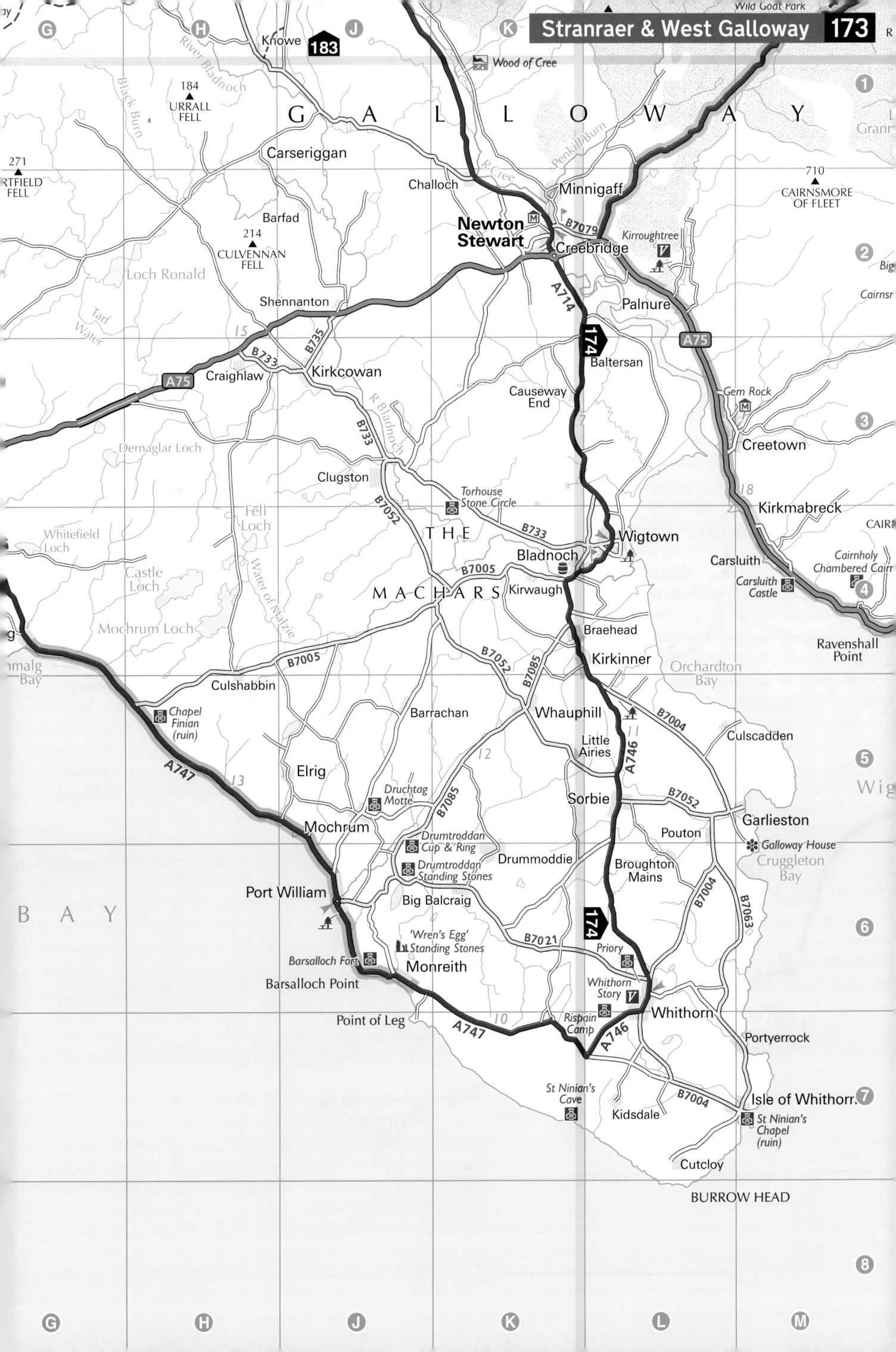

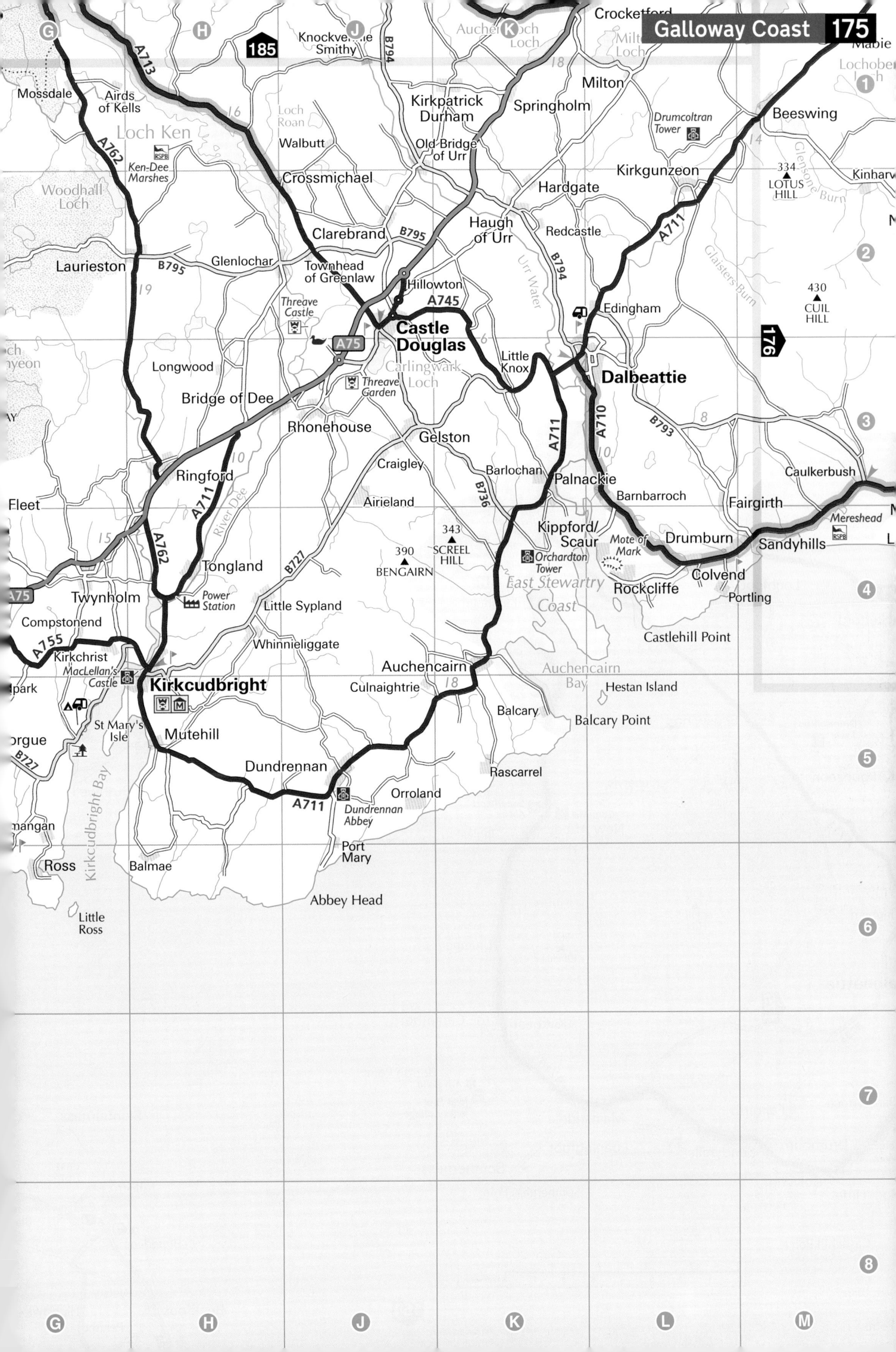

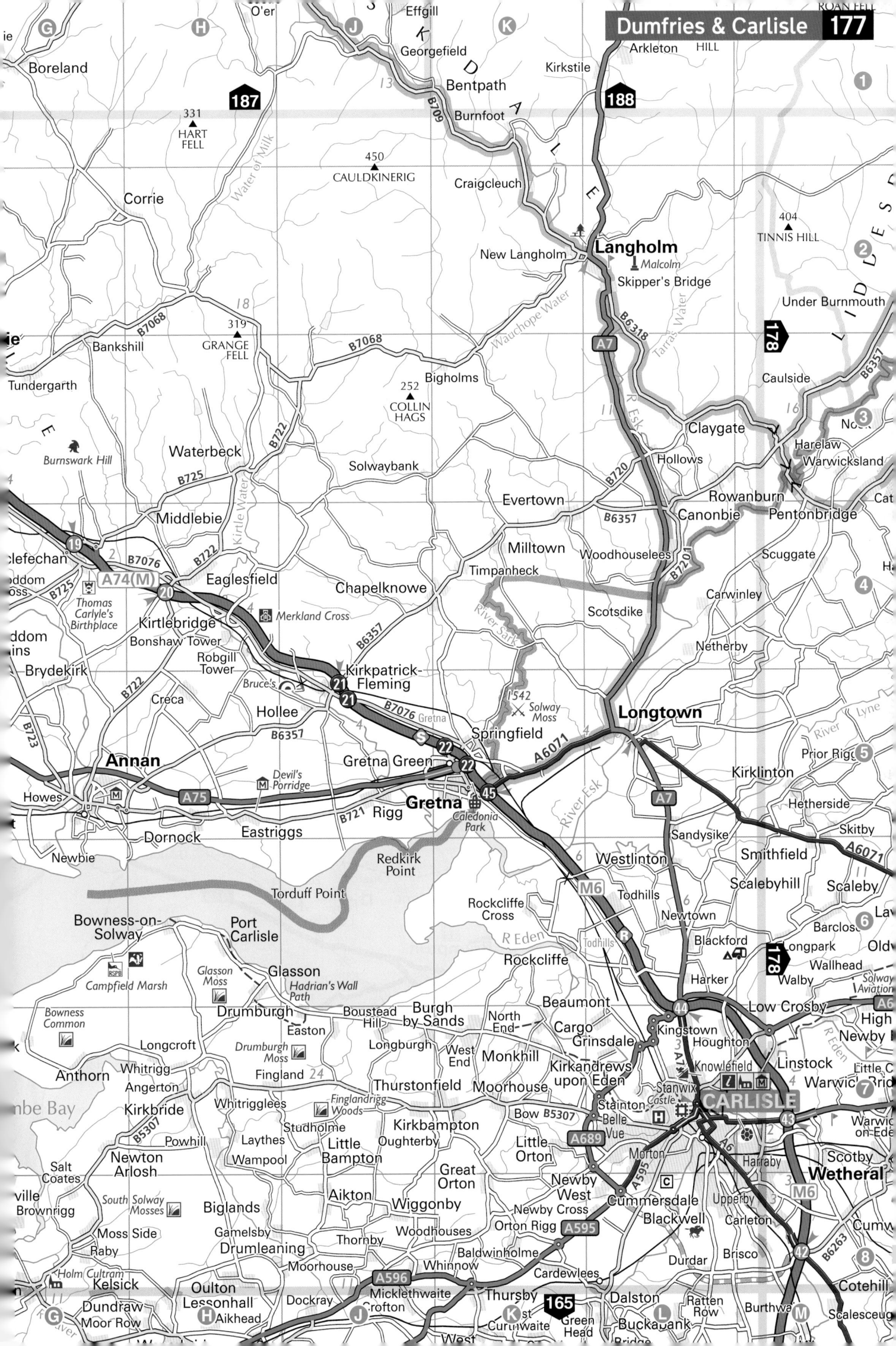

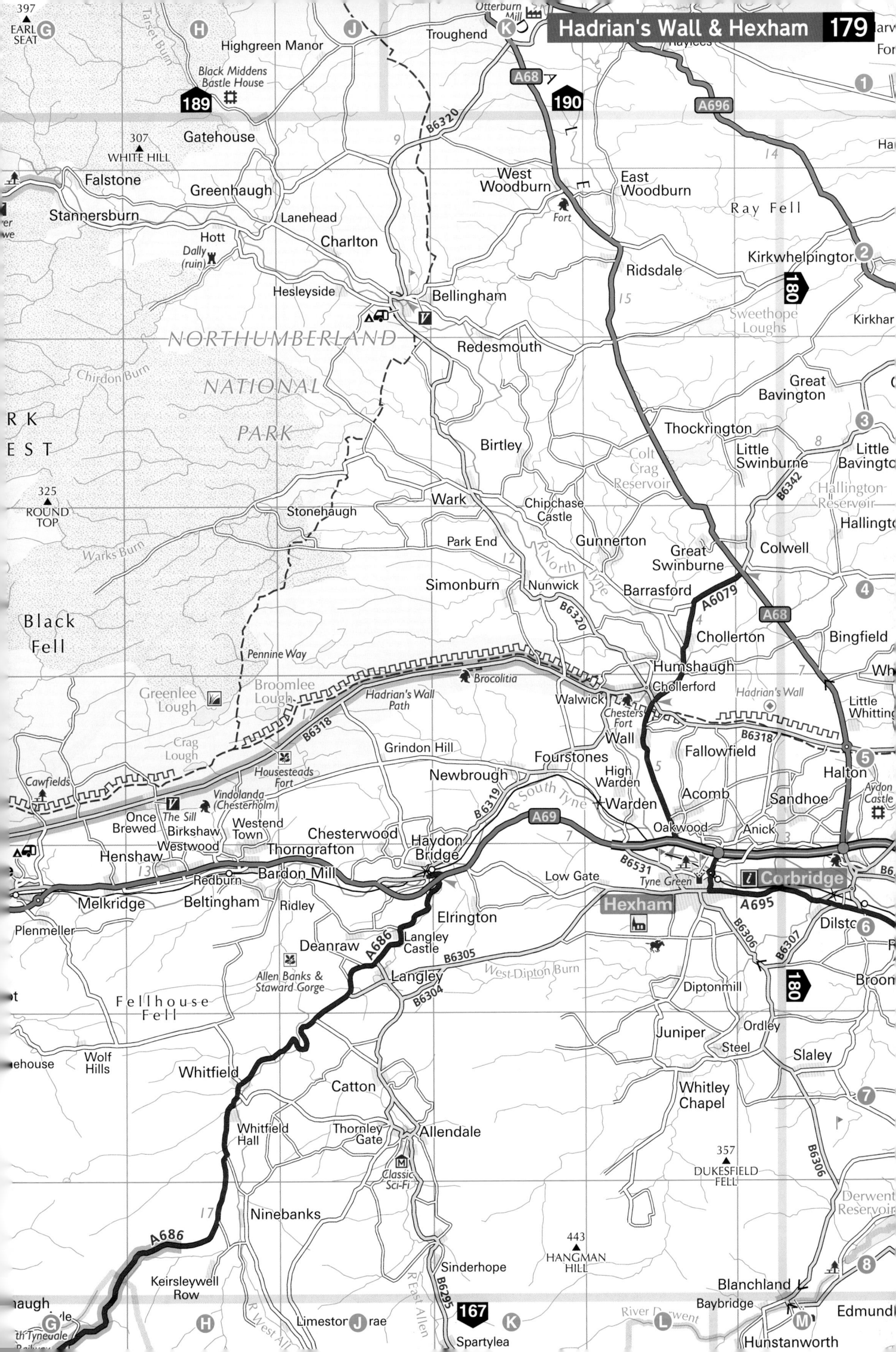

G H J K

1

2

3

4

5

6

7

8

M

A1068
Ellington
Lynemouth
191

A189 Woodhorn   Beacon Point
QE2
A197   M
Woodhorn Demesne

Hirst   H
North
Seaton   **Newbiggin-by-the-Sea**

Wansbeck
Riverside
pwash   Stakeford
B1334
North Seaton Colliery
Guide
Post   A1141
West Sleekburn
Bomarsund
7
Cambois
East
Sleekburn   North Blyth
lington

B1331   A193   C   Cowpen
Bebside   **Blyth**
A189

East   B1505   Newsham
Hartford   New   South
A192   Delaval   Newsham

Shankhouse   A1061
A192   A193   Seaton Sluice
gton   New   Hartley   Seaton
East   Seaton   Hartley
Cramlington   A190
Seaton   St Mary's
Hall
B1326   **Seaton**
H   **Delaval**   Holywell
Seghill
S   9
Annitsford
A192   B1325   C
Dudley
pen   4   B1322   A1148
Burradon   Backworth   Earsdon   A193   **Whitley**
Camperdown   Monkseaton   **Bay**
A1056   Shiremoor   Cullercoats
Killingworth   B1317   Murton
A191   A193
Forest Hall   New   H
P+R   A191   York   C   **Tynemouth**
A19   i   Tynemouth Priory   Amsterdam
Rising   4   & Castle   (IJmuiden)
Sun
Longbenton   **North**   A187
A1058   **Shields**
forth   5   Willington   Int. Ferry   **SOUTH**
Jesmond   Terminal   **SHIELDS**
Wallsend   Tyne Tunnel   i   M
Heaton   A187   Toll   (Electronic Toll)   Westoe   A183
Jarrow   Jarrow   Harton   **Marsden**
Walker   Hall   M   **Bay**
Byker   B1313   A185   A1300   H   Marsden
Hebburn   Souter Lighthouse
Sage   Monkton   Cleadon   & The Leas
A184   A19   C   Park   Whitburn Coastal Park
Felling   Wardley   A194   Cleadon   Souter Point
A184   Boldon   West   A183   **Whitburn**
TESHEAD   Colliery   Boldon
4   B1288   3   A184   East   A1018   Whitburn
A167   2   B1206   Boldon   A184   Bay
H   North-East   A1018
Low Wrekenton   Land Sea   Hylton   B1299   Seaburn
Fell Bowes   & Air   Castle   M
Railway   A194(M)   Southwick   Roker
M   A1290   A19   P+R
Springwell   Wetland   Castletown   Monkwearmouth
1   Centre
Usworth   South
65   C   A1231   Hylton   H
Birtley   A183
Portobello   **WASHINGTON**   Pennywell   B1522   **SUNDERLAND**
Washington   Offerton   Hendon
rpeth   S   Penshaw
Ouston   64   A195   Monument   A183   High Newport   Grangetown
kinsville   Fatfield   Mount   Herrington   A690   Tunstall
Pleasant   New   Durham
A782   Penshaw   Silksworth   B1286   Ryhope   Heritage Coast
R Wear   Herrington   B1287
Pelton   A183   Shiney Row   New Herrington
Fell   Houghton   Philadelphia   A19   A1018
on   63   Gate   Newbottle   B1287
Chester-   Bournmoor   High   East Durham H ge
Street   B1284   Dubmire   & Lifeboat Cent
169   Fence   Colliery   **Houghton-   A19   **Seaham**
hes   G   H   Ho   J   le-Spring**   K   L

S   B1333
B1313

B1310

A690
Hylton
Castle

A1231

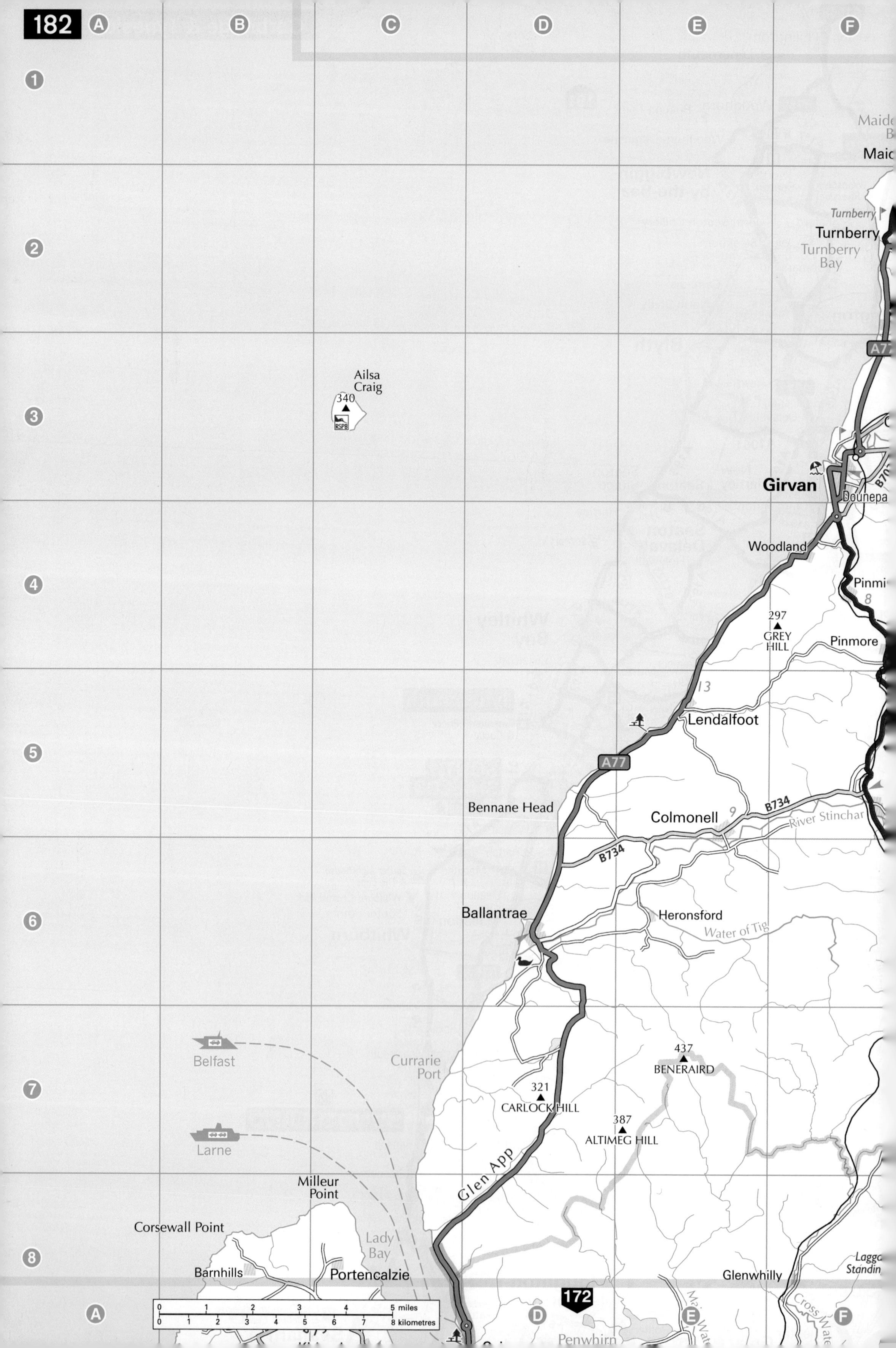

A   B   C   D   E   F

1

2

Maide
Bay
Maid
Turnberry
Turnberry
Turnberry
Bay
A77

3
Ailsa
Craig
340
▲
RSPB
Girvan
Dounepa

Woodland
Pinmi
8
4
297
▲
GREY
HILL
Pinmore

13
Lendalfoot
5
A77
Colmonell   9   B734
Bennane Head   River Stinchar

B734
6
Ballantrae
Heronsford
Water of Tig

437
▲
BENERAIRD
7
Belfast   Currarie
Port
321
▲
CARLOCK HILL
387
▲
ALTIMEG HILL
Larne
Glen App
Milleur
Point
Corsewall Point
Lady
Bay
Lagga
Standin
8
Barnhills   **Portencalzie**   Glenwhilly

A   **172**   D   E   F

0   1   2   3   4   5 miles
0   1   2   3   4   5   6   7   8 kilometres

Penwhirn   Cross Wate

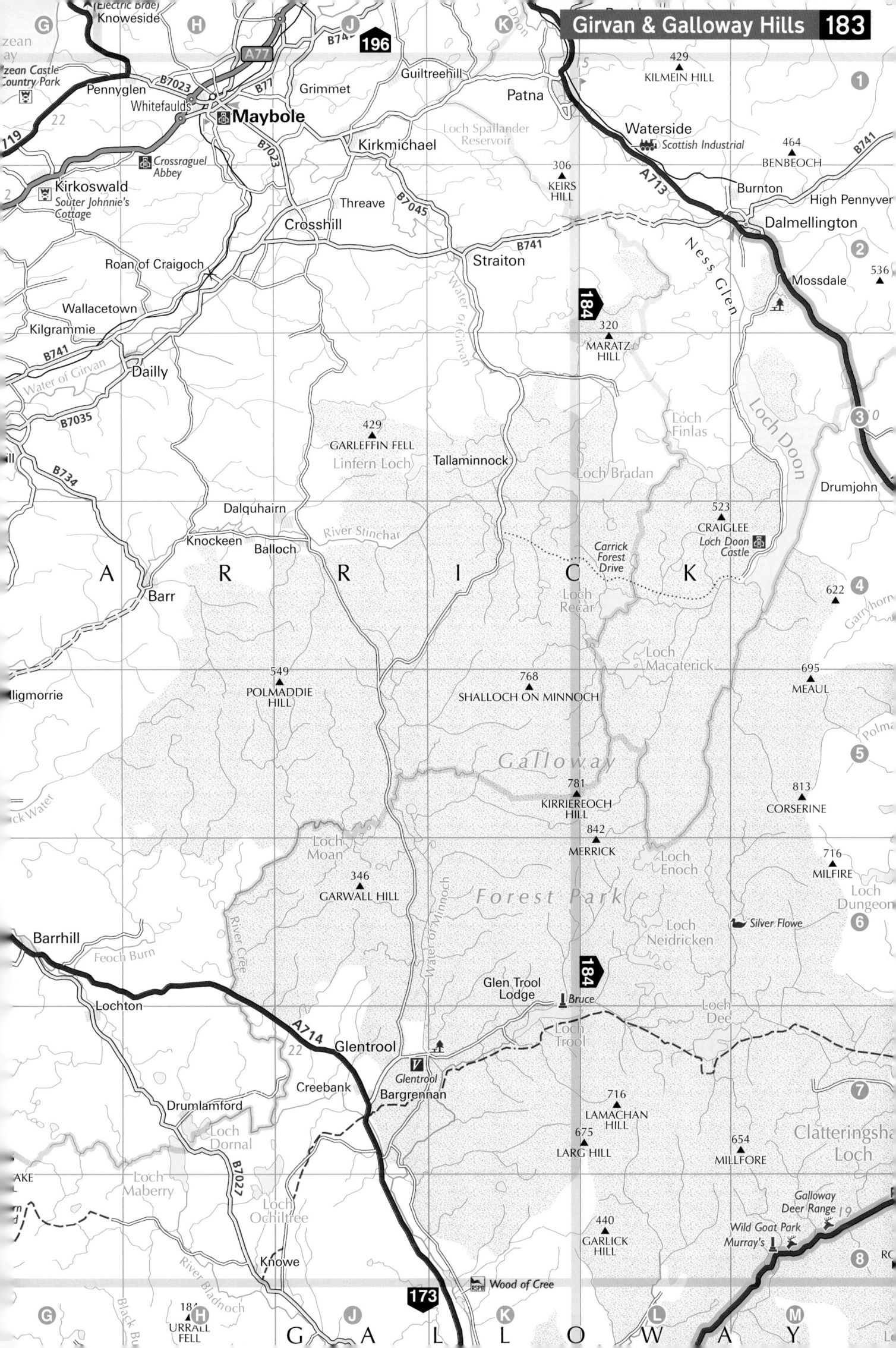

(Electric Brae)
Knoweside
G   H   J   **196**   K

zean   Guiltreehill   Doon
ay   Grimmet   Patna
zean Castle   429
Country Park   A77   KILMEIN HILL   1
            Pennyglen   B7023   Whitefaulds   B77   Waterside
                    Maybole   Scottish Industrial   464
Kirkoswald   Loch Spallander   BENBEOCH   B741
            Crossraguel   Kirkmichael   Reservoir   306   Burnton
            Abbey   KEIRS   Dalmellington   High Pennyver   2
2   Souter Johnnie's   Threave   HILL
    Cottage   Crosshill   B741   536
719   B7045   Straiton   Mossdale
                    Roan of Craigoch   184
                                                                              320   3
    Wallacetown   MARATZ   Drumjohn
    Kilgrammie   HILL
B741   Water of Girvan   Dailly   Loch
B7035   Finlas   Loch Doon
                                    429   Loch Bradan
                            GARLEFFIN FELL   523
                    Dalquhairn   Linfern Loch   Tallaminnock   CRAIGLEE
    Knockeen   River Stinchar   Carrick   Loch Doon
            Balloch   Forest   Castle
A   R   R   I   C   Drive   K
    Barr   Loch   622   4
                                    Recar   Garryhorn
                                        Loch
                                    Macaterick
ligmorrie   549   768   695
        POLMADDIE   SHALLOCH ON MINNOCH   MEAUL
        HILL
                                    Galloway   5
                                781   813
                            KIRRIEREOCH   CORSERINE
                            HILL
                                842   Loch
                    Loch   MERRICK   Enoch
                    Moan   346   716
                        GARWALL HILL   MILFIRE
                                                            Loch
                                Forest Park   Dungeon
Barrhill   6
    Feoch Burn   Loch
ck Water   Neidricken   Silver Flowe
    Lochton   Glen Trool   Loch
                    A714   Lodge   184   Dee
            Glentrool   Bruce
        Creebank   Glentrool   Loch
                    Bargrennan   Trool   7
    Drumlamford   716
                Loch   LAMACHAN   654
                Dornal   HILL   MILLFORE   Clatteringsha
                                675   Loch
                B7027   Loch   LARG HILL
AKE   Maberry   Galloway
                                                    Deer Range
                    Loch   Wild Goat Park
                    Ochiltree   440   Murray's
                                        GARLICK   8
            Knowe   HILL
                            173   Wood of Cree
                                        RSPB
G   184   H   J   K   L   M
    URRALL
    FELL   River Bladnoch   G   A   L   L   O   W   A   Y

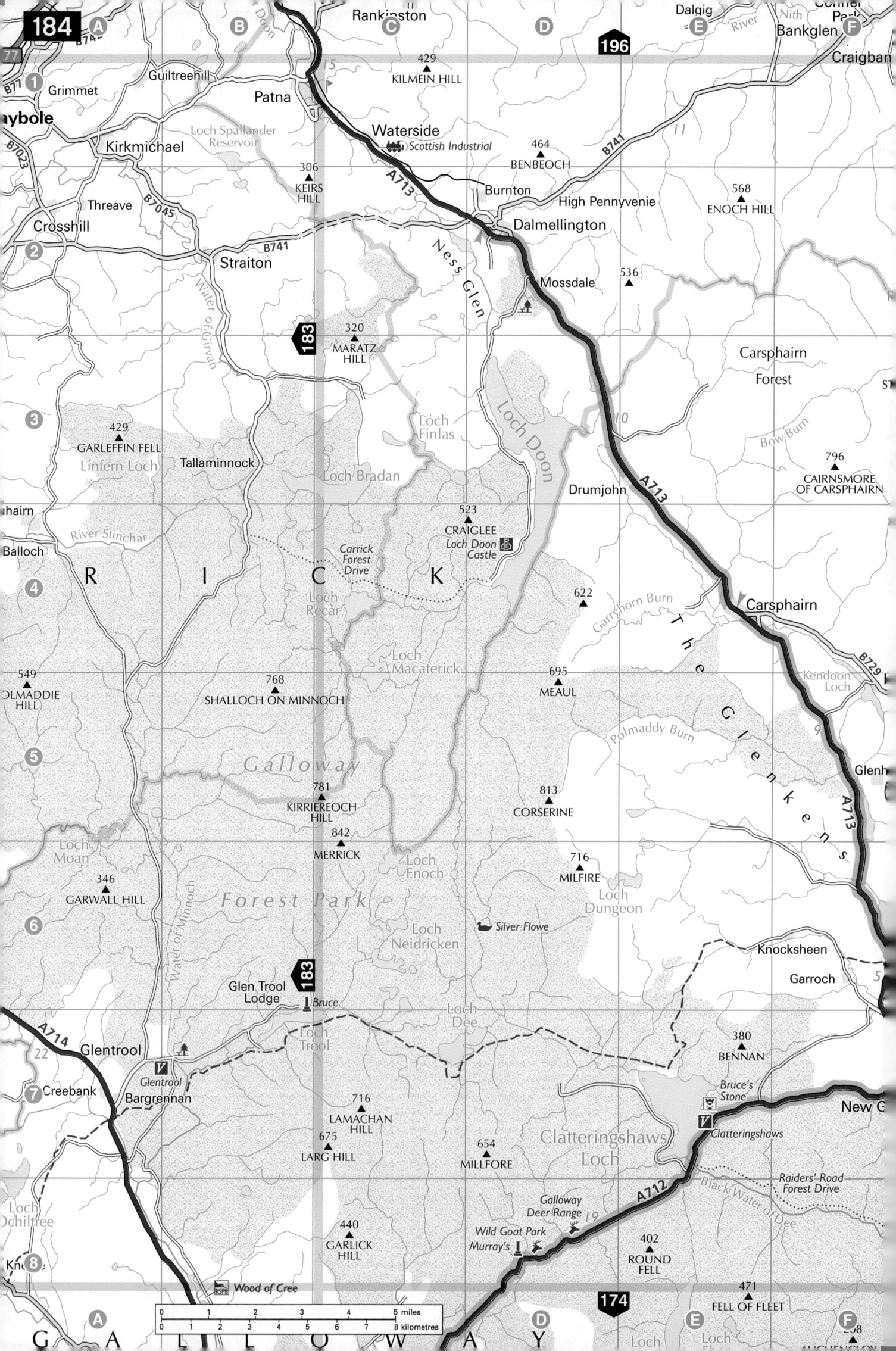

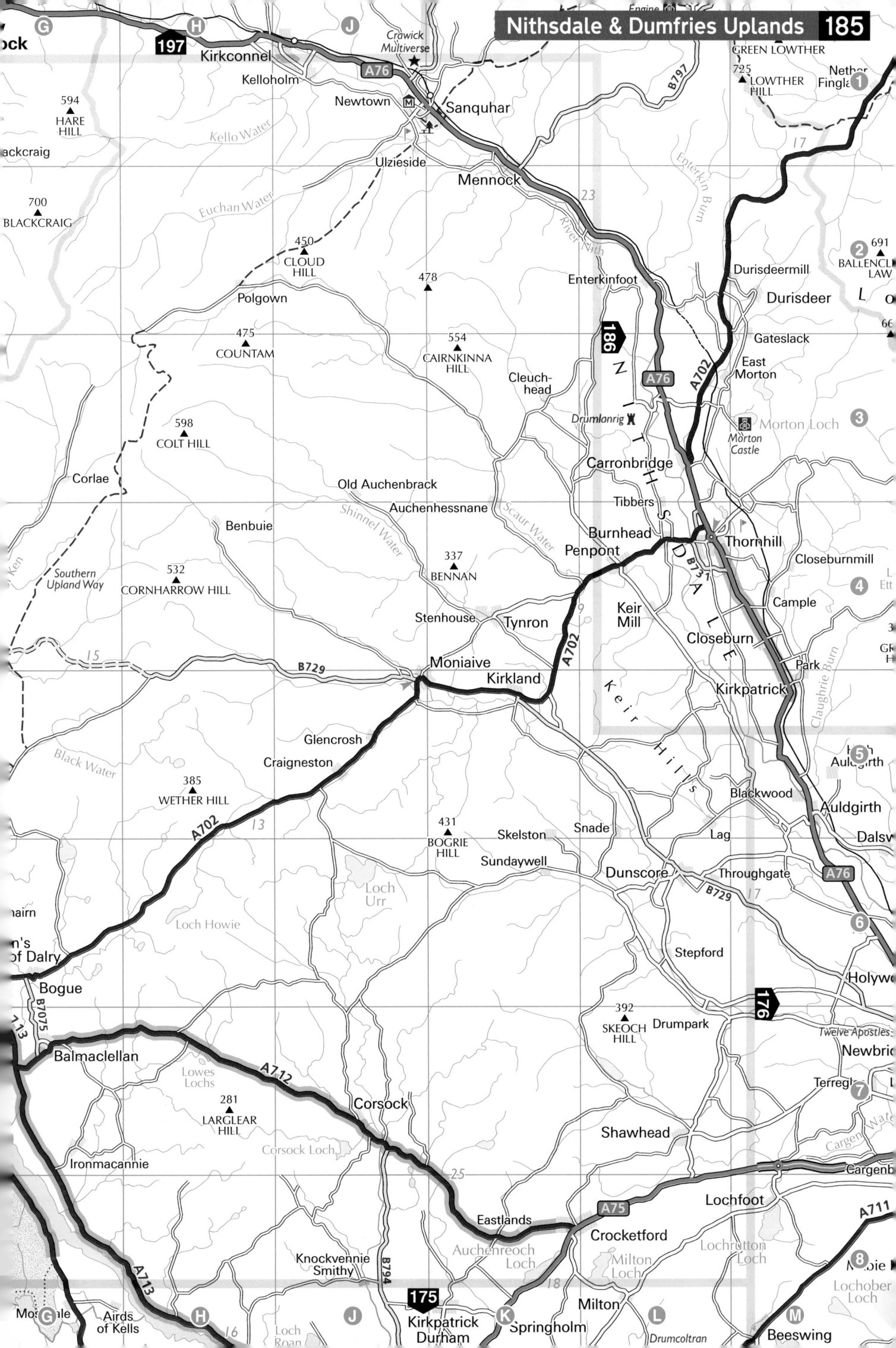

G
H **197** Kirkconnel
J
Crawick Multiverse
GREEN LOWTHER
725 ▲ LOWTHER HILL
Nether Fingla
1

Kelloholm
A76
Newtown M
Sanquhar
B797

594 ▲ HARE HILL
ackcraig

Mennock
23
Durisdeermill
691 ▲ BALLENCL LAW **2**
L

700 ▲ BLACKCRAIG

Ulzieside
River Nith
Enterkinfoot
Durisdeer
66

Euchan Water
Enterkin Burn

450 ▲ CLOUD HILL
478 ▲
Gateslack
East Morton

Polgown
186
A76
A702
3

475 ▲ COUNTAM
554 ▲ CAIRNKINNA HILL
Cleuch-head
Morton Loch
Morton Castle

598 ▲ COLT HILL
Old Auchenbrack
Drumlanrig
Carronbridge

Corlae
Auchenhessnane
Tibbers
Closeburnmill
4

Benbuie
Scaur Water
Burnhead
Penpont
Thornhill

Southern Upland Way
532 ▲ CORNHARROW HILL
Shinnel Water
337 ▲ BENNAN
Keir Mill
Cample

15
Stenhouse
Tynron
A702
9
Closeburn
Park

Ken
B729
Moniaive
Kirkland
Keir Hills
Kirkpatrick

Glencrosh
Auldgirth **5**
L Ett

Black Water
Craigneston
385 ▲ WETHER HILL
Blackwood
Auldgirth

A702
13
431 ▲ BOGRIE HILL
Skelston
Snade
Lag
Dalsw

Loch Urr
Sundaywell
Dunscore
B729
17
6

n's of Dalry
Loch Howie
Stepford
Holyw

Bogue
B7075
392 ▲ SKEOCH HILL
Drumpark
176
Twelve Apostles

13
Balmaclellan
A712
Newbri

Lowes Lochs
281 ▲ LARGLEAR HILL
Corsock
Shawhead
Terregl **7**

Ironmacannie
Corsock Loch
Cargen Wat

A713
25
Lochfoot
A711

A75
Lochrutton Loch
Cargenb

Mo dale
Airds of Kells
G
H
16
Knockvennie Smithy
B794
Eastlands
Crocketford
Auchenreoch Loch
Milton Loch
18
Milton
Lochober Loch **8**

175 Kirkpatrick Durham
J
K Springholm
L Drumcoltran
M Beeswing
Loch Roan

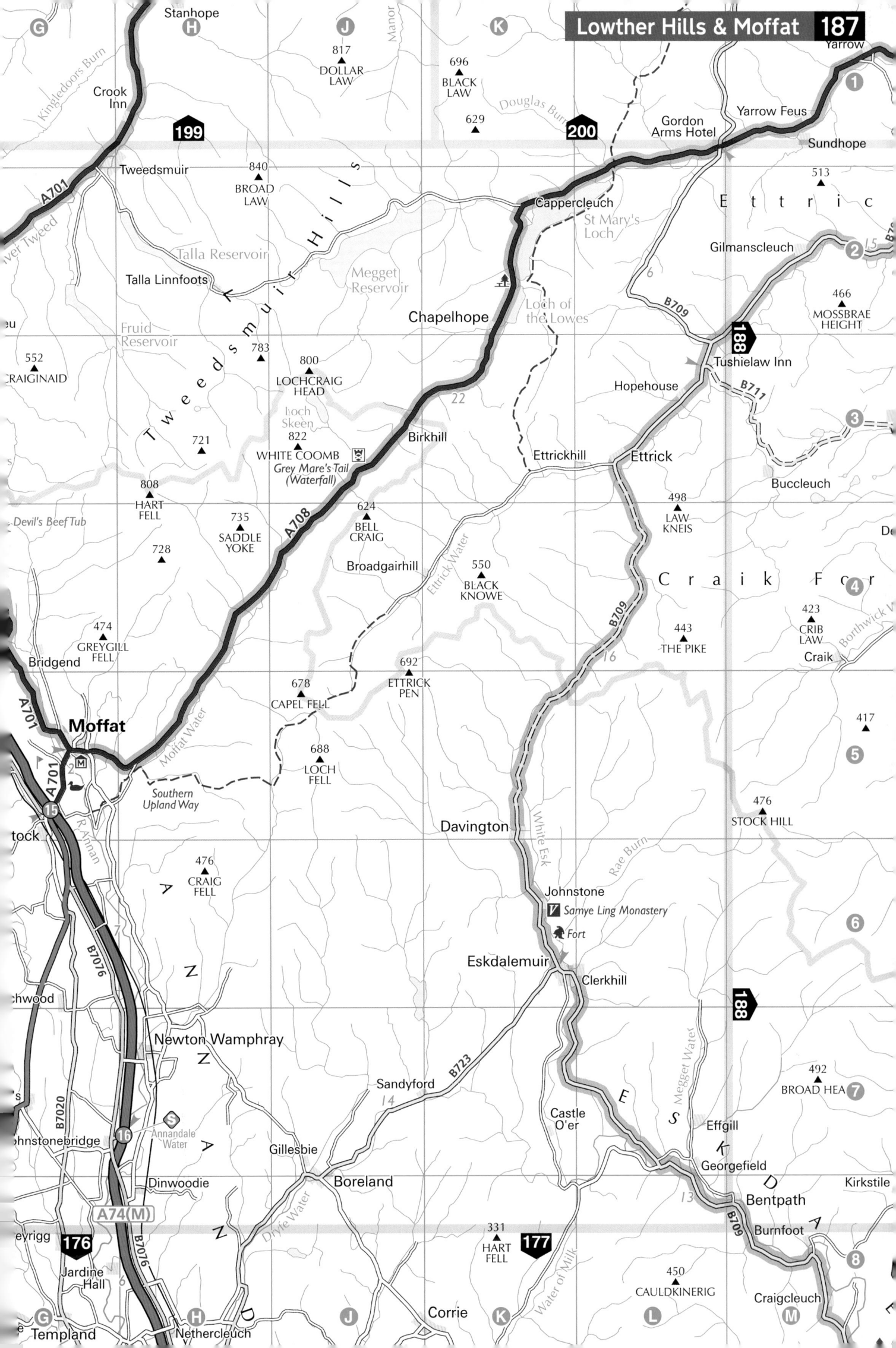

Stanhope

G **H** **J** **K**

817
DOLLAR
LAW

696
BLACK
LAW

Yarrow

1

Crook
Inn

629

199 **200**

Douglas Burn

Gordon
Arms Hotel

Yarrow Feus

Sundhope

Tweedsmuir

840
BROAD
LAW

River Tweed

A701

Cappercleuch

St Mary's
Loch

513

E t t r i c

Talla Reservoir

Talla Linnfoots

Megget
Reservoir

Gilmanscleuch

2

15

B7

552
CRAIGINAID

Fruid
Reservoir

Chapelhope

Loch of
the Lowes

B709

466
MOSSBRAE
HEIGHT

783

800
LOCHCRAIG
HEAD

188

Tushielaw Inn

Hopehouse

B711

721

Loch
Skeen

822
WHITE COOMB
*Grey Mare's Tail
(Waterfall)*

Birkhill

22

Ettrickhill

Ettrick

B709

Buccleuch

3

808
HART
FELL

Devil's Beef Tub

735
SADDLE
YOKE

A708

624
BELL
CRAIG

498
LAW
KNEIS

Ettrick Water

C r a i k   F o r

4

728

Broadgairhill

550
BLACK
KNOWE

423
CRIB
LAW

Borthwick W

474
GREYGILL
FELL

THE PIKE

Craik

Bridgend

692
ETTRICK
PEN

B709

443

417

A701

Moffat Water

678
CAPEL FELL

16

5

A701

Moffat

M

688
LOCH
FELL

476
STOCK HILL

*Southern
Upland Way*

White Esk

Davington

Rae Burn

15

R. Annan

476
CRAIG
FELL

tock

Johnstone

Samye Ling Monastery

6

A

B7076

Fort

Z

Eskdalemuir

Clerkhill

188

N

Newton Wamphray

Z

Z

Megget Water

492
BROAD HEA

7

B7020

Sandyford

B723

14

E
S

Effgill

ohnstonebridge

16

Annandale
Water

Castle
O'er

K

Georgefield

Kirkstile

Dinwoodie

Gillesbie

Boreland

Dryfe Water

13

B709

Bentpath

Burnfoot

A

A74(M)

B7076

eyrigg

176

331
HART
FELL

177

Water of Milk

D
A

M

Jardine
Hall

450
CAULDKINERIG

Craigcleuch

Templand

G **H** **J** **K** **L** **M**

Nethercleuch

Corrie

8

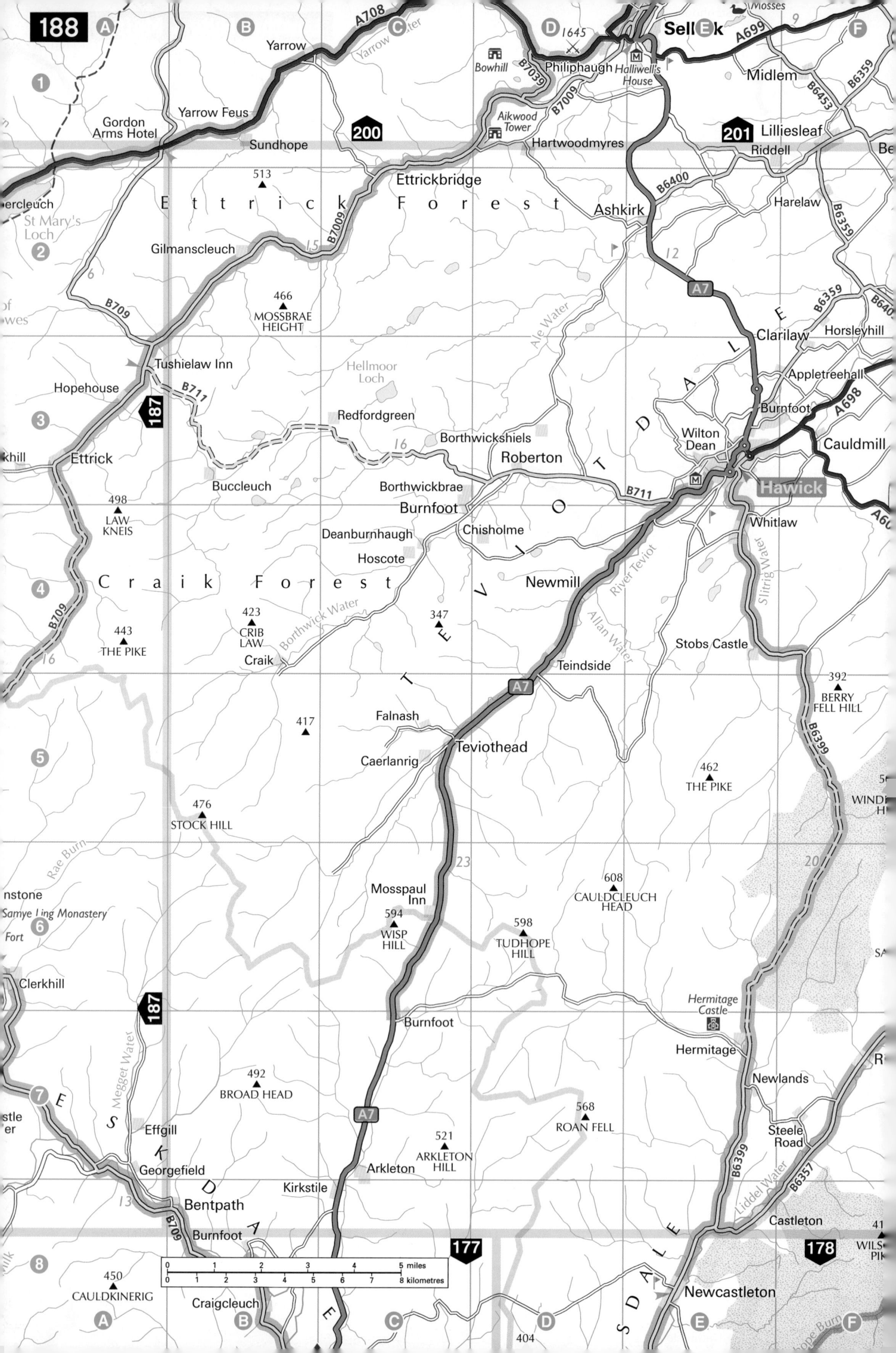

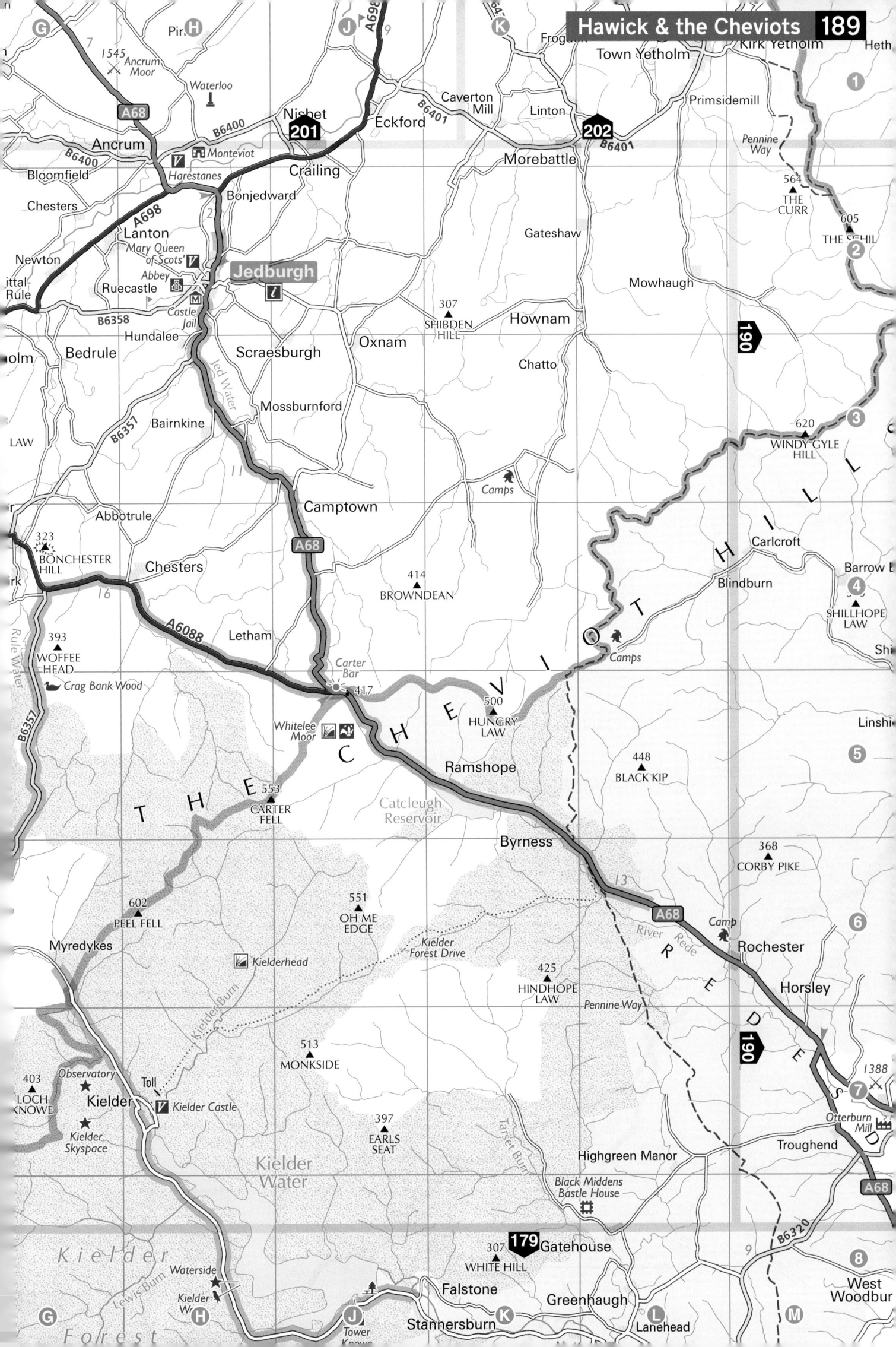

205

Muasdale

Glenacardoch
Point

Belloch

Carradale
Br

Glenbarr

Barr Water

454
▲
BEINN AN TUIRC

To

Cleongart

319
▲

408
▲
BORD
MOR

194
N

Sado

Bellochantuy Bay

Bellochantuy

Lussa
Loch

396
▲
SGREADAN
HILL

Ugadale

Tangy Loch

Glen Lussa

Kilkenzie

A83

Kilmichael

Peninver

Ardna
Ba

B842

Machrihanish
Bay

Campbeltown

Machrihanish

B842

Campbeltown

Island D

Drumlemble

B843

6

Stewarton

Campbeltown
Loch

Kilkerran

Kildalloig

Earadale Point

352
▲
BEINN GHUILEAN

385
▲
THE
STATE

Achinhoan

446
▲
CNOC
MOY

Conie Glen

Glen Kerran

R

Dalsmeran

10

Glen Breakerie

Strone Glen

Cattadale

B842

Polliwilline Bay

Southend

Macharioch

BEINN NA LICE
428
▲

Carskey

MULL
OF
KINTYRE

Dunaverty

Sound of Sanda

Sheep Island

Borgadalemore
Point

Carskey Bay

Sanda Island

0	1	2	3	4	5 miles
0	1 2 3 4 5 6 7				8 kilometres

Imachar

Balliekine

792
BEINN
NUIS

Glen Rosa

Merkland Point

Brodick Castle, Garden
& Country Park

Brodick
Bay

A R R A N

Auchagallon
Stone Circle

Machrie

Brodick

Strathwhillan

Corriegills

A'CHRUACH 512

Clauchlands
Point

Machrie
Bay

Tormore

Machrie Moor
Stone Circles

503
BEINN BHREAC

Margnaheglish

Moss Farm Road
Stone Circle

Balmichael

Lamlash

Lamlash
Bay

Holy Island

Torbeg

Shiskine

Cordon

Drumadoon
Point

Blackwaterfoot

Auchencairn

Kingscross

Knockenkelly

Drumadoon
Bay

Kilpatrick

Glen Scorrodale

Carn Ban

Whiting
Bay

194 Brown Head

Kilpatrick Dun

Whiting Bay

Glenashdale

Corriecravie

Largymore

Torr a' Chaisteal Fort

Sliddery

Kilmory Water

(May-Sept,
Sat only)

Largybeg

Dippin Head

Dippin

Kilmory

Torrylin
Cairn

Lagg

Bennan

Kildonan

Bennan Head

Pladda

195

Ballycastle
(Apr-Sept)

Ailsa
Craig

340

RSPB

K I L B R A N

Carradale

Port Right

3879

Waterfoot

Carradale
Point

Carradale
Bay

dell
ay

Iorsa Water

A841

6

4

4

G H J K L M
1 2 3 4 5 6 7 8

A · B · C · D · E · F

Cock of Arran

Loch Cìaran

Loch Garasdale

Crossaig

Lochranza

Castle

Catacol

Isle of Arran

Glen Chalmadale

A841

8

247
CRUACH MHIC GOUGAIN

264
CNOC AN T-SAMHLAIDH

Rhunahaorine

38

Cour Bay

Cour

Penrioch

North Arran

834
CAISTEAL ABHAIL

Glen Catacol

205

Grogport
Barmollack

Pirnmill

Whitefarland

715
BEINN BHARRAIN

Loch Tanna

Glen Iorsa

874
GOATFELL

354
CRUACH NAN GABHAR

39

B842

Imachar

Balliekine

792
BEINN NUIS

Glen Rosa

dale

Water

Carradale Water

B879

Carradale

Port Righ

Iorsa Water

192

454
BEINN AN TUIRC

Carradale Village
Bridgend
Dippen

Waterfoot

Carradale Point

A R R A N

Torrisdale

Carradale Bay

Auchagallon Stone Circle

Machrie

B

319

408
BÒRD MOR

Saddell Water

Saddell Bay

Machrie Bay

Tormore

Machrie Moor Stone Circles

B880

512
A'CHRUACH

Saddell

Moss Farm Road Stone Circle

503
BEINN BHREAC

Lussa Loch

396
SGREADAN HILL

Ugadale

Balmichael

Torbeg

Shiskine

Glen Lussa

Drumadoon Point

Blackwaterfoot

Glen Scorrodale

Peninver

B842

Ardnacross Bay

Drumadoon Bay

Kilpatrick

Kilpatrick Dun

Carn Ban

193

Brown Head

Corriecravie

Kilmory Water

Ki chael

Torr a' Chaisteal Fort

Sliddery

Campbeltown

B842

Stewarton

Campbeltown Loch

Island Davaar

Kilmory

Lagg

Torrylin Cairn

Bennan

Kilkerran

Kildalloig

Bennan Head

352
BEINN GHUILEAN

Achinhoan

Glen Kerran

Ru Stafnish

Ballycastle
(Apr–Sept)

0 1 2 3 4 5 miles
0 1 2 3 4 5 6 7 8 kilometres

Polliwilline Bay

G H J 207 K

Gar H ity

Garroch Head

Little
Cumbrae
Island

Fairlie Ro

Hunterston
Power Station

12

Drakemyre

1

Dalry

High

Munnoch

Dalgarven

Portencross

B7048

B781

B780

7

Dalgarven
Mill

Farland Head

**West
Kilbride**

B7047

B780

C

B714

U

2

Seamill

Dalgarven

B78

Horse Isle

A78

A738

Kilwinning

annox

A78

Ardrossan

A738

B78

A737

Stevenston

Corrie

B780

B779

Ardeer

6 Merkland Point

Saltcoats

196

B780

3

Brodick Castle, Garden
& Country Park

Irvine

Maritime

Brodick
Bay

V

M

Fulla

i

FIRTH

Irvine

Strathwhillan

Bay

Corriegills

OF

4

4

CLYDE

Bara

H

Clauchlands
Point

Margnaheglish

V

Troon

Lamlash
Bay

Holy Island

Lady Isle

Roy

Cordon

5

chencairn

Kingscross

(May–Sept, Sat only)

(May–Sept)

Knockenkelly

V

P

Whiting
Bay

4

hiting Bay

Bay

Largymore

6

ashdale

Largybeg

Dippin
Dippin Head

196

Kildonan

Doonfo

Burns Cott

Heads of Ayr
Heads
of Ayr

da

Fisherton

A719

All

7

Dunure

Culroy

Drumshang

Croy Brae
(Electric Brae)

Knoweside

8

Culzean
Bay

Culzean Castle
& Country Park

Pennyglen

B70

M

B7

A77

182

Whitefaulds

Mayl

G H J K L

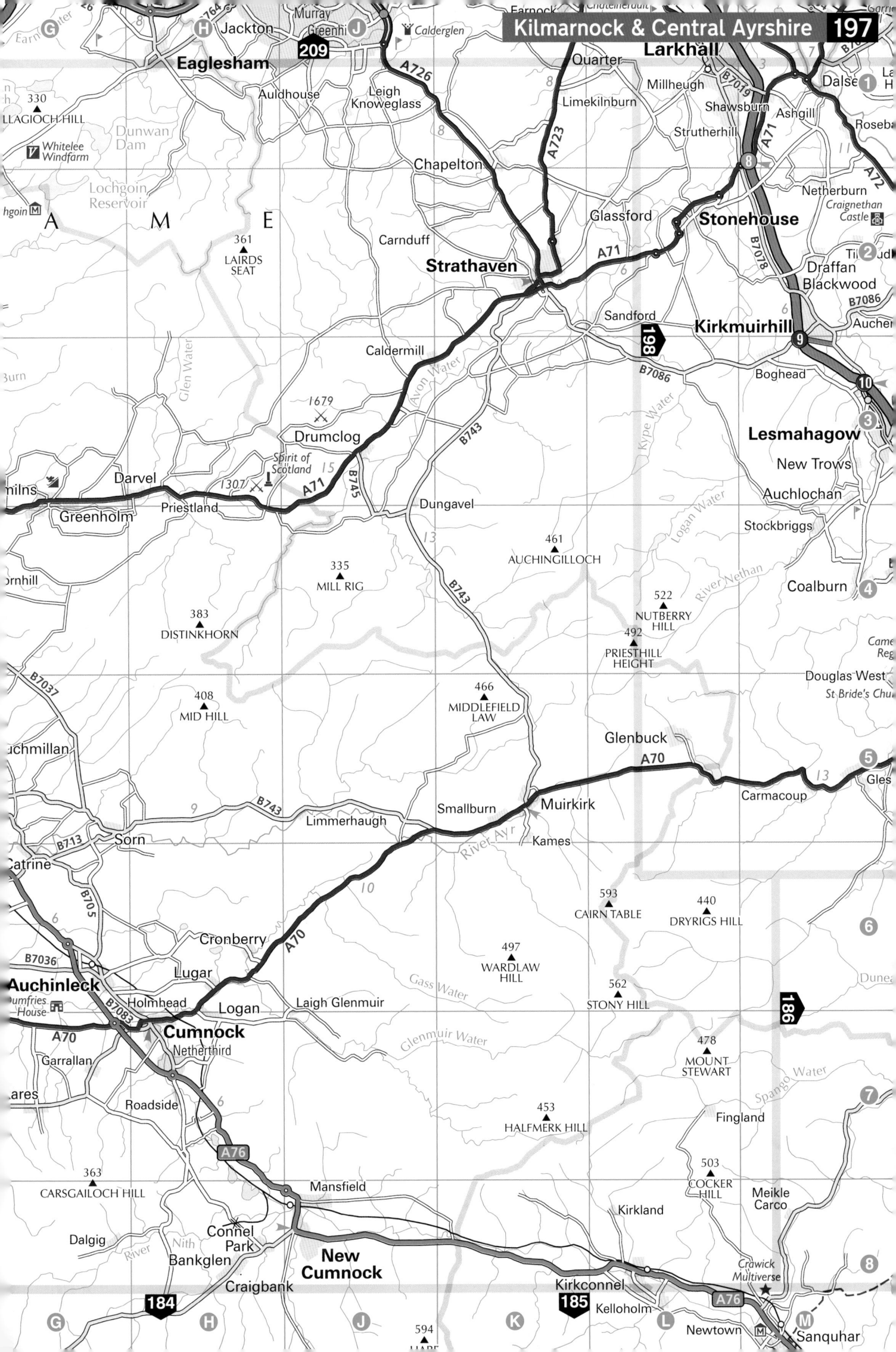

G H J

Murray
Greenhi
Jackton
Eaglesham
209
Auldhouse
Leigh
Knoweglass
Calderglen
A726

Farnock
Quarter
Larkhall
Dalse 1
B7019
Millheugh
Limekilnburn
Shawsburn
Ashgill
Roseba
A71
Netherburn
Craignethan Castle
Chapelton
A723
A71

LLAGIOCH HILL 330
Dunwan Dam
Whitelee Windfarm
Lochgoin Reservoir
hgoin M
A M E
Carnduff
LAIRDS SEAT 361
Strathaven
Glassford
A71
Stonehouse
Til 2
Draffan
Blackwood
B7078
B7086

Caldermill
Sandford
198
B7086
Kirkmuirhill
9
Aucher

1679
Drumclog
B743
Avon Water
Kype Water
Boghead
10
Lesmahagow
3

Spirit of Scotland
15
A71
1307
B745
Darvel
Priestland
Greenholm
milns
Dungavel
13
B743

New Trows
Auchlochan
Stockbriggs
Logan Water
River Nethan
Coalburn
4
Came Reg

MILL RIG 335
AUCHINGILLOCH 461
NUTBERRY HILL 522
PRIESTHILL HEIGHT 492

DISTINKHORN 383
ornhill

MID HILL 408
MIDDLEFIELD LAW 466
Douglas West
St Bride's Chu

uchmillan
Glenbuck
A70
5
Gles
Carmacoup
13

B7037
B743
Limmerhaugh
Smallburn
Muirkirk
Kames
River Ayr
9
Sorn
B713
CAIRN TABLE 593
DRYRIGS HILL 440
6
Catrine
B705
10
A70
Cronberry
Lugar
WARDLAW HILL 497
Dune

B7036
Auchinleck
Holmhead
Logan
Laigh Glenmuir
STONY HILL 562
186

Dumfries House
B7083
Cumnock
Netherthird
Gass Water
A70
Garrallan
Glenmuir Water
MOUNT STEWART 478

ares
Roadside
6
7
Spango Water

A76
HALFMERK HILL 453
Fingland

CARSGAILOCH HILL 363
Mansfield
Kirkland
COCKER HILL 503
Meikle Carco

Dalgig
Nith River
Connel Park
Bankglen
New Cumnock
Craigbank
Crawick Multiverse
8

184
185
Kirkconnel
Kelloholm
Newtown M
A76
Sanquhar

G H J K L M

594

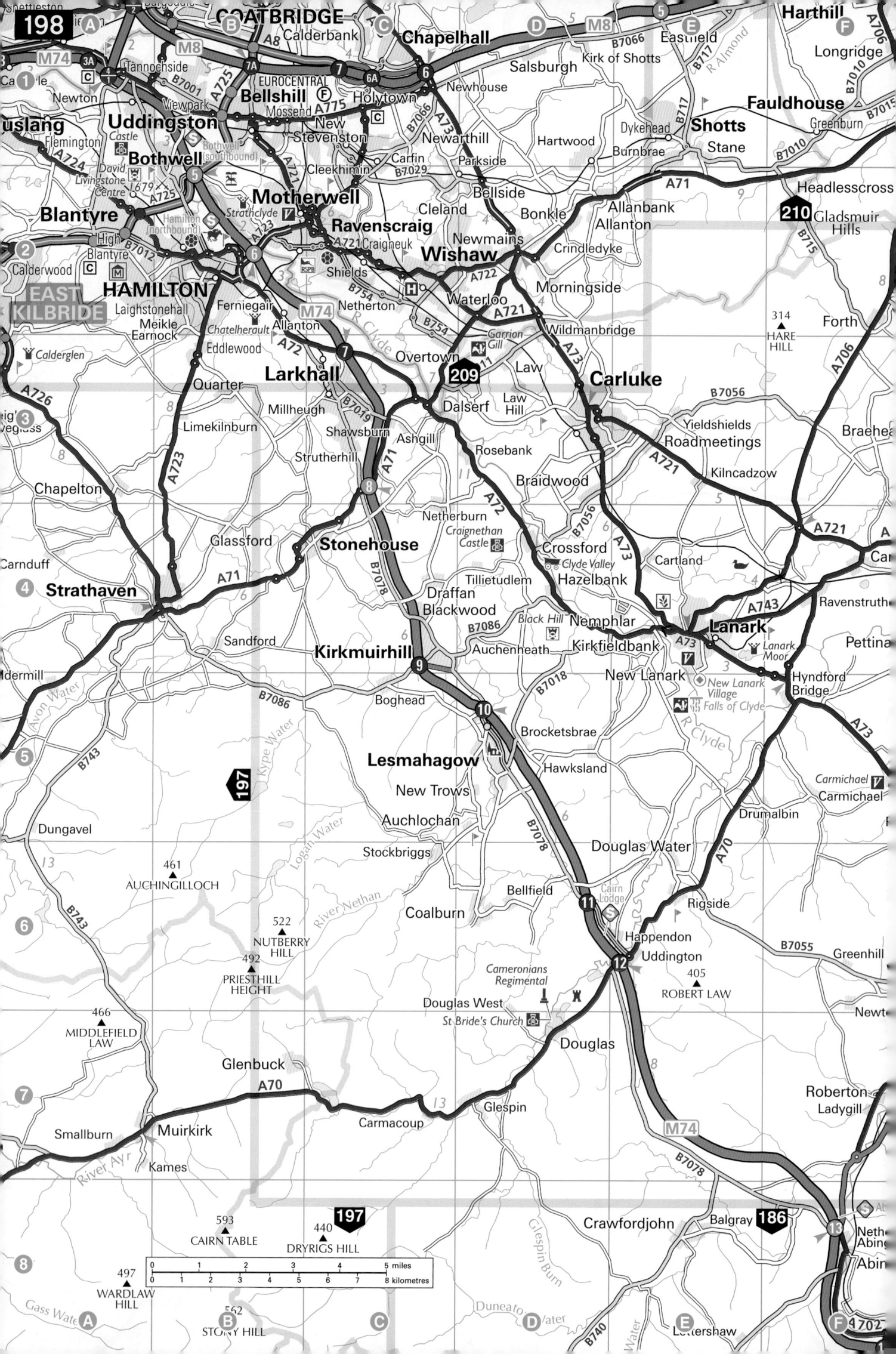

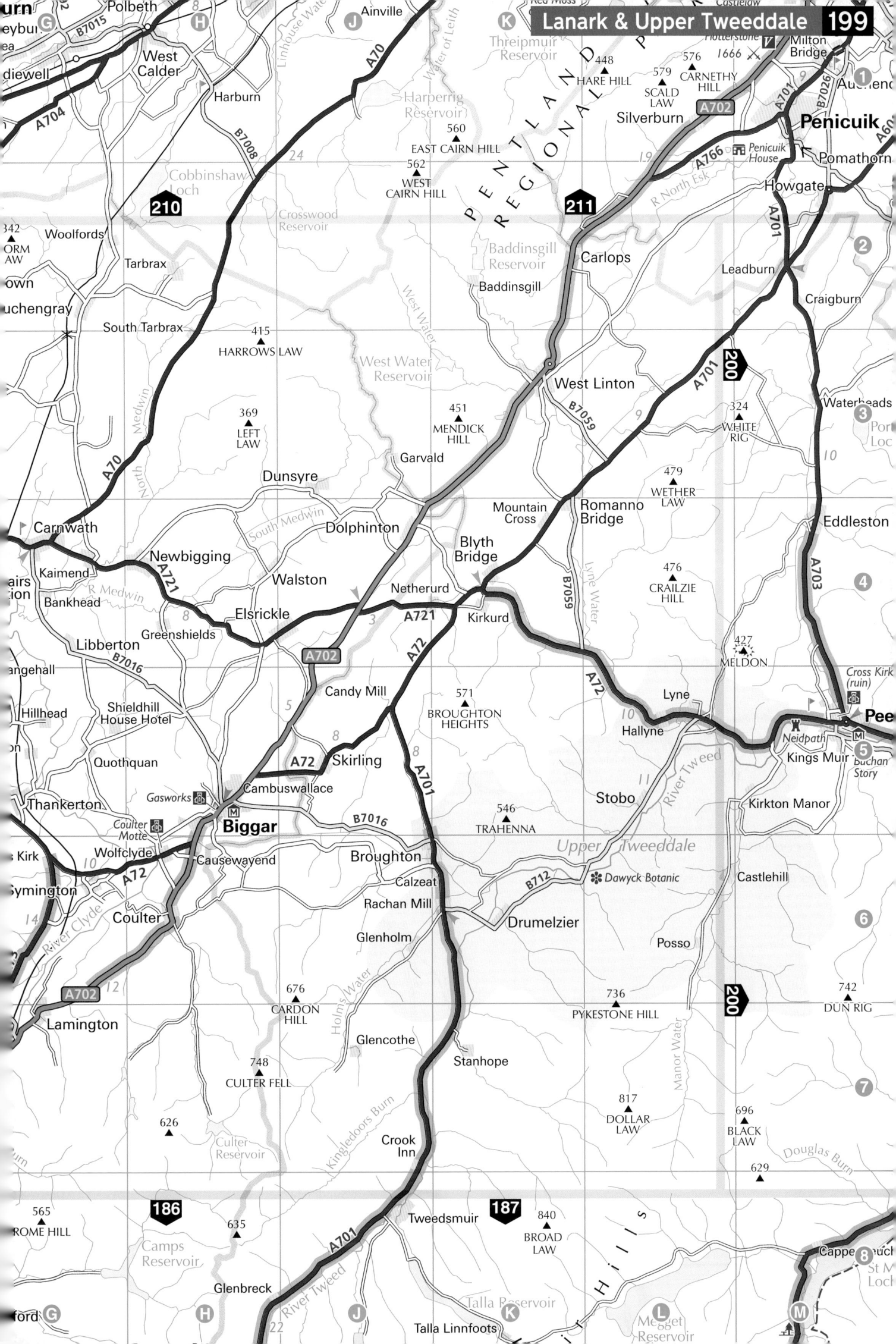

G B7015 Polbeth 8 H J Ainville K Red Moss Castlelaw Hottisfone V Milton Bridge

eyburn West Calder Harburn A70 Threipmuir Reservoir 448 HARE HILL 576 1666 579 CARNETHY HILL A702 9 A701 B7026 Auchend

diewell

A704 B7008 24 560 EAST CAIRN HILL SCALD LAW Silverburn A702 A766 1.9 A701 Penicuik House A60

210 Cobbinshaw Loch Harperrig Reservoir 562 WEST CAIRN HILL 211 Pomathorn Howgate A701

342 Woolfords Crosswood Reservoir PENTLAND Baddinsgill Reservoir Carlops Leadburn Craigburn 2

ORM AW Tarbrax REGIONAL Baddinsgill A701 200 A701 3

own South Tarbrax West Water Reservoir REGIONAL West Water Reservoir P 324 WHITE RIG Waterheads Port Loc

uchengray 415 HARROWS LAW West Linton B7059 9 10

A70 North Medwin 369 LEFT LAW 451 MENDICK HILL 479 WETHER LAW Eddleston A703

Carnwath South Medwin Dunsyre Garvald Mountain Cross Romanno Bridge 476 CRAILZIE HILL 4

Kaimend Newbigging Dolphinton Blyth Bridge B7059 427 MELDON Cross Kirk (ruin)

Bankhead A721 Walston Netherurd Kirkurd Lyne Water Pee

airs R Medwin 8 Elsrickle A721 A72 Lyne 5

Libberton Greenshields A702 3 A72 10 Hallyne Neidpath Buchan Story

B7016 Candy Mill 571 BROUGHTON HEIGHTS 10 Kings Muir 5

Hillhead Shieldhill House Hotel 5 A72 Skirling 8 A701 Stobo Kirkton Manor

Quothquan Cambuswallace 546 TRAHENNA River Tweed

Thankerton Gasworks Biggar B7016 Upper Tweeddale Castlehill

Coulter Motte Wolfclyde Causewayend Broughton B712 Dawyck Botanic 6

Kirk 10 A72 Calzeat Drumelzier Posso

ymington Coulter Rachan Mill Glenholm 736 PYKESTONE HILL 200 742 DUN RIG

14 River Clyde A702 12 676 CARDON HILL Glencothe Stanhope 817 DOLLAR LAW 696 BLACK LAW 7

Lamington 748 CULTER FELL 629

626 Culter Reservoir Crook Inn Douglas Burn 8

565 ROME HILL 186 635 187 840 BROAD LAW Cappe

ford Camps Reservoir A701 Tweedsmuir L Megget Reservoir M

G H Glenbreck 22 J River Tweed K Talla Linnfoots Talla Reservoir Hills

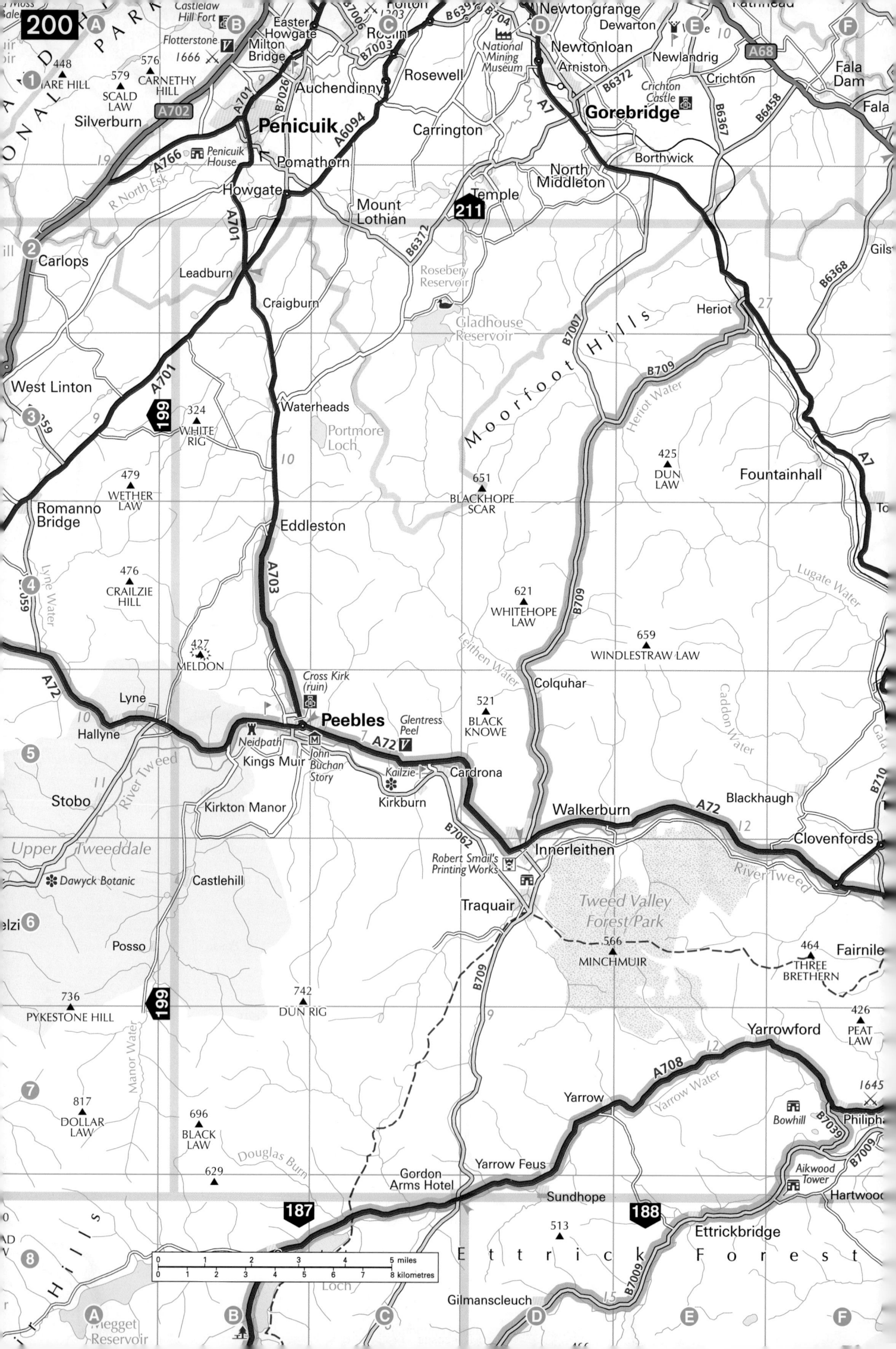

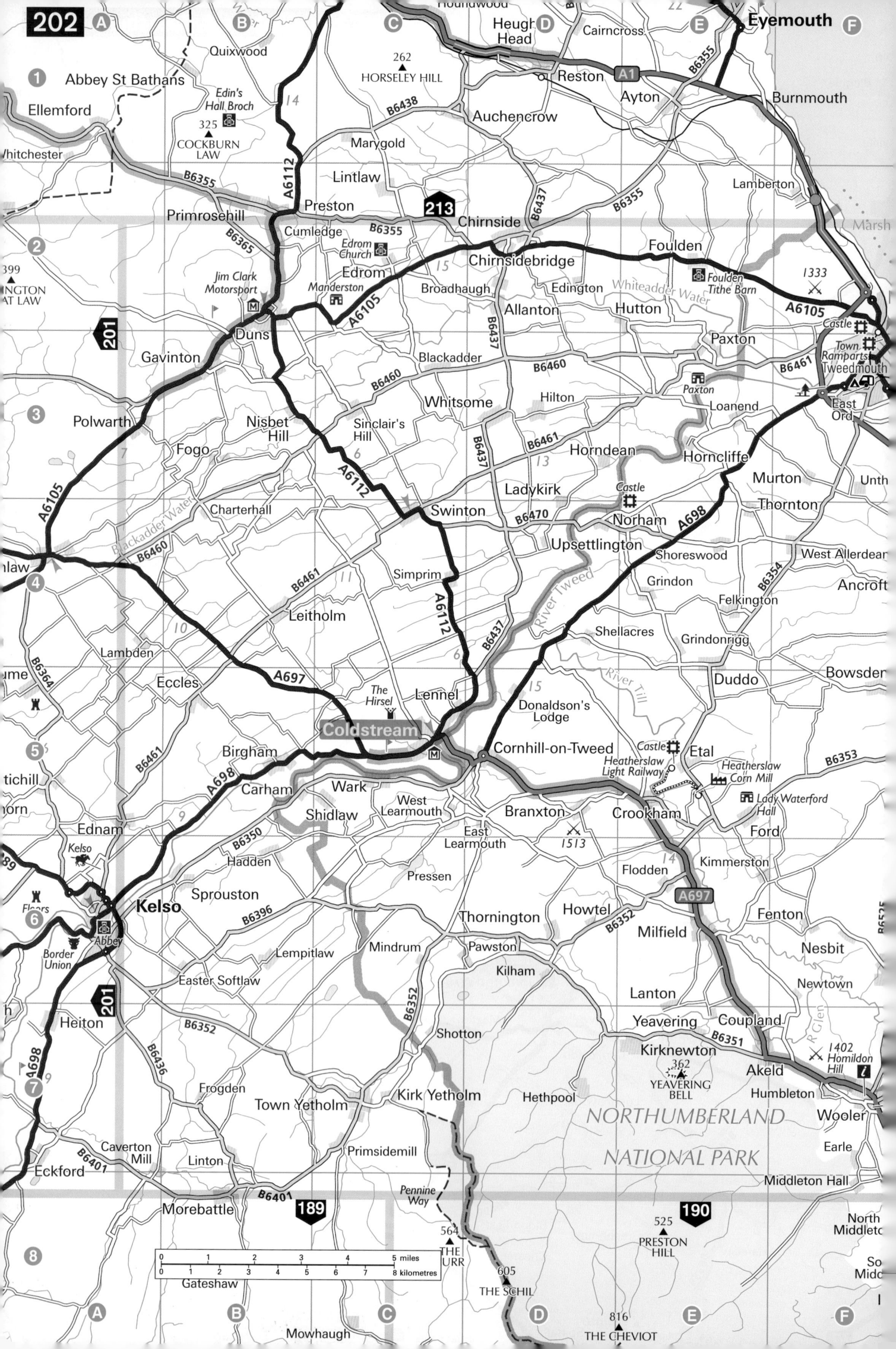

G   H   J

1

2

vs Bay

thumberland
ge Coast

ck-upon-Tweed
ℹ M
rd

3
uds
ead
erston

Cheswick

Causeway
flooded at
high tide

4
Goswick

Haggerston
Beal
HOLY ISLAND

Holy
Island
Fenham
Castle Point
Lindisfarne
Castle
Lindisfarne
Priory
Guile Point

West
Kyloe
Fenwick

5
Longstone
FARNE
ISLANDS

Buckton
North Northumberland
Heritage Coast

owick
Smeafield
Elwick
Ross
Staple
Sound
Inner
Sound

Holburn
Low
Middleton
Budle
Bay
Bamburgh

Detchant
St Cuthbert's
Cave
Middleton
Easington
Budle
B1342
Bamburgh

6
Hetton
Steads
Belford
Waren
Mill
Budle
Grace
Darling
New
Shoreston

North
Hazelrigg
Outchester
Spindlestone
Burton
B1340
Seahouses
ℹ

South
Hazelrigg
B6349
Bradford
B1341
North Sunderland

East
Horton
Bellshill
Lucker
Elford
Newham
Beadnell

7
Chatton
Warenton
B6348
Adderstone
Warenford
Swinhoe
B1340
Beadnell
Bay

A1
Chathill
Tughall

ead
Chillingham
Wild Cattle
Park
Ros Castle
Newstead
Ellingham
Preston
High Newton-by-the-Sea

ewtown
190
Hepburn
Preston
Tower
191
Brunton
Low Newton-by-the-Sea
Embleton &
Newton Links

8
267
CATERAN
HILL
Brownieside
North
Charlton
Doxford
Christon
Bank
Embleton
Embleton
Bay

Old Bewick
West
Ditchburn
South
Charlton
Fallodon
Dunstan
Steads
Dunstanburgh
Castle

G   H   B6346   Harehope   J   K   K347   Dunstan   L   ℹ   M

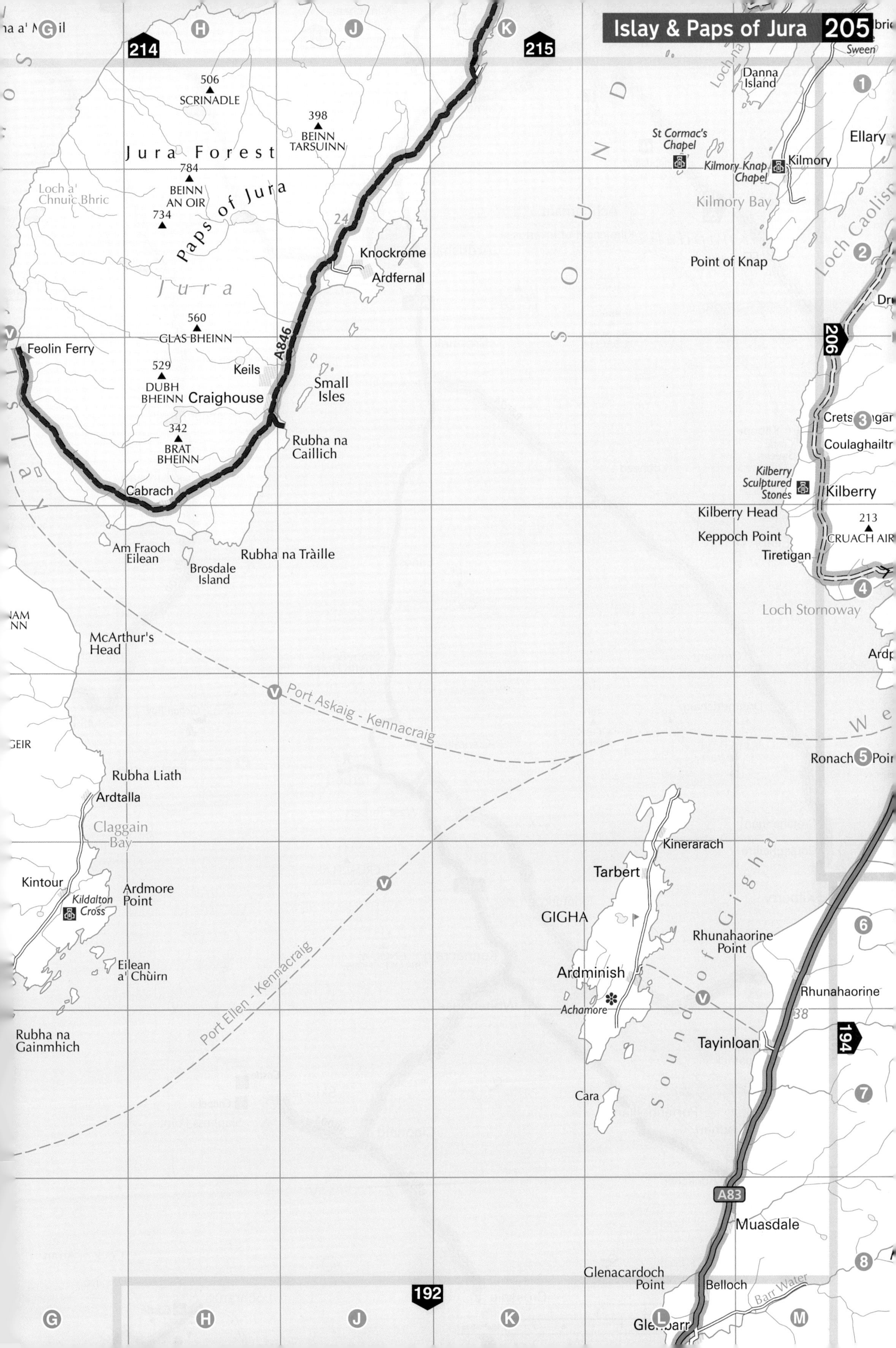

G H J K

214 215 206

Sween

Danna
Island

1

St Cormac's
Chapel

Ellary

Kilmory Knap
Chapel

Kilmory

506
SCRINADLE

Jura Forest

398
BEINN
TARSUINN

Kilmory Bay

Loch a'
Chnuic Bhric

784
BEINN
AN OIR

Point of Knap 2

Paps of Jura

734

Knockrome

Jura

Ardfernal

Crets gar 3

Coulaghailtr

560
GLAS BHEINN

Feolin Ferry

529
DUBH
BHEINN

Keils

A846

Small
Isles

Kilberry
Sculptured
Stones

Kilberry

Dr

Kilberry Head

342
BRAT
BHEINN

Craighouse

Rubha na
Caillich

Keppoch Point

213
CRUACH AIR

Cabrach

Tiretigan

4

Am Fraoch
Eilean

Rubha na Tràille

Brosdale
Island

Loch Stornoway

Ardp

McArthur's
Head

NAM
NN

Port Askaig - Kennacraig

Ronach 5 Poin

GEIR

Rubha Liath

Ardtalla

Claggain
Bay

Kinerarach

Kintour

Ardmore
Point

Tarbert

Kildalton
Cross

GIGHA

Rhunahaorine
Point

Eilean
a' Chùirn

6

Ardminish

Rhunahaorine

Rubha na
Gainmhich

Port Ellen - Kennacraig

Achamore

Tayinloan

194

Cara

7

A83

Muasdale

Glenacardoch
Point

Belloch

8

Gle arr

G H J K L M

192

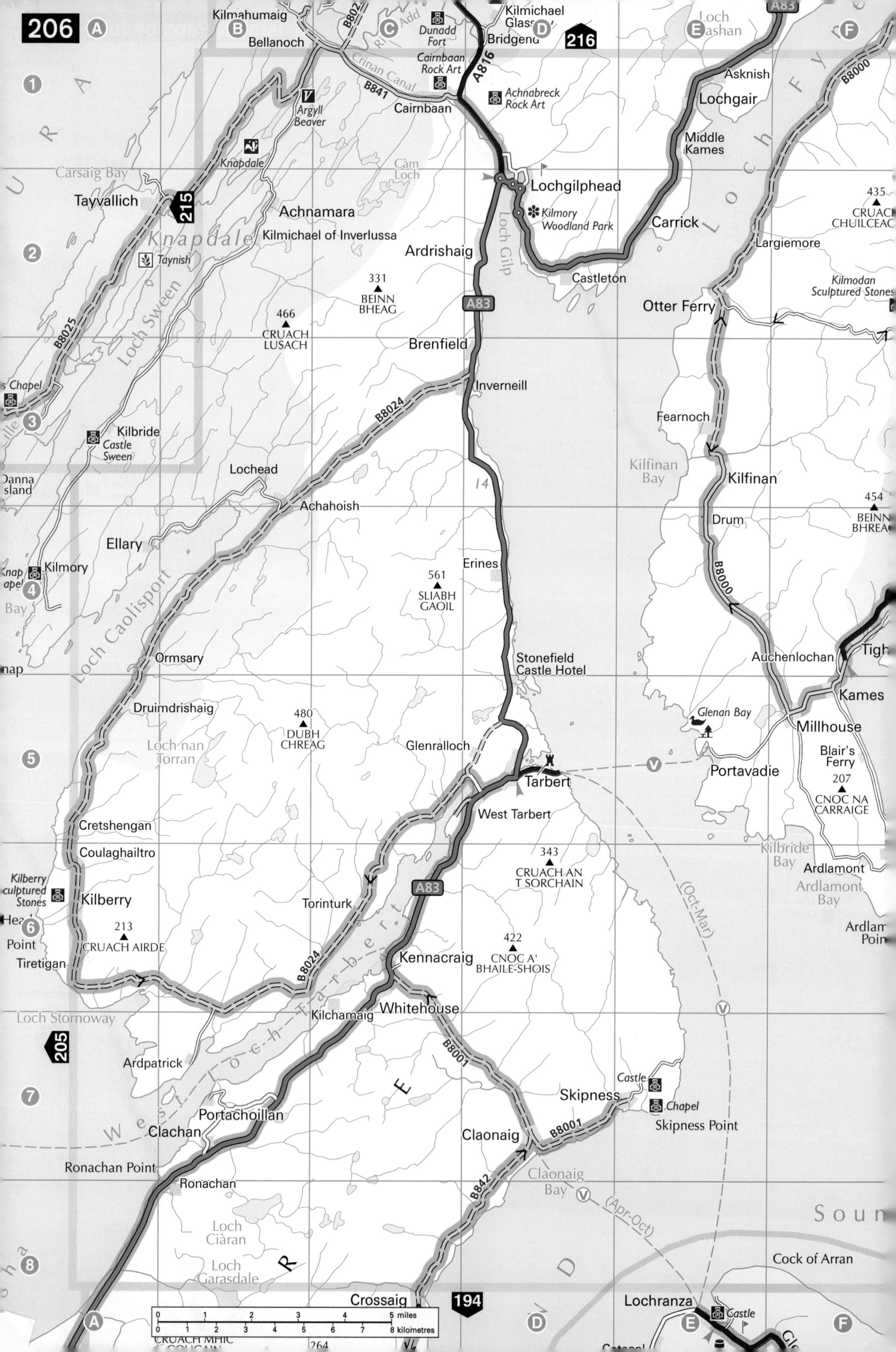

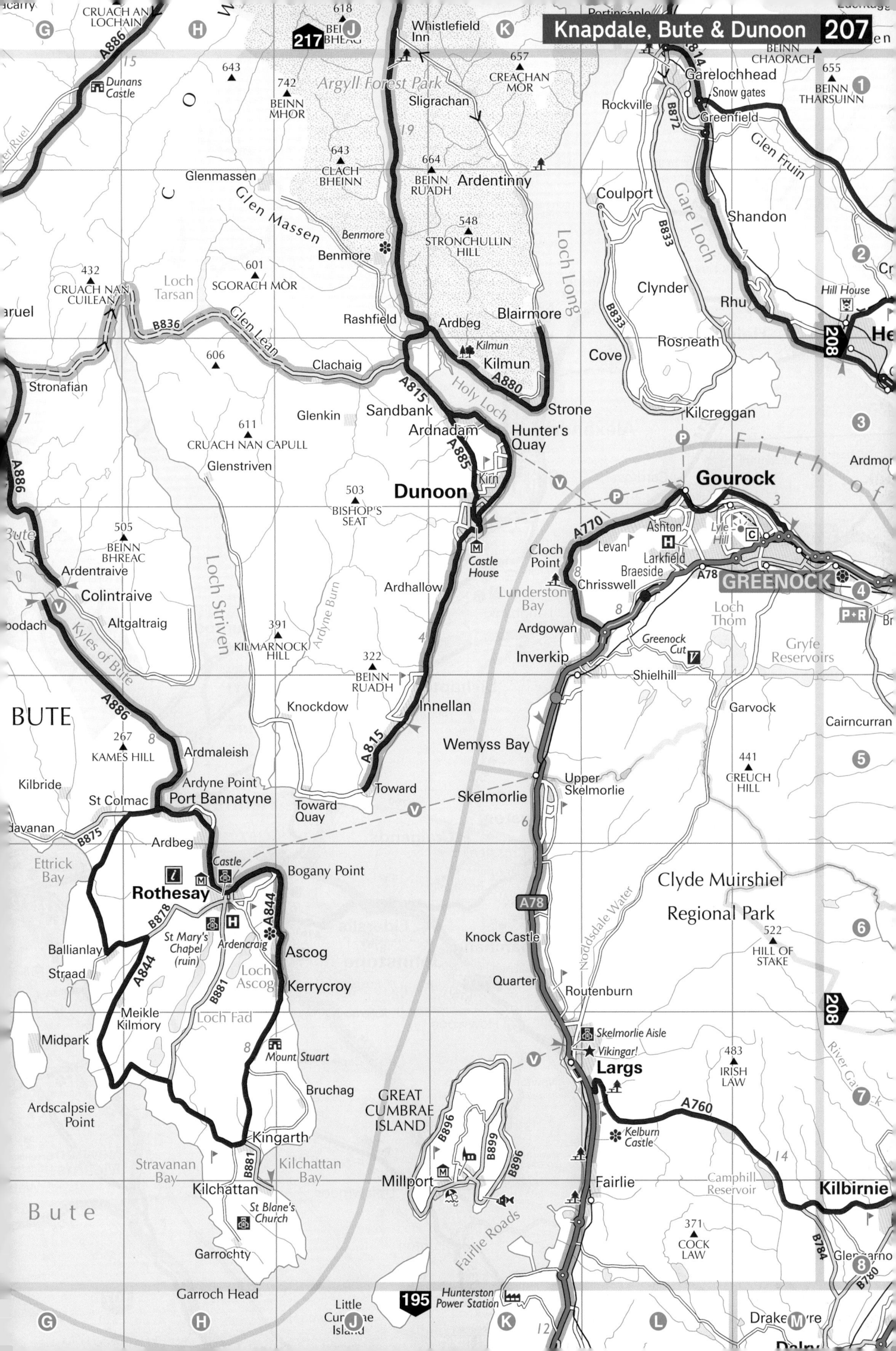

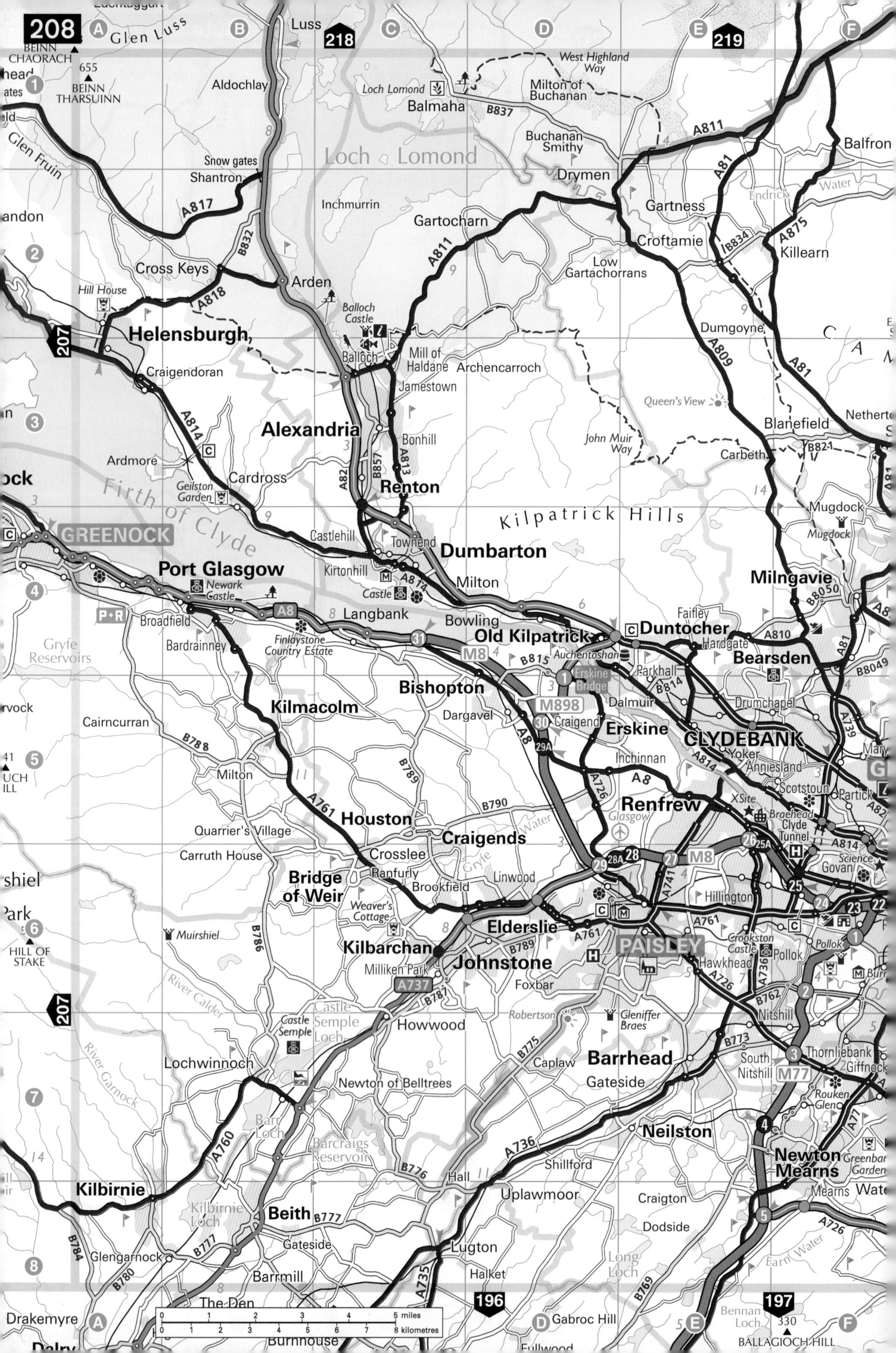

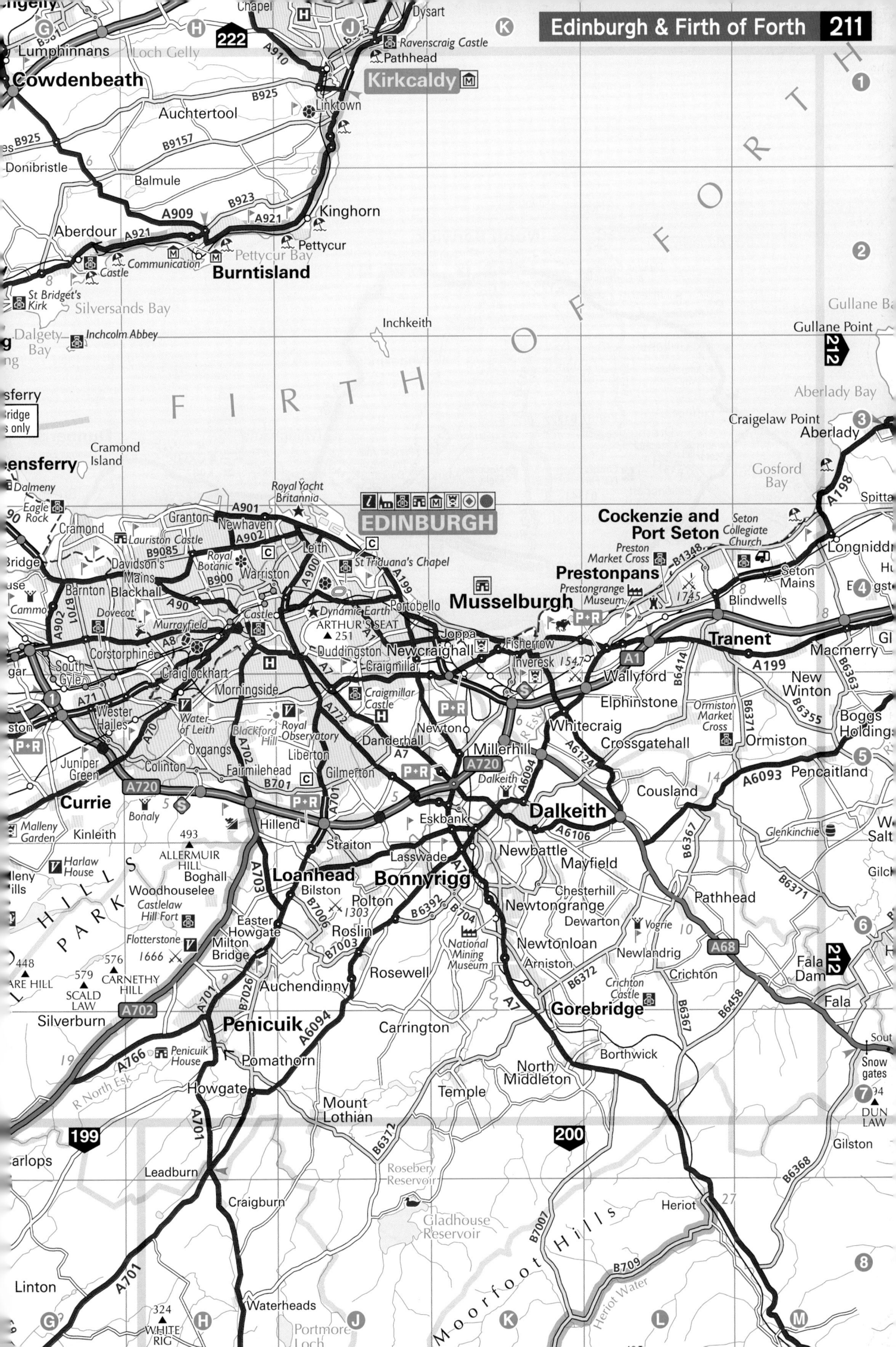

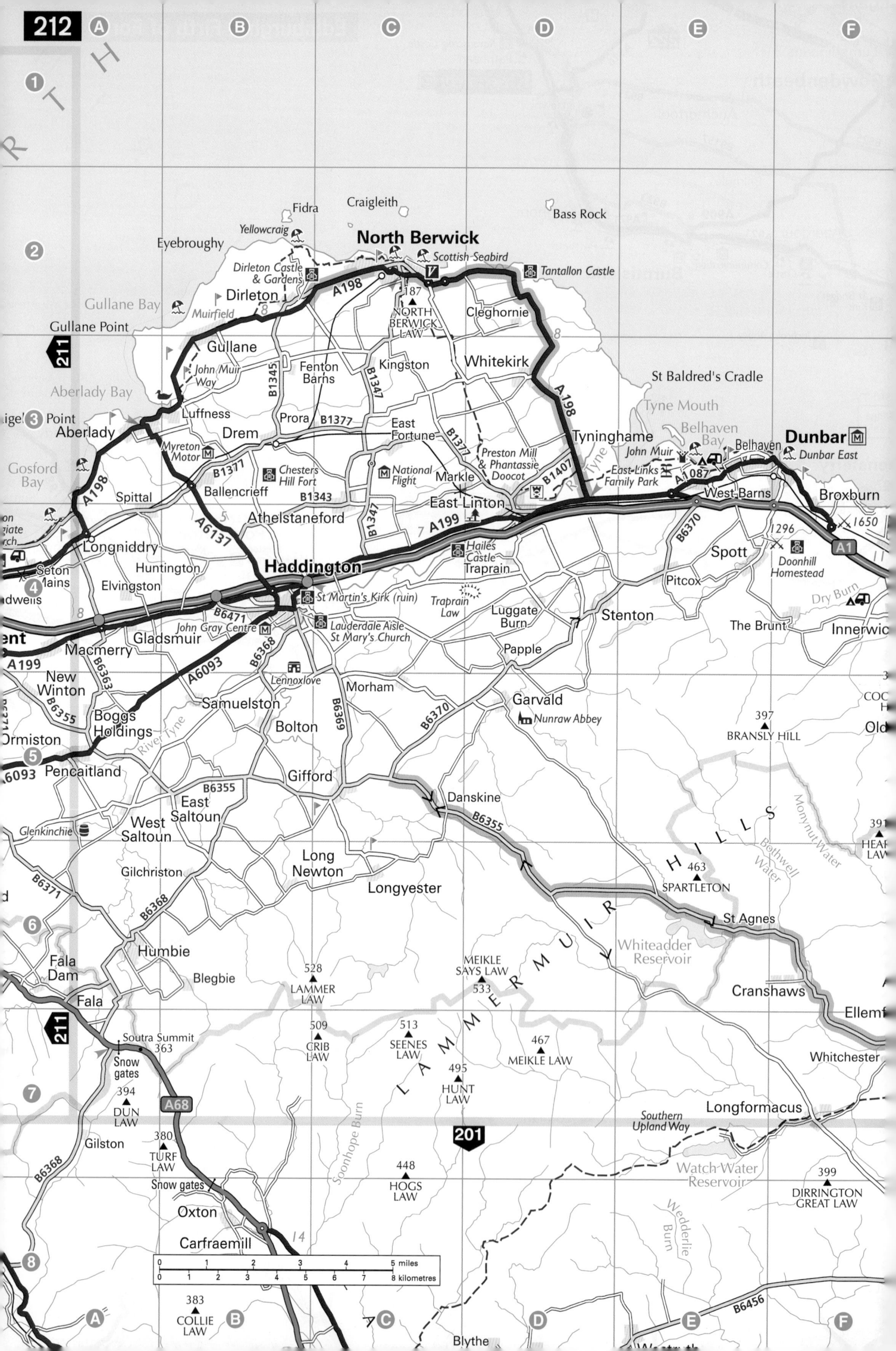

G H J

①
②
③
④
⑤
⑥
⑦
⑧

Chapel Point

Torness
Power Station
Thorntonloch

whill

Dunglass
Collegiate
Church

Reed
Point
Cove Pease
Bay Siccar
Point

Fast Castle Head

ST ABB'S HEAD

Cockburnspath

A1107

Pease Dean

196
▲
BROWN
RIG

Coldingham
Loch

Ecclaw

St Abbs

Coldingham
Bay

Grantshouse

Southern
Upland Way

Coldingham

A1107

22

Butterdean

Eye Water

21

Houndwood

B6438

Eyemouth

Heugh
Head

Cairncross

Quixwood

262
▲
HORSELEY HILL

B6355

athans

Edin's
Hall Broch

14

B6438

Reston

A1

Ayton

Burnmouth

325
▲
COCKBURN
LAW

Auchencrow

A6112

Marygold

Lintlaw

B6437

B6355

Lamberton

B6355

Preston

B6355

Chirnside

Marshall Meadows Bay

Primrosehill

B6365

Cumledge

B6355

Edrom
Church

15

Chirnsidebridge

202

Foulden

1333

North Northumberland
Heritage Coast

Jim Clark
Motorsport

Edrom

Manderston

Broadhaugh

Edington

Whiteadder Water

Hutton

Foulden
Tithe Barn

A6105

Berwick-upon

Castle

Barracks &
Main Guard

Duns

A6105

Allanton

B6437

Paxton

Town
Ramparts

Gavinton

Blackadder

B6460

Hilton

Loanend

Tweedmouth

Spittal

Huds
Head

Nisbet
Hill

Sinclair's
Hill

Whitsome

B6461

Paxton

East
Ord

A1167

Scremerston

G H J K L M

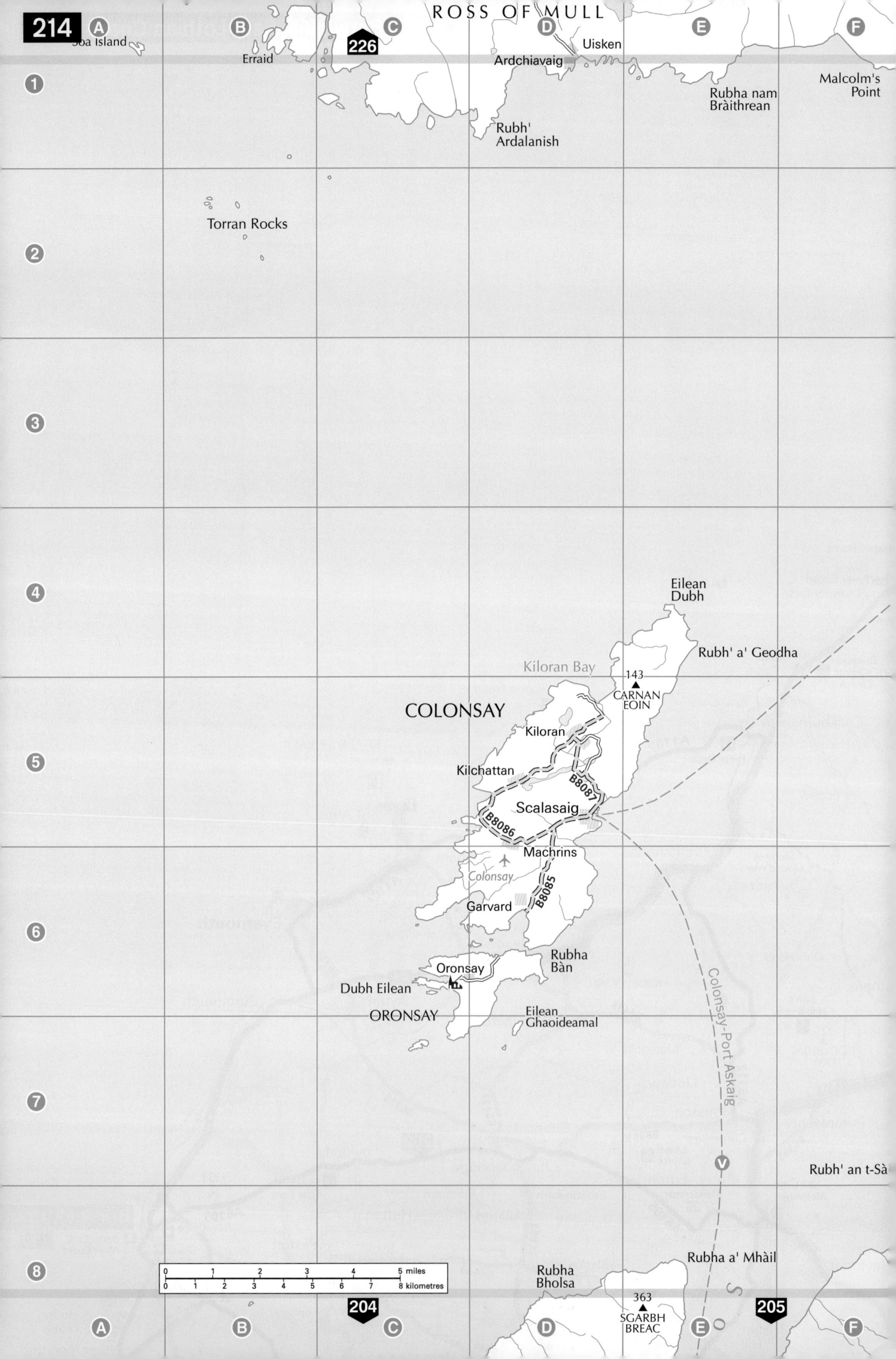

A B C D E F

1

Sòa Island
Erraid
226
Uisken
Ardchiavaig
Rubha nam
Bràithrean
Malcolm's
Point

Rubh'
Ardalanish

2

Torran Rocks

3

4

Eilean
Dubh

Kiloran Bay
Rubh' a' Geodha

143
CARNAN
EOIN

COLONSAY

Kiloran

5

Kilchattan
B8087

Scalasaig

B8086

Machrins
Colonsay

B8085

Garvard

6

Rubha
Bàn

Oronsay

Dubh Eilean

ORONSAY
Eilean
Ghaoideamal

Colonsay-Port Askaig

7

V
Rubh' an t-Sà

Rubha a' Mhàil

8

0   1   2   3   4   5 miles
0 1 2 3 4 5 6 7 8 kilometres

204

Rubha
Bholsa

363
SGARBH
BREAC

205

A B C D E F

G H J K

227

1

Insh
Island
Ellenabeich
Easdale
P
Folk
B844
B8003
Clachan
Clachan-Seil
SEIL
Balvicar
Ardmaddy

V

Colonsay - Oban

F I R T H

Cuan
Cullipool
Torsa
Degnish
LUING
Seil Sound
Loch Melfort
A81
2

Garbh Eileach

Eilean
Dubh Mòr
Arduaine
Garden
Arduaine

GARVELLACHS
Monastery &
Beehive Cells
Eileach
an Naoimh

LUNGA
Scarba, Lunga
and the
Garvellachs
SCARBA
448
CRUACH SCARBA

Sound of Luing
Shuna Sound
216
SHUNA
Shuna
Point
Craobh
Haven
3
Craigdhu
Ardfern
Kintr
En Mhic
B8002
En Righ
4
Carr
Aird

Gulf of Corryvreckan

Craignish Point
Island
Macaskin
Slockavullin
Temple Wood
Stone Circles
Ri Cruin Cai
Poltalloch
5

Glengarrisdale
Bay
295
CRUACH NA
SEILCHEIG

Glendebadel Bay

364
BEN
GARRISDALE

Lussa River
Lealt Burn
Loch Craignish

Loch Crinan
Crinan
Kilmahumaig
B8025
Crinan C
B841
Argyll
Beaver
6
Bellanoch
Knapdale

Corpach Bay

466
BEINN
BHREAC
Glen Grundale

J U R A

Carsaig Bay
Tayvallich
Achnamara
Kilmichael of Inverlussa

ian
Bay
453
RAINBERG MÒR

Ardlussa
Lussa Point
Lussagiven
A846

Knapdale
B8025
Taynish
206
7 31
BEINN
BHEAC
466
CRUACH
LUSACH

Loch Sween

och
n Mòr

F I R T H

Keills Chapel

Kilbride
Castle
Sween
Lochead

rbert

205

B80

8

G 398 H J K L M chahoish

Loch na Cille
Danna
Island

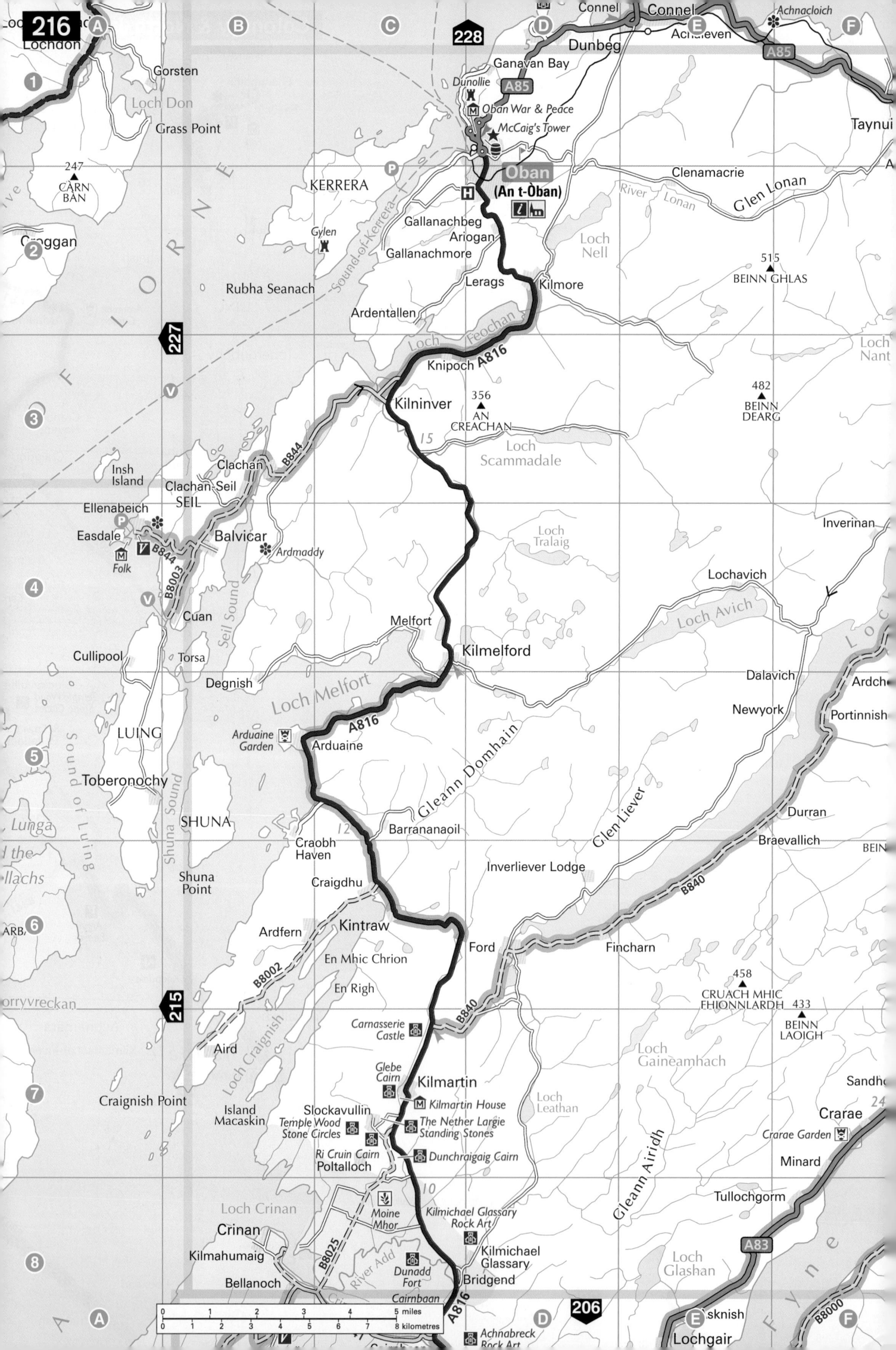

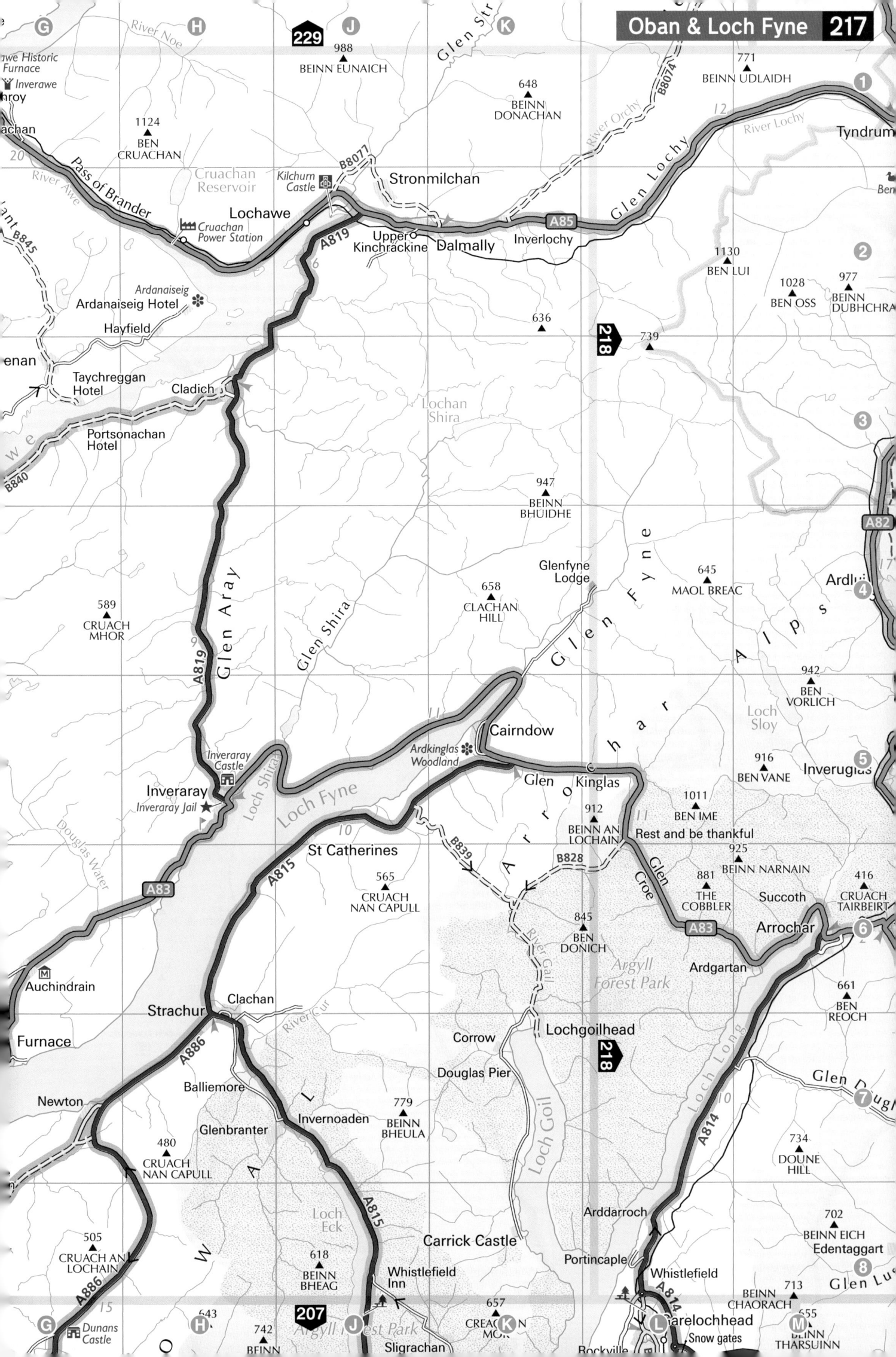

G H **229** J K

988
▲ BEINN EUNAICH

1

771
▲ BEINN UDLAIDH

648
▲ BEINN DONACHAN

River Noe

Glen Str

Glen Orchy

B8074

River Lochy

12

Tyndrum

1124
▲ BEN CRUACHAN

Pass of Brander

River Awe

B845

Cruachan Reservoir

Kilchurn Castle

B8077

Lochawe

Cruachan Power Station

Upper Kinchrackine

A819

Stronmilchan

A85

Inverlochy

Dalmally

Glen Lochy

1130
▲ BEN LUI

A82

2

1028
▲ BEN OSS

977
▲ BEINN DUBHCHRA

Ardanaiseig Hotel

Hayfield

Taychreggan Hotel

Cladich

Portsonachan Hotel

B840

6

636
▲

218 ▶

739
▲

3

Lochan Shira

947
▲ BEINN BHUIDHE

589
▲ CRUACH MHOR

Glen Aray

A819

9

Glen Shira

658
▲ CLACHAN HILL

Glenfyne Lodge

Glen Fyne

645
▲ MAOL BREAC

Ardlui

4

A82

Inveraray Castle

Inveraray

Inveraray Jail ★

Loch Shira

11

Ardkinglas Woodland

Cairndow

Glen Kinglas

942
▲ BEN VORLICH

Loch Sloy

916
▲ BEN VANE

Inveruglas

5

Douglas Water

Loch Fyne

10

A815

St Catherines

565
▲ CRUACH NAN CAPULL

B839

B828

912
▲ BEINN AN LOCHAIN

Glen Kinglas

Rest and be thankful

1011
▲ BEN IME

Arrochar Alps

925
▲ BEINN NARNAIN

881
▲ THE COBBLER

416
▲ CRUACH TAIRBEIRT

Succoth

6

A83

Auchindrain

Furnace

A83

Clachan

Strachur

A886

River Cur

Newton

Balliemore

Glenbranter

Invernoaden

480
▲ CRUACH NAN CAPULL

A

W

L

779
▲ BEINN BHEULA

River Gail

845
▲ BEN DONICH

Argyll Forest Park

Loch Goil

Corrow

Douglas Pier

218 ▶

Ardgartan

A814

Loch Long

10

Arddarroch

Portincaple

Glen Dougl

Glen Lu

7

702
▲ BEINN EICH

Edentaggart

734
▲ DOUNE HILL

661
▲ BEN REOCH

Arrochar

505
▲ CRUACH AN LOCHAIN

A886

15

Dunans Castle

643
▲

G H **207** J

742
▲ BEINN

BEINN BHEAG
618
▲

Loch Eck

A815

Carrick Castle

Whistlefield Inn

657
▲ CREAC

K

N MOR

Sligrachan

Whistlefield

A814

Garelochhead

Snow gates

L

Rockville

713
▲ BEINN CHAORACH

555
▲ BEINN THARSUINN

M

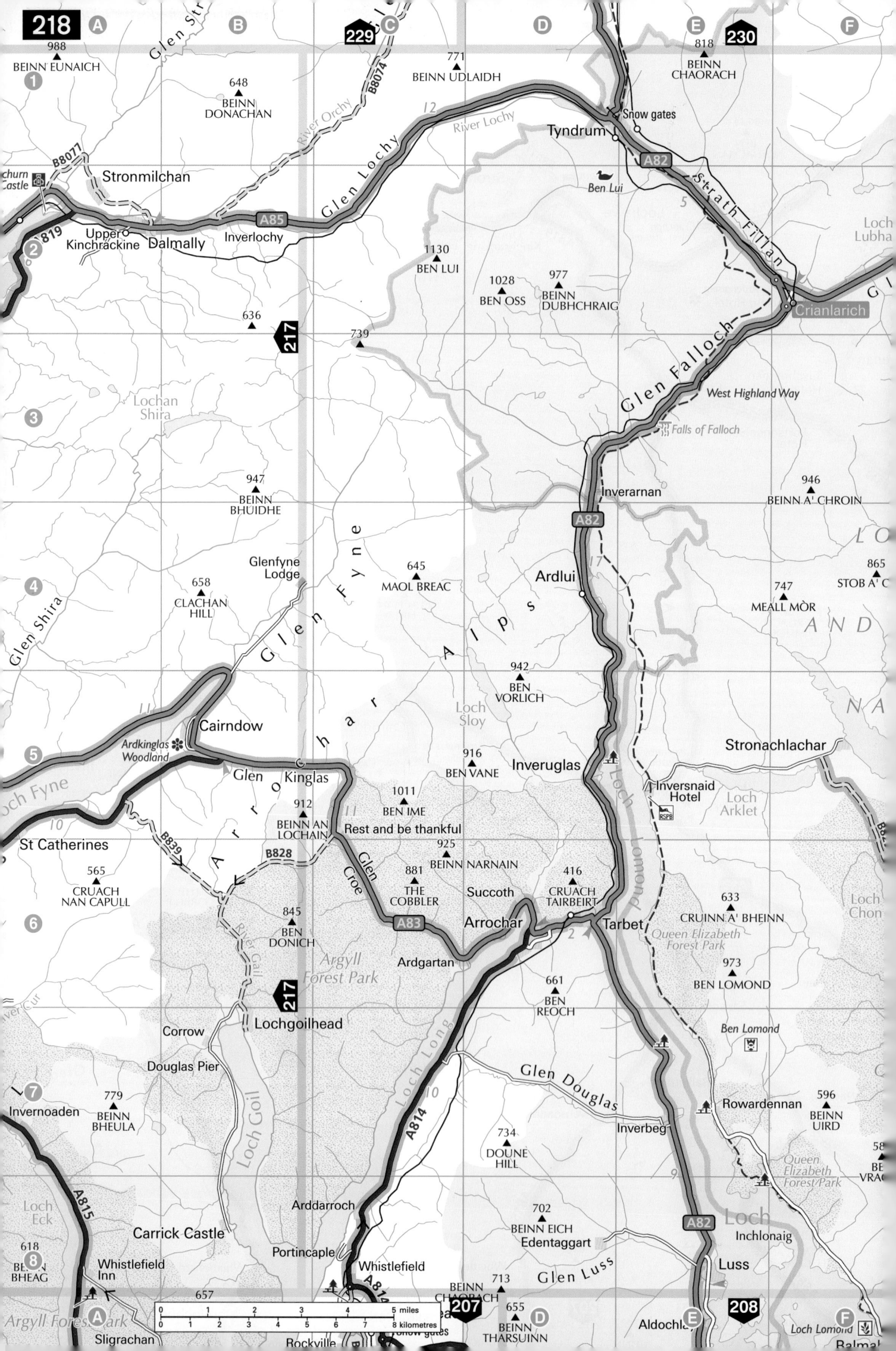

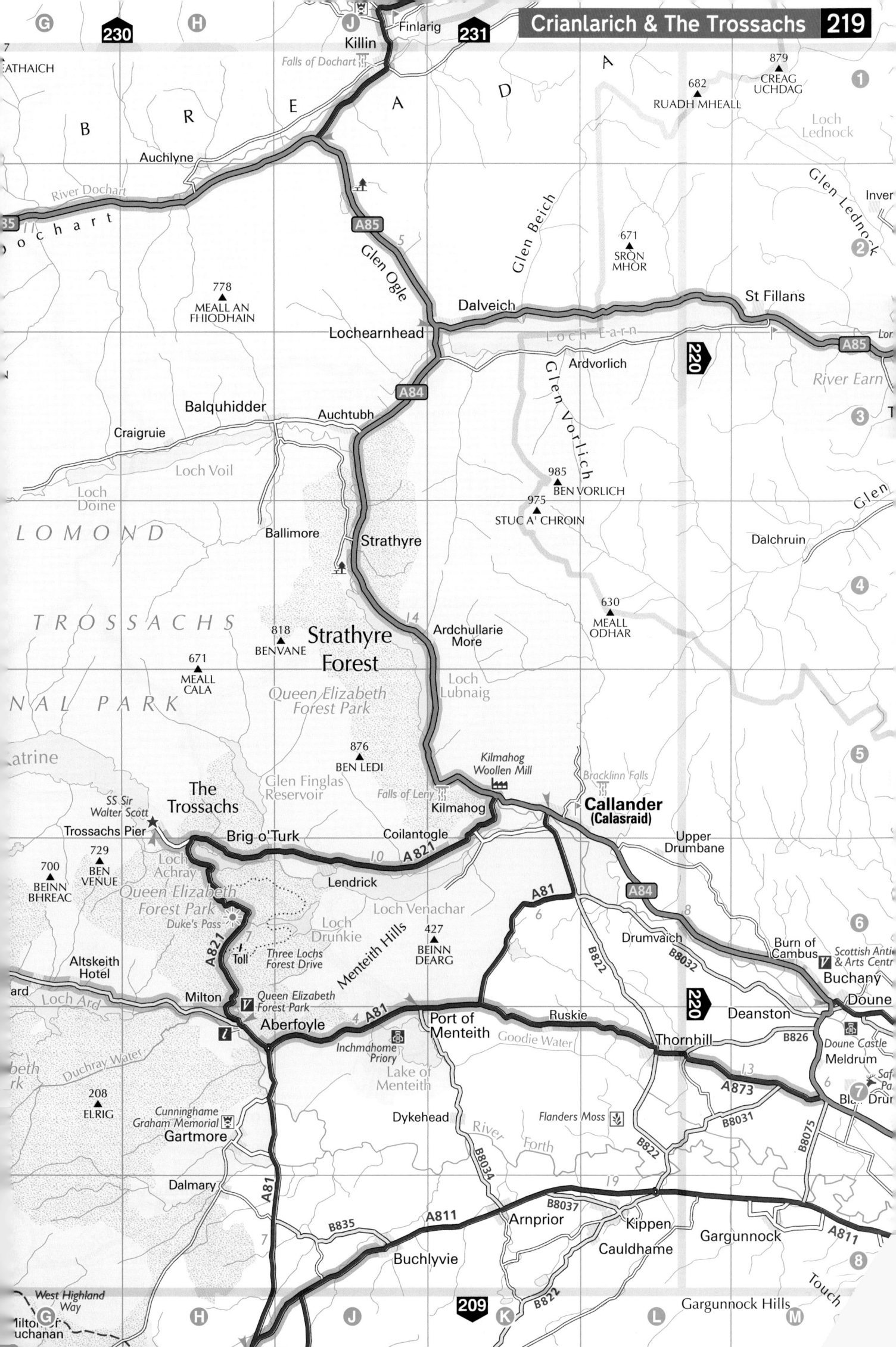

G 230 H J Finlarig 231
Killin
Falls of Dochart

EATHAICH

879
CREAG
UCHDAG
682
RUADH MHEALL
Loch
Lednock

B R E A D A D
Auchlyne

River Dochart

671
SRON
MHOR

Glen Beich

Inver
Glen Lednock

35
Dochart

778
MEALL AN
FHIODHAIN

A85
Glen Ogle

5

Dalveich
Lochearnhead

St Fillans

A85
Lor

220

River Earn

Balquhidder
Craigruie
Auchtubh
A84

Ardvorlich

Glen Vorlich

3

L O M O N D
Loch Voil
Loch
Doine

Ballimore
Strathyre

985
BEN VORLICH
975
STUC A' CHROIN

Dalchruin

Glen

T R O S S A C H S
818
BENVANE
14
Ardchullarie
More

630
MEALL
ODHAR

4

671
MEALL
CALA

*Strathyre
Forest*

*Queen Elizabeth
Forest Park*

Loch
Lubnaig

N A L   P A R K

atrine

876
BEN LEDI

*Glen Finglas
Reservoir*

Kilmahog
Woollen Mill

Bracklinn Falls

5

SS Sir
Walter Scott
The
Trossachs
Trossachs Pier

Falls of Leny
Kilmahog

Callander
(Calasraid)

Brig o'Turk
Coilantogle

Upper
Drumbane

700
BEINN
BHREAC
729
BEN
VENUE

*Loch
Achray*

Lendrick
10
A821

A81

A84

8

*Queen Elizabeth
Forest Park*
Duke's Pass

*Loch
Drunkie*
Menteith Hills

427
BEINN
DEARG

Loch Venachar

6

Drumvaich

Burn of
Cambus

Scottish Anti
& Arts Centr

6

Buchany

Altskeith
Hotel

A821
Toll

Three Lochs
Forest Drive

B822

B8032

Deanston

Doune

Milton
Loch Ard
ard

208
ELRIG

Aberfoyle

*Queen Elizabeth
Forest Park*

4 A81

Port of
Menteith

Duchray Water

*Inchmahome
Priory*

Ruskie

Goodie Water

Thornhill

220

B826

Doune Castle
Meldrum

Safa
Pa

beth
rk

Cunninghame
Graham Memorial

Gartmore

*Lake of
Menteith*

Dykehead

*River
Forth*

Flanders Moss

13

A873

6

Bla Drun

7

Dalmary

A81

B835

A811
Buchlyvie

B8034

B8037

Arnprior

Kippen
Cauldhame

B822

Gargunnock

B8031

B8075

A811

G
*West Highland
Way*
iltor f
uchanan

H

J

209

K

B822

Gargunnock Hills

L

M

8

Touch

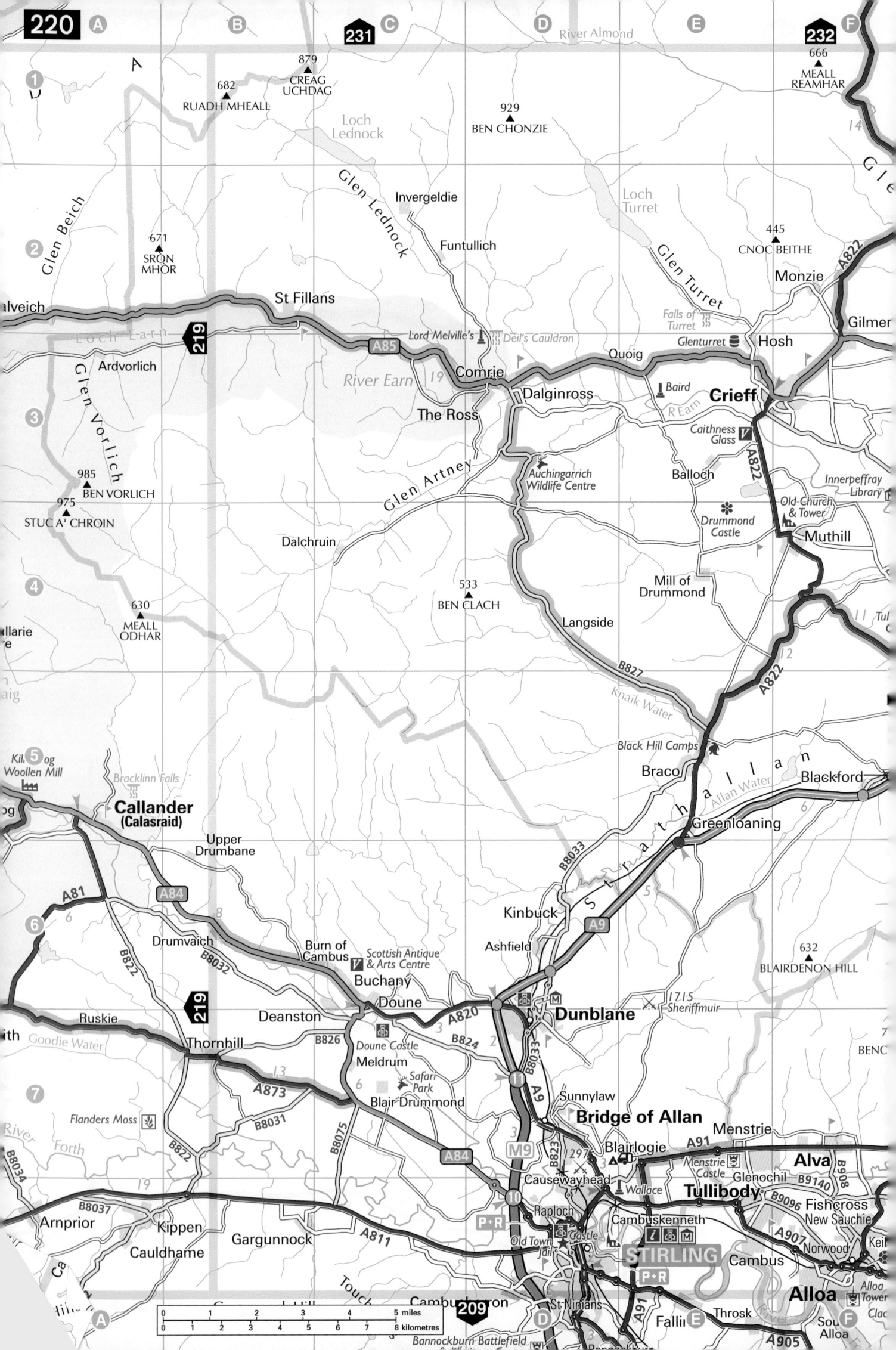

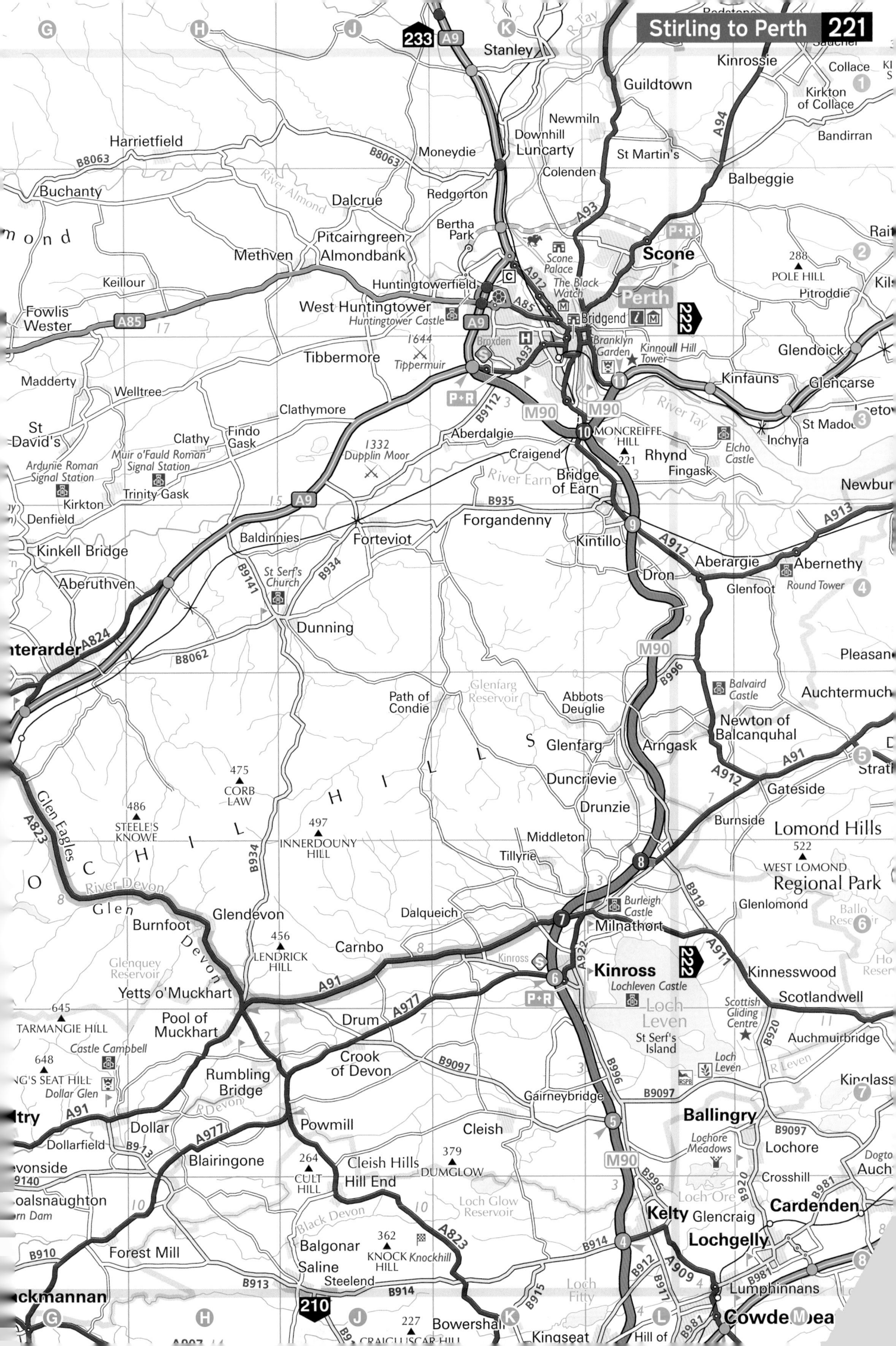

A B C D E F

1
2
3

Gris
Clabhach

Hogh Bay   Bally

Totrona

4 Bàgh a' Chaisteil
(Castlebay)
Ⓥ   Feall   Coll
                                        Bay   Ac
                    (Apr-Oct, Weds only)   Arileod
                                                    Uig
                                        RSPB
                    Calgary Point   Crossapol   Rubl
                                         Bay   Fàsac
                                                   Loch Breachacha
5   Gunna

                                   Caoles   Rubha Dubh
Rubha Port   Balephetrish   B8069
Bhiosd   Clachan   Bay   Ruaig
          Mor   Balephetrish
          Loch   B8068
Hough   Bhasapoll   Gott
Bay   Bay
     Ballevullin   Cornoigmore   Kenovay
6 Kilkenneth   B8068   Tiree
        Moss   Scarinish
Middleton   Heylipoll   B8065
                    Crossapol   TIREE
Barrapoll   B8065
                    Hynish Bay
          B8067   Balemartine
Loch a'
Phuill   Mannal
7 Rinn   Ⓥ
Thorbhais Balephuill   Hynish
          Bay

8
   0   1   2   3   4   5 miles
   0 1 2 3 4 5 6 7 8 kilometres

A B C D E F

G   H   J   K   L

1

Sanna Point

Sanna
Sanna Bay

Ardnamurchan Point

Portuairk   Achnaha

Achosnich   2

MEALL   4

236   B8007

Eilean Mòr   342
▲
BEINN
NA SEILG
Ormsaigmore   Kilcl

Rubha Mòr

Rubha Sgor-innis   Bàgh a' Chaisteil
(Castlebay)
Loch Baghasdail
(Lochboisdale)
(Oct-Mar)   3

Bousd   Sorisdale

B8072   236

Cliad Bay   Ardmore Point

B8071   Sorne Point

Coll - Oban   V   Quinish Point   Glengorm Castle   Rub nan

st   V

rinagour   Tober ory   4

COLL   Mul

292
▲
'S AIRDE BEINN

B8070   Caliach Point   5

Eilean Ornsay   SPEINNE   444

Dervaig   Achnadrish   Loch Frisa

5   B8073   6

Calgary
Art in
Nature   Old Byre   V

Calgary Bay

Treshnish Point   Ensay   342
▲
CÀRN MÒR

Rubh' a' Chaoil   Burg

Fanmore   390
▲
CNOC AN
DÀ CHINN

Ballygown   6

Fladda   Loch   BE NAN

226   Eas Fors   19

Lunga   Tuath

Gometra   P   Oskamull   3

TRESHNISH
ISLES   ULVA   7

Eorsa

Bac Mòr or Dutchman's Cap

Bac Beag   Little Colonsay   Loch n

Staffa   Inch Kenneth
Inchkenneth Chapel
(ruin)   B8035   17

Fingal's   Loch na Keal
Isle of Mull   Balnahard   8

G   H   J   K   L   M
226

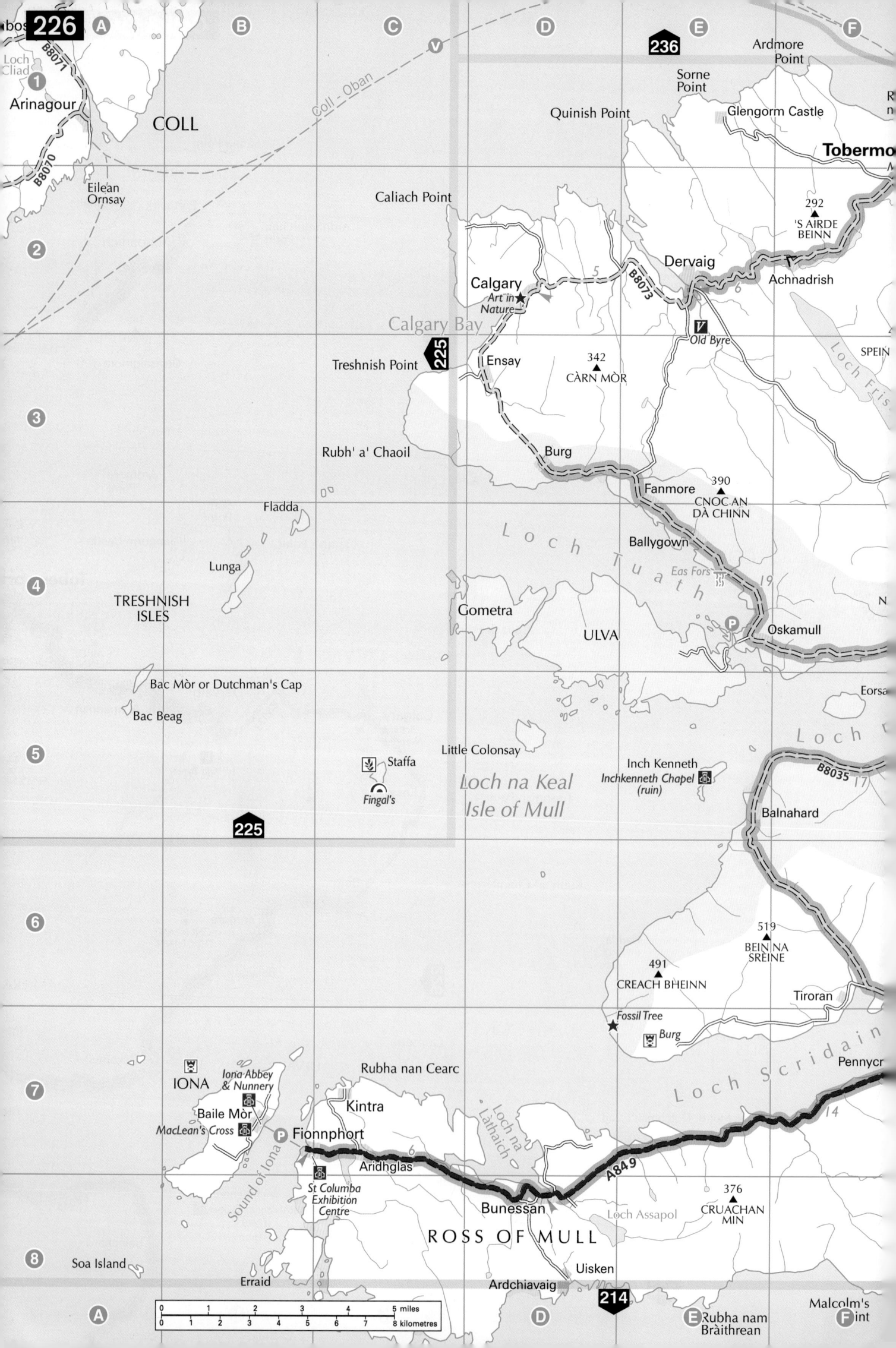

A   B   C   D   **236** E   F

1

bos

Loch
Cliad

Arinagour

COLL

Coll - Oban

Eilean
Ornsay

2

Caliach Point

Quinish Point

Ardmore
Point

Sorne
Point

Glengorm Castle

Tobermo

292 ▲
'S AIRDE
BEINN

Calgary
Art in
Nature ★

Dervaig

Achnadrish

Calgary Bay

B8073

Old Byre ⓥ

SPEIN

225

Treshnish Point

Ensay

342 ▲
CÀRN MÒR

Loch Fris

3

Rubh' a' Chaoil

Burg

Fanmore

390 ▲
CNOC AN
DÀ CHINN

Fladda

Ballygown

Loch Tuath

Eas Fors ♨

4

Lunga

TRESHNISH
ISLES

Gometra

ULVA

19

P

Oskamull

N

Eorsa

Bac Mòr or Dutchman's Cap

Bac Beag

Little Colonsay

Inch Kenneth
Inchkenneth Chapel 🏛
(ruin)

Loch

5

☘ Staffa

Loch na Keal

B8035   17

Fingal's

Isle of Mull

Balnahard

6

519 ▲
BEINN NA
SRÈINE

491 ▲
CREACH BHEINN

Tiroran

Fossil Tree
★

🏛 Burg

Loch Scridain

Pennycr

Rubha nan Cearc

7

🏛
IONA

Iona Abbey
& Nunnery 🏛

Baile Mòr

MacLean's Cross 🏛

P Fionnphort

Kintra

Aridhglas

Loch na Lathaich

A849

14

St Columba
Exhibition
Centre 🏛

Bunessan

Loch Assapol

376 ▲
CRUACHAN
MIN

8

Soa Island

ROSS OF MULL

Erraid

Ardchiavaig

Uisken

214

Malcolm's
int

A   B   D   Rubha nam E   Braithrean   F

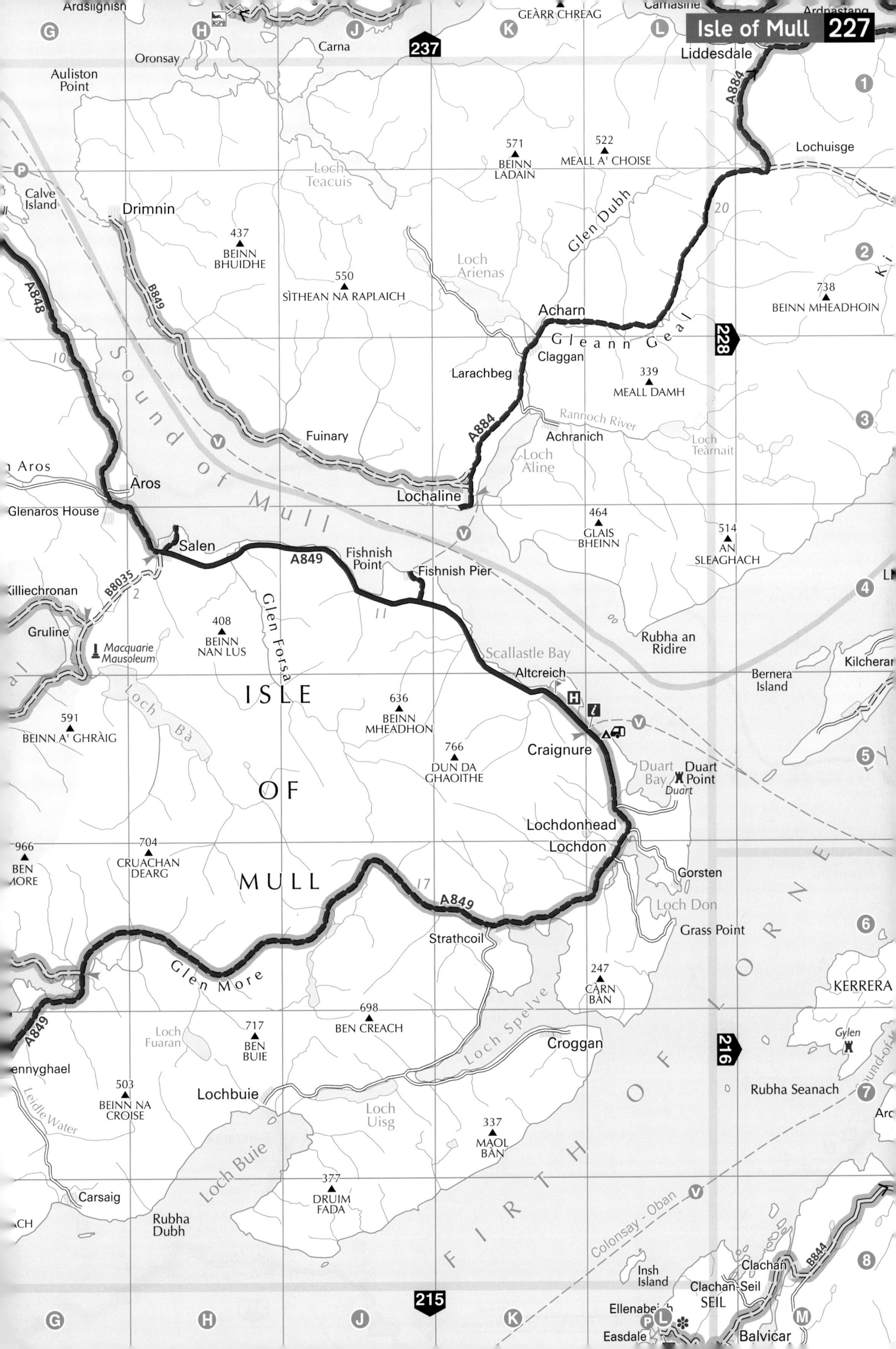

Ardslignish

GEÀRR CHREAG

Camasine

Ardnastang

G

H RSPB

J 237

K

L

1

Oronsay

Carna

Liddesdale

A884

Auliston
Point

MEALL A' CHOISE

Lochuisge

522

571
BEINN
LADAIN

Glen Dubh

20

Calve
Island

Loch
Teacuis

2

Drimnin

A848

437
BEINN
BHUIDHE

BEINN MHEADHOIN

738

P

B849

550
SÌTHEAN NA RAPLAICH

Loch
Arienas

Acharn

Gleann Geal

228

2

10

Claggan

339
MEALL DAMH

3

Sound

Fuinary

Larachbeg

A884

Rannoch River

Achranich

of

Loch
Aline

Loch
Tearnait

n Aros

Mull

Aros

Lochaline

Achranich

3

Glenaros House

464
GLAIS
BHEINN

514
AN
SLEAGHACH

4

Salen

Fishnish
Point

Fishnish Pier

V

L

Killiechronan

B8035

A849

2

Glen Forsa

11

Rubha an
Ridire

Bernera
Island

Kilcheran

Gruline

Macquarie
Mausoleum

408
BEINN
NAN LUS

Scallastle Bay

Altcreich

5

Loch Bà

ISLE

H

i

Loch

591
BEINN A' GHRÀIG

636
BEINN
MHEADHON

V

766
DUN DA
GHAOITHE

Craignure

Duart
Bay

Duart
Point

OF

Duart

966
BEN
MORE

704
CRUACHAN
DEARG

MULL

Lochdonhead

Lochdon

Gorsten

5

A849

17

Loch Don

Grass Point

6

Glen More

Strathcoil

247
CÀRN
BÀN

KERRERA

717
BEN
BUIE

698
BEN CREACH

Loch
Fuaran

Loch Spelve

216

Gylen

ennyghael

503
BEINN NA
CROISE

Croggan

Rubha Seanach

7

Leidle Water

Lochbuie

Loch
Uisg

337
MAOL
BÀN

Carsaig

Rubha
Dubh

377
DRUIM
FADA

Loch Buie

Colonsay - Oban

V

Clachan

B844

Insh
Island

8

Ellenabeich

Clachan-Seil
SEIL

Easdale

P L

Balvicar

M

G

H

J 215

K

L

M

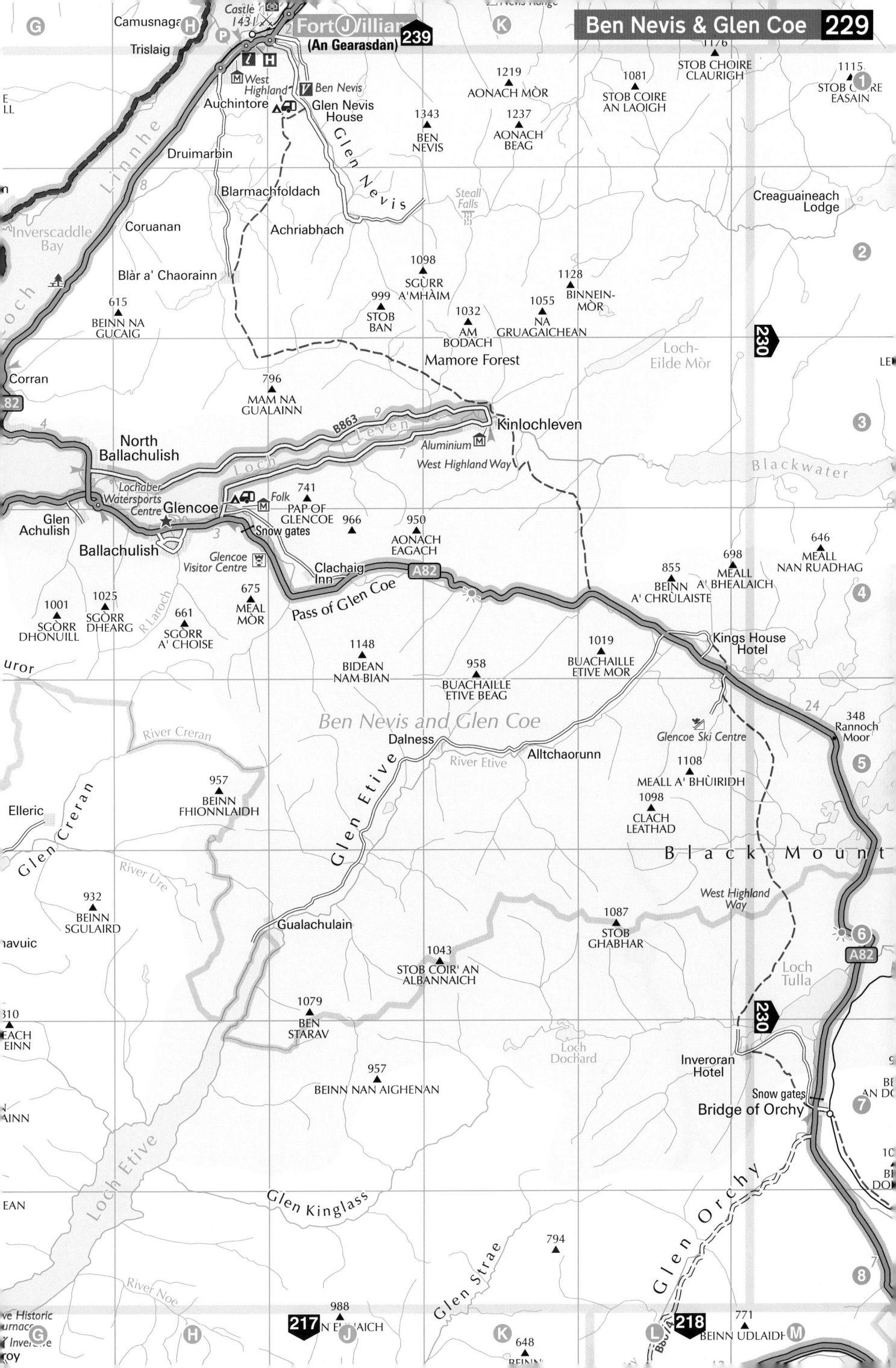

A | B | C | 240 | D | E | F

1176
STOB CHOIRE
CLAURIGH

1046
CHNO
DEARG

Loch
Gulbin

1101
BEINN
EIBHINN

1145
BEN
ALDER

1
TOB COIRE
N LAOIGH

1115
STOB COIRE
EASAIN

844
MEALL A'BHEALAICH

Glen Ossian

Creaguaineach
Lodge

Loch Treig

Loch Ossian

952
SGÒR
GAIBHRE

626
SRON A
CHLAONAID

2

Corrour
Station

229

Loch-
Eilde Mòr

906
LEUM UILLEIM

864
BEINN PHARIAGAIN

R Ericht

3

B l a c k w a t e r   R e s e r v o i r

Bridge
of Erich

646
MEALL
NAN RUADHAG

738
A' CHRUACH

Rannoch
Station

Dunan
B846

Finna

698
MEALL
A'BHEALAICH

Loch
Laidon

Loch
Eigheach

Bridge
of Gaur

855
BEINN
CHRÙLAISTE

4

Kings House
Hotel

Glencoe Ski Centre

24

348
Rannoch
Moor

R a n n o c h   M o o r

931
MEALL
BUIDHE

1108
MEALL A' BHÙIRIDH

5

Loch Bà

1098
CLACH
LEATHAD

B l a c k   M o u n t

Water of Tulla

Loch an
Daimh

West Highland
Way

087
TOE
ABHA

6

Loch
Tulla

A82

1079
BEINN
A' CHREACHAIN

Pubil

229

Inveroran
Hotel

996
BEINN
AN DÒTHAIDH

953
BEINN
MHANACH

Loch
Lyon

1038
MEALL
GHAORDIE

Snow gates
Bridge of Orchy

7

1074
BEN
DORAIN

1076
BEINN HEASGARNICH

G l e n   O r c h y

7

River Lochay

Falls

G l e n   L o c h a y

8

818

937
BEINN CHEATHAICH

771
INN UDL

B8074

0 1 2 3 4 5 miles
0 1 2 3 4 5 6 7 8 kilometres

A | 218 | D | E | 219 | F

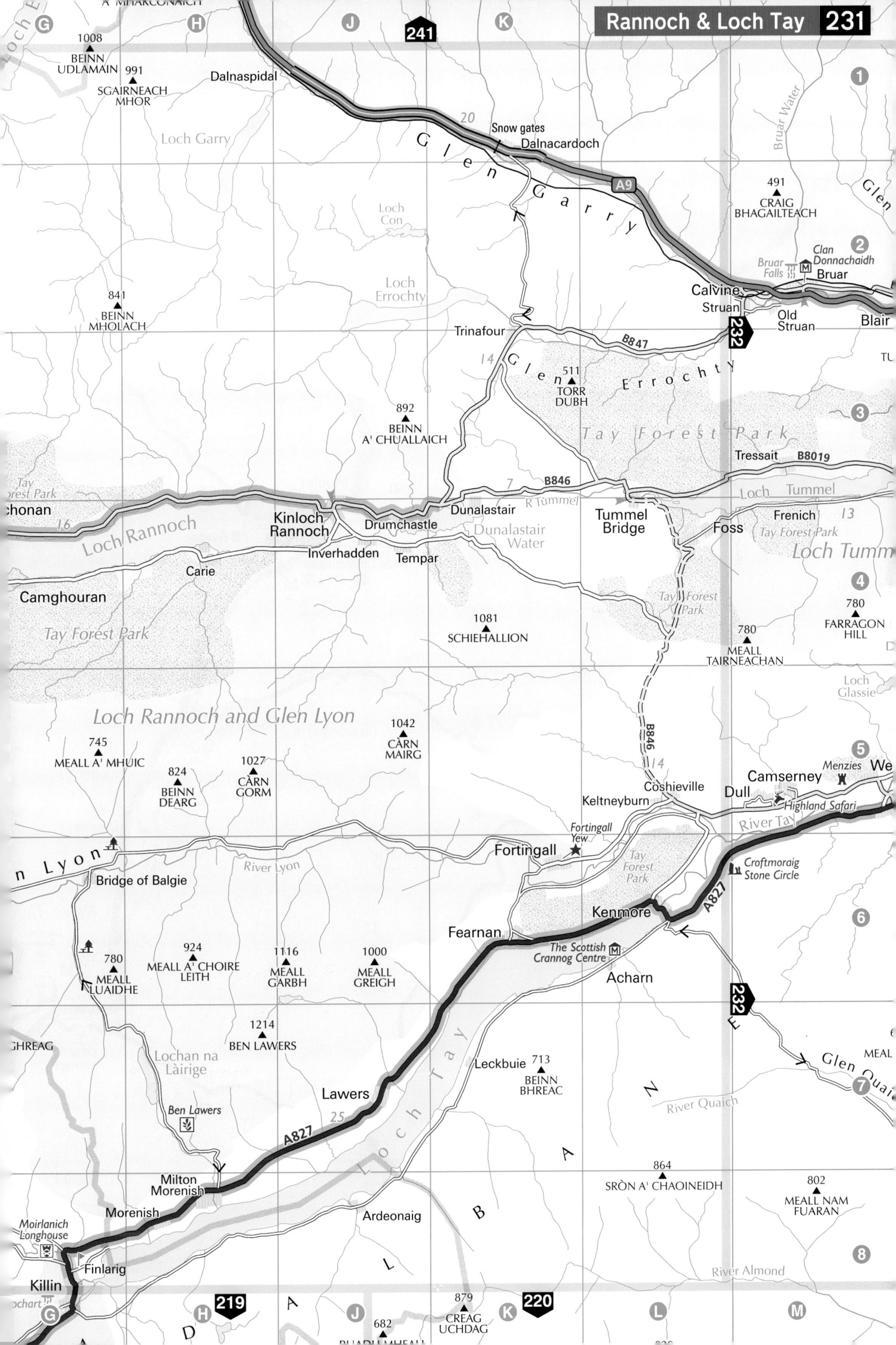

G   H   J   241   K

1

BEINN
UDLAMAIN
1008

SGAIRNEACH
MHOR
991

Dalnaspidal

Loch Garry

Glen   Garry

20

A9

Snow gates
Dalnacardoch

CRAIG
BHAGAILTEACH
491

Glen

2

Loch
Con

Bruar
Falls

Clan
Donnachaidh
M
Bruar

Loch
Errochty

Calvine
Struan
Old
Struan
Blair

232

BEINN
MHOLACH
841

Trinafour

B8 47

Glen   Errochty

TU

Tay Forest Park

3

TORR
DUBH
511

BEINN
A' CHUALLAICH
892

Tressait   B8019

Tay
orest Park

chonan

16

Loch Rannoch

Kinloch
Rannoch

Drumchastle

Dunalastair

B846

7

R Tummel

Tummel
Bridge

Loch Tummel

Frenich

Foss   Tay Forest Park   13

Loch Tumm

Inverhadden

Tempar

Dunalastair
Water

Carie

Camghouran

Tay Forest Park

SCHIEHALLION
1081

Tay Forest
Park

MEALL
TAIRNEACHAN
780

FARRAGON
HILL
780

4

Loch
Glassie

Loch Rannoch and Glen Lyon

MEALL A' MHUIC
745

BEINN
DEARG
824

CÀRN
GORM
1027

CÀRN
MAIRG
1042

B846

14

5

Menzies

Camserney

We

Coshieville

Dull

Highland Safari

n Lyon

Bridge of Balgie

River Lyon

Keltneyburn

Fortingall
Yew
★

Fortingall

Tay
Forest Park

Croftmoraig
Stone Circle

River Tay

A827

6

MEALL
LUAIDHE
780

MEALL A' CHOIRE
LEITH
924

MEALL
GARBH
1116

MEALL
GREICH
1000

Fearnan

The Scottish
Crannog Centre
M

Kenmore

Acharn

232

Glen Quai

MEAL

GHREAG

BEN LAWERS
1214

Lochan na
Làirige

Leckbuie

BEINN
BHREAC
713

N

River Quaich

7

Lawers

A827

25

Loch Tay

SRÒN A' CHAOINEIDH
864

MEALL NAM
FUARAN
802

Ben Lawers

Milton
Morenish

Morenish

Ardeonaig

A

B

L

8

Moirlanich
Longhouse

Finlarig

River Almond

Killin

ochart

G

H   219

A

J   682

K   220   CREAG
UCHDAG
879

L

M

BUADH MHFALL

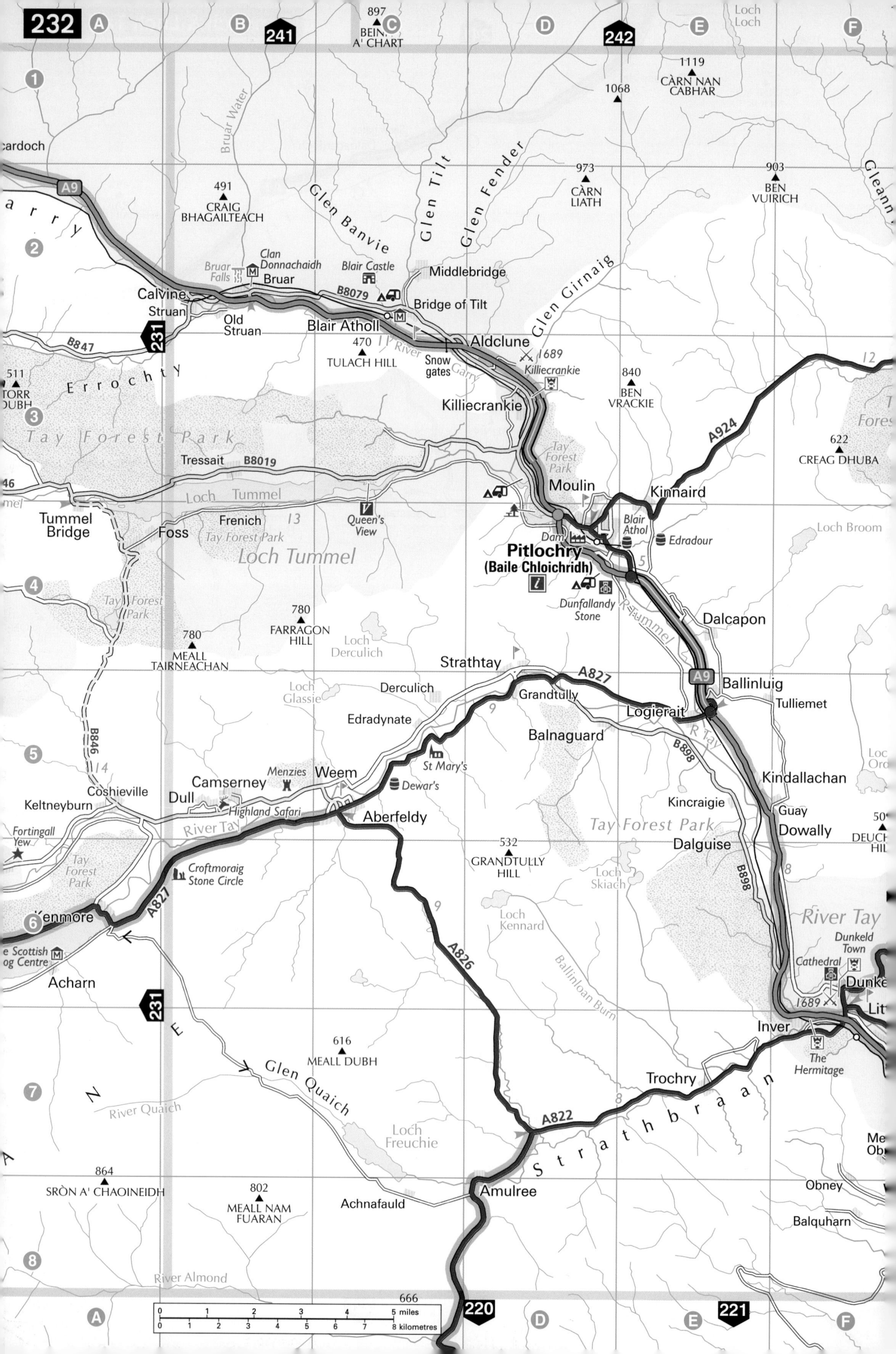

Lochsie
G 242 H 34 J River Isla 243 K Corrie L
A93

928 MAYAR
946 DRIESH
Clova 1
Glen Clova

Ben Gulabin 805
Snow gates

LA' HUIDHE

649 CAIRN OF BAMS
2
508

Spittal of Glenshee

861 CARN AIT
807 MONAMEANOCH

603 CAIRN DAUNIE
Runtaleave
Cormuir
Pitcarity
234
Glen Prosen

MEALL UAINE 792

700 DUCHRAY HILL
740 BADENDUN HILL
Presnerb
Glen Damff
Glen Finlet
3 Gl

Enochdhu
B951
Cray
Folda
Backwater Reservoir
Balintore

Milton
River Ardle

MOUNT BLAIR 744
Bridge of Brewlands
Kirkton of Glenisla

Blacklunans
B950
MEALL MOR 550
Bellaty
Dykends
Braes of Coul
B951
River Isla

michael
Strathardle 13

Ballintuim
Forest of Alyth
Loch of Lintrathen
Bridge of Craigisla
Bridgend of Lintrathen
B951
Kinnord
Loch of
4

A93

479
Alyth Burn

Netherton
Tullymurdoch
Dykehead
Reekie Linn Falls
Kirkton of Kingoldrum
Westmuir
Kirkton of Airlie
A926
M
5

Loch Benachally

A924
Bridge of Cally
Gauldswell
425 BALDUFF HILL
Airlie
Littleton of Airlie
Craigton of Airlie
Round

294 HILL OF ALYTH
B954
River Isla
H

Achalader 11
River Ericht
Lornty
Westfields of Rattray
Ruthven
A94
7
Eass Sculp Stone
Char

Concraigie
A923
Kinloch
Blairgowrie
Rattray
Alyth
New Alyth
B952
A926
Balhary
B954
T
Balkeerie
Kirkinch
Eassie and Nevay
6

Clunie
Rosemount
Longleys
A
Meigle
Sculptured Stone Museum

Craigie
Kirkton of Lethendy
B947
Muirton of Ardblair
A923
Newbigging
345 KINPURNEY HILL
B954
Ne Han

Spittalfield
A984
5
Ardler
Newtyle
7

Caputh Gellyburn
Meikleour
A93
A984
R
A94
Coupar Angus
Kettins
Bonnyton
Kirkton o Auchterhou

Murthly
Kinclaven
Meikleour Beech Hedge
Keithick
Woodside
Leys
Auchterhouse
Dronley

Cargill
Balholmie
B9099
Strelitz
Campmuir
Burrelton
Lundie
Piperdam
A923
Muirhead
rkh
8

Airntully
Loch Tay
15
Gallowhill
Saucher
376
Sidlaw Hills
15
Fowlis
Camperdo

A9
221
G
Stanley
H
Guildtown
Redstone
Wolfhill 13
Collace
KINGS SE
K 222
J Kinrossie
Kirkton of Collace
Abernyte
L
M
Liff
Gourdie
enhead of Gray
7

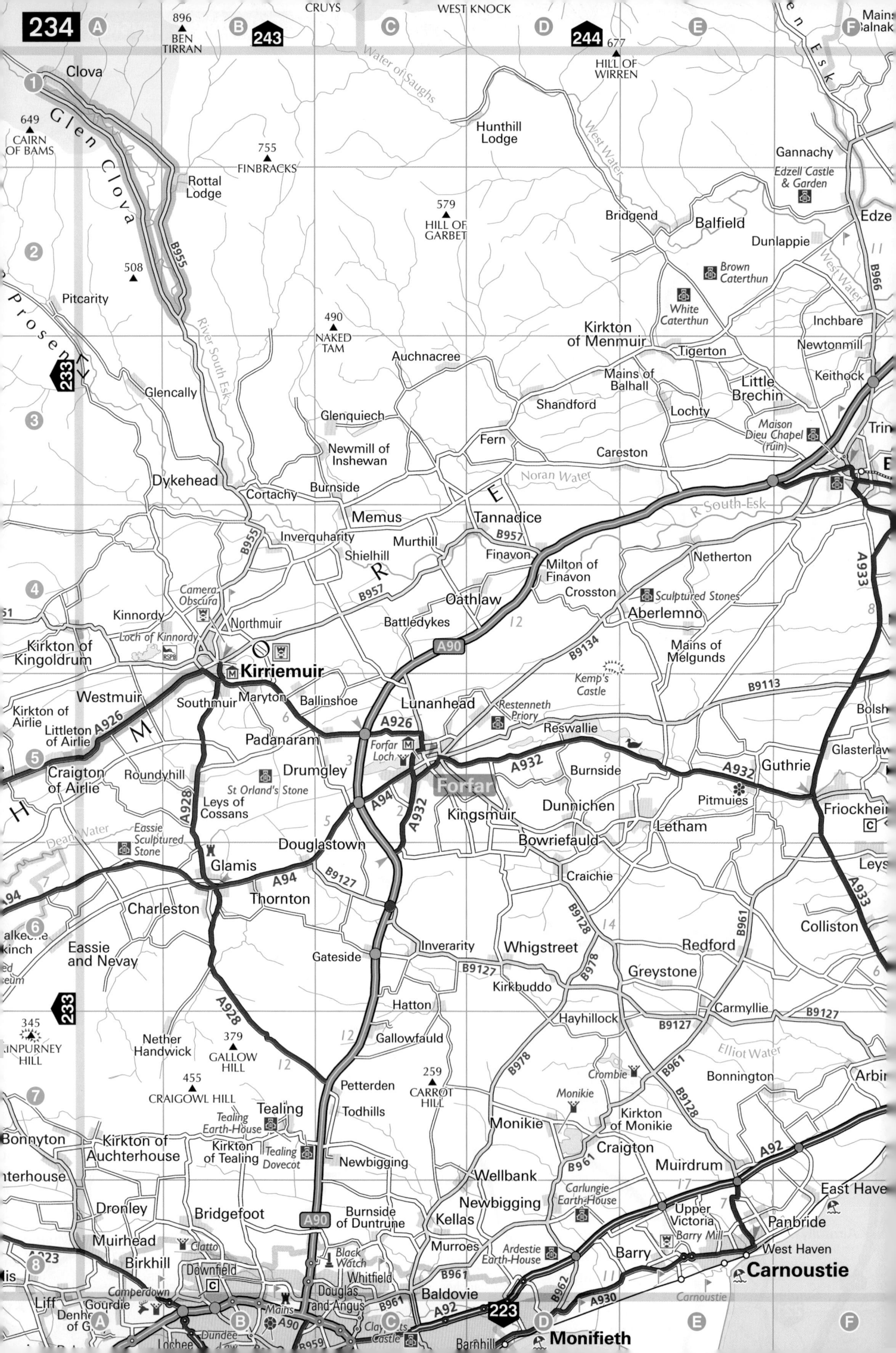

G H 244 J Redmyre Arbuthnott K 245
Pittarrow
Centre

1

Mains of
Haulkerton
Inverbervie
Bervie
Bay
Laurencekirk
Maritime
Gourdon

muir

B9120

B9120

auchieburn

B974

2

A90
North
Esk
Redford
Dykelands
Benholm
ermuir
A937
B974
Johnshaven
13

Marykirk
Bush
Logie
Pert
Craigo
Lochside
Milton Ness
Logie
Morphie
St Cyrus
3

Hillside
A92

House of
Dun
Montrose Air Station
Dun
A935
9
Montrose
Bridge of Dun
Montrose
Basin
M
4

Barnhead
Scurdie Ness
Maryton
Ferryden
A934
Craig
Usan

Westerton
of Rossie
Boddin Point
Braehead
Lunan
5

Lunan Bay

Inverkeilor
elton
13
uldcots
Red Head
6

A92
Marywell
Auchmithie
Carlingheugh
Bay
Arbroath Abbey
The Deil's
Head
7

Arbroath
Signal Tower

G H J K L M

8

0 1 2 3 4 5 miles
0 1 2 3 4 5 6 7 8 kilometres

A   B   C   D   E   F

1

A' Bhrìdeanach

570 ▲ ORVAL

MULLACH MÒR

246

Kinloch

Rubha na Ròinne

Loch-Scresort

RÙM

810 ▲ ASKIVAL

2

Harris Bay

763 ▲ SGÙRR NAN GILLEAN

> All vehicles must have the relevant island permit prior to travel to The Small Isles. Services are seasonal, day & weather dependent.

The Small Isles

Rubha nam Meirleach

Sound of Rùm

3

Rubha an Fhasaidh

Bay of Laig

Cleadale

Laig

299 ▲ AN CRUACHAN

EIGG

Kild

Sound of Eigg

393 ▲ AN SGÙRR

Galmis

4

Eilean nan Each

MUCK

Eilea Cha

Port Mòr

5

6

Sanna Point

Sanna Bay

Sanna

Portuairk

Achnaha

Ardnamurchan Point

Achosnich

ME

B8007

7

Eilean Mòr

Ⓥ

Bàgh a' Chaisteil (Castlebay)
Loch Baghasdail (Lochboisdale)
(Oct–Mar)

Rubha Mòr

Rubha Sgor-innis

225

342 ▲ BEINN NA SEILG

Ormsaigmore

Bousd

Sorisdale

Cliad Bay

B8072

COLL

| 0 | 1 | 2 | 3 | 4 | 5 miles |
| 0 | 1 2 3 4 5 6 7 | | | | 8 kilometres |

Ardmore Point

8

abost

B8071

Arinagour

Loch Cliad

A   B

Coll - Oban

C

Quinish Point

D

Sorne Po

226

E

Glengorm Castle

F

A   B   C   D   E   F

1

BEINN NA
SEAMRAIG

Gleann Beag
Brochs   Glen Beag

Glen Shiel

SOUTH
FHU

Loch na Dal

Ornsay

Ornsay

Sandaig Islands

1011
THE SADDLE

▲ 974
BEINN
SGRITHEAL

▲ 773
BEINN
NAN CAORACH

945
SGURR
NA SGINE

2

Rubha
Buidhe

Loch Hourn

Arnisdale

Glen Arnisdale

Rubha Àrd
Slisneach

Corran

Kinloch
Hourn

Inverguseran

▲ 614

709
DRUM
FADA

SOUND OF SLEAT

247

Glen Guseran

784
BEINN NA
CAILLICH

Barrisdale
Bay

S
MH

Airor

3

518
DRUIM NA
CLUAIN-AIRIDHE

1019
LADHAR
BHEINN

Knoydart

Sandaig

KNOYDART

Sandaig Bay

Loch Nevis

940
LUINNE BHEINN

Inverie

Inverie
Bay

Loch an
Dubh-Lochain

Rubha
Raonuill

P

946
MEALL BUIDHE

1003
SGURR MÒR

4

Mallaigvaig

547
CÀRN A'GHOBHAIR

854
BEINN BHUIDHE

1039
SGURR NA CICHE

Loch an
Nostaire

437
SGÙRR BHUIDHE

Beoraidbeg

P

Glen Dessar

5

Morar

Bracorina

Kylesmorar

859
SGURR NAH-AIDE

Bracora

723
SGURR BREAC

cross

Tarbet

Glen Pean

Swordland

Loch   Morar

503
CÀRN A'
MHÀDAIDH-RUAIDH

716
AN STAC

949
SGURR NAN
COIREACHAN

964
SGÙRR
THUILM

6

Meoble

600
SIDHEAN
MÒR

237

710
MEITH BHEINN

River Meoble

Prince's Cairn

796
SGÙRR
AN UTHA

Glen Finnan

Gleann Dubh Lighe

Gleann Fionnlig

Arisaig
House

Kinlochnanuagh

Loch Beoriad

633

Loch nan Uamh

Polnish

Lochailort

Loch
Eilt

A830

14

Glenfinnan
Viaduct

M

Glenfinnan

Kinloch

7

Ardnish

Inverailort

V

Rubha
oalais

Loch Ailort

A861

Glenfinnan
Monument

Drimsallie

877
ROIS-BHEINN

882
BEINN
ODHAR BHEAG

Garvan

nuig

712

8

Kirhmoid

664
BEINN GAIRE

718
MEALL
NAM DAMH

Glen Garvan

Seven Men
of Maidart

Brunery

| 0 | 1 | 2 | 3 | 4 | 5 miles |
| 0 | 1 2 3 4 | 5 | 6 | 7 | 8 kilometres |

A   Scamodale   D   228   E   758   F   Cona Gl
MEALL

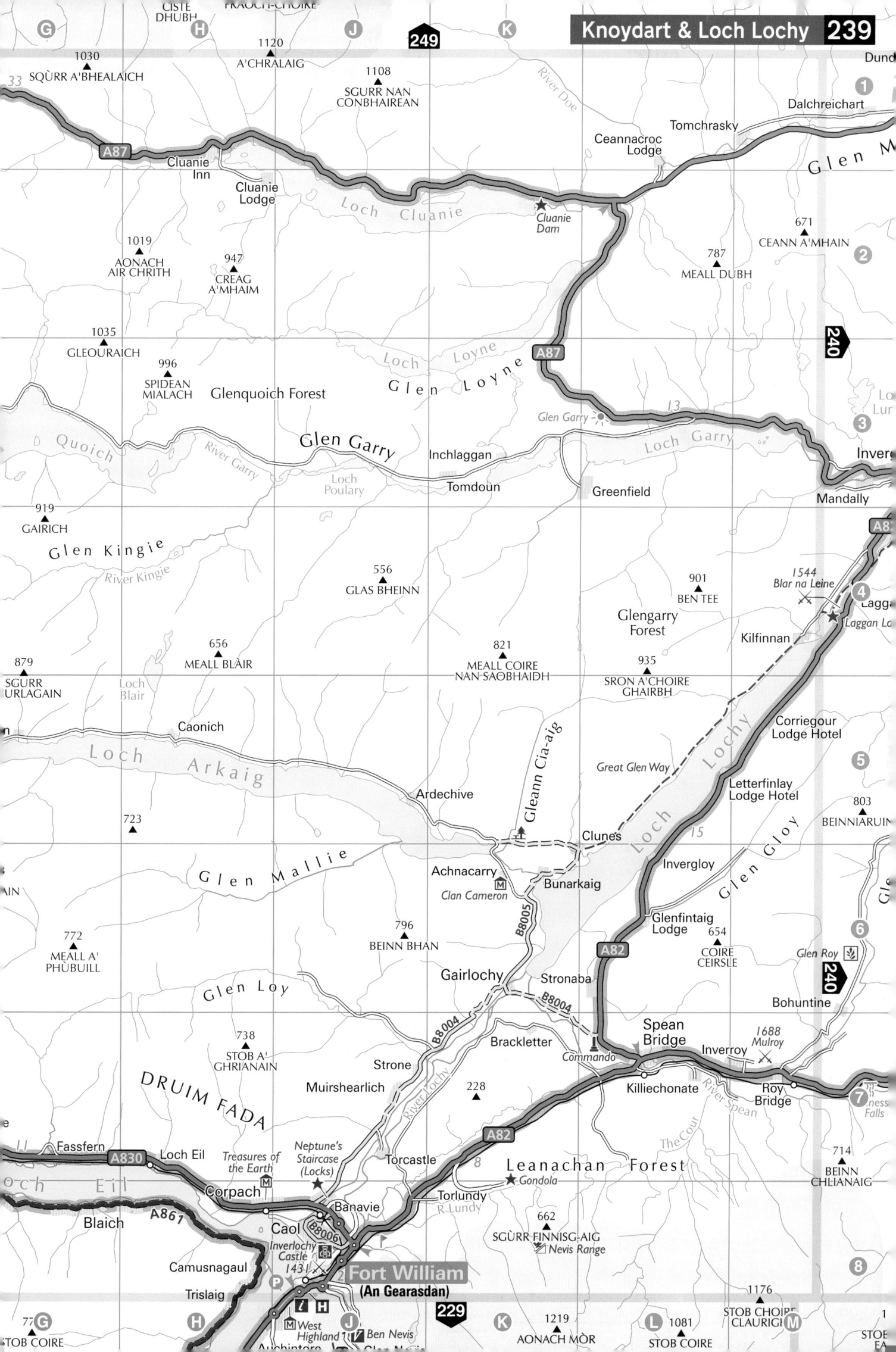

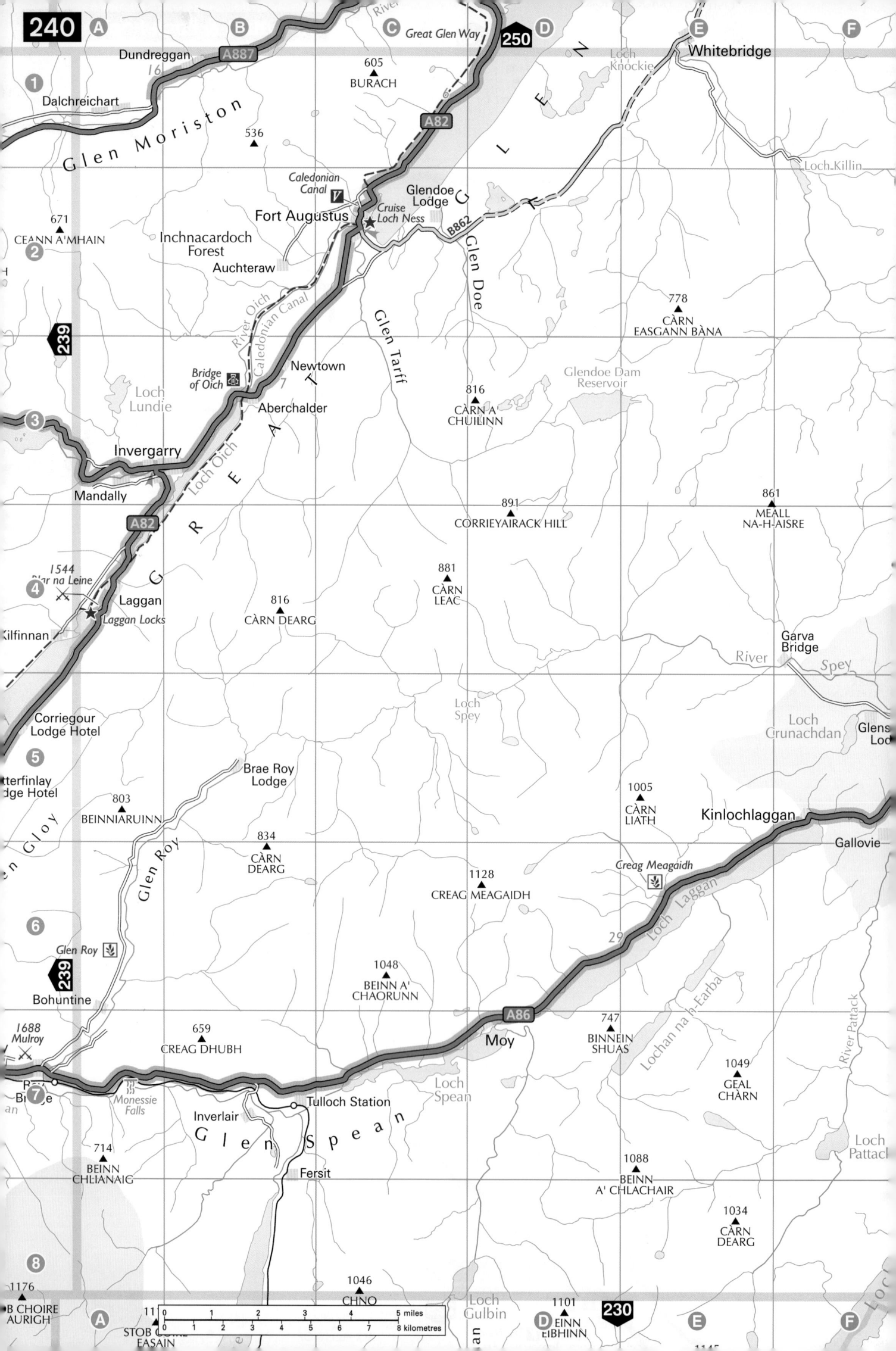

G 251 **H** **J** 252

810
CÀRN NA SAOBHAIDHE ▲

790
CÀRN COIRE
NA H-EASGAINN ▲

745
CNOC
FRAING ▲

712 Aviem ▲ **1**

810
RN NA
CHE MAOILE ▲

824
GEAL-CHÀRN MÒR ▲

Craigellachie

Loch
Alvie

River Eskin

729
CAIRN
DULNAN ▲

A9

B9152

B9970 **2**

813
CALPA
MÒR ▲

Monadhliath Mountains

878
CÀRN AN
FHREICEADAIN ▲

Raitts Burn

Highland
Wildlife Park

Kincraig

Feshiebridge

Lagganlia **3**

855
SGARAMAN
NAM FIADH ▲

928
A CHAILLEACH ▲

10

Loch
Insh

242 Invereshie &
Inshriach

941
CÀRN
BÀN ▲

Farr

Insh

Inveruglass

Markie

Kingussie

Lynchat

842
CÀRN AN
LETH-CHOIN ▲

Pitmain

Ruthven

Drumguish

Auchlean **4**

Newtonmore
(Baile Ur an t-Sleibh)

M Highland
Folk

Insh Marshes

RSPB

Ruthven
Barracks

Glen Feshie

River Feshie

12

A9

Ralia

C A I R N G O R M S

627
MEALL
BUIDHE ▲

Blargie

Laggan

Balgowan

A86

Glentruim

N A T I O N A L

River Tromie

MULLAC
A BH **5**

Catlodge

Snow gates

Etteridge

593
GARBH-
MHEALL MÒR ▲

857
CÀRN
DEARG MÒR ▲

Glenfes

Strathmashie
House

A86

Crubenmore

768
MEALLACH
MHÒR ▲

P A R K

15

Loch
Caoldair

A9

Loch na
Cuaich

898
BAGHA-
CLOICHE ▲

Loch an
t-Seilich

910
LEATHAD AN
TOABHAIN ▲ **6**

9

A889

Snow gates

Gaick Forest

Dalwhinnie

Glen Truim

242 R

G **7**

Snow gates

941
CÀRN NA CAIM ▲

Loch an Dùin

769
CREAGAN
MÒR ▲

1007
BEINN
DEARG ▲

975
A' MHARCONAICH ▲

926
GLAS
MHEALL MÒR ▲

814
SRON A'
CHLEIRICH ▲

459
Drumochter
Summit

897
BEINN
A' CHART ▲ **8**

N
SGAIRNEACH
MHOR

Dalnaspidal

G **H** **J** 231 **K** **L** 232 **M**

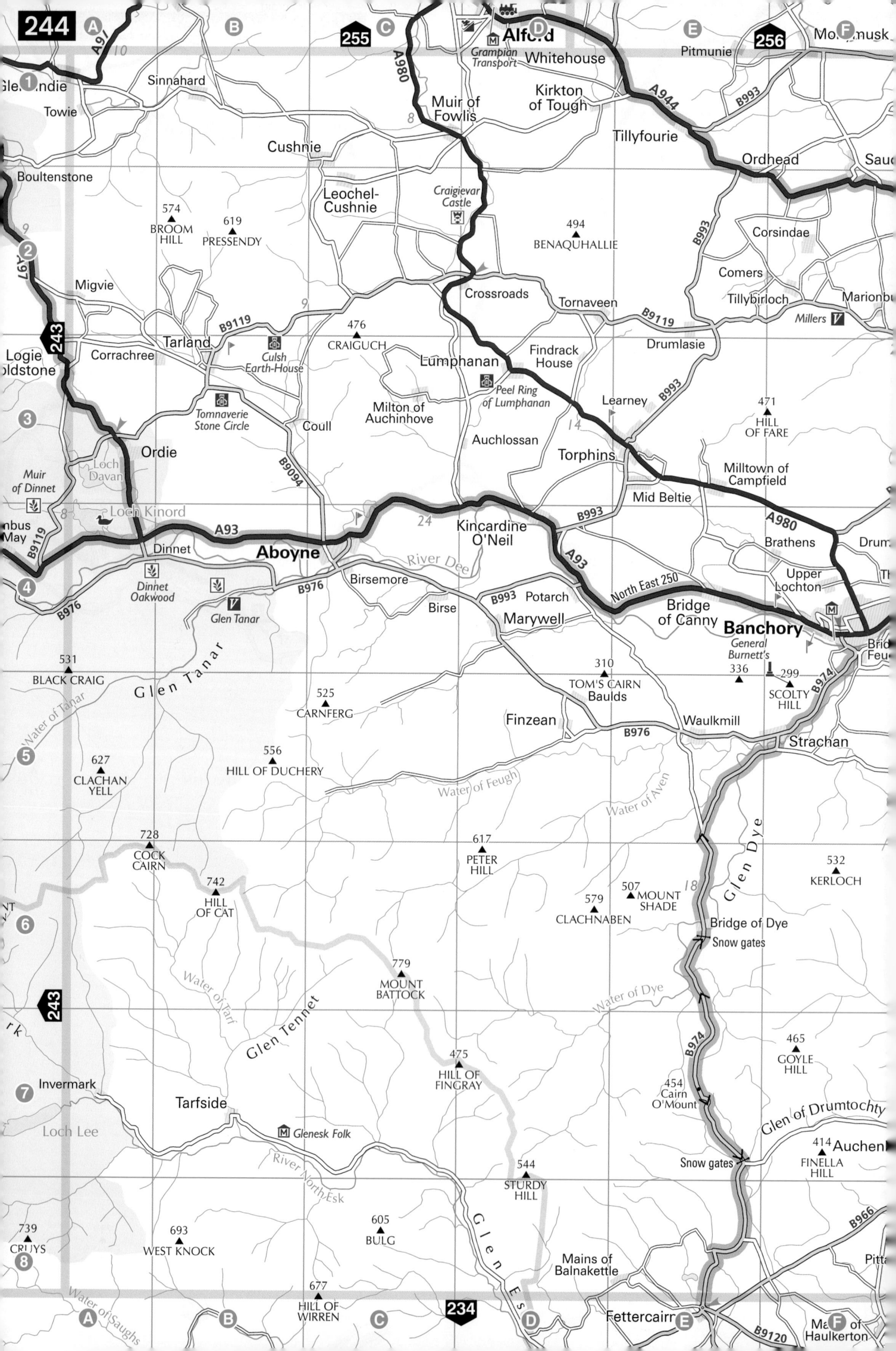

BHFAG

B
258
Colbost
Point
Harlosh
Island
Tarner
Island

C

Loch

Osе D

Dun
Beag
Bracadale
Coillore

E

Loch
Duagrich

F
Glen

Mug

1

368
▲
BEINN NA
BOINEID

Loch Bracadale

Wiay

Struan
23

Idrigill
Point

Oronsay
Portnalong
Fiskavaig

Loch Harport

B8009

439
▲
ROINEVAL

2

Rubha nan Clach

Fernilea

369
▲
ARNAVAL
Carbost

Talisker
Merkadale

Talisker
Drynoch

A863

Glen Dryn

Talisker
Bay

Talisker

Minginish

Glen Eynort

Glen
Brittle

369
▲
BEINN BHRE

3

447
▲
BEINN
BHREAC

Grula

Forest

Fairy

4

Loch Eynort

434
▲
AN CRUACHIN

Glenbrittle
Bualintur

97
SGU
A' GHE

C u

SC
ALA

5

Rubha an Dùnain

Loch Brittle

225
▲
CEANN NA BEINNE

Soay Sound

6

V
Loch Baghasdail
(Lochboisdale)

Ru
Aong

C U I L L I N

7

CANNA

Garrisdale Point

210
▲
CÀRN A' GHAILL

A'Chill

Canna
Harbour

Sanday

Kilmory
Bay

Rubha
Shamhnan
Insir

8

0   1   2   3   4   5 miles
0 1 2 3 4 5 6 7 8 kilometres

A'Bhrdealach

RÙM

302
▲
MULLACH
MÒR

Rubha
na Roinne

Sound of Canna

236

570
▲
ORVAL

Kinloch

Loch Scresort

Penifiler 412
BEN
TIANAVAIG
H
Camustianavaig
Tianavaig
Bay
Oskaig
J
DÙN CAAN 444
259
Camustorrach
Culduie
1
Ollach
Clachan
Inverarish
BEINN NA LEAC 310
Rubha na' Leac
River Toscaig
Toscaig

A87
Glen Varragill
B8883
The Braes
BEN LEE 444
Peinchorran
Suisnish Point
Eyre Point
V
SCALPAY
Eilean
Meadhonach
Eilean
Mòr
CROWLIN
ISLANDS

Sconser
Sligachan
Moll
Loch Ainort
Ard
Dorch
MULLACH
NA CARN 396
Longay 67
Port-an-Eor
Drumbu
2

GLAMAIG 773
A87
Luib
Dunan
Caolas Scalpay
Pabay
27
248
Badicaul

ISLE OF
SKYE
GLAS BHEIN MHÒR 564
Strollamus
Broadford
Bay
Kyle of Lochalsh
(Caol Loch Aillse)
Skye Bridge
3

URR
GILLEAN 65
BEINN NA CAILLICH 732
BEINN DEORG MHÒR 708
Corry
H
Broadford
Waterloo
Lower Breakish
Breakish
A87
Kyleakin

The Cuillin Hills
Hills
BLAVEN 927
B8083
Torrin 14
Harrapool
Skulamus
SGURR NA COINNICH
4

Loch na Crèithéach
Kirkibost
B8083
Loch Slapin
A851
BEN ASLAK 605
Kyl

Loch
ruisk
BEN MEABOST 344
BEINN NAN CARN 300
Heaste
BEINN NA SEAMRAIG 561
5

Loch Scavaig
Elgol
Glasnakille
Rubha
Suisnish
Suisnish
Loch Eishort
Drumfearn
Loch na Dal
Sandaig
Islands

Strathaird
Point
SGÒRACH BREAC 298
Tokavaig
Duisdalemore
Isleornsay
Ornsay
SOUND OF SLEAT
Rubha Àrd
Slisneach
6

Tarskavaig
Ord River
17
238

Tarskavaig Bay
Achnacloich
Loch nam
Uamph
Teangue
Knock
Knock
Bay
Invergusera
7

Ferrindonald
Kilmore
Airor

Kilbeg
A851

Armadale
Castle M
Ardvasar
Calligarry
Armadale
A851
Sandaig
DRUIM NA
CLUAIN-AIRIDHE 518

Aird
V
Sandaig Bay
8

Ard
Thurinish
237
Point
of Sleat
Courteachan
Rubha
Raonuill
Inverié
Bay

G
H
J
K
L P
M

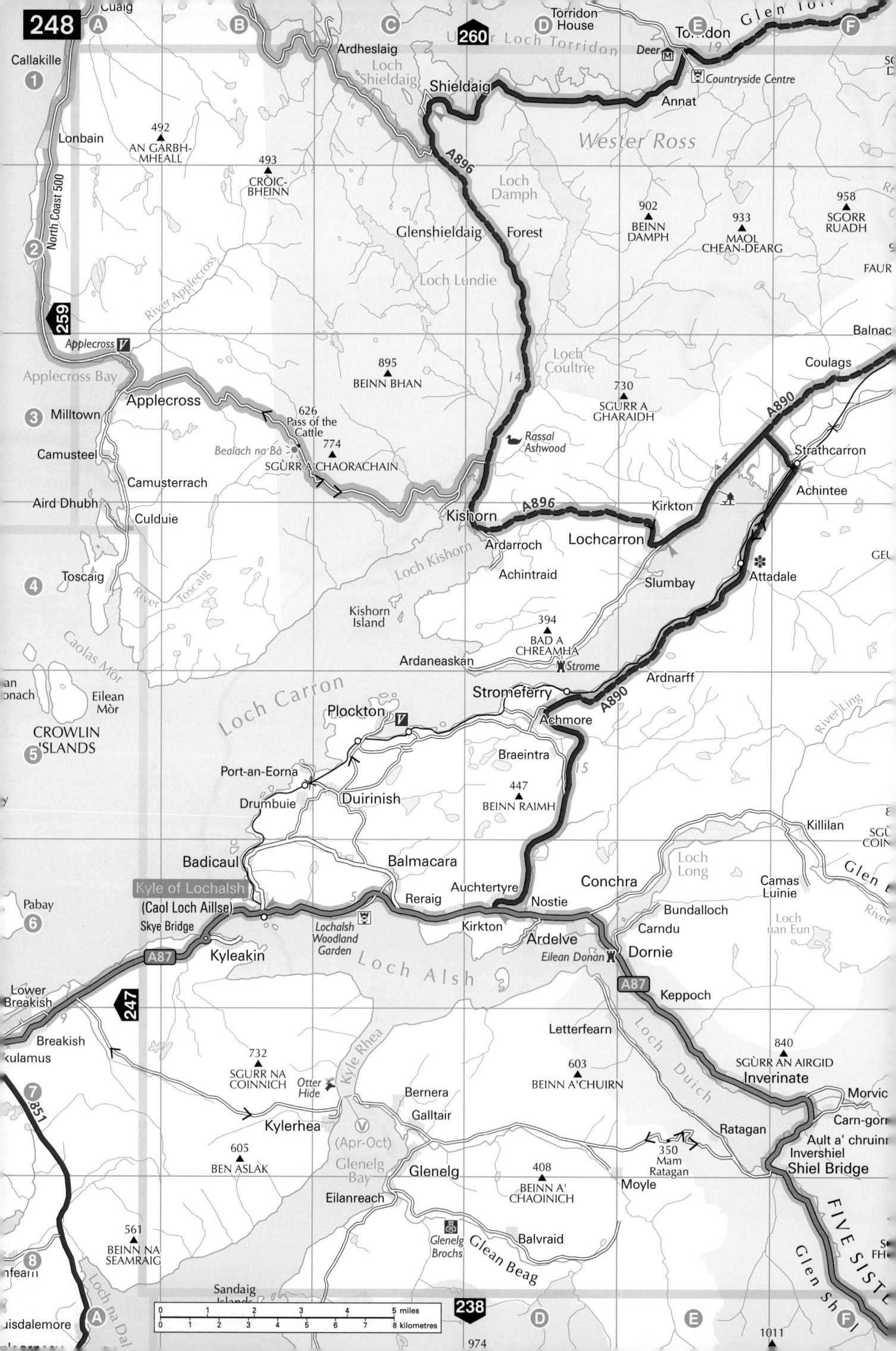

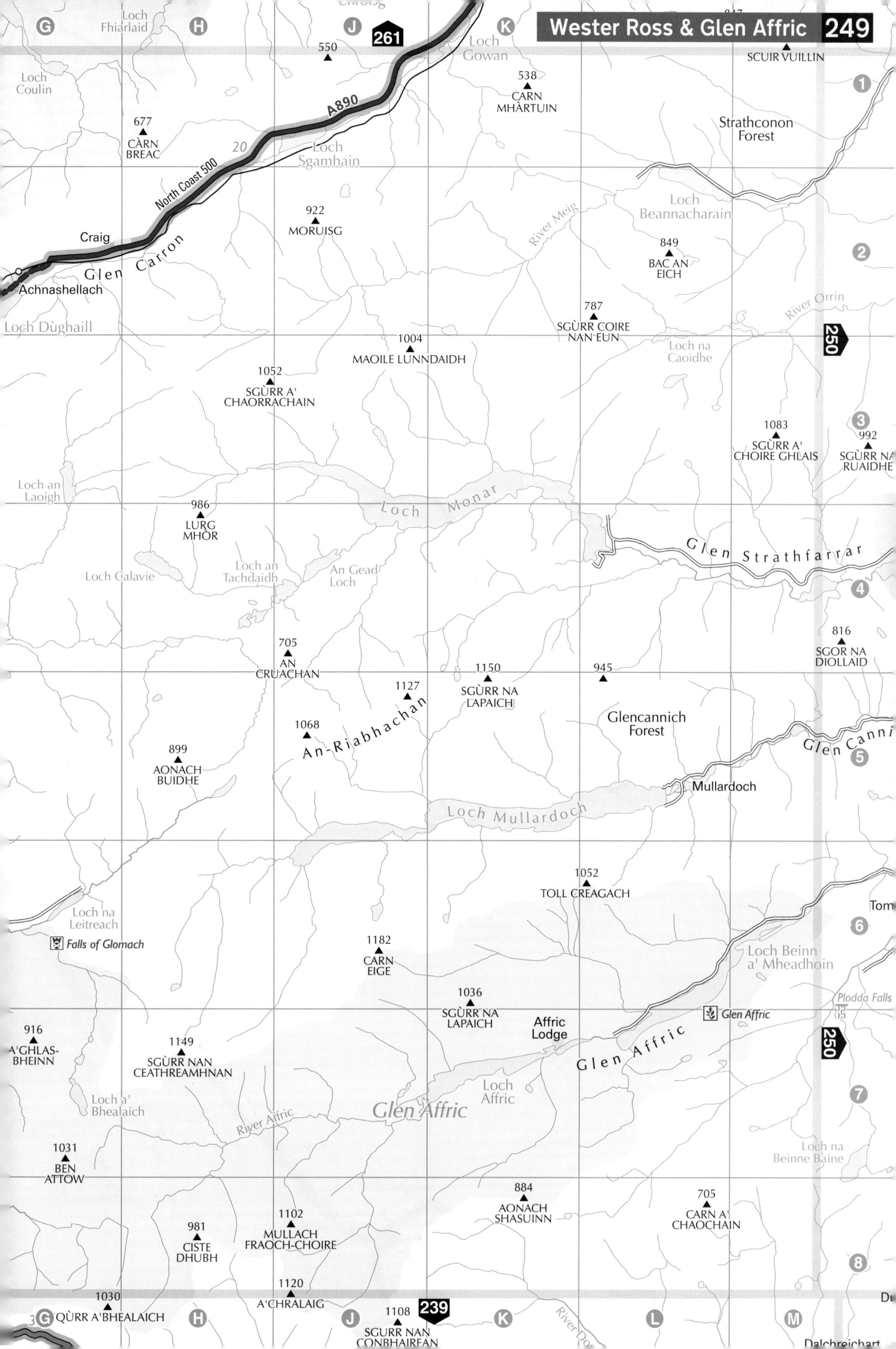

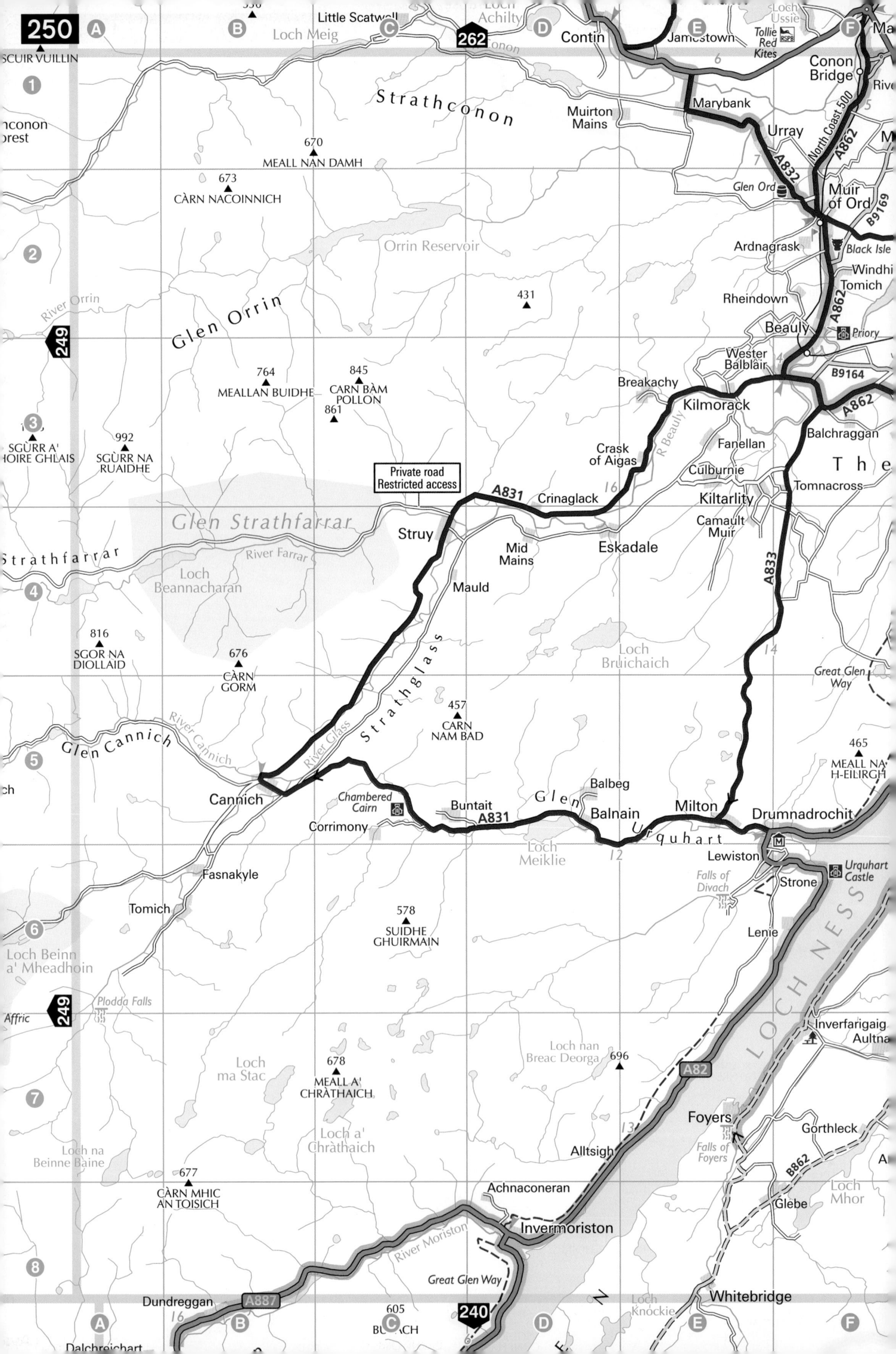

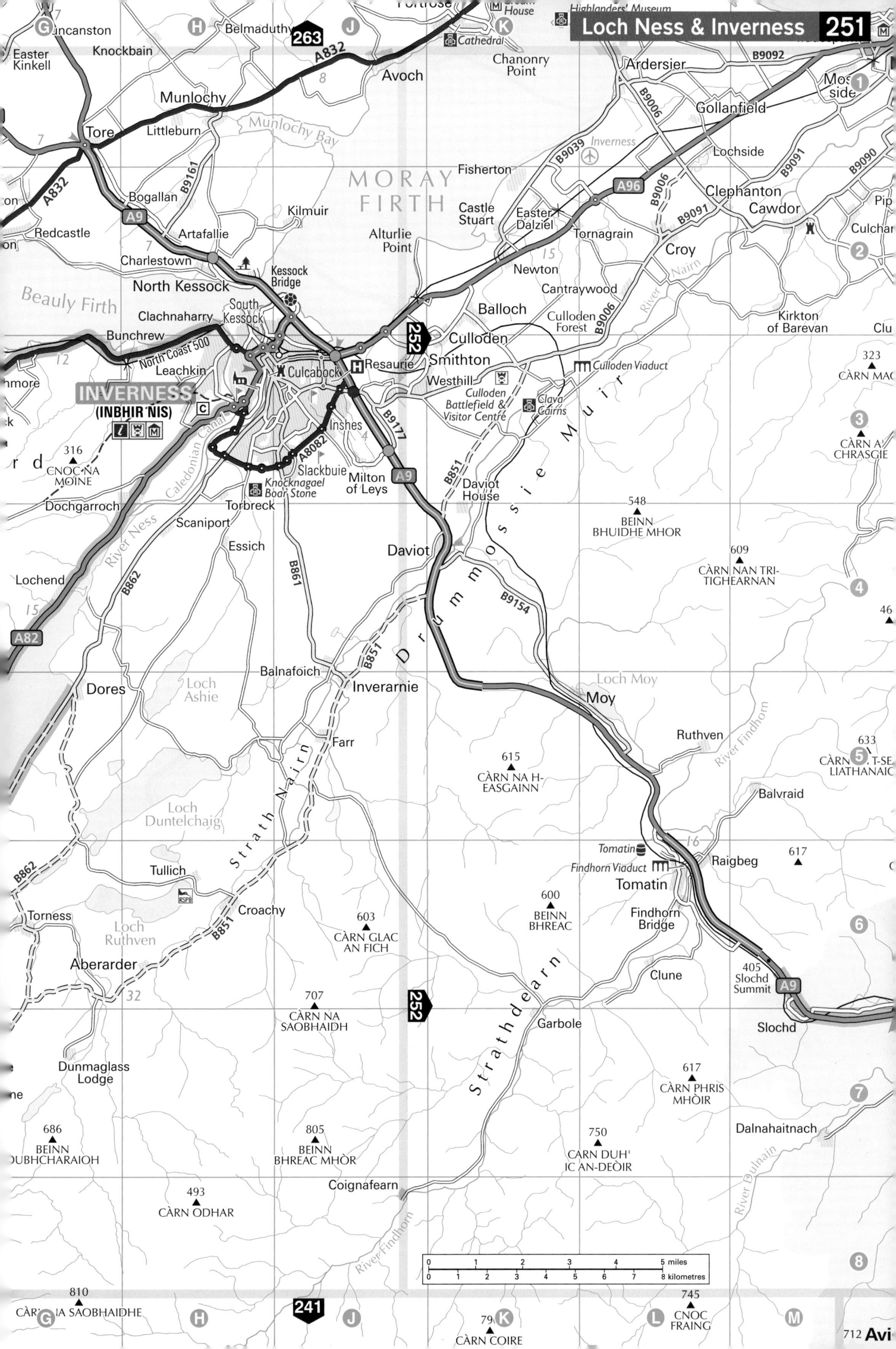

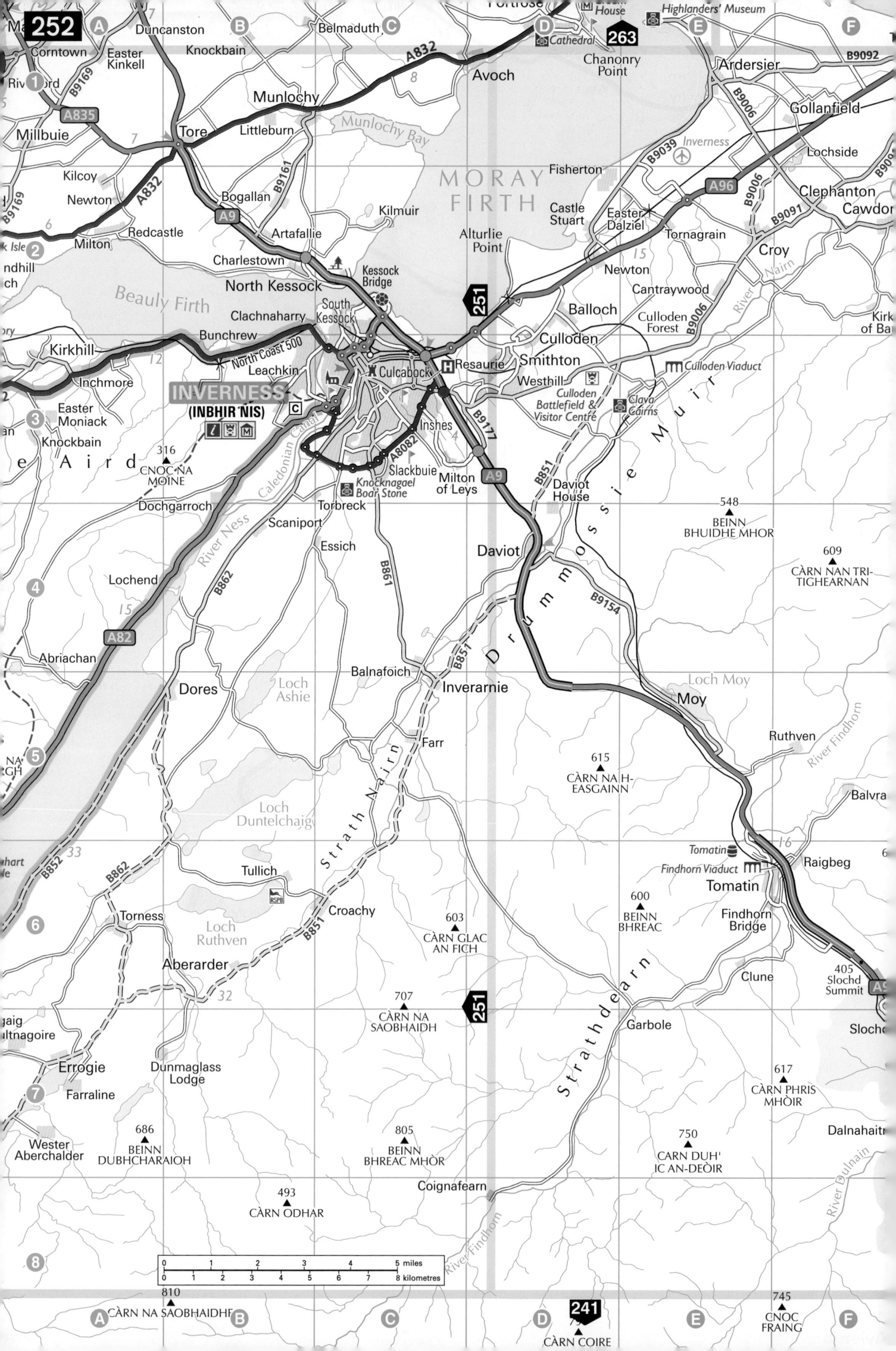

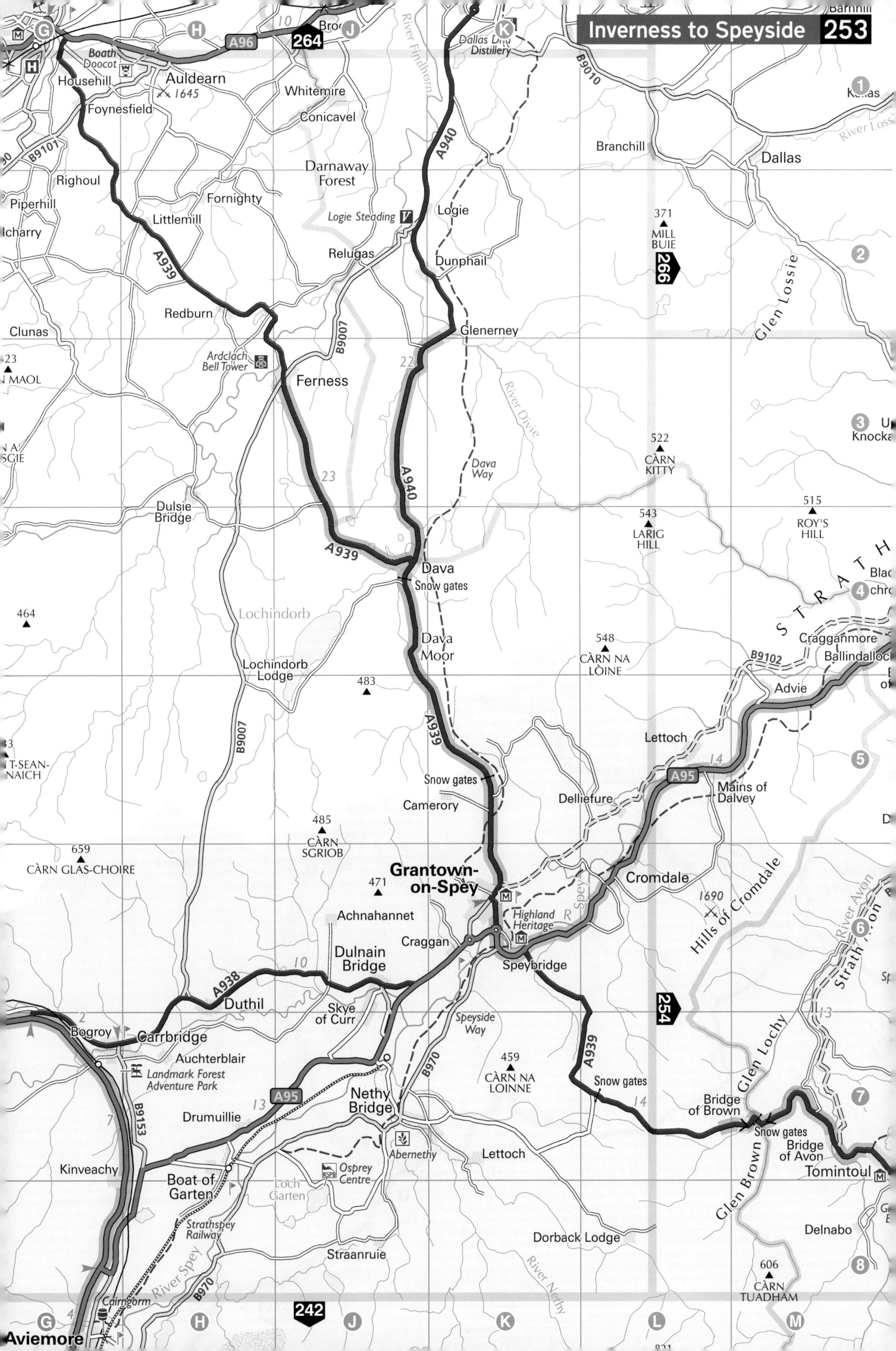

Barnhill

1

Kellas

River Lossie

Dallas

Branchill

266

371
▲
MILL
BUIE

2

3 U
Knocka

522
▲
CÀRN
KITTY

515
▲
ROY'S
HILL

543
▲
LARIG
HILL

S T R A T H

4 Blac
chro

Cragganmore

B9102

Ballindalloch
o

548
▲
CÀRN NA
LÒINE

Advie

5

Lettoch

A95

14

Mains of
Dalvey

Delliefure

River Avon

6

1690
×

Hills of Cromdale

Cromdale

R Spey

Speybridge

254

Glen Lochy

113

7

Bridge
of Brown

Snow gates

Bridge
of Avon

Tomintoul

Glen Brown

Delnabo

606
▲
CÀRN
TUADHAM

8

Barnhill

River Findhorn

Dallas Dhu
Distillery

K

B9010

A940

Logie Steading ⓥ

Logie

Dunphail

Glenerney

22

River Divie

Dava
Way

Dava

Snow gates

Dava
Moor

483
▲

A939

Snow gates

Camerory

**Grantown-
on-Spey**

471
▲

Achnahannet

Craggan

M ▶

Highland
Heritage

M

Dulnain
Bridge

10

A938

Skye
of Curr

459
▲
CÀRN NA
LOINNE

Speyside
Way

Lettoch

A939

Snow gates

14

242 J

K

L

M

Boath
Doocot

G

H

J

A96

10

Bro

264

Househill

H
M
H

Auldearn

× 1645

Whitemire

Conicavel

Foynesfield

Righoul

Darnaway
Forest

B9101

Piperhill

Fornighty

Littlemill

Icharry

Clunas

Redburn

A939

B9007

Relugas

Ferness

Ardclach
Bell Tower 🔔

23 ▲
N MAOL

23

Dulsie
Bridge

Lochindorb

Lochindorb
Lodge

464
▲

B9007

3
T-SEAN-
NAICH

485
▲
CÀRN
SGRIOB

659
▲
CÀRN GLAS-CHOIRE

Bogroy ▶

B9153

Carrbridge

Duthil

Auchterblair

Landmark Forest
Adventure Park

13

A95

Drumuillie

7

Kinveachy

Boat of
Garten

Strathspey
Railway

River Spey

B970

Cairngorm

4

G

H

Aviemore

B970

Nethy
Bridge

Abernethy

Osprey
Centre RSPB

Loch
Garten

Straanruie

Dorback Lodge

River Nethy

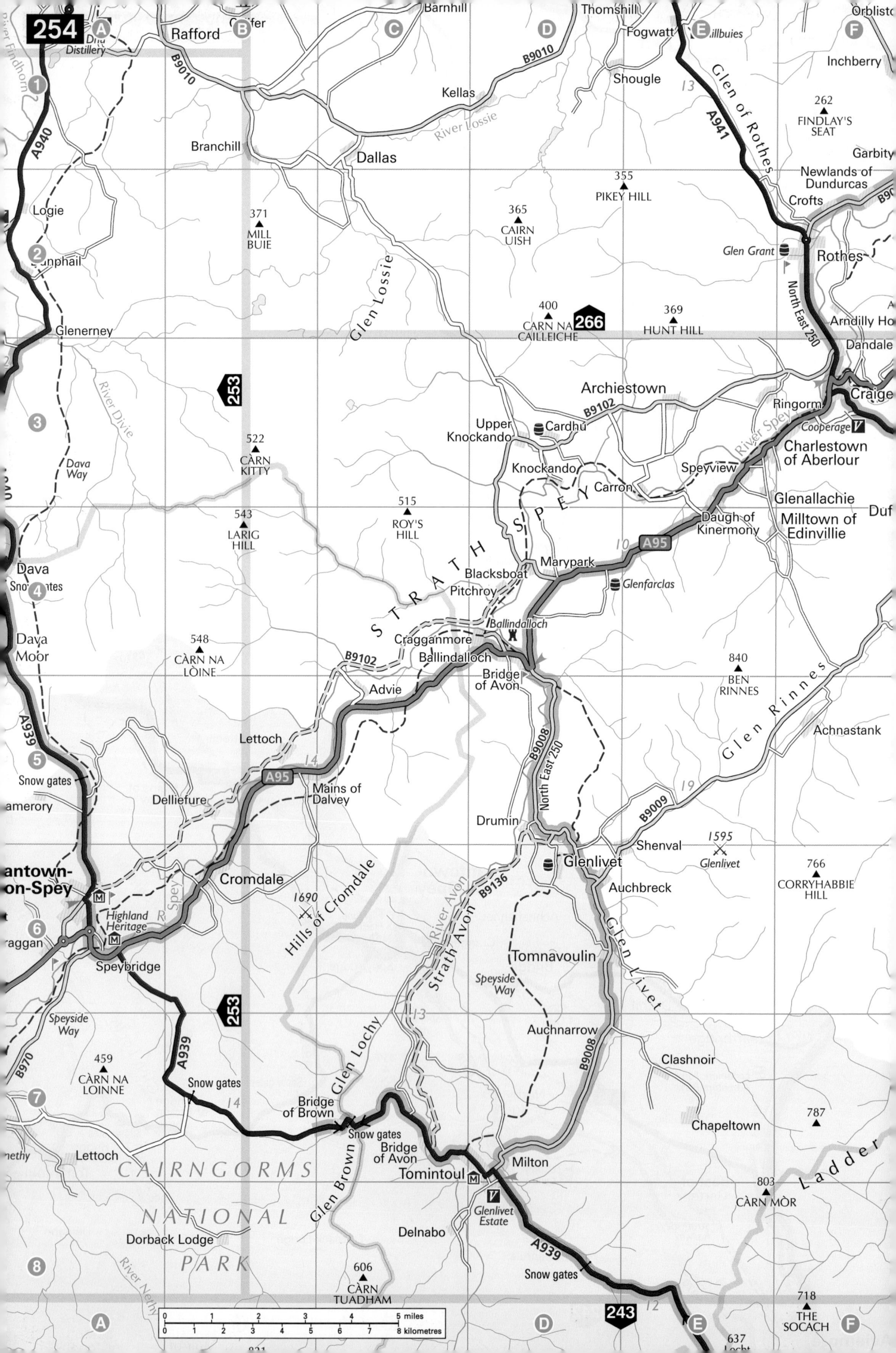

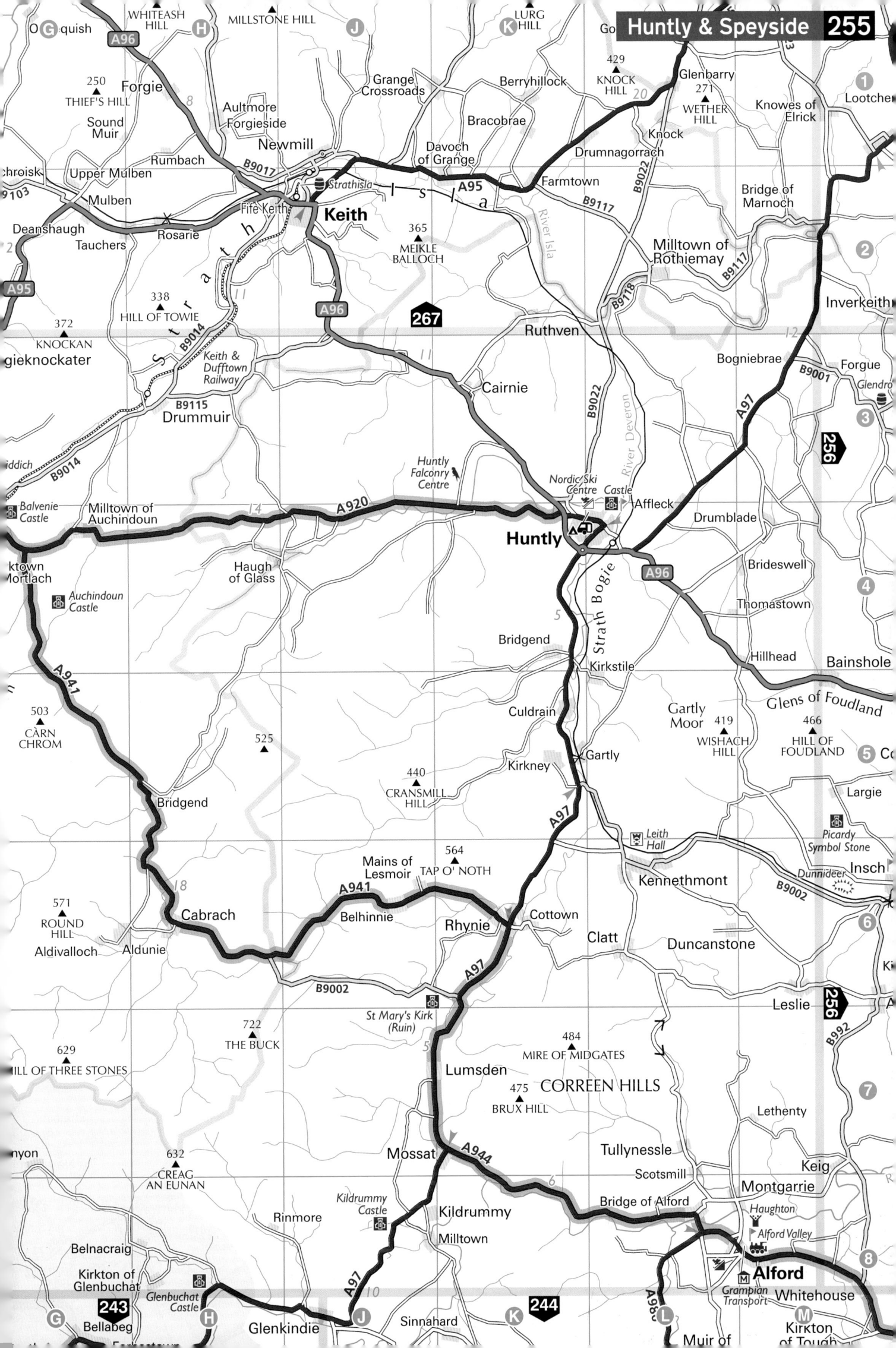

O**G**quish
WHITEASH HILL **H**
MILLSTONE HILL **J**
LURG HILL **K**
Go
1 Lootche

A96
429
Glenbarry

250
THIEF'S HILL
Forgie
Grange Crossroads
Berryhillock
KNOCK HILL 20
271
WETHER HILL
Knowes of Elrick

Sound Muir
Aultmore Forgieside
Bracobrae
Knock

chroisk
Rumbach
B9017
Davoch of Grange
Drumnagorrach
Bridge of Marnoch

9103
Upper Mulben
Newmill
Farmtown
B9022
B9117

Mulben
A95

Deanshaugh
Rosarie
Fife Keith
Strathisla
I s l a
A95
Milltown of Rothiemay
2

Tauchers
Keith
B9117

A95
365
MEIKLE BALLOCH
River Isla
Inverkeith

338
HILL OF TOWIE
A96
267
Ruthven
Bogniebrae
B9001
Forgue

372
KNOCKAN
B9014
Keith & Dufftown Railway
Cairnie
B9022
A97
Glendro
3
256

gieknockater
B9115
Drummuir
Huntly Falconry Centre
Nordic Ski Centre
Castle
Affleck
Drumblade

iddich
B9014
A920
Milltown of Auchindoun
14
Huntly
Strath Bogie
A96
Brideswell
4

Balvenie Castle
Haugh of Glass
Bridgend
Kirkstile
Thomastown

ktown Mortlach
Auchindoun Castle
5
Culdrain
Hillhead
Bainshole

503
CÀRN CHROM
A941
525
Gartly Moor
419
WISHACH HILL
466
HILL OF FOUNDLAND
Glens of Foundland
5 Co

440
CRANSMILL HILL
Kirkney
Gartly
A97
Largie

Bridgend
Leith Hall
Picardy Symbol Stone
Insch

564
TAP O' NOTH
Mains of Lesmoir
Kennethmont
Dunnideer
B9002

571
ROUND HILL
18
Cabrach
Belhinnie
A941
Rhynie
Cottown
Clatt
Duncanstone
256
Leslie

Aldivalloch
Aldunie
A97
B9992

B9002
484
MIRE OF MIDGATES
Lethenty
7

722
THE BUCK
St Mary's Kirk (Ruin)
5
Lumsden
475
BRUX HILL
CORREEN HILLS

629
ILL OF THREE STONES
632
CREAG AN EUNAN
A944
Mossat
6
Tullynessle
Scotsmill
Bridge of Alford
Keig
Montgarrie
8

nyon
Rinmore
Kildrummy Castle
Kildrummy
Milltown
Haughton
Alford Valley

Belnacraig
A97
Kirkton of Glenbuchat
Glenbuchat Castle
10
243
H
Glenkindie
J
Sinnahard
244 K
A944
Grampian Transport
M **Alford**
A980 **L**
Whitehouse **M**

Bellabeg
Muir of
Kirkton of Tough

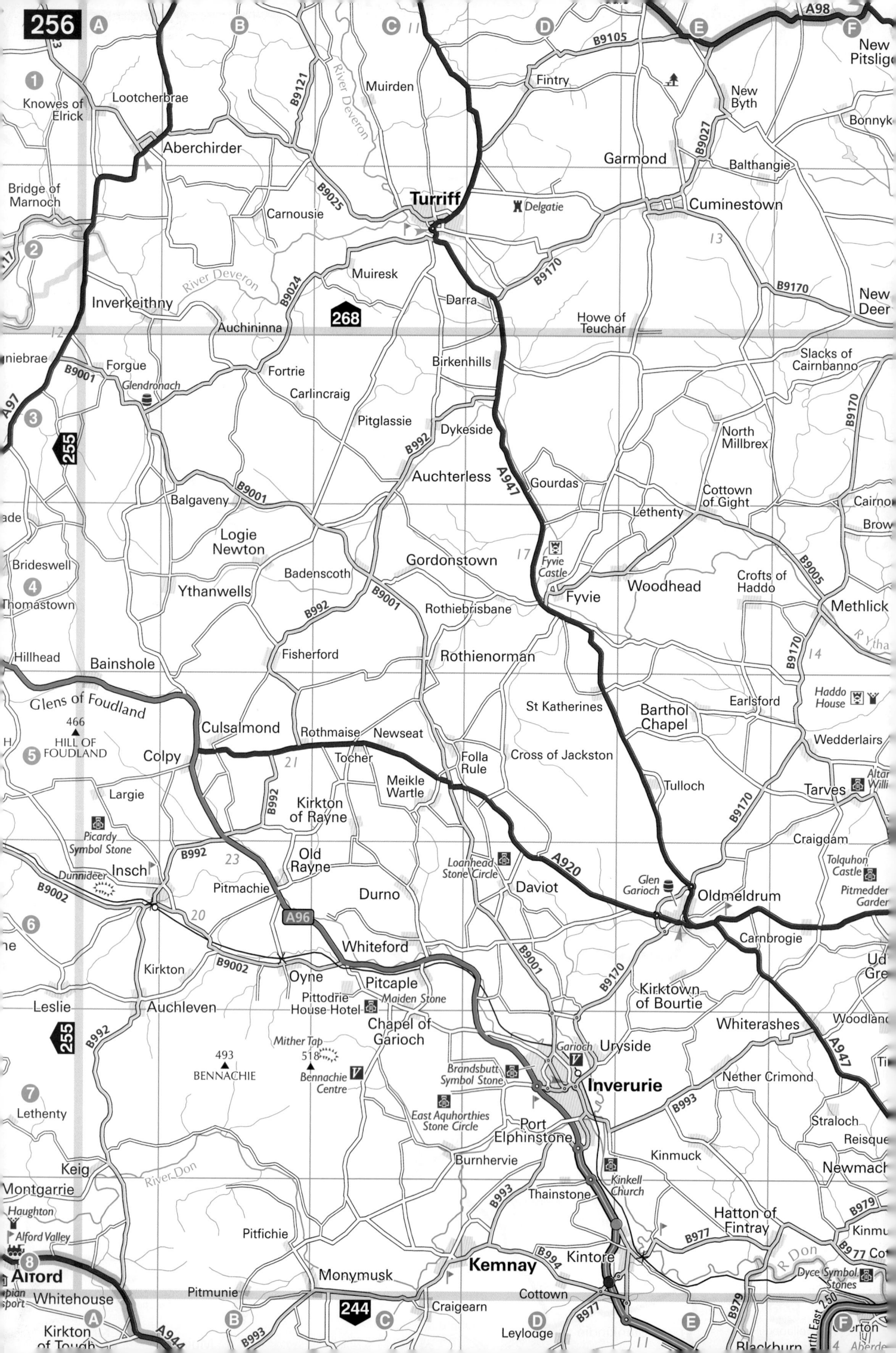

Crimond
Blackhill
North East 250
St Fergus
Scotstown Head

Strichen
WAUGHTON HILL
New Leeds
Leys
Backfolds
Kirktown
Rora
Denhead
Fetterangus
Maud
Deer Abbey
Dunshillock
Mintlaw
Longside
Inverugie
Buchanhaven
Peterhead
Old Deer
Railway
Inverquhomery
Peterhead
Arbuthnot
Blackhill of Clackriach
Stuartfield
Drymuir
Bulwark
Millbreck
Nether Kinmundy
Hillhead of Cocklaw
Peterhead Bay
Prison
Invernettie
Nethermuir
Clola
Boddam
Kinnadie
Blackhill
Stirling
Auchnagatt
Lendrum Terrace
Buchan Ness
Inkhorn
Kinknockie
Ardallie
Longhaven
Coldwells
Hatton
Auchiries
Bullers of Buchan
Arthrath
Muirtack
North Haven
Slains
Toll of Birness
Bogbrae
Cruden Bay
Birness
Chapel Hill
Bay of Cruden
Ythanbank
Whinnyfold
The Skares
Artrochie
Kinharrachie
Ellon
Kirkton of Logie Buchan
Kirktown of Slains
Esslemont
Collieston
nedden
Logierieve
Forvie
usieside
Udny Station
Newburgh
Cultercullen
Foveran
Delfrigs
Causeyend
seat
Whitecairns
Belhelvie
Balmedie
Potterton
245
Blackdog

0 ... 5 miles
0 ... 8 kilometres

A · B · C · D · E · F

1
2
3
4
5
6
7
8

The Little Minch

Fladda-chùain

Rubha Hu

An Tairbeart
(Tarbert)

Lùb Score

Borneskitaig
Kilmuir
Kilva
Balgown
Kilv
Li

Loch nam Madadh
(Lochmaddy)

Totscore

Rubha Bhatairnis

Idrigill

Uig Bay

Ascrib
Islands

283 ▲
BEN
GEARY

Geary

Loch Snizort

A87
16

Trumpan

Gillen

Earlish

Ardmore
Point

Hallin

Waternish

DUNVEGAN
HEAD

Isay   Mingay

Stein   Lusta

Loch
Bay

214 ▲
BEN
DIUBAIG

Greshornish

Loch Greshornish

Loch Snizo
K

Boreraig

Claigan

Bay

327 ▲
BEINN
BHREAC

B886

Upperglen

Flashader

Treaslane

22

A850

Loch Dunvegan

Uig

Loch
Pooltiel

Feriniquarrie

Totaig

Edinbane   Bernisdal

Oisgill
Bay

Glendale   Glasphein

Milovaig

B884

Colbost

🏰 *Dunvegan*

A850

ISLE OF

Lephin

Colbost Croft Ⓜ

Waterstein

Skinidin

Ⓜ *Giant Angus MacAskill*
Kilmuir

Dunvegan

Neist
Point

Lonmore

Caroy River

265 ▲
BEN
AKETIL

271 ▲
CRUACHAN BEINN
A' CHEARCAILL

SKYE

Moonen Bay

Duirnish

Roskhill

Ramasaig

469 ▲
HEALAVAL
MORE

Roag

Orbost

Vatten

Hoe
Rape

Loch Caroy

A863

Glen Ose

Ose

488 ▲
HEALAVAL
BHEAG

Harlosh

Hoe Point

368 ▲
BEINN NA

246

Harlosh
Island

Colbost
Point

*Dun
Beag*

Bracadale

Ⓓ Tarner
Island

Ⓔ

Ⓕ

St

Coillore

0 1 2 3 4 5 miles
0 1 2 3 4 5 6 7 8 kilometres

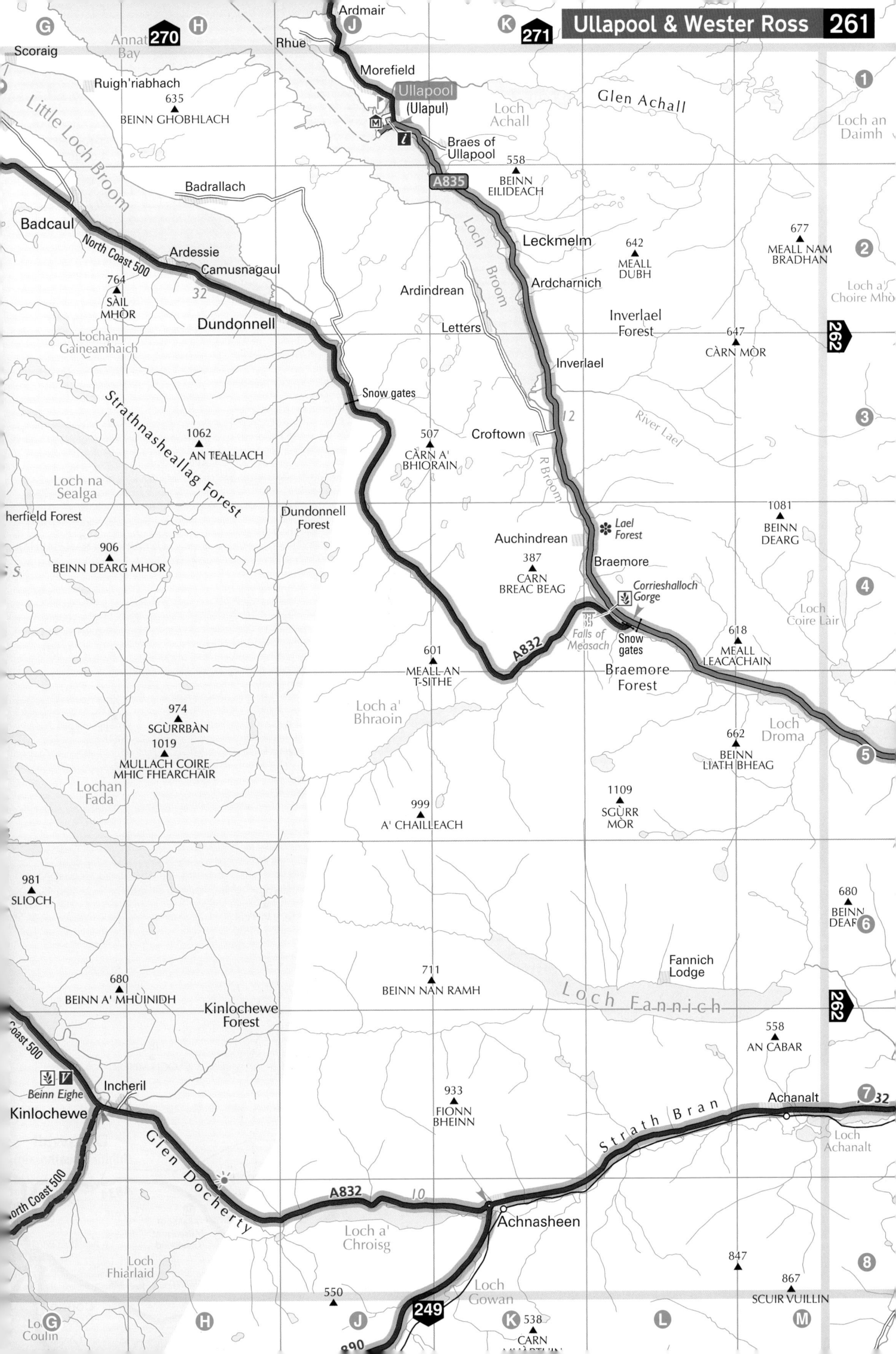

G 270 H J K 271 1

Scoraig
Annat Bay
Ardmair
Rhue
Morefield
Ullapool
(Ulapul)
Loch Achall
Glen Achall
Loch an Daimh

Ruigh'riabhach
635 ▲ BEINN GHOBHLACH

Braes of Ullapool
A835
558 ▲ BEINN EILIDEACH

Badrallach
Leckmelm
642 ▲ MEALL DUBH
677 ▲ MEALL NAM BRADHAN
2
Loch a' Choire Mhò

Badcaul
North Coast 500
Ardessie
Camusnagaul
32
Ardcharnich
Ardindrean
Inverlael Forest
647 ▲ CÀRN MÒR
262

764 ▲ SÀIL MHÒR
Dundonnell
Letters
Inverlael

Lochan Gaineamhaich
Strathnasheallag Forest
Snow gates
507 ▲ CÀRN A' BHIORAIN
Croftown
River Lael
R Broom
12
3

Loch na Sealga
1062 ▲ AN TEALLACH
Dundonnell Forest
1081 ▲ BEINN DEARG

...herfield Forest
906 ▲ BEINN DEARG MHOR
Auchindrean
387 ▲ CARN BREAC BEAG
Braemore
Lael Forest
Corrieshalloch Gorge
4
Loch Coire Làir
Loch...

A832
Falls of Measach
Snow gates
618 ▲ MEALL LEACACHAIN

601 ▲ MEALL-AN T-SITHE
Braemore Forest

Loch a' Bhraoin
974 ▲ SGÙRRBÀN
1019 ▲ MULLACH COIRE MHIC FHEARCHAIR
Loch Droma
662 ▲ BEINN LIATH BHEAG
5

Lochan Fada
999 ▲ A' CHAILLEACH
1109 ▲ SGÙRR MÒR

981 ▲ SLIOCH
680 ▲ BEINN DEAR...
6

711 ▲ BEINN NAN RAMH
Fannich Lodge
Loch Fannich

680 ▲ BEINN A' MHÙINIDH
Kinlochewe Forest
262

558 ▲ AN CABAR

Beinn Eighe
Incheril
933 ▲ FIONN BHEINN
Strath Bran
Achanalt
7 32

Kinlochewe
Glen Docherty
A832
10
Achnasheen
847 ▲
Loch Achanalt

Loch Fhiarlaid
Loch a' Chroisg
249
Loch Gowan
867 ▲ SCUIR VUILLIN
8

Lo... Coulin
G H J K 538 ▲ CARN... L M

North Coast 500

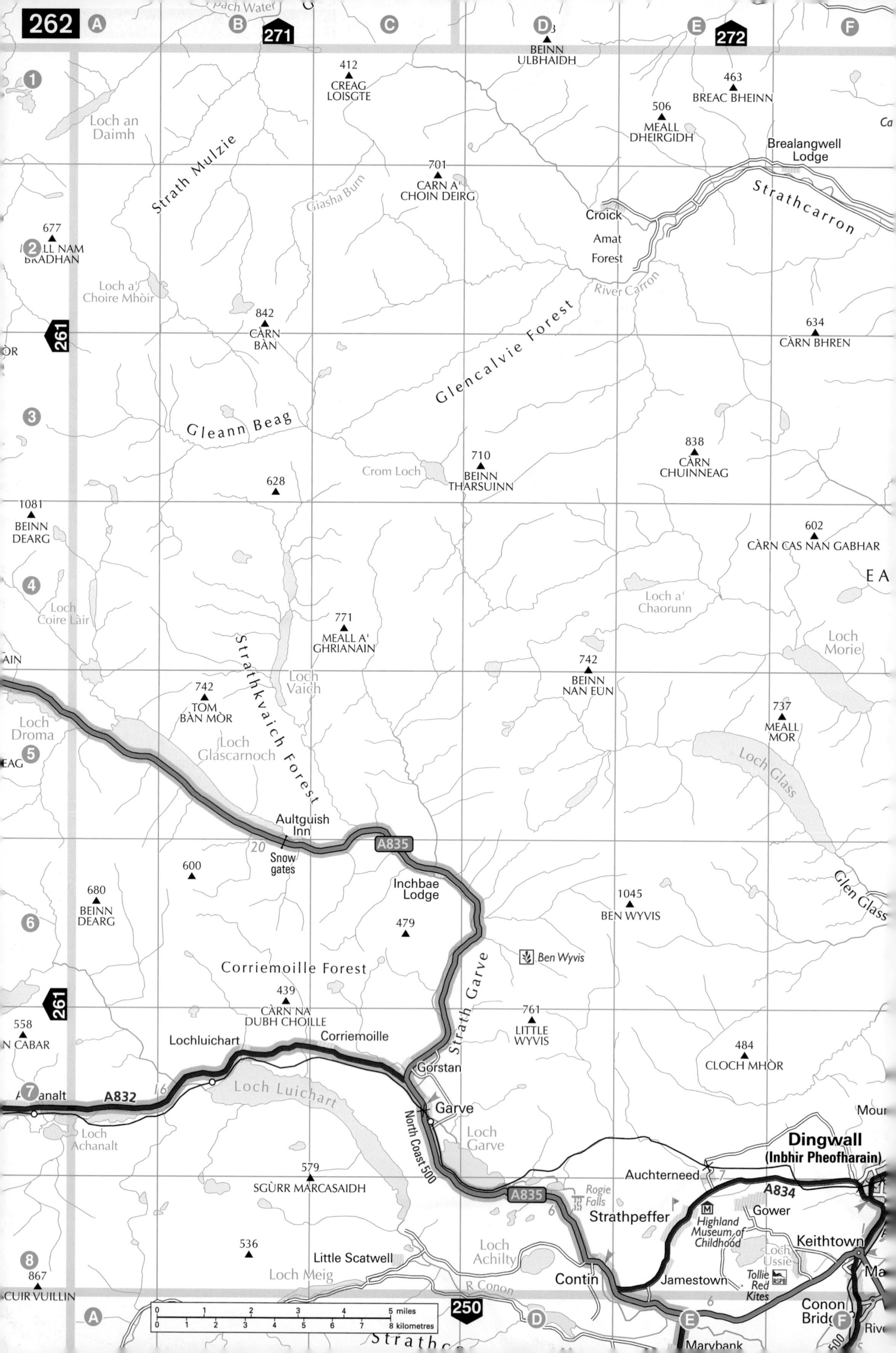

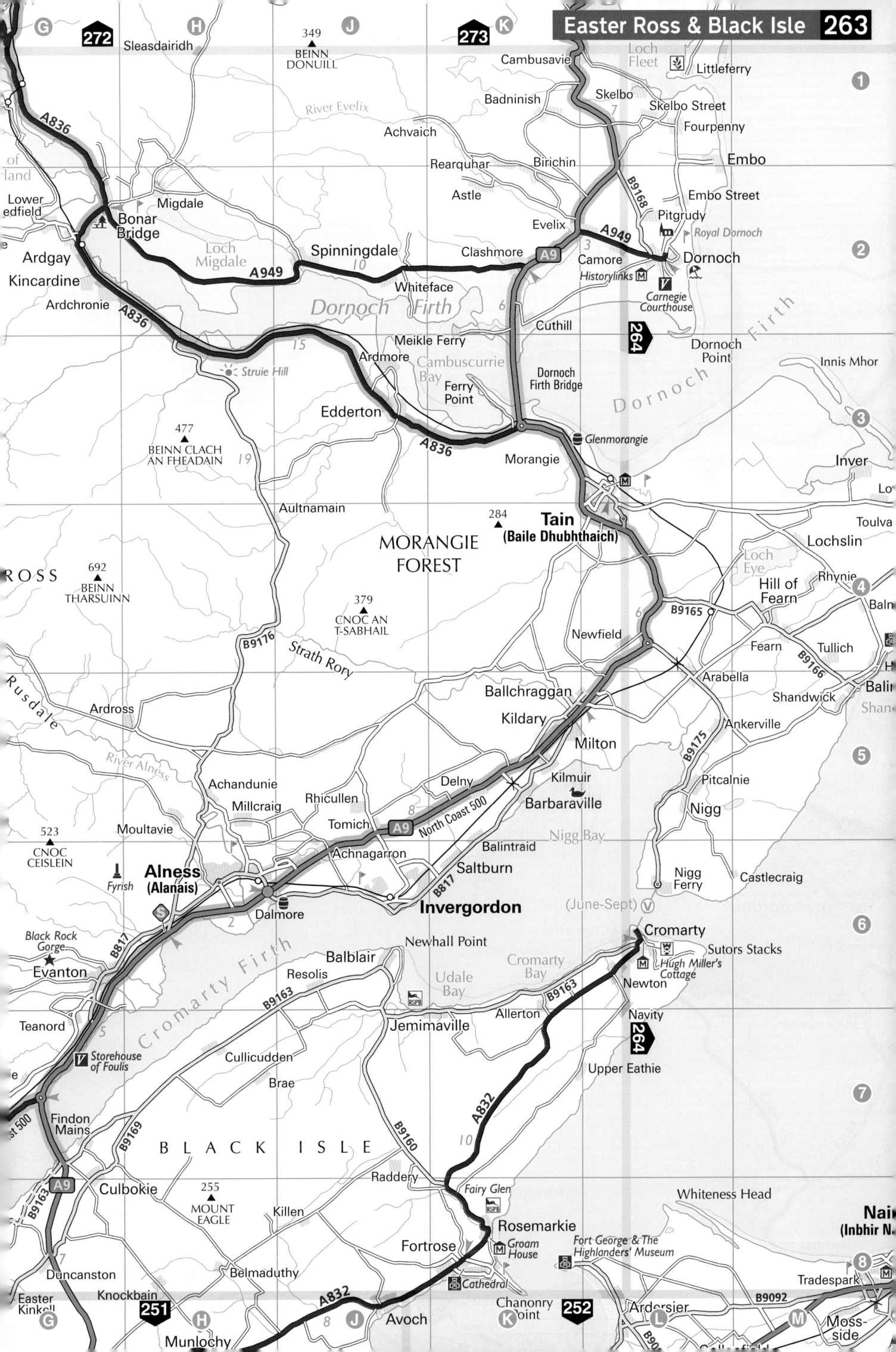

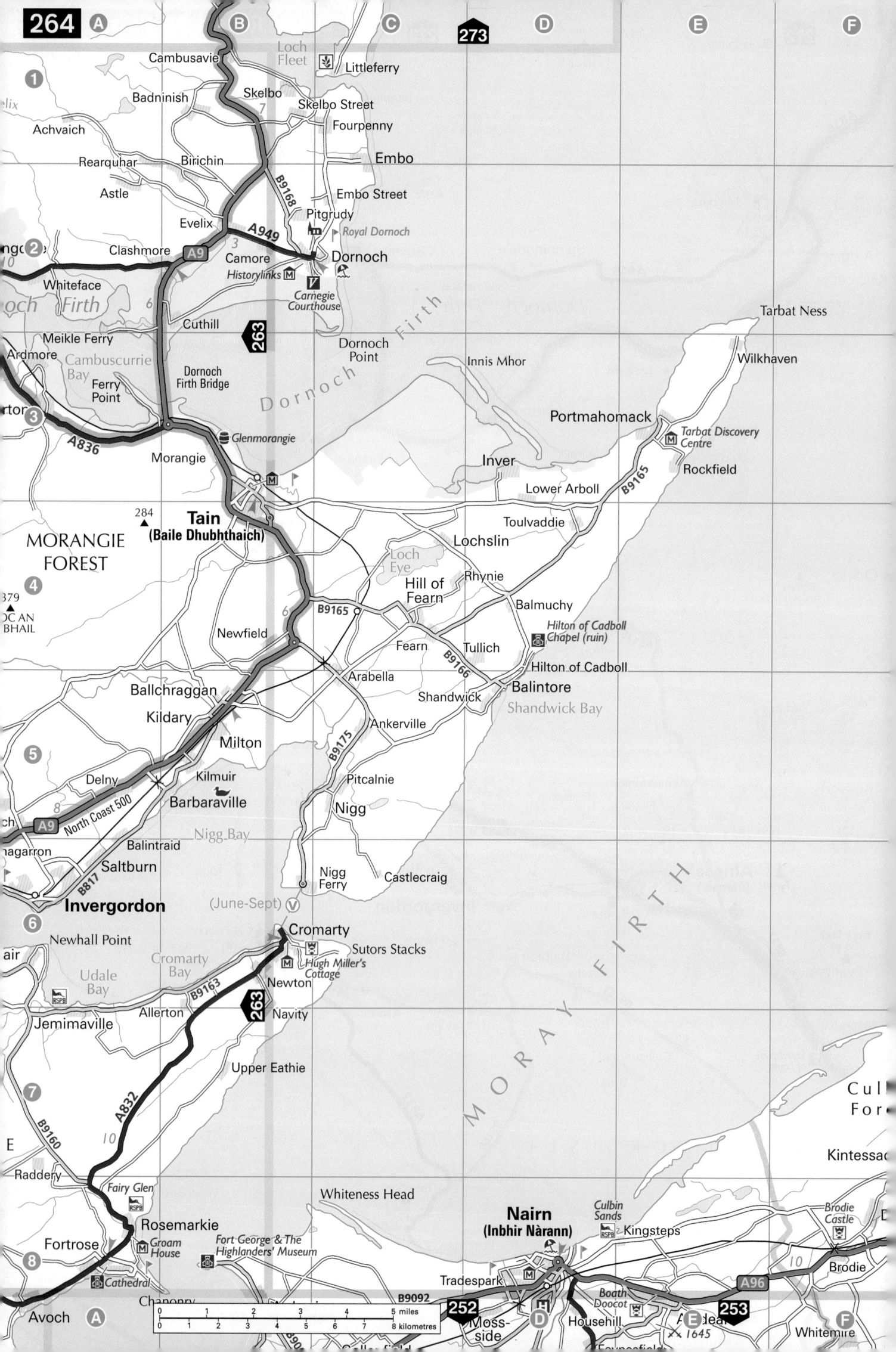

G H J K L

1
2
3
4
5
6
7
8

Fisheries & Community

Branderburgh

Stotfield

Lossiemouth

Seatown

B9040

Burghead Well

Hopeman

Burghead

Burnside

Duffus

St Peter's Kirk & Parish Cross

B9012

Cummingston

Roseisle

B9013

B9012

Duffus Castle

Loch Spynie

6

B9135

A941

Spynie Palace

B9103

Stonewells

Lochill

King on S

Burghead Bay

College of Roseisle

Quarrywood

Viewfield

Calcots

Innesmill

Findhorn

Hempriggs

B9089

Newton

Bishopmill

Elgin

Urquhart

A96

B9011

Kinloss

Coltfield

Glen Moray

New Elgin

Lhanbryde

The Lochs

Findhorn Bay

Alves

Linkwood

9

corth ouse

Grange Hall

266

Kilbuiack

12

Muir of Miltonduff

A96

Mosstodloc

Crofts of Dipple

eno's Stone

Falconer

Clackmarras

B9103

Forres

Pluscarden

Longmorn

Orbliston

B9013

Rafford

Califer

Barnhill

Thomshill

Fogwatt

Millbuies

Inchberry

8

Dallas Dhu Distillery

253

B9010

Kellas

Shougle

L Glen

M

G H J K

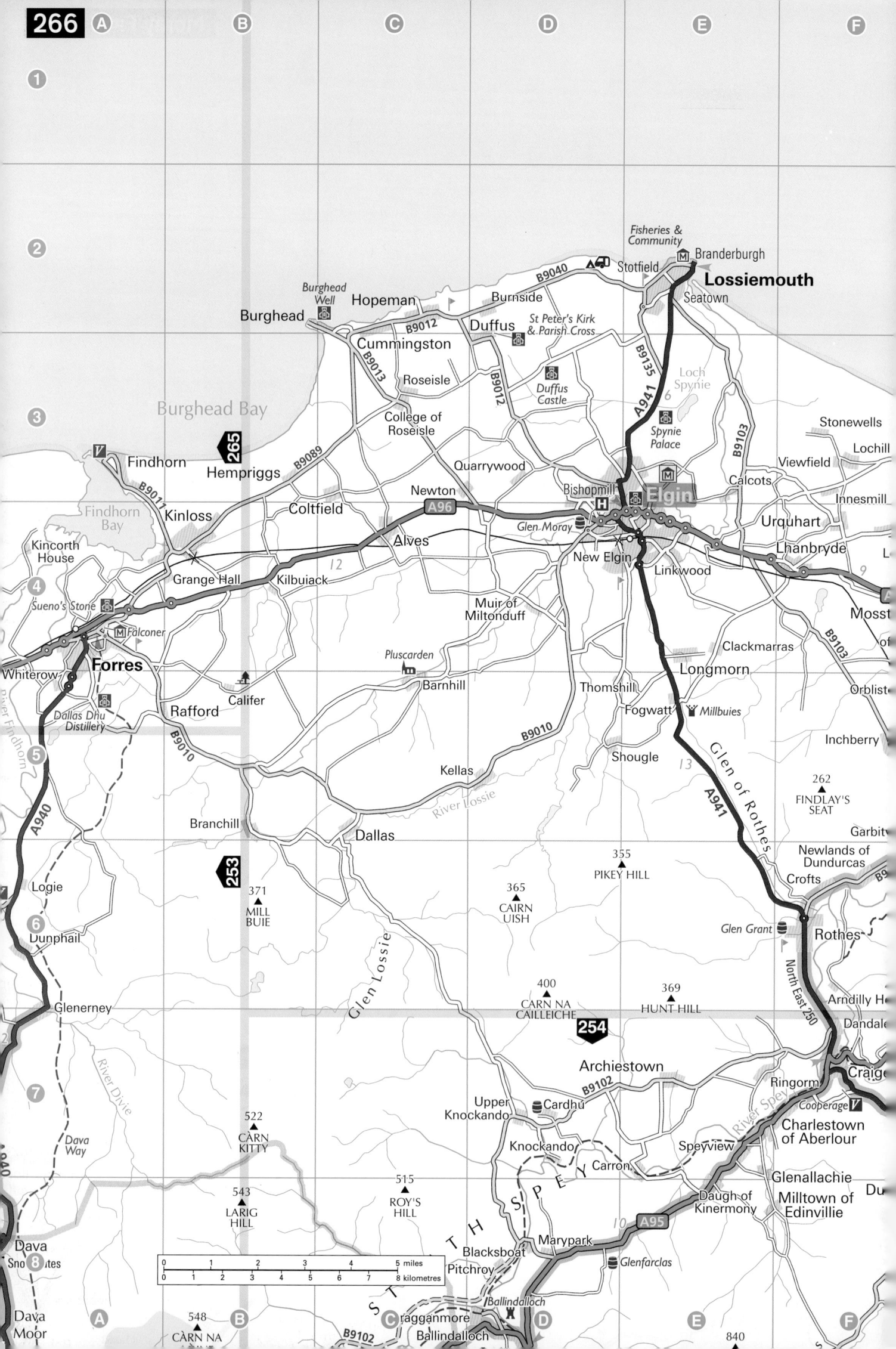

G   H   J   K   L

Spey Bay

Scottish Dolphin Centre
Spey Bay
Moray Firth

Portknockie
Findochty   ★ Bow-Fiddle-Rock
A942   Cullen Bay
North East 250   Cullen
Portessie   Lintmill   Findlater   Sandend Bay
Buckie   Sandend   Portsoy
Buckpool   A98   Birkenbog   B9139
Rathven   Tochieneal   North Ea
Fishing A98 12   Fordyce
Nether Dallachy   Milton   Boync
A990 Portgordon
Upper Dallachy   321   Kirktown of
Bogmoor   BIN OF   Deskford
B9104   Newton   CULLEN   Deskford
Broadley   Drybridge   Church   Windsole
Stynie   Auchenhalrig   Women's Land   Berryhillock
C Bridge   Army Scotland
of Tynet   Clochan   B9022
Gordon Castle   272   Cornhill
Fochabers   ADDIE   Craibstone   B9025
Dipple   HILL   B9018 12
Ordiequish   264 Braes of Enzie   313   A95
WHITEASH   301   LURG   Gordonstown   B9023
A96 Forgie   HILL   MILLSTONE HILL   HILL   268
250   429   Glenbarry
THIEF'S HILL   Grange   Berryhillock KNOCK 20   271   Knowes of
Sound Aultmore   Crossroads   HILL   WETHER   Lootcher
Muir   Forgieside   Bracobrae   HILL Knock
Upper Mulben   Newmill B9017   Davoch   Drumnagorrach   Bridge of
Rumbach   of Grange   Marnoch
A103 Mulben   Strathisla I s l a A95 Farmtown B9022
Deanshaugh   Fife Keith   B9117   Milltown of
Tauchers   Rosarie   t h a   Rothiemay B9117
A95   **Keith**   365   Inverkeithn
338   MEIKLE   River Isla
HILL OF TOWIE   BALLOCH   Bogniebrae
372   S   Ruthven   B9001
KNOCKAN   Keith &   t   Forgue
ieknockater Dufftown   r   255   Cairnie   B9022   Glendro
Railway   B9115   a   A97
Drummuir   t   Nordic Ski
h   Huntly   Centre Castle
B9014   Falconry   Affleck   Drumblade
Balvenie   Milltown of   A920   Centre   **Huntly**
Castle   Auchindoun 14   A96
wn   Haugh   Brideswell
rtlach   Auchindoun   of Glass   Strath Bogie Thomastown
Castle   Legend   A96
Hillhead

G   H   J   K   L   M

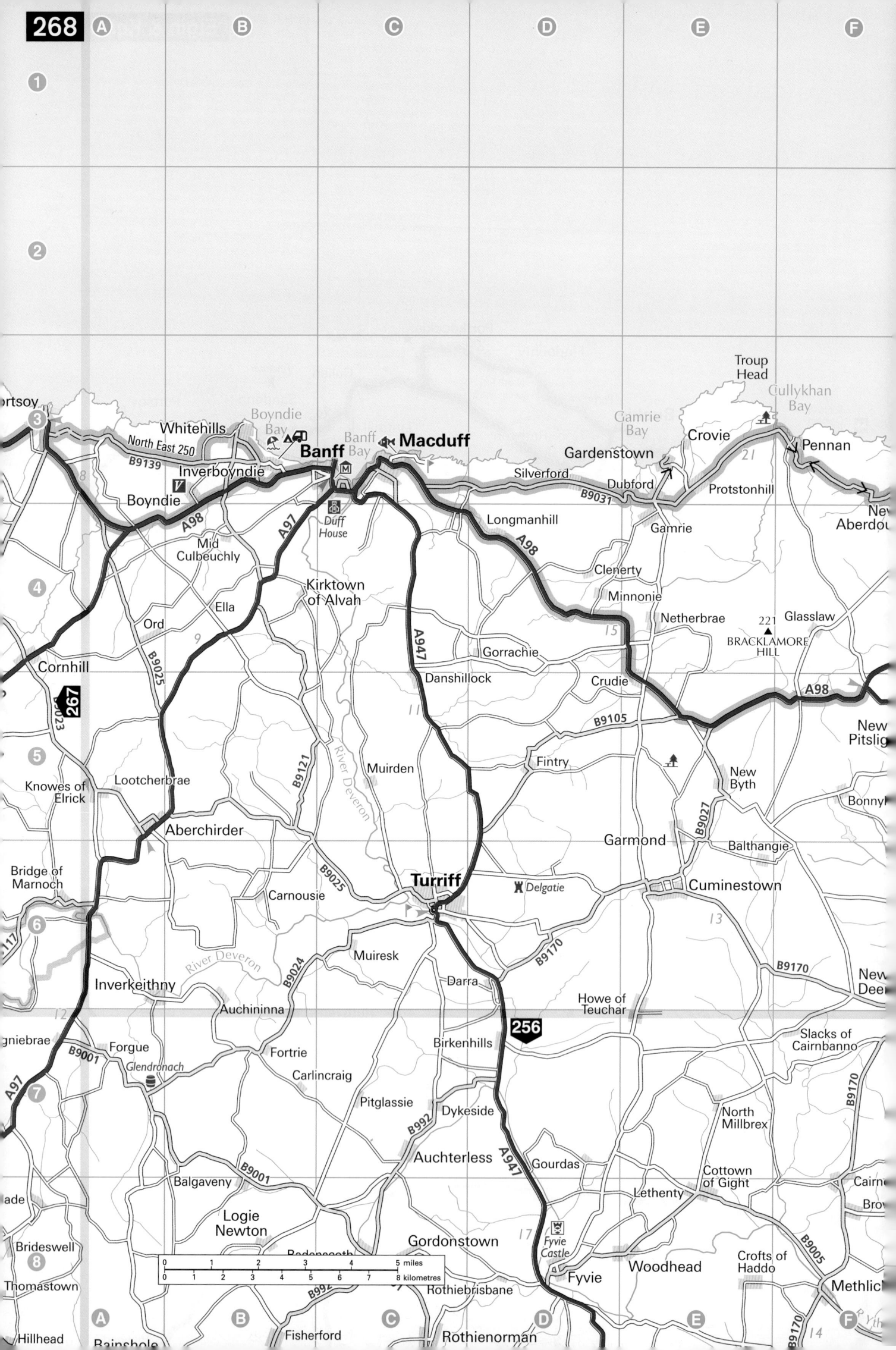

G   H   J   K

1

2

3

4

5

6

7

8

Rosehearty   Pittulie
B9031   Sandhaven   Castle, Lighthouse & Museum   Kinnaird Head
Pitsligo   Fraserburgh
igiefold   Peathill   Kirktown   Fraserburgh Bay
Percyhorner   Pitblae   Cairnbulg   Inverallochy
B9031   Coburby   Maggie's Hoosie   Whitelinks Bay
250   Mid Ardlaw   A90   B9033   St Combs
dlie   Tyrie   B9032   Memsie
A98   10   Rathen   Crofts of Savoch
Memsie Cairn   Lonmay
B9032   Newburgh   A981   RSPB   Loch of Strathbeg   Rattray Head
234   WAUGHTON HILL   12   Crimond
A952   North East 250   Blackhill
B9093   Strichen   18
New Leeds   Leys   Kirktown   St Fergus
B9093   Scotstown Head
Denhead   Backfolds   A90
Fetterangus   Rora
A981   A950   River Ugie
6   Deer Abbey   Dunshillock   Inverugie
Maud   B9106   Buchanhaven   V   Peterhead
B9029   Railway   B9029   Old Deer   Mintlaw   Longside   H   Peterhead   Arbuthnot
Blackhill of Clackriach   A950   Inverquhomery   9   A982   Peterhead Bay
Drymuir   Bulwark   Stuartfield   257   M   Prison
Nethermuir   Millbreck   Nether Kinmundy   Hillhead of Cocklaw   Invernettie
B9030   Kinnadie   Clola   Boddam
Auchnagatt   Blackhill   Stirling   Buchan Ness
12   Kinknockie   Lendrum Terrace
Inkhorn   Ardallie   Longhaven
A948   Coldwells   A952   A90   Bullers of Buchan
Hatton   Auchiries   North Haven
Arthrath   Muirtack   14   Slains   L   M
J   17   K   Cruden Bay

A B C D E F

1

Point of Stoer

Old Man
of Stoer

OLDANY
ISLAND

Eddrach
Bay

Culkein

Culkein
Drumbeg

Clashnessie
Bay

Achnacarnin

Oldany

Drumbeg

2

Clashmore

Nedd

Clashnessie

Loch
Poll

Stoer

B869

Loch
Beanna

North Coast 500

Clachtoll

3

Bay of Clachtoll

Rhicarn

Achmelvich
Bay

A837

Achmelvich

Baddidarrach

Lochinver

Soyea Island

Loch Inver

Assyn

4

Strathan

Inverkirkaig

River Kirkaig

Fionn
Loch

Rubha
Còigeach

Eilean Mòr

Enard Bay

Rubha Mòr

5

Reiff

Achnahaird

Loch
Siònas

Altandhu

Eilean Mullagrach

Loch
Osgaig

Isle Ristol

612

Polbain

STAC POLLAIDH

Glas-leac Mòr

Badentarbet

Loch Bad
a' Ghaill

769

SUMMER ISLES

Achiltibuie

CÙL B

6

Loch
Lurgainn

Badentarbat
Bay

Polglass

Tanera
Beg

Ben Mor
Coigach

Steòrnabhagh
(Stornoway)

Tanera
Mòr

Horse
Island

Horse
Sound

COIGACH

743

Glas-leac Beag

BEN MORE
COIGACH

Eilean Dubh

Achduart

Priest
Island

Culnacraig

Strathcana

7

Greenstone
Point

Leac Dhonn

Isle
Martin

Strath

Cailleach Head

North Coast 500

Rubha Beag

Ardmair

8

Rhue

Mor ld

ellon
drigle

0   1   2   3   4   5 miles
0   1   2   3   4   5   6   7   8 kilometres

Scoraig

Annat
Bay

Ullap

A   P   D Ruigh'riabhach   E   F

635

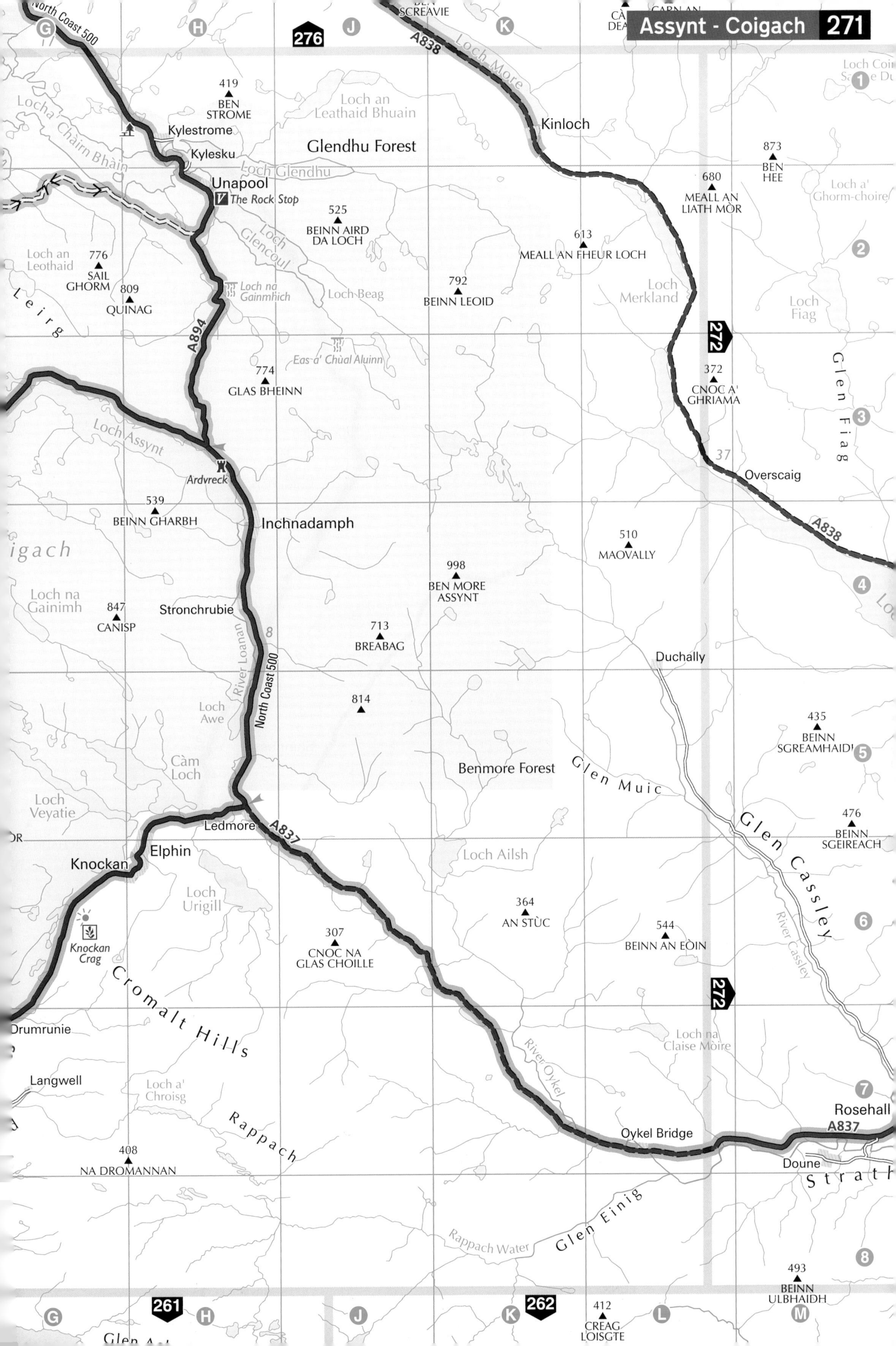

G North Coast 500

H

276 J

K

Loch More

A838

BEN SCREAVIE

CÀRNAN DEA...

CARNAN

Loch Coir Sa...le Du.. 1

419 ▲ BEN STROME

Loch an Leathaid Bhuain

Kinloch

873 ▲ BEN HEE

Loch a' Ghorm-choire

Kylestrome

Kylesku

Glendhu Forest

680 ▲ MEALL AN LIATH MÒR

Loch Glendhu

Unapool
V The Rock Stop

525 ▲ BEINN AIRD DA LOCH

613 ▲ MEALL AN FHEUR LOCH

2

Loch an Leothaid

776 ▲ SAIL GHORM

Loch Glencoul

Loch Beag

792 ▲ BEINN LEOID

Loch Merkland

Loch Fiag

809 ▲ QUINAG

Loch na Gainmhich

A894

272

Glen Fiag

Leirg

774 ▲ GLAS BHEINN

Eas-a' Chùal Aluinn

372 ▲ CNOC A' GHRIAMA

3

37

Loch Assynt

Overscaig

Ardvreck

539 ▲ BEINN GHARBH

Inchnadamph

igach

Loch na Gainimh

847 ▲ CANISP

Stronchrubie

510 ▲ MAOVALLY

A838

4

998 ▲ BEN MORE ASSYNT

North Coast 500

River Loanan

8

713 ▲ BREABAG

Duchally

435 ▲ BEINN SGREAMHAIDH

5

Loch Awe

814 ▲

Càm Loch

Benmore Forest

Glen Muic

Glen Cassley

476 ▲ BEINN SGEIREACH

Loch Veyatie

Ledmore A837

Loch Ailsh

River Cassley

6

Knockan

Elphin

364 ▲ AN STÙC

544 ▲ BEINN AN EÒIN

OR

Loch Urigill

307 ▲ CNOC NA GLAS CHOILLE

272

Knockan Crag

Cromalt Hills

Loch na Claise Mòire

7

Drumrunie

Rosehall A837

Langwell

Loch a' Chroisg

River Oykel

Oykel Bridge

Doune

Strath

Rappach

408 ▲ NA DROMANNAN

Glen Einig

Glen A...

Rappach Water

493 ▲ BEINN ULBHAIDH

412 ▲ CREAG LOISGTE

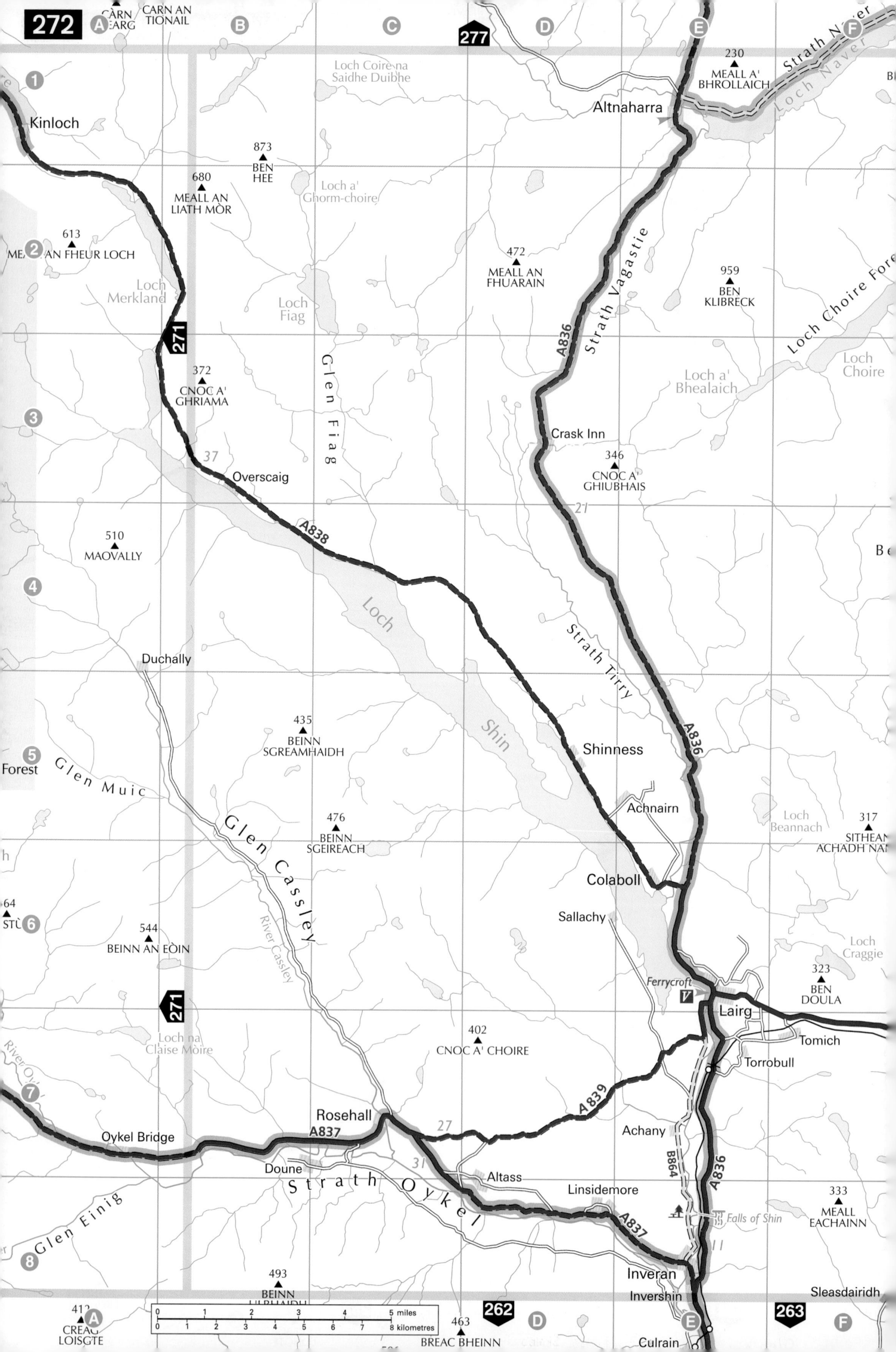

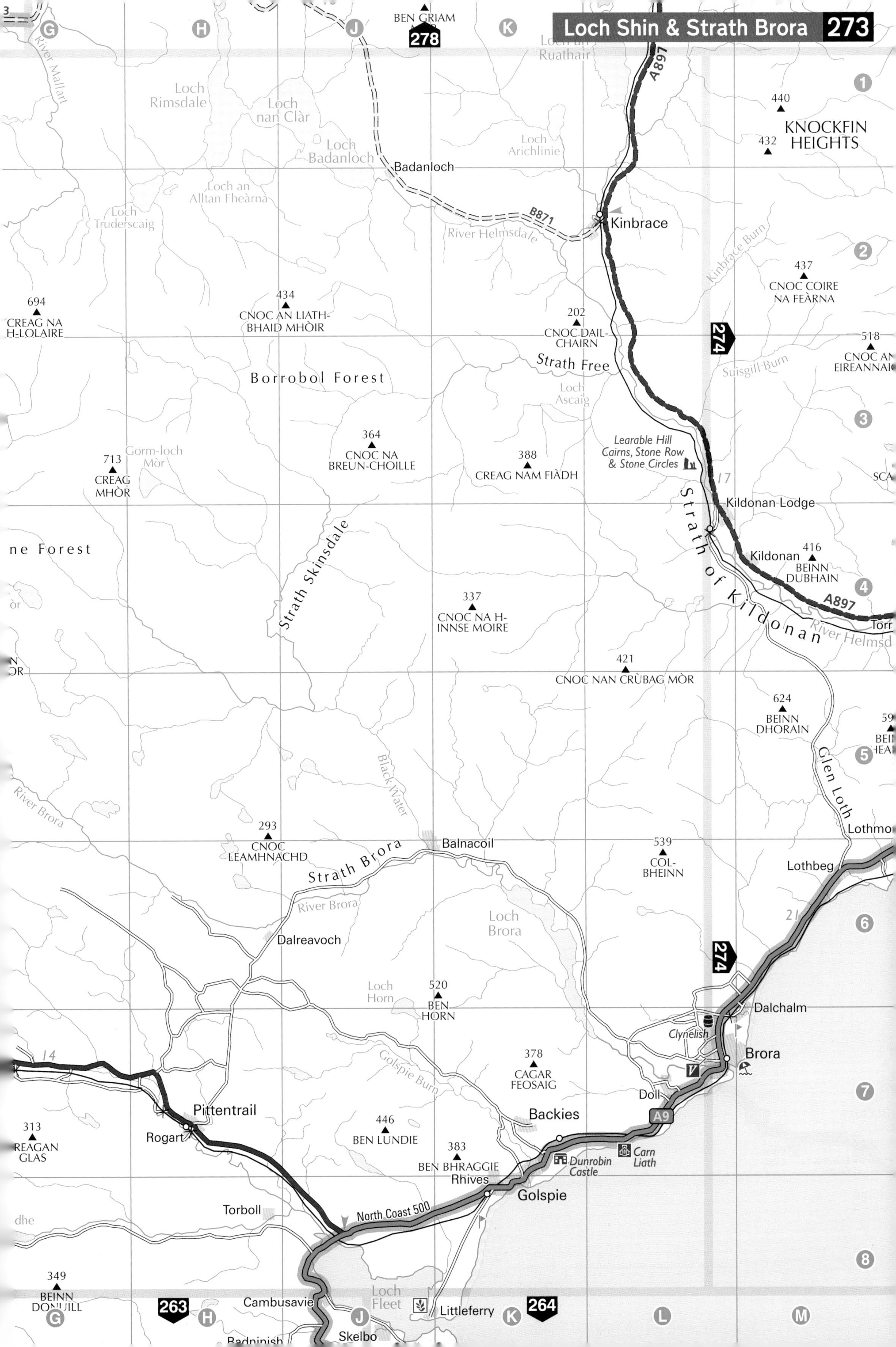

G   H   J   K

278

BEN GRIAM

Loch an
Ruathair

A897

1

440 ▲

Loch
Rimsdale

Loch
nan Clàr

**KNOCKFIN
HEIGHTS**

432 ▲

Loch
Badanloch

Badanloch

Loch
Arichlinie

B871

2

437 ▲
CNOC COIRE
NA FEÀRNA

River Helmsdale

Kinbrace

Loch an
Alltan Fheàrna

Loch
Truderscaig

694 ▲
CREAG NA
H-LOLAIRE

434 ▲
CNOC AN LIATH-
BHAID MHÒIR

202 ▲
CNOC DAIL-
CHAIRN

Strath Free

274

518 ▲
CNOC AN
EIREANNA

3

Borrobol Forest

Loch
Ascaig

Suisgill Burn

Gorm-loch
Mòr

364 ▲
CNOC NA
BREUN-CHOILLE

388 ▲
CREAG NAM FIÀDH

Learable Hill
Cairns, Stone Row
& Stone Circles

17

SCA

713 ▲
CREAG
MHÒR

Kildonan Lodge

ne Forest

òr

Strath Skinsdale

337 ▲
CNOC NA H-
INNSE MOIRE

Kildonan
BEINN
DUBHAIN

416 ▲

Strath of Kildonan

A897

Torr

River Helmsd

4

421 ▲
CNOC NAN CRÙBAG MÒR

624 ▲
BEINN
DHORAIN

59 ▲
BEI
HEA

5

River Brora

Black Water

293 ▲
CNOC
LEAMHNACHD

Balnacoil

539 ▲
COL-
BHEINN

Glen Loth

Lothmo

Lothbeg

Strath Brora

River Brora

Loch
Brora

21

6

Dalreavoch

Loch
Horn

520 ▲
BEN
HORN

274

Dalchalm

Clynelish

Brora

Doll

7

14

378 ▲
CAGAR
FEOSAIG

Backies

A9

Pittentrail

446 ▲
BEN LUNDIE

Carn
Liath

313 ▲
REAGAN
GLAS

Rogart

383 ▲
BEN BHRAGGIE
Rhives

Dunrobin
Castle

North Coast 500

Golspie

Torboll

dhe

349 ▲
BEINN
DONUILL

263

264

8

Cambusavie

Loch
Fleet

Littleferry

Badninish

Skelbo

G   H   J   K   L   M

A B C D 279 E F

348
BEN
ALISKY

1

264
CNOCAN
CONACHREAG

Loch an
Ruathair

Loch
ichlinie

Glutt Water

Glutt Lodge

440
KNOCKFIN
HEIGHTS

432

Dunbeath Wat

317
CNOC LOCH
MHADADH

B871
Kinbrace

2

273

437
CNOC COIRE
NA FEÀRNA

Berriedale Water

484
MAIDEN
PAP

Braemore

Knocka

Ramscra

202
CNOC-DAIL-
CHAIRN

Strath Free

518
CNOC AN
EIREANNAICH

705
MORVEN

626
SCARABEN

Loch
Ascaig

3

Langwell Forest

Newport

88
ÀM FIÀDH

Learable Hill
Cairns, Stone Row
& Stone Circles

Strath of Kildonan

17

554
CREAG
SCALABSDALE

20

Langwell
House

Berried

Kildonan Lodge

Kildonan

416
BEINN
DUBHAIN

A897

River Helmsdale

Torrish

401
CNOC NA
MAOILE

North Coast 500

A9

Badbea
Historic Village

4

421
CNOC NAN CRÙBAG MÒR

404
CREAG
THORARAIDH

Ord of Caithness

624
BEINN
DHORAIN

591
BEINN
MHEALAICH

Navidale
Timespan M

Snow gates

West
Helmsdale

East Helmsdale

Helmsdale

5

Gartymore

Portgower

Glen Loth

Lothmore

Lothbeg

539
COL-
BHEINN

21

6

273

Dalchalm

Clynelish

Brora

378
AGAR
OSA

7

V

Doll

Backies

A9

Carn
Liath

Dunrobin
Castle

Golspie

8

| 0 | 1 | 2 | 3 | 4 | 5 miles |
| 0 | 1 | 2 | 3 | 4 | 5 | 6 | 7 | 8 kilometres |

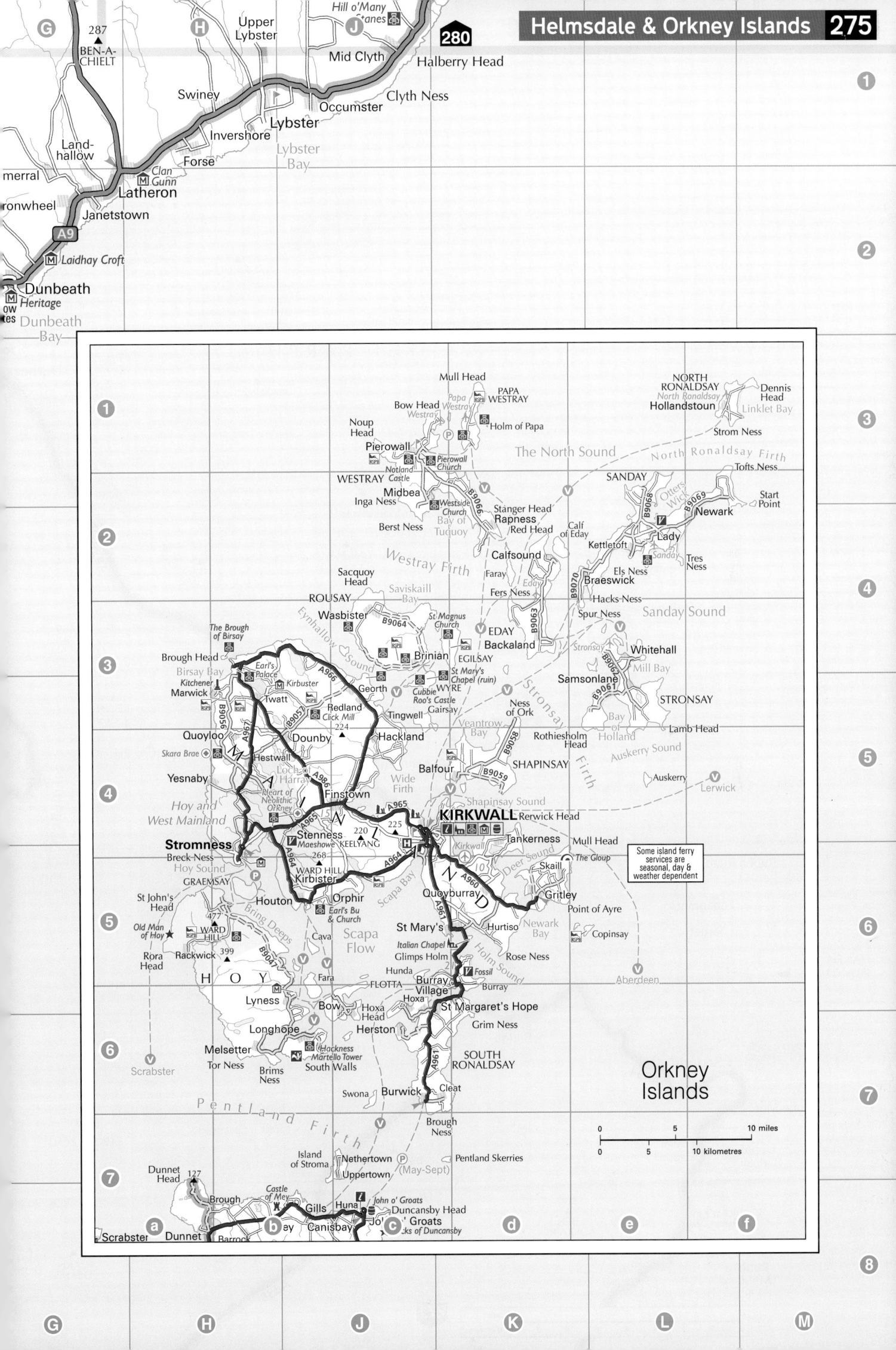

Orkney Islands

Some island ferry services are seasonal, day & weather dependent

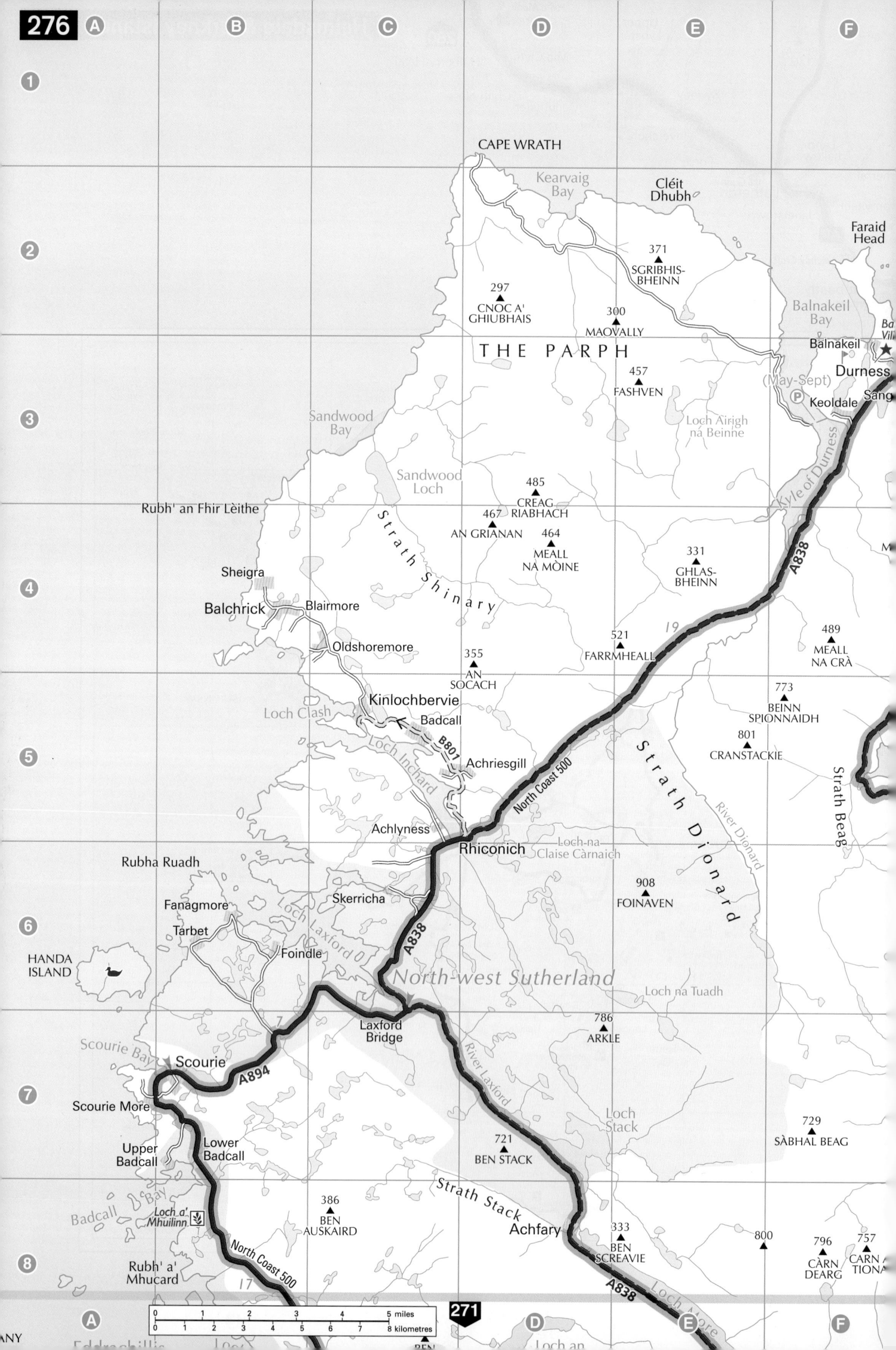

CAPE WRATH

Kearvaig
Bay

Cléit
Dhubh

Faraid
Head

371 ▲
SGRIBHIS-
BHEINN

Balnakeil
Bay

Ba
Vill

297 ▲
CNOC A'
GHIUBHAIS

300 ▲
MAOVALLY

T H E   P A R P H

Balnakeil

Durness

(May–Sept)

457 ▲
FASHVEN

Loch Àirigh
ná Beinne

Keoldale

Sang

Sandwood
Bay

Sandwood
Loch

Rubh' an Fhir Lèithe

485 ▲
CREAG
RIABHACH

467 ▲
AN GRIANAN

464 ▲
MEALL
NA MÒINE

331 ▲
GHLAS-
BHEINN

Sheigra

489 ▲
MEALL
NA CRÀ

Balchrick

Blairmore

521 ▲
FARRMHEALL

19

773 ▲
BEINN
SPIONNAIDH

Oldshoremore

355 ▲
AN
SOCACH

Kinlochbervie

801 ▲
CRANSTACKIE

Loch Clash

Badcall

B807

Loch Inchard

Achriesgill

North Coast 500

Strath Beag

Achlyness

Loch-na-
Claise Càrnaich

Rhiconich

Rubha Ruadh

Skerricha

908 ▲
FOINAVEN

Fanagmore

Tarbet

A838

Foindle

North-west Sutherland

Loch na Tuadh

HANDA
ISLAND

Loch Laxford

7

786 ▲
ARKLE

Laxford
Bridge

River Laxford

Scourie Bay

Scourie

A894

Loch
Stack

Scourie More

729 ▲
SÀBHAL BEAG

Upper
Badcall

Lower
Badcall

721 ▲
BEN STACK

Badcall
Bay

Loch a'
Mhuilinn

386 ▲
BEN
AUSKAIRD

Strath Stack

Achfary

333 ▲
BEN
SCREAVIE

800 ▲

796 ▲
CÀRN
DEARG

757 ▲
CARN
TIONA

North Coast 500

17

Rubh' a'
Mhucard

A838

Loch Mòre

| 0 | 1 | 2 | 3 | 4 | 5 miles |
| 0 | 1 2 3 4 | 5 6 7 | 8 kilometres |

A   B   C   D   E   F

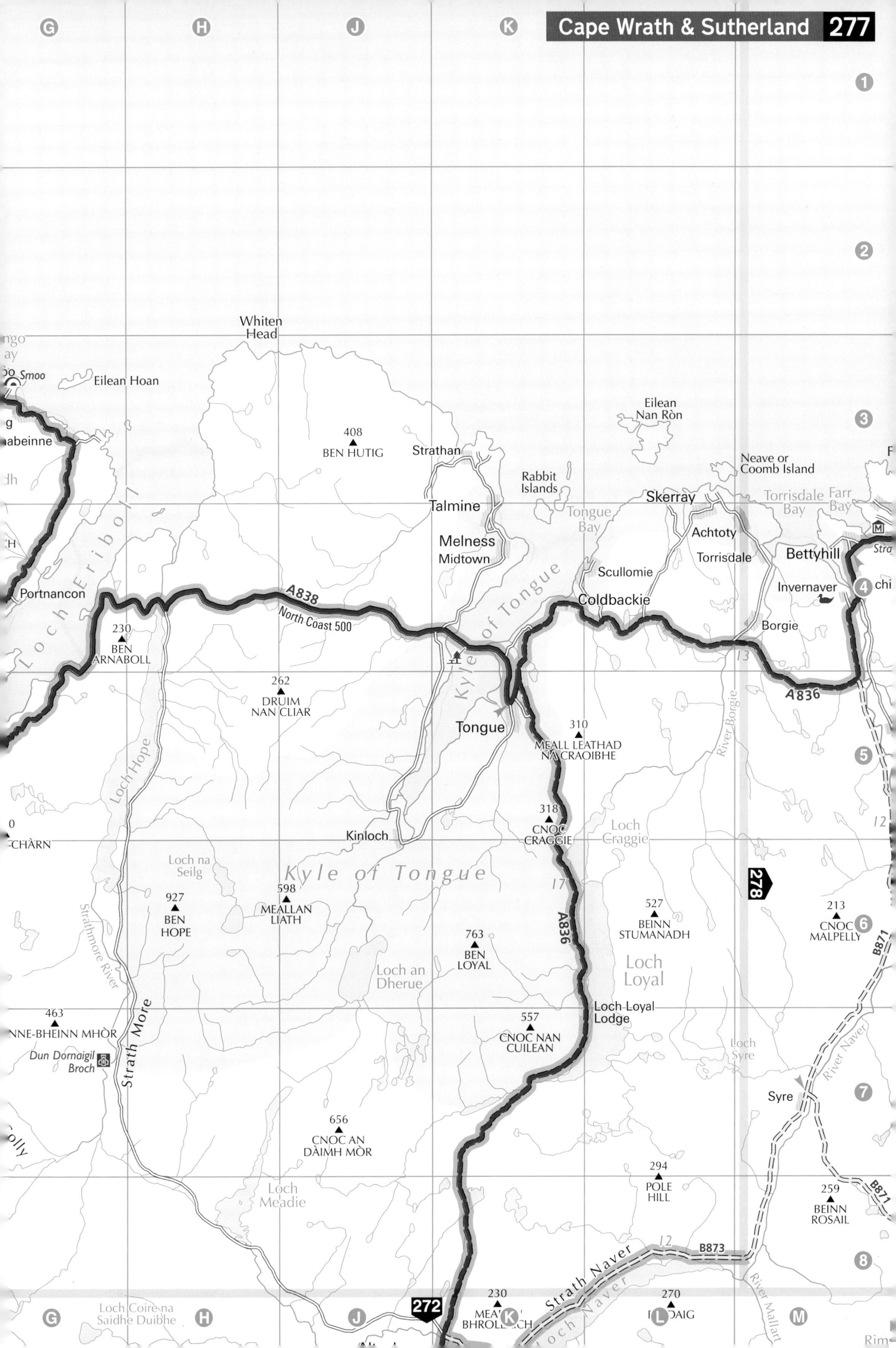

G   H   J   K

1
2
3
4
5
6
7
8

Whiten
Head

Smoo
Eilean Hoan

Portnancon

Loch Eriboll

408
▲
BEN HUTIG

Strathan

Rabbit
Islands

Talmine

Melness
Midtown

Tongue
Bay

Eilean
Nan Ròn

Neave or
Coomb Island

Skerray

Achtoty
Torrisdale

Scullomie

Torrisdale
Bay

Farr
Bay

Bettyhill

Invernaver

A838

North Coast 500

230
▲
BEN
ARNABOLL

262
▲
DRUIM
NAN CLIAR

Kyle of Tongue

Tongue

310
▲
MEALL LEATHAD
NA CRAOIBHE

Coldbackie

Borgie

13

A836

318
▲
CNOC
CRAGGIE

Loch
Craggie

278

213
▲
CNOC
MALPELLY

B871

Kinloch

Loch na
Seilg

Kyle of Tongue

927
▲
BEN
HOPE

598
▲
MEALLAN
LIATH

763
▲
BEN
LOYAL

Loch an
Dherue

17

A836

527
▲
BEINN
STUMANADH

Loch
Loyal

463
▲
NNE-BHEINN MHÒR

Dun Dornaigil
Broch

Strath More

Strathmore River

557
▲
CNOC NAN
CUILEAN

Loch-Loyal
Lodge

Loch
Syre

Syre

River Naver

Loch-
CHÀRN

656
▲
CNOC AN
DÀIMH MÒR

294
▲
POLE
HILL

259
▲
BEINN
ROSAIL

B871

Loch
Meadie

Strath Naver

12

B873

230
▲
MEA...
BHROLL...

270
▲
...DAIG

Strath Naver

River Mallart

Loch Coire na
Saidhe Duibhe

272

Loch Naver

G   H   J   K   L   M

Rim...

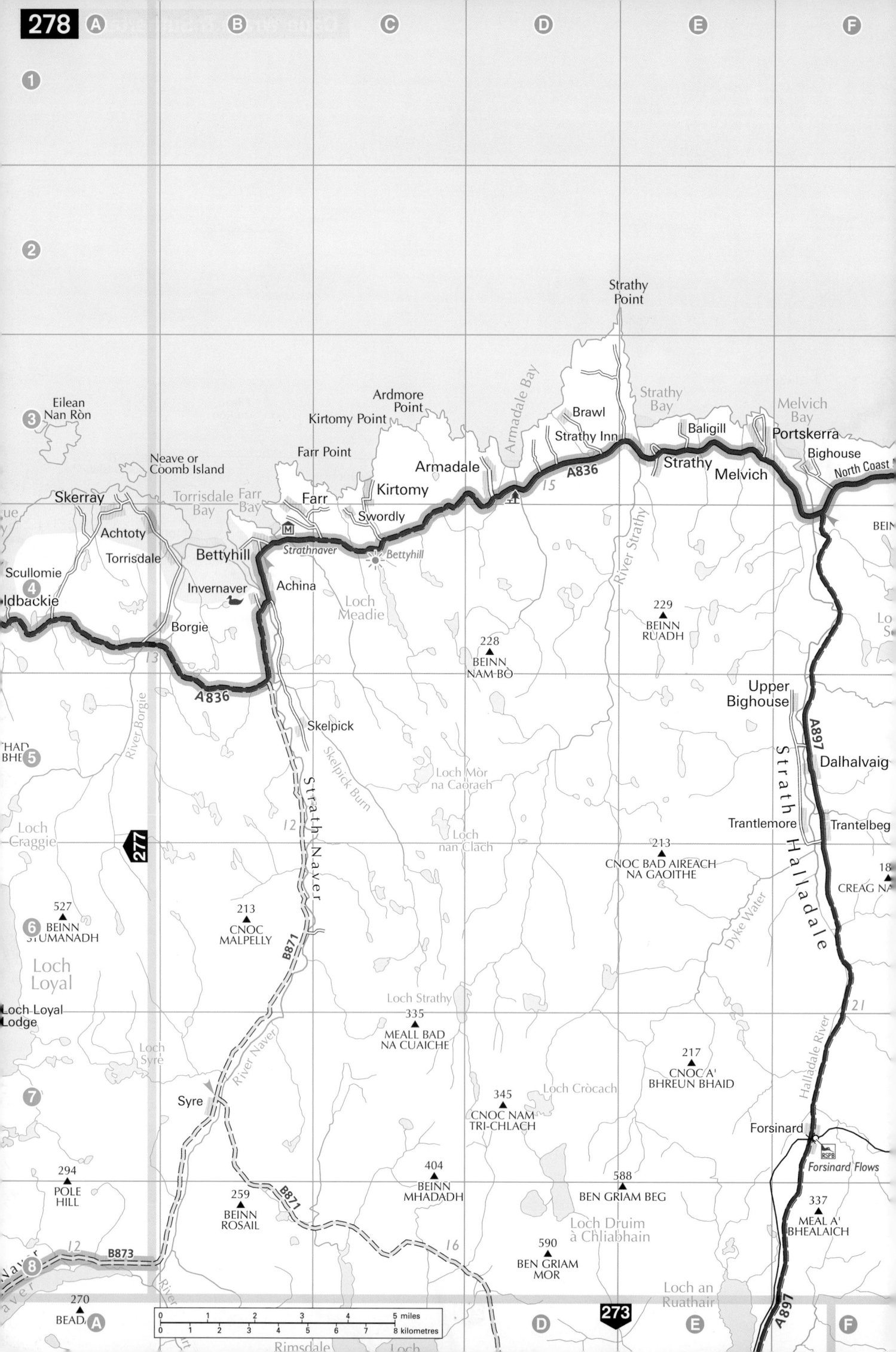

A B C D E F

Strathy Point

Eilean
Nan Ròn

Ardmore
Point
Kirtomy Point

Neave or
Coomb Island

Farr Point

Skerray

Achtoty

Torrisdale Farr
Bay Bay

Torrisdale

Scullomie

Idbackie

Borgie

Armadale Bay

Brawl
Strathy Inn

Baligill

Portskerra
Bighouse

Strathy   Melvich

North Coast

A836

15

Armadale

Kirtomy

Farr

Swordly

Bettyhill

Strathnaver

Bettyhill

Invernaver

Achina

Loch
Meadie

River Strathy

228
BEINN
NAM-BÒ

229
BEINN
RUADH

HAD
BHE

Loch
Craggie

A836

13

River Borgie

Skelpick

Skelpick Burn

Loch Mòr
na Caoraeh

Loch
nan Clach

Strath Naver

12

277

527
BEINN
STUMANADH

Loch
Loyal

213
CNOC
MALPELLY

B871

Upper
Bighouse

Dalhalvaig

Strath Halladale

A897

Trantlemore   Trantelbeg

213
CNOC BAD AIREACH
NA GAOITHE

18
CREAG NA

Dyke Water

Loch Loyal
Lodge

Loch
Syre

Syre

River Naver

Loch Strathy

335
MEALL BAD
NA CUAICHE

345
CNOC NAM
TRI-CHLACH

Loch Cròcach

217
CNOC A'
BHREUN BHAID

21

Forsinard

Forsinard Flows

RSPB

Halladale River

294
POLE
HILL

259
BEINN
ROSAIL

B871

404
BEINN
MHADADH

588
BEN GRIAM BEG

337
MEAL A'
BHEALAICH

12

River
Naver

B873

270
BEAD

16

590
BEN GRIAM
MOR

Loch Druim
à Chliabhain

Loch an
Ruathair

A897

273

Rimsdale   Loch

| 0 | 1 | 2 | 3 | 4 | 5 miles |
| 0 | 1 | 2 | 3 | 4 | 5 | 6 | 7 | 8 kilometres |

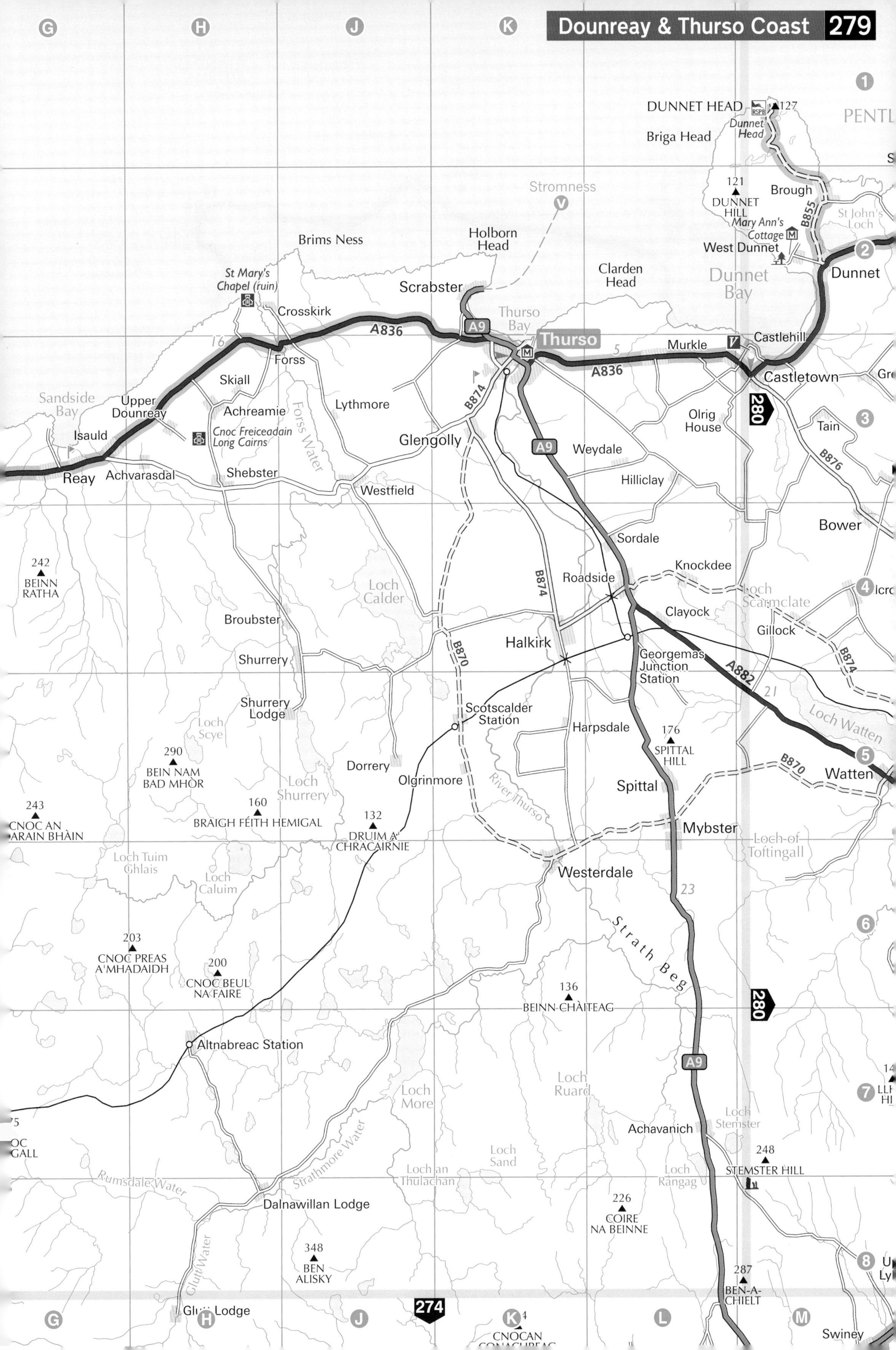

G | H | J | K

1

DUNNET HEAD ▲ 127
Briga Head
Dunnet
Head
PENTL

Stromness
V

121
▲ DUNNET
HILL
Mary Ann's
Cottage Ⓜ
West Dunnet

Brough

St John's
Loch
B855

Dunnet

2

Brims Ness

Holborn
Head

St Mary's
Chapel (ruin)
Crosskirk

Scrabster

Clarden
Head

Thurso
Bay

Thurso
Ⓜ

Murkle
V

Castlehill

A836
16
Forss

A9

5

Castletown
A836

280

Skiall

Sandside
Bay
Upper
Dounreay

Achreamie
Cnoc Freiceadain
Long Cairns

Lythmore

B874

Olrig
House

Tain

Gre

3

Isauld

Glengolly

A9

Weydale

B876

Reay
Achvarasdal
Shebster

Westfield

Hilliclay

Bower

242
▲
BEINN
RATHA

Broubster

Loch
Calder

Sordale

Knockdee

Loch
Scarmclate

Icro

4

Shurrery

B874

Roadside

Clayock

Gillock

B874

Shurrery
Lodge

Loch
Scye

B870

Halkirk

Georgemas
Junction
Station

A882
21

Loch Watten

290
▲
BEIN NAM
BAD MHÒR

Dorrery

Loch
Shurrery

Scotscalder
Station

Harpsdale

176
▲ SPITTAL
HILL

B870

Watten

5

243
▲
CNOC AN
ARAIN BHÀIN

160
▲
BRAIGH FÉITH HEMIGAL

Olgrinmore

132
▲ DRUIM A'
CHRACAIRNIE

River Thurso

Spittal

Mybster

Loch-of-
Toftingall

Loch Tuim
Ghlais

Loch
Caluim

Westerdale

23

6

203
▲
CNOC PREAS
A'MHADAIDH

200
▲
CNOC BEUL
NA FAIRE

136
▲
BEINN CHÀITEAG

Strath Beg

280

75

OC
GALL

Altnabreac Station

Loch
More

Loch
Ruard

A9

Achavanich

Loch
Stemster

7

LLI
HI

Rumsdale Water

Strathmore Water

Loch an
Thulachan

Loch
Sand

Loch
Rangag

248
▲ STEMSTER HILL

Dalnawillan Lodge

226
▲
COIRE
NA BEINNE

Clyth Water

348
▲
BEN
ALISKY

287
▲
BEN-A-
CHIELT

8

U
Ly

Glut Lodge

274

K 4
CNOCAN
CONACHREAG

Swiney

G | H | J | K | L | M

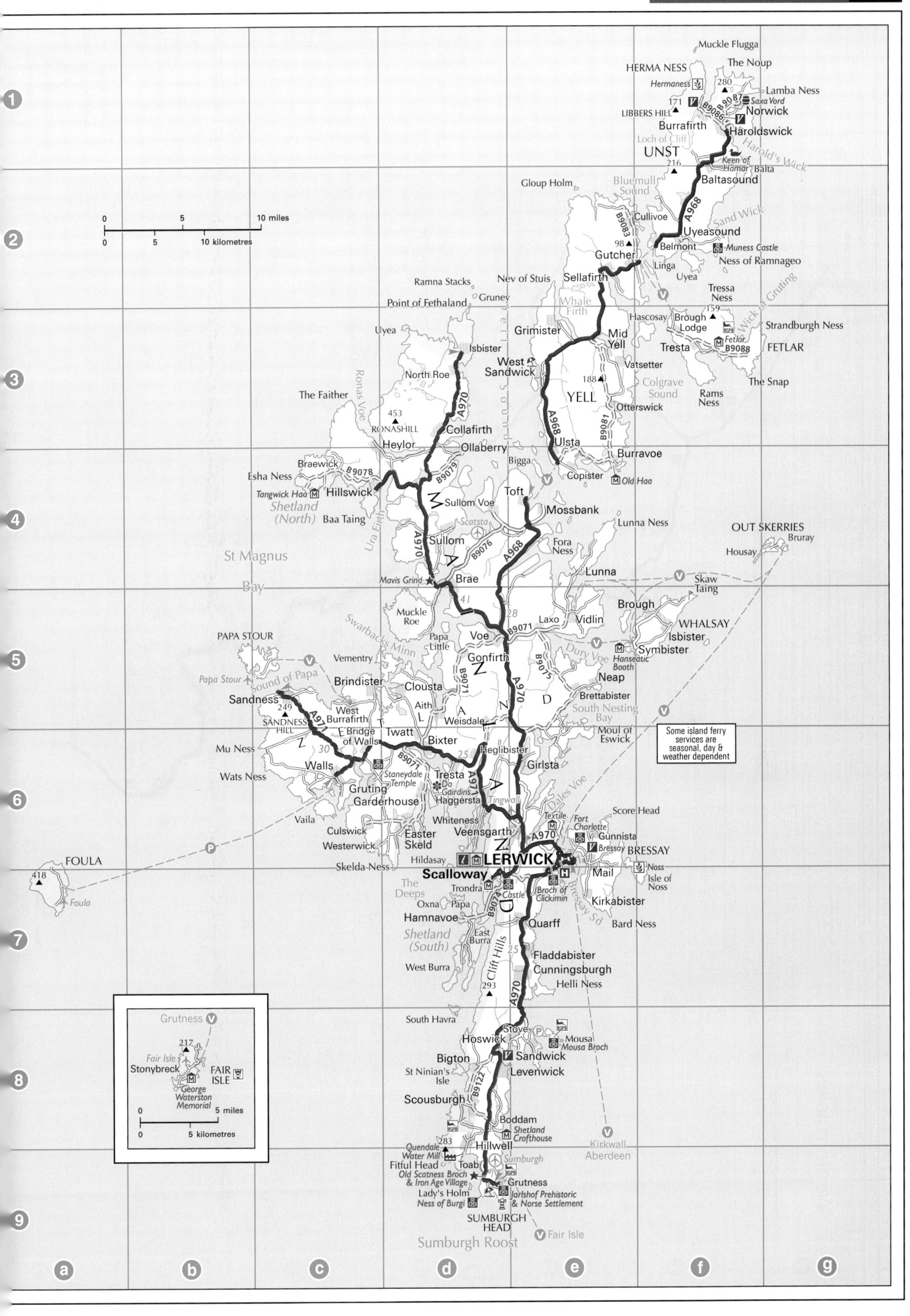

0   5   10 miles

0   5   10 kilometres

Muckle Flugga
The Noup
HERMA NESS
Hermaness   280
171   Lamba Ness
LIBBERS HILL   Saxa Vord
Norwick
Burrafirth   Haroldswick
Loch of Cliff
UNST   Keen of
Hamar   Balta
216
Baltasound
Gloup Holm   Bluemull
Sound   Cullivoe   Uyeasound
Nev of Stuis   B9083   Belmont   Muness Castle
Ramna Stacks   Sellafirth   98   Linga   Ness of Ramnageo
Point of Fethaland   Gruney   Uyea
Grimister   Tressa
Uyea   Ness
West   Mid   Hascosay   Brough
Isbister   Sandwick   Yell   Lodge   159
North Roe   Vatsetter   Tresta   FETLAR
The Faither   B9088
453   YELL   188   The Snap
RONASHILL   Collafirth   Otterswick   Rams
Heylor   Ollaberry   Ness
Braewick   B9078   Bigga   Burravoe
Esha Ness   B9079   Ulsta   Copister   Old Haa
Tangwick Haa   Hillswick   Toft   OUT SKERRIES
Shetland   Sullom Voe   Mossbank   Bruray
(North)   Baa Taing   Scatsta   Lunna Ness   Housay
St Magnus   Sullom   B9076   Fora   Skaw
Bay   A970   Ness   Taing
Mavis Grind   Brae   A968   Lunna
41   Brough
Muckle   28   WHALSAY
PAPA STOUR   Roe   Laxo   Vidlin   Isbister
Papa   Voe   B9071   Symbister
Little   Hanseatic
Vementry   Gonfirth   Booth
Papa Stour   Brindister   Clousta   Neap
Sandness   A971   Aith   Weisdale   Brettabister
249   West   Moul of
SANDNESS   Burrafirth   South Nesting   Eswick
HILL   Twatt   Bixter   Heglibister   Bay
Mu Ness   30   Bridge   B9071   Some island ferry
of Walls   25   services are
Wats Ness   Walls   Tresta   Girlsta   seasonal, day &
Gruting   Da   weather dependent
Garderhouse   Staneydale   Gairdins
Vaila   Temple   Haggersta   Tingwall
Whiteness   Textile   Score Head
Culswick   Easter   Veensgarth   Fort   Gunnista
Westerwick   Skeld   A970   Charlotte   BRESSAY
Hildasay   Bressay
Skelda-Ness   LERWICK
FOULA   Scalloway   Mail   Isle of Noss
418   Castle   Broch of   Noss
Foula   The   Trondra   Clickimin   Kirkabister
Deeps   Oxna   Papa   Bard Ness
Hamnavoe   Quarff
Shetland   East   Fladdabister
(South)   Burra   Cunningsburgh
West Burra   Cliff Hills   25   Helli Ness
293   A970
South Havra   Stove   Mousa
Hoswick   Mousa Broch
Grutness   Bigton   Sandwick
217   St Ninian's   Levenswick
Fair Isle   Isle   B9122   Scousburgh
Stonybreck   FAIR   Boddam
ISLE   Hillwell   Shetland
George   Quendale   283   Crofthouse
Waterston   Water Mill   Kirkwall
Memorial   Fitful Head   Toab   Aberdeen
0   5 miles   Old Scatness Broch   Sumburgh
& Iron Age Village   Jarlshof Prehistoric
0   5 kilometres   Lady's Holm   & Norse Settlement
Ness of Burgi   Grutness
SUMBURGH
HEAD   Fair Isle
Sumburgh Roost

a   b   c   d   e   f   g

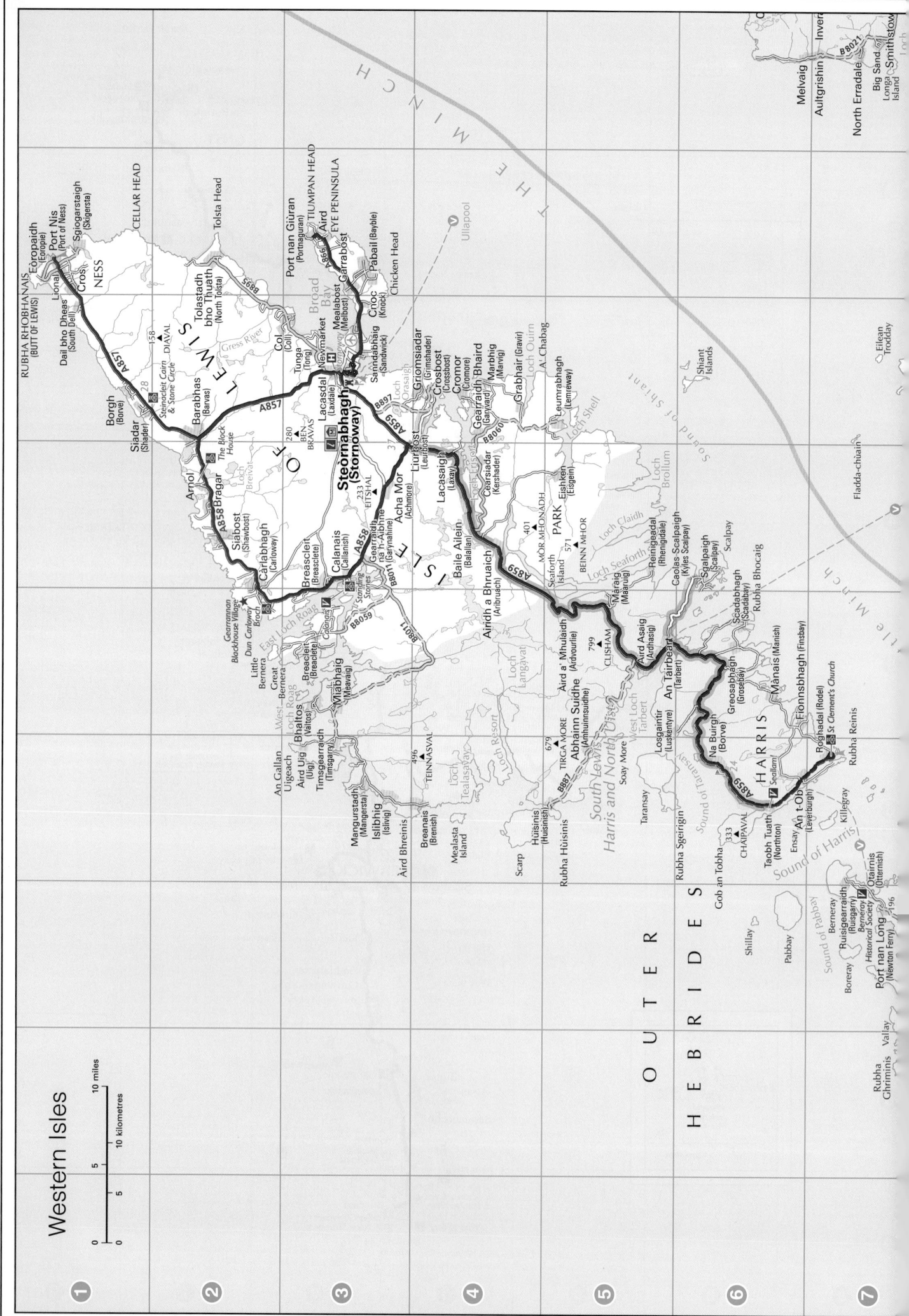

Western Isles

THE MINCH

Sound of Shiant

The Minch

RUBHA RHOBHANAIS
(BUTT OF LEWIS)
Eòropaidh
(Eoropie)
Port Nis
(Port of Ness)
Sgiogarstaigh
(Skigersta)
Lional
(Lionel)
Cros
(Cross)
NESS
Dail bho Dheas
(South Dell)

CELLAR HEAD

Tolsta Head

Tolastadh bho Thuath
(North Tolsta)

TIUMPAN HEAD
Port nan Giùran
(Portnaguran)
Aird
EYE PENINSULA
Mealabost
(Melbost)
Garrabost
Pabail
(Bayble)
Cnoc
(Knock)
CHICKEN HEAD

Ullapool

Eilean
Trodday

Borgh
(Borve)
Siadar
(Shader)
Arnol
Barabhas
(Barvas)
A857
Steinacleit Cairn
& Stone Circle
DIAVAL
158
Col
(Coll)
Tunga
(Tong)
LEWIS
BEN
BRAGAR
280
Gress River
A857
Newmarket
Steòrnabhagh
(Stornoway)
Lacasdal
(Laxdale)
Sanndabhaig
(Sandwick)
Griomsiadar
(Grimshader)
Crosbost
(Crossbost)
Cromor
(Cromore)
Gearraidh Bhaird
(Garyvard)
Marbhig
(Marvig)
Grabhair
(Gravir)
A' Chabag
Leumrabhagh
(Lemreway)
Shiant
Islands

A858
Bragar
Loch
Breivat
The Block
House
233
EITSHAL
A858
A857
Loch
Orasaigh
B887
A859
B8060
Loch Shell
Fladda-chùain

Siabost
(Shawbost)
Càrlabhagh
(Carloway)
Breascleit
(Breasclete)
Calanais
(Callanish)
Gearraidh
na h-Aibhne
(Garynahine)
Liurbost
(Leurbost)
Lacasaigh
(Laxay)
Cearsiadar
(Kershader)
Eishken
(Eisgein)
BEINN MHOR
Loch Brollum

Gearrannan
Blackhouse Village
Dun Carloway
Broch
B8011
Calanais
Standing
Stones
ISLE
Acha Mor
(Achmore)
Baile Ailein
(Balallan)
PARK
Loch
Claidh
Loch Ouirn

Little
Bernera
Great
Bernera
Miabhaig
(Meavaig)
B8059
OF
Airidh a Bhruaich
(Aribruach)
MOR MHONADH
Seaforth
Island
401
571
Loch Seaforth
Reinigeadal
(Rhenigidale)
Caolas Scalpaigh
(Kyles Scalpay)
Scalpaigh
(Scalpay)
Scalpay
Rubha Bhocaig

An Gallan
Uigeach
Àird Uig
(Ardroil)
Timsgearraidh
(Timsgarry)
Mangurstadh
(Mangersta)
Islibhig
(Islivig)
West
Loch
Roag
B8011
L1087
496
TEINNASVAL
Loch
Tealasavay
Ard a' Mhulaidh
(Ardvourlie)
799
CLISHAM
Àird Asaig
(Ardhasig)
An Tairbeart
(Tarbert)
Scadabhagh
(Scadabay)
Màraig
(Maaruig)

Àrd Bhreinis
Breanais
(Brenish)
Mealasta
Island
Loch
Langavat
679
TIRGA MORE
B887
Abhainn Suidhe
(Amhuinnsuidhe)
West Loch
Tarbert
Losgaintir
(Luskentyre)
Na Buirgh
(Borve)
Greosabhagh
(Grosebay)
Manais
(Manish)
Fionnsbhagh
(Finsbay)

Scarp
Huisinis
(Husinish)
Rubha Hùisinis
Soay More
Taransay
Rubha
Sgeirigin
HARRIS
24
A859
Seilam
Ròghadal
(Rodel)
St Clement's Church
Rubha Reinis

OUTER
South Lewis,
Harris and North Uist
Sound of Taransay
Gob an Tobha
CHAIPAVAL
333
Taobh Tuath
(Northton)
Ensay
An t-Ob
(Leverburgh)
Sound of Harris
Killegray
Otairnis
(Otternish)
196

Shillay
Pabbay
HEBRIDES
Sound of Pabbay
Bearaidh
Berneray
Bhearnaraigh
Ruisigearraidh
(Ruisgarry)
Berneray
Historical Society
Port nan Long
(Newton Ferry)

Rubha
Ghriminis
Valtay
Rubha
Ghriminis
INNER

Melvaig
Aultgrishin
North Erradale
Big Sand
Longa
Smithstow
Inver
B8021
Loch

10 miles
10 kilometres
5
5
0
0

Motorway and primary route junctions which have access or exit restrictions are shown on the map pages thus:

M1 London - Leeds

Junction	Northbound	Southbound
2	Access only from A1 (northbound)	Exit only to A1 (southbound)
4	Access only from A41 (northbound)	Exit only to A41 (southbound)
6A	Access only from M25 (no link from A405)	Exit only to M25 (no link from A405)
7	Access only from A414	Exit only to A414
17	Exit only to M45	Access only from M45
19	Exit only to M6 (northbound)	Exit only to A14 (southbound)
21A	Exit only, no access	Access only, no exit
24A	Access only, no exit	Access only from A50 (eastbound)
35A	Exit only, no access	Access only, no exit
43	Exit only to M621	Access only from M621
48	Exit only to A1(M) (northbound)	Access only from A1(M) (southbound)

M2 Rochester - Faversham

Junction	Westbound	Eastbound
1	No exit to A2 (eastbound)	No access from A2 (westbound)

M3 Sunbury - Southampton

Junction	Northeastbound	Southwestbound
8	Access only from A303, no exit	Exit only to A303, no access
10	Exit only, no access	Access only, no exit
14	Access from M27 only, no exit	No access to M27 (westbound)

M4 London - South Wales

Junction	Westbound	Eastbound
1	Access only from A4 (westbound)	Exit only to A4 (eastbound)
2	Access only from A4 (westbound)	Access only from A4 (eastbound)
21	Exit only to M48	Access only from M48
23	Access only from M48	Exit only to M48
25	Exit only, no access	Access only, no exit
25A	Exit only, no access	Access only, no exit
29	Exit only to A48(M)	Access only from A48(M)
38	Exit only, no access	No restriction
39	Access only, no exit	No access or exit
42	Exit only to A483	Access only from A483

M5 Birmingham - Exeter

Junction	Northeastbound	Southwestbound
10	Access only, no exit	Exit only, no access
11A	Access only from A417 (westbound)	Exit only to A417 (eastbound)
18A	Exit only to M49	Access only from M49
18	Exit only, no access	Access only, no exit

M6 Toll Motorway

Junction	Northwestbound	Southeastbound
T1	Access only, no exit	No access or exit
T2	No access or exit	Exit only, no access
T5	Access only, no exit	Exit only to A5148 (northbound), no access
T7	Exit only, no access	Access only, no exit
T8	Exit only, no access	Access only, no exit

M6 Rugby - Carlisle

Junction	Northbound	Southbound
3A	Exit only to M6 Toll	Access only from M6 Toll
4	Exit only to M42 (southbound) & A446	Exit only to A446
4A	Access only from M42 (southbound)	Exit only to M42
5	Exit only, no access	Access only, no exit
10A	Exit only to M54	Access only from M54
11A	Access only from M6 Toll	Exit only to M6 Toll
with M56 (jct 20A)	No restriction	Access only from M56 (eastbound)
20	Exit only to M56 (westbound)	Access only from M56 (eastbound)
24	Access only, no exit	Exit only, no access
25	Exit only, no access	Access only, no exit
30	Access only from M61	Exit only to M61

	31A	Exit only, no access	Access only, no exit
	45	Exit only, no access	Access only, no exit

M8 Edinburgh - Bishopton

Junction	Westbound	Eastbound
6	Exit only, no access	Access only, no exit
6A	Access only, no exit	Exit only, no access
7	Access only, no exit	Exit only, no access
7A	Exit only, no access	Access only from A725 (northbound), no exit
8	No access from M73 (southbound) or from A8 (eastbound) & A89	No exit to M73 (northbound) or to A8 (westbound) & A89
9	Access only, no exit	Exit only, no access
13	Access only from M80 (southbound)	Exit only to M80 (northbound)
14	Access only, no exit	Exit only, no access
16	Exit only to A804	Access only from A879
17	Exit only to A82	No restriction
18	Access only from A82 (eastbound)	Exit only to A814
19	No access from A814 (westbound)	Exit only to A814 (westbound)
20	Exit only, no access	Access only, no exit
21	Access only, no exit	Exit only to A8
22	Exit only to M77 (southbound)	Access only from M77 (northbound)
23	Exit only to B768	Access only from B768
25	No access or exit from or to A8	No access or exit from or to A8
25A	Exit only, no access	Access only, no exit
28	Exit only, no access	Access only, no exit
28A	Exit only to A737	Access only from A737
29A	Exit only to A8	Access only, no exit

M9 Edinburgh - Dunblane

Junction	Northwestbound	Southeastbound
2	Access only, no exit	Exit only, no access
3	Exit only, no access	Access only, no exit
6	Access only, no exit	Exit only to A905
8	Exit only to M876 (southwestbound)	Access only from M876 (northeastbound)

M11 London - Cambridge

Junction	Northbound	Southbound
4	Access only from A406 (eastbound)	Exit only to A406
5	Exit only, no access	Access only, no exit
8A	Exit only, no access	No direct access, use jct 8
9	Exit only to A11	Access only from A11
13	Exit only, no access	Access only, no exit
14	Exit only, no access	Access only, no exit

M20 Swanley - Folkestone

Junction	Northwestbound	Southeastbound
2	Staggered junction; follow signs - access only	Staggered junction; follow signs - exit only
3	Exit only to M26 (westbound)	Access only from M26 (eastbound)
5	Access only from A20	For access follow signs - exit only to A20
6	No restriction	For exit follow signs
10	Access only, no exit	Exit only, no access
11A	Access only, no exit	Exit only, no access

M23 Hooley - Crawley

Junction	Northbound	Southbound
7	Exit only to A23 (northbound)	Access only from A23 (southbound)
10A	Access only, no exit	Exit only, no access

M25 London Orbital

Junction	Clockwise	Anticlockwise
1B	No direct access, use slip road to jct 2 Exit only	Access only, no exit
5	No exit to M26 (eastbound)	No access from M26
19	Exit only, no access	Access only, no exit
21	Access only from M1 (southbound) Exit only to M1 (northbound)	Access only from M1 (southbound) Exit only to M1 (northbound)
31	No exit (use slip road via jct 30), access only	No access (use slip road via jct 30), exit only

M26 Sevenoaks - Wrotham

Junction	Westbound	Eastbound
with M25 (jct 5)	Exit only to clockwise M25 (westbound)	Access only from anticlockwise M25 (eastbound)
with M20 (jct 3)	Access only from M20 (northwestbound)	Exit only to M20 (southeastbound)

M27 Cadnam - Portsmouth

Junction	Westbound	Eastbound
4	Staggered junction; follow signs - access only from M3 (southbound). Exit only to M3 (northbound)	Staggered junction; follow signs - access only from M3 (southbound). Exit only to M3 (northbound)
10	Exit only, no access	Access only, no exit
12	Staggered junction; follow signs - exit only to M275 (southbound)	Staggered junction; follow signs - access only from M275 (northbound)

M40 London - Birmingham

Junction	Northwestbound	Southeastbound
3	Exit only, no access	Access only, no exit
7	Exit only, no access	Access only, no exit
8	Exit only to M40/A40	Access only from M40/A40
13	Exit only, no access	Access only, no exit
14	Access only, no exit	Exit only, no access
16	Access only, no exit	Exit only, no access

M42 Bromsgrove - Measham

Junction	Northeastbound	Southwestbound
1	Access only, no exit	Exit only, no access
7	Exit only to M6 (northwestbound)	Access only from M6 (northwestbound)
7A	Exit only to M6 (southeastbound)	No access or exit
8	Access only from M6 (southeastbound)	Exit only to M6 (northwestbound)

M45 Coventry - M1

Junction	Westbound	Eastbound
Dunchurch (unnumbered)	Access only from A45	Exit only, no access
with M1 (jct 17)	Access only from M1 (northbound)	Exit only to M1 (southbound)

M48 Chepstow

Junction	Westbound	Eastbound
21	Access only from M4 (westbound)	Exit only to M4 (eastbound)
23	No exit to M4 (eastbound)	No access from M4 (westbound)

M53 Mersey Tunnel - Chester

Junction	Northbound	Southbound
11	Access only from M56 (westbound) Exit only to M56 (eastbound)	Access only from M5 (westbound) Exit only to M56 (eastbound)

M54 Telford - Birmingham

Junction	Westbound	Eastbound
with M6 (jct 10A)	Access only from M6 (northbound)	Exit only to M6 (southbound)

M56 Chester - Manchester

Junction	Westbound	Eastbound
1	Access only from M60 (westbound)	Exit only to M60 (eastbound) & A34 (northbound)
2	Exit only, no access	Access only, no exit
3	Access only, no exit	Exit only, no access
4	Exit only, no access	Access only, no exit
7	Exit only, no access	No restriction
8	Access only, no exit	No access or exit
9	No exit to M6 (southbound)	No access from M6 (northbound)
15	Exit only to M53	Access only from M5
16	No access or exit	No restriction

M57 Liverpool Outer Ring Road

Junction	Northwestbound	Southeastbound
3	Access only, no exit	Exit only, no access
5	Access only from A580 (westbound)	Exit only, no access

M60 Manchester Orbital

Junction	Clockwise	Anticlockwise
2	Access only, no exit	Exit only, no access
3	No access from M56	Access only from A34 (northbound)
4	Access only from A34 (northbound). Exit only to M56	Access only from M56 (eastbound). Exit only to A34 (southbound)
5	Access and exit only from and to A5103 (northbound)	Access and exit only from and to A5103 (southbound)
7	No direct access, use slip road to jct 8. Exit only to A56	Access only from A56. No exit, use jct 8
14	Access from A580 (eastbound)	Exit only to A580 (westbound)
16	Access only, no exit	Exit only, no access
20	Exit only, no access	Access only, no exit
22	No restriction	Exit only, no access
25	Exit only, no access	No restriction
26	No restriction	Exit only, no access
27	Access only, no exit	Exit only, no access

M61 Manchester - Preston

Junction	Northwestbound	Southeastbound
3	No access or exit	Exit only, no access
with M6 (jct 30)	Exit only to M6 (northbound)	Access only from M6 (southbound)

M62 Liverpool - Kingston upon Hull

Junction	Westbound	Eastbound
23	Access only, no exit	Exit only, no access
32A	No access to A1(M) (southbound)	No restriction

M65 Preston - Colne

Junction	Northeastbound	Southwestbound
9	Exit only, no access	Access only, no exit
11	Access only, no exit	Exit only, no access

M66 Bury

Junction	Northbound	Southbound
with A56	Exit only to A56 (northbound)	Access only from A56 (southbound)
1	Exit only, no access	Access only, no exit

M67 Hyde Bypass

Junction	Westbound	Eastbound
1A	Access only, no exit	Exit only, no access
2	Exit only, no access	Access only, no exit

M69 Coventry - Leicester

Junction	Northbound	Southbound
2	Access only, no exit	Exit only, no access

M73 East of Glasgow

Junction	Northbound	Southbound
1	No exit to A74 & A721	No exit to A74 & A721
2	No access from or exit to A89. No access from M8 (eastbound)	No access from or exit to A89. No exit to M8 (westbound)

M74 and A74(M) Glasgow - Gretna

Junction	Northbound	Southbound
3	Exit only, no access	Access only, no exit
3A	Access only, no exit	Exit only, no access
4	No access from A74 & A721	Access only, no exit to A74 & A721
7	Access only, no exit	Exit only, no access
9	No access or exit	Exit only, no access
10	No restriction	Access only, no exit
11	Access only, no exit	Exit only, no access
12	Exit only, no access	Access only, no exit
18	Exit only, no access	Access only, no exit

M77 Glasgow - Kilmarnock

Junction	Northbound	Southbound
with M8 (jct 22)	No exit to M8 (westbound)	No access from M8 (eastbound)
4	Access only, no exit	Exit only, no access
6	Access only, no exit	Exit only, no access
7	Access only, no exit	No restriction
8	Exit only, no access	Exit only, no access

M80 Glasgow - Stirling

Junction	Northbound	Southbound
4A	Exit only, no access	Access only, no exit
6A	Exit only, no access	Exit only, no access
8	Exit only to M876 (northeastbound)	Access only from M876 (southwestbound)

M90 Edinburgh - Perth

Junction	Northbound	Southbound
1	No exit, access only	Exit only to A90 (eastbound)
2A	Exit only to A92 (eastbound)	Access only from A92 (westbound)
7	Access only, no exit	Exit only, no access
8	Access only, no exit	Access only, no exit
10	No access from A912. No exit to A912 (southbound)	No access from A912 (northbound). No exit to A912

M180 Doncaster - Grimsby

Junction	Westbound	Eastbound
1	Access only, no exit	Exit only, no access

M606 Bradford Spur

Junction	Northbound	Southbound
2	Exit only, no access	No restriction

M621 Leeds - M1

Junction	Clockwise	Anticlockwise
2A	Access only, no exit	Exit only, no access
4	No exit or access	No restriction
5	Access only, no exit	Exit only, no access
6	Exit only, no access	Access only, no exit
with M1 (jct 43)	Exit only to M1 (southbound)	Access only from M1 (northbound)

M876 Bonnybridge - Kincardine Bridge

Junction	Northeastbound	Southwestbound
with M80 (jct 5)	Access only from M80 (northeastbound)	Exit only to M80 (southwestbound)
with M9 (jct 8)	Exit only to M9 (eastbound)	Access only from M9 (westbound)

A1(M) South Mimms - Baldock

Junction	Northbound	Southbound
2	Exit only, no access	Access only, no exit
3	No restriction	Exit only, no access
5	Access only, no exit	No access or exit

A1(M) Pontefract - Bedale

Junction	Northbound	Southbound
41	No access to M62 (eastbound)	No restriction
43	Access only from M1 (northbound)	Exit only to M1 (southbound)

A1(M) Scotch Corner - Newcastle upon Tyne

Junction	Northbound	Southbound
57	Exit only to A66(M) (eastbound)	Access only from A66(M) (westbound)
65	No access Exit only to A194(M) & A1 (northbound)	No exit Access only from A194(M) & A1 (southbound)

A3(M) Horndean - Havant

Junction	Northbound	Southbound
1	Access only from A3	Exit only to A3
4	Exit only, no access	Access only, no exit

A38(M) Birmingham, Victoria Road (Park Circus)

Junction	Northbound	Southbound
with B4132	No exit	No access

A48(M) Cardiff Spur

Junction	Westbound	Eastbound
29	Access only from M4 (westbound)	Exit only to M4 (eastbound)
29A	Exit only to A48 (westbound)	Access only from A48 (eastbound)

A57(M) Manchester, Brook Street (A34)

Junction	Westbound	Eastbound
with A34	No exit	No access

A58(M) Leeds, Park Lane and Westgate

Junction	Northbound	Southbound
with A58	No restriction	No access

A64(M) Leeds, Clay Pit Lane (A58)

Junction	Westbound	Eastbound
with A58	No exit (to Clay Pit Lane)	No access (from Clay Pit Lane)

A66(M) Darlington Spur

Junction	Westbound	Eastbound
with A1(M) (jct 57)	Exit only to A1(M) (southbound)	Access only from A1(M) (northbound)

A74(M) Gretna - Abington

Junction	Northbound	Southbound
18	Exit only, no access	Access only, no exit

A194(M) Newcastle upon Tyne

Junction	Northbound	Southbound
with A1(M) (jct 65)	Access only from A1(M) (northbound)	Exit only to A1(M) (southbound)

A12 M25 - Ipswich

Junction	Northeastbound	Southwestbound
13	Access only, no exit	No restriction
14	Exit only, no access	Access only, no exit
20A	Exit only, no access	Access only, no exit
20B	Access only, no exit	Exit only, no access
21	No restriction	Access only, no exit
23	Access only, no exit	Access only, no exit
24	Access only, no exit	Exit only, no access
27	Exit only, no access	Access only, no exit
Dedham & Stratford St Mary (unnumbered)	Exit only	Access only

A14 M1 - Felixstowe

Junction	Westbound	Eastbound
with M1/M6 (jct19)	Exit only to M6 and M1 (northbound)	Access only from M6 and M1 (southbound)
4	Exit only, no access	Access only, no exit
21	Access only, no exit	Exit only, no access
22	Exit only, no access	Access only from A1 (southbound)
23	Access only, no exit	Exit only, no access
26	No restriction	Access only, no exit
34	Access only, no exit	Exit only, no access
36	Exit only to A11, access only from A1303	Access only from A11
38	Access only from A11	Exit only to A11
39	Exit only, no access	Access only, no exit
61	Access only, no exit	Exit only, no access

A55 Holyhead - Chester

Junction	Westbound	Eastbound
8A	Exit only, no access	Access only, no exit
23A	Access only, no exit	Exit only, no access
24A	Exit only, no access	No access or exit
27A	No restriction	No access or exit
33A	Exit only, no access	No access or exit
33B	Exit only, no access	Access only, no exit
36A	Exit only to A5104	Access only from A5104

This index lists places appearing in the main map section of the atlas in alphabetical order. The reference following each name gives the atlas page number and grid reference of the square in which the place appears. The map shows counties, unitary authorities and administrative areas, together with a list of the abbreviated name forms used in the index. In addition World Heritage sites are indexed in green, motorway services areas in blue, airports in blue *italic* and National Parks in green *italic*.

Scotland

Abers	Aberdeenshire
Ag & B	Argyll and Bute
Angus	Angus
Border	Scottish Borders
C Aber	City of Aberdeen
C Dund	City of Dundee
C Edin	City of Edinburgh
C Glas	City of Glasgow
Clacks	Clackmannanshire (1)
D & G	Dumfries & Galloway
E Ayrs	East Ayrshire
E Duns	East Dunbartonshire (2)
E Loth	East Lothian
E Rens	East Renfrewshire (3)
Falk	Falkirk
Fife	Fife
Highld	Highland
Inver	Inverclyde (4)
Mdloth	Midlothian (5)
Moray	Moray
N Ayrs	North Ayrshire
N Lans	North Lanarkshire (6)
Ork	Orkney Islands
P & K	Perth & Kinross
Rens	Renfrewshire (7)
S Ayrs	South Ayrshire
S Lans	South Lanarkshire
Shet	Shetland Islands
Stirlg	Stirling
W Duns	West Dunbartonshire (8)
W Isls	Western Isles (Na h-Eileanan an Iar)
W Loth	West Lothian

Wales

Blae G	Blaenau Gwent (9)
Brdgnd	Bridgend (10)
Caerph	Caerphilly (11)
Cardif	Cardiff
Carmth	Carmarthenshire
Cerdgn	Ceredigion
Conwy	Conwy
Denbgs	Denbighshire
Flints	Flintshire
Gwynd	Gwynedd
IoA	Isle of Anglesey
Mons	Monmouthshire
Myr Td	Merthyr Tydfil (12)
Neath	Neath Port Talbot (13)
Newpt	Newport (14)
Pembks	Pembrokeshire
Powys	Powys
Rhondd	Rhondda Cynon Taf (15)
Swans	Swansea
Torfn	Torfaen (16)
V Glam	Vale of Glamorgan (17)
Wrexhm	Wrexham

Channel Islands & Isle of Man

Guern	Guernsey
Jersey	Jersey
IoM	Isle of Man

England

BaNES	Bath & N E Somerset (18)
Barns	Barnsley (19)
BCP	Bournemouth, Christchurch and Poole (20)
Bed	Bedford
Birm	Birmingham
Bl w D	Blackburn with Darwen (21)
Bolton	Bolton (22)
Bpool	Blackpool
Br & H	Brighton & Hove (23)
Br For	Bracknell Forest (24)
Bristl	City of Bristol
Bucks	Buckinghamshire
Bury	Bury (25)
C Beds	Central Bedfordshire
C Brad	City of Bradford
C Derb	City of Derby
C KuH	City of Kingston upon Hull
C Leic	City of Leicester
C Nott	City of Nottingham
C Pete	City of Peterborough
C Plym	City of Plymouth
C Port	City of Portsmouth
C Sotn	City of Southampton
C Stke	City of Stoke-on-Trent
C York	City of York
Calder	Calderdale (26)
Cambs	Cambridgeshire
Ches E	Cheshire East
Ches W	Cheshire West and Chester
Cnwll	Cornwall
Covtry	Coventry
Cumb	Cumbria
Darltn	Darlington (27)
Derbys	Derbyshire
Devon	Devon
Donc	Doncaster (28)
Dorset	Dorset
Dudley	Dudley (29)
Dur	Durham
E R Yk	East Riding of Yorkshire
E Susx	East Sussex
Essex	Essex
Gatesd	Gateshead (30)
Gloucs	Gloucestershire
Gt Lon	Greater London
Halton	Halton (31)
Hants	Hampshire
Hartpl	Hartlepool (32)
Herefs	Herefordshire
Herts	Hertfordshire
IoS	Isles of Scilly
IoW	Isle of Wight
Kent	Kent
Kirk	Kirklees (33)
Knows	Knowsley (34)
Lancs	Lancashire
Leeds	Leeds
Leics	Leicestershire
Lincs	Lincolnshire
Lpool	Liverpool
Luton	Luton

M Keyn	Milton Keynes
Manch	Manchester
Medway	Medway
Middsb	Middlesbrough
N Linc	North Lincolnshire
N Som	North Somerset
N Tyne	North Tyneside (35)
N u Ty	Newcastle upon Tyne
N York	North Yorkshire
NE Lin	North East Lincolnshire
Nhants	Northamptonshire
Norfk	Norfolk
Notts	Nottinghamshire
Nthumb	Northumberland
Oldham	Oldham (36)
Oxon	Oxfordshire
R & Cl	Redcar & Cleveland
Readg	Reading
Rochdl	Rochdale (37)
Rothm	Rotherham (38)
Rutlnd	Rutland
S Glos	South Gloucestershire (39)
S on T	Stockton-on-Tees (40)
S Tyne	South Tyneside (41)
Salfd	Salford (42)
Sandw	Sandwell (43)
Sefton	Sefton (44)
Sheff	Sheffield
Shrops	Shropshire
Slough	Slough (45)
Solhll	Solihull (46)
Somset	Somerset
St Hel	St Helens (47)
Staffs	Staffordshire
Sthend	Southend-on-Sea
Stockp	Stockport (48)
Suffk	Suffolk
Sundld	Sunderland
Surrey	Surrey
Swindn	Swindon
Tamesd	Tameside (49)
Thurr	Thurrock (50)
Torbay	Torbay
Traffd	Trafford (51)
W & M	Windsor & Maidenhead (52)
W Berk	West Berkshire
W Susx	West Sussex
Wakefd	Wakefield (53)
Warrtn	Warrington (54)
Warwks	Warwickshire
Wigan	Wigan (55)
Wilts	Wiltshire
Wirral	Wirral (56)
Wokham	Wokingham (57)
Wolves	Wolverhampton (58)
Worcs	Worcestershire
Wrekin	Telford & Wrekin (59)
Wsall	Walsall (60)

ORKNEY ISLANDS

SHETLAND ISLANDS

WESTERN ISLES (Na h-Eileanan an Iar)

HIGHLAND

MORAY

S C O T L A N D

ABERDEENSHIRE

Aberdeen

ANGUS

PERTH & KINROSS

Dundee

ARGYLL AND BUTE

STIRLING

FIFE

1

8
2
FALK
W LOTH
Edinburgh
E LOTH

4
Glasgow
6
7
3
5

NORTH AYRSHIRE

S LANS

SCOTTISH BORDERS

E AYRS

S AYRS

DUMFRIES & GALLOWAY

NORTHUMBERLAND

Newcastle upon Tyne
35
30
41
Sunderland

CUMBRIA

DURHAM
32
27 40 R & CL
Middlesbrough

IoM

NORTH YORKSHIRE

Bradford
York
EAST RIDING OF YORKSHIRE
Kingston upon Hull

Blackpool
LANCASHIRE
Leeds
26
53
N LINC
NE LIN

21
37
33
25
36
19
28
55
22
42
49
44
34
47
54
51
48
Manchester
38
Sheffield
56
31

Liverpool

IoA

CONWY
FLINTS
CHES W
CHES E
DERBYS
NOTTS
LINCOLNSHIRE

DENBGS
Stoke-on-Trent
Derby
Nottingham

WREXHAM

GWYNEDD

59
STAFFS
LEICS
RUTLAND
NORFOLK
Peterborough

SHROPSHIRE
58 60
43
Birmingham
Leicester
CAMBS

29
46
Coventry
SUFFOLK

POWYS

WORCS
WARWKS
NHANTS
BED

CERDGN
HEREFS
Milton Keynes

W A L E S   E N G L A N D

PEMBKS
CARMTH
9
MONS
GLOUCS
OXON
BUCKS
BEDS
Luton
HERTS
ESSEX

12
16
11
Southend-on-Sea

13
15
GREATER LONDON
50

10
Cardiff
14
39
Swindon
Reading
52 45
MEDWAY

17
Bristol
W BERK
57 24

N SOM
18
WILTSHIRE
SURREY
KENT

Swansea

SOMERSET
HAMPSHIRE

DEVON
DORSET
20
W SUSX
E SUSX
23

Southampton
Portsmouth
IoW

CORNWALL
CHANNEL ISLANDS
Guernsey
Jersey

Torbay
Plymouth

IoS

A

Abbas Combe Somset 32 B6
Abberley Worcs 81 H2
Abberley Common Worcs 81 G2
Abberton Essex 72 E3
Abberton Worcs 82 A4
Abberwick Nthumb 191 G3
Abbess Roding Essex 70 E5
Abbey Devon 14 D1
Abbeycwmhir Powys 78 E1
Abbeydale Sheff 132 F3
Abbey Dore Herefs 62 D1
Abbey Green Staffs 131 J8
Abbey Hill Somset 30 D7
Abbey St Bathans Border 213 G6
Abbeystead Lancs 147 L5
Abbeytown Cumb 177 G8
Abbey Village Lancs 139 J3
Abbey Wood Gt Lon 52 A3
Abbotrule Border 189 G4
Abbots Bickington Devon 27 G8
Abbots Bromley Staffs 115 H6
Abbotsbury Dorset 16 A5
Abbot's Chair Derbys 131 K2
Abbots Deuglie P & K 221 K5
Abbotsham Devon 27 G5
Abbotskerswell Devon 8 C1
Abbots Langley Herts 68 E6
Abbotsleigh Devon 8 B5
Abbots Leigh N Som 45 G4
Abbotsley Cambs 86 E4
Abbots Morton Worcs 82 B4
Abbots Ripton Cambs 102 E7
Abbot's Salford Warwks 82 C5
Abbotstone Hants 35 H4
Abbotswood Hants 34 D6
Abbots Worthy Hants 35 G4
Abbotts Ann Hants 34 D2
Abbott Street Dorset 17 J3
Abcott Shrops 95 J7
Abdon Shrops 96 D6
Abenhall Gloucs 63 K4
Aberaeron Cerdgn 76 E3
Aberaman Rhondd 60 F7
Aberangell Gwynd 93 J2
Aber-arad Carmth 76 B7
Aberarder Highld 251 H6
Aberargie P & K 222 B4
Aberarth Cerdgn 76 E3
Aberavon Neath 57 K7
Aber-banc Cerdgn 76 C7
Aberbargoed Caerph 61 J7
Aberbeeg Blae G 61 K6
Abercanaid Myr Td 61 G6
Abercarn Caerph 43 K3
Abercastle Pembks 74 D5
Abercegir Powys 93 H3
Aberchalder Highld 240 B3
Aberchirder Abers 268 A5
Aber Clydach Powys 61 H3
Abercorn W Loth 210 E3
Abercraf Powys 59 M6
Abercregan Neath 42 C2
Abercwmboi Rhondd 60 F7
Abercych Pembks 75 M4
Abercynon Rhondd 43 G3
Aberdalgie P & K 221 K3
Aberdare Rhondd 60 F6
Aberdaron Gwynd 108 C6
Aberdeen C Aber 245 L2
Aberdeen Airport C Aber 245 J1
Aberdesach Gwynd 109 G1
Aberdour Fife 211 G2
Aberdulais Neath 57 L5
Aberdyfi Gwynd 92 D4
Aberedw Powys 78 F6
Abereiddy Pembks 74 C6
Abererch Gwynd 109 G4
Aberfan Myr Td 61 G7
Aberfeldy P & K 232 C5
Aberffraw IoA 124 F6
Aberffrwd Cerdgn 92 E7
Aberford Leeds 150 F8
Aberfoyle Stirlg 219 H7
Abergarw Brdgnd 42 D5
Abergarwed Neath 60 B6
Abergavenny Mons 62 C4
Abergele Conwy 127 J4
Aber-giar Carmth 76 F7
Abergorlech Carmth 59 G2
Abergwesyn Powys 78 A4
Abergwili Carmth 58 D5
Abergwydol Powys 93 G3
Abergwynfi Neath 42 D3
Abergwyngregyn Gwynd 126 C5
Abergynolwyn Gwynd 92 E2
Aberhafesp Powys 94 C5
Aberhosan Powys 93 H4

Aberkenfig Brdgnd 42 D5
Aberlady E Loth 212 A3
Aberlemno Angus 234 E4
Aberllefenni Gwynd 93 G2
Aberllynfi Powys 79 H7
Aberlour, Charlestown of Moray 254 E3
Abermagwr Cerdgn 92 E8
Aber-meurig Cerdgn 77 G4
Abermorddu Flints 129 G8
Abermule Powys 94 E4
Abernant Carmth 58 C4
Abernant Rhondd 60 F6
Abernethy P & K 222 C4
Abernyte P & K 222 D1
Aberporth Cerdgn 76 A5
Abersoch Gwynd 108 E6
Abersychan Torfn 62 B6
Aberthin V Glam 42 F6
Abertillery Blae G 61 K6
Abertridwr Caerph 43 H4
Abertridwr Powys 111 K7
Abertysswg Caerph 61 H6
Aberuthven P & K 221 H4
Aberwheeler Denbgs 128 C6
Aberyscir Powys 60 F1
Aberystwyth Cerdgn 92 C7
Abingdon-on-Thames Oxon 66 C7
Abinger Common Surrey 37 H2
Abinger Hammer Surrey 37 G2
Abington Nhants 84 F3
Abington S Lans 186 D2
Abington Pigotts Cambs 86 F6
Abington Services S Lans 186 D1
Abingworth W Susx 21 J3
Ab Kettleby Leics 117 J7
Ab Lench Worcs 82 B5
Ablington Gloucs 65 G5
Ablington Wilts 33 K2
Abney Derbys 132 D4
Above Church Staffs 115 G2
Aboyne Abers 244 C4
Abram Wigan 139 J7
Abriachan Highld 250 F1
Abridge Essex 70 C7
Abronhill N Lans 209 L4
Abson S Glos 45 L4
Abthorpe Nhants 84 C6
Aby Lincs 137 H4
Acaster Malbis C York 151 J6
Acaster Selby N York 151 J6
Accrington Lancs 139 M2
Acha Ag & B 224 F4
Achahoish Ag & B 206 B3
Achalader P & K 233 H6
Achaleven Ag & B 228 E8
Acha Mor W Isls 282 f3
Achanalt Highld 261 M7
Achandunie Highld 263 H5
Achany Highld 272 E7
Acharacle Highld 237 K7
Acharn Highld 227 K2
Acharn P & K 231 L6
Achavanich Highld 279 L7
Achduart Highld 270 D7
Achfary Highld 276 D8
Achgarve Highld 260 E1
A'Chill Highld 246 C2
Achiltibuie Highld 270 D6
Achina Highld 278 B4
Achinhoan Ag & B 192 F5
Achintee Highld 248 D4
Achintraid Highld 248 D4
Achlyness Highld 276 C5
Achmelvich Highld 270 C4
Achmore Highld 248 D5
Achmore W Isls 282 f3
Achnacarnin Highld 270 D2
Achnacarry Highld 239 K6
Achnacloich Highld 247 J6
Achnaconeran Highld 250 D8
Achnacroish Ag & B 228 C7
Achnadrish Ag & B 226 F2
Achnafauld P & K 232 C8
Achnagarron Highld 263 J6
Achnaha Highld 236 F6
Achnahaird Highld 270 D6
Achnahannet Highld 253 J6
Achnairn Highld 272 E5
Achnalea Highld 228 C3
Achnamara Ag & B 206 B2
Achnasheen Highld 261 K8
Achnashellach Highld 249 G2
Achnastank Moray 254 F5
Achosnich Highld 236 F7
Achranich Highld 227 K3
Achreamie Highld 279 H3
Achriabhach Highld 229 J2
Achriesgill Highld 276 D5

Achtoty Highld 277 M4
Achurch Nhants 102 A6
Achvaich Highld 263 J1
Achvarasdal Highld 279 H3
Ackergill Highld 280 E5
Acklam Middsb 170 C7
Acklam N York 152 B3
Acklington Nthumb 191 J6
Ackton Wakefd 142 C3
Ackworth Moor Top Wakefd 142 C4
Acle Norfk 107 H1
Acock's Green Birm 98 E6
Acol Kent 41 J2
Acomb C York 151 J5
Acomb Nthumb 179 L5
Acombe Somset 30 B8
Aconbury Herefs 80 C8
Acre Lancs 140 B3
Acrefair Wrexhm 112 D3
Acresford Derbys 99 J1
Acton Ches E 113 K1
Acton Dorset 17 J7
Acton Gt Lon 51 G3
Acton Shrops 95 H6
Acton Staffs 114 C1
Acton Suffk 89 H6
Acton Worcs 81 J2
Acton Beauchamp Herefs 80 F5
Acton Bridge Ches W 130 B4
Acton Burnell Shrops 96 C3
Acton Green Herefs 81 G5
Acton Pigott Shrops 96 C3
Acton Round Shrops 96 E4
Acton Scott Shrops 95 L5
Acton Trussell Staffs 114 C7
Acton Turville S Glos 46 A3
Adbaston Staffs 114 B6
Adber Dorset 31 K6
Adbolton Notts 117 G4
Adderbury Oxon 83 L8
Adderley Shrops 113 L3
Adderstone Nthumb 203 J7
Addiewell W Loth 210 C6
Addingham C Brad 149 K6
Addington Bucks 67 H2
Addington Gt Lon 51 K6
Addington Kent 52 E7
Addiscombe Gt Lon 51 J5
Addlestone Surrey 50 D6
Addlestonemoor Surrey 50 D6
Addlethorpe Lincs 137 K6
Adeney Wrekin 113 M7
Adeyfield Herts 68 D5
Adfa Powys 94 C3
Adforton Herefs 79 M1
Adisham Kent 41 H4
Adlestrop Gloucs 65 K2
Adlingfleet E R Yk 143 L3
Adlington Ches E 131 H4
Adlington Lancs 139 J5
Admaston Staffs 115 G7
Admaston Wrekin 96 E1
Admington Warwks 82 E6
Adpar Cerdgn 76 B7
Adsborough Somset 30 D5
Adscombe Somset 30 B3
Adstock Bucks 67 H1
Adstone Nhants 84 B5
Adswood Stockp 131 H2
Adversane W Susx 37 G6
Advie Highld 254 C5
Adwalton Leeds 141 K2
Adwell Oxon 67 G7
Adwick le Street Donc 142 E6
Adwick upon Dearne Donc 142 D7
Ae D & G 176 C1
Ae Bridgend D & G 176 D2
Afan Forest Park Neath 42 C2
Affetside Bury 139 M5
Affleck Abers 255 L4
Affpuddle Dorset 16 F4
Affric Lodge Highld 249 K7
Afon-wen Flints 128 D5
Afon Wen Gwynd 109 H4
Afton Devon 8 C2
Afton IoW 18 E6
Agglethorpe N York 159 K5
Aigburth Lpool 129 J2
Aike E R Yk 153 G6
Aiketgate Cumb 166 B1
Aikhead Cumb 165 H1
Aikton Cumb 177 J8
Ailby Lincs 137 H4
Ailey Herefs 79 H5
Ailsworth C Pete 102 C4
Ainderby Quernhow N York 160 E6
Ainderby Steeple N York 160 E4
Aingers Green Essex 73 G3

Ainsdale Sefton 138 C
Ainsdale-on-Sea Sefton 138 C
Ainstable Cumb 166 C
Ainsworth Bury 139 M
Ainthorpe N York 162 C
Aintree Sefton 138 D8
Aird Ag & B 216 B
Aird D & G 172 C
Aird Highld 247 J8
Aird W Isls 282
Àird a' Mhulaidh W Isls 282 e
Aird Asaig W Isls 282 e
Aird Dhubh Highld 248 A4
Airdeny Ag & B 216 B
Airdrie N Lans 209 K
Airdriehill N Lans 209 K
Airds of Kells D & G 175 G
Àird Uig W Isls 282 d
Airidh a bhruaich W Isls 282 f
Airieland D & G 175 J
Airlie Angus 233 M
Airmyn E R Yk 143 J
Airntully P & K 233 G
Airor Highld 247 M
Airth Falk 210 B
Airton N York 148 D
Aisby Lincs 118 D
Aisby Lincs 135 H
Aisgill Cumb 158 D
Aish Devon 7
Aish Devon 8
Aisholt Somset 30 B
Aiskew N York 160 C
Aislaby N York 162 C
Aislaby N York 162 F
Aislaby S on T 169 L
Aisthorpe Lincs 135 J
Aith Shet 281 d
Akeld Nthumb 202 F
Akeley Bucks 84 D
Akenham Suffk 90 D
Albaston Cnwll 12 A
Alberbury Shrops 112 E
Albourne W Susx 22 C
Albourne Green W Susx 22 C
Albrighton Shrops 97 G
Albrighton Shrops 113 H
Alburgh Norfk 106 B
Albury Herts 70 B
Albury Oxon 67 G
Albury Surrey 37 G
Albury End Herts 70 B
Albury Heath Surrey 37 G
Alby Hill Norfk 122 D
Alcaig Highld 263 G
Alcaston Shrops 95 K
Alcester Warwks 82 C
Alciston E Susx 23 H
Alcombe Somset 29 H
Alcombe Wilts 46 A
Alconbury Cambs 102 D
Alconbury Weald Cambs 102 D
Alconbury Weston Cambs 102 D
Aldborough N York 150 F
Aldborough Norfk 122 D
Aldbourne Wilts 47 K
Aldbrough E R Yk 153 L
Aldbrough St John N York 169 G
Aldbury Herts 68 J
Aldcliffe Lancs 147 J
Aldclune P & K 232 D
Aldeburgh Suffk 91 K
Aldeby Norfk 107
Aldenham Herts 68 F
Alderbury Wilts 33 L
Aldercar Derbys 116 D
Alderford Norfk 122 C
Alderholt Dorset 33 K
Alderley Gloucs 45 M
Alderley Edge Ches E 131
Aldermans Green Covtry 99
Aldermaston W Berk 48
Alderminster Warwks 82
Alder Moor Staffs 115
Aldersey Green Ches W 129
Aldershot Hants 36
Alderton Gloucs 82
Alderton Nhants 84
Alderton Shrops 113
Alderton Suffk 91
Alderton Wilts 46
Alderwasley Derbys 116
Aldfield N York 150
Aldford Ches W 129
Aldgate Rutlnd 101
Aldham Essex 72
Aldham Suffk 90
Aldingbourne W Susx 20
Aldingham Cumb 146

Place	County	Page	Grid
Aldington	Kent	40	E8
Aldington	Worcs	82	C6
Aldington Corner	Kent	40	E7
Aldivalloch	Moray	255	G6
Aldochlay	Ag & B	208	B1
Aldon	Shrops	95	K7
Aldoth	Cumb	164	F1
Aldreth	Cambs	103	J8
Aldridge	Wsall	98	D3
Aldringham	Suffk	91	K3
Aldro	N York	152	B3
Aldsworth	Gloucs	65	H5
Aldsworth	W Susx	20	C5
Aldunie	Moray	255	G6
Aldwark	Derbys	132	E8
Aldwark	N York	151	G3
Aldwick	W Susx	20	E7
Aldwincle	Nhants	101	M7
Aldworth	W Berk	48	E3
Alexandria	W Duns	208	C3
Aley	Somset	30	B3
Alfardisworthy	Devon	26	E8
Alfington	Devon	14	D3
Alfold	Surrey	36	F4
Alfold Bars	W Susx	36	F4
Alfold Crossways	Surrey	36	F4
Alford	Abers	255	M8
Alford	Lincs	137	H4
Alford	Somset	31	K4
Alfreton	Derbys	133	H8
Alfrick	Worcs	81	H4
Alfrick Pound	Worcs	81	G5
Alfriston	E Susx	23	H4
Algarkirk	Lincs	119	J4
Alhampton	Somset	31	K4
Alkborough	N Linc	143	M3
Alkerton	Gloucs	63	M6
Alkerton	Oxon	83	J6
Alkham	Kent	41	H6
Alkington	Shrops	113	H4
Alkmonton	Derbys	115	K4
Allaleigh	Devon	8	B4
Allanaquoich	Abers	242	F5
Allanbank	N Lans	209	M7
Allanton	Border	202	D2
Allanton	N Lans	209	M7
Allanton	S Lans	209	K8
Allaston	Gloucs	63	J6
Allbrook	Hants	34	F6
All Cannings	Wilts	46	F6
Allendale	Nthumb	179	J7
Allen End	Warwks	98	F4
Allenheads	Nthumb	167	K4
Allensford	Dur	168	D1
Allen's Green	Herts	70	C4
Allensmore	Herefs	80	B8
Allenton	C Derb	116	B5
Aller	Devon	28	D5
Aller	Somset	30	F5
Allerby	Cumb	164	E3
Allercombe	Devon	14	B4
Aller Cross	Devon	28	B5
Allerford	Somset	28	F2
Allerston	N York	162	F6
Allerthorpe	E R Yk	152	B6
Allerton	C Brad	141	H1
Allerton	Highld	263	K6
Allerton	Lpool	129	J2
Allerton Bywater	Leeds	142	C2
Allerton Mauleverer	N York	150	F4
Allesley	Covtry	99	J7
Allestree	C Derb	116	B4
Allet	Cnwll	4	C5
Allexton	Leics	101	H3
Allgreave	Ches E	131	J6
Allhallows	Medway	53	H3
Allhallows-on-Sea	Medway	53	H3
Alligin Shuas	Highld	260	D8
Allimore Green	Staffs	114	D7
Allington	Dorset	15	K4
Allington	Kent	53	G7
Allington	Lincs	117	M3
Allington	Wilts	33	L3
Allington	Wilts	46	C4
Allington	Wilts	46	F6
Allithwaite	Cumb	156	E7
Alloa	Clacks	220	F8
Allonby	Cumb	164	E2
Allostock	Ches W	130	E5
Alloway	S Ayrs	196	C7
Allowenshay	Somset	30	F8
All Saints South Elmham	Suffk	107	G4
Allscott	Shrops	97	G4
Allscott	Wrekin	96	E1
All Stretton	Shrops	95	L4
Alltami	Flints	129	G6
Alltchaorunn	Highld	229	K5
Alltmawr	Powys	78	F6
Alltsigh	Highld	250	D7
Alltwalis	Carmth	58	E3
Alltwen	Neath	57	K4
Alltyblaca	Cerdgn	76	F6
Allwood Green	Suffk	90	B1
Almeley	Herefs	79	L5
Almeley Wooton	Herefs	79	L5
Almer	Dorset	17	H3
Almholme	Donc	142	F6
Almington	Staffs	113	M4
Almodington	W Susx	20	D7
Almondbank	P & K	221	J2
Almondbury	Kirk	141	J5
Almondsbury	S Glos	45	J2
Alne	N York	151	H2
Alness	Highld	263	H6
Alnham	Nthumb	190	E4
Alnmouth	Nthumb	191	J4
Alnwick	Nthumb	191	H3
Alperton	Gt Lon	50	F2
Alphamstone	Essex	89	H8
Alpheton	Suffk	89	H5
Alphington	Devon	13	L4
Alpington	Norfk	106	F3
Alport	Derbys	132	D6
Alpraham	Ches E	130	B7
Alresford	Essex	72	F3
Alrewas	Staffs	115	K8
Alsager	Ches E	130	F8
Alsagers Bank	Staffs	114	C2
Alsop en le Dale	Derbys	132	C8
Alston	Cumb	167	G2
Alston	Devon	15	G2
Alstone	Gloucs	64	E1
Alstone	Somset	30	D2
Alstonefield	Staffs	132	C8
Alston Sutton	Somset	44	E8
Alswear	Devon	28	C6
Alt	Oldham	140	E7
Altandhu	Highld	270	C5
Altarnun	Cnwll	11	J6
Altass	Highld	272	D8
Altcreich	Ag & B	227	K5
Altgaltraig	Ag & B	207	G4
Altham	Lancs	140	A1
Althorne	Essex	72	D7
Althorpe	N Linc	143	L6
Altnabreac Station	Highld	279	H7
Altnaharra	Highld	272	E1
Altofts	Wakefd	142	B3
Alton	Derbys	133	G6
Alton	Hants	35	L3
Alton	Staffs	115	H3
Alton	Wilts	33	K2
Alton Barnes	Wilts	47	G6
Alton Pancras	Dorset	16	D2
Alton Priors	Wilts	47	G6
Altrincham	Traffd	130	E2
Altskeith Hotel	Stirlg	219	G6
Alva	Clacks	220	F7
Alvanley	Ches W	129	L5
Alvaston	C Derb	116	C5
Alvechurch	Worcs	82	E1
Alvecote	Warwks	99	H3
Alvediston	Wilts	33	G6
Alveley	Shrops	97	G6
Alverdiscott	Devon	27	J6
Alverstoke	Hants	19	K4
Alverstone	IoW	19	K6
Alverthorpe	Wakefd	141	M3
Alverton	Notts	117	L3
Alves	Moray	266	C4
Alvescot	Oxon	65	K6
Alveston	S Glos	45	J1
Alveston	Warwks	82	F4
Alvingham	Lincs	137	G2
Alvington	Gloucs	63	J7
Alwalton	C Pete	102	C4
Alweston	Dorset	31	L8
Alwinton	Nthumb	190	C5
Alwoodley	Leeds	150	C7
Alwoodley Gates	Leeds	150	D7
Alyth	P & K	233	K5
Am Bàgh a Tuath	W Isls	283	b13
Ambergate	Derbys	116	B1
Amber Hill	Lincs	119	H2
Amberley	Gloucs	64	B6
Amberley	W Susx	21	H4
Amber Row	Derbys	133	G8
Amberstone	E Susx	23	K5
Amble	Nthumb	191	K5
Amblecote	Dudley	97	K6
Ambler Thorn	C Brad	141	H2
Ambleside	Cumb	156	E2
Ambleston	Pembks	75	G7
Ambrosden	Oxon	66	F3
Amcotts	N Linc	143	L5
America	Cambs	103	J7
Amersham	Bucks	68	B7
Amersham Common	Bucks	68	B7
Amersham Old Town	Bucks	68	B7
Amersham on the Hill	Bucks	68	B7
Amerton	Staffs	114	F6
Amesbury	Wilts	33	K3
Amhuinnsuidhe	W Isls	282	d5
Amington	Staffs	99	G3
Amisfield	D & G	176	D2
Amlwch	IoA	125	H1
Ammanford	Carmth	59	H6
Amotherby	N York	162	C7
Ampfield	Hants	34	E6
Ampleforth	N York	161	J7
Ampney Crucis	Gloucs	64	F6
Ampney St Mary	Gloucs	65	G6
Ampney St Peter	Gloucs	65	G6
Amport	Hants	34	C2
Ampthill	C Beds	85	K7
Ampton	Suffk	89	H1
Amroth	Pembks	55	K5
Amulree	P & K	232	D8
Amwell	Herts	68	F4
Anaheilt	Highld	228	C3
Ancaster	Lincs	118	C3
Ancells Farm	Hants	49	K7
Anchor	Shrops	94	E6
Ancroft	Nthumb	202	F4
Ancrum	Border	189	H1
Ancton	W Susx	21	G6
Anderby	Lincs	137	K4
Anderby Creek	Lincs	137	K4
Andersea	Somset	30	C4
Andersfield	Somset	30	C4
Anderson	Dorset	17	G3
Anderton	Ches W	130	C4
Anderton	Cnwll	6	E4
Andover	Hants	34	D2
Andover Down	Hants	34	E2
Andoversford	Gloucs	64	F3
Andreas	IoM	154	f2
Anelog	Gwynd	108	B6
Anerley	Gt Lon	51	J5
Anfield	Lpool	129	J1
Angarrack	Cnwll	2	F4
Angarrick	Cnwll	3	K4
Angelbank	Shrops	96	D8
Angersleigh	Somset	30	B7
Angerton	Cumb	177	H2
Angle	Pembks	54	D6
Anglesey	IoA	125	G3
Angmering	W Susx	21	H6
Angram	N York	151	H6
Angram	N York	158	F3
Angrouse	Cnwll	3	H7
Anick	Nthumb	179	L5
Ankerville	Highld	264	C5
Ankle Hill	Leics	117	K7
Anlaby	E R Yk	144	C2
Anmer	Norfk	121	G5
Anmore	Hants	19	L1
Annan	D & G	177	G5
Annandale Water Services	D & G	187	H7
Annaside	Cumb	155	K5
Annat	Highld	248	E1
Annathill	N Lans	209	J5
Anna Valley	Hants	34	D2
Annbank	S Ayrs	196	E6
Annesley	Notts	116	E1
Annesley Woodhouse	Notts	116	E1
Annfield Plain	Dur	180	E8
Anniesland	C Glas	208	F5
Annitsford	N Tyne	181	G4
Annscroft	Shrops	95	L2
Ansdell	Lancs	138	D2
Ansford	Somset	31	L4
Ansley	Warwks	99	J5
Anslow	Staffs	115	L6
Anslow Gate	Staffs	115	K6
Anslow Lees	Staffs	115	K6
Ansteadbrook	Surrey	36	D4
Anstey	Hants	35	L3
Anstey	Herts	87	H8
Anstey	Leics	100	C2
Anstruther	Fife	223	K6
Ansty	W Susx	37	L6
Ansty	Warwks	99	L6
Ansty	Wilts	33	G5
Ansty Cross	Dorset	16	E2
An Tairbeart	W Isls	282	e5
Anthill Common	Hants	19	L1
Anthonys	Surrey	50	C6
Anthorn	Cumb	177	G7
Antingham	Norfk	122	E5
An t-Ob	W Isls	282	d6
Antonine Wall		209	M3
Anton's Gowt	Lincs	119	J2
Antony	Cnwll	6	D4
Antrobus	Ches W	130	C4
Anvil Corner	Devon	11	M2
Anvil Green	Kent	40	E5
Anwick	Lincs	118	F2
Anwoth	D & G	174	F4
Aperfield	Gt Lon	51	L7
Apes Dale	Worcs	82	A1
Apethorpe	Nhants	102	A4
Apeton	Staffs	114	D7
Apley	Lincs	136	B5
Apperknowle	Derbys	133	H4
Apperley	Gloucs	64	B2
Apperley Bridge	C Brad	150	B8
Apperley Dene	Nthumb	180	C7
Appersett	N York	158	E4
Appin	Ag & B	228	E6
Appleby	N Linc	144	B5
Appleby-in-Westmorland	Cumb	166	F6
Appleby Magna	Leics	99	J2
Appleby Parva	Leics	99	J2
Appleby Street	Herts	69	J6
Applecross	Highld	248	A3
Appledore	Devon	27	H5
Appledore	Devon	29	K7
Appledore	Kent	25	H2
Appledore Heath	Kent	25	H1
Appleford	Oxon	66	D8
Applegarth Town	D & G	176	F2
Applehaigh	Wakefd	142	A5
Applemore	Hants	18	F2
Appleshaw	Hants	34	C1
Applethwaite	Cumb	165	J5
Appleton	Halton	129	M2
Appleton	Oxon	66	C6
Appleton	Warrtn	130	B3
Appleton-le-Moors	N York	162	C5
Appleton-le-Street	N York	162	C7
Appleton Roebuck	N York	151	J7
Appleton Thorn	Warrtn	130	C3
Appleton Wiske	N York	160	F2
Appletreehall	Border	188	F3
Appletreewick	N York	149	J4
Appley	Somset	29	K6
Appley Bridge	Lancs	139	G6
Apse Heath	IoW	19	J7
Apsley End	C Beds	86	C8
Apuldram	W Susx	20	D6
Arabella	Highld	264	C5
Arbirlot	Angus	234	F7
Arborfield	Wokham	49	H5
Arborfield Cross	Wokham	49	J5
Arborfield Green	Wokham	49	J6
Arbourthorne	Sheff	133	G3
Arbroath	Angus	235	G7
Arbuthnott	Abers	245	H8
Arcadia	Kent	39	L6
Archddu	Carmth	56	E4
Archdeacon Newton	Darltn	169	H7
Archencarroch	W Duns	208	C3
Archiestown	Moray	254	E3
Archirondel	Jersey	9	f2
Arclid	Ches E	130	F7
Ardallie	Abers	257	J4
Ardanaiseig Hotel	Ag & B	217	H2
Ardaneaskan	Highld	248	D4
Ardarroch	Highld	248	D4
Ardbeg	Ag & B	204	F7
Ardbeg	Ag & B	207	H5
Ardbeg	Ag & B	207	K2
Ardcharnich	Highld	261	K2
Ardchiavaig	Ag & B	214	D1
Ardchonnell	Ag & B	216	F5
Ardchronie	Highld	263	G2
Ardchullarie More	Stirlg	219	K4
Arddarroch	Ag & B	218	C8
Arddleen	Powys	112	C8
Ard Dorch	Highld	247	J3
Ardechive	Highld	239	J5
Ardeer	N Ayrs	196	B3
Ardeley	Herts	69	J2
Ardelve	Highld	248	D6
Arden	Ag & B	208	B2
Ardens Grafton	Warwks	82	D4
Ardentallen	Ag & B	216	C2
Ardentinny	Ag & B	207	K2
Ardentraive	Ag & B	207	G4
Ardeonaig	Stirlg	231	J8
Ardersier	Highld	252	E1
Ardessie	Highld	261	H2
Ardfern	Ag & B	216	C2
Ardfernal	Ag & B	205	J2
Ardgartan	Ag & B	218	D6
Ardgay	Highld	263	G2
Ardgour	Highld	229	G3
Ardgowan	Inver	207	L4
Ardhallow	Ag & B	207	K4
Ardhasig	W Isls	282	e5
Ardheslaig	Highld	260	C8
Ardindrean	Highld	261	K2
Ardingly	W Susx	38	A7
Ardington	Oxon	48	B1
Ardington Wick	Oxon	48	B1
Ardlamont	Ag & B	206	F6
Ardleigh	Essex	72	F1

Ardleigh Heath Essex 72 F1
Ardler P & K 233 L7
Ardley Oxon 66 D2
Ardley End Essex 70 D4
Ardlui Ag & B 218 D4
Ardlussa Ag & B 215 J6
Ardmair Highld 270 F8
Ardmaleish Ag & B 207 H5
Ardminish Ag & B 205 L6
Ardmolich Highld 237 K6
Ardmore Ag & B 208 A3
Ardmore Highld 263 J3
Ardnadam Ag & B 207 K3
Ardnagrask Highld 250 F2
Ardnamurchan Highld 237 H7
Ardnarff Highld 248 E4
Ardnastang Highld 228 B3
Ardpatrick Ag & B 206 B7
Ardrishaig Ag & B 206 D2
Ardross Highld 263 H5
Ardrossan N Ayrs 195 L3
Ardsley Barns 142 B6
Ardslignish Highld 237 H8
Ardtalla Ag & B 205 G5
Ardtoe Highld 237 J6
Arduaine Ag & B 216 B5
Ardullie Highld 263 G7
Ardvasar Highld 247 K7
Ardvorlich P & K 219 K3
Ardvourlie W Isls 282 e5
Ardwell D & G 172 D5
Ardwick Manch 140 C8
Areley Kings Worcs 81 H1
Arevegaig Highld 237 J7
Arford Hants 36 B3
Arglam E R Yk 152 B8
Argoed Caerph 61 J7
Argoed Shrops 112 E7
Argoed Mill Powys 78 D3
Argos Hill E Susx 23 J2
Argyll Forest Park Ag & B 218 C6
Aribruach W Isls 282 f4
Aridhglas Ag & B 226 C7
Arileod Ag & B 224 F4
Arinagour Ag & B 225 G4
Ariogan Ag & B 216 D2
Arisaig Highld 237 J3
Arisaig House Highld 237 K4
Arkendale N York 150 E4
Arkesden Essex 87 K8
Arkholme Lancs 147 L2
Arkleby Cumb 164 F3
Arkleton D & G 188 C7
Arkle Town N York 159 H2
Arkley Gt Lon 69 G7
Arksey Donc 142 F6
Arkwright Town Derbys 133 H5
Arle Gloucs 64 D2
Arlecdon Cumb 164 D7
Arlescote Warwks 83 J5
Arlesey C Beds 86 D7
Arleston Wrekin 96 F1
Arley Ches E 130 C3
Arlingham Gloucs 63 L5
Arlington Devon 27 L3
Arlington E Susx 23 J5
Arlington Gloucs 65 G5
Arlington Beccott Devon 27 L3
Armadale Highld 247 K7
Armadale Highld 278 D3
Armadale W Loth 210 B5
Armaside Cumb 164 F5
Armathwaite Cumb 166 C2
Arminghall Norfk 106 E3
Armitage Staffs 115 H8
Armitage Bridge Kirk 141 H5
Armley Leeds 141 L1
Armscote Warwks 82 F6
Armshead Staffs 114 E2
Armston Nhants 102 B6
Armthorpe Donc 143 G6
Arnabost Ag & B 225 G3
Arnaby Cumb 156 A5
Arncliffe N York 149 G2
Arncliffe Cote N York 149 G2
Arncroach Fife 223 J6
Arndilly House Moray 266 F6
Arne Dorset 17 J5
Arnesby Leics 100 D5
Arngask P & K 221 L5
Arnisdale Highld 238 D2
Arnish Highld 259 K7
Arniston Mdloth 211 K6
Arnol W Isls 282 f2
Arnold E R Yk 153 H7
Arnold Notts 117 J2
Arnprior Stirlg 219 K8
Arnside Cumb 157 G7
Aros Ag & B 227 G3
Arowry Wrexhm 113 G4

Arrad Foot Cumb 156 D6
Arram E R Yk 153 G7
Arran N Ayrs 194 E4
Arrathorne N York 160 B4
Arreton IoW 19 H6
Arrina Highld 260 B8
Arrington Cambs 87 G5
Arrochar Ag & B 218 D6
Arrow Warwks 82 C4
Arrowfield Top Worcs 98 C8
Arscott Shrops 95 K2
Artafallie Highld 251 H2
Arthington Leeds 150 C6
Arthingworth Nhants 101 G7
Arthog Gwynd 110 C8
Arthrath Abers 257 H4
Arthursdale Leeds 150 E8
Artrochie Abers 257 J5
Arundel W Susx 21 G5
Asby Cumb 164 E6
Ascog Ag & B 207 J4
Ascot W & M 50 A5
Ascott Warwks 83 H8
Ascott Earl Oxon 65 L3
Ascott-under-Wychwood Oxon 65 L3
Asenby N York 160 F7
Asfordby Leics 117 J7
Asfordby Hill Leics 117 J7
Asgarby Lincs 118 F3
Asgarby Lincs 136 F6
Ash Devon 8 C5
Ash Devon 12 C1
Ash Dorset 32 E8
Ash Kent 41 J4
Ash Kent 52 D6
Ash Somset 30 C6
Ash Somset 31 G6
Ash Surrey 36 D1
Ashampstead W Berk 48 E4
Ashampstead Green W Berk 48 E3
Ashbocking Suffk 90 E4
Ashbourne Derbys 115 K2
Ashbrittle Somset 29 J6
Ashburnham Place E Susx 24 C4
Ashburton Devon 13 H8
Ashbury Devon 12 C3
Ashbury Oxon 47 K2
Ashby N Linc 143 M6
Ashby by Partney Lincs 137 H6
Ashby cum Fenby NE Lin 145 H7
Ashby de la Launde Lincs 135 L8
Ashby-de-la-Zouch Leics 116 B8
Ashby Folville Leics 100 F1
Ashby Magna Leics 100 C5
Ashby Parva Leics 100 C5
Ashby Puerorum Lincs 136 F5
Ashby St Ledgers Nhants 84 B2
Ashby St Mary Norfk 107 G3
Ashchurch Gloucs 81 L3
Ashcombe Devon 13 L6
Ashcombe N Som 44 C6
Ashcott Somset 31 G3
Ashdon Essex 88 B6
Ashdown Forest E Susx 38 C7
Ashe Hants 35 H1
Asheldham Essex 72 E6
Ashen Essex 88 C4
Ashendon Bucks 67 H4
Asheridge Bucks 68 B6
Ashfield Hants 34 E7
Ashfield Herefs 63 H6
Ashfield Stirlg 220 D6
Ashfield cum Thorpe Suffk 90 F3
Ashfield Green Suffk 88 F4
Ashfield Green Suffk 106 F8
Ashfold Crossways W Susx 37 K5
Ashford Devon 7 K5
Ashford Devon 27 J4
Ashford Kent 40 D6
Ashford Surrey 50 D4
Ashford Bowdler Shrops 80 C1
Ashford Carbonell Shrops 80 C1
Ashford Hill Hants 48 E6
Ashford in the Water Derbys 132 D5
Ashgill S Lans 198 C3
Ash Green Surrey 36 D1
Ash Green Warwks 99 J6
Ashill Devon 29 K8
Ashill Norfk 105 H3
Ashill Somset 30 D7
Ashingdon Essex 72 C8
Ashington BCP 17 K3
Ashington Nthumb 181 G1
Ashington Somset 31 J6
Ashington W Susx 21 K4
Ashkirk Border 188 E2
Ashlett Hants 19 G3
Ashleworth Gloucs 64 A2
Ashleworth Quay Gloucs 64 B2

Ashley Cambs 88 D3
Ashley Ches E 130 F3
Ashley Devon 28 B8
Ashley Dorset 18 A3
Ashley Gloucs 64 D8
Ashley Hants 18 C4
Ashley Hants 34 E4
Ashley Kent 41 J5
Ashley Nhants 101 H5
Ashley Staffs 114 B8
Ashley Wilts 46 B5
Ashley Green Bucks 68 B6
Ashleyhay Derbys 115 M1
Ashley Heath Dorset 17 M2
Ashley Moor Herefs 80 B2
Ash Magna Shrops 113 J4
Ashmansworth Hants 48 B7
Ashmansworthy Devon 26 F7
Ashmead Green Gloucs 63 M7
Ashmill Devon 11 M3
Ash Mill Devon 28 D6
Ashmore Dorset 32 F7
Ashmore Green W Berk 48 D5
Ashorne Warwks 83 G4
Ashover Derbys 133 G7
Ashover Hay Derbys 133 G7
Ashow Warwks 83 H1
Ash Parva Shrops 113 J4
Ashperton Herefs 80 C7
Ashprington Devon 8 B3
Ash Priors Somset 29 L5
Ashreigney Devon 27 L8
Ash Street Suffk 89 K6
Ashtead Surrey 50 F7
Ash Thomas Devon 29 H8
Ashton C Pete 102 B2
Ashton Cnwll 2 F5
Ashton Devon 13 K5
Ashton Hants 35 H7
Ashton Herefs 80 C2
Ashton Inver 207 L4
Ashton Nhants 84 E5
Ashton Nhants 102 B5
Ashton Somset 30 F1
Ashton Common Wilts 46 C7
Ashton Hayes Ches W 129 L6
Ashton Hill Wilts 46 C7
Ashton-in-Makerfield Wigan 139 H7
Ashton Keynes Wilts 64 F8
Ashton-on-Ribble Lancs 139 G2
Ashton under Hill Worcs 82 A7
Ashton-under-Lyne Tamesd 140 E7
Ashton upon Mersey Traffd 130 F1
Ashton Vale Bristl 45 H5
Ashurst Hants 18 E2
Ashurst Kent 38 D5
Ashurst Lancs 138 F6
Ashurst W Susx 21 L4
Ashurst Wood W Susx 38 B6
Ash Vale Surrey 49 L8
Ashwater Devon 11 M4
Ashwell Herts 86 F7
Ashwell Rutlnd 101 J1
Ashwell Somset 30 E7
Ashwell End Herts 86 E7
Ashwellthorpe Norfk 106 C4
Ashwick Somset 31 K1
Ashwicken Norfk 120 F7
Ashwood Staffs 97 K5
Askam in Furness Cumb 156 B7
Askern Donc 142 F5
Askerswell Dorset 15 M4
Askett Bucks 67 K6
Askham Cumb 166 C6
Askham Notts 134 E5
Askham Bryan C York 151 H6
Askham Richard C York 151 H6
Asknish Ag & B 206 E1
Askrigg N York 159 G4
Askwith N York 149 L6
Aslackby Lincs 118 E5
Aslacton Norfk 106 D5
Aslockton Notts 117 K3
Asney Somset 31 G3
Aspall Suffk 90 E2
Aspatria Cumb 164 F2
Aspenden Herts 69 K2
Aspenshaw Derbys 131 K2
Asperton Lincs 119 J4
Aspley Staffs 114 C5
Aspley Guise C Beds 85 J8
Aspley Heath C Beds 85 J8
Aspley Heath Warwks 82 C1
Aspull Wigan 139 J6
Aspull Common Wigan 139 J8
Asselby E R Yk 143 H2
Asserby Lincs 137 J4
Asserby Turn Lincs 137 J4
Assington Suffk 89 J7
Assington Green Suffk 88 F5

Astbury Ches E .....131 G
Astcote Nhants .....84 H
Asterby Lincs .....136 G
Asterley Shrops .....95 L
Asterton Shrops .....95 L
Asthall Oxon .....65 L
Asthall Leigh Oxon .....65 L
Astle Highld .....263 K
Astley Shrops .....113 H
Astley Warwks .....99 J
Astley Wigan .....139 J
Astley Worcs .....81 J
Astley Abbots Shrops .....96 K
Astley Bridge Bolton .....139 L
Astley Cross Worcs .....81 J
Astley Green Wigan .....139 J
Aston Birm .....98 D
Aston Ches E .....113 K
Aston Ches W .....130 A
Aston Derbys .....132 D
Aston Flints .....129 K
Aston Herefs .....80 B
Aston Herts .....69 B
Aston Oxon .....65 M
Aston Rothm .....133 J
Aston Shrops .....97 H
Aston Shrops .....113 H
Aston Staffs .....114 B
Aston Staffs .....114 B
Aston Wokham .....49 J
Aston Wrekin .....96 E
Aston Abbotts Bucks .....67 K
Aston Botterell Shrops .....96 K
Aston-by-Stone Staffs .....114 B
Aston Cantlow Warwks .....82 E
Aston Clinton Bucks .....67 L
Aston Crews Herefs .....63 K
Aston Cross Gloucs .....81 L
Aston End Herts .....69 H
Aston-Eyre Shrops .....96 E
Aston Fields Worcs .....81 M
Aston Flamville Leics .....100 A
Aston Heath Ches W .....130 A
Aston Ingham Herefs .....63 K
Aston juxta Mondrum Ches E .....130 A
Aston le Walls Nhants .....83 L
Aston Magna Gloucs .....82 E
Aston Munslow Shrops .....96 E
Aston-on-Carrant Gloucs .....81 L
Aston on Clun Shrops .....95 J
Aston Pigott Shrops .....95 H
Aston Rogers Shrops .....95 H
Aston Rowant Oxon .....67 J
Aston Sandford Bucks .....67 J
Aston Somerville Worcs .....82 D
Aston-sub-Edge Gloucs .....82 D
Aston Tirrold Oxon .....48 E
Aston-upon-Trent Derbys .....116 E
Aston Upthorpe Oxon .....48 E
Astrop Nhants .....83 J
Astrope Herts .....67 L
Astwick C Beds .....86 E
Astwith Derbys .....133 J
Astwood M Keyn .....85 J
Astwood Worcs .....81 L
Astwood Bank Worcs .....82 C
Aswarby Lincs .....118 E
Aswardby Lincs .....137 G
Atcham Shrops .....96 C
Atch Lench Worcs .....82 E
Athelhampton Dorset .....16 E
Athelington Suffk .....90 F
Athelney Somset .....30 C
Athelstaneford E Loth .....212 C
Atherfield Green IoW .....19 G
Atherington Devon .....27 K
Atherington W Susx .....21 G
Atherstone Somset .....30 F
Atherstone Warwks .....99 J
Atherstone on Stour Warwks .....82 E
Atherton Wigan .....139 K
Atley Hill N York .....160 D
Atlow Derbys .....115 L
Attadale Highld .....248 D
Attenborough Notts .....116 K
Atterby Lincs .....135 K
Attercliffe Sheff .....133 G
Atterley Shrops .....96 E
Atterton Leics .....99 L
Attleborough Norfk .....105 L
Attleborough Warwks .....99 K
Attlebridge Norfk .....122 D
Attleton Green Suffk .....88 E
Atwick E R Yk .....153 K
Atworth Wilts .....46 B
Auberrow Herefs .....80 B
Aubourn Lincs .....135 L
Auchbreck Moray .....254 D
Auchedly Abers .....257 G
Auchenblae Abers .....244 D

Auchenbowie Stirlg	209	L2
Auchencairn D & G	175	K4
Auchencairn D & G	176	C2
Auchencairn N Ayrs	195	G5
Auchencrow Border	213	J7
Auchendinny Mdloth	211	H4
Auchengray S Lans	199	G2
Auchenhalrig Moray	267	H4
Auchenheath S Lans	198	D4
Auchenhessnane D & G	185	K4
Auchenlochan Ag & B	206	F4
Auchenmade N Ayrs	196	C2
Auchenmalg D & G	173	G4
Auchentiber N Ayrs	196	D2
Auchindrain Ag & B	217	G6
Auchindrean Highld	261	K4
Auchininna Abers	268	B6
Auchinleck E Ayrs	197	G6
Auchinloch N Lans	209	H5
Auchinstarry N Lans	209	J4
Auchintore Highld	229	H1
Auchiries Abers	257	K4
Auchlean Highld	241	M4
Auchlee Abers	245	K4
Auchleven Abers	256	A6
Auchlochan S Lans	198	D5
Auchlossan Abers	244	D3
Auchlyne Stirlg	219	H1
Auchmillan E Ayrs	197	G5
Auchmithie Angus	235	G6
Auchmuirbridge Fife	222	C7
Auchnacree Angus	234	C3
Auchnagatt Abers	257	G3
Auchnarrow Moray	254	D7
Auchnotteroch D & G	172	B3
Auchroisk Moray	267	G6
Auchterarder P & K	221	G4
Auchteraw Highld	240	B2
Auchterblair Highld	253	H7
Auchtercairn Highld	260	C4
Auchterderran Fife	222	C8
Auchterhouse Angus	233	M7
Auchterless Abers	256	C3
Auchtermuchty Fife	222	D5
Auchterneed Highld	262	E7
Auchtertool Fife	211	H1
Auchtertyre Highld	248	D6
Auchtubh Stirlg	219	J3
Auckengill Highld	280	C2
Auckley Donc	143	G7
Audenshaw Tamesd	140	D8
Audlem Ches E	113	L3
Audley Staffs	114	C2
Audley End Essex	87	L7
Audley End Essex	89	G7
Audley End Suffk	89	G4
Audmore Staffs	114	C7
Audnam Dudley	97	K6
Aughertree Cumb	165	H3
Aughton E R Yk	151	L8
Aughton Lancs	138	E6
Aughton Lancs	147	L2
Aughton Rothm	133	J2
Aughton Wilts	47	K7
Aughton Park Lancs	138	E6
Auldearn Highld	253	H1
Aulden Herefs	80	B4
Auldgirth D & G	176	B2
Auldhouse S Lans	197	H1
Ault a' chruinn Highld	248	F7
Aultbea Highld	260	D2
Aultgrishin Highld	260	B3
Aultguish Inn Highld	262	B4
Ault Hucknall Derbys	133	J6
Aultmore Moray	267	H5
Aultnagoire Highld	250	F7
Aultnamain Highld	263	J4
Aunby Lincs	118	D8
Aunk Devon	14	B3
Aunsby Lincs	118	D4
Aust S Glos	45	H1
Austendike Lincs	119	J7
Austerfield Donc	134	D1
Austerlands Oldham	140	E6
Austhorpe Leeds	142	B1
Austonley Kirk	141	H6
Austrey Warwks	99	J2
Austwick N York	148	B7
Authorpe Lincs	137	G3
Authorpe Row Lincs	137	K5
Avebury Wilts	47	G5
Avebury Wilts	47	G5
Avebury Trusloe Wilts	47	G5
Aveley Thurr	52	C3
Avening Gloucs	64	C7
Averham Notts	117	K1
Aveton Gifford Devon	7	K5
Aviemore Highld	242	B1
Avington W Berk	48	A5
Avoch Highld	251	J1
Avon Hants	18	A4
Avonbridge Falk	210	B4
Avon Dassett Warwks	83	K5
Avonmouth Bristl	45	G3
Avonwick Devon	7	K3
Awbridge Hants	34	D6
Awkley S Glos	45	H2
Awliscombe Devon	14	D2
Awre Gloucs	63	L5
Awsworth Notts	116	E3
Axborough Worcs	97	J7
Axbridge Somset	44	E8
Axford Hants	35	J2
Axford Wilts	47	K5
Axmansford Hants	48	E6
Axminster Devon	15	G3
Axmouth Devon	14	F4
Axton Flints	128	D4
Aycliffe Dur	169	H6
Aydon Nthumb	180	B5
Aylburton Gloucs	63	J6
Ayle Nthumb	167	G1
Aylesbeare Devon	14	B4
Aylesbury Bucks	67	K4
Aylesby NE Lin	145	G6
Aylesford Kent	52	F7
Aylesham Kent	41	H5
Aylestone C Leic	100	C3
Aylestone Park C Leic	100	C3
Aylmerton Norfk	122	D4
Aylsham Norfk	122	D6
Aylton Herefs	80	F7
Aylworth Gloucs	65	G3
Aymestrey Herefs	80	A2
Aynho Nhants	83	L8
Ayot Green Herts	69	G4
Ayot St Lawrence Herts	69	G4
Ayot St Peter Herts	69	G4
Ayr S Ayrs	196	C6
Aysgarth N York	159	H5
Ayshford Devon	29	J7
Ayside Cumb	156	F6
Ayston Rutlnd	101	J3
Aythorpe Roding Essex	70	E4
Ayton Border	213	K6
Azerley N York	160	C7

B

Babbacombe Torbay	8	D2
Babbington Notts	116	E3
Babbinswood Shrops	112	E5
Babbs Green Herts	69	K4
Babcary Somset	31	J5
Babel Carmth	59	M2
Babel Green Suffk	88	E5
Babell Flints	128	E5
Babeny Devon	12	F7
Bablock Hythe Oxon	66	B6
Babraham Cambs	87	K5
Babworth Notts	134	D3
Bachau IoA	125	H3
Bache Shrops	95	L7
Bacheldre Powys	94	F5
Bachelor's Bump E Susx	24	F5
Backaland Ork	275	d3
Backbarrow Cumb	156	E5
Backe Carmth	58	A5
Backfolds Abers	269	J5
Backford Ches W	129	J5
Backford Cross Ches W	129	J5
Backies Highld	273	K7
Back of Keppoch Highld	237	J3
Back o' th' Brook Staffs	115	J1
Back Street Suffk	88	E3
Backwell N Som	44	F5
Backworth N Tyne	181	H4
Bacon's End Solhll	98	F6
Baconsthorpe Norfk	122	D4
Bacton Herefs	62	D1
Bacton Norfk	123	G5
Bacton Suffk	90	C2
Bacton Green Suffk	90	B2
Bacup Lancs	140	C3
Badachro Highld	260	C5
Badanloch Highld	273	J2
Badbury Swindn	47	J3
Badby Nhants	84	A3
Badcall Highld	276	C5
Badcaul Highld	261	G2
Baddeley Edge C Stke	114	E1
Baddeley Green C Stke	114	E1
Baddesley Clinton Warwks	82	F1
Baddesley Ensor Warwks	99	H4
Baddidarrach Highld	270	E3
Baddinsgill Border	199	K2
Badenscoth Abers	256	C4
Badentarbet Highld	270	D6
Badenyon Abers	255	G7
Badersfield Norfk	122	E6
Badgall Cnwll	11	J5
Badgeney Cambs	103	J4
Badger Shrops	97	H3
Badger's Cross Cnwll	2	D4
Badgers Mount Kent	52	B6
Badgeworth Gloucs	64	C3
Badgworth Somset	44	E8
Badharlick Cnwll	11	J5
Badicaul Highld	248	B6
Badingham Suffk	91	G2
Badlesmere Kent	40	D4
Badlieu Border	187	G2
Badlipster Highld	280	B6
Badluarach Highld	261	G1
Badninish Highld	263	K1
Badrallach Highld	261	H2
Badsey Worcs	82	C6
Badshot Lea Surrey	36	C1
Badsworth Wakefd	142	C5
Badwell Ash Suffk	89	K2
Badwell Green Suffk	89	K2
Bagber Dorset	32	C8
Bagby N York	161	G6
Bag Enderby Lincs	136	F5
Bagendon Gloucs	64	E5
Bagginswood Shrops	96	F7
Baggrow Cumb	165	G2
Bàgh a' Chaisteil W Isls	283	b13
Bagham Kent	40	E4
Bagillt Flints	128	F4
Baginton Warwks	99	K8
Baglan Neath	57	K6
Bagley Leeds	141	K1
Bagley Shrops	112	F6
Bagley Somset	31	G2
Bagmore Hants	35	K2
Bagnall Staffs	114	E1
Bagnor W Berk	48	C5
Bagshot Surrey	49	M6
Bagshot Wilts	47	L6
Bagstone S Glos	45	K2
Bagthorpe Notts	116	D1
Bagworth Leics	99	M2
Bagwyllydiart Herefs	62	F2
Baildon C Brad	149	L7
Baildon Green C Brad	149	L7
Baile Ailein W Isls	282	f4
Baile a' Mhanaich W Isls	283	c9
Baile Mòr Ag & B	226	B7
Bailey Green Hants	35	K5
Baileyhead Cumb	178	C3
Bailiff Bridge Calder	141	J3
Baillieston C Glas	209	H6
Bailrigg Lancs	147	J4
Bainbridge N York	159	G4
Bainshole Abers	256	A5
Bainton C Pete	102	B2
Bainton E R Yk	152	E5
Bainton Oxon	66	E2
Baintown Fife	222	F6
Bairnkine Border	189	H3
Baker's End Herts	69	L4
Baker Street Thurr	52	D3
Bakewell Derbys	132	D6
Bala Gwynd	111	H4
Balallan W Isls	282	f4
Balbeg Highld	250	D5
Balbeggie P & K	222	B1
Balblair Highld	263	J6
Balby Donc	142	E7
Balcary D & G	175	K5
Balchraggan Highld	250	F3
Balchrick Highld	276	B4
Balcombe W Susx	37	M5
Balcombe Lane W Susx	37	M4
Balcomie Links Fife	223	L5
Baldersby N York	160	E7
Baldersby St James N York	160	E7
Balderstone Lancs	139	J1
Balderstone Rochdl	140	D5
Balderton Notts	117	L1
Baldhu Cnwll	4	C6
Baldinnie Fife	223	G5
Baldinnies P & K	221	J4
Baldock Herts	86	E8
Baldock Services Herts	86	E7
Baldovie C Dund	234	C8
Baldrine IoM	154	f5
Baldslow E Susx	24	E4
Baldwin IoM	154	e6
Baldwinholme Cumb	177	K8
Baldwin's Gate Staffs	114	B3
Baldwin's Hill W Susx	38	B5
Bale Norfk	121	M4
Baledgarno P & K	222	D1
Balemartine Ag & B	224	C7
Balerno C Edin	211	G5
Balfarg Fife	222	D6
Balfield Angus	234	E2
Balfour Ork	275	d4
Balfron Stirlg	208	F1
Balgaveny Abers	256	B4
Balgonar Fife	221	J8
Balgowan D & G	172	E6
Balgowan Highld	241	H4
Balgown Highld	258	F3
Balgracie D & G	172	B3
Balgray S Lans	186	C2
Balham Gt Lon	51	H4
Balhary P & K	233	L6
Balholmie P & K	233	H8
Baligill Highld	278	E3
Balintore Angus	233	L4
Balintore Highld	264	D5
Balintraid Highld	263	K5
Balivanich W Isls	283	c9
Balk N York	161	G6
Balkeerie Angus	233	M6
Balkholme E R Yk	143	K2
Ballabeg IoM	154	c7
Ballachulish Highld	229	H4
Ballafesson IoM	154	b7
Ballajora IoM	154	g4
Ballakilpheric IoM	154	b7
Ballamodha IoM	154	c7
Ballantrae S Ayrs	182	D6
Ballards Gore Essex	72	C8
Ballards Green Warwks	99	H5
Ballasalla IoM	154	c7
Ballater Abers	243	L4
Ballaugh IoM	154	d3
Ballchraggan Highld	263	K5
Ballencrieff E Loth	212	B3
Ballevullin Ag & B	224	B6
Ball Green C Stke	114	D1
Ball Haye Green Staffs	131	K8
Ball Hill Hants	48	B6
Ballianlay Ag & B	207	G6
Ballidon Derbys	115	K1
Balliekine N Ayrs	194	D3
Balliemore Ag & B	217	H7
Balligmorrie S Ayrs	183	G5
Ballimore Stirlg	219	H4
Ballindalloch Moray	254	D4
Ballindean P & K	222	D2
Ballingdon Suffk	89	H7
Ballinger Common Bucks	67	M6
Ballingham Herefs	63	H1
Ballingry Fife	222	B7
Ballinluig P & K	232	E5
Ballinshoe Angus	234	B5
Ballintuim P & K	233	G4
Balloch Highld	252	D2
Balloch N Lans	209	K4
Balloch P & K	220	E3
Balloch S Ayrs	183	J4
Balloch W Duns	208	C3
Balls Cross W Susx	36	E5
Balls Green E Susx	38	D6
Ball's Green Gloucs	64	B7
Ballygown Ag & B	226	E4
Ballygrant Ag & B	204	F3
Ballyhaugh Ag & B	224	F4
Balmacara Highld	248	C6
Balmaclellan D & G	185	G7
Balmae D & G	175	H6
Balmaha Stirlg	208	C1
Balmalcolm Fife	222	E5
Balmangan D & G	175	G5
Balmedie Abers	257	H8
Balmer Heath Shrops	113	G4
Balmerino Fife	222	F2
Balmerlawn Hants	18	D3
Balmichael N Ayrs	194	E5
Balmore E Duns	209	G4
Balmuchy Highld	264	D4
Balmule Fife	211	H2
Balmullo Fife	223	G3
Balnacoil Highld	273	K6
Balnacra Highld	248	F3
Balnacroft Abers	243	J5
Balnafoich Highld	251	J4
Balnaguard P & K	232	D5
Balnahard Ag & B	226	E5
Balnain Highld	250	D5
Balnakeil Highld	276	F3
Balne N York	142	F4
Balquharn P & K	232	F8
Balquhidder Stirlg	219	H3
Balsall Common Solhll	99	G8
Balsall Heath Birm	98	D6
Balsall Street Solhll	99	G8
Balscote Oxon	83	J6
Balsham Cambs	88	B5
Baltasound Shet	281	f1
Balterley Staffs	114	B2
Balterley Green Staffs	114	B2
Balterley Heath Staffs	114	B2

Baltersan D & G 174 C3
Balthangie Abers 268 E6
Baltonsborough Somset 31 J4
Balvicar Ag & B 216 B4
Balvraid Highld 248 D8
Balvraid Highld 252 F5
Balwest Cnwll 2 F5
Bamber Bridge Lancs 139 H3
Bamber's Green Essex 70 E3
Bamburgh Nthumb 203 K6
Bamford Derbys 132 D3
Bamford Rochdl 140 C5
Bampton Cumb 166 C7
Bampton Devon 29 G6
Bampton Oxon 65 L6
Bampton Grange Cumb 166 C7
Banavie Highld 239 J8
Banbury Oxon 83 K7
Bancffosfelen Carmth 58 E6
Banchory Abers 244 F4
Banchory-Devenick Abers .245 K3
Bancycapel Carmth 58 D6
Bancyfelin Carmth 58 B5
Banc-y-ffordd Carmth 76 D7
Bandirran P & K 222 C1
Bandrake Head Cumb 156 D5
Banff Abers 268 C3
Bangor Gwynd 125 K5
Bangor-on-Dee Wrexhm 112 F2
Bangors Cnwll 11 H3
Bangor's Green Lancs 138 D6
Bangour Village W Loth 210 D5
Bangrove Suffk 89 J1
Banham Norfk 106 B6
Bank Hants 18 D2
Bankend D & G 176 D5
Bankfoot P & K 233 G8
Bankglen E Ayrs 197 H8
Bank Ground Cumb 156 D3
Bankhead C Aber 245 K2
Bankhead S Lans 199 G4
Bank Newton N York 148 F5
Banknock Falk 209 K3
Banks Cumb 178 D6
Banks Lancs 138 E4
Banks Green Worcs 82 A2
Bankshill D & G 177 G3
Bank Street Worcs 80 E3
Bank Top Calder 141 H3
Bank Top Lancs 139 G6
Banningham Norfk 122 E5
Bannister Green Essex 71 G3
Bannockburn Stirlg 209 L1
Banstead Surrey 51 H7
Bantham Devon 7 K6
Banton N Lans 209 K3
Banwell N Som 44 E7
Bapchild Kent 40 B3
Bapton Wilts 33 G3
Barabhas W Isls 282 g2
Barassie S Ayrs 196 C4
Barbaraville Highld 263 K5
Barber Booth Derbys 132 B3
Barber Green Cumb 156 F6
Barbieston S Ayrs 196 E7
Barbon Cumb 157 K6
Barbridge Ches E 130 B8
Barbrook Devon 28 C2
Barby Nhants 84 A1
Barcaldine Ag & B 228 F7
Barcheston Warwks 83 G7
Barclose Cumb 178 B6
Barcombe E Susx 22 F4
Barcombe Cross E Susx 23 G4
Barcroft C Brad 149 J8
Barden N York 159 L4
Barden Park Kent 38 F4
Bardfield End Green Essex ...70 F1
Bardfield Saling Essex 71 G2
Bardney Lincs 136 B6
Bardon Leics 99 M1
Bardon Mill Nthumb 179 H6
Bardowie E Duns 209 G4
Bardown E Susx 39 G7
Bardrainney Inver 208 B4
Bardsea Cumb 156 D7
Bardsey Leeds 150 E7
Bardsey Island Gwynd 108 A7
Bardsley Oldham 140 D7
Bardwell Suffk 105 J8
Bare Lancs 147 J3
Bareppa Cnwll 3 K5
Barfad D & G 173 J2
Barford Norfk 106 C2
Barford Warwks 83 G3
Barford St John Oxon 83 K8
Barford St Martin Wilts 33 J4
Barford St Michael Oxon 83 K8
Barfrestone Kent 41 H5
Bargate Derbys 116 B2

Bargeddie N Lans 209 J6
Bargoed Caerph 61 J7
Bargrennan D & G 183 J7
Barham Cambs 102 C8
Barham Kent 41 G5
Barham Suffk 90 D5
Bar Hill Cambs 87 H3
Barholm Lincs 102 B1
Barkby Leics 100 E2
Barkby Thorpe Leics 100 E2
Barkers Green Shrops 113 H6
Barkestone-le-Vale Leics 117 K4
Barkham Wokham 49 J5
Barking Gt Lon 51 L2
Barking Suffk 90 C4
Barking Riverside Gt Lon 52 A2
Barkingside Gt Lon 51 L1
Barking Tye Suffk 90 C5
Barkisland Calder 141 G4
Barkston Lincs 118 B3
Barkston Ash N York 151 G8
Barkway Herts 87 H8
Barlanark C Glas 209 H6
Barlaston Staffs 114 D4
Barlavington W Susx 21 G4
Barlborough Derbys 133 J4
Barlby N York 143 G1
Barlestone Leics 99 L3
Barley Herts 87 H7
Barley Lancs 148 E7
Barleycroft End Herts 70 B2
Barley Hole Rothm 142 B8
Barleythorpe Rutlnd 101 J2
Barling Essex 53 K1
Barlings Lincs 135 M5
Barlochan D & G 175 K3
Barlow Derbys 133 G5
Barlow Gatesd 180 E6
Barlow N York 143 G2
Barmby Moor E R Yk 152 B6
Barmby on the Marsh E R Yk ..143 H2
Barmer Norfk 121 H5
Barming Heath Kent 39 J2
Barmollack Ag & B 194 C2
Barmouth Gwynd 109 L8
Barmpton Darltn 169 J7
Barmston E R Yk 153 J4
Barnaby Green Suffk 107 K7
Barnacarry Ag & B 216 F8
Barnack C Pete 102 B2
Barnacle Warwks 99 K6
Barnard Castle Dur 168 D7
Barnard Gate Oxon 66 B5
Barnardiston Suffk 88 E5
Barnbarroch D & G 175 L3
Barnburgh Donc 142 D7
Barnby Suffk 107 K5
Barnby Dun Donc 142 F6
Barnby in the Willows Notts ..117 M1
Barnby Moor Notts 134 D3
Barncorkrie D & G 172 D7
Barnehurst Gt Lon 52 B4
Barnes Gt Lon 51 G4
Barnes Street Kent 39 G4
Barnet Gt Lon 69 H7
Barnetby le Wold N Linc 144 D6
Barnet Gate Gt Lon 69 G8
Barney Norfk 121 M5
Barnham Suffk 105 H7
Barnham W Susx 20 F6
Barnham Broom Norfk 106 B2
Barnhead Angus 235 G4
Barnhill C Dund 223 H1
Barnhill Ches W 113 H1
Barnhill Moray 266 C5
Barnhills D & G 182 B8
Barningham Dur 168 D8
Barningham Suffk 105 K8
Barnoldby le Beck NE Lin 145 G7
Barnoldswick Lancs 148 F6
Barnsdale Bar Donc 142 D5
Barns Green W Susx 37 H5
Barnsley Barns 142 A6
Barnsley Gloucs 65 G4
Barnsole Kent 41 J4
Barnstaple Devon 27 K4
Barnston Essex 70 F3
Barnston Wirral 129 G3
Barnstone Notts 117 J4
Barnt Green Worcs 98 C8
Barnton C Edin 211 G4
Barnton Ches W 130 C5
Barnwell All Saints Nhants ..102 A6
Barnwell St Andrew Nhants .102 A6
Barnwood Gloucs 64 B3
Baron's Cross Herefs 80 B4
Baronwood Cumb 166 C2
Barr S Ayrs 183 H4
Barra W Isls 283 b13

Barra Airport W Isls 283 b12
Barrachan D & G 173 J5
Barraigh W Isls 283 b13
Barrananaoil Ag & B 216 C5
Barrapoll Ag & B 224 B6
Barras Cumb 167 J8
Barrasford Nthumb 179 L4
Barregarrow IoM 154 d4
Barrets Green Ches E 130 B7
Barrhead E Rens 208 E7
Barrhill S Ayrs 183 G6
Barrington Cambs 87 H5
Barrington Somset 30 F7
Barripper Cnwll 3 G3
Barrmill N Ayrs 196 D1
Barrock Highld 280 C2
Barrow Gloucs 64 C2
Barrow Lancs 148 C8
Barrow Rutlnd 118 A8
Barrow Shrops 96 E3
Barrow Somset 32 B4
Barrow Suffk 88 F3
Barroway Drove Norfk 104 B3
Barrow Bridge Bolton 139 K5
Barrow Burn Nthumb 190 B4
Barrowby Lincs 118 A4
Barrow Common N Som 45 H5
Barrowden Rutlnd 101 L3
Barrowford Lancs 148 E7
Barrow Gurney N Som 45 G5
Barrow Haven N Linc 144 D3
Barrow Hill Derbys 133 H4
Barrow-in-Furness Cumb 146 D2
Barrow Island Cumb 146 D2
Barrow Nook Lancs 138 F7
Barrow's Green Ches E 130 D8
Barrows Green Cumb 157 H5
Barrow Street Wilts 32 D5
Barrow-upon-Humber N Linc ..144 D4
Barrow upon Soar Leics 116 F8
Barrow upon Trent Derbys ...116 B6
Barrow Vale BaNES 45 J7
Barry Angus 234 E8
Barry V Glam 43 H7
Barry Island V Glam 43 H8
Barsby Leics 100 F1
Barsham Suffk 107 H5
Barston Solhll 99 G7
Bartestree Herefs 80 D7
Barthol Chapel Abers 256 E5
Bartholomew Green Essex 71 H3
Barthomley Ches E 114 B1
Bartley Hants 18 D1
Bartley Green Birm 98 C7
Bartlow Cambs 88 B6
Barton Cambs 87 H4
Barton Ches W 113 G1
Barton Gloucs 65 G2
Barton Herefs 79 K4
Barton Lancs 138 D6
Barton Lancs 147 K8
Barton N York 160 C1
Barton Oxon 66 E5
Barton Torbay 8 D2
Barton Warwks 82 D5
Barton Bendish Norfk 104 E2
Barton End Gloucs 64 B7
Barton Green Staffs 115 K7
Barton Hartshorn Bucks 66 F1
Barton Hill N York 151 L3
Barton in Fabis Notts 116 E5
Barton in the Beans Leics 99 L2
Barton-le-Clay C Beds 68 D1
Barton-le-Street N York 162 C7
Barton-le-Willows N York 151 M3
Barton Mills Suffk 104 E8
Barton-on-Sea Hants 18 C5
Barton-on-the-Heath Warwks ..65 K1
Barton St David Somset 31 J4
Barton Seagrave Nhants 101 J7
Barton Stacey Hants 34 F3
Barton Town Devon 28 B3
Barton Turf Norfk 123 G7
Barton-under-Needwood
  Staffs 115 K7
Barton-upon-Humber N Linc ..144 C3
Barton upon Irwell Salfd 140 A8
Barton Waterside N Linc 144 C3
Barugh Barns 141 M6
Barugh Green Barns 141 M6
Barvas W Isls 282 g2
Barway Cambs 103 L8
Barwell Leics 99 L4
Barwick Devon 12 E1
Barwick Herts 69 K3
Barwick Somset 31 J8
Barwick in Elmet Leeds 150 F8
Baschurch Shrops 112 F7
Bascote Warwks 83 J3
Bascote Heath Warwks 83 J3

Base Green Suffk 89 L3
Basford Green Staffs 114 F1
Bashall Eaves Lancs 148 B7
Bashall Town Lancs 148 C7
Bashley Hants 18 C4
Basildon Essex 52 F1
Basingstoke Hants 48 F8
Baslow Derbys 132 E5
Bason Bridge Somset 30 E2
Bassaleg Newpt 44 B2
Bassendean Border 201 K4
Bassenthwaite Cumb 165 H4
Bassett C Sotn 34 F7
Bassingbourn-cum-
  Kneesworth Cambs 87 G6
Bassingfield Notts 117 G4
Bassingham Lincs 135 H7
Bassingthorpe Lincs 118 C8
Bassus Green Herts 69 J2
Basted Kent 38 F2
Baston Lincs 102 C1
Bastwick Norfk 123 K8
Batch Somset 44 C7
Batchworth Herts 68 D8
Batchworth Heath Herts 68 D8
Batcombe Dorset 16 B2
Batcombe Somset 31 M3
Bate Heath Ches E 130 D4
Batford Herts 68 F4
Bath BaNES 45 L6
Bath BaNES 45 L6
Bathampton BaNES 45 M5
Bathealton Somset 29 J6
Batheaston BaNES 45 M5
Bathford BaNES 46 A5
Bathgate W Loth 210 C5
Bathley Notts 134 E8
Bathpool Cnwll 11 K2
Bathpool Somset 30 C6
Bath Side Essex 73 K1
Bathville W Loth 210 B5
Bathway Somset 45 H8
Batley Kirk 141 K3
Batsford Gloucs 82 E8
Batson Devon 7 L2
Battersby N York 161 K1
Battersea Gt Lon 51 H4
Battisborough Cross Devon 7 H5
Battisford Suffk 90 D7
Battisford Tye Suffk 89 L8
Battle E Susx 24 D3
Battle Powys 60 F1
Battleborough Somset 30 E1
Battledown Gloucs 64 D2
Battledykes Angus 234 C8
Battlefield Shrops 113 H8
Battlesbridge Essex 71 J4
Battlesden C Beds 68 B2
Battleton Somset 29 G5
Battlies Green Suffk 89 H3
Battram Leics 99 L2
Battramsley Cross Hants 18 E5
Batt's Corner Hants 36 B3
Baughton Worcs 81 K5
Baughurst Hants 48 E7
Baulds Abers 244 F4
Baulking Oxon 47 L3
Baumber Lincs 136 D5
Baunton Gloucs 64 E4
Baveney Wood Shrops 96 F7
Baverstock Wilts 33 J5
Bawburgh Norfk 106 D2
Bawdeswell Norfk 122 C6
Bawdrip Somset 30 E4
Bawdsey Suffk 91 H7
Bawsey Norfk 120 E7
Bawtry Donc 134 C2
Baxenden Lancs 140 A3
Baxterley Warwks 99 H4
Baxter's Green Suffk 88 E4
Bay Highld 258 D6
Bayble W Isls 282 h3
Baybridge Hants 35 H5
Baybridge Nthumb 168 B2
Baycliff Cumb 146 E2
Baydon Wilts 47 L4
Bayford Herts 69 J5
Bayford Somset 32 B5
Bayhead W Isls 283 b8
Bay Horse Lancs 147 K4
Bayley's Hill Kent 38 D3
Baylham Suffk 90 D6
Baynard's Green Oxon 66 E2
Baysdale Abbey N York 161 K2
Baysham Herefs 63 H2
Bayston Hill Shrops 96 B3
Baythorne End Essex 88 E6
Bayton Worcs 96 E8
Bayton Common Worcs 81 G1
Bayworth Oxon 66 D6

Beach S Glos	45	L5
Beachampton Bucks	84	E7
Beachamwell Norfk	104	E2
Beachley Gloucs	45	H1
Beachy Head E Susx	23	K8
Beacon Devon	14	E2
Beacon End Essex	72	D2
Beacon Hill Kent	39	K6
Beacon Hill Notts	117	L1
Beacon Hill Surrey	36	C3
Beacon's Bottom Bucks	67	J8
Beaconsfield Bucks	50	B1
Beaconsfield Services Bucks	50	B1
Beadlam N York	161	L5
Beadlow C Beds	86	C7
Beadnell Nthumb	203	L7
Beaford Devon	27	K7
Beal N York	142	E3
Beal Nthumb	203	H4
Bealbury Cnwll	6	D2
Bealsmill Cnwll	11	L7
Beam Hill Staffs	115	L6
Beamhurst Staffs	115	H4
Beaminster Dorset	15	L2
Beamish Dur	180	F8
Beamsley N York	149	K5
Bean Kent	52	C4
Beanacre Wilts	46	C5
Beanley Nthumb	190	F3
Beardon Devon	12	C5
Beardwood Bl w D	139	K2
Beare Devon	14	A2
Beare Green Surrey	37	J2
Bearley Warwks	82	E3
Bearley Cross Warwks	82	E3
Bearpark Dur	169	G2
Bearsden E Duns	208	F4
Bearsted Kent	39	K2
Bearstone Shrops	114	A4
Bearwood BCP	17	L3
Bearwood Birm	98	C6
Bearwood Herefs	79	M4
Beattock D & G	187	G5
Beauchamp Roding Essex	70	E5
Beauchief Sheff	132	F3
Beaudesert Warwks	82	E2
Beaufort Blae G	61	J5
Beaulieu Essex	71	H5
Beaulieu Hants	18	F3
Beaulieu Road Station Hants	18	E2
Beauly Highld	250	F2
Beaumaris IoA	126	B4
Beaumaris Castle IoA	126	B4
Beaumont Cumb	177	K7
Beaumont Essex	73	H2
Beaumont Jersey	9	c3
Beaumont Hill Darltn	169	J7
Beaumont Leys C Leic	100	C2
Beausale Warwks	82	F1
Beauworth Hants	35	J5
Beaworthy Devon	12	B3
Beazley End Essex	71	H1
Bebington Wirral	129	H3
Bebside Nthumb	181	G4
Beccles Suffk	107	J5
Becconsall Lancs	138	F3
Beckbury Shrops	97	H3
Beckenham Gt Lon	51	K5
Beckermet Cumb	155	J1
Beckett End Norfk	104	F4
Beckfoot Cumb	155	L3
Beckfoot Cumb	156	B5
Beck Foot Cumb	157	K3
Beckfoot Cumb	164	E1
Beckford Worcs	82	A8
Beckhampton Wilts	47	G5
Beck Hole N York	162	E2
Beckingham Lincs	118	A1
Beckingham Notts	134	F2
Beckington Somset	46	B8
Beckjay Shrops	95	J7
Beckley E Susx	24	F3
Beckley Hants	18	C4
Beckley Oxon	66	E5
Beck Row Suffk	104	D7
Becks C Brad	149	J6
Beck Side Cumb	156	B6
Beck Side Cumb	156	L6
Beckton Gt Lon	51	L3
Beckwithshaw N York	150	C5
Becontree Gt Lon	52	A2
Becquet Vincent Jersey	9	d2
Bedale N York	160	C5
Bedburn Dur	168	E4
Bedchester Dorset	32	E7
Beddau Rhondd	43	G4
Beddgelert Gwynd	109	L2
Beddingham E Susx	23	G5
Beddington Gt Lon	51	J6
Beddington Corner Gt Lon	51	H5

Bedfield Suffk	90	F2
Bedfield Little Green Suffk	90	F2
Bedford Bed	85	L5
Bedgebury Cross Kent	39	H6
Bedgrove Bucks	67	K4
Bedham W Susx	36	F6
Bedhampton Hants	20	A5
Bedingfield Suffk	90	E2
Bedingfield Green Suffk	90	E2
Bedlam N York	150	C3
Bedlington Nthumb	181	G3
Bedlinog Myr Td	61	H6
Bedminster Bristl	45	H5
Bedminster Down Bristl	45	H5
Bedmond Herts	68	E6
Bednall Staffs	114	F7
Bedrule Border	189	G3
Bedstone Shrops	95	J8
Bedwas Caerph	43	J4
Bedwellty Caerph	61	J7
Bedworth Warwks	99	K6
Bedworth Woodlands Warwks	99	K6
Beeby Leics	100	E2
Beech Hants	35	L3
Beech Staffs	114	D4
Beech Hill W Berk	49	G6
Beechingstoke Wilts	47	G7
Beedon W Berk	48	C3
Beedon Hill W Berk	48	C3
Beeford E R Yk	153	H5
Beeley Derbys	132	E6
Beelsby NE Lin	145	G7
Beenham W Berk	48	E5
Beenham's Heath W & M	49	K4
Beeny Cnwll	11	G4
Beer Devon	14	F5
Beer Somset	30	F4
Beercrocombe Somset	30	D6
Beer Hackett Dorset	31	K8
Beesands Devon	8	B6
Beesby Lincs	137	J4
Beeson Devon	8	B6
Beeston C Beds	86	D5
Beeston Ches W	129	M7
Beeston Leeds	141	L2
Beeston Norfk	121	K8
Beeston Notts	116	E4
Beeston Regis Norfk	122	D3
Beeswing D & G	176	A5
Beetham Cumb	157	H6
Beetham Somset	30	D8
Beetley Norfk	121	L8
Began Cardif	43	K5
Begbroke Oxon	66	C4
Begdale Cambs	103	J2
Begelly Pembks	55	J5
Beggarington Hill Leeds	141	L3
Beggar's Bush Powys	79	J2
Beguildy Powys	94	F7
Beighton Norfk	107	H2
Beighton Sheff	133	J3
Beinn Na Faoghla W Isls	283	c9
Beith N Ayrs	208	B8
Bekesbourne Kent	41	G4
Bekesbourne Hill Kent	41	G4
Belaugh Norfk	122	F7
Belbroughton Worcs	97	L7
Belchalwell Dorset	16	F1
Belchalwell Street Dorset	16	F1
Belchamp Otten Essex	88	F6
Belchamp St Paul Essex	88	F6
Belchamp Walter Essex	89	G7
Belchford Lincs	136	E4
Belford Nthumb	203	H6
Belgrave C Leic	100	D2
Belhaven E Loth	212	E3
Belhelvie Abers	257	H8
Belhinnie Abers	255	J6
Bellabeg Abers	243	K1
Bellamore Herefs	79	M7
Bellanoch Ag & B	216	B8
Bellasize E R Yk	143	K2
Bellaty Angus	233	K3
Bell Bar Herts	69	H6
Bell Busk N York	148	F4
Belleau Lincs	137	G4
Bell End Worcs	97	L7
Bellerby N York	159	K4
Bellever Devon	12	F7
Belle Vue Cumb	177	L7
Belle Vue Wakefd	142	A4
Bellfield S Lans	198	D6
Bellfields Surrey	50	C8
Bell Heath Worcs	97	L7
Bell Hill Hants	35	M6
Bellingdon Bucks	68	B6
Bellingham Nthumb	179	J2
Belloch Ag & B	192	D1
Bellochantuy Ag & B	192	D2
Bell o' th' Hill Ches W	113	H2

Bellows Cross Dorset	33	J8
Bells Cross Suffk	90	D5
Bellshill N Lans	209	J7
Bellshill Nthumb	203	J7
Bellside N Lans	209	L7
Bellsquarry W Loth	210	E6
Bells Yew Green E Susx	38	F6
Belluton BaNES	45	J6
Belmaduthy Highld	263	H8
Belmesthorpe Rutlnd	102	A2
Belmont Bl w D	139	K4
Belmont Gt Lon	51	H6
Belmont S Ayrs	196	C7
Belmont Shet	281	f2
Belnacraig Abers	255	H8
Belowda Cnwll	4	F3
Belper Derbys	116	B2
Belper Lane End Derbys	116	B2
Belph Derbys	133	L4
Belsay Nthumb	180	D3
Belses Border	201	J8
Belsford Devon	7	L3
Belsize Herts	68	D7
Belstead Suffk	90	D7
Belstone Devon	12	E4
Belthorn Bl w D	139	L3
Beltinge Kent	41	G2
Beltingham Nthumb	179	H6
Beltoft N Linc	143	K6
Belton Leics	116	D7
Belton Lincs	118	B3
Belton N Linc	143	K6
Belton Norfk	107	K3
Belton in Rutland Rutlnd	101	H3
Beltring Kent	39	H4
Belvedere Gt Lon	52	B3
Belvoir Leics	117	L5
Bembridge IoW	19	L6
Bemerton Wilts	33	K5
Bempton E R Yk	153	K2
Benacre Suffk	107	L6
Benbecula W Isls	283	c9
Benbecula Airport W Isls	283	c9
Benbuie D & G	185	H4
Benderloch Ag & B	228	D7
Benenden Kent	39	K6
Benfieldside Dur	180	D8
Benfleet Essex	53	G2
Bengate Norfk	122	F6
Bengeo Herts	69	J4
Bengeworth Worcs	82	B6
Benhall Green Suffk	91	J3
Benhall Street Suffk	91	H3
Benholm Abers	235	K2
Beningbrough N York	151	H4
Benington Herts	69	J2
Benington Lincs	119	L2
Benington Sea End Lincs	119	L2
Benllech IoA	125	J3
Benmore Ag & B	207	J2
Bennacott Cnwll	11	K4
Bennan N Ayrs	193	K4
Bennet Head Cumb	166	B6
Bennetland E R Yk	143	L2
Bennett End Bucks	67	J7
Ben Nevis Highld	229	K1
Benniworth Lincs	136	D3
Benover Kent	39	H4
Ben Rhydding C Brad	149	L6
Benslie N Ayrs	196	C2
Benson Oxon	66	F8
Bentfield Green Essex	70	D2
Benthall Shrops	96	F3
Bentham Gloucs	64	C4
Benthoul C Aber	245	H3
Bentlawnt Shrops	95	H3
Bentley Donc	142	E6
Bentley E R Yk	152	F8
Bentley Hants	36	A2
Bentley Suffk	90	D7
Bentley Warwks	99	H4
Bentley Heath Herts	69	H7
Bentley Heath Solhll	98	F8
Benton Devon	28	B4
Bentpath D & G	188	B8
Bentwichen Devon	28	C4
Bentworth Hants	35	K3
Benvie Angus	222	E1
Benville Dorset	15	M2
Benwick Cambs	103	G5
Beoley Worcs	82	C1
Beoraidbeg Highld	237	K2
Bepton W Susx	20	D3
Berden Essex	70	C1
Berea Pembks	74	C6
Bere Alston Devon	6	E2
Bere Ferrers Devon	6	E2
Berepper Cnwll	3	G6
Bere Regis Dorset	17	G4
Bergh Apton Norfk	106	F3

Berhill Somset	31	G4
Berinsfield Oxon	66	E7
Berkeley Gloucs	63	K7
Berkeley Heath Gloucs	63	K7
Berkeley Road Gloucs	63	L7
Berkhamsted Herts	68	C5
Berkley Somset	32	D1
Berkswell Solhll	99	H7
Bermondsey Gt Lon	51	J3
Bermuda Warwks	99	K5
Bernera Highld	248	C7
Bernisdale Highld	258	F6
Berrick Prior Oxon	66	F8
Berrick Salome Oxon	66	F8
Berriedale Highld	274	F3
Berrier Cumb	165	L5
Berriew Powys	94	E3
Berrington Nthumb	202	F4
Berrington Shrops	96	C2
Berrington Worcs	80	D2
Berrington Green Worcs	80	D2
Berrow Somset	44	C8
Berrow Worcs	81	H8
Berrow Green Worcs	81	H3
Berry Brow Kirk	141	H5
Berry Cross Devon	27	H7
Berry Down Cross Devon	27	K2
Berryfield Wilts	46	C6
Berryfields Bucks	67	J4
Berry Hill Gloucs	63	H4
Berry Hill Pembks	75	H4
Berryhillock Moray	267	K4
Berryhillock Moray	267	K5
Berrynarbor Devon	27	K2
Berry Pomeroy Devon	8	B3
Berry's Green Gt Lon	51	L7
Bersham Wrexhm	112	D2
Bersted W Susx	20	F6
Bertha Park P & K	221	K2
Berthengam Flints	128	D4
Berwick E Susx	23	H6
Berwick Bassett Wilts	47	G4
Berwick Hill Nthumb	180	E4
Berwick St James Wilts	33	J3
Berwick St John Wilts	32	F6
Berwick St Leonard Wilts	32	F4
Berwick Station E Susx	23	J6
Berwick-upon-Tweed Nthumb	202	F3
Bescaby Leics	117	L6
Bescar Lancs	138	E5
Besford Shrops	113	J6
Besford Worcs	81	L6
Bessacarr Donc	142	F7
Bessels Leigh Oxon	66	C6
Besses o' th' Barn Bury	140	B6
Bessingby E R Yk	153	J3
Bessingham Norfk	122	D4
Bestbeech Hill E Susx	38	F7
Besthorpe Norfk	106	B4
Besthorpe Notts	135	G6
Bestwood Village Notts	116	F2
Beswick E R Yk	152	F6
Betchcott Shrops	95	K4
Betchworth Surrey	37	K1
Bethania Cerdgn	77	G3
Bethania Gwynd	110	D3
Bethel Gwynd	111	J4
Bethel Gwynd	125	J6
Bethel IoA	125	L6
Bethel Powys	111	L7
Bethersden Kent	40	B7
Bethesda Gwynd	126	C6
Bethesda Gwynd	126	C6
Bethesda Pembks	55	J3
Bethlehem Carmth	59	J4
Bethnal Green Gt Lon	51	K2
Betley Staffs	114	B2
Betsham Kent	52	D4
Betteshanger Kent	41	J5
Bettiscombe Dorset	15	J3
Bettisfield Wrexhm	113	J4
Betton Shrops	113	M4
Betton Strange Shrops	96	C2
Bettws Brdgnd	42	D4
Bettws Newpt	44	C1
Bettws Cedewain Powys	94	D4
Bettws Ifan Cerdgn	76	B5
Bettws-Newydd Mons	62	D6
Bettyhill Highld	278	D2
Betws Carmth	59	H6
Betws Bledrws Cerdgn	77	H5
Betws Garmon Gwynd	125	K8
Betws Gwerfil Goch Denbgs	111	K2
Betws-y-Coed Conwy	126	F8
Betws-yn-Rhos Conwy	127	H5
Beulah Cerdgn	76	B6
Beulah Powys	78	C5
Bevendean Br & H	22	E6
Bevercotes Notts	134	D5
Beverley E R Yk	153	G7

Place	County	Page	Grid
Beverston	Gloucs	64	B8
Bevington	Gloucs	63	K7
Bewaldeth	Cumb	165	H4
Bewcastle	Cumb	178	D4
Bewdley	Worcs	97	H8
Beverley	N York	149	L3
Bewholme	E R Yk	153	J6
Bewlbridge	Kent	39	H6
Bexhill-on-Sea	E Susx	24	D5
Bexley	Gt Lon	52	B4
Bexleyheath	Gt Lon	52	A4
Bexleyhill	W Susx	36	D6
Bexon	Kent	53	J7
Bexwell	Norfk	104	C3
Beyton	Suffk	89	J3
Beyton Green	Suffk	89	J3
Bhaltos	W Isls	282	e3
Bhatarsaigh	W Isls	283	b13
Bibstone	S Glos	45	K1
Bibury	Gloucs	65	G5
Bicester	Oxon	66	E3
Bickenhill	Solhll	99	G7
Bicker	Lincs	119	H4
Bicker Bar	Lincs	119	H4
Bicker Gauntlet	Lincs	119	H4
Bickershaw	Wigan	139	J7
Bickerstaffe	Lancs	138	F7
Bickerton	Ches E	113	H1
Bickerton	Devon	8	B7
Bickerton	N York	151	G5
Bickerton	Nthumb	190	E6
Bickford	Staffs	114	D8
Bickington	Devon	13	J8
Bickington	Devon	27	J4
Bickleigh	Devon	7	G2
Bickleigh	Devon	13	M1
Bickleton	Devon	27	J5
Bickley	Ches W	113	J2
Bickley	Gt Lon	51	L5
Bickley	N York	163	G4
Bickley	Worcs	80	E1
Bickley Moss	Ches W	113	J2
Bicknacre	Essex	71	J6
Bicknoller	Somset	29	K3
Bicknor	Kent	53	J7
Bickton	Hants	33	K8
Bicton	Herefs	80	B2
Bicton	Shrops	95	G6
Bicton	Shrops	113	G8
Bidborough	Kent	38	E5
Bidden	Hants	35	L1
Biddenden	Kent	39	L5
Biddenden Green	Kent	39	M5
Biddenham	Bed	85	K5
Biddestone	Wilts	46	B4
Biddisham	Somset	44	D8
Biddlesden	Bucks	84	C7
Biddlestone	Nthumb	190	D4
Biddulph	Staffs	131	H7
Biddulph Moor	Staffs	131	H8
Bideford	Devon	27	H5
Bidford-on-Avon	Warwks	82	D5
Bidston	Wirral	129	G2
Bielby	E R Yk	152	B7
Bieldside	C Aber	245	K3
Bierley	IoW	19	H8
Bierton	Bucks	67	K4
Big Balcraig	D & G	173	K6
Bigbury	Devon	7	K5
Bigbury-on-Sea	Devon	7	J6
Bigby	Lincs	144	D6
Biggar	Cumb	146	D3
Biggar	S Lans	199	H5
Biggin	Derbys	115	L2
Biggin	Derbys	132	C7
Biggin	N York	142	E1
Biggin Hill	Gt Lon	51	L7
Biggleswade	C Beds	86	D6
Bigholms	D & G	177	K3
Bighouse	Highld	278	H3
Bighton	Hants	35	J4
Biglands	Cumb	177	H8
Bignall End	Staffs	114	C1
Bignor	W Susx	21	G4
Bigrigg	Cumb	164	D8
Big Sand	Highld	260	B4
Bigton	Shet	281	d8
Bilborough	C Nott	116	E3
Bilbrook	Somset	29	J3
Bilbrook	Staffs	97	K3
Bilbrough	N York	151	H6
Bilbster	Highld	280	C5
Bildershaw	Dur	169	G6
Bildeston	Suffk	89	K5
Billacott	Cnwll	11	J4
Billericay	Essex	71	G6
Billesdon	Leics	100	F3
Billesley	Warwks	82	D4
Billingborough	Lincs	118	F5
Billinge	St Hel	139	G7
Billingford	Norfk	106	D7
Billingford	Norfk	121	M7
Billingham	S on T	170	B6
Billinghay	Lincs	136	C8
Billingley	Barns	142	C6
Billingshurst	W Susx	37	G5
Billingsley	Shrops	97	G6
Billington	C Beds	68	B3
Billington	Lancs	148	C8
Billington	Staffs	114	D7
Billockby	Norfk	107	J1
Billy Row	Dur	168	F3
Bilsborrow	Lancs	147	K7
Bilsby	Lincs	137	J4
Bilsham	W Susx	21	G6
Bilsington	Kent	40	D8
Bilsthorpe	Notts	134	C7
Bilsthorpe Moor	Notts	134	C7
Bilston	Mdloth	211	J6
Bilston	Wolves	98	B4
Bilstone	Leics	99	K2
Bilting	Kent	40	D5
Bilton	E R Yk	144	F1
Bilton	N York	150	D4
Bilton	Nthumb	191	J4
Bilton	Warwks	100	B8
Bilton Banks	Nthumb	191	J4
Bilton-in-Ainsty	N York	151	G6
Binbrook	Lincs	136	D1
Binchester Blocks	Dur	169	G4
Bincombe	Dorset	16	D5
Binegar	Somset	31	K1
Bines Green	W Susx	21	L3
Binfield	Br For	49	K4
Binfield Heath	Oxon	49	H3
Bingfield	Nthumb	180	A4
Bingham	Notts	117	J3
Bingham's Melcombe	Dorset	16	E2
Bingley	C Brad	149	K7
Bings Heath	Shrops	113	J7
Binham	Norfk	121	L4
Binley	Covtry	99	K7
Binley	Hants	48	B8
Binley Woods	Warwks	99	L7
Binnegar	Dorset	17	G5
Binniehill	Falk	209	M4
Binscombe	Surrey	36	E2
Binsey	Oxon	66	C5
Binstead	IoW	19	K5
Binsted	Hants	36	A3
Binsted	W Susx	21	G5
Binton	Warwks	82	D4
Bintree	Norfk	121	M7
Binweston	Shrops	95	H3
Birch	Essex	72	D3
Birch	Rochdl	140	C6
Birchall	Staffs	131	K8
Bircham Newton	Norfk	121	G5
Bircham Tofts	Norfk	121	G5
Birchanger	Essex	70	D3
Birchanger Green Services	Essex	70	D3
Birch Cross	Staffs	115	J5
Birchencliffe	Kirk	141	H4
Bircher	Herefs	80	B2
Birchett's Green	E Susx	39	G7
Birchfield	Birm	98	D5
Birch Green	Essex	72	D3
Birch Green	Herts	69	J5
Birch Green	Worcs	81	K6
Birchgrove	Cardif	43	J5
Birchgrove	Swans	57	K5
Birchgrove	W Susx	38	B7
Birch Heath	Ches W	130	A7
Birch Hill	Ches W	129	M5
Birchington	Kent	41	J2
Birchington-on-Sea	Kent	41	J2
Birchley Heath	Warwks	99	H4
Birchmoor	Warwks	99	H3
Birchmoor Green	C Beds	85	J8
Birchover	Derbys	132	E7
Birch Services	Rochdl	140	C6
Birch Vale	Derbys	131	K2
Birchwood	Lincs	135	J6
Birch Wood	Somset	30	C8
Birchwood	Warrtn	130	C2
Bircotes	Notts	134	C2
Birdbrook	Essex	88	E7
Birdforth	N York	161	G7
Birdham	W Susx	20	D6
Birdingbury	Warwks	83	K2
Birdlip	Gloucs	64	D4
Birdoswald	Cumb	178	E5
Birdsall	N York	152	B3
Birds Edge	Kirk	141	K6
Birds Green	Essex	70	E5
Birdsgreen	Shrops	97	H6
Birdsmoorgate	Dorset	15	J3
Bird Street	Suffk	89	K5
Birdwell	Barns	142	A7
Birdwood	Gloucs	63	L3
Birgham	Border	202	B5
Birichin	Highld	263	K2
Birkacre	Lancs	139	H5
Birkby	N York	160	D2
Birkdale	Sefton	138	C5
Birkenbog	Abers	267	L3
Birkenhead	Wirral	129	H2
Birkenhead (Queensway) Tunnel	Lpool	129	H2
Birkenhills	Abers	256	D3
Birkenshaw	Kirk	141	K2
Birkhall	Abers	243	K5
Birkhill	Angus	234	A8
Birkhill	D & G	187	J3
Birkholme	Lincs	118	C6
Birkin	N York	142	E2
Birks	Leeds	141	L2
Birkshaw	Nthumb	179	H5
Birley	Herefs	80	B4
Birley Carr	Sheff	133	G1
Birling	Kent	52	E6
Birling	Nthumb	191	K5
Birling Gap	E Susx	23	J8
Birlingham	Worcs	81	L6
Birmingham	Birm	98	D6
Birmingham Airport	*Solhll*	*98*	*F6*
Birnam	P & K	232	F7
Birness	Abers	257	H5
Birse	Abers	244	C4
Birsemore	Abers	244	C4
Birstall	Kirk	141	K3
Birstall	Leics	100	D2
Birstwith	N York	150	B4
Birthorpe	Lincs	118	E5
Birtley	Gatesd	181	G7
Birtley	Herefs	79	L2
Birtley	Nthumb	179	K3
Birts Street	Worcs	81	H7
Bisbrooke	Rutlnd	101	J3
Biscathorpe	Lincs	136	D3
Biscovey	Cnwll	5	H4
Bisham	W & M	49	K2
Bishampton	Worcs	82	A5
Bish Mill	Devon	28	C6
Bishop Auckland	Dur	169	G5
Bishopbridge	Lincs	135	L2
Bishopbriggs	E Duns	209	G5
Bishop Burton	E R Yk	152	F7
Bishop Middleham	Dur	169	J4
Bishopmill	Moray	266	E3
Bishop Monkton	N York	150	D3
Bishop Norton	Lincs	135	K1
Bishopsbourne	Kent	41	G5
Bishops Cannings	Wilts	46	F6
Bishop's Castle	Shrops	95	H5
Bishop's Caundle	Dorset	32	B8
Bishop's Cleeve	Gloucs	64	D2
Bishop's Frome	Herefs	80	F5
Bishops Gate	Surrey	50	B5
Bishop's Green	Essex	70	F3
Bishop's Green	Hants	48	D6
Bishop's Hull	Somset	30	B6
Bishop's Itchington	Warwks	83	J4
Bishops Lydeard	Somset	29	M5
Bishop's Norton	Gloucs	64	B2
Bishop's Nympton	Devon	28	D6
Bishop's Offley	Staffs	114	B5
Bishop's Stortford	Herts	70	C3
Bishop's Sutton	Hants	35	J4
Bishop's Tachbrook	Warwks	83	H3
Bishop's Tawton	Devon	27	K5
Bishopsteignton	Devon	13	L7
Bishopstoke	Hants	34	F7
Bishopston	Swans	57	G7
Bishopstone	Bucks	67	J5
Bishopstone	E Susx	23	J7
Bishopstone	Herefs	80	A6
Bishopstone	Kent	41	G2
Bishopstone	Swindn	47	K2
Bishopstone	Wilts	33	J5
Bishopstrow	Wilts	32	E2
Bishop Sutton	BaNES	45	H7
Bishop's Waltham	Hants	35	H7
Bishopswood	Somset	30	C8
Bishop's Wood	Staffs	97	J2
Bishopsworth	Bristl	45	H5
Bishop Thornton	N York	150	C3
Bishopthorpe	C York	151	J6
Bishopton	Darltn	169	K6
Bishopton	Rens	208	D5
Bishopton	Warwks	82	E4
Bishop Wilton	E R Yk	152	B5
Bishton	Newpt	44	D2
Bishton	Staffs	115	G7
Bisley	Gloucs	64	C6
Bisley	Surrey	50	B7
Bisley Camp	Surrey	50	B7
Bispham	Bpool	146	F7
Bispham Green	Lancs	138	F5
Bissoe	Cnwll	3	
Bisterne	Hants	18	
Bitchet Green	Kent	38	
Bitchfield	Lincs	118	
Bittadon	Devon	27	
Bittaford	Devon	7	
Bittering	Norfk	121	
Bitterley	Shrops	96	
Bitterne	C Sotn	34	
Bitteswell	Leics	100	
Bitton	S Glos	45	
Bix	Oxon	49	
Bixter	Shet	281	
Blaby	Leics	100	
Blackadder	Border	202	
Blackawton	Devon	8	
Blackbeck	Cumb	155	
Blackborough	Devon	14	
Blackborough End	Norfk	120	
Black Bourton	Oxon	65	
Blackboys	E Susx	23	
Blackbrook	Derbys	116	
Blackbrook	St Hel	139	
Blackbrook	Staffs	114	
Blackbrook	Surrey	37	
Blackburn	Abers	245	
Blackburn	Bl w D	139	
Blackburn	Rothm	133	
Blackburn	W Loth	210	
Blackburn with Darwen Services	Bl w D	139	
Black Callerton	N u Ty	180	
Black Carr	Norfk	106	
Black Corner	W Susx	37	
Blackcraig	E Ayrs	185	
Black Crofts	Ag & B	228	
Black Cross	Cnwll	4	
Blackden Heath	Ches E	130	
Blackdog	Abers	245	
Black Dog	Devon	13	
Blackdown	Devon	12	
Blackdown	Dorset	15	
Blackdyke	Cumb	176	
Blacker	Barns	142	
Blacker Hill	Barns	142	
Blackfen	Gt Lon	51	
Blackfield	Hants	19	
Blackford	Cumb	177	
Blackford	P & K	220	
Blackford	Somset	30	
Blackford	Somset	31	
Blackfordby	Leics	116	
Blackgang	IoW	19	
Blackhall	C Edin	211	
Blackhall Colliery	Dur	170	
Blackhall Mill	Gatesd	180	
Blackhall Rocks	Dur	170	
Blackham	E Susx	38	
Blackhaugh	Border	200	
Blackheath	Essex	72	
Blackheath	Gt Lon	51	
Blackheath	Sandw	98	
Blackheath	Suffk	107	
Blackheath	Surrey	36	
Black Heddon	Nthumb	180	
Blackhill	Abers	257	
Blackhill	Abers	269	
Blackhill	Dur	180	
Blackhill of Clackriach	Abers	269	
Blackjack	Lincs	119	
Blackland	Wilts	46	
Black Lane Ends	Lancs	149	
Blacklaw	D & G	186	
Blackley	Manch	140	
Blacklunans	P & K	233	
Blackmarstone	Herefs	80	
Blackmill	Brdgnd	42	
Blackmoor	Hants	36	
Black Moor	Leeds	150	
Blackmoor	N Som	44	
Blackmoorfoot	Kirk	141	
Blackmoor Gate	Devon	28	
Blackmore	Essex	70	
Blackmore End	Essex	71	
Blackmore End	Herts	68	
Black Mountains		61	
Blackness	Falk	210	
Blacknest	Hants	36	
Blacknest	W & M	50	
Black Notley	Essex	71	
Blacko	Lancs	148	
Black Pill	Swans	57	
Blackpool	Bpool	146	
Blackpool	Devon	8	
Blackpool	Devon	13	
Blackpool Gate	Cumb	178	
Blackridge	W Loth	210	
Blackrock	Cnwll	3	
Blackrock	Mons	61	
Blackrod	Bolton	139	

Blacksboat Moray 254 D4
Blackshaw D & G 176 D5
Blackshaw Head Calder 140 E2
Blacksmith's Green Suffk 90 D2
Blacksnape Bl w D 139 L3
Blackstone W Susx 22 C4
Black Street Suffk 107 K6
Black Tar Pembks 55 G5
Blackthorn Oxon 66 F3
Blackthorpe Suffk 89 H3
Blacktoft E R Yk 143 L3
Blacktop C Aber 245 J3
Black Torrington Devon 12 B2
Blackwall Derbys 115 L2
Blackwall Tunnel Gt Lon 51 K3
Blackwater Cnwll 4 B5
Blackwater Hants 49 K7
Blackwater IoW 19 H6
Blackwater Somset 30 C7
Blackwaterfoot N Ayrs 194 D5
Blackwell Cumb 177 L8
Blackwell Darltn 169 H8
Blackwell Derbys 132 C5
Blackwell Derbys 133 J7
Blackwell Warwks 82 F6
Blackwell Worcs 82 A1
Blackwellsend Green Gloucs 63 M2
Blackwood Caerph 43 J2
Blackwood D & G 176 B2
Blackwood S Lans 198 C4
Blackwood Hill Staffs 131 H8
Blacon Ches W 129 J6
Bladbean Kent 41 G6
Bladnoch D & G 174 C4
Bladon Oxon 66 C4
Bladon Somset 30 F6
Blaenannerch Cerdgn 75 M2
Blaenau Ffestiniog Gwynd 110 D2
Blaenau Ffestiniog Gwynd 110 D2
Blaenavon Torfn 61 L5
Blaenavon Industrial Landscape Torfn 61 K5
Blaencwm Rhondd 60 D7
Blaen Dyryn Powys 78 C7
Blaenffos Pembks 75 L5
Blaengarw Brdgnd 42 D3
Blaengeuffordd Cerdgn 92 E7
Blaengwrach Neath 60 C6
Blaengwynfi Neath 42 D2
Blaenllechau Rhondd 42 F2
Blaenpennal Cerdgn 77 H2
Blaenplwyf Cerdgn 92 C2
Blaenporth Cerdgn 76 A5
Blaenrhondda Rhondd 60 D7
Blaenwaun Carmth 75 M6
Blaen-y-coed Carmth 58 C3
Blaen-y-cwm Blae G 61 H5
Blaenycwm Cerdgn 93 H8
Blagdon N Som 45 G7
Blagdon Somset 30 B7
Blagdon Torbay 8 C3
Blagdon Hill Somset 30 B7
Blagill Cumb 167 G1
Blaguegate Lancs 138 F6
Blaich Highld 239 G8
Blain Highld 237 K6
Blaina Blae G 61 K5
Blair Atholl P & K 232 C2
Blair Drummond Stirlg 220 C7
Blairgowrie P & K 233 J6
Blairhall Fife 210 D1
Blairingone P & K 221 H1
Blairlogie Stirlg 220 E7
Blairmore Ag & B 207 K2
Blairmore Highld 276 B4
Blair's Ferry Ag & B 206 E7
Blaisdon Gloucs 63 K4
Blakebrook Worcs 97 J8
Blakedown Worcs 97 K7
Blake End Essex 71 H3
Blakeley Lane Staffs 114 F2
Blakemere Ches W 130 A5
Blakemere Herefs 79 L7
Blakemore Devon 7 M3
Blakenall Heath Wsall 98 C3
Blakeney Gloucs 63 K5
Blakeney Norfk 122 A3
Blakenhall Ches E 114 A2
Blakenhall Wolves 97 K4
Blakeshall Worcs 97 J7
Blakesley Nhants 84 C5
Blanchland Nthumb 180 A8
Blandford Camp Dorset 17 H1
Blandford Forum Dorset 17 G1
Blandford St Mary Dorset 17 G2
Bland Hill N York 150 C4
Blanefield Stirlg 208 F3
Blankney Lincs 135 L7
Blantyre S Lans 209 J7
Blàr a' Chaorainn Highld 229 H2

Blarghour Ag & B 216 F4
Blargie Highld 241 G4
Blarmachfoldach Highld 229 H2
Blashford Hants 18 A2
Blaston Leics 101 H4
Blatherwycke Nhants 101 L4
Blawith Cumb 156 C5
Blawquhairn D & G 184 F6
Blaxhall Suffk 91 J4
Blaxton Donc 143 H7
Blaydon Gatesd 180 F6
Bleadney Somset 31 H2
Bleadon N Som 44 C7
Bleak Street Somset 32 C4
Blean Kent 40 F3
Bleasby Lincs 136 B3
Bleasby Notts 117 J3
Bleasdale Lancs 147 L6
Bleatarn Cumb 167 G7
Bleathwood Herefs 80 D1
Blebocraigs Fife 223 J4
Bleddfa Powys 79 H2
Bledington Gloucs 65 K3
Bledlow Bucks 67 J6
Bledlow Ridge Bucks 67 J7
Bleet Wilts 46 C7
Blegbie E Loth 212 B6
Blencarn Cumb 166 E4
Blencogo Cumb 165 G1
Blendworth Hants 35 L8
Blenheim Palace Oxon 66 B4
Blennerhasset Cumb 165 G2
Bletchingdon Oxon 66 D4
Bletchingley Surrey 38 A3
Bletchley M Keyn 85 G8
Bletchley Shrops 113 K5
Bletherston Pembks 55 H3
Bletsoe Bed 85 K4
Blewbury Oxon 48 D2
Blickling Norfk 122 D6
Blidworth Notts 134 B8
Blidworth Bottoms Notts 117 G1
Blindburn Nthumb 189 L4
Blindcrake Cumb 164 F4
Blindley Heath Surrey 38 A4
Blindwells E Loth 211 L4
Blisland Cnwll 10 F8
Blissford Hants 33 L8
Bliss Gate Worcs 81 G1
Blisworth Nhants 84 D4
Blithbury Staffs 115 H7
Blitterlees Cumb 176 F8
Blockley Gloucs 82 E8
Blofield Norfk 107 G2
Blofield Heath Norfk 107 G1
Blo Norton Norfk 105 K7
Bloomfield Border 189 G2
Blore Staffs 114 A4
Blore Staffs 115 J2
Blounce Hants 35 L2
Blounts Green Staffs 115 H5
Blowick Sefton 138 D4
Bloxham Oxon 83 K8
Bloxholm Lincs 118 E1
Bloxwich Wsall 98 C3
Bloxworth Dorset 17 G4
Blubberhouses N York 149 L5
Blue Anchor Cnwll 4 E3
Blue Anchor Somset 29 J2
Blue Bell Hill Kent 52 F6
Blundellsands Sefton 138 C7
Blundeston Suffk 107 L4
Blunham C Beds 86 C5
Blunsdon St Andrew Swindn 47 H1
Bluntington Worcs 97 K8
Bluntisham Cambs 103 H8
Blunts Cnwll 6 C2
Blunts Green Warwks 82 D2
Blurton C Stke 114 D3
Blyborough Lincs 135 J1
Blyford Suffk 107 J8
Blymhill Staffs 97 H1
Blymhill Lawn Staffs 97 J1
Blyth Notts 134 C2
Blyth Nthumb 181 H3
Blyth Bridge Border 199 K4
Blythburgh Suffk 107 J8
Blythe Border 201 J3
Blythe Bridge Staffs 114 F3
Blythe End Warwks 99 G5
Blythe Marsh Staffs 114 F3
Blyth Services Notts 134 C2
Blyton Lincs 135 G1
Boarhills Fife 223 K4
Boarhunt Hants 19 K2
Boarley Kent 53 G2
Boarsgreave Lancs 140 C4
Boarshead E Susx 38 E6
Boar's Head Wigan 139 H6
Boars Hill Oxon 66 D6

Boarstall Bucks 66 F4
Boasley Cross Devon 12 C4
Boath Highld 263 G5
Boat of Garten Highld 253 H7
Bobbing Kent 53 J6
Bobbington Staffs 97 H5
Bobbingworth Essex 70 D6
Bocaddon Cnwll 5 L3
Bocking Essex 71 J2
Bocking Churchstreet Essex 71 J2
Bockleton Worcs 80 D3
Boconnoc Cnwll 5 K3
Boddam Abers 257 L3
Boddam Shet 281 d8
Boddington Gloucs 64 C2
Bodedern IoA 124 F4
Bodelwyddan Denbgs 127 K5
Bodenham Herefs 80 C5
Bodenham Wilts 33 L5
Bodenham Moor Herefs 80 D5
Bodewryd IoA 125 G2
Bodfari Denbgs 128 C5
Bodffordd IoA 125 G4
Bodham Norfk 122 C3
Bodiam E Susx 24 E2
Bodicote Oxon 83 K7
Bodieve Cnwll 10 D7
Bodinnick Cnwll 5 K4
Bodle Street Green E Susx 23 L4
Bodmin Cnwll 5 H2
Bodmin Moor Cnwll 11 H7
Bodney Norfk 105 G4
Bodorgan IoA 125 G6
Bodsham Kent 40 E6
Boduan Gwynd 108 E4
Bodwen Cnwll 5 H3
Bodymoor Heath Warwks 99 G4
Bogallan Highld 251 H2
Bogbrae Abers 257 J4
Bogend S Ayrs 196 D4
Boggs Holdings E Loth 212 A5
Boghall Mdloth 211 H6
Boghall W Loth 210 C5
Boghead S Lans 198 C5
Bogmoor Moray 267 G4
Bogmuir Abers 235 G1
Bogniebrae Abers 255 M3
Bognor Regis W Susx 20 F7
Bogroy Highld 253 G7
Bogue D & G 185 G6
Bohetherick Cnwll 6 E1
Bohortha Cnwll 3 L4
Bohuntine Highld 240 F4
Bojewyan Cnwll 2 B4
Bokiddick Cnwll 5 H2
Bolam Dur 169 G6
Bolam Nthumb 180 D2
Bolberry Devon 7 K7
Bold Heath St Hel 129 M2
Boldmere Birm 98 E4
Boldon Colliery S Tyne 181 J6
Boldre Hants 18 E4
Boldron Dur 168 C7
Bole Notts 134 F2
Bolehill Derbys 132 F8
Bole Hill Derbys 133 G5
Bolenowe Cnwll 3 H3
Bolham Devon 29 G7
Bolham Water Devon 29 L8
Bolingey Cnwll 4 C4
Bollington Ches E 131 J4
Bollington Cross Ches E 131 H4
Bollow Gloucs 63 L4
Bolney W Susx 37 L6
Bolnhurst Bed 86 B3
Bolnore W Susx 22 E3
Bolshan Angus 234 F5
Bolsover Derbys 133 J5
Bolster Moor Kirk 141 G5
Bolsterstone Sheff 141 L8
Boltby N York 161 H5
Bolter End Bucks 67 J8
Bolton Bolton 139 L6
Bolton Cumb 166 G6
Bolton E Loth 212 B5
Bolton E R Yk 152 B3
Bolton Nthumb 191 G3
Bolton Abbey N York 149 K5
Bolton Bridge N York 149 K5
Bolton-by-Bowland Lancs 148 D6
Boltonfellend Cumb 178 C6
Boltongate Cumb 165 H3
Bolton-le-Sands Lancs 147 J2
Bolton Low Houses Cumb 165 H2
Bolton New Houses Cumb 165 H2
Bolton-on-Swale N York 160 C3
Bolton Percy N York 151 H7
Bolton Town End Lancs 147 J2
Bolton upon Dearne Barns 142 C7
Bolventor Cnwll 11 H7

Bomarsund Nthumb 181 G2
Bomere Heath Shrops 113 G7
Bonar Bridge Highld 263 G2
Bonawe Ag & B 228 F8
Bonby N Linc 144 C5
Boncath Pembks 75 L4
Bonchester Bridge Border 189 G4
Bonchurch IoW 19 K8
Bondleigh Devon 12 F2
Bonds Lancs 147 J6
Bonehill Devon 13 G7
Bonehill Staffs 99 G3
Bo'ness Falk 210 D3
Boney Hay Staffs 98 D2
Bonhill W Duns 208 C3
Boningale Shrops 97 J3
Bonjedward Border 189 H2
Bonkle N Lans 209 M7
Bonnington Angus 234 F7
Bonnington Kent 40 D8
Bonnybank Fife 222 F6
Bonnybridge Falk 209 L3
Bonnykelly Abers 268 F5
Bonnyrigg Mdloth 211 J6
Bonnyton Angus 233 M7
Bonsall Derbys 132 E8
Bonshaw Tower D & G 177 H4
Bont Mons 62 D3
Bontddu Gwynd 110 C7
Bont-Dolgadfan Powys 93 J3
Bont-goch Cerdgn 92 E6
Bonthorpe Lincs 137 J5
Bontnewydd Cerdgn 77 H2
Bontnewydd Gwynd 125 J7
Bontuchel Denbgs 128 C8
Bonvilston V Glam 43 G7
Bonwm Denbgs 111 L3
Bon-y-maen Swans 57 J6
Boode Devon 27 J3
Booker Bucks 49 K1
Booley Shrops 113 J6
Boon Border 201 J4
Boon Hill Staffs 114 C2
Boorley Green Hants 35 G8
Boosbeck R & Cl 170 F7
Boose's Green Essex 71 K1
Boot Cumb 155 M3
Booth Calder 141 G2
Boothby Graffoe Lincs 135 K7
Boothby Pagnell Lincs 118 C5
Boothferry E R Yk 143 J3
Booth Green Ches E 131 H3
Boothstown Salfd 139 L7
Boothtown Calder 141 G2
Boothville Nhants 84 F2
Bootle Cumb 155 K5
Bootle Sefton 138 D8
Boots Green Ches W 130 E5
Boot Street Suffk 90 F5
Booze N York 159 H2
Boraston Shrops 80 E1
Bordeaux Guern 9 k2
Borden Kent 53 J6
Borden W Susx 36 B6
Border Cumb 177 G8
Bordesley Worcs 82 B1
Bordley N York 149 G3
Bordon Hants 36 B4
Boreham Essex 71 J5
Boreham Wilts 32 E2
Boreham Street E Susx 24 B5
Borehamwood Herts 69 G7
Boreland D & G 187 J8
Boreraig Highld 258 B6
Boreton Shrops 96 C2
Borgh W Isls 282 g1
Borgh W Isls 283 b13
Borgie Highld 278 B4
Borgue D & G 175 G5
Borgue Highld 274 F3
Borley Essex 89 G6
Borley Green Essex 89 G6
Borley Green Suffk 89 K3
Borneskitaig Highld 258 F2
Borness D & G 174 F5
Boroughbridge N York 150 E3
Borough Green Kent 38 F2
Borras Head Wrexhm 112 E1
Borrowash Derbys 116 C4
Borrowby N York 160 F5
Borrowby N York 171 H7
Borrowdale Cumb 165 J7
Borrowstoun Falk 210 D3
Borstal Medway 52 F5
Borth Cerdgn 92 D5
Borthwick Mdloth 211 L7
Borthwickbrae Border 188 C3
Borthwickshiels Border 188 D3
Borth-y-Gest Gwynd 109 K4
Borve Highld 259 G7

Borve W Isls....282 d6
Borve W Isls....282 g1
Borve W Isls....283 b13
Borwick Lancs....147 K1
Borwick Lodge Cumb....156 E3
Borwick Rails Cumb....156 A6
Bosavern Cnwll....2 B5
Bosbury Herefs....80 F6
Boscarne Cnwll....5 H1
Boscastle Cnwll....10 F4
Boscombe BCP....17 M4
Boscombe Wilts....33 L3
Boscoppa Cnwll....5 H4
Bosham W Susx....20 C6
Bosham Hoe W Susx....20 D6
Bosherston Pembks....54 F7
Boskednan Cnwll....2 C4
Boskenna Cnwll....2 C6
Bosley Ches E....131 H6
Bosoughan Cnwll....4 E3
Bossall N York....151 M4
Bossiney Cnwll....10 F5
Bossingham Kent....40 F5
Bossington Somset....28 F1
Bostock Green Ches W....130 C6
Boston Lincs....119 K3
Boston Spa Leeds....150 F6
Boswarthan Cnwll....2 C4
Boswinger Cnwll....5 G6
Botallack Cnwll....2 B4
Botany Bay Gt Lon....69 J7
Botcheston Leics....100 B2
Botesdale Suffk....105 L8
Bothal Nthumb....180 F2
Bothampstead W Berk....48 D4
Bothamsall Notts....134 D5
Bothel Cumb....165 G3
Bothenhampton Dorset....15 L4
Bothwell S Lans....209 J7
Bothwell Services
  (southbound) S Lans....209 J7
Botley Bucks....68 B6
Botley Hants....35 G8
Botley Oxon....66 C6
Botolph Claydon Bucks....67 H2
Botolphs W Susx....21 L5
Botolph's Bridge Kent....40 F8
Bottesford Leics....117 L4
Bottesford N Linc....143 M6
Bottisham Cambs....87 L3
Bottomcraig Fife....222 F2
Bottom of Hutton Lancs....138 F2
Bottom o' th' Moor Bolton....139 K5
Bottoms Calder....140 D3
Bottoms Cnwll....2 B6
Botts Green Warwks....99 H5
Botusfleming Cnwll....6 E3
Botwnnog Gwynd....108 D5
Bough Beech Kent....38 D4
Boughrood Powys....79 G7
Boughspring Gloucs....63 H7
Boughton Nhants....84 E2
Boughton Norfk....104 D3
Boughton Notts....134 D6
Boughton Aluph Kent....40 D6
Boughton End C Beds....85 J7
Boughton Green Kent....39 J3
Boughton Lees Kent....40 D6
Boughton Malherbe Kent....39 M3
Boughton Monchelsea Kent....39 J3
Boughton Street Kent....40 D3
Boulby R & Cl....171 H7
Boulder Clough Calder....140 F3
Bouldnor IoW....18 F5
Bouldon Shrops....96 C6
Boulmer Nthumb....191 K3
Boulston Pembks....55 G4
Boultenstone Abers....243 M2
Boultham Lincs....135 J6
Boundary Staffs....114 F3
Bourn Cambs....87 G4
Bournbrook Birm....98 D6
Bourne Lincs....118 E7
Bournebridge Essex....70 D8
Bourne End Bed....85 K3
Bourne End Bucks....49 L2
Bourne End C Beds....85 J6
Bourne End Herts....68 C6
Bournemouth BCP....17 L4
Bournemouth Airport BCP....17 M3
Bournes Green Gloucs....64 C6
Bournes Green Sthend....53 K2
Bournheath Worcs....98 B8
Bournmoor Dur....181 H8
Bournville Birm....98 D7
Bourton Dorset....32 C5
Bourton N Som....44 D6
Bourton Oxon....47 K2
Bourton Shrops....96 D4

Bourton Wilts....46 F6
Bourton on Dunsmore Warwks....83 K1
Bourton-on-the-Hill Gloucs....65 J1
Bourton-on-the-Water Gloucs....65 H3
Bousd Ag & B....225 J4
Boustead Hill Cumb....177 J7
Bouth Cumb....156 D5
Bouthwaite N York....149 L2
Bouts Worcs....82 B3
Boveney Bucks....50 B3
Boveridge Dorset....33 J7
Bovey Tracey Devon....13 J7
Bovingdon Herts....68 C6
Bovingdon Green Bucks....49 K2
Bovinger Essex....70 D6
Bovington Dorset....16 F5
Bovington Camp Dorset....16 F5
Bow Cumb....177 K7
Bow Devon....8 B3
Bow Devon....13 G2
Bow Gt Lon....51 K2
Bow Ork....275 c6
Bowbank Dur....168 B6
Bow Brickhill M Keyn....85 H8
Bowbridge Gloucs....64 B6
Bowburn Dur....169 J3
Bowcombe IoW....19 H6
Bowd Devon....14 D4
Bowden Border....201 H7
Bowden Devon....8 C5
Bowden Hill Wilts....46 D5
Bowdon Traffd....130 E2
Bower Highld....280 B4
Bowerchalke Wilts....33 H6
Bowerhill Wilts....46 C6
Bower Hinton Somset....31 G7
Bower House Tye Suffk....89 K7
Bowermadden Highld....280 B3
Bowers Staffs....114 C4
Bowers Gifford Essex....53 G1
Bowershall Fife....210 E1
Bower's Row Leeds....142 B2
Bowes Dur....168 C7
Bowgreave Lancs....147 K7
Bowhouse D & G....176 D5
Bowithick Cnwll....11 H6
Bowker's Green Lancs....138 E6
Bowland Border....200 F5
Bowland Bridge Cumb....156 F5
Bowley Herefs....80 C5
Bowley Town Herefs....80 C5
Bowlhead Green Surrey....36 D3
Bowling C Brad....141 J2
Bowling W Duns....208 D4
Bowling Bank Wrexhm....112 F2
Bowling Green Worcs....81 J5
Bowmanstead Cumb....156 D3
Bowmore Ag & B....204 D4
Bowness-on-Solway Cumb....177 H6
Bowness-on-Windermere
  Cumb....156 F3
Bow of Fife Fife....222 E4
Bowriefauld Angus....234 D6
Bowscale Cumb....165 K4
Bowsden Nthumb....202 F5
Bowston Cumb....157 H3
Bow Street Cerdgn....92 D6
Bow Street Norfk....105 K4
Bowthorpe Norfk....106 D2
Box Gloucs....64 B7
Box Wilts....46 B5
Boxbush Gloucs....63 K3
Boxbush Gloucs....63 L4
Box End Bed....85 K5
Boxford Suffk....89 K7
Boxford W Berk....48 B4
Boxgrove W Susx....20 E5
Box Hill Surrey....51 G8
Boxley Kent....53 G7
Boxmoor Herts....68 D6
Box's Shop Cnwll....11 H2
Boxted Essex....72 E1
Boxted Suffk....89 G5
Boxted Cross Essex....72 E1
Boxwell Gloucs....64 A8
Boxworth Cambs....87 G2
Boyden End Suffk....88 E4
Boyden Gate Kent....41 K2
Boylestone Derbys....115 K4
Boyndie Abers....268 B3
Boyndlie Abers....269 G4
Boynton E R Yk....153 J2
Boysack Angus....234 F5
Boys Hill Dorset....16 C1
Boythorpe Derbys....133 G5
Boyton Cnwll....11 L4
Boyton Suffk....91 J6
Boyton Wilts....32 F3
Boyton Cross Essex....70 F5
Boyton End Suffk....88 E6

Bozeat Nhants....85 H3
Braaid IoM....154 d6
Brabling Green Suffk....91 G2
Brabourne Kent....40 E7
Brabourne Lees Kent....40 E7
Brabstermire Highld....280 D2
Bracadale Highld....246 E1
Braceborough Lincs....102 B1
Bracebridge Heath Lincs....135 K6
Bracebridge Low Fields Lincs....135 J6
Braceby Lincs....118 D4
Bracewell Lancs....148 F6
Brackenfield Derbys....133 G7
Brackenhirst N Lans....209 K5
Brackenthwaite Cumb....165 J1
Brackenthwaite N York....150 C5
Brackla Brdgnd....42 D5
Bracklesham W Susx....20 C7
Brackletter Highld....239 K7
Brackley Nhants....84 B7
Brackley Hatch Nhants....84 C7
Bracknell Br For....49 L5
Braco P & K....220 E5
Bracobrae Moray....267 K5
Bracon Ash Norfk....106 D3
Bracora Highld....237 L2
Bracorina Highld....237 L2
Bradaford Devon....11 M4
Bradbourne Derbys....115 K1
Bradbury Dur....169 J5
Bradden Nhants....84 C5
Braddock Cnwll....5 K2
Bradeley C Stke....114 D1
Bradenham Bucks....67 K7
Bradenstoke Wilts....46 E3
Bradfield Devon....14 B1
Bradfield Essex....73 H1
Bradfield Norfk....122 F5
Bradfield Sheff....132 E1
Bradfield W Berk....48 F4
Bradfield Combust Suffk....89 H4
Bradfield Green Ches E....130 D7
Bradfield Heath Essex....73 H1
Bradfield St Clare Suffk....89 H4
Bradfield St George Suffk....89 H3
Bradfield Southend W Berk....48 E5
Bradford C Brad....141 J1
Bradford Cnwll....11 G7
Bradford Devon....12 A1
Bradford Nthumb....180 C3
Bradford Nthumb....203 J6
Bradford Abbas Dorset....31 K8
Bradford Leigh Wilts....46 B6
Bradford-on-Avon Wilts....46 B6
Bradford-on-Tone Somset....30 B6
Bradford Peverell Dorset....16 C4
Bradiford Devon....27 K4
Brading IoW....19 K6
Bradley Ches W....113 H2
Bradley Derbys....115 L2
Bradley Hants....35 K3
Bradley Kirk....141 J4
Bradley N York....159 J6
Bradley NE Lin....145 G6
Bradley Staffs....114 D7
Bradley Wolves....98 B4
Bradley Worcs....82 A3
Bradley Wrexhm....112 F2
Bradley Green Somset....30 C3
Bradley Green Warwks....99 H3
Bradley Green Worcs....82 A3
Bradley in the Moors Staffs....115 H3
Bradley Stoke S Glos....45 J3
Bradmore Notts....117 G5
Bradney Somset....30 E3
Bradninch Devon....14 A2
Bradninch Devon....27 L4
Bradnop Staffs....131 K8
Bradnor Green Herefs....79 K4
Bradpole Dorset....15 L4
Bradshaw Bolton....139 L5
Bradshaw Calder....141 G2
Bradshaw Kirk....141 G5
Bradstone Devon....11 M6
Bradwall Green Ches E....130 E7
Bradwell Derbys....132 C3
Bradwell Devon....27 J2
Bradwell Essex....71 K3
Bradwell M Keyn....85 G7
Bradwell Norfk....107 K3
Bradwell-on-Sea Essex....72 E5
Bradwell Waterside Essex....72 E5
Bradworthy Devon....26 E8
Brae Highld....263 H7
Brae Shet....281 d4
Braeface Falk....209 K3
Braehead Angus....235 H5
Braehead D & G....173 K4
Braehead S Lans....198 F3
Braeintra Highld....248 D5

Braemar Abers....243 G5
Braemore Highld....261 L4
Braemore Highld....274 E2
Brae Roy Lodge Highld....240 B5
Braeside Inver....207 L4
Braes of Coul Angus....233 L4
Braes of Enzie Moray....267 H4
Braes of Ullapool Highld....261 K1
Braeswick Ork....275 e2
Braevallich Ag & B....216 E5
Braewick Shet....281 c4
Brafferton Darltn....169 H6
Brafferton N York....150 F3
Brafield-on-the-Green Nhants....84 F3
Bragar W Isls....282 f2
Bragbury End Herts....69 H3
Braidwood S Lans....198 D3
Brailsford Derbys....115 L3
Brailsford Green Derbys....115 L3
Brain's Green Gloucs....63 K5
Braintree Essex....71 J2
Braiseworth Suffk....90 D1
Braishfield Hants....34 E6
Braiswick Essex....72 E2
Braithwaite C Brad....149 L6
Braithwaite Cumb....165 H4
Braithwell Donc....133 K1
Braken Hill Wakefd....142 C4
Bramber W Susx....21 L5
Brambridge Hants....35 G6
Bramcote Notts....116 E4
Bramcote Warwks....99 L5
Bramdean Hants....35 J5
Bramerton Norfk....106 F2
Bramfield Herts....69 H4
Bramfield Suffk....107 H8
Bramford Suffk....90 D6
Bramhall Stockp....131 H3
Bramham Leeds....150 F7
Bramhope Leeds....150 C7
Bramley Hants....49 G8
Bramley Leeds....141 K1
Bramley Rothm....133 K1
Bramley Surrey....36 F2
Bramley Corner Hants....48 F7
Bramley Green Hants....49 G7
Bramley Head N York....149 L4
Bramling Kent....41 J4
Brampford Speke Devon....13 L4
Brampton Cambs....86 E1
Brampton Cumb....166 F6
Brampton Cumb....178 C6
Brampton Lincs....135 G5
Brampton Norfk....122 E6
Brampton Rothm....142 C5
Brampton Suffk....107 J7
Brampton Abbotts Herefs....63 J3
Brampton Ash Nhants....101 H5
Brampton Bryan Herefs....79 L8
Brampton-en-le-Morthen
  Rothm....133 J2
Bramshall Staffs....115 H5
Bramshaw Hants....34 C6
Bramshill Hants....49 G6
Bramshott Hants....36 C4
Bramwell Somset....31 G5
Branault Highld....237 G7
Brancaster Norfk....121 G3
Brancaster Staithe Norfk....121 H3
Brancepeth Dur....169 G3
Branchill Moray....266 B5
Brand End Lincs....119 L2
Branderburgh Moray....266 B2
Brandesburton E R Yk....153 H7
Brandeston Suffk....90 F3
Brand Green Gloucs....63 L3
Brandis Corner Devon....12 A1
Brandiston Norfk....122 C7
Brandon Dur....169 G3
Brandon Lincs....118 B2
Brandon Nthumb....190 F4
Brandon Suffk....104 F8
Brandon Warwks....99 L8
Brandon Bank Norfk....104 C8
Brandon Creek Norfk....104 C8
Brandon Parva Norfk....106 B2
Brandsby N York....151 J2
Brandy Wharf Lincs....144 C8
Brane Cnwll....2 C5
Bran End Essex....71 G2
Branksome BCP....17 G4
Branksome Park BCP....17 F4
Bransbury Hants....34 F3
Bransby Lincs....135 H4
Branscombe Devon....14 C5
Bransford Worcs....81 H5
Bransgore Hants....18 B4
Bransholme C KuH....144 D1
Bransley Shrops....96 H8
Branson's Cross Worcs....82 D8

ranston Leics 117 L6
ranston Lincs 135 L6
ranston Staffs 115 L6
ranston Booths Lincs 135 L6
ranstone IoW 19 J7
rant Broughton Lincs 118 B1
rantham Suffk 90 D8
ranthwaite Cumb 164 E5
ranthwaite Cumb 165 J3
rantingham E R Yk 144 B2
ranton Donc 143 G7
ranton Nthumb 190 F3
ranton Green N York 150 F3
ranxton Nthumb 202 D5
rassey Green Ches W 129 M7
rasside Dur 169 H2
rassington Derbys 115 L1
rasted Kent 38 D2
rasted Chart Kent 51 M8
rathens Abers 244 F4
ratoft Lincs 137 J6
rattleby Lincs 135 J3
ratton Somset 29 G2
ratton Wilts 46 C8
ratton Wrekin 96 E1
ratton Clovelly Devon 12 B4
ratton Fleming Devon 27 M3
ratton Seymour Somset 31 L5
raughing Herts 69 K2
raughing Friars Herts 70 B2
raunston Nhants 84 A2
raunston Rutlnd 101 H2
raunstone Town Leics 100 C3
raunton Devon 27 J4
rawby N York 162 C7
rawl Highld 278 D3
raworth N York 161 H1
ray W & M 49 L3
raybrooke Nhants 101 G6
raydon Wilts 46 F1
raydon Brook Wilts 64 E8
raydon Side Wilts 46 E2
rayford Devon 28 B4
ray's Hill E Susx 24 B4
ray Shop Cnwll 11 L7
raystones Cumb 155 H2
raythorn N York 150 C6
rayton N York 142 F2
raywick W & M 49 L3
raywoodside W & M 49 L4
razacott Cnwll 11 K4
reach Kent 41 G4
reach Kent 53 H6
reachwood Green Herts 68 F3
reacleit W Isls 282 e3
reaclete W Isls 282 e3
readen Heath Shrops 113 G4
readsall Derbys 116 B4
readstone Gloucs 63 L7
reage Cnwll 3 G5
reakachy Highld 250 E3
reakish Highld 247 L4
realangwell Lodge Highld 262 F1
ream Gloucs 63 J6
reamore Hants 33 L7
rean Somset 44 C7
reanais W Isls 282 d4
rearley Calder 140 F3
rearton N York 150 D4
reascleit W Isls 282 f3
reasclete W Isls 282 f3
reaston Derbys 116 D5
rechfa Carmth 58 F3
rechin Angus 234 F3
reckles Norfk 105 J4
recon Powys 61 G2
recon Beacons National Park 60 F2
redbury Stockp 131 H2
rede E Susx 24 E4
redenbury Herefs 80 E4
redfield Suffk 91 G4
redgar Kent 53 J7
redhurst Kent 53 G6
redon Worcs 81 L7
redon's Hardwick Worcs 81 L8
redon's Norton Worcs 81 L7
redward Herefs 79 K4
redwardine Herefs 79 L6
reedon on the Hill Leics 116 C7
reich W Loth 210 C7
reightmet Bolton 139 L6
reighton E R Yk 143 H1
reinton Herefs 80 B7
remhill Wilts 46 E4
remridge Devon 28 B5
renchley Kent 39 H5
rendon Devon 11 L1
rendon Devon 28 D1
rendon Hill Somset 29 J4

Brenfield Ag & B 206 D3
Brenish W Isls 282 d4
Brenkley N u Ty 180 F4
Brent Cross Gt Lon 51 G2
Brent Eleigh Suffk 89 J5
Brentford Gt Lon 50 F3
Brentingby Leics 117 K7
Brent Knoll Somset 30 E1
Brent Mill Devon 7 K3
Brent Pelham Herts 70 B1
Brentwood Essex 70 E8
Brenzett Kent 25 J2
Brenzett Green Kent 25 J2
Brereton Staffs 115 G8
Brereton Green Ches E 130 F6
Brereton Heath Ches E 130 F6
Brereton Hill Staffs 115 G8
Bressay Shet 281 e6
Bressingham Norfk 106 B7
Bressingham Common Norfk 106 B7
Bretby Derbys 116 A7
Bretford Warwks 99 L7
Bretforton Worcs 82 C6
Bretherton Lancs 138 F4
Brettabister Shet 281 e5
Brettenham Norfk 105 J6
Brettenham Suffk 89 K4
Bretton C Pete 102 D3
Bretton Derbys 132 D4
Bretton Flints 129 H7
Brewers End Essex 70 E3
Brewer Street Surrey 51 J8
Brewood Staffs 97 K2
Briantspuddle Dorset 16 F4
Brick End Essex 70 E2
Brickendon Herts 69 J5
Bricket Wood Herts 68 E6
Brick Houses Sheff 132 F3
Brickkiln Green Essex 71 H1
Bricklehampton Worcs 82 A6
Bride IoM 154 f2
Bridekirk Cumb 164 F4
Bridell Pembks 75 L4
Bridestowe Devon 12 C5
Brideswell Abers 255 M4
Bridford Devon 13 J5
Bridge Kent 41 G4
Bridge End Cumb 156 A6
Bridge End Cumb 165 L1
Bridge End Devon 7 K5
Bridge End Dur 168 C3
Bridge End Essex 71 G1
Bridge End Lincs 118 F4
Bridgefoot Angus 234 B8
Bridgefoot Cumb 164 E5
Bridge Green Essex 87 K7
Bridgehampton Somset 31 J6
Bridge Hewick N York 150 D2
Bridgehill Dur 180 D8
Bridgehouse Gate N York 149 L3
Bridgemary Hants 19 K3
Bridgemere Ches E 113 M2
Bridgend Abers 255 K4
Bridgend Ag & B 194 B3
Bridgend Ag & B 204 E4
Bridgend Ag & B 216 C8
Bridgend Angus 234 E2
Bridgend Brdgnd 42 D5
Bridgend Cerdgn 75 L3
Bridgend Cumb 165 L7
Bridgend D & G 187 G4
Bridgend Devon 7 G5
Bridgend Fife 223 G5
Bridgend Moray 255 H5
Bridgend P & K 221 L2
Bridgend W Loth 210 D4
Bridgend of Lintrathen Angus 233 L4
Bridge of Alford Abers 255 L8
Bridge of Allan Stirlg 220 D7
Bridge of Avon Moray 254 C7
Bridge of Avon Moray 254 D4
Bridge of Balgie P & K 231 G6
Bridge of Brewlands Angus 233 J3
Bridge of Brown Highld 254 C7
Bridge of Cally P & K 233 H5
Bridge of Canny Abers 244 E4
Bridge of Craigisla Angus 233 K4
Bridge of Dee D & G 175 J3
Bridge of Don C Aber 245 L2
Bridge of Dun Angus 235 G4
Bridge of Dye Abers 244 E6
Bridge of Earn P & K 221 L3
Bridge of Ericht P & K 230 F4
Bridge of Feugh Abers 244 F4
Bridge of Gairn Abers 243 K4
Bridge of Gaur P & K 230 F4
Bridge of Marnoch Abers 267 M6
Bridge of Muchalls Abers 245 K5
Bridge of Orchy Ag & B 230 B7

Bridge of Tilt P & K 232 C2
Bridge of Tynet Moray 267 H4
Bridge of Walls Shet 281 c6
Bridge of Weir Rens 208 C6
Bridge Reeve Devon 28 B8
Bridgerule Devon 11 K2
Bridges Shrops 95 J4
Bridge Sollers Herefs 80 A6
Bridge Street Suffk 89 H5
Bridgetown Cnwll 11 L5
Bridgetown Somset 29 G4
Bridge Trafford Ches W 129 K5
Bridge Yate S Glos 45 K4
Bridgham Norfk 105 J6
Bridgnorth Shrops 97 G5
Bridgwater Somset 30 D3
Bridgwater Services Somset 30 D4
Bridlington E R Yk 153 K3
Bridport Dorset 15 K4
Bridstow Herefs 63 H2
Brierfield Lancs 148 E8
Brierley Barns 142 B5
Brierley Gloucs 63 J4
Brierley Herefs 80 C4
Brierley Hill Dudley 97 L6
Brierlow Bar Derbys 132 B5
Brierton Hartpl 170 B5
Briery Cumb 165 J6
Brigg N Linc 144 C6
Briggate Norfk 123 G6
Briggswath N York 162 F1
Brigham Cumb 164 E4
Brigham Cumb 165 J6
Brigham E R Yk 153 H5
Brighouse Calder 141 J3
Brighstone IoW 19 G7
Brightgate Derbys 132 E7
Brighthampton Oxon 66 A6
Brightholmlee Sheff 132 F1
Brightley Devon 12 E3
Brightling E Susx 24 C3
Brightlingsea Essex 73 G4
Brighton Br & H 22 D6
Brighton Cnwll 4 E4
Brighton City Airport W Susx 22 B6
Brighton le Sands Sefton 138 C7
Brightons Falk 210 B3
Brightwalton W Berk 48 B3
Brightwalton Green W Berk 48 B3
Brightwalton Holt W Berk 48 B3
Brightwell Suffk 90 F6
Brightwell Baldwin Oxon 67 G8
Brightwell-cum-Sotwell Oxon 48 E1
Brightwell Upperton Oxon 67 G8
Brignall Dur 168 D8
Brig o'Turk Stirlg 219 J6
Brigsley NE Lin 145 H7
Brigsteer Cumb 157 G5
Brigstock Nhants 101 L6
Brill Bucks 67 G4
Brill Cnwll 3 J5
Brilley Herefs 79 J5
Brimfield Herefs 80 C2
Brimfield Cross Herefs 80 C2
Brimington Derbys 133 H5
Brimley Devon 13 J7
Brimpsfield Gloucs 64 D4
Brimpton W Berk 48 E6
Brimpton Common W Berk 48 E6
Brimscombe Gloucs 64 C6
Brimstage Wirral 129 G3
Brincliffe Sheff 132 F3
Brind E R Yk 143 J2
Brindham Somset 31 H3
Brindister Shet 281 c5
Brindle Lancs 139 J3
Brindley Ches E 113 K1
Brineton Staffs 97 H1
Bringhurst Leics 101 J5
Bringsty Common Herefs 81 G4
Brington Cambs 102 B8
Brinian Ork 275 c3
Briningham Norfk 122 A5
Brinkely Notts 117 J3
Brinkhill Lincs 137 G5
Brinkley Cambs 88 C4
Brinklow Warwks 99 L7
Brinkworth Wilts 46 E2
Brinscall Lancs 139 J3
Brinscombe Somset 44 E8
Brinsea N Som 44 F6
Brinsley Notts 116 D2
Brinsop Herefs 80 B6
Brinsworth Rothm 133 H2
Brinton Norfk 122 A4
Brisco Cumb 178 A8
Brisley Norfk 121 L7
Brislington Bristl 45 J5
Brissenden Green Kent 40 B7
Bristol Bristl 45 H4

Bristol Airport N Som 45 G6
Briston Norfk 122 B5
Brisworthy Devon 7 G2
Britannia Lancs 140 C3
Britford Wilts 33 L5
Brithdir Caerph 61 J6
Brithdir Gwynd 110 E7
British Legion Village Kent 52 F7
Briton Ferry Neath 57 K6
Britwell Salome Oxon 67 G8
Brixham Torbay 8 D4
Brixton Devon 7 G4
Brixton Gt Lon 51 J4
Brixton Deverill Wilts 32 E3
Brixworth Nhants 84 E1
Brize Norton Oxon 65 L5
Brize Norton Airport Oxon 65 L6
Broad Alley Worcs 81 K2
Broad Blunsdon Swindn 47 H1
Broadbottom Tamesd 131 K1
Broadbridge W Susx 20 D6
Broadbridge Heath W Susx 37 H4
Broad Campden Gloucs 82 E7
Broad Carr Calder 141 H4
Broad Chalke Wilts 33 H5
Broad Clough Lancs 140 C3
Broadclyst Devon 14 A3
Broadfield Inver 208 B4
Broadfield Pembks 55 K6
Broadford Highld 247 K4
Broad Ford Kent 39 H5
Broadford Bridge W Susx 37 G6
Broadgairhill Border 187 K4
Broadgrass Green Suffk 89 K3
Broad Green Cambs 88 D3
Broad Green Essex 72 C2
Broad Green Worcs 81 H4
Broad Green Worcs 82 A1
Broadhaugh Border 202 D2
Broad Haven Pembks 54 D4
Broadheath Traffd 130 E2
Broadhembury Devon 14 C2
Broadhempston Devon 8 B2
Broad Hill Cambs 104 B8
Broad Hinton Wilts 47 G4
Broadholme Lincs 135 H5
Broadland Row E Susx 24 F3
Broadlay Carmth 56 C3
Broad Layings Hants 48 B6
Broadley Essex 70 B5
Broadley Lancs 140 C4
Broadley Moray 267 H4
Broadley Common Essex 70 B5
Broad Marston Worcs 82 D6
Broadmayne Dorset 16 D5
Broad Meadow Staffs 114 C2
Broadmere Hants 35 J4
Broadmoor Gloucs 63 J4
Broadmoor Pembks 55 J5
Broadnymett Devon 13 G2
Broad Oak Carmth 59 G4
Broad Oak Cumb 155 K4
Broadoak Dorset 15 K3
Broad Oak E Susx 23 K3
Broad Oak E Susx 24 F3
Broadoak Gloucs 63 K4
Broad Oak Hants 49 H8
Broad Oak Herefs 62 F3
Broad Oak Kent 41 G4
Broad Oak St Hel 139 G8
Broadoak Wrexhm 129 J7
Broad Road Suffk 106 F8
Broadsands Torbay 8 D3
Broad's Green Essex 71 G4
Broadstairs Kent 41 L2
Broadstone BCP 17 K3
Broadstone Mons 63 G6
Broadstone Shrops 96 C5
Broad Street E Susx 24 F4
Broad Street Essex 70 E4
Broad Street Kent 39 L2
Broad Street Kent 40 F7
Broad Street Medway 53 G4
Broad Street Wilts 47 G7
Broad Street Green Essex 71 L5
Broad Town Wilts 47 G3
Broadwas Worcs 81 H4
Broadwater Herts 69 H3
Broadwater W Susx 21 K6
Broadwaters Worcs 97 J7
Broadway Carmth 56 B3
Broadway Carmth 56 E4
Broadway Pembks 54 E4
Broadway Somset 30 D7
Broadway Suffk 107 H7
Broadway Worcs 82 C7
Broadwell Gloucs 63 H5
Broadwell Gloucs 65 J2
Broadwell Oxon 65 K6
Broadwell Warwks 83 K2

Place	County	Page	Grid
Broadwey	Dorset	16	C6
Broadwindsor	Dorset	15	K2
Broadwood Kelly	Devon	12	E2
Broadwoodwidger	Devon	12	A5
Brobury	Herefs	79	L6
Brochel	Highld	259	K7
Brochroy	Ag & B	216	F1
Brock	Lancs	147	K7
Brockamin	Worcs	81	H4
Brockbridge	Hants	35	J7
Brockdish	Norfk	106	E7
Brockencote	Worcs	97	K8
Brockenhurst	Hants	18	D3
Brocketsbrae	S Lans	198	D5
Brockford Green	Suffk	90	D2
Brockford Street	Suffk	90	D2
Brockhall	Nhants	84	C3
Brockhall Village	Lancs	148	B8
Brockham	Surrey	37	J1
Brockhampton	Gloucs	64	D2
Brockhampton	Gloucs	64	F3
Brockhampton	Hants	20	B5
Brockhampton	Herefs	63	H1
Brockhampton Green	Dorset	16	D2
Brockholes	Kirk	141	J5
Brockhurst	Derbys	133	G6
Brockhurst	Warwks	100	A6
Brocklebank	Cumb	165	J2
Brocklesby	Lincs	144	E5
Brockley	N Som	44	F5
Brockley	Suffk	89	G1
Brockley Green	Suffk	88	E6
Brockley Green	Suffk	89	G4
Brockleymoor	Cumb	166	C3
Brockmoor	Dudley	97	K5
Brockscombe	Devon	12	B4
Brock's Green	Hants	48	D6
Brockton	Shrops	95	H3
Brockton	Shrops	95	H6
Brockton	Shrops	96	D4
Brockton	Shrops	97	G3
Brockton	Staffs	114	C5
Brockweir	Gloucs	63	G6
Brockwood Park	Hants	35	K5
Brockworth	Gloucs	64	C4
Brocton	Cnwll	5	G1
Brocton	Staffs	114	F7
Brodick	N Ayrs	195	G4
Brodie	Moray	264	F8
Brodsworth	Donc	142	D6
Brogaig	Highld	259	H3
Brogborough	C Beds	85	J7
Brokenborough	Wilts	46	D1
Broken Cross	Ches E	131	H5
Broken Cross	Ches W	130	D5
Brokerswood	Wilts	46	B8
Bromborough	Wirral	129	H3
Brome	Suffk	106	C8
Brome Street	Suffk	106	C8
Bromeswell	Suffk	91	G5
Bromfield	Cumb	165	G1
Bromfield	Shrops	96	B8
Bromham	Bed	85	K5
Bromham	Wilts	46	D6
Bromley	Barns	141	M7
Bromley	Dudley	97	K5
Bromley	Gt Lon	51	L5
Bromley	Shrops	97	G4
Bromley Common	Gt Lon	51	L5
Bromley Cross	Bolton	139	L5
Bromley Cross	Essex	72	F2
Bromley Green	Kent	40	C8
Bromlow	Shrops	95	H3
Brompton	Medway	53	G5
Brompton	N York	160	E3
Brompton-by-Sawdon	N York	163	G6
Brompton-on-Swale	N York	160	B3
Brompton Ralph	Somset	29	K4
Brompton Regis	Somset	29	G4
Bromsash	Herefs	63	J2
Bromsberrow	Gloucs	81	G8
Bromsberrow Heath	Gloucs	81	G8
Bromsgrove	Worcs	81	M1
Bromstead Heath	Staffs	114	B8
Bromyard	Herefs	80	F4
Bromyard Downs	Herefs	80	F4
Bronaber	Gwynd	110	D5
Bronant	Cerdgn	77	H2
Broncroft	Shrops	96	C6
Brongest	Cerdgn	76	B6
Bronington	Wrexhm	113	H3
Bronllys	Powys	79	G8
Bronwydd	Carmth	58	D4
Bronydd	Powys	79	J6
Brongarth	Shrops	112	C4
Brook	Carmth	56	A3
Brook	Hants	34	C8
Brook	Hants	34	D5
Brook	IoW	18	F6
Brook	Kent	40	E6
Brook	Surrey	36	D3
Brook	Surrey	37	G2
Brooke	Norfk	106	F3
Brooke	Rutlnd	101	J2
Brookenby	Lincs	145	G8
Brook End	Bed	86	B3
Brook End	C Beds	86	D5
Brook End	Cambs	86	B1
Brook End	M Keyn	85	H6
Brookfield	Rens	208	C6
Brookhampton	Oxon	66	F7
Brookhampton	Somset	31	K5
Brook Hill	Hants	34	C7
Brookhouse	Denbgs	128	C6
Brookhouse	Lancs	147	K3
Brookhouse	Rothm	133	K2
Brookhouse Green	Ches E	130	F7
Brookhouses	Derbys	131	K2
Brookland	Kent	25	J2
Brooklands	Traffd	130	F2
Brookmans Park	Herts	69	H6
Brooks	Powys	94	E3
Brooksby	Leics	117	H8
Brooks End	Kent	41	J2
Brooks Green	W Susx	37	H6
Brook Street	Essex	70	E8
Brook Street	Kent	40	B8
Brook Street	Suffk	89	G5
Brook Street	W Susx	22	D2
Brookthorpe	Gloucs	64	B4
Brookville	Norfk	104	E4
Brookwood	Surrey	50	B7
Broom	C Beds	86	D6
Broom	Rothm	133	J1
Broom	Warwks	82	C4
Broombank	Worcs	80	F1
Broome	Norfk	107	G5
Broome	Shrops	95	K7
Broome	Worcs	97	K7
Broomedge	Warrtn	130	D3
Broome Park	Nthumb	191	G4
Broomer's Corner	W Susx	37	H6
Broomershill	W Susx	21	H3
Broomfield	Essex	71	H5
Broomfield	Kent	39	L3
Broomfield	Kent	41	G2
Broomfield	Somset	30	B4
Broomfields	Shrops	112	F7
Broomfleet	E R Yk	143	M2
Broom Green	Norfk	121	L6
Broomhall	W & M	50	B5
Broomhaugh	Nthumb	180	B6
Broom Hill	Barns	142	C7
Broom Hill	Dorset	17	K2
Broom Hill	Notts	116	F2
Broomhill	Nthumb	191	J6
Broom Hill	Worcs	97	L8
Broomhill Green	Ches E	113	K2
Broomley	Nthumb	180	C6
Broompark	Dur	169	H2
Broom's Green	Gloucs	81	G8
Broomsthorpe	Norfk	121	J6
Broom Street	Kent	40	D3
Brora	Highld	274	B7
Broseley	Shrops	96	F3
Brotherhouse Bar	Lincs	119	J8
Brotherlee	Dur	167	L3
Brothertoft	Lincs	119	J2
Brotherton	N York	142	D3
Brotton	R & Cl	170	F6
Broubster	Highld	279	J4
Brough	Cumb	167	J7
Brough	Derbys	132	D3
Brough	E R Yk	144	B2
Brough	Highld	280	B2
Brough	Notts	135	G2
Brough	Shet	281	f5
Broughall	Shrops	113	J3
Brough Lodge	Shet	281	f3
Brough Sowerby	Cumb	167	J8
Broughton	Border	199	K6
Broughton	Bucks	67	K4
Broughton	Cambs	102	F7
Broughton	Flints	129	H7
Broughton	Hants	34	C4
Broughton	Lancs	139	G1
Broughton	M Keyn	85	H7
Broughton	N Linc	144	B6
Broughton	N York	149	G5
Broughton	N York	162	D8
Broughton	Nhants	101	J4
Broughton	Oxon	83	K7
Broughton	Salfd	140	B7
Broughton	Staffs	114	B5
Broughton	V Glam	42	D7
Broughton Astley	Leics	100	B5
Broughton Beck	Cumb	156	C6
Broughton Gifford	Wilts	46	C6
Broughton Green	Worcs	81	M3
Broughton Hackett	Worcs	81	L4
Broughton-in-Furness	Cumb	156	B5
Broughton Mains	D & G	174	C6
Broughton Mills	Cumb	156	B4
Broughton Moor	Cumb	164	E4
Broughton Poggs	Oxon	65	K6
Broughton Tower	Cumb	156	B5
Broughty Ferry	C Dund	223	H1
Brough with St Giles	N York	160	B3
Brow End	Cumb	156	C7
Brownber	Cumb	158	F3
Brown Candover	Hants	35	J3
Brown Edge	Lancs	138	D5
Brown Edge	Staffs	114	E1
Brown Heath	Ches W	129	K6
Brownheath	Shrops	113	G5
Brownhill	Abers	256	F4
Brownhills	Fife	223	J6
Brownhills	Wsall	98	D2
Brownieside	Nthumb	191	H2
Browninghill Green	Hants	48	E7
Brown Knowl	Ches W	113	K6
Brown Lees	Staffs	131	G8
Brownlow Heath	Ches E	131	G7
Brownrigg	Cumb	164	D6
Brownrigg	Cumb	177	G6
Brownsea Island	Dorset	17	K5
Brown's Green	Birm	98	D5
Brownsham	Devon	26	E5
Browns Hill	Gloucs	64	C6
Brownsover	Warwks	100	B7
Brownston	Devon	7	K4
Brown Street	Suffk	90	C3
Browston Green	Norfk	107	K3
Broxa	N York	163	G4
Broxbourne	Herts	69	K5
Broxburn	E Loth	212	F3
Broxburn	W Loth	210	E4
Broxfield	Nthumb	191	J3
Broxted	Essex	70	E2
Broxton	Ches W	113	H1
Broyle Side	E Susx	23	G4
Bruan	Highld	280	D8
Bruar	P & K	232	B2
Bruchag	Ag & B	207	J2
Bruera	Ches W	129	K7
Bruern Abbey	Oxon	65	K3
Bruichladdich	Ag & B	204	C4
Bruisyard	Suffk	91	H2
Bruisyard Street	Suffk	91	H2
Brumby	N Linc	143	M6
Brund	Staffs	132	B7
Brundall	Norfk	107	G2
Brundish	Suffk	91	G1
Brundish Street	Suffk	91	G1
Brunery	Highld	237	L6
Brunnion	Cnwll	2	D4
Brunslow	Shrops	95	J6
Brunswick Village	N u Ty	180	F4
Bruntcliffe	Leeds	141	L2
Brunthwaite	C Brad	149	J6
Bruntingthorpe	Leics	100	D5
Brunton	Fife	222	E3
Brunton	Nthumb	191	J1
Brunton	Wilts	47	K7
Brushford	Devon	12	F1
Brushford	Somset	29	G5
Bruton	Somset	31	L4
Bryan's Green	Worcs	81	K2
Bryanston	Dorset	17	G1
Bryant's Bottom	Bucks	67	L7
Brydekirk	D & G	177	G5
Bryher	IoS	10	b2
Brymbo	Wrexhm	112	D1
Brympton	Somset	31	H7
Bryn	Carmth	57	G5
Bryn	Ches W	130	B5
Bryn	Neath	42	B3
Bryn	Shrops	95	H6
Bryn	Wigan	139	H7
Brynamman	Carmth	59	K6
Brynberian	Pembks	75	J5
Brynbryddan	Neath	57	L6
Bryn Bwbach	Gwynd	110	B4
Bryncae	Rhondd	42	F5
Bryncethin	Brdgnd	42	D5
Bryncir	Gwynd	109	H3
Bryn-côch	Neath	57	K5
Bryncroes	Gwynd	108	C5
Bryncrug	Gwynd	92	D3
Bryn Du	IoA	124	F5
Bryn-Eden	Gwynd	110	D5
Bryneglwys	Denbgs	112	A2
Bryneglwys & Abergynolwyn Slate Landscape	Gwynd	92	E2
Brynfields	Wrexhm	112	D3
Brynford	Flints	128	E5
Bryn Gates	Wigan	139	J7
Bryn Golau	Rhondd	42	F4
Bryngwran	IoA	124	F4
Bryngwyn	Mons	62	D5
Bryngwyn	Powys	79	H
Bryn-Henllan	Pembks	75	G
Brynhoffnant	Cerdgn	76	E
Bryning	Lancs	138	E
Brynithel	Blae G	61	K
Brynmawr	Blae G	61	H
Bryn-mawr	Gwynd	108	M
Brynmenyn	Brdgnd	42	M
Brynmill	Swans	57	H
Brynna	Rhondd	42	M
Brynnau Gwynion	Rhondd	42	M
Bryn-penarth	Powys	94	C
Brynrefail	Gwynd	125	K
Brynrefail	IoA	125	H
Brynsadler	Rhondd	42	F
Bryn Saith Marchog	Denbgs	111	L
Brynsiencyn	IoA	125	H
Brynteg	IoA	125	H
Bryn-y-bal	Flints	128	M
Bryn-y-Maen	Conwy	127	G
Bryn-yr-Eos	Wrexhm	112	G
Bualintur	Highld	246	F
Buarth-draw	Flints	128	E
Bubbenhall	Warwks	83	J
Bubwith	E R Yk	151	M
Buccleuch	Border	188	B
Buchanan Smithy	Stirlg	208	F
Buchanhaven	Abers	269	K
Buchanty	P & K	221	G
Buchany	Stirlg	220	C
Buchlyvie	Stirlg	219	J
Buckabank	Cumb	165	J
Buckden	Cambs	86	D
Buckden	N York	159	G
Buckenham	Norfk	107	G
Buckerell	Devon	14	C
Buckfast	Devon	7	L
Buckfastleigh	Devon	7	L
Buckhaven	Fife	222	F
Buckholt	Mons	63	G
Buckhorn	Devon	11	M
Buckhorn Weston	Dorset	32	C
Buckhurst Hill	Essex	69	L
Buckie	Moray	267	J
Buckingham	Bucks	84	E
Buckland	Bucks	67	L
Buckland	Devon	7	L
Buckland	Gloucs	82	C
Buckland	Hants	18	E
Buckland	Herts	87	H
Buckland	Kent	41	M
Buckland	Oxon	65	M
Buckland	Surrey	37	K
Buckland Brewer	Devon	27	G
Buckland Common	Bucks	68	A
Buckland Dinham	Somset	32	C
Buckland Filleigh	Devon	12	E
Buckland in the Moor	Devon	13	H
Buckland Monachorum	Devon	6	M
Buckland Newton	Dorset	16	E
Buckland Ripers	Dorset	16	E
Buckland St Mary	Somset	30	C
Buckland-Tout-Saints	Devon	7	H
Bucklebury	W Berk	48	E
Bucklers Hard	Hants	18	E
Bucklesham	Suffk	90	F
Buckley	Flints	129	G
Buckley Green	Warwks	82	E
Bucklow Hill	Ches E	130	E
Buckminster	Leics	118	A
Bucknall	C Stke	114	E
Bucknall	Lincs	136	C
Bucknell	Oxon	66	E
Bucknell	Shrops	95	H
Buckpool	Moray	267	H
Bucksburn	C Aber	245	K
Buck's Cross	Devon	26	E
Bucks Green	W Susx	37	H
Bucks Hill	Herts	68	H
Bucks Horn Oak	Hants	36	B
Buck's Mills	Devon	26	E
Buckton	E R Yk	153	G
Buckton	Herefs	95	H
Buckton	Nthumb	203	H
Buckworth	Cambs	102	E
Budby	Notts	134	E
Buddileigh	Staffs	114	E
Bude	Cnwll	11	H
Budge's Shop	Cnwll	6	E
Budlake	Devon	14	M
Budle	Nthumb	203	H
Budleigh Salterton	Devon	14	E
Budlett's Common	E Susx	23	H
Budock Water	Cnwll	3	H
Buerton	Ches E	113	E
Bugbrooke	Nhants	84	E
Bugford	Devon	8	E
Buglawton	Ches E	131	G
Bugle	Cnwll	5	G

Place	Region	Page	Grid
Bugley	Dorset	32	C6
Bugthorpe	E R Yk	152	B4
Buildwas	Shrops	96	E2
Builth Road	Powys	78	E4
Builth Wells	Powys	78	E5
Bulbourne	Herts	68	B4
Bulbridge	Wilts	33	J5
Bulby	Lincs	118	D6
Bulcote	Notts	117	H3
Bulford	Wilts	33	L2
Bulford Camp	Wilts	33	L2
Bulkeley	Ches E	113	J1
Bulkington	Warwks	99	K6
Bulkington	Wilts	46	D7
Bulkworthy	Devon	27	G8
Bullamoor	N York	160	F4
Bull Bay	IoA	125	G1
Bullbridge	Derbys	116	B1
Bullbrook	Br For	49	L5
Bullen's Green	Herts	69	G6
Bulley	Gloucs	63	M3
Bullgill	Cumb	164	E3
Bullingham	Herefs	80	C7
Bullinghope	Herefs	80	C7
Bullington	Hants	34	F3
Bullington	Lincs	136	A4
Bullockstone	Kent	41	G2
Bull's Green	Herts	69	H4
Bull's Green	Norfk	107	J4
Bulmer	Essex	89	G7
Bulmer	N York	151	L2
Bulmer Tye	Essex	89	G7
Bulphan	Thurr	52	D2
Bulstone	Devon	14	E4
Bulstrode	Herts	68	C6
Bulverhythe	E Susx	24	D5
Bulwark	Abers	257	G3
Bulwell	C Nott	116	F3
Bulwick	Nhants	101	L4
Bumble's Green	Essex	69	L6
Bunacaimb	Highld	237	J2
Bunarkaig	Highld	239	K6
Bunbury	Ches E	130	A8
Bunbury Heath	Ches E	130	A8
Bunchrew	Highld	251	H3
Buncton	W Susx	21	K4
Bundalloch	Highld	248	E6
Bunessan	Ag & B	226	D8
Bungay	Suffk	107	G5
Bunker's Hill	Lincs	119	J1
Bunnahabhain	Ag & B	204	F2
Bunny	Notts	117	G5
Buntait	Highld	250	C5
Buntingford	Herts	69	K1
Bunwell	Norfk	106	C4
Bunwell Hill	Norfk	106	C5
Bupton	Derbys	115	L4
Burbage	Derbys	131	L5
Burbage	Leics	99	L5
Burbage	Wilts	47	K6
Burcher	Herefs	79	L3
Burchett's Green	W & M	49	K3
Burcombe	Wilts	33	J5
Burcot	Oxon	66	E7
Burcot	Worcs	82	A1
Burcote	Shrops	97	G4
Burcott	Bucks	67	K4
Burcott	Bucks	67	L2
Burdale	N York	152	F2
Bures	Essex	89	H8
Burford	Oxon	65	D2
Burford	Shrops	80	D2
Burg	Ag & B	226	D3
Burgate	Suffk	106	B8
Burgates	Hants	36	A5
Burge End	Herts	68	F1
Burgess Hill	W Susx	22	E3
Burgh	Suffk	90	F5
Burgh by Sands	Cumb	177	K7
Burgh Castle	Norfk	107	K2
Burghclere	Hants	48	C6
Burghead	Moray	266	C2
Burghfield	W Berk	49	G5
Burghfield Common	W Berk	49	G5
Burgh Heath	Surrey	51	H7
Burgh Hill	E Susx	24	C2
Burghill	Herefs	80	B6
Burgh Island	Devon	7	J7
Burgh le Marsh	Lincs	137	J6
Burgh next Aylsham	Norfk	122	E6
Burgh on Bain	Lincs	136	D2
Burgh St Margaret	Norfk	123	J8
Burgh St Peter	Norfk	107	K5
Burghwallis	Donc	142	E5
Burham	Kent	52	F6
Buriton	Hants	20	B3
Burland	Ches E	113	K1
Burlawn	Cnwll	10	D8
Burleigh	Gloucs	64	C6
Burlescombe	Devon	29	K7
Burleston	Dorset	16	E4
Burlestone	Devon	8	B5
Burley	Hants	18	C3
Burley	Rutlnd	101	J1
Burley	Shrops	96	B7
Burleydam	Ches E	113	K3
Burley Gate	Herefs	80	E6
Burley in Wharfedale	C Brad	149	L6
Burley Lawn	Hants	18	C3
Burley Street	Hants	18	B3
Burley Wood Head	C Brad	149	L7
Burlingham Green	Norfk	107	H1
Burlingjobb	Powys	79	J4
Burlington	Shrops	97	H1
Burlton	Shrops	113	G6
Burmarsh	Kent	25	L1
Burmington	Warwks	83	G7
Burn	N York	142	F2
Burnage	Manch	131	G1
Burnaston	Derbys	115	M5
Burnbanks	Cumb	166	C7
Burnbrae	N Lans	210	A7
Burn Bridge	N York	150	D5
Burnby	E R Yk	152	C6
Burn Cross	Sheff	142	A4
Burndell	W Susx	21	G6
Burnden	Bolton	139	L6
Burnedge	Rochdl	140	D5
Burneside	Cumb	157	H6
Burneston	N York	160	D5
Burnett	BaNES	45	K6
Burnfoot	Border	188	C4
Burnfoot	Border	188	E3
Burnfoot	D & G	177	K1
Burnfoot	D & G	186	E7
Burnfoot	D & G	188	C6
Burnfoot	P & K	221	H6
Burnham	Bucks	50	A3
Burnham	N Linc	144	D4
Burnham Deepdale	Norfk	121	H3
Burnham Green	Herts	69	H4
Burnham Market	Norfk	121	H3
Burnham Norton	Norfk	121	H3
Burnham-on-Crouch	Essex	72	D7
Burnham-on-Sea	Somset	30	D1
Burnham Overy	Somset	121	J3
Burnham Overy Staithe	Norfk	121	J3
Burnham Thorpe	Norfk	121	J3
Burnhead	D & G	186	C7
Burnhervie	Abers	256	C7
Burnhill Green	Staffs	97	H3
Burnhope	Dur	169	G1
Burnhouse	N Ayrs	196	D1
Burniston	N York	163	H4
Burnley	Lancs	140	C1
Burnmouth	Border	213	L6
Burn Naze	Lancs	147	H2
Burn of Cambus	Stirlg	220	C6
Burnopfield	Dur	180	E7
Burnrigg	Cumb	178	C7
Burnsall	N York	149	J3
Burnside	Angus	234	C3
Burnside	Angus	234	D5
Burnside	Fife	222	B5
Burnside	Moray	266	D2
Burnside	W Loth	210	E4
Burnside of Duntrune	Angus	234	C8
Burntcommon	Surrey	50	D8
Burnt Heath	Essex	72	F2
Burnt Hill	W Berk	48	E4
Burnthouse	Cnwll	3	K4
Burnt Houses	Dur	168	D3
Burntisland	Fife	211	H2
Burnt Oak	E Susx	23	H2
Burnton	E Ayrs	184	D2
Burntwood	Flints	129	G6
Burntwood	Staffs	98	D2
Burntwood Green	Staffs	98	D2
Burnt Yates	N York	150	C4
Burnworthy	Somset	30	B7
Burpham	Surrey	50	C8
Burpham	W Susx	21	H5
Burradon	N Tyne	181	G4
Burradon	Nthumb	190	D5
Burrafirth	Shet	281	f1
Burras	Cnwll	3	H4
Burraton	Cnwll	6	D3
Burravoe	Shet	281	e4
Burray Village	Ork	275	d6
Burrells	Cumb	166	F7
Burrelton	P & K	233	J8
Burridge	Devon	15	H2
Burridge	Devon	27	K4
Burridge	Hants	19	J2
Burrill	N York	160	C5
Burringham	N Linc	143	M4
Burrington	Devon	27	L7
Burrington	Herefs	80	B1
Burrington	N Som	44	F7
Burrough End	Cambs	88	C4
Burrough Green	Cambs	88	C4
Burrough on the Hill	Leics	101	G1
Burrow	Lancs	157	K7
Burrow	Somset	29	G2
Burrow Bridge	Somset	30	E5
Burrowhill	Surrey	50	B6
Burrows Cross	Surrey	37	G2
Burry	Swans	56	E6
Burry Green	Swans	56	E6
Burry Port	Carmth	56	E5
Burscough	Lancs	138	F5
Burscough Bridge	Lancs	138	F5
Bursea	E R Yk	143	K1
Burshill	E R Yk	153	H6
Bursledon	Hants	19	H2
Burslem	C Stke	114	D2
Burstall	Suffk	90	C6
Burstock	Dorset	15	K2
Burston	Norfk	106	C6
Burston	Staffs	114	E5
Burstow	Surrey	37	M3
Burstwick	E R Yk	145	G2
Burtersett	N York	158	F5
Burtholme	Cumb	178	D6
Burthorpe Green	Suffk	88	F2
Burthwaite	Cumb	165	M1
Burthy	Cnwll	4	E4
Burtle	Somset	30	F2
Burtle Hill	Somset	30	F2
Burtoft	Lincs	119	J4
Burton	BCP	18	B5
Burton	Ches E	129	H5
Burton	Ches W	129	L7
Burton	Dorset	16	D4
Burton	Nthumb	203	K6
Burton	Pembks	55	G5
Burton	Somset	30	B2
Burton	Somset	31	H8
Burton	Wilts	32	D4
Burton	Wilts	46	B3
Burton Agnes	E R Yk	153	H3
Burton Bradstock	Dorset	15	L5
Burton-by-Lincoln	Lincs	135	J5
Burton Coggles	Lincs	118	C6
Burton Dassett	Warwks	83	J5
Burton End	Essex	70	D2
Burton End	Suffk	88	D6
Burton Fleming	E R Yk	153	H2
Burton Green	Warwks	99	H8
Burton Green	Wrexhm	129	H7
Burton Hastings	Warwks	99	L5
Burton-in-Kendal	Cumb	157	H7
Burton-in-Kendal Services	Cumb	157	H7
Burton in Lonsdale	N York	148	A2
Burton Joyce	Notts	117	H3
Burton Latimer	Nhants	101	K8
Burton Lazars	Leics	117	K8
Burton Leonard	N York	150	D3
Burton on the Wolds	Leics	117	G7
Burton Overy	Leics	100	E4
Burton Pedwardine	Lincs	118	F3
Burton Pidsea	E R Yk	145	H2
Burton Salmon	N York	142	D2
Burton's Green	Essex	71	K2
Burton upon Stather	N Linc	143	L4
Burton upon Trent	Staffs	115	L6
Burton Waters	Lincs	135	J5
Burtonwood	Warrtn	130	A1
Burtonwood Services	Warrtn	130	B2
Burwardsley	Ches W	129	L8
Burwarton	Shrops	96	E6
Burwash	E Susx	24	B2
Burwash Common	E Susx	23	L3
Burwash Weald	E Susx	23	L3
Burwell	Cambs	88	B2
Burwell	Lincs	137	G4
Burwen	IoA	125	G1
Burwick	Ork	275	c6
Bury	Bury	140	B5
Bury	Cambs	102	F6
Bury	Somset	29	G5
Bury	W Susx	21	G4
Bury End	C Beds	86	C8
Bury Green	Herts	70	C3
Bury St Edmunds	Suffk	89	G2
Burythorpe	N York	152	B3
Busby	E Rens	208	F7
Busby Stoop	N York	160	E6
Buscot	Oxon	65	J7
Bush	Abers	235	J2
Bush	Cnwll	11	J1
Bush Bank	Herefs	80	B5
Bushbury	Wolves	97	G3
Bushby	Leics	100	E3
Bushey	Herts	68	E8
Bushey Heath	Herts	68	F8
Bush Green	Norfk	106	E6
Bush Green	Suffk	89	H4
Bush Hill Park	Gt Lon	69	J7
Bushley	Worcs	81	K8
Bushley Green	Worcs	81	K8
Bushmead	Bed	86	C3
Bushmoor	Shrops	95	K6
Bushton	Wilts	46	F3
Busk	Cumb	166	E2
Buslingthorpe	Lincs	135	M3
Bussage	Gloucs	64	C6
Bussex	Somset	30	E4
Bute	Ag & B	207	G5
Butleigh	Somset	31	H4
Butleigh Wootton	Somset	31	H4
Butler's Cross	Bucks	67	K5
Butler's Hill	Notts	116	F2
Butlers Marston	Warwks	83	H5
Butley	Suffk	91	J5
Butley High Corner	Suffk	91	J5
Buttercrambe	N York	152	A4
Butterdean	Border	213	H6
Butterknowle	Dur	168	E5
Butterleigh	Devon	14	A1
Butterley	Derbys	116	C1
Buttermere	Cumb	165	G7
Buttermere	Wilts	47	M6
Buttershaw	C Brad	141	H2
Butterstone	P & K	233	G6
Butterton	Staffs	114	C3
Butterton	Staffs	131	L8
Butterwick	Dur	169	K5
Butterwick	Lincs	119	L3
Butterwick	N York	152	F2
Butterwick	N York	162	C7
Butt Green	Ches E	113	L1
Buttington	Powys	95	G2
Buttonbridge	Shrops	97	G7
Buttonoak	Shrops	97	G7
Buttsash	Hants	19	G2
Buttsbear Cross	Cnwll	11	K2
Butt's Green	Essex	71	J6
Buxhall	Suffk	89	K4
Buxhall Fen Street	Suffk	89	K3
Buxted	E Susx	23	H3
Buxton	Derbys	131	L5
Buxton	Norfk	122	E7
Buxton Heath	Norfk	122	D7
Buxworth	Derbys	131	K3
Bwlch	Powys	61	J3
Bwlchgwyn	Wrexhm	112	C1
Bwlchllan	Cerdgn	77	G3
Bwlchnewydd	Carmth	58	C4
Bwlchtocyn	Gwynd	108	E6
Bwlch-y-cibau	Powys	112	B8
Bwlch-y-Ddar	Powys	112	B7
Bwlchyfadfa	Cerdgn	76	D5
Bwlch-y-ffridd	Powys	94	C4
Bwlch-y-groes	Pembks	75	M5
Bwlchymyrdd	Swans	57	G5
Bwlch-y-sarnau	Powys	94	B8
Byermoor	Gatesd	180	F7
Byers Green	Dur	169	G4
Byfield	Nhants	83	M4
Byfleet	Surrey	50	D6
Byford	Herefs	79	M6
Bygrave	Herts	86	F7
Byker	N u Ty	181	G6
Byland Abbey	N York	161	J6
Bylaugh	Norfk	122	A7
Bylchau	Conwy	127	K7
Byley	Ches W	130	E6
Bynea	Carmth	57	G5
Byrness	Nthumb	189	K5
Bystock	Devon	14	B6
Bythorn	Cambs	102	B8
Byton	Herefs	79	L2
Bywell	Nthumb	180	C6
Byworth	W Susx	36	E6

C

Place	Region	Page	Grid
Cabbacott	Devon	27	G6
Cabourne	Lincs	144	E7
Cabrach	Ag & B	205	H3
Cabrach	Moray	255	H6
Cabus	Lancs	147	J6
Cackle Street	E Susx	23	G2
Cackle Street	E Susx	24	C3
Cackle Street	E Susx	24	E3
Cadbury	Devon	13	L2
Cadbury Barton	Devon	28	B7
Cadder	E Duns	209	G4
Caddington	C Beds	68	D3
Caddonfoot	Border	200	F6
Cadeby	Donc	142	E7

Cadeby Leics..............99 L3
Cadeleigh Devon..............13 L1
Cade Street E Susx..............23 K3
Cadgwith Cnwll..............3 J8
Cadham Fife..............222 D6
Cadishead Salfd..............130 D1
Cadle Swans..............57 H5
Cadley Lancs..............139 G2
Cadley Wilts..............47 J5
Cadley Wilts..............47 K8
Cadmore End Bucks..............67 J8
Cadnam Hants..............34 C8
Cadney N Linc..............144 C7
Cadole Flints..............128 E7
Cadoxton V Glam..............43 H7
Cadoxton Juxta-Neath Neath..............57 L5
Cadwst Denbgs..............111 K4
Caeathro Gwynd..............125 J7
Caehopkin Powys..............59 M6
Caenby Lincs..............135 K2
Caerau Brdgnd..............42 C3
Caerau Cardif..............43 H6
Cae'r-bont Powys..............59 M6
Cae'r bryn Carmth..............59 H6
Caerdeon Gwynd..............110 C7
Caer Farchell Pembks..............74 C6
Caergeiliog IoA..............124 E4
Caergwrle Flints..............129 G8
Caerhun Conwy..............126 F5
Caerlanrig Border..............188 C5
Caerleon Newpt..............44 D1
Caernarfon Gwynd..............125 H7
Caernarfon Castle Gwynd..............125 H7
Caerphilly Caerph..............43 J4
Caersws Powys..............94 B5
Caerwedros Cerdgn..............76 C4
Caerwent Mons..............44 F1
Caerwys Flints..............128 D5
Caerynwch Gwynd..............110 E8
Caggle Street Mons..............62 D4
Caim IoA..............126 C3
Caio Carmth..............77 J7
Cairinis W Isls..............283 c8
Cairnbaan Ag & B..............206 C1
Cairnbulg Abers..............269 J3
Cairncross Border..............213 K6
Cairncurran Inver..............208 A5
Cairndow Ag & B..............217 K5
Cairneyhill Fife..............210 D2
Cairngarroch D & G..............172 C5
Cairngorms National Park..............242 E3
Cairnie Abers..............255 K3
Cairn Lodge Services S Lans..............198 D6
Cairnorrie Abers..............256 F3
Cairnryan D & G..............172 D1
Cairnty Moray..............267 G5
Caister-on-Sea Norfk..............107 L1
Caistor Lincs..............144 E7
Caistor St Edmund Norfk..............106 E3
Cakebole Worcs..............81 K1
Cake Street Norfk..............106 B5
Calais Street Suffk..............89 K7
Calanais W Isls..............282 f3
Calbourne IoW..............19 G6
Calceby Lincs..............137 G4
Calcoed Flints..............128 E5
Calcot Gloucs..............65 G5
Calcot W Berk..............49 G4
Calcot Row W Berk..............49 G4
Calcots Moray..............266 E3
Calcott Kent..............41 G3
Calcott Shrops..............113 G8
Calcutt N York..............150 E4
Calcutt Wilts..............65 G8
Caldbeck Cumb..............165 K3
Caldbergh N York..............159 K5
Caldecote Cambs..............87 G4
Caldecote Cambs..............102 C5
Caldecote Herts..............86 E1
Caldecote Nhants..............84 D5
Caldecott Nhants..............85 K2
Caldecott Oxon..............66 D7
Caldecott Rutlnd..............101 J4
Caldecotte M Keyn..............85 H8
Calder Cumb..............155 J2
Calderbank N Lans..............209 K6
Calder Bridge Cumb..............155 J2
Calderbrook Rochdl..............140 E4
Caldercruix N Lans..............209 L5
Calder Grove Wakefd..............141 M4
Caldermill S Lans..............197 J3
Caldermore Rochdl..............140 D4
Calder Vale Lancs..............147 K6
Calderwood S Lans..............209 H7
Caldey Island Pembks..............55 K7
Caldicot Mons..............44 F1
Caldmore Wsall..............98 C4
Caldwell N York..............168 F8
Caldy Wirral..............128 F3
Calenick Cnwll..............4 D6

Calf of Man IoM..............154 a8
Calford Green Suffk..............88 D6
Calfsound Ork..............275 d2
Calgary Ag & B..............226 D2
Califer Moray..............265 H8
California Falk..............210 B4
California Norfk..............123 K8
California Cross Devon..............7 K4
Calke Derbys..............116 B7
Callakille Highld..............259 M5
Callander Stirlg..............219 K5
Callanish W Isls..............282 f3
Callaughton Shrops..............96 E4
Callerton N u Ty..............180 E5
Callestick Cnwll..............4 C5
Calligarry Highld..............247 K7
Callington Cnwll..............6 D1
Callingwood Staffs..............115 K6
Callow Herefs..............80 C8
Callow End Worcs..............81 J5
Callow Hill Wilts..............46 F2
Callow Hill Worcs..............82 B2
Callow Hill Worcs..............97 G8
Callows Grave Worcs..............80 D2
Calmore Hants..............34 D7
Calmsden Gloucs..............64 F5
Calne Wilts..............46 E5
Calow Derbys..............133 H5
Calshot Hants..............19 H3
Calstock Cnwll..............6 E1
Calstone Wellington Wilts..............46 F5
Calthorpe Norfk..............122 D5
Calthorpe Street Norfk..............123 H6
Calthwaite Cumb..............166 B3
Calton N York..............148 F4
Calton Staffs..............115 H2
Calveley Ches E..............130 B7
Calver Derbys..............132 E5
Calverhall Shrops..............113 K4
Calver Hill Herefs..............79 L5
Calverleigh Devon..............29 G8
Calverley Leeds..............150 B8
Calver Sough Derbys..............132 E5
Calvert Bucks..............67 G2
Calverton M Keyn..............84 F7
Calverton Notts..............117 G2
Calvine P & K..............232 B2
Calvo Cumb..............176 F8
Calzeat Border..............199 K6
Cam Gloucs..............63 M7
Camasachoirce Highld..............228 B3
Camasine Highld..............237 L8
Camas Luinie Highld..............248 F6
Camastianavaig Highld..............247 G1
Camault Muir Highld..............250 E4
Camber E Susx..............25 H3
Camberley Surrey..............49 L6
Camberwell Gt Lon..............51 J4
Camblesforth N York..............143 G3
Cambo Nthumb..............180 B2
Cambois Nthumb..............181 H2
Camborne Cnwll..............3 G3
Camborne & Redruth Mining
District Cnwll..............3 G3
Cambourne Cambs..............87 G3
Cambridge Cambs..............87 J3
Cambridge Gloucs..............63 L6
Cambridge Airport Cambs..............87 K4
Cambrose Cnwll..............4 A5
Cambus Clacks..............220 E8
Cambusavie Highld..............263 L1
Cambusbarron Stirlg..............209 K1
Cambuskenneth Stirlg..............220 D8
Cambuslang S Lans..............209 H7
Cambus o' May Abers..............243 M4
Cambuswallace S Lans..............199 H5
Camden Town Gt Lon..............51 H2
Cameley BaNES..............45 J7
Camelford Cnwll..............10 F6
Camelon Falk..............209 M3
Camerory Highld..............253 K5
Camer's Green Worcs..............81 H8
Camerton BaNES..............45 K7
Camerton Cumb..............164 D4
Camghouran P & K..............231 G4
Camieston Border..............201 J7
Cammachmore Abers..............245 K4
Cammeringham Lincs..............135 J3
Camore Highld..............263 L2
Campbeltown Ag & B..............192 E4
Campbeltown Airport Ag & B..............192 D4
Camperdown N Tyne..............181 G4
Cample D & G..............186 D7
Campmuir P & K..............233 K7
Camps W Loth..............210 E5
Campsall Donc..............142 E5
Campsea Ash Suffk..............91 H4
Camps End Cambs..............88 C6
Campton C Beds..............86 C7
Camptown Border..............189 J4

Camrose Pembks..............54 F3
Camserney P & K..............232 B5
Camusnagaul Highld..............239 H8
Camusnagaul Highld..............261 H2
Camusteel Highld..............248 A3
Camusterrach Highld..............248 A3
Canada Hants..............34 C7
Canal Foot Cumb..............156 D7
Canaston Bridge Pembks..............55 H4
Candacraig Abers..............243 K4
Candlesby Lincs..............137 H6
Candle Street Suffk..............105 L8
Candover Green Shrops..............96 C2
Candy Mill Border..............199 J5
Cane End Oxon..............49 G3
Canewdon Essex..............72 C8
Canford Bottom Dorset..............17 K3
Canford Cliffs BCP..............17 L5
Canford Heath BCP..............17 K4
Canford Magna BCP..............17 K3
Canhams Green Suffk..............90 C2
Canisbay Highld..............280 D2
Canklow Rothm..............133 H2
Canley Covtry..............99 J7
Cann Dorset..............32 E6
Canna Highld..............246 B7
Cann Common Dorset..............32 E6
Cannich Highld..............250 B5
Cannington Somset..............30 C3
Canning Town Gt Lon..............51 L3
Cannock Staffs..............98 B2
Cannock Chase Staffs..............114 F7
Cannock Wood Staffs..............98 D1
Cannon Bridge Herefs..............80 A7
Canonbie D & G..............177 L4
Canon Frome Herefs..............80 F6
Canon Pyon Herefs..............80 B5
Canons Ashby Nhants..............84 B5
Canonstown Cnwll..............2 E4
Canterbury Kent..............40 F4
Canterbury Cathedral Kent..............40 F4
Cantley Norfk..............107 H3
Cantlop Shrops..............96 C2
Canton Cardif..............43 J6
Cantraywood Highld..............252 E2
Cantsfield Lancs..............147 M1
Canvey Island Essex..............53 G2
Canwick Lincs..............135 K6
Canworthy Water Cnwll..............11 J4
Caol Highld..............239 J8
Caolas Scalpaigh W Isls..............282 f6
Caoles Ag & B..............224 D5
Caonich Highld..............239 H5
Capel Kent..............39 G4
Capel Surrey..............37 J3
Capel Bangor Cerdgn..............92 E7
Capel Betws Lleucu Cerdgn..............77 H4
Capel Coch IoA..............125 H3
Capel Curig Conwy..............126 E8
Capel Cynon Cerdgn..............76 C5
Capel Dewi Carmth..............58 E5
Capel Dewi Cerdgn..............76 E6
Capel-Dewi Cerdgn..............92 D7
Capel Garmon Conwy..............127 G8
Capel Green Suffk..............91 J5
Capel Gwyn Carmth..............58 E4
Capel Gwyn IoA..............124 F4
Capel Gwynfe Carmth..............59 K4
Capel Hendre Carmth..............59 G6
Capel Isaac Carmth..............59 G3
Capel Iwan Carmth..............58 B2
Capel-le-Ferne Kent..............41 H7
Capelles Guern..............9 j2
Capel Llanilltern Cardif..............43 H5
Capel Mawr IoA..............125 G5
Capel Parc IoA..............125 H2
Capel St Andrew Suffk..............91 J5
Capel St Mary Suffk..............90 C7
Capel Seion Cerdgn..............92 D7
Capel Trisant Cerdgn..............92 F7
Capeluchaf Gwynd..............109 H2
Capelulo Conwy..............126 E4
Capel-y-ffin Powys..............61 L1
Capel-y-graig Gwynd..............125 K6
Capenhurst Ches W..............129 J5
Capernwray Lancs..............147 K2
Cape Wrath Highld..............276 D1
Capheaton Nthumb..............180 C3
Caplaw E Rens..............208 D7
Capon's Green Suffk..............91 G2
Cappercleuch Border..............187 K2
Capstone Medway..............53 G6
Capton Devon..............8 C4
Capton Somset..............29 K3
Caputh P & K..............233 G7
Caradon Mining District Cnwll..............11 K7
Caradon Town Cnwll..............11 K8
Carbeth Stirlg..............208 E3
Carbis Cnwll..............5 G3
Carbis Bay Cnwll..............2 E3

Carbost Highld..............246 E
Carbost Highld..............259 G
Carbrook Sheff..............133 H
Carbrooke Norfk..............105 A
Carburton Notts..............134 C
Carclaze Cnwll..............5 E
Car Colston Notts..............117 J
Carcroft Donc..............142 F
Cardenden Fife..............222 E
Cardeston Shrops..............95 J
Cardewlees Cumb..............177 H
Cardhu Moray..............254 E
Cardiff Cardif..............43 J
Cardiff Airport V Glam..............43 E
Cardiff Gate Services Cardif..............43 E
Cardiff West Services Cardif..............43 E
Cardigan Cerdgn..............75 L
Cardinal's Green Cambs..............88 C
Cardington Bed..............86 E
Cardington Shrops..............96 C
Cardinham Cnwll..............5 J
Cardrain D & G..............172 E
Cardrona Border..............200 B
Cardross Ag & B..............208 D
Cardryne D & G..............172 E
Cardurnock Cumb..............177 H
Careby Lincs..............118 E
Careston Angus..............234 E
Carew Pembks..............55 H
Carew Cheriton Pembks..............55 H
Carew Newton Pembks..............55 H
Carey Herefs..............63 J
Carfin N Lans..............209 K
Carfraemill Border..............201 H
Cargate Green Norfk..............107 H
Cargenbridge D & G..............176 C
Cargill P & K..............233 J
Cargo Cumb..............177 H
Cargreen Cnwll..............6 E
Cargurrel Cnwll..............3 K
Carham Nthumb..............202 F
Carhampton Somset..............29 H
Carharrack Cnwll..............4 C
Carie P & K..............231 H
Carinish W Isls..............283 c
Carisbrooke IoW..............19 H
Cark Cumb..............156 D
Carkeel Cnwll..............6 E
Càrlabhagh W Isls..............282 f
Carland Cross Cnwll..............4 C
Carlbury Darltn..............169 G
Carlby Lincs..............102 A
Carlcroft Nthumb..............190 B
Carlecotes Barns..............141 J
Carleen Cnwll..............3 G
Carlesmoor N York..............160 B
Carleton Cumb..............155 J
Carleton Cumb..............166 C
Carleton Cumb..............178 D
Carleton Lancs..............146 E
Carleton Wakefd..............142 C
Carleton Forehoe Norfk..............106 C
Carleton-in-Craven N York..............149 G
Carleton Rode Norfk..............106 C
Carleton St Peter Norfk..............107 H
Carlidnack Cnwll..............3 K
Carlincraig Abers..............256 E
Carlingcott BaNES..............45 K
Carlin How R & Cl..............171 J
Carlisle Cumb..............177 L
Carlisle Lake District Airport
Cumb..............178 B
Carloggas Cnwll..............4 E
Carlops Border..............199 K
Carloway W Isls..............282 f
Carlton Barns..............142 B
Carlton Bed..............85 K
Carlton Cambs..............88 C
Carlton Leeds..............142 A
Carlton Leics..............99 L
Carlton N York..............143 G
Carlton N York..............159 G
Carlton N York..............161 J
Carlton Notts..............117 G
Carlton S on T..............169 L
Carlton Suffk..............91 J
Carlton Colville Suffk..............107 L
Carlton Curlieu Leics..............100 E
Carlton Green Cambs..............88 C
Carlton Husthwaite N York..............161 H
Carlton-in-Cleveland N York..............161 J
Carlton in Lindrick Notts..............134 C
Carlton-le-Moorland Lincs..............135 J
Carlton Miniott N York..............160 F
Carlton-on-Trent Notts..............134 F
Carlton Scroop Lincs..............118 C
Carluke S Lans..............198 C
Carlyon Bay Cnwll..............5 J
Carmacoup S Lans..............198 C
Carmarthen Carmth..............58 E

armel Carmth 59 G5	Castle Acre Norfk 121 H8	Catshill Worcs 98 B8	Cemmaes Road Powys 93 H3
armel Flints 128 E4	Castle Ashby Nhants 85 G3	Catstree Shrops 97 G4	Cenarth Cerdgn 76 A7
armel Gwynd 125 J8	Castlebay W Isls 283 b13	Cattadale Ag & B 192 D6	Cerbyd Pembks 74 D6
armichael S Lans 198 F5	Castle Bolton N York 159 J4	Cattal N York 150 F5	Ceres Fife 223 G5
armunnock C Glas 209 G7	Castle Bromwich Solhll 98 F5	Cattawade Suffk 90 C8	Cerne Abbas Dorset 16 C2
armyle C Glas 209 H6	Castle Bytham Lincs 118 C7	Catterall Lancs 147 K7	Cerney Wick Gloucs 65 G7
armyllie Angus 234 E6	Castlebythe Pembks 75 H6	Catteralslane Shrops 113 J3	Cerrigceinwen IoA 125 G5
arnaby E R Yk 153 J3	Castle Caereinion Powys 94 E2	Catterick N York 160 C3	Cerrigydrudion Conwy 111 J2
arnbee Fife 223 J6	Castle Camps Cambs 88 C6	Catterick Bridge N York 160 B3	Cess Norfk 123 J7
arnbo P & K 221 J6	Castle Carrock Cumb 178 D7	Catterick Garrison N York 160 B3	Ceunant Gwynd 125 J2
arn Brea Cnwll 3 H3	Castlecary N Lans 209 K3	Catterlen Cumb 166 B4	Chaceley Gloucs 64 B1
arnbrogie Abers 256 F6	Castle Cary Somset 31 L4	Catterline Abers 245 J7	Chacewater Cnwll 4 B6
arndu Highld 248 E6	Castle Combe Wilts 46 B3	Catterton N York 151 H6	Chackmore Bucks 84 D8
arnduff S Lans 197 J2	Castlecraig Highld 264 C6	Catteshall Surrey 36 E2	Chacombe Nhants 83 L6
arne Cnwll 3 K6	Castle Donington Leics 116 D6	Catthorpe Leics 100 C7	Chadbury Worcs 82 B6
arne Cnwll 4 E7	Castle Douglas D & G 175 J2	Cattishall Suffk 89 H2	Chadderton Oldham 140 D6
arne Cnwll 4 F3	Castle Eaton Swindn 65 H7	Cattistock Dorset 16 B3	Chadderton Fold Oldham 140 D6
arnell E Ayrs 196 F4	Castle Eden Dur 169 L3	Catton N York 160 E7	Chaddesden C Derb 116 C4
arnewas Cnwll 4 D1	Castle End C Pete 102 C2	Catton Nthumb 179 J7	Chaddesley Corbett Worcs 81 K1
arnforth Lancs 147 K2	Castleford Wakefd 142 C3	Catwick E R Yk 153 J6	Chaddlehanger Devon 12 B7
arn-gorm Highld 248 F7	Castle Frome Herefs 80 F6	Catworth Cambs 86 B1	Chaddleworth W Berk 48 B3
arnhedryn Pembks 74 C6	Castle Gate Cnwll 2 D4	Caudle Green Gloucs 64 D5	Chadlington Oxon 65 M3
arnhell Green Cnwll 3 G4	Castle Green Cumb 157 H4	Caulcott C Beds 85 K6	Chadshunt Warwks 83 H5
arnie Abers 245 H2	Castle Green Surrey 50 B6	Caulcott Oxon 66 D2	Chadwell Leics 117 K6
arnkie Cnwll 3 H3	Castle Gresley Derbys 115 M7	Cauldcots Angus 235 G6	Chadwell Shrops 114 B8
arnkie Cnwll 3 H4	Castle Hedingham Essex 88 F8	Cauldhame Stirlg 219 L8	Chadwell End Bed 86 B2
arnkief Cnwll 4 C4	Castlehill Border 200 B6	Cauldmill Border 188 F3	Chadwell Heath Gt Lon 52 A1
arno Powys 93 L4	Castlehill Highld 280 B3	Cauldon Staffs 115 H2	Chadwell St Mary Thurr 52 E3
arnock Fife 210 D1	Castle Hill Kent 39 H5	Cauldon Lowe Staffs 115 H2	Chadwick Worcs 81 J2
arnon Downs Cnwll 3 K3	Castle Hill Suffk 90 D6	Cauldwell Derbys 115 L8	Chadwick End Solhll 99 G8
arnousie Abers 268 B6	Castlehill W Duns 208 C4	Caulkerbush D & G 176 B7	Chadwick Green St Hel 139 G7
arnoustie Angus 234 E8	Castle Kennedy D & G 172 D3	Caulside D & G 178 B3	Chaffcombe Somset 15 H1
arnsmerry Cnwll 5 G3	Castle Lachlan Ag & B 217 G8	Caundle Marsh Dorset 31 L8	Chafford Hundred Thurr 52 D3
arnwath S Lans 199 G4	Castlemartin Pembks 54 E7	Caunsall Worcs 97 J7	Chagford Devon 13 G5
arnyorth Cnwll 2 B4	Castlemilk C Glas 209 G7	Caunton Notts 134 E7	Chailey E Susx 22 F3
arol Green Solhll 99 H7	Castle Morris Pembks 74 E6	Causeway Hants 35 M6	Chainbridge Cambs 103 J3
arpalla Cnwll 4 F4	Castlemorton Worcs 81 H7	Causeway End Cumb 157 G5	Chainhurst Kent 39 J4
arperby N York 159 H4	Castlemorton Common Worcs 81 H7	Causeway End D & G 173 K3	Chalbury Dorset 17 K1
arr Rothm 133 K2	Castle O'er D & G 187 K7	Causeway End Essex 71 G3	Chalbury Common Dorset 17 K2
arradale Ag & B 194 C3	Castle Rising Norfk 120 E6	Causewayend S Lans 199 H6	Chaldon Surrey 51 J7
arradale Village Ag & B 194 B3	Castleside Dur 168 D1	Causewayhead Cumb 176 F8	Chaldon Herring Dorset 16 F6
arrbridge Highld 253 D2	Castle Stuart Highld 252 D2	Causewayhead Stirlg 220 D8	Chale IoW 19 H8
arrbrook Tamesd 140 E7	Castlethorpe M Keyn 84 F6	Causeyend Abers 257 H7	Chale Green IoW 19 H7
arrefour Jersey 9 c2	Castlethorpe N Linc 144 B6	Causey Park Nthumb 191 H7	Chalfont Common Bucks 68 C8
arreglefn IoA 125 G2	Castleton Ag & B 206 D2	Causey Park Bridge Nthumb 191 H7	Chalfont St Giles Bucks 68 C8
arr Gate Wakefd 141 M3	Castleton Border 188 E8	Cavendish Suffk 88 F6	Chalfont St Peter Bucks 50 C1
arrhouse N Linc 143 K6	Castleton Derbys 132 C3	Cavenham Suffk 88 F1	Chalford Gloucs 64 C6
arrick Ag & B 206 E2	Castleton N York 162 B1	Caversfield Oxon 66 E2	Chalford Oxon 67 H7
arrick Castle Ag & B 217 K8	Castleton Newpt 43 L5	Caversham Readg 49 H4	Chalford Wilts 32 E1
arriden Falk 210 D3	Castleton Rochdl 140 C5	Caverswall Staffs 114 F3	Chalgrave C Beds 68 C2
arrington Lincs 136 F8	Castletown Ches W 113 G1	Caverton Mill Border 202 A7	Chalgrove Oxon 66 F7
arrington Mdloth 211 K7	Castletown Dorset 16 D7	Cavil E R Yk 143 J2	Chalk Kent 52 E4
arrington Traffd 130 E2	Castletown Highld 280 A3	Cawdor Highld 252 F2	Chalk End Essex 70 F5
arrog Conwy 110 E2	Castletown IoM 154 c8	Cawkwell Lincs 136 E4	Chalkhouse Green Oxon 49 H3
arrog Denbgs 111 L3	Castletown Sundld 181 J7	Cawood N York 151 J8	Chalkway Somset 15 J1
arron Falk 210 A3	Castley N York 150 C6	Cawsand Cnwll 6 E5	Chalkwell Kent 53 J6
arron Moray 254 E3	Caston Norfk 105 J4	Cawston Norfk 122 C6	Challaborough Devon 7 J6
arronbridge D & G 186 C6	Castor C Pete 102 C4	Cawston Warwks 100 A8	Challacombe Devon 28 B3
arron Bridge Stirlg 209 K2	Caswell Bay Swans 57 G7	Cawthorn N York 162 D5	Challoch D & G 173 K2
arronshore Falk 210 A2	Catacol N Ayrs 194 E1	Cawthorne Barns 141 L6	Challock Kent 40 C5
arrow Hill Mons 44 E1	Cat and Fiddle Derbys 131 K5	Cawton N York 161 K7	Chalmington Dorset 16 B2
arr Shield Nthumb 167 J1	Catbrain S Glos 45 H3	Caxton Cambs 86 F3	Chalton C Beds 68 C2
arrutherstown D & G 176 E4	Catbrook Mons 63 G6	Caxton End Cambs 87 G4	Chalton C Beds 86 C5
arruth House Inver 208 B6	Catch Flints 128 F5	Caxton Gibbet Cambs 86 F3	Chalton Hants 20 B4
arr Vale Derbys 133 J5	Catchall Cnwll 2 C5	Caynham Shrops 80 D1	Chalvey Slough 50 B3
arrville Dur 169 J2	Catchem's Corner Solhll 99 H8	Caythorpe Lincs 118 B2	Chalvington E Susx 23 H5
arsaig Ag & B 227 G8	Catchgate Dur 180 E8	Caythorpe Notts 117 J2	Chambers Green Kent 40 B6
arseriggan D & G 173 H1	Catcliffe Rothm 133 H2	Cayton N York 163 J6	Chandler's Cross Herts 68 D7
arsethorn D & G 176 C7	Catcomb Wilts 46 B3	Ceannabeinne Highld 277 J2	Chandlers Cross Worcs 81 H7
arshalton Gt Lon 51 H6	Catcott Somset 30 F3	Ceann a Bhaigh W Isls 283 b8	Chandler's Ford Hants 34 F7
arsington Derbys 115 L1	Caterham Surrey 51 J7	Ceannacroc Lodge Highld 239 L1	Channel's End Bed 86 C4
arskey Ag & B 192 D6	Catfield Norfk 123 H7	Cearsiadar W Isls 282 f4	Channel Tunnel Terminal Kent 41 G7
arsluith D & G 174 D4	Catfield Common Norfk 123 H7	Ceciliford Mons 63 G6	Chantry Somset 32 B2
arsphairn D & G 184 E4	Catford Gt Lon 51 K4	Cefn Newpt 44 B1	Chantry Suffk 90 D6
arstairs S Lans 198 F4	Catforth Lancs 138 F1	Cefn Berain Conwy 127 K6	Chapel Cumb 165 H4
arstairs Junction S Lans 198 F4	Cathcart C Glas 209 G7	Cefn-brîth Conwy 111 H2	Chapel Fife 222 D8
arswell Marsh Oxon 65 L7	Cathedine Powys 61 J2	Cefn-bryn-brain Carmth 59 K6	Chapel Allerton Leeds 150 D8
arter's Clay Hants 34 C6	Catherine-de-Barnes Solhll 98 F7	Cefn Byrle Powys 60 C5	Chapel Allerton Somset 30 F1
arters Green Essex 70 D5	Catherine Slack C Brad 141 G2	Cefn Canel Powys 112 C5	Chapel Amble Cnwll 10 D7
arterton Oxon 65 L5	Catherington Hants 35 L8	Cefn Coch Powys 111 L6	Chapel Brampton Nhants 84 E2
arterway Heads Nthumb 180 C4	Catherston Leweston Dorset 15 J4	Cefn-coed-y-cymmer	Chapelbridge Cambs 102 F4
arthew Cnwll 5 G4	Catherton Shrops 96 E7	Myr Td 60 F5	Chapel Chorlton Staffs 114 C4
arthorpe N York 160 D6	Catisfield Hants 19 J2	Cefn Cribwr Brdgnd 42 C5	Chapel Cross E Susx 23 K3
artington Nthumb 190 E5	Catley Herefs 80 F6	Cefn Cross Brdgnd 42 C5	Chapel End Bed 86 B4
artland S Lans 198 F4	Catley Lane Head Rochdl 140 C4	Cefn-ddwysarn Gwynd 111 J4	Chapel End C Beds 85 L6
artledge Derbys 132 F4	Catlodge Highld 241 H5	Cefn-Einion Shrops 95 G6	Chapel End Cambs 102 C6
artmel Cumb 156 E7	Catlow Lancs 148 F8	Cefneithin Carmth 59 G6	Chapel End Warwks 99 J5
artmel Fell Cumb 156 F5	Catlowdy Cumb 178 B3	Cefngorwydd Powys 78 B6	Chapelend Way Essex 88 E7
arway Carmth 56 E5	Catmere End Essex 87 K7	Cefn-mawr Wrexhm 112 D3	Chapel-en-le-Frith Derbys 131 L3
arwinley Cumb 177 L4	Catmore W Berk 48 C3	Cefnpennar Rhondd 61 G7	Chapel-Field Bury 140 B6
ashe's Green Gloucs 64 B3	Caton Devon 13 H8	Cefn-y-bedd Flints 129 H8	Chapelgate Lincs 119 L6
ashmoor Dorset 33 G8	Caton Lancs 147 K3	Cefn-y-pant Carmth 75 L7	Chapel Green Warwks 83 L3
assington Oxon 66 C5	Caton Green Lancs 147 L3	Ceint IoA 125 J4	Chapel Green Warwks 99 H6
assop Dur 169 K3	Cator Court Devon 13 G7	Cellan Cerdgn 77 H5	Chapel Haddlesey N York 142 F3
astallack Cnwll 2 C6	Catrine E Ayrs 197 G6	Cellardyke Fife 223 K6	Chapelhall N Lans 209 K6
astel Guern 9 j3	Cat's Ash Newpt 44 D1	Cellarhead Staffs 114 F2	Chapel Hill Abers 257 K4
astell Conwy 126 F6	Catsfield E Susx 24 C4	Celleron Cumb 166 C5	Chapel Hill Lincs 119 G1
astell-y-bwch Torfn 62 B8	Catsfield Stream E Susx 24 C4	Celynen Caerph 43 K3	Chapel Hill Mons 63 G7
asterton Cumb 157 K6	Catsgore Somset 31 H5	Cemaes IoA 124 F1	Chapel Hill N York 150 D6
astle Cnwll 5 J3	Catsham Somset 31 J4	Cemmaes Powys 93 H2	Chapelhope Border 187 K2

Chapelknowe D & G 177 K4
Chapel Lawn Shrops 95 H8
Chapel-le-Dale N York 158 C7
Chapel Leigh Somset 29 L5
Chapel Milton Derbys 131 L3
Chapel of Garioch Abers 256 C7
Chapel Rossan D & G 172 D6
Chapel Row E Susx 23 L5
Chapel Row Essex 71 J7
Chapel Row W Berk 48 E5
Chapels Cumb 156 B6
Chapel St Leonards Lincs 137 K5
Chapel Stile Cumb 156 D2
Chapelton Abers 245 K5
Chapelton Angus 234 F6
Chapelton Devon 27 K5
Chapelton S Lans 197 K1
Chapeltown Bl w D 139 L4
Chapel Town Cnwll 4 E4
Chapeltown Moray 254 E7
Chapeltown Sheff 142 A8
Chapmanslade Wilts 32 D1
Chapmans Well Devon 11 L4
Chapmore End Herts 69 J4
Chappel Essex 72 C2
Charaton Cnwll 6 B1
Chard Somset 15 H1
Chard Junction Somset 15 H2
Chardleigh Green Somset 30 D8
Chardstock Devon 15 G2
Charfield S Glos 63 L8
Chargrove Gloucs 64 D3
Charing Kent 40 B5
Charing Heath Kent 40 B5
Charing Hill Kent 40 B5
Charingworth Gloucs 82 E7
Charlbury Oxon 66 A3
Charlcombe BaNES 45 L5
Charlcutt Wilts 46 E4
Charlecote Warwks 83 G4
Charlemont Sandw 98 C4
Charles Devon 28 B4
Charleshill Surrey 36 D2
Charleston Angus 234 B6
Charlestown C Aber 245 L3
Charlestown C Brad 149 L8
Charlestown Calder 140 E2
Charlestown Cnwll 5 H4
Charlestown Cnwll 5 H4
Charlestown Derbys 131 L1
Charlestown Dorset 16 C6
Charlestown Fife 210 E2
Charlestown Highld 251 H2
Charlestown Highld 260 C5
Charlestown Salfd 140 B7
Charlestown of Aberlour
  Moray 254 E3
Charles Tye Suffk 89 L5
Charlesworth Derbys 131 K1
Charlinch Somset 30 C3
Charlottetown Fife 222 E5
Charlton Gt Lon 51 L3
Charlton Hants 34 D2
Charlton Herts 68 F2
Charlton Nhants 83 M8
Charlton Nthumb 179 J2
Charlton Oxon 48 B1
Charlton Somset 30 D5
Charlton Somset 31 K2
Charlton Somset 45 K8
Charlton Surrey 50 D5
Charlton W Susx 20 E4
Charlton Wilts 32 F6
Charlton Wilts 46 D1
Charlton Worcs 81 J1
Charlton Worcs 82 B6
Charlton Wrekin 96 D1
Charlton Abbots Gloucs 64 F2
Charlton Adam Somset 31 J5
Charlton All Saints Wilts 33 L6
Charlton Down Dorset 16 C4
Charlton Hill Shrops 96 D2
Charlton Horethorne Somset 31 L6
Charlton Kings Gloucs 64 D3
Charlton Mackrell Somset 31 H5
Charlton Marshall Dorset 17 H2
Charlton Musgrove Somset 32 B5
Charlton-on-Otmoor Oxon 66 E4
Charlton on the Hill Dorset 17 H2
Charlton St Peter Wilts 47 G7
Charlwood Hants 35 K4
Charlwood Surrey 37 K3
Charminster Dorset 16 C4
Charmouth Dorset 15 H4
Charndon Bucks 67 G2
Charney Bassett Oxon 66 A8
Charnock Green Lancs 139 H4
Charnock Richard Lancs 139 H4
Charnock Richard Services
  Lancs 139 H5

Charsfield Suffk 90 F4
Chart Corner Kent 39 K3
Charter Alley Hants 48 E7
Charterhall Border 202 B4
Charterhouse Somset 45 G7
Chartershall Stirlg 209 L1
Charterville Allotments Oxon 65 L5
Chartham Kent 40 E4
Chartham Hatch Kent 40 E4
Chart Hill Kent 39 K3
Chartridge Bucks 68 B6
Chart Sutton Kent 39 K3
Chartway Street Kent 39 L3
Charvil Wokham 49 J4
Charwelton Nhants 83 M4
Chase Cross Gt Lon 52 B1
Chase Terrace Staffs 98 D2
Chasetown Staffs 98 D2
Chastleton Oxon 65 K1
Chasty Devon 11 L2
Chatburn Lancs 148 D7
Chatcull Staffs 114 B4
Chatham Caerph 43 K4
Chatham Medway 53 G5
Chatham Green Essex 71 H4
Chathill Nthumb 203 K7
Chatley Worcs 81 J3
Chattenden Medway 53 G4
Chatter End Essex 70 C2
Chatteris Cambs 103 H6
Chatterton Lancs 140 B4
Chattisham Suffk 90 C6
Chatto Border 189 K3
Chatton Nthumb 203 G7
Chaul End C Beds 68 D3
Chawleigh Devon 28 C8
Chawley Oxon 66 C6
Chawston Bed 86 C4
Chawton Hants 35 L3
Chaxhill Gloucs 63 L4
Chazey Heath Oxon 49 G3
Cheadle Staffs 115 G3
Cheadle Stockp 131 G2
Cheadle Heath Stockp 131 H2
Cheadle Hulme Stockp 131 G2
Cheam Gt Lon 51 H6
Cheapside W & M 50 B5
Chearsley Bucks 67 H5
Chebsey Staffs 114 D6
Checkendon Oxon 49 G2
Checkley Ches E 114 A2
Checkley Herefs 80 E7
Checkley Staffs 115 G4
Checkley Green Ches E 114 A2
Chedburgh Suffk 88 F4
Cheddar Somset 44 F8
Cheddington Bucks 68 A4
Cheddleton Staffs 114 F1
Cheddleton Heath Staffs 114 F1
Cheddon Fitzpaine Somset 30 C5
Chedglow Wilts 64 D8
Chedgrave Norfk 107 H3
Chedington Dorset 15 L2
Chediston Suffk 107 G7
Chediston Green Suffk 107 G7
Chedworth Gloucs 64 F5
Chedzoy Somset 30 E3
Cheeseman's Green Kent 40 D7
Cheetham Hill Manch 140 C7
Cheldon Devon 28 C8
Chelford Ches E 130 F5
Chellaston C Derb 116 C5
Chellington Bed 85 J4
Chelmarsh Shrops 97 G5
Chelmer Village Essex 71 H5
Chelmick Shrops 95 L5
Chelmondiston Suffk 90 F6
Chelmorton Derbys 132 B5
Chelmsford Essex 71 H5
Chelmsley Wood Solhll 98 F6
Chelsea Gt Lon 51 H3
Chelsfield Gt Lon 52 A6
Chelsham Surrey 51 K7
Chelston Somset 29 L6
Chelsworth Suffk 89 K5
Cheltenham Gloucs 64 D3
Chelveston Nhants 85 K1
Chelvey N Som 44 F5
Chelwood BaNES 45 J6
Chelwood Common E Susx 38 B7
Chelwood Gate E Susx 38 B7
Chelworth Wilts 64 E8
Chelworth Lower Green Wilts 65 G8
Chelworth Upper Green Wilts 65 G8
Cheney Longville Shrops 95 K6
Chenies Bucks 68 C7
Chepstow Mons 63 G8
Chequerbent Bolton 139 K6
Chequers Corner Norfk 103 K2
Cherhill Wilts 46 F5

Cherington Gloucs 64 C7
Cherington Warwks 83 G7
Cheriton Devon 28 C2
Cheriton Hants 35 J5
Cheriton Kent 41 G7
Cheriton Pembks 55 G2
Cheriton Swans 56 E6
Cheriton Bishop Devon 13 H4
Cheriton Fitzpaine Devon 13 K2
Cherrington Wrekin 113 L7
Cherry Burton E R Yk 152 F7
Cherry Hinton Cambs 87 K4
Cherry Orchard Worcs 81 K4
Cherry Willingham Lincs 135 L5
Chertsey Surrey 50 D5
Cherwell Valley Services Oxon 66 E2
Cheselbourne Dorset 16 E3
Chesham Bucks 68 B6
Chesham Bury 140 B5
Chesham Bois Bucks 68 B7
Cheshunt Herts 69 K6
Chesil Beach Dorset 16 B6
Chesley Kent 53 J6
Cheslyn Hay Staffs 98 B2
Chessetts Wood Warwks 99 G8
Chessington Gt Lon 50 F6
Chester Ches W 129 J6
Chesterblade Somset 31 L3
Chesterfield Derbys 133 G5
Chesterfield Staffs 98 E2
Chesterhill Mdloth 211 L6
Chester-le-Street Dur 181 G8
Chester Moor Dur 169 H1
Chesters Border 189 G2
Chesters Border 189 H4
Chester Services Ches W 129 K5
Chesterton Cambs 87 K3
Chesterton Cambs 102 C4
Chesterton Gloucs 64 E7
Chesterton Oxon 66 E3
Chesterton Shrops 97 H4
Chesterton Staffs 114 C2
Chesterton Green Warwks 83 H4
Chesterwood Nthumb 179 J6
Chestfield Kent 40 F2
Chestnut Street Kent 53 J6
Cheston Devon 7 K3
Cheswardine Shrops 114 A5
Cheswick Nthumb 203 G4
Cheswick Green Solhll 98 E8
Chetnole Dorset 16 B1
Chettiscombe Devon 29 H7
Chettisham Cambs 103 L6
Chettle Dorset 32 F8
Chetton Shrops 96 F5
Chetwode Bucks 66 F1
Chetwynd Wrekin 114 A7
Chetwynd Aston Wrekin 114 B8
Cheveley Cambs 88 D3
Chevening Kent 52 A7
Cheverton IoW 19 G6
Chevington Suffk 88 F3
Cheviot Hills 189 K5
Chevithorne Devon 29 H7
Chew Magna BaNES 45 H6
Chew Moor Bolton 139 K6
Chew Stoke BaNES 45 H6
Chewton Keynsham BaNES 45 K5
Chewton Mendip Somset 45 H8
Chichacott Devon 12 E3
Chicheley M Keyn 85 H6
Chichester W Susx 20 E6
Chickerell Dorset 16 C6
Chickering Suffk 106 E8
Chicklade Wilts 32 F4
Chicksands C Beds 86 C7
Chickward Herefs 79 K4
Chidden Hants 35 K7
Chiddingfold Surrey 36 E4
Chiddingly E Susx 23 J4
Chiddingstone Kent 38 D4
Chiddingstone Causeway Kent 38 D4
Chiddingstone Hoath Kent 38 D5
Chideock Dorset 15 K4
Chidham W Susx 20 C6
Chidswell Kirk 141 L3
Chieveley W Berk 48 C4
Chieveley Services W Berk 48 C4
Chignall St James Essex 71 G5
Chignall Smealy Essex 71 G5
Chigwell Essex 70 B8
Chigwell Row Essex 70 C8
Chilbolton Hants 34 E2
Chilcomb Hants 35 G5
Chilcombe Dorset 15 M4
Chilcompton Somset 45 J8
Chilcote Leics 99 H1
Childer Thornton Ches W 129 J4
Child Okeford Dorset 32 D8
Childrey Oxon 48 A2

Child's Ercall Shrops .... 113 L
Childswickham Worcs .... 82 C
Childwall Lpool .... 129 K
Childwick Bury Herts 68
Childwick Green Herts 68
Chilfrome Dorset .... 16 B
Chilgrove W Susx .... 20 D
Chilham Kent .... 40 E
Chilla Devon .... 12 B
Chillaton Devon .... 12 B
Chillenden Kent .... 41 J
Chillerton IoW .... 19 H
Chillesford Suffk .... 91 H
Chillingham Nthumb .... 203 H
Chillington Devon 8
Chillington Somset .... 30 C
Chilmark Wilts .... 33 G
Chilmington Green Kent .... 40 C
Chilson Oxon .... 65 L
Chilsworthy Cnwll .... 12 C
Chilsworthy Devon .... 11 K
Chiltern Green C Beds .... 68 E
Chiltern Hills .... 67 J
Chilthorne Domer Somset .... 31 G
Chilton Bucks 67
Chilton Devon .... 13 K
Chilton Dur .... 169 H
Chilton Kent 41
Chilton Oxon .... 48 C
Chilton Suffk .... 89 H
Chilton Candover Hants .... 35 J
Chilton Cantelo Somset .... 31 J
Chilton Foliat Wilts .... 47 L
Chilton Polden Somset 30
Chilton Street Suffk 88
Chilton Trinity Somset .... 30 C
Chilwell Notts .... 116 E
Chilworth Hants .... 34 E
Chilworth Surrey .... 36 F
Chimney Oxon .... 65 M
Chineham Hants .... 49 J
Chingford Gt Lon .... 69 K
Chinley Derbys 131
Chinnor Oxon .... 67 J
Chipchase Castle Nthumb .... 179 K
Chipnall Shrops .... 114 A
Chippenham Cambs .... 88 D
Chippenham Wilts .... 46 D
Chipperfield Herts .... 68 D
Chipping Herts .... 69 K
Chipping Lancs .... 147 M
Chipping Campden Gloucs .... 82 E
Chipping Hill Essex 71
Chipping Norton Oxon .... 65 L
Chipping Ongar Essex .... 70 E
Chipping Sodbury S Glos .... 45 L
Chipping Warden Nhants 83
Chipshop Devon 12
Chipstable Somset 29
Chipstead Kent 38
Chipstead Surrey 51
Chirbury Shrops 95
Chirk Wrexhm 112
Chirnside Border .... 202 D
Chirnsidebridge Border .... 202 D
Chirton Wilts .... 47 K
Chisbury Wilts .... 47 K
Chiselborough Somset 31
Chiseldon Swindn .... 47 H
Chiselhampton Oxon .... 66 F
Chiserley Calder .... 140 F
Chisholme Border .... 188 D
Chislehurst Gt Lon 51
Chislet Kent 41
Chiswell Green Herts 68
Chiswick Gt Lon .... 51 G
Chiswick End Cambs 87
Chisworth Derbys 131
Chitcombe E Susx 24
Chithurst W Susx 36
Chittering Cambs 87
Chitterne Wilts 33
Chittlehamholt Devon 28
Chittlehampton Devon 27
Chittoe Wilts 46
Chivelstone Devon 8
Chivenor Devon 27
Chiverton Cross Cnwll 4
Chlenry D & G 172
Chobham Surrey 50
Cholderton Wilts 34
Cholesbury Bucks 68
Chollerford Nthumb 179
Chollerton Nthumb 179
Cholmondeston Ches E 130
Cholsey Oxon 48
Cholstrey Herefs 80
Chop Gate N York 161
Choppington Nthumb 181
Chopwell Gatesd 180

Chorley Ches E	113 J1	Church Street Essex	88 F6	Clarach Cerdgn	92 D6	Clench Common Wilts	47 H6
Chorley Lancs	139 H4	Church Street Kent	52 F4	Claravale Gatesd	180 E6	Clenchwarton Norfk	120 D7
Chorley Shrops	96 F6	Church Street Suffk	107 K6	Clarbeston Pembks	55 H3	Clenerty Abers	268 D4
Chorley Staffs	98 D1	Church Stretton Shrops	95 L4	Clarbeston Road Pembks	55 G3	Clent Worcs	97 L7
Chorleywood Herts	68 C7	Churchthorpe Lincs	145 J8	Clarborough Notts	134 E3	Cleobury Mortimer Shrops	96 F8
Chorleywood West Herts	68 C7	Churchtown Bpool	146 F7	Clare Suffk	88 F6	Cleobury North Shrops	96 E6
Chorlton Ches E	114 A2	Churchtown Cnwll	10 F7	Clarebrand D & G	175 J2	Cleongart Ag & B	192 D2
Chorlton-cum-Hardy Manch	130 F1	Churchtown Derbys	132 E7	Clarencefield D & G	176 E5	Clephanton Highld	252 F2
Chorlton Lane Ches W	113 G2	Churchtown Devon	28 B2	Clarewood Nthumb	180 B5	Clerkhill D & G	187 L6
Choulton Shrops	95 J5	Churchtown IoM	154 f3	Clarilaw Border	188 F3	Cleuch-head D & G	185 K3
Chowley Ches W	129 L8	Churchtown Lancs	147 J7	Clark's Green Surrey	37 J3	Clevancy Wilts	46 F4
Chrishall Essex	87 J7	Churchtown Sefton	138 D6	Clarkston E Rens	208 F7	Clevedon N Som	44 E5
Chrisswell Inver	207 L4	Church Town N Linc	143 K6	Clashmore Highld	263 K2	Cleveley Oxon	66 B2
Christchurch BCP	18 B5	Church Village Rhondd	43 G4	Clashmore Highld	270 D2	Cleveleys Lancs	146 F7
Christchurch Cambs	103 K4	Church Warsop Notts	133 L6	Clashnessie Highld	270 E2	Cleverton Wilts	46 E2
Christchurch Gloucs	63 H4	Church Wilne Derbys	116 D5	Clashnoir Moray	254 E7	Clewer Somset	31 G1
Christchurch Newpt	44 D1	Churnsike Lodge Nthumb	178 D4	Clathy P & K	221 H3	Cley next the Sea Norfk	122 A3
Christian Malford Wilts	46 D3	Churston Ferrers Torbay	8 D4	Clathymore P & K	221 H3	Cliburn Cumb	166 E5
Christleton Ches W	129 K6	Churt Surrey	36 C3	Clatt Abers	255 L6	Cliddesden Hants	35 K1
Christmas Common Oxon	67 H8	Churton Ches W	129 K8	Clatter Powys	94 B4	Cliff Warwks	99 G4
Christmas Pie Surrey	36 D1	Churwell Leeds	141 L1	Clatterford End Essex	70 F4	Cliffe Lancs	139 L1
Christon N Som	44 D7	Chwilog Gwynd	109 H4	Clatworthy Somset	29 J4	Cliffe Medway	52 F4
Christon Bank Nthumb	191 J2	Chyandour Cnwll	2 D5	Claughton Lancs	147 K7	Cliffe N York	143 G2
Christow Devon	13 J5	Chyanvounder Cnwll	3 G6	Claughton Lancs	147 L3	Cliffe N York	169 G7
Christ's Hospital W Susx	37 H5	Chyeowling Cnwll	3 K3	Claughton Wirral	129 G2	Cliff End E Susx	25 G4
Chuck Hatch E Susx	38 D4	Chyvarloe Cnwll	3 G6	Clavelshay Somset	30 C4	Cliffe Woods Medway	52 F4
Chudleigh Devon	13 K6	Cîl Powys	94 E3	Claverdon Warwks	82 E2	Clifford Herefs	79 J6
Chudleigh Knighton Devon	13 K7	Cilcain Flints	128 E6	Claverham N Som	44 F5	Clifford Leeds	150 F7
Chulmleigh Devon	28 B8	Cilcennin Cerdgn	76 F3	Clavering Essex	70 C1	Clifford Chambers Warwks	82 E5
Chunal Derbys	131 L2	Cilcewydd Powys	94 F3	Claverley Shrops	97 H5	Clifford's Mesne Gloucs	63 K2
Church Lancs	139 L2	Cilfrew Neath	57 L5	Claverton BaNES	46 A6	Cliffsend Kent	41 K2
Churcham Gloucs	63 M3	Cilfynydd Rhondd	43 H3	Claverton Down BaNES	45 M6	Clifton Bristl	45 H4
Church Aston Wrekin	114 A8	Cilgerran Pembks	75 L4	Clawdd-coch V Glam	43 G6	Clifton C Beds	86 D7
Church Brampton Nhants	84 D2	Cilgwyn Carmth	59 K3	Clawdd-newydd Denbgs	111 L1	Clifton C Nott	116 F4
Church Brough Cumb	167 J7	Cilgwyn Gwynd	109 J1	Clawthorpe Cumb	157 H7	Clifton C York	151 J5
Church Broughton Derbys	115 K5	Ciliau-Aeron Cerdgn	76 F4	Clawton Devon	11 L3	Clifton Calder	141 J3
Church Cove Cnwll	3 J8	Cilmaengwyn Neath	57 K4	Claxby Lincs	136 B1	Clifton Cumb	166 C5
Church Crookham Hants	49 K8	Cilmery Powys	78 D5	Claxby Lincs	137 H5	Clifton Derbys	115 K3
Churchdown Gloucs	64 C3	Cilrhedyn Pembks	58 A2	Claxton N York	151 L4	Clifton Devon	27 L3
Church Eaton Staffs	114 C8	Cilsan Carmth	59 H4	Claxton Norfk	107 G3	Clifton Donc	142 E8
Church End Bed	85 L3	Ciltalgarth Gwynd	111 G3	Claybrooke Magna Leics	100 B5	Clifton Lancs	138 F2
Church End Bed	86 C3	Cilycwm Carmth	77 L7	Clay Common Suffk	107 K7	Clifton N York	150 B6
Church End Bucks	67 H5	Cimla Neath	57 L5	Clay Coton Nhants	100 D8	Clifton Nthumb	180 F2
Church End C Beds	68 C3	Cinderford Gloucs	63 K4	Clay Cross Derbys	133 H7	Clifton Oxon	66 C1
Church End C Beds	68 C3	Cinder Hill Wolves	97 L4	Claydon Oxon	83 K5	Clifton Salfd	140 A7
Church End C Beds	85 J8	Cippenham Slough	50 B3	Claydon Suffk	90 D5	Clifton Worcs	81 J6
Church End C Beds	85 K8	Cirencester Gloucs	64 F6	Clay End Herts	69 J2	Clifton Campville Staffs	99 H1
Church End C Beds	86 D4	Citadilla N York	160 B3	Claygate D & G	177 L3	Clifton Hampden Oxon	66 D7
Church End C Beds	86 D7	City Gt Lon	51 J3	Claygate Kent	39 H4	Clifton Reynes M Keyn	85 H5
Church End Cambs	102 B8	City V Glam	42 F6	Claygate Surrey	50 F6	Clifton upon Dunsmore	
Church End Cambs	102 E6	City Airport Gt Lon	51 L3	Claygate Cross Kent	38 F2	Warwks	100 C8
Church End Cambs	103 G7	City Dulas IoA	125 H2	Clayhall Gt Lon	51 L1	Clifton upon Teme Worcs	81 G3
Church End Essex	70 F4	Clabhach Ag & B	224 F3	Clayhanger Devon	29 J6	Cliftonville Kent	41 L1
Church End Essex	71 H2	Clachaig Ag & B	207 J3	Clayhanger Wsall	98 D3	Climping W Susx	21 G6
Church End Essex	71 H4	Clachaig Inn Highld	229 J4	Clayhidon Devon	29 L7	Clink Somset	32 C1
Churchend Essex	72 E8	Clachan Ag & B	206 B7	Clayhill E Susx	24 F3	Clint N York	150 C4
Church End Gloucs	81 K8	Clachan Ag & B	216 B3	Clayhill Hants	18 D2	Clinterty C Aber	245 J1
Church End Gt Lon	51 H1	Clachan Ag & B	217 H6	Clayhithe Cambs	87 K2	Clint Green Norfk	105 L1
Church End Herts	68 E5	Clachan Ag & B	228 D6	Clayock Highld	279 L4	Clintmains Border	201 J6
Church End Herts	69 H1	Clachan Highld	247 H1	Claypit Hill Cambs	87 G4	Clipiau Gwynd	93 H1
Church End Herts	70 C3	Clachan-a-Luib W Isls	283 c8	Claypits Gloucs	63 M6	Clippesby Norfk	123 J8
Church End Lincs	119 H5	Clachan Mor Ag & B	224 C5	Claypole Lincs	117 M2	Clipsham Rutlnd	118 C8
Church End Lincs	145 L8	Clachan na Luib W Isls	283 c8	Claythorpe Lincs	137 H4	Clipston Nhants	100 F7
Church End Suffk	90 F8	Clachan of Campsie E Duns	209 G3	Clayton C Brad	141 J3	Clipston Notts	117 H5
Churchend Warwks	99 H5	Clachan-Seil Ag & B	216 B3	Clayton Donc	142 C6	Clipstone C Beds	68 B2
Church End Warwks	99 H5	Clachnaharry Highld	251 H2	Clayton W Susx	22 D4	Clipstone Notts	134 B7
Church Enstone Oxon	66 A2	Clachtoll Highld	270 D3	Clayton Green Lancs	139 H3	Clitheroe Lancs	148 C7
Church Fenton N York	151 H8	Clacket Lane Services		Clayton-le-Moors Lancs	139 M2	Clive Shrops	113 H6
Churchfield Sandw	98 C6	Surrey	51 L8	Clayton-le-Woods Lancs	139 H3	Clixby Lincs	144 E7
Churchgate Herts	69 K6	Clackmannan Clacks	210 B1	Clayton West Kirk	141 L5	Cloatley Wilts	46 E1
Churchgate Street Essex	70 C5	Clackmannanshire Bridge		Clayworth Notts	134 E2	Clocaenog Denbgs	111 L1
Church Green Devon	14 E3	Fife	210 B2	Cleadale Highld	236 F3	Clochan Moray	267 H4
Church Gresley Derbys	115 M7	Clackmarras Moray	266 E4	Cleadon S Tyne	181 J6	Clock Face St Hel	129 M2
Church Hanborough Oxon	66 B4	Clacton-on-Sea Essex	73 J4	Cleadon Park S Tyne	181 J6	Cloddiau Powys	94 F2
Church Hill Staffs	98 C1	Cladich Ag & B	217 H3	Clearbrook Devon	7 G2	Clodock Herefs	62 C2
Church Houses N York	161 L3	Cladswell Worcs	82 C5	Clearwell Gloucs	63 H5	Cloford Somset	32 B2
Churchill Devon	15 G2	Claggan Highld	227 K3	Cleasby N York	169 H8	Clola Abers	257 J3
Churchill Devon	27 L3	Claigan Highld	258 C6	Cleat Ork	275 c6	Clophill C Beds	86 B7
Churchill N Som	44 E7	Clandown BaNES	45 K7	Cleatlam Dur	168 E7	Clopton Nhants	102 B7
Churchill Oxon	65 L2	Clanfield Hants	35 L7	Cleator Cumb	164 D7	Clopton Suffk	90 F4
Churchill Worcs	81 L4	Clanfield Oxon	65 L6	Cleator Moor Cumb	164 D7	Clopton Corner Suffk	90 F4
Churchill Worcs	97 K7	Clannaborough Devon	13 H2	Cleckheaton Kirk	141 J3	Clopton Green Suffk	88 F4
Churchinford Somset	30 B8	Clanville Hants	34 D1	Cleedownton Shrops	96 D7	Clopton Green Suffk	89 K3
Church Knowle Dorset	17 H6	Clanville Somset	31 K4	Cleehill Shrops	96 D8	Clos du Valle Guern	9 k1
Church Laneham Notts	135 G4	Claonaig Ag & B	206 D7	Cleekhimin N Lans	209 K7	Closeburn D & G	186 D7
Church Langton Leics	100 F5	Clapgate Dorset	17 K2	Clee St Margaret Shrops	96 D6	Closeburnmill D & G	186 D7
Church Lawford Warwks	99 M8	Clapgate Herts	70 C2	Cleestanton Shrops	96 D7	Closeclark IoM	154 c7
Church Lawton Ches E	130 F4	Clapham Bed	85 K4	Cleethorpes NE Lin	145 J4	Closworth Somset	16 A1
Church Leigh Staffs	115 G4	Clapham Devon	13 L5	Cleeton St Mary Shrops	96 E7	Clothall Herts	69 H1
Church Lench Worcs	82 B5	Clapham Gt Lon	51 H4	Cleeve N Som	44 F5	Clotton Ches W	129 M6
Church Mayfield Staffs	115 J3	Clapham N York	148 C2	Cleeve Oxon	48 F3	Cloudesley Bush Warwks	100 A6
Church Minshull Ches E	130 C7	Clapham W Susx	21 J5	Cleeve Hill Gloucs	64 C2	Clouds Herefs	80 D7
Church Norton W Susx	20 E7	Clapham Green Bed	85 K4	Cleeve Prior Worcs	82 C5	Clough Oldham	140 E6
Churchover Warwks	100 B7	Clap Hill Kent	40 D7	Cleghornie E Loth	212 D2	Clough Foot Calder	140 D3
Church Preen Shrops	96 C4	Clappersgate Cumb	156 E2	Clehonger Herefs	80 B7	Clough Head Calder	141 H4
Church Pulverbatch Shrops	95 K3	Clapton Somset	15 J1	Cleish P & K	221 K7	Cloughton N York	163 H4
Churchstanton Somset	30 B7	Clapton Somset	45 J8	Cleland N Lans	209 L7	Cloughton Newlands N York	163 H3
Churchstoke Powys	95 G4	Clapton-in-Gordano N Som	44 F4	Clement's End C Beds	68 C4	Clousta Shet	281 d5
Churchstow Devon	7 K5	Clapton-on-the-Hill Gloucs	65 H3	Clement Street Kent	52 B5	Clova Angus	233 M1
Church Stowe Nhants	84 C4	Clapworthy Devon	28 B6	Clenamacrie Ag & B	216 E2	Clovelly Devon	26 E6

Clovenfords Border......200 F6
Clovulin Highld......228 F3
Clow Bridge Lancs......140 B2
Clowne Derbys......133 K4
Clows Top Worcs......81 G1
Cloy Wrexhm......112 F3
Cluanie Inn Highld......239 H1
Cluanie Lodge Highld......239 H2
Clubworthy Cnwll......11 K4
Clugston D & G......173 J3
Clun Shrops......95 H7
Clunas Highld......253 G2
Clunbury Shrops......95 J7
Clunderwen Carmth......55 J3
Clune Highld......252 E6
Clunes Highld......239 K6
Clungunford Shrops......95 K7
Clunie P & K......233 H6
Clunton Shrops......95 H7
Cluny Fife......222 D8
Clutton BaNES......45 J7
Clutton Ches W......113 G1
Clutton Hill BaNES......45 J7
Clwt Conwy......127 J7
Clwt-y-bont Gwynd......125 K7
Clydach Mons......61 K4
Clydach Swans......57 J4
Clydach Vale Rhondd......42 E3
Clydebank W Duns......208 E5
Clydey Pembks......75 M5
Clyffe Pypard Wilts......47 G3
Clynder Ag & B......207 L2
Clyne Neath......60 B7
Clynnog Fawr Gwynd......109 G2
Clyro Powys......79 H6
Clyst Honiton Devon......14 A4
Clyst Hydon Devon......14 B2
Clyst St George Devon......14 A5
Clyst St Lawrence Devon......14 B3
Clyst St Mary Devon......14 A4
Cnoc W Isls......282 g3
Cnwch Coch Cerdgn......92 E8
Coad's Green Cnwll......11 K7
Coal Aston Derbys......133 G4
Coalbrookvale Blae G......61 K5
Coalburn S Lans......198 D6
Coalburns Gatesd......180 D6
Coaley Gloucs......63 M6
Coalhill Essex......71 J7
Coalmoor Wrekin......96 F2
Coalpit Heath S Glos......45 K3
Coal Pool Wsall......98 C3
Coalport Wrekin......96 F3
Coalsnaughton Clacks......221 G8
Coal Street Suffk......90 F1
Coaltown of Balgonie Fife......222 E7
Coaltown of Wemyss Fife......222 E8
Coalville Leics......99 L1
Coanwood Nthumb......178 F7
Coat Somset......31 G6
Coatbridge N Lans......209 J6
Coatdyke N Lans......209 K6
Coate Swindn......47 J2
Coate Wilts......46 F6
Coates Cambs......102 F4
Coates Gloucs......64 E5
Coates Lincs......135 H3
Coates Notts......135 G3
Coates W Susx......21 G3
Coatham R & Cl......170 E5
Coatham Mundeville Darltn......169 H6
Cobbaton Devon......27 L5
Coberley Gloucs......64 D4
Cobhall Common Herefs......80 B8
Cobham Kent......52 E5
Cobham Surrey......50 E7
Cobham Services Surrey......50 E7
Coblers Green Essex......71 G3
Cobley Dorset......33 H6
Cobnash Herefs......80 B3
Cobo Guern......9 j2
Cobridge C Stke......114 D2
Coburby Abers......269 G3
Cock Alley Derbys......133 H5
Cockayne N York......161 K3
Cockayne Hatley C Beds......86 F5
Cock Bank Wrexhm......112 E2
Cock Bevington Warwks......82 C5
Cock Bridge Abers......243 J2
Cockburnspath Border......213 G5
Cock Clarks Essex......71 K6
Cock & End Suffk......88 E4
Cockenzie and Port Seton
    E Loth......211 L4
Cocker Bar Lancs......139 G3
Cocker Brook Lancs......139 L3
Cockerham Lancs......147 J5
Cockermouth Cumb......164 F4
Cockernhoe Herts......68 E2
Cockersdale Leeds......141 K2

Cockett Swans......57 H6
Cockfield Dur......168 E6
Cockfield Suffk......89 H4
Cockfosters Gt Lon......69 H7
Cock Green Essex......71 G3
Cocking W Susx......20 E3
Cocking Causeway W Susx......20 E3
Cockington Torbay......8 D2
Cocklake Somset......31 G1
Cockley Beck Cumb......156 C2
Cockley Cley Norfk......104 C3
Cock Marling E Susx......24 F3
Cockpole Green Wokham......49 J3
Cocks Cnwll......4 C4
Cockshutford Shrops......96 D6
Cockshutt Shrops......113 G5
Cock Street Kent......39 K3
Cockthorpe Norfk......121 L3
Cockwells Cnwll......2 E4
Cockwood Devon......14 A6
Cockwood Somset......30 B2
Cockyard Derbys......131 L4
Cockyard Herefs......80 A8
Coddenham Suffk......90 D4
Coddington Ches W......129 K8
Coddington Herefs......81 G6
Coddington Notts......117 L1
Codford St Mary Wilts......33 G3
Codford St Peter Wilts......33 G3
Codicote Herts......69 G3
Codmore Hill W Susx......21 H3
Codnor Derbys......116 C2
Codrington S Glos......45 L3
Codsall Staffs......97 K3
Codsall Wood Staffs......97 J2
Coed Darcy Neath......57 K5
Coedely Rhondd......42 F4
Coed Hirwaun Neath......42 B5
Coedkernew Newpt......44 B2
Coed Morgan Mons......62 D5
Coedpoeth Wrexhm......112 D1
Coed Talon Flints......129 G7
Coedway Powys......112 E8
Coed-y-Bryn Cerdgn......76 C6
Coed-y-caerau Newpt......44 D1
Coed-y-Cwm Rhondd......43 G3
Coed-y-paen Mons......62 C7
Coed-yr-ynys Powys......61 J3
Coed Ystumgwern Gwynd......109 H6
Coelbren Powys......60 C5
Coffinswell Devon......8 D1
Coffle End Bed......85 K3
Cofton Devon......13 M6
Cofton Hackett Worcs......98 C8
Cogan V Glam......43 J7
Cogenhoe Nhants......84 F3
Cogges Oxon......65 M5
Coggeshall Essex......71 K3
Coggin's Mill E Susx......23 K2
Coignafearn Highld......251 J8
Coilacriech Abers......243 K4
Coilantogle Stirlg......219 K5
Coillore Highld......246 E1
Coity Brdgnd......42 D5
Col W Isls......282 g3
Colaboll Highld......272 E6
Colan Cnwll......4 E3
Colaton Raleigh Devon......14 C5
Colbost Highld......258 C7
Colburn N York......160 B3
Colby Cumb......166 F6
Colby IoM......154 b7
Colby Norfk......122 E5
Colchester Essex......72 E2
Cold Ash W Berk......48 D5
Cold Ashby Nhants......100 E8
Cold Ashton S Glos......45 L4
Cold Aston Gloucs......65 H3
Coldbackie Highld......277 K4
Coldbeck Cumb......158 C2
Cold Blow Pembks......55 J4
Cold Brayfield M Keyn......85 H5
Cold Cotes N York......148 C2
Coldean Br & H......22 E5
Coldeast Devon......13 J7
Colden Calder......140 E2
Colden Common Hants......35 G6
Coldfair Green Suffk......91 K3
Coldham Cambs......103 J3
Cold Hanworth Lincs......135 L3
Coldharbour Cnwll......4 B5
Coldharbour Devon......29 J4
Coldharbour Gloucs......63 H6
Cold Harbour Herts......68 F4
Cold Harbour Oxon......48 F3
Coldharbour Surrey......37 H2
Cold Hatton Wrekin......113 K7
Cold Hatton Heath Wrekin......113 K7
Cold Hesledon Dur......169 L2
Cold Hiendley Wakefd......142 B5

Cold Higham Nhants......84 C4
Coldingham Border......213 K6
Cold Kirby N York......161 H6
Coldmeece Staffs......114 D5
Cold Newton Leics......100 F2
Cold Northcott Cnwll......11 G1
Cold Norton Essex......71 K7
Cold Overton Leics......101 H2
Coldred Kent......41 J6
Coldridge Devon......13 G1
Coldstream Border......202 C5
Coldwaltham W Susx......21 H3
Coldwell Herefs......80 A8
Coldwells Abers......257 K4
Cold Weston Shrops......96 C6
Cole Somset......31 L4
Colebatch Shrops......95 H6
Colebrook C Plym......7 G3
Colebrook Devon......14 B2
Colebrooke Devon......13 H3
Coleby Lincs......135 K7
Coleby N Linc......143 M4
Cole End Warwks......99 G5
Coleford Devon......13 H2
Coleford Gloucs......63 H5
Coleford Somset......31 L1
Coleford Water Somset......29 L4
Colegate End Norfk......106 D6
Cole Green Herts......69 H5
Cole Green Herts......70 B1
Cole Henley Hants......34 F1
Colehill Dorset......17 K2
Coleman Green Herts......69 G4
Coleman's Hatch E Susx......38 C6
Colemere Shrops......113 G5
Colemore Hants......35 L5
Colemore Green Shrops......97 G4
Colenden P & K......221 K1
Colerne Wilts......46 B5
Colesbourne Gloucs......64 C4
Cole's Cross Devon......8 A5
Coles Cross Dorset......15 J2
Colesden Bed......86 C4
Coles Green Suffk......90 C7
Coleshill Bucks......68 B8
Coleshill Oxon......65 K8
Coleshill Warwks......99 G5
Colestocks Devon......14 C3
Coley BaNES......45 H7
Colgate W Susx......37 K4
Colinsburgh Fife......223 H6
Colinton C Edin......211 H5
Colintraive Ag & B......207 G4
Colkirk Norfk......121 K6
Coll Ag & B......225 G4
Coll W Isls......282 g3
Collace P & K......222 C1
Collafirth Shet......281 d3
Coll Airport Ag & B......224 F4
Collaton Devon......7 L7
Collaton St Mary Torbay......8 C3
College of Roseisle Moray......266 C3
College Town Br For......49 K6
Collessie Fife......222 D4
Colleton Mills Devon......28 B7
Collier Row Gt Lon......52 B1
Collier's End Herts......69 K3
Collier's Green E Susx......24 E3
Colliers Green Kent......39 J5
Collier Street Kent......39 H4
Colliery Row Sundld......169 J1
Collieston Abers......257 J6
Collin D & G......176 D4
Collingbourne Ducis Wilts......47 K8
Collingbourne Kingston
    Wilts......47 K7
Collingham Leeds......150 E6
Collingham Notts......135 G7
Collington Herefs......80 F3
Collingtree Nhants......84 E4
Collins Green Warrtn......130 A1
Collins Green Worcs......81 G4
Colliston Angus......234 F6
Colliton Devon......14 C2
Collyweston Nhants......101 M3
Colmonell S Ayrs......182 E5
Colmworth Bed......86 C4
Colnabaichin Abers......243 J2
Colnbrook Slough......50 C3
Colne Cambs......103 H8
Colne Lancs......148 F7
Colne Bridge Kirk......141 J4
Colne Edge Lancs......148 F7
Colne Engaine Essex......71 K1
Colney Norfk......106 D2
Colney Heath Herts......69 G6
Colney Street Herts......68 F6
Coln Rogers Gloucs......65 G5
Coln St Aldwyns Gloucs......65 H6

Coln St Dennis Gloucs......65 G5
Colonsay Ag & B......214 D5
Colonsay Airport Ag & B......214 D6
Colpy Abers......256 B5
Colquhar Border......200 D5
Colquite Cnwll......10 E8
Colscott Devon......26 F7
Colsterdale N York......159 L6
Colsterworth Lincs......118 B6
Colston Bassett Notts......117 J5
Coltfield Moray......266 C3
Colt Hill Hants......49 H8
Coltishall Norfk......122 F7
Colton Cumb......156 D5
Colton Leeds......142 B1
Colton N York......151 H6
Colton Norfk......106 C2
Colton Staffs......115 G7
Colt's Hill Kent......39 G4
Columbjohn Devon......13 M3
Colva Powys......79 H4
Colvend D & G......175 L6
Colwall Herefs......81 H6
Colwell Nthumb......179 M6
Colwich Staffs......115 G3
Colwick Notts......117 G2
Colwinston V Glam......42 E6
Colworth W Susx......20 F6
Colwyn Bay Conwy......127 G4
Colyford Devon......14 F4
Colyton Devon......14 F4
Combe Devon......7 L4
Combe Herefs......79 L2
Combe Oxon......66 B4
Combe W Berk......48 A7
Combe Almer Dorset......17 J2
Combe Common Surrey......36 E4
Combe Down BaNES......45 M6
Combe Fishacre Devon......8 C3
Combe Florey Somset......29 L4
Combe Hay BaNES......45 L7
Combeinteignhead Devon......13 L7
Combe Martin Devon......27 K3
Combe Raleigh Devon......14 E3
Comberbach Ches W......130 C5
Comberford Staffs......99 G3
Comberton Cambs......87 H4
Comberton Herefs......80 B3
Combe St Nicholas Somset......30 C3
Combpyne Devon......15 J4
Combridge Staffs......115 H5
Combrook Warwks......83 G4
Combs Derbys......131 L4
Combs Suffk......90 B4
Combs Ford Suffk......90 B4
Combwich Somset......30 C3
Comers Abers......244 F2
Comeytrowe Somset......30 B7
Comhampton Worcs......81 J8
Commercial End Cambs......87 L2
Commins Coch Powys......93 J2
Commondale N York......170 F7
Common Edge Bpool......138 D2
Common End Cumb......164 D5
Common Moor Cnwll......6 A2
Common Platt Wilts......47 J2
Commonside Ches W......130 A5
Commonside Derbys......115 L3
Common Side Derbys......133 G4
Commonwood Shrops......113 H4
Commonwood Wrexhm......112 F2
Compass Somset......30 D5
Compstall Stockp......131 L2
Compstonend D & G......175 G5
Compton Devon......8 C3
Compton Hants......34 D5
Compton Hants......34 F6
Compton Staffs......97 J6
Compton Surrey......36 E2
Compton W Berk......48 D3
Compton W Susx......20 C4
Compton Wilts......47 H6
Compton Abbas Dorset......32 E6
Compton Abdale Gloucs......64 F3
Compton Bassett Wilts......46 F4
Compton Beauchamp Oxon......47 L2
Compton Bishop Somset......44 D8
Compton Chamberlayne Wilts......33 H5
Compton Dando BaNES......45 K6
Compton Dundon Somset......31 H5
Compton Durville Somset......30 F7
Compton Greenfield S Glos......45 H2
Compton Martin BaNES......45 H7
Compton Pauncefoot Somset......31 L6
Compton Valence Dorset......16 C4
Comrie Fife......210 E2
Comrie P & K......220 D4
Conaglen House Highld......229 K2
Conchra Highld......248 B6
Concraigie P & K......233

Conder Green Lancs...............147 J4
Conderton Worcs....................81 M7
Condicote Gloucs....................65 H2
Condorrat N Lans..................209 K4
Condover Shrops.....................96 B2
Coney Hill Gloucs....................64 B3
Coneyhurst W Susx..................37 H6
Coneysthorpe N York.............151 M2
Coneythorpe N York...............150 E4
Coney Weston Suffk...............105 J7
Congdon's Shop Cnwll..............11 K7
Congerstone Leics....................99 K2
Congham Norfk......................120 F6
Congleton Ches E...................131 G7
Congl-y-wal Gwynd.................110 D3
Congresbury N Som..................44 E6
Congreve Staffs.......................97 K1
Conheath D & G.....................176 C5
Conicavel Moray....................253 J1
Coningsby Lincs.....................136 D8
Conington Cambs.....................87 G2
Conington Cambs....................102 D6
Conisbrough Donc..................142 D8
Conisholme Lincs...................145 K8
Coniston Cumb......................156 D3
Coniston E R Yk.....................144 F1
Coniston Cold N York.............148 F5
Conistone N York...................149 H2
Connah's Quay Flints..............129 G5
Connel Ag & B.......................228 E8
Connel Park E Ayrs.................197 H8
Connor Downs Cnwll..................2 F3
Cononbridge Highld.................250 F1
Cononley N York.....................149 H6
Consall Staffs........................114 F2
Consett Dur...........................180 D8
Constable Burton N York..........159 L4
Constable Lee Lancs...............140 B3
Constantine Cnwll.....................3 J5
Constantine Bay Cnwll.............10 B7
Contin Highld........................262 D8
Conwy Conwy........................126 F4
Conwy Castle Conwy...............126 F4
Conyer Kent...........................40 C2
Conyer's Green Suffk................89 H2
Cooden E Susx........................24 C6
Cookbury Devon......................12 A2
Cookbury Wick Devon..............11 M2
Cookham W & M......................49 L2
Cookham Dean W & M.............49 L2
Cookham Rise W & M...............49 L2
Cookhill Worcs.......................82 C3
Cookley Suffk........................107 G8
Cookley Worcs........................97 J7
Cookley Green Oxon.................49 G1
Cookney Abers......................245 J5
Cooksbridge E Susx..................22 F4
Cooksey Green Worcs...............81 L1
Cook's Green Essex..................73 J3
Cooks Green Suffk...................89 K4
Cookshill Staffs.....................114 E3
Cooksland Cnwll.......................5 J1
Cooksmill Green Essex..............70 F6
Cookson Green Ches W.............130 B5
Coolham W Susx......................37 H6
Cooling Medway......................53 G4
Cooling Street Medway..............52 F4
Coombe Cnwll...........................3 G5
Coombe Cnwll...........................3 L3
Coombe Cnwll...........................4 F4
Coombe Devon.........................13 J6
Coombe Devon.........................13 L7
Coombe Devon.........................14 C4
Coombe Gloucs.......................63 M8
Coombe Hants.........................35 K6
Coombe Wilts..........................33 K1
Coombe Bissett Wilts...............33 K5
Coombe Cellars Devon..............13 L8
Coombe Cross Hants.................35 K6
Coombe Hill Gloucs..................64 C2
Coombe Keynes Dorset.............17 G6
Coombe Pafford Torbay...............8 D2
Coombes W Susx......................21 L5
Coombes-Moor Herefs...............79 L3
Coombe Street Somset...............32 C4
Coombeswood Dudley...............98 B6
Coopersale Common Essex.........70 C6
Coopersale Street Essex.............70 C6
Cooper's Corner Kent................38 D3
Coopers Green E Susx................23 H3
Coopers Green Herts.................69 G5
Cooper Street Kent...................41 J3
Cooper Turning Bolton............139 J6
Cootham W Susx......................21 J4
Copdock Suffk.........................90 D7
Copford Essex.........................72 D2
Copford Green Essex.................72 D3
Copgrove N York....................150 D3
Copister Shet.........................281 e4

Cople Bed...............................86 C5
Copley Calder........................141 G3
Copley Dur............................168 D5
Copley Tamesd.......................140 E8
Coplow Dale Derbys................132 C4
Copmanthorpe C York..............151 J5
Copmere End Staffs................114 C5
Copp Lancs...........................147 H7
Coppathorne Cnwll...................11 H3
Coppenhall Staffs...................114 E7
Coppenhall Moss Ches E..........130 D8
Copperhouse Cnwll....................2 F3
Coppicegate Shrops..................97 G7
Coppingford Cambs.................102 D7
Coppins Corner Kent.................40 B5
Copplestone Devon...................13 H2
Coppull Lancs........................139 H5
Coppull Moor Lancs................139 H5
Copsale W Susx.......................37 J6
Copster Green Lancs................139 K1
Copston Magna Warwks.............99 M5
Cop Street Kent........................41 J3
Copthall Green Essex.................70 B7
Copt Heath Solhll.....................98 F7
Copt Hewick N York................150 D2
Copthorne Cnwll......................11 K4
Copthorne W Susx.....................37 M3
Copt Oak Leics......................100 B1
Copy's Green Norfk.................121 L4
Copythorne Hants.....................34 C8
Coram Street Suffk...................89 K6
Corbets Tey Gt Lon...................52 C2
Corbière Jersey..........................9 a3
Corbridge Nthumb..................180 B6
Corby Nhants.........................101 K5
Corby Glen Lincs....................118 C6
Corby Hill Cumb....................178 B7
Cordon N Ayrs.......................195 G5
Cordwell Derbys.....................132 F4
Coreley Shrops.........................96 E8
Cores End Bucks......................49 L2
Corfe Somset...........................30 C7
Corfe Castle Dorset...................17 J6
Corfe Mullen Dorset..................17 J3
Corfton Shrops.........................96 B6
Corgarff Abers.......................243 J2
Corhampton Hants....................35 J6
Corks Pond Kent......................39 G5
Corlae D & G.........................185 G3
Corley Warwks........................99 J6
Corley Ash Warwks...................99 J6
Corley Moor Warwks.................99 H6
Corley Services Warwks..............99 J6
Cormuir Angus......................233 L2
Cornard Tye Suffk.....................89 H7
Corndon Devon........................13 G5
Corner Row Lancs...................138 E1
Corney Cumb.........................155 K4
Cornforth Dur........................169 J4
Cornhill Abers.......................267 M4
Cornhill-on-Tweed Nthumb.......202 D5
Cornholme Calder...................140 D3
Cornish Hall End Essex..............88 D7
Cornoigmore Ag & B................224 C6
Cornriggs Dur.........................167 K2
Cornsay Dur...........................168 F2
Cornsay Colliery Dur................168 F2
Corntown Highld.....................262 F8
Corntown V Glam......................42 D6
Cornwall Airport Newquay
   Cnwll....................................4 E2
Cornwell Oxon.........................65 K2
Cornwood Devon........................7 H3
Cornworthy Devon......................8 B4
Corpach Highld......................239 H8
Corpusty Norfk......................122 C5
Corrachree Abers...................244 B3
Corran Highld........................229 G3
Corran Highld........................238 D2
Corrany IoM..........................154 f4
Corrie D & G.........................177 G2
Corrie N Ayrs.........................195 G2
Corriecravie N Ayrs.................193 J4
Corriegills N Ayrs...................195 G4
Corriegour Lodge Hotel
   Highld...............................239 M5
Corriemoille Highld.................262 C7
Corrimony Highld...................250 C5
Corringham Lincs...................135 H2
Corringham Thurr.....................52 F2
Corris Gwynd...........................93 G2
Corris Uchaf Gwynd..................92 F2
Corrow Ag & B.......................217 K7
Corry Highld.........................247 K4
Corscombe Devon.....................12 E3
Corscombe Dorset.....................15 L2
Corse Gloucs...........................64 A2
Corse Lawn Gloucs....................64 B1
Corsham Wilts..........................46 C5
Corsindae Abers.....................244 F2

Corsley Wilts...........................32 D2
Corsley Heath Wilts...................32 D2
Corsock D & G.......................185 J7
Corston BaNES.........................45 K6
Corston Wilts...........................46 D2
Corstorphine C Edin................211 G4
Cors-y-Gedol Gwynd................109 L7
Cortachy Angus......................234 B3
Corton Suffk..........................107 L4
Corton Wilts............................32 F3
Corton Denham Somset.............31 K6
Coruanan Highld....................229 H2
Corwen Denbgs......................111 L3
Coryates Dorset........................16 B5
Coryton Devon.........................12 B6
Coryton Thurr..........................52 F2
Cosby Leics...........................100 C4
Coseley Dudley........................97 L4
Cosford Shrops.........................97 H2
Cosgrove Nhants......................84 F6
Cosham C Port.........................19 L3
Cosheston Pembks.....................55 G6
Coshieville P & K....................231 L5
Cossall Notts.........................116 E3
Cossall Marsh Notts................116 E3
Cossington Leics....................100 D1
Cossington Somset....................30 E3
Costessey Norfk.....................106 D1
Costock Notts........................116 F6
Coston Leics.........................117 M7
Coston Norfk.........................106 B2
Cote Oxon..............................65 M6
Cote Somset............................30 L2
Cotebrook Ches W...................130 B6
Cotehill Cumb.......................166 B1
Cotes Cumb..........................157 G5
Cotes Leics..........................116 F7
Cotes Staffs..........................114 C4
Cotesbach Leics.....................100 C7
Cotes Heath Staffs...................114 C4
Cotford St Luke Somset.............30 A5
Cotgrave Notts......................117 H4
Cothal Abers.........................256 F8
Cotham Notts........................117 L2
Cothelstone Somset...................30 B4
Cotherstone Dur.....................168 C6
Cothill Oxon...........................66 C7
Cotleigh Devon........................14 E2
Cotmanhay Derbys..................116 D3
Coton Cambs...........................87 H3
Coton Nhants...........................84 D1
Coton Shrops.........................113 J4
Coton Staffs............................98 F2
Coton Staffs.........................114 C7
Coton Staffs.........................114 F5
Coton Clanford Staffs..............114 D7
Coton Hayes Staffs..................114 F5
Coton Hill Shrops.....................96 B1
Coton in the Clay Staffs...........115 K5
Coton in the Elms Derbys.........115 L8
Coton Park Derbys..................115 M7
Cotswold Airport Wilts...............64 D7
Cotswolds...............................64 E5
Cott Devon...............................8 B3
Cottam E R Yk.......................152 F3
Cottam Lancs........................139 G1
Cottam Notts.........................135 G4
Cottenham Cambs.....................87 J2
Cotterdale N York...................158 E4
Cottered Herts.........................69 J1
Cotteridge Birm.......................98 D7
Cotterstock Nhants..................102 A5
Cottesbrooke Nhants...............100 F8
Cottesmore Rutlnd..................101 K1
Cottingham E R Yk..................144 D1
Cottingham Nhants..................101 J5
Cottingley C Brad...................149 K8
Cottisford Oxon.......................66 E1
Cotton Suffk............................90 C2
Cotton End Bed........................86 B6
Cotton Tree Lancs...................148 F7
Cottown Abers.......................255 K6
Cottown Abers.......................256 D8
Cottown of Gight Abers............256 K6
Cotts Devon..............................6 E2
Cotwall Wrekin.......................113 K8
Cotwalton Staffs.....................114 E4
Couch's Mill Cnwll.....................5 K3
Coughton Herefs......................63 H3
Coughton Warwks.....................82 C3
Coulaghailtro Ag & B..............206 A6
Coulags Highld......................248 F3
Coulby Newham Middsb............170 C7
Coulderton Cumb....................155 H1
Coull Abers...........................244 B3
Coulport Ag & B.....................207 L2
Coulsdon Gt Lon......................51 J7
Coulston Wilts.........................46 D8
Coulter S Lans.......................199 H6
Coultershaw Bridge W Susx........21 G3

Coultings Somset......................30 C3
Coulton N York......................161 K7
Coultra Fife...........................222 F3
Cound Shrops..........................96 D2
Coundlane Shrops.....................96 D2
Coundon Dur.........................169 G5
Coundon Grange Dur...............169 G5
Countersett N York.................159 G5
Countess Wilts.........................33 K2
Countess Cross Essex................72 C1
Countess Wear Devon................13 M5
Countesswells C Aber...............245 J3
Countesthorpe Leics................100 D4
Countisbury Devon....................28 C1
Coupar Angus P & K................233 K7
Coupe Green Lancs..................139 H2
Coupland Cumb......................167 G7
Coupland Nthumb...................202 E7
Cour Ag & B..........................194 C2
Court-at-Street Kent..................40 E8
Courteachan Highld.................237 K1
Courteenhall Nhants..................84 E4
Court Henry Carmth..................59 G4
Courtsend Essex.......................72 F8
Courtway Somset......................30 B4
Cousland Mdloth....................211 L5
Cousley Wood E Susx.................39 G6
Cove Ag & B.........................207 L3
Cove Border..........................213 G4
Cove Devon.............................29 G7
Cove Hants.............................49 L7
Cove Highld...........................260 C2
Cove Bay C Aber.....................245 L3
Cove Bottom Suffk..................107 K7
Covehithe Suffk.....................107 L7
Coven Staffs............................97 K2
Coveney Cambs......................103 K7
Covenham St Bartholomew
   Lincs................................136 F1
Covenham St Mary Lincs...........136 F1
Coven Heath Staffs...................97 K2
Coventry Covtry........................99 J7
Coverack Cnwll..........................3 K7
Coverack Bridges Cnwll..............3 H5
Coverham N York....................159 K5
Covington Cambs......................85 L1
Covington S Lans....................199 G5
Cowan Bridge Lancs................157 L2
Cowbeech E Susx......................23 K4
Cowbit Lincs.........................119 H7
Cowbridge V Glam.....................42 F6
Cowdale Derbys......................132 B5
Cowden Kent...........................38 C5
Cowdenbeath Fife...................211 G1
Cowden Pound Kent..................38 C5
Cowden Station Kent..................38 D5
Cowers Lane Derbys.................116 A2
Cowes IoW..............................19 H4
Cowesby N York......................161 G5
Cowesfield Green Wilts..............34 B6
Cowfold W Susx........................37 K6
Cowgill Cumb........................158 C5
Cow Green Suffk.......................90 C2
Cowhill S Glos.........................45 J1
Cowie Stirlg..........................209 M1
Cowlam E R Yk.......................152 E3
Cowley Devon..........................13 L3
Cowley Gloucs.........................64 D4
Cowley Gt Lon..........................50 D3
Cowley Oxon...........................66 D6
Cowling Lancs.......................139 J4
Cowling N York......................149 H7
Cowling N York......................160 C5
Cowlinge Suffk........................88 E4
Cowmes Kirk.........................141 J4
Cowpe Lancs.........................140 C4
Cowpen Nthumb.....................181 H3
Cowpen Bewley S on T.............170 B5
Cowplain Hants........................19 M2
Cowshill Dur.........................167 K3
Cowslip Green N Som.................44 F6
Cowthorpe N York...................150 F5
Coxall Herefs...........................95 J8
Coxbank Ches E......................113 L3
Coxbench Derbys....................116 C3
Coxbridge Somset.....................31 J3
Cox Common Suffk..................107 H7
Coxford Cnwll..........................11 H3
Coxford Norfk........................121 J5
Coxgreen Staffs........................97 H6
Cox Green Surrey......................37 G4
Coxheath Kent..........................39 J3
Coxhoe Dur..........................169 J3
Coxley Somset..........................31 H2
Coxley Wakefd......................141 L4
Coxley Wick Somset..................31 H2
Coxpark Cnwll..........................12 A8
Coxtie Green Essex....................70 E7
Coxwold N York......................161 H7
Coychurch Brdgnd.....................42 E6

Coylton S Ayrs 196 E7
Coylumbridge Highld 242 B1
Coytrahen Brdgnd 42 D4
Crabbs Cross Worcs 82 B2
Crab Orchard Dorset 17 L1
Crabtree W Susx 37 K6
Crabtree Green Wrexhm 112 E3
Crackenthorpe Cumb 166 F6
Crackington Haven Cnwll 11 G3
Crackley Staffs 114 C2
Crackley Warwks 99 J8
Crackleybank Shrops 97 G1
Crackpot N York 159 H3
Cracoe N York 149 H4
Craddock Devon 29 K8
Cradle End Herts 70 C3
Cradley Dudley 97 L6
Cradley Herefs 81 G6
Cradley Heath Sandw 97 L6
Cradoc Powys 60 F1
Crafthole Cnwll 6 D4
Crafton Bucks 67 L3
Crag Foot Lancs 157 G7
Craggan Highld 253 K6
Cragganmore Moray 254 D7
Cragg Hill Leeds 150 B8
Cragg Vale Calder 140 F3
Craghead Dur 180 F8
Crai Powys 60 D2
Craibstone Moray 267 K4
Craichie Angus 234 D6
Craig Angus 235 H4
Craig Highld 249 H2
Craigbank E Ayrs 197 H8
Craigburn Border 200 B2
Craig-cefn-parc Swans 57 J4
Craigcleuch D & G 177 K2
Craigdam Abers 256 F5
Craigearn Abers 245 G1
Craigellachie Moray 254 D7
Craigend P & K 221 K3
Craigend Rens 208 D5
Craigendoran Ag & B 208 A3
Craigends Rens 208 C6
Craighlaw D & G 173 H3
Craighouse Ag & B 205 H3
Craigie P & K 233 H6
Craigie S Ayrs 196 E4
Craigiefold Abers 269 G3
Craigley D & G 175 J3
Craig Llangiwg Neath 57 K4
Craiglockhart C Edin 211 H5
Craigmillar C Edin 211 J4
Craignant Shrops 112 C4
Craigneston D & G 185 J5
Craigneuk N Lans 209 K6
Craigneuk N Lans 209 K7
Craignure Ag & B 227 L5
Craigo Angus 235 H4
Craig Penllyn V Glam 42 E6
Craigrothie Fife 222 F5
Craigruie Stirlg 219 H3
Craig's End Essex 88 E7
Craigton Angus 234 D7
Craigton C Aber 245 J3
Craigton E Rens 208 E8
Craigton of Airlie Angus 233 M5
Craig-y-Duke Neath 57 K4
Craig-y-nos Powys 60 C4
Craik Border 188 B4
Crail Fife 223 L5
Crailing Border 189 J1
Craiselound N Linc 143 J8
Crakehall N York 160 C5
Crakehill N York 160 F7
Crakemarsh Staffs 115 H4
Crambe N York 151 M3
Crambeck N York 151 M2
Cramlington Nthumb 181 G3
Cramond C Edin 211 G4
Cramond Bridge C Edin 211 G4
Crampmoor Hants 34 E6
Cranage Ches E 130 C6
Cranberry Staffs 114 C4
Cranborne Dorset 33 H8
Cranbourne Br For 50 A4
Cranbrook Devon 14 A4
Cranbrook Kent 39 J6
Cranbrook Common Kent 39 K5
Crane Moor Barns 141 M7
Crane's Corner Norfk 105 J1
Cranfield C Beds 85 J6
Cranford Devon 26 F6
Cranford Gt Lon 50 E4
Cranford St Andrew Nhants 101 K7
Cranford St John Nhants 101 K7
Cranham Gloucs 64 C4
Cranham Gt Lon 52 C2
Cranhill Warwks 82 D4

Crank St Hel 139 G7
Cranleigh Surrey 37 G3
Cranmer Green Suffk 89 L1
Cranmore IoW 18 F5
Cranmore Somset 31 L2
Cranoe Leics 101 G4
Cransford Suffk 91 H2
Cranshaws Border 212 F6
Cranstal IoM 154 f2
Cranswick E R Yk 152 F5
Crantock Cnwll 4 C3
Cranwell Lincs 118 D2
Cranwich Norfk 104 F4
Cranworth Norfk 105 K3
Craobh Haven Ag & B 216 B5
Crapstone Devon 6 F1
Crarae Ag & B 216 F7
Crask Inn Highld 272 D3
Crask of Aigas Highld 250 E3
Craster Nthumb 191 K2
Craswall Herefs 79 K8
Crateford Staffs 97 K2
Cratfield Suffk 107 G8
Crathes Abers 245 G4
Crathie Abers 243 J4
Crathie Highld 241 G5
Crathorne N York 161 G1
Craven Arms Shrops 95 K6
Crawcrook Gatesd 180 D6
Crawford Lancs 139 G7
Crawford S Lans 186 E2
Crawfordjohn S Lans 186 C2
Crawley Hants 34 F4
Crawley Oxon 65 M4
Crawley W Susx 37 L4
Crawley Down W Susx 38 A6
Crawleyside Dur 168 C3
Crawshawbooth Lancs 140 B3
Crawton Abers 245 J7
Craxe's Green Essex 72 D3
Cray N York 159 G6
Cray P & K 233 H3
Crayford Gt Lon 52 B4
Crayke N York 151 J2
Craymere Beck Norfk 122 B5
Crays Hill Essex 71 H8
Cray's Pond Oxon 48 F3
Craythorne Staffs 115 L6
Craze Lowman Devon 29 H8
Crazies Hill Wokham 49 J3
Creacombe Devon 28 E7
Creagan Inn Ag & B 228 F6
Creag Ghoraidh W Isls 283 c9
Creagorry W Isls 283 c9
Creaguaineach Lodge
    Highld 230 B2
Creamore Bank Shrops 113 H5
Creaton Nhants 84 D1
Creca D & G 177 H5
Credenhill Herefs 80 B6
Crediton Devon 13 J3
Creebank D & G 183 J7
Creebridge D & G 173 K2
Creech Dorset 17 H6
Creech Heathfield Somset 30 D5
Creech St Michael Somset 30 C6
Creed Cnwll 4 F5
Creekmoor BCP 17 K4
Creekmouth Gt Lon 51 M3
Creeksea Essex 72 D7
Creeting St Mary Suffk 90 C4
Creeting St Peter Suffk 90 C3
Creeton Lincs 118 D7
Creetown D & G 174 D3
Cregneash IoM 154 b8
Creg ny Baa IoM 154 e5
Cregrina Powys 79 H3
Creich Fife 222 E3
Creigiau Cardif 43 G5
Cremyll Cnwll 6 D4
Cressage Shrops 96 D3
Cressbrook Derbys 132 C5
Cresselly Pembks 55 H5
Cressex Bucks 67 K8
Cressing Essex 71 J3
Cresswell Nthumb 191 K7
Cresswell Pembks 55 H5
Cresswell Staffs 114 F4
Creswell Derbys 133 K5
Creswell Green Staffs 98 D1
Cretingham Suffk 90 F3
Cretshengan Ag & B 206 A5
Crewe Ches E 130 D8
Crewe-by-Farndon Ches W 112 F1
Crewe Green Ches E 130 E8
Crew Green Powys 112 D8
Crewkerne Somset 15 K1
Crews Hill Gt Lon 69 J7
Crewton C Derb 116 C5
Crianlarich Stirlg 218 F2

Cribyn Cerdgn 76 F5
Criccieth Gwynd 109 J4
Crich Derbys 116 B1
Crich Carr Derbys 116 B1
Crichton Mdloth 211 L6
Crick Mons 44 F1
Crick Nhants 84 B1
Crickadarn Powys 78 F6
Cricket St Thomas Somset 15 J1
Crickheath Shrops 112 D7
Crickhowell Powys 61 K3
Cricklade Wilts 65 G8
Cricklewood Gt Lon 51 G2
Cridling Stubbs N York 142 B3
Crieff P & K 220 F3
Criggan Cnwll 5 G3
Criggion Powys 112 D8
Crigglestone Wakefd 141 M4
Crimble Rochdl 140 C5
Crimond Abers 269 K5
Crimplesham Norfk 104 C3
Crimscote Warwks 82 F5
Crinaglack Highld 250 D4
Crinan Ag & B 216 B8
Crindledyke N Lans 209 L7
Cringleford Norfk 106 D2
Cringles C Brad 149 J6
Crinow Pembks 55 K4
Cripplesease Cnwll 2 D4
Cripplestyle Dorset 33 J8
Cripp's Corner E Susx 24 D3
Croachy Highld 251 H6
Croanford Cnwll 10 E8
Crockenhill Kent 52 B5
Crocker End Oxon 49 H2
Crockerhill W Susx 20 F5
Crockernwell Devon 13 H4
Crocker's Ash Herefs 63 G4
Crockerton Wilts 32 E2
Crocketford D & G 185 K8
Crockey Hill C York 151 K6
Crockham Hill Kent 38 C3
Crockhurst Street Kent 39 G4
Crockleford Heath Essex 72 F2
Crock Street Somset 30 D8
Croeserw Neath 42 C3
Croes-goch Pembks 74 D6
Croes-lan Cerdgn 76 C6
Croesor Gwynd 110 B3
Croesyceiliog Carmth 58 D5
Croesyceiliog Torfn 62 C7
Croes-y-mwyalch Torfn 62 C8
Croes-y-pant Mons 62 C6
Croft Leics 100 B4
Croft Lincs 137 J7
Croft Warrtn 130 C1
Croftamie Stirlg 208 E2
Croft Mitchell Cnwll 3 H4
Crofton Cumb 165 J1
Crofton Wakefd 142 B4
Crofton Wilts 47 K6
Croft-on-Tees N York 160 D1
Croftown Highld 261 K3
Crofts Moray 266 F6
Crofts Bank Traffd 139 M8
Crofts of Dipple Moray 267 G4
Crofts of Haddo Abers 256 E4
Crofts of Savoch Abers 269 J4
Crofty Swans 56 F6
Crogen Gwynd 111 K4
Croggan Ag & B 227 K7
Croglin Cumb 166 D1
Croick Highld 262 D2
Cromarty Highld 264 B6
Crombie Fife 210 E2
Cromdale Highld 253 L6
Cromer Herts 69 J2
Cromer Norfk 122 E3
Cromford Derbys 132 F8
Cromhall S Glos 45 K1
Cromhall Common S Glos 45 K1
Cromor W Isls 282 g4
Crompton Fold Oldham 140 E6
Cromwell Notts 134 F7
Cronberry E Ayrs 197 H6
Crondall Hants 36 B1
Cronkbourne IoM 154 e6
Cronk-y-Voddy IoM 154 d5
Cronton Knows 129 L2
Crook Cumb 157 G4
Crook Dur 168 F4
Crookdake Cumb 165 G2
Crooke Wigan 139 H6
Crooked End Gloucs 63 J3
Crookedholm E Ayrs 196 K6
Crooked Soley Wilts 47 L4
Crookes Sheff 132 F2
Crookhall Dur 180 D8
Crookham Nthumb 202 E5

Crookham W Berk 48 D6
Crookham Village Hants 49 J8
Crook Inn Border 199 J7
Crooklands Cumb 157 H6
Crook of Devon P & K 221 J7
Cropper Derbys 115 L4
Cropredy Oxon 83 L6
Cropston Leics 100 C1
Cropthorne Worcs 82 B6
Cropton N York 162 D5
Cropwell Bishop Notts 117 H4
Cropwell Butler Notts 117 J4
Cros W Isls 282 h1
Crosbost W Isls 282 g4
Crosby Cumb 164 C8
Crosby IoM 154 d6
Crosby N Linc 143 M5
Crosby Sefton 138 C8
Crosby Garret Cumb 158 C1
Crosby Ravensworth Cumb 166 E7
Crosby Villa Cumb 164 C3
Croscombe Somset 31 K2
Crosemere Shrops 113 G5
Crosland Edge Kirk 141 H5
Crosland Hill Kirk 141 H5
Cross Somset 44 E8
Crossaig Ag & B 194 C1
Crossapol Ag & B 224 C6
Cross Ash Mons 62 E3
Cross-at-Hand Kent 39 K4
Crossbost W Isls 282 g4
Crossbush W Susx 21 H5
Crosscanonby Cumb 164 E3
Cross Coombe Cnwll 4 B4
Crossdale Street Norfk 122 E4
Cross End Bed 85 L4
Cross End Essex 89 G8
Crossens Sefton 138 D4
Cross Flatts C Brad 149 K2
Crossford Fife 210 E2
Crossford S Lans 198 C3
Crossgate Cnwll 11 L5
Crossgate Lincs 119 H6
Crossgate Staffs 114 E4
Crossgatehall E Loth 211 L1
Crossgates E Ayrs 196 D2
Crossgates Fife 210 F1
Cross Gates Leeds 142 B1
Crossgates N York 163 J6
Crossgates Powys 78 D2
Crossgill Lancs 147 L1
Cross Green Devon 11 M5
Cross Green Leeds 141 M2
Cross Green Staffs 97 K3
Cross Green Suffk 89 G4
Cross Green Suffk 89 H4
Cross Green Suffk 89 K4
Crosshands Carmth 55 L2
Cross Hands Carmth 59 G4
Crosshands E Ayrs 196 F5
Cross Hands Pembks 55 H4
Cross Hill Derbys 116 C2
Crosshill Fife 222 B7
Crosshill S Ayrs 183 J2
Cross Hills N York 149 H6
Crosshouse E Ayrs 196 D2
Cross Houses Shrops 96 C2
Cross Houses Shrops 96 F3
Cross in Hand E Susx 23 J1
Cross Inn Cerdgn 76 G2
Cross Inn Cerdgn 77 G3
Cross Inn Pembks 55 G1
Cross Inn Rhondd 43 G2
Cross Keys Ag & B 208 B2
Crosskeys Caerph 43 K4
Cross Keys Wilts 46 C5
Crosskirk Highld 279 H2
Crosslands Cumb 156 F3
Cross Lane IoW 19 H5
Cross Lane Head Shrops 97 G4
Cross Lanes Cnwll 3 H6
Cross Lanes Cnwll 4 C4
Cross Lanes N York 151 J3
Crosslanes Shrops 112 E7
Cross Lanes Wrexhm 112 E2
Crosslee Rens 208 C6
Crossley Kirk 141 K3
Crossmichael D & G 175 J2
Cross Oak Powys 61 J3
Cross of Jackston Abers 256 D5
Cross o' th' hands Derbys 115 M3
Crosspost W Susx 37 L6
Crossroads Abers 244 C3
Crossroads Abers 245 G5
Cross Roads C Brad 149 J8
Cross Street Suffk 106 D8
Crosston Angus 234 E4
Cross Town Ches E 130 E5
Crossway Mons 62 F4
Crossway Powys 78 E3

Crossway Green Mons 63 G8
Crossway Green Worcs 81 J2
Crossways Dorset 16 E5
Crosswell Pembks 75 J5
Crosthwaite Cumb 156 F4
Croston Lancs 138 F4
Crostwick Norfk 122 E8
Crostwight Norfk 123 G5
Crouch Kent 38 F2
Crouch Kent 40 D4
Crouch End Gt Lon 51 J1
Croucheston Wilts 33 J6
Crouch Hill Dorset 32 B8
Crough House Green Kent 38 C4
Croughton Nhants 84 A8
Crovie Abers 268 E3
Crow Hants 18 B3
Crowan Cnwll 3 G4
Crowborough E Susx 38 D7
Crowborough Warren E Susx 38 D7
Crowcombe Somset 29 L3
Crowdecote Derbys 132 B6
Crowden Derbys 141 G7
Crowden Devon 12 C3
Crowdhill Hants 35 G6
Crowdleham Kent 52 C7
Crow Edge Barns 141 J6
Crowell Oxon 67 H7
Crow End Cambs 87 G4
Crowfield Nhants 84 B7
Crowfield Suffk 90 D4
Crowfield Green Suffk 90 D4
Crowgate Street Norfk 123 G7
Crow Green Essex 70 E7
Crowhill E Loth 213 G4
Crow Hill Herefs 63 J2
Crowhole Derbys 133 G4
Crowhurst E Susx 24 D5
Crowhurst Surrey 38 B4
Crowhurst Lane End Surrey 38 B4
Crowland Lincs 102 E2
Crowland Suffk 89 K1
Crowlas Cnwll 2 E4
Crowle N Linc 143 K5
Crowle Worcs 81 L4
Crowle Green Worcs 81 L4
Crowmarsh Gifford Oxon 48 F1
Crown Corner Suffk 90 F1
Crownhill C Plym 6 C5
Crownpits Surrey 36 E2
Crownthorpe Norfk 106 B3
Crowntown Cnwll 3 G5
Crows-an-Wra Cnwll 2 B7
Crow's Green Essex 71 G2
Crowshill Norfk 105 J2
Crow's Nest Cnwll 6 B1
Crowsnest Shrops 95 J3
Crowthorne Wokham 49 K6
Crowton Ches W 130 B5
Croxall Staffs 99 G1
Croxby Lincs 144 F8
Croxdale Dur 169 H3
Croxden Staffs 115 H4
Croxley Green Herts 68 D7
Croxteth Lpool 138 E8
Croxton Cambs 86 E3
Croxton N Linc 144 E5
Croxton Norfk 105 H6
Croxton Norfk 121 L5
Croxton Staffs 114 B5
Croxtonbank Staffs 114 B5
Croxton Green Ches E 113 J1
Croxton Kerrial Leics 117 L5
Croy Highld 252 E2
Croy N Lans 209 J4
Croyde Devon 27 H3
Croyde Bay Devon 27 G3
Croydon Cambs 87 G5
Croydon Gt Lon 51 J6
Crubenmore Highld 241 J5
Cruckmeole Shrops 95 K2
Cruckton Shrops 95 K1
Cruden Bay Abers 257 K4
Crudgington Wrekin 113 K7
Crudie Abers 268 E5
Crudwell Wilts 64 D8
Cruft Devon 12 C3
Crûg Powys 79 H1
Crugmeer Cnwll 10 C7
Crugybar Carmth 77 J7
Crug-y-byddar Powys 94 E7
Crumlin Caerph 43 K2
Crumplehorn Cnwll 5 L4
Crumpsall Manch 140 C7
Crundale Kent 40 E5
Crundale Pembks 54 F3
Crunwere Pembks 55 L5
Cruwys Morchard Devon 28 F8
Crux Easton Hants 48 B7
Cruxton Dorset 16 B3

Crwbin Carmth 58 E6
Cryers Hill Bucks 67 L7
Crymych Pembks 75 L5
Crynant Neath 60 B6
Crystal Palace Gt Lon 51 J5
Cuaig Highld 260 A8
Cuan Ag & B 215 L2
Cubbington Warwks 83 H2
Cubert Cnwll 4 C3
Cubley Barns 141 K7
Cublington Bucks 67 K3
Cublington Herefs 79 M7
Cuckfield W Susx 22 D2
Cucklington Somset 32 C5
Cuckney Notts 133 L5
Cuckoo Bridge Lincs 119 G7
Cuckoo's Corner Hants 35 M3
Cuckoo's Nest Ches W 129 J7
Cuddesdon Oxon 66 F6
Cuddington Bucks 67 H5
Cuddington Ches W 130 B5
Cuddington Heath Ches W 113 G2
Cuddy Hill Lancs 147 J8
Cudham Gt Lon 51 L7
Cudliptown Devon 12 C6
Cudnell BCP 17 L3
Cudworth Barns 142 B6
Cudworth Somset 30 F8
Cuerdley Cross Warrtn 130 A2
Cufaude Hants 49 G7
Cuffley Herts 69 J6
Cuil Highld 228 F4
Culbokie Highld 263 H7
Culbone Somset 28 E1
Culburnie Highld 250 E3
Culcabock Highld 251 J3
Culcharry Highld 253 G2
Culcheth Warrtn 130 C1
Culdrain Abers 255 K5
Culduie Highld 248 A4
Culford Suffk 89 G1
Culgaith Cumb 166 E5
Culham Oxon 66 D8
Culkein Highld 270 D2
Culkein Drumbeg Highld 270 F1
Culkerton Gloucs 64 D7
Cullen Moray 267 K3
Cullercoats N Tyne 181 J4
Cullerlie Abers 245 G3
Cullicudden Highld 263 H7
Cullingworth C Brad 149 J8
Cuillin Hills Highld 247 G4
Cullipool Ag & B 215 L2
Cullivoe Shet 281 e2
Culloden Highld 252 D3
Cullompton Devon 14 B1
Cullompton Services Devon 14 B1
Culm Davy Devon 29 L7
Culmington Shrops 96 B7
Culmstock Devon 29 K8
Culnacraig Highld 270 E7
Culnaightrie D & G 175 J5
Culnaknock Highld 259 J4
Culpho Suffk 90 F5
Culrain Highld 263 G1
Culross Fife 210 C2
Culroy S Ayrs 196 C8
Culsalmond Abers 256 B5
Culscadden D & G 174 D5
Culshabbin D & G 173 H4
Culswick Shet 281 c6
Cultercullen Abers 257 G7
Cults C Aber 245 K3
Culverstone Green Kent 52 D6
Culverthorpe Lincs 118 D3
Culworth Nhants 84 A6
Cumbernauld N Lans 209 K4
Cumbernauld Village N Lans 209 K4
Cumberworth Lincs 137 J5
Cumdivock Cumb 165 K1
Cuminestown Abers 268 E6
Cumledge Border 202 B2
Cummersdale Cumb 177 L8
Cummertrees D & G 176 F5
Cummingston Moray 266 C2
Cumnock E Ayrs 197 H7
Cumnor Oxon 66 C6
Cumrew Cumb 178 D8
Cumrue D & G 176 E2
Cumwhinton Cumb 178 B8
Cumwhitton Cumb 178 C8
Cundall N York 150 F1
Cunninghamhead N Ayrs 196 D3
Cunningsburgh Shet 281 e7
Cupar Fife 222 F4
Cupar Muir Fife 222 F4
Curbar Derbys 132 E5
Curbridge Hants 19 J1
Curbridge Oxon 65 M5
Curdridge Hants 35 H8

Curdworth Warwks 98 F5
Curland Somset 30 C7
Curridge W Berk 48 C4
Currie C Edin 211 G5
Curry Mallet Somset 30 E6
Curry Rivel Somset 30 F6
Curteis Corner Kent 39 L5
Curtisden Green Kent 39 J5
Curtisknowle Devon 7 L4
Cury Cnwll 3 H6
Cushnie Abers 244 C1
Cushuish Somset 30 B5
Cusop Herefs 79 J7
Cusworth Donc 142 E7
Cutcloy D & G 174 C7
Cutcombe Somset 29 G3
Cutgate Rochdl 140 C5
Cuthill Highld 263 K2
Cutiau Gwynd 110 B8
Cutler's Green Essex 70 E1
Cutmadoc Cnwll 5 J2
Cutmere Cnwll 6 C3
Cutnall Green Worcs 81 K2
Cutsdean Gloucs 65 G1
Cutthorpe Derbys 133 G5
Cuttivett Cnwll 6 D2
Cuxham Oxon 67 G8
Cuxton Medway 52 F5
Cuxwold Lincs 144 F7
Cwm Blae G 61 J6
Cwm Denbgs 128 C4
Cwmafan Neath 57 L6
Cwmaman Rhondd 60 F7
Cwmann Carmth 77 G6
Cwmavon Torfn 62 B6
Cwmbach Carmth 56 E4
Cwmbach Carmth 75 M7
Cwmbâch Powys 79 G7
Cwmbach Rhondd 60 F6
Cwmbach Llechrhyd Powys 78 E4
Cwmbelan Powys 93 J2
Cwmbran Torfn 62 C8
Cwmbrwyno Cerdgn 92 F7
Cwm Capel Carmth 56 E4
Cwmcarn Caerph 43 K3
Cwmcarvan Mons 62 F5
Cwm-celyn Blae G 61 K5
Cwm-Cewydd Gwynd 93 J1
Cwm-cou Cerdgn 76 B4
Cwm Crawnon Powys 61 J3
Cwmdare Rhondd 60 F6
Cwmdu Carmth 59 H3
Cwmdu Powys 61 J2
Cwmdu Swans 57 H6
Cwmduad Carmth 58 C3
Cwm Dulais Swans 57 H4
Cwmdwr Carmth 59 K2
Cwmfelin Brdgnd 42 C4
Cwmfelin Myr Td 61 H6
Cwmfelin Boeth Carmth 55 L3
Cwmfelinfach Caerph 43 J3
Cwmfelin Mynach Carmth 75 L7
Cwmffrwd Carmth 58 D5
Cwmgiedd Powys 59 L4
Cwmgorse Carmth 57 K3
Cwm Gwaun Pembks 75 H5
Cwmgwili Carmth 57 G3
Cwmgwrach Neath 60 C4
Cwmhiraeth Carmth 76 C7
Cwmifor Carmth 59 J4
Cwm Irfon Powys 78 A5
Cwmisfael Carmth 58 F7
Cwm Llinau Powys 93 J2
Cwmllynfell Neath 59 K6
Cwmmawr Carmth 58 F6
Cwm Morgan Carmth 58 B2
Cwmparc Rhondd 42 E3
Cwmpengraig Carmth 58 C2
Cwm Penmachno Conwy 110 E2
Cwmpennar Rhondd 61 G2
Cwmrhos Powys 61 J2
Cwmrhydyceirw Swans 57 J5
Cwmsychbant Cerdgn 76 E6
Cwmtillery Blae G 61 K6
Cwm-twrch Isaf Powys 57 L3
Cwm-twrch Uchaf Powys 59 L6
Cwm-y-glo Carmth 59 G6
Cwm-y-glo Gwynd 125 K7
Cwmyoy Mons 62 C3
Cwmystwyth Cerdgn 93 G8
Cwrt Gwynd 92 E3
Cwrtnewydd Cerdgn 76 E6
Cwrt-y-gollen Powys 61 K4
Cyffylliog Denbgs 128 C8
Cyfronydd Powys 94 E2
Cylibebyll Neath 57 K4
Cymau Flints 129 G8
Cymmer Neath 42 C3
Cymmer Rhondd 42 F3
Cyncoed Cardif 43 K5

Cynghordy Carmth 77 M7
Cynheidre Carmth 56 E5
Cynonville Neath 42 C3
Cynwyd Denbgs 111 K3
Cynwyl Elfed Carmth 58 C3

D

Daccombe Devon 8 D1
Dacre Cumb 166 B5
Dacre N York 150 B4
Dacre Banks N York 150 B3
Daddry Shield Dur 167 K3
Dadford Bucks 84 C7
Dadlington Leics 99 J3
Dafen Carmth 56 F4
Daffy Green Norfk 105 J2
Dagenham Gt Lon 52 B2
Daglingworth Gloucs 64 D6
Dagnall Bucks 68 C4
Dagworth Suffk 89 L3
Dail bho Dheas W Isls 282 g1
Dailly S Ayrs 183 H3
Dainton Devon 8 C2
Dairsie Fife 223 G4
Daisy Hill Bolton 139 K6
Daisy Hill Leeds 141 L2
Dalabrog W Isls 283 b11
Dalavich Ag & B 216 F5
Dalbeattie D & G 175 L3
Dalbury Derbys 115 M5
Dalby IoM 154 b6
Dalby Lincs 137 H5
Dalby N York 151 K2
Dalcapon P & K 232 E4
Dalchalm Highld 274 B6
Dalchreichart Highld 240 A1
Dalchruin P & K 220 C4
Dalcrue P & K 221 J2
Dalderby Lincs 136 E6
Dalditch Devon 14 B6
Dale Cumb 166 D2
Dale Pembks 54 C5
Dale Abbey Derbys 116 D4
Dale Bottom Cumb 165 J6
Dale End Derbys 132 D7
Dale End N York 149 G6
Dale Hill E Susx 39 H7
Dalehouse N York 171 H7
Dalelia Highld 237 L6
Dalgarven N Ayrs 196 B2
Dalgety Bay Fife 211 G2
Dalgig E Ayrs 197 G8
Dalginross P & K 220 D3
Dalguise P & K 232 E6
Dalhalvaig Highld 278 F5
Dalham Suffk 88 E3
Daliburgh W Isls 283 b11
Dalkeith Mdloth 211 K5
Dallas Moray 266 C5
Dallinghoo Suffk 91 G4
Dallington E Susx 24 B3
Dallington Nhants 84 E3
Dallow N York 150 B2
Dalmally Ag & B 217 K2
Dalmary Stirlg 219 H8
Dalmellington E Ayrs 184 D2
Dalmeny C Edin 210 F3
Dalmore Highld 263 H6
Dalmuir W Duns 208 E5
Dalnabreck Highld 237 K6
Dalnacardoch P & K 231 K1
Dalnahaitnach Highld 252 F7
Dalnaspidal P & K 231 J1
Dalnawillan Lodge Highld 279 H8
Dalness Highld 229 K5
Dalqueich P & K 221 K6
Dalquhairn S Ayrs 183 J4
Dalreavoch Highld 273 H6
Dalry N Ayrs 196 B1
Dalrymple E Ayrs 196 D8
Dalserf S Lans 198 C3
Dalsmeran Ag & B 192 D5
Dalston Cumb 165 L1
Dalston Gt Lon 51 J2
Dalswinton D & G 176 B2
Dalton Cumb 157 H7
Dalton D & G 176 F4
Dalton Lancs 139 G6
Dalton N York 159 K1
Dalton N York 160 F7
Dalton Nthumb 180 D4
Dalton Rothm 133 J1
Dalton-in-Furness Cumb 156 B7
Dalton-le-Dale Dur 169 L1
Dalton Magna Rothm 133 J1
Dalton-on-Tees N York 160 D1
Dalton Parva Rothm 133 J1

Dalton Piercy Hartpl 170 B4
Dalveich Stirlg 219 K2
Dalwhinnie Highld 241 H6
Dalwood Devon 14 F3
Damask Green Herts 69 H1
Damerham Hants 33 J7
Damgate Norfk 107 H2
Dam Green Norfk 105 L6
Damnaglaur D & G 172 E7
Danaway Kent 53 J6
Danbury Essex 71 J6
Danby N York 162 C1
Danby Bottom N York 162 B2
Danby Wiske N York 160 E3
Dandaleith Moray 254 F3
Danderhall Mdloth 211 J5
Danebridge Ches E 131 J6
Dane End Herts 69 J3
Danegate E Susx 38 E6
Danehill E Susx 22 F2
Dane Hills C Leic 100 C3
Danemoor Green Norfk 105 L2
Danesford Shrops 97 G5
Danesmoor Derbys 133 H7
Dane Street Kent 40 D5
Daniel's Water Kent 40 C7
Danshillock Abers 268 C5
Danskine E Loth 212 C5
Danthorpe E R Yk 145 H1
Danzey Green Warwks 82 D2
Dapple Heath Staffs 115 G6
Darby Green Hants 49 K7
Darcy Lever Bolton 139 L6
Dardy Powys 61 K3
Darenth Kent 52 C4
Daresbury Halton 130 B3
Darfield Barns 142 C6
Darfoulds Notts 133 L4
Dargate Kent 40 E3
Dargavel Rens 208 D5
Darite Cnwll 6 B1
Darland Medway 53 G6
Darland Wrexhm 129 J8
Darlaston Wsall 98 B4
Darlaston Green Wsall 98 B4
Darley N York 150 B4
Darley Abbey C Derb 116 B4
Darley Bridge Derbys 132 E7
Darley Dale Derbys 132 E7
Darley Green Solhll 98 F8
Darleyhall Herts 68 F3
Darley Head N York 150 B4
Darlingscott Warwks 82 F6
Darlington Darltn 169 H7
Darliston Shrops 113 J5
Darlton Notts 134 F5
Darnford Staffs 98 E2
Darnick Border 201 H6
Darowen Powys 93 H3
Darra Abers 268 D6
Darracott Devon 26 D7
Darracott Devon 27 H3
Darras Hall Nthumb 180 E5
Darrington Wakefd 142 D4
Darsham Suffk 91 K1
Darshill Somset 31 K2
Dartford Kent 52 B4
Dartford Crossing Kent 52 C4
Dartington Devon 8 B2
Dartmeet Devon 12 F7
Dartmoor National Park Devon 13 G6
Dartmouth Devon 8 C4
Darton Barns 141 M5
Darvel E Ayrs 197 H3
Darwell Hole E Susx 24 C3
Darwen Bl w D 139 K3
Datchet W & M 50 C3
Datchworth Herts 69 H3
Datchworth Green Herts 69 H3
Daubhill Bolton 139 L6
Daugh of Kinermony Moray 254 E3
Dauntsey Wilts 46 E3
Dava Highld 253 J4
Davenham Ches W 130 C5
Davenport Stockp 131 H2
Davenport Green Ches E 131 G4
Davenport Green Traffd 130 F2
Daventry Nhants 84 B3
Davidson's Mains C Edin 211 H4
Davidstow Cnwll 11 G5
David Street Kent 52 E6
Davington D & G 187 K5
Davington Kent 40 D3
Daviot Abers 256 D6
Daviot Highld 252 D4
Daviot House Highld 252 D4
Davis's Town E Susx 23 J4
Davoch of Grange Moray 267 K6
Davyhulme Traffd 139 M8
Daw End Wsall 98 C3

Dawesgreen Surrey 37 K2
Dawley Wrekin 96 F2
Dawlish Devon 13 M7
Dawlish Warren Devon 14 A7
Dawn Conwy 127 G5
Daws Green Somset 30 B6
Daws Heath Essex 53 H1
Daw's House Cnwll 11 K6
Dawsmere Lincs 120 A5
Daybrook Notts 116 F3
Day Green Ches E 130 F8
Dayhills Staffs 114 F5
Dayhouse Bank Worcs 98 B7
Daylesford Gloucs 65 K2
Ddol Flints 128 D5
Ddol-Cownwy Powys 111 K8
Deal Kent 41 L5
Dean Cumb 164 E5
Dean Devon 7 L2
Dean Devon 27 L2
Dean Devon 28 C1
Dean Dorset 33 G7
Dean Hants 34 F4
Dean Hants 35 H7
Dean Lancs 140 C3
Dean Oxon 65 M3
Dean Somset 31 L2
Dean Bottom Kent 52 C5
Deanburnhaugh Border 188 C4
Deancombe Devon 7 L2
Dean Court Oxon 66 C6
Deane Bolton 139 K6
Deane Hants 35 H1
Dean End Dorset 33 G7
Dean Head Barns 141 L7
Deanhead Kirk 141 G4
Deanland Dorset 33 G7
Deanlane End W Susx 20 B4
Dean Prior Devon 7 L2
Deanraw Nthumb 179 J6
Dean Row Ches E 131 G3
Deans W Loth 210 D5
Deanscales Cumb 164 E5
Deanshanger Nhants 84 E7
Deanshaugh Moray 267 G6
Deanston Stirlg 220 C6
Dean Street Kent 39 J3
Dearham Cumb 164 E3
Dearnley Rochdl 140 D4
Debach Suffk 90 F4
Debden Essex 70 C7
Debden Essex 87 L8
Debden Green Essex 70 C7
Debenham Suffk 90 E3
Deblin's Green Worcs 81 J5
Dechmont W Loth 210 D5
Deddington Oxon 66 C1
Dedham Essex 90 C8
Dedham Heath Essex 72 F1
Dedworth W & M 50 B4
Deene Nhants 101 L5
Deenethorpe Nhants 101 L5
Deepcar Sheff 141 L8
Deepcut Surrey 49 L7
Deepdale Cumb 158 C5
Deepdale N York 158 F6
Deeping Gate C Pete 102 C2
Deeping St James Lincs 102 D2
Deeping St Nicholas Lincs 119 H8
Deerhurst Gloucs 64 C1
Deerhurst Walton Gloucs 64 C2
Deerton Street Kent 40 C3
Defford Worcs 81 L6
Defynnog Powys 60 D2
Deganwy Conwy 126 F4
Degnish Ag & B 216 B5
Deighton C York 151 K7
Deighton N York 160 E2
Deiniolen Gwynd 125 K7
Delabole Cnwll 10 F6
Delamere Ches W 130 A6
Delamere Park Ches W 130 B5
Delfrigs Abers 257 H7
Delley Devon 27 L6
Delliefure Highld 253 L5
Dell Quay W Susx 20 D6
Delly End Oxon 65 M4
Delnabo Moray 254 C8
Delny Highld 263 K5
Delph Oldham 140 E6
Delves Dur 168 E1
Delvin End Essex 88 F4
Dembleby Lincs 118 D4
Demelza Cnwll 5 G2
Denaby Donc 142 D7
Denaby Main Donc 142 D7
Denbies Surrey 37 H1
Denbigh Denbgs 128 C6
Denbrae Fife 222 F3
Denbury Devon 8 B1

Denby Derbys 116 C2
Denby Bottles Derbys 116 C2
Denby Dale Kirk 141 K6
Denchworth Oxon 48 A1
Dendron Cumb 146 E2
Denel End C Beds 85 K8
Denfield P & K 221 G4
Denford Nhants 101 L8
Dengie Essex 72 E6
Denham Bucks 50 D2
Denham Suffk 88 E3
Denham Suffk 106 D8
Denham End Suffk 88 F3
Denham Green Bucks 50 D1
Denham Green Suffk 106 D8
Denhead Abers 269 J5
Denhead Fife 223 H4
Denhead of Gray C Dund 222 F1
Denholm Border 189 G3
Denholme C Brad 141 G1
Denholme Clough C Brad 141 G1
Denio Gwynd 108 F4
Denmead Hants 19 L1
Denmore C Aber 245 L1
Denne Park W Susx 37 J5
Dennington Suffk 91 G2
Denny Falk 209 L3
Dennyloanhead Falk 209 L3
Den of Lindores Fife 222 D4
Denshaw Oldham 140 E5
Denside of Durris Abers 245 H4
Densole Kent 41 G7
Denston Suffk 88 F5
Denstone Staffs 115 H3
Denstroude Kent 40 E3
Dent Cumb 158 B5
Denton Cambs 102 C5
Denton Darltn 169 G7
Denton E Susx 23 G6
Denton Kent 41 G6
Denton Kent 52 E4
Denton Lincs 117 M5
Denton N York 149 L6
Denton Nhants 85 G4
Denton Norfk 106 F5
Denton Oxon 66 E6
Denton Tamesd 131 H1
Denver Norfk 104 C3
Denwick Nthumb 191 J3
Deopham Norfk 105 L3
Deopham Green Norfk 105 L4
Depden Suffk 88 F4
Depden Green Suffk 88 F4
Deptford Gt Lon 51 K3
Deptford Wilts 33 H3
Derby C Derb 116 B4
Derby Devon 27 K4
Derbyhaven IoM 154 c8
Derculich P & K 232 C5
Dereham Norfk 105 K1
Deri Caerph 61 K6
Derril Devon 11 K2
Derringstone Kent 41 G5
Derrington Staffs 114 D7
Derriton Devon 11 L2
Derry Hill Wilts 46 D5
Derrythorpe N Linc 143 L6
Dersingham Norfk 120 F5
Dervaig Ag & B 226 G2
Derwen Denbgs 111 L2
Derwenlas Powys 92 F4
Derwent Valley Mills Derbys 132 F8
Derwent Water Cumb 165 J6
Derwydd Carmth 59 H5
Desborough Nhants 101 H6
Desford Leics 100 B3
Detchant Nthumb 203 H6
Detling Kent 53 G7
Deuxhill Shrops 96 F6
Devauden Mons 62 F7
Devil's Bridge Cerdgn 92 F4
Devitts Green Warwks 99 H5
Devizes Wilts 46 E6
Devonport C Plym 6 C6
Devonside Clacks 221 G7
Devoran Cnwll 3 K3
Devoran & Perran Cnwll 3 K3
Dewarton Mdloth 211 L6
Dewlish Dorset 16 F3
Dewsbury Kirk 141 K3
Dewsbury Moor Kirk 141 K3
Deytheur Powys 112 F2
Dial N Som 45 G5
Dial Green W Susx 36 D5
Dial Post W Susx 21 K3
Dibberford Dorset 15 K3
Dibden Hants 18 F2
Dibden Purlieu Hants 18 F2
Dickens Heath Solhll 98 E8
Dickleburgh Norfk 106 D7

Didbrook Gloucs 64 F1
Didcot Oxon 48 D1
Diddington Cambs 86 D2
Diddlebury Shrops 96 F1
Didley Herefs 62 F1
Didling W Susx 20 B3
Didmarton Gloucs 46 B2
Didsbury Manch 131 G4
Didworthy Devon 7 H1
Digby Lincs 118 D1
Digg Highld 259 H2
Diggle Oldham 140 F6
Digmoor Lancs 139 G6
Digswell Herts 69 H4
Digswell Water Herts 69 H4
Dihewyd Cerdgn 76 A2
Dilham Norfk 123 G6
Dilhorne Staffs 114 F1
Dill Hall Lancs 139 M2
Dillington Cambs 86 D2
Dilston Nthumb 180 A6
Dilton Wilts 32 E1
Dilton Marsh Wilts 32 D1
Dilwyn Herefs 80 L4
Dimple Bolton 139 L4
Dimple Derbys 132 F7
Dinas Carmth 58 A3
Dinas Cnwll 10 D4
Dinas Gwynd 108 D4
Dinas Gwynd 125 M2
Dinas Rhondd 42 F3
Dinas Cross Pembks 75 J3
Dinas Dinlle Gwynd 125 H8
Dinas-Mawddwy Gwynd 111 G8
Dinas Powys V Glam 43 J7
Dinder Somset 31 J4
Dinedor Herefs 80 C7
Dingestow Mons 62 F5
Dingle Lpool 129 J4
Dingleden Kent 39 K7
Dingley Nhants 101 K6
Dingwall Highld 262 F8
Dinmael Conwy 111 J3
Dinnet Abers 244 C4
Dinnington N u Ty 180 F5
Dinnington Rothm 133 K3
Dinnington Somset 30 F8
Dinorwig Gwynd 125 L7
Dinorwig Slate Landscape Gwynd 125 L7
Dinton Bucks 67 J5
Dinton Wilts 33 H4
Dinwoodie D & G 187 H8
Dinworthy Devon 26 E7
Dipford Somset 30 B6
Dipley Hants 49 H7
Dippen Ag & B 194 B3
Dippenhall Surrey 36 B2
Dippermill Devon 12 B3
Dippertown Devon 12 B5
Dippin N Ayrs 195 G6
Dipple Moray 267 G4
Dipple S Ayrs 182 F2
Diptford Devon 7 L3
Dipton Dur 180 E8
Diptonmill Nthumb 179 L6
Dirleton E Loth 212 B2
Dirt Pot Nthumb 167 K2
Discoed Powys 79 K2
Diseworth Leics 116 D6
Dishforth N York 160 E8
Disley Ches E 131 J3
Diss Norfk 106 C7
Disserth Powys 78 E4
Distington Cumb 164 D6
Ditchampton Wilts 33 J4
Ditcheat Somset 31 K4
Ditchingham Norfk 107 G5
Ditchling E Susx 22 F4
Ditherington Shrops 113 H8
Ditteridge Wilts 46 B5
Dittisham Devon 8 C4
Ditton Kent 52 F7
Ditton Green Cambs 88 D4
Ditton Priors Shrops 96 E5
Dixton Gloucs 64 C8
Dixton Mons 63 G4
Dizzard Cnwll 11 H3
Dobcross Oldham 140 F6
Dobwalls Cnwll 5 L2
Doccombe Devon 13 H5
Dochgarroch Highld 251 H3
Dockenfield Surrey 36 B3
Docker Lancs 157 J7
Docking Norfk 121 G4
Docklow Herefs 80 D4
Dockray Cumb 165 J1
Dockray Cumb 165 L6
Doddinghurst Essex 70 E7

Place	Region	Page	Grid
Doddington	Cambs	103	H5
Doddington	Kent	40	B4
Doddington	Lincs	135	H5
Doddington	Nthumb	202	F6
Doddington	Shrops	96	E8
Doddiscombsleigh	Devon	13	K5
Dodd's Green	Ches E	113	K3
Doddshill	Norfk	120	F5
Doddy Cross	Cnwll	6	C2
Dodford	Nhants	84	B3
Dodford	Worcs	97	L8
Dodington	S Glos	45	L3
Dodington	Somset	30	A3
Dodleston	Ches W	129	J7
Dodscott	Devon	27	K7
Dodside	E Rens	208	E8
Dod's Leigh	Staffs	115	G4
Dodworth	Barns	141	M6
Dodworth Bottom	Barns	141	M7
Dodworth Green	Barns	141	M6
Doe Bank	Birm	98	C4
Doe Lea	Derbys	133	J6
Dogdyke	Lincs	136	D8
Dogley Lane	Kirk	141	J5
Dogmersfield	Hants	49	J8
Dogridge	Wilts	47	G2
Dogsthorpe	C Pete	102	D3
Dog Village	Devon	14	A3
Dolanog	Powys	94	C1
Dolau	Powys	79	G2
Dolaucothi	Carmth	77	J7
Dolbenmaen	Gwynd	109	J3
Doley	Staffs	114	A5
Dolfach	Powys	93	K3
Dol-fôr	Powys	93	H2
Dolfor	Powys	94	D6
Dolgarrog	Conwy	126	F6
Dolgellau	Gwynd	110	D7
Dolgoch	Gwynd	92	E3
Dol-gran	Carmth	58	D2
Doll	Highld	273	L7
Dollar	Clacks	221	G7
Dollarfield	Clacks	221	G7
Dolley Green	Powys	79	K2
Dollwen	Cerdgn	92	F2
Dolphin	Flints	128	E5
Dolphinholme	Lancs	147	K5
Dolphinton	S Lans	199	J4
Dolton	Devon	27	K8
Dolwen	Conwy	127	H5
Dolwyddelan	Conwy	110	D1
Dolybont	Cerdgn	92	D5
Dolyhir	Powys	79	J4
Domgay	Powys	112	D7
Donaldson's Lodge	Nthumb	202	D5
Doncaster	Donc	142	F7
Doncaster Carr	Donc	142	F7
Doncaster North Services	Donc	143	G5
Doncaster Sheffield Airport	Donc	143	G8
Donhead St Andrew	Wilts	32	F6
Donhead St Mary	Wilts	32	F6
Donibristle	Fife	211	J1
Doniford	Somset	29	K2
Donington	Lincs	119	H4
Donington on Bain	Lincs	136	D3
Donington Park Services	Leics	116	D6
Donington Southing	Lincs	119	G5
Donisthorpe	Leics	99	J1
Donkey Street	Kent	25	L1
Donkey Town	Surrey	50	B6
Donnington	Gloucs	65	J2
Donnington	Herefs	81	G8
Donnington	Shrops	96	E2
Donnington	W Berk	48	C5
Donnington	W Susx	20	D6
Donnington	Wrekin	113	M8
Donnington Wood	Wrekin	97	G2
Donyatt	Somset	30	E8
Doomsday Green	W Susx	37	J5
Doonfoot	S Ayrs	196	C7
Dora's Green	Hants	36	B1
Dorback Lodge	Highld	253	L8
Dorchester	Dorset	16	D4
Dorchester-on-Thames	Oxon	66	E8
Dordon	Warwks	99	H3
Dore	Sheff	132	F3
Dores	Highld	251	G5
Dorking	Surrey	37	J1
Dorking Tye	Suffk	89	J4
Dormansland	Surrey	38	B5
Dormans Park	Surrey	38	B5
Dormington	Herefs	80	D7
Dormston	Worcs	82	A4
Dorn	Gloucs	82	F8
Dorney	Bucks	50	B3
Dorney Reach	Bucks	50	A3
Dornie	Highld	248	D6
Dornoch	Highld	264	B2
Dornock	D & G	177	H5
Dorrery	Highld	279	J5
Dorridge	Solhll	98	F8
Dorrington	Lincs	118	E1
Dorrington	Shrops	96	B3
Dorrington	Shrops	114	A3
Dorsington	Warwks	82	D5
Dorstone	Herefs	79	K7
Dorton	Bucks	67	G4
Dosthill	Staffs	99	G3
Dothan	IoA	124	F5
Dottery	Dorset	15	K4
Doublebois	Cnwll	5	L2
Doughton	Gloucs	46	C1
Douglas	IoM	154	e6
Douglas	S Lans	198	D7
Douglas and Angus	C Dund	234	C8
Douglas Pier	Ag & B	217	K7
Douglastown	Angus	234	B6
Douglas Water	S Lans	198	D6
Douglas West	S Lans	198	D7
Doulting	Somset	31	L2
Dounby	Ork	275	b4
Doune	Highld	272	B7
Doune	Stirlg	220	C6
Dounepark	S Ayrs	182	F3
Dounie	Highld	263	G2
Dousland	Devon	7	G1
Dovaston	Shrops	112	E7
Dove Dale	Derbys	115	J1
Dove Green	Notts	116	D1
Dove Holes	Derbys	131	L4
Dovenby	Cumb	164	E4
Dover	Kent	41	K7
Dover	Wigan	139	J7
Dovercourt	Essex	73	K1
Doverdale	Worcs	81	K2
Doveridge	Derbys	115	J5
Doversgreen	Surrey	37	L1
Dowally	P & K	232	F5
Dowbridge	Lancs	138	E2
Dowdeswell	Gloucs	64	E3
Dowlais	Myr Td	61	G5
Dowland	Devon	12	D1
Dowlish Ford	Somset	30	E8
Dowlish Wake	Somset	30	E8
Down Ampney	Gloucs	65	G4
Downderry	Cnwll	6	C4
Downe	Gt Lon	51	L6
Downend	Gloucs	64	B7
Downend	IoW	19	J6
Downend	S Glos	45	K3
Downend	W Berk	48	C4
Downfield	C Dund	234	B8
Downgate	Cnwll	11	K8
Downgate	Cnwll	11	L8
Downham	Essex	71	H7
Downham	Gt Lon	51	K4
Downham	Lancs	148	D1
Downham Market	Norfk	104	C3
Down Hatherley	Gloucs	64	C3
Downhead	Somset	31	J6
Downhead	Somset	32	A2
Downhill	Cnwll	4	D1
Downhill	P & K	221	K1
Downholland Cross	Lancs	138	D6
Downholme	N York	159	K3
Downicarey	Devon	11	M4
Downies	Abers	245	K4
Downing	Flints	128	D4
Downley	Bucks	67	K8
Down St Mary	Devon	13	H2
Downside	Somset	31	K2
Downside	Somset	31	L1
Downside	Surrey	50	E7
Down Thomas	Devon	6	F5
Downton	Hants	18	D5
Downton	Wilts	33	L6
Dowsby	Lincs	118	E5
Dowsdale	Lincs	102	F2
Doxey	Staffs	114	D6
Doxford	Nthumb	191	H2
Doynton	S Glos	45	L4
Draethen	Caerph	43	K4
Draffan	S Lans	198	C4
Dragonby	N Linc	143	M5
Dragons Green	W Susx	37	H6
Drakeholes	Notts	134	D2
Drakelow	Worcs	97	J7
Drakemyre	N Ayrs	196	B1
Drakes Broughton	Worcs	81	L5
Drakewalls	Cnwll	12	B8
Draughton	N York	149	J5
Draughton	Nhants	101	G8
Drax	N York	143	H3
Drax Hales	N York	143	H3
Draycote	Warwks	83	K1
Draycot Foliat	Swindn	47	J3
Draycott	Derbys	116	D5
Draycott	Gloucs	82	E8
Draycott	Shrops	97	H5
Draycott	Somset	31	G1
Draycott	Somset	31	J6
Draycott	Worcs	81	K5
Draycott in the Clay	Staffs	115	J6
Draycott in the Moors	Staffs	114	F3
Drayford	Devon	28	D8
Drayton	C Port	19	L3
Drayton	Leics	101	H5
Drayton	Lincs	119	H4
Drayton	Norfk	106	D1
Drayton	Oxon	66	C6
Drayton	Oxon	83	K7
Drayton	Somset	30	F6
Drayton	Somset	31	G7
Drayton	Worcs	97	K8
Drayton Bassett	Staffs	99	G3
Drayton Beauchamp	Bucks	67	L5
Drayton Parslow	Bucks	67	K2
Drayton St Leonard	Oxon	66	E7
Drebley	N York	149	J4
Dreemskerry	IoM	154	g4
Dreen Hill	Pembks	54	F4
Drefach	Carmth	58	F6
Drefach	Carmth	76	C7
Drefach	Cerdgn	76	F6
Drefelin	Carmth	76	C7
Dreghorn	N Ayrs	196	C3
Drellingore	Kent	41	H7
Drem	E Loth	212	B3
Dresden	C Stke	114	E3
Drewsteignton	Devon	13	H4
Driby	Lincs	137	G5
Driffield	E R Yk	152	F4
Driffield	Gloucs	65	G7
Driffield Cross Roads	Gloucs	64	F7
Drift	Cnwll	2	C5
Drigg	Cumb	155	K3
Drighlington	Leeds	141	K4
Drimnin	Highld	227	G2
Drimpton	Dorset	15	K2
Drimsallie	Highld	238	F7
Dringhouses	C York	151	J6
Drinkstone	Suffk	89	J3
Drinkstone Green	Suffk	89	J3
Drive End	Dorset	16	B1
Driver's End	Herts	69	G3
Drointon	Staffs	115	G6
Droitwich Spa	Worcs	81	K3
Dron	P & K	221	L4
Dronfield	Derbys	133	G4
Dronfield Woodhouse	Derbys	133	G4
Drongan	E Ayrs	196	E7
Dronley	Angus	234	A8
Droop	Dorset	16	E1
Dropping Well	Rothm	133	H1
Droxford	Hants	35	J7
Droylsden	Tamesd	140	D8
Druid	Denbgs	111	K3
Druidston	Pembks	54	E3
Druimarbin	Highld	229	H1
Druimavuic	Ag & B	229	G6
Druimdrishaig	Ag & B	206	A5
Druimindarroch	Highld	237	K4
Drum	Ag & B	206	E4
Drum	P & K	221	J7
Drumalbin	S Lans	198	F5
Drumbeg	Highld	270	F2
Drumblade	Abers	255	M4
Drumbreddon	D & G	172	D6
Drumbuie	Highld	248	B5
Drumburgh	Cumb	177	J7
Drumburn	D & G	175	L4
Drumburn	D & G	176	C6
Drumchapel	C Glas	208	E5
Drumchastle	P & K	231	J4
Drumclog	S Lans	197	J3
Drumeldrie	Fife	223	G6
Drumelzier	Border	199	K6
Drumfearn	Highld	247	L5
Drumfrennie	Abers	244	F4
Drumgley	Angus	234	C5
Drumguish	Highld	241	L4
Drumin	Moray	254	D5
Drumjohn	D & G	184	E3
Drumlamford	S Ayrs	183	H7
Drumlasie	Abers	244	E2
Drumleaning	Cumb	177	J8
Drumlemble	Ag & B	192	D4
Drumlithie	Abers	245	H7
Drummoddie	D & G	173	K6
Drummore	D & G	172	E7
Drummuir	Moray	255	H3
Drumnadrochit	Highld	250	E5
Drumnagorrach	Moray	267	L5
Drumoak	Abers	245	H4
Drumpark	D & G	185	L7
Drumrunie	Highld	271	G7
Drumshang	S Ayrs	195	L8
Drumuie	Highld	259	G7
Drumuillie	Highld	253	H7
Drumvaich	Stirlg	220	B6
Drunzie	P & K	221	L5
Druridge	Nthumb	191	K7
Drury	Flints	129	G6
Drws-y-coed	Gwynd	109	K1
Drybeck	Cumb	166	F7
Drybridge	Moray	267	J4
Drybridge	N Ayrs	196	D4
Drybrook	Gloucs	63	J4
Dryburgh	Border	201	J6
Dry Doddington	Lincs	117	M2
Dry Drayton	Cambs	87	H3
Dryhill	Kent	38	D2
Drymen	Stirlg	208	E1
Drymuir	Abers	257	G3
Drynoch	Highld	246	F2
Dry Sandford	Oxon	66	C7
Dryslwyn	Carmth	59	G5
Dry Street	Essex	52	E2
Dryton	Shrops	96	D2
Dubford	Abers	268	E3
Dublin	Suffk	90	E1
Duchally	Highld	271	L4
Duck End	Bed	85	L6
Duck End	Cambs	86	E2
Duck End	Essex	71	G2
Duck End	Essex	88	D8
Duckend Green	Essex	71	H3
Duckington	Ches W	113	H1
Ducklington	Oxon	65	M5
Duck's Cross	Bed	86	C4
Duddenhoe End	Essex	87	J7
Duddingston	C Edin	211	J4
Duddington	Nhants	101	L3
Duddlestone	Somset	30	C6
Duddleswell	E Susx	38	C7
Duddlewick	Shrops	96	F6
Duddo	Nthumb	202	E4
Duddon	Ches W	129	L6
Duddon Bridge	Cumb	156	B5
Duddon Common	Ches W	129	M6
Dudleston	Shrops	112	E4
Dudleston Heath	Shrops	112	E4
Dudley	Dudley	97	L5
Dudley	N Tyne	181	G4
Dudley Hill	C Brad	141	J2
Dudley Port	Sandw	98	B5
Dudnill	Shrops	96	E8
Dudsbury	Dorset	17	L3
Dudswell	Herts	68	B5
Duffield	Derbys	116	B3
Duffryn	Neath	42	C3
Dufftown	Moray	255	G4
Duffus	Moray	266	D3
Dufton	Cumb	166	F5
Duggleby	N York	152	D2
Duirinish	Highld	248	C5
Duisdalemore	Highld	247	L6
Duisky	Highld	239	G8
Dukestown	Blae G	61	J5
Duke Street	Suffk	90	C6
Dukinfield	Tamesd	140	E8
Dulas	IoA	125	H2
Dulcote	Somset	31	J2
Dulford	Devon	14	C2
Dull	P & K	232	B5
Dullatur	N Lans	209	K4
Dullingham	Cambs	88	C4
Dullingham Ley	Cambs	88	C4
Dulnain Bridge	Highld	253	J6
Duloe	Bed	86	D3
Duloe	Cnwll	5	M3
Dulsie Bridge	Highld	253	H3
Dulverton	Somset	29	G5
Dulwich	Gt Lon	51	J4
Dumbarton	W Duns	208	C4
Dumbleton	Gloucs	82	B8
Dumfries	D & G	176	C4
Dumgoyne	Stirlg	208	E2
Dummer	Hants	35	J2
Dumpton	Kent	41	L2
Dun	Angus	235	G3
Dunalastair	P & K	231	K4
Dunan	Highld	247	J3
Dunan	P & K	230	E4
Dunaverty	Ag & B	192	E6
Dunball	Somset	30	D3
Dunbar	E Loth	212	E3
Dunbeath	Highld	275	G2
Dunbeg	Ag & B	228	D8
Dunblane	Stirlg	220	D7
Dunbog	Fife	222	D4
Dunbridge	Hants	34	D5
Duncanston	Highld	263	G8
Duncanstone	Abers	255	L6
Dunchideock	Devon	13	K5
Dunchurch	Warwks	83	L1
Duncote	Nhants	84	C5

Duncow D & G....176 C2
Duncrievie P & K....221 L5
Duncton W Susx....20 F3
Dundee C Dund....223 G1
Dundee Airport C Dund....222 F2
Dundon Somset....31 G4
Dundonald S Ayrs....196 D4
Dundonnell Highld....261 J2
Dundraw Cumb....165 H1
Dundreggan Highld....240 B1
Dundrennan D & G....175 J5
Dundry N Som....45 H5
Dunecht Abers....245 G2
Dunfermline Fife....210 E2
Dunfield Gloucs....65 H7
Dunford Bridge Barns....141 J7
Dungate Kent....40 B3
Dungavel S Lans....197 J3
Dunge Wilts....46 C8
Dungeness Kent....25 L4
Dungworth Sheff....132 E2
Dunham-on-the-Hill Ches W....129 L5
Dunham-on-Trent Notts....135 G5
Dunhampstead Worcs....81 L3
Dunhampton Worcs....81 J2
Dunham Town Traffd....130 E2
Dunham Woodhouses Traffd....130 E2
Dunholme Lincs....135 L4
Dunino Fife....223 J5
Dunipace Falk....209 L2
Dunkeld P & K....232 F6
Dunkerton BaNES....45 L7
Dunkeswell Devon....14 D1
Dunkeswick N York....150 D6
Dunkirk Ches W....129 J5
Dunkirk Kent....40 E3
Dunkirk S Glos....46 A2
Dunkirk Wilts....46 E6
Dunk's Green Kent....38 F3
Dunlappie Angus....234 F2
Dunley Hants....48 C8
Dunley Worcs....81 H2
Dunlop E Ayrs....196 E1
Dunmaglass Highld....251 G7
Dunmere Cnwll....5 H1
Dunmore Falk....210 A1
Dunnet Highld....280 B2
Dunnichen Angus....234 D5
Dunning P & K....221 J4
Dunnington C York....151 L5
Dunnington E R Yk....153 J5
Dunnington Warwks....82 C4
Dunnockshaw Lancs....140 B2
Dunn Street Kent....53 G6
Dunoon Ag & B....207 K4
Dunphail Moray....253 J2
Dunragit D & G....172 E3
Duns Border....202 B2
Dunsa Derbys....132 E5
Dunsby Lincs....118 E6
Dunscar Bolton....139 L5
Dunscore D & G....185 L6
Dunscroft Donc....143 G6
Dunsdale R & Cl....170 E6
Dunsden Green Oxon....49 H3
Dunsdon Devon....11 K1
Dunsfold Surrey....36 F4
Dunsford Devon....13 J5
Dunshalt Fife....222 D5
Dunshillock Abers....269 H6
Dunsill Notts....133 J7
Dunsley N York....171 K8
Dunsley Staffs....97 J6
Dunsmore Bucks....67 L6
Dunsop Bridge Lancs....148 B6
Dunstable C Beds....68 C3
Dunstall Staffs....115 K7
Dunstall Common Worcs....81 K6
Dunstall Green Suffk....88 E3
Dunstan Nthumb....191 K2
Dunstan Steads Nthumb....191 J2
Dunster Somset....29 H2
Duns Tew Oxon....66 C2
Dunston Gatesd....180 F6
Dunston Lincs....135 L7
Dunston Norfk....106 E3
Dunston Staffs....114 E8
Dunstone Devon....7 H4
Dunstone Devon....13 G7
Dunston Heath Staffs....114 E8
Dunsville Donc....143 G6
Dunswell E R Yk....144 D1
Dunsyre S Lans....199 J3
Dunterton Devon....11 M6
Dunthrop Oxon....65 M2
Duntisbourne Abbots Gloucs....64 E5
Duntisbourne Leer Gloucs....64 E5
Duntisbourne Rouse Gloucs....64 E6
Duntish Dorset....16 D2
Duntocher W Duns....208 E4

Dunton Bucks....67 K2
Dunton C Beds....86 E6
Dunton Norfk....121 J5
Dunton Bassett Leics....100 C5
Dunton Green Kent....38 D2
Dunton Wayletts Essex....52 E1
Duntulm Highld....259 G2
Dunure S Ayrs....195 L7
Dunvant Swans....57 G6
Dunvegan Highld....258 C7
Dunwich Suffk....91 L1
Dunwood Staffs....131 J8
Durdar Cumb....177 L8
Durgan Cnwll....3 K5
Durgates E Susx....39 G7
Durham Dur....169 H2
Durham Cathedral Dur....169 H2
Durham Services Dur....169 J3
Durisdeer D & G....186 C5
Durisdeermill D & G....186 C5
Durkar Wakefd....141 M4
Durleigh Somset....30 C4
Durley Hants....35 G7
Durley Wilts....47 K6
Durley Street Hants....35 H7
Durlock Kent....41 J2
Durlock Kent....41 J4
Durlow Common Herefs....80 E7
Durn Rochdl....140 E4
Durness Highld....276 F3
Durno Abers....256 C6
Duror Highld....228 F4
Durran Ag & B....216 F5
Durrington W Susx....21 J6
Durrington Wilts....33 K2
Dursley Gloucs....63 M7
Dursley Cross Gloucs....63 K4
Durston Somset....30 D5
Durweston Dorset....17 G1
Duston Nhants....84 D3
Duthil Highld....253 H6
Dutlas Powys....94 F7
Duton Hill Essex....70 F2
Dutson Cnwll....11 L5
Dutton Ches W....130 B4
Duxford Cambs....87 K6
Duxford Oxon....66 A7
Dwygyfylchi Conwy....126 E4
Dwyran IoA....125 H6
Dyce C Aber....245 K1
Dyer's End Essex....88 E7
Dyfatty Carmth....56 E5
Dyffrydan Gwynd....110 D8
Dyffryn Brdgnd....42 C3
Dyffryn Myr Td....61 G6
Dyffryn V Glam....43 H7
Dyffryn Ardudwy Gwynd....109 K7
Dyffryn Castell Cerdgn....93 G7
Dyffryn Cellwen Neath....60 C5
Dyke Lincs....118 L2
Dyke Moray....264 F8
Dykehead Angus....233 K4
Dykehead Angus....234 B3
Dykehead N Lans....210 A4
Dykehead Stirlg....219 K7
Dykelands Abers....235 H2
Dykends Angus....233 K4
Dykeside Abers....256 C3
Dykes of Gray C Dund....222 F1
Dylife Powys....93 J4
Dymchurch Kent....25 L1
Dymock Gloucs....63 K1
Dyrham S Glos....45 L4
Dysart Fife....222 E8
Dyserth Denbgs....128 C4

E

Eachway Worcs....98 C8
Eachwick Nthumb....180 D4
Eagland Hill Lancs....147 H6
Eagle Lincs....135 H6
Eagle Barnsdale Lincs....135 H6
Eagle Moor Lincs....135 H6
Eaglescliffe S on T....169 L7
Eaglesfield Cumb....164 E6
Eaglesfield D & G....177 H4
Eaglesham E Rens....208 F8
Eagley Bolton....139 L5
Eairy IoM....154 d6
Eakring Notts....134 D7
Ealand N Linc....143 K5
Ealing Gt Lon....50 F3
Eals Nthumb....178 F7
Eamont Bridge Cumb....166 C5
Earby Lancs....148 F6
Earcroft Bl w D....139 K3
Eardington Shrops....97 G5

Eardisland Herefs....80 A4
Eardisley Herefs....79 K5
Eardiston Shrops....112 E6
Eardiston Worcs....80 F2
Earith Cambs....103 H8
Earle Nthumb....202 F7
Earlestown St Hel....130 B1
Earley Wokham....49 H4
Earlham Norfk....106 D2
Earlish Highld....258 F4
Earls Barton Nhants....85 G3
Earls Colne Essex....71 L1
Earls Common Worcs....81 M3
Earl's Croome Worcs....81 K6
Earlsditton Shrops....96 E8
Earlsdon Covtry....99 J7
Earl's Down E Susx....23 L3
Earlsferry Fife....223 H7
Earlsfield Gt Lon....51 H4
Earlsford Abers....256 E5
Earl's Green Suffk....90 B2
Earlsheaton Kirk....141 L3
Earl Shilton Leics....100 A4
Earl Soham Suffk....90 F3
Earl Sterndale Derbys....132 B6
Earlston Border....201 J5
Earlston E Ayrs....196 D4
Earl Stonham Suffk....90 D3
Earlswood Surrey....37 L1
Earlswood Warwks....98 E8
Earlswood Common Mons....62 F8
Earnley W Susx....20 D7
Earnshaw Bridge Lancs....139 G3
Earsdon N Tyne....181 H4
Earsdon Nthumb....191 J7
Earsham Norfk....107 G5
Earswick York....151 K4
Eartham W Susx....20 F5
Earthcott S Glos....45 K2
Easby N York....161 J1
Easdale Ag & B....215 L1
Easebourne W Susx....36 D6
Easenhall Warwks....100 A7
Eashing Surrey....36 E2
Easington Bucks....67 G5
Easington Dur....169 L2
Easington E R Yk....145 K4
Easington Nthumb....203 J6
Easington Oxon....67 G7
Easington R & Cl....171 H7
Easington Colliery Dur....169 L2
Easington Lane Sundld....169 K2
Easingwold N York....151 H2
Easole Street Kent....41 H5
Eassie and Nevay Angus....233 M6
East Aberthaw V Glam....42 F8
East Allington Devon....7 M5
East Anstey Devon....28 F5
East Anton Hants....34 E1
East Appleton N York....160 C3
East Ardsley Leeds....141 M3
East Ashey IoW....19 K6
East Ashling W Susx....20 D5
East Aston Hants....34 F2
East Ayton N York....163 H5
East Balsdon Cnwll....11 K3
East Bank Blae G....61 K6
East Barkwith Lincs....136 C3
East Barming Kent....39 H3
East Barnby N York....171 J8
East Barnet Gt Lon....69 H8
East Barns E Loth....212 F4
East Barsham Norfk....121 K5
East Beckham Norfk....122 D4
East Bedfont Gt Lon....50 D4
East Bergholt Suffk....90 C8
East Bierley Kirk....141 J2
East Bilney Norfk....121 L7
East Blatchington E Susx....23 H7
East Bloxworth Dorset....17 H4
East Boldon S Tyne....181 J6
East Boldre Hants....18 F4
East Bolton Nthumb....191 G3
Eastbourne Darltn....169 J7
Eastbourne E Susx....23 K7
East Bower Somset....30 D3
East Bradenham Norfk....105 J2
East Brent Somset....44 D8
Eastbridge Suffk....91 K2
East Bridgford Notts....117 J3
East Briscoe Dur....168 B6
Eastbrook V Glam....43 J7
East Buckland Devon....28 B4
East Budleigh Devon....14 C5
Eastburn C Brad....149 J7
Eastburn E R Yk....152 F4
East Burnham Bucks....50 B2
East Burton Dorset....16 F5
Eastbury W Berk....47 M3
East Butsfield Dur....168 E2

East Butterwick N Linc....143 L6
Eastby N York....149 J5
East Calder W Loth....210 E5
East Carleton Norfk....106 D3
East Carlton Leeds....150 B7
East Carlton Nhants....101 H5
East Chaldon Dorset....16 F6
East Challow Oxon....48 A1
East Charleton Devon....7 L6
East Chelborough Dorset....16 C2
East Chiltington E Susx....22 F4
East Chinnock Somset....31 H8
East Chisenbury Wilts....47 M3
East Cholderton Hants....34 C2
Eastchurch Kent....53 L5
East Clandon Surrey....50 D8
East Claydon Bucks....67 H4
East Clevedon N Som....44 E5
East Coker Somset....31 J8
Eastcombe Gloucs....64 C6
Eastcombe Somset....29 L4
East Compton Somset....31 K3
East Cornworthy Devon....8 C4
East Cote Cumb....176 F7
Eastcote Gt Lon....50 E3
Eastcote Nhants....84 D4
Eastcote Solhll....99 G7
Eastcott Cnwll....26 D7
Eastcott Wilts....46 L1
East Cottingwith E R Yk....151 L7
Eastcourt Wilts....47 K6
Eastcourt Wilts....64 E6
East Cowes IoW....19 H4
East Cowick E R Yk....143 G3
East Cowton N York....160 D2
East Cramlington Nthumb....181 G4
East Cranmore Somset....31 L2
East Creech Dorset....17 H6
East Curthwaite Cumb....165 K3
East Dean E Susx....23 J7
East Dean Gloucs....63 K6
East Dean Hants....34 C1
East Dean W Susx....20 E5
Eastdown Devon....8 B5
East Down Devon....27 L2
East Drayton Notts....134 F4
East Dulwich Gt Lon....51 J4
East Dundry N Som....45 H6
East Ella C KuH....144 D2
East End Bed....86 C
East End C Beds....85 J
East End E R Yk....145 G
East End E R Yk....145 H
East End Essex....70 B
Eastend Essex....72 D
East End Hants....18 D
East End Hants....48 B
East End Herts....70 C
East End Kent....39 L
East End Kent....53 L
East End M Keyn....85 J
East End Oxon....66 B
East End Somset....31 L
East End Suffk....90 C
Easter Balmoral Abers....243 J
Easter Compton S Glos....45 H
Easter Dalziel Highld....252 E
Eastergate W Susx....20 F
Easterhouse C Glas....209 J
Easter Howgate Mdloth....211 J
Easter Kinkell Highld....251 G
Easter Moniack Highld....250 F
Eastern Green Covtry....99 H
Easter Ord Abers....245 J
Easter Pitkierie Fife....223 K
Easter Skeld Shet....281 d
Easter Softlaw Border....202 B
Easterton Wilts....46 F
Eastertown Somset....44 D
East Everleigh Wilts....47 J
East Farleigh Kent....39 J
East Farndon Nhants....100 F
East Ferry Lincs....143 K
Eastfield N Lans....210 A
Eastfield N York....163 H
East Firsby Lincs....135 J
East Fortune E Loth....212 C
East Garforth Leeds....142 C
East Garston W Berk....47 C
Eastgate Dur....168 B
Eastgate Lincs....118 F
Eastgate Norfk....122 C
East Ginge Oxon....48 C
East Goscote Leics....100 E
East Grafton Wilts....47 J
East Green Suffk....91 L
East Grimstead Wilts....34 C
East Grinstead W Susx....38 C
East Guldeford E Susx....25 J
East Haddon Nhants....84 E

Place	Area	Page	Ref
East Hagbourne	Oxon	48	D1
East Halton	N Linc	144	E4
East Ham	Gt Lon	51	L2
Eastham	Wirral	129	H4
Eastham Ferry	Wirral	129	J3
Easthampton	Herefs	80	A4
East Hanney	Oxon	66	B8
East Hanningfield	Essex	71	J6
East Hardwick	Wakefd	142	D4
East Harling	Norfk	105	K6
East Harlsey	N York	160	F3
East Harnham	Wilts	33	K5
East Harptree	BaNES	45	H7
East Hartford	Nthumb	181	G3
East Harting	W Susx	20	C3
East Hatch	Wilts	32	F5
East Hatley	Cambs	86	F5
East Hauxwell	N York	159	L4
East Haven	Angus	234	F8
Eastheath	Wokham	49	J5
East Heckington	Lincs	119	G3
East Hedleyhope	Dur	168	F3
East Helmsdale	Highld	274	D5
East Hendred	Oxon	48	C1
East Heslerton	N York	163	G7
East Hewish	N Som	44	E6
East Hoathly	E Susx	23	H4
East Holme	Dorset	17	H5
East Hope	Dur	159	J1
Easthope	Shrops	96	D4
Easthorpe	Essex	72	C3
Easthorpe	Notts	117	J1
East Horrington	Somset	31	J2
East Horsley	Surrey	50	E8
East Horton	Nthumb	203	G7
East Howe	BCP	17	L3
East Huntspill	Somset	30	E4
East Hyde	C Beds	68	E4
East Ilkerton	Devon	28	C2
East Ilsley	W Berk	48	D3
Eastington	Devon	13	H1
Eastington	Gloucs	63	M6
Eastington	Gloucs	65	H4
East Keal	Lincs	137	G7
East Kennett	Wilts	47	G5
East Keswick	Leeds	150	E7
East Kilbride	S Lans	209	H8
East Kimber	Devon	12	C3
East Kirkby	Lincs	136	F7
East Knighton	Dorset	16	F5
East Knowstone	Devon	28	E6
East Knoyle	Wilts	32	E5
East Lambrook	Somset	31	J4
Eastlands	D & G	185	K8
East Langdon	Kent	41	K6
East Langton	Leics	100	F5
East Lavant	W Susx	20	D5
East Lavington	W Susx	20	F4
East Layton	N York	159	L1
Eastleach Martin	Gloucs	65	J6
Eastleach Turville	Gloucs	65	J6
East Leake	Notts	116	F6
East Learmouth	Nthumb	202	D5
East Leigh	Devon	7	K4
East Leigh	Devon	13	L3
East Leigh	Devon	13	G2
Eastleigh	Devon	27	J5
Eastleigh	Hants	34	F7
East Lexham	Norfk	121	J8
Eastling	Kent	40	C4
East Linton	E Loth	212	D3
East Liss	Hants	36	A5
East Lockinge	Oxon	48	B2
East Lound	N Linc	143	K7
East Lulworth	Dorset	17	G6
East Lutton	N York	152	E2
East Lydeard	Somset	30	B5
East Lydford	Somset	31	J4
East Malling	Kent	39	H2
East Malling Heath	Kent	39	H2
East Marden	W Susx	20	C4
East Markham	Notts	134	E5
East Martin	Hants	33	J7
East Marton	N York	148	F3
East Meon	Hants	35	L6
East Mere	Devon	29	H7
East Mersea	Essex	72	F4
East Midlands Airport	Leics	116	
East Molesey	Surrey	50	F5
Eastmoor	Norfk	104	E3
East Morden	Dorset	17	H4
East Morton	C Brad	149	K4
East Morton	D & G	186	C6
East Ness	N York	162	B7
East Newton	E R Yk	153	L8
Eastney	C Port	19	L4
Eastnor	Herefs	81	G7
East Norton	Leics	101	G3
Eastoft	N Linc	143	K4
East Ogwell	Devon	13	J8
Easton	Cambs	86	C1
Easton	Cumb	177	J7
Easton	Devon	13	G5
Easton	Dorset	16	D8
Easton	Hants	35	G4
Easton	Lincs	118	B6
Easton	Norfk	106	C1
Easton	Somset	31	H2
Easton	Suffk	91	G3
Easton	W Berk	48	B4
Easton	Wilts	46	C5
Easton Grey	Wilts	46	C2
Easton-in-Gordano	N Som	45	G4
Easton Maudit	Nhants	85	H3
Easton-on-the-Hill	Nhants	101	M3
Easton Royal	Wilts	47	J7
East Orchard	Dorset	32	D7
East Ord	Nthumb	202	F3
East Panson	Devon	11	L4
East Parley	BCP	17	M3
East Peckham	Kent	39	G4
East Pennard	Somset	31	K3
East Portlemouth	Devon	7	L7
East Prawle	Devon	8	A7
East Preston	W Susx	21	H4
East Pulham	Dorset	16	D1
East Putford	Devon	26	F7
East Quantoxhead	Somset	29	L2
East Rainham	Medway	53	H5
East Rainton	Sundld	169	J1
East Ravendale	NE Lin	145	G7
East Raynham	Norfk	121	J6
Eastrea	Cambs	102	F4
Eastriggs	D & G	177	H5
East Rigton	Leeds	150	E7
Eastrington	E R Yk	143	K2
East Rolstone	N Som	44	E6
Eastrop	Swindn	65	J8
East Rounton	N York	160	F2
East Rudham	Norfk	121	H6
East Runton	Norfk	122	D3
East Ruston	Norfk	123	G6
Eastry	Kent	41	J4
East Saltoun	E Loth	212	B5
Eastshaw	W Susx	36	C6
East Sheen	Gt Lon	51	G4
East Shefford	W Berk	48	A4
East Sleekburn	Nthumb	181	G2
East Somerton	Norfk	123	K7
East Stockwith	Lincs	134	F1
East Stoke	Dorset	17	G5
East Stoke	Notts	117	K2
East Stour	Dorset	32	D6
East Stour Common	Dorset	32	D6
East Stourmouth	Kent	41	H3
East Stowford	Devon	27	L5
East Stratton	Hants	35	H3
East Studdal	Kent	41	J5
East Sutton	Kent	39	L3
East Taphouse	Cnwll	5	L2
East-the-Water	Devon	27	H5
East Thirston	Nthumb	191	J6
East Tilbury	Thurr	52	E3
East Tilbury Village	Thurr	52	E3
East Tisted	Hants	35	L4
East Torrington	Lincs	136	B3
East Tuddenham	Norfk	106	B1
East Tytherley	Hants	34	C5
East Tytherton	Wilts	46	D4
East Village	Devon	13	K2
Eastville	Bristl	45	J4
Eastville	Lincs	137	H8
East Wall	Shrops	96	C4
East Walton	Norfk	121	G8
East Water	Somset	31	J1
East Week	Devon	12	F4
Eastwell	Leics	117	K6
East Wellow	Hants	34	C6
East Wemyss	Fife	222	F7
East Whitburn	W Loth	210	C6
Eastwick	Herts	70	B5
East Wickham	Gt Lon	51	M3
East Williamston	Pembks	55	J6
East Winch	Norfk	120	F8
East Winterslow	Wilts	34	B4
East Wittering	W Susx	20	C7
East Witton	N York	159	L5
Eastwood	Notts	116	D2
Eastwood	Sthend	53	H1
East Woodburn	Nthumb	179	L2
Eastwood End	Cambs	103	J5
East Woodhay	Hants	48	B6
East Woodlands	Somset	32	C2
East Worldham	Hants	35	M3
East Worthing	W Susx	21	K6
East Wretham	Norfk	105	J5
East Youlstone	Devon	26	D7
Eathorpe	Warwks	83	J2
Eaton	Ches E	131	G6
Eaton	Ches W	130	B7
Eaton	Leics	117	L5
Eaton	Norfk	106	E2
Eaton	Notts	134	E4
Eaton	Oxon	66	C6
Eaton	Shrops	95	J5
Eaton	Shrops	96	B5
Eaton Bishop	Herefs	80	B7
Eaton Bray	C Beds	68	B3
Eaton Constantine	Shrops	96	D2
Eaton Ford	Cambs	86	D3
Eaton Green	C Beds	68	B3
Eaton Hastings	Oxon	65	K7
Eaton Mascott	Shrops	96	C2
Eaton Socon	Cambs	86	D3
Eaton upon Tern	Shrops	113	L7
Eaves Brow	Warrtn	130	C1
Eaves Green	Solhll	99	H6
Ebberston	N York	162	F6
Ebbesborne Wake	Wilts	33	G6
Ebbsfleet	Kent	52	D4
Ebbw Vale	Blae G	61	J5
Ebchester	Dur	180	D7
Ebdon	N Som	44	D6
Ebernoe	W Susx	36	E5
Ebford	Devon	14	A5
Ebley	Gloucs	64	B6
Ebnal	Ches W	113	H2
Ebnall	Herefs	80	B3
Ebrington	Gloucs	82	E7
Ebsworthy	Devon	12	C4
Ecchinswell	Hants	48	D7
Ecclaw	Border	213	G5
Ecclefechan	D & G	177	G4
Eccles	Border	202	B5
Eccles	Kent	52	F6
Eccles	Salfd	140	A8
Ecclesall	Sheff	132	F3
Ecclesfield	Sheff	133	G1
Eccles Green	Herefs	79	L5
Eccleshall	Staffs	114	C5
Eccleshill	C Brad	149	M8
Ecclesmachan	W Loth	210	E4
Eccles on Sea	Norfk	123	H5
Eccles Road	Norfk	105	L5
Eccleston	Ches W	129	J7
Eccleston	Lancs	139	G4
Eccleston	St Hel	138	F8
Eccleston Green	Lancs	139	G4
Echt	Abers	245	G2
Eckford	Border	201	L7
Eckington	Derbys	133	H4
Eckington	Worcs	81	L7
Ecton	Nhants	84	F3
Ecton	Staffs	132	B8
Edale	Derbys	132	B3
Eday	Ork	275	d3
Eday Airport	Ork	275	d2
Edburton	W Susx	22	C5
Edderside	Cumb	164	E2
Edderton	Highld	263	J3
Eddington	Cambs	87	J3
Eddington	Kent	41	G2
Eddleston	Border	200	B4
Eddlewood	S Lans	209	J8
Edenbridge	Kent	38	C4
Edenfield	Lancs	140	B4
Edenhall	Cumb	166	D4
Edenham	Lincs	118	E7
Eden Mount	Cumb	156	F7
Eden Park	Gt Lon	51	K5
Edensor	Derbys	132	E5
Edentaggart	Ag & B	218	D8
Edenthorpe	Donc	143	G6
Edern	Gwynd	108	E4
Edgarley	Somset	31	H3
Edgbaston	Birm	98	D6
Edgcott	Bucks	67	G3
Edgcott	Somset	28	E3
Edgcumbe	Cnwll	3	J4
Edge	Gloucs	64	B5
Edge	Shrops	95	K2
Edgebolton	Shrops	113	J7
Edge End	Gloucs	63	H4
Edgefield	Norfk	122	B5
Edgefield Green	Norfk	122	B4
Edgefold	Bolton	139	L6
Edge Green	Ches W	113	H1
Edgehill	Warwks	83	J5
Edgerley	Shrops	112	E7
Edgerton	Kirk	141	H4
Edgeside	Lancs	140	C3
Edgeworth	Gloucs	64	D6
Edgeworthy	Devon	28	E8
Edginswell	Torbay	8	C2
Edgiock	Worcs	82	B3
Edgmond	Wrekin	114	A7
Edgmond Marsh	Wrekin	114	A7
Edgton	Shrops	95	J6
Edgware	Gt Lon	51	G1
Edgworth	Bl w D	139	L4
Edinbane	Highld	258	E6
Edinburgh	C Edin	211	J4
Edinburgh Airport	C Edin	210	F4
Edinburgh Old & New Town	C Edin	211	H4
Edingale	Staffs	99	G1
Edingham	D & G	175	L2
Edingley	Notts	134	D8
Edingthorpe	Norfk	123	G5
Edingthorpe Green	Norfk	122	F5
Edington	Border	202	D2
Edington	Nthumb	180	E2
Edington	Somset	30	F3
Edington	Wilts	46	D8
Edingworth	Somset	44	D8
Edistone	Devon	26	D6
Edithmead	Somset	30	E1
Edith Weston	Rutlnd	101	K2
Edlesborough	Bucks	68	B3
Edlingham	Nthumb	191	G4
Edlington	Lincs	136	D5
Edmond Castle	Cumb	178	C7
Edmondsham	Dorset	33	J8
Edmondsley	Dur	169	G1
Edmondstown	Rhondd	42	F4
Edmondthorpe	Leics	117	M8
Edmonton	Cnwll	10	D8
Edmonton	Gt Lon	69	J8
Edmundbyers	Dur	168	C1
Ednam	Border	202	A5
Ednaston	Derbys	115	L3
Edney Common	Essex	71	G6
Edradynate	P & K	232	C5
Edrom	Border	202	C2
Edstaston	Shrops	113	H5
Edstone	Warwks	82	E3
Edvin Loach	Herefs	80	F3
Edwalton	Notts	117	G4
Edwardstone	Suffk	89	J6
Edwardsville	Myr Td	43	G2
Edwinsford	Carmth	59	H2
Edwinstowe	Notts	134	C6
Edworth	C Beds	86	E7
Edwyn Ralph	Herefs	80	F4
Edzell	Angus	234	F2
Edzell Woods	Abers	234	F2
Efail-fach	Neath	57	L6
Efail Isaf	Rhondd	43	H5
Efailnewydd	Gwynd	108	F4
Efail-Rhyd	Powys	112	A6
Efailwen	Carmth	75	K7
Efenechtyd	Denbgs	128	D8
Effgill	D & G	187	L7
Effingham	Surrey	50	E8
Effingham Junction	Surrey	50	E7
Efflinch	Staffs	115	K8
Efford	Devon	13	K2
Egbury	Hants	48	B8
Egdean	W Susx	21	G3
Egerton	Bolton	139	L5
Egerton	Kent	40	B6
Egerton Forstal	Kent	40	A6
Eggborough	N York	142	E3
Eggbuckland	C Plym	6	F3
Eggesford	Devon	28	B8
Eggington	C Beds	68	B2
Egginton	Derbys	115	M6
Egglescliffe	S on T	169	L7
Eggleston	Dur	168	C6
Egham	Surrey	50	C5
Egham Wick	Surrey	50	B5
Egleton	Rutlnd	101	J2
Eglingham	Nthumb	191	G2
Egloshayle	Cnwll	10	D8
Egloskerry	Cnwll	11	K5
Eglwysbach	Conwy	126	F5
Eglwys-Brewis	V Glam	42	F7
Eglwys Cross	Wrexhm	113	G3
Eglwys Fach	Cerdgn	92	F4
Eglwyswrw	Pembks	75	K4
Egmanton	Notts	134	E6
Egremont	Cumb	164	D8
Egremont	Wirral	129	H1
Egton	N York	162	E2
Egton Bridge	N York	162	D2
Egypt	Bucks	50	B2
Egypt	Hants	34	F3
Eigg	Highld	236	F3
Eight Ash Green	Essex	72	D2
Eilanreach	Highld	248	C8
Eisgein	W Isls	282	f5
Eishken	W Isls	282	f5
Eisteddfa Gurig	Cerdgn	93	H6
Elan Valley	Powys	78	B2
Elan Village	Powys	78	C2
Elberton	S Glos	45	J1
Elbridge	W Susx	20	F6
Elburton	C Plym	7	G4
Elcombe	Swindn	47	H3
Elcot	W Berk	48	B5

Eldernell Cambs 103 G4
Eldersfield Worcs 64 A1
Elderslie Rens 208 D6
Elder Street Essex 88 B8
Eldon Dur 169 G5
Eldwick C Brad 149 L7
Elerch Cerdgn 92 E6
Elfhill Abers 245 H6
Elford Nthumb 203 K7
Elford Staffs 98 F1
Elgin Moray 266 E4
Elgol Highld 247 H6
Elham Kent 41 G6
Elie Fife 223 J7
Elilaw Nthumb 190 D4
Elim IoA 124 F3
Eling Hants 18 F1
Elkesley Notts 134 D4
Elkstone Gloucs 64 D4
Ella Abers 268 B4
Ellacombe Torbay 8 D2
Elland Calder 141 H4
Elland Lower Edge Calder 141 H3
Ellary Ag & B 206 A4
Ellastone Staffs 115 J3
Ellel Lancs 147 J4
Ellemford Border 212 F7
Ellenabeich Ag & B 215 L1
Ellenborough Cumb 164 D3
Ellenbrook Salfd 139 L7
Ellenhall Staffs 114 C6
Ellen's Green Surrey 37 G4
Ellerbeck N York 160 F3
Ellerby N York 171 J7
Ellerdine Heath Wrekin 113 K7
Ellerhayes Devon 14 A2
Elleric Ag & B 229 G5
Ellerker E R Yk 144 A2
Ellers N York 149 H7
Ellerton E R Yk 151 L7
Ellerton N York 160 C3
Ellerton Shrops 114 A6
Ellesborough Bucks 67 K6
Ellesmere Shrops 112 F4
Ellesmere Port Ches W 129 J4
Ellicombe Somset 29 H2
Ellingham Hants 18 A2
Ellingham Norfk 107 H5
Ellingham Nthumb 203 K8
Ellingstring N York 159 M6
Ellington Cambs 86 D1
Ellington Nthumb 191 K7
Ellington Thorpe Cambs 86 D1
Elliots Green Somset 32 D2
Ellisfield Hants 35 K2
Ellishader Highld 259 H3
Ellistown Leics 99 L1
Ellon Abers 257 H5
Ellonby Cumb 166 A4
Ellough Suffk 107 J6
Elloughton E R Yk 144 B2
Ellwood Gloucs 63 H5
Elm Cambs 103 K2
Elmbridge Worcs 81 K2
Elmdon Essex 87 J7
Elmdon Solhll 98 F6
Elmdon Heath Solhll 98 F7
Elmer W Susx 21 G6
Elmers End Gt Lon 51 K5
Elmer's Green Lancs 139 G6
Elmesthorpe Leics 100 A4
Elm Green Essex 71 J6
Elmhurst Staffs 98 E1
Elmington Nhants 102 B5
Elmley Castle Worcs 82 A7
Elmley Lovett Worcs 81 K1
Elmore Gloucs 64 A4
Elmore Back Gloucs 63 M4
Elm Park Gt Lon 52 B2
Elmscott Devon 26 D6
Elmsett Suffk 90 C6
Elms Green Worcs 81 G2
Elmstead Heath Essex 72 F3
Elmstead Market Essex 72 F2
Elmstead Row Essex 72 F3
Elmsted Kent 40 F6
Elmstone Kent 41 H3
Elmstone Hardwicke Gloucs 64 D2
Elmswell E R Yk 152 F4
Elmswell Suffk 89 K3
Elmton Derbys 133 K5
Elphin Highld 271 H6
Elphinstone E Loth 211 L5
Elrick Abers 245 H2
Elrig D & G 173 J5
Elrington Nthumb 179 K6
Elsdon Nthumb 190 C7
Elsecar Barns 142 B7
Elsenham Essex 70 D2
Elsfield Oxon 66 D5

Elsham N Linc 144 C5
Elsing Norfk 122 B8
Elslack N York 149 G6
Elson Hants 19 K3
Elson Shrops 112 F4
Elsrickle S Lans 199 J4
Elstead Surrey 36 D2
Elsted W Susx 20 D3
Elsted Marsh W Susx 20 D3
Elsthorpe Lincs 118 E6
Elstob Dur 169 J6
Elston Lancs 139 J1
Elston Notts 117 K2
Elston Wilts 33 J2
Elstone Devon 28 B7
Elstow Bed 85 L6
Elstree Herts 68 F8
Elstronwick E R Yk 145 G1
Elswick Lancs 147 H8
Elswick N u Ty 180 F6
Elsworth Cambs 87 G3
Elterwater Cumb 156 D2
Eltham Gt Lon 51 L4
Eltisley Cambs 86 F3
Elton Bury 140 B5
Elton Cambs 102 B4
Elton Ches W 129 K4
Elton Derbys 132 D7
Elton Gloucs 63 K4
Elton Herefs 80 B1
Elton S on T 169 L7
Elton Green Ches W 129 K5
Elton-on-the-Hill Notts 117 K4
Eltringham Nthumb 180 C6
Elvanfoot S Lans 186 E3
Elvaston Derbys 116 C5
Elveden Suffk 105 G6
Elvetham Heath Hants 49 K7
Elvingston E Loth 212 A4
Elvington C York 151 L6
Elvington Kent 41 J5
Elwell Devon 28 B4
Elwick Hartpl 170 B4
Elwick Nthumb 203 J5
Elworth Ches E 130 E7
Elworthy Somset 29 K4
Ely Cambs 103 L7
Ely Cardif 43 J6
Emberton M Keyn 85 H5
Embleton Cumb 165 G4
Embleton Dur 169 L5
Embleton Nthumb 191 J4
Embo Highld 264 C1
Emborough Somset 31 K1
Embo Street Highld 264 C2
Embsay N York 149 H5
Emery Down Hants 18 D2
Emley Kirk 141 K5
Emley Moor Kirk 141 K5
Emmbrook Wokham 49 J5
Emmer Green Readg 49 H4
Emmett Carr Derbys 133 J4
Emmington Oxon 67 H6
Emneth Norfk 103 K2
Emneth Hungate Norfk 103 K2
Empingham Rutlnd 101 L2
Empshott Hants 35 M4
Empshott Green Hants 35 M5
Emsworth Hants 20 B5
Enborne W Berk 48 B6
Enborne Row W Berk 48 C6
Enchmarsh Shrops 96 B4
Enderby Leics 100 C3
Endmoor Cumb 157 H5
Endon Staffs 114 E1
Endon Bank Staffs 114 E1
Enfield Gt Lon 69 K7
Enfield Lock Gt Lon 69 K7
Enfield Wash Gt Lon 69 K7
Enford Wilts 47 H8
Engine Common S Glos 45 K2
England's Gate Herefs 80 D5
Englefield W Berk 48 F4
Englefield Green Surrey 50 C4
Engleseabrook Ches E 114 B1
English Bicknor Gloucs 63 H4
Englishcombe BaNES 45 L6
English Frankton Shrops 113 J6
Engollan Cnwll 10 B8
Enham Alamein Hants 34 D1
Enmore Somset 30 C4
Enmore Green Dorset 32 E6
Ennerdale Bridge Cumb 164 E7
Enniscaven Cnwll 4 F3
Enochdhu P & K 233 G3
Ensay Ag & B 226 D3
Ensbury BCP 17 L3
Ensdon Shrops 112 F8
Ensis Devon 27 K5
Enson Staffs 114 E6

Enstone Oxon 66 A2
Enterkinfoot D & G 186 C5
Enterpen N York 161 G2
Enville Staffs 97 J6
Eochar W Isls 283 b9
Eòlaigearraidh W Isls 283 b12
Eoligarry W Isls 283 b12
Eòropaidh W Isls 282 h1
Eoropie W Isls 282 h1
Epney Gloucs 63 M5
Epperstone Notts 117 H2
Epping Essex 70 C6
Epping Green Essex 70 B6
Epping Green Herts 69 J5
Epping Upland Essex 70 C6
Eppleby N York 168 F8
Eppleworth E R Yk 144 C2
Epsom Surrey 51 G6
Epwell Oxon 83 H7
Epworth N Linc 143 K7
Epworth Turbary N Linc 143 J7
Erbistock Wrexhm 112 E3
Erdington Birm 98 E5
Eridge Green E Susx 38 E6
Eridge Station E Susx 38 E6
Erines Ag & B 206 D4
Eriska Ag & B 228 D6
Eriswell Suffk 104 E7
Erith Gt Lon 52 B3
Erlestoke Wilts 46 D8
Ermington Devon 7 J4
Ernesettle C Plym 6 E3
Erpingham Norfk 122 D5
Erriottwood Kent 40 B3
Errogie Highld 250 F7
Errol P & K 222 D3
Erskine Rens 208 D5
Erskine Bridge Rens 208 D4
Ervie D & G 172 B1
Erwarton Suffk 90 F8
Erwood Powys 78 F6
Eryholme N York 160 D1
Eryrys Denbgs 128 E8
Escalls Cnwll 2 B5
Escomb Dur 168 F4
Escott Somset 29 K3
Escrick N York 151 K7
Esgair Carmth 58 C3
Esgair Cerdgn 77 G2
Esgairgeiliog Powys 93 G2
Esgerdawe Carmth 77 H7
Esgyryn Conwy 126 F4
Esh Dur 169 G2
Esher Surrey 50 E6
Esholt C Brad 150 A7
Eshott Nthumb 191 J6
Eshton N York 149 G6
Esh Winning Dur 169 G2
Eskadale Highld 250 D4
Eskbank Mdloth 211 K5
Eskdale Green Cumb 155 L3
Eskdalemuir D & G 187 K6
Eske E R Yk 153 G7
Eskham Lincs 145 K5
Eskholme Donc 143 G4
Esperley Lane Ends Dur 168 E6
Esprick Lancs 147 H8
Essendine Rutlnd 102 A1
Essendon Herts 69 H5
Essich Highld 251 H4
Essington Staffs 98 B3
Esslemont Abers 257 G6
Eston R & Cl 170 D7
Etal Nthumb 202 E5
Etchilhampton Wilts 46 F7
Etchingham E Susx 24 C2
Etchinghill Kent 41 G7
Etchinghill Staffs 115 G7
Etchingwood E Susx 23 H3
Etling Green Norfk 121 M8
Etloe Gloucs 63 K6
Eton W & M 50 B3
Eton Wick W & M 50 B3
Etruria C Stke 114 D2
Etteridge Highld 241 J5
Ettersgill Dur 167 K5
Ettiley Heath Ches E 130 E7
Ettingshall Wolves 97 L4
Ettington Warwks 83 G5
Etton C Pete 102 C2
Etton E R Yk 152 F7
Ettrick Border 187 L3
Ettrickbridge Border 188 C1
Ettrickhill Border 187 L3
Etwall Derbys 115 M5
Eudon George Shrops 96 F5
Euston Suffk 105 H7
Euximoor Drove Cambs 103 K4
Euxton Lancs 139 H4
Evancoyd Powys 79 J3

Evanton Highld 263 G...
Evedon Lincs 118 E...
Evelith Shrops 97 G...
Evelix Highld 263 L...
Evenjobb Powys 79 J...
Evenley Nhants 84 B...
Evenlode Gloucs 65 J...
Evenwood Dur 168 F...
Evenwood Gate Dur 168 F...
Evercreech Somset 31 K...
Everingham E R Yk 152 B...
Everleigh Wilts 47 J...
Everley N York 163 J...
Eversholt C Beds 85 J...
Evershot Dorset 16 A...
Eversley Hants 49 J...
Eversley Cross Hants 49 J...
Everthorpe E R Yk 144 B...
Everton C Beds 86 E...
Everton Hants 18 D...
Everton Lpool 129 H...
Everton Notts 134 D...
Evertown D & G 177 J...
Evesbatch Herefs 80 F...
Evesham Worcs 82 B...
Evington C Leic 100 D...
Ewden Village Sheff 141 L...
Ewell Surrey 51 G...
Ewell Minnis Kent 41 H...
Ewelme Oxon 48 F...
Ewen Gloucs 64 C...
Ewenny V Glam 42 D...
Ewerby Lincs 118 E...
Ewerby Thorpe Lincs 118 F...
Ewhurst Surrey 37 J...
Ewhurst Green E Susx 24 E...
Ewhurst Green Surrey 37 G...
Ewloe Flints 129 G...
Ewloe Green Flints 129 G...
Ewood Bl w D 139 K...
Ewood Bridge Lancs 140 B...
Eworthy Devon 12 B...
Ewshot Hants 36 B...
Ewyas Harold Herefs 62 D...
Exbourne Devon 12 E...
Exbury Hants 19 G...
Exceat E Susx 23 H...
Exebridge Somset 29 G...
Exelby N York 160 D...
Exeter Devon 13 L...
Exeter Airport Devon 14 A...
Exeter Services Devon 13 M...
Exford Somset 28 E...
Exfordsgreen Shrops 95 J...
Exhall Warwks 82 D...
Exhall Warwks 99 K...
Exlade Street Oxon 49 G...
Exley Head C Brad 149 J...
Exminster Devon 13 M...
Exmoor National Park 28 E...
Exmouth Devon 14 A...
Exning Suffk 88 C...
Exted Kent 41 G...
Exton Devon 14 A...
Exton Hants 35 J...
Exton Rutlnd 101 K...
Exton Somset 29 G...
Exwick Devon 13 L...
Eyam Derbys 132 D...
Eydon Nhants 83 M...
Eye C Pete 102 E...
Eye Herefs 80 C...
Eye Suffk 106 E...
Eye Green C Pete 102 E...
Eyemouth Border 213 L...
Eyeworth C Beds 86 E...
Eyhorne Street Kent 39 H...
Eyke Suffk 91 H...
Eynesbury Cambs 86 E...
Eynsford Kent 52 B...
Eynsham Oxon 66 B...
Eype Dorset 15 K...
Eyre Highld 259 H...
Eythorne Kent 41 H...
Eyton Herefs 80 B...
Eyton Shrops 95 J...
Eyton Shrops 112 E...
Eyton Shrops 113 G...
Eyton Wrexhm 112 E...
Eyton on Severn Shrops 96 D...
Eyton upon the Weald Moors Wrekin 113 L...

F

Faccombe Hants 48 A...
Faceby N York 161 H...
Fachwen Powys 111 L...

Facit Lancs 140 D4
Fackley Notts 133 J7
Faddiley Ches E 113 K1
Fadmoor N York 161 L5
Faerdre Swans 57 J4
Faifley W Duns 208 G4
Failand N Som 45 G4
Failford S Ayrs 196 F5
Failsworth Oldham 140 D7
Fairbourne Gwynd 92 D1
Fairburn N York 142 D2
Fairfield Derbys 131 L5
Fairfield Kent 25 L1
Fairfield Worcs 97 L8
Fairfield Park Herts 86 D8
Fairford Gloucs 65 H6
Fairford Park Gloucs 65 H6
Fairgirth D & G 175 L3
Fair Green Norfk 120 E8
Fairhaven Lancs 138 C2
Fair Isle Shet 281 b8
Fair Isle Airport Shet 281 b8
Fairlands Surrey 50 B8
Fairlie N Ayrs 207 L8
Fairlight E Susx 24 F5
Fairlight Cove E Susx 24 F5
Fairmile Devon 14 C3
Fairmile Surrey 50 E6
Fairmilehead C Edin 211 H5
Fairnilee Border 200 F6
Fair Oak Hants 35 G7
Fairoak Staffs 114 B5
Fair Oak Green Hants 49 G6
Fairseat Kent 52 D6
Fairstead Essex 71 J4
Fairstead Norfk 120 E7
Fairstead Norfk 122 F6
Fairwarp E Susx 23 G2
Fairwater Cardif 43 J6
Fairy Cross Devon 27 G6
Fakenham Norfk 121 K5
Fakenham Magna Suffk 105 H8
Fala Mdloth 211 M6
Fala Dam Mdloth 211 M6
Falcut Nhants 84 B6
Faldingworth Lincs 135 L3
Faldouët Jersey 9 f2
Falfield S Glos 63 K8
Falkenham Suffk 91 G7
Falkirk Falk 210 A3
Falkland Fife 222 D5
Fallburn S Lans 199 G5
Fallgate Derbys 133 G2
Fallin Stirlg 209 L1
Fallodon Nthumb 191 H2
Fallowfield Manch 131 G1
Fallowfield Nthumb 179 L5
Falmer E Susx 22 E5
Falmouth Cnwll 3 K4
Falnash Border 188 C5
Falsgrave N York 163 J5
Falstone Nthumb 179 G2
Fanagmore Highld 276 B6
Fancott C Beds 68 C2
Fanellan Highld 250 E3
Fangdale Beck N York 161 J4
Fangfoss E R Yk 152 A5
Fanmore Ag & B 226 E3
Fannich Lodge Highld 261 L6
Fans Border 201 J5
Far Bletchley M Keyn 85 G8
Farcet Cambs 102 D4
Far Cotton Nhants 84 E3
Farden Shrops 96 D8
Fareham Hants 19 K2
Farewell Staffs 98 D1
Far Forest Worcs 97 G8
Farforth Lincs 136 F4
Far Green Gloucs 63 M7
Faringdon Oxon 65 L8
Farington Lancs 139 G3
Farlam Cumb 178 D7
Farleigh N Som 45 G5
Farleigh Surrey 51 K7
Farleigh Hungerford Somset 46 A7
Farleigh Wallop Hants 35 J2
Farlesthorpe Lincs 137 J5
Farleton Cumb 157 H6
Farleton Lancs 147 L2
Farley Derbys 132 F7
Farley Staffs 115 H3
Farley Wilts 34 B5
Farley Green Suffk 88 E4
Farley Green Surrey 37 G2
Farley Hill Wokham 49 H6
Farleys End Gloucs 63 M4
Farlington C Port 19 M3
Farlington N York 151 K2
Farlow Shrops 96 E7
Farmborough BaNES 45 K7

Farmbridge End Essex 70 F5
Farmcote Gloucs 64 F1
Farmcote Shrops 97 H5
Farmington Gloucs 65 H4
Farmoor Oxon 66 C5
Far Moor Wigan 139 G2
Farms Common Cnwll 3 H4
Farm Town Leics 116 C8
Farmtown Moray 267 K6
Farnah Green Derbys 116 B2
Farnborough Gt Lon 51 L6
Farnborough Hants 49 L8
Farnborough W Berk 48 B1
Farnborough Warwks 83 K5
Farnborough Park Hants 49 L7
Farncombe Surrey 36 E2
Farndish Bed 85 H3
Farndon Ches W 112 F1
Farndon Notts 117 K1
Farne Islands Nthumb 203 L5
Farnell Angus 235 G4
Farnham Dorset 33 G7
Farnham Essex 70 C2
Farnham N York 150 E4
Farnham Suffk 91 H3
Farnham Surrey 36 B2
Farnham Common Bucks 50 B2
Farnham Green Essex 70 C2
Farnham Royal Bucks 50 B2
Farningham Kent 52 C5
Farnley Leeds 141 L1
Farnley N York 150 B6
Farnley Tyas Kirk 141 J5
Farnsfield Notts 134 C8
Farnworth Bolton 139 L6
Farnworth Halton 129 L2
Far Oakridge Gloucs 64 D6
Farr Highld 241 L3
Farr Highld 251 J5
Farr Highld 278 B4
Farraline Highld 251 G7
Farringdon Devon 14 B4
Farrington Gurney BaNES 45 J7
Far Sawrey Cumb 156 E4
Farsley Leeds 141 K1
Farther Howegreen Essex 71 K6
Farthing Green Kent 39 K4
Farthinghoe Nhants 83 M7
Farthingloe Kent 41 J7
Farthingstone Nhants 84 B4
Farthing Street Gt Lon 51 L6
Fartown Kirk 141 J4
Farway Devon 14 E3
Fasnacloich Ag & B 229 G6
Fasnakyle Highld 250 B6
Fassfern Highld 239 G7
Fatfield Sundld 181 H7
Faugh Cumb 178 C7
Fauld Staffs 115 K6
Fauldhouse W Loth 210 B6
Faulkbourne Essex 71 J4
Faulkland Somset 45 L8
Fauls Shrops 113 K5
Faversham Kent 40 D3
Fawdington N York 150 F1
Fawdon N u Ty 180 F5
Fawdon Nthumb 190 E3
Fawfieldhead Staffs 131 L7
Fawkham Green Kent 52 C6
Fawler Oxon 66 A4
Fawley Bucks 49 J2
Fawley Hants 19 J3
Fawley W Berk 48 B3
Fawley Chapel Herefs 63 H1
Fawnog Flints 128 F6
Fawsley Nhants 84 A4
Faxfleet E R Yk 143 L3
Faygate W Susx 37 K4
Fazakerley Lpool 138 D8
Fazeley Staffs 99 G3
Fearby N York 160 B6
Fearn Highld 264 C4
Fearnan P & K 231 K6
Fearnbeg Highld 260 B7
Fearnhead Warrtn 130 C2
Fearnmore Highld 260 A7
Fearnoch Ag & B 206 E3
Featherstone Staffs 97 L2
Featherstone Wakefd 142 C4
Feckenham Worcs 82 B3
Feering Essex 72 C3
Feetham N York 159 H3
Feizor N York 148 D2
Felbridge Surrey 38 B5
Felbrigg Norfk 122 E4
Felcourt Surrey 38 B5
Felden Herts 68 D6
Felindre Carmth 59 G4
Felindre Carmth 59 K3
Felindre Carmth 76 C7

Felindre Cerdgn 77 G4
Felindre Powys 61 J2
Felindre Powys 94 E7
Felindre Swans 57 H4
Felindre Farchog Pembks 75 J4
Felinfach Cerdgn 76 F4
Felinfach Powys 78 F8
Felinfoel Carmth 56 F4
Felingwmisaf Carmth 58 F4
Felingwmuchaf Carmth 58 F4
Felin-newydd Powys 78 F8
Felixkirk N York 161 G5
Felixstowe Suffk 91 G8
Felixstowe Ferry Suffk 91 H7
Felkington Nthumb 202 E4
Felkirk Wakefd 142 B5
Felling Gatesd 181 G6
Fell Lane C Brad 149 J7
Fell Side Cumb 165 J3
Felmersham Bed 85 K4
Felmingham Norfk 122 E5
Felpham W Susx 20 F7
Felsham Suffk 89 J4
Felsted Essex 71 G3
Feltham Gt Lon 50 E4
Felthamhill Surrey 50 E5
Felthorpe Norfk 122 D7
Felton Herefs 80 D5
Felton N Som 45 G6
Felton Nthumb 191 H6
Felton Butler Shrops 112 F8
Feltwell Norfk 104 E5
Fenay Bridge Kirk 141 J4
Fence Lancs 148 E8
Fence Rothm 133 J3
Fence Houses Sundld 169 J1
Fencott Oxon 66 E4
Fendike Corner Lincs 137 H7
Fen Ditton Cambs 87 K3
Fen Drayton Cambs 87 G2
Fen End Lincs 119 H7
Fen End Solhll 99 G8
Fenham Nthumb 203 H5
Feniscliffe Bl w D 139 K2
Feniscowles Bl w D 139 K3
Feniton Devon 14 C3
Feniton Court Devon 14 D3
Fenn Green Shrops 97 H6
Fenn Street Medway 53 G4
Fenny Bentley Derbys 115 K2
Fenny Bridges Devon 14 D3
Fenny Compton Warwks 83 K5
Fenny Drayton Leics 99 K4
Fenny Stratford M Keyn 85 G8
Fenrother Nthumb 191 H7
Fenstanton Cambs 87 G2
Fenstead End Suffk 88 F5
Fen Street Norfk 105 K4
Fen Street Suffk 90 E3
Fenton C Stke 114 D3
Fenton Cambs 103 G7
Fenton Cumb 178 C7
Fenton Lincs 118 A1
Fenton Lincs 135 G4
Fenton Notts 134 F3
Fenton Nthumb 202 F6
Fenton Barns E Loth 212 B3
Fenwick Donc 142 F4
Fenwick E Ayrs 196 F2
Fenwick Nthumb 180 C4
Fenwick Nthumb 203 H5
Feock Cnwll 3 L3
Feolin Ferry Ag & B 205 G2
Fergushill N Ayrs 196 C2
Feriniquarrie Highld 258 B6
Fermain Bay Guern 9 k3
Fern Angus 234 D3
Ferndale Rhondd 42 F2
Ferndown Dorset 17 L3
Ferness Highld 253 J3
Fernham Oxon 65 L8
Fernhill Heath Worcs 81 K3
Fernhurst W Susx 36 D5
Fernie Fife 222 E4
Ferniegair S Lans 209 K8
Fernilea Highld 246 E2
Fernilee Derbys 131 K4
Fernwood Notts 117 L2
Ferrensby N York 150 E4
Ferriby Sluice N Linc 144 B4
Ferrindonald Highld 247 L7
Ferring W Susx 21 J6
Ferrybridge Wakefd 142 D3
Ferrybridge Services Wakefd 142 D3
Ferryden Angus 235 H4
Ferryhill Dur 169 H4
Ferryhill Station Dur 169 J4
Ferry Point Highld 263 K3
Ferryside Carmth 56 C3
Fersfield Norfk 106 B6

Fersit Highld 240 B7
Feshiebridge Highld 241 M3
Fetcham Surrey 50 F7
Fetlar Shet 281 f3
Fetterangus Abers 269 H6
Fettercairn Abers 235 G1
Fewcott Oxon 66 D2
Fewston N York 150 B5
Ffairfach Carmth 59 H4
Ffair Rhos Cerdgn 77 K2
Ffald-y-Brenin Carmth 77 H6
Ffarmers Carmth 77 J6
Ffawyddog Powys 61 K3
Ffordd-las Denbgs 128 D6
Fforest Carmth 57 G4
Fforest Gôch Neath 57 K4
Ffostrasol Cerdgn 76 C5
Ffrith Flints 129 G8
Ffynnonddewi Cerdgn 76 C4
Ffynnongroyw Flints 128 D3
Ffynnon-oer Cerdgn 76 F4
Fickleshole Surrey 51 K6
Fiddington Gloucs 64 D1
Fiddington Somset 30 B3
Fiddleford Dorset 32 D8
Fiddlers Green Cnwll 4 D4
Fiddlers Hamlet Essex 70 C6
Field Staffs 115 G5
Field Broughton Cumb 156 E6
Field Dalling Norfk 121 M4
Fieldhead Cumb 166 B3
Field Head Leics 100 B2
Fifehead Magdalen Dorset 32 C6
Fifehead Neville Dorset 32 C8
Fifehead St Quintin Dorset 16 E1
Fife Keith Moray 267 J6
Fifield Oxon 65 K3
Fifield W & M 49 L4
Fifield Wilts 33 K1
Figheldean Wilts 33 K2
Filands Wilts 46 D1
Filby Norfk 107 K1
Filey N York 163 L6
Filgrave M Keyn 85 G5
Filkins Oxon 65 K6
Filleigh Devon 28 B4
Filleigh Devon 28 C8
Fillingham Lincs 135 J3
Fillongley Warwks 99 H5
Filmore Hill Hants 35 K5
Filton S Glos 45 J3
Fimber E R Yk 152 D4
Finavon Angus 234 D4
Fincham Norfk 104 D2
Finchampstead Wokham 49 J6
Fincharn Ag & B 216 D6
Finchdean Hants 20 B4
Finchingfield Essex 88 D8
Finchley Gt Lon 51 H1
Findern Derbys 116 A5
Findhorn Moray 265 G7
Findhorn Bridge Highld 252 E6
Findochty Moray 267 J3
Findo Gask P & K 221 H3
Findon Abers 245 L4
Findon W Susx 21 J5
Findon Mains Highld 263 G7
Findon Valley W Susx 21 K5
Findrack House Abers 244 D3
Finedon Nhants 85 H1
Fingal Street Suffk 90 F1
Fingask P & K 222 B3
Fingest Bucks 49 J1
Finghall N York 160 B5
Fingland Cumb 177 H7
Fingland D & G 197 L7
Finglesham Kent 41 K4
Fingringhoe Essex 72 F3
Finkle Green Essex 88 D7
Finkle Street Barns 141 M7
Finlake Devon 13 K6
Finlarig Stirlg 231 G8
Finmere Oxon 84 C8
Finnart P & K 230 F4
Finningham Suffk 90 C2
Finningley Donc 143 H7
Finsbay W Isls 282 e6
Finstall Worcs 82 A1
Finsthwaite Cumb 156 E5
Finstock Oxon 66 A4
Finstown Ork 275 c4
Fintry Abers 268 D5
Fintry Stirlg 209 G2
Finzean Abers 244 D5
Fionnphort Ag & B 226 B7
Fionnsbhagh W Isls 282 e6
Firbank Cumb 157 K4
Firbeck Rothm 133 L2
Firby N York 152 A3

Place	County	Page	Grid
Firby	N York	160	C5
Firgrove	Rochdl	140	D5
Firle	E Susx	23	G6
Firsby	Lincs	137	H7
Firsdown	Wilts	34	B4
Fir Tree	Dur	168	F4
Fishbourne	IoW	19	J5
Fishbourne	W Susx	20	D6
Fishburn	Dur	169	K4
Fishcross	Clacks	220	F8
Fisher	W Susx	20	E6
Fisherford	Abers	256	B4
Fisherrow	E Loth	211	K4
Fisher's Pond	Hants	35	G6
Fisher's Row	Lancs	147	H6
Fisherstreet	W Susx	36	E4
Fisherton	Highld	252	D2
Fisherton	S Ayrs	196	B7
Fisherton de la Mere	Wilts	33	G3
Fisherwick	Staffs	98	F2
Fishery	W & M	49	L3
Fishguard	Pembks	74	F5
Fishlake	Donc	143	G5
Fishleigh	Devon	12	D2
Fishmere End	Lincs	119	J4
Fishnish Pier	Ag & B	227	J4
Fishpond Bottom	Dorset	15	J3
Fishponds	Bristl	45	J4
Fishtoft	Lincs	119	K3
Fishtoft Drove	Lincs	119	K2
Fishwick	Lancs	139	H2
Fiskavaig	Highld	246	D2
Fiskerton	Lincs	135	L5
Fiskerton	Notts	117	K1
Fitling	E R Yk	145	H1
Fittleton	Wilts	33	K1
Fittleworth	W Susx	21	G3
Fitton End	Cambs	103	J1
Fitz	Shrops	113	G7
Fitzhead	Somset	29	L5
Fitzroy	Somset	30	B5
Fitzwilliam	Wakefd	142	C5
Five Ash Down	E Susx	23	H3
Five Ashes	E Susx	23	J2
Five Bells	Somset	29	K2
Five Bridges	Herefs	80	F6
Fivecrosses	Ches W	129	M4
Fivehead	Somset	30	E6
Fivelanes	Cnwll	11	J6
Five Lanes	Mons	44	F1
Five Oak Green	Kent	39	G4
Five Oaks	Jersey	9	e3
Five Oaks	W Susx	37	G5
Five Roads	Carmth	56	E4
Five Wents	Kent	39	K3
Flack's Green	Essex	71	J4
Flackwell Heath	Bucks	49	L1
Fladbury	Worcs	82	A6
Fladdabister	Shet	281	e7
Flagg	Derbys	132	C6
Flamborough	E R Yk	153	K2
Flamborough Head	E R Yk	153	L2
Flamstead	Herts	68	D4
Flamstead End	Herts	69	J6
Flansham	W Susx	20	F6
Flanshaw	Wakefd	141	M4
Flappit Spring	C Brad	149	J8
Flasby	N York	149	G4
Flash	Staffs	131	K6
Flashader	Highld	258	E6
Flaunden	Herts	68	C7
Flawborough	Notts	117	K3
Flawith	N York	151	G3
Flax Bourton	N Som	45	G5
Flaxby	N York	150	E4
Flaxley	Gloucs	63	K4
Flaxmere	Ches W	130	A5
Flaxpool	Somset	29	L4
Flaxton	N York	151	L3
Fleckney	Leics	100	E5
Flecknoe	Warwks	83	M3
Fledborough	Notts	134	F5
Fleet	Dorset	16	C6
Fleet	Hants	20	B6
Fleet	Hants	49	K8
Fleet	Lincs	119	L6
Fleetend	Hants	19	H3
Fleet Hargate	Lincs	119	L6
Fleet Services	Hants	49	J7
Fleetwood	Lancs	146	F6
Fleggburgh	Norfk	123	J8
Flemingston	V Glam	42	F7
Flemington	S Lans	209	H7
Flempton	Suffk	89	G1
Fletchersbridge	Cnwll	5	J2
Fletcher's Green	Kent	38	E3
Fletchertown	Cumb	165	G2
Fletching	E Susx	23	G3
Fleur-de-lis	Caerph	43	J3
Flexbury	Cnwll	11	J1
Flexford	Surrey	36	D1
Flimby	Cumb	164	D4
Flimwell	E Susx	39	H7
Flint	Flints	128	F5
Flintham	Notts	117	K2
Flint Mountain	Flints	128	F5
Flinton	E R Yk	153	K8
Flint's Green	Solhll	99	H7
Flishinghurst	Kent	39	J6
Flitcham	Norfk	120	F6
Flitch Green	Essex	71	G3
Flitton	C Beds	85	L8
Flitwick	C Beds	85	K8
Flixborough	N Linc	143	L5
Flixborough Stather	N Linc	143	L5
Flixton	N York	163	J6
Flixton	Suffk	107	G6
Flixton	Traffd	130	E1
Flockton	Kirk	141	K5
Flockton Green	Kirk	141	L5
Flodden	Nthumb	202	E6
Flodigarry	Highld	259	H2
Flookburgh	Cumb	156	E7
Flordon	Norfk	106	D4
Flore	Nhants	84	C3
Flotterton	Nthumb	190	E5
Flowers Green	E Susx	23	L5
Flowton	Suffk	90	C6
Flushdyke	Wakefd	141	L4
Flushing	Cnwll	3	K4
Fluxton	Devon	14	C4
Flyford Flavell	Worcs	82	A4
Fobbing	Thurr	52	F2
Fochabers	Moray	267	G4
Fochriw	Caerph	61	H6
Fockerby	N Linc	143	L4
Foddington	Somset	31	J5
Foel	Powys	94	B1
Foelgastell	Carmth	59	G6
Foel y Dyffryn	Brdgnd	42	C3
Foggathorpe	E R Yk	152	A8
Fogo	Border	202	B3
Fogwatt	Moray	266	E5
Foindle	Highld	276	B6
Folda	Angus	233	J4
Fole	Staffs	115	G4
Foleshill	Covtry	99	K7
Folke	Dorset	31	L8
Folkestone	Kent	41	H8
Folkestone Services	Kent	40	F7
Folkingham	Lincs	118	E5
Folkington	E Susx	23	J6
Folksworth	Cambs	102	C5
Folkton	N York	163	J6
Folla Rule	Abers	256	C5
Follifoot	N York	150	D5
Folly Gate	Devon	12	D3
Folly Hill	Surrey	36	B1
Fonmon	V Glam	43	G8
Fonthill Bishop	Wilts	32	F4
Fonthill Gifford	Wilts	32	F4
Fontmell Magna	Dorset	32	E7
Fontmell Parva	Dorset	32	D7
Fontwell	W Susx	20	F5
Font-y-gary	V Glam	43	G8
Foolow	Derbys	132	D4
Foots Cray	Gt Lon	52	A5
Forbestown	Abers	243	L1
Forcett	N York	168	F8
Ford	Ag & B	216	D6
Ford	Bucks	67	J5
Ford	Derbys	133	H4
Ford	Devon	7	J5
Ford	Devon	8	B6
Ford	Devon	27	G6
Ford	Gloucs	65	G1
Ford	Nthumb	202	E5
Ford	Shrops	95	K1
Ford	Somset	29	K5
Ford	Somset	45	H8
Ford	Staffs	115	H1
Ford	W Susx	21	G6
Ford	Wilts	33	L4
Ford	Wilts	46	B4
Forda	Devon	12	D4
Fordcombe	Kent	38	E5
Fordell	Fife	211	G1
Forden	Powys	94	F3
Ford End	Essex	71	G4
Forder Green	Devon	8	B2
Ford Green	Lancs	147	J6
Fordham	Cambs	88	C1
Fordham	Essex	72	D2
Fordham	Norfk	104	C3
Fordham Heath	Essex	72	D2
Ford Heath	Shrops	95	K1
Fordingbridge	Hants	33	K8
Fordon	E R Yk	163	J7
Fordoun	Abers	245	G8
Ford's Green	Suffk	90	C2
Fordstreet	Essex	72	D2
Ford Street	Somset	29	L7
Fordton	Devon	13	J3
Fordwells	Oxon	65	L4
Fordwich	Kent	41	G3
Fordyce	Abers	267	L3
Forebridge	Staffs	114	E7
Foremark	Derbys	116	B6
Forest	Guern	9	j4
Forest	N York	160	C3
Forest Becks	Lancs	148	D5
Forestburn Gate	Nthumb	190	F7
Forest Chapel	Ches E	131	J5
Forest Coal Pit	Mons	62	B3
Forest Gate	Gt Lon	51	L2
Forest Green	Surrey	37	H3
Forest Hall	N Tyne	181	G5
Forest Head	Cumb	178	D7
Forest Hill	Gt Lon	51	K4
Forest Hill	Oxon	66	E5
Forest-in-Teesdale	Dur	167	K4
Forest Lane Head	N York	150	D4
Forest Mill	Clacks	221	G8
Forest of Bowland	Lancs	148	A5
Forest of Dean	Gloucs	63	J5
Forest Row	E Susx	38	C6
Forest Side	IoW	19	H5
Forestside	W Susx	20	C4
Forest Town	Notts	133	L7
Forfar	Angus	234	C5
Forgandenny	P & K	221	K3
Forge	Powys	93	G3
Forge Hammer	Torfn	62	B7
Forge Side	Torfn	61	L5
Forgie	Moray	267	H5
Forgieside	Moray	267	H5
Forgue	Abers	256	C4
Forhill	Worcs	98	D8
Formby	Sefton	138	C6
Forncett End	Norfk	106	C4
Forncett St Mary	Norfk	106	D4
Forncett St Peter	Norfk	106	D5
Fornham All Saints	Suffk	89	G2
Fornham St Martin	Suffk	89	G2
Fornham St Genevieve	Suffk	89	G2
Fornighty	Highld	253	H2
Forres	Moray	265	G8
Forsbrook	Staffs	114	F3
Forse	Highld	275	H1
Forshaw Heath	Warwks	98	E8
Forsinard	Highld	278	F7
Forss	Highld	279	J3
Forston	Dorset	16	C3
Fort Augustus	Highld	240	C2
Forteviot	P & K	221	J4
Forth	S Lans	198	F2
Forthampton	Gloucs	64	D1
Fort Hommet	Guern	9	i2
Forth Rail Bridge	C Edin	210	F3
Forth Road Bridge	Fife	210	F3
Fortingall	P & K	231	K6
Forton	Hants	34	F2
Forton	Lancs	147	J5
Forton	Shrops	113	G8
Forton	Somset	15	H1
Forton	Staffs	114	B7
Fort Richmond	Guern	9	i2
Fortrie	Abers	256	B3
Fortrose	Highld	263	K8
Fortuneswell	Dorset	16	D7
Fort William	Highld	239	J8
Forty Green	Bucks	68	B8
Forty Hill	Gt Lon	69	J7
Forward Green	Suffk	90	C3
Fosbury	Wilts	47	L7
Foscot	Oxon	65	K3
Foscote	Nhants	84	C6
Fosdyke	Lincs	119	K5
Fosdyke Bridge	Lincs	119	K5
Foss	P & K	231	L4
Fossebridge	Gloucs	65	G5
Foss-y-ffin	Cerdgn	76	E3
Fosterhouses	Donc	143	G5
Foster Street	Essex	70	C5
Foston	Derbys	115	K5
Foston	Leics	100	D4
Foston	Lincs	117	M3
Foston	N York	151	L3
Foston on the Wolds	E R Yk	153	H4
Fotherby	Lincs	136	F2
Fothergill	Cumb	164	D4
Fotheringhay	Nhants	102	B5
Foula	Shet	281	a7
Foula Airport	Shet	281	a7
Foul Anchor	Cambs	120	A7
Foulbridge	Cumb	165	M1
Foulby	Wakefd	142	B4
Foulden	Border	202	E2
Foulden	Norfk	104	C4
Foul End	Warwks	99	H4
Foul Mile	E Susx	23	K
Foulness Island	Essex	53	K
Foulridge	Lancs	148	
Foulsham	Norfk	122	
Fountainhall	Border	200	
Four Ashes	Solhll	98	
Four Ashes	Staffs	97	
Four Ashes	Staffs	97	
Four Ashes	Suffk	89	K
Four Cabots	Guern	9	ja
Four Crosses	Powys	112	
Four Crosses	Staffs	98	
Four Elms	Kent	38	
Four Foot	Somset	30	
Four Forks	Somset	30	
Four Gates	Bolton	139	
Four Gotes	Cambs	120	
Four Lane End	Barns	141	
Four Lane Ends	Ches W	130	
Four Lanes	Cnwll	3	
Fourlanes End	Ches E	130	
Four Marks	Hants	35	
Four Mile Bridge	IoA	124	
Four Oaks	Birm	98	
Four Oaks	E Susx	24	
Four Oaks	Gloucs	63	
Four Oaks	Solhll	99	
Fourpenny	Highld	264	
Four Points	W Berk	48	
Four Roads	Carmth	56	
Four Shire Stone	Warwks	65	
Fourstones	Nthumb	179	
Four Throws	Kent	39	
Four Wents	Kent	38	
Fovant	Wilts	33	
Foveran	Abers	257	
Fowey	Cnwll	5	
Fowley Common	Warrtn	139	
Fowlhall	Kent	39	
Fowlis	Angus	233	M
Fowlis Wester	P & K	221	
Fowlmere	Cambs	87	
Fownhope	Herefs	80	
Foxbar	Rens	208	
Foxcombe	Devon	12	
Fox Corner	Surrey	50	
Foxcote	Gloucs	64	
Foxcote	Somset	45	
Foxdale	IoM	154	
Foxearth	Essex	89	
Foxendown	Kent	52	
Foxfield	Cumb	156	
Foxham	Wilts	46	
Fox Hatch	Essex	70	
Foxhills	Hants	18	
Foxhole	Cnwll	4	
Foxholes	N York	163	
Foxhunt Green	E Susx	23	
Foxley	Nhants	84	
Foxley	Norfk	122	
Foxley	Wilts	46	
Foxlydiate	Worcs	82	
Fox Street	Essex	72	
Foxt	Staffs	115	
Foxton	Cambs	87	
Foxton	Dur	169	
Foxton	Leics	100	
Foxton	N York	160	
Foxup	N York	158	
Foxwist Green	Ches W	130	
Foxwood	Shrops	96	
Foy	Herefs	63	
Foyers	Highld	250	
Foynesfield	Highld	253	
Fraddam	Cnwll	2	
Fraddon	Cnwll	4	
Fradley	Staffs	98	
Fradswell	Staffs	114	
Fraisthorpe	E R Yk	153	
Framfield	E Susx	23	
Framingham Earl	Norfk	106	
Framingham Pigot	Norfk	106	
Framlingham	Suffk	91	
Frampton	Dorset	16	
Frampton	Lincs	119	
Frampton Cotterell	S Glos	45	
Frampton Mansell	Gloucs	64	
Frampton-on-Severn	Gloucs	63	
Frampton West End	Lincs	119	
Framsden	Suffk	90	
Framwellgate Moor	Dur	169	
Franche	Worcs	97	
Frandley	Ches W	130	
Frankaborough	Devon	11	
Frankby	Wirral	128	
Frankfort	Norfk	122	
Franklands Gate	Herefs	80	
Frankley	Worcs	98	
Frankley Services	Worcs	98	
Franksbridge	Powys	78	

Frankton Warwks 83 K1
Frant E Susx 38 F6
Fraserburgh Abers 269 J3
Frating Essex 73 G3
Frating Green Essex 73 G2
Fratton C Port 19 L4
Freathy Cnwll 6 D4
Freckenham Suffk 88 D1
Freckleton Lancs 138 E2
Freebirch Derbys 132 F5
Freeby Leics 117 L7
Freefolk Hants 35 G1
Freehay Staffs 115 G3
Freeland Oxon 66 B4
Freethorpe Norfk 107 H2
Freethorpe Common Norfk 107 H2
Freiston Lincs 119 L3
Fremington Devon 27 J4
Fremington N York 159 J3
Frenchay S Glos 45 J3
Frenchbeer Devon 12 F5
French Street Kent 51 M8
Frenich P & K 232 B4
Frensham Surrey 36 C3
Freshfield Sefton 138 C6
Freshford Wilts 46 A4
Freshwater IoW 18 E6
Freshwater Bay IoW 18 E6
Freshwater East Pembks 55 G7
Fressingfield Suffk 106 F7
Freston Suffk 90 E7
Freswick Highld 280 E3
Fretherne Gloucs 63 L5
Frettenham Norfk 122 E8
Freuchie Fife 222 D6
Freystrop Pembks 54 F4
Friar Park Sandw 98 C4
Friar's Gate E Susx 38 D6
Friars' Hill N York 162 C5
Friar Waddon Dorset 16 C5
Friday Bridge Cambs 103 K2
Friday Street Suffk 90 F3
Friday Street Suffk 91 H5
Friday Street Suffk 91 J3
Friday Street Surrey 37 H2
Fridaythorpe E R Yk 152 D4
Friden Derbys 132 C7
Friendly Calder 141 G3
Friern Barnet Gt Lon 69 H4
Friesthorpe Lincs 135 M3
Frieston Lincs 118 B2
Frieth Bucks 49 J1
Friezeland Notts 116 D2
Frilford Oxon 66 B7
Frilsham W Berk 48 E4
Frimley Surrey 49 L7
Frimley Green Surrey 49 L7
Frindsbury Medway 52 F5
Fring Norfk 121 G4
Fringford Oxon 66 F1
Frinsted Kent 40 A4
Frinton-on-Sea Essex 73 K3
Friockheim Angus 234 F5
Friog Gwynd 92 D1
Frisby on the Wreake Leics 117 J8
Friskney Lincs 137 J8
Friskney Eaudike Lincs 137 J8
Friston E Susx 23 J7
Friston Suffk 91 J3
Fritchley Derbys 116 B1
Fritham Hants 34 B8
Frith Bank Lincs 119 K2
Frith Common Worcs 80 F1
Frithelstock Devon 27 H7
Frithelstock Stone Devon 27 H7
Frithend Hants 36 B3
Frithsden Herts 68 C5
Frithville Lincs 119 K2
Frittenden Kent 39 K5
Frittiscombe Devon 8 B6
Fritton Norfk 106 E5
Fritton Norfk 107 K3
Fritwell Oxon 66 D1
Frizinghall C Brad 149 L8
Frizington Cumb 164 D7
Frocester Gloucs 63 M6
Frodesley Shrops 96 C3
Frodsham Ches W 129 M4
Frogden Border 202 B7
Frog End Cambs 87 H6
Frog End Cambs 87 L3
Froggatt Derbys 132 E4
Froghall Staffs 115 G3
Frogham Hants 33 L8
Frogham Kent 41 H5
Frogmore Devon 7 M6
Frognall Lincs 102 D2
Frogpool Cnwll 3 J3
Frog Pool Worcs 81 J2
Frogwell Cnwll 6 C1

Frolesworth Leics 100 B5
Frome Somset 32 C1
Frome St Quintin Dorset 16 B2
Fromes Hill Herefs 80 F6
Fron Gwynd 108 F4
Fron Gwynd 109 J1
Fron Powys 94 E4
Fron Powys 94 F3
Froncysyllte Wrexhm 112 C3
Fron-goch Gwynd 111 H4
Fron Isaf Wrexhm 112 C3
Frostenden Suffk 107 K7
Frosterley Dur 168 C3
Froxfield C Beds 85 J4
Froxfield Wilts 47 L5
Froxfield Green Hants 35 L5
Fryern Hill Hants 34 F6
Fryerning Essex 70 F7
Fryton N York 162 B7
Fuinary Highld 227 J3
Fulbeck Lincs 118 B2
Fulbourn Cambs 87 L4
Fulbrook Oxon 65 K4
Fulflood Hants 35 G5
Fulford C York 151 K6
Fulford Somset 30 B5
Fulford Staffs 114 F4
Fulham Gt Lon 51 H4
Fulking W Susx 22 C5
Fullaford Devon 28 B3
Fullarton N Ayrs 196 C3
Fuller's End Essex 70 D2
Fuller's Moor Ches W 113 H1
Fuller Street Essex 71 H4
Fuller Street Kent 38 E2
Fullerton Hants 34 E3
Fulletby Lincs 136 E5
Fullready Warwks 83 G6
Full Sutton E R Yk 152 A5
Fullwood E Ayrs 196 E1
Fulmer Bucks 50 C2
Fulmodeston Norfk 121 M5
Fulnetby Lincs 136 B4
Fulney Lincs 119 J6
Fulstone Kirk 141 J6
Fulstow Lincs 145 J8
Fulwell Oxon 66 A3
Fulwell Sundld 181 J7
Fulwood Lancs 139 H2
Fulwood Notts 133 J8
Fulwood Sheff 132 F3
Fulwood Somset 30 B6
Fundenhall Norfk 106 C4
Funtington W Susx 20 C5
Funtley Hants 19 J2
Funtullich P & K 220 C2
Furley Devon 15 G2
Furnace Ag & B 217 G7
Furnace Carmth 56 F4
Furnace Cerdgn 92 E4
Furnace End Warwks 99 H5
Furner's Green E Susx 22 F2
Furness Vale Derbys 131 K3
Furneux Pelham Herts 70 B2
Further Quarter Kent 39 M5
Furtho Nhants 84 E6
Furzehill Devon 28 C2
Furzehill Dorset 17 K2
Furzehills Lincs 136 E5
Furzeley Corner Hants 19 L2
Furze Platt W & M 49 L3
Furzley Hants 34 C7
Fyfett Somset 30 C7
Fyfield Essex 70 E5
Fyfield Hants 34 C2
Fyfield Oxon 66 B7
Fyfield Wilts 47 H5
Fyfield Wilts 47 H6
Fyfield Bavant Wilts 33 H6
Fylingthorpe N York 163 G2
Fyning W Susx 36 B6
Fyvie Abers 256 D4

G

Gabroc Hill E Ayrs 196 E1
Gaddesby Leics 100 F1
Gaddesden Row Herts 68 D4
Gadfa IoA 125 H2
Gadgirth S Ayrs 196 E6
Gadlas Shrops 112 E4
Gaer Powys 61 J3
Gaerllwyd Mons 62 F7
Gaerwen IoA 125 H5
Gagingwell Oxon 66 B2
Gailes N Ayrs 196 C4
Gailey Staffs 97 K1
Gainford Dur 168 F7

Gainsborough Lincs 135 G2
Gainsborough Suffk 90 C1
Gainsford End Essex 88 E8
Gairloch Highld 260 C4
Gairlochy Highld 239 K6
Gairneybridge P & K 221 L7
Gaisgill Cumb 157 K2
Gaitsgill Cumb 165 L1
Galashiels Border 201 G6
Galgate Lancs 147 J6
Galhampton Somset 31 K5
Gallanachbeg Ag & B 216 C2
Gallanachmore Ag & B 216 C2
Gallantry Bank Ches E 113 H1
Gallatown Fife 222 E8
Galley Common Warwks 99 J5
Galleywood Essex 71 H6
Gallovie Highld 240 F5
Galloway Forest Park 184 C6
Gallowfauld Angus 234 C7
Gallowhill P & K 233 J8
Gallows Green Essex 72 D2
Gallows Green Worcs 81 L3
Gallowstree Common Oxon 49 G3
Galltair Highld 248 C7
Gallt-y-foel Gwynd 125 K6
Gallypot Street E Susx 38 D6
Galmisdale Highld 236 F4
Galmpton Devon 7 K6
Galmpton Torbay 8 D4
Galphay N York 150 C1
Galston E Ayrs 196 F4
Gamballs Green Staffs 131 L6
Gamblesby Cumb 166 E3
Gambles Green Essex 71 J4
Gamelsby Cumb 177 H8
Gamesley Derbys 131 K1
Gamlingay Cambs 86 E5
Gamlingay Cinques Cambs 86 E4
Gamlingay Great Heath Cambs 86 E5
Gammersgill N York 159 J6
Gamrie Abers 268 E4
Gamston Notts 117 G4
Gamston Notts 134 E4
Ganarew Herefs 63 G4
Ganavan Bay Ag & B 216 D1
Gang Cnwll 6 C1
Ganllwyd Gwynd 110 D6
Gannachy Angus 234 F1
Ganstead E R Yk 144 F1
Ganthorpe N York 151 L2
Ganton N York 163 H7
Ganwick Corner Herts 69 H7
Gappah Devon 13 K7
Garbity Moray 266 F5
Garboldisham Norfk 105 K7
Garbole Highld 252 E7
Garchory Abers 243 J2
Garden City Flints 129 H6
Gardeners Green Wokham 49 K5
Gardenstown Abers 268 E3
Garden Village Sheff 141 L8
Garderhouse Shet 281 d6
Gardham E R Yk 152 E2
Gare Hill Somset 32 C3
Garelochhead Ag & B 207 L1
Garford Oxon 66 B7
Garforth Leeds 142 B1
Gargrave N York 149 G5
Gargunnock Stirlg 220 B8
Garlic Street Norfk 106 E6
Garlieston D & G 174 D5
Garlinge Kent 41 K2
Garlinge Green Kent 40 F5
Garlogie Abers 245 H2
Garmond Abers 268 E4
Garmouth Moray 267 H3
Garmston Shrops 96 E2
Garnant Carmth 59 J6
Garndolbenmaen Gwynd 109 J3
Garnett Bridge Cumb 157 H3
Garnfadryn Gwynd 108 E5
Garnlydan Blae G 61 J4
Garnswllt Swans 57 H3
Garn-yr-erw Torfn 61 K5
Garrabost W Isls 282 h3
Garrallan E Ayrs 197 G7
Garras Cnwll 3 H6
Garreg Gwynd 109 L3
Garrigill Cumb 167 H2
Garriston N York 159 L4
Garroch D & G 184 F6
Garrochtrie D & G 172 D7
Garrochty Ag & B 207 H8
Garros Highld 259 H4
Garsdale Cumb 158 C5
Garsdale Head Cumb 158 D4
Garsdon Wilts 46 D2
Garshall Green Staffs 114 F5
Garsington Oxon 66 E6

Garstang Lancs 147 J6
Garston Herts 68 E7
Garston Lpool 129 J3
Garswood St Hel 139 H7
Gartachossan Ag & B 204 E4
Gartcosh N Lans 209 J5
Garth Brdgnd 42 C4
Garth Mons 62 D8
Garth Powys 78 C5
Garth Powys 79 J1
Garth Wrexhm 112 C3
Garthamlock C Glas 209 H5
Garthbrengy Powys 78 E8
Gartheli Cerdgn 77 G4
Garthmyl Powys 94 F3
Garthorpe Leics 117 L7
Garthorpe N Linc 143 L4
Garth Row Cumb 157 H3
Garths Cumb 157 H5
Gartly Abers 255 K5
Gartmore Stirlg 219 H7
Gartness N Lans 209 K6
Gartness Stirlg 208 E2
Gartocharn W Duns 208 D2
Garton E R Yk 145 H1
Garton-on-the-Wolds E R Yk 152 F4
Gartymore Highld 274 D5
Garva Bridge Highld 240 F4
Garvald Border 199 J3
Garvald E Loth 212 D5
Garvan Highld 238 F8
Garvard Ag & B 214 D6
Garve Highld 262 C7
Garvellachs Ag & B 215 J2
Garvestone Norfk 105 L2
Garvock Inver 207 L5
Garway Herefs 62 F3
Garway Common Herefs 62 F3
Garway Hill Herefs 62 F2
Garynahine W Isls 282 f3
Garyvard W Isls 282 g4
Gasper Wilts 32 C4
Gastard Wilts 46 C5
Gasthorpe Norfk 105 K7
Gaston Green Essex 70 C4
Gatcombe IoW 19 H6
Gateacre Lpool 129 K2
Gatebeck Cumb 157 J5
Gate Burton Lincs 135 G3
Gateford Notts 134 B3
Gateforth N York 142 E2
Gatehead E Ayrs 196 D4
Gate Helmsley N York 151 L5
Gatehouse Nthumb 179 H1
Gatehouse of Fleet D & G 174 F4
Gateley Norfk 121 L6
Gatenby N York 160 D5
Gatesgarth Cumb 165 G7
Gateshaw Border 189 L2
Gateshead Gatesd 181 G6
Gates Heath Ches W 129 L7
Gateside Angus 234 C6
Gateside E Rens 208 E7
Gateside Fife 222 B5
Gateside N Ayrs 208 B8
Gateslack D & G 186 C5
Gathurst Wigan 139 G6
Gatley Stockp 131 G2
Gatton Surrey 51 H8
Gattonside Border 201 H6
Gatwick Airport W Susx 37 L3
Gaufron Powys 78 D2
Gaulby Leics 100 F3
Gauldry Fife 222 F2
Gauldswell P & K 233 K5
Gaulkthorn Lancs 139 M3
Gaultree Norfk 103 K2
Gaunton's Bank Ches E 113 J2
Gaunt's Common Dorset 17 K2
Gaunt's End Essex 70 E2
Gautby Lincs 136 C5
Gavinton Border 202 B3
Gawber Barns 141 M6
Gawcott Bucks 67 G1
Gawsworth Ches E 131 H5
Gawthorpe Wakefd 141 L3
Gawthrop Cumb 158 B5
Gawthwaite Cumb 156 C5
Gay Bowers Essex 71 J6
Gaydon Warwks 83 J4
Gayhurst M Keyn 85 G6
Gayle N York 158 F5
Gayles N York 159 L1
Gay Street W Susx 21 J3
Gayton Nhants 84 D4
Gayton Norfk 120 F7
Gayton Staffs 114 F6
Gayton Wirral 129 G4
Gayton le Marsh Lincs 137 H3
Gayton Thorpe Norfk 121 G7

Gaywood Norfk 120 E7
Gazeley Suffk 88 E2
Gear Cnwll 3 J6
Gearraidh Bhaird W Isls 282 g4
Gearraidh na h-Aibhne W Isls 282 f3
Geary Highld 258 D4
Gedding Suffk 89 J4
Geddington Nhants 101 K6
Gedling Notts 117 G3
Gedney Lincs 119 L6
Gedney Broadgate Lincs 119 L7
Gedney Drove End Lincs 120 A5
Gedney Dyke Lincs 119 L6
Gedney Hill Lincs 103 G1
Gee Cross Tamesd 131 J1
Geeston Rutlnd 101 L3
Geirinis W Isls 283 c10
Geldeston Norfk 107 H5
Gelli Rhondd 42 E3
Gelli Torfn 62 B8
Gellideg Myr Td 60 F5
Gellifor Denbgs 128 D7
Gelligaer Caerph 43 H2
Gelligroes Caerph 43 J3
Gelligron Neath 57 K4
Gellilydan Gwynd 110 C4
Gellinudd Neath 57 K4
Gelly Pembks 55 J3
Gellyburn P & K 233 G7
Gellywen Carmth 58 A4
Gelston D & G 175 J3
Gelston Lincs 118 B3
Gembling E R Yk 153 H4
Gentleshaw Staffs 98 D1
Georgefield D & G 187 L7
George Green Bucks 50 C3
Georgeham Devon 27 H3
Georgemas Junction Station Highld 279 L4
George Nympton Devon 28 B6
Georgetown Blae G 61 J5
Georgia Cnwll 2 D4
Georth Ork 275 c3
Gerinish W Isls 283 c10
Gerlan Gwynd 126 C6
Germansweek Devon 12 B4
Germoe Cnwll 2 F5
Gerrans Cnwll 3 M4
Gerrards Cross Bucks 50 C1
Gerrick R & Cl 171 G8
Gestingthorpe Essex 89 G7
Gethsemane Pembks 75 J4
Geuffordd Powys 112 B8
Gib Hill Ches W 130 C4
Gibraltar Lincs 137 K7
Gibsmere Notts 117 J2
Giddeahall Wilts 46 B4
Giddy Green Dorset 16 F5
Gidea Park Gt Lon 52 B1
Gidleigh Devon 12 F5
Giffnock E Rens 208 F7
Gifford E Loth 212 C5
Giffordtown Fife 222 E5
Giggleswick N York 148 D3
Gigha Ag & B 205 L6
Gilberdyke E R Yk 143 L2
Gilbert's End Worcs 81 J6
Gilbert Street Hants 35 K4
Gilchriston E Loth 212 B6
Gilcrux Cumb 164 F3
Gildersome Leeds 141 K2
Gildingwells Rothm 133 L3
Gilesgate Moor Dur 169 J2
Gileston V Glam 42 F8
Gilfach Caerph 43 J2
Gilfach Goch Brdgnd 42 E4
Gilfachrheda Cerdgn 76 D3
Gilgarran Cumb 164 D6
Gill Cumb 166 B3
Gillamoor N York 162 B6
Gillan Cnwll 3 K6
Gillen Highld 258 D5
Gillesbie D & G 187 J7
Gilling East N York 161 K7
Gillingham Dorset 32 D5
Gillingham Medway 53 G5
Gillingham Norfk 107 H5
Gilling West N York 160 B2
Gillock Highld 280 B4
Gillow Heath Staffs 131 H7
Gills Highld 280 D2
Gill's Green Kent 39 J7
Gilmanscleuch Border 188 B2
Gilmerton C Edin 211 J5
Gilmerton P & K 220 F2
Gilmonby Dur 168 C8
Gilmorton Leics 100 C6
Gilsland Nthumb 178 C5
Gilson Warwks 99 G5
Gilstead C Brad 149 L7

Gilston Border 200 F2
Gilston Herts 70 C4
Gilston Park Herts 70 B4
Giltbrook Notts 116 E2
Gilwern Mons 61 L4
Gimingham Norfk 122 F4
Ginclough Ches E 131 J4
Gingers Green E Susx 23 K5
Gipping Suffk 90 C3
Gipsey Bridge Lincs 119 J2
Girdle Toll N Ayrs 196 C3
Girlington C Brad 141 H1
Girlsta Shet 281 e6
Girsby N York 160 E1
Girtford C Beds 86 D5
Girthon D & G 174 F4
Girton Cambs 87 J3
Girton Notts 135 G6
Girvan S Ayrs 182 F3
Gisburn Lancs 148 E6
Gisleham Suffk 107 K5
Gislingham Suffk 90 C1
Gissing Norfk 106 C6
Gittisham Devon 14 D3
Givons Grove Surrey 50 F7
Gladestry Powys 79 J4
Gladsmuir E Loth 212 A4
Glais Swans 57 K5
Glaisdale N York 162 D2
Glamis Angus 234 B6
Glanaber Gwynd 110 B1
Glanaman Carmth 59 J6
Glandford Norfk 122 A3
Glan-Duar Carmth 76 F6
Glandwr Pembks 75 L6
Glan-Dwyfach Gwynd 109 J3
Glandy Cross Carmth 75 K6
Glandyfi Cerdgn 92 F4
Glangrwyney Powys 61 K4
Glanllynfi Brdgnd 42 C3
Glanmule Powys 94 E5
Glanrhyd Pembks 75 K4
Glan-rhyd Powys 57 L3
Glanton Nthumb 190 F3
Glanton Pike Nthumb 190 F3
Glanvilles Wootton Dorset 16 C1
Glan-y-don Flints 128 E4
Glan-y-llyn Cardif 43 H5
Glan-y-nant Powys 93 K6
Glan-yr-afon Gwynd 111 H3
Glan-yr-afon Gwynd 111 K3
Glan-yr-afon IoA 126 B4
Glan-yr-afon Swans 57 H4
Glan-y-wern Gwynd 109 L4
Glapthorn Nhants 101 M5
Glapwell Derbys 133 J6
Glasbury Powys 79 H7
Glascoed Denbgs 127 K5
Glascoed Mons 62 C6
Glascote Staffs 99 G3
Glascwm Powys 79 G5
Glasfryn Conwy 111 H2
Glasgow C Glas 209 G6
Glasgow Airport Rens 208 E5
Glasgow Prestwick Airport S Ayrs 196 D5
Glasinfryn Gwynd 125 K6
Glasnacardoch Bay Highld 237 K2
Glasnakille Highld 247 H6
Glasphein Highld 258 B6
Glaspwll Powys 92 F4
Glassenbury Kent 39 J6
Glassford S Lans 197 L2
Glasshoughton Wakefd 142 C3
Glasshouse Gloucs 63 L3
Glasshouse Hill Gloucs 63 L3
Glasshouses N York 149 L3
Glaslaw Abers 268 F4
Glasson Cumb 177 H6
Glassonby Cumb 166 D3
Glasson Dock Lancs 147 J4
Glasterlaw Angus 234 F5
Glaston Rutlnd 101 K3
Glastonbury Somset 31 H3
Glatton Cambs 102 C6
Glazebrook Warrtn 130 D1
Glazebury Warrtn 139 K8
Glazeley Shrops 96 F5
Gleadless Sheff 133 G3
Gleadsmoss Ches E 130 F6
Gleaston Cumb 146 E2
Glebe Highld 250 F8
Gledhow Leeds 150 D8
Gledpark D & G 175 G5
Gledrid Shrops 112 D4
Glemsford Suffk 89 G5
Glen Achulish Highld 229 G4
Glenallachie Moray 254 E3
Glenancross Highld 237 K2
Glenaros House Ag & B 227 G4

Glen Auldyn IoM 154 f4
Glenbarr Ag & B 192 D1
Glenbarry Abers 267 L5
Glenbeg Highld 237 H8
Glenbervie Abers 245 G7
Glenboig N Lans 209 J5
Glenborrodale Highld 237 H8
Glenbranter Ag & B 217 J7
Glenbreck Border 187 G2
Glenbrittle Highld 246 E3
Glenbuck E Ayrs 198 B7
Glencally Angus 234 A3
Glencaple D & G 176 C5
Glencarse P & K 222 C3
Glencothe Border 199 J7
Glencraig Fife 222 B8
Glencrosh D & G 185 J5
Glendale Highld 258 B6
Glendaruel Ag & B 206 F2
Glendevon P & K 221 H6
Glendoe Lodge Highld 240 C2
Glendoick P & K 222 C3
Glenduckie Fife 222 D3
Glenegedale Ag & B 204 E6
Glenelg Highld 248 C7
Glenerney Moray 253 K2
Glenfarg P & K 221 L5
Glenfield Leics 100 C2
Glenfinnan Highld 238 E7
Glenfintaig Lodge Highld 239 L6
Glenfoot P & K 222 B4
Glenfyne Lodge Ag & B 217 L4
Glengarnock N Ayrs 208 B8
Glengolly Highld 279 K3
Glengorm Castle Ag & B 226 E1
Glengrasco Highld 259 G7
Glenholm Border 199 J6
Glenhoul D & G 184 F5
Glenkin Ag & B 207 J3
Glenkindie Abers 243 M1
Glenlivet Moray 254 D6
Glenlochar D & G 175 J2
Glenlomond P & K 222 B6
Glenluce D & G 172 F3
Glenmassen Ag & B 207 H2
Glenmavis N Lans 209 K5
Glen Maye IoM 154 b6
Glen Mona IoM 154 f4
Glenmore Highld 259 G8
Glenmore Lodge Highld 242 C2
Glen Nevis House Highld 229 J1
Glenochil Clacks 220 F8
Glen Parva Leics 100 C4
Glenquiech Angus 234 C3
Glenralloch Ag & B 206 D5
Glenridding Cumb 165 L7
Glenrothes Fife 222 D7
Glenshero Lodge Highld 240 F5
Glenstriven Ag & B 207 H3
Glentham Lincs 135 K2
Glentrool D & G 183 J7
Glen Trool Lodge D & G 183 K7
Glentruim Highld 241 J4
Glentworth Lincs 135 J2
Glenuig Highld 237 K5
Glenvarragill Highld 259 H8
Glen Vine IoM 154 d6
Glenwhilly D & G 182 F8
Glespin S Lans 198 D7
Glewstone Herefs 63 H3
Glinton C Pete 102 C2
Glooston Leics 101 G4
Glossop Derbys 131 L1
Gloster Hill Nthumb 191 K5
Gloucester Gloucs 64 B3
Gloucester Services Gloucs 64 B4
Gloucestershire Airport Gloucs 64 C3
Glusburn N York 149 H6
Glutt Lodge Highld 274 D1
Gluvian Cnwll 4 F2
Glympton Oxon 66 B3
Glynarthen Cerdgn 76 B5
Glyn Ceiriog Wrexhm 112 D4
Glyncoch Rhondd 43 G3
Glyncorrwg Neath 60 C7
Glynde E Susx 23 G5
Glyndebourne E Susx 23 G5
Glyndyfrdwy Denbgs 112 A3
Glynneath Neath 60 D5
Glynogwr Brdgnd 42 E4
Glyntaff Rhondd 43 H4
Glyntawe Powys 60 C4
Glynteg Carmth 76 C7
Gnosall Staffs 114 C7
Gnosall Heath Staffs 114 C7
Goadby Leics 101 G4
Goadby Marwood Leics 117 K6
Goatacre Wilts 46 F4
Goatham Green E Susx 24 E3

Goathill Dorset 31
Goathland N York 162
Goathurst Somset 30
Goathurst Common Kent 38
Goat Lees Kent 40
Gobowen Shrops 112
Godalming Surrey 36
Goddard's Corner Suffk 91
Goddard's Green Kent 39
Goddards Green W Susx 22
Godden Green Kent 38
Godford Cross Devon 14
Godington Oxon 66
Godley Tamesd 140
Godmanchester Cambs 86
Godmanstone Dorset 16
Godmersham Kent 40
Godney Somset 31
Godolphin Cross Cnwll 2
Godre'r-graig Neath 57
Godshill Hants 33
Godshill IoW 19
Godstone Staffs 115
Godstone Surrey 51
Godsworthy Devon 12
Godwinscroft Hants 18
Goetre Mons 62
Goff's Oak Herts 69
Gogar C Edin 211
Goginan Cerdgn 92
Golan Gwynd 109
Golant Cnwll 5
Golberdon Cnwll 11
Golborne Wigan 139
Golcar Kirk 141
Goldcliff Newpt 44
Golden Cross E Susx 23
Golden Green Kent 39
Golden Grove Carmth 59
Goldenhill C Stke 114
Golden Hill Pembks 55
Golden Pot Hants 35
Golden Valley Derbys 116
Golders Green Gt Lon 51
Goldfinch Bottom W Berk 48
Goldhanger Essex 72
Gold Hill Cambs 103
Gold Hill Dorset 32
Golding Shrops 96
Goldington Bed 86
Goldsborough N York 150
Goldsborough N York 171
Goldsithney Cnwll 2
Goldstone Kent 41
Goldstone Shrops 113
Goldthorpe Barns 142
Goldworthy Devon 27
Golford Kent 39
Golford Green Kent 39
Gollanfield Highld 252
Gollinglith Foot N York 159
Golly Wrexhm 129
Golsoncott Somset 29
Golspie Highld 273
Gomeldon Wilts 33
Gomersal Kirk 141
Gomshall Surrey 37
Gonalston Notts 117
Gonerby Hill Foot Lincs 118
Gonerby Moor Lincs 118
Gonfirth Shet 281
Goodamoor Devon 7
Good Easter Essex 70
Gooderstone Norfk 104
Goodleigh Devon 27
Goodmanham E R Yk 152
Goodmayes Gt Lon 51
Goodnestone Kent 40
Goodnestone Kent 41
Goodrich Herefs 63
Goodrington Torbay 8
Goodshaw Lancs 140
Goodshaw Fold Lancs 140
Goodstone Devon 13
Goodwick Pembks 74
Goodwood W Susx 20
Goodworth Clatford Hants 34
Goodyers End Warwks 99
Goole E R Yk 143
Goole Fields E R Yk 143
Goom's Hill Worcs 82
Goonbell Cnwll 4
Goonhavern Cnwll 4
Goonvrea Cnwll 4
Goosecruives Abers 245
Gooseford Devon 12
Goose Green Essex 73
Goose Green Kent 39
Goose Green Kent 39
Goose Green S Glos 45

Goose Green W Susx 21 J3
Goose Green Wigan 139 H7
Gooseham Cnwll 26 D7
Gooseham Mill Cnwll 26 D7
Goosehill Green Worcs 81 L3
Goose Pool Herefs 80 B7
Goosey Oxon 47 M1
Goosnargh Lancs 147 L8
Goostrey Ches E 130 F5
Gordano Services N Som 45 G4
Gorddinog Conwy 126 D5
Gordon Border 201 K4
Gordon Arms Hotel Border 200 C8
Gordonstown Abers 256 C6
Gordonstown Abers 267 L5
Gore Powys 79 J3
Gorebridge Mdloth 211 K6
Gorefield Cambs 103 J1
Gore Pit Essex 72 C3
Gores Wilts 47 G7
Gore Street Kent 41 J2
Gorey Jersey 9 f3
Goring Oxon 48 F3
Goring-by-Sea W Susx 21 J6
Goring Heath Oxon 49 G3
Gorleston-on-Sea Norfk 107 L3
Gorrachie Abers 268 D4
Gorran Churchtown Cnwll 5 G6
Gorran Haven Cnwll 5 G6
Gorran High Lanes Cnwll 5 G6
Gorrig Cerdgn 76 D6
Gors Cerdgn 92 D7
Gorsedd Flints 128 D4
Gorseddau Slate Landscape Gwynd 109 K3
Gorse Hill Swindn 47 H2
Gorseinon Swans 57 G5
Gorseybank Derbys 115 M1
Gorsgoch Cerdgn 76 E5
Gorslas Carmth 59 G6
Gorsley Gloucs 63 K2
Gorsley Common Herefs 63 K2
Gorstage Ches W 130 B5
Gorstan Highld 262 C7
Gorstella Ches W 129 H7
Gorsten Ag & B 227 L6
Gorst Hill Worcs 81 G1
Gorsty Hill Staffs 115 H6
Gorthleck Highld 250 F1
Gorton Manch 140 C8
Gosbeck Suffk 90 D4
Gosberton Lincs 119 H5
Gosberton Clough Lincs 119 G5
Gosfield Essex 71 J1
Gosford Devon 14 C3
Gosford Oxon 66 D4
Gosforth Cumb 155 J2
Gosforth N u Ty 180 F5
Gosling Street Somset 31 J4
Gosmore Herts 68 F2
Gospel End Staffs 97 K4
Gospel Green W Susx 36 D4
Gosport Hants 19 K4
Gossard's Green C Beds 85 J6
Gossington Gloucs 63 L4
Goswick Nthumb 203 G4
Gotham Notts 116 F5
Gotherington Gloucs 64 D1
Gotton Somset 30 C5
Goudhurst Kent 39 H6
Goulceby Lincs 136 E4
Gourdas Abers 256 D3
Gourdie C Dund 222 F1
Gourdon Abers 235 K1
Gourock Inver 207 L3
Govan C Glas 208 F6
Goveton Devon 7 L1
Govilon Mons 61 L4
Gowdall E R Yk 143 G3
Gower Highld 262 E8
Gower Swans 56 F6
Gowerton Swans 57 G5
Gowkhall Fife 210 E1
Gowthorpe E R Yk 152 A5
Goxhill E R Yk 153 K6
Goxhill N Linc 144 E3
Goytre Neath 57 L7
Grabhair W Isls 282 g4
Graby Lincs 118 E5
Grade Cnwll 3 H8
Gradeley Green Ches E 113 K1
Graffham W Susx 20 F3
Grafham Cambs 86 D2
Grafham Surrey 36 F3
Grafton Herefs 80 C7
Grafton Oxon 65 K7
Grafton Shrops 113 G7
Grafton Worcs 80 D3
Grafton Worcs 82 A7
Grafton Flyford Worcs 81 M4

Grafton Regis Nhants 84 E6
Grafton Underwood Nhants 101 K7
Grafty Green Kent 39 L4
Graianrhyd Denbgs 128 F8
Graig Conwy 126 F5
Graig Denbgs 128 C5
Graigfechan Denbgs 112 A1
Grain Medway 53 J4
Grains Bar Oldham 140 E6
Grainsby Lincs 145 H7
Grainthorpe Lincs 145 K8
Grampound Cnwll 4 F5
Grampound Road Cnwll 4 E5
Gramsdal W Isls 283 c9
Gramsdale W Isls 283 c9
Granborough Bucks 67 J2
Granby Notts 117 K4
Grandborough Warwks 83 L2
Grand Chemins Jersey 9 e3
Grandes Rocques Guern 9 j2
Grandtully P & K 232 D5
Grange Cumb 165 H7
Grange Medway 53 G5
Grange P & K 222 D2
Grange Wirral 128 F2
Grange Crossroads Moray 267 K5
Grange Hall Moray 265 H7
Grangehall S Lans 199 G4
Grange Hill Essex 70 C5
Grangemill Derbys 132 E8
Grange Moor Kirk 141 K4
Grangemouth Falk 210 B3
Grange of Lindores Fife 222 D6
Grange-over-Sands Cumb 156 F7
Grangepans Falk 210 D3
Grange Park Nhants 84 E4
Grangetown R & Cl 170 D6
Grangetown Sundld 181 K8
Grange Villa Dur 180 F8
Gransmoor E R Yk 153 H4
Gransmore Green Essex 71 G2
Granston Pembks 74 E5
Grantchester Cambs 87 J4
Grantham Lincs 118 B4
Granton C Edin 211 H4
Grantown-on-Spey Highld 253 K6
Grantsfield Herefs 80 C3
Grantshouse Border 213 H6
Grappenhall Warrtn 130 C2
Grasby Lincs 144 D6
Grasmere Cumb 156 D1
Grasscroft Oldham 140 E6
Grassendale Lpool 129 J3
Grassgarth Cumb 165 K2
Grass Green Essex 88 E7
Grassington N York 149 H3
Grassmoor Derbys 133 H6
Grassthorpe Notts 134 F6
Grateley Hants 34 C3
Gratwich Staffs 115 G5
Graveley Cambs 86 E2
Graveley Herts 69 G2
Gravelly Hill Birm 98 E5
Gravelsbank Shrops 95 H3
Graveney Kent 40 D3
Gravesend Kent 52 E4
Gravir W Isls 282 g4
Grayingham Lincs 144 E8
Grayrigg Cumb 157 J3
Grays Thurr 52 D3
Grayshott Hants 36 C4
Grayson Green Cumb 164 C5
Grayswood Surrey 36 D4
Graythorpe Hartpl 170 C5
Grazeley Wokham 49 G5
Greasbrough Rothm 142 C8
Greasby Wirral 128 F2
Greasley Notts 116 E2
Great Abington Cambs 87 L5
Great Addington Nhants 101 L1
Great Alne Warwks 82 D3
Great Altcar Lancs 138 C6
Great Amwell Herts 69 K4
Great Asby Cumb 166 A2
Great Ashfield Suffk 89 K2
Great Ayton N York 170 D8
Great Baddow Essex 71 H6
Great Badminton S Glos 46 A2
Great Bardfield Essex 71 G1
Great Barford Bed 86 C5
Great Barr Sandw 98 D4
Great Barrington Gloucs 65 J4
Great Barrow Ches W 129 L6
Great Barton Suffk 89 H2
Great Barugh N York 162 C6
Great Bavington Nthumb 180 B3
Great Bealings Suffk 90 F5
Great Bedwyn Wilts 47 K6
Great Bentley Essex 73 G3
Great Billing Nhants 84 F3

Great Bircham Norfk 121 G5
Great Blakenham Suffk 90 D5
Great Blencow Cumb 166 B4
Great Bolas Wrekin 113 L7
Great Bookham Surrey 50 E8
Great Bosullow Cnwll 2 C4
Great Bourton Oxon 83 K6
Great Bowden Leics 101 G5
Great Bradley Suffk 88 D4
Great Braxted Essex 72 B4
Great Bricett Suffk 90 B5
Great Brickhill Bucks 67 L1
Great Bridge Sandw 98 C5
Great Bridgeford Staffs 114 D6
Great Brington Nhants 84 C2
Great Bromley Essex 73 G2
Great Broughton Cumb 164 E4
Great Broughton N York 161 J2
Great Budworth Ches W 130 C4
Great Burdon Darltn 169 J7
Great Burstead Essex 71 G8
Great Busby N York 161 H2
Great Canfield Essex 70 E3
Great Carlton Lincs 137 H3
Great Casterton Rutlnd 101 L2
Great Chalfield Wilts 46 B6
Great Chart Kent 40 C7
Great Chatwell Staffs 114 B8
Great Chell C Stke 114 D1
Great Chesterford Essex 87 K6
Great Cheverell Wilts 46 E8
Great Chishill Cambs 87 J7
Great Clacton Essex 73 J4
Great Cliff Wakefd 141 M4
Great Clifton Cumb 164 D5
Great Coates NE Lin 145 G6
Great Comberton Worcs 81 L5
Great Comp Kent 39 G2
Great Corby Cumb 178 B7
Great Cornard Suffk 89 H7
Great Cowden E R Yk 153 L3
Great Coxwell Oxon 65 K8
Great Cransley Nhants 101 H8
Great Cressingham Norfk 105 G3
Great Crosthwaite Cumb 165 J6
Great Cubley Derbys 115 K4
Great Cumbrae Island N Ayrs 207 K7
Great Dalby Leics 117 K8
Great Denham Bed 85 K5
Great Doddington Nhants 85 H2
Great Doward Herefs 63 G4
Great Dunham Norfk 121 J2
Great Dunmow Essex 70 F3
Great Durnford Wilts 33 K3
Great Easton Essex 70 F2
Great Easton Leics 101 J5
Great Eccleston Lancs 147 H7
Great Edstone N York 162 C6
Great Ellingham Norfk 105 L4
Great Elm Somset 32 C1
Great Everdon Nhants 84 B4
Great Eversden Cambs 87 H4
Great Fencote N York 160 D4
Greatfield Wilts 47 G2
Great Finborough Suffk 89 K4
Greatford Lincs 102 B1
Great Fransham Norfk 105 H1
Great Gaddesden Herts 68 C5
Greatgate Staffs 115 G3
Great Gidding Cambs 102 C6
Great Givendale E R Yk 152 B5
Great Glemham Suffk 91 H3
Great Glen Leics 100 E4
Great Gonerby Lincs 118 B4
Great Gransden Cambs 86 F4
Great Green Cambs 86 F4
Great Green Norfk 106 F5
Great Green Suffk 89 J2
Great Green Suffk 89 J4
Great Habton N York 162 D7
Great Hale Lincs 118 F3
Great Hallingbury Essex 70 D3
Greatham Hants 36 A5
Greatham Hartpl 170 C5
Greatham W Susx 21 H4
Great Hampden Bucks 67 K6
Great Harrowden Nhants 85 G1
Great Harwood Lancs 139 L1
Great Haseley Oxon 66 F6
Great Hatfield E R Yk 153 K7
Great Haywood Staffs 114 F7
Great Heck N York 142 F4
Great Henny Essex 89 H7
Great Hinton Wilts 46 C7
Great Hockham Norfk 105 J5
Great Holland Essex 73 J3
Great Hollands Br For 49 L5
Great Horkesley Essex 72 E1
Great Hormead Herts 69 L1
Great Horton C Brad 141 J2

Great Horwood Bucks 67 J1
Great Houghton Barns 142 C6
Great Houghton Nhants 84 F3
Great Hucklow Derbys 132 D4
Great Kelk E R Yk 153 H4
Great Kimble Bucks 67 K6
Great Kingshill Bucks 67 L7
Great Langdale Cumb 156 D2
Great Langton N York 160 D3
Great Leighs Essex 71 H4
Great Limber Lincs 144 E6
Great Linford M Keyn 85 G6
Great Livermere Suffk 89 H1
Great Longstone Derbys 132 D5
Great Lumley Dur 169 J1
Great Lyth Shrops 95 L2
Great Malvern Worcs 81 H6
Great Maplestead Essex 89 G8
Great Marton Bpool 138 C1
Great Massingham Norfk 121 H7
Great Melton Norfk 106 C2
Great Meols Wirral 128 F2
Great Milton Oxon 66 F6
Great Missenden Bucks 67 L6
Great Mitton Lancs 148 C8
Great Mongeham Kent 41 K5
Great Moulton Norfk 106 D5
Great Munden Herts 69 K2
Great Musgrave Cumb 167 H7
Great Ness Shrops 112 F7
Great Notley Essex 71 H3
Great Oak Mons 62 D5
Great Oakley Essex 73 J2
Great Oakley Nhants 101 J6
Great Offley Herts 68 F2
Great Ormside Cumb 167 G7
Great Orton Cumb 177 K7
Great Ouseburn N York 150 F3
Great Oxendon Nhants 100 F6
Great Oxney Green Essex 71 G6
Great Palgrave Norfk 105 G1
Great Parndon Essex 70 B5
Great Pattenden Kent 39 J4
Great Paxton Cambs 86 E3
Great Plumpton Lancs 138 D1
Great Plumstead Norfk 106 F2
Great Ponton Lincs 118 B5
Great Potheridge Devon 27 J7
Great Preston Leeds 142 B2
Great Purston Nhants 83 M7
Great Raveley Cambs 102 E7
Great Rissington Gloucs 65 J4
Great Rollright Oxon 65 L1
Great Ryburgh Norfk 121 L6
Great Ryle Nthumb 190 E4
Great Ryton Shrops 96 B3
Great Saling Essex 71 G2
Great Salkeld Cumb 166 D3
Great Sampford Essex 88 C8
Great Saredon Staffs 98 B2
Great Saughall Ches W 129 H5
Great Saxham Suffk 88 F3
Great Shefford W Berk 48 A4
Great Shelford Cambs 87 J5
Great Smeaton N York 160 E2
Great Snoring Norfk 121 L4
Great Somerford Wilts 46 D2
Great Soudley Shrops 114 A5
Great Stainton Darltn 169 J6
Great Stambridge Essex 53 J1
Great Staughton Cambs 86 C2
Great Steeping Lincs 137 H6
Great Stonar Kent 41 K3
Greatstone-on-Sea Kent 25 K3
Great Strickland Cumb 166 D6
Great Stukeley Cambs 102 E8
Great Sturton Lincs 136 D4
Great Sutton Ches W 129 J4
Great Sutton Shrops 96 C6
Great Swinburne Nthumb 179 L4
Great Tew Oxon 66 B1
Great Tey Essex 72 C2
Great Thurlow Suffk 88 D5
Great Torrington Devon 27 J7
Great Tosson Nthumb 190 E6
Great Totham Essex 72 B5
Great Totham Essex 72 C4
Great Tows Lincs 136 D2
Great Urswick Cumb 156 C7
Great Wakering Essex 53 K2
Great Waldingfield Suffk 89 H6
Great Walsingham Norfk 121 L4
Great Waltham Essex 71 G4
Great Warford Ches E 130 F4
Great Warley Essex 52 C1
Great Washbourne Gloucs 82 A8
Great Weeke Devon 13 G5
Great Welnetham Suffk 89 H3
Great Wenham Suffk 90 C7
Great Whittington Nthumb 180 B5

Great Wigborough Essex	72 D4	Green Street Green Kent	52 C5
Great Wilbraham Cambs	87 L4	Greenstreet Green Suffk	90 B5
Great Wilne Derbys	116 D5	Green Tye Herts	70 C3
Great Wishford Wilts	33 J4	Greenway Gloucs	81 G8
Great Witchingham Norfk	122 C7	Greenway Somset	30 D6
Great Witcombe Gloucs	64 D4	Greenway V Glam	43 F3
Great Witley Worcs	81 H2	Greenway Worcs	81 G1
Great Wolford Warwks	82 F8	Greenwich Gt Lon	51 K3
Greatworth Nhants	84 A6	Greenwich Maritime Gt Lon	51 K3
Great Wratting Suffk	88 D5	Greet Gloucs	64 F1
Great Wymondley Herts	69 G2	Greete Shrops	80 D1
Great Wyrley Staffs	98 C2	Greetham Lincs	136 F5
Great Wytheford Shrops	113 J7	Greetham Rutlnd	118 E8
Great Yarmouth Norfk	107 L2	Greetland Calder	141 G3
Great Yeldham Essex	88 F7	Gregson Lane Lancs	139 J2
Grebby Lincs	137 H6	Greinton Somset	30 F4
Greeba IoM	154 d6	Grenaby IoM	154 c7
Green Denbgs	128 C6	Grendon Nhants	85 G3
Green Bank Cumb	156 E6	Grendon Warwks	99 H3
Greenbottom Cnwll	4 C6	Grendon Green Herefs	80 E4
Greenburn W Loth	210 B7	Grendon Underwood Bucks	67 J3
Greencroft Hall Dur	168 F1	Grenofen Devon	12 C8
Green Cross Surrey	36 C3	Grenoside Sheff	133 G1
Green Down Somset	45 H8	Greosabhagh W Isls	282 e6
Green End Bed	85 K5	Gresford Wrexhm	112 E1
Green End Bed	86 B2	Gresham Norfk	122 D4
Green End Bed	86 B3	Greshornish Highld	258 E6
Green End Bed	86 C5	Gressenhall Norfk	121 L8
Green End Cambs	87 H4	Gressenhall Green Norfk	121 L8
Green End Cambs	87 K2	Gressingham Lancs	147 L2
Green End Cambs	87 K3	Gresty Green Ches E	113 M1
Green End Cambs	102 D6	Greta Bridge Dur	168 D8
Green End Cambs	102 E8	Gretna D & G	177 K5
Green End Herts	69 H1	Gretna Green D & G	177 K5
Green End Herts	69 J3	Gretna Services D & G	177 J5
Green End Herts	87 G8	Gretton Gloucs	64 E1
Greenend Oxon	65 L3	Gretton Nhants	101 K4
Green End Warwks	99 H6	Gretton Shrops	96 C4
Greenfield Ag & B	207 L1	Grewelthorpe N York	160 C7
Greenfield C Beds	85 L8	Grey Friars Suffk	91 L1
Greenfield Flints	128 E4	Greygarth N York	150 A1
Greenfield Highld	239 L3	Grey Green N Linc	143 K6
Greenfield Oldham	140 F7	Greylake Somset	30 F4
Greenfield Oxon	49 H1	Greylees Lincs	118 D3
Greenford Gt Lon	50 F3	Greyrigg D & G	176 E1
Greengairs N Lans	209 L5	Greys Green Oxon	49 H2
Greengates C Brad	150 B8	Greysouthen Cumb	164 E5
Greengill Cumb	164 F3	Greystoke Cumb	166 B4
Greenhalgh Lancs	147 H8	Greystone Angus	234 E6
Greenham Somset	29 K6	Greywell Hants	35 L1
Greenham W Berk	48 C6	Gribb Dorset	15 J2
Green Hammerton N York	151 G4	Gribthorpe E R Yk	143 J1
Greenhaugh Nthumb	179 J2	Griff Warwks	99 K5
Green Head Cumb	165 L1	Griffithstown Torfn	62 C7
Greenhead Nthumb	178 F6	Griffydam Leics	116 C7
Green Heath Staffs	98 C1	Griggs Green Hants	36 B4
Greenheys Salfd	139 L7	Grimeford Village Lancs	139 J5
Greenhill D & G	176 F3	Grimesthorpe Sheff	133 G2
Greenhill Falk	209 L3	Grimethorpe Barns	142 C6
Greenhill Herefs	81 G5	Grimister Shet	281 e3
Greenhill Kent	40 F2	Grimley Worcs	81 J3
Greenhill Leics	99 M1	Grimmet S Ayrs	183 J1
Greenhill S Lans	198 F6	Grimoldby Lincs	137 G2
Green Hill Wilts	46 F2	Grimpo Shrops	112 E6
Greenhillocks Derbys	116 C2	Grimsargh Lancs	139 H1
Greenhills S Lans	209 G8	Grimsby NE Lin	145 H5
Greenhithe Kent	52 C4	Grimscote Nhants	84 C4
Greenholm E Ayrs	197 G3	Grimscott Cnwll	11 J1
Greenholme Cumb	157 J2	Grimshader W Isls	282 g4
Greenhouse Border	188 F2	Grimshaw Bl w D	139 L3
Greenhow Hill N York	149 K3	Grimshaw Green Lancs	139 G5
Greenland Highld	280 B3	Grimsthorpe Lincs	118 D6
Greenland Sheff	133 H2	Grimston E R Yk	145 H1
Greenlands Bucks	49 J2	Grimston Leics	117 J7
Green Lane Devon	13 H7	Grimston Norfk	120 F7
Green Lane Worcs	82 C2	Grimstone Dorset	16 C4
Greenlaw Border	201 L4	Grimstone End Suffk	89 J2
Greenlea D & G	176 D4	Grinacombe Moor Devon	12 A4
Greenloaning P & K	220 E5	Grindale E R Yk	153 J2
Green Moor Barns	141 L7	Grindle Shrops	97 G3
Greenmount Bury	140 A5	Grindleford Derbys	132 E4
Green Oak E R Yk	143 K2	Grindleton Lancs	148 D6
Greenock Inver	207 M4	Grindley Brook Shrops	113 H3
Greenodd Cumb	156 D6	Grindlow Derbys	132 D4
Green Ore Somset	31 J1	Grindon Nthumb	202 E4
Green Park Readg	49 H5	Grindon S on T	169 K5
Green Quarter Cumb	157 G2	Grindon Staffs	115 H1
Greensgate Norfk	122 B8	Grindon Hill Nthumb	179 J5
Greenshields S Lans	199 H4	Grindonrigg Nthumb	202 E4
Greenside Gatesd	180 E6	Gringley on the Hill Notts	134 E2
Greenside Kirk	141 J4	Grinsdale Cumb	177 L2
Greens Norton Nhants	84 C4	Grinshill Shrops	113 H6
Greenstead Green Essex	71 K2	Grinton N York	159 J3
Greensted Essex	70 D6	Griomsiadar W Isls	282 g4
Green Street E Susx	24 D5	Grishipoll Ag & B	224 F3
Green Street Gloucs	64 C4	Grisling Common E Susx	23 G3
Green Street Herts	69 G7	Gristhorpe N York	163 K6
Green Street Herts	70 C3	Griston Norfk	105 J4
Green Street Worcs	81 K5	Gritley Ork	275 d5
Green Street Green Gt Lon	51 M6	Grittenham Wilts	46 F2

Grittleton Wilts	46 B3	Gurnos Powys	57 L3
Grizebeck Cumb	156 C5	Gushmere Kent	40 D4
Grizedale Cumb	156 D4	Gussage All Saints Dorset	33 J8
Groby Leics	100 B2	Gussage St Andrew Dorset	33 G8
Groes Conwy	127 K6	Gussage St Michael Dorset	33 G8
Groes-faen Rhondd	43 G5	Guston Kent	41 K6
Groesffordd Gwynd	108 D4	Gutcher Shet	281 f2
Groesffordd Powys	61 G2	Guthrie Angus	234 E4
Groesffordd Marli Denbgs	127 K5	Guyhirn Cambs	103 H3
Groeslon Gwynd	125 H8	Guyhirn Gull Cambs	103 H3
Groeslon Gwynd	125 J7	Guy's Marsh Dorset	32 D4
Groes-lwyd Powys	94 F1	Guyzance Nthumb	191 J5
Groes-Wen Caerph	43 H4	Gwaenysgor Flints	128 C3
Grogarry W Isls	283 c10	Gwalchmai IoA	125 H3
Grogport Ag & B	194 C2	Gwastadnant Gwynd	126 C8
Groigearraidh W Isls	283 c10	Gwaun-Cae-Gurwen Carmth	59 J6
Gromford Suffk	91 J3	Gwbert on Sea Cerdgn	75 K2
Gronant Flints	128 C3	Gwealavellan Cnwll	2 F3
Groombridge E Susx	38 E6	Gweek Cnwll	3 H5
Grosebay W Isls	282 e6	Gwehelog Mons	62 D6
Grosmont Mons	62 E2	Gwenddwr Powys	78 E6
Grosmont N York	162 E2	Gwennap Cnwll	3 J3
Groton Suffk	89 J7	Gwennap Mining District Cnwll	4 B6
Grotton Oldham	140 E6	Gwenter Cnwll	3 J7
Grouville Jersey	9 e3	Gwernaffield Flints	128 F6
Grove Bucks	67 M3	Gwernesney Mons	62 E6
Grove Dorset	16 D8	Gwernogle Carmth	58 F2
Grove Kent	41 H3	Gwernymynydd Flints	128 F6
Grove Notts	134 E4	Gwersyllt Wrexhm	112 D1
Grove Oxon	48 B1	Gwespyr Flints	128 C3
Grove Pembks	55 G6	Gwindra Cnwll	4 F4
Grove Green Kent	39 K2	Gwinear Cnwll	2 F4
Grovenhurst Kent	39 H5	Gwithian Cnwll	2 F3
Grove Park Gt Lon	51 L4	Gwredog IoA	125 G3
Grovesend S Glos	45 K1	Gwrhay Caerph	61 J7
Grovesend Swans	57 G5	Gwyddelwern Denbgs	111 L2
Grubb Street Kent	52 C5	Gwyddgrug Carmth	58 E2
Gruinard Highld	260 F2	Gwynfryn Wrexhm	112 C1
Gruinart Ag & B	204 D3	Gwystre Powys	78 D3
Grula Highld	246 E3	Gwytherin Conwy	127 H7
Gruline Ag & B	227 G4	Gyfelia Wrexhm	112 E3
Grumbla Cnwll	2 C5	Gyrn Goch Gwynd	109 G2
Grundisburgh Suffk	90 F5		
Gruting Shet	281 c6		
Grutness Shet	281 d9		
Gualachulain Highld	229 J6	**H**	
Guanockgate Lincs	103 H2		
Guardbridge Fife	223 H3	Habberley Shrops	95 K3
Guarlford Worcs	81 J6	Habberley Worcs	97 H7
Guay P & K	232 F5	Habergham Lancs	140 B1
Guernsey Guern	9 j3	Habertoft Lincs	137 J6
Guernsey Airport Guern	9 i3	Habin W Susx	36 B6
Guestling Green E Susx	24 F4	Habrough NE Lin	144 F5
Guestling Thorn E Susx	24 F4	Hacconby Lincs	118 E6
Guestwick Norfk	122 B6	Haceby Lincs	118 D4
Guide Bridge Tamesd	140 D8	Hacheston Suffk	91 G3
Guide Post Nthumb	181 G2	Hackbridge Gt Lon	51 H5
Guilden Morden Cambs	86 F6	Hackenthorpe Sheff	133 H4
Guilden Sutton Ches W	129 K6	Hackford Norfk	106 B3
Guildford Surrey	36 F1	Hackforth N York	160 C4
Guildstead Kent	53 H6	Hack Green Ches E	113 L2
Guildtown P & K	221 L1	Hackland Ork	275 c4
Guilsborough Nhants	84 D1	Hackleton Nhants	84 F4
Guilsfield Powys	94 F1	Hacklinge Kent	41 K4
Guilton Kent	41 J4	Hackman's Gate Worcs	97 K7
Guiltreehill S Ayrs	183 J1	Hackness N York	163 H4
Guineaford Devon	27 K3	Hackness Somset	30 E2
Guisborough R & Cl	170 E7	Hackney Gt Lon	51 K2
Guiseley Leeds	150 B7	Hackthorn Lincs	135 K3
Guist Norfk	121 M6	Hackthorpe Cumb	166 D6
Guiting Power Gloucs	65 G2	Hacton Gt Lon	52 C2
Gullane E Loth	212 C2	Hadden Border	202 B6
Gulling Green Suffk	89 G4	Haddenham Bucks	67 H5
Gulval Cnwll	2 D5	Haddenham Cambs	103 J8
Gulworthy Devon	12 B8	Haddington E Loth	212 B4
Gumfreston Pembks	55 J6	Haddington Lincs	135 H7
Gumley Leics	100 F5	Haddiscoe Norfk	107 L4
Gummow's Shop Cnwll	4 E3	Haddon Cambs	102 C5
Gunby E R Yk	143 H1	Hade Edge Kirk	141 J6
Gunby Lincs	118 B7	Hadfield Derbys	140 F8
Gundleton Hants	35 J4	Hadham Cross Herts	70 B3
Gun Green Kent	39 J7	Hadham Ford Herts	70 B3
Gun Hill E Susx	23 J4	Hadleigh Essex	53 H2
Gun Hill Warwks	99 H5	Hadleigh Suffk	89 L6
Gunn Devon	27 L4	Hadleigh Heath Suffk	89 K7
Gunnerside N York	159 G3	Hadley Worcs	81 J3
Gunnerton Nthumb	179 L4	Hadley Wrekin	96 F1
Gunness N Linc	143 L5	Hadley End Staffs	115 J7
Gunnislake Cnwll	12 B8	Hadley Wood Gt Lon	69 H7
Gunnista Shet	281 e6	Hadlow Kent	39 G3
Gunthorpe C Pete	102 D3	Hadlow Down E Susx	23 J2
Gunthorpe N Linc	143 K8	Hadnall Shrops	113 H7
Gunthorpe Norfk	121 M4	Hadrian's Wall	179 M5
Gunthorpe Notts	117 H3	Hadstock Essex	88 B6
Gunton Suffk	107 L4	Hadston Nthumb	191 K6
Gunwalloe Cnwll	3 G6	Hadzor Worcs	81 L3
Gupworthy Somset	29 H4	Haffenden Quarter Kent	39 M5
Gurnard IoW	19 H4	Hafodunos Conwy	127 H6
Gurnett Ches E	131 H5	Hafod-y-bwch Wrexhm	112 D2
Gurney Slade Somset	31 K1	Hafod-y-coed Blae G	61 K7

Hafodyrynys Caerph....61 K7
Haggate Lancs....140 C1
Haggbeck Cumb....178 B4
Haggersta Shet....281 d6
Haggerston Nthumb....203 G4
Haggington Hill Devon....27 K2
Haggs Falk....209 L3
Hagley Herefs....80 D7
Hagley Worcs....97 K7
Hagmore Green Suffk....89 J7
Hagnaby Lincs....136 F7
Hagnaby Lincs....137 J4
Hagworthingham Lincs....136 F6
Haigh Wigan....139 J6
Haighton Green Lancs....139 H1
Haile Cumb....155 J1
Hailes Gloucs....64 F1
Hailey Herts....69 K5
Hailey Oxon....48 F2
Hailey Oxon....65 M4
Hailsham E Susx....23 K5
Hail Weston Cambs....86 D3
Hainault Gt Lon....70 C8
Haine Kent....41 K2
Hainford Norfk....122 E7
Hainton Lincs....136 C3
Hainworth C Brad....149 J8
Haisthorpe E R Yk....153 H3
Hakin Pembks....54 E5
Halam Notts....117 H1
Halbeath Fife....210 F1
Halberton Devon....29 H8
Halcro Highld....280 B4
Hale Cumb....157 H7
Hale Halton....129 L3
Hale Hants....33 L7
Hale Somset....32 C5
Hale Surrey....36 C1
Hale Traffd....130 F2
Hale Bank Halton....129 L3
Hale Barns Traffd....130 F3
Hale Green E Susx....23 J4
Hale Nook Lancs....147 G7
Hales Norfk....107 H4
Hales Staffs....113 M5
Halesgate Lincs....119 K6
Hales Green Derbys....115 K3
Halesowen Dudley....98 B6
Hales Place Kent....40 F3
Hale Street Kent....39 G3
Halesville Essex....72 C8
Halesworth Suffk....107 H7
Halewood Knows....129 K3
Halford Devon....13 J7
Halford Shrops....95 K6
Halford Warwks....83 G6
Halfpenny Cumb....157 H5
Halfpenny Green Staffs....97 J5
Halfpenny Houses N York....160 B5
Halfway Carmth....59 J3
Halfway Carmth....59 M2
Halfway Sheff....133 J3
Halfway W Berk....48 B5
Halfway Bridge W Susx....36 D6
Halfway House Shrops....95 H1
Halfway Houses Kent....53 K4
Halifax Calder....141 H3
Halket E Ayrs....208 D8
Halkirk Highld....279 K4
Halkyn Flints....128 F5
Hall E Rens....208 C8
Hallam Fields Derbys....116 D4
Halland E Susx....23 H4
Hallaton Leics....101 H4
Hallatrow BaNES....45 J7
Hallbankgate Cumb....178 D7
Hallbeck Cumb....157 K5
Hall Cliffe Wakefd....141 L4
Hall Cross Lancs....138 E2
Hall Dunnerdale Cumb....156 B3
Hallen S Glos....45 H3
Hall End Bed....85 K6
Hall End C Beds....86 B7
Hallfield Gate Derbys....133 H8
Hallgarth Dur....169 J2
Hallglen Falk....210 A3
Hall Green Birm....98 E7
Hallin Highld....258 C5
Halling Medway....52 F6
Hallington Lincs....136 F3
Hallington Nthumb....180 B4
Halliwell Bolton....139 L5
Halloughton Notts....117 J1
Hallow Worcs....81 J3
Hallow Heath Worcs....81 J3
Hallsands Devon....8 B7
Hall's Green Essex....69 L5
Hall's Green Herts....69 H2
Hallthwaites Cumb....156 A5
Hallworthy Cnwll....11 H5

Hallyne Border....199 L5
Halmer End Staffs....114 B2
Halmond's Frome Herefs....80 F5
Halmore Gloucs....63 K6
Halnaker W Susx....20 E5
Halsall Lancs....138 D5
Halse Nhants....84 A7
Halse Somset....29 L5
Halsetown Cnwll....2 D1
Halsham E R Yk....145 H2
Halsinger Devon....27 J3
Halstead Essex....71 K1
Halstead Kent....52 A6
Halstead Leics....101 G2
Halstock Dorset....15 M1
Halsway Somset....29 L3
Haltcliff Bridge Cumb....165 L3
Haltham Lincs....136 D7
Haltoft End Lincs....119 L3
Halton Bucks....67 L5
Halton Halton....129 M3
Halton Lancs....147 K3
Halton Leeds....142 A1
Halton Nthumb....180 B5
Halton Wrexhm....112 D3
Halton East N York....149 J5
Halton Fenside Lincs....137 H7
Halton Gill N York....158 F7
Halton Green Lancs....147 K3
Halton Holegate Lincs....137 H6
Halton Lea Gate Nthumb....178 F7
Halton Quay Cnwll....6 E2
Halton Shields Nthumb....180 B5
Halton West N York....148 E5
Haltwhistle Nthumb....179 G6
Halvana Cnwll....11 J6
Halvergate Norfk....107 J2
Halwell Devon....8 A4
Halwill Devon....12 B3
Halwill Junction Devon....12 B3
Ham Devon....14 F2
Ham Gloucs....63 K7
Ham Gloucs....64 E3
Ham Gt Lon....50 F4
Ham Kent....41 K4
Ham Somset....30 D6
Ham Somset....31 L1
Ham Wilts....47 L6
Hambleden Bucks....49 J2
Hambledon Hants....35 K7
Hambledon Surrey....36 E3
Hamble-le-Rice Hants....19 H4
Hambleton Lancs....147 G7
Hambleton N York....142 E2
Hambleton Moss Side Lancs....147 G7
Hambridge Somset....30 F6
Hambrook S Glos....45 J3
Hambrook W Susx....20 C5
Ham Common Dorset....32 D5
Hameringham Lincs....136 F6
Hamerton Cambs....102 C7
Ham Green Herefs....81 H6
Ham Green Kent....25 G2
Ham Green Kent....53 H5
Ham Green N Som....45 G4
Ham Green Worcs....82 B3
Ham Hill Kent....52 F6
Hamilton S Lans....209 J7
Hamilton Services
(northbound) S Lans....209 J7
Hamlet Dorset....16 B1
Hammer W Susx....36 C4
Hammerpot W Susx....21 H5
Hammersmith Gt Lon....51 G3
Hammer Vale Hants....36 C4
Hammerwich Staffs....98 D2
Hammerwood E Susx....38 C5
Hammond Street Herts....69 J6
Hammoon Dorset....32 D7
Hamnavoe Shet....281 d7
Hampden Park E Susx....23 K6
Hamperden End Essex....70 E1
Hampnett Gloucs....65 G4
Hampole Donc....142 D5
Hampreston Dorset....17 L3
Hampsfield Cumb....156 F6
Hampson Green Lancs....147 J5
Hampstead Gt Lon....51 H2
Hampstead Norreys W Berk....48 D4
Hampsthwaite N York....150 C4
Hampton Devon....15 G3
Hampton Gt Lon....50 F5
Hampton Kent....40 F2
Hampton Shrops....97 G6
Hampton Swindn....65 J8
Hampton Worcs....82 B6
Hampton Bishop Herefs....80 D7
Hampton Fields Gloucs....64 C7
Hampton Green Ches W....113 H2
Hampton Hargate C Pete....102 D4

Hampton Heath Ches W....113 H2
Hampton-in-Arden Solhll....99 G7
Hampton Loade Shrops....97 G6
Hampton Lovett Worcs....81 K2
Hampton Lucy Warwks....83 G3
Hampton Magna Warwks....83 G2
Hampton on the Hill Warwks....82 F2
Hampton Park Wilts....33 K4
Hampton Poyle Oxon....66 C6
Hampton Vale C Pete....102 D4
Hampton Wick Gt Lon....50 F5
Hamptworth Wilts....34 B7
Hamrow Norfk....121 K6
Hamsey E Susx....22 F5
Hamsey Green Surrey....51 K7
Hamstall Ridware Staffs....115 H7
Hamstead Birm....98 D5
Hamstead IoW....18 F5
Hamstead Marshall W Berk....48 B6
Hamsterley Dur....168 E4
Hamsterley Dur....180 D7
Hamsterley Mill Dur....180 E7
Hamstreet Kent....40 C8
Ham Street Somset....31 J4
Hamwood N Som....44 D7
Hamworthy BCP....17 K4
Hanbury Staffs....115 K6
Hanbury Worcs....81 M2
Hanby Lincs....118 D5
Hanchet End Suffk....88 C6
Hanchurch Staffs....114 C3
Handa Island Highld....276 A6
Handale R & Cl....171 G7
Hand and Pen Devon....14 B3
Handbridge Ches W....129 J6
Handcross W Susx....37 L5
Handforth Ches E....131 G3
Hand Green Ches W....130 A7
Handley Ches W....129 L8
Handley Derbys....133 G7
Handley Green Essex....71 G6
Handsacre Staffs....115 H8
Handsworth Birm....98 D5
Handsworth Sheff....133 H2
Handy Cross Bucks....49 K1
Hanford C Stke....114 D3
Hanford Dorset....32 D8
Hanging Heaton Kirk....141 L3
Hanging Houghton Nhants....84 E1
Hanging Langford Wilts....33 H3
Hangleton Br & H....22 D6
Hangleton W Susx....21 J4
Hanham S Glos....45 J4
Hankelow Ches E....113 L2
Hankerton Wilts....46 E1
Hankham E Susx....23 K5
Hanley C Stke....114 D2
Hanley Broadheath Worcs....80 F2
Hanley Castle Worcs....81 J6
Hanley Child Worcs....80 F2
Hanley Swan Worcs....81 J6
Hanley William Worcs....80 F2
Hanlith N York....148 F3
Hanmer Wrexhm....113 G4
Hannaford Devon....27 L5
Hannah Lincs....137 J4
Hannington Hants....48 D7
Hannington Nhants....84 F1
Hannington Swindn....65 H8
Hannington Wick Swindn....65 H8
Hanscombe End C Beds....86 C8
Hanslope M Keyn....84 F6
Hanthorpe Lincs....118 D7
Hanwell Gt Lon....50 F3
Hanwell Oxon....83 K6
Hanwood Shrops....95 K2
Hanworth Gt Lon....50 E5
Hanworth Norfk....122 D4
Happendon S Lans....198 E6
Happisburgh Norfk....123 H4
Happisburgh Common Norfk....123 H5
Hapsford Ches W....129 L5
Hapton Lancs....140 B2
Hapton Norfk....106 D4
Harberton Devon....8 A3
Harbertonford Devon....8 A4
Harbledown Kent....40 F4
Harborne Birm....98 C6
Harborough Magna Warwks....100 B7
Harbottle Nthumb....190 C5
Harbourneford Devon....7 K2
Harbours Hill Worcs....81 M2
Harbridge Hants....18 A2
Harbridge Green Hants....33 K8
Harburn W Loth....210 D6
Harbury Warwks....83 J3
Harby Leics....117 K5
Harby Notts....135 H5
Harcombe Devon....13 K6
Harcombe Devon....14 D4

Harcombe Bottom Devon....15 H3
Harden C Brad....149 K8
Harden Wsall....98 C3
Hardendale Cumb....166 D7
Hardenhuish Wilts....46 C4
Hardgate Abers....245 H3
Hardgate D & G....175 K2
Hardgate N York....150 C3
Hardgate W Duns....208 E4
Hardham W Susx....21 H3
Hardhorn Lancs....147 G8
Hardingham Norfk....105 L3
Hardingstone Nhants....84 E4
Hardington Somset....45 L8
Hardington Mandeville Somset....31 H8
Hardington Marsh Somset....15 L1
Hardington Moor Somset....31 H8
Hardisworthy Devon....26 D6
Hardley Hants....19 G3
Hardley Street Norfk....107 H3
Hardmead M Keyn....85 H5
Hardraw N York....158 F4
Hardsough Lancs....140 B4
Hardstoft Derbys....133 J7
Hardway Hants....19 K3
Hardway Somset....32 B4
Hardwick Bucks....67 K3
Hardwick Cambs....87 H3
Hardwick Nhants....85 G1
Hardwick Norfk....106 E5
Hardwick Oxon....66 A6
Hardwick Oxon....66 E1
Hardwick Rothm....133 K2
Hardwick Wsall....98 D4
Hardwicke Gloucs....64 A4
Hardwicke Gloucs....64 C2
Hardwick Village Notts....134 C4
Hardy's Green Essex....72 D3
Harebeating E Susx....23 K5
Hareby Lincs....136 F6
Hare Croft C Brad....149 K8
Harefield Gt Lon....50 D1
Hare Green Essex....73 G2
Hare Hatch Wokham....49 J3
Harehill Derbys....115 K4
Harehills Leeds....141 M1
Harehope Nthumb....191 G2
Harelaw Border....188 F2
Harelaw D & G....178 B3
Harelaw Dur....180 E8
Hareplain Kent....39 L5
Haresceugh Cumb....166 E2
Harescombe Gloucs....64 B5
Haresfield Gloucs....64 A5
Harestock Hants....34 F4
Hare Street Essex....70 E5
Hare Street Essex....70 D7
Hare Street Herts....69 K1
Harewood Leeds....150 D6
Harewood End Herefs....63 G2
Harford Devon....7 J3
Hargate Norfk....106 C5
Hargatewall Derbys....132 B4
Hargrave Ches W....129 L7
Hargrave Nhants....85 K1
Hargrave Suffk....88 F3
Harker Cumb....177 L6
Harkstead Suffk....90 E8
Harlaston Staffs....99 G1
Harlaxton Lincs....118 A5
Harlech Gwynd....109 K5
Harlech Castle Gwynd....109 K5
Harlescott Shrops....113 H8
Harlesden Gt Lon....51 G2
Harlesthorpe Derbys....133 K4
Harleston Devon....8 B6
Harleston Norfk....106 E6
Harleston Suffk....89 L3
Harlestone Nhants....84 D2
Harle Syke Lancs....140 C1
Harley Rothm....142 B8
Harley Shrops....96 D3
Harling Road Norfk....105 K6
Harlington C Beds....68 D1
Harlington Donc....142 D7
Harlington Gt Lon....50 E3
Harlosh Highld....258 D8
Harlow Essex....70 C5
Harlow Hill Nthumb....180 C5
Harlthorpe E R Yk....151 M8
Harlton Cambs....87 H5
Harlyn Cnwll....10 B7
Harman's Cross Dorset....17 J6
Harmby N York....159 L5
Harmer Green Herts....69 H4
Harmer Hill Shrops....113 H5
Harmondsworth Gt Lon....50 D3
Harmston Lincs....135 K7
Harnage Shrops....96 D3
Harnham Nthumb....180 C3

Harnhill Gloucs 64 F7
Harold Hill Gt Lon 70 D8
Haroldston West Pembks 54 D4
Haroldswick Shet 281 f1
Harold Wood Gt Lon 52 C1
Harome N York 161 L6
Harpenden Herts 68 E4
Harpford Devon 14 C4
Harpham E R Yk 153 H3
Harpley Norfk 121 H6
Harpley Worcs 80 F3
Harpole Nhants 84 D3
Harpsdale Highld 279 K5
Harpsden Oxon 49 J3
Harpswell Lincs 135 J2
Harpurhey Manch 140 C7
Harpur Hill Derbys 131 L5
Harraby Cumb 177 M7
Harracott Devon 27 K5
Harrapool Highld 247 K4
Harras Cumb 164 C7
Harrietfield P & K 221 H1
Harrietsham Kent 39 L3
Harringay Gt Lon 51 J1
Harrington Cumb 164 C5
Harrington Lincs 137 G5
Harrington Nhants 101 G7
Harringworth Nhants 101 K4
Harris W Isls 282 e6
Harriseahead Staffs 131 G8
Harriston Cumb 165 G2
Harrogate N York 150 D5
Harrold Bed 85 J4
Harrop Dale Oldham 140 F6
Harrow Gt Lon 50 F1
Harrowbarrow Cnwll 11 M8
Harrowden Bed 86 B5
Harrowgate Village Darltn 169 H7
Harrow Green Suffk 89 H4
Harrow Hill Gloucs 63 H4
Harrow on the Hill Gt Lon 50 F2
Harrow Weald Gt Lon 50 F1
Harston Cambs 87 J5
Harston Leics 117 L5
Harswell E R Yk 152 C7
Hart Hartpl 170 B4
Hartburn Nthumb 180 D2
Hartburn S on T 169 L7
Hartest Suffk 89 G5
Hartfield E Susx 38 D6
Hartford Cambs 86 E1
Hartford Ches W 130 C5
Hartford Somset 29 C4
Hartfordbridge Hants 49 J7
Hartford End Essex 71 G3
Hartforth N York 159 L2
Hartgrove Dorset 32 D7
Harthill Ches W 129 L8
Harthill N Lans 210 B6
Harthill Rothm 133 K3
Harthope D & G 186 F4
Hartington Derbys 132 C7
Hartington Nthumb 180 B1
Hartland Devon 26 D6
Hartland Quay Devon 26 C6
Hartlebury Worcs 81 J1
Hartlepool Hartpl 170 C4
Hartley Cumb 158 D1
Hartley Kent 39 J6
Hartley Kent 52 D5
Hartley Nthumb 181 H4
Hartley Green Kent 52 D5
Hartley Green Staffs 114 F5
Hartley Wespall Hants 49 G7
Hartley Wintney Hants 49 J7
Hartlip Kent 53 H6
Hartoft End N York 162 C4
Harton N York 151 L3
Harton S Tyne 181 J4
Harton Shrops 96 B5
Hartpury Gloucs 64 A2
Hartshead Kirk 141 J3
Hartshead Moor Services
    Calder 141 J3
Hartshead Moor Top Kirk 141 J3
Hartshill C Stke 114 D2
Hartshill Warwks 99 J3
Hartshorne Derbys 116 B7
Hartside Nthumb 190 D3
Hartsop Cumb 165 L8
Hart Station Hartpl 170 B3
Hartswell Somset 29 K5
Hartwell Nhants 84 F5
Hartwith N York 150 B3
Hartwood N Lans 209 M7
Hartwoodmyres Border 188 D1
Harvel Kent 52 E6
Harvington Worcs 82 C5
Harvington Worcs 97 K8
Harwell Notts 134 D2

Harwell Oxon 48 C1
Harwich Essex 73 K1
Harwood Bolton 139 L5
Harwood Dur 167 J4
Harwood Nthumb 190 E8
Harwood Dale N York 163 H3
Harwood Lee Bolton 139 L5
Harworth Notts 134 C2
Hasbury Dudley 98 B6
Hascombe Surrey 36 F3
Haselbech Nhants 100 F7
Haselbury Plucknett Somset 31 G8
Haseley Warwks 82 E1
Haseley Green Warwks 82 F1
Haseley Knob Warwks 82 F1
Haselor Warwks 82 D4
Hasfield Gloucs 64 B2
Hasguard Pembks 54 D5
Hasholme E R Yk 143 L1
Haskayne Lancs 138 D6
Hasketon Suffk 90 F5
Hasland Derbys 133 H5
Haslemere Surrey 36 D4
Haslingden Lancs 140 B3
Haslingfield Cambs 87 H5
Haslington Ches E 130 E8
Hassall Ches E 130 E8
Hassall Green Ches E 130 F7
Hassell Street Kent 40 E6
Hassingham Norfk 107 H2
Hassness Cumb 165 G7
Hassocks W Susx 22 D4
Hassop Derbys 132 D5
Haste Hill Surrey 36 D4
Haster Highld 280 D6
Hasthorpe Lincs 137 J5
Hastingleigh Kent 40 E6
Hastings E Susx 24 E5
Hastings Somset 30 D7
Hastingwood Essex 70 C5
Hastoe Herts 68 A5
Haswell Dur 169 K2
Haswell Plough Dur 169 K2
Hatch C Beds 86 D5
Hatch Beauchamp Somset 30 D6
Hatch End Bed 86 B3
Hatch End Gt Lon 50 E1
Hatchet Gate Hants 18 F3
Hatching Green Herts 68 E4
Hatchmere Ches W 130 A5
Hatch Warren Hants 35 J1
Hatcliffe NE Lin 145 G6
Hatfield Donc 143 G6
Hatfield Herefs 80 E3
Hatfield Herts 69 G5
Hatfield Worcs 81 K5
Hatfield Broad Oak Essex 70 E4
Hatfield Heath Essex 70 D4
Hatfield Peverel Essex 71 J5
Hatfield Woodhouse Donc 143 H6
Hatford Oxon 65 M8
Hatherden Hants 34 D1
Hatherleigh Devon 12 D2
Hathern Leics 116 E7
Hatherop Gloucs 65 H6
Hathersage Derbys 132 E3
Hathersage Booths Derbys 132 E3
Hatherton Ches E 113 L2
Hatherton Staffs 98 B1
Hatley St George Cambs 86 F5
Hatt Cnwll 6 D2
Hattersley Tamesd 131 K1
Hattingley Hants 35 K3
Hatton Abers 257 K4
Hatton Angus 234 C6
Hatton Derbys 115 L5
Hatton Gt Lon 50 E4
Hatton Lincs 136 C4
Hatton Shrops 95 L5
Hatton Warrtn 130 B3
Hatton Warwks 82 F2
Hatton Heath Ches W 129 K7
Hatton of Fintray Abers 256 F8
Hatton Park Warwks 82 F2
Haugh E Ayrs 196 F6
Haugh Lincs 137 H4
Haugh Rochdl 140 E5
Haugham Lincs 136 F3
Haughhead E Duns 209 G3
Haugh Head Nthumb 202 F7
Haughley Suffk 89 L3
Haughley Green Suffk 89 L2
Haugh of Glass Moray 255 H4
Haugh of Urr D & G 175 K2
Haughs of Kinnaird Angus 235 G4
Haughton Ches E 130 B8
Haughton Notts 134 D5
Haughton Powys 112 D7
Haughton Shrops 96 F4
Haughton Shrops 97 G2

Haughton Shrops 112 F6
Haughton Shrops 113 J8
Haughton Staffs 114 D7
Haughton Green Tamesd 131 J1
Haughton le Skerne Darltn 169 J7
Haultwick Herts 69 J3
Haunton Staffs 99 G1
Hautes Croix Jersey 9 d1
Hauxton Cambs 87 J5
Havannah Ches E 131 G6
Havant Hants 20 B5
Haven Herefs 79 M4
Haven Bank Lincs 119 H1
Haven Side E R Yk 144 F2
Havenstreet IoW 19 J5
Havercroft Wakefd 142 B5
Haverfordwest Pembks 54 F4
Haverhill Suffk 88 D6
Haverigg Cumb 155 L7
Havering-atte-Bower Gt Lon 70 D8
Haversham M Keyn 84 F6
Haverthwaite Cumb 156 E6
Haverton Hill S on T 170 C6
Havyatt N Som 44 F6
Havyatt Somset 31 H3
Hawarden Flints 129 H6
Hawbridge Worcs 81 L5
Hawbush Green Essex 71 J3
Hawcoat Cumb 146 D2
Hawen Cerdgn 76 C6
Hawes N York 158 F5
Hawe's Green Norfk 106 E4
Hawford Worcs 81 J3
Hawick Border 188 E3
Hawkchurch Devon 15 H3
Hawkedon Suffk 88 F4
Hawkenbury Kent 39 K4
Hawkeridge Wilts 46 B8
Hawkerland Devon 14 C5
Hawker's Cove Cnwll 10 C7
Hawkesbury S Glos 45 M2
Hawkesbury Warwks 99 K6
Hawkesbury Upton S Glos 45 M2
Hawkes End Covtry 99 J6
Hawk Green Stockp 131 J2
Hawkhead Rens 208 E6
Hawkhill Nthumb 191 J4
Hawkhurst Kent 39 J7
Hawkhurst Common E Susx 23 J4
Hawkinge Kent 41 H7
Hawkley Hants 35 M5
Hawkley Wigan 139 H4
Hawkridge Somset 28 F5
Hawksdale Cumb 165 L1
Hawkshaw Bury 139 M5
Hawkshead Cumb 156 E3
Hawkshead Hill Cumb 156 D3
Hawksland S Lans 198 D5
Hawkspur Green Essex 71 G1
Hawkstone Shrops 113 J5
Hawkswick N York 149 G2
Hawksworth Leeds 149 L7
Hawksworth Notts 117 K3
Hawkwell Essex 53 J1
Hawkwell Nthumb 180 C4
Hawley Hants 49 K7
Hawley Kent 52 C4
Hawling Gloucs 64 F3
Hawnby N York 161 J5
Haworth C Brad 149 J8
Hawridge Bucks 68 B6
Hawstead Suffk 89 G5
Hawstead Green Suffk 89 H3
Hawthorn Dur 169 L2
Hawthorn Hants 35 K4
Hawthorn Rhondd 43 H4
Hawthorn Hill Br For 49 L4
Hawthorn Hill Lincs 136 D8
Hawthorpe Lincs 118 D6
Hawton Notts 117 L1
Haxby C York 151 K4
Haxby Gates C York 151 K4
Haxey N Linc 143 J7
Haxey Carr N Linc 143 J7
Haxted Surrey 38 C4
Haxton Wilts 33 K1
Hay Cnwll 4 F4
Hay Cnwll 10 D8
Haydock St Hel 139 H8
Haydon BaNES 45 K8
Haydon Dorset 31 L7
Haydon Somset 30 C6
Haydon Bridge Nthumb 179 J6
Haydon Wick Swindn 47 H2
Haye Cnwll 11 L8
Hayes Gt Lon 50 E3
Hayes Gt Lon 51 L5
Hayes End Gt Lon 50 D3
Hayfield Ag & B 217 H2
Hayfield Derbys 131 L2

Hayfield Green Donc 143 G7
Haygate Wrekin 96 E1
Hay Green Norfk 120 C7
Hayhillock Angus 234 E7
Hayle Cnwll 2 E4
Hayle Port Cnwll 2 F4
Hayley Green Dudley 98 B6
Hayling Island Hants 20 B6
Haymoor Green Ches E 113 L2
Hayne Devon 13 H5
Hayne Devon 29 G7
Haynes C Beds 86 B6
Haynes Church End C Beds 86 B7
Haynes West End C Beds 85 L7
Hay-on-Wye Powys 79 J6
Hayscastle Pembks 74 E7
Hayscastle Cross Pembks 74 E7
Hay Street Herts 69 K2
Hayton Cumb 164 F2
Hayton Cumb 178 C7
Hayton E R Yk 152 C6
Hayton Notts 134 E3
Hayton's Bent Shrops 96 C7
Haytor Vale Devon 13 H7
Haytown Devon 26 F7
Haywards Heath W Susx 22 E2
Haywood Donc 142 F5
Haywood Herefs 80 B8
Haywood Oaks Notts 134 D4
Hazards Green E Susx 24 C5
Hazelbank S Lans 198 D4
Hazelbury Bryan Dorset 16 E1
Hazeleigh Essex 71 K6
Hazeley Hants 49 H7
Hazelford Notts 117 J2
Hazel Grove Stockp 131 H2
Hazelhurst Tamesd 140 E7
Hazelslade Staffs 98 C1
Hazel Street Kent 39 H5
Hazel Stub Suffk 88 D6
Hazelton Walls Fife 222 E3
Hazelwood Derbys 116 B2
Hazlemere Bucks 67 L8
Hazlerigg N u Ty 180 F4
Hazles Staffs 114 F2
Hazleton Gloucs 65 G3
Heacham Norfk 120 E4
Headbourne Worthy Hants 35 G4
Headbrook Herefs 79 K4
Headcorn Kent 39 L4
Headingley Leeds 150 C8
Headington Oxon 66 D5
Headlam Dur 168 F7
Headlesscross N Lans 210 B7
Headless Cross Worcs 82 B2
Headley Hants 36 B4
Headley Hants 48 D6
Headley Surrey 51 G8
Headley Down Hants 36 B4
Headley Heath Worcs 98 D8
Headon Devon 11 M2
Headon Notts 134 E4
Heads Nook Cumb 178 C7
Heage Derbys 116 B2
Healaugh N York 151 G6
Healaugh N York 159 H3
Heald Green Stockp 131 G3
Heale Devon 28 A2
Heale Somset 30 C6
Heale Somset 30 F5
Healey N York 160 B6
Healey Nthumb 180 B7
Healey Rochdl 140 D4
Healey Wakefd 141 L4
Healeyfield Dur 168 D1
Healing NE Lin 145 G5
Heamoor Cnwll 2 D5
Heanor Derbys 116 D2
Heanton Punchardon Devon 27 J4
Heapham Lincs 135 H2
Hearn Hants 36 B4
Heart of Scotland Services
    N Lans 210 B6
Hearts Delight Kent 53 J6
Heasley Mill Devon 28 C4
Heaste Highld 247 K5
Heath Derbys 133 J6
Heath Wakefd 142 A4
Heath and Reach C Beds 68 B3
Heath Common W Susx 21 J4
Heathcote Derbys 132 C7
Heathcote Shrops 113 L6
Heath End Bucks 67 L7
Heath End Hants 48 B6
Heath End Leics 116 B7
Heath End Warwks 82 E1
Heather Leics 99 K1
Heathfield Cambs 87 J6
Heathfield Devon 13 J7
Heathfield E Susx 23 K3

Heathfield N York 149 L2
Heathfield Somset 29 L5
Heathfield Village Oxon 66 D4
Heath Green Worcs 82 C1
Heath Hall D & G 176 C3
Heath Hayes & Wimblebury Staffs 98 C2
Heath Hill Shrops 97 H1
Heath House Somset 30 F2
Heathrow Airport Gt Lon 50 D4
Heathstock Devon 14 F2
Heathton Shrops 97 H5
Heath Town Wolves 97 L3
Heathwaite N York 161 G2
Heatley Staffs 115 H6
Heatley Warrtn 130 D2
Heaton Bolton 139 L6
Heaton C Brad 149 L8
Heaton Lancs 147 J4
Heaton N u Ty 181 G5
Heaton Staffs 131 J7
Heaton Chapel Stockp 131 H1
Heaton Mersey Stockp 131 G2
Heaton Norris Stockp 131 H2
Heaton's Bridge Lancs 138 E5
Heaverham Kent 52 C7
Heaviley Stockp 131 H2
Heavitree Devon 13 L4
Hebburn S Tyne 181 H6
Hebden N York 149 J3
Hebden Bridge Calder 140 F2
Hebden Green Ches W 130 C6
Hebing End Herts 69 J3
Hebron Carmth 75 L6
Hebron IoA 125 H3
Hebron Nthumb 191 J8
Heckfield Hants 49 H6
Heckfield Green Suffk 106 D8
Heckfordbridge Essex 72 D3
Heckington Lincs 118 F3
Heckmondwike Kirk 141 K1
Heddington Wilts 46 E5
Heddon-on-the-Wall Nthumb 180 D5
Hedenham Norfk 107 G5
Hedge End Hants 19 H1
Hedgerley Bucks 50 B2
Hedgerley Green Bucks 50 B2
Hedging Somset 30 D5
Hedley on the Hill Nthumb 180 C7
Hednesford Staffs 98 C1
Hedon E R Yk 145 F2
Hedsor Bucks 49 L2
Heeley Sheff 133 G3
Hegdon Hill Herefs 80 D4
Heglibister Shet 281 d6
Heighington Darltn 169 H6
Heighington Lincs 135 L4
Heightington Worcs 81 H1
Heiton Border 201 L7
Hele Devon 13 H8
Hele Devon 14 A2
Hele Devon 27 J2
Hele Somset 30 B6
Helebridge Cnwll 11 J2
Hele Lane Devon 28 D8
Helensburgh Ag & B 208 A3
Helenton S Ayrs 196 D5
Helford Cnwll 3 J5
Helford Passage Cnwll 3 J5
Helhoughton Norfk 121 J6
Helions Bumpstead Essex 88 C7
Hellaby Rothm 133 K1
Helland Cnwll 10 F8
Hellandbridge Cnwll 10 F8
Hell Corner W Berk 48 A6
Hellescott Cnwll 11 K5
Hellesdon Norfk 106 E1
Hellesveor Cnwll 2 D3
Hellidon Nhants 83 M4
Hellifield N York 148 E4
Hellingly E Susx 23 K5
Hellington Norfk 107 G3
Helm Nthumb 191 H7
Helmdon Nhants 84 B6
Helme Kirk 141 H5
Helmingham Suffk 90 E4
Helmington Row Dur 168 F4
Helmsdale Highld 274 D1
Helmshore Lancs 140 B3
Helmsley N York 161 K6
Helperby N York 150 F2
Helperthorpe N York 152 E2
Helpringham Lincs 118 F3
Helpston C Pete 102 C2
Helsby Ches W 129 L4
Helsey Lincs 137 L6
Helston Cnwll 3 G5
Helstone Cnwll 10 F6
Helton Cumb 166 C6
Helwith N York 159 K2

Helwith Bridge N York 148 D2
Hemblington Norfk 107 G1
Hembridge Somset 31 K3
Hemel Hempstead Herts 68 D5
Hemerdon Devon 7 H3
Hemingbrough N York 143 H2
Hemingby Lincs 136 D5
Hemingfield Barns 142 B7
Hemingford Abbots Cambs 86 F1
Hemingford Grey Cambs 86 F1
Hemingstone Suffk 90 D4
Hemington Leics 116 D6
Hemington Nhants 102 A6
Hemington Somset 45 L8
Hemley Suffk 91 G6
Hemlington Middsb 170 C7
Hempholme E R Yk 153 H5
Hempnall Norfk 106 E4
Hempnall Green Norfk 106 E5
Hempriggs Moray 266 B3
Hempstead Essex 88 C7
Hempstead Medway 53 G6
Hempstead Norfk 122 C4
Hempstead Norfk 123 H6
Hempsted Gloucs 64 B4
Hempton Norfk 121 K5
Hempton Oxon 66 C1
Hemsby Norfk 123 K8
Hemswell Lincs 135 J2
Hemswell Cliff Lincs 135 J2
Hemsworth Wakefd 142 C5
Hemyock Devon 29 L8
Henbury Bristl 45 H3
Henbury Ches E 131 H5
Hendham Devon 7 L5
Hendomen Powys 94 F4
Hendon Gt Lon 51 G1
Hendon Sundld 181 K7
Hendra Cnwll 3 J4
Hendra Cnwll 10 E7
Hendre Brdgnd 42 E5
Hendre Flints 128 E6
Hendredenny Caerph 43 H4
Hendy Carmth 57 G4
Heneglwys IoA 125 G4
Henfield W Susx 22 C4
Henford Devon 11 M4
Henfynyw Cerdgn 76 E3
Henghurst Kent 40 B8
Hengoed Caerph 43 J3
Hengoed Powys 79 J4
Hengoed Shrops 112 D5
Hengrave Suffk 89 G2
Henham Essex 70 E2
Heniarth Powys 94 D2
Henlade Somset 30 C6
Henley Dorset 16 D2
Henley Gloucs 64 C4
Henley Shrops 95 L5
Henley Shrops 96 C8
Henley Somset 30 F4
Henley Suffk 90 E5
Henley W Susx 36 D5
Henley Green Covtry 99 K7
Henley-in-Arden Warwks 82 E2
Henley-on-Thames Oxon 49 J2
Henley Park Surrey 50 B8
Henley's Down E Susx 24 D5
Henley Street Kent 52 E5
Henllan Cerdgn 76 C7
Henllan Denbgs 127 L6
Henllan Amgoed Carmth 55 L3
Henllys Torfn 44 B1
Henlow C Beds 86 D7
Henlow Camp C Beds 86 D8
Hennock Devon 13 J4
Henny Street Essex 89 H7
Henryd Conwy 126 F5
Henry's Moat (Castell Hendre) Pembks 75 H6
Hensall N York 142 F3
Henshaw Nthumb 179 H6
Hensingham Cumb 164 C7
Henstead Suffk 107 K4
Hensting Hants 35 G6
Henstridge Somset 32 B7
Henstridge Ash Somset 32 B6
Henstridge Marsh Somset 32 B6
Henton Oxon 67 J6
Henton Somset 31 H2
Henwick Worcs 81 J4
Henwood Cnwll 11 K1
Henwood Oxon 66 C6
Heolgerrig Myr Td 60 F6
Heol-las Swans 57 J5
Heol Senni Powys 60 D2
Heol-y-Cyw Brdgnd 42 E5
Hepburn Nthumb 190 F1
Hepple Nthumb 190 E6
Hepscott Nthumb 180 F2

Heptonstall Calder 140 E2
Hepworth Kirk 141 J6
Hepworth Suffk 105 K8
Herbrandston Pembks 54 E5
Hereford Herefs 80 C7
Hereson Kent 41 L2
Heribusta Highld 258 F3
Heriot Border 200 E2
Hermiston C Edin 211 G5
Hermitage Border 188 E7
Hermitage Dorset 16 C1
Hermitage W Berk 48 D4
Hermitage W Susx 20 B5
Hermit Hill Barns 141 M7
Hermon Carmth 58 C3
Hermon IoA 125 G6
Hermon Pembks 75 L6
Herne Kent 41 G2
Herne Bay Kent 41 G2
Herne Common Kent 41 G2
Herne Hill Gt Lon 51 J4
Herne Pound Kent 39 G3
Herner Devon 27 K5
Hernhill Kent 40 E3
Herodsfoot Cnwll 5 L3
Heronden Kent 41 J4
Herongate Essex 52 D1
Heronsford S Ayrs 182 E6
Heronsgate Herts 68 C8
Herriard Hants 35 K2
Herringfleet Suffk 107 K4
Herring's Green Bed 86 B6
Herringswell Suffk 88 E1
Herringthorpe Rothm 133 J1
Herrington Sundld 181 J8
Hersden Kent 41 G3
Hersham Cnwll 11 J1
Hersham Surrey 50 E6
Herstmonceux E Susx 23 L5
Herston Dorset 17 K6
Herston Ork 275 c6
Hertford Herts 69 J4
Hertford Heath Herts 69 K5
Hertingfordbury Herts 69 J5
Hesketh Bank Lancs 138 F3
Hesketh Lane Lancs 147 M7
Hesket Newmarket Cumb 165 K3
Heskin Green Lancs 139 G4
Hesleden Dur 170 B3
Hesleden N York 158 F7
Hesley Donc 134 C1
Hesleyside Nthumb 179 J2
Heslington C York 151 K5
Hessay C York 151 H5
Hessenford Cnwll 6 C3
Hessett Suffk 89 J3
Hessle E R Yk 144 C3
Hessle Wakefd 142 C4
Hest Bank Lancs 147 J3
Hestley Green Suffk 90 D2
Heston Gt Lon 50 E3
Heston Services Gt Lon 50 E3
Hestwall Ork 275 b4
Heswall Wirral 129 G3
Hethe Oxon 66 E1
Hethersett Norfk 106 C2
Hethersgill Cumb 178 B5
Hetherside Cumb 178 B5
Hetherson Green Ches W 113 H2
Hethpool Nthumb 202 D7
Hett Dur 169 H3
Hetton N York 149 G4
Hetton-le-Hole Sundld 169 K1
Hetton Steads Nthumb 203 G6
Heugh Nthumb 180 D4
Heughhead Abers 243 L1
Heugh Head Border 213 J6
Heveningham Suffk 91 H1
Hever Kent 38 D4
Heversham Cumb 157 H6
Hevingham Norfk 122 D7
Hewas Water Cnwll 4 F5
Hewelsfield Gloucs 63 H6
Hewenden C Brad 149 K8
Hewish N Som 44 E6
Hewish Somset 15 K1
Hewood Dorset 15 H2
Hexham Nthumb 179 L6
Hextable Kent 52 B5
Hexthorpe Donc 142 F7
Hexton Herts 68 E1
Hexworthy Cnwll 11 L6
Hexworthy Devon 12 F8
Hey Lancs 148 F7
Heybridge Essex 70 F7
Heybridge Essex 71 L5
Heybridge Basin Essex 72 C5
Heybrook Bay Devon 6 D6
Heydon Cambs 87 J7
Heydon Norfk 122 C6

Heydour Lincs 118 D4
Hey Houses Lancs 138 D2
Heylipoll Ag & B 224 B6
Heylor Shet 281 d4
Heyrod Tamesd 140 E7
Heysham Lancs 147 H4
Heyshaw N York 149 L3
Heyshott W Susx 20 E3
Heyside Oldham 140 D6
Heytesbury Wilts 32 F2
Heythrop Oxon 65 M2
Heywood Rochdl 140 C5
Heywood Wilts 46 C8
Hibaldstow N Linc 144 B7
Hickleton Donc 142 D6
Hickling Norfk 123 J6
Hickling Notts 117 J6
Hickling Green Norfk 123 H6
Hickling Heath Norfk 123 H7
Hickling Pastures Notts 117 H6
Hickmans Green Kent 40 E4
Hicks Forstal Kent 41 G3
Hickstead W Susx 22 D3
Hidcote Bartrim Gloucs 82 E6
Hidcote Boyce Gloucs 82 E6
High Ackworth Wakefd 142 C4
Higham Barns 141 M6
Higham Derbys 133 H7
Higham Kent 38 F4
Higham Kent 52 F5
Higham Lancs 148 E8
Higham Suffk 88 E2
Higham Suffk 89 L8
Higham Dykes Nthumb 180 D4
Higham Ferrers Nhants 85 J2
Higham Gobion C Beds 86 C8
Higham Hill Gt Lon 51 K1
Higham on the Hill Leics 99 K4
Highampton Devon 12 C2
Highams Park Gt Lon 69 K8
High Angerton Nthumb 180 D2
High Ardwell D & G 172 D5
High Auldgirth D & G 176 B1
High Bankhill Cumb 166 D2
High Barnet Gt Lon 69 H7
High Beach Essex 69 L7
High Bentham N York 148 B2
High Bewaldeth Cumb 165 H4
High Bickington Devon 27 L6
High Biggins Cumb 157 K7
High Birkwith N York 158 D7
High Blantyre S Lans 209 H7
High Bonnybridge Falk 209 L3
High Borrans Cumb 156 F3
High Bradley N York 149 H6
High Bray Devon 28 B4
Highbridge Hants 34 F6
Highbridge Somset 30 D2
Highbrook W Susx 38 A7
High Brooms Kent 38 F5
High Bullen Devon 27 J6
Highburton Kirk 141 J5
Highbury Gt Lon 51 J2
Highbury Somset 31 M1
High Buston Nthumb 191 J4
High Callerton Nthumb 180 E5
High Casterton Cumb 157 K7
High Catton E R Yk 151 M5
Highclere Hants 48 B7
Highcliffe BCP 18 C5
High Close Dur 168 F7
High Cogges Oxon 66 A5
High Common Norfk 105 K2
High Coniscliffe Darltn 169 G7
High Crosby Cumb 178 B6
High Cross Cnwll 3 J5
High Cross E Ayrs 196 D2
High Cross Hants 35 L5
High Cross Herts 69 K3
Highcross Lancs 147 G8
High Cross W Susx 22 C4
High Cross Warwks 82 E2
High Drummore D & G 172 E7
High Dubmire Sundld 169 J1
High Easter Essex 70 F4
High Eggborough N York 142 F3
High Ellington N York 160 B6
Higher Alham Somset 31 L3
Higher Ansty Dorset 16 E2
Higher Ballam Lancs 138 D2
Higher Bartle Lancs 139 G1
Higher Berry End C Beds 85 J8
Higher Bockhampton Dorset 16 D4
Higher Brixham Torbay 8 D4
Higher Burrowton Devon 14 B3
Higher Burwardsley Ches W 129 M8
High Ercall Wrekin 113 K8
Higher Chillington Somset 15 J1
Higher Clovelly Devon 26 E6
Highercombe Somset 28 F5

Higher Coombe Dorset 15 M4
Higher Disley Ches E 131 J3
Higher Folds Wigan 139 K7
Higherford Lancs 148 F7
Higher Gabwell Devon 8 D1
Higher Halstock Leigh Dorset 15 L1
Higher Harpers Lancs 148 E8
Higher Heysham Lancs 147 H4
Higher Hurdsfield Ches E 131 J5
Higher Irlam Salfd 130 E1
Higher Kingcombe Dorset 15 M3
Higher Kinnerton Flints 129 H7
Higher Marston Ches W 130 C4
Higher Muddiford Devon 27 K3
Higher Nyland Dorset 32 B6
Higher Ogden Rochdl 140 E5
Higher Pentire Cnwll 3 G6
Higher Penwortham Lancs 139 G2
Higher Prestacott Devon 11 M3
Higher Studfold N York 148 E2
Higher Town Cnwll 4 C6
Higher Town Cnwll 5 G3
Higher Town IoS 10 c2
Higher Tregantle Cnwll 6 D4
Higher Walton Lancs 139 H2
Higher Walton Warrtn 130 B3
Higher Wambrook Somset 15 G1
Higher Waterston Dorset 16 D3
Higher Whatcombe Dorset 17 G2
Higher Wheelton Lancs 139 J3
Higher Whitley Ches W 130 B4
Higher Wincham Ches W 130 D4
Higher Wraxhall Dorset 16 A2
Higher Wych Ches W 113 H3
High Etherley Dur 168 F5
High Ferry Lincs 119 K2
Highfield E R Yk 151 M8
Highfield Gatesd 180 E7
Highfield N Ayrs 196 C1
Highfields Donc 142 E6
Highfields Caldecote Cambs 87 G3
High Flats Kirk 141 K6
High Garrett Essex 71 J2
Highgate E Susx 38 C6
Highgate Gt Lon 51 H2
Highgate Kent 39 J7
Highgate Lincs 119 L2
High Grange Dur 168 F4
High Grantley N York 150 B2
High Green Cumb 156 F2
High Green Kirk 141 K5
High Green Norfk 106 C2
High Green Norfk 106 D5
High Green Sheff 142 A8
High Green Shrops 96 F6
High Green Suffk 89 G3
High Green Worcs 81 K6
Highgreen Manor Nthumb 189 L7
High Halden Kent 40 A7
High Halstow Medway 53 G4
High Ham Somset 30 F4
High Harrington Cumb 164 D5
High Harrogate N York 150 D5
High Haswell Dur 169 K2
High Hatton Shrops 113 K6
High Hauxley Nthumb 191 K5
High Hawsker N York 163 G1
High Hesket Cumb 166 B2
High Hoyland Barns 141 L5
High Hunsley E R Yk 144 B1
High Hurstwood E Susx 23 H2
High Hutton N York 152 A2
High Ireby Cumb 165 H3
High Kelling Norfk 122 C3
High Kilburn N York 161 H6
High Killerby N York 163 J6
High Knipe Cumb 166 C6
High Lands Dur 168 E5
Highlane Ches E 131 H6
Highlane Derbys 133 H3
High Lane Stockp 131 J3
High Lanes Cnwll 2 F4
High Laver Essex 70 D5
Highlaws Cumb 164 F1
Highleadon Gloucs 63 M2
High Legh Ches E 130 D3
Highleigh W Susx 20 D7
High Leven S on T 170 B8
Highley Shrops 97 G6
High Littleton BaNES 45 J7
High Lorton Cumb 165 G5
High Marishes N York 162 E7
High Marnham Notts 134 F5
High Melton Donc 142 D7
High Mickley Nthumb 180 C6
Highmoor Cumb 165 J1
Highmoor Oxon 49 H2
Highmoor Cross Oxon 49 H2
Highmoor Hill Mons 44 F1
High Moorsley Sundld 169 J2

Highnam Gloucs 63 M3
High Newport Sundld 181 J8
High Newton Cumb 156 F6
High Newton-by-the-Sea
   Nthumb 203 L8
High Nibthwaite Cumb 156 D5
High Offley Staffs 114 B6
High Ongar Essex 70 E6
High Onn Staffs 114 C8
High Park Corner Essex 72 F3
High Pennyvenie E Ayrs 184 D2
High Pittington Dur 169 J2
High Post Wilts 33 K4
Highridge N Som 45 H5
High Roding Essex 70 F4
High Row Cumb 165 K3
High Row Cumb 165 K6
High Salter Lancs 147 M3
High Salvington W Susx 21 K5
High Scales Cumb 165 G2
High Seaton Cumb 164 D4
High Shaw N York 158 F4
High Side Cumb 165 H4
High Spen Gatesd 180 E7
Highstead Kent 41 G8
Highsted Kent 40 B3
High Stoop Dur 168 E3
High Street Cnwll 5 G4
High Street Kent 39 J7
Highstreet Kent 40 B3
High Street Suffk 91 J1
High Street Suffk 91 K4
Highstreet Green Essex 88 F8
Highstreet Green Surrey 36 F3
Hightae D & G 176 E3
Highter's Heath Birm 98 E7
High Throston Hartpl 170 C4
Hightown Ches E 131 G7
Hightown Hants 18 B3
Hightown Sefton 138 C7
High Town Staffs 98 C1
Hightown Green Suffk 89 K4
High Toynton Lincs 136 E5
High Trewhitt Nthumb 190 E5
High Urpeth Dur 181 G8
High Valleyfield Fife 210 D2
High Warden Nthumb 179 L5
Highway Herefs 80 B5
Highway Wilts 46 F4
Highweek Devon 13 K6
High Westwood Dur 180 D7
Highwood Essex 70 F6
Highwood Staffs 115 H5
Highwood W Susx 37 J5
Highwood Hill Gt Lon 69 G8
Highwoods Essex 72 E2
High Woolaston Gloucs 63 H7
High Worsall N York 160 F1
Highworth Swindn 65 J8
High Wray Cumb 156 E3
High Wych Herts 70 C4
High Wycombe Bucks 67 L8
Hilborough Norfk 105 G3
Hilcote Derbys 133 J8
Hilcott Wilts 47 G7
Hildenborough Kent 38 E4
Hilden Park Kent 38 F4
Hildersham Cambs 87 L5
Hilderstone Staffs 114 E4
Hilderthorpe E R Yk 153 J3
Hilfield Dorset 16 C2
Hilgay Norfk 104 C4
Hill S Glos 63 J8
Hill Warwks 83 K2
Hillam N York 142 D2
Hillbeck Cumb 167 H7
Hillborough Kent 41 G8
Hill Brow Hants 36 B5
Hillbutts Dorset 17 K2
Hill Chorlton Staffs 114 B4
Hillclifflane Derbys 115 M2
Hill Common Norfk 123 H7
Hill Common Somset 29 L5
Hill Deverill Wilts 32 E3
Hilldyke Lincs 119 K2
Hill End Dur 168 C3
Hillend Fife 210 F2
Hill End Fife 221 H4
Hill End Gloucs 81 K7
Hillend Mdloth 211 H5
Hillend N Lans 209 L5
Hillend Swans 56 D6
Hillersland Gloucs 63 H4
Hillerton Devon 13 G3
Hillesden Bucks 67 G1
Hillesley Gloucs 45 M1
Hillfarrance Somset 29 L6
Hill Green Kent 53 H6
Hillgrove W Susx 36 D5
Hillhampton Herefs 80 D6

Hillhead Abers 255 M4
Hillhead Devon 8 D4
Hill Head Hants 19 J3
Hillhead S Lans 199 G5
Hillhead of Cocklaw Abers 257 K3
Hilliard's Cross Staffs 98 F1
Hilliclay Highld 279 L3
Hillingdon Gt Lon 50 D2
Hillington C Glas 208 E6
Hillington Norfk 120 F6
Hillis Corner IoW 19 H5
Hillmorton Warwks 100 C8
Hillock Vale Lancs 140 A2
Hill of Beath Fife 210 F1
Hill of Fearn Highld 264 C4
Hillowton D & G 175 J2
Hillpool Worcs 97 K8
Hillpound Hants 35 J7
Hill Ridware Staffs 115 H8
Hillside Abers 245 K4
Hillside Angus 235 H3
Hillside Devon 7 K3
Hill Side Kirk 141 J4
Hill Side Worcs 81 H3
Hills Town Derbys 133 J5
Hillstreet Hants 34 D7
Hillswick Shet 281 c4
Hill Top Dur 168 C6
Hill Top Hants 18 F3
Hill Top Kirk 141 G5
Hill Top Rothm 133 H1
Hill Top Sandw 98 C5
Hill Top Wakefd 142 A4
Hillwell Shet 281 d8
Hilmarton Wilts 46 E4
Hilperton Wilts 46 C7
Hilperton Marsh Wilts 46 C7
Hilsea C Port 19 L3
Hilston E R Yk 145 H1
Hiltingbury Hants 34 F6
Hilton Border 202 D3
Hilton Cambs 86 F2
Hilton Cumb 167 G6
Hilton Derbys 115 L5
Hilton Dorset 16 E2
Hilton Dur 168 F6
Hilton S on T 170 B8
Hilton Shrops 97 H4
Hilton of Cadboll Highld 264 D4
Hilton Park Services Staffs 98 B2
Himbleton Worcs 81 L3
Himley Staffs 97 K5
Hincaster Cumb 157 H5
Hinchley Wood Surrey 50 F6
Hinckley Leics 99 L4
Hinderclay Suffk 105 L8
Hinderwell N York 171 J7
Hindford Shrops 112 E5
Hindhead Surrey 36 C4
Hindhead Tunnel Surrey 36 D4
Hindle Fold Lancs 139 L1
Hindley Nthumb 180 C7
Hindley Wigan 139 J6
Hindley Green Wigan 139 J7
Hindlip Worcs 81 K3
Hindolveston Norfk 122 A5
Hindon Wilts 32 F4
Hindringham Norfk 121 L4
Hingham Norfk 105 L3
Hinksford Staffs 97 K5
Hinstock Shrops 113 M6
Hintlesham Suffk 90 C6
Hinton Gloucs 63 K6
Hinton Hants 18 C4
Hinton Herefs 79 L7
Hinton Nhants 83 M5
Hinton S Glos 45 L4
Hinton Shrops 95 K2
Hinton Shrops 96 E7
Hinton Admiral Hants 18 C4
Hinton Ampner Hants 35 J5
Hinton Blewett BaNES 45 H7
Hinton Charterhouse BaNES 45 M7
Hinton Cross Worcs 82 B7
Hinton-in-the-Hedges Nhants 84 A7
Hinton Marsh Hants 35 J5
Hinton Martell Dorset 17 K2
Hinton on the Green Worcs 82 B7
Hinton Parva Swindn 47 K2
Hinton St George Somset 30 F8
Hinton St Mary Dorset 32 C7
Hinton Waldrist Oxon 66 A2
Hints Shrops 96 E8
Hints Staffs 98 F3
Hinwick Bed 85 J3
Hinxhill Kent 40 D6
Hinxton Cambs 87 K6
Hinxworth Herts 86 E7
Hipperholme Calder 141 H3
Hipsburn Nthumb 191 J4

Hipswell N York 160 B3
Hirn Abers 245 G3
Hirnant Powys 111 K7
Hirst Nthumb 181 G2
Hirst Courtney N York 142 F3
Hirwaen Denbgs 128 D2
Hirwaun Rhondd 60 E6
Hiscott Devon 27 K5
Histon Cambs 87 J3
Hitcham Suffk 89 K5
Hitcham Causeway Suffk 89 K5
Hitcham Street Suffk 89 K5
Hitchin Herts 68 F1
Hither Green Gt Lon 51 K4
Hittisleigh Devon 13 G3
Hive E R Yk 143 K2
Hixon Staffs 114 F6
Hoaden Kent 41 J3
Hoar Cross Staffs 115 J7
Hoarwithy Herefs 63 G1
Hoath Kent 41 G2
Hoathly Kent 39 G6
Hobarris Shrops 95 H7
Hobbles Green Suffk 88 C4
Hobbs Cross Essex 70 C7
Hobbs Cross Essex 70 D5
Hobkirk Border 189 G4
Hobland Hall Norfk 107 K3
Hobsick Notts 116 F2
Hobson Dur 180 E7
Hoby Leics 117 H8
Hoccombe Somset 29 K5
Hockering Norfk 106 C8
Hockerton Notts 134 E8
Hockley Ches E 131 J2
Hockley Covtry 99 H2
Hockley Essex 71 K7
Hockley Staffs 99 G3
Hockley Heath Solhll 82 F8
Hockliffe C Beds 68 B2
Hockwold cum Wilton Norfk 104 C7
Hockworthy Devon 29 J1
Hoddesdon Herts 69 K5
Hoddlesden Bl w D 139 L2
Hoddom Cross D & G 177 G2
Hoddom Mains D & G 177 G2
Hodgehill Ches E 131 G8
Hodgeston Pembks 55 G7
Hodnet Shrops 113 K6
Hodsock Notts 134 C4
Hodsoll Street Kent 52 E6
Hodson Swindn 47 H2
Hodthorpe Derbys 133 L5
Hoe Hants 35 J4
Hoe Norfk 121 M8
Hoe Benham W Berk 48 C5
Hoe Gate Hants 35 K4
Hoff Cumb 166 F7
Hogben's Hill Kent 40 D4
Hoggards Green Suffk 89 H4
Hoggeston Bucks 67 L3
Hoggrill's End Warwks 99 G6
Hog Hill E Susx 25 G5
Hoghton Lancs 139 J2
Hoghton Bottoms Lancs 139 J2
Hognaston Derbys 115 M2
Hogsthorpe Lincs 137 K5
Holbeach Lincs 119 K6
Holbeach Bank Lincs 119 K6
Holbeach Clough Lincs 119 K6
Holbeach Drove Lincs 103 G8
Holbeach Hurn Lincs 119 L5
Holbeach St Johns Lincs 119 K7
Holbeach St Mark's Lincs 119 L4
Holbeach St Matthew Lincs 119 L4
Holbeck Notts 133 L5
Holbeck Woodhouse Notts 133 L5
Holberrow Green Worcs 82 B3
Holbeton Devon 7 G5
Holborn Gt Lon 51 J3
Holborough Kent 52 F6
Holbrook Derbys 116 B3
Holbrook Sheff 133 G3
Holbrook Suffk 90 E7
Holbrook Moor Derbys 116 B3
Holbrooks Covtry 99 J7
Holburn Nthumb 203 G5
Holbury Hants 19 G4
Holcombe Devon 13 M5
Holcombe Somset 31 L7
Holcombe Rogus Devon 29 J2
Holcot Nhants 84 F7
Holden Lancs 148 G3
Holdenby Nhants 84 D7
Holden Gate Calder 140 D3
Holder's Green Essex 70 F2
Holdgate Shrops 96 E6
Holdingham Lincs 118 E2
Holditch Dorset 15 H2
Holdsworth Calder 141 G2

Holehouse Derbys 131 K1
Hole-in-the-Wall Herefs 63 J2
Holemoor Devon 12 A2
Hole Street W Susx 21 K4
Holford Somset 29 L3
Holgate C York 151 J5
Holker Cumb 156 E7
Holkham Norfk 121 K3
Hollacombe Devon 11 M2
Holland Fen Lincs 119 H2
Holland Lees Lancs 139 G6
Holland-on-Sea Essex 73 J4
Hollandstoun Ork 275 f1
Hollee D & G 177 J5
Hollesley Suffk 91 H6
Hollicombe Torbay 8 D2
Hollingbourne Kent 39 L2
Hollingbury Br & H 22 D5
Hollingdon Bucks 67 L2
Hollingrove E Susx 24 C3
Hollingthorpe Leeds 142 B2
Hollington Derbys 115 L4
Hollington Staffs 115 G4
Hollingworth Tamesd 140 F8
Hollins Bury 140 B6
Hollins Derbys 132 F5
Hollins Staffs 114 F2
Hollinsclough Staffs 131 L6
Hollins End Sheff 133 H3
Hollins Green Warrtn 130 D2
Hollins Lane Lancs 147 K5
Hollinswood Wrekin 96 F2
Hollinwood Shrops 113 H4
Hollocombe Devon 27 L8
Holloway Derbys 132 F8
Holloway Gt Lon 51 J2
Holloway Wilts 32 E5
Hollowell Nhants 84 D1
Hollowmoor Heath Ches W 129 L6
Hollows D & G 177 L3
Hollybush Caerph 61 J6
Hollybush E Ayrs 196 D7
Hollybush Herefs 81 H7
Holly End Norfk 103 K2
Holly Green Worcs 81 K6
Hollyhurst Ches E 113 J3
Hollym E R Yk 145 J3
Hollywater Hants 36 B4
Hollywood Worcs 98 D7
Holmbridge Kirk 141 H6
Holmbury St Mary Surrey 37 H2
Holmbush Cnwll 5 H4
Holmcroft Staffs 114 E6
Holme Cambs 102 D6
Holme Cumb 157 H7
Holme Kirk 141 H6
Holme N Linc 144 A6
Holme N York 160 E6
Holme Notts 134 F7
Holme Chapel Lancs 140 C2
Holme Green N York 151 J6
Holme Hale Norfk 105 H2
Holme Lacy Herefs 80 D8
Holme Marsh Herefs 79 L4
Holme next the Sea Norfk 120 F3
Holme on the Wolds E R Yk 152 E6
Holme Pierrepont Notts 117 G4
Holmer Herefs 80 C6
Holmer Green Bucks 67 L2
Holme St Cuthbert Cumb 164 F1
Holmes Chapel Ches E 130 E6
Holmesfield Derbys 132 F4
Holmes Hill E Susx 23 J4
Holmeswood Lancs 138 E4
Holmethorpe Surrey 51 H8
Holme upon Spalding Moor
  E R Yk 152 B8
Holmewood Derbys 133 H6
Holmfield Calder 141 G2
Holmfirth Kirk 141 H6
Holmgate Derbys 133 G6
Holmhead E Ayrs 197 H7
Holmpton E R Yk 145 K3
Holmrook Cumb 155 K3
Holmshurst E Susx 23 L2
Holmside Dur 169 G1
Holmwrangle Cumb 166 C1
Holne Devon 7 H5
Holnest Dorset 16 C1
Holnicote Somset 29 G2
Holsworthy Devon 11 L2
Holsworthy Beacon Devon 11 L1
Holt Dorset 17 K2
Holt Norfk 122 B4
Holt Wilts 46 B6
Holt Worcs 81 J2
Holt Wrexhm 112 F1
Holtby C York 151 L5
Holt End Worcs 82 C1
Holt Fleet Worcs 81 J3

Holt Green Lancs 138 E6
Holt Heath Dorset 17 L2
Holt Heath Worcs 81 J3
Holton Oxon 66 F5
Holton Somset 31 L5
Holton Suffk 107 H7
Holton cum Beckering Lincs 136 B3
Holton Heath Dorset 17 J4
Holton Hill E Susx 24 B2
Holton le Clay Lincs 145 H7
Holton le Moor Lincs 144 D8
Holton St Mary Suffk 90 C7
Holt Street Kent 41 H5
Holtye E Susx 38 C5
Holway Flints 128 E4
Holwell Dorset 32 B8
Holwell Herts 86 D3
Holwell Leics 117 J6
Holwell Oxon 65 K5
Holwick Dur 167 L5
Holworth Dorset 16 D8
Holybourne Hants 35 M3
Holy Cross Worcs 97 L7
Holyfield Essex 69 K6
Holyhead IoA 124 D3
Holy Island IoA 124 D3
Holy Island Nthumb 203 J4
Holy Island Nthumb 203 J5
Holymoorside Derbys 133 G6
Holyport W & M 49 L3
Holystone Nthumb 190 D5
Holytown N Lans 209 K6
Holywell C Beds 68 C4
Holywell Cambs 87 G1
Holywell Cnwll 4 C3
Holywell Dorset 16 B2
Holywell Flints 128 E4
Holywell Nthumb 181 H4
Holywell Warwks 82 E2
Holywell Green Calder 141 G4
Holywell Lake Somset 29 K6
Holywell Row Suffk 104 E7
Holywood D & G 176 B3
Holywood Village D & G 176 C3
Homer Shrops 96 E3
Homer Green Sefton 138 D7
Homersfield Suffk 106 F6
Homescales Cumb 157 J5
Hom Green Herefs 63 H3
Homington Wilts 33 K5
Honeyborough Pembks 54 F5
Honeybourne Worcs 82 D6
Honeychurch Devon 12 E2
Honey Hill Kent 40 F3
Honeystreet Wilts 47 G6
Honey Tye Suffk 89 J8
Honiley Warwks 82 F1
Honing Norfk 123 G6
Honingham Norfk 106 C1
Honington Lincs 118 B3
Honington Suffk 105 H8
Honington Warwks 83 G6
Honiton Devon 14 E3
Honley Kirk 141 H5
Honnington Wrekin 114 A8
Hoo Kent 41 J2
Hoobrook Worcs 97 J8
Hood Green Barns 141 M7
Hood Hill Rothm 142 B4
Hooe C Plym 6 F4
Hooe E Susx 24 C5
Hoo End Herts 68 F3
Hoo Green Ches E 130 D3
Hoohill Bpool 146 F8
Hook Cambs 103 J5
Hook Devon 15 G2
Hook E R Yk 143 J3
Hook Gt Lon 50 F6
Hook Hants 19 H3
Hook Hants 49 H8
Hook Pembks 55 G5
Hook Wilts 47 G2
Hook-a-Gate Shrops 95 L2
Hook Bank Worcs 81 J7
Hooke Dorset 15 M3
Hook End Essex 70 E7
Hookgate Staffs 114 A4
Hook Green Kent 39 G6
Hook Green Kent 52 D5
Hook Norton Oxon 83 H8
Hook Street Gloucs 63 K7
Hook Street Wilts 47 G2
Hookway Devon 13 K3
Hookwood Surrey 37 L2
Hooley Surrey 51 H7
Hooley Bridge Rochdl 140 C5
Hoo Meavy Devon 7 H7
Hoo St Werburgh Medway 53 G4
Hooton Ches W 129 J4
Hooton Levitt Rothm 133 K2

Hooton Pagnell Donc 142 D6
Hooton Roberts Rothm 142 D8
Hopcrofts Holt Oxon 66 C2
Hope Derbys 132 C3
Hope Devon 7 K6
Hope Flints 129 G7
Hope Powys 95 G2
Hope Shrops 95 H3
Hope Staffs 132 B8
Hope Bagot Shrops 96 D8
Hope Bowdler Shrops 95 L5
Hope End Green Essex 70 E3
Hopehouse Border 187 L3
Hopeman Moray 266 C2
Hope Mansell Herefs 63 J3
Hopesay Shrops 95 J6
Hopetown Wakefd 142 B3
Hope under Dinmore Herefs 80 C5
Hopgrove C York 151 K5
Hopperton N York 150 F4
Hop Pole Lincs 102 D1
Hopsford Warwks 99 L6
Hopstone Shrops 97 H4
Hopton Derbys 115 L1
Hopton Shrops 112 F7
Hopton Staffs 114 E6
Hopton Suffk 105 K7
Hopton Cangeford Shrops 96 C7
Hopton Castle Shrops 95 J7
Hoptonheath Shrops 95 J7
Hopton on Sea Norfk 107 L3
Hopton Wafers Shrops 96 E8
Hopwas Staffs 98 F2
Hopwood Rochdl 140 C6
Hopwood Worcs 98 C8
Hopwood Park Services Worcs 98 D8
Horam E Susx 23 K4
Horbling Lincs 118 F4
Horbury Wakefd 141 L4
Horcott Gloucs 65 H7
Horden Dur 170 B3
Horderley Shrops 95 K6
Hordle Hants 18 D4
Hordley Shrops 112 F5
Horeb Carmth 56 F4
Horeb Cerdgn 76 D6
Horfield Bristl 45 H4
Horham Suffk 90 F1
Horkesley Heath Essex 72 E1
Horkstow N Linc 144 B4
Horley Oxon 83 K6
Horley Surrey 37 L2
Hornblotton Green Somset 31 K4
Hornby Lancs 147 L2
Hornby N York 160 B4
Hornby N York 160 E6
Horncastle Lincs 136 E6
Hornchurch Gt Lon 52 B2
Horncliffe Nthumb 202 E3
Horndean Border 202 D3
Horndean Hants 35 L8
Horndon Devon 12 C6
Horndon on the Hill Thurr 52 E2
Horne Surrey 38 A4
Horner Somset 28 F2
Horne Row Essex 71 J6
Horners Green Suffk 89 K7
Horney Common E Susx 23 G2
Horn Hill Bucks 68 C8
Horning Norfk 123 G8
Horninghold Leics 101 H4
Horninglow Staffs 115 L6
Horningsea Cambs 87 K3
Horningsham Wilts 32 D3
Horningtoft Norfk 121 K6
Horningtops Cnwll 6 B3
Hornsbury Somset 30 E8
Hornsby Cumb 166 C1
Hornsbygate Cumb 166 C1
Horns Cross Devon 27 G6
Horns Cross E Susx 24 E3
Hornsea E R Yk 153 K6
Hornsey Gt Lon 51 J1
Horn's Green Gt Lon 51 M7
Horn Street Kent 41 G8
Hornton Oxon 83 J6
Horpit Swindn 47 J2
Horrabridge Devon 7 G2
Horringer Suffk 89 G3
Horringford IoW 19 J6
Horrocks Fold Bolton 139 L5
Horrocksford Lancs 148 C5
Horsacott Devon 27 J4
Horsebridge Devon 12 A7
Horsebridge E Susx 23 K5
Horsebridge Hants 34 D4
Horsebridge Shrops 95 J2
Horsebridge Staffs 114 F1
Horsebrook Staffs 97 K1
Horsecastle N Som 44 E5

Horsedown Cnwll 3 G4
Horsehay Wrekin 96 F2
Horseheath Cambs 88 C5
Horsehouse N York 159 J6
Horsell Surrey 50 C7
Horseman's Green Wrexhm 113 G3
Horsenden Bucks 67 J6
Horsey Norfk 123 J7
Horsey Somset 30 D3
Horsey Corner Norfk 123 J7
Horsford Norfk 122 D8
Horsforth Leeds 150 B8
Horsham W Susx 37 J5
Horsham Worcs 81 G4
Horsham St Faith Norfk 122 E8
Horsington Lincs 136 C6
Horsington Somset 32 B6
Horsley Derbys 116 C3
Horsley Gloucs 64 B7
Horsley Nthumb 180 D5
Horsley Nthumb 190 B6
Horsley Cross Essex 73 H2
Horsleycross Street Essex 73 G1
Horsley-Gate Derbys 132 F4
Horsleyhill Border 188 F2
Horsley's Green Bucks 67 J8
Horsley Woodhouse Derbys 116 C3
Horsmonden Kent 39 H5
Horspath Oxon 66 E6
Horstead Norfk 122 F7
Horsted Keynes W Susx 22 F2
Horton Bucks 68 A3
Horton Dorset 17 K1
Horton Lancs 148 E6
Horton Nhants 84 F4
Horton S Glos 45 M2
Horton Shrops 113 H5
Horton Somset 30 D7
Horton Staffs 131 J8
Horton Surrey 51 G6
Horton Swans 56 E7
Horton W & M 50 C4
Horton Wilts 46 F6
Horton Wrekin 113 L8
Horton Cross Somset 30 E7
Horton-cum-Studley Oxon 66 F4
Horton Green Ches W 113 G2
Horton Heath Hants 35 G7
Horton-in-Ribblesdale N York 148 D2
Horton Kirby Kent 52 C5
Horwich Bolton 139 J5
Horwich End Derbys 131 K3
Horwood Devon 27 J5
Hoscar Lancs 138 F5
Hoscote Border 188 C4
Hose Leics 117 J5
Hosey Hill Kent 51 M8
Hosh P & K 220 E3
Hoswick Shet 281 e8
Hotham E R Yk 143 M1
Hothfield Kent 40 C6
Hoton Leics 116 F7
Hott Nthumb 179 H2
Hough Ches E 113 M1
Hough Ches E 131 G4
Hougham Lincs 118 A3
Hough End Leeds 141 K1
Hough Green Halton 129 L2
Hough-on-the-Hill Lincs 118 B2
Houghton Cambs 86 F1
Houghton Cumb 177 L7
Houghton Hants 34 D4
Houghton Nthumb 180 D5
Houghton Pembks 55 G5
Houghton W Susx 21 H4
Houghton Conquest C Beds 85 L7
Houghton Gate Dur 181 H8
Houghton Green E Susx 25 G3
Houghton Green Warrtn 130 C1
Houghton le Side Darltn 169 G6
Houghton-le-Spring Sundld 169 J1
Houghton on the Hill Leics 100 E3
Houghton Regis C Beds 68 C2
Houghton St Giles Norfk 121 K4
Houlton Warwks 100 C8
Hound Green Hants 49 H7
Houndslow Border 201 K4
Houndsmoor Somset 29 L5
Houndwood Border 213 J6
Hounslow Gt Lon 50 F4
Househill Highld 253 G1
Houses Hill Kirk 141 K4
Housieside Abers 257 G6
Houston Rens 208 C5
Houstry Highld 275 G1
Houton Ork 275 b5
Hove Br & H 22 D6
Hove Edge Calder 141 H3
Hoveringham Notts 117 J2
Hoveton Norfk 122 F7

Place	County	Page	Grid
Hovingham	N York	161	L7
Howbrook	Barns	141	M8
How Caple	Herefs	63	J1
Howden	E R Yk	143	J2
Howden-le-Wear	Dur	168	F4
Howe	Highld	280	D4
Howe	IoM	154	b8
Howe	N York	160	E6
Howe	Norfk	106	F3
Howe Bridge	Wigan	139	K7
Howe Green	Essex	71	H6
Howegreen	Essex	71	K6
Howell	Lincs	118	F2
How End	C Beds	85	K7
Howe of Teuchar	Abers	268	E6
Howes	D & G	177	G5
Howe Street	Essex	71	G4
Howe Street	Essex	88	D8
Howey	Powys	78	E3
Howgate	Cumb	164	C6
Howgate	Mdloth	211	H7
Howgill	Lancs	148	E6
Howick	Nthumb	191	K3
Howle	Wrekin	113	M6
Howle Hill	Herefs	63	J3
Howlett End	Essex	88	B8
Howley	Somset	15	G1
How Mill	Cumb	178	C7
Howmore	W Isls	283	b10
Hownam	Border	189	L2
Hownam	Border	189	L2
Howrigg	Cumb	165	K1
Howsham	N Linc	144	D6
Howsham	N York	151	M3
Howtel	Nthumb	202	D6
Howt Green	Kent	53	J6
Howton	Herefs	62	E1
Howtown	Cumb	166	B6
How Wood	Herts	68	F6
Howwood	Rens	208	C7
Hoxa	Ork	275	c6
Hoxne	Suffk	106	D7
Hoy	Ork	275	b5
Hoylake	Wirral	128	F2
Hoyland	Barns	142	B7
Hoyland Common	Barns	142	B7
Hoylandswaine	Barns	141	L6
Hoyle	W Susx	20	E3
Hoyle Mill	Barns	142	B6
Hubberholme	N York	159	G7
Hubberston	Pembks	54	E5
Hubbert's Bridge	Lincs	119	J3
Huby	N York	150	C6
Huby	N York	151	J3
Huccaby	Devon	12	F8
Hucclecote	Gloucs	64	C4
Hucking	Kent	53	H7
Hucknall	Notts	116	F2
Huddersfield	Kirk	141	H4
Huddington	Worcs	81	L4
Hudnall	Herts	68	C4
Hudswell	N York	159	L3
Huggate	E R Yk	152	D5
Hugglescote	Leics	99	L1
Hughenden Valley	Bucks	67	L7
Hughley	Shrops	96	D4
Hugh Town	IoS	10	c3
Huish	Devon	27	J8
Huish	Wilts	47	H6
Huish Champflower	Somset	29	J5
Huish Episcopi	Somset	31	G5
Hùisinis	W Isls	282	d5
Huisinish	W Isls	282	d5
Hulcote	C Beds	85	J7
Hulcote	Nhants	84	D5
Hulcott	Bucks	67	K4
Hulham	Devon	14	B6
Hulland	Derbys	115	L2
Hulland Ward	Derbys	115	L2
Hullavington	Wilts	46	C3
Hull Bridge	E R Yk	153	G7
Hullbridge	Essex	71	K8
Hull, Kingston upon	C KuH	144	D2
Hulme	Manch	140	C8
Hulme	Staffs	114	E2
Hulme	Warrtn	130	B2
Hulme End	Staffs	132	E2
Hulme Walfield	Ches E	131	G6
Hulse Heath	Ches E	130	E3
Hulton Lane Ends	Bolton	139	K6
Hulverstone	IoW	18	F6
Hulver Street	Norfk	105	J1
Hulver Street	Suffk	107	K6
Humber	Devon	13	L7
Humber	Herefs	80	C4
Humber Bridge	N Linc	144	C3
Humberside Airport	N Linc	144	E5
Humberston	NE Lin	145	J6
Humberstone	C Leic	100	E2
Humberton	N York	150	F2
Humbie	E Loth	212	A6
Humbleton	E R Yk	145	G1
Humbleton	Nthumb	202	F7
Humby	Lincs	118	D5
Hume	Border	201	L5
Humshaugh	Nthumb	179	L4
Huna	Highld	280	D2
Huncoat	Lancs	140	A2
Huncote	Leics	100	B4
Hundalee	Border	189	H3
Hundall	Derbys	133	H4
Hunderthwaite	Dur	168	C6
Hundleby	Lincs	137	G6
Hundle Houses	Lincs	119	H1
Hundleton	Pembks	54	F6
Hundon	Suffk	88	E5
Hundred End	Lancs	138	E3
Hundred House	Powys	78	F4
Hungarton	Leics	100	F2
Hungerford	Hants	33	L8
Hungerford	Somset	29	J3
Hungerford	W Berk	47	M5
Hungerford Newtown	W Berk	47	M4
Hunger Hill	Bolton	139	K6
Hunger Hill	Lancs	139	G5
Hungerstone	Herefs	80	B8
Hungerton	Lincs	118	A5
Hungryhatton	Shrops	113	L6
Hunmanby	N York	163	K7
Hunningham	Warwks	83	J2
Hunnington	Worcs	98	B7
Hunsbury Hill	Nhants	84	E4
Hunsdon	Herts	69	L4
Hunsdonbury	Herts	69	L4
Hunsingore	N York	150	F5
Hunslet	Leeds	141	M2
Hunsonby	Cumb	166	D4
Hunstanton	Norfk	120	E3
Hunstanworth	Dur	168	B1
Hunsterson	Ches E	113	M2
Hunston	Suffk	89	K2
Hunston	W Susx	20	D6
Hunston Green	Suffk	89	K2
Hunstrete	BaNES	45	J6
Hunsworth	Kirk	141	J2
Hunt End	Worcs	82	B2
Hunter's Inn	Devon	28	B1
Hunter's Quay	Ag & B	207	K3
Huntham	Somset	30	E5
Hunthill Lodge	Angus	234	D1
Huntingdon	Cambs	86	E1
Huntingfield	Suffk	107	G8
Huntingford	Dorset	32	D5
Huntington	C York	151	K4
Huntington	Ches W	129	K6
Huntington	E Loth	212	B4
Huntington	Herefs	79	J4
Huntington	Herefs	80	B6
Huntington	Staffs	98	B1
Huntingtowerfield	P & K	221	K2
Huntley	Gloucs	63	L3
Huntly	Abers	255	L1
Hunton	Hants	35	G3
Hunton	Kent	39	H3
Hunton	N York	160	B4
Hunton Bridge	Herts	68	D7
Hunt's Corner	Norfk	105	L5
Huntscott	Somset	29	G2
Hunt's Cross	Lpool	129	K3
Hunts Green	Bucks	67	L6
Hunts Green	Warwks	98	H4
Huntsham	Devon	29	H6
Huntshaw	Devon	27	J6
Huntshaw Cross	Devon	27	J6
Huntspill	Somset	30	D2
Huntstile	Somset	30	C4
Huntworth	Somset	30	D4
Hunwick	Dur	168	F4
Hunworth	Norfk	122	B4
Hurcott	Somset	30	F7
Hurdcott	Wilts	33	L4
Hurdsfield	Ches E	131	H5
Hurley	W & M	49	K2
Hurley	Warwks	99	H4
Hurley Bottom	W & M	49	K2
Hurley Common	Warwks	99	H4
Hurlford	E Ayrs	196	F4
Hurlston Green	Lancs	138	E5
Hurn	BCP	18	A4
Hurn's End	Lincs	119	M2
Hursley	Hants	34	F6
Hurst	Dorset	16	F4
Hurst	N York	159	J4
Hurst	Somset	31	G7
Hurst	Wokham	49	J4
Hurstbourne Priors	Hants	34	F2
Hurstbourne Tarrant	Hants	48	A8
Hurst Green	E Susx	24	D7
Hurst Green	Essex	73	G4
Hurst Green	Lancs	148	B8
Hurst Green	Surrey	38	B3
Hurst Hill	Dudley	97	L4
Hurstley	Herefs	79	L5
Hurstpierpoint	W Susx	22	D4
Hurst Wickham	W Susx	22	D4
Hurstwood	Lancs	140	C2
Hurtiso	Ork	275	d5
Hurtmore	Surrey	36	F2
Hurworth Burn	Dur	169	L4
Hurworth-on-Tees	Darltn	169	J8
Hurworth Place	Darltn	160	D1
Hury	Dur	168	B6
Husbands Bosworth	Leics	100	E6
Husborne Crawley	C Beds	85	J8
Husthwaite	N York	161	H7
Hutcherleigh	Devon	8	A5
Hut Green	N York	142	F3
Huthwaite	Notts	133	J7
Huttoft	Lincs	137	K4
Hutton	Border	202	E4
Hutton	Cumb	166	B5
Hutton	E R Yk	152	F5
Hutton	Essex	70	F8
Hutton	Lancs	139	G2
Hutton	N Som	44	D7
Hutton Bonville	N York	160	E3
Hutton Buscel	N York	163	H6
Hutton Conyers	N York	160	D7
Hutton Cranswick	E R Yk	153	G5
Hutton End	Cumb	166	B3
Hutton Hang	N York	159	L5
Hutton Henry	Dur	169	L3
Hutton-le-Hole	N York	162	B4
Hutton Lowcross	R & Cl	170	E7
Hutton Magna	Dur	168	E8
Hutton Mulgrave	N York	162	E1
Hutton Roof	Cumb	157	J7
Hutton Roof	Cumb	165	L4
Hutton Rudby	N York	161	G2
Hutton Sessay	N York	161	G7
Hutton Wandesley	N York	151	H5
Huxham	Devon	13	M3
Huxham Green	Somset	31	K4
Huxley	Ches W	129	L7
Huyton	Knows	129	K2
Hycemoor	Cumb	155	K5
Hyde	Gloucs	64	C6
Hyde	Hants	33	L8
Hyde	Tamesd	131	J1
Hyde Heath	Bucks	68	B7
Hyde Lea	Staffs	114	E7
Hydestile	Surrey	36	E3
Hykeham Moor	Lincs	135	J6
Hyndford Bridge	S Lans	198	F5
Hynish	Ag & B	224	C7
Hyssington	Powys	95	H4
Hystfield	Gloucs	63	K7
Hythe	Essex	72	E2
Hythe	Hants	19	G2
Hythe	Kent	41	G8
Hythe	Somset	44	F8
Hythe End	W & M	50	C4
Hyton	Cumb	155	K5

I

Place	County	Page	Grid
Ibberton	Dorset	16	F1
Ible	Derbys	132	E8
Ibsley	Hants	18	A2
Ibstock	Leics	99	L2
Ibstone	Bucks	67	J8
Ibthorpe	Hants	48	A8
Iburndale	N York	162	F1
Ibworth	Hants	48	E7
Icelton	N Som	44	D6
Ichrachan	Ag & B	217	G1
Ickburgh	Norfk	105	G4
Ickenham	Gt Lon	50	D2
Ickford	Bucks	66	F5
Ickham	Kent	41	H4
Ickleford	Herts	68	F2
Icklesham	E Susx	24	F4
Ickleton	Cambs	87	K6
Icklingham	Suffk	88	C1
Ickornshaw	N York	149	G7
Ickwell Green	C Beds	86	C6
Icomb	Gloucs	65	J3
Idbury	Oxon	65	K3
Iddesleigh	Devon	12	D1
Ide	Devon	13	L4
Ideford	Devon	13	K7
Ide Hill	Kent	38	D3
Iden	E Susx	25	G3
Iden Green	Kent	39	J6
Iden Green	Kent	39	M7
Idle	C Brad	149	M8
Idless	Cnwll	4	D5
Idlicote	Warwks	83	G6
Idmiston	Wilts	33	L3
Idole	Carmth	58	D5
Idridgehay	Derbys	115	M2
Idrigill	Highld	258	D5
Idstone	Oxon	47	K2
Iffley	Oxon	66	D6
Ifield	W Susx	37	K3
Ifold	W Susx	36	F4
Iford	BCP	18	A5
Iford	E Susx	22	F5
Ifton	Mons	44	F1
Ifton Heath	Shrops	112	F1
Ightfield	Shrops	113	K4
Ightham	Kent	38	F2
Iken	Suffk	91	J4
Ilam	Staffs	115	J2
Ilchester	Somset	31	H6
Ilderton	Nthumb	190	E2
Ilford	Gt Lon	51	L2
Ilford	Somset	30	E7
Ilfracombe	Devon	27	J2
Ilkeston	Derbys	116	D3
Ilketshall St Andrew	Suffk	107	H6
Ilketshall St John	Suffk	107	H6
Ilketshall St Lawrence	Suffk	107	H6
Ilketshall St Margaret	Suffk	107	G6
Ilkley	C Brad	149	K6
Illand	Cnwll	11	K7
Illey	Dudley	98	B7
Illidge Green	Ches E	130	F7
Illingworth	Calder	141	G2
Illogan	Cnwll	3	H2
Illston on the Hill	Leics	100	F3
Ilmer	Bucks	67	J6
Ilmington	Warwks	82	F5
Ilminster	Somset	30	E7
Ilsington	Devon	13	H7
Ilsington	Dorset	16	E4
Ilston	Swans	57	G6
Ilton	N York	160	B7
Ilton	Somset	30	E7
Imachar	N Ayrs	194	D3
Immingham	NE Lin	144	F5
Immingham Dock	NE Lin	145	G4
Impington	Cambs	87	J3
Ince	Ches W	129	K4
Ince Blundell	Sefton	138	C2
Ince-in-Makerfield	Wigan	139	J6
Inchbae Lodge	Highld	262	C
Inchbare	Angus	234	F2
Inchberry	Moray	266	F5
Incheril	Highld	261	G2
Inchinnan	Rens	208	E5
Inchlaggan	Highld	239	L2
Inchmichael	P & K	222	D2
Inchmore	Highld	251	G2
Inchnadamph	Highld	271	H
Inchture	P & K	222	D2
Inchyra	P & K	222	C3
Indian Queens	Cnwll	4	E
Ingatestone	Essex	70	F
Ingbirchworth	Barns	141	K4
Ingerthorpe	N York	150	C
Ingestre	Staffs	114	F
Ingham	Lincs	135	J
Ingham	Norfk	123	G
Ingham	Suffk	89	G
Ingham Corner	Norfk	123	H
Ingleborough	Norfk	120	B
Ingleby	Derbys	116	B
Ingleby Arncliffe	N York	161	G
Ingleby Barwick	S on T	170	B
Ingleby Cross	N York	161	G
Ingleby Greenhow	N York	161	J
Ingleigh Green	Devon	12	E
Inglesbatch	BaNES	45	L
Ingleston	D & G	176	C
Ingleton	Dur	168	F
Ingleton	N York	158	B
Inglewhite	Lancs	147	L
Ingmanthorpe	N York	150	F
Ingoe	Nthumb	180	C
Ingol	Lancs	139	G
Ingoldisthorpe	Norfk	120	F
Ingoldmells	Lincs	137	L
Ingoldsby	Lincs	118	D
Ingram	Nthumb	190	E
Ingrave	Essex	52	D
Ingrow	C Brad	149	J
Ings	Cumb	157	G
Ingst	S Glos	45	H
Ingthorpe	RutInd	101	M
Ingworth	Norfk	122	D
Inkberrow	Worcs	82	B
Inkerman	Dur	168	E
Inkersall Green	Derbys	133	K
Inkhorn	Abers	257	G
Inkpen	W Berk	48	A
Inkstack	Highld	280	C
Inmarsh	Wilts	46	E

Innellan Ag & B......................207 J5
Innerleithen Border................200 D6
Innerleven Fife.....................222 F7
Innermessan D & G................172 D2
Innerwick E Loth...................212 F4
Innesmill Moray.....................266 F3
Innsworth Gloucs....................64 B3
Insch Abers..........................256 A6
Insh Highld..........................241 H7
Inshes Highld.......................251 J3
Inskip Lancs........................147 J8
Inskip Moss Side Lancs............147 J8
Instow Devon..........................27 H5
Insworke Cnwll.........................6 E7
Intake Sheff.........................133 H3
Inver Abers..........................243 H5
Inver Highld.........................264 J3
Inver P & K..........................232 F7
Inverailort Highld..................238 B7
Inveralligin Highld.................260 D8
Inverallochy Abers..................269 J3
Inveran Highld......................272 E8
Inveraray Ag & B....................217 H5
Inverarish Highld...................247 H2
Inverarity Angus....................234 C6
Inverarnan Stirlg...................218 B1
Inverarnie Highld...................251 J5
Inverasdale Highld..................260 C3
Inverbeg Ag & B.....................218 E4
Inverbervie Abers...................235 K1
Inverboyndie Abers..................268 B3
Invercreran Lodge Ag & B...........229 G6
Inverdruie Highld...................242 B1
Inveresk E Loth.....................211 K5
Inveresragan Ag & B.................228 F8
Inverey Abers.......................242 E5
Inverfarigaig Highld................250 F7
Inverfolla Ag & B...................228 E6
Invergarry Highld...................240 A3
Invergeldie P & K...................220 C2
Invergloy Highld....................239 L6
Invergordon Highld..................263 J6
Invergowrie P & K...................222 F1
Inverguseran Highld.................238 B2
Inverhadden P & K...................231 J4
Inverie Highld......................238 B3
Inverinan Ag & B....................216 F4
Inverinate Highld...................248 E7
Inverkeilor Angus...................235 G5
Inverkeithing Fife..................210 F2
Inverkeithny Abers..................268 A6
Inverkip Inver......................207 K4
Inverkirkaig Highld.................270 E4
Inverlael Highld....................261 K3
Inverlair Highld....................240 B7
Inverliever Lodge Ag & B...........216 D6
Inverlochy Ag & B...................217 K2
Invermark Angus.....................244 A7
Invermoriston Highld................250 D8
Invernaver Highld...................278 B4
Inverneill Ag & B...................206 D3
Inverness Highld....................251 H3
Inverness Airport Highld..........252 E1
Invernettie Abers...................257 L3
Invernoaden Ag & B..................217 J7
Inveroran Hotel Ag & B.............229 M7
Inverquharity Angus.................234 B4
Inverquhomery Abers.................257 J2
Inverroy Highld.....................239 M7
Inversanda Highld...................228 E3
Invershiel Highld...................248 F7
Invershin Highld....................272 E6
Invershore Highld...................275 H1
Inversnaid Hotel Stirlg.............218 E5
Inverugie Abers.....................269 L6
Inveruglas Ag & B...................218 D5
Inveruglass Highld..................241 L3
Inverurie Abers.....................256 D7
Inwardleigh Devon....................12 D3
Inworth Essex........................72 C3
Iochdar W Isls......................283 b9
Iona Ag & B.........................226 B7
Iping W Susx.........................36 C6
Port Logistics Park Donc...........142 F8
Ipplepen Devon........................8 B2
Ipsden Oxon...........................48 F2
Ipstones Staffs.....................115 G2
Ipswich Suffk.........................90 E6
Irby Wirral.........................128 F3
Irby in the Marsh Lincs............137 J7
Irby upon Humber NE Lin............145 G6
Irchester Nhants.....................85 J2
Ireby Cumb.........................165 H3
Ireby Lancs........................157 L7
Ireland C Beds.......................86 C7
Ireleth Cumb.......................156 B2
Ireshopeburn Dur...................167 K3
Ireton Wood Derbys.................115 M2
Irlam Salfd.........................130 E1
Irnham Lincs.......................118 D6

Iron Acton S Glos....................45 K2
Iron Bridge Cambs...................103 K4
Ironbridge Wrekin....................96 F3
Ironbridge Gorge Wrekin............96 F3
Iron Cross Warwks....................82 C5
Ironmacannie D & G..................185 G7
Irons Bottom Surrey..................37 K2
Ironville Derbys....................116 D1
Irstead Norfk......................123 H7
Irthington Cumb....................178 C6
Irthlingborough Nhants..............85 J1
Irton N York.......................163 H6
Irvine N Ayrs......................196 C3
Isauld Highld......................279 G3
Isbister Shet......................281 d3
Isbister Shet......................281 f5
Isfield E Susx.......................23 G4
Isham Nhants.......................101 J8
Isington Hants.......................36 A2
Islandpool Worcs.....................97 K7
Islay Ag & B.......................204 F5
Islay Airport Ag & B..............204 E6
Isle Abbotts Somset..................30 E6
Isle Brewers Somset..................30 E6
Isleham Cambs......................104 C8
Isle of Dogs Gt Lon..................51 K3
Isle of Grain Medway.................53 J4
Isle of Lewis W Isls...............282 f3
Isle of Man IoM....................154 e5
Isle of Man Ronaldsway
  Airport IoM....................154 c8
Isle of Mull Ag & B................227 H5
Isle of Purbeck Dorset...............17 K6
Isle of Sheppey Kent.................40 C2
Isle of Skye Highld................246 F1
Isle of Thanet Kent..................41 K2
Isle of Walney Cumb................146 D3
Isle of Whithorn D & G.............174 D7
Isle of Wight IoW....................19 J6
Isleornsay Highld..................247 L6
Isles of Scilly IoS..................10 c2
Isles of Scilly St Mary's
  Airport IoS.....................10 c3
Islesteps D & G....................176 C4
Islet Village Guern...................9 k2
Isleworth Gt Lon.....................50 F4
Isley Walton Leics.................116 C6
Islibhig W Isls....................282 d3
Islington Gt Lon.....................51 J3
Islip Nhants.......................101 L7
Islip Oxon...........................66 D4
Islivig W Isls.....................282 d3
Isombridge Wrekin....................96 E1
Istead Rise Kent.....................52 D5
Itchen Abbas Hants...................35 H4
Itchen Stoke Hants...................35 H4
Itchingfield W Susx..................37 H5
Itchington S Glos....................45 K2
Itteringham Norfk...................122 C5
Itton Devon..........................12 F3
Itton Mons...........................62 F8
Itton Common Mons....................62 F7
Ivegill Cumb.......................165 M2
Ivelet N York......................159 G3
Iver Bucks...........................50 B3
Iver Heath Bucks.....................50 C2
Iveston Dur........................168 E1
Ivinghoe Bucks.......................68 B4
Ivinghoe Aston Bucks.................68 B3
Ivington Herefs......................80 B4
Ivington Green Herefs................80 B4
Ivybridge Devon.......................7 J4
Ivychurch Kent.......................25 J2
Ivy Cross Dorset.....................32 E6
Ivy Hatch Kent.......................38 F3
Ivy Todd Norfk.....................105 H2
Iwade Kent...........................40 A2
Iwerne Courtney Dorset...............32 E8
Iwerne Minster Dorset................32 E8
Ixworth Suffk........................89 J1
Ixworth Thorpe Suffk.................89 J1

J

Jack Green Lancs...................139 J3
Jack Hill N York...................150 B5
Jack-in-the-Green Devon..............14 B3
Jack's Bush Hants....................34 C3
Jacksdale Notts....................116 D1
Jackson Bridge Kirk................141 J4
Jackton S Lans.....................209 G8
Jacobstow Cnwll......................11 H3
Jacobstowe Devon.....................12 E2
Jacobs Well Surrey...................50 C8
Jameston Pembks......................55 H7
Jamestown Highld...................262 E8
Jamestown W Duns...................208 C3
Janetstown Highld..................275 G2

Jardine Hall D & G.................176 E1
Jarrow S Tyne......................181 H6
Jarvis Brook E Susx..................38 E7
Jasper's Green Essex.................71 H2
Jawcraig Falk......................209 M4
Jaywick Essex........................73 H4
Jealott's Hill Br For................49 L4
Jeater Houses N York...............160 F4
Jedburgh Border....................189 H7
Jeffreyston Pembks...................55 J5
Jemimaville Highld.................263 K7
Jerbourg Guern........................9 k4
Jersey Jersey..........................9 d2
Jersey Airport Jersey................9 b2
Jersey Marine Neath..................57 K6
Jerusalem Lincs....................135 J5
Jesmond N u Ty.....................181 H5
Jevington E Susx.....................23 J7
Jingle Street Mons...................62 F5
Jockey End Herts.....................68 D4
Jodrell Bank Ches E...............130 F5
Jodrell Bank Ches E................130 F5
Johnby Cumb........................166 B4
John Lennon Airport Lpool.........129 K3
John o' Groats Highld..............280 E2
Johns Cross E Susx...................24 D3
Johnshaven Abers...................235 K2
Johnson Street Norfk...............123 H8
Johnston Pembks......................54 F5
Johnstone D & G....................187 K6
Johnstone Rens.....................208 D6
Johnstonebridge D & G..............187 G7
Johnstown Carmth.....................58 D5
Johnstown Wrexhm...................112 D2
Joppa C Edin.......................211 K4
Joppa Cerdgn.........................77 G2
Joppa S Ayrs.......................196 E7
Jordans Bucks........................50 B1
Jordanston Pembks....................74 F5
Jordanthorpe Sheff.................133 G3
Joyden's Wood Kent...................52 B4
Jubilee Corner Kent..................39 L4
Jump Barns.........................142 B7
Jumper's Town E Susx.................38 C6
Juniper Nthumb.....................179 L7
Juniper Green C Edin...............211 G5
Jura Ag & B........................215 G7
Jurassic Coast Devon...............15 H5
Jurby IoM..........................154 e3
Jurston Devon........................13 G5

K

Kaber Cumb.........................167 J8
Kaimend S Lans.....................199 G4
Kames Ag & B.......................206 F5
Kames E Ayrs.......................197 K5
Kea Cnwll.............................4 C6
Keadby N Linc......................143 L5
Keal Cotes Lincs...................137 G7
Kearby Town End N York.............150 E6
Kearsley Bolton....................139 M6
Kearsley Nthumb....................180 B4
Kearsney Kent.......................41 J6
Kearstwick Cumb....................157 K6
Kearton N York.....................159 H3
Keasden N York.....................148 C3
Keaton Devon..........................7 J4
Keckwick Halton....................130 B3
Keddington Lincs...................136 F2
Keddington Corner Lincs............137 G2
Kedington Suffk......................88 E6
Kedleston Derbys...................116 A3
Keelby Lincs.......................144 F5
Keele Staffs.......................114 C3
Keele Services Staffs.............114 C3
Keele University Staffs............114 C3
Keeley Green Bed.....................85 H6
Keelham C Brad.....................141 G1
Keeres Green Essex...................70 F4
Keeston Pembks.......................54 E3
Keevil Wilts.........................46 D7
Kegworth Leics.....................116 E6
Kehelland Cnwll.......................3 G3
Keig Abers.........................256 A7
Keighley C Brad....................149 J7
Keilarsbrae Clacks.................220 F8
Keillour P & K.....................221 H2
Keiloch Abers......................243 G6
Keils Ag & B.......................205 H3
Keinton Mandeville Somset...........31 J5
Keir Mill D & G....................186 C7
Keirsleywell Row Nthumb............179 H8
Keisby Lincs.......................118 D6
Keisley Cumb.......................167 G6
Keiss Highld.......................280 D4
Keith Moray........................267 J6
Keithick P & K.....................233 J7

Keithock Angus.....................234 F3
Keithtown Highld...................262 F8
Kelbrook Lancs.....................148 F7
Kelby Lincs........................118 D3
Keld Cumb..........................166 D7
Keld N York........................158 F3
Keld Head N York...................162 D5
Keldholme N York...................162 C5
Kelfield N Linc....................143 L7
Kelfield N York....................151 J8
Kelham Notts.......................134 F8
Kellacott Devon......................12 A5
Kellamergh Lancs...................138 E2
Kellas Angus.......................234 C8
Kellas Moray.......................266 D5
Kellaton Devon........................8 B7
Kelleth Cumb.......................157 L2
Kelling Norfk......................122 B3
Kellingley N York..................142 E3
Kellington N York..................142 E3
Kelloe Dur.........................169 K3
Kelloholm D & G....................185 J1
Kells Cumb.........................164 C7
Kelly Devon.........................11 M6
Kelly Bray Cnwll....................11 L8
Kelmarsh Nhants....................101 G7
Kelmscott Oxon.......................65 K7
Kelsale Suffk........................91 J2
Kelsall Ches W.....................129 M6
Kelshall Herts......................87 G7
Kelsick Cumb.......................165 G1
Kelso Border.......................201 M6
Kelstedge Derbys...................133 G7
Kelstern Lincs.....................136 D2
Kelsterton Flints..................129 G5
Kelston BaNES........................45 K5
Keltneyburn P & K..................231 L5
Kelton D & G.......................176 C5
Kelty Fife.........................221 L8
Kelvedon Essex.......................72 C3
Kelvedon Hatch Essex.................70 E7
Kelvinhead N Lans..................209 K3
Kelynack Cnwll........................2 B5
Kemacott Devon.......................28 B2
Kemback Fife.......................223 G4
Kemberton Shrops.....................97 G3
Kemble Gloucs........................64 E7
Kemble Wick Gloucs...................64 E7
Kemerton Worcs.......................81 L7
Kemeys Commander Mons................62 D6
Kemnay Abers.......................256 D8
Kempe's Corner Kent..................40 D6
Kempley Gloucs.......................63 K1
Kempley Green Gloucs.................63 K1
Kempsey Worcs........................81 J5
Kempsford Gloucs.....................65 H7
Kemps Green Warwks...................82 D1
Kempshott Hants......................35 J1
Kempston Bed........................85 K5
Kempston Hardwick Bed................85 K6
Kempton Shrops.......................95 J6
Kemp Town Br & H.....................22 E6
Kemsing Kent.........................52 C7
Kemsley Kent.........................40 B2
Kemsley Street Kent..................53 H6
Kenardington Kent....................25 H1
Kenchester Herefs....................80 B6
Kencot Oxon..........................65 K6
Kendal Cumb........................157 H4
Kenderchurch Herefs..................62 E2
Kendleshire S Glos...................45 K3
Kenfig Brdgnd........................42 B5
Kenfig Hill Brdgnd...................42 C5
Kenilworth Warwks....................83 G1
Kenley Gt Lon........................51 J7
Kenley Shrops........................96 D3
Kenmore Highld.....................260 B8
Kenmore P & K......................231 L6
Kenn Devon..........................13 L5
Kenn N Som...........................44 E5
Kennacraig Ag & B..................206 C6
Kennall Vale Cnwll..................3 J3
Kennards House Cnwll.................11 K6
Kenneggy Cnwll........................2 F5
Kennerleigh Devon....................13 J1
Kennet Clacks......................210 B1
Kennethmont Abers..................255 L6
Kennett Cambs........................88 D2
Kennford Devon.......................13 L5
Kenninghall Norfk..................105 L6
Kennington Kent......................40 D6
Kennington Oxon......................66 D6
Kennington Lees Kent.................40 D6
Kennoway Fife......................222 F6
Kenny Somset.........................30 D7
Kenny Hill Suffk...................104 D7
Kennythorpe N York.................152 B3
Kenovay Ag & B.....................224 C6
Kensaleyre Highld..................259 G6

Kensington Gt Lon 51 H3
Kensworth Common C Beds 68 C3
Kentallen Highld 228 F4
Kentchurch Herefs 62 E2
Kentford Suffk 88 E2
Kent Green Ches E 131 G8
Kentisbeare Devon 14 C1
Kentisbury Devon 27 L2
Kentisbury Ford Devon 27 L2
Kentish Town Gt Lon 51 H2
Kentmere Cumb 157 G2
Kenton Devon 13 M6
Kenton Gt Lon 50 F1
Kenton N u Ty 180 F5
Kenton Suffk 90 E2
Kenton Bankfoot N u Ty 180 F5
Kentra Highld 237 J6
Kents Bank Cumb 156 F7
Kentsboro Hants 34 C3
Kent's Green Gloucs 63 L2
Kent's Oak Hants 34 D6
Kent Street E Susx 24 E4
Kent Street Kent 39 G2
Kenwick Shrops 112 F5
Kenwyn Cnwll 4 D5
Kenyon Warrtn 139 J8
Keoldale Highld 276 F3
Keppoch Highld 248 E6
Kepwick N York 161 G4
Keresley Covtry 99 J6
Kermincham Ches E 130 F6
Kernborough Devon 8 B6
Kerne Bridge Herefs 63 H3
Kerrera Ag & B. 216 C2
Kerridge Ches E 131 J4
Kerridge-end Ches E 131 J4
Kerris Cnwll 2 C5
Kerry Powys 94 E5
Kerrycroy Ag & B. 207 J6
Kersall Notts 134 E7
Kersbrook Devon 14 C6
Kerscott Devon 27 L5
Kersey Suffk 89 K6
Kersey Tye Suffk 89 K6
Kersey Upland Suffk 89 K6
Kershader W Isls 282 f4
Kershopefoot Cumb 178 B2
Kersoe Worcs 82 A7
Kerswell Devon 14 C2
Kerswell Green Worcs 81 K6
Kerthen Wood Cnwll 2 F4
Kesgrave Suffk 90 F6
Kessingland Suffk 107 L6
Kessingland Beach Suffk 107 L6
Kestle Cnwll 5 G5
Kestle Mill Cnwll 4 D3
Keston Gt Lon 51 L6
Keswick Cumb 165 J6
Keswick Norfk 106 E2
Ketsby Lincs 137 G4
Kettering Nhants 101 J7
Ketteringham Norfk 106 D3
Kettins P & K. 233 K7
Kettlebaston Suffk 89 K5
Kettlebridge Fife 222 E5
Kettlebrook Staffs 99 G3
Kettleburgh Suffk 91 G3
Kettle Green Herts 69 L3
Kettleholm D & G 176 F3
Kettleness N York 171 J7
Kettleshulme Ches E. 131 K4
Kettlesing N York 150 B4
Kettlesing Bottom N York 150 B4
Kettlestone Norfk 121 L5
Kettlethorpe Lincs 135 G4
Kettletoft Ork 275 e2
Kettlewell N York 149 H2
Ketton Rutlnd 101 L3
Kew Gt Lon 50 F4
Kew Royal Botanic Gardens Gt Lon 50 F4
Kewstoke N Som 44 C6
Kexbrough Barns 141 M6
Kexby C York 151 L5
Kexby Lincs 135 H3
Key Green Ches E 131 H7
Key Green N York 162 D2
Keyham Leics 100 E2
Keyhaven Hants 18 D5
Keyingham E R Yk 145 H3
Keymer W Susx 22 D4
Keynsham BaNES 45 K5
Keysoe Bed 86 B3
Keysoe Row Bed 86 B3
Keyston Cambs 102 A8
Key Street Kent 53 J6
Keyworth Notts 117 G5
Kibbear Somset 30 B6
Kibblesworth Gatesd 181 G7
Kibworth Beauchamp Leics 100 F4

Kibworth Harcourt Leics 100 F4
Kidbrooke Gt Lon 51 L4
Kidburngill Cumb 164 E6
Kiddemore Green Staffs 97 J2
Kidderminster Worcs 97 J8
Kiddington Oxon 66 B3
Kidd's Moor Norfk 106 C3
Kidlington Oxon 66 D4
Kidmore End Oxon 49 G3
Kidsdale D & G 174 C7
Kidsgrove Staffs 131 G8
Kidstones N York 159 G6
Kidwelly Carmth 56 D3
Kiel Crofts Ag & B. 228 D7
Kielder Nthumb 189 H7
Kielder Forest 178 E2
Kiells Ag & B. 204 F3
Kilbarchan Rens 208 C6
Kilbeg Highld 247 K7
Kilberry Ag & B. 206 A6
Kilbirnie N Ayrs 208 A8
Kilbride Ag & B. 207 G5
Kilbride Ag & B. 215 L8
Kilbuiack Moray 266 B4
Kilburn Derbys 116 C2
Kilburn Gt Lon 51 H2
Kilburn N York 161 H6
Kilby Leics 100 D4
Kilchamaig Ag & B. 206 C6
Kilchattan Ag & B. 207 H8
Kilchattan Ag & B. 214 D5
Kilcheran Ag & B. 228 C7
Kilchoan Highld 236 F7
Kilchoman Ag & B. 204 B4
Kilchrenan Ag & B. 217 G3
Kilconquhar Fife 223 H6
Kilcot Gloucs 63 K2
Kilcoy Highld 251 G2
Kilcreggan Ag & B. 207 L3
Kildale N York 161 K1
Kildalloig Ag & B. 192 F4
Kildary Highld 263 K5
Kildavaig Ag & B. 206 F6
Kildavanan Ag & B. 207 G5
Kildonan Highld 274 B4
Kildonan N Ayrs 195 G6
Kildonan Lodge Highld 274 B4
Kildonnan Highld 236 F3
Kildrochet House D & G. 172 D4
Kildrummy Abers 255 J8
Kildwick N York 149 H6
Kilfinan Ag & B. 206 E3
Kilfinnan Highld 239 M4
Kilford Denbgs 128 C6
Kilgetty Pembks 55 K5
Kilgrammie S Ayrs 183 G3
Kilgwrrwg Common Mons 62 F7
Kilham E R Yk 153 G3
Kilham Nthumb 202 D6
Kilkenneth Ag & B. 224 B6
Kilkenzie Ag & B. 192 D3
Kilkerran Ag & B. 192 E4
Kilkhampton Cnwll 26 D8
Killamarsh Derbys 133 J3
Killay Swans 57 H6
Killearn Stirlg 208 E2
Killen Highld 263 J8
Killerby Darltn 169 G6
Killerton Devon 14 A3
Killichonan P & K. 231 G4
Killiechonate Highld 239 L7
Killiechronan Ag & B 227 G4
Killiecrankie P & K. 232 D3
Killilan Highld 248 F5
Killimster Highld 280 D5
Killin Stirlg 231 G8
Killinghall N York 150 C4
Killington Cumb 157 K5
Killington Devon 28 B2
Killington Lake Services Cumb 157 J4
Killingworth N Tyne 181 G5
Killiow Cnwll 4 C6
Killochyett Border 200 F4
Kilmacolm Inver 208 B5
Kilmahog Stirlg 219 M3
Kilmahumaig Ag & B 216 B8
Kilmaluag Highld 259 G2
Kilmany Fife 222 F3
Kilmarnock E Ayrs 196 E3
Kilmartin Ag & B 216 C7
Kilmaurs E Ayrs 196 E3
Kilmelford Ag & B 216 C4
Kilmersdon Somset 45 K8
Kilmeston Hants 35 J5
Kilmichael Ag & B. 192 E4
Kilmichael Glassary Ag & B. 216 D8
Kilmichael of Inverlussa Ag & B 206 B2
Kilmington Devon 15 G3
Kilmington Wilts 32 C4

Kilmington Common Wilts 32 C4
Kilmington Street Wilts 32 C4
Kilmorack Highld 250 E3
Kilmore Ag & B. 216 D2
Kilmore Highld 247 K7
Kilmory Ag & B. 205 M2
Kilmory Highld 237 G6
Kilmory N Ayrs 193 K4
Kilmuir Highld 251 J2
Kilmuir Highld 258 D7
Kilmuir Highld 258 F3
Kilmuir Highld 263 K5
Kilmun Ag & B. 207 K3
Kilnave Ag & B. 204 D2
Kilncadzow S Lans 198 E3
Kilndown Kent 39 H6
Kiln Green Wokham 49 K3
Kilnhill Cumb 165 H4
Kilnhurst Rothm 142 C8
Kilninver Ag & B. 216 C3
Kiln Pit Hill Nthumb 180 C7
Kilnsea E R Yk 145 L4
Kilnsey N York 149 H2
Kilnwick E R Yk 152 F6
Kilnwick Percy E R Yk 152 C6
Kilnwood Vale W Susx 37 K4
Kiloran Ag & B. 214 D5
Kilpatrick N Ayrs 194 D5
Kilpeck Herefs 62 F1
Kilpin E R Yk 143 K2
Kilpin Pike E R Yk 143 J2
Kilrenny Fife 223 K6
Kilsby Nhants 84 A1
Kilspindie P & K. 222 C2
Kilstay D & G 172 E7
Kilsyth N Lans 209 J3
Kiltarlity Highld 250 E3
Kilton R & Cl. 171 G7
Kilton Somset 29 L2
Kilton Thorpe R & Cl. 171 G7
Kilvaxter Highld 258 F3
Kilve Somset 29 L2
Kilvington Notts 117 L3
Kilwinning N Ayrs 196 B2
Kimberley Norfk 106 B3
Kimberley Notts 116 E3
Kimberworth Rothm 133 H1
Kimblesworth Dur 169 H1
Kimble Wick Bucks 67 J5
Kimbolton Cambs 86 B2
Kimbolton Herefs 80 C3
Kimcote Leics 100 D6
Kimmeridge Dorset 17 H6
Kimmerston Nthumb 202 E6
Kimpton Hants 34 C2
Kimpton Herts 68 F3
Kimworthy Devon 26 E8
Kinbrace Highld 273 L2
Kinbuck Stirlg 220 D6
Kincaple Fife 223 H3
Kincardine Fife 210 B2
Kincardine Highld 263 G2
Kincardine Bridge Fife 210 B2
Kincardine O'Neil Abers 244 D4
Kinclaven P & K 233 H7
Kincorth C Aber 245 L3
Kincorth House Moray 265 G7
Kincraig Highld 241 M2
Kincraigie P & K 232 E5
Kindallachan P & K 232 E5
Kinerarach Ag & B. 205 L5
Kineton Gloucs 65 G2
Kineton Warwks 83 H5
Kinfauns P & K 222 B3
Kingarth Ag & B 207 H7
Kingcausie Abers 245 J3
Kingcoed Mons 62 E6
Kingerby Lincs 135 L1
Kingford Devon 11 K2
Kingham Oxon 65 K2
Kingholm Quay D & G 176 C4
Kinghorn Fife 211 J2
Kinglassie Fife 222 C7
Kingoodie P & K 222 F1
King's Acre Herefs 80 B7
Kingsand Cnwll 6 E5
Kingsash Bucks 67 L6
Kingsbarns Fife 223 K5
Kingsborough Kent 53 L4
Kingsbridge Devon 7 L6
Kingsbridge Somset 29 H3
Kings Bromley Staffs 115 J8
Kingsbrook Bucks 67 K4
Kingsburgh Highld 258 F5
Kingsbury Gt Lon 51 G1
Kingsbury Warwks 99 G5
Kingsbury Episcopi Somset 31 G6
King's Caple Herefs 63 H2
Kingsclere Hants 48 D7

Kings Cliffe Nhants 101 M4
Kings Clipstone Notts 134 C6
Kingscote Gloucs 64
Kingscott Devon 27
King's Coughton Warwks 82
Kingscross N Ayrs 195 G5
Kingsdon Somset 31
Kingsdown Kent 41
Kingsdown Swindn 47
Kingsdown Wilts 46 A5
Kingseat Abers 257
Kingseat Fife 210
Kingsey Bucks 67
Kingsfold W Susx 37
Kingsford C Aber 245
Kingsford E Ayrs 196
Kingsford Worcs 97
Kingsgate Kent 41
Kings Green Gloucs 81 H8
Kingshall Street Suffk 89 J3
Kingsheanton Devon 27 K3
King's Heath Birm 98
Kings Hill Kent 39
King's Hill Wsall 98
Kings House Hotel Highld 229
Kingshurst Solhll 98
Kingside Hill Cumb 177
Kingskerswell Devon 8
Kingskettle Fife 222
Kingsland Dorset 15
Kingsland Herefs 80
Kingsland IoA 124
Kings Langley Herts 68
Kingsley Ches W 130
Kingsley Hants 36
Kingsley Staffs 115
Kingsley Green W Susx 36
Kingsley Holt Staffs 115
Kingsley Park Nhants 84
Kingslow Shrops 97
King's Lynn Norfk 120
Kings Meaburn Cumb 166
Kingsmead Hants 35
King's Mills Guern 9
King's Moss St Hel 139
Kingsmuir Angus 234
Kings Muir Border 200
Kingsmuir Fife 223
Kings Newnham Warwks 99
King's Newton Derbys 116
Kingsnorth Kent 40
King's Norton Birm 98
King's Norton Leics 100
Kings Nympton Devon 28
King's Pyon Herefs 80
Kings Ripton Cambs 102
King's Somborne Hants 34
King's Stag Dorset 32
King's Stanley Gloucs 64
King's Sutton Nhants 83
Kingstanding Birm 98
Kingsteignton Devon 13
Kingsteps Highld 264
King Sterndale Derbys 132
Kingsthorne Herefs 63
Kingsthorpe Nhants 84
Kingston Cambs 87
Kingston Cnwll 11
Kingston Devon 7
Kingston Devon 14
Kingston Dorset 16
Kingston Dorset 17
Kingston E Loth 212
Kingston Hants 18
Kingston IoW 19
Kingston Kent 41
Kingston W Susx 21
Kingston Bagpuize Oxon 66
Kingston Blount Oxon 67
Kingston by Sea W Susx 22
Kingston Deverill Wilts 32
Kingstone Herefs 80
Kingstone Somset 30
Kingstone Staffs 115
Kingstone Winslow Oxon 47
Kingston Lisle Oxon 47
Kingston near Lewes E Susx 22
Kingston on Soar Notts 116
Kingston on Spey Moray 267
Kingston Russell Dorset 16
Kingston St Mary Somset 30
Kingston Seymour N Som 44
Kingston Stert Oxon 67
Kingston upon Hull C KuH 144
Kingston upon Thames Gt Lon 50
Kingstown Cumb 177
King's Walden Herts 68
Kingswear Devon 8
Kingswells C Aber 245
Kings Weston Bristl 45 G

Kingswinford Dudley 97 K5
Kingswood Bucks 67 G3
Kingswood C KuH 144 D1
Kingswood Gloucs 63 L8
Kingswood Kent 39 L3
Kingswood Powys 94 F3
Kingswood S Glos 45 J4
Kingswood Somset 29 K3
Kingswood Surrey 51 H7
Kingswood Warwks 82 E1
Kingswood Brook Warwks 82 E1
Kingswood Common Herefs 79 K4
Kingswood Common Staffs 97 J3
Kings Worthy Hants 35 G4
Kingthorpe Lincs 136 B4
Kington Herefs 79 K4
Kington S Glos 45 J1
Kington Worcs 82 A4
Kington Langley Wilts 46 D3
Kington Magna Dorset 32 C6
Kington St Michael Wilts 46 C3
Kingussie Highld 241 K3
Kingweston Somset 31 H5
Kinharrachie Abers 257 G5
Kinharvie D & G 176 B5
Kinkell Bridge P & K 221 G4
Kinknockie Abers 257 J3
Kinleith C Edin 211 G5
Kinlet Shrops 97 G7
Kinloch Highld 246 E8
Kinloch Highld 271 K1
Kinloch Highld 277 J5
Kinloch P & K 233 H6
Kinlochard Stirlg 219 G6
Kinlochbervie Highld 276 C5
Kinlocheil Highld 238 F7
Kinlochewe Highld 261 G7
Kinloch Hourn Highld 238 F2
Kinlochlaggan Highld 240 F5
Kinlochleven Highld 229 K3
Kinlochmoidart Highld 237 K6
Kinlochnanuagh Highld 237 L4
Kinloch Rannoch P & K 231 J4
Kinloss Moray 265 H7
Kinmel Bay Conwy 127 K4
Kinmuck Abers 256 E7
Kinmundy Abers 256 F8
Kinnabus Ag & B 204 D7
Kinnadie Abers 257 H3
Kinnaird P & K 232 E4
Kinneff Abers 245 J8
Kinnelhead D & G 186 F6
Kinnell Angus 234 F5
Kinnerley Shrops 112 E7
Kinnersley Herefs 79 L5
Kinnersley Worcs 81 K6
Kinnerton Powys 79 J3
Kinnerton Shrops 95 J4
Kinnerton Green Flints 129 H7
Kinnesswood P & K 222 B6
Kinninvie Dur 168 D6
Kinnordy Angus 234 B4
Kinoulton Notts 117 H5
Kinross P & K 221 K6
Kinrossie P & K 222 C1
Kinross Services P & K 221 K6
Kinsbourne Green Herts 68 E4
Kinsey Heath Ches E 113 L3
Kinsham Herefs 79 L2
Kinsham Worcs 81 L8
Kinsley Wakefd 142 C5
Kinson BCP 17 L3
Kintail Highld 249 G8
Kintbury W Berk 48 A5
Kintessack Moray 264 F7
Kintillo P & K 221 L4
Kinton Herefs 95 K8
Kinton Shrops 112 E7
Kintore Abers 256 E8
Kintour Ag & B 205 G6
Kintra Ag & B 204 D6
Kintra Ag & B 226 C7
Kintraw Ag & B 216 C6
Kintyre Ag & B 194 A3
Kinveachy Highld 253 G7
Kinver Staffs 97 J6
Kiplin N York 160 C3
Kippax Leeds 142 C2
Kippen Stirlg 219 L8
Kippford D & G 175 L4
Kipping's Cross Kent 39 G5
Kirbister Ork 275 c5
Kirby Bedon Norfk 106 F2
Kirby Bellars Leics 117 J7
Kirby Cane Norfk 107 H5
Kirby Corner Covtry 99 J8
Kirby Cross Essex 73 J3
Kirby Fields Leics 100 B3
Kirby Green Norfk 107 H4
Kirby Grindalythe N York 152 D2

Kirby Hill N York 150 E2
Kirby Hill N York 159 L2
Kirby Knowle N York 161 G5
Kirby-le-Soken Essex 73 J3
Kirby Misperton N York 162 D6
Kirby Muxloe Leics 100 B3
Kirby Sigston N York 160 F4
Kirby Underdale E R Yk 152 B4
Kirby Wiske N York 160 E5
Kirdford W Susx 36 F5
Kirk Highld 280 C4
Kirkabister Shet 281 e7
Kirkandrews D & G 174 F5
Kirkandrews upon Eden Cumb ..177 K7
Kirkbampton Cumb 177 J7
Kirkbean D & G 176 C7
Kirk Bramwith Donc 143 H5
Kirkbride Cumb 177 H7
Kirkbridge N York 160 C4
Kirkbuddo Angus 234 D6
Kirkburn Border 200 C5
Kirkburn E R Yk 152 F5
Kirkburton Kirk 141 K5
Kirkby Knows 138 E7
Kirkby Lincs 135 L1
Kirkby N York 161 H2
Kirkby Fleetham N York 160 D4
Kirkby Green Lincs 136 A8
Kirkby-in-Ashfield Notts 133 K8
Kirkby-in-Furness Cumb 156 B6
Kirkby la Thorpe Lincs 118 E2
Kirkby Lonsdale Cumb 157 K7
Kirkby Malham N York 148 F4
Kirkby Mallory Leics 99 M3
Kirkby Malzeard N York 160 C7
Kirkby Mills N York 162 C5
Kirkbymoorside N York 162 B5
Kirkby on Bain Lincs 136 D7
Kirkby Overblow N York 150 D6
Kirkby Stephen Cumb 158 D1
Kirkby Thore Cumb 166 E5
Kirkby Underwood Lincs 118 E6
Kirkby Wharf N York 151 H7
Kirkby Woodhouse Notts 116 E1
Kirkcaldy Fife 211 J1
Kirkcambeck Cumb 178 C5
Kirkchrist D & G 175 G4
Kirkcolm D & G 172 C1
Kirkconnel D & G 197 L8
Kirkconnell D & G 176 C5
Kirkcowan D & G 173 J3
Kirkcudbright D & G 175 H5
Kirkdale Lpool 129 H1
Kirk Deighton N York 150 F5
Kirk Ella E R Yk 144 C2
Kirkfieldbank S Lans 198 E4
Kirkgunzeon D & G 175 L2
Kirk Hallam Derbys 116 D3
Kirkham Lancs 138 E1
Kirkham N York 151 M3
Kirkhamgate Wakefd 141 L3
Kirk Hammerton N York 151 G5
Kirkharle Nthumb 180 B2
Kirkhaugh Nthumb 167 G1
Kirkheaton Kirk 141 J4
Kirkheaton Nthumb 180 B3
Kirkhill Highld 250 F3
Kirkhope S Lans 186 E5
Kirkhouse Cumb 178 D7
Kirkhouse Green Donc 143 G5
Kirkibost Highld 247 H5
Kirkinch P & K 233 L6
Kirkinner D & G 174 C4
Kirkintilloch E Duns 209 H4
Kirk Ireton Derbys 115 M2
Kirkland Cumb 164 E7
Kirkland Cumb 166 F4
Kirkland D & G 185 K5
Kirkland D & G 186 F8
Kirkland D & G 197 L8
Kirkland Guards Cumb 165 G3
Kirk Langley Derbys 115 M4
Kirkleatham R & Cl. 170 E6
Kirklevington S on T 160 F1
Kirkley Suffk 107 L5
Kirklington N York 160 D6
Kirklington Notts 134 D8
Kirklinton Cumb 178 B5
Kirkliston C Edin 210 F4
Kirkmabreck D & G 174 D4
Kirkmaiden D & G 172 E7
Kirk Merrington Dur 169 H4
Kirk Michael IoM 154 d4
Kirkmichael P & K 233 G3
Kirkmichael S Ayrs 183 J1
Kirkmuirhill S Lans 198 C4
Kirknewton Nthumb 202 E7
Kirknewton W Loth 210 F5
Kirkney Abers 255 K5
Kirk of Shotts N Lans 209 M6

Kirkoswald Cumb 166 D3
Kirkoswald S Ayrs 183 G2
Kirkpatrick D & G 186 D8
Kirkpatrick Durham D & G 175 K1
Kirkpatrick-Fleming D & G 177 J2
Kirk Sandall Donc 142 F6
Kirksanton Cumb 155 L6
Kirk Smeaton N York 142 E4
Kirkstall Leeds 150 C8
Kirkstead Lincs 136 C7
Kirkstile Abers 255 L5
Kirkstile D & G 188 C8
Kirkstone Pass Inn Cumb 156 F1
Kirkstyle Highld 280 D2
Kirkthorpe Wakefd 142 B3
Kirkton Abers 256 B6
Kirkton D & G 176 C3
Kirkton Fife 222 F2
Kirkton Highld 248 C6
Kirkton Highld 248 E3
Kirkton P & K 221 G3
Kirkton Manor Border 200 B5
Kirkton of Airlie Angus 233 M5
Kirkton of Auchterhouse
  Angus 234 A7
Kirkton of Barevan Highld 252 F2
Kirkton of Collace P & K 222 C1
Kirkton of Durris Abers 245 G4
Kirkton of Glenbuchat Abers ...255 H8
Kirkton of Glenisla Angus 233 K3
Kirkton of Kingoldrum Angus ..233 M4
Kirkton of Lethendy P & K 233 H7
Kirkton of Logie Buchan Abers ..257 H6
Kirkton of Maryculter Abers 245 J4
Kirkton of Menmuir Angus 234 E3
Kirkton of Monikie Angus 234 D7
Kirkton of Rayne Abers 256 C5
Kirkton of Skene Abers 245 H2
Kirkton of Tealing Angus 234 B7
Kirkton of Tough Abers 244 D1
Kirktown Abers 269 J3
Kirktown Abers 269 K6
Kirktown of Alvah Abers 268 B4
Kirktown of Bourtie Abers 256 E6
Kirktown of Deskford Moray 267 G3
Kirktown of Fetteresso Abers ...245 J6
Kirktown of Mortlach Moray 255 G4
Kirktown of Slains Abers 257 J6
Kirkurd Border 199 J3
Kirkwall Ork 275 c4
Kirkwall Airport Ork 275 d5
Kirkwhelpington Nthumb 180 B2
Kirk Yetholm Border 202 C7
Kirmington N Linc 144 E5
Kirmond le Mire Lincs 136 C1
Kirn Ag & B 207 K3
Kirriemuir Angus 234 D4
Kirstead Green Norfk 106 F4
Kirtlebridge D & G 177 H4
Kirtling Cambs 88 D4
Kirtling Green Cambs 88 D4
Kirtlington Oxon 66 D3
Kirtomy Highld 278 C3
Kirton Lincs 119 J2
Kirton Notts 134 D6
Kirton Suffk 91 G7
Kirton End Lincs 119 J3
Kirtonhill W Duns 208 C4
Kirton Holme Lincs 119 J3
Kirton in Lindsey N Linc 144 A8
Kirwaugh D & G 173 K4
Kishorn Highld 248 D2
Kislingbury Nhants 84 D3
Kitebrook Warwks 65 K1
Kite Green Warwks 82 E2
Kites Hardwick Warwks 83 L2
Kitleigh Cnwll 11 J3
Kitt Green Wigan 139 H6
Kittisford Somset 29 K6
Kittle Swans 57 G7
Kitt's Green Birm 98 F6
Kittybrewster C Aber 245 K2
Kitwood Hants 35 K4
Kivernoll Herefs 62 F1
Kiveton Park Rothm 133 K3
Knaith Lincs 135 G3
Knaith Park Lincs 135 G3
Knap Corner Dorset 32 D6
Knaphill Surrey 50 B7
Knapp Somset 30 D5
Knapp Hill Hants 34 E6
Knapthorpe Notts 134 E7
Knapton C York 151 J5
Knapton N York 162 F7
Knapton Norfk 122 F5
Knapton Green Herefs 80 B5
Knapwell Cambs 87 J3
Knaresborough N York 150 E4
Knarsdale Nthumb 178 F8
Knaven Abers 257 G3

Knayton N York 160 F5
Knebworth Herts 69 H3
Knedlington E R Yk 143 J2
Kneesall Notts 134 D6
Kneeton Notts 117 J2
Knelston Swans 56 E7
Knenhall Staffs 114 E4
Knettishall Suffk 105 K7
Knightacott Devon 28 B3
Knightcote Warwks 83 J4
Knightley Staffs 114 C6
Knightley Dale Staffs 114 C6
Knighton BCP 17 L3
Knighton C Leic 100 D3
Knighton Devon 7 G5
Knighton Dorset 31 K8
Knighton Powys 79 K1
Knighton Somset 30 B2
Knighton Staffs 114 A3
Knighton Staffs 114 B6
Knighton Wilts 47 L4
Knighton on Teme Worcs 80 E1
Knightsbridge Gloucs 64 C2
Knightsmill Cnwll 10 F6
Knightwick Worcs 81 G4
Knill Herefs 79 K3
Knipoch Ag & B 216 C3
Knipton Leics 117 L5
Knitsley Dur 168 E1
Kniveton Derbys 115 K2
Knock Cumb 166 F5
Knock Highld 247 L6
Knock Moray 267 L5
Knock W Isls 282 g3
Knockally Highld 274 F2
Knockan Highld 271 H6
Knockando Moray 254 D3
Knockbain Highld 250 F3
Knockbain Highld 263 H8
Knock Castle N Ayrs 207 K6
Knockdee Highld 279 L4
Knockdow Ag & B 207 J5
Knockdown Wilts 46 B1
Knockeen S Ayrs 183 H4
Knockenkelly N Ayrs 195 G5
Knockentiber E Ayrs 196 D3
Knockhall Kent 52 C4
Knockholt Kent 51 M7
Knockholt Pound Kent 52 A7
Knockin Shrops 112 E7
Knockinlaw E Ayrs 196 E3
Knockmill Kent 52 C6
Knocknain D & G 172 B2
Knockrome Ag & B 205 J2
Knocksharry IoM 154 c5
Knocksheen D & G 184 F6
Knockvennie Smithy D & G 185 J8
Knodishall Suffk 91 K3
Knodishall Common Suffk 91 K3
Knole Somset 31 G6
Knole Park S Glos 45 H2
Knolls Green Ches E 130 F4
Knolton Wrexhm 112 F4
Knook Wilts 32 F3
Knossington Leics 101 H2
Knott End-on-Sea Lancs 147 G6
Knotting Bed 85 K3
Knotting Green Bed 85 K3
Knottingley Wakefd 142 D3
Knotty Ash Lpool 129 J1
Knotty Green Bucks 68 B8
Knowbury Shrops 96 D8
Knowe D & G 183 H8
Knowehead D & G 184 F5
Knoweside S Ayrs 195 L8
Knowes of Elrick Abers 268 A3
Knowle Bristl 45 J5
Knowle Devon 13 H2
Knowle Devon 14 B1
Knowle Devon 14 B6
Knowle Devon 27 J3
Knowle Shrops 96 D8
Knowle Solhll 98 F8
Knowle Somset 29 H2
Knowle Cross Devon 14 B3
Knowlefield Cumb 177 L7
Knowle Green Lancs 148 A8
Knowle Hill Surrey 50 C5
Knowle St Giles Somset 30 E8
Knowle Village Hants 19 J2
Knowle Wood Calder 140 D3
Knowl Green Essex 88 F7
Knowl Hill W & M 49 K3
Knowlton Dorset 17 K1
Knowlton Kent 41 J4
Knowsley Knows 138 E8
Knowstone Devon 28 E6
Knox N York 150 C4
Knox Bridge Kent 39 K5
Knoydart Highld 238 C3

Knucklas Powys ...95 G8
Knuston Nhants ...85 H2
Knutsford Ches E ...130 E4
Knutsford Services Ches E ...130 E4
Knutton Staffs ...114 C2
Krumlin Calder ...141 G4
Kuggar Cnwll ...3 J7
Kyleakin Highld ...248 B6
Kyle of Lochalsh Highld ...248 B6
Kylerhea Highld ...248 C7
Kylesku Highld ...271 H1
Kylesmorar Highld ...238 C5
Kyles Scalpay W Isls ...282 f6
Kylestrome Highld ...271 H1
Kynaston Herefs ...80 E8
Kynaston Shrops ...112 E7
Kynnersley Wrekin ...113 L8
Kyre Green Worcs ...80 E3
Kyre Park Worcs ...80 E3
Kyrewood Worcs ...80 E2
Kyrle Somset ...29 J6

L

La Bellieuse Guern ...9 j3
Lacasaigh W Isls ...282 f4
Lacasdal W Isls ...282 g3
Laceby NE Lin ...145 G6
Lacey Green Bucks ...67 K7
Lach Dennis Ches W ...130 D5
Lackenby R & Cl ...170 D6
Lackford Suffk ...88 F1
Lackford Green Suffk ...88 F1
Lacock Wilts ...46 C5
Ladbroke Warwks ...83 K3
Ladderedge Staffs ...114 F1
Laddingford Kent ...39 H4
Lade Bank Lincs ...119 L1
Ladock Cnwll ...4 E5
Lady Ork ...275 e2
Ladybank Fife ...222 E5
Ladycross Cnwll ...11 L5
Ladygill S Lans ...198 F7
Lady Hall Cumb ...156 B5
Ladykirk Border ...202 D3
Ladyridge Herefs ...63 H1
Lady's Green Suffk ...88 E3
Ladywood Birm ...98 D6
Ladywood Worcs ...81 K3
La Fontenelle Guern ...9 k1
La Fosse Guern ...9 j4
Lag D & G ...185 L5
Laga Highld ...237 J8
Lagavulin Ag & B ...204 F7
Lagg N Ayrs ...193 K4
Laggan Highld ...240 A4
Laggan Highld ...241 G5
Lagganlia Highld ...241 M3
La Greve Guern ...9 k2
La Grève de Lecq Jersey ...9 b1
La Hougue Bie Jersey ...9 e3
La Houguette Guern ...9 h3
Laid Highld ...277 G4
Laide Highld ...260 E2
Laig Highld ...236 F3
Laigh Clunch E Ayrs ...196 F2
Laigh Fenwick E Ayrs ...196 F3
Laigh Glenmuir E Ayrs ...197 J7
Laighstonehall S Lans ...209 J8
Laindon Essex ...52 E1
Lairg Highld ...272 E6
Laisterdyke C Brad ...141 J1
Laithes Cumb ...166 B4
Lake Devon ...12 C5
Lake Devon ...27 K4
Lake IoW ...19 K7
Lake Wilts ...33 K3
Lake District Cumb ...165 H8
Lake District National Park Cumb ...165 H8
Lakenham Norfk ...106 E2
Lakenheath Suffk ...104 E6
Laker's Green Surrey ...36 F4
Lakes End Norfk ...103 L4
Lakeside Cumb ...156 E5
Laleham Surrey ...50 D5
Laleston Brdgnd ...42 C5
Lamanva Cnwll ...3 J5
Lamarsh Essex ...89 H8
Lamas Norfk ...122 E7
Lambden Border ...202 A4
Lamberhurst Kent ...39 H6
Lamberhurst Down Kent ...39 G6
Lamberton Border ...213 L7
Lambeth Gt Lon ...51 J3
Lambfair Green Suffk ...88 E4
Lambley Notts ...117 H2
Lambley Nthumb ...178 F7

Lambourn W Berk ...47 L3
Lambourne End Essex ...70 C8
Lambourn Woodlands W Berk ...47 L4
Lamb Roe Lancs ...148 C8
Lambs Green W Susx ...37 K3
Lambston Pembks ...54 E3
Lamellion Cnwll ...6 A2
Lamerton Devon ...12 B7
Lamesley Gatesd ...181 G7
Lamington S Lans ...199 G7
Lamlash N Ayrs ...195 G5
Lamonby Cumb ...165 L3
Lamorick Cnwll ...5 H2
Lamorna Cnwll ...2 C6
Lamorran Cnwll ...4 E6
Lampen Cnwll ...5 L2
Lampeter Cerdgn ...77 G5
Lampeter Velfrey Pembks ...55 K4
Lamphey Pembks ...55 G6
Lamplugh Cumb ...164 E6
Lamport Nhants ...101 G8
Lamyatt Somset ...31 L4
Lana Devon ...11 K1
Lana Devon ...11 L3
Lanark S Lans ...198 E4
Lancaster Lancs ...147 J3
Lancaster Services Lancs ...147 K5
Lancaut Gloucs ...63 G7
Lanchester Dur ...168 F1
Lancing W Susx ...21 L6
L'Ancresse Guern ...9 k1
Landbeach Cambs ...87 K2
Landcross Devon ...27 H6
Landerberry Abers ...245 G3
Landford Wilts ...34 B7
Land-hallow Highld ...275 G4
Landimore Swans ...56 E6
Landkey Devon ...27 L4
Landore Swans ...57 J5
Landrake Cnwll ...6 D3
Landscove Devon ...7 M2
Land's End Cnwll ...2 A6
Land's End Airport Cnwll ...2 B5
Landshipping Pembks ...55 G4
Landue Cnwll ...11 L6
Landulph Cnwll ...6 E3
Landwade Suffk ...88 C2
Lane Cnwll ...4 D3
Laneast Cnwll ...11 J6
Lane Bottom Lancs ...140 C1
Lane End Bucks ...49 K1
Lane End Cnwll ...5 H1
Lane End Hants ...35 H5
Lane End Kent ...52 C4
Lane End Lancs ...148 F6
Lane End Warrtn ...130 D2
Lane End Wilts ...32 D2
Lane Ends Derbys ...115 L4
Lane Ends Lancs ...140 B2
Lane Ends N York ...149 H7
Lane Green Staffs ...97 K3
Laneham Notts ...134 F4
Lanehead Dur ...167 J2
Lane Head Dur ...168 E8
Lanehead Nthumb ...179 H2
Lane Head Wigan ...139 J8
Lane Head Wsall ...98 B3
Lane Heads Lancs ...147 H1
Lanercost Cumb ...178 D6
Laneshaw Bridge Lancs ...149 G7
Lane Side Lancs ...140 B3
Langaford Devon ...12 A3
Langal Highld ...237 K6
Langaller Somset ...30 C5
Langar Notts ...117 J4
Langbank Rens ...208 C4
Langbar N York ...149 K5
Langbaurgh N York ...170 D8
Langcliffe N York ...148 E3
Langdale End N York ...163 G4
Langdon Cnwll ...11 K5
Langdon Beck Dur ...167 K4
Langdon Hills Essex ...52 E2
Langdown Hants ...19 G2
Langdyke Fife ...222 E6
Langenhoe Essex ...72 E3
Langford C Beds ...86 D7
Langford Devon ...14 B2
Langford Essex ...71 K5
Langford N Som ...44 F6
Langford Notts ...135 G7
Langford Oxon ...65 K6
Langford Somset ...30 B5
Langford Budville Somset ...29 K6
Langham Dorset ...32 C5
Langham Essex ...72 F1
Langham Norfk ...121 M3
Langham Rutlnd ...101 J1
Langham Suffk ...89 K1
Langho Lancs ...139 L1

Langholm D & G ...177 L2
Langland Swans ...57 H7
Langlee Border ...201 G6
Langley Ches E ...131 J5
Langley Derbys ...116 D2
Langley Gloucs ...64 E2
Langley Hants ...19 G3
Langley Herts ...69 G3
Langley Kent ...39 K3
Langley Nthumb ...179 J6
Langley Oxon ...65 L4
Langley Rochdl ...140 C6
Langley Slough ...50 C5
Langley Somset ...29 K5
Langley W Susx ...36 B5
Langley Warwks ...82 E3
Langley Burrell Wilts ...46 D4
Langley Castle Nthumb ...179 J6
Langley Common Derbys ...115 M4
Langley Green Derbys ...115 M4
Langley Green Essex ...72 C3
Langley Green Warwks ...82 E3
Langley Heath Kent ...39 K3
Langley Lower Green Essex ...87 J8
Langley Marsh Somset ...29 K5
Langley Mill Derbys ...116 D2
Langley Moor Dur ...169 H3
Langley Park Dur ...169 G2
Langley Street Norfk ...107 H3
Langley Upper Green Essex ...87 J8
Langley Vale Surrey ...51 G7
Langney E Susx ...23 L6
Langold Notts ...134 B2
Langore Cnwll ...11 K5
Langport Somset ...30 F5
Langrick Lincs ...119 J2
Langridge BaNES ...45 L5
Langridgeford Devon ...27 K6
Langrigg Cumb ...165 G2
Langrish Hants ...35 L6
Langsett Barns ...141 K7
Langside P & K ...220 D4
Langstone Hants ...20 B6
Langstone Newpt ...44 D1
Langthorne N York ...160 C4
Langthorpe N York ...150 E2
Langthwaite N York ...159 H2
Langtoft E R Yk ...152 F3
Langtoft Lincs ...102 C1
Langton Dur ...168 F6
Langton Lincs ...136 D6
Langton Lincs ...137 G5
Langton N York ...152 B2
Langton by Wragby Lincs ...136 C4
Langton Green Kent ...38 E5
Langton Green Suffk ...106 C8
Langton Herring Dorset ...16 B6
Langton Long Blandford Dorset ...17 H2
Langton Matravers Dorset ...17 K6
Langtree Devon ...27 H7
Langtree Week Devon ...27 H7
Langwathby Cumb ...166 D4
Langwell Highld ...271 K6
Langwell House Highld ...274 F3
Langwith Derbys ...133 K5
Langwith Junction Derbys ...133 K6
Langworth Lincs ...135 L4
Lanivet Cnwll ...5 H2
Lanjeth Cnwll ...5 G4
Lank Cnwll ...10 F7
Lanlivery Cnwll ...5 J3
Lanner Cnwll ...3 J3
Lanoy Cnwll ...11 K7
Lanreath Cnwll ...5 L3
Lansallos Cnwll ...5 K4
Lanteglos Cnwll ...10 F6
Lanteglos Highway Cnwll ...5 K4
Lanton Border ...189 G2
Lanton Nthumb ...202 F6
La Passee Guern ...9 j2
Lapford Devon ...13 G1
Laphroaig Ag & B ...204 F7
Lapley Staffs ...97 K1
La Pulente Jersey ...9 a3
Lapworth Warwks ...82 E1
Larachbeg Highld ...227 K3
Larbert Falk ...209 M3
Larbreck Lancs ...147 H7
Largie Abers ...256 A5
Largiemore Ag & B ...206 E2
Largoward Fife ...223 H5
Largs N Ayrs ...207 K7
Largybeg N Ayrs ...195 G6
Largymore N Ayrs ...195 G6
Larkbeare Devon ...14 C3
Larkfield Inver ...207 L4
Larkfield Kent ...52 F7
Larkhall S Lans ...198 C3
Larkhill Wilts ...33 K2

Larling Norfk ...105 K5
La Rocque Jersey ...9 f4
La Rousaillerie Guern ...9 j2
Lartington Dur ...168 C7
Lasborough Gloucs ...64 B2
Lasham Hants ...35 K2
Lashbrook Devon ...12 A1
Lashbrook Devon ...12 B2
Lashenden Kent ...39 L5
Lask Edge Staffs ...131 H8
Lasswade Mdloth ...211 J6
Lastingham N York ...162 C4
Latcham Somset ...31 G2
Latchford Herts ...69 K3
Latchford Oxon ...67 G6
Latchford Warrtn ...130 C2
Latchingdon Essex ...72 E5
Latchley Cnwll ...12 A7
Lately Common Warrtn ...139 K8
Lathbury M Keyn ...85 G6
Latheron Highld ...275 G2
Latheronwheel Highld ...275 G2
Lathom Lancs ...138 F5
Lathones Fife ...223 H5
Latimer Bucks ...68 C8
Latteridge S Glos ...45 K2
Lattiford Somset ...32 B5
Latton Wilts ...65 G2
Lauder Border ...201 L5
Laugharne Carmth ...56 B3
Laughterton Lincs ...135 G4
Laughton E Susx ...23 H4
Laughton Leics ...100 E5
Laughton Lincs ...118 E5
Laughton Lincs ...143 L5
Laughton Common Rothm ...133 K2
Laughton-en-le-Morthen Rothm ...133 K2
Launcells Cnwll ...11 J2
Launcells Cross Cnwll ...11 K2
Launceston Cnwll ...11 L4
Launton Oxon ...66 F2
Laurencekirk Abers ...235 H6
Laurieston D & G ...175 H2
Laurieston Falk ...210 B3
Lavendon M Keyn ...85 H5
Lavenham Suffk ...89 H5
Lavernock V Glam ...43 H6
Laversdale Cumb ...178 C6
Laverstock Wilts ...33 L3
Laverstoke Hants ...35 G2
Laverton Gloucs ...82 C8
Laverton N York ...160 C6
Laverton Somset ...45 M8
La Villette Guern ...9 j3
Lavister Wrexhm ...129 J1
Law S Lans ...209 L8
Lawers P & K ...231 J7
Lawford Essex ...73 G8
Lawford Somset ...29 K6
Law Hill S Lans ...209 L8
Lawhitton Cnwll ...11 L6
Lawkland N York ...148 D3
Lawkland Green N York ...148 D3
Lawley Wrekin ...96 F2
Lawnhead Staffs ...114 C6
Lawrence Weston Bristl ...45 H3
Lawrenny Pembks ...55 G5
Lawrenny Quay Pembks ...55 G5
Lawshall Suffk ...89 H4
Lawshall Green Suffk ...89 H4
Lawton Herefs ...80 B3
Laxay W Isls ...282 f5
Laxdale W Isls ...282 g3
Laxey IoM ...154 f4
Laxfield Suffk ...91 G8
Laxford Bridge Highld ...276 C6
Laxo Shet ...281 e5
Laxton E R Yk ...143 K2
Laxton Nhants ...101 L4
Laxton Notts ...134 E6
Laycock C Brad ...149 J7
Layer Breton Essex ...72 D3
Layer-de-la-Haye Essex ...72 D3
Layer Marney Essex ...72 D4
Layham Suffk ...89 L7
Laymore Dorset ...15 J2
Layter's Green Bucks ...50 C2
Laytham E R Yk ...152 A8
Laythes Cumb ...177 H8
Lazenby R & Cl ...170 D6
Lazonby Cumb ...166 D2
Lea Derbys ...132 F8
Lea Herefs ...63 K4
Lea Lincs ...135 G4
Lea Shrops ...95 J5
Lea Shrops ...95 K3
Lea Wilts ...46 D2
Leachkin Highld ...251 H3
Leadburn Border ...200 B2

eadenham Lincs ... 118 B1
eaden Roding Essex ... 70 E4
eadgate Cumb ... 167 G2
eadgate Dur ... 180 D8
eadgate Nthumb ... 180 D6
eadhills S Lans ... 186 C3
eadingcross Green Kent ... 39 M3
eadmill Derbys ... 132 E4
eafield Oxon ... 65 L4
eagrave Luton ... 68 D2
eahead Ches W ... 130 D6
ea Heath Staffs ... 115 G6
eake N York ... 160 F4
eake Common Side Lincs ... 119 L1
ealholm N York ... 162 D1
ealholm Side N York ... 162 D1
ealt Highld ... 259 H4
eam Derbys ... 132 E4
ea Marston Warwks ... 99 G5
eamington Hastings Warwks ... 83 K2
eamington Spa Warwks ... 83 H2
eamside Dur ... 169 J1
eap Cross E Susx ... 23 K5
earney Abers ... 244 E3
easgill Cumb ... 157 H6
easingham Lincs ... 118 E2
easingthorne Dur ... 169 H4
eatherhead Surrey ... 50 F7
eathley N York ... 150 B6
eaton Shrops ... 113 G7
eaton Wrekin ... 96 E1
ea Town Lancs ... 138 F2
eaveland Kent ... 40 C4
eavenheath Suffk ... 89 J7
eavening N York ... 152 B3
eaves Green Gt Lon ... 51 L6
ea Yeat Cumb ... 158 D5
ebberston N York ... 163 K6
e Bigard Guern ... 9 i4
e Bourg Guern ... 9 j4
e Bourg Guern ... 9 f4
echlade on Thames Gloucs ... 65 J7
echt Gruinart Ag & B ... 204 D3
eck Lancs ... 157 K7
eckbuie P & K ... 231 K2
eckford Hants ... 34 E3
eckhampstead Bucks ... 84 D7
eckhampstead W Berk ... 48 B4
eckhampstead Thicket W Berk ... 48 B4
eckhampton Gloucs ... 64 D3
eckmelm Highld ... 261 K2
eckwith V Glam ... 43 J6
econfield E R Yk ... 152 F7
edaig Ag & B ... 228 E7
edburn Bucks ... 67 L3
edbury Herefs ... 81 K7
eddington Gloucs ... 80 F8
edgemoor Herefs ... 79 M5
edicot Herefs ... 80 A3
edmore Highld ... 271 H6
edsham Ches W ... 129 H5
edsham Leeds ... 142 C2
edston Leeds ... 142 C2
edstone Devon ... 7 L5
edston Luck Leeds ... 142 C2
edwell Oxon ... 66 B2
ee Devon ... 27 H2
ee Gt Lon ... 51 K4
ee Hants ... 34 D7
ee Shrops ... 112 F5
eebotwood Shrops ... 96 B4
ee Brockhurst Shrops ... 113 L4
eece Cumb ... 146 E2
ee Chapel Essex ... 52 E2
ee Clump Bucks ... 67 M6
ee Common Bucks ... 67 M6
eeds Kent ... 39 K3
eeds Leeds ... 141 L1
eeds Bradford Airport Leeds ... 150 B7
eeds Skelton Lake Services Leeds ... 142 A2
eedstown Cnwll ... 2 F4
ee Green Ches E ... 130 C7
eek Staffs ... 131 K8
eek Wootton Warwks ... 83 G2
ee Mill Devon ... 7 H4
eeming C Brad ... 141 G1
eeming N York ... 160 D4
eeming Bar N York ... 160 D4
eeming Bar Rest Area N York ... 160 D5
ee Moor Devon ... 7 H3
ee-on-the-Solent Hants ... 19 J4
ees C Brad ... 149 J8
ees Derbys ... 115 L4
ees Oldham ... 140 E6
ees Green Derbys ... 115 L4
eesthorpe Leics ... 101 H1
eeswood Flints ... 129 G7
eetown P & K ... 222 C3
eftwich Ches W ... 130 C5

Legar Powys ... 61 K4
Legbourne Lincs ... 137 G3
Legburthwaite Cumb ... 165 K6
Legerwood Border ... 201 J4
Le Gron Guern ... 9 i3
Legsby Lincs ... 136 B3
Le Haguais Jersey ... 9 e4
Le Hocq Jersey ... 9 e4
Leicester C Leic ... 100 D3
Leicester Forest East Leics ... 100 B3
Leicester Forest East Services Leics ... 100 C3
Leigh Devon ... 28 C8
Leigh Dorset ... 16 B1
Leigh Gloucs ... 64 C2
Leigh Kent ... 38 E4
Leigh Shrops ... 95 H3
Leigh Surrey ... 37 K2
Leigh Wigan ... 139 K7
Leigh Wilts ... 64 F8
Leigh Worcs ... 81 H4
Leigh Beck Essex ... 53 H2
Leigh Delamere Wilts ... 46 C3
Leigh Delamere Services Wilts ... 46 C3
Leigh Green Kent ... 40 A8
Leigh Knoweglass S Lans ... 197 J1
Leighland Chapel Somset ... 29 J4
Leigh-on-Sea Sthend ... 53 H2
Leigh Park Dorset ... 17 K4
Leigh Park Hants ... 20 B5
Leigh Sinton Worcs ... 81 H5
Leighswood Wsall ... 98 D3
Leighterton Gloucs ... 46 B1
Leighton N York ... 159 L6
Leighton Powys ... 94 F2
Leighton Shrops ... 96 K3
Leighton Somset ... 32 B2
Leighton Bromswold Cambs ... 102 C8
Leighton Buzzard C Beds ... 68 A2
Leigh upon Mendip Somset ... 31 M2
Leigh Woods N Som ... 45 H4
Leinthall Earls Herefs ... 80 B2
Leinthall Starkes Herefs ... 80 A1
Leintwardine Herefs ... 95 K8
Leire Leics ... 100 B5
Leiston Suffk ... 91 K3
Leith C Edin ... 211 J4
Leitholm Border ... 202 B4
Lelant Cnwll ... 2 E4
Lelley E R Yk ... 145 G1
Lem Hill Worcs ... 97 G8
Lempitlaw Border ... 202 B6
Lemreway W Isls ... 282 g5
Lemsford Herts ... 69 G4
Lenchwick Worcs ... 82 B6
Lendalfoot S Ayrs ... 182 E5
Lendrick Stirlg ... 219 J6
Lendrum Terrace Abers ... 257 L3
Lenham Kent ... 40 A5
Lenham Heath Kent ... 40 B5
Lenie Highld ... 250 F6
Lennel Border ... 202 C5
Lennox Plunton D & G ... 174 F4
Lennoxtown E Duns ... 209 G3
Lent Bucks ... 50 A3
Lenton C Nott ... 116 F4
Lenton Lincs ... 118 D5
Lenwade Norfk ... 122 B7
Lenzie E Duns ... 209 H4
Leochel-Cushnie Abers ... 244 C2
Leomansley Staffs ... 98 E2
Leominster Herefs ... 80 C3
Leonard Stanley Gloucs ... 64 A6
Leoville Jersey ... 9 b1
Lepe Hants ... 19 G4
Lephin Highld ... 258 B6
Leppington N York ... 152 A4
Lepton Kirk ... 141 K5
Lerags Ag & B ... 216 C2
L'Erée Guern ... 9 h3
Lerryn Cnwll ... 5 K3
Lerwick Shet ... 281 e6
Les Arquêts Guern ... 9 h3
Lesbury Nthumb ... 191 J4
Les Hubits Guern ... 9 k3
Leslie Abers ... 255 M6
Leslie Fife ... 222 D6
Les Lohiers Guern ... 9 i3
Lesmahagow S Lans ... 198 D5
Les Murchez Guern ... 9 i4
Lesnewth Cnwll ... 11 G4
Les Nicolles Guern ... 9 j4
Les Quartiers Guern ... 9 j2
Les Quennevais Jersey ... 9 b3
Les Sages Guern ... 9 i4
Lessingham Norfk ... 123 H6
Lessonhall Cumb ... 165 H1
Lestowder Cnwll ... 3 K6
Les Villets Guern ... 9 i4
Leswalt D & G ... 172 C2

L'Etacq Jersey ... 9 a2
Letchmore Heath Herts ... 68 F7
Letchworth Garden City Herts ... 86 E8
Letcombe Bassett Oxon ... 48 A2
Letcombe Regis Oxon ... 48 A2
Letham Angus ... 234 E5
Letham Border ... 189 J4
Letham Falk ... 210 B2
Letham Fife ... 222 E4
Letham Grange Angus ... 235 G6
Lethenty Abers ... 255 M7
Lethenty Abers ... 256 E4
Letheringham Suffk ... 91 G4
Letheringsett Norfk ... 122 B4
Lettaford Devon ... 13 G6
Letterewe Highld ... 260 F5
Letterfearn Highld ... 248 D7
Letterfinlay Lodge Hotel Highld ... 239 L5
Letters Highld ... 261 K2
Lettershaw S Lans ... 186 D2
Letterston Pembks ... 74 F6
Lettoch Highld ... 253 K7
Lettoch Highld ... 254 B5
Letton Herefs ... 79 L1
Letton Herefs ... 79 L6
Lett's Green Kent ... 51 M7
Letty Green Herts ... 69 H5
Letwell Rothm ... 133 L2
Leuchars Fife ... 223 H3
Leumrabhagh W Isls ... 282 g5
Leurbost W Isls ... 282 g4
Levalsa Meor Cnwll ... 5 G5
Levan Inver ... 207 L4
Levedale Staffs ... 114 D8
Leven E R Yk ... 153 H6
Leven Fife ... 222 F7
Levens Cumb ... 157 G5
Levens Green Herts ... 69 K3
Levenshulme Manch ... 131 G1
Levenwick Shet ... 281 d8
Leverburgh W Isls ... 282 d6
Leverington Cambs ... 103 J1
Leverstock Green Herts ... 68 D5
Leverton Lincs ... 119 L2
Le Villocq Guern ... 9 j2
Levington Suffk ... 90 F7
Levisham N York ... 162 E1
Lew Oxon ... 65 L6
Lewannick Cnwll ... 11 K6
Lewdown Devon ... 12 B5
Lewes E Susx ... 22 F5
Leweston Pembks ... 54 F2
Lewisham Gt Lon ... 51 K4
Lewiston Highld ... 250 F6
Lewistown Brdgnd ... 42 E4
Lewis Wych Herefs ... 79 L4
Lewknor Oxon ... 67 H7
Leworthy Devon ... 11 L2
Leworthy Devon ... 28 B3
Lewson Street Kent ... 40 C3
Lewth Lancs ... 147 J8
Lewtrenchard Devon ... 12 B5
Lexden Essex ... 72 D2
Lexworthy Somset ... 30 C4
Ley Cnwll ... 5 K2
Leybourne Kent ... 52 E7
Leyburn N York ... 159 K4
Leycett Staffs ... 114 B2
Leygreen Herts ... 68 F2
Ley Hill Bucks ... 68 C6
Leyland Lancs ... 139 H3
Leyland Green St Hel ... 139 H7
Leylodge Abers ... 245 G1
Leys Abers ... 269 J5
Leys P & K ... 233 K2
Leysdown-on-Sea Kent ... 53 M5
Leysmill Angus ... 234 F6
Leys of Cossans Angus ... 234 B5
Leysters Herefs ... 80 D2
Leyton Gt Lon ... 51 K2
Leytonstone Gt Lon ... 51 K2
Lezant Cnwll ... 11 L6
Lezerea Cnwll ... 3 H4
Leziate Norfk ... 120 E7
Lhanbryde Moray ... 266 F4
Libanus Powys ... 60 F2
Libberton S Lans ... 199 G4
Libbery Worcs ... 81 L4
Liberton C Edin ... 211 J5
Lichfield Staffs ... 98 E2
Lickey Worcs ... 98 C8
Lickey End Worcs ... 81 M1
Lickey Rock Worcs ... 98 B8
Lickfold W Susx ... 36 D5
Liddaton Green Devon ... 12 B6
Liddesdale Highld ... 228 B3
Liddington Swindn ... 47 J3
Lidgate Derbys ... 132 F4
Lidgate Suffk ... 88 E4

Lidget Donc ... 143 G7
Lidgett Notts ... 134 C6
Lidham Hill E Susx ... 24 F4
Lidlington C Beds ... 85 K7
Lidsey W Susx ... 20 F6
Lidsing Kent ... 53 G6
Liff Angus ... 222 E1
Lifford Birm ... 98 D7
Lifton Devon ... 11 M5
Liftondown Devon ... 11 M5
Lighthorne Warwks ... 83 H4
Lighthorne Heath Warwks ... 83 H4
Lightwater Surrey ... 50 B6
Lightwood C Stke ... 114 E3
Lightwood Green Ches E ... 113 L3
Lightwood Green Wrexhm ... 112 F3
Lilbourne Nhants ... 100 C8
Lilburn Tower Nthumb ... 190 E1
Lilford Nhants ... 102 A6
Lilleshall Wrekin ... 114 A8
Lilley Herts ... 68 E2
Lilley W Berk ... 48 C3
Lilliesleaf Border ... 201 H8
Lillingstone Dayrell Bucks ... 84 D7
Lillingstone Lovell Bucks ... 84 D7
Lillington Dorset ... 31 K8
Lilliput BCP ... 17 K5
Lilstock Somset ... 29 L2
Lilyhurst Shrops ... 97 G1
Limbrick Lancs ... 139 J4
Limbury Luton ... 68 D2
Limebrook Herefs ... 79 L2
Limefield Bury ... 140 B5
Limekilnburn S Lans ... 197 K1
Limekilns Fife ... 210 E2
Limerigg Falk ... 209 M5
Limerstone IoW ... 19 G7
Limestone Brae Nthumb ... 167 J1
Lime Street Worcs ... 64 A1
Limington Somset ... 31 J6
Limmerhaugh E Ayrs ... 197 J5
Limpenhoe Norfk ... 107 H3
Limpley Stoke Wilts ... 45 M6
Limpsfield Surrey ... 51 L8
Limpsfield Chart Surrey ... 51 L8
Linby Notts ... 116 F1
Linchmere W Susx ... 36 C5
Lincluden D & G ... 176 C3
Lincoln Lincs ... 135 K5
Lincomb Worcs ... 81 J2
Lincombe Devon ... 7 L6
Lincombe Devon ... 27 J2
Lindale Cumb ... 156 F6
Lindal in Furness Cumb ... 156 C7
Lindfield W Susx ... 22 E2
Lindford Hants ... 36 B4
Lindley Kirk ... 141 H4
Lindley N York ... 150 B6
Lindores Fife ... 222 D4
Lindow End Ches E ... 130 F4
Lindridge Worcs ... 80 F2
Lindsell Essex ... 70 F2
Lindsey Suffk ... 89 K6
Lindsey Tye Suffk ... 89 K6
Liney Somset ... 30 E4
Linford Hants ... 18 B2
Linford Thurr ... 52 E3
Lingbob C Brad ... 149 K8
Lingdale R & Cl ... 170 F7
Lingen Herefs ... 79 L2
Lingfield Surrey ... 38 B4
Lingfield Common Surrey ... 38 B4
Lingwood Norfk ... 107 G2
Liniclate W Isls ... 283 c9
Linicro Highld ... 258 F3
Linkend Worcs ... 64 B1
Linkenholt Hants ... 48 A7
Linkhill Kent ... 24 E2
Linkinhorne Cnwll ... 11 L7
Linktown Fife ... 211 J1
Linkwood Moray ... 266 E4
Linley Shrops ... 95 J5
Linley Green Herefs ... 80 F4
Linleygreen Shrops ... 96 F4
Linlithgow W Loth ... 210 C4
Linshiels Nthumb ... 190 C5
Linsidemore Highld ... 272 D8
Linslade C Beds ... 67 M2
Linstead Parva Suffk ... 107 G7
Linstock Cumb ... 178 A7
Linthurst Worcs ... 82 B1
Linthwaite Kirk ... 141 H5
Lintlaw Border ... 213 H7
Lintmill Moray ... 267 K3
Linton Border ... 202 B7
Linton Cambs ... 88 B6
Linton Derbys ... 115 M8
Linton Herefs ... 63 K2
Linton Kent ... 39 J3
Linton Leeds ... 150 E6

Linton N York 149 H3
Linton Nthumb 191 K7
Linton Heath Derbys 115 M8
Linton Hill Herefs 63 K2
Linton-on-Ouse N York 151 G4
Linwood Hants 18 B2
Linwood Lincs 136 B2
Linwood Rens 208 D6
Lionacleit W Isls 283 c9
Lional W Isls 282 h1
Lions Green E Susx 23 J4
Liphook Hants 36 C4
Lipley Shrops 114 A5
Liscard Wirral 129 G1
Liscombe Somset 28 F4
Liskeard Cnwll 6 B2
Lismore Ag & B 228 C7
Liss Hants 36 A5
Lissett E R Yk 153 J4
Liss Forest Hants 36 A5
Lissington Lincs 136 B3
Liston Essex 89 G6
Lisvane Cardif 43 J5
Liswerry Newpt 44 D2
Litcham Norfk 121 J8
Litchborough Nhants 84 C4
Litchfield Hants 48 C8
Litherland Sefton 138 D8
Litlington Cambs 87 G6
Litlington E Susx 23 J7
Little Abington Cambs 87 L5
Little Addington Nhants 101 L8
Little Airies D & G 173 K5
Little Almshoe Herts 69 G2
Little Alne Warwks 82 D3
Little Altcar Sefton 138 C6
Little Amwell Herts 69 K5
Little Asby Cumb 158 B1
Little Aston Staffs 98 E3
Little Atherfield IoW 19 G7
Little Ayton N York 170 D8
Little Baddow Essex 71 J5
Little Badminton S Glos 46 A2
Little Bampton Cumb 177 J7
Little Bardfield Essex 71 G1
Little Barford Bed 86 D4
Little Barningham Norfk 122 C5
Little Barrington Gloucs 65 J4
Little Barrow Ches W 129 L5
Little Barugh N York 162 D6
Little Bavington Nthumb 180 B3
Little Bealings Suffk 90 F5
Littlebeck N York 162 F2
Little Bedwyn Wilts 47 L5
Little Bentley Essex 73 G2
Little Berkhamsted Herts 69 H5
Little Billing Nhants 84 F3
Little Billington C Beds 68 B3
Little Birch Herefs 63 G1
Little Bispham Bpool 146 F7
Little Blakenham Suffk 90 C5
Little Blencow Cumb 166 B4
Little Bloxwich Wsall 98 C3
Little Bognor W Susx 21 G3
Little Bolehill Derbys 116 A1
Little Bollington Ches E 130 E2
Little Bookham Surrey 50 E8
Littleborough Devon 28 E8
Littleborough Notts 135 G3
Littleborough Rochdl 140 E4
Littlebourne Kent 41 G4
Little Bourton Oxon 83 K6
Little Bowden Leics 101 G6
Little Bradley Suffk 88 D5
Little Brampton Herefs 79 K3
Little Brampton Shrops 95 J7
Little Braxted Essex 71 K4
Little Brechin Angus 234 F3
Littlebredy Dorset 16 B5
Little Brickhill M Keyn 67 L1
Little Bridgeford Staffs 114 D6
Little Brington Nhants 84 C3
Little Bromley Essex 73 G2
Little Broughton Cumb 164 E4
Little Budworth Ches W 130 B6
Littleburn Highld 251 H1
Little Burstead Essex 71 G8
Littlebury Essex 87 L7
Littlebury Green Essex 87 K7
Little Bytham Lincs 118 D7
Little Canfield Essex 70 E3
Little Carlton Lincs 137 G3
Little Carlton Notts 134 F8
Little Casterton Rutlnd 101 M2
Little Catwick E R Yk 153 H6
Little Catworth Cambs 86 B1
Little Cawthorpe Lincs 137 G3
Little Chalfont Bucks 68 C7
Little Chart Kent 40 B6
Little Chesterford Essex 87 L7

Little Cheveney Kent 39 H4
Little Cheverell Wilts 46 E8
Little Chishill Cambs 87 J7
Little Clacton Essex 73 H3
Little Clanfield Oxon 65 K6
Little Clifton Cumb 164 E5
Little Coates NE Lin 145 H6
Little Comberton Worcs 81 M6
Little Common E Susx 24 C5
Little Comp Kent 39 G2
Little Compton Warwks 65 K1
Little Corby Cumb 178 B7
Little Cornard Suffk 89 H7
Littlecott Wilts 47 H8
Little Cowarne Herefs 80 E5
Little Coxwell Oxon 65 L8
Little Crakehall N York 160 C4
Little Cransley Nhants 101 H8
Little Cressingham Norfk 105 H3
Little Crosby Sefton 138 C7
Little Crosthwaite Cumb 165 H5
Little Cubley Derbys 115 J4
Little Dalby Leics 117 K8
Littledean Gloucs 63 K4
Little Dewchurch Herefs 63 G1
Little Ditton Cambs 88 D3
Little Doward Herefs 63 G4
Littledown Hants 47 M7
Little Downham Cambs 103 L6
Little Driffield E R Yk 152 F4
Little Dunham Norfk 105 H1
Little Dunkeld P & K 232 F7
Little Dunmow Essex 71 G3
Little Durnford Wilts 33 K4
Little Easton Essex 70 F2
Little Eaton Derbys 116 B3
Little Ellingham Norfk 105 K3
Little Elm Somset 32 B2
Little Everdon Nhants 84 B4
Little Eversden Cambs 87 H4
Little Faringdon Oxon 65 J6
Little Fencote N York 160 D4
Little Fenton N York 142 E1
Littleferry Highld 264 C1
Little Fransham Norfk 105 H1
Little Gaddesden Herts 68 C4
Little Garway Herefs 62 F2
Little Gidding Cambs 102 C7
Little Glemham Suffk 91 H4
Little Gorsley Herefs 63 K2
Little Gransden Cambs 86 F4
Little Green Notts 117 J3
Little Green Somset 32 B1
Little Grimsby Lincs 136 F2
Little Gringley Notts 134 E3
Little Habton N York 162 C7
Little Hadham Herts 70 B3
Little Hale Lincs 118 F3
Little Hallam Derbys 116 D3
Little Hallingbury Essex 70 D4
Littleham Devon 14 B6
Littleham Devon 27 H6
Little Hampden Bucks 67 L6
Littlehampton W Susx 21 H6
Little Hanford Dorset 32 D8
Little Harrowden Nhants 85 G1
Little Haseley Oxon 66 F7
Little Hatfield E R Yk 153 J7
Little Hautbois Norfk 122 E7
Little Haven Pembks 54 D4
Littlehaven W Susx 37 J4
Little Hay Staffs 98 E3
Little Hayfield Derbys 131 K2
Little Haywood Staffs 115 G7
Little Heath Staffs 114 D8
Little Heath W Berk 49 G6
Littlehempston Devon 8 B2
Little Hereford Herefs 80 D2
Little Horkesley Essex 72 D1
Little Hormead Herts 69 L2
Little Horsted E Susx 23 G4
Little Horton C Brad 141 J2
Little Horton Wilts 46 F6
Little Horwood Bucks 67 J1
Little Houghton Barns 142 C6
Little Houghton Nhants 84 F3
Littlehoughton Nthumb 191 J3
Little Hucklow Derbys 132 C4
Little Hulton Salfd 139 L7
Little Hungerford W Berk 48 D4
Little Hutton N York 161 G7
Little Irchester Nhants 85 H4
Little Kelk E R Yk 153 H4
Little Keyford Somset 32 C2
Little Kimble Bucks 67 K5
Little Kineton Warwks 83 H5
Little Kingshill Bucks 67 L7
Little Knox D & G 175 K3
Little Langdale Cumb 156 D2
Little Langford Wilts 33 H4

Little Laver Essex 70 E5
Little Leigh Ches W 130 B4
Little Leighs Essex 71 H4
Little Lever Bolton 139 M6
Little Linford M Keyn 85 G6
Little Load Somset 31 G6
Little London Bucks 66 F4
Little London Cambs 103 J4
Little London E Susx 23 J3
Little London Essex 70 C1
Little London Essex 88 D8
Little London Gloucs 63 L3
Little London Hants 34 E1
Little London Hants 48 F7
Little London Leeds 150 B7
Little London Lincs 119 H7
Little London Lincs 119 M6
Little London Lincs 136 F5
Little London Norfk 120 C7
Little London Powys 94 C5
Little Longstone Derbys 132 D5
Little Madeley Staffs 114 B3
Little Malvern Worcs 81 H7
Little Mancot Flints 129 H6
Little Maplestead Essex 89 G8
Little Marcle Herefs 80 F7
Little Marland Devon 27 J8
Little Marlow Bucks 49 L2
Little Massingham Norfk 121 H6
Little Melton Norfk 106 D2
Littlemill Abers 243 K4
Littlemill Highld 253 H2
Little Mill Mons 62 C6
Little Milton Oxon 66 F7
Little Missenden Bucks 68 A7
Little Mongeham Kent 41 K5
Littlemoor Derbys 133 G7
Little Moor Somset 30 D4
Littlemore Oxon 66 D6
Little Musgrave Cumb 167 H8
Little Ness Shrops 112 F7
Little Neston Ches W 129 G4
Little Newcastle Pembks 75 G6
Little Newsham Dur 168 E7
Little Norton Somset 31 G7
Little Oakley Essex 73 J1
Little Oakley Nhants 101 K6
Little Odell Bed 85 J4
Little Offley Herts 68 E2
Little Ormside Cumb 167 G7
Little Orton Cumb 177 K7
Little Ouse Cambs 104 C5
Little Ouseburn N York 150 F4
Littleover C Derb 116 B5
Little Oxendon Nhants 100 F6
Little Packington Warwks 99 G6
Little Pattenden Kent 39 J4
Little Paxton Cambs 86 D3
Little Petherick Cnwll 10 C8
Little Plumpton Lancs 138 D1
Little Plumstead Norfk 107 G1
Little Ponton Lincs 118 B5
Littleport Cambs 104 B6
Littleport Bridge Cambs 104 B6
Little Posbrook Hants 19 J3
Little Potheridge Devon 27 J8
Little Preston Leeds 142 B2
Little Preston Nhants 84 B4
Littler Ches W 130 C6
Little Raveley Cambs 102 E7
Little Reedness E R Yk 143 K3
Little Ribston N York 150 E3
Little Rissington Gloucs 65 J3
Little Rollright Oxon 65 L1
Little Rowsley Derbys 132 E6
Little Ryburgh Norfk 121 L6
Little Ryle Nthumb 190 E4
Little Ryton Shrops 96 B3
Little Salkeld Cumb 166 D3
Little Sampford Essex 88 C8
Little Sandhurst Br For 49 K6
Little Saredon Staffs 97 L2
Little Saughall Ches W 129 J6
Little Saxham Suffk 88 F2
Little Scatwell Highld 262 C8
Little Shelford Cambs 87 J5
Little Shrewley Warwks 82 F2
Little Silver Devon 13 L1
Little Singleton Lancs 147 G7
Little Skipwith N York 151 K8
Little Smeaton N York 142 E4
Little Snoring Norfk 121 L5
Little Sodbury S Glos 45 M2
Little Sodbury End S Glos 45 L2
Little Somborne Hants 34 E4
Little Somerford Wilts 46 D2
Little Soudley Shrops 114 A6
Little Stainforth N York 148 E2
Little Stainton Darltn 169 G6
Little Stanion Nhants 101 K6

Little Stanney Ches W 129 J5
Little Staughton Bed 86 B3
Little Steeping Lincs 137 H7
Little Stoke Staffs 114 E5
Littlestone-on-Sea Kent 25 K2
Little Stonham Suffk 90 D3
Little Stretton Leics 100 E5
Little Stretton Shrops 95 K5
Little Strickland Cumb 166 D6
Little Stukeley Cambs 102 E8
Little Sugnall Staffs 114 C6
Little Sutton Ches W 129 J4
Little Sutton Lincs 96 C6
Little Swinburne Nthumb 179 M3
Little Sypland D & G 175 H4
Little Tew Oxon 66 A2
Little Tey Essex 72 C2
Little Thetford Cambs 103 L8
Little Thirkleby N York 161 G7
Little Thornage Norfk 122 B4
Little Thornton Lancs 147 G7
Little Thorpe Dur 169 L2
Littlethorpe Leics 100 C4
Littlethorpe N York 150 D2
Little Thurlow Suffk 88 D5
Little Thurlow Green Suffk 88 D5
Little Thurrock Thurr 52 D3
Littleton BaNES 45 H6
Littleton Ches W 129 K6
Littleton D & G 175 G4
Littleton Dorset 17 H2
Littleton Hants 34 F4
Littleton Somset 31 H5
Littleton Surrey 36 E2
Littleton Surrey 50 D5
Littleton Drew Wilts 46 B2
Littleton of Airlie Angus 234 A5
Littleton-on-Severn S Glos 45 H1
Littleton Panell Wilts 46 F8
Little Torrington Devon 27 J7
Little Totham Essex 72 C4
Little Town Cumb 165 H5
Littletown Dur 169 J2
Little Town Lancs 148 B8
Little Town Warrtn 130 C2
Little Twycross Leics 99 K2
Little Urswick Cumb 156 C6
Little Wakering Essex 53 K2
Little Walden Essex 87 L6
Little Waldingfield Suffk 89 J6
Little Walsingham Norfk 121 K5
Little Waltham Essex 71 H4
Little Warley Essex 52 D1
Little Washbourne Gloucs 82 A8
Little Weighton E R Yk 144 B1
Little Welnetham Suffk 89 H3
Little Welton Lincs 136 F2
Little Wenham Suffk 90 C7
Little Wenlock Wrekin 96 E3
Little Weston Somset 31 K5
Little Whitefield IoW 19 K5
Little Whittingham Green Suffk 106 E7
Little Whittington Nthumb 180 B5
Littlewick Green W & M 49 K3
Little Wilbraham Cambs 87 L4
Littlewindsor Dorset 15 J2
Little Witcombe Gloucs 64 C4
Little Witley Worcs 81 H2
Little Wittenham Oxon 66 D8
Little Wolford Warwks 83 J7
Littlewood Staffs 98 C2
Little Woodcote Gt Lon 51 H7
Littleworth Bucks 67 L4
Littleworth Oxon 65 L7
Littleworth Staffs 98 C2
Littleworth Staffs 114 E7
Littleworth W Susx 21 L4
Littleworth Worcs 81 H4
Littleworth Worcs 82 B5
Littleworth Common Bucks 50 B3
Little Wratting Suffk 88 D6
Little Wymington Bed 85 J3
Little Wymondley Herts 69 G2
Little Wyrley Staffs 98 C2
Little Wytheford Shrops 113 K7
Little Yeldham Essex 88 F7
Littley Green Essex 71 G4
Litton Derbys 132 C5
Litton N York 158 F6
Litton Somset 45 H8
Litton Cheney Dorset 15 M4
Liurbost W Isls 282 h4
Liverpool Lpool 129 J4
Liversedge Kirk 141 J3
Liverton Devon 13 L8
Liverton R & Cl 171 G6
Liverton Mines R & Cl 171 G6
Liverton Street Kent 39 L4
Livingston W Loth 210 D5
Livingston Village W Loth 210 D5

Lixwm Flints 128 E5
Lizard Cnwll 3 H8
Llaingoch IoA 124 D3
Llaithddu Powys 94 C7
Llan Powys 93 J3
Llanaber Gwynd 109 L7
Llanaelhaearn Gwynd 109 G3
Llanafan Cerdgn 77 J1
Llanafan-Fawr Powys 78 D4
Llanallgo IoA 125 J3
Llanarmon Gwynd 109 G4
Llanarmon Dyffryn Ceiriog
  Wrexhm 112 A5
Llanarmon-yn-Ial Denbgs 128 E8
Llanarth Cerdgn 76 D4
Llanarth Mons 62 D5
Llanarthne Carmth 58 F5
Llanasa Flints 128 D3
Llanbabo IoA 124 F2
Llanbadarn Fawr Cerdgn 92 D7
Llanbadarn Fynydd Powys 94 D7
Llanbadarn-y-garreg Powys 78 F5
Llanbadoc Mons 62 D7
Llanbadrig IoA 124 F1
Llanbeder Newpl 44 D1
Llanbedr Gwynd 109 K6
Llanbedr Powys 61 K3
Llanbedr Powys 79 G6
Llanbedr-Dyffryn-Clwyd
  Denbgs 128 D7
Llanbedrgoch IoA 125 J4
Llanbedrog Gwynd 108 E5
Llanbedr-y-Cennin Conwy 126 E6
Llanberis Gwynd 125 K7
Llanbethêry V Glam 43 G7
Llanbister Powys 94 D8
Llanblethian V Glam 42 F7
Llanboidy Carmth 55 L2
Llanbradach Caerph 43 J4
Llanbrynmair Powys 93 K3
Llancadle V Glam 42 F8
Llancarfan V Glam 43 G7
Llancayo Mons 62 D6
Llancloudy Herefs 63 G3
Llancynfelyn Cerdgn 92 C2
Llandaff Cardif 43 J6
Llandanwg Gwynd 109 K6
Llandarcy Neath 57 K6
Llandawke Carmth 58 A6
Llanddaniel Fab IoA 125 J5
Llanddarog Carmth 58 F5
Llanddeiniol Cerdgn 77 G1
Llanddeiniolen Gwynd 125 K6
Llandderfel Gwynd 111 J4
Llanddeusant Carmth 59 L4
Llanddeusant IoA 124 F3
Llanddew Powys 61 G1
Llanddewi Swans 56 E7
Llanddewi Brefi Cerdgn 77 J4
Llanddewi'r Cwm Powys 78 E5
Llanddewi Rhydderch Mons 62 D4
Llanddewi Velfrey Pembks 55 K3
Llanddewi Ystradenni Powys 78 F2
Llanddoged Conwy 126 F7
Llanddona IoA 125 K4
Llanddowror Carmth 58 A6
Llanddulas Conwy 127 H4
Llanddwywe Gwynd 109 K7
Llanddyfnan IoA 125 J4
Llandecwyn Gwynd 110 B4
Llandefaelog Powys 60 F1
Llandefaelog-Tre'r-Graig
  Powys 61 H1
Llandefalle Powys 78 F8
Llandegfan IoA 125 K5
Llandegla Denbgs 112 B1
Llandegley Powys 79 G3
Llandegveth Mons 62 C8
Llandegwning Gwynd 108 D5
Llandeilo Carmth 59 H4
Llandeilo Graban Powys 78 F6
Llandeilo'r Fan Powys 78 B8
Llandeloy Pembks 74 D6
Llandenny Mons 62 E6
Llandevaud Newpt 44 E1
Llandevenny Mons 44 E2
Llandinabo Herefs 63 G2
Llandinam Powys 94 B5
Llandissilio Pembks 55 J3
Llandogo Mons 63 G6
Llandough V Glam 42 F7
Llandough V Glam 43 J7
Llandovery Carmth 59 L2
Llandow V Glam 42 E7
Llandre Carmth 77 J6
Llandre Cerdgn 92 D6
Llandre Isaf Pembks 75 K6
Llandrillo Denbgs 111 K4
Llandrillo-yn-Rhôs Conwy 127 G4
Llandrindod Wells Powys 78 E3

Llandrinio Powys 112 D8
Llandudno Conwy 126 F3
Llandudno Junction Conwy 126 F4
Llandulas Powys 78 B7
Llandwrog Gwynd 125 H6
Llandybie Carmth 59 H6
Llandyfaelog Carmth 58 D6
Llandyfan Carmth 59 H5
Llandyfriog Cerdgn 76 B7
Llandyfrydog IoA 125 H3
Llandygai Gwynd 126 B5
Llandygwydd Cerdgn 75 M3
Llandynan Denbgs 112 B3
Llandyrnog Denbgs 128 D6
Llandyssil Powys 94 F4
Llandysul Cerdgn 76 D7
Llanedeyrn Cardif 43 K5
Llanedi Carmth 57 G3
Llaneglwys Powys 78 E7
Llanegryn Gwynd 92 D2
Llanegwad Carmth 58 F4
Llaneilian IoA 125 H1
Llanelian-yn-Rhôs Conwy 127 G4
Llanelidan Denbgs 111 L2
Llanelieu Powys 79 H8
Llanellen Mons 62 C5
Llanelli Carmth 56 F5
Llanelltyd Gwynd 110 D7
Llanelly Mons 61 K4
Llanelly Hill Mons 61 K4
Llanelwedd Powys 78 E5
Llanenddwyn Gwynd 109 L6
Llanengan Gwynd 108 E6
Llanerch Gwynd 111 G8
Llanerch Powys 95 H4
Llanerchymedd IoA 125 G3
Llanerfyl Powys 94 B4
Llanfabon Caerph 43 H3
Llanfachraeth IoA 124 E3
Llanfachreth Gwynd 110 E7
Llanfaelog IoA 124 F5
Llanfaelrhys Gwynd 108 C6
Llanfaenor Mons 62 E4
Llanfaes IoA 126 B4
Llanfaes Powys 61 G2
Llanfaethlu IoA 124 E2
Llanfair Gwynd 109 K5
Llanfair Caereinion Powys 94 D2
Llanfair Clydogau Cerdgn 77 H5
Llanfair Dyffryn Clwyd Denbgs 128 D8
Llanfairfechan Conwy 126 D5
Llanfair Kilgeddin Mons 62 D5
Llanfair-Nant-Gwyn Pembks 75 K5
Llanfairpwllgwyngyll IoA 125 J5
Llanfair Talhaiarn Conwy 127 J5
Llanfair Waterdine Shrops 94 F8
Llanfairynghornwy IoA 124 E2
Llanfair-yn-Neubwll IoA 124 E4
Llanfallteg Carmth 55 K3
Llanfallteg West Carmth 55 K3
Llanfarian Cerdgn 92 D7
Llanfechain Powys 112 B7
Llanfechan Powys 78 D5
Llanfechell IoA 124 F2
Llanferres Denbgs 128 E7
Llan Ffestiniog Gwynd 110 D3
Llanfflewyn IoA 124 F2
Llanfigael IoA 124 F2
Llanfihangel-ar-arth Carmth 76 E7
Llanfihangel Glyn Myfyr
  Conwy 111 J2
Llanfihangel Nant Bran Powys 78 C8
Llanfihangel-nant-Melan
  Powys 79 H4
Llanfihangel Rhydithon Powys 79 G2
Llanfihangel Rogiet Mons 44 F2
Llanfihangel Tal-y-llyn Powys 61 H2
Llanfihangel-uwch-Gwili
  Carmth 58 E4
Llanfihangel-y-Creuddyn
  Cerdgn 92 E8
Llanfihangel-yng-Ngwynfa
  Powys 111 L8
Llanfihangel yn Nhowyn IoA 124 E4
Llanfihangel-y-pennant Gwynd 92 E2
Llanfihangel-y-pennant
  Gwynd 109 J3
Llanfilo Powys 78 F8
Llanfoist Mons 62 B4
Llanfor Gwynd 111 H4
Llanfrechfa Torfn 62 C8
Llanfrothen Gwynd 110 B3
Llanfrynach Powys 61 G2
Llanfwrog Denbgs 128 D8
Llanfwrog IoA 124 E3
Llanfyllin Powys 112 A7
Llanfynydd Carmth 59 G3
Llanfynydd Flints 129 G8
Llanfyrnach Pembks 75 L6
Llangadfan Powys 94 B1

Llangadog Carmth 56 D3
Llangadog Carmth 59 K3
Llangadwaladr IoA 125 G6
Llangadwaladr Powys 112 B5
Llangaffo IoA 125 H6
Llangain Carmth 58 C5
Llangammarch Wells Powys 78 C6
Llangan V Glam 42 E6
Llangarron Herefs 63 G3
Llangasty-Talyllyn Powys 61 H2
Llangathen Carmth 59 G4
Llangattock Powys 61 K3
Llangattock Lingoed Mons 62 D3
Llangattock-Vibon-Avel Mons 62 F4
Llangedwyn Powys 112 B6
Llangefni IoA 125 H4
Llangeinor Brdgnd 42 D4
Llangeitho Cerdgn 77 H3
Llangeler Carmth 76 C7
Llangelynin Gwynd 92 C2
Llangennech Carmth 57 G4
Llangennith Swans 56 D6
Llangenny Powys 61 K3
Llangernyw Conwy 127 H6
Llangian Gwynd 108 C6
Llangiwg Neath 57 K4
Llangloffan Pembks 74 E5
Llanglydwen Carmth 75 L6
Llangoed IoA 126 C4
Llangoedmor Cerdgn 75 L3
Llangollen Denbgs 112 B3
Llangolman Pembks 75 J6
Llangors Powys 61 H2
Llangorwen Cerdgn 92 D6
Llangovan Mons 62 F6
Llangower Gwynd 111 G5
Llangrannog Cerdgn 76 B4
Llangristiolus IoA 125 H5
Llangrove Herefs 63 G3
Llangua Mons 62 D2
Llangunllo Powys 79 H1
Llangunnor Carmth 58 D5
Llangurig Powys 93 K7
Llangwm Conwy 111 J3
Llangwm Mons 62 E7
Llangwm Pembks 55 G5
Llangwnnadl Gwynd 108 C5
Llangwyfan Denbgs 128 D6
Llangwyllog IoA 125 H4
Llangwyryfon Cerdgn 77 H1
Llangybi Cerdgn 77 H4
Llangybi Gwynd 109 G3
Llangybi Mons 62 D7
Llangyfelach Swans 57 H5
Llangyndeyrn Carmth 58 E6
Llangynhafal Denbgs 128 D7
Llangynidr Powys 61 J3
Llangynin Carmth 55 M3
Llangynllo Carmth 76 C6
Llangynog Carmth 58 C5
Llangynog Powys 111 K6
Llangynwyd Brdgnd 42 C4
Llanhamlach Powys 61 H2
Llanharan Rhondd 42 F5
Llanharry Rhondd 42 F5
Llanhennock Mons 62 D8
Llanhilleth Blae G 61 K7
Llanidan IoA 125 J6
Llanidloes Powys 93 L6
Llaniestyn Gwynd 108 D5
Llanigon Powys 79 H7
Llanilar Cerdgn 92 D8
Llanilid Rhondd 42 E5
Llanina Cerdgn 76 D3
Llanio Cerdgn 77 H4
Llanishen Cardif 43 J5
Llanishen Mons 62 F6
Llanllechid Gwynd 126 C6
Llanlleonfel Powys 78 C5
Llanllowell Mons 62 D7
Llanllugan Powys 94 C3
Llanllwch Carmth 58 C5
Llanllwchaiarn Powys 94 D5
Llanllwni Carmth 76 D6
Llanllyfni Gwynd 109 H1
Llanmadoc Swans 56 D6
Llanmaes V Glam 42 E7
Llanmartin Newpt 44 E1
Llanmerewig Powys 94 E5
Llanmihangel V Glam 42 E7
Llanmiloe Carmth 55 M5
Llanmorlais Swans 56 F6
Llannefydd Conwy 127 K5
Llannon Carmth 56 F3
Llannor Gwynd 108 F4
Llanon Cerdgn 76 F2
Llanover Mons 62 C5
Llanpumsaint Carmth 58 D3
Llanrhaeadr-ym-Mochnant
  Powys 111 M6

Llanrhian Pembks 74 D6
Llanrhidian Swans 56 F6
Llanrhos Conwy 126 F4
Llanrhychwyn Conwy 126 F7
Llanrhyddlad IoA 124 F2
Llanrhystud Cerdgn 76 F1
Llanrothal Herefs 62 F3
Llanrug Gwynd 125 J7
Llanrumney Cardif 43 K5
Llanrwst Conwy 126 F7
Llansadurnen Carmth 56 A3
Llansadwrn Carmth 59 J3
Llansadwrn IoA 125 K4
Llansaint Carmth 56 C3
Llansamlet Swans 57 J5
Llansanffraid Glan Conwy
  Conwy 126 F4
Llansannan Conwy 127 J6
Llansannor V Glam 42 F6
Llansantffraed Powys 61 H2
Llansantffraed-Cwmdeuddwr
  Powys 78 D2
Llansantffraed-in-Elvel Powys 78 F4
Llansantffraid Cerdgn 76 F2
Llansantffraid-ym-Mechain
  Powys 112 C7
Llansawel Carmth 59 H2
Llansilin Powys 112 B6
Llansoy Mons 62 E6
Llanspyddid Powys 60 F2
Llanstadwell Pembks 54 F6
Llansteffan Carmth 56 C3
Llanstephan Powys 78 F6
Llantarnam Torfn 62 C8
Llanteg Pembks 55 L5
Llanthewy Skirrid Mons 62 D4
Llanthony Mons 62 B2
Llantilio-Crossenny Mons 62 E4
Llantilio Pertholey Mons 62 C4
Llantood Pembks 75 K4
Llantrisant IoA 124 F3
Llantrisant Mons 62 D7
Llantrisant Rhondd 43 G5
Llantrithyd V Glam 43 G7
Llantwit Fardre Rhondd 43 G4
Llantwit Major V Glam 42 E7
Llantysilio Denbgs 112 B3
Llanuwchllyn Gwynd 111 G6
Llanvaches Newpt 44 E1
Llanvair Discoed Mons 62 F8
Llanvapley Mons 62 D4
Llanvetherine Mons 62 D4
Llanveynoe Herefs 62 C1
Llanvihangel Crucorney Mons 62 C3
Llanvihangel Gobion Mons 62 D5
Llanvihangel-Ystern-Llewern
  Mons 62 E4
Llanwarne Herefs 63 G2
Llanwddyn Powys 111 K7
Llanwenarth Mons 62 B4
Llanwenog Cerdgn 76 F6
Llanwern Newpt 44 D2
Llanwinio Carmth 58 A4
Llanwnda Gwynd 125 H8
Llanwnda Pembks 74 F4
Llanwnnen Cerdgn 76 F6
Llanwnog Powys 94 B3
Llanwonno Rhondd 42 F3
Llanwrda Carmth 59 K3
Llanwrin Powys 93 G3
Llanwrthwl Powys 78 D3
Llanwrtyd Powys 78 B5
Llanwrtyd Wells Powys 78 B6
Llanwyddelan Powys 94 C3
Llanyblodwel Shrops 112 C7
Llanybri Carmth 58 B6
Llanybydder Carmth 76 F6
Llanycefn Pembks 55 J2
Llanychaer Pembks 75 G5
Llanycil Gwynd 111 H4
Llanycrwys Carmth 77 H6
Llanymawddwy Gwynd 111 G7
Llanymynech Powys 112 C7
Llanynghenedl IoA 124 E3
Llanynys Denbgs 128 C7
Llan-y-pwll Wrexhm 112 F1
Llanyre Powys 78 E3
Llanystumdwy Gwynd 109 H4
Llanywern Powys 61 H2
Llawhaden Pembks 55 H3
Llawnt Shrops 112 C5
Llawryglyn Powys 93 K5
Llay Wrexhm 129 H8
Llechcynfarwy IoA 125 G3
Llechfaen Powys 61 G2
Llechrhyd Caerph 61 H5
Llechryd Cerdgn 75 L3
Llechylched IoA 124 F4
Lledrod Cerdgn 77 H1
Llidiardau Gwynd 111 G4

Llidiartnenog Carmth 77 G7
Llidiart-y-parc Denbgs 111 M3
Llithfaen Gwynd 108 F3
Lloc Flints 128 D4
Llowes Powys 79 H7
Llwydcoed Rhondd 60 F6
Llwydiarth Powys 111 K8
Llwyn Denbgs 128 C6
Llwyncelyn Cerdgn 76 E3
Llwyndafydd Cerdgn 76 C4
Llwynderw Powys 94 F3
Llwyn-drain Pembks 58 A2
Llwyn-du Mons 62 C4
Llwyndyrys Gwynd 108 F3
Llwyngwril Gwynd 92 D2
Llwynhendy Carmth 56 F5
Llwynmawr Wrexhm 112 C4
Llwyn-on Myr Td 60 F5
Llwyn-y-brain Carmth 55 L4
Llwyn-y-groes Cerdgn 77 G4
Llwynypia Rhondd 42 F3
Llynclys Shrops 112 D6
Llynfaes IoA 125 G4
Llŷn Peninsula Gwynd 108 E4
Llyn-y-pandy Flints 128 E6
Llysfaen Conwy 127 H4
Llyswen Cerdgn 76 E3
Llyswen Powys 79 G7
Llysworney V Glam 42 E6
Llys-y-frân Pembks 55 H2
Llywel Powys 60 C1
Load Brook Sheff 132 E2
Loan Falk 210 C4
Loanend Nthumb 202 E3
Loanhead Mdloth 211 J6
Loaningfoot D & G 176 C7
Loans S Ayrs 196 C4
Lobb Devon 27 H3
Lobhillcross Devon 12 B5
Lochailort Highld 238 B7
Lochaline Highld 227 K3
Lochans D & G 172 D3
Locharbriggs D & G 176 C3
Lochavich Ag & B 216 E4
Lochawe Ag & B 217 J2
Loch Baghasdail W Isls 283 c11
Lochboisdale W Isls 283 c11
Lochbuie Ag & B 227 H7
Lochcarron Highld 248 E4
Lochdon Ag & B 227 L6
Lochdonhead Ag & B 227 L5
Lochead Ag & B 206 B3
Lochearnhead Stirlg 219 K2
Lochee C Dund 222 F1
Loch Eil Highld 239 H7
Locheilside Station Highld 239 G7
Lochend Highld 251 G4
Locheport W Isls 283 c8
Loch Euphort W Isls 283 c8
Lochfoot D & G 176 B4
Lochgair Ag & B 206 E1
Lochgelly Fife 222 C8
Lochgilphead Ag & B 206 D2
Lochgoilhead Ag & B 217 K7
Lochieheads Fife 222 D4
Lochill Moray 266 F3
Lochindorb Lodge Highld 253 J4
Lochinver Highld 270 E4
Loch Lomond and The Trossachs National Park 219 G4
Loch Loyal Lodge Highld 277 L7
Lochluichart Highld 262 B7
Lochmaben D & G 176 E2
Lochmaddy W Isls 283 d8
Loch nam Madadh W Isls 283 d8
Loch Ness Highld 250 F6
Lochore Fife 222 B7
Loch Portain W Isls 283 d8
Lochportain W Isls 283 d8
Lochranza N Ayrs 194 E1
Loch Sgioport W Isls 283 c10
Lochside Abers 235 J3
Lochside D & G 176 C3
Lochside Highld 252 D1
Lochskipport W Isls 283 c10
Lochslin Highld 264 C4
Lochton S Ayrs 183 G7
Lochty Angus 234 E3
Lochty Fife 223 J5
Lochuisge Highld 228 B4
Lochwinnoch Rens 208 B7
Lochwood D & G 187 G6
Lockengate Cnwll 5 H3
Lockerbie D & G 176 F3
Lockeridge Wilts 47 H5
Lockerley Hants 34 C5
Locking N Som 44 D7
Locking Stumps Warrtn 130 C1
Lockington E R Yk 152 F6
Lockington Leics 116 D6

Lockleywood Shrops 113 M6
Locksbottom Gt Lon 51 L6
Locksgreen IoW 19 G5
Locks Heath Hants 19 H2
Lockton N York 162 E5
Loddington Leics 101 H3
Loddington Nhants 101 H7
Loddiswell Devon 7 L5
Loddon Norfk 107 H4
Lode Cambs 87 L3
Lode Heath Solhll 98 F7
Loders Dorset 15 L4
Lodsworth W Susx 36 D6
Lofthouse Leeds 142 A3
Lofthouse N York 159 K8
Lofthouse Gate Wakefd 142 A3
Loftus R & Cl 171 G7
Logan E Ayrs 197 H6
Loganbeck Cumb 156 A4
Loganlea W Loth 210 C6
Loggerheads Staffs 114 A4
Logie Angus 235 H3
Logie Fife 223 G3
Logie Moray 253 K2
Logie Coldstone Abers 243 M3
Logie Newton Abers 256 B4
Logie Pert Angus 235 G3
Logierait P & K 232 E5
Logierieve Abers 257 G2
Login Carmth 55 K2
Lolworth Cambs 87 H2
Lonbain Highld 259 M6
Londesborough E R Yk 152 C6
London Gt Lon 51 J3
London Apprentice Cnwll 5 G5
London Ashford Airport Kent 25 K3
London Beach Kent 39 M6
London City Airport Gt Lon 51 L3
London Colney Herts 68 F6
Londonderry N York 160 D5
London Gateway Services Gt Lon 69 G8
London Gatwick Airport W Susx 37 L3
London Heathrow Airport Gt Lon 50 D4
London Luton Airport Luton 68 E3
London Oxford Airport Oxon 66 C4
London Southend Airport Essex 53 J1
London Stansted Airport Essex 70 E2
Londonthorpe Lincs 118 C4
Londubh Highld 260 D4
Lonemore Highld 260 C4
Long Ashton N Som 45 H5
Long Bank Worcs 97 H8
Long Bennington Lincs 117 L3
Longbenton N Tyne 181 H6
Longborough Gloucs 65 J1
Long Bredy Dorset 16 A4
Longbridge Birm 98 C7
Longbridge Warwks 83 E3
Longbridge Deverill Wilts 32 E3
Long Buckby Nhants 84 C2
Longburgh Cumb 177 J2
Longburton Dorset 31 L8
Long Cause Devon 8 B3
Long Clawson Leics 117 J6
Longcliffe Derbys 132 D8
Longcombe Devon 8 C8
Long Common Hants 35 G7
Long Compton Staffs 114 D7
Long Compton Warwks 83 G8
Longcot Oxon 47 K1
Long Crendon Bucks 67 G5
Long Crichel Dorset 17 J1
Longcroft Cumb 177 H7
Longcross Surrey 50 C6
Longden Shrops 95 K2
Longden Common Shrops 95 K2
Long Ditton Surrey 50 H8
Longdon Staffs 115 H8
Longdon Worcs 81 J7
Longdon Green Staffs 98 D1
Longdon Heath Worcs 81 J7
Longdon upon Tern Wrekin 113 K8
Longdown Devon 13 K4
Longdowns Cnwll 3 J4
Long Drax N York 143 H2
Long Duckmanton Derbys 133 J5
Long Eaton Derbys 116 E5
Longfield Kent 52 D5
Longford Covtry 99 K6
Longford Derbys 115 L4
Longford Gloucs 64 B3
Longford Gt Lon 50 D4
Longford Kent 38 D2
Longford Shrops 113 L5
Longford Wrekin 114 A7
Longforgan P & K 222 E1
Longformacus Border 212 F7

Longframlington Nthumb 191 G6
Long Green Ches W 129 L5
Long Green Worcs 81 J8
Longham Dorset 17 L3
Longham Norfk 121 L8
Long Hanborough Oxon 66 B4
Longhaven Abers 257 L4
Long Hedges Lincs 119 K2
Longhirst Nthumb 191 J8
Longhope Gloucs 63 K3
Longhope Ork 275 b6
Longhorsley Nthumb 191 H7
Longhoughton Nthumb 191 J3
Long Itchington Warwks 83 K2
Longlands Cumb 165 J3
Longlane Derbys 115 L4
Long Lawford Warwks 100 A8
Longlevens Gloucs 64 B3
Longley Calder 141 G3
Longley Kirk 141 J6
Longley Green Worcs 81 G5
Longleys P & K 233 L6
Long Load Somset 31 G6
Longmanhill Abers 268 D4
Long Marston Herts 67 L4
Long Marston N York 151 H5
Long Marston Warwks 82 E5
Long Marton Cumb 166 F5
Long Meadowend Shrops 95 K7
Long Melford Suffk 89 H6
Longmoor Camp Hants 36 B4
Longmorn Moray 266 E4
Longmoss Ches E 131 H5
Long Newnton Gloucs 64 C8
Longnewton Border 201 J7
Long Newton E Loth 212 B6
Longnewton S on T 169 K7
Longney Gloucs 63 M4
Longniddry E Loth 212 A4
Longnor Shrops 96 B3
Longnor Staffs 132 B6
Longparish Hants 34 F2
Longpark Cumb 178 A6
Long Preston N York 148 E4
Longridge Lancs 147 M8
Longridge Staffs 114 E8
Longridge W Loth 210 C6
Longriggend N Lans 209 L5
Long Riston E R Yk 153 H7
Longrock Cnwll 2 D5
Longsdon Staffs 114 F1
Longshaw Wigan 139 G7
Longside Abers 269 J6
Long Sight Oldham 140 D6
Longslow Shrops 113 L4
Longstanton Cambs 87 H2
Longstock Hants 34 D3
Longstone Pembks 55 K5
Longstowe Cambs 86 F4
Long Stratton Norfk 106 D5
Long Street M Keyn 84 F5
Longstreet Wilts 47 H8
Long Sutton Hants 35 M2
Long Sutton Lincs 119 M7
Long Sutton Somset 31 K5
Longthorpe C Pete 102 D4
Long Thurlow Suffk 89 K2
Longthwaite Cumb 166 B6
Longton C Stke 114 E3
Longton Lancs 138 F3
Longtown Cumb 177 L5
Longtown Herefs 62 C1
Longueville Jersey 9 e3
Longville in the Dale Shrops 96 C4
Long Waste Wrekin 113 K8
Long Whatton Leics 116 D6
Longwick Bucks 67 J6
Long Wittenham Oxon 66 E8
Longwitton Nthumb 180 C1
Longwood D & G 175 J3
Longwood Shrops 96 D2
Longworth Oxon 66 A7
Longyester E Loth 212 C6
Lôn-las Swans 57 K5
Lonmay Abers 269 J4
Lonmore Highld 258 D7
Looe Cnwll 6 B4
Loose Kent 39 J3
Loosebeare Devon 13 G2
Loosegate Lincs 119 K6
Loosley Row Bucks 67 K7
Lootcherbrae Abers 268 A5
Lopcombe Corner Wilts 34 B4
Lopen Somset 30 F8
Loppington Shrops 113 G5
Lorbottle Nthumb 190 E6
Lordington W Susx 20 C5
Lordsbridge Norfk 104 B1
Lordshill C Sotn 34 E7
Lords Wood Medway 53 G6

Lornty P & K 233 J6
Loscoe Derbys 116 C2
Loscombe Dorset 15 L3
Losgaintir W Isls 282 e6
Lossiemouth Moray 266 E2
Lostford Shrops 113 K5
Lostock Gralam Ches W 130 D5
Lostock Green Ches W 130 D5
Lostock Hall Lancs 139 H4
Lostock Hall Fold Bolton 139 K6
Lostock Junction Bolton 139 K6
Lostwithiel Cnwll 5 J3
Lothbeg Highld 274 C6
Lothersdale N York 149 G6
Lothmore Highld 274 C6
Loudwater Bucks 49 L1
Loudwater Herts 49 A8
Loughborough Leics 116 F7
Loughor Swans 57 G5
Loughton Essex 70 B7
Loughton M Keyn 85 G7
Loughton Shrops 96 E6
Lound Lincs 118 E7
Lound Notts 134 D2
Lound Suffk 107 K4
Lounston Devon 13 J7
Lount Leics 116 C7
Louth Lincs 136 F2
Loveclough Lancs 140 B2
Lovedean Hants 19 M1
Lover Wilts 34 B6
Loversall Donc 142 F8
Loves Green Essex 70 F6
Lovesome Hill N York 160 E3
Loveston Pembks 55 J5
Lovington Somset 31 K5
Low Ackworth Wakefd 142 C4
Low Angerton Nthumb 180 D2
Lowbands Gloucs 63 M1
Low Barbeth D & G 172 C2
Low Barlings Lincs 136 A5
Low Bell End N York 162 C3
Low Bentham N York 148 A2
Low Biggins Cumb 157 K7
Low Borrowbridge Cumb 157 K2
Low Bradfield Sheff 132 E2
Low Bradley N York 149 H6
Low Braithwaite Cumb 166 A2
Low Burnham N Linc 143 K7
Low Buston Nthumb 191 J5
Lowca Cumb 164 C6
Low Catton E R Yk 151 L5
Low Coniscliffe Darltn 169 H7
Low Crosby Cumb 178 B7
Lowdham Notts 117 H2
Low Dinsdale Darltn 169 K8
Lowe Shrops 113 H5
Lowe Hill Staffs 131 K8
Low Ellington N York 160 B6
Lower Aisholt Somset 30 B4
Lower Ansty Dorset 16 E2
Lower Apperley Gloucs 64 B2
Lower Arboll Highld 264 D3
Lower Arncott Oxon 66 F4
Lower Ashton Devon 13 K6
Lower Assendon Oxon 49 H2
Lower Badcall Highld 276 B5
Lower Ballam Lancs 138 D2
Lower Bartle Lancs 139 G1
Lower Basildon W Berk 48 F3
Lower Bearwood Herefs 79 M4
Lower Beeding W Susx 37 K5
Lower Benefield Nhants 101 L5
Lower Bentley Worcs 82 A2
Lower Beobridge Shrops 97 H5
Lower Birchwood Derbys 116 D2
Lower Boddington Nhants 83 L5
Lower Boscaswell Cnwll 2 B4
Lower Bourne Surrey 36 C2
Lower Brailes Warwks 83 H2
Lower Breakish Highld 247 L4
Lower Bredbury Stockp 131 H2
Lower Broadheath Worcs 81 J4
Lower Broxwood Herefs 79 L4
Lower Buckenhill Herefs 80 E8
Lower Bullingham Herefs 80 C7
Lower Burgate Hants 33 K7
Lower Burrowton Devon 14 B3
Lower Burton Herefs 80 A4
Lower Caldecote C Beds 86 D6
Lower Cam Gloucs 63 L2
Lower Canada N Som 44 A5
Lower Catesby Nhants 83 M4
Lower Chapel Powys 78 E5
Lower Chicksgrove Wilts 33 G3
Lower Chute Wilts 47 L8
Lower Clapton Gt Lon 51 K2
Lower Clent Worcs 97 L7
Lower Common Hants 49 J8
Lower Compton Wilts 46 E5

Lower Creedy Devon 13 K2
Lower Crossings Derbys 131 L4
Lower Cumberworth Kirk 141 K6
Lower Darwen Bl w D 139 K3
Lower Dean Bed..........................85 L2
Lower Denby Kirk 141 K6
Lower Diabaig Highld............260 C7
Lower Dicker E Susx 23 J5
Lower Dinchope Shrops............95 L6
Lower Down Shrops....................95 H6
Lower Dunsforth N York 150 F3
Lower Egleton Herefs................80 E6
Lower Elkstone Staffs 131 L8
Lower Ellastone Staffs 115 J3
Lower End Bucks........................67 G5
Lower End M Keyn......................85 H7
Lower End Nhants......................84 F3
Lower End Nhants......................85 H3
Lower Everleigh Wilts..............47 J8
Lower Exbury Hants 19 G4
Lower Eythorne Kent................41 J5
Lower Failand N Som................45 G4
Lower Farringdon Hants..........35 L4
Lower Feltham Gt Lon..............50 F4
Lower Fittleworth W Susx 21 G3
Lower Foxdale IoM 154 c6
Lower Frankton Shrops..........112 E5
Lower Freystrop Pembks..........54 F4
Lower Froyle Hants 35 M2
Lower Gabwell Devon..................8 D1
Lower Gledfield Highld..........263 G2
Lower Godney Somset..............31 G2
Lower Gornal Dudley................97 L5
Lower Gravenhurst C Beds......86 C8
Lower Green Herts....................86 D8
Lower Green Herts....................87 J8
Lower Green Kent......................38 E5
Lower Green Kent......................39 G5
Lower Green Norfk 121 L4
Lower Green Staffs..................97 K2
Lower Green Suffk 88 E2
Lower Hacheston Suffk............91 H4
Lower Halstock Leigh Dorset..15 M1
Lower Halstow Kent..................53 J5
Lower Hamworthy BCP..............17 K4
Lower Hardres Kent..................40 F5
Lower Harpton Herefs..............79 K3
Lower Hartlip Kent....................53 H6
Lower Hartshay Derbys..........116 C1
Lower Hartwell Bucks..............67 J4
Lower Hatton Staffs 114 C4
Lower Hawthwaite Cumb........156 B5
Lower Haysden Kent..................38 F4
Lower Hergest Herefs..............79 K4
Lower Heyford Oxon..................66 C2
Lower Heysham Lancs............147 H4
Lower Higham Kent 52 F4
Lower Holbrook Suffk..............90 E8
Lower Hordley Shrops............112 F5
Lower Horncroft W Susx..........21 G3
Lowerhouse Lancs....................140 B1
Lower Houses Kirk 141 J5
Lower Howsell Worcs................81 H5
Lower Irlam Salfd....................130 D1
Lower Kilburn Derbys............116 C3
Lower Kilcott Gloucs................46 A1
Lower Killeyan Ag & B 204 D7
Lower Kingcombe Dorset..........16 A3
Lower Kingswood Surrey..........51 H8
Lower Kinnerton Ches W 129 H7
Lower Langford N Som..............44 F6
Lower Largo Fife....................223 G6
Lower Leigh Staffs 115 G4
Lower Lemington Gloucs..........82 F8
Lower Llanfadog Powys............78 C2
Lower Lovacott Devon..............27 J5
Lower Loxhore Devon................27 L3
Lower Lydbrook Gloucs............63 H4
Lower Lye Herefs 79 M2
Lower Machen Newpt................43 K4
Lower Maes-coed Herefs..........62 D1
Lower Mannington Dorset........17 L2
Lower Marston Somset............32 C2
Lower Meend Gloucs..................63 H6
Lower Merridge Somset............30 B4
Lower Middleton Cheney
     Nhants................................83 L7
Lower Milton Somset................31 J2
Lower Moor Worcs......................82 A6
Lower Morton S Glos..................63 J8
Lower Nazeing Essex................69 K6
Lower Norton Warwks................82 F3
Lower Nyland Dorset................32 C6
Lower Oddington Gloucs..........65 K2
Lower Penarth V Glam..............43 J7
Lower Penn Staffs....................97 K4
Lower Pennington Hants..........18 E5
Lower Penwortham Lancs........139 G2
Lower Peover Ches E................130 E5
Lower Place Rochdl..................140 D5

Lower Pollicott Bucks..............67 H4
Lower Quinton Warwks..............82 E6
Lower Rainham Medway............53 H5
Lower Raydon Suffk..................90 B7
Lower Roadwater Somset..........29 J3
Lower Salter Lancs................147 M3
Lower Seagry Wilts..................46 D3
Lower Sheering Essex................70 C4
Lower Shelton C Beds................85 K6
Lower Shiplake Oxon................49 J3
Lower Shuckburgh Warwks......83 L3
Lower Slaughter Gloucs..........65 H3
Lower Soothill Kirk 141 L3
Lower Soudley Gloucs..............63 K5
Lower Standen Kent..................41 H7
Lower Stanton St Quintin Wilts..46 D3
Lower Stoke Medway..................53 H4
Lower Stondon C Beds..............86 C8
Lower Stone Gloucs..................63 K8
Lower Stonnall Staffs..............98 D3
Lower Stow Bedon Norfk 105 K4
Lower Street Dorset..................17 G3
Lower Street E Susx..................24 C5
Lower Street Norfk 122 F4
Lower Street Suffk....................88 F5
Lower Street Suffk....................90 D5
Lower Stretton Warrtn............130 C3
Lower Stroud Dorset................15 K3
Lower Sundon C Beds................68 D2
Lower Swanwick Hants..............19 H2
Lower Swell Gloucs..................65 H2
Lower Tadmarton Oxon............83 J7
Lower Tale Devon......................14 C2
Lower Tasburgh Norfk............106 D4
Lower Tean Staffs 115 G4
Lower Thurlton Norfk............107 J3
Lower Town Cnwll........................3 G8
Lower Town Devon 13 G8
Lower Town Herefs....................80 E6
Lower Town IoS..........................10 c1
Lower Town Pembks..................74 F5
Lower Trebullett Cnwll............11 L7
Lower Treluswell Cnwll............3 K4
Lower Tysoe Warwks..................83 H6
Lower Ufford Suffk..................91 G5
Lower Upcott Devon..................13 K6
Lower Upham Hants..................35 H7
Lower Upnor Medway................53 G5
Lower Vexford Somset..............29 L4
Lower Walton Warrtn..............130 B3
Lower Waterston Dorset..........16 E4
Lower Weare Somset..................44 E8
Lower Weedon Nhants..............84 C3
Lower Welson Herefs................79 K5
Lower Westmancote Worcs 81 L7
Lower Whatcombe Dorset........17 G2
Lower Whatley Somset..............32 B3
Lower Whitley Ches W............130 B4
Lower Wick Gloucs....................63 L7
Lower Wick Worcs......................81 J5
Lower Wield Hants 35 K3
Lower Willingdon E Susx........23 K6
Lower Withington Ches E 130 F5
Lower Woodend Bucks..............49 K2
Lower Woodford Wilts..............33 K4
Lower Wraxhall Dorset............16 A2
Lower Wyche Worcs....................81 H6
Lower Wyke C Brad..................141 J3
Lowesby Leics..........................100 F2
Lowestoft Suffk......................107 L5
Loweswater Cumb....................164 F6
Low Etherley Dur....................168 F5
Low Fell Gatesd......................181 G7
Lowfield Heath W Susx............37 L3
Low Gartachorrans Stirlg 208 D2
Low Gate Nthumb....................179 L6
Low Gettbridge Cumb............178 C7
Lowgill Cumb..........................157 K3
Lowgill Lancs..........................148 A3
Low Grantley N York..............150 B2
Low Green N York....................150 B4
Low Habberley Worcs................97 H7
Low Ham Somset........................30 F5
Low Harrogate N York............150 C5
Low Hawkser N York................163 G1
Low Hesket Cumb....................166 B2
Low Hutton N York..................152 A2
Lowick Cumb............................156 D5
Lowick Nhants..........................101 L7
Lowick Nthumb........................203 G5
Lowick Bridge Cumb..............156 D5
Lowick Green Cumb................156 D5
Low Knipe Cumb......................166 C6
Low Laithe N York..................150 B3
Lowlands Dur..........................168 E5
Lowlands Torfn..........................62 C7
Low Langton Lincs..................136 C4
Low Leighton Derbys..............131 K3
Low Lorton Cumb....................164 F5
Low Marishes N York..............162 E7

Low Marnham Notts................134 F6
Low Middleton Nthumb..........203 J1
Low Mill N York........................161 L4
Low Moor C Brad......................141 J2
Low Moorsley Sundld..............169 J2
Low Moresby Cumb..................164 C6
Low Newton Cumb..................156 F6
Low Newton-by-the-Sea
     Nthumb............................191 J1
Low Pittington Dur................169 J2
Low Row Cumb........................165 G2
Low Row Cumb........................165 K3
Low Row Cumb........................178 D6
Low Row N York......................159 H3
Low Salchrie D & G................172 C2
Low Santon N Linc..................144 B5
Lowsonford Warwks..................82 E2
Low Street Norfk....................123 G6
Low Street Thurr......................52 E3
Low Tharston Norfk................106 D4
Lowther Cumb..........................166 D6
Lowthorpe E R Yk....................153 H4
Lowton Devon............................12 F2
Lowton Somset..........................30 B7
Lowton Wigan..........................139 J8
Lowton Common Wigan..........139 J8
Lowton St Mary's Wigan........139 J8
Low Torry Fife........................210 D2
Low Toynton Lincs..................136 G5
Low Valley Barns......................142 B7
Low Wood Cumb......................156 E6
Low Worsall N York................160 F1
Low Wray Cumb........................156 E2
Loxbeare Devon..........................29 G7
Loxhill Surrey............................36 F3
Loxhore Devon............................27 L3
Loxhore Cott Devon..................27 L3
Loxley Warwks............................83 G4
Loxley Green Staffs 115 H5
Loxter Herefs..............................81 G7
Loxton N Som..............................44 D7
Loxwood W Susx........................36 F4
Lubenham Leics........................100 F6
Lucasgate Lincs......................119 M2
Lucas Green Surrey....................50 B7
Luccombe Somset......................29 G2
Luccombe Village IoW..............19 K7
Lucker Nthumb........................203 J7
Luckett Cnwll............................11 M7
Lucking Street Essex................89 G8
Luckington Wilts......................46 B2
Lucklawhill Fife......................223 G3
Lucknam Wilts............................46 B4
Luckwell Bridge Somset..........28 F3
Lucton Herefs..............................80 B2
Lucy Cross N York....................169 G8
Ludag W Isls............................283 c12
Ludborough Lincs..................145 H8
Ludbrook Devon............................7 J4
Ludchurch Pembks....................55 K4
Luddenden Calder..................141 G3
Luddenden Foot Calder..........140 F3
Luddenham Court Kent............40 C3
Luddesdown Kent......................52 E5
Luddington N Linc..................143 L4
Luddington Warwks..................82 E5
Luddington in the Brook
     Nhants..............................102 C6
Ludford Lincs..........................136 D2
Ludford Shrops..........................96 C8
Ludgershall Bucks....................67 G4
Ludgershall Wilts......................34 B1
Ludgvan Cnwll..............................2 D7
Ludham Norfk..........................123 H7
Ludlow Shrops............................96 C8
Ludney Somset............................30 F8
Ludwell Wilts..............................32 F6
Ludworth Dur..........................169 K2
Luffenhall Herts........................69 J1
Luffincott Devon........................11 L4
Luffness E Loth......................212 B3
Lugar E Ayrs............................197 H6
Luggate Burn E Loth..............212 D4
Lugg Green Herefs....................80 B3
Luggiebank N Lans..................209 K4
Lugton E Ayrs..........................208 C8
Lugwardine Herefs....................80 D7
Luib Highld..............................247 J3
Luing Ag & B............................215 L2
Lulham Herefs............................80 A7
Lullington Derbys......................99 H1
Lullington E Susx......................23 K6
Lullington Somset......................45 M8
Lulsgate Bottom N Som............45 G6
Lulsley Worcs..............................81 G4
Lulworth Camp Dorset..............16 F6
Lumb Calder..............................140 F3
Lumb Lancs..............................140 C3
Lumbutts Calder......................140 E3
Lumby N York..........................142 D2

Lumphanan Abers....................244 D3
Lumphinnans Fife..................222 B8
Lumsden Abers........................255 K7
Lunan Angus............................235 H5
Lunanhead Angus....................234 D5
Luncarty P & K........................221 K1
Lund E R Yk..............................152 E6
Lund N York..............................143 G1
Lundie Angus..........................233 L8
Lundin Links Fife..................223 G6
Lundin Mill Fife......................223 G6
Lundy Devon................................26 B2
Lundy Green Norfk..................106 E5
Lunga Ag & B............................215 K3
Lunna Shet................................281 e4
Lunsford Kent............................52 F7
Lunsford's Cross E Susx..........24 C5
Lunt Sefton..............................138 D7
Luntley Herefs............................79 M4
Luppitt Devon............................14 E1
Lupridge Devon............................7 L2
Lupset Wakefd..........................141 M4
Lupton Cumb............................157 J6
Lurgashall W Susx......................36 D5
Lurley Devon..............................29 G7
Lusby Lincs..............................136 F6
Luscombe Devon............................8 B3
Luskentyre W Isls....................282 e6
Luson Devon..................................7 H5
Luss Ag & B..............................218 E8
Lussagiven Ag & B..................215 J7
Lusta Highld............................258 D5
Lustleigh Devon..........................13 H6
Luston Herefs..............................80 B3
Luthermuir Abers....................235 G2
Luthrie Fife..............................222 E3
Lutley Dudley..............................97 L6
Luton Devon................................13 L7
Luton Devon................................14 C2
Luton Luton................................68 E3
Luton Medway............................53 G5
Luton Airport Luton................68 E3
Lutterworth Leics..................100 C6
Lutton Devon..................................7 H3
Lutton Devon..................................7 K3
Lutton Lincs............................119 M6
Lutton Nhants..........................102 C6
Luxborough Somset..................29 H3
Luxulyan Cnwll............................5 H3
Luxulyan Valley Cnwll..............5 H3
Luzley Tamesd........................140 E7
Lybster Highld........................275 H1
Lydbury North Shrops..............95 J6
Lydcott Devon............................28 B4
Lydd Kent....................................25 K3
Lydd Airport Kent....................25 K3
Lydden Kent................................41 H6
Lydden Kent................................41 K2
Lyddington Rutlnd..................101 J4
Lydd-on-Sea Kent......................25 K3
Lydeard St Lawrence Somset..29 L4
Lyde Green Hants......................49 H7
Lyde Green S Glos......................45 K3
Lydford Devon............................12 C5
Lydford on Fosse Somset..........31 J5
Lydgate Calder........................140 D3
Lydgate Rochdl........................140 E4
Lydham Shrops............................95 H5
Lydiard Green Wilts..................47 G2
Lydiard Millicent Wilts............47 G2
Lydiard Tregoze Swindn..........47 G2
Lydiate Sefton........................138 D3
Lydiate Ash Worcs......................98 B8
Lydlinch Dorset..........................32 B8
Lydney Gloucs............................63 J6
Lydstep Pembks..........................55 J7
Lye Dudley..................................97 L6
Lye Cross N Som........................44 F6
Lye Green Bucks........................68 B6
Lye Green E Susx........................38 C6
Lye Green Warwks......................82 E2
Lye Head Worcs..........................97 G8
Lye's Green Wilts......................32 D2
Lyford Oxon................................66 B8
Lymbridge Green Kent..............40 F6
Lyme Regis Dorset......................15 H4
Lyminge Kent..............................40 F7
Lymington Hants........................18 E4
Lyminster W Susx......................21 H6
Lymm Warrtn............................130 D2
Lymm Services Warrtn............130 C3
Lympne Kent................................40 F7
Lympsham Somset......................44 C8
Lympstone Devon........................14 A6
Lynbridge Devon........................28 C1
Lynchat Highld........................241 L3
Lynch Green Norfk..................106 C2
Lyndhurst Hants........................18 D2
Lyndon Rutlnd........................101 K3
Lyndon Green Birm....................98 F6

Lyne Border 199 L5
Lyne Surrey 50 C5
Lyneal Shrops 113 G5
Lyne Down Herefs 63 J1
Lyneham Oxon 65 K3
Lyneham Wilts 46 F3
Lyneholmford Cumb 178 C4
Lynemouth Nthumb 191 K7
Lyne of Skene Abers 245 G2
Lynesack Dur 168 E5
Lyness Ork 275 b6
Lyng Norfk 122 B7
Lyng Somset 30 E5
Lynmouth Devon 28 C1
Lynn Staffs 98 D3
Lynn Wrekin 114 B8
Lynsted Kent 40 B3
Lynstone Cnwll 11 H2
Lynton Devon 28 C1
Lynton Cross Devon 27 K2
Lyon's Gate Dorset 16 C2
Lyonshall Herefs 79 L4
Lytchett Matravers Dorset ...17 J3
Lytchett Minster Dorset 17 J4
Lyth Highld 280 C4
Lytham Lancs 138 D2
Lytham St Annes Lancs 138 D2
Lythbank Shrops 95 L2
Lythe N York 171 K8
Lythmore Highld 279 J3

M

Maaruig W Isls 282 e5
Mabe Burnthouse Cnwll 3 J4
Mablethorpe Lincs 137 J3
Macclesfield Ches E 131 H5
Macduff Abers 268 C3
Macharioch Ag & B 192 E6
Machen Caerph 43 K4
Machrie N Ayrs 194 D4
Machrihanish Ag & B 192 D4
Machrins Ag & B 214 D5
Machroes Gwynd 108 E6
Machynlleth Powys 93 G3
Machynys Carmth 56 F5
Mackworth Derbys 116 A4
Macmerry E Loth 211 M4
Maddaford Devon 12 D4
Madderty P & K 221 G3
Maddington Wilts 33 J2
Maddiston Falk 210 B4
Madehurst W Susx 21 G5
Madeley Staffs 114 B3
Madeley Wrekin 96 F3
Madeley Heath Staffs 114 B2
Madeley Park Wood Staffs ...114 B3
Madford Devon 29 L8
Madingley Cambs 87 H3
Madley Herefs 80 A7
Madresfield Worcs 81 J5
Madron Cnwll 2 C5
Maenaddwyn IoA 125 H4
Maenan Conwy 126 F6
Maenclochog Pembks 75 J6
Maendy V Glam 42 F6
Maenporth Cnwll 3 K5
Maentwrog Gwynd 110 E3
Maen-y-groes Cerdgn 76 C3
Maer Cnwll 11 H1
Maer Staffs 114 B4
Maerdy Carmth 59 J3
Maerdy Conwy 111 K3
Maerdy Rhondd 42 E2
Maesbrook Shrops 112 D7
Maesbury Shrops 112 D6
Maesbury Marsh Shrops 112 D6
Maes-glas Newpt 44 C2
Maesgwynne Carmth 55 L2
Maeshafn Denbgs 128 E7
Maesllyn Cerdgn 76 C6
Maesmynis Powys 78 D6
Maesmynis Powys 78 E5
Maesteg Brdgnd 42 C3
Maesybont Carmth 59 G5
Maesycwmmer Caerph 43 J3
Magdalen Laver Essex 70 D5
Maggieknockater Moray 254 F3
Maggots End Essex 70 C2
Magham Down E Susx 23 K5
Maghull Sefton 138 D7
Magna Park Leics 100 B6
Magor Mons 44 E2
Magor Services Mons 44 E1
Maidenbower W Susx 37 L4
Maiden Bradley Wilts 32 D3
Maidencombe Torbay 8 D1
Maidenhayne Devon 15 G3

Maiden Head N Som 45 H5
Maidenhead W & M 49 L3
Maiden Law Dur 168 F1
Maiden Newton Dorset 16 B3
Maidens S Ayrs 182 F1
Maiden's Green Br For 49 L4
Maidenwell Lincs 136 F4
Maiden Wells Pembks 55 G7
Maidford Nhants 84 B5
Maids Moreton Bucks 84 D8
Maidstone Kent 39 J2
Maidstone Services Kent 39 K2
Maidwell Nhants 101 G8
Mail Shet 281 e6
Maindee Newpt 44 C1
Mainland Ork 275 c4
Mainland Shet 281 d6
Mainsforth Dur 169 J4
Mains of Balhall Angus 234 D3
Mains of Balnakettle Abers ...244 E8
Mains of Dalvey Highld 254 B5
Mains of Haulkerton Abers ...235 H1
Mains of Lesmoir Abers 255 J6
Mains of Melgunds Angus ...234 E4
Mainsriddle D & G 176 B7
Mainstone Shrops 95 G6
Maisemore Gloucs 64 A3
Major's Green Worcs 98 E7
Makeney Derbys 116 B3
Malborough Devon 7 K7
Malcoff Derbys 131 L3
Malden Rushett Gt Lon 50 F6
Maldon Essex 71 K5
Malham N York 148 F3
Maligar Highld 259 H4
Mallaig Highld 237 K1
Mallaigvaig Highld 237 K1
Malleny Mills C Edin 211 G6
Mallows Green Essex 70 C2
Mallwyd Gwynd 93 J1
Malmesbury Wilts 46 D2
Malmsmead Devon 28 D1
Malpas Ches W 113 H2
Malpas Cnwll 4 D5
Malpas Newpt 44 C1
Malshanger Hants 48 E8
Malswick Gloucs 63 L2
Maltby Lincs 136 F3
Maltby Rothm 133 K1
Maltby S on T 170 B7
Maltby le Marsh Lincs 137 J3
Malting Green Essex 72 E3
Maltman's Hill Kent 40 A6
Malton N York 152 B2
Malvern Worcs 81 H6
Malvern Hills Worcs 81 H6
Malvern Link Worcs 81 H5
Malvern Wells Worcs 81 H6
Mamble Worcs 80 F1
Mamhilad Mons 62 C6
Manaccan Cnwll 3 J6
Manafon Powys 94 D3
Mànais W Isls 282 e6
Manaton Devon 13 H6
Manby Lincs 137 G2
Mancetter Warwks 99 J4
Manchester Manch 140 C8
Manchester Airport Manch ...130 F3
Mancot Flints 129 H6
Mandally Highld 240 A3
Manea Cambs 103 K5
Maney Birm 98 E4
Manfield N York 169 G8
Mangersta W Isls 282 d3
Mangerton Dorset 15 L3
Mangotsfield S Glos 45 K4
Mangrove Green Herts 68 E2
Mangurstadh W Isls 282 d3
Manhay Cnwll 3 H5
Manish W Isls 282 e6
Mankinholes Calder 140 E3
Manley Ches W 129 L5
Manmoel Caerph 61 J6
Mannal Ag & B 224 C7
Manningford Bohune Wilts ...47 H7
Manningford Bruce Wilts 47 H7
Manningham C Brad 141 J1
Mannings Heath W Susx 37 K5
Mannington Dorset 17 L2
Manningtree Essex 73 G1
Mannofield C Aber 245 K3
Manorbier Pembks 55 H7
Manorbier Newton Pembks ...55 H6
Manordeilo Carmth 59 J4
Manorhill Border 201 L6
Manorowen Pembks 74 F5
Manor Park Gt Lon 51 L2
Mansell Gamage Herefs 79 M6
Mansell Lacy Herefs 80 A6

Mansergh Cumb 157 K6
Mansfield E Ayrs 197 J8
Mansfield Notts 133 K7
Mansfield Woodhouse Notts ...133 K7
Mansriggs Cumb 156 D6
Manston Dorset 32 D7
Manston Kent 41 K2
Manston Leeds 142 B1
Manswood Dorset 17 J1
Manthorpe Lincs 118 B4
Manthorpe Lincs 118 E8
Manton N Linc 144 A7
Manton Notts 134 C4
Manton Rutlnd 101 J3
Manton Wilts 47 H5
Manuden Essex 70 C2
Manwood Green Essex 70 E4
Maperton Somset 31 L5
Maplebeck Notts 134 E7
Maple Cross Herts 68 C8
Mapledurham Oxon 49 G4
Mapledurwell Hants 49 G8
Maplehurst W Susx 37 J6
Maplescombe Kent 52 C6
Mapleton Derbys 115 K2
Mapleton Kent 38 C3
Mapperley Derbys 116 D3
Mapperley Park C Nott 117 G3
Mapperton Dorset 15 L3
Mappleborough Green Warwks ...82 C2
Mappleton E R Yk 153 K7
Mapplewell Barns 141 M5
Mappowder Dorset 16 E2
Màraig W Isls 282 e5
Marazanvose Cnwll 4 C5
Marazion Cnwll 2 E5
Marbhig W Isls 282 g4
Marbury Ches E 113 J2
March Cambs 103 J4
March S Lans 186 E3
Marcham Oxon 66 C7
Marchamley Shrops 113 K5
Marchamley Wood Shrops ...113 K5
Marchington Staffs 115 J5
Marchington Woodlands
  Staffs 115 J6
Marchwiel Wrexhm 112 E2
Marchwood Hants 18 F2
Marcross V Glam 42 D7
Marden Herefs 80 C6
Marden Kent 39 J4
Marden Wilts 47 G7
Marden Ash Essex 70 E6
Marden Beech Kent 39 J5
Marden's Hill E Susx 38 D7
Marden Thorn Kent 39 J5
Mardlebury Herts 69 H3
Mardy Mons 62 C4
Marefield Leics 101 G2
Mareham le Fen Lincs 136 E7
Mareham on the Hill Lincs ...136 E6
Marehay Derbys 116 C2
Marehill W Susx 21 H3
Maresfield E Susx 23 G2
Marfleet C KuH 144 E2
Marford Wrexhm 129 H8
Margam Neath 57 L7
Margaret Marsh Dorset 32 D7
Margaret Roding Essex 70 F5
Margaretting Essex 71 G6
Margaretting Tye Essex 71 G7
Margate Kent 41 K1
Margnaheglish N Ayrs 195 G4
Margrie D & G 174 F5
Margrove Park R & Cl 170 F7
Marham Norfk 104 E2
Marhamchurch Cnwll 11 J3
Marham Park Suffk 89 G2
Marholm C Pete 102 C3
Marian-glas IoA 125 J3
Mariansleigh Devon 28 C6
Marine Town Kent 53 K4
Marionburgh Abers 244 F2
Marishader Highld 259 H4
Maristow Devon 6 F2
Marjoriebanks D & G 176 E2
Mark Somset 30 F1
Markbeech Kent 38 D5
Markby Lincs 137 J4
Mark Causeway Somset 30 E2
Mark Cross E Susx 38 F7
Markeaton C Derb 116 B4
Market Bosworth Leics 99 L3
Market Deeping Lincs 102 C2
Market Drayton Shrops 113 L5
Market Harborough Leics 100 F6
Market Lavington Wilts 46 E8
Market Overton Rutlnd 118 A8
Market Rasen Lincs 136 B2
Market Stainton Lincs 136 D4

Market Warsop Notts 133 L6
Market Weighton E R Yk 152 D7
Market Weston Suffk 105 K7
Markfield Leics 100 B2
Markham Caerph 61 J6
Markham Moor Notts 134 E5
Markinch Fife 222 E6
Markington N York 150 C3
Markle E Loth 212 C3
Marksbury BaNES 45 K4
Mark's Corner IoW 19 H5
Marks Tey Essex 72 C2
Markwell Cnwll 6 D3
Markyate Herts 68 D4
Marlborough Wilts 47 J5
Marlbrook Herefs 80 C4
Marlbrook Worcs 98 B8
Marlcliff Warwks 82 C5
Marldon Devon 8 C2
Marle Green E Susx 23 K4
Marlesford Suffk 91 H3
Marley Kent 41 G5
Marley Kent 41 K4
Marley Green Ches E 113 J2
Marley Hill Gatesd 180 F7
Marlingford Norfk 106 C2
Marloes Pembks 54 C5
Marlow Bucks 49 K2
Marlow Herefs 95 K8
Marlow Bottom Bucks 49 K1
Marlpit Hill Kent 38 C4
Marlpits E Susx 24 C4
Marlpits E Susx 38 C7
Marlpool Derbys 116 D3
Marnhull Dorset 32 C7
Marple Stockp 131 J2
Marple Bridge Stockp 131 J2
Marr Donc 142 E6
Marrick N York 159 K3
Marros Carmth 55 L5
Marsden Kirk 141 G5
Marsden S Tyne 181 K6
Marsden Height Lancs 148 F8
Marsett N York 158 F5
Marsh Bucks 67 K5
Marsh C Brad 149 J8
Marsh Devon 30 C8
Marshall's Heath Herts 68 F4
Marshalswick Herts 68 F5
Marsham Norfk 122 D6
Marsh Baldon Oxon 66 E7
Marsh Benham W Berk 48 B5
Marshborough Kent 41 K4
Marshbrook Shrops 95 K5
Marshchapel Lincs 145 K7
Marsh Farm Luton 68 D2
Marshfield Newpt 43 L5
Marshfield S Glos 45 M4
Marshgate Cnwll 11 G4
Marsh Gibbon Bucks 66 F3
Marsh Green Devon 14 B4
Marsh Green Kent 38 C4
Marsh Green Wrekin 113 K8
Marshland St James Norfk ...103 L2
Marsh Lane Derbys 133 H4
Marsh Lane Gloucs 63 H5
Marshside Sefton 138 D4
Marsh Street Somset 29 H2
Marshwood Dorset 15 J3
Marske N York 159 K3
Marske-by-the-Sea R & Cl ...170 E6
Marsland Green Wigan 139 K7
Marston Ches W 130 D5
Marston Herefs 79 L4
Marston Lincs 118 A3
Marston Oxon 66 D5
Marston Staffs 97 J1
Marston Staffs 114 E6
Marston Warwks 99 G4
Marston Wilts 46 D7
Marston Green Solhll 98 F6
Marston Jabbet Warwks 99 K5
Marston Magna Somset 31 K6
Marston Meysey Wilts 65 H2
Marston Montgomery Derbys ...115 J4
Marston Moretaine C Beds 85 K7
Marston on Dove Derbys 115 L5
Marston St Lawrence Nhants ...84 A7
Marston Stannett Herefs 80 D4
Marston Trussell Nhants 100 F6
Marstow Herefs 63 H3
Marsworth Bucks 68 A4
Marten Wilts 47 L5
Marthall Ches E 130 F4
Martham Norfk 123 J7
Martin Hants 33 J7
Martin Kent 41 K6
Martin Lincs 136 B7
Martin Lincs 136 D6
Martindale Cumb 166 B6

Martin Dales Lincs......................136 C7
Martin Drove End Hants..............33 H6
Martinhoe Devon..........................28 B1
Martin Hussingtree Worcs..........81 K3
Martinscroft Warrtn...................130 C2
Martinstown Dorset......................16 C5
Martlesham Suffk..........................90 F6
Martlesham Heath Suffk.............90 F6
Martletwy Pembks..........................55 H5
Martley Worcs.................................81 H3
Martock Somset.............................31 G7
Marton Ches E.............................131 G6
Marton Ches W............................130 C6
Marton Cumb................................156 C7
Marton E R Yk.............................153 J7
Marton E R Yk.............................153 K2
Marton Lincs................................135 G3
Marton Middsb.............................170 C7
Marton N York.............................162 C6
Marton Shrops................................95 G3
Marton Warwks...............................83 J2
Marton-cum-Grafton N York......150 F3
Marton-le-Moor N York..............150 E2
Martyr's Green Surrey..................50 E7
Martyr Worthy Hants....................35 G4
Marvig W Isls..............................282 g4
Marwick Ork.................................275 b3
Marwood Devon..............................27 K3
Marybank Highld..........................250 E1
Maryburgh Highld.........................262 F8
Marygold Border...........................213 H7
Maryhill C Glas............................208 F5
Marykirk Abers.............................235 K2
Maryland Mons................................63 G6
Marylebone Gt Lon..........................51 H3
Marylebone Wigan........................139 H6
Marypark Moray............................254 D4
Maryport Cumb.............................164 D3
Maryport D & G............................172 E7
Marystow Devon..............................12 B6
Mary Tavy Devon.............................12 C6
Maryton Angus..............................234 B5
Maryton Angus..............................235 H4
Marywell Abers............................244 D4
Marywell Abers............................245 L4
Marywell Angus............................235 G6
Masham N York.............................160 B6
Mashbury Essex...............................71 G5
Masongill N York..........................157 K7
Mastin Moor Derbys.....................133 J4
Matching Essex................................70 D5
Matching Green Essex....................70 D5
Matching Tye Essex.........................70 D5
Matfen Nthumb.............................180 C4
Matfield Kent..................................39 G5
Mathern Mons.................................45 G1
Mathon Herefs.................................81 G6
Mathry Pembks................................74 E6
Matlask Norfk...............................122 C4
Matlock Derbys.............................132 F7
Matlock Bank Derbys...................132 F7
Matlock Bath Derbys....................132 F8
Matlock Dale Derbys....................132 F7
Matson Gloucs.................................64 B4
Matterdale End Cumb...................165 L6
Mattersey Notts............................134 D2
Mattersey Thorpe Notts...............134 D2
Mattingley Hants............................49 H7
Mattishall Norfk...........................105 L1
Mattishall Burgh Norfk...............105 L1
Mauchline E Ayrs..........................196 F5
Maud Abers...................................269 G6
Maufant Jersey..................................9 e2
Maugersbury Gloucs........................65 J2
Maughold IoM...............................154 g4
Mauld Highld................................250 C4
Maulden C Beds...............................85 L7
Maulds Meaburn Cumb.................166 E7
Maunby N York.............................160 E5
Maund Bryan Herefs.......................80 D5
Maundown Somset...........................29 J5
Mautby Norfk................................107 K1
Mavesyn Ridware Staffs...............115 H8
Mavis Enderby Lincs.....................137 G6
Mawbray Cumb..............................164 E1
Mawdesley Lancs...........................139 G5
Mawdlam Brdgnd.............................42 B5
Mawgan Cnwll...................................3 J6
Mawgan Porth Cnwll........................4 D2
Maw Green Ches E........................130 D8
Mawla Cnwll......................................4 A5
Mawnan Cnwll....................................3 K5
Mawnan Smith Cnwll........................3 K5
Mawsley Nhants.............................101 H8
Mawthorpe Lincs...........................137 J5
Maxey C Pete................................102 C2
Maxstoke Warwks............................99 G6
Maxted Street Kent.........................40 F6
Maxton Border...............................201 J7
Maxton Kent.....................................41 J7

Maxwelltown D & G.....................176 C4
Maxworthy Cnwll.............................11 J4
Mayals Swans...................................57 H6
May Bank Staffs............................114 D2
Maybole S Ayrs.............................183 H1
Maybury Surrey...............................50 C7
Mayes Green Surrey.........................37 H3
Mayfield E Susx...............................23 K2
Mayfield Mdloth.............................211 K6
Mayfield Staffs..............................115 J2
Mayford Surrey................................50 C7
May Hill Gloucs................................63 L3
Mayland Essex..................................72 D6
Maylandsea Essex............................72 C6
Maynard's Green E Susx.................23 K3
Maypole Birm...................................98 D7
Maypole Kent...................................41 G2
Maypole Mons..................................62 F4
Maypole Green Norfk....................107 J4
Maypole Green Suffk.......................89 J3
Maypole Green Suffk.......................91 J2
May's Green Oxon............................49 H3
May's Green Surrey.........................50 E7
Mead Devon.....................................26 C7
Meadgate BaNES.............................45 K7
Meadle Bucks...................................67 K6
Meadowfield Dur...........................169 H3
Meadowtown Shrops........................95 H3
Meadwell Devon...............................12 A6
Meaford Staffs...............................114 D4
Mealabost W Isls..........................282 g3
Meal Bank Cumb............................157 H4
Mealrigg Cumb..............................164 F2
Mealsgate Cumb.............................165 H2
Meanwood Leeds...........................150 C8
Mearbeck N York..........................148 E4
Meare Somset...................................31 G3
Meare Green Somset........................30 D6
Meare Green Somset........................30 E5
Mearns E Rens...............................208 F7
Mears Ashby Nhants........................85 G2
Measham Leics.................................99 J1
Meath Green Surrey.........................37 L2
Meathop Cumb...............................156 F6
Meaux E R Yk................................153 H7
Meavaig W Isls.............................282 e3
Meavy Devon.....................................7 G2
Medbourne Leics...........................101 H5
Medburn Nthumb..........................180 D5
Meddon Devon..................................26 D7
Meden Vale Notts..........................134 B5
Medlam Lincs................................136 F8
Medlar Lancs.................................147 H8
Medmenham Bucks..........................49 K2
Medomsley Dur..............................180 D7
Medstead Hants...............................35 K3
Medway Services Medway............53 H6
Meerbrook Staffs...........................131 K7
Meer Common Herefs.......................79 L5
Meesden Herts.................................70 B1
Meeson Wrekin..............................113 L7
Meeth Devon....................................12 D1
Meeting Green Suffk........................88 E4
Meeting House Hill Norfk............122 F6
Meidrim Carmth...............................58 B5
Meifod Powys...................................94 E1
Meigle P & K.................................233 L6
Meikle Carco D & G.....................186 A3
Meikle Earnock S Lans.................209 J8
Meikle Ferry Highld......................263 K2
Meikle Kilmory Ag & B................207 G6
Meikle Obney P & K......................232 F7
Meikleour P & K...........................233 J7
Meikle Wartle Abers.....................256 C5
Meinciau Carmth.............................56 E3
Meir C Stke...................................114 E3
Meir Heath Staffs..........................114 E3
Melbost W Isls..............................282 g3
Melbourn Cambs..............................87 H5
Melbourne Derbys.........................116 C6
Melbourne E R Yk.........................152 A7
Melbourne Essex..............................71 G5
Melbur Cnwll......................................4 F4
Melbury Cnwll...................................26 F7
Melbury Abbas Dorset.....................32 E6
Melbury Bubb Dorset.......................16 B2
Melbury Osmond Dorset..................16 A1
Melbury Sampford Dorset...............16 A2
Melchbourne Bed.............................85 K2
Melcombe Bingham Dorset.............16 E2
Meldon Devon...................................12 D4
Meldon Nthumb..............................180 D2
Meldon Park Nthumb.....................180 D2
Meldreth Cambs...............................87 H6
Meldrum Stirlg..............................220 C7
Melfort Ag & B.............................216 C4
Meliden Denbgs..............................128 D3
Melinau Pembks...............................55 L4
Melin-byrhedyn Powys.....................93 H4
Melincourt Neath.............................60 B6

Melin-y-coed Conwy......................127 G7
Melin-y-ddol Powys........................94 D2
Melin-y-wîg Denbgs.......................111 K2
Melkinthorpe Cumb......................166 D5
Melkridge Nthumb........................179 G6
Melksham Wilts...............................46 C6
Mell Green W Berk..........................48 C3
Mellguards Cumb..........................166 C3
Melling Lancs................................147 M2
Melling Sefton...............................138 E7
Melling Mount Sefton...................138 E7
Mellis Suffk..................................106 B8
Mellon Charles Highld..................260 D2
Mellon Udrigle Highld..................260 E1
Mellor Lancs.................................139 K2
Mellor Stockp................................131 K2
Mellor Brook Lancs.......................139 J2
Mells Somset...................................32 B1
Mells Suffk...................................107 H8
Melmerby Cumb.............................166 C3
Melmerby N York..........................159 K5
Melmerby N York..........................160 E7
Melness Highld..............................277 K4
Melon Green Suffk...........................89 G4
Melplash Dorset...............................15 L3
Melrose Border..............................201 H6
Melsetter Ork................................275 b6
Melsonby N York...........................160 B1
Meltham Kirk.................................141 H5
Meltham Mills Kirk........................141 H5
Melton E R Yk...............................144 B2
Melton Suffk....................................91 G5
Meltonby E R Yk...........................152 B5
Melton Constable Norfk...............122 A5
Melton Mowbray Leics..................117 K7
Melton Ross N Linc.......................144 D5
Melvaig Highld..............................260 B3
Melverley Shrops...........................112 E8
Melverley Green Shrops................112 E7
Melvich Highld..............................278 E3
Membury Devon................................15 G2
Membury Services W Berk.............47 L4
Memsie Abers................................269 H4
Memus Angus.................................234 C4
Menabilly Cnwll.................................5 J4
Menagissey Cnwll..............................4 B5
Menai Bridge IoA...........................125 K5
Mendham Suffk.............................106 F6
Mendip Hills....................................45 G8
Mendlesham Suffk...........................90 D2
Mendlesham Green Suffk................90 C3
Menheniot Cnwll................................6 B2
Menithwood Worcs..........................81 G2
Menna Cnwll......................................4 E4
Mennock D & G.............................185 K2
Menston C Brad.............................149 L7
Menstrie Clacks.............................220 E7
Menthorpe N York.........................143 H1
Mentmore Bucks..............................67 M3
Meoble Highld................................238 C6
Meole Brace Shrops.........................96 B1
Meonstoke Hants.............................35 J7
Meon Vale Warwks...........................82 E6
Meopham Kent.................................52 D5
Meopham Green Kent......................52 D6
Meopham Station Kent...................52 D5
Mepal Cambs.................................103 J7
Meppershall C Beds.........................86 C8
Merbach Herefs................................79 K6
Mere Ches E..................................130 E3
Mere Wilts..32 D4
Mere Brow Lancs...........................138 E4
Mereclough Lancs.........................140 C2
Mere Green Birm.............................98 E4
Mere Green Worcs...........................81 J3
Mere Heath Ches W.......................130 C5
Meresborough Medway...................53 H6
Mereworth Kent...............................39 G3
Meriden Solhll..................................99 G7
Merkadale Highld..........................246 E2
Merley BCP.......................................17 K3
Merlin's Bridge Pembks...................54 F4
Merrington Shrops.........................113 G7
Merrion Pembks................................54 F7
Merriott Somset...............................31 G8
Merrivale Devon...............................12 D7
Merrow Surrey..................................36 F1
Merry Field Hill Dorset...................17 K2
Merry Hill Herts...............................68 E8
Merryhill Wolves..............................97 K4
Merry Lees Leics............................100 A2
Merrymeet Cnwll...............................6 B2
Mersea Island Essex.........................72 F4
Mersey Gateway Bridge
   Halton......................................129 M3
Mersham Kent..................................40 D7
Merstham Surrey..............................51 H8
Merston W Susx...............................20 E6
Merstone IoW...................................19 J6

Merther Cnwll.....................................4 D6
Merthyr Carmth................................58 C5
Merthyr Cynog Powys.....................78 D7
Merthyr Dyfan V Glam.....................43 H7
Merthyr Mawr Brdgnd.....................42 D4
Merthyr Tydfil Myr Td....................61 G6
Merthyr Vale Myr Td.......................61 G7
Merton Devon...................................27 J8
Merton Gt Lon..................................51 H5
Merton Norfk................................105 H4
Merton Oxon....................................66 E3
Meshaw Devon..................................28 D7
Messing Essex...................................72 C3
Messingham N Linc.......................143 M6
Metal Bridge Dur...........................169 J4
Metfield Suffk...............................106 F7
Metherell Cnwll..................................6 E1
Metheringham Lincs.....................135 L7
Methil Fife.....................................222 F7
Methilhill Fife...............................222 F7
Methley Leeds...............................142 B2
Methley Junction Leeds................142 B3
Methlick Abers..............................256 F4
Methven P & K..............................221 J2
Methwold Norfk............................104 E4
Methwold Hythe Norfk.................104 E4
Mettingham Suffk.........................107 H5
Metton Norfk................................122 D4
Mevagissey Cnwll...............................5 G6
Mexborough Donc.........................142 D7
Mey Highld....................................280 C2
Meysey Hampton Gloucs................65 G7
Miabhaig W Isls............................282 e3
Michaelchurch Herefs......................63 G2
Michaelchurch Escley Herefs.........79 K8
Michaelchurch-on-Arrow
   Powys..79 J5
Michaelstone-y-Fedw Newpt........43 K5
Michaelston-le-Pit V Glam...........43 J7
Michaelstow Cnwll..........................10 E7
Michaelwood Services Gloucs......63 L8
Michelcombe Devon...........................7 K1
Micheldever Hants..........................35 G3
Micheldever Station Hants.............35 G2
Michelmersh Hants..........................34 C7
Mickfield Suffk.................................90 D3
Micklebring Donc..........................133 K1
Mickleby N York............................171 J8
Micklefield Leeds...........................142 C1
Micklefield Green Herts..................68 D7
Mickleham Surrey............................50 F8
Mickleover C Derb........................116 A5
Micklethwaite C Brad....................149 K7
Micklethwaite Cumb.....................165 J1
Mickleton Dur................................168 B6
Mickleton Gloucs.............................82 E6
Mickletown Leeds..........................142 B2
Mickle Trafford Ches W................129 K5
Mickley Derbys..............................132 F4
Mickley N York..............................160 C5
Mickley Green Suffk........................89 G4
Mickley Square Nthumb...............180 C6
Mid Ardlaw Abers.........................269 H3
Midbea Ork...................................275 c2
Mid Beltie Abers...........................244 E3
Mid Bockhampton BCP...................18 B4
Mid Calder W Loth.......................210 E5
Mid Clyth Highld..........................280 C8
Mid Culbeuchly Abers...................268 B4
Middle Assendon Oxon...................49 H2
Middle Aston Oxon..........................66 C2
Middle Barton Oxon........................66 B2
Middlebie D & G............................177 H4
Middlebridge P & K.......................232 C2
Middle Chinnock Somset................31 G8
Middle Claydon Bucks....................67 H2
Middlecliffe Barns.........................142 C6
Middlecott Devon.............................13 G5
Middlecroft Derbys........................133 H5
Middle Duntisbourne Gloucs.........64 D6
Middleham N York.........................159 L5
Middle Handley Derbys.................133 H4
Middle Harling Norfk...................105 K6
Middlehill Cnwll.................................6 B1
Middlehill Wilts................................46 B5
Middlehope Shrops...........................96 B5
Middle Kames Ag & B...................206 E1
Middle Littleton Worcs...................82 C6
Middle Madeley Staffs..................114 B3
Middle Maes-coed Herefs..............79 L8
Middlemarsh Dorset........................16 C1
Middle Mayfield Staffs..................115 J3
Middle Mill Pembks.........................74 C7
Middlemoor Devon...........................12 C8
Middle Quarter Kent.......................40 A7
Middle Rasen Lincs.......................136 A2
Middle Rocombe Devon.....................8 D1
Middle Salter Lancs......................147 M3
Middlesbrough Middsb..................170 C6
Middlesceugh Cumb......................165 L2

Middleshaw Cumb......157 J5
Middlesmoor N York......159 K7
Middle Stoford Somset......30 B6
Middle Stoke Medway......53 H4
Middlestone Dur......169 H4
Middlestone Moor Dur......169 H4
Middle Stoughton Somset......30 F1
Middlestown Wakefd......141 L4
Middle Street Gloucs......63 M6
Middle Taphouse Cnwll......5 K2
Middlethird Border......201 L4
Middleton Ag & B......224 B6
Middleton Cumb......157 K5
Middleton Derbys......132 D7
Middleton Derbys......132 E8
Middleton Essex......89 H7
Middleton Hants......34 F2
Middleton Herefs......80 D1
Middleton Lancs......147 H4
Middleton Leeds......141 M2
Middleton N York......149 L6
Middleton N York......162 D5
Middleton Nhants......101 J5
Middleton Norfk......120 E8
Middleton Nthumb......180 C2
Middleton Nthumb......203 H6
Middleton P & K......221 L6
Middleton Rochdl......140 C6
Middleton Shrops......96 C7
Middleton Shrops......112 D5
Middleton Suffk......91 K2
Middleton Swans......56 D7
Middleton Warwks......98 F4
Middleton Cheney Nhants......83 L7
Middleton Green Staffs......114 F4
Middleton Hall Nthumb......202 F8
Middleton-in-Teesdale Dur......168 B5
Middleton Moor Suffk......91 J2
Middleton One Row Darltn......169 K8
Middleton-on-Leven N York......161 G1
Middleton-on-Sea W Susx......20 F6
Middleton on the Hill Herefs......80 C2
Middleton on the Wolds
    E R Yk......152 E6
Middleton Park C Aber......245 K1
Middleton Priors Shrops......96 E5
Middleton Quernhow N York......160 E7
Middleton St George Darltn......169 K8
Middleton Scriven Shrops......96 F6
Middleton Stoney Oxon......66 D2
Middleton Tyas N York......160 B2
Middletown Cumb......155 H1
Middle Town IoS......10 b3
Middletown N Som......44 F4
Middletown Powys......95 H1
Middle Tysoe Warwks......83 H6
Middle Wallop Hants......34 C3
Middlewich Ches E......130 D6
Middle Winterslow Wilts......34 B4
Middlewood Cnwll......11 K7
Middlewood Herefs......79 K6
Middle Woodford Wilts......33 K4
Middlewood Green Suffk......90 C3
Middle Yard Gloucs......64 B6
Middlezoy Somset......30 E4
Middridge Dur......169 H5
Midford BaNES......45 M6
Midge Hall Lancs......139 G3
Midgeholme Cumb......178 E7
Midgham W Berk......48 E5
Midgley Calder......140 F3
Midgley Wakefd......141 L5
Mid Holmwood Surrey......37 J2
Midhopestones Sheff......141 K7
Midhurst W Susx......36 C6
Mid Lavant W Susx......20 D5
Midlem Border......201 H7
Mid Mains Highld......250 D4
Midney Somset......31 H5
Midpark Ag & B......207 G7
Midsomer Norton BaNES......45 K8
Midtown Highld......277 K4
Midville Lincs......137 G8
Midway Ches E......131 H3
Mid Yell Shet......281 e3
Migdale Highld......263 H2
Migvie Abers......244 A2
Milborne Port Somset......31 L7
Milborne St Andrew Dorset......16 F3
Milborne Wick Somset......31 L6
Milbourne Nthumb......180 D4
Milbourne Wilts......46 D2
Milburn Cumb......166 F5
Milbury Heath S Glos......45 K1
Milby N York......150 F2
Milcombe Oxon......83 K8
Milden Suffk......89 J6
Mildenhall Suffk......104 E8
Mildenhall Wilts......47 J5
Milebrook Powys......79 K1

Milebush Kent......39 J4
Mile Elm Wilts......46 E5
Mile End Gloucs......63 H5
Mile End Suffk......107 G5
Mileham Norfk......121 K7
Mile Oak Br & H......22 C5
Mile Oak Kent......39 H4
Mile Oak Staffs......98 F3
Miles Green Staffs......114 C2
Miles Hope Herefs......80 D2
Milesmark Fife......210 E1
Miles Platting Manch......140 C7
Mile Town Kent......53 K4
Milfield Nthumb......202 E6
Milford Derbys......116 B3
Milford Devon......26 D6
Milford Powys......94 D5
Milford Staffs......114 F7
Milford Surrey......36 E2
Milford Haven Pembks......54 E5
Milford on Sea Hants......18 D5
Milkwall Gloucs......63 H5
Millais Jersey......9 a1
Milland W Susx......36 B5
Milland Marsh W Susx......36 C5
Mill Bank Calder......140 F3
Millbeck Cumb......165 H5
Millbreck Abers......257 J3
Millbridge Surrey......36 C2
Millbrook C Beds......85 K7
Millbrook C Sotn......34 E8
Millbrook Cnwll......6 E4
Millbrook Jersey......9 c3
Millbrook Tamesd......140 E7
Mill Brow Stockp......131 J2
Millbuie Abers......245 H2
Millbuie Highld......250 F1
Millcombe Devon......8 B5
Mill Common Norfk......107 G3
Mill Common Suffk......107 H7
Millcorner E Susx......24 E3
Millcraig Highld......263 H5
Mill Cross Devon......7 L3
Milldale Staffs......115 J1
Mill End Bucks......49 J2
Millend Gloucs......63 L7
Mill End Herts......87 G8
Millerhill Mdloth......211 K5
Miller's Dale Derbys......132 C5
Millers Green Derbys......115 M1
Miller's Green Essex......70 E5
Millerston C Glas......209 H5
Millgate Lancs......140 D4
Mill Green Cambs......88 C6
Mill Green Essex......70 F6
Mill Green Herts......69 G5
Mill Green Lincs......119 H6
Mill Green Norfk......106 C6
Millgreen Shrops......113 L6
Mill Green Staffs......98 D3
Mill Green Staffs......115 H7
Mill Green Suffk......89 J6
Mill Green Suffk......89 K4
Mill Green Suffk......90 D3
Mill Green Suffk......91 H3
Millhalf Herefs......79 K5
Millhayes Devon......14 F2
Millhead Lancs......147 K2
Millheugh S Lans......198 B3
Mill Hill E Susx......23 L6
Mill Hill Gt Lon......69 G8
Millhouse Ag & B......206 F5
Millhouse Cumb......165 K3
Millhousebridge D & G......176 F2
Millhouse Green Barns......141 K7
Millhouses Barns......142 C6
Millhouses Sheff......133 G3
Milliken Park Rens......208 C6
Millin Cross Pembks......55 G4
Millington E R Yk......152 C5
Mill Lane Hants......36 A1
Millmeece Staffs......114 C5
Millness Cumb......157 H6
Mill of Drummond P & K......220 E4
Mill of Haldane W Duns......208 C3
Millom Cumb......155 M6
Millook Cnwll......11 H3
Millpool Cnwll......2 F5
Millpool Cnwll......11 G8
Millport N Ayrs......207 K8
Mill Side Cumb......157 G6
Mill Street Kent......39 H2
Mill Street Norfk......122 B7
Mill Street Suffk......90 C1
Millthorpe Derbys......132 F4
Millthrop Cumb......157 L4
Milltimber C Aber......245 J3
Milltown Abers......243 J2
Milltown Abers......255 J8
Milltown Cnwll......5 J3

Milltown D & G......177 K4
Milltown Derbys......133 G7
Milltown Devon......27 K3
Milltown Highld......248 A3
Milltown of Auchindoun
    Moray......255 G4
Milltown of Campfield Abers......244 E3
Milltown of Edinvillie Moray......254 F4
Milltown of Rothiemay
    Moray......267 L6
Milnathort P & K......221 K6
Milngavie E Duns......208 F4
Milnrow Rochdl......140 D5
Milnthorpe Cumb......157 H6
Milnthorpe Wakefd......142 A4
Milovaig Highld......258 B6
Milson Shrops......80 E1
Milstead Kent......40 A3
Milston Wilts......33 L2
Milthorpe Lincs......118 F5
Milthorpe Nhants......84 B6
Milton C Stke......114 E2
Milton Cambs......87 K3
Milton Cumb......178 D6
Milton D & G......172 F4
Milton D & G......175 L1
Milton Derbys......116 A6
Milton Highld......250 E5
Milton Highld......251 G2
Milton Highld......263 K5
Milton Highld......280 D6
Milton Inver......208 B5
Milton Kent......52 E4
Milton Moray......254 D7
Milton Moray......267 K4
Milton N Som......44 D6
Milton Newpt......44 B1
Milton Notts......134 E5
Milton Oxon......66 C8
Milton Oxon......83 K8
Milton P & K......233 G3
Milton Pembks......55 H6
Milton Somset......31 G6
Milton Stirlg......219 H7
Milton W Duns......208 D4
Milton Abbas Dorset......16 F2
Milton Abbot Devon......12 A6
Milton Bridge Mdloth......211 H6
Milton Bryan C Beds......68 B1
Milton Clevedon Somset......31 L3
Milton Combe Devon......6 F2
Milton Common Oxon......67 G6
Milton Damerel Devon......27 G8
Milton End Gloucs......63 L5
Milton End Gloucs......65 H7
Milton Ernest Bed......85 K4
Milton Green Ches W......129 K7
Milton Hill Oxon......48 C1
Milton Keynes M Keyn......85 G7
Milton Lilbourne Wilts......47 J7
Milton Malsor Nhants......84 E4
Milton Morenish P & K......231 H8
Milton of Auchinhove Abers......244 C3
Milton of Balgonie Fife......222 E7
Milton of Buchanan Stirlg......208 D1
Milton of Campsie E Duns......209 H4
Milton of Finavon Angus......234 D4
Milton of Leys Highld......251 J3
Milton of Murtle C Aber......245 J3
Milton on Stour Dorset......32 D5
Milton Regis Kent......40 A2
Milton Street E Susx......23 J6
Milton-under-Wychwood
    Oxon......65 K3
Milverton Somset......29 L5
Milverton Warwks......83 H2
Milwich Staffs......114 F5
Milwr Flints......128 E5
Minard Ag & B......216 F7
Minchington Dorset......33 G2
Minchinhampton Gloucs......64 C7
Mindenhurst Surrey......49 M7
Mindrum Nthumb......202 C6
Minehead Somset......29 H2
Minera Wrexhm......112 C1
Minety Wilts......46 F1
Minffordd Gwynd......109 L4
Mingarrypark Highld......237 J5
Miningsby Lincs......136 F6
Minions Cnwll......11 J8
Minishant S Ayrs......196 C8
Minllyn Gwynd......111 J6
Minnigaff D & G......173 K2
Minnonie Abers......268 D4
Minshull Vernon Ches E......130 D7
Minskip N York......150 E3
Minstead Hants......18 D2
Minsted W Susx......20 D3
Minster Kent......41 J2
Minsterley Shrops......95 J2

Minster Lovell Oxon......65 L5
Minster-on-Sea Kent......53 L4
Minsterworth Gloucs......64 A4
Minterne Magna Dorset......16 C2
Minterne Parva Dorset......16 C2
Minting Lincs......136 C5
Mintlaw Abers......269 J6
Minto Border......188 F2
Minton Shrops......95 K5
Minwear Pembks......55 H4
Minworth Birm......98 F5
Mirehouse Cumb......164 C7
Mireland Highld......280 D4
Mirfield Kirk......141 K4
Miserden Gloucs......64 D5
Miskin Rhondd......43 G2
Miskin Rhondd......43 G5
Misson Notts......134 D1
Misterton Leics......100 C6
Misterton Notts......134 F1
Misterton Somset......15 K1
Mistley Essex......73 G1
Mistley Heath Essex......73 H1
Mitcham Gt Lon......51 H5
Mitcheldean Gloucs......63 K3
Mitchell Cnwll......4 D4
Mitchellslacks D & G......186 E7
Mitchel Troy Mons......62 F5
Mitford Nthumb......180 D2
Mithian Cnwll......4 B5
Mitton Staffs......114 D8
Mixbury Oxon......84 B8
Mixenden Calder......141 G2
Moats Tye Suffk......90 B4
Mobberley Ches E......130 F4
Mobberley Staffs......115 G3
Moccas Herefs......79 L6
Mochdre Conwy......127 G4
Mochdre Powys......94 C5
Mochrum D & G......173 J5
Mockbeggar Hants......18 B2
Mockbeggar Kent......39 H4
Mockerkin Cumb......164 E6
Modbury Devon......7 J4
Moddershall Staffs......114 E4
Moelfre IoA......125 J2
Moelfre Powys......112 B6
Moel Tryfan Gwynd......125 J8
Moffat D & G......187 G5
Mogador Surrey......51 H8
Moggerhanger C Beds......86 C5
Moira Leics......116 A8
Molash Kent......40 D5
Mol-chlach Highld......246 F6
Mold Flints......128 F7
Moldgreen Kirk......141 J4
Molehill Green Essex......70 E2
Molehill Green Essex......71 H3
Molescroft E R Yk......152 F7
Molesden Nthumb......180 E2
Molesworth Cambs......102 B8
Moll Highld......247 J3
Molland Devon......28 E5
Mollington Ches W......129 J5
Mollington Oxon......83 K5
Mollinsburn N Lans......209 J5
Monachty Cerdgn......76 F3
Mondynes Abers......245 H7
Monewden Suffk......90 F3
Moneydie P & K......221 J1
Moneyrow Green W & M......49 L3
Moniaive D & G......185 J5
Monifieth Angus......223 J1
Monikie Angus......234 D7
Monimail Fife......222 E4
Monington Pembks......75 K3
Monk Bretton Barns......142 B6
Monken Hadley Gt Lon......69 H7
Monk Fryston N York......142 D2
Monkhide Herefs......80 E6
Monkhill Cumb......177 K2
Monkhopton Shrops......96 E5
Monkland Herefs......80 B4
Monkleigh Devon......27 H6
Monknash V Glam......42 D7
Monkokehampton Devon......12 E2
Monkseaton N Tyne......181 J4
Monks Eleigh Suffk......89 K5
Monk's Gate W Susx......37 K5
Monks Heath Ches E......131 G5
Monk Sherborne Hants......48 F7
Monks Horton Kent......29 K3
Monksilver Somset......29 K3
Monks Kirby Warwks......100 A6
Monk Soham Suffk......90 F2
Monkspath Solhll......98 E8
Monks Risborough Bucks......67 K6
Monksthorpe Lincs......137 H6
Monk Street Essex......70 F2
Monkswood Mons......62 D6

Monkton Devon 14 E2
Monkton Kent 41 J2
Monkton S Ayrs 196 D5
Monkton S Tyne 181 H6
Monkton V Glam 42 D7
Monkton Combe BaNES 45 M6
Monkton Deverill Wilts 32 E3
Monkton Farleigh Wilts 46 A6
Monkton Heathfield Somset 30 C5
Monkton Up Wimborne Dorset 33 H8
Monkton Wyld Dorset 15 H3
Monkwearmouth Sundld 181 K7
Monkwood Hants 35 K5
Monmore Green Wolves 97 L4
Monmouth Mons 63 G4
Monnington on Wye Herefs 79 L6
Monreith D & G 173 J6
Montacute Somset 31 H7
Montcliffe Bolton 139 K5
Montford Shrops 112 F8
Montford Bridge Shrops 113 G8
Montgarrie Abers 255 L8
Montgomery Powys 94 F4
Monton Salfd 140 A7
Montrose Angus 235 H4
Mont Saint Guern 9 i3
Monxton Hants 34 C2
Monyash Derbys 132 C6
Monymusk Abers 256 C8
Monzie P & K 220 F2
Moodiesburn N Lans 209 J5
Moonzie Fife 222 F4
Moor Allerton Leeds 150 D8
Moorbath Dorset 15 K4
Moorby Lincs 136 E6
Moorcot Herefs 79 L4
Moor Crichel Dorset 17 K1
Moordown BCP 17 L4
Moore Halton 130 B3
Moor End C Beds 68 B3
Moor End Calder 141 G2
Moor End Devon 12 F1
Moorend Gloucs 63 L6
Moor End Lancs 147 G6
Moor End N York 151 J8
Moorends Donc 143 H4
Moorgreen Hants 35 G7
Moor Green Herts 69 J2
Moorgreen Notts 116 E2
Moorhall Derbys 132 F5
Moorhampton Herefs 79 M6
Moorhead C Brad 149 L8
Moor Head Leeds 141 K2
Moorhouse Cumb 177 H8
Moorhouse Cumb 177 K7
Moorhouse Donc 142 D5
Moorhouse Notts 134 E6
Moorhouse Bank Surrey 51 L8
Moorland Somset 30 E4
Moorlinch Somset 30 F3
Moor Monkton N York 151 H4
Moor Row Cumb 164 D7
Moor Row Cumb 165 H1
Moorsholm R & Cl 170 F7
Moorside Dorset 32 D7
Moorside Dur 168 D1
Moor Side Lancs 138 E1
Moor Side Lancs 147 K8
Moorside Leeds 150 C8
Moor Side Lincs 136 E8
Moorside Oldham 140 E6
Moorstock Kent 40 E7
Moor Street Medway 53 H6
Moorswater Cnwll 5 M2
Moorthorpe Wakefd 142 C5
Moortown Devon 12 C7
Moortown Hants 18 A3
Moortown IoW 19 G7
Moortown Leeds 150 D7
Moortown Lincs 144 D7
Moortown Wrekin 113 K7
Morangie Highld 263 K3
Morar Highld 237 K2
Morborne Cambs 102 C5
Morchard Bishop Devon 13 H1
Morchard Road Devon 13 H2
Morcombelake Dorset 15 J4
Morcott Rutlnd 101 K3
Morda Shrops 112 D6
Morden Dorset 17 H3
Morden Gt Lon 51 H5
Mordiford Herefs 80 D7
Mordon Dur 169 J5
More Shrops 95 H5
Morebath Devon 29 G6
Morebattle Border 189 K1
Morecambe Lancs 147 H3
Moredon Swindn 47 H2
Morefield Highld 261 J1
Morehall Kent 41 G7

Moreleigh Devon 7 L4
Morenish P & K 231 H8
Moresby Parks Cumb 164 C6
Morestead Hants 35 G6
Moreton Dorset 16 F5
Moreton Essex 70 D5
Moreton Herefs 80 C2
Moreton Oxon 67 G6
Moreton Staffs 114 B8
Moreton Staffs 115 J5
Moreton Wirral 129 G2
Moreton Corbet Shrops 113 J6
Moreton Hall Suffk 89 H2
Moretonhampstead Devon 13 H5
Moreton-in-Marsh Gloucs 65 J1
Moreton Jeffries Herefs 80 E5
Moretonmill Shrops 113 J5
Moreton Morrell Warwks 83 H4
Moreton on Lugg Herefs 80 C6
Moreton Paddox Warwks 83 H4
Moreton Pinkney Nhants 84 B3
Moreton Say Shrops 113 K4
Moreton Valence Gloucs 63 M5
Morfa Cerdgn 76 B4
Morfa Bychan Gwynd 109 K4
Morfa Dinlle Gwynd 125 H8
Morfa Glas Neath 60 C6
Morfa Nefyn Gwynd 108 E3
Morganstown Cardif 43 H5
Morgan's Vale Wilts 33 L6
Morham E Loth 212 C5
Moriah Cerdgn 92 D7
Morland Cumb 166 E6
Morley Ches E 130 F3
Morley Derbys 116 C3
Morley Dur 168 E5
Morley Leeds 141 L2
Morley Green Ches E 130 F3
Morley St Botolph Norfk 106 B3
Mornick Cnwll 11 L8
Morningside C Edin 211 H5
Morningside N Lans 209 L7
Morningthorpe Norfk 106 E5
Morpeth Nthumb 180 F2
Morphie Abers 235 H3
Morrey Staffs 115 J7
Morridge Side Staffs 115 G1
Morriston Swans 57 J5
Morston Norfk 121 M3
Mortehoe Devon 27 H2
Morthen Rothm 133 J2
Mortimer W Berk 49 G6
Mortimer Common W Berk 49 G6
Mortimer's Cross Herefs 80 A3
Mortimer West End Hants 48 F6
Mortlake Gt Lon 51 L4
Morton Cumb 166 B3
Morton Cumb 177 L7
Morton Derbys 133 H7
Morton IoW 19 K6
Morton Lincs 118 E6
Morton Lincs 134 F1
Morton Lincs 135 H7
Morton Notts 117 J1
Morton Shrops 112 D6
Morton-on-Swale N York 160 D4
Morton on the Hill Norfk 122 C8
Morton Tinmouth Dur 168 F6
Morvah Cnwll 2 B4
Morval Cnwll 6 B3
Morvich Highld 248 F7
Morville Shrops 96 F4
Morville Heath Shrops 96 F4
Morwenstow Cnwll 26 C7
Mosborough Sheff 133 H3
Moscow E Ayrs 196 F3
Mose Shrops 97 G5
Mosedale Cumb 165 K4
Moseley Birm 98 D6
Moseley Wolves 97 L4
Moseley Worcs 81 J3
Moses Gate Bolton 139 L6
Moss Ag & B 224 B6
Moss Donc 142 F5
Moss Wrexhm 112 D1
Mossat Abers 255 K7
Mossbank Shet 281 e4
Moss Bank St Hel 139 G8
Mossbay Cumb 164 C5
Mossblown S Ayrs 196 D6
Mossbrow Traffd 130 D2
Mossburnford Border 189 H3
Mossdale D & G 175 G1
Mossdale E Ayrs 184 D2
Moss Edge Lancs 147 H7
Moss End Ches E 130 D4
Mossend N Lans 209 K7
Mosser Mains Cumb 164 F5
Mossley Ches E 131 H7
Mossley Tamesd 140 E7

Mosspaul Inn Border 188 C6
Moss Side Cumb 177 G8
Moss-side Highld 253 G1
Moss Side Lancs 138 D2
Moss Side Sefton 138 D7
Mosstodloch Moray 267 G4
Mossyard D & G 174 E4
Mossy Lea Lancs 139 G5
Mosterton Dorset 15 K2
Moston Manch 140 C7
Moston Shrops 113 J6
Moston Green Ches E 130 E7
Mostyn Flints 128 E4
Motcombe Dorset 32 E6
Mothecombe Devon 7 H5
Motherby Cumb 166 A5
Motherwell N Lans 209 K6
Motspur Park Gt Lon 51 G5
Mottingham Gt Lon 51 L4
Mottisfont Hants 34 D5
Mottistone IoW 18 F7
Mottram in Longdendale
Tamesd 140 F8
Mottram St Andrew Ches E 131 G4
Mouilpied Guern 9 j3
Mouldsworth Ches W 129 L5
Moulin P & K 232 D3
Moulsecoomb Br & H 22 E6
Moulsford Oxon 48 E2
Moulsoe M Keyn 85 H7
Moultavie Highld 263 H5
Moulton Ches W 130 C5
Moulton Lincs 119 J6
Moulton N York 160 C2
Moulton Nhants 84 F2
Moulton Suffk 88 D2
Moulton V Glam 43 G7
Moulton Chapel Lincs 119 J7
Moulton St Mary Norfk 107 H2
Moulton Seas End Lincs 119 K6
Mount Cnwll 4 C4
Mount Cnwll 5 K1
Mount Kirk 141 H4
Mountain C Brad 141 G2
Mountain Ash Rhondd 61 G7
Mountain Cross Border 199 K4
Mountain Street Kent 40 E5
Mount Ambrose Cnwll 4 B5
Mount Bures Essex 89 H8
Mountfield E Susx 24 D3
Mountgerald Highld 263 G7
Mount Hawke Cnwll 4 B5
Mount Hermon Cnwll 3 H7
Mountjoy Cnwll 4 E3
Mount Lothian Mdloth 200 C2
Mountnessing Essex 70 F7
Mounton Mons 63 G8
Mount Pleasant Ches E 131 G8
Mount Pleasant Derbys 115 M8
Mount Pleasant Derbys 116 B2
Mount Pleasant Dur 169 H4
Mount Pleasant E R Yk 153 L7
Mount Pleasant E Susx 23 G4
Mount Pleasant Norfk 105 K4
Mount Pleasant Suffk 88 E5
Mount Pleasant Sundld 181 H8
Mount Pleasant Worcs 82 B2
Mountsorrel Leics 116 F8
Mount Sorrel Wilts 33 H6
Mount Tabor Calder 141 G2
Mousehole Cnwll 2 D5
Mouswald D & G 176 E4
Mow Cop Ches E 131 G8
Mowhaugh Border 189 L2
Mowmacre Hill C Leic 100 D2
Mowsley Leics 100 E5
Moy Highld 240 D7
Moy Highld 252 E5
Moyle Highld 248 D7
Moylegrove Pembks 75 J3
Muasdale Ag & B 205 L8
Muchalls Abers 245 K5
Much Birch Herefs 63 G1
Much Cowarne Herefs 80 E5
Much Dewchurch Herefs 62 F1
Muchelney Somset 30 F6
Muchelney Ham Somset 31 G6
Much Hadham Herts 70 B3
Much Hoole Lancs 138 F3
Much Hoole Town Lancs 138 F3
Muchlarnick Cnwll 5 L3
Much Marcle Herefs 63 K1
Much Wenlock Shrops 96 E3
Muck Highld 236 E4
Mucking Thurr 52 F2
Muckleford Dorset 16 C4
Mucklestone Staffs 114 A4
Muckley Shrops 96 E4
Muckton Lincs 137 G3
Muddiford Devon 27 K3

Muddles Green E Susx 23 J4
Mudeford BCP 18 B5
Mudford Somset 31 J7
Mudford Sock Somset 31 J7
Mudgley Somset 31 G2
Mud Row Kent 53 M4
Mugdock Stirlg 208 F4
Mugeary Highld 246 F1
Mugginton Derbys 115 M3
Muggintonlane End Derbys 115 M3
Muggleswick Dur 168 D1
Muirden Abers 268 C5
Muirdrum Angus 234 E7
Muiresk Abers 268 C6
Muirhead Angus 233 M8
Muirhead Fife 222 D6
Muirhead N Lans 209 J5
Muirhouses Falk 210 D3
Muirkirk E Ayrs 197 K5
Muirmill Stirlg 209 J2
Muir of Fowlis Abers 244 C1
Muir of Miltonduff Moray 266 D4
Muir of Ord Highld 250 F2
Muirshearlich Highld 239 J7
Muirtack Abers 257 J4
Muirton P & K 221 G5
Muirton Mains Highld 250 E1
Muirton of Ardblair P & K 233 J6
Muker N York 158 F3
Mulbarton Norfk 106 D3
Mulben Moray 267 G6
Mulfra Cnwll 2 C4
Mull Ag & B 227 H5
Mullacott Cross Devon 27 J2
Mullardoch Highld 249 L5
Mullion Cnwll 3 H7
Mullion Cove Cnwll 3 H7
Mumby Lincs 137 K5
Munderfield Row Herefs 80 F5
Munderfield Stocks Herefs 80 F5
Mundesley Norfk 123 G4
Mundford Norfk 104 F4
Mundham Norfk 107 G4
Mundon Essex 72 C6
Mungrisdale Cumb 165 L4
Munlochy Highld 251 H1
Munnoch N Ayrs 195 L1
Munsley Herefs 80 F7
Munslow Shrops 96 C6
Murchington Devon 13 G5
Murcot Worcs 82 C7
Murcott Oxon 66 E4
Murcott Wilts 46 D1
Murkle Highld 279 L3
Murlaggan Highld 239 G5
Murrell Green Hants 49 H7
Murroes Angus 234 C8
Murrow Cambs 103 H2
Mursley Bucks 67 K2
Murston Kent 40 B3
Murthill Angus 234 C4
Murthly P & K 233 G7
Murton C York 151 K5
Murton Cumb 167 G6
Murton Dur 169 K1
Murton N Tyne 181 H5
Murton Nthumb 202 F3
Murton Swans 57 G7
Musbury Devon 15 G4
Muscoates N York 162 B6
Musselburgh E Loth 211 K4
Muston Leics 117 L4
Muston N York 163 K6
Mustow Green Worcs 97 K8
Muswell Hill Gt Lon 51 H1
Mutehill D & G 175 H5
Mutford Suffk 107 K5
Muthill P & K 220 F4
Mutterton Devon 14 B2
Muxton Wrekin 114 A8
Mybster Highld 279 L5
Myddfai Carmth 59 L3
Myddle Shrops 113 G6
Mydroilyn Cerdgn 76 E4
Myerscough Lancs 147 K7
Myland Essex 72 E2
Mylor Cnwll 3 L4
Mylor Bridge Cnwll 3 K4
Mynachlog ddu Pembks 75 K6
Myndd-llan Flints 128 D5
Myndtown Shrops 95 J5
Mynydd Bach Cerdgn 92 F8
Mynydd-bach Mons 62 F8
Mynydd-Bach Swans 57 J3
Mynyddgarreg Carmth 56 D3
Mynydd Isa Flints 128 D7
Mynydd Llandygai Gwynd 126 B6
Mynydd Mechell IoA 124 F2
Mynytho Gwynd 108 E5

Myrebird Abers 245 G4
Myredykes Border 189 G6
Mytchett Surrey 49 L7
Mytholm Calder 140 E2
Mytholmroyd Calder 140 F3
Mythop Lancs 138 D1
Myton-on-Swale N York 150 F3

N

Naast Highld 260 C3
Nab's Head Lancs 139 J2
Na Buirgh W Isls 282 d6
Naburn C York 151 J6
Naccolt Kent 40 D6
Nackington Kent 40 F4
Nacton Suffk 90 F7
Nafferton E R Yk 153 G4
Nag's Head Gloucs 64 C7
Nailbridge Gloucs 63 J4
Nailsbourne Somset 30 B5
Nailsea N Som 44 F5
Nailstone Leics 99 L2
Nailsworth Gloucs 64 B7
Nairn Highld 264 D8
Nalderswood Surrey 37 K2
Nancegollan Cnwll 3 G4
Nancledra Cnwll 2 D4
Nanhoron Gwynd 108 E5
Nannerch Flints 128 E5
Nanpantan Leics 116 E8
Nanpean Cnwll 4 F4
Nanquidno Cnwll 2 B5
Nanstallon Cnwll 5 H2
Nant-ddu Powys 60 F4
Nanternis Cerdgn 76 C4
Nantgaredig Carmth 58 F4
Nantgarw Rhondd 43 H4
Nant-glas Powys 78 D2
Nantglyn Denbgs 127 K7
Nantgwyn Powys 93 L8
Nant Gwynant Gwynd 110 B2
Nantlle Gwynd 109 J1
Nantlle Valley Slate
   Landscape Gwynd 109 J1
Nantmawr Shrops 112 C6
Nantmel Powys 78 E2
Nantmor Gwynd 109 L2
Nant Peris Gwynd 126 B7
Nantwich Ches E 113 L1
Nant-y-Bwch Blae G 61 H5
Nantycaws Carmth 58 E5
Nant-y-derry Mons 62 C6
Nant-y-ffin Carmth 59 G3
Nantyffyllon Brdgnd 42 C3
Nantyglo Blae G 61 K5
Nant-y-gollen Shrops 112 C5
Nant-y-moel Brdgnd 42 D3
Nant-y-pandy Conwy 126 D5
Naphill Bucks 67 K7
Napleton Worcs 81 K5
Nappa N York 148 E5
Napton on the Hill Warwks 83 L3
Narberth Pembks 55 J4
Narborough Leics 100 C4
Narborough Norfk 104 E1
Narkurs Cnwll 6 C4
Nasareth Gwynd 109 H2
Naseby Nhants 100 F7
Nash Bucks 84 F8
Nash Gt Lon 51 L6
Nash Herefs 79 K3
Nash Newpt 44 D2
Nash Shrops 80 E1
Nash End Worcs 97 H7
Nashes Green Hants 35 K2
Nash Lee Bucks 67 K5
Nash Street Kent 52 D5
Nassington Nhants 102 B4
Nastend Gloucs 64 A6
Nasty Herts 69 K2
Nateby Cumb 158 D1
Nateby Lancs 147 J7
Natland Cumb 157 H5
Naughton Suffk 89 L5
Naunton Gloucs 65 K4
Naunton Worcs 81 K7
Naunton Beauchamp Worcs 81 M5
Navenby Lincs 135 K8
Navestock Essex 70 D7
Navestock Side Essex 70 E7
Navidale Highld 274 D5
Navity Highld 264 B7
Nawton N York 161 L1
Nayland Suffk 89 K8
Nazeing Essex 69 L6
Nazeing Gate Essex 69 L6
Neacroft Hants 18 B4

Neal's Green Warwks 99 J6
Neap Shet 281 e5
Near Cotton Staffs 115 H2
Near Sawrey Cumb 156 E3
Neasden Gt Lon 51 G2
Neasham Darltn 169 J8
Neath Neath 57 L5
Neatham Hants 35 M3
Neatishead Norfk 123 G7
Nebo Cerdgn 77 G2
Nebo Conwy 127 G8
Nebo Gwynd 109 H2
Nebo IoA 125 H2
Necton Norfk 105 H2
Nedd Highld 270 F2
Nedderton Nthumb 180 F2
Nedging Suffk 89 K5
Nedging Tye Suffk 89 L5
Needham Norfk 106 E7
Needham Market Suffk 90 C4
Needham Street Suffk 88 E2
Needingworth Cambs 87 G1
Neen Savage Shrops 96 F7
Neen Sollars Shrops 80 F1
Neenton Shrops 96 E6
Nefyn Gwynd 108 E3
Neilston E Rens 208 E7
Nemphlar S Lans 198 E4
Nempnett Thrubwell BaNES 45 G7
Nenthall Cumb 167 H2
Nenthead Cumb 167 H2
Nenthorn Border 201 L5
Neopardy Devon 13 J3
Nep Town W Susx 22 B4
Nerabus Ag & B 204 C5
Nercwys Flints 128 F7
Nerston S Lans 209 H7
Nesbit Nthumb 202 F6
Nesfield N York 149 K6
Ness Ches W 129 G4
Nesscliffe Shrops 112 F7
Neston Ches W 129 G4
Neston Wilts 46 B5
Netchwood Shrops 96 E5
Nether Abington S Lans 186 D2
Nether Alderley Ches E 131 G4
Netheravon Wilts 33 K1
Nether Blainslie Border 201 H4
Netherbrae Abers 268 E4
Nether Broughton Leics 117 J6
Netherburn S Lans 198 C4
Netherbury Dorset 15 L3
Netherby Cumb 177 L4
Netherby N York 150 D6
Nether Cerne Dorset 16 C3
Nethercleuch D & G 176 F2
Nether Compton Dorset 31 K7
Nethercote Warwks 83 M2
Nethercott Devon 11 L3
Nethercott Devon 27 H3
Nether Crimond Abers 256 E7
Nether Dallachy Moray 267 G3
Netherend Gloucs 63 H7
Nether Exe Devon 13 L3
Netherfield E Susx 24 C3
Netherfield Leics 117 G3
Netherfield Notts 117 G3
Nether Fingland S Lans 186 D4
Nethergate N Linc 143 J7
Nethergate Norfk 122 B5
Netherhampton Wilts 33 K5
Nether Handley Derbys 133 H4
Nether Handwick Angus 234 B7
Nether Haugh Rothm 142 C8
Netherhay Dorset 15 J2
Nether Headon Notts 134 E4
Nether Heage Derbys 116 B2
Nether Heyford Nhants 84 C3
Nether Kellet Lancs 147 K2
Nether Kinmundy Abers 257 K3
Netherland Green Staffs 115 H5
Nether Langwith Notts 133 L5
Netherley Abers 245 J5
Netherley Lpool 129 K2
Nethermill D & G 176 D1
Nethermuir Abers 257 G3
Netherne-on-the-Hill Surrey 51 J7
Netheroyd Hill Kirk 141 H4
Nether Padley Derbys 132 E4
Nether Poppleton C York 151 J5
Nether Row Cumb 165 K3
Netherseal Derbys 99 H1
Nether Silton N York 161 G4
Nether Skyborry Shrops 95 J8
Nether Stowey Somset 30 B3
Nether Street Essex 70 E5
Netherstreet Wilts 46 E6
Netherthird E Ayrs 197 H7

Netherthong Kirk 141 H6
Netherthorpe Derbys 133 J5
Netherton Angus 234 E4
Netherton Devon 13 L8
Netherton Dudley 97 L5
Netherton Hants 48 A7
Netherton Herefs 63 G2
Netherton Kirk 141 H5
Netherton N Lans 209 K8
Netherton Nthumb 190 E4
Netherton Oxon 66 B7
Netherton P & K 233 H5
Netherton Sefton 138 D7
Netherton Shrops 97 G6
Netherton Stirlg 208 F3
Netherton Wakefd 141 L4
Netherton Worcs 82 A7
Nethertown Cumb 155 H1
Nethertown Highld 280 E1
Nethertown Lancs 148 C8
Nethertown Staffs 115 J8
Netherurd Border 199 J4
Nether Wallop Hants 34 C4
Nether Wasdale Cumb 155 L2
Nether Welton Cumb 165 K2
Nether Westcote Gloucs 65 J3
Nether Whitacre Warwks 99 G5
Nether Whitecleuch S Lans 186 B2
Nether Winchendon Bucks 67 H4
Netherwitton Nthumb 191 G8
Nethy Bridge Highld 253 J7
Netley Hants 19 G2
Netley Marsh Hants 34 D8
Nettlebed Oxon 49 G2
Nettlebridge Somset 31 L1
Nettlecombe Dorset 15 L3
Nettlecombe IoW 19 J8
Nettleden Herts 68 C5
Nettleham Lincs 135 K4
Nettlestead Kent 39 H3
Nettlestead Green Kent 39 H3
Nettlestone IoW 19 L5
Nettlesworth Dur 169 H1
Nettleton Lincs 144 E7
Nettleton Wilts 46 B3
Nettleton Shrub Wilts 46 B3
Netton Devon 7 G5
Netton Wilts 33 K3
Neuadd Carmth 59 K4
Neuadd-ddu Powys 93 K8
Nevendon Essex 53 G1
Nevern Pembks 75 J4
Nevill Holt Leics 101 H4
New Abbey D & G 176 C5
New Aberdour Abers 268 F3
New Addington Gt Lon 51 K6
Newall Leeds 150 B6
New Alresford Hants 35 J4
New Alyth P & K 233 K6
Newark C Pete 102 E3
Newark Ork 275 f2
Newark-on-Trent Notts 117 L1
New Arley Warwks 99 J5
New Arram E R Yk 153 G7
Newarthill N Lans 209 L7
New Ash Green Kent 52 D6
New Balderton Notts 117 L1
Newbarn Kent 40 F7
New Barn Kent 52 D5
New Barnet Gt Lon 69 H7
New Barnetby N Linc 144 D5
New Barton Nhants 85 G2
Newbattle Mdloth 211 K6
New Bewick Nthumb 190 F2
Newbie D & G 177 G6
Newbiggin Cumb 146 E2
Newbiggin Cumb 155 K4
Newbiggin Cumb 166 B5
Newbiggin Cumb 166 D1
Newbiggin Cumb 166 E5
Newbiggin Dur 167 L5
Newbiggin Dur 168 F1
Newbiggin N York 159 G4
Newbiggin N York 159 H5
Newbiggin-by-the-Sea
   Nthumb 181 H1
Newbigging Angus 233 L7
Newbigging Angus 234 C7
Newbigging Angus 234 D8
Newbigging S Lans 199 H4
Newbiggin-on-Lune Cumb 158 C2
New Bilton Warwks 100 B8
Newbold Derbys 133 G5
Newbold Leics 116 C7
Newbold on Avon Warwks 100 B7
Newbold on Stour Warwks 82 F6
Newbold Pacey Warwks 83 G4
Newbold Revel Warwks 99 M7
Newbold Verdon Leics 99 L3
New Bolingbroke Lincs 136 F8

Newborough C Pete 102 D2
Newborough IoA 125 G6
Newborough Staffs 115 J6
Newbottle Nhants 83 M7
Newbottle Sundld 181 H8
New Boultham Lincs 135 K5
Newbourne Suffk 91 G6
New Bradwell M Keyn 84 F7
New Brampton Derbys 133 G5
New Brancepeth Dur 169 G2
Newbridge C Edin 210 F4
Newbridge Caerph 43 K2
Newbridge Cerdgn 76 F3
Newbridge Cnwll 2 C5
Newbridge Cnwll 4 C6
Newbridge D & G 176 C3
Newbridge Hants 34 C7
Newbridge IoW 18 F6
New Bridge N York 162 D5
Newbridge Oxon 66 B6
Newbridge Wrexhm 112 D3
Newbridge Green Worcs 81 J7
Newbridge-on-Usk Mons 62 D8
Newbridge-on-Wye Powys 78 E4
New Brighton Flints 128 F6
New Brighton Wirral 129 G1
New Brinsley Notts 116 D2
Newbrough Nthumb 179 K5
New Broughton Wrexhm 112 D1
New Buckenham Norfk 106 B5
Newbuildings Devon 13 J2
Newburgh Abers 257 J6
Newburgh Abers 269 H4
Newburgh Fife 222 C3
Newburgh Lancs 138 F5
Newburn N u Ty 180 E6
New Bury Bolton 139 L6
Newbury Somset 32 B1
Newbury W Berk 48 C5
Newbury Wilts 32 D3
Newbury Park Gt Lon 51 L1
Newby Cumb 166 E6
Newby Lancs 148 E6
Newby N York 148 C2
Newby N York 163 J5
Newby N York 170 C8
Newby Bridge Cumb 156 E5
Newby Cross Cumb 177 L6
Newby East Cumb 178 B7
Newby Head Cumb 166 E6
New Byth Abers 268 E5
Newby West Cumb 177 L8
Newby Wiske N York 160 E5
Newcastle Mons 62 F4
Newcastle Shrops 95 G7
Newcastle Airport Nthumb 180 E4
Newcastle Emlyn Carmth 76 B2
Newcastle Great Park N u Ty ... 180 F5
Newcastleton Border 178 C2
Newcastle-under-Lyme
   Staffs 114 D2
Newcastle upon Tyne N u Ty ... 181 G6
Newchapel Pembks 75 L4
Newchapel Staffs 131 G8
Newchapel Surrey 38 A5
Newchurch Blae G 61 J5
Newchurch Herefs 79 L5
Newchurch IoW 19 J6
Newchurch Kent 25 K3
Newchurch Mons 62 F7
Newchurch Powys 79 H5
Newchurch Staffs 115 J7
Newchurch in Pendle Lancs 148 E7
New Costessey Norfk 106 D2
New Cowper Cumb 164 F2
Newcraighall C Edin 211 K4
New Crofton Wakefd 142 B4
New Cross Cerdgn 92 D8
New Cross Gt Lon 51 K4
New Cross Somset 30 F2
New Cumnock E Ayrs 197 J8
New Cut E Susx 24 E4
New Deer Abers 268 F6
New Delaval Nthumb 181 H5
New Delph Oldham 140 F5
New Denham Bucks 50 D2
Newdigate Surrey 37 J3
New Duston Nhants 84 D3
New Earswick C York 151 K5
New Eastwood Notts 116 D2
New Edlington Donc 142 E2
New Elgin Moray 266 C3
New Ellerby E R Yk 153 J7
Newell Green Br For 49 L5
New Eltham Gt Lon 51 L4
New End Worcs 82 C2
Newenden Kent 24 F4
New England C Pete 102 D3
New England Essex 88 E6
Newent Gloucs 63 L2

New Farnley Leeds 141 L2
New Ferry Wirral 129 H3
Newfield Dur 169 G4
Newfield Dur 181 G8
Newfield Highld 264 B4
New Fletton C Pete 102 D4
New Forest National Park 18 D2
Newfound Hants 48 E8
New Fryston Wakefd 142 C2
Newgale Pembks 54 D2
New Galloway D & G 185 G7
Newgate Norfk 122 A3
Newgate Street Herts 69 J6
New Gilston Fife 223 G6
New Grimsby IoS 10 b2
Newhall Ches E 113 K2
Newhall Derbys 115 M7
Newham Nthumb 203 K7
New Hartley Nthumb 181 H3
Newhaven C Edin 211 H4
Newhaven Derbys 132 C7
Newhaven E Susx 23 G7
New Haw Surrey 50 D6
New Hedges Pembks 55 K6
New Herrington Sundld 181 H8
Newhey Rochdl 140 D5
New Holkham Norfk 121 J4
New Holland N Linc 144 D3
Newholm N York 171 K8
New Houghton Derbys 133 K6
New Houghton Norfk 121 H6
Newhouse N Lans 209 L6
New Houses N York 158 D7
New Hutton Cumb 157 J4
New Hythe Kent 52 F7
Newick E Susx 22 F3
Newingreen Kent 40 F8
Newington Kent 41 G7
Newington Kent 53 J6
Newington Oxon 66 F7
Newington Shrops 95 K6
Newington Bagpath Gloucs 64 B8
New Inn Carmth 58 E2
New Inn Pembks 75 H6
New Inn Torfn 62 C7
New Invention Shrops 95 H8
New Lanark S Lans 198 E4
New Lanark Village S Lans 198 E5
Newland C KuH 144 D2
Newland Cumb 156 D6
Newland E R Yk 143 K2
Newland Gloucs 63 H5
Newland N York 143 H2
Newland Oxon 66 A5
Newland Somset 28 E3
Newland Worcs 81 H5
Newlandrig Mdloth 211 L6
Newlands Border 188 E7
Newlands Cumb 165 K3
Newlands Nthumb 180 D7
Newlands of Dundurcas
  Moray 266 F6
New Lane Lancs 138 E5
New Lane End Warrtn 130 C1
New Langholm D & G 177 K2
New Leake Lincs 137 G8
New Leeds Abers 269 H5
New Lodge Barns 142 A6
New Longton Lancs 139 G3
New Luce D & G 172 F2
Newlyn Cnwll 2 D5
Newmachar Abers 256 F7
Newmains N Lans 209 L7
New Malden Gt Lon 51 G5
Newman's End Essex 70 D4
Newman's Green Suffk 89 H6
Newmarket Suffk 88 C3
Newmarket W Isls 282 g3
New Marske R & Cl 170 E6
New Marston Oxon 66 D5
New Marton Shrops 112 E4
New Mill Abers 245 H7
Newmill Border 188 D4
New Mill Cnwll 2 D5
New Mill Herts 68 A4
New Mill Kirk 141 J6
Newmill Moray 267 J5
Newmillerdam Wakefd 142 A4
Newmill of Inshewan Angus 234 C3
Newmills C Edin 211 G5
New Mills Cnwll 4 E4
New Mills Derbys 131 K3
Newmills Fife 210 D2
Newmills Mons 63 G5
New Mills Powys 94 D3
Newmiln P & K 221 L1
Newmilns E Ayrs 197 G3
New Milton Hants 18 C4
New Mistley Essex 73 H1
New Moat Pembks 75 H7

Newnes Shrops 112 F5
Newney Green Essex 71 G5
Newnham Hants 49 H8
Newnham Herts 86 E7
Newnham Kent 40 B4
Newnham Nhants 84 B3
Newnham Bridge Worcs 80 E2
Newnham on Severn Gloucs 63 K5
New Ollerton Notts 134 D6
New Oscott Birm 98 E4
New Pitsligo Abers 268 F5
New Polzeath Cnwll 10 C6
Newport Cnwll 11 L5
Newport Dorset 17 G4
Newport E R Yk 143 L2
Newport Essex 87 L8
Newport Gloucs 63 K7
Newport Highld 274 F3
Newport IoW 19 H6
Newport Newpt 44 C1
Newport Norfk 123 K8
Newport Pembks 75 H4
Newport Wrekin 114 A7
Newport-on-Tay Fife 223 G2
Newport Pagnell M Keyn 85 G6
Newport Pagnell Services
  M Keyn 85 G6
Newpound Common W Susx 37 G5
New Prestwick S Ayrs 196 C6
New Quay Cerdgn 76 D3
Newquay Cnwll 4 D3
New Quay Essex 72 F2
New Rackheath Norfk 106 F1
New Radnor Powys 79 H3
New Rent Cumb 166 B3
New Ridley Nthumb 180 C7
New Road Side N York 149 H7
New Romney Kent 25 K2
New Rossington Donc 143 G8
New Row Cerdgn 92 F8
New Row Lancs 148 A8
New Sauchie Clacks 220 F8
Newsbank Ches E 131 G6
Newseat Abers 256 C5
Newsham Lancs 147 K8
Newsham N York 160 E5
Newsham N York 168 E8
Newsham Nthumb 181 H3
New Sharlston Wakefd 142 B4
Newsholme E R Yk 143 H2
Newsholme Lancs 148 E5
New Shoreston Nthumb 203 K6
New Silksworth Sundld 181 J8
New Skelton R & Cl 170 F7
Newsome Kirk 141 J5
New Somerby Lincs 118 B4
New Springs Wigan 139 J6
Newstead Border 201 H6
Newstead Notts 116 E1
Newstead Nthumb 203 J7
New Stevenston N Lans 209 K7
New Street Herefs 79 L4
New Swanage Dorset 17 K6
New Swannington Leics 116 D8
Newthorpe N York 142 D1
Newthorpe Notts 116 E2
New Thundersley Essex 53 G1
Newtimber W Susx 22 D4
Newtoft Lincs 135 L2
Newton Ag & B 217 G7
Newton Border 189 G2
Newton Brdgnd 42 C6
Newton C Beds 86 E6
Newton Cambs 87 J5
Newton Cambs 119 M8
Newton Cardif 43 K6
Newton Ches W 129 J6
Newton Ches W 129 L7
Newton Ches W 129 M4
Newton Cumb 146 D2
Newton Derbys 133 J7
Newton Herefs 79 L1
Newton Herefs 79 L8
Newton Herefs 80 C7
Newton Highld 251 G2
Newton Highld 252 D2
Newton Highld 263 L6
Newton Highld 280 D6
Newton Lancs 147 G8
Newton Lancs 157 J7
Newton Lincs 118 D4
Newton Mdloth 211 K5
Newton Moray 266 C3
Newton Moray 267 G4
Newton N York 152 D1
Newton Nhants 101 J6
Newton Norfk 121 H8
Newton Notts 117 J3
Newton Nthumb 180 C6
Newton Nthumb 190 D5

Newton S Lans 198 F6
Newton S Lans 209 H6
Newton Sandw 98 C4
Newton Shrops 112 F4
Newton Somset 29 K3
Newton Staffs 115 G6
Newton Suffk 89 J7
Newton W Loth 210 E3
Newton Warwks 100 C3
Newton Wilts 34 B6
Newton Abbot Devon 13 K8
Newton Arlosh Cumb 177 G7
Newton Aycliffe Dur 169 H5
Newton Bewley Hartpl 170 B5
Newton Blossomville M Keyn 85 H5
Newton Bromswold Nhants 85 K2
Newton Burgoland Leics 99 K3
Newton by Toft Lincs 135 L2
Newton Ferrers Devon 7 G5
Newton Ferry W Isls 282 c7
Newton Flotman Norfk 106 D1
Newtongrange Mdloth 211 K6
Newton Green Mons 45 G1
Newton Harcourt Leics 100 E4
Newton Heath Manch 140 C2
Newtonhill Abers 245 K5
Newton Hill Wakefd 141 M3
Newton-in-Bowland Lancs 148 B5
Newton Kyme N York 151 G2
Newton-le-Willows N York 160 B5
Newton-le-Willows St Hel 139 H8
Newtonloan Mdloth 211 K6
Newton Longville Bucks 67 K3
Newton Mearns E Rens 208 F7
Newtonmill Angus 234 F3
Newtonmore Highld 241 J4
Newton Morrell N York 160 C1
Newton Mountain Pembks 55 G5
Newton Mulgrave N York 171 H7
Newton of Balcanquhal P & K 222 B5
Newton of Balcormo Fife 223 J6
Newton of Belltrees Rens 208 C7
Newton-on-Ayr S Ayrs 196 C6
Newton-on-Ouse N York 151 H4
Newton-on-Rawcliffe N York 162 E4
Newton on the Hill Shrops 113 H7
Newton-on-the-Moor
  Nthumb 191 H5
Newton on Trent Lincs 135 G5
Newton Poppleford Devon 14 C5
Newton Purcell Oxon 66 F1
Newton Regis Warwks 99 H2
Newton Reigny Cumb 166 B2
Newton St Cyres Devon 13 K3
Newton St Faith Norfk 122 E8
Newton St Loe BaNES 45 L6
Newton St Petrock Devon 27 G6
Newton Solney Derbys 115 M6
Newton Stacey Hants 34 E3
Newton Stewart D & G 173 K2
Newton Tony Wilts 34 B3
Newton Tracey Devon 27 J5
Newton under Roseberry
  R & Cl 170 D8
Newton Underwood Nthumb 180 E2
Newton upon Derwent E R Yk 151 M6
Newton Valence Hants 35 L4
Newton Wamphray D & G 187 G2
Newton with Scales Lancs 138 F2
Newtown BCP 17 K4
Newtown Blae G 61 J5
Newtown Ches W 129 M4
Newtown Cnwll 2 F5
Newtown Cnwll 11 K7
Newtown Cumb 164 E1
Newtown Cumb 166 C6
Newtown Cumb 177 L6
Newtown Cumb 178 C6
Newtown D & G 185 J1
Newtown Derbys 131 K3
Newtown Devon 14 C3
Newtown Devon 28 D6
Newtown Dorset 15 L2
New Town Dorset 17 K1
New Town Dorset 32 F7
New Town Dorset 33 G7
New Town E Susx 23 H3
Newtown Gloucs 63 K6
Newtown Hants 18 D2
Newtown Hants 35 J8
Newtown Hants 48 C6
Newtown Herefs 80 B4
Newtown Herefs 80 C8
Newtown Herefs 80 E6
Newtown Highld 240 B3
Newtown IoW 19 G6
Newtown Nthumb 190 E6
Newtown Nthumb 202 F6
Newtown Nthumb 203 G8
Newtown Powys 94 D5

Newtown Rhondd 61 G7
Newtown Shrops 112 F7
Newtown Shrops 113 H5
Newtown Somset 30 C8
Newtown Staffs 98 C3
Newtown Staffs 131 H7
Newtown Wigan 139 H6
Newtown Wilts 32 F5
Newtown Wilts 47 L6
Newtown Worcs 81 K4
Newtown Worcs 98 B7
Newtown-in-St Martin Cnwll 3 J6
Newtown Linford Leics 100 B2
Newtown St Boswells Border 201 J6
Newtown Unthank Leics 100 B3
New Tredegar Caerph 61 J6
New Trows S Lans 198 D5
New Tupton Derbys 133 H6
Newtyle Angus 233 L7
New Walsoken Cambs 103 K2
New Waltham NE Lin 145 H6
New Whittington Derbys 133 H4
New Winton E Loth 211 M5
New Yatt Oxon 66 A4
Newyears Green Gt Lon 50 D1
Newyork Ag & B 216 F5
New York Lincs 136 D8
New York N Tyne 181 H5
New York N York 150 B3
New Zealand Wilts 46 E3
Nextend Herefs 79 L4
Neyland Pembks 54 F6
Niarbyl IoM 154 b6
Nibley Gloucs 63 K5
Nibley S Glos 45 K3
Nibley Green Gloucs 63 L7
Nicholashayne Devon 29 K4
Nicholaston Swans 56 F7
Nickies Hill Cumb 178 D5
Nidd N York 150 D4
Nigg C Aber 245 L3
Nigg Highld 264 C5
Nigg Ferry Highld 264 B6
Nimlet BaNES 45 L5
Ninebanks Nthumb 179 H8
Nine Elms Swindn 47 G2
Nine Wells Pembks 74 C7
Ninfield E Susx 24 C5
Ningwood IoW 18 F6
Nisbet Border 201 L8
Nisbet Hill Border 202 B3
Niton IoW 19 H8
Nitshill C Glas 208 E7
Noah's Ark Kent 52 C7
Noak Bridge Essex 52 E1
Noak Hill Gt Lon 70 D8
Nobelthorpe Barns 141 L6
Nobold Shrops 95 L2
Nobottle Nhants 84 C3
Nocton Lincs 135 L6
Nogdam End Norfk 107 J2
Noke Oxon 66 E4
Nolton Pembks 54 E3
Nolton Haven Pembks 54 D3
No Man's Heath Ches W 113 H2
No Man's Heath Warwks 99 H2
No Man's Land Cnwll 6 B3
Nomansland Devon 28 E8
Nomansland Wilts 34 B7
Noneley Shrops 113 H6
Nonington Kent 41 H5
Nook Cumb 157 H6
Nook Cumb 178 B3
Norbiton Gt Lon 51 G5
Norbreck Bpool 146 F7
Norbridge Herefs 81 G6
Norbury Ches E 113 J2
Norbury Derbys 115 J3
Norbury Gt Lon 51 J5
Norbury Shrops 95 J5
Norbury Staffs 114 B6
Norbury Common Ches E 113 J2
Norbury Junction Staffs 114 B7
Norchard Worcs 81 J2
Norcott Brook Ches W 130 B4
Norcross Lancs 146 F7
Nordelph Norfk 103 L3
Norden Rochdl 140 C5
Nordley Shrops 96 F4
Norfolk Broads Norfk 107 J2
Norham Nthumb 202 D4
Norland Calder 141 G3
Norley Ches W 130 B5
Norleywood Hants 18 E4
Norlington E Susx 23 G4
Normanby Lincs 135 K2
Normanby N Linc 143 M4
Normanby N York 162 C6
Normanby R & Cl 170 D7
Normanby le Wold Lincs 136 B1

Norman Cross Cambs......102 D5
Normandy Surrey......50 B8
Normans Bay E Susx......24 C6
Norman's Green Devon......14 C2
Normanton C Derb......116 B5
Normanton Leics......117 L3
Normanton Notts......134 E8
Normanton Rutlnd......101 K2
Normanton Wakefd......142 B3
Normanton Wilts......33 K3
Normanton le Heath Leics......99 K1
Normanton on Cliffe Lincs......118 B2
Normanton on Soar Notts......116 E7
Normanton on the Wolds Notts......117 G5
Normanton on Trent Notts......134 F6
Normoss Lancs......147 G8
Norney Surrey......36 D2
Norrington Common Wilts......46 C6
Norris Green Cnwll......6 E1
Norris Green Lpool......129 J1
Norris Hill Leics......116 B8
Norristhorpe Kirk......141 K3
Northacre Norfk......105 J4
Northall Bucks......68 B3
Northall Green Norfk......121 M8
Northam C Sotn......19 G1
Northam Devon......27 H5
Northampton Nhants......84 E3
Northampton Worcs......81 J2
Northampton Services Nhants......84 D4
North Anston Rothm......133 K3
North Ascot Br For......49 M5
North Aston Oxon......66 C1
Northaw Herts......69 H6
Northay Somset......30 D8
North Baddesley Hants......34 E6
North Ballachulish Highld......229 G3
North Barrow Somset......31 K5
North Barsham Norfk......121 K4
Northbay W Isls......283 b13
North Benfleet Essex......53 G1
North Berwick E Loth......212 C2
North Bitchburn Dur......168 F4
North Blyth Nthumb......181 H2
North Boarhunt Hants......19 K2
North Bockhampton BCP......18 B4
Northborough C Pete......102 C2
Northbourne Kent......41 K5
North Bovey Devon......13 H6
North Bradley Wilts......46 B7
North Brentor Devon......12 C6
North Brewham Somset......32 B3
North Bridge Surrey......36 E3
Northbridge Street E Susx......24 D2
Northbrook Hants......35 G3
Northbrook Oxon......66 D3
North Brook End Cambs......86 F6
North Buckland Devon......27 H3
North Burlingham Norfk......107 H2
North Cadbury Somset......31 K5
North Carlton Lincs......135 J4
North Carlton Notts......134 B3
North Cave E R Yk......143 M1
North Cerney Gloucs......64 E5
North Chailey E Susx......22 F3
Northchapel W Susx......36 E5
North Charford Hants......33 L7
North Charlton Nthumb......191 H2
North Cheam Gt Lon......51 G6
North Cheriton Somset......31 M5
North Chideock Dorset......15 K4
Northchurch Herts......68 B5
North Cliffe E R Yk......152 D8
North Clifton Notts......135 G5
North Close Dur......169 H4
North Cockerington Lincs......137 G2
North Connel Ag & B......228 E8
North Cornelly Brdgnd......42 B5
North Corner Cnwll......3 K7
North Cotes Lincs......145 J7
Northcott Devon......11 L4
Northcott Devon......14 D1
Northcott Devon......29 K8
North Country Cnwll......4 A6
Northcourt Oxon......66 D7
North Cove Suffk......107 K5
North Cowton N York......160 D2
North Crawley M Keyn......85 H6
North Cray Gt Lon......52 A4
North Creake Norfk......121 J4
North Curry Somset......30 D6
North Dalton E R Yk......152 E5
North Deighton N York......150 E5
Northdown Kent......41 L1
North Downs......40 B4
North Duffield N York......151 L8
Northedge Derbys......133 G6
North Elham Kent......41 G6

North Elkington Lincs......136 E2
North Elmham Norfk......121 L7
North Elmsall Wakefd......142 D5
Northend Bucks......67 H8
North End C Port......19 L3
North End Cumb......177 K7
North End Dorset......32 D5
North End E R Yk......145 H2
North End E R Yk......153 K7
North End Essex......71 G3
North End Hants......33 J7
North End Hants......35 J5
North End Leics......116 F8
North End Lincs......119 H3
North End Lincs......137 H2
North End Lincs......144 D7
North End Lincs......145 J7
North End N Linc......144 E5
North End N Som......44 E5
North End Nhants......85 J2
North End Norfk......105 K5
North End Nthumb......191 G6
North End Sefton......138 C6
North End W Susx......21 G6
North End W Susx......21 J5
Northend Warwks......83 J5
Northenden Manch......131 G2
Northend Woods Bucks......49 L1
North Erradale Highld......260 B4
North Evington C Leic......100 D3
North Fambridge Essex......71 K7
North Featherstone Wakefd......142 C3
North Ferriby E R Yk......144 B3
Northfield Birm......98 C7
Northfield C Aber......245 K2
Northfield E R Yk......144 C2
Northfields Lincs......102 A2
Northfleet Kent......52 D4
North Frodingham E R Yk......153 H5
Northgate Lincs......119 G6
North Gorley Hants......33 L8
North Green Norfk......106 E5
North Green Suffk......91 G3
North Green Suffk......91 J2
North Greetwell Lincs......135 K5
North Grimston N York......152 C2
North Halling Medway......52 F6
North Hayling Hants......20 B6
North Hazelrigg Nthumb......203 G6
North Heasley Devon......28 C4
North Heath W Susx......37 G6
North Hele Devon......29 J6
North Hill Cnwll......11 K7
North Hillingdon Gt Lon......50 D2
North Hinksey Village Oxon......66 D6
North Holmwood Surrey......37 J2
North Huish Devon......7 K3
North Hykeham Lincs......135 J6
Northiam E Susx......24 E2
Northill C Beds......86 C6
Northington Gloucs......63 L5
Northington Hants......35 H3
North Kelsey Lincs......144 D7
North Kessock Highld......251 H2
North Killingholme N Linc......144 F4
North Kilvington N York......160 F5
North Kilworth Leics......100 D6
North Kingston Hants......18 B3
North Kyme Lincs......118 F1
North Lancing W Susx......21 L5
North Landing E R Yk......153 L2
Northlands Lincs......119 K1
Northleach Gloucs......65 G4
North Lee Bucks......67 K5
North Lees N York......160 D7
Northleigh Devon......14 E3
Northleigh Devon......27 L4
North Leigh Kent......40 F6
North Leigh Oxon......66 A4
North Leverton with Habblesthorpe Notts......134 F3
Northlew Devon......12 C3
North Littleton Worcs......82 C5
Northload Bridge Somset......31 H3
North Lopham Norfk......105 L6
North Luffenham Rutlnd......101 K3
North Marden W Susx......20 C4
North Marston Bucks......67 J3
North Middleton Mdloth......211 K7
North Middleton Nthumb......190 E1
North Millbrex Abers......256 E3
North Milmain D & G......172 D4
North Molton Devon......28 C5
Northmoor Oxon......66 B6
North Moreton Oxon......48 E1
Northmuir Angus......234 B4
North Mundham W Susx......20 E6
North Muskham Notts......134 F7
North Newbald E R Yk......152 D8
North Newington Oxon......83 K7

North Newnton Wilts......47 H7
North Newton Somset......30 D4
Northney Hants......20 B6
North Nibley Gloucs......63 L7
North Oakley Hants......48 D8
North Ockendon Gt Lon......52 C2
Northolt Gt Lon......50 E2
Northolt Airport Gt Lon......50 E2
Northop Flints......128 F6
Northop Hall Flints......129 G6
North Ormesby Middsb......170 C6
North Ormsby Lincs......136 E1
Northorpe Kirk......141 K3
Northorpe Lincs......118 E8
Northorpe Lincs......119 G4
Northorpe Lincs......143 M8
North Otterington N York......160 E5
Northover Somset......31 H3
Northover Somset......31 H6
North Owersby Lincs......135 L1
Northowram Calder......141 H2
North Perrott Somset......15 L1
North Petherton Somset......30 D4
North Petherwin Cnwll......11 K5
North Pickenham Norfk......105 H2
North Piddle Worcs......81 M4
North Poorton Dorset......15 M3
Northport Dorset......17 H5
North Poulner Hants......18 B2
North Queensferry Fife......210 F3
North Radworthy Devon......28 C4
North Rauceby Lincs......118 D2
Northrepps Norfk......122 E4
North Reston Lincs......137 G3
North Rigton N York......150 C6
North Ripley Hants......18 B4
North Rode Ches E......131 H6
North Roe Shet......281 d3
North Ronaldsay Ork......275 f1
North Ronaldsay Airport Ork......275 f1
North Row Cumb......165 H4
North Runcton Norfk......120 E8
North Scale Cumb......146 C2
North Scarle Lincs......135 G6
North Seaton Nthumb......181 H2
North Seaton Colliery Nthumb......181 H2
North Shian Ag & B......228 E6
North Shields N Tyne......181 J5
North Shoebury Sthend......53 K2
North Shore Bpool......146 F8
North Side C Pete......102 F3
North Side Cumb......164 C5
North Skelton R & Cl......170 F7
North Somercotes Lincs......145 L8
North Stainley N York......160 D7
North Stainmore Cumb......167 J7
North Stifford Thurr......52 D3
North Stoke BaNES......45 L5
North Stoke Oxon......48 F2
North Stoke W Susx......21 H5
Northstowe Cambs......87 K2
North Street Cambs......88 B2
North Street Hants......33 K7
North Street Hants......35 K4
North Street Kent......40 D4
North Street Medway......53 H4
North Street W Berk......48 F4
North Sunderland Nthumb......203 K6
North Tamerton Cnwll......11 K3
North Tawton Devon......12 F2
North Third Stirlg......209 K1
North Thoresby Lincs......145 H8
North Togston Nthumb......191 K5
North Tolsta W Isls......282 h2
Northton W Isls......282 d6
North Town Devon......12 C1
North Town Somset......31 J2
North Town W & M......49 L3
North Tuddenham Norfk......122 A8
North Uist W Isls......283 b8
Northumberland National Park Nthumb......179 J3
North Walbottle N u Ty......180 E5
North Walsham Norfk......122 F5
North Waltham Hants......35 H1
North Warnborough Hants......35 M1
Northway Somset......29 L5
North Weald Bassett Essex......70 D6
North Wheatley Notts......134 F3
North Whilborough Devon......8 C2
Northwich Ches W......130 C5
North Wick BaNES......45 H6
Northwick S Glos......45 H2
Northwick Somset......30 E1
Northwick Worcs......81 J4
North Widcombe BaNES......45 H7
North Willingham Lincs......136 C2
North Wingfield Derbys......133 H6
North Witham Lincs......118 B7
Northwold Norfk......104 E4

Northwood C Stke......114 D2
Northwood Derbys......132 E6
Northwood Gt Lon......50 E1
Northwood IoW......19 H5
Northwood Shrops......113 G5
Northwood Worcs......97 H5
Northwood Green Gloucs......63 L4
North Wootton Dorset......31 L7
North Wootton Norfk......120 E6
North Wootton Somset......31 J3
North Wraxall Wilts......46 A3
North Wroughton Swindn......47 H3
North York Moors National Park......162 C3
Norton Donc......142 E5
Norton E Susx......23 G7
Norton Gloucs......64 B2
Norton Halton......130 A3
Norton Hants......34 F3
Norton Herts......86 E8
Norton IoW......18 E6
Norton Mons......62 F3
Norton N Som......44 D6
Norton Nhants......84 B3
Norton Notts......133 L5
Norton Powys......79 K2
Norton S on T......170 B6
Norton Sheff......133 G3
Norton Shrops......95 L7
Norton Shrops......96 D2
Norton Shrops......96 E6
Norton Shrops......97 G3
Norton Suffk......89 J2
Norton Swans......57 H7
Norton W Susx......21 F5
Norton Wilts......46 C2
Norton Worcs......81 K5
Norton Worcs......82 B5
Norton Bavant Wilts......32 F2
Norton Bridge Staffs......114 D5
Norton Canes Staffs......98 C2
Norton Canes Services Staffs......98 C2
Norton Canon Herefs......79 M6
Norton Corner Norfk......122 B6
Norton Disney Lincs......135 H7
Norton Ferris Wilts......32 C4
Norton Fitzwarren Somset......30 B5
Norton Green IoW......18 E6
Norton Hawkfield BaNES......45 H6
Norton Heath Essex......70 F6
Norton in Hales Shrops......113 M4
Norton-Juxta-Twycross Leics......99 J2
Norton-le-Clay N York......150 F2
Norton-le-Moors C Stke......114 D1
Norton Lindsey Warwks......82 F3
Norton Little Green Suffk......89 K2
Norton Malreward BaNES......45 J6
Norton Mandeville Essex......70 E6
Norton-on-Derwent N York......152 B2
Norton St Philip Somset......45 M7
Norton Subcourse Norfk......107 H4
Norton sub Hamdon Somset......31 G7
Norton Wood Herefs......79 L5
Norwell Notts......134 F7
Norwell Woodhouse Notts......134 F7
Norwich Norfk......106 E2
Norwich Airport Norfk......106 E1
Norwick Shet......281 f1
Norwood Clacks......220 F8
Norwood Derbys......133 J3
Norwood Kent......25 K3
Norwood End Essex......70 E5
Norwood Green Calder......141 H3
Norwood Green Gt Lon......50 E3
Norwood Hill Surrey......37 K2
Norwoodside Cambs......103 H4
Noseley Leics......101 G4
Noss Mayo Devon......7 G5
Nosterfield N York......160 C6
Nosterfield End Cambs......88 C6
Nostie Highld......248 D6
Notgrove Gloucs......65 G3
Nottage Brdgnd......42 B6
Notter Cnwll......6 D3
Nottingham C Nott......116 F4
Nottington Dorset......16 C6
Notton Wakefd......142 A5
Notton Wilts......46 C5
Nounsley Essex......71 J5
Noutard's Green Worcs......81 J2
Nowton Suffk......89 H3
Nox Shrops......95 K1
Nuffield Oxon......49 G2
Nunburnholme E R Yk......152 C6
Nuncargate Notts......116 E1
Nunclose Cumb......166 C2
Nuneaton Warwks......99 K5
Nuneham Courtenay Oxon......66 D6
Nunhead Gt Lon......51 K4
Nunkeeling E R Yk......153 J6

Nun Monkton N York 151 H4
Nunney Somset 32 B2
Nunney Catch Somset 32 B2
Nunnington Herefs 80 D6
Nunnington N York 161 L6
Nunsthorpe NE Lin 145 H6
Nunthorpe C York 151 J6
Nunthorpe Middsb 170 C7
Nunthorpe Village Middsb 170 D8
Nunton Wilts 33 K5
Nunwick N York 160 D7
Nunwick Nthumb 179 K4
Nupdown S Glos 63 J7
Nup End Bucks 67 L3
Nupend Gloucs 64 A5
Nuptown Br For 49 L4
Nursling Hants 34 E7
Nursted Hants 36 A6
Nursteed Wilts 46 F6
Nurton Staffs 97 J3
Nutbourne W Susx 20 C6
Nutbourne W Susx 21 J3
Nutfield Surrey 37 M1
Nuthall Notts 116 E3
Nuthampstead Herts 87 H8
Nuthurst W Susx 37 J5
Nutley E Susx 23 G2
Nutley Hants 35 J2
Nuttall Bury 140 B4
Nutwell Donc 143 G7
Nybster Highld 280 E3
Nyetimber W Susx 20 E7
Nyewood W Susx 36 B6
Nymet Rowland Devon 13 G1
Nymet Tracey Devon 13 G3
Nympsfield Gloucs 64 A7
Nynehead Somset 29 L6
Nythe Somset 30 F4
Nyton W Susx 20 F5

O

Oadby Leics 100 D3
Oad Street Kent 53 J6
Oakall Green Worcs 81 J3
Oakamoor Staffs 115 G3
Oakbank W Loth 210 E5
Oak Cross Devon 12 D3
Oakdale Caerph 43 J2
Oake Somset 29 L6
Oaken Staffs 97 J3
Oakenclough Lancs 147 K6
Oakengates Wrekin 96 F1
Oakenholt Flints 129 G5
Oakenshaw Dur 169 G3
Oakenshaw Kirk 141 J2
Oakerthorpe Derbys 133 H8
Oakford Cerdgn 76 E4
Oakford Devon 29 G6
Oakfordbridge Devon 29 G6
Oakgrove Ches E 131 H6
Oakham Rutlnd 101 J2
Oakhanger Ches E 114 B1
Oakhanger Hants 36 A4
Oakhill Somset 31 K2
Oakhurst Kent 38 C3
Oakington Cambs 87 H2
Oaklands Herts 69 H3
Oaklands Powys 78 E5
Oakle Street Gloucs 63 M4
Oakley BCP 17 K5
Oakley Bed 85 K4
Oakley Bucks 66 F4
Oakley Fife 210 D1
Oakley Hants 35 H1
Oakley Oxon 67 H7
Oakley Suffk 106 D7
Oakley Green W & M 50 L4
Oakley Park Powys 93 L6
Oakridge Lynch Gloucs 64 C6
Oaks Lancs 139 K1
Oaks Shrops 95 K4
Oaksey Wilts 64 E8
Oaks Green Derbys 115 J5
Oakshaw Ford Cumb 178 C4
Oakshott Hants 35 M5
Oakthorpe Leics 99 J1
Oak Tree Darltn 169 K8
Oakwood C Derb 116 C4
Oakwood Nthumb 179 L6
Oakworth C Brad 149 J8
Oare Kent 40 C3
Oare Somset 28 D2
Oare Wilts 47 H6
Oasby Lincs 118 D4
Oath Somset 30 F5
Oathlaw Angus 234 D4
Oatlands Park Surrey 50 E6

Oban Ag & B 216 D1
Oban Airport Ag & B 228 E8
Obley Shrops 95 H7
Obney P & K 232 F8
Oborne Dorset 31 L7
Obthorpe Lincs 118 E8
Occold Suffk 90 D1
Occumster Highld 275 J1
Ochiltree E Ayrs 196 F6
Ockbrook Derbys 116 C4
Ocker Hill Sandw 98 B4
Ockeridge Worcs 81 H3
Ockham Surrey 50 D7
Ockle Highld 237 G6
Ockley Surrey 37 H3
Ocle Pychard Herefs 80 E6
Octon E R Yk 153 G2
Odcombe Somset 31 H7
Odd Down BaNES 45 L6
Oddendale Cumb 166 E8
Oddingley Worcs 81 L3
Oddington Oxon 66 E4
Odell Bed 85 J4
Odham Devon 12 C2
Odiham Hants 35 M1
Odsal C Brad 141 J2
Odsey Cambs 86 F7
Odstock Wilts 33 K5
Odstone Leics 99 K2
Offchurch Warwks 83 J2
Offenham Worcs 82 C6
Offerton Stockp 131 H2
Offerton Sundld 181 J7
Offham E Susx 22 F5
Offham Kent 39 G2
Offham W Susx 21 H5
Offleymarsh Staffs 114 B5
Offord Cluny Cambs 86 E2
Offord D'Arcy Cambs 86 E2
Offton Suffk 90 C5
Offwell Devon 14 E3
Ogbourne Maizey Wilts 47 J4
Ogbourne St Andrew Wilts 47 J4
Ogbourne St George Wilts 47 J4
Ogden Calder 141 G2
Ogle Nthumb 180 E3
Oglet Lpool 129 K3
Ogmore V Glam 42 D6
Ogmore-by-Sea V Glam 42 C6
Ogmore Vale Brdgnd 42 E4
Ogwen Bank Gwynd 126 C6
Okeford Fitzpaine Dorset 32 D8
Okehampton Devon 12 E4
Oker Side Derbys 132 E7
Okewood Hill Surrey 37 H3
Olchard Devon 13 K7
Old Nhants 84 F1
Old Aberdeen C Aber 245 L2
Old Alresford Hants 35 J4
Oldany Highld 270 L2
Old Arley Warwks 99 H5
Old Auchenbrack D & G 185 J3
Old Basford C Nott 116 F3
Old Basing Hants 49 G8
Old Beetley Norfk 121 L7
Oldberrow Warwks 82 D2
Old Bewick Nthumb 190 F2
Old Bolingbroke Lincs 136 F6
Old Boxted Essex 89 K8
Old Bramhope Leeds 150 B7
Old Brampton Derbys 133 G5
Old Bridge of Urr D & G 175 J2
Old Buckenham Norfk 106 B5
Old Burghclere Hants 48 C7
Oldbury Kent 38 F2
Oldbury Sandw 98 C5
Oldbury Shrops 97 G5
Oldbury Warwks 99 J4
Oldbury Naite S Glos 63 J8
Oldbury-on-Severn S Glos 63 J8
Oldbury on the Hill Gloucs 46 B1
Old Byland N York 161 J5
Old Cantley Donc 143 G7
Old Cassop Dur 169 J3
Oldcastle Mons 62 C2
Oldcastle Heath Ches W 113 G2
Old Catton Norfk 106 E1
Old Clee NE Lin 145 H6
Old Cleeve Somset 29 J3
Old Colwyn Conwy 127 H4
Oldcotes Notts 134 B2
Old Churchstoke Powys 95 G4
Old Coulsdon Gt Lon 51 J7
Old Dailly S Ayrs 183 G3
Old Dalby Leics 117 H6
Old Dam Derbys 132 B4
Old Deer Abers 269 H6
Old Ditch Somset 31 H1
Old Edlington Donc 142 E8
Old Eldon Dur 169 H5

Old Ellerby E R Yk 153 J8
Old Felixstowe Suffk 91 H8
Oldfield C Brad 149 H8
Oldfield Worcs 81 J2
Old Fletton C Pete 102 D4
Oldford Somset 32 C1
Old Forge Herefs 63 H3
Old Furnace Herefs 62 F2
Old Glossop Derbys 131 L1
Old Goole E R Yk 143 J3
Old Grimsby IoS 10 b2
Old Hall Green Herts 69 K3
Oldhall Green Suffk 89 H4
Old Hall Street Norfk 122 F5
Oldham Oldham 140 D6
Oldhamstocks E Loth 213 G5
Old Harlow Essex 70 C5
Old Heath Essex 72 E3
Old Hunstanton Norfk 120 F3
Old Hurst Cambs 102 F7
Old Hutton Cumb 157 J5
Old Inns Services N Lans 209 K4
Old Kea Cnwll 4 D6
Old Kilpatrick W Duns 208 D4
Old Knebworth Herts 69 G3
Old Lakenham Norfk 106 E2
Oldland S Glos 45 K4
Old Langho Lancs 148 B8
Old Laxey IoM 154 f5
Old Leake Lincs 119 L2
Old Malton N York 152 B1
Oldmeldrum Abers 256 E6
Oldmill Cnwll 11 M7
Old Milverton Warwks 83 G2
Oldmixon N Som 44 C7
Old Newton Suffk 90 B3
Old Oxted Surrey 51 K8
Old Portlethen Abers 245 L4
Old Quarrington Dur 169 J3
Old Radford C Nott 116 F3
Old Radnor Powys 79 J3
Old Rayne Abers 256 B6
Old Romney Kent 25 J2
Old Shoreham W Susx 22 F5
Oldshoremore Highld 276 C4
Old Soar Kent 38 F3
Old Sodbury S Glos 45 L3
Old Somerby Lincs 118 C5
Oldstead N York 161 H6
Old Stratford Nhants 84 E7
Old Struan P & K 232 B2
Old Swarland Nthumb 191 H6
Old Swinford Dudley 97 K6
Old Tebay Cumb 157 K2
Old Thirsk N York 160 F6
Old Town Calder 140 F2
Old Town Cumb 157 J6
Old Town Cumb 166 B2
Old Town E Susx 23 K7
Old Town IoS 10 c3
Old Trafford Traffd 140 B8
Old Tupton Derbys 133 H6
Oldwall Cumb 178 B6
Oldwalls Swans 56 E6
Old Warden C Beds 86 C6
Oldways End Somset 28 F6
Old Weston Cambs 102 B7
Old Wick Highld 280 L6
Old Windsor W & M 50 C4
Old Wives Lees Kent 40 E4
Old Woking Surrey 50 C7
Old Wolverton M Keyn 84 F7
Old Woodhall Lincs 136 D6
Old Woods Shrops 113 G7
Olgrinmore Highld 279 K5
Olive Green Staffs 115 J7
Oliver's Battery Hants 34 F5
Ollaberry Shet 281 d4
Ollach Highld 247 H1
Ollerton Ches E 130 F4
Ollerton Notts 134 D6
Ollerton Shrops 113 L6
Olmarch Cerdgn 77 H4
Olmstead Green Cambs 88 C7
Olney M Keyn 85 H5
Olrig House Highld 279 L3
Olton Solhll 98 E7
Olveston S Glos 45 J2
Ombersley Worcs 81 J2
Ompton Notts 134 D6
Once Brewed Nthumb 179 H5
Onchan IoM 154 e6
Onecote Staffs 131 L8
Onehouse Suffk 89 K3
Onen Mons 62 E4
Ongar Street Herefs 79 M2
Onibury Shrops 95 L7
Onich Highld 229 G3
Onllwyn Neath 60 C5
Onneley Staffs 114 B3

Onslow Green Essex 71 G3
Onslow Village Surrey 36 E1
Onston Ches W 130 B5
Openwoodgate Derbys 116 B2
Opinan Highld 260 B5
Orbliston Moray 266 F5
Orbost Highld 258 D7
Orby Lincs 137 J6
Orchard Portman Somset 30 C6
Orcheston Wilts 33 J2
Orcop Herefs 62 F2
Orcop Hill Herefs 62 F2
Ord Abers 268 A4
Ordhead Abers 244 E2
Ordie Abers 244 A3
Ordiequish Moray 267 G5
Ordley Nthumb 179 L7
Ordsall Notts 134 D4
Ore E Susx 24 F5
Oreleton Common Herefs 80 B2
Oreton Shrops 96 E7
Orford Suffk 91 K5
Orford Warrtn 130 B2
Organford Dorset 17 H4
Orgreave Staffs 115 J8
Orkney Islands Ork 275 c4
Orkney Neolithic Ork 275 b4
Orlestone Kent 40 C8
Orleton Herefs 80 C2
Orleton Worcs 81 G2
Orlingbury Nhants 85 G1
Ormathwaite Cumb 165 J5
Ormesby R & Cl 170 C7
Ormesby St Margaret Norfk 123 K8
Ormesby St Michael Norfk 123 K8
Ormiscaig Highld 260 D2
Ormiston E Loth 211 M5
Ormsaigmore Highld 236 F7
Ormsary Ag & B 206 A4
Ormskirk Lancs 138 E6
Ornsby Hill Dur 168 F1
Oronsay Ag & B 214 C6
Orphir Ork 275 b5
Orpington Gt Lon 51 M5
Orrell Sefton 138 D8
Orrell Wigan 139 G7
Orrell Post Wigan 139 G6
Orrisdale IoM 154 d4
Orroland D & G 175 J5
Orsett Thurr 52 D3
Orsett Heath Thurr 52 D3
Orslow Staffs 114 C8
Orston Notts 117 K3
Orthwaite Cumb 165 H4
Ortner Lancs 147 K5
Orton Cumb 157 K1
Orton Nhants 101 H7
Orton Staffs 97 K4
Orton Longueville C Pete 102 D4
Orton-on-the-Hill Leics 99 J3
Orton Rigg Cumb 177 K8
Orton Waterville C Pete 102 C4
Orwell Cambs 87 H5
Osbaldeston Lancs 139 K2
Osbaldeston Green Lancs 139 K1
Osbaldwick C York 151 K5
Osbaston Leics 99 L3
Osbaston Mons 63 G4
Osbaston Shrops 112 D7
Osborne IoW 19 H5
Osbournby Lincs 118 E4
Oscroft Ches W 129 L6
Ose Highld 258 E8
Osgathorpe Leics 116 D7
Osgodby Lincs 135 M1
Osgodby N York 143 G1
Osgodby N York 163 J5
Oskaig Highld 247 H1
Oskamull Ag & B 226 E4
Osmaston Derbys 115 K3
Osmington Dorset 16 D6
Osmington Mills Dorset 16 D6
Osmondthorpe Leeds 142 A1
Osmotherley N York 161 G3
Osney Oxon 66 D6
Ospringe Kent 40 C3
Ossett Wakefd 141 L4
Ossington Notts 134 E6
Ostend Essex 72 D7
Osterley Gt Lon 50 F3
Oswaldkirk N York 161 K6
Oswaldtwistle Lancs 139 L2
Oswestry Shrops 112 D5
Otairnis W Isls 282 c7
Otford Kent 52 B7
Otham Kent 39 K3
Otham Hole Kent 39 K3
Othery Somset 30 F4
Otley Leeds 150 B6
Otley Suffk 90 E4

Otley Green Suffk...90 F4
Otterbourne Hants...34 F6
Otterburn N York...148 F4
Otterburn Nthumb...190 C7
Otter Ferry Ag & B...206 E2
Otterham Cnwll...11 H4
Otterhampton Somset...30 C2
Otterham Quay Kent...53 H5
Otterham Station Cnwll...11 G5
Otternish W Isls...282 c7
Ottershaw Surrey...50 C6
Otterswick Shet...281 e3
Otterton Devon...14 C5
Otterwood Hants...18 F3
Ottery St Mary Devon...14 C3
Ottinge Kent...41 G6
Ottringham E R Yk...145 H3
Oughterby Cumb...177 J7
Oughtershaw N York...158 F6
Oughterside Cumb...164 F3
Oughtibridge Sheff...132 F1
Oughtrington Warrtn...130 D2
Oulston N York...161 J7
Oulton Cumb...177 H8
Oulton Leeds...142 B2
Oulton Norfk...122 C6
Oulton Staffs...114 B7
Oulton Staffs...114 E4
Oulton Suffk...107 L4
Oulton Broad Suffk...107 L5
Oulton Street Norfk...122 C6
Oundle Nhants...102 A5
Ounsdale Staffs...97 K5
Ousby Cumb...166 E4
Ousden Suffk...88 E3
Ousefleet E R Yk...143 L3
Ouston Dur...181 G8
Outchester Nthumb...203 J6
Out Elmstead Kent...41 G5
Outgate Cumb...156 E3
Outhgill Cumb...158 D2
Outhill Warwks...82 D2
Outlands Staffs...114 B5
Outlane Kirk...141 G4
Out Newton E R Yk...145 K3
Out Rawcliffe Lancs...147 H7
Out Skerries Shet...281 g4
Outwell Norfk...103 K3
Outwick Hants...33 K7
Outwood Surrey...37 M2
Outwood Wakefd...142 A3
Outwood Gate Bury...140 B6
Outwoods Leics...116 C7
Outwoods Staffs...114 B7
Ouzlewell Green Leeds...142 A3
Ovenden Calder...141 G2
Over Cambs...87 H1
Over Ches W...130 C6
Over Gloucs...64 A3
Over S Glos...45 H2
Over Burrows Derbys...115 L4
Overbury Worcs...81 M7
Overcombe Dorset...16 D6
Over Compton Dorset...31 K7
Overgreen Derbys...132 F5
Over Green Warwks...98 F4
Over Haddon Derbys...132 D6
Over Hulton Bolton...139 K6
Over Kellet Lancs...147 K2
Over Kiddington Oxon...66 B3
Overleigh Somset...31 G4
Overley Staffs...115 J8
Over Monnow Mons...63 G4
Over Norton Oxon...65 L2
Over Peover Ches E...130 F5
Overpool Ches W...129 J4
Overscaig Highld...272 B3
Overseal Derbys...115 M8
Over Silton N York...161 G4
Oversland Kent...40 D4
Oversley Green Warwks...82 C4
Overstone Nhants...84 F2
Over Stowey Somset...30 B3
Overstrand Norfk...122 E3
Over Stratton Somset...31 G7
Overstreet Wilts...33 J3
Over Tabley Ches E...130 E4
Overthorpe Nhants...83 L7
Overton C Aber...245 J1
Overton Ches W...129 M4
Overton Hants...35 G1
Overton Lancs...147 H4
Overton N York...151 J5
Overton Shrops...80 C1
Overton Swans...56 E7
Overton Wakefd...141 L4
Overton Wrexhm...112 E3
Overton Bridge Wrexhm...112 E3
Overton Green Ches E...130 F7

Overtown Lancs...140 C2
Overtown Lancs...157 K7
Overtown N Lans...209 L8
Overtown Swindn...47 H3
Overtown Wakefd...142 A4
Over Wallop Hants...34 C3
Over Whitacre Warwks...99 H5
Over Woodhouse Derbys...133 J5
Over Worton Oxon...66 B1
Overy Oxon...66 E8
Oving Bucks...67 J3
Oving W Susx...20 E6
Ovingdean Br & H...22 E6
Ovingham Nthumb...180 D6
Ovington Dur...168 E7
Ovington Essex...88 F6
Ovington Hants...35 H4
Ovington Norfk...105 J3
Ovington Nthumb...180 C6
Ower Hants...19 H3
Ower Hants...34 D7
Owermoigne Dorset...16 E5
Owlbury Shrops...95 H5
Owlerton Sheff...133 G2
Owlpen Gloucs...64 A7
Owl's Green Suffk...91 G1
Owlsmoor Br For...49 K6
Owlswick Bucks...67 J6
Owmby Lincs...135 K2
Owmby Lincs...144 D6
Owslebury Hants...35 G6
Owston Donc...142 E5
Owston Leics...101 A2
Owston Ferry N Linc...143 K7
Owstwick E R Yk...145 H1
Owthorne E R Yk...145 J2
Owthorpe Notts...117 H5
Owton Manor Hartpl...170 C5
Oxborough Norfk...104 E3
Oxbridge Dorset...15 L3
Oxcombe Lincs...136 F4
Oxcroft Derbys...133 J5
Oxen End Essex...71 G1
Oxenholme Cumb...157 H5
Oxenhope C Brad...140 F1
Oxen Park Cumb...156 D5
Oxenpill Somset...31 G3
Oxenton Gloucs...64 D1
Oxenwood Wilts...47 L7
Oxford Oxon...66 D6
Oxford Airport Oxon...66 C4
Oxford Services Oxon...66 F6
Oxgangs C Edin...211 H5
Oxhey Herts...68 E8
Oxhill Dur...180 F8
Oxhill Warwks...83 H6
Oxley Wolves...97 K3
Oxley Green Essex...72 C4
Oxley's Green E Susx...24 C3
Oxlode Cambs...103 K6
Oxnam Border...189 J3
Oxnead Norfk...122 E6
Oxshott Surrey...50 F6
Oxshott Heath Surrey...50 E6
Oxspring Barns...141 L7
Oxted Surrey...51 K8
Oxton Border...201 G2
Oxton N York...151 H7
Oxton Notts...117 G1
Oxton Wirral...129 G2
Oxwich Swans...56 F7
Oxwich Green Swans...56 F7
Oxwick Norfk...121 K6
Oykel Bridge Highld...271 L7
Oyne Abers...256 B6
Oystermouth Swans...57 H7
Ozleworth Gloucs...64 A8

P

Pabail W Isls...282 h3
Packers Hill Dorset...16 D1
Packington Leics...116 B8
Packmoor C Stke...114 D1
Packmores Warwks...83 G2
Padanaram Angus...234 D2
Padbury Bucks...67 H1
Paddington Gt Lon...51 H3
Paddington Warrtn...130 C2
Paddlesworth Kent...41 G7
Paddlesworth Kent...52 E6
Paddock Wood Kent...39 G4
Paddolgreen Shrops...113 H5
Padfield Derbys...140 F8
Padgate Warrtn...130 C2
Padhams Green Essex...70 F7
Padiham Lancs...140 B1
Padside N York...149 L4

Padstow Cnwll...10 C7
Padworth W Berk...48 F5
Page Bank Dur...169 G4
Pagham W Susx...20 E7
Paglesham Essex...72 D8
Paignton Torbay...8 C3
Pailton Warwks...100 A7
Paine's Cross E Susx...23 K3
Painleyhill Staffs...115 G5
Painscastle Powys...79 G6
Painshawfield Nthumb...180 C6
Painsthorpe E R Yk...152 B4
Painswick Gloucs...64 C5
Painter's Forstal Kent...40 C3
Paisley Rens...208 E6
Pakefield Suffk...107 L5
Pakenham Suffk...89 J2
Pale Gwynd...111 J4
Pale Green Essex...88 D6
Palestine Hants...34 B3
Paley Street W & M...49 L4
Palfrey Wsall...98 C4
Palgrave Suffk...106 C7
Pallington Dorset...16 F4
Palmarsh Kent...40 F8
Palmers Green Gt Lon...69 J8
Palmerston E Ayrs...196 F7
Palmerstown V Glam...43 H7
Palnackie D & G...175 K3
Palnure D & G...174 C2
Palterton Derbys...133 J6
Pamber End Hants...48 F7
Pamber Green Hants...48 F7
Pamber Heath Hants...48 F6
Pamington Gloucs...81 L8
Pamphill Dorset...17 K3
Pampisford Cambs...87 K5
Panborough Somset...31 G2
Panbride Angus...234 E8
Pancrasweek Devon...11 K2
Pancross V Glam...43 G7
Pandy Gwynd...92 D3
Pandy Gwynd...111 G5
Pandy Mons...62 C3
Pandy Powys...93 K3
Pandy Wrexhm...112 B4
Pandy Wrexhm...112 E1
Pandy'r Capel Denbgs...111 L2
Pandy Tudur Conwy...127 G6
Panfield Essex...71 H2
Pangbourne W Berk...48 F4
Pangdean W Susx...22 D5
Panks Bridge Herefs...80 E5
Pannal N York...150 D5
Pannal Ash N York...150 C5
Pant Shrops...112 D7
Pantasaph Flints...128 E4
Panteg Pembks...74 F5
Pantersbridge Cnwll...5 K1
Pant-ffrwyth Brdgnd...42 E5
Pant Glas Gwynd...109 H2
Pantglas Powys...93 G4
Pant-Gwyn Carmth...59 G4
Pant-lasau Swans...57 J5
Pant Mawr Powys...93 J7
Panton Lincs...136 C4
Pant-pastynog Denbgs...128 B7
Pantperthog Gwynd...93 G3
Pantside Caerph...43 K2
Pant-y-caws Carmth...75 K7
Pant-y-dwr Powys...93 L8
Pant-y-ffridd Powys...94 E3
Pantyffynnon Carmth...57 H3
Pantygaseg Torfn...61 L7
Pantygelli Mons...62 C3
Pant-y-gog Brdgnd...42 D2
Pantymwyn Flints...128 E6
Panxworth Norfk...107 G1
Papa Stour Shet...281 c5
Papa Stour Airport Shet...281 c5
Papa Westray Ork...275 d1
Papa Westray Airport Ork...275 d1
Papcastle Cumb...164 F4
Papigoe Highld...280 D6
Papple E Loth...212 D4
Papplewick Notts...116 F1
Papworth Everard Cambs...86 F3
Papworth St Agnes Cambs...86 F2
Par Cnwll...5 H4
Paramour Street Kent...41 J3
Parbold Lancs...139 G5
Parbrook Somset...31 J4
Parbrook W Susx...37 G6
Parc Gwynd...111 G5
Parcllyn Cerdgn...75 M2
Parc Seymour Newpt...44 E1
Pardown Hants...35 J1
Pardshaw Cumb...164 E5
Parham Suffk...91 G3
Park D & G...186 D7

Park Nthumb...178 F6
Park Bottom Cnwll...3 H3
Park Bridge Tamesd...140 E7
Park Corner E Susx...38 E6
Park Corner Oxon...49 G5
Park Corner W & M...49 K2
Park End Bed...85 K4
Parkend Gloucs...63 J5
Park End Nthumb...179 K4
Parker's Green Kent...38 F4
Parkeston Essex...73 K1
Parkeston Quay Essex...90 F8
Park Farm Kent...40 D4
Parkgate Ches W...129 G4
Parkgate Cumb...165 H1
Parkgate D & G...176 D1
Parkgate E Susx...24 C5
Parkgate Essex...71 G1
Park Gate Hants...19 J2
Parkgate Kent...39 L6
Parkgate Kent...52 B6
Park Gate Leeds...150 A7
Parkgate Surrey...37 K2
Park Gate Worcs...81 L1
Park Green Essex...70 C2
Park Green Suffk...90 D2
Parkhall W Duns...208 E4
Parkham Devon...27 G6
Parkham Ash Devon...26 F6
Park Head Derbys...116 B1
Parkhill Dur...169 J3
Park Hill Gloucs...63 H7
Parkhouse Mons...63 G6
Parkmill Swans...57 G7
Park Royal Gt Lon...51 G3
Parkside Dur...169 L1
Parkside N Lans...209 L7
Parkside Wrexhm...129 J8
Parkstone BCP...17 K4
Park Street Herts...68 F6
Park Street W Susx...37 H4
Parkway Herefs...81 G8
Parley Green BCP...17 M3
Parmoor Bucks...49 J1
Parracombe Devon...28 B2
Parrog Pembks...75 H4
Parsonby Cumb...164
Parson Cross Sheff...133 G1
Parson Drove Cambs...103 H2
Parson's Heath Essex...72 F
Parson's Hill Derbys...116 A
Partick C Glas...208 F
Partington Traffd...130 D
Partney Lincs...137 H
Parton Cumb...164 C
Partridge Green W Susx...22 B
Partrishow Powys...62 B
Parwich Derbys...115 K
Paslow Wood Common Essex...70 E
Passenham Nhants...84 F
Passfield Hants...36 B
Passingford Bridge Essex...70 D
Paston C Pete...102 D
Paston Norfk...123 G
Pasturefields Staffs...114 F
Patchacott Devon...12 B
Patcham Br & H...22 D
Patchetts Green Herts...68 F
Patching W Susx...21 J
Patchole Devon...27 L
Patchway S Glos...45 J
Pateley Bridge N York...149 L
Paternoster Heath Essex...72 D
Pathe Somset...30 F
Pathhead Fife...222 E
Pathhead Mdloth...211 L
Pathlow Warwks...82 E
Path of Condie P & K...221 K
Patmore Heath Herts...70 B
Patna E Ayrs...183 K
Patney Wilts...47 G
Patrick IoM...154 c
Patrick Brompton N York...160 B
Patricroft Salfd...139 M
Patrington E R Yk...145 J
Patrington Haven E R Yk...145 J
Patrixbourne Kent...41 G
Patterdale Cumb...165 J
Pattingham Staffs...97 J
Pattishall Nhants...84 C
Pattiswick Green Essex...71 K
Patton Shrops...96 D
Patton Bridge Cumb...157 J
Paul Cnwll...2 D
Paulerspury Nhants...84 D
Paull E R Yk...144 F
Paulton BaNES...45 K
Paunton Herefs...80 C
Pauperhaugh Nthumb...191 G
Pave Lane Wrekin...114 B

Pavenham Bed....85 K4
Pawlett Somset....30 D2
Pawston Nthumb....202 C6
Paxford Gloucs....82 E7
Paxton Border....202 A6
Payden Street Kent....40 B4
Payhembury Devon....14 C2
Paynter's Lane End Cnwll....3 H2
Paythorne Lancs....148 E5
Paytoe Herefs....80 A1
Peacehaven E Susx....22 F7
Peak Dale Derbys....132 B4
Peak District National Park....132 D2
Peak Forest Derbys....132 B4
Peak Hill Lincs....119 J8
Peakirk C Pete....102 D2
Pearson's Green Kent....39 H4
Peartree Green Herefs....80 E8
Peasedown St John BaNES....45 K7
Peasehill Derbys....116 C2
Peaseland Green Norfk....122 B8
Peasemore W Berk....48 C3
Peasenhall Suffk....91 H2
Pease Pottage W Susx....37 L4
Pease Pottage Services
 W Susx....37 L4
Peaslake Surrey....37 G2
Peasley Cross St Hel....129 M1
Peasmarsh E Susx....25 G3
Peasmarsh Somset....30 E8
Peasmarsh Surrey....36 E2
Peathill Abers....269 G3
Peat Inn Fife....223 H5
Peatling Magna Leics....100 D5
Peatling Parva Leics....100 D5
Peaton Shrops....96 C6
Pebmarsh Essex....89 G8
Pebsham E Susx....24 D5
Pebworth Worcs....82 D6
Pecket Well Calder....140 F2
Peckforton Ches E....129 M8
Peckham Gt Lon....51 J4
Peckleton Leics....100 A3
Pedairffordd Powys....111 M6
Pedlinge Kent....40 F8
Pedmore Dudley....97 K7
Pedwell Somset....30 F4
Peebles Border....200 B5
Peel IoM....154 c5
Peel Lancs....138 D2
Peel Common Hants....19 K3
Peene Kent....41 G7
Peening Quarter Kent....39 M7
Peggs Green Leics....116 C7
Pegsdon C Beds....68 E1
Pegswood Nthumb....180 F2
Pegwell Kent....41 K3
Peinchorran Highld....247 H2
Peinlich Highld....259 G5
Pelcomb Pembks....54 F3
Pelcomb Bridge Pembks....54 F3
Pelcomb Cross Pembks....54 F3
Peldon Essex....72 E4
Pell Green E Susx....39 G6
Pelsall Wsall....98 C3
Pelsall Wood Wsall....98 C3
Pelton Dur....181 G8
Pelton Fell Dur....181 G8
Pelutho Cumb....164 F1
Pelynt Cnwll....5 L4
Pemberton Carmth....56 F5
Pemberton Wigan....139 H7
Pembles Cross Kent....39 M4
Pembrey Carmth....56 D4
Pembridge Herefs....79 M4
Pembroke Pembks....55 G6
Pembroke Dock Pembks....54 F6
Pembrokeshire Coast
 National Park Pembks....54 D3
Pembury Kent....39 G5
Pen-allt Herefs....63 H1
Penallt Mons....63 G5
Penally Pembks....55 J7
Penare Cnwll....5 G2
Penarth V Glam....43 J7
Penblewin Pembks....55 J4
Pen-bont Rhydybeddau Cerdgn....92 E6
Penbryn Cerdgn....76 B5
Pencader Carmth....58 E2
Pencaenewydd Gwynd....109 G3
Pencaitland E Loth....212 A5
Pencarnisiog IoA....124 F5
Pencarreg Carmth....76 D6
Pencarrow Cnwll....10 F6
Pencelli Powys....61 H2
Penclawdd Swans....57 G5
Pencoed Brdgnd....42 E5
Pencombe Herefs....80 E5
Pencoyd Herefs....63 G2
Pencraig Herefs....63 H3

Pencraig Powys....111 K6
Pendeen Cnwll....2 B4
Penderyn Rhondd....60 E5
Pendine Carmth....55 L5
Pendlebury Salfd....140 B7
Pendleton Lancs....148 D7
Pendock Worcs....81 H8
Pendoggett Cnwll....10 E6
Pendomer Somset....31 H8
Pendoylan V Glam....43 G6
Penegoes Powys....93 G3
Penelewey Cnwll....3 K3
Pen-ffordd Pembks....55 J2
Pengam Caerph....43 K6
Pengam Cardif....43 K6
Penge Gt Lon....51 K5
Pengelly Cnwll....10 F6
Pengenffordd Powys....61 J1
Pengorffwysfa IoA....125 H1
Pengover Green Cnwll....6 B2
Pen-groes-oped Mons....62 C5
Pengwern Denbgs....127 K4
Penhale Cnwll....3 H7
Penhale Cnwll....4 E3
Penhale Cnwll....5 J3
Penhale Cnwll....6 E4
Penhallow Cnwll....4 C4
Penhalurick Cnwll....3 H3
Penhalvean Cnwll....3 H3
Penhill Swindn....47 H1
Penhow Newpt....44 E1
Penhurst E Susx....24 C4
Peniarth Gwynd....92 D2
Penicuik Mdloth....211 H7
Peniel Carmth....58 D4
Peniel Denbgs....127 L7
Penifiler Highld....259 H8
Peninver Ag & B....192 F3
Penisarwaun Gwynd....125 K7
Penistone Barns....141 K8
Penjerrick Cnwll....3 K5
Penketh Warrtn....130 A2
Penkill S Ayrs....183 G3
Penkridge Staffs....97 L1
Penlean Cnwll....11 H3
Penleigh Wilts....32 E1
Penley Wrexhm....112 F3
Penllergaer Swans....57 H5
Pen-llyn IoA....124 F3
Penllyn V Glam....42 E6
Pen-lôn IoA....125 G6
Penmachno Conwy....110 D2
Penmaen Caerph....43 J2
Penmaen Swans....56 F7
Penmaenan Conwy....126 E4
Penmaenmawr Conwy....126 E4
Penmaenpool Gwynd....110 C7
Penmark V Glam....43 G7
Penmon IoA....126 C3
Penmorfa Gwynd....109 K3
Penmynydd IoA....125 J5
Penn Bucks....67 M8
Penn Wolves....97 K4
Pennal Gwynd....92 F3
Pennan Abers....268 E3
Pennant Cerdgn....76 F3
Pennant Denbgs....111 K5
Pennant Powys....93 J4
Pennant-Melangell Powys....111 K6
Pennar Pembks....54 F6
Pennard Swans....57 G7
Pennerley Shrops....95 J3
Pennicott Devon....13 K2
Pennines....140 E1
Pennington Cumb....156 C7
Pennington Hants....18 D4
Pennington Green Wigan....139 J6
Pennorth Powys....61 H2
Penn Street Bucks....68 A7
Pennsylvania S Glos....45 L4
Penny Bridge Cumb....156 D6
Pennycross Ag & B....226 F7
Pennygate Norfk....123 G7
Pennyghael Ag & B....227 G2
Pennyglen S Ayrs....183 H1
Penny Green Derbys....133 L4
Penny Hill Lincs....119 K6
Pennymoor Devon....28 F8
Pennywell Sundld....181 J7
Penparc Cerdgn....75 L3
Penparcau Cerdgn....92 D7
Penpedairheol Caerph....43 J2
Penpedairheol Mons....62 C6
Penpergwm Mons....62 C5
Penperlleni Mons....62 C6
Penpethy Cnwll....10 D5
Penpillick Cnwll....5 J4
Penpol Cnwll....3 K3
Penpoll Cnwll....5 K4
Penponds Cnwll....3 G3

Penpont Cnwll....10 F7
Penpont D & G....186 C7
Penpont Powys....60 E2
Penquit Devon....7 J4
Penrest Cnwll....11 L7
Penrherber Carmth....76 B7
Pen-rhiw Pembks....75 M4
Penrhiwceiber Rhondd....43 G2
Pen Rhiwfawr Neath....57 K3
Penrhiwgoch Carmth....59 G5
Penrhiwllan Cerdgn....76 C6
Penrhiwpal Cerdgn....76 C6
Penrhos Gwynd....108 F5
Penrhos IoA....124 D3
Penrhos Mons....62 E5
Penrhos Powys....59 L6
Penrhos garnedd Gwynd....125 K5
Penrhyn Bay Conwy....127 G3
Penrhyn-coch Cerdgn....92 E6
Penrhyndeudraeth Gwynd....109 L4
Penrhyn-side Conwy....126 F3
Penrhyn Slate Landscape
 Gwynd....126 C6
Penrhys Rhondd....42 F3
Penrice Swans....56 F7
Penrioch N Ayrs....194 D2
Penrith Cumb....166 C4
Penrose Cnwll....10 B8
Penruddock Cumb....166 A5
Penryn Cnwll....3 K4
Pensarn Conwy....127 J4
Pensax Worcs....81 G2
Pensby Wirral....129 G3
Penselwood Somset....32 C4
Pensford BaNES....45 J6
Pensham Worcs....81 L6
Penshaw Sundld....181 H8
Penshurst Kent....38 E4
Penshurst Station Kent....38 E4
Pensilva Cnwll....11 L4
Pensnett Dudley....97 K5
Penstone Devon....13 H3
Penstrowed Powys....94 C5
Pentewan Cnwll....5 G5
Pentir Gwynd....125 K6
Pentire Cnwll....4 C3
Pentlepoir Pembks....55 J5
Pentlow Essex....89 G6
Pentlow Street Essex....89 G6
Pentney Norfk....120 F8
Penton Grafton Hants....34 D2
Penton Mewsey Hants....34 D2
Pentraeth IoA....125 J4
Pentre Denbgs....128 C7
Pentre Flints....129 H6
Pentre Mons....62 C6
Pentre Mons....62 E7
Pentre Powys....94 C6
Pentre Powys....94 E5
Pentre Powys....95 G5
Pentre Rhondd....42 E2
Pentre Shrops....112 E7
Pentre Shrops....112 D3
Pentre-bâch Cerdgn....77 G6
Pentre Bach Flints....128 F4
Pentrebach Myr Td....61 G6
Pentre-bach Powys....78 B8
Pentrebeirdd Powys....94 E1
Pentre Berw IoA....125 H5
Pentre-bont Conwy....110 D1
Pentre-cagel Carmth....76 C7
Pentrecelyn Denbgs....112 A1
Pentre-celyn Powys....93 J2
Pentre-chwyth Swans....57 J6
Pentre-clawdd Shrops....112 D5
Pentre-cwrt Carmth....76 D7
Pentredwr Denbgs....112 B2
Pentrefelin Gwynd....109 J4
Pentrefelin IoA....125 H1
Pentre Ffwrndan Flints....128 F5
Pentrefoelas Conwy....111 G1
Pentregalar Pembks....75 L6
Pentregat Cerdgn....76 C5
Pentre-Gwenlais Carmth....59 H5
Pentre Gwynfryn Gwynd....109 L6
Pentre Halkyn Flints....128 E5
Pentre Hodrey Shrops....95 H7
Pentre Isaf Conwy....127 K5
Pentre Llanrhaeadr Denbgs....128 C7
Pentre Llifior Powys....94 E4
Pentre-llwyn-llwyd Powys....78 C4
Pentre-llyn Cerdgn....92 D8
Pentre-llyn-cymmer Conwy....111 J1
Pentre-Maw Powys....93 J3
Pentre Meyrick V Glam....42 E6
Pentre-piod Torfn....62 B6
Pentre-poeth Newpt....44 B2
Pentre'rbryn Cerdgn....76 D4
Pentre'r-felin Cerdgn....77 H5

Pentre'r Felin Conwy....126 F6
Pentre'r-felin Powys....60 D1
Pentre Saron Denbgs....127 L7
Pentre-tafarn-y-fedw Conwy....126 F7
Pentre ty gwyn Carmth....59 M2
Pentrich Derbys....116 C1
Pentridge Dorset....33 H7
Pen-twyn Caerph....61 K7
Pentwyn Cardif....43 K5
Pen-twyn Mons....63 G5
Pen-twyn Torfn....61 L6
Pentwynmaur Caerph....43 K2
Pentyrch Cardif....43 H5
Penwithick Cnwll....5 H4
Penwood Hants....48 C6
Penwyllt Powys....60 C4
Penybanc Carmth....59 H4
Penybont Powys....78 F2
Pen-y-bont Powys....112 B6
Penybontfawr Powys....111 L6
Pen-y-bryn Pembks....75 L4
Pen-y-cae Powys....60 C4
Penycae Wrexhm....112 D3
Pen-y-cae-mawr Mons....62 E8
Penycaerau Gwynd....108 C6
Pen-y-cefn Flints....128 D4
Pen-y-clawdd Mons....62 F5
Pen-y-coedcae Rhondd....43 G4
Penycwn Pembks....54 D2
Pen-y-fai Brdgnd....42 D5
Pen-y-felin Flints....128 D5
Pen-y-ffordd Flints....128 D3
Penyffordd Flints....129 G7
Penyffridd Gwynd....125 J8
Pen-y-garn Cerdgn....92 D6
Pen-y-Garnedd Powys....111 L6
Pen-y-graig Gwynd....108 C5
Penygraig Rhondd....42 F3
Penygroes Carmth....59 G6
Penygroes Gwynd....109 H1
Penygroeslon Gwynd....108 C5
Pen-y-Gwryd Gwynd....126 D8
Pen-y-lan V Glam....42 F6
Pen-y-Mynydd Carmth....56 E4
Penymynydd Flints....129 G7
Pen-y-pass Gwynd....126 C8
Pen-yr-Heol Mons....62 E5
Penysarn IoA....125 H2
Pen-y-stryt Denbgs....112 B1
Penywaun Rhondd....60 E6
Penzance Cnwll....2 D5
Peopleton Worcs....81 L5
Peover Heath Ches E....130 F5
Peper Harow Surrey....36 D2
Peplow Shrops....113 K6
Pepper's Green Essex....70 F5
Pepperstock C Beds....68 D3
Perceton N Ayrs....196 C3
Percyhorner Abers....269 H3
Perelle Guern....9 i3
Perham Down Wilts....34 B1
Periton Somset....29 G2
Perivale Gt Lon....50 F2
Perkins Village Devon....14 B4
Perkinsville Dur....181 G8
Perlethorpe Notts....134 C5
Perranarworthal Cnwll....3 K3
Perranporth Cnwll....4 B4
Perranuthnoe Cnwll....2 E5
Perranwell Cnwll....3 K3
Perranwell Cnwll....4 C4
Perran Wharf Cnwll....3 K3
Perranzabuloe Cnwll....4 C4
Perrott's Brook Gloucs....64 E6
Perry Birm....98 D5
Perry Cambs....86 C2
Perry Barr Birm....98 D5
Perry Green Essex....71 K3
Perry Green Herts....70 B4
Perry Green Wilts....46 F2
Perrystone Hill Herefs....63 J1
Perry Street Somset....15 H2
Pershall Staffs....114 C5
Pershore Worcs....81 L6
Pertenhall Bed....86 B2
Perth P & K....221 K3
Perthy Shrops....112 E5
Perton Herefs....80 E7
Perton Staffs....97 J3
Pertwood Wilts....32 E4
Peterborough C Pete....102 D4
Peterborough Services Cambs....102 C5
Peterchurch Herefs....79 L7
Peterculter C Aber....245 J3
Peterhead Abers....257 L2
Peterlee Dur....169 L2
Petersfield Hants....35 M6
Peter's Green Herts....68 F3
Petersham Gt Lon....50 F4
Peters Marland Devon....27 H8

Peterstone Wentlooge Newpt...43 L5
Peterston-super-Ely V Glam...43 G6
Peterstow Herefs...63 H2
Peters Village Kent...52 F6
Peter Tavy Devon...12 C7
Petham Kent...40 F5
Petherwin Gate Cnwll...11 K5
Petrockstow Devon...12 C1
Petsoe End M Keyn...85 H5
Pet Street Kent...40 E6
Pett E Susx...24 F4
Pettaugh Suffk...90 E3
Pett Bottom Kent...40 F5
Petterden Angus...234 C7
Pettinain S Lans...198 F4
Pettistree Suffk...91 G4
Petton Devon...29 H6
Petton Shrops...113 G6
Petts Wood Gt Lon...51 M5
Pettycur Fife...211 J2
Petty France S Glos...46 A2
Pettymuk Abers...257 G7
Petworth W Susx...36 E6
Pevensey E Susx...23 L6
Pevensey Bay E Susx...24 B6
Pewsey Wilts...47 H7
Pewsham Wilts...46 D4
Pheasant's Hill Bucks...49 J2
Phepson Worcs...81 L3
Philadelphia Sundld...181 H8
Philham Devon...26 D6
Philiphaugh Border...200 F7
Phillack Cnwll...2 F3
Philleigh Cnwll...3 L3
Philpot End Essex...70 F3
Philpstoun W Loth...210 E4
Phocle Green Herefs...63 J2
Phoenix Green Hants...49 J7
Pibsbury Somset...31 G5
Pica Cumb...164 D6
Piccadilly Warwks...99 G4
Piccotts End Herts...68 D5
Pickburn Donc...142 E6
Pickering N York...162 D6
Picket Piece Hants...34 E2
Picket Post Hants...18 B2
Picket Twenty Hants...34 E2
Pickford Covtry...99 H7
Pickford Green Covtry...99 H7
Pickhill N York...160 E6
Picklescott Shrops...95 K3
Pickmere Ches E...130 D4
Pickney Somset...30 B5
Pickstock Wrekin...114 A6
Pickup Bank Bl w D...139 L3
Pickwell Devon...27 H3
Pickwell Leics...101 G1
Pickwick Wilts...46 B5
Pickworth Lincs...118 D5
Pickworth Rutlnd...101 L1
Picton Ches W...129 K5
Picton Flints...128 D3
Picton N York...160 F1
Piddinghoe E Susx...23 L6
Piddington Bucks...67 K8
Piddington Nhants...84 F4
Piddington Oxon...66 F4
Piddlehinton Dorset...16 D3
Piddletrenthide Dorset...16 D3
Pidley Cambs...103 G7
Piercebridge Darltn...169 G7
Pierowall Ork...275 c1
Piff's Elm Gloucs...64 C2
Pigdon Nthumb...180 E1
Pigeon Green Warwks...82 F3
Pig Oak Dorset...17 K2
Pig Street Herefs...79 L5
Pikehall Derbys...132 D7
Pilford Dorset...17 K2
Pilgrims Hatch Essex...70 F7
Pilham Lincs...135 H1
Pill N Som...45 G4
Pillaton Cnwll...6 D2
Pillatonmill Cnwll...6 D2
Pillerton Hersey Warwks...83 G5
Pillerton Priors Warwks...83 G5
Pilleth Powys...79 J2
Pilley Barns...142 A7
Pilley Hants...18 E4
Pilley Bailey Hants...18 E4
Pillgwenlly Newpt...44 C2
Pillhead Devon...27 H5
Pilling Lancs...147 H6
Pilling Lane Lancs...147 G6
Pilning S Glos...45 H2
Pilot Inn Kent...25 K4
Pilsbury Derbys...132 B7
Pilsdon Dorset...15 J3
Pilsgate C Pete...102 B2
Pilsley Derbys...132 E5

Pilsley Derbys...133 H7
Pilson Green Norfk...107 H1
Piltdown E Susx...23 G3
Pilton Devon...27 K4
Pilton Nhants...101 M6
Pilton Rutlnd...101 K3
Pilton Somset...31 K3
Pilton Green Swans...56 E7
Pimbo Lancs...139 G7
Pimlico Herts...68 E6
Pimlico Lancs...148 C7
Pimlico Nhants...84 B7
Pimperne Dorset...17 H1
Pinchbeck Lincs...119 H6
Pinchbeck Bars Lincs...119 G6
Pincheon Green Donc...143 G4
Pinchinthorpe R & Cl...170 D7
Pincock Lancs...139 H4
Pinfold Lancs...138 E5
Pinford End Suffk...89 G3
Pinged Carmth...56 D4
Pingewood W Berk...49 G5
Pin Green Herts...69 H2
Pinhoe Devon...13 M4
Pinkett's Booth Covtry...99 H7
Pinkney Wilts...46 B2
Pinkneys Green W & M...49 L3
Pinley Covtry...99 K7
Pinley Green Warwks...82 F2
Pin Mill Suffk...90 E7
Pinminnoch S Ayrs...182 F4
Pinmore S Ayrs...182 F4
Pinn Devon...14 C5
Pinner Gt Lon...50 E1
Pinner Green Gt Lon...50 E1
Pinsley Green Ches E...113 K2
Pinvin Worcs...81 M5
Pinwherry S Ayrs...182 F5
Pinxton Derbys...133 J8
Pipe and Lyde Herefs...80 C6
Pipe Aston Herefs...80 B1
Pipe Gate Shrops...114 A3
Pipehill Staffs...98 E2
Piperdam Angus...233 L8
Piperhill Highld...253 G2
Pipers Pool Cnwll...11 J6
Pipewell Nhants...101 J6
Pippacott Devon...27 J3
Pippin Street Lancs...139 H3
Pipton Powys...79 G7
Pirbright Surrey...50 B7
Pirbright Camp Surrey...50 B7
Pirnie Border...201 K7
Pirnmill N Ayrs...194 D2
Pirton Herts...68 F1
Pirton Worcs...81 K5
Pisgah Cerdgn...92 E7
Pishill Oxon...49 H1
Pistyll Gwynd...108 E3
Pitblae Abers...269 H3
Pitcairngreen P & K...221 J2
Pitcalnie Highld...264 C5
Pitcaple Abers...256 C6
Pitcarity Angus...233 M2
Pitchcombe Gloucs...64 B5
Pitchcott Bucks...67 J3
Pitcher Row Lincs...119 J5
Pitchford Shrops...96 C3
Pitch Green Bucks...67 J6
Pitch Place Surrey...36 C3
Pitch Place Surrey...50 B8
Pitchroy Moray...254 D4
Pitcombe Somset...31 L4
Pitcot V Glam...42 D6
Pitcox E Loth...212 E4
Pitfichie Abers...256 B8
Pitglassie Abers...256 C3
Pitgrudy Highld...264 B2
Pitlessie Fife...222 E5
Pitlochry P & K...232 D4
Pitmachie Abers...256 B6
Pitmain Highld...241 K3
Pitmedden Abers...256 F6
Pitminster Somset...30 B7
Pitmuies Angus...234 E5
Pitmunie Abers...256 B8
Pitney Somset...31 G5
Pitroddie P & K...222 C2
Pitscottie Fife...223 G4
Pitsea Essex...52 F1
Pitses Oldham...140 E7
Pitsford Nhants...84 E2
Pitstone Bucks...68 B4
Pitt Devon...29 J7
Pitt Hants...34 F5
Pittarrow Abers...245 G8
Pitt Court Gloucs...63 L7
Pittentrail Highld...273 H7
Pittenweem Fife...223 K6
Pitteuchar Fife...222 D7

Pittodrie House Hotel Abers...256 C6
Pitton Wilts...34 B4
Pitt's Wood Kent...38 F3
Pittulie Abers...269 H3
Pityme Cnwll...10 C7
Pity Me Dur...169 H2
Pivington Kent...40 B6
Pixey Green Suffk...106 E8
Pixham Surrey...37 J1
Plains N Lans...209 L5
Plain Street Cnwll...10 D6
Plaish Shrops...96 C4
Plaistow Gt Lon...51 L2
Plaistow W Susx...36 F5
Plaitford Hants...34 C7
Plank Lane Wigan...139 J7
Plas Cymyran IoA...124 C4
Plastow Green Hants...48 D6
Platt Bridge Wigan...139 J7
Platt Lane Shrops...113 H4
Platts Heath Kent...39 L3
Plawsworth Dur...169 H1
Plaxtol Kent...38 F3
Playden E Susx...25 G3
Playford Suffk...90 F5
Play Hatch Oxon...49 H4
Playing Place Cnwll...4 C6
Playley Green Gloucs...63 M1
Plealey Shrops...95 K2
Plean Stirlg...209 M2
Pleasance Fife...222 C4
Pleasington Bl w D...139 J2
Pleasley Derbys...133 K6
Pleasleyhill Notts...133 K6
Pleck Dorset...32 B8
Pledgdon Green Essex...70 E2
Pledwick Wakefd...142 A4
Pleinheaume Guern...9 j2
Plemont Jersey...9 a1
Plemstall Ches W...129 K5
Plenmeller Nthumb...179 G6
Pleshey Essex...71 G4
Plockton Highld...248 C5
Plowden Shrops...95 J6
Plox Green Shrops...95 J3
Pluckley Kent...40 B6
Pluckley Station Kent...40 B6
Pluckley Thorne Kent...40 B6
Plucks Gutter Kent...41 J3
Plumbland Cumb...164 F3
Plumgarths Cumb...157 G4
Plumley Ches E...130 E5
Plump Hill Gloucs...63 K4
Plumpton Cumb...156 D7
Plumpton Cumb...166 C3
Plumpton E Susx...22 E4
Plumpton Nhants...84 B5
Plumpton End Nhants...84 D6
Plumpton Green E Susx...22 E4
Plumpton Head Cumb...166 C4
Plumstead Gt Lon...51 L3
Plumstead Norfk...122 C4
Plumstead Green Norfk...122 C4
Plumtree Notts...117 G5
Plumtree Green Kent...39 K4
Plungar Leics...117 K5
Plurenden Kent...40 B7
Plush Dorset...16 D2
Plusha Cnwll...11 J6
Plushabridge Cnwll...11 K8
Plwmp Cerdgn...76 C5
Plymouth C Plym...6 F4
Plympton C Plym...7 G4
Plymstock C Plym...7 G4
Plymtree Devon...14 B2
Pockley N York...161 K5
Pocklington E R Yk...152 B6
Pode Hole Lincs...119 H7
Podimore Somset...31 J6
Podington Bed...85 J3
Podmore Staffs...114 B4
Point Clear Essex...73 G4
Pointon Lincs...118 F5
Pokesdown BCP...18 A5
Polbain Highld...270 C6
Polbathic Cnwll...6 C3
Polbeth W Loth...210 D6
Polbrock Cnwll...5 G1
Poldark Mine Cnwll...3 H5
Polebrook Nhants...102 B6
Pole Elm Worcs...81 J5
Polegate E Susx...23 K6
Pole Moor Kirk...141 G4
Polesworth Warwks...99 H3
Polgigga Cnwll...2 B6
Polglass Highld...270 D6
Polgooth Cnwll...5 G5
Polgown D & G...185 H2
Poling W Susx...21 H6
Poling Corner W Susx...21 H5

Polkerris Cnwll...5 J4
Pollard Street Norfk...123 G5
Pollington E R Yk...142 F4
Polloch Highld...228 B2
Pollok C Glas...208 F6
Pollokshaws C Glas...208 F6
Pollokshields C Glas...208 F6
Polmassick Cnwll...5 G5
Polmear Cnwll...5 J4
Polmont Falk...210 B3
Polnish Highld...237 L4
Polperro Cnwll...5 L4
Polruan Cnwll...5 K5
Polsham Somset...31 H2
Polstead Suffk...89 K7
Polstead Heath Suffk...89 K7
Poltalloch Ag & B...216 C2
Poltescoe Cnwll...3 J7
Poltimore Devon...13 M3
Polton Mdloth...211 J6
Polwarth Border...202 A3
Polyphant Cnwll...11 J3
Polzeath Cnwll...10 C6
Pomathorn Mdloth...211 H7
Pomeroy Derbys...132 B6
Ponde Powys...78 F3
Pondersbridge Cambs...102 F5
Ponders End Gt Lon...69 K7
Ponsanooth Cnwll...3 J3
Ponsonby Cumb...155 J3
Ponsongath Cnwll...3 J7
Ponsworthy Devon...13 G7
Pont Abraham Services
  Carmth...57 G3
Pontac Jersey...9 e4
Pontamman Carmth...59 H6
Pontantwn Carmth...58 E6
Pontardawe Neath...57 K4
Pontarddulais Swans...57 G4
Pont-ar-gothi Carmth...58 F4
Pont-ar-Hydfer Powys...60 C2
Pont-ar-llechau Carmth...59 K4
Pontarsais Carmth...58 E3
Pontblyddyn Flints...129 G7
Pont Cyfyng Conwy...126 E8
Pontcysyllte Aqueduct
  Wrexhm...112 C3
Pont Dolgarrog Conwy...126 F6
Pontdolgoch Powys...94 B3
Pont-Ebbw Newpt...44 C2
Pontefract Wakefd...142 C3
Ponteland Nthumb...180 E4
Ponterwyd Cerdgn...93 G7
Pontesbury Shrops...95 K2
Pontesbury Hill Shrops...95 K2
Pontesford Shrops...95 K2
Pontfadog Wrexhm...112 C4
Pontfaen Pembks...75 G5
Pont-faen Powys...78 D3
Pontgarreg Cerdgn...76 B6
Pontgarreg Pembks...75 K4
Pont Henri Carmth...56 E3
Ponthir Torfn...62 C4
Ponthirwaun Cerdgn...76 A6
Pontllanfraith Caerph...43 J3
Pontlliw Swans...57 H5
Pontllyfni Gwynd...109 H1
Pontlottyn Caerph...61 H6
Pont Morlais Carmth...56 F3
Pontnêddféchan Neath...60 D5
Pontnewydd Torfn...62 B2
Pontnewynydd Torfn...62 B6
Pont Pen-y-benglog Gwynd...126 C7
Pontrhydfendigaid Cerdgn...77 K2
Pont Rhyd-sarn Gwynd...111 G5
Pont Rhyd-y-cyff Brdgnd...42 C4
Pontrhydyfen Neath...42 B2
Pont-rhyd-y-groes Cerdgn...77 K1
Pontrhydyrun Torfn...62 C2
Pontrilas Herefs...62 F2
Pont Robert Powys...94 D1
Pont-rug Gwynd...125 J7
Ponts Green E Susx...24 B4
Pontshill Herefs...63 J1
Pontsian Cerdgn...76 D6
Pontsticill Myr Td...61 G5
Pont Walby Neath...60 D6
Pontwelly Carmth...76 D7
Pontyates Carmth...56 E3
Pontyberem Carmth...58 F6
Pont-y-blew Wrexhm...112 D4
Pontybodkin Flints...129 G7
Pontyclun Rhondd...42 F5
Pontycymer Brdgnd...42 D3
Pontyglasier Pembks...75 K3
Pontygwaith Rhondd...42 F3
Pontygynon Pembks...75 K3
Pontymister Caerph...43 K2
Pont-y-pant Conwy...110 E1
Pontypool Torfn...62 C3

Name	County	Page	Grid
Pontypridd	Rhondd	43	G4
Pont-yr-hafod	Pembks	74	E7
Pont-yr-Rhyl	Brdgnd	42	D4
Pontywaun	Caerph	43	K3
Pool	Cnwll	3	H3
Poole	BCP	17	K4
Poole Keynes	Gloucs	64	E8
Poolewe	Highld	260	D4
Pooley Bridge	Cumb	166	B6
Pooley Street	Norfk	105	L7
Poolfold	Staffs	131	H7
Pool Head	Herefs	80	D5
Poolhill	Gloucs	63	L1
Pool in Wharfedale	Leeds	150	C6
Pool of Muckhart	Clacks	221	H7
Pool Quay	Powys	95	G1
Pool Street	Essex	88	F7
Pootings	Kent	38	C3
Popes Hill	Gloucs	63	K4
Popham	Hants	35	H2
Poplar	Gt Lon	51	K3
Poplar Street	Suffk	91	K2
Porchfield	IoW	19	G5
Poringland	Norfk	106	F3
Porkellis	Cnwll	3	H4
Porlock	Somset	28	F2
Porlock Weir	Somset	28	F1
Portachoillan	Ag & B	206	B7
Port-an-Eorna	Highld	248	M1
Port Appin	Ag & B	228	D6
Port Askaig	Ag & B	205	G3
Portavadie	Ag & B	206	E5
Port Bannatyne	Ag & B	207	H5
Portbury	N Som	45	G4
Port Carlisle	Cumb	177	H6
Port Charlotte	Ag & B	204	C4
Portchester	Hants	19	K3
Port Clarence	S on T	170	C6
Port Driseach	Ag & B	206	F4
Port Ellen	Ag & B	204	E7
Port Elphinstone	Abers	256	D7
Portencalzie	D & G	182	C8
Portencross	N Ayrs	195	K1
Port Erin	IoM	154	b8
Portesham	Dorset	16	B5
Portessie	Moray	267	J3
Port e Vullen	IoM	154	g4
Port Eynon	Swans	56	E7
Portfield Gate	Pembks	54	F4
Portgate	Devon	12	A5
Port Gaverne	Cnwll	10	D6
Port Glasgow	Inver	208	B4
Portgordon	Moray	267	J3
Portgower	Highld	274	D5
Porth	Cnwll	4	D2
Porth	Rhondd	42	F3
Porthallow	Cnwll	3	K6
Porthallow	Cnwll	5	L4
Porthcawl	Brdgnd	42	B6
Porthcothan	Cnwll	10	B8
Porthcurno	Cnwll	2	B7
Porthdinllaen	Gwynd	108	D3
Port Henderson	Highld	260	B5
Porthgain	Pembks	74	D5
Porthgwarra	Cnwll	2	B7
Porthill	Staffs	114	D2
Porthkea	Cnwll	4	D6
Porthkerry	V Glam	43	G8
Porthleven	Cnwll	2	H2
Porthmadog	Gwynd	109	K4
Porthmadog	Gwynd	109	K4
Porthmeor	Cnwll	2	C4
Porth Navas	Cnwll	3	J5
Portholland	Cnwll	4	F6
Porthoustock	Cnwll	3	K6
Porthpean	Cnwll	5	H5
Porthtowan	Cnwll	3	H2
Porthwgan	Wrexhm	112	F2
Porthyrhyd	Carmth	58	F5
Porth-y-Waen	Shrops	112	C6
Portincaple	Ag & B	218	C8
Portinfer	Jersey	9	a1
Portington	E R Yk	143	K2
Portinnisherrich	Ag & B	216	F5
Portinscale	Cumb	165	H6
Port Isaac	Cnwll	10	D6
Portishead	N Som	44	F4
Portknockie	Moray	267	J3
Portland	Dorset	16	D8
Portlethen	Abers	245	K4
Portling	D & G	175	L4
Portloe	Cnwll	4	F7
Port Logan	D & G	172	D6
Portlooe	Cnwll	6	A4
Portmahomack	Highld	264	E3
Port Mary	D & G	175	J5
Portmellon	Cnwll	5	G6
Port Mòr	Highld	236	E4
Portmore	Hants	18	E4
Port Mulgrave	N York	171	J7
Portnacroish	Ag & B	228	E6
Portnaguran	W Isls	282	h3
Portnahaven	Ag & B	204	B6
Portnalong	Highld	246	D2
Portnancon	Highld	277	G4
Port nan Giùran	W Isls	282	h3
Port nan Long	W Isls	282	c7
Port Nis	W Isls	282	h1
Portobello	C Edin	211	J4
Portobello	Gatesd	181	G7
Portobello	Wolves	98	B4
Port of Menteith	Stirlg	219	J7
Port of Ness	W Isls	282	h1
Porton	Wilts	33	L4
Portontown	Devon	12	A7
Portpatrick	D & G	172	B4
Port Quin	Cnwll	10	D6
Port Ramsay	Ag & B	228	C6
Portreath	Cnwll	3	G2
Portreath Harbour	Cnwll	3	G2
Portree	Highld	259	H7
Port Righ	Ag & B	194	C3
Port St Mary	IoM	154	b8
Portscatho	Cnwll	3	M4
Portsea	C Port	19	L4
Portskerra	Highld	278	E3
Portskewett	Mons	45	G1
Portslade	Br & H	22	C6
Portslade-by-Sea	Br & H	22	C6
Portslogan	D & G	172	B3
Portsmouth	C Port	19	L4
Portsmouth	Calder	140	D3
Portsmouth Arms	Devon	27	L7
Port Soderick	IoM	154	d7
Port Solent	C Port	19	L3
Portsonachan Hotel	Ag & B	217	G3
Portsoy	Abers	267	M3
Port Sunlight	Wirral	129	H3
Portswood	C Sotn	34	F8
Port Talbot	Neath	57	L7
Port Tennant	Swans	57	J6
Portuairk	Highld	236	E7
Portway	Herefs	80	B6
Portway	Herefs	80	C8
Portway	Sandw	98	B6
Portway	Worcs	82	C1
Port Wemyss	Ag & B	204	B6
Port William	D & G	173	J6
Portwrinkle	Cnwll	6	D4
Portyerrock	D & G	174	D7
Posbury	Devon	13	J3
Posenhall	Shrops	96	E3
Poslingford	Suffk	88	F5
Posso	Border	199	L6
Postbridge	Devon	12	F6
Postcombe	Oxon	67	H7
Post Green	Dorset	17	J4
Postling	Kent	40	F7
Postwick	Norfk	106	F2
Potarch	Abers	244	D4
Potsgrove	C Beds	68	B1
Potten End	Herts	68	C5
Potten Street	Kent	41	H2
Potter Brompton	N York	163	H7
Pottergate Street	Norfk	106	D5
Potterhanworth	Lincs	135	L6
Potterhanworth Booths	Lincs	135	M6
Potter Heigham	Norfk	123	J7
Potterne	Wilts	46	E7
Potterne Wick	Wilts	46	E7
Potter Row	Bucks	67	L6
Potters Bar	Herts	69	H6
Potters Brook	Lancs	147	J5
Potters Corner	Kent	40	C6
Potter's Cross	Staffs	97	J6
Potters Crouch	Herts	68	E4
Potter's Forstal	Kent	39	M4
Potters Green	Covtry	99	K7
Potter's Green	E Susx	23	H3
Potter's Green	Herts	69	K4
Pottersheath	Herts	69	G3
Potters Marston	Leics	100	B4
Potter Somersal	Derbys	115	J4
Potterspury	Nhants	84	E6
Potter Street	Essex	70	C5
Potterton	Abers	257	G8
Potterton	Leeds	150	F8
Potthorpe	Norfk	121	L7
Pottle Street	Wilts	32	D3
Potto	N York	161	G2
Potton	C Beds	86	E5
Pott Row	Norfk	120	F7
Pott's Green	Essex	72	C3
Pott Shrigley	Ches E	131	J4
Poughill	Cnwll	11	J1
Poughill	Devon	13	K1
Poulner	Hants	18	B2
Poulshot	Wilts	46	E7
Poulton	Gloucs	65	G7
Poulton	Wirral	129	G2
Poulton-le-Fylde	Lancs	147	G7
Poulton Priory	Gloucs	65	G7
Pound Bank	Worcs	97	G8
Poundbury	Dorset	16	C4
Poundffald	Swans	57	G6
Poundgate	E Susx	38	D7
Pound Green	E Susx	23	H3
Pound Green	Suffk	88	E4
Pound Green	Worcs	97	G7
Pound Hill	W Susx	37	L3
Poundon	Bucks	66	F2
Poundsbridge	Kent	38	E5
Poundsgate	Devon	13	G6
Poundstock	Cnwll	11	H3
Pound Street	Hants	48	C6
Pounsley	E Susx	23	J3
Pouton	D & G	174	C5
Pouy Street	Suffk	91	H1
Povey Cross	Surrey	37	L3
Powburn	Nthumb	190	F3
Powderham	Devon	13	M5
Powerstock	Dorset	15	L3
Powfoot	D & G	176	F5
Pow Green	Herefs	81	G6
Powhill	Cumb	177	H7
Powick	Worcs	81	J5
Powmill	P & K	221	J7
Poxwell	Dorset	16	E6
Poyle	Slough	50	C4
Poynings	W Susx	22	C5
Poyntington	Dorset	31	L6
Poynton	Ches E	131	H3
Poynton	Wrekin	113	J8
Poynton Green	Wrekin	113	J7
Poyston Cross	Pembks	55	G3
Poystreet Green	Suffk	89	K4
Praa Sands	Cnwll	2	F5
Pratt's Bottom	Gt Lon	52	A6
Praze-an-Beeble	Cnwll	3	G4
Predannack Wollas	Cnwll	3	H7
Prees	Shrops	113	J5
Preesall	Lancs	147	G6
Prees Green	Shrops	113	J5
Preesgweene	Shrops	112	D4
Prees Heath	Shrops	113	J4
Prees Higher Heath	Shrops	113	J4
Prees Lower Heath	Shrops	113	J5
Prendwick	Nthumb	190	E4
Pren-gwyn	Cerdgn	76	D6
Prenteg	Gwynd	109	K3
Prenton	Wirral	129	G2
Prescot	Knows	129	L1
Prescott	Devon	29	K8
Prescott	Shrops	96	F7
Prescott	Shrops	112	F7
Presnerb	Angus	233	J2
Pressen	Nthumb	202	C6
Prestatyn	Denbgs	128	C3
Prestbury	Ches E	131	H4
Prestbury	Gloucs	64	E2
Presteigne	Powys	79	K2
Prestleigh	Somset	31	K3
Prestolee	Bolton	139	M6
Preston	Border	213	H7
Preston	Br & H	22	D6
Preston	Devon	13	K7
Preston	Dorset	16	D6
Preston	E R Yk	144	F2
Preston	Gloucs	64	F7
Preston	Herts	68	F2
Preston	Kent	40	D3
Preston	Kent	41	H3
Preston	Lancs	139	G2
Preston	Nthumb	203	K8
Preston	Rutlnd	101	J3
Preston	Shrops	96	C1
Preston	Somset	29	K4
Preston	Torbay	8	D3
Preston	Wilts	46	F3
Preston	Wilts	47	K4
Preston Bagot	Warwks	82	E2
Preston Bissett	Bucks	67	G1
Preston Bowyer	Somset	29	L5
Preston Brockhurst	Shrops	113	J6
Preston Brook	Halton	130	B4
Preston Candover	Hants	35	J3
Preston Capes	Nhants	84	B4
Preston Crowmarsh	Oxon	48	F1
Preston Deanery	Nhants	84	F4
Preston Green	Warwks	82	E2
Preston Gubbals	Shrops	113	H7
Preston Montford	Shrops	113	H7
Preston on Stour	Warwks	82	F5
Preston on Tees	S on T	169	L7
Preston on the Hill	Halton	130	B3
Preston on Wye	Herefs	79	M7
Prestonpans	E Loth	211	L4
Preston Patrick	Cumb	157	H6
Preston Plucknett	Somset	31	H7
Preston St Mary	Suffk	89	J5
Preston Street	Kent	41	H3
Preston-under-Scar	N York	159	K4
Preston upon the Weald Moors	Wrekin	113	L8
Preston Wynne	Herefs	80	D6
Prestwich	Bury	140	B6
Prestwick	Nthumb	180	E4
Prestwick	S Ayrs	196	C6
Prestwick Airport	S Ayrs	196	D5
Prestwood	Bucks	67	L7
Prestwood	Staffs	97	K6
Price Town	Brdgnd	42	E3
Prickwillow	Cambs	104	B7
Priddy	Somset	31	H1
Priestacott	Devon	12	B1
Priestcliffe	Derbys	132	C5
Priestcliffe Ditch	Derbys	132	C5
Priest Hutton	Lancs	157	H7
Priestland	E Ayrs	197	H3
Priestley Green	Calder	141	H3
Priest Weston	Shrops	95	H4
Priestwood Green	Kent	52	E6
Primethorpe	Leics	100	B5
Primrose Green	Norfk	122	B8
Primrosehill	Border	213	H7
Primrose Hill	Cambs	103	H5
Primrose Hill	Derbys	133	J8
Primrose Hill	Dudley	97	L6
Primrose Hill	Lancs	138	E6
Primsidemill	Border	202	C7
Prince of Wales Bridge	Mons	45	G2
Princes Gate	Pembks	55	K4
Princes Risborough	Bucks	67	K6
Princethorpe	Warwks	83	J1
Princetown	Devon	12	E7
Prinsted	W Susx	20	C5
Prion	Denbgs	128	C7
Prior Rigg	Cumb	178	B5
Priors Halton	Shrops	96	B8
Priors Hardwick	Warwks	83	L4
Priorslee	Wrekin	97	G1
Priors Marston	Warwks	83	L4
Priors Norton	Gloucs	64	C2
Priors Park	Gloucs	64	C1
Priory Wood	Herefs	79	J6
Prisk	V Glam	42	F6
Priston	BaNES	45	K7
Pristow Green	Norfk	106	C5
Prittlewell	Sthend	53	J2
Privett	Hants	35	L5
Prixford	Devon	27	K3
Probus	Cnwll	4	E5
Prora	E Loth	212	B3
Prospect	Cumb	164	F3
Prospidnick	Cnwll	3	G5
Protstonhill	Abers	268	E3
Prudhoe	Nthumb	180	D6
Prussia Cove	Cnwll	2	E5
Pubil	P & K	230	E7
Publow	BaNES	45	J6
Puckeridge	Herts	69	K2
Puckington	Somset	30	E7
Pucklechurch	S Glos	45	K4
Puckrup	Gloucs	81	K7
Puddinglake	Ches W	130	E5
Puddington	Ches W	129	H5
Puddington	Devon	28	E8
Puddledock	Norfk	105	L5
Puddletown	Dorset	16	E4
Pudleston	Herefs	80	D3
Pudsey	Leeds	141	K1
Pulborough	W Susx	21	H3
Puleston	Wrekin	114	A7
Pulford	Ches W	129	J7
Pulham	Dorset	16	D1
Pulham Market	Norfk	106	D6
Pulham St Mary	Norfk	106	E6
Pullens Green	S Glos	63	J8
Pulloxhill	C Beds	85	L8
Pulverbatch	Shrops	95	K3
Pumpherston	W Loth	210	E5
Pumsaint	Carmth	77	J7
Puncheston	Pembks	75	G6
Puncknowle	Dorset	15	M5
Punnett's Town	E Susx	23	K3
Purbrook	Hants	19	M2
Purfleet-on-Thames	Thurr	52	C3
Puriton	Somset	30	D3
Purleigh	Essex	71	K6
Purley	Gt Lon	51	J6
Purley on Thames	W Berk	49	G4
Purlogue	Shrops	95	G7
Purlpit	Wilts	46	C5
Purls Bridge	Cambs	103	K6
Purse Caundle	Dorset	32	B7
Purshull Green	Worcs	81	K1
Purslow	Shrops	95	J7
Purston Jaglin	Wakefd	142	C4
Purtington	Somset	15	J1
Purton	Gloucs	63	K6

Purton Gloucs 63 K6
Purton Wilts 47 G2
Purton Stoke Wilts 47 G1
Pury End Nhants 84 D6
Pusey Oxon 65 M7
Putley Herefs 80 E7
Putley Green Herefs 80 F7
Putloe Gloucs 64 A5
Putney Gt Lon 51 G4
Putsborough Devon 27 H3
Puttenham Herts 67 L4
Puttenham Surrey 36 D2
Puttock End Essex 89 G7
Putton Dorset 16 C6
Putts Corner Devon 14 D3
Puxley Nhants 84 E6
Puxton N Som 44 E6
Pwll Carmth 56 E4
Pwllcrochan Pembks 54 F6
Pwll-du Mons 61 L5
Pwll-glâs Denbgs 111 M1
Pwllgloyw Powys 78 E8
Pwllheli Gwynd 108 F4
Pwllmeyric Mons 63 G8
Pwll-trap Carmth 58 A5
Pwll-y-glaw Neath 42 B3
Pydew Conwy 126 F4
Pye Bridge Derbys 116 D1
Pyecombe W Susx 22 D4
Pye Corner Newpt 44 D2
Pye Green Staffs 114 F8
Pyle Brdgnd 42 B5
Pyleigh Somset 29 L5
Pylle Somset 31 K3
Pymoor Cambs 103 K6
Pymore Dorset 15 L4
Pyrford Surrey 50 D7
Pyrton Oxon 67 G7
Pytchley Nhants 101 J8
Pyworthy Devon 11 K2

Q

Quabbs Shrops 94 F7
Quadring Lincs 119 H5
Quadring Eaudike Lincs 119 H5
Quainton Bucks 67 H3
Quaker's Yard Myr Td 43 H3
Quaking Houses Dur 180 F8
Quantock Hills Somset 30 A3
Quarff Shet 281 e7
Quarley Hants 34 C2
Quarndon Derbys 116 B3
Quarr Hill IoW 19 K5
Quarrier's Village Inver 208 B5
Quarrington Lincs 118 E3
Quarrington Hill Dur 169 J3
Quarrybank Ches W 130 A6
Quarry Bank Dudley 97 L6
Quarrywood Moray 266 D3
Quarter N Ayrs 207 K6
Quarter S Lans 197 L1
Quatford Shrops 97 G5
Quatt Shrops 97 G5
Quebec Dur 168 F2
Quedgeley Gloucs 64 A4
Queen Adelaide Cambs 104 B7
Queenborough Kent 53 K4
Queen Camel Somset 31 K6
Queen Charlton BaNES 45 J5
Queen Dart Devon 28 E7
Queen Elizabeth Forest Park Stirlg 219 H6
Queen Elizabeth II Bridge Thurr 52 C4
Queenhill Worcs 81 K7
Queen Oak Dorset 32 C4
Queen's Bower IoW 19 J6
Queensbury C Brad 141 H2
Queensferry Flints 129 H6
Queensferry Crossing Fife 210 F3
Queen's Head Shrops 112 E6
Queen's Hills Norfk 106 D1
Queenslie C Glas 209 H6
Queen's Park Bed 85 L5
Queen's Park Essex 71 G7
Queen's Park Nhants 84 E3
Queen Street Kent 39 H4
Queen Street Wilts 46 F2
Queenzieburn N Lans 209 J3
Quendon Essex 70 D1
Queniborough Leics 100 E1
Quenington Gloucs 65 H6
Quernmore Lancs 147 K4
Queslett Birm 98 D4
Quethiock Cnwll 6 C2
Quick's Green W Berk 48 E4
Quidenham Norfk 105 L6

Quidhampton Hants 35 G1
Quidhampton Wilts 33 K5
Quina Brook Shrops 113 H5
Quinbury End Nhants 84 B5
Quinton Dudley 98 C6
Quinton Nhants 84 E4
Quinton Green Nhants 84 F4
Quintrell Downs Cnwll 4 D3
Quixhall Staffs 115 H3
Quixwood Border 213 H5
Quoditch Devon 12 A3
Quoig P & K 220 E3
Quorn Leics 116 F8
Quothquan S Lans 199 G5
Quoyburray Ork 275 d5
Quoyloo Ork 275 b4

R

Raasay Highld 259 K8
Rabbit's Cross Kent 39 K4
Rableyheath Herts 69 G3
Raby Cumb 177 G8
Raby Wirral 129 H4
Rachan Mill Border 199 K6
Rachub Gwynd 126 C6
Rackenford Devon 28 E7
Rackham W Susx 21 H4
Rackheath Norfk 106 F1
Racks D & G 176 D4
Rackwick Ork 275 a5
Radbourne Derbys 115 M4
Radcliffe Bury 140 B6
Radcliffe Nthumb 191 K5
Radcliffe on Trent Notts 117 H4
Radclive Bucks 84 D8
Radcot Oxon 65 L7
Raddery Highld 263 J7
Raddington Somset 29 J5
Radernie Fife 223 H5
Radford Covtry 99 J7
Radford Semele Warwks 83 H2
Radlet Somset 30 B3
Radlett Herts 68 F7
Radley Devon 28 C6
Radley Oxon 66 D7
Radley W Berk 48 A5
Radley Green Essex 70 F6
Radmore Green Ches E 130 B8
Radnage Bucks 67 J7
Radstock BaNES 45 K8
Radstone Nhants 84 B7
Radway Warwks 83 J5
Radwell Bed 85 K4
Radwell Herts 86 E8
Radwinter Essex 88 C7
Radwinter End Essex 88 C7
Radyr Cardif 43 H5
RAF College (Cranwell) Lincs 118 D2
Rafford Moray 265 H8
Ragdale Leics 117 H7
Ragdon Shrops 95 L5
Raginnis Cnwll 2 D6
Raglan Mons 62 E5
Ragnall Notts 134 F5
Raigbeg Highld 252 F6
Rainbow Hill Worcs 81 K4
Rainford St Hel 138 F7
Rainford Junction St Hel 138 F7
Rainham Gt Lon 52 B3
Rainham Medway 53 H6
Rainhill St Hel 129 L2
Rainhill Stoops St Hel 129 L2
Rainow Ches E 131 J4
Rainsough Bury 140 B7
Rainton N York 160 E7
Rainworth Notts 134 B8
Raisbeck Cumb 157 K1
Raise Cumb 167 G2
Raisthorpe N York 152 C3
Rait P & K 222 C2
Raithby Lincs 136 F3
Raithby Lincs 137 G6
Raithwaite N York 171 K8
Rake Hants 36 B5
Rakewood Rochdl 140 E5
Ralia Highld 241 J4
Ram Carmth 77 G6
Ramasaig Highld 258 B7
Rame Cnwll 3 J4
Rame Cnwll 6 E5
Ram Hill S Glos 45 K3
Ram Lane Kent 40 C6
Rampisham Dorset 16 A2
Rampside Cumb 146 D3
Rampton Cambs 87 J2
Rampton Notts 134 F4
Ramsbottom Bury 140 B4

Ramsbury Wilts 47 K4
Ramscraigs Highld 274 F3
Ramsdean Hants 35 L6
Ramsdell Hants 48 E7
Ramsden Oxon 65 M4
Ramsden Worcs 81 L6
Ramsden Bellhouse Essex 71 H8
Ramsden Heath Essex 71 H7
Ramsey Cambs 102 F6
Ramsey Essex 73 J1
Ramsey IoM 154 f3
Ramsey Forty Foot Cambs 102 F6
Ramsey Heights Cambs 102 E6
Ramsey Island Pembks 74 A7
Ramsey Mereside Cambs 102 F5
Ramsey St Mary's Cambs 102 E6
Ramsgate Kent 41 L2
Ramsgill N York 149 K2
Ramshaw Dur 168 B1
Ramshaw Dur 168 F5
Ramsholt Suffk 91 H7
Ramshope Nthumb 189 K5
Ramshorn Staffs 115 H3
Ramsley Devon 12 F4
Ramsnest Common Surrey 36 E4
Ranby Lincs 136 D4
Ranby Notts 134 C3
Rand Lincs 136 B4
Randwick Gloucs 64 B5
Ranfurly Rens 208 C6
Rangemore Staffs 115 K7
Rangeworthy S Glos 45 K2
Rankinston E Ayrs 196 E8
Ranksborough Rutlnd 101 H1
Rank's Green Essex 71 H3
Rannoch Station P & K 230 D4
Ranscombe Somset 29 G2
Ranskill Notts 134 C2
Ranton Staffs 114 D6
Ranton Green Staffs 114 D7
Ranworth Norfk 123 G8
Raploch Stirlg 220 D8
Rapness Ork 275 d2
Rapps Somset 30 E7
Rascarrel D & G 175 K5
Rashfield Ag & B 207 J2
Rashwood Worcs 81 L2
Raskelf N York 151 G2
Rassau Blae G 61 J5
Rastrick Calder 141 H3
Ratagan Highld 248 E7
Ratby Leics 100 B2
Ratcliffe Culey Leics 99 J3
Ratcliffe on Soar Notts 116 E6
Ratcliffe on the Wreake Leics 117 G8
Rathen Abers 269 J4
Rathillet Fife 222 F3
Rathmell N York 148 D4
Ratho C Edin 210 F5
Ratho Station C Edin 210 F4
Rathven Moray 267 J2
Ratlake Hants 34 E6
Ratley Warwks 83 J5
Ratling Kent 41 H4
Ratlinghope Shrops 95 K4
Rattar Highld 280 C2
Ratten Row Cumb 165 K3
Ratten Row Cumb 165 L1
Ratten Row Lancs 147 H7
Rattery Devon 7 J4
Rattlesden Suffk 89 K3
Ratton Village E Susx 23 K7
Rattray P & K 233 J6
Raughton Cumb 165 L1
Raughton Head Cumb 165 L2
Raunds Nhants 85 K1
Ravenfield Rothm 133 J1
Ravenglass Cumb 155 K3
Ravenhills Green Worcs 81 G4
Raveningham Norfk 107 H3
Ravenscar N York 163 H2
Ravenscraig N Lans 209 K7
Ravensdale IoM 154 e4
Ravensden Bed 86 B4
Ravenseat N York 158 E2
Ravenshead Notts 133 L8
Ravensmoor Ches E 113 K2
Ravensthorpe Kirk 141 K4
Ravensthorpe Nhants 84 C1
Ravenstone Leics 99 L1
Ravenstone M Keyn 85 G5
Ravenstonedale Cumb 158 C2
Ravenstruther S Lans 198 F4
Ravensworth N York 159 L1
Raw N York 163 G2
Rawcliffe C York 151 J5
Rawcliffe E R Yk 143 H3
Rawcliffe Bridge E R Yk 143 H3
Rawdon Leeds 150 B7
Rawling Street Kent 40 B3

Rawmarsh Rothm 142 C8
Rawnsley Staffs 98 C1
Rawreth Essex 71 J8
Rawridge Devon 14 E2
Rawtenstall Lancs 140 B3
Raydon Suffk 90 B7
Raylees Nthumb 190 C7
Rayleigh Essex 53 H1
Raymond's Hill Devon 15 H3
Rayne Essex 71 H3
Raynes Park Gt Lon 51 G5
Reach Cambs 88 B2
Read Lancs 140 A1
Reading Readg 49 H4
Reading Services W Berk 49 G5
Reading Street Kent 25 G1
Reading Street Kent 41 L2
Reagill Cumb 166 E2
Rearquhar Highld 263 K1
Rearsby Leics 117 H8
Rease Heath Ches E 113 L1
Reawla Cnwll 2
Reay Highld 279 G3
Reculver Kent 41 H2
Red Ball Devon 29 K7
Redberth Pembks 55 J6
Redbourn Herts 68 E4
Redbourne N Linc 144 B7
Redbrook Gloucs 63 G5
Redbrook Wrexhm 113 H3
Redbrook Street Kent 40 B8
Redburn Highld 253 H2
Redburn Nthumb 179 H6
Redcar R & Cl 170 E6
Redcastle D & G 175 K2
Redcastle Highld 251 G2
Red Dial Cumb 165 H2
Redding Falk 210 B3
Reddingmuirhead Falk 210 B3
Reddish Stockp 131 H1
Redditch Worcs 82 B2
Rede Suffk 88 F4
Redenhall Norfk 106 F6
Redenham Hants 34 C1
Redesmouth Nthumb 179 K3
Redford Abers 235 J2
Redford Angus 234 E6
Redford W Susx 36 C5
Redfordgreen Border 188 C3
Redgate Rhondd 42 F4
Redgorton P & K 221 K2
Redgrave Suffk 105 L7
Redhill Abers 245 H3
Red Hill BCP 17 L3
Redhill Herts 86 F8
Redhill N Som 45 G6
Redhill Surrey 37 L1
Red Hill Warwks 82 D4
Redisham Suffk 107 H6
Redland Bristl 45 H4
Redland Ork 275 c3
Redlingfield Suffk 90 E5
Redlingfield Green Suffk 90 E5
Red Lodge Suffk 88 D1
Red Lumb Rochdl 140 C4
Redlynch Somset 32 B4
Redlynch Wilts 33 L6
Redmain Cumb 164 F4
Redmarley Worcs 81 H2
Redmarley D'Abitot Gloucs 63 L1
Redmarshall S on T 169 K6
Redmile Leics 117 L4
Redmire N York 159 L2
Redmyre Abers 245 G8
Rednal Birm 98 C8
Rednal Shrops 112 E6
Redpath Border 201 H2
Red Point Highld 260 B4
Red Post Cnwll 11 K2
Red Rice Hants 34 D2
Red Rock Wigan 139 H6
Red Roses Carmth 55 L4
Red Row Nthumb 191 K5
Redruth Cnwll 4 D6
Redstocks Wilts 46 D6
Redstone P & K 233 J8
Redstone Cross Pembks 55 J5
Red Street Staffs 114 C8
Redvales Bury 140 B6
Red Wharf Bay IoA 125 J2
Redwick Newpt 44 E4
Redwick S Glos 45 H2
Redworth Darltn 169 G6
Reed Herts 87 H8
Reedham Norfk 107 J2
Reedness E R Yk 143 H3
Reeds Beck Lincs 136 D6
Reeds Holme Lancs 140 B3
Reepham Lincs 135 H6
Reepham Norfk 122 D7

Reeth N York 159 J3
Reeves Green Solhll 99 H7
Regaby IoM 154 f3
Regil N Som 45 G6
Reiff Highld 270 C5
Reigate Surrey 37 L1
Reighton N York 163 L7
Reinigeadal W Isls 282 f5
Reisque Abers 256 F7
Reiss Highld 280 D5
Rejerrah Cnwll 4 C4
Releath Cnwll 3 G4
Relubbus Cnwll 2 F4
Relugas Moray 253 J2
Remenham Wokham 49 J2
Remenham Hill Wokham 49 J2
Rempstone Notts 116 F6
Rendcomb Gloucs 64 E5
Rendham Suffk 91 H2
Rendlesham Suffk 91 H4
Renfrew Rens 208 E5
Renhold Bed 86 B5
Renishaw Derbys 133 J4
Rennington Nthumb 191 J3
Renton W Duns 208 C3
Renwick Cumb 166 E2
Repps Norfk 123 J8
Repton Derbys 116 A6
Reraig Highld 248 C6
Resaurie Highld 251 J3
Rescassa Cnwll 5 G6
Rescorla Cnwll 5 G5
Resipole Burn Highld 237 L7
Reskadinnick Cnwll 3 G3
Resolis Highld 263 J6
Resolven Neath 60 C6
Rest and be thankful Ag & B 218 C5
Reston Border 213 J6
Restronguet Cnwll 3 K4
Reswallie Angus 234 D5
Reterth Cnwll 4 F2
Retford Notts 134 D3
Retire Cnwll 5 G2
Rettendon Common Essex 71 J7
Rettendon Village Essex 71 J7
Retyn Cnwll 4 E3
Revesby Lincs 136 E7
Rew Devon 7 K7
Rew Devon 13 H8
Rewe Devon 13 M3
Rew Street IoW 19 H5
Rexon Devon 12 A5
Reydon Suffk 107 K7
Reymerston Norfk 105 L2
Reynalton Pembks 55 J5
Reynoldston Swans 56 E6
Rezare Cnwll 11 L7
Rhadyr Mons 62 D6
Rhandirmwyn Carmth 77 L6
Rhayader Powys 78 D2
Rheindown Highld 250 F2
Rhenigidale W Isls 282 f5
Rhes-y-cae Flints 128 E5
Rhewl Denbgs 112 B3
Rhewl Denbgs 128 D7
Rhewl Mostyn Flints 128 D4
Rhicarn Highld 270 E3
Rhiconich Highld 276 D5
Rhicullen Highld 263 J4
Rhigos Rhondd 60 D6
Rhives Highld 273 K7
Rhiwbina Cardif 43 J5
Rhiwbryfdir Gwynd 110 D2
Rhiwderyn Newpt 43 L4
Rhiwen Gwynd 125 K7
Rhiwinder Rhondd 42 F4
Rhiwlas Gwynd 111 H4
Rhiwlas Gwynd 125 K6
Rhiwlas Powys 112 B5
Rhiwsaeson Rhondd 43 G5
Rhode Somset 30 C4
Rhoden Green Kent 39 H4
Rhodesia Notts 133 L4
Rhodes Minnis Kent 40 F6
Rhodiad-y-brenin Pembks 74 C6
Rhonehouse D & G 175 J3
Rhoose V Glam 43 G8
Rhos Carmth 58 C2
Rhos Denbgs 128 D7
Rhos Neath 57 K4
Rhosaman Carmth 59 K6
Rhosbeirio IoA 125 G2
Rhoscefnhir IoA 125 J4
Rhoscolyn IoA 124 D4
Rhoscrowther Pembks 54 E6
Rhosesmor Flints 128 F6
Rhos-fawr Gwynd 109 G4
Rhosgadfan Gwynd 125 J8
Rhosgoch IoA 125 G2
Rhosgoch Powys 79 H5

Rhos Haminiog Cerdgn 76 F2
Rhoshill Pembks 75 L4
Rhoshirwaun Gwynd 108 C5
Rhoslan Gwynd 109 H3
Rhoslefain Gwynd 92 C2
Rhosllanerchrugog Wrexhm 112 D2
Rhôs Lligwy IoA 125 J2
Rhosmaen Carmth 59 H4
Rhosmeirch IoA 125 H4
Rhosneigr IoA 124 E5
Rhosnesni Wrexhm 112 E2
Rhôs-on-Sea Conwy 127 G4
Rhosrobin Wrexhm 112 E1
Rhossili Swans 56 D7
Rhostrehwfa IoA 125 H5
Rhostryfan Gwynd 125 J8
Rhostyllen Wrexhm 112 D2
Rhosybol IoA 125 G2
Rhos-y-brithdir Powys 111 M7
Rhosygadfa Shrops 112 D4
Rhos-y-garth Cerdgn 77 H1
Rhos-y-gwaliau Gwynd 111 H4
Rhos-y-llan Gwynd 108 D4
Rhosymedre Wrexhm 112 D3
Rhos-y-meirch Powys 79 K1
Rhu Ag & B 207 M2
Rhuallt Denbgs 128 C5
Rhubodach Ag & B 207 G4
Rhuddall Heath Ches W 130 A7
Rhuddlan Cerdgn 76 F6
Rhuddlan Denbgs 127 L4
Rhue Highld 270 E8
Rhulen Powys 79 G5
Rhunahaorine Ag & B 205 M6
Rhyd Gwynd 110 B3
Rhydargaeau Carmth 58 D4
Rhydcymerau Carmth 77 G7
Rhydd Worcs 81 J6
Rhyd-Ddu Gwynd 109 K1
Rhydding Neath 57 K5
Rhydgaled Conwy 127 K6
Rhydlanfair Conwy 110 F1
Rhydlewis Cerdgn 76 C5
Rhydlios Gwynd 108 C5
Rhydlydan Conwy 111 G2
Rhydowen Cerdgn 76 E6
Rhydroser Cerdgn 77 G2
Rhydspence Herefs 79 J5
Rhydtalog Flints 128 F8
Rhyd-uchaf Gwynd 111 G4
Rhyd-y-clafdy Gwynd 108 E4
Rhydycroesau Shrops 112 C5
Rhydyfelin Cerdgn 92 D7
Rhydyfelin Rhondd 43 H4
Rhyd-y-foel Conwy 127 H4
Rhydyfro Neath 57 K4
Rhyd-y-groes Gwynd 125 K6
Rhydymain Gwynd 110 F7
Rhyd-y-meirch Mons 62 C5
Rhydymwyn Flints 128 E6
Rhyd-y-pennau Cerdgn 92 D6
Rhyd-yr-onnen Gwynd 92 D3
Rhyd-y-sarn Gwynd 110 C3
Rhyl Denbgs 127 K3
Rhymney Caerph 61 H5
Rhynd P & K 222 B3
Rhynie Abers 255 K6
Rhynie Highld 264 C4
Ribbesford Worcs 97 H8
Ribbleton Lancs 139 H2
Ribby Lancs 138 E2
Ribchester Lancs 139 K1
Riber Derbys 132 F7
Riby Lincs 144 F6
Riccall N York 151 K8
Riccarton Border 188 F7
Riccarton E Ayrs 196 E4
Richards Castle Herefs 80 C1
Richings Park Bucks 50 D3
Richmond Gt Lon 50 F4
Richmond N York 159 M2
Richmond Sheff 133 H3
Rich's Holford Somset 29 L4
Rickerscote Staffs 114 E7
Rickford N Som 44 F7
Rickham Devon 7 L7
Rickinghall Suffk 105 L8
Rickling Essex 70 D1
Rickling Green Essex 70 D1
Rickmansworth Herts 68 D8
Riddell Border 188 E1
Riddings Derbys 116 C1
Riddlecombe Devon 27 L8
Riddlesden C Brad 149 K7
Ridge BaNES 45 H7
Ridge Dorset 17 H5
Ridge Herts 69 G7
Ridge Wilts 33 G4
Ridgebourne Powys 78 E3
Ridge Green Surrey 37 L1

Ridge Lane Warwks 99 J4
Ridge Row Kent 41 G6
Ridgeway Derbys 133 H3
Ridgeway Worcs 82 B3
Ridgeway Cross Herefs 81 G5
Ridgewell Essex 88 E7
Ridgewood E Susx 23 H3
Ridgmont C Beds 85 J8
Riding Mill Nthumb 180 B6
Ridley Kent 52 D6
Ridley Nthumb 179 H6
Ridley Green Ches E 113 J1
Ridlington Norfk 123 G5
Ridlington Rutlnd 101 J3
Ridlington Street Norfk 123 G5
Ridsdale Nthumb 179 L2
Rievaulx N York 161 J5
Rigg D & G 177 J5
Riggend N Lans 209 K5
Righoul Highld 253 G2
Rigmadon Park Cumb 157 K5
Rigsby Lincs 137 H4
Rigside S Lans 198 L6
Riley Green Lancs 139 J3
Rileyhill Staffs 115 J8
Rilla Mill Cnwll 11 K7
Rillaton Cnwll 11 K7
Rillington N York 162 E7
Rimington Lancs 148 D6
Rimpton Somset 31 K6
Rimswell E R Yk 145 J2
Rinaston Pembks 75 G7
Rindleford Shrops 97 G4
Ringford D & G 175 H3
Ringinglow Sheff 132 F3
Ringland Norfk 106 C1
Ringles Cross E Susx 23 H3
Ringlestone Kent 39 L2
Ringley Bolton 139 M6
Ringmer E Susx 23 G5
Ringmore Devon 7 J5
Ringmore Devon 13 L8
Ringorm Moray 254 E3
Ring's End Cambs 103 H3
Ringsfield Suffk 107 H5
Ringsfield Corner Suffk 107 H6
Ringshall Herts 68 C4
Ringshall Suffk 90 B4
Ringshall Stocks Suffk 90 B5
Ringstead Nhants 101 L8
Ringstead Norfk 120 F3
Ringwood Hants 18 A3
Ringwould Kent 41 K5
Rinmore Abers 255 H8
Rinsey Cnwll 2 F5
Rinsey Croft Cnwll 2 F5
Ripe E Susx 23 H5
Ripley Derbys 116 C2
Ripley Hants 18 B4
Ripley N York 150 C4
Ripley Surrey 50 D7
Riplingham E R Yk 144 B2
Riplington Hants 35 K6
Ripon N York 150 D2
Rippingale Lincs 118 E6
Ripple Kent 41 K5
Ripple Worcs 81 K7
Ripponden Calder 140 F4
Risabus Ag & B 204 D7
Risbury Herefs 80 D4
Risby N Linc 144 A5
Risby Suffk 88 F2
Risca Caerph 43 K3
Rise E R Yk 153 J7
Riseden E Susx 38 F7
Riseden Kent 39 H6
Risegate Lincs 119 H5
Riseholme Lincs 135 K5
Risehow Cumb 164 D4
Riseley Bed 85 L3
Riseley Wokham 49 H6
Rishangles Suffk 90 E2
Rishton Lancs 139 L2
Rishworth Calder 140 F4
Rising Bridge Lancs 140 A3
Risley Derbys 116 D4
Risley Warrtn 130 C1
Risplith N York 150 B2
Rivar Wilts 47 L6
Rivenhall End Essex 71 K4
River Kent 41 J6
River W Susx 36 D6
River Bank Cambs 87 L2
Riverford Highld 250 F1
Riverhead Kent 38 D2
Rivers Corner Dorset 32 C8
Rivington Lancs 139 J5
Rivington Services Lancs 139 J5
Roachill Devon 28 E6
Roade Nhants 84 E5

Road Green Norfk 106 F4
Roadhead Cumb 178 C4
Roadmeetings S Lans 198 E3
Roadside E Ayrs 197 H7
Roadside Highld 279 L4
Roadwater Somset 29 J3
Roag Highld 258 D7
Roa Island Cumb 146 D3
Roan of Craigoch S Ayrs 183 H2
Roast Green Essex 87 J8
Roath Cardif 43 K6
Roberton Border 188 D3
Roberton S Lans 198 F7
Robertsbridge E Susx 24 D3
Roberttown Kirk 141 J3
Robeston Wathen Pembks 55 J4
Robgill Tower D & G 177 H4
Robin Hill Staffs 131 H8
Robin Hood Lancs 139 G5
Robin Hood Leeds 141 M2
Robinhood End Essex 88 E7
Robin Hood's Bay N York 163 G2
Roborough Devon 6 F2
Roborough Devon 27 K7
Robroyston C Glas 209 H5
Roby Knows 129 K2
Roby Mill Lancs 139 G6
Rocester Staffs 115 J4
Roch Pembks 54 E3
Rochdale Rochdl 140 D5
Roche Cnwll 5 G3
Rochester Medway 52 F5
Rochester Nthumb 189 M6
Rochford Essex 53 J1
Rochford Worcs 80 E2
Roch Gate Pembks 54 E3
Rock Cnwll 10 C7
Rock Neath 57 L6
Rock Nthumb 191 J2
Rock W Susx 21 K4
Rock Worcs 81 G1
Rockbeare Devon 14 B4
Rockbourne Hants 33 K7
Rockcliffe Cumb 177 K6
Rockcliffe D & G 175 L4
Rockcliffe Cross Cumb 177 K6
Rock End Staffs 131 H8
Rockend Torbay 8 D2
Rock Ferry Wirral 129 H2
Rockfield Highld 264 E3
Rockfield Mons 62 F4
Rockford Devon 28 D1
Rockford Hants 18 B2
Rockgreen Shrops 96 C8
Rockhampton S Glos 63 K8
Rockhead Cnwll 10 F5
Rockhill Shrops 95 G7
Rock Hill Worcs 81 L1
Rockingham Nhants 101 J5
Rockland All Saints Norfk 105 K4
Rockland St Mary Norfk 107 G3
Rockland St Peter Norfk 105 K4
Rockley Notts 134 E5
Rockley Wilts 47 H4
Rockliffe Lancs 140 C3
Rockville Ag & B 207 L1
Rockwell End Bucks 49 J1
Rockwell Green Somset 29 L6
Rodborough Gloucs 64 B6
Rodbourne Swindn 47 H2
Rodbourne Wilts 46 D2
Rodd Herefs 79 K3
Roddam Nthumb 190 E2
Rodden Dorset 16 B5
Roddymoor Dur 168 F3
Rode Somset 46 A8
Rode Heath Ches E 130 F8
Rode Heath Ches E 131 G6
Rodel W Isls 282 d7
Roden Wrekin 113 J8
Rodhuish Somset 29 J3
Rodington Wrekin 113 K8
Rodington Heath Wrekin 113 K8
Rodley Gloucs 63 L5
Rodley Leeds 150 B8
Rodmarton Gloucs 64 D7
Rodmell E Susx 22 F6
Rodmersham Kent 40 B3
Rodmersham Green Kent 40 B3
Rodney Stoke Somset 31 H1
Rodsley Derbys 115 K3
Rodway Somset 30 C3
Roecliffe N York 150 E3
Roe Cross Tamesd 140 E8
Roe Green Herts 69 G5
Roe Green Herts 87 G8
Roe Green Salfd 139 L7
Roehampton Gt Lon 51 G4
Roffey W Susx 37 J4
Rogart Highld 273 H7

Rogate W Susx......36 B6
Roger Ground Cumb......156 E3
Rogerstone Newpt......44 B2
Roghadal W Isls......282 d7
Rogiet Mons......44 F2
Roke Oxon......66 F8
Roker Sundld......181 K7
Rollesby Norfk......123 J8
Rolleston Leics......100 F3
Rolleston Notts......117 K1
Rollestone Wilts......33 J2
Rolleston on Dove Staffs......115 L6
Rolston E R Yk......153 K6
Rolstone N Som......44 D6
Rolvenden Kent......39 L7
Rolvenden Layne Kent......39 L7
Romaldkirk Dur......168 C6
Romanby N York......160 E4
Romanno Bridge Border......199 K3
Romansleigh Devon......28 C6
Romden Castle Kent......40 A7
Romesdal Highld......258 F6
Romford Dorset......17 L1
Romford Gt Lon......52 B1
Romiley Stockp......131 J2
Romney Street Kent......52 C6
Romsey Cambs......87 K4
Romsey Hants......34 D6
Romsley Shrops......97 H6
Romsley Worcs......98 B7
Rona Highld......259 L5
Ronachan Ag & B......206 B8
Rood Ashton Wilts......46 C7
Rookhope Dur......167 L2
Rookley IoW......19 H6
Rookley Green IoW......19 H7
Rooks Bridge Somset......44 D8
Rooks Nest Somset......29 K4
Rookwith N York......160 B5
Roos E R Yk......145 H2
Roose Cumb......146 D2
Roosebeck Cumb......146 E2
Roothams Green Bed......86 B4
Ropley Hants......35 K4
Ropley Dean Hants......35 K4
Ropley Soke Hants......35 K4
Ropsley Lincs......118 C5
Rora Abers......269 K6
Rorrington Shrops......95 H3
Rosarie Moray......267 H6
Rose Cnwll......4 C4
Roseacre Lancs......147 H8
Rose Ash Devon......28 D6
Rosebank S Lans......198 D3
Rosebush Pembks......75 J6
Rosecare Cnwll......11 H3
Rosecliston Cnwll......4 D3
Rosedale Abbey N York......162 C3
Rose Green Essex......72 C2
Rose Green Suffk......89 J7
Rose Green Suffk......89 K6
Rose Green W Susx......20 E7
Rosehall Highld......272 C7
Rosehearty Abers......269 K6
Rose Hill E Susx......23 G4
Rose Hill Lancs......140 B2
Rosehill Shrops......113 G8
Roseisle Moray......266 C3
Roselands E Susx......23 K7
Rosemarket Pembks......54 F5
Rosemarkie Highld......263 K8
Rosemary Lane Devon......29 L7
Rosemount P & K......233 J6
Rosenannon Cnwll......4 F2
Rosenithon Cnwll......3 K6
Roser's Cross E Susx......23 J3
Rosevean Cnwll......5 H3
Rosevine Cnwll......3 M4
Rosewarne Cnwll......2 F4
Rosewell Mdloth......211 J6
Roseworth S on T......169 L6
Roseworthy Cnwll......3 G3
Rosgill Cumb......166 D7
Roskestal Cnwll......2 B6
Roskhill Highld......258 D7
Roskorwell Cnwll......3 K6
Rosley Cumb......165 K2
Roslin Mdloth......211 J6
Rosliston Derbys......115 L8
Rosneath Ag & B......207 L2
Ross D & G......175 G6
Ross Nthumb......203 J5
Rossett Wrexhm......129 J8
Rossett Green N York......150 D5
Rossington Donc......143 G8
Ross-on-Wye Herefs......63 J3
Roster Highld......280 C8
Rostherne Ches E......130 E3
Rosthwaite Cumb......165 H7
Roston Derbys......115 J3

Rosudgeon Cnwll......2 E5
Rosyth Fife......210 F2
Rothbury Nthumb......190 F6
Rotherby Leics......117 H8
Rotherfield E Susx......38 E7
Rotherfield Greys Oxon......49 H3
Rotherfield Peppard Oxon......49 H3
Rotherham Rothm......133 H1
Rothersthorpe Nhants......84 D4
Rotherwick Hants......49 H7
Rothes Moray......266 F6
Rothesay Ag & B......207 H6
Rothiebrisbane Abers......256 D6
Rothiemurchus Lodge Highld......242 C2
Rothienorman Abers......256 C4
Rothley Leics......100 D1
Rothley Nthumb......180 C1
Rothmaise Abers......256 B5
Rothwell Leeds......142 A2
Rothwell Lincs......144 F7
Rothwell Nhants......101 H7
Rotsea E R Yk......153 G5
Rottal Lodge Angus......234 B2
Rottingdean Br & H......22 F6
Rottington Cumb......164 C8
Roucan D & G......176 D3
Roud IoW......19 H7
Rougham Norfk......121 H7
Rougham Suffk......89 H3
Rough Close Staffs......114 E4
Rough Common Kent......40 F3
Roughlee Lancs......148 E7
Roughpark Abers......243 K1
Roughton Lincs......136 D6
Roughton Norfk......122 E4
Roughton Shrops......97 G4
Roughway Kent......38 F3
Roundbush Essex......72 B6
Round Bush Herts......68 F7
Roundbush Green Essex......70 E3
Round Green Luton......68 E3
Roundham Somset......15 K1
Roundhay Leeds......150 D8
Rounds Green Sandw......98 C5
Round Street Kent......52 E5
Roundstreet Common W Susx......37 G5
Roundswell Devon......27 K4
Roundway Wilts......46 E6
Roundyhill Angus......234 B5
Rousay Ork......275 c3
Rousdon Devon......15 G4
Rousham Oxon......66 C2
Rous Lench Worcs......82 B4
Routenburn N Ayrs......207 K6
Routh E R Yk......153 H7
Rout's Green Bucks......67 J7
Row Cnwll......10 F7
Row Cumb......157 G5
Row Cumb......166 E4
Rowanburn D & G......177 L3
Rowardennan Stirlg......218 E7
Rowarth Derbys......131 K2
Row Ash Hants......35 H8
Rowberrow Somset......44 F7
Rowborough IoW......19 G6
Rowde Wilts......46 E6
Rowden Devon......12 F3
Rowen Conwy......126 E5
Rowfield Derbys......115 K2
Rowfoot Nthumb......178 F6
Rowford Somset......30 C5
Row Green Essex......71 H3
Rowhedge Essex......72 F3
Rowhook W Susx......37 H4
Rowington Warwks......82 F2
Rowland Derbys......132 D5
Rowland's Castle Hants......20 B5
Rowlands Gill Gatesd......180 E7
Rowledge Surrey......36 B2
Rowley Dur......168 C2
Rowley E R Yk......144 B1
Rowley Shrops......95 H2
Rowley Hill Kirk......141 J5
Rowley Regis Sandw......98 B6
Rowlstone Herefs......62 D2
Rowly Surrey......37 G3
Rowner Hants......19 K3
Rowney Green Worcs......82 B1
Rownhams Hants......34 E7
Rownhams Services Hants......34 E7
Rowrah Cumb......164 E7
Rowsham Bucks......67 K3
Rowsley Derbys......132 E6
Rowstock Oxon......48 C1
Rowston Lincs......136 A8
Rowthorne Derbys......133 J6
Rowton Ches W......129 K6
Rowton Shrops......95 J1
Rowton Shrops......95 K7
Rowton Wrekin......113 K7

Row Town Surrey......50 D6
Roxburgh Border......201 L7
Roxby N Linc......144 A4
Roxby N York......171 H7
Roxton Bed......86 C4
Roxwell Essex......70 F5
Royal Leamington Spa Warwks......83 H2
Royal Oak Darltn......169 G6
Royal Oak Lancs......138 E2
Royal's Green Ches E......113 K3
Royal Sutton Coldfield Birm......98 E4
Royal Tunbridge Wells Kent......38 F5
Royal Wootton Bassett Wilts......46 F3
Roy Bridge Highld......239 M7
Roydhouse Kirk......141 K5
Roydon Essex......69 L5
Roydon Norfk......106 C7
Roydon Norfk......120 F7
Roydon Hamlet Essex......69 L5
Royston Barns......142 B5
Royston Herts......87 G7
Royton Oldham......140 D6
Rozel Jersey......9 e2
Ruabon Wrexhm......112 D3
Ruaig Ag & B......224 D6
Ruan High Lanes Cnwll......4 E6
Ruan Lanihorne Cnwll......4 E6
Ruan Major Cnwll......3 H7
Ruan Minor Cnwll......3 J8
Ruardean Gloucs......63 J3
Ruardean Hill Gloucs......63 J4
Ruardean Woodside Gloucs......63 J4
Rubery Birm......98 C7
Rubha Ban W Isls......283 c12
Ruckcroft Cumb......166 C2
Ruckhall Herefs......80 B7
Ruckinge Kent......40 D8
Ruckland Lincs......136 F4
Ruckley Shrops......96 C3
Rudbaxton Pembks......54 F3
Rudby N York......161 G1
Rudchester Nthumb......180 D5
Ruddington Notts......116 F5
Ruddle Gloucs......63 K5
Ruddlemoor Cnwll......5 G4
Rudford Gloucs......63 M3
Rudge Somset......46 B8
Rudgeway S Glos......45 J2
Rudgwick W Susx......37 G4
Rudhall Herefs......63 J2
Rudheath Ches W......130 D5
Rudheath Woods Ches E......130 E5
Rudley Green Essex......71 K6
Rudloe Wilts......46 B5
Rudry Caerph......43 K4
Rudston E R Yk......153 H2
Rudyard Staffs......131 J8
Ruecastle Border......189 G2
Rufford Lancs......138 F4
Rufforth C York......151 H5
Rug Denbgs......111 K3
Rugby Warwks......100 B8
Rugby Services Warwks......100 B7
Rugeley Staffs......115 G2
Ruigh'riabhach Highld......261 G1
Ruisgarry W Isls......282 d7
Ruishton Somset......30 C6
Ruisigearraidh W Isls......282 d7
Ruislip Gt Lon......50 E2
Rùm Highld......236 D1
Rumbach Moray......267 H5
Rumbling Bridge P & K......221 J7
Rumburgh Suffk......107 G7
Rumby Hill Dur......168 F4
Rumford Cnwll......10 B8
Rumford Falk......210 B4
Rumney Cardif......43 K6
Rumwell Somset......30 B6
Runcorn Halton......129 L3
Runcton W Susx......20 E6
Runcton Holme Norfk......104 C2
Runfold Surrey......36 C2
Runhall Norfk......105 L2
Runham Norfk......107 J1
Runham Norfk......107 L2
Runnington Somset......29 L6
Runsell Green Essex......71 J6
Runshaw Moor Lancs......139 G4
Runswick N York......171 J7
Runtaleave Angus......233 L2
Runwell Essex......71 J8
Ruscombe Wokham......49 J4
Rushall Herefs......80 E8
Rushall Norfk......106 D6
Rushall Wilts......47 H7
Rushall Wsall......98 C3
Rushbrooke Suffk......89 H3
Rushbury Shrops......96 C5
Rushden Herts......69 J1
Rushden Nhants......85 J2

Rushenden Kent......53 K5
Rusher's Cross E Susx......38 F7
Rushford Devon......12 B7
Rushford Norfk......105 J7
Rush Green Essex......73 H4
Rush Green Gt Lon......52 B2
Rush Green Herts......69 G2
Rush Green Warrtn......130 D2
Rushlake Green E Susx......23 L3
Rushmere Suffk......107 K6
Rushmere St Andrew Suffk......90 E6
Rushmoor Surrey......36 C3
Rushock Herefs......79 K3
Rushock Worcs......81 K1
Rusholme Manch......131 G1
Rushton Ches W......130 B7
Rushton Nhants......101 J6
Rushton Shrops......96 D2
Rushton Spencer Staffs......131 J7
Rushwick Worcs......81 J4
Rushyford Dur......169 G5
Ruskie Stirlg......219 K7
Ruskington Lincs......118 E1
Rusland Cross Cumb......156 E5
Rusper W Susx......37 K3
Ruspidge Gloucs......63 K5
Russell Green Essex......71 H4
Russell's Water Oxon......49 H1
Russel's Green Suffk......90 F1
Russ Hill Surrey......37 K3
Rusthall Kent......38 E5
Rustington W Susx......21 H6
Ruston N York......163 G6
Ruston Parva E R Yk......153 G3
Ruswarp N York......162 F1
Ruthall Shrops......96 D5
Rutherford Border......201 K7
Rutherglen S Lans......209 G6
Ruthernbridge Cnwll......5 G2
Ruthin Denbgs......128 D8
Ruthrieston C Aber......245 K3
Ruthven Abers......267 K6
Ruthven Angus......233 L5
Ruthven Highld......241 K4
Ruthven Highld......252 F1
Ruthvoes Cnwll......4 F3
Ruthwaite Cumb......165 H3
Ruthwell D & G......176 E5
Ruxley Gt Lon......52 A5
Ruxton Green Herefs......63 G3
Ruyton-XI-Towns Shrops......112 F7
Ryal Nthumb......180 B4
Ryall Dorset......15 J4
Ryall Worcs......81 K7
Ryarsh Kent......52 E7
Rycote Oxon......67 G6
Rydal Cumb......156 E2
Ryde IoW......19 K5
Rye E Susx......25 G3
Ryebank Shrops......113 H5
Ryeford Herefs......63 J3
Rye Foreign E Susx......25 G3
Rye Harbour E Susx......25 H3
Ryehill E R Yk......145 G3
Ryeish Green Wokham......49 H5
Rye Street Worcs......81 H8
Ryhall Rutlnd......102 A1
Ryhill Wakefd......142 B5
Ryhope Sundld......181 K8
Rylah Derbys......133 J6
Ryland Lincs......135 K4
Rylands Notts......116 F4
Rylstone N York......149 H4
Ryme Intrinseca Dorset......31 J8
Ryther N York......151 J7
Ryton Gatesd......180 E6
Ryton N York......162 D7
Ryton Shrops......97 G3
Ryton Warwks......99 L6
Ryton-on-Dunsmore Warwks......99 K8
Ryton Woodside Gatesd......180 E6

S

Sabden Lancs......148 D8
Sabine's Green Essex......70 E7
Sacombe Herts......69 J3
Sacombe Green Herts......69 J3
Sacriston Dur......169 G1
Sadberge Darltn......169 J7
Saddell Ag & B......194 B4
Saddington Leics......100 E5
Saddlebow Norfk......120 D8
Saddlescombe W Susx......22 D5
Sadgill Cumb......157 G2
Saffron Walden Essex......87 L7
Sageston Pembks......55 H6
Saham Hills Norfk......105 H3

Place	Page	Grid
Saham Toney Norfk	105	H3
Saighton Ches W	129	K7
St Abbs Border	213	K5
St Agnes Border	212	F6
St Agnes Cnwll	4	B5
St Agnes IoS	10	b3
St Agnes Mining District Cnwll	4	B5
St Albans Herts	68	F5
St Allen Cnwll	4	D5
St Andrew Guern	9	j3
St Andrews Fife	223	J4
St Andrews Major V Glam	43	H7
St Andrews Well Dorset	15	L4
St Anne's Lancs	138	C2
St Ann's D & G	187	G7
St Ann's Chapel Cnwll	12	A8
St Ann's Chapel Devon	7	J5
St Anthony-in-Meneage Cnwll	3	K6
St Anthony's Hill E Susx	23	L7
St Arvans Mons	63	G7
St Asaph Denbgs	128	B5
St Athan V Glam	42	F8
St Aubin Jersey	9	c3
St Austell Cnwll	5	G4
St Bees Cumb	164	C8
St Blazey Cnwll	5	H4
St Blazey Gate Cnwll	5	H4
St Boswells Border	201	J7
St Brelade Jersey	9	b3
St Brelade's Bay Jersey	9	b3
St Breock Cnwll	10	D8
St Breward Cnwll	10	F7
St Briavels Gloucs	63	H6
St Brides Pembks	54	C5
St Brides Major V Glam	42	D6
St Brides Netherwent Mons	44	E1
St Brides-super-Ely V Glam	43	H6
St Brides Wentlooge Newpt	44	C3
St Budeaux C Plym	6	E3
Saintbury Gloucs	82	D7
St Buryan Cnwll	2	C6
St Catherine BaNES	45	M5
St Catherines Ag & B	217	J5
St Chloe Gloucs	64	B6
St Clears Carmth	58	A5
St Cleer Cnwll	6	A1
St Clement Cnwll	4	D6
St Clement Jersey	9	e4
St Clether Cnwll	11	H5
St Colmac Ag & B	207	G5
St Columb Major Cnwll	4	E2
St Columb Minor Cnwll	4	D2
St Columb Road Cnwll	4	E3
St Combs Abers	269	K4
St Cross South Elmham Suffk	106	F6
St Cyrus Abers	235	J2
St David's P & K	221	G3
St Davids Pembks	74	B7
St Day Cnwll	4	B6
St Decumans Somset	29	K2
St Dennis Cnwll	4	F3
St Devereux Herefs	62	E1
St Dogmaels Pembks	75	K3
St Dogwells Pembks	75	G6
St Dominick Cnwll	6	D1
St Donats V Glam	42	E8
St Edith's Marsh Wilts	46	E6
St Endellion Cnwll	10	D6
St Enoder Cnwll	4	E3
St Erme Cnwll	4	D5
St Erney Cnwll	6	D3
St Erth Cnwll	2	E4
St Erth Praze Cnwll	2	F4
St Ervan Cnwll	10	B8
St Eval Cnwll	4	E1
St Ewe Cnwll	5	G6
St Fagans Cardif	43	H6
St Fergus Abers	269	K6
St Fillans P & K	220	B2
St Florence Pembks	55	J6
St Gennys Cnwll	11	G3
St George Conwy	127	K4
St Georges N Som	44	D6
St George's V Glam	43	H6
St George's Hill Surrey	50	D6
St Germans Cnwll	6	D3
St Giles in the Wood Devon	27	J7
St Giles-on-the-Heath Devon	11	L4
St Gluvia's Cnwll	3	K4
St Harmon Powys	78	D1
St Helen Auckland Dur	168	F5
St Helens Cumb	164	D6
St Helen's E Susx	24	E5
St Helens IoW	19	L6
St Helens St Hel	139	G8
St Helier Gt Lon	51	H5
St Helier Jersey	9	d3
St Hilary Cnwll	2	E5
St Hilary V Glam	42	F7
Saint Hill Devon	14	C1
Saint Hill W Susx	38	B6
St Illtyd Blae G	61	K6
St Ippolyts Herts	69	G2
St Ishmael's Pembks	54	D5
St Issey Cnwll	10	C8
St Ive Cnwll	6	C2
St Ive Cross Cnwll	6	C2
St Ives Cambs	87	G1
St Ives Cnwll	2	E3
St Ives Dorset	17	M2
St James Norfk	122	F7
St James's End Nhants	84	E3
St James South Elmham Suffk	107	G7
St Jidgey Cnwll	4	F1
St John Cnwll	6	E4
St John Jersey	9	c1
St Johns Dur	168	D4
St John's E Susx	38	D7
St John's IoM	154	c5
St John's Kent	38	E2
St Johns Surrey	50	C7
St Johns Worcs	81	J4
St John's Chapel Devon	27	J5
St John's Chapel Dur	167	K3
St John's Fen End Norfk	103	L1
St John's Highway Norfk	120	C8
St John's Kirk S Lans	199	G6
St John's Town of Dalry D & G	184	F6
St John's Wood Gt Lon	51	H2
St Judes IoM	154	e3
St Just Cnwll	2	B5
St Just-in-Roseland Cnwll	3	L4
St Just Mining District Cnwll	2	B4
St Katherines Abers	256	D5
St Keverne Cnwll	3	K6
St Kew Cnwll	10	E7
St Kew Highway Cnwll	10	E7
St Keyne Cnwll	6	A3
St Lawrence Cnwll	5	H2
St Lawrence Essex	72	D6
St Lawrence IoW	19	J8
St Lawrence Jersey	9	c2
St Lawrence Kent	41	K2
St Lawrence Bay Essex	72	D6
St Leonards Bucks	67	M5
St Leonards Dorset	17	M2
St Leonards E Susx	24	E5
St Leonard's Street Kent	39	H2
St Levan Cnwll	2	B5
St Luke's Park Essex	71	J7
St Lythans V Glam	43	H7
St Mabyn Cnwll	10	E7
St Madoes P & K	222	C3
St Margarets Herefs	79	L8
St Margarets Herts	69	K5
St Margaret's at Cliffe Kent	41	K6
St Margaret's Hope Ork	275	c6
St Margaret South Elmham Suffk	107	G6
St Marks IoM	154	d7
St Martin Cnwll	3	J6
St Martin Cnwll	6	B4
St Martin Guern	9	j3
St Martin Jersey	9	e2
St Martin's IoS	10	c1
St Martin's P & K	221	L1
St Martin's Shrops	112	D4
St Martin's Moor Shrops	112	D4
St Mary Jersey	9	c2
St Mary Bourne Hants	34	F1
St Marychurch Torbay	8	D2
St Mary Church V Glam	42	F7
St Mary Cray Gt Lon	52	A5
St Mary Hill V Glam	42	E6
St Mary in the Marsh Kent	25	K2
St Mary's IoS	10	c3
St Mary's Ork	275	d5
St Mary's Bay Kent	25	K2
St Mary's Hoo Medway	53	H4
St Mary's Platt Kent	39	G2
St Maughans Mons	62	F4
St Maughans Green Mons	62	F4
St Mawes Cnwll	3	L4
St Mawgan Cnwll	4	E2
St Mellion Cnwll	6	D2
St Mellons Cardif	43	K5
St Merryn Cnwll	10	B7
St Mewan Cnwll	5	G4
St Michael Caerhays Cnwll	4	F6
St Michael Church Somset	30	D5
St Michael Penkevil Cnwll	4	D6
St Michaels Kent	39	M6
St Michaels Worcs	80	D2
St Michael's on Wyre Lancs	147	J7
St Michael South Elmham Suffk	107	G6
St Minver Cnwll	10	D7
St Monans Fife	223	J6
St Neot Cnwll	5	L1
St Neots Cambs	86	D3
St Newlyn East Cnwll	4	D3
St Nicholas Pembks	74	E5
St Nicholas V Glam	43	H6
St Nicholas-at-Wade Kent	41	J2
St Ninians Stirlg	209	L1
St Olaves Norfk	107	M3
St Osyth Essex	73	H4
St Ouen Jersey	9	b2
St Owen's Cross Herefs	63	G2
St Paul's Cray Gt Lon	52	A5
St Paul's Walden Herts	69	G3
St Peter Jersey	9	b2
St Peter Port Guern	9	k3
St Peter's Guern	9	i3
St Peter's Kent	41	L2
St Peter's Hill Cambs	86	E1
St Petrox Pembks	55	J6
St Pinnock Cnwll	5	L2
St Quivox S Ayrs	196	D6
St Ruan Cnwll	3	J8
St Sampson Guern	9	k2
St Saviour Guern	9	i3
St Saviour Jersey	9	d3
St Stephen Cnwll	4	F4
St Stephens Cnwll	6	E3
St Stephens Cnwll	11	L5
St Teath Cnwll	10	F6
St Thomas Devon	13	L4
St Margaret's Bay Kent	41	K6
St Tudy Cnwll	10	F7
St Twynnells Pembks	54	F7
St Veep Cnwll	5	K4
St Vigeans Angus	235	G6
St Wenn Cnwll	5	G2
St Weonards Herefs	63	G2
St Winnow Cnwll	5	J3
St y-Nyll V Glam	43	H6
Salcombe Devon	7	L7
Salcombe Regis Devon	14	D5
Salcott-cum-Virley Essex	72	D4
Sale Traffd	130	F2
Saleby Lincs	137	J4
Sale Green Worcs	81	L4
Salehurst E Susx	24	D2
Salem Carmth	59	H4
Salem Cerdgn	92	E6
Salen Ag & B	227	H4
Salen Highld	237	K7
Salesbury Lancs	139	K1
Salford C Beds	85	H7
Salford Oxon	65	L2
Salford Salfd	140	B8
Salford Priors Warwks	82	C5
Salfords Surrey	37	L2
Salhouse Norfk	123	G8
Saline Fife	221	J8
Salisbury Wilts	33	K5
Salisbury Plain Wilts	33	J2
Salkeld Dykes Cumb	166	D3
Sallachy Highld	272	D6
Salle Norfk	122	C6
Salmonby Lincs	136	F5
Salperton Gloucs	65	G3
Salph End Bed	86	B5
Salsburgh N Lans	209	L6
Salt Staffs	114	F6
Salta Cumb	164	E2
Saltaire C Brad	149	L8
Saltaire C Brad	149	L8
Saltash Cnwll	6	E3
Saltburn Highld	263	K6
Saltburn-by-the-Sea R & Cl	170	F6
Saltby Leics	117	M6
Salt Coates Cumb	177	G8
Saltcoats Cumb	155	K3
Saltcoats N Ayrs	195	L3
Saltcotes Lancs	138	D2
Saltdean Br & H	22	F6
Salterbeck Cumb	164	C5
Salterforth Lancs	148	F6
Salterswall Ches W	130	C6
Salterton Wilts	33	K4
Saltfleet Lincs	137	H1
Saltfleetby All Saints Lincs	137	H2
Saltfleetby St Clement Lincs	137	J1
Saltfleetby St Peter Lincs	137	H2
Saltford BaNES	45	K5
Salthouse Norfk	122	B3
Saltley Birm	98	E5
Saltmarsh Newpt	44	D2
Saltmarshe E R Yk	143	K3
Saltney Flints	129	J6
Salton N York	162	C6
Saltrens Devon	27	H6
Saltwick Nthumb	180	E3
Saltwood Kent	40	F8
Salvington W Susx	21	K6
Salwarpe Worcs	81	K3
Salway Ash Dorset	15	K3
Sambourne Warwks	82	C3
Sambrook Wrekin	113	M6
Samlesbury Lancs	139	H2
Samlesbury Bottoms Lancs	139	J2
Sampford Arundel Somset	29	K7
Sampford Brett Somset	29	K3
Sampford Courtenay Devon	12	F2
Sampford Moor Somset	29	K7
Sampford Peverell Devon	29	J8
Sampford Spiney Devon	12	D8
Samsonlane Ork	275	e3
Samson's Corner Essex	73	G3
Samuelston E Loth	212	B5
Sanaigmore Ag & B	204	C2
Sancreed Cnwll	2	C5
Sancton E R Yk	152	D7
Sand Somset	31	G2
Sandaig Highld	247	M8
Sandale Cumb	165	H3
Sandal Magna Wakefd	142	A4
Sanday Ork	275	e2
Sanday Airport Ork	275	e2
Sandbach Ches E	130	E7
Sandbach Services Ches E	130	F7
Sandbank Ag & B	207	K3
Sandbanks BCP	17	K5
Sandend Abers	267	L3
Sanderstead Gt Lon	51	J6
Sandford Cumb	167	G7
Sandford Devon	13	J2
Sandford Dorset	17	H5
Sandford Hants	18	B3
Sandford IoW	19	J7
Sandford N Som	44	E7
Sandford S Lans	197	L2
Sandford Shrops	112	E6
Sandford Shrops	113	J5
Sandford-on-Thames Oxon	66	D6
Sandford Orcas Dorset	31	K6
Sandford St Martin Oxon	66	B2
Sandgate Kent	41	G8
Sandhaven Abers	269	H3
Sandhead D & G	172	D5
Sandhill Rothm	142	C8
Sandhills Dorset	16	B3
Sandhills Dorset	31	L8
Sand Hills Leeds	150	E7
Sandhills Oxon	66	E5
Sandhills Surrey	36	D3
Sandhoe Nthumb	180	A5
Sandhole Ag & B	216	F7
Sand Hole E R Yk	152	B8
Sandholme E R Yk	143	L2
Sandholme Lincs	119	K4
Sandhurst Br For	49	K6
Sandhurst Gloucs	64	B2
Sandhurst Kent	39	K7
Sandhurst Cross Kent	24	E2
Sand Hutton N York	151	L4
Sandhutton N York	160	E6
Sandiacre Derbys	116	E4
Sandilands Lincs	137	K3
Sandiway Ches W	130	B5
Sandleheath Hants	33	K7
Sandleigh Oxon	66	C6
Sandley Dorset	32	C6
Sandling Kent	53	G7
Sandlow Green Ches E	130	F6
Sandness Shet	281	c5
Sandon Essex	71	H6
Sandon Herts	87	G8
Sandon Staffs	114	E5
Sandon Bank Staffs	114	E6
Sandown IoW	19	K6
Sandplace Cnwll	6	A3
Sandridge Herts	68	F5
Sandridge Wilts	46	D6
Sandringham Norfk	120	F5
Sands Bucks	67	K8
Sandsend N York	171	K8
Sand Side Cumb	156	B6
Sandside Cumb	157	G6
Sandtoft N Linc	143	J6
Sandway Kent	39	M3
Sandwich Kent	41	K4
Sandwich Bay Kent	41	K4
Sandwick Cumb	166	A6
Sandwick Shet	281	e8
Sandwick W Isls	282	g3
Sandwith Cumb	164	C7
Sandwith Newtown Cumb	164	C7
Sandy C Beds	86	D5
Sandy Bank Lincs	136	E8
Sandycroft Flints	129	H6
Sandy Cross E Susx	23	K3
Sandy Cross Herefs	80	F4
Sandyford D & G	187	J2
Sandygate Devon	13	K7
Sandygate IoM	154	e3
Sandy Haven Pembks	54	D5
Sandyhills D & G	175	M4

Sandylands Lancs	147	H3	
Sandy Lane C Brad	149	K8	
Sandylane Staffs	113	M4	
Sandylane Swans	57	G7	
Sandy Lane Wilts	46	D5	
Sandy Lane Wrexhm	112	F3	
Sandy Park Devon	13	G5	
Sandysike Cumb	177	L5	
Sandyway Herefs	63	G2	
Sangobeg Highld	277	G3	
Sangomore Highld	276	F3	
Sankey Bridges Warrtn	130	B2	
Sankyn's Green Worcs	81	H2	
Sanna Highld	236	E6	
Sanndabhaig W Isls	282	g3	
Sannox N Ayrs	195	G2	
Sanquhar D & G	185	K1	
Santon Cumb	155	K2	
Santon IoM	154	d7	
Santon Bridge Cumb	155	K2	
Santon Downham Suffk	105	G6	
Sapcote Leics	100	B5	
Sapey Common Herefs	81	G2	
Sapiston Suffk	105	J8	
Sapley Cambs	102	E8	
Sapperton Derbys	115	K4	
Sapperton Gloucs	64	D6	
Sapperton Lincs	118	D5	
Saracen's Head Lincs	119	K6	
Sarclet Highld	280	D7	
Sarisbury Hants	19	H2	
Sarn Brdgnd	42	D5	
Sarn Powys	94	F5	
Sarnau Carmth	58	B5	
Sarnau Cerdgn	76	B5	
Sarnau Gwynd	111	J4	
Sarnau Powys	78	E8	
Sarnau Powys	112	C8	
Sarn Bach Gwynd	108	E6	
Sarnesfield Herefs	79	L5	
Sarn Mellteyrn Gwynd	108	D5	
Sarn Park Services Brdgnd	42	D5	
Sarn-wen Powys	112	D7	
Saron Carmth	59	H6	
Saron Carmth	76	C7	
Saron Gwynd	125	H7	
Saron Gwynd	125	J6	
Sarratt Herts	68	D7	
Sarre Kent	41	H2	
Sarsden Oxon	65	L3	
Sarson Hants	34	C2	
Satley Dur	168	E2	
Satmar Kent	41	H7	
Satron N York	159	G3	
Satterleigh Devon	28	B6	
Satterthwaite Cumb	156	D4	
Satwell Oxon	49	H2	
Sauchen Abers	244	F1	
Saucher P & K	233	J8	
Sauchieburn Abers	235	G2	
Saul Gloucs	63	L5	
Saundby Notts	134	F2	
Saundersfoot Pembks	55	K6	
Saunderton Bucks	67	J6	
Saunderton Station Bucks	67	K7	
Saunton Devon	27	H3	
Sausthorpe Lincs	137	G6	
Saverley Green Staffs	114	F4	
Savile Town Kirk	141	K4	
Sawbridge Warwks	83	L2	
Sawbridgeworth Herts	70	C4	
Sawdon N York	163	G5	
Sawley Derbys	116	D5	
Sawley Lancs	148	D6	
Sawley N York	150	C2	
Sawston Cambs	87	K5	
Sawtry Cambs	102	D6	
Saxby Leics	117	L7	
Saxby Lincs	135	K3	
Saxby All Saints N Linc	144	C4	
Saxelbye Leics	117	J7	
Saxham Street Suffk	90	C3	
Saxilby Lincs	135	H4	
Saxlingham Norfk	122	A4	
Saxlingham Green Norfk	106	E4	
Saxlingham Nethergate Norfk	106	E4	
Saxlingham Thorpe Norfk	106	E4	
Saxmundham Suffk	91	J3	
Saxondale Notts	117	H3	
Saxon Street Cambs	88	D3	
Saxtead Suffk	91	G2	
Saxtead Green Suffk	90	F2	
Saxtead Little Green Suffk	90	F2	
Saxthorpe Norfk	122	C5	
Saxton N York	151	G8	
Sayers Common W Susx	22	D4	
Scackleton N York	161	L8	
Scadabay W Isls	282	e6	
Scadabhagh W Isls	282	e6	
Scafell Pike Cumb	156	B1	
Scaftworth Notts	134	D2	
Scagglethorpe N York	152	C1	
Scalasaig Ag & B	214	D5	
Scalby E R Yk	143	L2	
Scalby N York	163	H4	
Scald End Bed	85	L4	
Scaldwell Nhants	84	E1	
Scaleby Cumb	178	B6	
Scalebyhill Cumb	178	B6	
Scale Houses Cumb	166	E2	
Scales Cumb	146	E2	
Scales Cumb	165	K5	
Scalesceugh Cumb	166	B1	
Scalford Leics	117	K6	
Scaling N York	171	H7	
Scaling Dam R & Cl	171	H8	
Scalloway Shet	281	d7	
Scalpay Highld	247	J2	
Scalpay W Isls	282	f6	
Scamblesby Lincs	136	E4	
Scammonden Kirk	141	G4	
Scamodale Highld	228	C1	
Scampston N York	162	F7	
Scampton Lincs	135	J4	
Scaniport Highld	251	H4	
Scapegoat Hill Kirk	141	G4	
Scarba Ag & B	215	K3	
Scarborough N York	163	J5	
Scarcewater Cnwll	4		
Scarcliffe Derbys	133	K6	
Scarcroft Leeds	150	E7	
Scarfskerry Highld	280	C2	
Scargill Dur	168	D8	
Scarinish Ag & B	224	D6	
Scarisbrick Lancs	138	D5	
Scarness Cumb	165	H4	
Scarning Norfk	105	J1	
Scarrington Notts	117	J3	
Scarth Hill Lancs	138	E6	
Scarthingwell N York	151	G8	
Scartho NE Lin	145	H6	
Scethrog Powys	61	H2	
Scholar Green Ches E	131	G8	
Scholes Kirk	141	J3	
Scholes Kirk	141	J6	
Scholes Leeds	150	E8	
Scholes Rothm	142	B8	
Scholes Wigan	139	J6	
School Aycliffe Dur	169	H6	
School Green C Brad	141	H1	
School Green Ches W	130	C6	
Schoolgreen Wokham	49	H5	
School House Dorset	15	J2	
Scissett Kirk	141	K5	
Scleddau Pembks	74	F5	
Scofton Notts	134	C4	
Scole Norfk	106	C7	
Scone P & K	221	L2	
Sconser Highld	247	H2	
Scoonie Fife	222	F6	
Scopwick Lincs	135	M8	
Scoraig Highld	261	G1	
Scorborough E R Yk	152	F6	
Scorrier Cnwll	4	B6	
Scorriton Devon	7	K1	
Scorton Lancs	147	K6	
Scorton N York	160	C3	
Sco Ruston Norfk	122	F7	
Scotby Cumb	178	B7	
Scotch Corner N York	160	B2	
Scotch Corner Rest Area N York	160	B2	
Scotforth Lancs	147	J4	
Scot Hay Staffs	114	B2	
Scothern Lincs	135	L4	
Scotland Lincs	118	C5	
Scotland Gate Nthumb	181	G2	
Scotlandwell P & K	222	C7	
Scot Lane End Bolton	139	J6	
Scotscalder Station Highld	279	K5	
Scotsdike Cumb	177	L4	
Scot's Gap Nthumb	180	C2	
Scotsmill Abers	255	L7	
Scotstoun C Glas	208	F5	
Scotswood N u Ty	180	F6	
Scotter Lincs	143	M7	
Scotterthorpe Lincs	143	L7	
Scottlethorpe Lincs	118	D7	
Scotton Lincs	143	M7	
Scotton N York	150	D4	
Scotton N York	160	B3	
Scottow Norfk	122	F6	
Scott Willoughby Lincs	118	D4	
Scoulton Norfk	105	K3	
Scounslow Green Staffs	115	H5	
Scourie Highld	276	B7	
Scourie More Highld	276	A7	
Scousburgh Shet	281	d8	
Southead Oldham	140	D4	
Scrabster Highld	279	K2	
Scraesburgh Border	189	J3	
Scrafield Lincs	136	F6	
Scrainwood Nthumb	190	D4	
Scrane End Lincs	119	L3	
Scraptoft Leics	100	E2	
Scratby Norfk	123	K8	
Scrayingham N York	152	A4	
Scrays E Susx	24	D3	
Scredington Lincs	118	E3	
Scremby Lincs	137	H6	
Scremerston Nthumb	202	F3	
Screveton Notts	117	J3	
Scrivelsby Lincs	136	E6	
Scriven N York	150	E4	
Scrooby Notts	134	C2	
Scropton Derbys	115	K5	
Scrub Hill Lincs	136	D8	
Scruton N York	160	D4	
Scuggate Cumb	178	B4	
Scullomie Highld	277	L4	
Sculthorpe Norfk	121	K5	
Scunthorpe N Linc	143	M5	
Scurlage Swans	56	E7	
Sea Somset	30	E8	
Seaborough Dorset	15	K2	
Seabridge Staffs	114	C3	
Seabrook Kent	41	G8	
Seaburn Sundld	181	K6	
Seacombe Wirral	129	H2	
Seacroft Leeds	150	E8	
Seacroft Lincs	137	L7	
Seadyke Lincs	119	K4	
Seafield W Loth	210	D6	
Seaford E Susx	23	H7	
Seaforth Sefton	138	C4	
Seagrave Leics	117	G8	
Seagry Heath Wilts	46	D3	
Seaham Dur	169	L1	
Seahouses Nthumb	203	L6	
Seal Kent	38	E2	
Sealand Flints	129	H6	
Seale Surrey	36	D1	
Seamer N York	163	J6	
Seamer N York	170	C8	
Seamill N Ayrs	195	K2	
Sea Palling Norfk	123	K6	
Searby Lincs	144	D6	
Seasalter Kent	40	E2	
Seascale Cumb	155	J2	
Seathwaite Cumb	156	B3	
Seathwaite Cumb	165	H8	
Seatle Cumb	156	E6	
Seatoller Cumb	165	H7	
Seaton Cnwll	6	C4	
Seaton Cumb	164	D4	
Seaton Devon	14	F4	
Seaton Dur	169	L1	
Seaton E R Yk	153	J6	
Seaton Kent	41	H4	
Seaton Nthumb	181	H3	
Seaton Rutlnd	101	K4	
Seaton Burn N Tyne	181	G4	
Seaton Carew Hartpl	170	C5	
Seaton Delaval Nthumb	181	H4	
Seaton Ross E R Yk	152	B7	
Seaton Sluice Nthumb	181	H4	
Seatown Dorset	15	K4	
Seatown Moray	266	E2	
Seave Green N York	161	J3	
Seaview IoW	19	L5	
Seaville Cumb	177	G8	
Seavington St Mary Somset	30	F7	
Seavington St Michael Somset	30	F7	
Sebastopol Torfn	62	C7	
Sebergham Cumb	165	K2	
Seckington Warwks	99	H2	
Second Severn Crossing Mons	45	L2	
Sedbergh Cumb	157	L4	
Sedbury Gloucs	63	H8	
Sedbusk N York	158	F4	
Sedgeberrow Worcs	82	B7	
Sedgebrook Lincs	117	M4	
Sedge Fen Suffk	104	D6	
Sedgefield Dur	169	K5	
Sedgeford Norfk	120	F4	
Sedgehill Wilts	32	E5	
Sedgemoor Services Somset	44	D8	
Sedgley Dudley	97	L4	
Sedgley Park Bury	140	B2	
Sedgwick Cumb	157	H5	
Sedlescombe E Susx	24	E4	
Sedrup Bucks	67	J5	
Seed Kent	40	B4	
Seend Wilts	46	D6	
Seend Cleeve Wilts	46	D6	
Seer Green Bucks	68	B8	
Seething Norfk	107	G4	
Sefton Sefton	138	D7	
Seghill Nthumb	181	G4	
Seighford Staffs	114	D7	
Seion Gwynd	125	K6	
Seisdon Staffs	97	J4	
Selattyn Shrops	112	C5	
Selborne Hants	35	M4	
Selby N York	142	F1	
Selham W Susx	20	F3	
Selhurst Gt Lon	51	J5	
Selkirk Border	201	G7	
Sellack Herefs	63	H2	
Sellafield Station Cumb	155	J2	
Sellafirth Shet	281	e3	
Sellan Cnwll	2	C5	
Sellindge Kent	40	E7	
Selling Kent	40	E4	
Sells Green Wilts	46	D6	
Selly Oak Birm	98	D7	
Selmeston E Susx	23	H6	
Selsdon Gt Lon	51	K6	
Selsey W Susx	20	D8	
Selsfield Common W Susx	38	A6	
Selside Cumb	157	H3	
Selside N York	158	D7	
Selsley Gloucs	64	B6	
Selsted Kent	41	H6	
Selston Notts	116	D1	
Selworthy Somset	29	G2	
Semer Suffk	89	K6	
Semington Wilts	46	C6	
Semley Wilts	32	E5	
Sempringham Lincs	118	F5	
Send Surrey	50	C7	
Send Marsh Surrey	50	D7	
Senghenydd Caerph	43	H3	
Sennen Cnwll	2	B6	
Sennen Cove Cnwll	2	B6	
Sennybridge Powys	60	D2	
Serlby Notts	134	C2	
Sessay N York	161	G7	
Setchey Norfk	104	C1	
Setley Hants	18	D3	
Seton Mains E Loth	211	M4	
Settle N York	148	E3	
Settrington N York	152	C2	
Seven Ash Somset	29	L4	
Sevenhampton Gloucs	64	F3	
Sevenhampton Swindn	47	J1	
Seven Kings Gt Lon	51	M2	
Sevenoaks Kent	38	E2	
Sevenoaks Weald Kent	38	E3	
Seven Sisters Neath	60	B5	
Seven Springs Gloucs	64	D4	
Seven Star Green Essex	72	D2	
Severn Beach S Glos	45	G2	
Severn Bridge S Glos	45	H1	
Severn Stoke Worcs	81	K6	
Severn View Services S Glos	45	H1	
Sevick End Bed	86	B4	
Sevington Kent	40	D7	
Sewards End Essex	88	B7	
Sewardstonebury Essex	69	K7	
Sewell C Beds	68	C3	
Sewerby E R Yk	153	K2	
Seworgan Cnwll	3	H5	
Sewstern Leics	118	A7	
Sexhow N York	161	G2	
Sgalpaigh W Isls	282	f6	
Sgiogarstaigh W Isls	282	h1	
Shabbington Bucks	67	G5	
Shackerley Shrops	97	J2	
Shackerstone Leics	99	K2	
Shacklecross Derbys	116	C5	
Shackleford Surrey	36	D2	
Shade Calder	140	D7	
Shader W Isls	282	g1	
Shadforth Dur	169	J3	
Shadingfield Suffk	107	J6	
Shadoxhurst Kent	40	C7	
Shadwell Leeds	150	D7	
Shadwell Norfk	105	J6	
Shaftenhoe End Herts	87	H7	
Shaftesbury Dorset	32	E6	
Shaftholme Donc	142	F6	
Shafton Barns	142	B5	
Shafton Two Gates Barns	142	B5	
Shakerley Wigan	139	K7	
Shalbourne Wilts	47	L6	
Shalcombe IoW	18	F6	
Shalden Hants	35	L3	
Shalden Green Hants	35	L2	
Shaldon Devon	13	L8	
Shalfleet IoW	18	F6	
Shalford Essex	71	H1	

Shalford Surrey 36 F2
Shalford Green Essex 71 H2
Shallowford Staffs 114 D5
Shalmsford Street Kent 40 E4
Shalstone Bucks 84 C7
Shamley Green Surrey 36 F2
Shandford Angus 234 D3
Shandon Ag & B 207 L2
Shandwick Highld 264 D5
Shangton Leics 100 F4
Shankhouse Nthumb 181 G3
Shanklin IoW 19 K7
Shantron Ag & B 208 B2
Shap Cumb 166 D7
Shapinsay Ork 275 d4
Shapwick Dorset 17 H2
Shapwick Somset 30 F3
Shard End Birm 98 F5
Shardlow Derbys 116 D5
Shareshill Staffs 97 L2
Sharlston Wakefd 142 B4
Sharlston Common Wakefd 142 B4
Sharmans Cross Solhll 98 E7
Sharnal Street Medway 53 G4
Sharnbrook Bed 85 K3
Sharneyford Lancs 140 C3
Sharnford Leics 100 B5
Sharnhill Green Dorset 16 D2
Sharoe Green Lancs 139 G1
Sharow N York 150 D2
Sharpenhoe C Beds 68 D1
Sharperton Nthumb 190 D5
Sharp Green Norfk 123 H7
Sharpness Gloucs 63 K6
Sharpthorne W Susx 38 B6
Sharptor Cnwll 11 J8
Sharpway Gate Worcs 81 L2
Sharrington Norfk 122 A4
Shatterford Worcs 97 H7
Shatterling Kent 41 J4
Shatton Derbys 132 D3
Shaugh Prior Devon 7 G2
Shave Cross Dorset 15 J3
Shavington Ches E 113 M1
Shaw C Brad 140 F1
Shaw Oldham 140 D6
Shaw Swindn 47 G2
Shaw W Berk 48 C5
Shaw Wilts 46 G4
Shawbirch Wrekin 113 L8
Shawbost W Isls 282 f2
Shawbury Shrops 113 J7
Shawclough Rochdl 140 D5
Shaw Common Gloucs 63 K2
Shawdon Hill Nthumb 190 F3
Shawell Leics 100 C7
Shawford Hants 34 F6
Shawforth Lancs 140 D4
Shaw Green Herts 69 J1
Shaw Green Lancs 139 G4
Shaw Green N York 150 C5
Shawhead D & G 185 L7
Shaw Mills N York 150 C3
Shawsburn S Lans 198 C3
Shear Cross Wilts 32 E3
Shearington D & G 176 D5
Shearsby Leics 100 D5
Shearston Somset 30 D5
Shebbear Devon 12 B1
Shebdon Staffs 114 B6
Shebster Highld 279 H3
Shedfield Hants 35 H8
Sheen Staffs 132 B7
Sheepbridge Derbys 133 G5
Sheep Hill Dur 180 E7
Sheepridge Kirk 141 J4
Sheepscar Leeds 141 M1
Sheepscombe Gloucs 64 C5
Sheepstor Devon 7 G1
Sheepwash Devon 12 C2
Sheepwash Nthumb 181 G4
Sheepway N Som 45 G4
Sheepy Magna Leics 99 J3
Sheepy Parva Leics 99 J3
Sheering Essex 70 D4
Sheerness Kent 53 K4
Sheerwater Surrey 50 C6
Sheet Hants 36 A6
Sheffield Cnwll 2 D5
Sheffield Sheff 133 G2
Sheffield Bottom W Berk 49 G5
Sheffield Green E Susx 22 F2
Shefford C Beds 86 C7
Shefford Woodlands W Berk 48 A4
Sheigra Highld 276 B4
Sheinton Shrops 96 E3
Shelderton Shrops 95 K7
Sheldon Birm 98 F6
Sheldon Derbys 132 C6
Sheldon Devon 14 D1

Sheldwich Kent 40 D4
Sheldwich Lees Kent 40 D4
Shelf Calder 141 H2
Shelfanger Norfk 106 C6
Shelfield Warwks 82 D3
Shelfield Wsall 98 C3
Shelfield Green Warwks 82 D3
Shelford Notts 117 H3
Shelford Warwks 99 L5
Shellacres Nthumb 202 D4
Shelley Essex 70 E6
Shelley Kirk 141 K5
Shelley Suffk 89 L7
Shelley Far Bank Kirk 141 K5
Shellingford Oxon 65 L8
Shellow Bowells Essex 70 F5
Shelsley Beauchamp Worcs 81 G3
Shelsley Walsh Worcs 81 G3
Shelton Bed 85 K2
Shelton Norfk 106 E5
Shelton Notts 117 K3
Shelton Shrops 95 L1
Shelton Green Norfk 106 E5
Shelton Lock C Derb 116 C5
Shelton Under Harley Staffs 114 C4
Shelve Shrops 95 H4
Shelwick Herefs 80 C6
Shenfield Essex 70 F8
Shenington Oxon 83 J6
Shenley Herts 68 F7
Shenley Brook End M Keyn 85 G8
Shenleybury Herts 68 F6
Shenley Church End M Keyn 85 G7
Shenmore Herefs 79 M7
Shennanton D & G 173 J2
Shenstone Staffs 98 E3
Shenstone Worcs 97 J8
Shenstone Woodend Staffs 98 E3
Shenton Leics 99 K3
Shenval Moray 254 E6
Shepeau Stow Lincs 102 F1
Shephall Herts 69 H2
Shepherd's Bush Gt Lon 51 G3
Shepherd's Green Oxon 49 H2
Shepherds Patch Gloucs 63 L6
Shepherdswell Kent 41 H5
Shepley Kirk 141 J6
Shepperdine S Glos 63 J8
Shepperton Surrey 50 D5
Shepperton Green Surrey 50 D5
Shepreth Cambs 87 H5
Shepshed Leics 116 E7
Shepton Beauchamp Somset 30 F7
Shepton Mallet Somset 31 K2
Shepton Montague Somset 31 L4
Shepway Kent 39 J3
Sheraton Dur 170 B4
Sherborne Dorset 31 L7
Sherborne Gloucs 65 H4
Sherborne Somset 45 H7
Sherborne St John Hants 48 F7
Sherbourne Warwks 83 G3
Sherburn Dur 169 J2
Sherburn N York 163 G7
Sherburn Hill Dur 169 J2
Sherburn in Elmet N York 142 D1
Shere Surrey 37 G1
Shereford Norfk 121 K5
Sherfield English Hants 34 C6
Sherfield on Loddon Hants 49 G7
Sherfin Lancs 140 B3
Sherford Devon 7 G4
Sherford Devon 8 A6
Sherford Dorset 17 H4
Sheriffhales Shrops 97 G1
Sheriff Hutton N York 151 K3
Sheringham Norfk 122 E3
Sherington M Keyn 85 H6
Shermanbury W Susx 22 B3
Shernborne Norfk 120 F5
Sherrington Wilts 33 G3
Sherston Wilts 46 B2
Sherwood C Nott 116 F3
Sherwood Forest Notts 134 D2
Shetland Islands Shet 281 d6
Shettleston C Glas 209 H6
Shevington Wigan 139 H6
Shevington Moor Wigan 139 H6
Shevington Vale Wigan 139 G6
Sheviock Cnwll 6 D4
Shibden Head C Brad 141 H2
Shide IoW 19 H6
Shidlaw Nthumb 202 C5
Shiel Bridge Highld 248 F7
Shieldaig Highld 248 C1
Shieldhill D & G 176 D2
Shieldhill Falk 210 B4
Shieldhill House Hotel S Lans 199 G5
Shields N Lans 209 K7
Shielfoot Highld 237 J6

Shielhill Angus 234 C4
Shielhill Inver 207 L4
Shifford Oxon 66 A6
Shifnal Shrops 97 G2
Shilbottle Nthumb 191 J4
Shildon Dur 169 G5
Shillford E Rens 208 D7
Shillingford Devon 29 H6
Shillingford Oxon 66 E8
Shillingford Abbot Devon 13 L5
Shillingford St George Devon 13 L5
Shillingstone Dorset 32 D8
Shillington C Beds 86 C8
Shillmoor Nthumb 190 B6
Shilton Oxon 65 K5
Shilton Warwks 99 L6
Shimpling Norfk 106 D6
Shimpling Suffk 89 H5
Shimpling Street Suffk 89 H4
Shincliffe Dur 169 H3
Shiney Row Sundld 181 H8
Shinfield Wokham 49 H5
Shingay Cambs 86 F6
Shingle Street Suffk 91 J6
Shinnersbridge Devon 8 B2
Shinness Highld 272 E5
Shipbourne Kent 38 F3
Shipdham Norfk 105 J2
Shipham Somset 44 E7
Shiphay Torbay 8 D2
Shiplake Oxon 49 J3
Shiplake Row Oxon 49 H3
Shiplate N Som 44 D7
Shipley C Brad 149 L8
Shipley Derbys 116 D3
Shipley Shrops 97 H4
Shipley W Susx 37 H6
Shipley Bridge Surrey 37 M3
Shipley Hatch Kent 40 C7
Shipmeadow Suffk 107 H5
Shippea Hill Station Cambs 104 C6
Shippon Oxon 66 C7
Shipston-on-Stour Warwks 83 G7
Shipton Bucks 67 J2
Shipton Gloucs 64 F3
Shipton N York 151 H4
Shipton Shrops 96 D5
Shipton Bellinger Hants 34 B2
Shipton Gorge Dorset 15 L4
Shipton Green W Susx 20 C7
Shipton Moyne Gloucs 46 C1
Shipton-on-Cherwell Oxon 66 C4
Shiptonthorpe E R Yk 152 C7
Shipton-under-Wychwood
  Oxon 65 L3
Shirburn Oxon 67 G7
Shirdley Hill Lancs 138 D5
Shire Cumb 166 E4
Shirebrook Derbys 133 K6
Shiregreen Sheff 133 G1
Shirehampton Bristl 45 G4
Shiremoor N Tyne 181 H4
Shirenewton Mons 62 F8
Shire Oak Wsall 98 D3
Shireoaks Notts 133 L3
Shirkoak Kent 40 B8
Shirland Derbys 133 H8
Shirlett Shrops 96 E4
Shirley C Sotn 34 E8
Shirley Derbys 115 L3
Shirley Gt Lon 51 K6
Shirley Solhll 98 E7
Shirl Heath Herefs 80 A3
Shirrell Heath Hants 35 H8
Shirwell Devon 27 L3
Shiskine N Ayrs 194 E5
Shittlehope Dur 168 C3
Shobdon Herefs 79 M3
Shobley Hants 18 B2
Shobrooke Devon 13 K2
Shoby Leics 117 H7
Shocklach Ches W 113 G2
Shocklach Green Ches W 113 G2
Shoeburyness Sthend 53 K2
Sholden Kent 41 K5
Sholing C Sotn 19 G2
Shoot Hill Shrops 95 K1
Shop Cnwll 10 B7
Shop Cnwll 26 D7
Shopwyke W Susx 20 E6
Shore Rochdl 140 D4
Shoreditch Gt Lon 51 J2
Shoreditch Somset 30 C6
Shoreham Kent 52 B6
Shoreham-by-Sea W Susx 22 C6
Shoreswood Nthumb 202 E4
Shorley Hants 35 J5
Shorncote Gloucs 64 F7
Shorne Kent 52 E5
Shortacross Cnwll 6 B3

Shortbridge E Susx 23 G3
Shortfield Common Surrey 36 C2
Shortgate E Susx 23 H4
Short Heath Birm 98 E5
Shortheath Hants 36 A4
Short Heath Wsall 98 C3
Shortlanesend Cnwll 4 C5
Shortlees E Ayrs 196 E4
Shortstown Bed 86 B6
Shorwell IoW 19 G7
Shoscombe BaNES 45 L7
Shotesham Norfk 106 E4
Shotgate Essex 71 J8
Shotley Suffk 90 F8
Shotley Bridge Dur 180 D8
Shotleyfield Nthumb 180 C8
Shotley Gate Suffk 90 F8
Shottenden Kent 40 D4
Shottermill Surrey 36 C4
Shottery Warwks 82 E4
Shotteswell Warwks 83 K6
Shottisham Suffk 91 H6
Shottle Derbys 116 A2
Shottlegate Derbys 116 A2
Shotton Dur 169 K5
Shotton Dur 169 L3
Shotton Flints 129 H6
Shotton Nthumb 180 F3
Shotton Nthumb 202 C7
Shotton Colliery Dur 169 K3
Shotts N Lans 210 A7
Shotwick Ches W 129 H5
Shougle Moray 266 D5
Shouldham Norfk 104 D2
Shouldham Thorpe Norfk 104 D2
Shoulton Worcs 81 J3
Shover's Green E Susx 39 G7
Shraleybrook Staffs 114 B2
Shrawardine Shrops 112 F8
Shrawley Worcs 81 J2
Shreding Green Bucks 50 C3
Shrewley Warwks 82 F2
Shrewsbury Shrops 96 B1
Shrewton Wilts 33 J2
Shripney W Susx 20 F6
Shrivenham Oxon 47 K1
Shropham Norfk 105 K5
Shroton Dorset 32 E8
Shrub End Essex 72 E2
Shucknall Herefs 80 D6
Shudy Camps Cambs 88 C6
Shuna Ag & B 216 B5
Shurdington Gloucs 64 D3
Shurlock Row W & M 49 K4
Shurnock Worcs 82 B3
Shurrery Highld 279 J4
Shurrery Lodge Highld 279 J5
Shurton Somset 30 B2
Shustoke Warwks 99 G5
Shute Devon 13 L3
Shute Devon 14 F3
Shutford Oxon 83 J7
Shut Heath Staffs 114 D7
Shuthonger Gloucs 81 K8
Shutlanger Nhants 84 E5
Shutterton Devon 13 M6
Shutt Green Staffs 97 K2
Shuttington Warwks 99 H2
Shuttlewood Derbys 133 J5
Shuttleworth Bury 140 B4
Siabost W Isls 282 f2
Siadar W Isls 282 g1
Sibbertoft Nhants 100 E6
Sibdon Carwood Shrops 95 K6
Sibford Ferris Oxon 83 H7
Sibford Gower Oxon 83 H7
Sible Hedingham Essex 88 F8
Sibley's Green Essex 70 F2
Siblyback Cnwll 11 J8
Sibsey Lincs 119 K2
Sibsey Fenside Lincs 119 K1
Sibson Cambs 102 B4
Sibson Leics 99 K3
Sibster Highld 280 D5
Sibthorpe Notts 117 K2
Sibthorpe Notts 134 E5
Sibton Suffk 91 J2
Sicklesmere Suffk 89 H3
Sicklinghall N York 150 E6
Sidbrook Somset 30 C5
Sidbury Devon 14 D4
Sidbury Shrops 96 F6
Sid Cop Barns 142 B6
Sidcot N Som 44 E7
Sidcup Gt Lon 51 M4
Siddick Cumb 164 D4
Siddington Ches E 131 G5
Siddington Gloucs 64 F7
Sidemoor Worcs 81 L1
Sidestrand Norfk 122 F3

Sidford Devon 14 D4
Sidlesham W Susx 20 D7
Sidlesham Common W Susx 20 D6
Sidley E Susx 24 D5
Sidmouth Devon 14 D5
Siefton Shrops 96 B6
Sigford Devon 13 H7
Sigglesthorne E R Yk 153 J6
Sigingstone V Glam 42 E7
Signet Oxon 65 K5
Silchester Hants 48 F6
Sileby Leics 117 G8
Silecroft Cumb 155 L6
Silfield Norfk 106 C3
Silian Cerdgn 77 G5
Silkstead Hants 34 F6
Silkstone Barns 141 L6
Silkstone Common Barns 141 L6
Silk Willoughby Lincs 118 E3
Silloth Cumb 176 F8
Silpho N York 163 H4
Silsden C Brad 149 J6
Silsoe C Beds 86 B8
Silton Dorset 32 C5
Silverburn Mdloth 211 G7
Silverdale Lancs 157 G7
Silverdale Staffs 114 C2
Silver End Essex 71 K3
Silverford Abers 268 D3
Silvergate Norfk 122 D6
Silver Jubilee Bridge Halton 129 L3
Silverlace Green Suffk 91 H3
Silverley's Green Suffk 106 F8
Silverstone Nhants 84 C6
Silver Street Kent 53 J7
Silver Street Somset 31 J4
Silverton Devon 13 M2
Silverwell Cnwll 4 B5
Silvington Shrops 96 E7
Simister Bury 140 C6
Simmondley Derbys 131 K1
Simonburn Nthumb 179 K4
Simonsbath Somset 28 D3
Simonsburrow Devon 29 L7
Simonstone Lancs 140 A1
Simonstone N York 158 F4
Simprim Border 202 C4
Simpson M Keyn 85 H8
Simpson Cross Pembks 54 E3
Sinclair's Hill Border 202 C3
Sinclairston E Ayrs 196 F7
Sinderby N York 160 E6
Sinderhope Nthumb 179 K8
Sinderland Green Traffd 130 E2
Sindlesham Wokham 49 J5
Sinfin C Derb 116 B5
Singleborough Bucks 67 J1
Single Street Gt Lon 51 L7
Singleton Kent 40 C7
Singleton Lancs 147 G8
Singleton W Susx 20 E4
Singlewell Kent 52 E5
Sinkhurst Green Kent 39 K5
Sinnahard Abers 244 B1
Sinnington N York 162 C5
Sinope Leics 116 C8
Sinton Worcs 81 J3
Sinton Worcs 81 J3
Sinton Green Worcs 81 J3
Sipson Gt Lon 50 D3
Sirhowy Blae G 61 J5
Sissinghurst Kent 39 K6
Siston S Glos 45 K4
Sitcott Devon 11 L4
Sithney Cnwll 3 G5
Sithney Common Cnwll 3 G5
Sithney Green Cnwll 3 G5
Sittingbourne Kent 40 B3
Six Ashes Shrops 97 H5
Six Bells Blae G 61 J5
Six Hills Leics 117 H7
Sixhills Lincs 136 C2
Six Mile Bottom Cambs 88 B4
Sixmile Cottages Kent 40 F6
Sixpenny Handley Dorset 33 G7
Six Rues Jersey 9 c2
Sizewell Suffk 91 L3
Skaill Ork 275 d5
Skara Brae Ork 275 b4
Skares E Ayrs 197 G7
Skateraw Abers 245 K5
Skateraw E Loth 213 L4
Skeabost Highld 259 G7
Skeeby N York 160 B2
Skeffington Leics 101 G3
Skeffling E R Yk 145 K4
Skegby Notts 133 K7
Skegby Notts 134 F5
Skegness Lincs 137 L7
Skelbo Highld 264 B1

Skelbo Street Highld 264 B1
Skelbrooke Donc 142 D5
Skeldyke Lincs 119 K4
Skellingthorpe Lincs 135 J5
Skellorn Green Ches E 131 H3
Skellow Donc 142 E5
Skelmanthorpe Kirk 141 K5
Skelmersdale Lancs 138 F6
Skelmorlie N Ayrs 207 K5
Skelpick Highld 278 B5
Skelston D & G 185 K6
Skelton C York 151 J4
Skelton Cumb 166 B4
Skelton E R Yk 143 J3
Skelton N York 159 K3
Skelton R & Cl 170 F7
Skelton on Ure N York 150 E2
Skelwith Bridge Cumb 156 E2
Skendleby Lincs 137 H5
Skene House Abers 245 G2
Skenfrith Mons 62 F3
Skerne E R Yk 153 G5
Skerray Highld 277 L4
Skerricha Highld 276 C6
Skerton Lancs 147 J3
Sketchley Leics 99 L5
Sketty Swans 57 H6
Skewen Neath 57 K5
Skewsby N York 151 K2
Skeyton Norfk 122 E6
Skeyton Corner Norfk 122 E6
Skiall Highld 279 H3
Skidbrooke Lincs 137 H1
Skidbrooke North End Lincs 137 H1
Skidby E R Yk 144 C1
Skigersta W Isls 282 h1
Skilgate Somset 29 H5
Skillington Lincs 118 A6
Skinburness Cumb 176 F7
Skinflats Falk 210 B2
Skinidin Highld 258 C7
Skinners Green W Berk 48 C6
Skinningrove R & Cl 171 G6
Skipness Ag & B 206 E7
Skipper's Bridge D & G 177 L2
Skiprigg Cumb 165 L2
Skipsea E R Yk 153 J5
Skipsea Brough E R Yk 153 J5
Skipton N York 149 H5
Skipton-on-Swale N York 160 E6
Skipwith N York 151 L8
Skirbeck Lincs 119 K3
Skirlaugh E R Yk 153 J7
Skirling Border 199 J5
Skirmett Bucks 49 J1
Skirpenbeck E R Yk 152 A4
Skirwith Cumb 166 C4
Skirwith N York 158 C7
Skirza Highld 280 E3
Skitby Cumb 178 B5
Skittle Green Bucks 67 J6
Skokholm Island Pembks 54 B6
Skomer Island Pembks 54 B5
Skulamus Highld 247 L4
Skyborry Green Shrops 95 G8
Skye Green Essex 72 C3
Skye of Curr Highld 253 J6
Skyreholme N York 149 J4
Slack Calder 140 E2
Slackbuie Highld 251 J3
Slackcote Oldham 140 E6
Slack Head Cumb 157 G6
Slackholme End Lincs 137 K5
Slacks of Cairnbanno Abers 256 F3
Slad Gloucs 64 C5
Slade Devon 14 D1
Slade Devon 27 J2
Slade Devon 28 E5
Slade End Oxon 48 E1
Slade Green Gt Lon 52 B4
Slade Heath Staffs 97 L2
Slade Hooton Rothm 133 K2
Sladesbridge Cnwll 10 E8
Slades Green Worcs 81 J8
Slaggyford Nthumb 178 F8
Slaidburn Lancs 148 C5
Slaithwaite Kirk 141 G5
Slaley Derbys 132 E7
Slaley Nthumb 180 A7
Slamannan Falk 209 M4
Slapton Bucks 68 B3
Slapton Devon 8 B6
Slapton Nhants 84 C6
Slattocks Rochdl 140 D6
Slaugham W Susx 37 L5
Slaughterford Wilts 46 B4
Slawston Leics 101 G4
Sleaford Hants 36 B3
Sleaford Lincs 118 E2
Sleagill Cumb 166 E6

Sleap Shrops 113 H6
Sleapford Wrekin 113 L8
Sleapshyde Herts 69 G5
Sleasdairidh Highld 272 F8
Slebech Pembks 55 H4
Sledge Green Worcs 81 J8
Sledmere E R Yk 152 E3
Sleetbeck Cumb 178 C3
Sleight Dorset 17 J3
Sleightholme Dur 168 B8
Sleights N York 162 F1
Slepe Dorset 17 H4
Slickly Highld 280 C3
Sliddery N Ayrs 193 J4
Sligachan Highld 247 G3
Sligrachan Ag & B 207 K1
Slimbridge Gloucs 63 L6
Slindon Staffs 114 C5
Slindon W Susx 20 F5
Slinfold W Susx 37 H4
Sling Gloucs 63 H5
Sling Gwynd 126 B6
Slingsby N York 162 B7
Slip End C Beds 68 D3
Slip End Herts 86 F7
Slipton Nhants 101 L7
Slitting Mill Staffs 115 G8
Slochd Highld 252 F7
Slockavullin Ag & B 216 C7
Sloley Norfk 122 F6
Sloncombe Devon 13 H5
Sloothby Lincs 137 J5
Slough Slough 50 C3
Slough Green Somset 30 C7
Slough Green W Susx 37 L5
Slumbay Highld 248 E4
Slyfield Surrey 50 C8
Slyne Lancs 147 J3
Smailholm Border 201 K6
Smallbridge Rochdl 140 D5
Smallbrook Devon 13 K3
Smallbrook Gloucs 63 H7
Smallburgh Norfk 123 G6
Smallburn E Ayrs 197 K5
Smalldale Derbys 132 B4
Smalldale Derbys 132 C3
Small Dole W Susx 22 C5
Smalley Derbys 116 C3
Smalley Common Derbys 116 C3
Smalley Green Derbys 116 C3
Smallfield Surrey 37 M2
Smallford Herts 69 G5
Small Heath Birm 98 C6
Small Hythe Kent 25 G1
Smallridge Devon 15 G2
Smallthorne C Stke 114 D2
Smallways N York 168 E8
Smallwood Ches E 130 F7
Small Wood Hey Lancs 147 H6
Smallworth Norfk 105 K7
Smannell Hants 34 E1
Smardale Cumb 158 C1
Smarden Kent 39 L5
Smarden Bell Kent 39 L5
Smart's Hill Kent 38 E5
Smeafield Nthumb 203 H5
Smeatharpe Devon 14 E1
Smeeth Kent 40 E7
Smeeton Westerby Leics 100 E5
Smelthouses N York 150 B3
Smerral Highld 275 G2
Smestow Staffs 97 J5
Smethwick Sandw 98 C6
Smethwick Green Ches E 130 F7
Smirisary Highld 237 J5
Smisby Derbys 116 B7
Smith End Green Worcs 81 H5
Smithfield Cumb 178 B6
Smith Green Lancs 147 J5
Smithies Barns 142 A6
Smithincott Devon 29 J8
Smith's End Herts 87 H7
Smith's Green Essex 70 E3
Smith's Green Essex 88 D7
Smithstown Highld 260 C4
Smithton Highld 252 D3
Smithy Bridge Rochdl 140 D5
Smithy Green Ches E 130 E5
Smithy Green Stockp 131 G3
Smithy Houses Derbys 116 C2
Smockington Leics 99 M5
Smoo Highld 277 G3
Smythe's Green Essex 72 D3
Snade D & G 185 L5
Snailbeach Shrops 95 J3
Snailwell Cambs 88 C2
Snainton N York 163 G6
Snaith E R Yk 143 G3
Snake Pass Inn Derbys 132 B2
Snape N York 160 C6

Snape Suffk 91 J3
Snape Green Lancs 138 D5
Snape Street Suffk 91 J3
Snaresbrook Gt Lon 51 L1
Snarestone Leics 99 K2
Snarford Lincs 135 L3
Snargate Kent 25 J2
Snave Kent 25 J1
Sneachill Worcs 81 L4
Snead Powys 95 H5
Sneath Common Norfk 106 D5
Sneaton N York 162 F1
Sneatonthorpe N York 162 F2
Snelland Lincs 135 M4
Snelson Ches E 130 F5
Snelston Derbys 115 J3
Snetterton Norfk 105 K5
Snettisham Norfk 120 F4
Snibston Leics 116 C8
Snig's End Gloucs 64 A1
Snitter Nthumb 190 E5
Snitterby Lincs 135 K1
Snitterfield Warwks 82 F3
Snitterton Derbys 132 E7
Snitton Shrops 96 D8
Snoadhill Kent 40 E6
Snodhill Herefs 79 K7
Snodland Kent 52 F6
Snoll Hatch Kent 39 G4
Snowden Hill Barns 141 L4
Snowdon Gwynd 109 L1
Snowdon Kent 41 H5
Snowdonia National Park 110 F5
Snow End Herts 69 L1
Snowshill Gloucs 82 C8
Snow Street Norfk 106 B7
Soake Hants 19 L2
Soar Cardif 43 H5
Soar Devon 7 K7
Soar Powys 60 E1
Soay Highld 246 F6
Soberton Hants 35 J7
Soberton Heath Hants 35 J8
Sockbridge Cumb 166 C5
Sockburn Darltn 160 E1
Sodom Denbgs 128 C5
Sodylt Bank Shrops 112 E3
Soham Cambs 104 B8
Soham Cotes Cambs 104 B8
Solas W Isls 282 c7
Solbury Pembks 54 E4
Soldon Devon 26 E8
Soldon Cross Devon 26 E8
Soldridge Hants 35 K4
Sole Street Kent 40 E5
Sole Street Kent 52 E5
Solihull Solhll 98 F7
Sollas W Isls 282 c7
Sollers Dilwyn Herefs 80 A4
Sollers Hope Herefs 80 E8
Sollom Lancs 138 E5
Solva Pembks 74 C7
Solwaybank D & G 177 J3
Somerby Leics 101 G1
Somerby Lincs 144 E6
Somercotes Derbys 116 C1
Somerford BCP 18 B5
Somerford Keynes Gloucs 64 E8
Somerley W Susx 20 E7
Somerleyton Suffk 107 K4
Somersal Herbert Derbys 115 J4
Somersby Lincs 136 F5
Somersham Cambs 103 J8
Somersham Suffk 90 C6
Somerton Oxon 66 D2
Somerton Somset 31 H7
Somerton Suffk 89 G4
Somerwood Shrops 113 J8
Sompting W Susx 21 K6
Sompting Abbotts W Susx 21 K5
Sonning Wokham 49 J4
Sonning Common Oxon 49 H3
Sonning Eye Oxon 49 H4
Sontley Wrexhm 112 E2
Sopley Hants 18 B5
Sopwell Herts 68 F6
Sopworth Wilts 46 B2
Sorbie D & G 174 C7
Sordale Highld 279 J3
Sorisdale Ag & B 225 H2
Sorn E Ayrs 197 G4
Sornhill E Ayrs 197 G3
Sortat Highld 280 C4
Sotby Lincs 136 D4
Sots Hole Lincs 136 B8
Sotterley Suffk 107 L5
Soughton Flints 128 F6
Soulbury Bucks 67 L2
Soulby Cumb 166 B6
Soulby Cumb 167 H5

Souldern Oxon 66 D1
Souldrop Bed 85 J3
Sound Ches E 113 K2
Sound Muir Moray 267 G5
Soundwell S Glos 45 J4
Sourton Devon 12 D4
Soutergate Cumb 156 B6
South Acre Norfk 121 H8
South Alkham Kent 41 H7
Southall Gt Lon 50 E3
South Allington Devon 8 B7
South Alloa Falk 210 A1
Southam Gloucs 64 E2
Southam Warwks 83 K3
South Ambersham W Susx 20 F3
Southampton C Sotn 19 G1
Southampton Airport Hants 34 F7
South Anston Rothm 133 K3
South Ascot W & M 50 A5
South Ashford Kent 40 C7
South Baddesley Hants 18 E4
South Bank C York 151 J5
South Bank R & Cl 170 C6
South Barrow Somset 31 K5
South Beddington Gt Lon 51 H6
South Beer Cnwll 11 K4
South Benfleet Essex 53 G2
South Bockhampton BCP 18 B4
Southborough Gt Lon 51 L5
Southborough Kent 38 F5
Southbourne BCP 18 A5
Southbourne W Susx 20 C5
South Bowood Dorset 15 K3
South Bramwith Donc 143 G5
South Brent Devon 7 K3
South Brewham Somset 32 B4
South Broomhill Nthumb 191 K6
Southburgh Norfk 105 K2
South Burlingham Norfk 107 H2
Southburn E R Yk 152 F5
South Cadbury Somset 31 K5
South Carlton Lincs 135 J4
South Carlton Notts 134 B3
South Cave E R Yk 144 A2
South Cerney Gloucs 64 F7
South Chailey E Susx 22 F4
South Chard Somset 15 H2
South Charlton Nthumb 191 K4
South Cheriton Somset 32 B6
South Church Dur 169 G5
Southchurch Sthend 53 J2
South Cleatlam Dur 168 E7
South Cliffe E R Yk 152 D8
South Clifton Notts 135 G5
South Cockerington Lincs 137 G2
South Cornelly Brdgnd 42 B5
Southcott Cnwll 11 H3
Southcott Devon 12 D4
Southcott Devon 13 H6
Southcott Devon 27 H7
Southcott Wilts 47 H7
Southcourt Bucks 67 K5
South Cove Suffk 107 K7
South Creake Norfk 121 J4
South Crosland Kirk 141 H5
South Croxton Leics 100 F2
South Dalton E R Yk 152 E6
South Darenth Kent 52 C5
South Dell W Isls 282 g1
South Downs National Park 22 E5
South Duffield N York 143 H1
South Earlswood Surrey 37 L1
Southease E Susx 23 G6
South Elkington Lincs 136 E2
South Elmsall Wakefd 142 D5
South End Ag & B 192 E6
South End E R Yk 145 K4
South End Hants 33 J7
South End Herefs 81 G6
South End N Linc 144 K4
South End Norfk 105 K5
Southend Wilts 47 J4
Southend Airport Essex 53 J1
Southend-on-Sea Sthend 53 J2
Southernby Cumb 165 L3
Southernden Kent 39 L4
Southerndown V Glam 42 D7
Southerness D & G 176 C2
South Erradale Highld 260 B5
Southerton Devon 14 C4
Southery Norfk 104 C4
South Fambridge Essex 72 B8
South Fawley W Berk 48 A3
South Ferriby N Linc 144 B4
South Field E R Yk 144 C3
Southfield Falk 209 M4
Southfleet Kent 52 D5
Southford IoW 19 J7
Southgate Gt Lon 69 J8
Southgate Norfk 120 E5

Southgate Norfk 121 J4
Southgate Norfk 122 C6
Southgate Swans 57 G7
South Godstone Surrey 38 A4
South Gorley Hants 18 B2
South Gosforth N u Ty 181 G5
South Green Essex 71 G8
South Green Essex 72 F3
South Green Kent 53 J7
South Green Norfk 105 L1
South Green Suffk 106 D8
South Gyle C Edin 211 G4
South Hanningfield Essex 71 H7
South Harting W Susx 20 C3
South Hayling Hants 20 B6
South Hazelrigg Nthumb 203 G6
South Heath Bucks 67 M6
South Heighton E Susx 23 D8
South Hetton Dur 169 K2
South Hiendley Wakefd 142 B5
South Hill Cnwll 11 L8
South Hill Somset 31 G5
South Hinksey Oxon 66 D6
South Hole Devon 26 C6
South Holmwood Surrey 37 J2
South Hornchurch Gt Lon 52 B2
South Horrington Somset 31 J2
South Huish Devon 7 K6
South Hykeham Lincs 135 J6
South Hylton Sundld 181 J7
Southill C Beds 86 C6
Southington Hants 35 G1
South Kelsey Lincs 144 D8
South Kessock Highld 251 H2
South Killingholme N Linc 144 F4
South Kilvington N York 160 F6
South Kilworth Leics 100 D7
South Kirkby Wakefd 142 C5
South Knighton Devon 13 J8
South Kyme Lincs 119 G2
Southleigh Devon 14 E4
South Leigh Oxon 66 B5
South Leverton Notts 134 F3
South Littleton Worcs 82 C6
South Lopham Norfk 105 L7
South Luffenham Rutlnd 101 K3
South Lynn Norfk 120 D7
South Malling E Susx 23 G6
South Marston Swindn 47 J2
South Merstham Surrey 51 H8
South Middleton Nthumb 190 E2
South Milford N York 142 D2
South Milton Devon 7 K6
South Mimms Herts 69 G6
South Mimms Services Herts 69 G7
Southminster Essex 72 D7
South Molton Devon 28 C5
South Moor Dur 180 F8
Southmoor Oxon 66 B7
South Moreton Oxon 48 E1
Southmuir Angus 234 B5
South Mundham W Susx 20 E6
South Muskham Notts 134 F8
South Newbald E R Yk 152 D8
South Newington Oxon 83 J8
South Newsham Nthumb 181 H3
South Newton Wilts 33 J4
South Nitshill C Glas 208 E1
South Normanton Derbys 133 J8
South Norwood Gt Lon 51 J5
South Nutfield Surrey 37 M1
South Ockendon Thurr 52 D2
Southoe Cambs 86 D2
Southolt Suffk 90 E2
South Ormsby Lincs 137 G4
Southorpe C Pete 102 B3
South Ossett Wakefd 141 L4
South Otterington N York 160 E5
Southover Dorset 16 B4
Southover E Susx 24 B2
South Owersby Lincs 135 L1
Southowram Calder 141 H3
South Park Surrey 37 K1
South Perrott Dorset 15 L1
South Petherton Somset 31 G7
South Petherwin Cnwll 11 K6
South Pickenham Norfk 105 G3
South Pill Cnwll 6 E4
South Pool Devon 7 M6
South Poorton Dorset 15 M3
Southport Sefton 138 D4
South Queensferry C Edin 210 F3
South Radworthy Devon 28 C4
South Rauceby Lincs 118 D2
South Raynham Norfk 121 J6
South Reddish Stockp 131 H1
Southrepps Norfk 122 E4
South Reston Lincs 137 G3
Southrey Lincs 136 B6
South Ronaldsay Ork 275 c6

Southrop Gloucs 65 J6
Southrope Hants 35 K2
South Runcton Norfk 104 C2
South Scarle Notts 135 G6
Southsea C Port 19 L4
Southsea Wrexhm 112 D1
South Shian Ag & B 228 E7
South Shields S Tyne 181 J5
South Shore Bpool 138 C2
Southside Dur 168 E5
South Somercotes Lincs 137 H1
South Stainley N York 150 D3
South Stifford Thurr 52 D3
South Stoke BaNES 45 L6
South Stoke Oxon 48 F2
South Stoke W Susx 21 H5
South Stour Kent 40 D7
South Street Kent 40 D4
South Street Kent 40 F2
South Street Kent 52 D6
South Tarbrax S Lans 199 H3
South Tawton Devon 12 F4
South Tehidy Cnwll 3 G3
South Thoresby Lincs 137 G4
South Thorpe Dur 168 E7
South Town Hants 35 K4
Southtown Norfk 107 L2
Southtown Somset 30 D7
South Uist W Isls 283 c10
Southwaite Cumb 166 B2
Southwaite Services Cumb 166 B2
South Walsham Norfk 107 H1
Southwark Gt Lon 51 J3
South Warnborough Hants 35 L2
Southwater W Susx 37 J5
Southwater Street W Susx 37 J5
Southway C Plym 6 F3
Southway Somset 31 H2
South Weald Essex 70 E8
Southwell Dorset 16 D8
Southwell Notts 117 J1
South Weston Oxon 67 H7
South Wheatley Cnwll 11 J4
South Wheatley Notts 134 F3
Southwick Hants 19 L2
Southwick Nhants 101 M5
Southwick Somset 30 E2
Southwick Sundld 181 J7
Southwick W Susx 22 C6
Southwick Wilts 46 B7
South Widcombe BaNES 45 H7
South Wigston Leics 100 D4
South Willingham Lincs 136 C3
South Wingate Dur 169 L4
South Wingfield Derbys 133 G8
South Witham Lincs 118 B7
Southwold Suffk 107 K8
South Wonston Hants 34 F4
Southwood Norfk 107 H2
Southwood Somset 31 H4
South Woodham Ferrers Essex 71 K7
South Wootton Norfk 120 E7
South Wraxall Wilts 46 B6
South Zeal Devon 12 F4
Sovereign Harbour E Susx 23 L6
Sowerby Calder 141 G3
Sowerby N York 160 F6
Sowerby Bridge Calder 141 G3
Sowerby Row Cumb 165 L3
Sower Carr Lancs 147 G7
Sowerhill Somset 28 F6
Sowhill Torfn 62 B7
Sowley Green Suffk 88 D5
Sowood Calder 141 G4
Sowton Devon 6 F2
Sowton Devon 14 A4
Soyland Town Calder 140 F4
Spa Common Norfk 122 F5
Spain's End Essex 88 D7
Spalding Lincs 119 H7
Spaldington E R Yk 143 J1
Spaldwick Cambs 86 C1
Spalford Notts 135 G6
Spanby Lincs 118 E4
Spanish Green Hants 49 G7
Sparham Norfk 122 B7
Sparhamill Norfk 122 B7
Spark Bridge Cumb 156 D5
Sparket Cumb 166 B5
Sparkford Somset 31 K5
Sparkhill Birm 98 E6
Sparkwell Devon 7 H3
Sparrow Green Norfk 121 L8
Sparrowpit Derbys 132 B4
Sparrows Green E Susx 39 G6
Sparsholt Hants 34 F4
Sparsholt Oxon 47 M2
Spartylea Nthumb 167 K1
Spath Staffs 115 H4
Spaunton N York 162 C5

Spaxton Somset 30 C3
Spean Bridge Highld 239 L7
Spear Hill W Susx 21 K3
Spearywell Hants 34 D5
Speen Bucks 67 K7
Speen W Berk 48 C5
Speeton N York 163 L7
Speke Lpool 129 K3
Speldhurst Kent 38 E5
Spellbrook Herts 70 C4
Spelmonden Kent 39 H6
Spelsbury Oxon 65 M3
Spen Kirk 141 K3
Spencers Wood Wokham 49 H5
Spen Green Ches E 130 F7
Spennithorne N York 159 L5
Spennymoor Dur 169 H4
Spernall Warwks 82 C3
Spetchley Worcs 81 K4
Spetisbury Dorset 17 H2
Spexhall Suffk 107 H7
Spey Bay Moray 267 G3
Speybridge Highld 253 K6
Speyview Moray 254 E3
Spilsby Lincs 137 G6
Spindlestone Nthumb 203 J6
Spinkhill Derbys 133 J4
Spinningdale Highld 263 J2
Spion Kop Notts 133 L6
Spirthill Wilts 46 E4
Spital Wirral 129 H3
Spital Hill Donc 134 C1
Spital in the Street Lincs 135 K2
Spithurst E Susx 23 G4
Spittal E Loth 212 A4
Spittal E R Yk 152 B5
Spittal Highld 279 L5
Spittal Nthumb 202 F3
Spittal Pembks 55 G2
Spittalfield P & K 233 H7
Spittal of Glenmuick Abers 243 K6
Spittal of Glenshee P & K 233 H2
Spittal-on-Rule Border 189 G2
Spixworth Norfk 122 E8
Splatt Cnwll 10 C7
Splatt Cnwll 11 J5
Splatt Devon 12 E2
Splayne's Green E Susx 23 G2
Splott Cardif 43 K6
Spofforth N York 150 E5
Spondon C Derb 116 C4
Spon Green Flints 129 G7
Spooner Row Norfk 106 B4
Sporle Norfk 105 G1
Spott E Loth 212 E4
Spottiswoode Border 201 J3
Spratton Nhants 84 D1
Spreakley Surrey 36 B3
Spreyton Devon 13 G3
Spriddlestone Devon 7 G4
Spridlington Lincs 135 K3
Springburn C Glas 209 G5
Springfield D & G 177 K5
Springfield Essex 71 H5
Springfield Fife 222 F5
Springhill Staffs 98 B3
Springhill Staffs 98 D2
Springholm D & G 175 K1
Springside N Ayrs 196 D3
Springthorpe Lincs 135 H2
Spring Vale Barns 141 L7
Springwell Sundld 181 G7
Sproatley E R Yk 145 F1
Sproston Green Ches W 130 E6
Sprotbrough Donc 142 E7
Sproughton Suffk 90 D6
Sprouston Border 202 B6
Sprowston Norfk 106 E1
Sproxton Leics 117 M6
Sproxton N York 161 K6
Spunhill Shrops 112 F5
Spurstow Ches E 130 A8
Spyway Dorset 15 M4
Square and Compass Pembks 74 D6
Stableford Shrops 97 G4
Stableford Staffs 114 C4
Stacey Bank Sheff 132 F2
Stackhouse N York 148 E3
Stackpole Pembks 55 G7
Stackpole Elidor Pembks 55 G7
Stacksford Norfk 105 L5
Stacksteads Lancs 140 C3
Staddiscombe C Plym 7 G4
Staddlethorpe E R Yk 143 L2
Staden Derbys 131 L5
Stadhampton Oxon 66 F7
Stadhlaigearraidh W Isls 283 b10
Staffield Cumb 166 D2
Staffin Highld 259 H3
Stafford Staffs 114 E7

Stafford Services (northbound) Staffs ... 114 D5
Stafford Services (southbound) Staffs ... 114 D5
Stagsden Bed ... 85 J5
Stainborough Barns ... 141 M7
Stainburn Cumb ... 164 D5
Stainburn N York ... 150 C6
Stainby Lincs ... 118 B7
Staincross Barns ... 141 M5
Staindrop Dur ... 168 E6
Staines-upon-Thames Surrey ... 50 D5
Stainfield Lincs ... 118 E6
Stainfield Lincs ... 136 B5
Stainforth Donc ... 143 G5
Stainforth N York ... 148 E2
Staining Lancs ... 147 G8
Stainland Calder ... 141 G4
Stainsacre N York ... 163 G1
Stainsby Derbys ... 133 J6
Stainton Cumb ... 157 H5
Stainton Cumb ... 166 C5
Stainton Cumb ... 177 L7
Stainton Donc ... 133 L1
Stainton Dur ... 168 D7
Stainton Middsb ... 170 B7
Stainton N York ... 159 K3
Stainton by Langworth Lincs ... 135 L4
Staintondale N York ... 163 H3
Stainton Grove Dur ... 168 D7
Stainton le Vale Lincs ... 136 C1
Stainton with Adgarley Cumb ... 146 E1
Stair Cumb ... 165 H6
Stair E Ayrs ... 196 E6
Stairfoot Barns ... 142 B6
Stairhaven D & G ... 172 F4
Staithes N York ... 171 H7
Stakeford Nthumb ... 181 G2
Stake Pool Lancs ... 147 H6
Stakes Hants ... 19 M2
Stalbridge Dorset ... 32 B7
Stalbridge Weston Dorset ... 32 B7
Stalham Norfk ... 123 H6
Stalham Green Norfk ... 123 H6
Stalisfield Green Kent ... 40 B5
Stalland Common Norfk ... 105 L4
Stallen Dorset ... 31 K7
Stallingborough NE Lin ... 145 G5
Stalling Busk N York ... 159 G6
Stallington Staffs ... 114 E4
Stalmine Lancs ... 147 G6
Stalmine Moss Side Lancs ... 147 G6
Stalybridge Tamesd ... 140 E8
Stambourne Essex ... 88 E7
Stambourne Green Essex ... 88 D7
Stamford Lincs ... 102 A2
Stamford Nthumb ... 191 J2
Stamford Bridge Ches W ... 129 L6
Stamford Bridge E R Yk ... 151 M5
Stamfordham Nthumb ... 180 C4
Stamford Hill Gt Lon ... 51 J2
Stanah Lancs ... 147 G7
Stanborough Herts ... 69 G5
Stanbridge C Beds ... 68 B2
Stanbridge Dorset ... 17 K2
Stanbury C Brad ... 149 H8
Stand Bury ... 140 B6
Stand N Lans ... 209 K5
Standburn Falk ... 210 B4
Standeford Staffs ... 97 K2
Standen Kent ... 39 L5
Standen Street Kent ... 39 K7
Standerwick Somset ... 32 D1
Standford Hants ... 36 B4
Standingstone Cumb ... 164 D4
Standish Gloucs ... 64 A5
Standish Wigan ... 139 H5
Standish Lower Ground Wigan ... 139 H6
Standlake Oxon ... 66 B6
Standon Hants ... 34 F5
Standon Herts ... 69 K3
Standon Staffs ... 114 C4
Standon Green End Herts ... 69 K3
Standwell Green Suffk ... 90 D1
Stane N Lans ... 210 A7
Stanfield Norfk ... 121 K7
Stanford C Beds ... 86 D7
Stanford Kent ... 40 F7
Stanford Shrops ... 95 H1
Stanford Bishop Herefs ... 80 F5
Stanford Bridge Worcs ... 81 G2
Stanford Bridge Wrekin ... 113 M6
Stanford Dingley W Berk ... 48 E4
Stanford in the Vale Oxon ... 65 M8
Stanford le Hope Thurr ... 52 E3
Stanford on Avon Nhants ... 100 D7
Stanford on Soar Notts ... 116 F7
Stanford on Teme Worcs ... 81 G2
Stanford Rivers Essex ... 70 D7

Stanfree Derbys ... 133 J5
Stanghow R & Cl ... 170 F7
Stanground C Pete ... 102 D4
Stanhill Lancs ... 139 L2
Stanhoe Norfk ... 121 H4
Stanhope Border ... 199 K7
Stanhope Dur ... 168 C3
Stanhope Kent ... 40 C7
Stanhope Bretby Derbys ... 116 A7
Stanion Nhants ... 101 K6
Stanklin Worcs ... 97 J8
Stanley Derbys ... 116 C3
Stanley Dur ... 180 F8
Stanley Notts ... 133 J7
Stanley P & K ... 221 K1
Stanley Shrops ... 97 G6
Stanley Staffs ... 114 E1
Stanley Wakefd ... 142 A3
Stanley Common Derbys ... 116 C3
Stanley Crook Dur ... 168 F3
Stanley Ferry Wakefd ... 142 A3
Stanley Gate Lancs ... 138 F6
Stanley Moor Staffs ... 114 E1
Stanley Pontlarge Gloucs ... 64 E1
Stanmer Br & H ... 22 E5
Stanmore Gt Lon ... 68 F8
Stanmore Hants ... 34 F5
Stanmore W Berk ... 48 C3
Stannersburn Nthumb ... 179 G2
Stanningfield Suffk ... 89 H4
Stanningley Leeds ... 141 K1
Stannington Nthumb ... 180 F3
Stannington Sheff ... 132 F2
Stannington Station Nthumb ... 180 F3
Stansbatch Herefs ... 79 L3
Stansfield Suffk ... 88 F5
Stanshope Staffs ... 115 J1
Stanstead Suffk ... 89 G5
Stanstead Abbotts Herts ... 69 K5
Stansted Kent ... 52 D6
Stansted Airport Essex ... 70 E2
Stansted Mountfitchet Essex ... 70 D2
Stanton Derbys ... 115 M7
Stanton Gloucs ... 82 C8
Stanton Mons ... 62 C3
Stanton Nthumb ... 191 G8
Stanton Staffs ... 115 J2
Stanton Suffk ... 105 K8
Stanton by Bridge Derbys ... 116 B6
Stanton by Dale Derbys ... 116 D4
Stanton Cross Nhants ... 85 H2
Stanton Drew BaNES ... 45 H6
Stanton Fitzwarren Swindn ... 47 J1
Stanton Harcourt Oxon ... 66 B6
Stanton Hill Notts ... 133 J7
Stanton in Peak Derbys ... 132 E6
Stanton Lacy Shrops ... 96 B7
Stanton Lees Derbys ... 132 E7
Stanton Long Shrops ... 96 D5
Stanton-on-the-Wolds Notts ... 117 G5
Stanton Prior BaNES ... 45 K6
Stanton St Bernard Wilts ... 47 G6
Stanton St John Oxon ... 66 E5
Stanton St Quintin Wilts ... 46 C3
Stanton Street Suffk ... 89 J2
Stanton under Bardon Leics ... 100 A1
Stanton upon Hine Heath Shrops ... 113 J6
Stanton Wick BaNES ... 45 J6
Stantway Gloucs ... 63 L4
Stanwardine in the Field Shrops ... 112 F6
Stanwardine in the Wood Shrops ... 113 G6
Stanway Essex ... 72 D2
Stanway Gloucs ... 64 F1
Stanway Green Essex ... 72 D2
Stanway Green Suffk ... 90 F1
Stanwell Surrey ... 50 D4
Stanwell Moor Surrey ... 50 D4
Stanwick Nhants ... 85 J1
Stanwick St John N York ... 168 F8
Stanwix Cumb ... 177 L7
Staoinebrig W Isls ... 283 b10
Stape N York ... 162 D4
Stapehill Dorset ... 17 L3
Stapeley Ches E ... 113 L2
Stapenhill Staffs ... 115 L7
Staple Kent ... 41 J4
Staple Cross Devon ... 29 J6
Staplecross E Susx ... 24 E3
Staplefield W Susx ... 37 L5
Staple Fitzpaine Somset ... 30 C7
Stapleford Cambs ... 87 K5
Stapleford Herts ... 69 J4
Stapleford Leics ... 117 L7
Stapleford Lincs ... 135 H8
Stapleford Notts ... 116 E4
Stapleford Wilts ... 33 J3
Stapleford Abbotts Essex ... 70 D8

Stapleford Tawney Essex ... 70 D7
Staplegrove Somset ... 30 B5
Staplehay Somset ... 30 B6
Staple Hill Worcs ... 98 B8
Staplehurst Kent ... 39 K5
Staplers IoW ... 19 H6
Staplestreet Kent ... 40 D3
Stapleton Cumb ... 178 C4
Stapleton Herefs ... 79 L2
Stapleton Leics ... 99 L4
Stapleton N York ... 169 H8
Stapleton Shrops ... 95 L3
Stapleton Somset ... 31 G6
Stapley Somset ... 30 B8
Staploe Bed ... 86 C3
Staplow Herefs ... 80 F7
Star Fife ... 222 G6
Star IoA ... 125 J5
Star Pembks ... 75 M5
Star Somset ... 44 E7
Starbeck N York ... 150 D4
Starbotton N York ... 159 G7
Starcross Devon ... 14 A6
Stareton Warwks ... 83 H1
Starkholmes Derbys ... 132 F7
Starlings Green Essex ... 70 C1
Starr's Green E Susx ... 24 D4
Starston Norfk ... 106 E6
Start Devon ... 8 L4
Startforth Dur ... 168 D7
Startley Wilts ... 46 D3
Statenborough Kent ... 41 J4
Statham Warrtn ... 130 D2
Stathe Somset ... 30 E5
Stathern Leics ... 117 K5
Station Town Dur ... 169 L3
Staughton Green Cambs ... 86 C2
Staughton Highway Cambs ... 86 C2
Staunton Gloucs ... 63 H4
Staunton Gloucs ... 64 A1
Staunton in the Vale Notts ... 117 L3
Staunton on Arrow Herefs ... 79 L3
Staunton on Wye Herefs ... 79 L6
Staveley Cumb ... 157 G3
Staveley Derbys ... 133 H5
Staveley N York ... 150 E3
Staveley-in-Cartmel Cumb ... 156 E5
Staverton Devon ... 8 B2
Staverton Gloucs ... 64 C2
Staverton Nhants ... 83 M3
Staverton Wilts ... 46 B6
Staverton Bridge Gloucs ... 64 C3
Stawell Somset ... 30 E3
Stawley Somset ... 29 J6
Staxigoe Highld ... 280 E5
Staxton N York ... 163 J6
Staylittle Cerdgn ... 92 E5
Staylittle Powys ... 93 J5
Staynall Lancs ... 147 G7
Staythorpe Notts ... 117 K1
Stead C Brad ... 149 L6
Stean N York ... 159 K8
Stearsby N York ... 151 K2
Steart Somset ... 30 C2
Stebbing Essex ... 71 G2
Stebbing Green Essex ... 71 G2
Stechford Birm ... 98 E6
Stede Quarter Kent ... 39 L5
Stedham W Susx ... 36 C6
Steel Nthumb ... 179 L7
Steel Cross E Susx ... 38 E7
Steelend Fife ... 210 D1
Steele Road Border ... 188 F7
Steel Green Cumb ... 155 L6
Steel Heath Shrops ... 113 J4
Steen's Bridge Herefs ... 80 C4
Steep Hants ... 35 M6
Steephill IoW ... 19 J8
Steep Lane Calder ... 140 F3
Steeple Dorset ... 17 H6
Steeple Essex ... 72 D6
Steeple Ashton Wilts ... 46 C7
Steeple Aston Oxon ... 66 C2
Steeple Barton Oxon ... 66 C2
Steeple Bumpstead Essex ... 88 D7
Steeple Claydon Bucks ... 67 H2
Steeple Gidding Cambs ... 102 C7
Steeple Langford Wilts ... 33 H3
Steeple Morden Cambs ... 86 F6
Steep Marsh Hants ... 35 M5
Steeton C Brad ... 149 J7
Stein Highld ... 258 D5
Stella Gatesd ... 180 E6
Stelling Minnis Kent ... 40 F6
Stembridge Somset ... 30 F6
Stenalees Cnwll ... 5 G3
Stenhouse D & G ... 185 K4
Stenhousemuir Falk ... 210 A2
Stenigot Lincs ... 136 D3
Stenness Ork ... 275 b4

Stenscholl Highld ... 259 H3
Stenson Fields Derbys ... 116 B5
Stenton E Loth ... 212 D4
Steòrnabhagh W Isls ... 282 g3
Stepaside Pembks ... 55 K5
Stepford D & G ... 185 K6
Stepney Gt Lon ... 51 K3
Stepping Hill Stockp ... 131 H2
Steppingley C Beds ... 85 K8
Stepps N Lans ... 209 H5
Sternfield Suffk ... 91 J3
Stert Wilts ... 46 F7
Stetchworth Cambs ... 88 C3
Stevenage Herts ... 69 G3
Steven's Crouch E Susx ... 24 C4
Stevenston N Ayrs ... 196 B3
Steventon Hants ... 35 H1
Steventon Oxon ... 66 C5
Steventon End Essex ... 88 B6
Stevington Bed ... 85 K4
Stewartby Bed ... 85 K6
Stewartfield S Lans ... 209 H7
Stewarton Ag & B ... 192 E4
Stewarton E Ayrs ... 196 E2
Stewkley Bucks ... 67 K2
Stewley Somset ... 30 D7
Stewton Lincs ... 137 G2
Steyne Cross IoW ... 19 L6
Steyning W Susx ... 21 L4
Steynton Pembks ... 54 E5
Stibb Cnwll ... 26 C8
Stibbard Norfk ... 121 L6
Stibb Cross Devon ... 27 G7
Stibb Green Wilts ... 47 J6
Stibbington Cambs ... 102 B4
Stichill Border ... 201 L5
Sticker Cnwll ... 5 G5
Stickford Lincs ... 136 F6
Sticklepath Devon ... 12 F4
Sticklepath Somset ... 29 J6
Stickling Green Essex ... 87 K5
Stickney Lincs ... 136 F8
Stiffkey Norfk ... 121 L4
Stifford Clays Thurr ... 52 D3
Stifford's Bridge Herefs ... 81 G5
Stiff Street Kent ... 53 J6
Stile Bridge Kent ... 39 J6
Stileway Somset ... 31 G2
Stilligarry W Isls ... 283 b10
Stillingfleet N York ... 151 J7
Stillington N York ... 151 J2
Stillington S on T ... 169 K6
Stilton Cambs ... 102 C5
Stinchcombe Gloucs ... 63 L7
Stinsford Dorset ... 16 D4
Stiperstones Shrops ... 95 J3
Stirchley Birm ... 98 D7
Stirchley Wrekin ... 96 F2
Stirling Abers ... 257 L3
Stirling Stirlg ... 220 D8
Stirling Services Stirlg ... 209 L1
Stirtloe Cambs ... 86 D3
Stirton N York ... 149 H6
Stisted Essex ... 71 J3
Stitchcombe Wilts ... 47 K5
Stithians Cnwll ... 3 J4
Stivichall Covtry ... 99 J7
Stixwould Lincs ... 136 C6
St Michaels Fife ... 223 H8
Stoak Ches W ... 129 K6
Stobo Border ... 199 L6
Stoborough Dorset ... 17 H5
Stoborough Green Dorset ... 17 H5
Stobs Castle Border ... 188 E4
Stobswood Nthumb ... 191 J7
Stock Essex ... 71 G8
Stock N Som ... 44 F6
Stockbridge Hants ... 34 D4
Stockbridge W Susx ... 20 D6
Stockbriggs S Lans ... 198 C4
Stockbury Kent ... 53 H8
Stockcross W Berk ... 48 B4
Stockdalewath Cumb ... 165 L2
Stocker's Head Kent ... 40 C4
Stockerston Leics ... 101 H4
Stock Green Worcs ... 82 A4
Stocking Herefs ... 63 J2
Stockingford Warwks ... 99 C6
Stocking Pelham Herts ... 70 C2
Stockland Devon ... 14 F2
Stockland Bristol Somset ... 30 C3
Stockland Green Kent ... 38 E4
Stockleigh English Devon ... 13 K2
Stockleigh Pomeroy Devon ... 13 K3
Stockley Wilts ... 46 E5
Stockley Hill Herefs ... 79 L7
Stocklinch Somset ... 30 F7
Stockmoor Herefs ... 79 M3
Stockport Stockp ... 131 H3
Stocksbridge Sheff ... 141 L5

Stocksfield Nthumb....180 C6
Stocksmoor Kirk....141 J5
Stockton Herefs....80 C3
Stockton Norfk....107 H4
Stockton Shrops....95 G3
Stockton Shrops....97 G3
Stockton Warwks....83 K3
Stockton Wilts....33 G3
Stockton Wrekin....114 B8
Stockton Brook Staffs....114 E1
Stockton Heath Warrtn....130 B3
Stockton-on-Tees S on T....170 B6
Stockton on Teme Worcs....81 G2
Stockton on the Forest C York....151 L4
Stockwell Gloucs....64 D4
Stockwell End Wolves....97 K3
Stockwell Heath Staffs....115 K7
Stockwood Bristl....45 J5
Stockwood Dorset....16 B1
Stock Wood Worcs....82 B3
Stodday Lancs....147 J4
Stodmarsh Kent....41 H3
Stody Norfk....122 B4
Stoer Highld....270 D2
Stoford Somset....31 J8
Stoford Wilts....33 J4
Stogumber Somset....29 K3
Stogursey Somset....30 B2
Stoke Covtry....99 K7
Stoke Devon....26 D6
Stoke Hants....20 B6
Stoke Hants....48 B8
Stoke Medway....53 H4
Stoke Abbott Dorset....15 K3
Stoke Albany Nhants....101 H5
Stoke Ash Suffk....90 D1
Stoke Bardolph Notts....117 H3
Stoke Bliss Worcs....80 F3
Stoke Bruerne Nhants....84 E5
Stoke-by-Clare Suffk....88 E6
Stoke-by-Nayland Suffk....89 K7
Stoke Canon Devon....13 L3
Stoke Charity Hants....35 G3
Stoke Climsland Cnwll....11 L7
Stoke Cross Herefs....80 E5
Stoke D'Abernon Surrey....50 E7
Stoke Doyle Nhants....102 M6
Stoke Dry Rutlnd....101 J4
Stoke Edith Herefs....80 E7
Stoke End Warwks....98 F4
Stoke Farthing Wilts....33 H5
Stoke Ferry Norfk....104 D3
Stoke Fleming Devon....8 C5
Stokeford Dorset....17 G5
Stoke Gabriel Devon....8 C3
Stoke Gifford S Glos....45 J3
Stoke Golding Leics....99 L4
Stoke Goldington M Keyn....85 G5
Stoke Green Bucks....50 B3
Stokeham Notts....134 F4
Stoke Hammond Bucks....67 L1
Stoke Heath Shrops....113 L5
Stoke Heath Worcs....81 L2
Stoke Holy Cross Norfk....106 D2
Stokeinteignhead Devon....13 L8
Stoke Lacy Herefs....80 E5
Stoke Lyne Oxon....66 E2
Stoke Mandeville Bucks....67 K5
Stokenchurch Bucks....67 J7
Stoke Newington Gt Lon....51 J2
Stokenham Devon....8 B6
Stoke-on-Trent C Stke....114 D2
Stoke Orchard Gloucs....64 D2
Stoke Poges Bucks....50 B2
Stoke Pound Worcs....81 M2
Stoke Prior Herefs....80 C4
Stoke Prior Worcs....81 L2
Stoke Rivers Devon....27 L4
Stoke Rochford Lincs....118 B6
Stoke Row Oxon....49 G2
Stoke St Gregory Somset....30 E5
Stoke St Mary Somset....30 C6
Stoke St Michael Somset....31 L2
Stoke St Milborough Shrops....96 D7
Stokesay Shrops....95 K7
Stokesby Norfk....107 J1
Stokesley N York....161 H1
Stoke sub Hamdon Somset....31 G7
Stoke Talmage Oxon....67 G7
Stoke Trister Somset....32 B5
Stoke upon Tern Shrops....113 L6
Stoke-upon-Trent C Stke....114 D3
Stoke Wake Dorset....16 E1
Stoke Wharf Worcs....81 L2
Stolford Somset....30 C2
Stondon Massey Essex....70 E7
Stone Bucks....67 J4
Stone Gloucs....63 K8
Stone Kent....52 C4
Stone Rothm....133 L2

Stone Somset....31 J4
Stone Staffs....114 E5
Stone Worcs....97 J8
Stonea Cambs....103 J5
Stone Allerton Somset....30 F1
Ston Easton Somset....45 J8
Stonebridge N Som....44 D7
Stonebridge Norfk....105 J5
Stonebridge Warwks....99 G6
Stone Bridge Corner C Pete....102 F3
Stonebroom Derbys....133 H7
Stone Chair Calder....141 H2
Stone Cross E Susx....23 K6
Stone Cross E Susx....38 D7
Stone Cross E Susx....39 G7
Stone Cross Kent....38 E5
Stone Cross Kent....40 D7
Stone Cross Kent....41 K4
Stonecross Green Suffk....89 G4
Stonecrouch Kent....39 H6
Stone-edge-Batch N Som....44 F4
Stoneferry C KuH....144 E2
Stonefield Castle Hotel Ag & B....206 D5
Stonegate E Susx....39 G7
Stonegate N York....162 D1
Stonegrave N York....161 L7
Stonehall Worcs....81 K5
Stonehaugh Nthumb....179 J4
Stonehaven Abers....245 J6
Stonehenge Wilts....33 K2
Stone Hill Donc....143 H6
Stonehouse C Plym....6 F4
Stone House Cumb....158 D5
Stonehouse Gloucs....64 A6
Stonehouse Nthumb....179 G7
Stonehouse S Lans....198 C4
Stone in Oxney Kent....25 H2
Stoneleigh Warwks....83 H1
Stoneley Green Ches E....113 K1
Stonely Cambs....86 C2
Stoner Hill Hants....35 M5
Stonesby Leics....117 L6
Stonesfield Oxon....66 B4
Stones Green Essex....73 H2
Stone Street Kent....38 F2
Stone Street Suffk....89 K6
Stone Street Suffk....89 K7
Stone Street Suffk....107 H7
Stonestreet Green Kent....40 E7
Stonethwaite Cumb....165 J7
Stonewells Moray....266 F3
Stonewood Kent....52 D4
Stoneybridge W Isls....283 b10
Stoneybridge Worcs....97 L8
Stoneyburn W Loth....210 C6
Stoney Cross Hants....18 D1
Stoneygate C Leic....100 D3
Stoneyhills Essex....72 D7
Stoneykirk D & G....172 D4
Stoney Middleton Derbys....132 E4
Stoney Stanton Leics....100 B4
Stoney Stoke Somset....32 B4
Stoney Stratton Somset....31 L3
Stoney Stretton Shrops....95 J2
Stoneywood C Aber....245 K1
Stoneywood Falk....209 L2
Stonham Aspal Suffk....90 D3
Stonnall Staffs....98 D3
Stonor Oxon....49 H1
Stonton Wyville Leics....101 G4
Stonybreck Shet....281 b8
Stony Cross Herefs....80 D2
Stony Cross Herefs....81 G5
Stonyford Hants....34 D7
Stony Houghton Derbys....133 K6
Stony Stratford M Keyn....84 F7
Stonywell Staffs....98 D1
Stoodleigh Devon....28 B4
Stoodleigh Devon....29 G7
Stopham W Susx....21 H3
Stopsley Luton....68 E2
Stoptide Cnwll....10 C7
Storeton Wirral....129 G3
Storeyard Green Herefs....81 G6
Storey Arms Powys....60 E3
Stornoway W Isls....282 g3
Stornoway Airport W Isls....282 g3
Storridge Herefs....81 H5
Storrington W Susx....21 J4
Storth Cumb....157 G6
Storwood E R Yk....151 M7
Stotfield Moray....266 E2
Stotfold C Beds....86 E7
Stottesdon Shrops....96 F6
Stoughton Leics....100 E3
Stoughton Surrey....50 C8
Stoughton W Susx....20 C4
Stoulton Worcs....81 L5
Stourbridge Dudley....97 K6

Stourpaine Dorset....17 G1
Stourport-on-Severn Worcs....81 J1
Stour Provost Dorset....32 C6
Stour Row Dorset....32 D6
Stourton Leeds....141 M2
Stourton Staffs....97 K6
Stourton Warwks....83 G7
Stourton Wilts....32 C4
Stourton Caundle Dorset....32 B7
Stout Somset....31 G4
Stove Shet....281 e8
Stoven Suffk....107 J7
Stow Border....200 F4
Stow Lincs....135 H3
Stow Bardolph Norfk....104 C2
Stow Bedon Norfk....105 J4
Stowbridge Norfk....104 B2
Stow-cum-Quy Cambs....87 L3
Stowe Gloucs....63 H5
Stowe Shrops....95 H8
Stowe-by-Chartley Staffs....114 F6
Stowehill Nhants....84 C3
Stowell Somset....31 L6
Stowey BaNES....45 H7
Stowford Devon....12 B3
Stowford Devon....12 B5
Stowford Devon....14 D5
Stowford Devon....28 B3
Stowlangtoft Suffk....89 J2
Stow Longa Cambs....86 C1
Stow Maries Essex....71 K7
Stowmarket Suffk....90 B3
Stow-on-the-Wold Gloucs....65 J2
Stowting Kent....40 F7
Stowting Common Kent....40 F6
Stowupland Suffk....90 C3
Straad Ag & B....207 G6
Straanruie Highld....253 J8
Strachan Abers....244 F5
Strachur Ag & B....217 H7
Stradbroke Suffk....106 E8
Stradishall Suffk....88 E5
Stradsett Norfk....104 D2
Stragglethorpe Lincs....118 B1
Stragglethorpe Notts....117 H4
Straight Soley Wilts....47 L4
Straiton Mdloth....211 J5
Straiton S Ayrs....183 K2
Straloch Abers....256 F7
Straloch P & K....232 F3
Stramshall Staffs....115 H4
Strang IoM....154 e6
Strangeways Salfd....140 B7
Strangford Herefs....63 H2
Stranraer D & G....172 C3
Strata Florida Cerdgn....77 K2
Stratfield Mortimer W Berk....49 G6
Stratfield Saye Hants....49 G6
Stratfield Turgis Hants....49 G7
Stratford C Beds....86 D5
Stratford Gt Lon....51 K2
Stratford St Andrew Suffk....91 H3
Stratford St Mary Suffk....90 B8
Stratford sub Castle Wilts....33 K4
Stratford Tony Wilts....33 J5
Stratford-upon-Avon Warwks....82 F4
Strath Highld....260 C4
Strathan Highld....270 E4
Strathan Highld....277 K3
Strathaven S Lans....197 K2
Strathblane Stirlg....208 F3
Strathcanaird Highld....270 F7
Strathcarron Highld....248 F3
Strathcoil Ag & B....227 K6
Strathdon Abers....243 K1
Strathkinness Fife....223 H4
Strathloanhead W Loth....210 B4
Strathmashie House Highld....241 G5
Strathmiglo Fife....222 C5
Strathpeffer Highld....262 E8
Strathtay P & K....232 D4
Strathwhillan N Ayrs....195 G4
Strathy Highld....278 C3
Strathy Inn Highld....278 E3
Strathyre Stirlg....219 J4
Stratton Cnwll....11 J1
Stratton Dorset....16 C4
Stratton Gloucs....64 E6
Stratton Audley Oxon....66 F2
Stratton-on-the-Fosse Somset....31 L1
Stratton St Margaret Swindn....47 H2
Stratton St Michael Norfk....106 D4
Stratton Strawless Norfk....122 E7
Stream Somset....29 K3
Streat E Susx....22 E5
Streatham Gt Lon....51 J4
Streatley C Beds....68 D2
Streatley W Berk....48 E3
Street Devon....14 E5

Street Lancs....147 K5
Street N York....162 C2
Street Somset....31 H3
Street Ashton Warwks....99 M7
Street Dinas Shrops....112 E4
Street End E Susx....23 K3
Street End Kent....40 F4
Street End W Susx....20 D7
Street Gate Gatesd....180 F7
Streethay Staffs....98 F1
Street Houses N York....151 H6
Streetlam N York....160 D3
Street Lane Derbys....116 C2
Streetly Wsall....98 D4
Streetly End Cambs....88 C5
Street on the Fosse Somset....31 K3
Strefford Shrops....95 K6
Strelitz P & K....233 J8
Strelley Notts....116 E3
Strensall C York....151 K4
Strensham Worcs....81 L7
Strensham Services (northbound) Worcs....81 K7
Strensham Services (southbound) Worcs....81 L7
Stretcholt Somset....30 D2
Strete Devon....8 C5
Stretford Herefs....80 B4
Stretford Herefs....80 C4
Stretford Traffd....130 F1
Strethall Essex....87 K7
Stretham Cambs....103 K8
Strettington W Susx....20 C5
Stretton Ches W....113 G1
Stretton Derbys....133 H7
Stretton Rutlnd....118 B8
Stretton Staffs....97 K1
Stretton Staffs....115 L6
Stretton Warrtn....130 C3
Stretton en le Field Leics....99 J1
Stretton Grandison Herefs....80 E6
Stretton-on-Dunsmore Warwks....83 J1
Stretton on Fosse Warwks....82 F7
Stretton Sugwas Herefs....80 B6
Stretton under Fosse Warwks....99 M7
Stretton Westwood Shrops....96 D4
Strichen Abers....269 H5
Strines Stockp....131 J2
Stringston Somset....30 B2
Strixton Nhants....85 H3
Stroat Gloucs....63 H7
Strollamus Highld....247 J3
Stroma Highld....280 E1
Stromeferry Highld....248 D5
Stromness Ork....275 b4
Stronaba Highld....239 L6
Stronachlachar Stirlg....218 F5
Stronafian Ag & B....207 G3
Stronchrubie Highld....271 H4
Strone Ag & B....207 K3
Strone Highld....239 J7
Strone Highld....250 F6
Stronmilchan Ag & B....217 J2
Stronsay Ork....275 e3
Stronsay Airport Ork....275 e3
Strontian Highld....228 C3
Strood Kent....39 L7
Strood Medway....52 F5
Strood Green Surrey....37 J1
Strood Green W Susx....36 F6
Stroud Gloucs....64 B6
Stroud Hants....35 L6
Stroude Surrey....50 C5
Stroud Green Essex....53 J1
Stroud Green Gloucs....64 A5
Stroxton Lincs....118 B5
Struan Highld....246 D1
Struan P & K....232 B2
Strubby Lincs....137 H3
Strumpshaw Norfk....107 H2
Strutherhill S Lans....198 C3
Struthers Fife....222 F5
Struy Highld....250 C4
Stryd-y-Facsen IoA....124 F3
Stuartfield Abers....257 H3
Stubbers Green Wsall....98 D3
Stubbington Hants....19 J3
Stubbins Lancs....140 B4
Stubbs Cross Kent....40 C7
Stubbs Green Norfk....106 E4
Stubhampton Dorset....32 F8
Stubley Derbys....133 G4
Stubshaw Cross Wigan....139 H7
Stubton Lincs....118 A2
Stuckton Hants....18 E2
Studfold N York....148 E2
Stud Green W & M....49 L3
Studham C Beds....68 C4
Studholme Cumb....177 H7

Studland Dorset	17	K6
Studlands Park Suffk	88	C2
Studley Warwks	82	C2
Studley Wilts	46	D4
Studley Common Warwks	82	C2
Studley Roger N York	150	C2
Studley Royal N York	150	C2
Studley Royal Park & Fountains Abbey N York	150	C2
Stuntney Cambs	103	L7
Stunts Green E Susx	23	K4
Sturbridge Staffs	114	C5
Sturgate Lincs	135	H2
Sturmer Essex	88	D6
Sturminster Common Dorset	32	C8
Sturminster Marshall Dorset	17	J3
Sturminster Newton Dorset	32	C8
Sturry Kent	41	G3
Sturton N Linc	144	B7
Sturton by Stow Lincs	135	H4
Sturton le Steeple Notts	134	F3
Stuston Suffk	106	C7
Stutton N York	151	G7
Stutton Suffk	90	D8
Styal Ches E	131	G3
Stydd Lancs	148	A8
Stynie Moray	267	G4
Styrrup Notts	134	C2
Succoth Ag & B	218	D6
Suckley Worcs	81	G5
Suckley Green Worcs	81	G4
Sudborough Nhants	101	L7
Sudbourne Suffk	91	J4
Sudbrook Lincs	118	C3
Sudbrook Mons	45	G2
Sudbrooke Lincs	135	L4
Sudbury Derbys	115	K5
Sudbury Gt Lon	50	F2
Sudbury Suffk	89	H7
Sudden Rochdl	140	C5
Sudgrove Gloucs	64	D5
Suffield N York	163	H4
Suffield Norfk	122	E5
Sugdon Wrekin	113	K4
Sugnall Staffs	114	B5
Sugwas Pool Herefs	80	B6
Suisnish Highld	247	J5
Sulby IoM	154	e3
Sulgrave Nhants	84	A6
Sulham W Berk	48	F4
Sulhamstead W Berk	48	F5
Sulhamstead Abbots W Berk	48	F5
Sulhamstead Bannister W Berk	48	F5
Sullington W Susx	21	J4
Sullom Shet	281	d4
Sullom Voe Shet	281	d4
Sully V Glam	43	J8
Sumburgh Airport Shet	281	d9
Summerbridge N York	150	B3
Summercourt Cnwll	4	E4
Summerfield Norfk	121	G4
Summerfield Worcs	97	J8
Summer Heath Bucks	49	H1
Summerhill Pembks	55	K5
Summerhill Staffs	98	D2
Summer Hill Wrexhm	112	D1
Summerhouse Darltn	169	G6
Summerlands Cumb	157	H5
Summerley Derbys	133	G4
Summersdale W Susx	20	D5
Summerseat Bury	140	B5
Summertown Oxon	66	D5
Summit Oldham	140	D6
Summit Rochdl	140	E4
Sunbiggin Cumb	157	L1
Sunbury-on-Thames Surrey	50	E5
Sundaywell D & G	185	K6
Sunderland Ag & B	204	C3
Sunderland Cumb	165	G4
Sunderland Lancs	147	H4
Sunderland Sundld	181	K7
Sunderland Bridge Dur	169	H3
Sundhope Border	200	D8
Sundon Park Luton	68	D2
Sundridge Kent	38	D2
Sunk Island E R Yk	145	H4
Sunningdale W & M	50	B5
Sunninghill W & M	50	B5
Sunningwell Oxon	66	D7
Sunniside Dur	168	F3
Sunniside Gatesd	180	F7
Sunny Brow Dur	169	G4
Sunnyhill C Derb	116	B5
Sunnyhurst Bl w D	139	K3
Sunnylaw Stirlg	220	D1
Sunnymead Oxon	66	D5
Sunton Wilts	47	K8
Surbiton Gt Lon	50	F5
Surfleet Lincs	119	H6
Surfleet Seas End Lincs	119	J6
Surlingham Norfk	107	G2
Surrex Essex	72	C3
Sustead Norfk	122	D4
Susworth Lincs	143	L7
Sutcombe Devon	26	F8
Sutcombemill Devon	26	F8
Suton Norfk	106	B4
Sutterby Lincs	137	G5
Sutterton Lincs	119	J4
Sutton C Beds	86	E5
Sutton C Pete	102	B4
Sutton Cambs	103	J7
Sutton Devon	7	K6
Sutton Devon	13	G2
Sutton Donc	142	E5
Sutton E Susx	23	H7
Sutton Gt Lon	51	H6
Sutton Kent	41	K5
Sutton N York	142	D3
Sutton Norfk	123	H6
Sutton Notts	117	K4
Sutton Oxon	66	B6
Sutton Pembks	54	E4
Sutton Shrops	96	C1
Sutton Shrops	97	G6
Sutton Shrops	112	E6
Sutton Shrops	113	L5
Sutton St Hel	129	M1
Sutton Staffs	114	B7
Sutton Suffk	91	G6
Sutton W Susx	21	G4
Sutton Abinger Surrey	37	J2
Sutton-at-Hone Kent	52	C5
Sutton Bassett Nhants	101	G5
Sutton Benger Wilts	46	D3
Sutton Bingham Somset	31	J8
Sutton Bonington Notts	116	E6
Sutton Bridge Lincs	120	B7
Sutton Cheney Leics	99	L3
Sutton Coldfield Birm	98	E4
Sutton Courtenay Oxon	66	D8
Sutton Crosses Lincs	119	M7
Sutton cum Lound Notts	134	D3
Sutton Fields Notts	116	E6
Sutton Green Surrey	50	C8
Sutton Green Wrexhm	112	F2
Sutton Heath Suffk	91	H5
Sutton Howgrave N York	160	D6
Sutton-in-Ashfield Notts	133	K7
Sutton-in-Craven N York	149	H7
Sutton in the Elms Leics	100	B4
Sutton Lane Ends Ches E	131	H5
Sutton Maddock Shrops	97	G3
Sutton Mallet Somset	30	E3
Sutton Mandeville Wilts	33	G5
Sutton Manor St Hel	129	L2
Sutton Marsh Herefs	80	D6
Sutton Montis Somset	31	K6
Sutton-on-Hull C KuH	144	E1
Sutton on Sea Lincs	137	K3
Sutton-on-the-Forest N York	151	J3
Sutton on the Hill Derbys	115	L5
Sutton on Trent Notts	134	F6
Sutton Poyntz Dorset	16	D6
Sutton St Edmund Lincs	103	H1
Sutton St James Lincs	119	L7
Sutton St Nicholas Herefs	80	C6
Sutton Scotney Hants	34	F3
Sutton Street Kent	39	K2
Sutton-under-Brailes Warwks	83	G7
Sutton-under-Whitestonecliffe N York	161	G6
Sutton upon Derwent E R Yk	151	L6
Sutton Valence Kent	39	K3
Sutton Veny Wilts	32	E3
Sutton Waldron Dorset	32	E7
Sutton Weaver Ches W	130	A4
Sutton Wick BaNES	45	H7
Sutton Wick Oxon	66	C8
Swaby Lincs	137	G4
Swadlincote Derbys	116	A7
Swaffham Norfk	105	G2
Swaffham Bulbeck Cambs	87	L3
Swaffham Prior Cambs	88	B2
Swafield Norfk	122	F5
Swainby N York	161	G2
Swainshill Herefs	80	B7
Swainsthorpe Norfk	106	E3
Swainswick BaNES	45	M5
Swalcliffe Oxon	83	J7
Swalecliffe Kent	40	F2
Swallow Lincs	144	F7
Swallow Beck Lincs	135	J6
Swallowcliffe Wilts	33	G5
Swallowfield Wokham	49	H6
Swallownest Rothm	133	J3
Swallows Cross Essex	70	F7
Swampton Hants	34	E1
Swanage Dorset	17	K6
Swanbourne Bucks	67	K2
Swanbridge V Glam	43	J8
Swancote Shrops	97	G4
Swan Green Ches W	130	E5
Swanland E R Yk	144	C2
Swanley Kent	52	B5
Swanley Village Kent	52	B5
Swanmore Hants	35	J7
Swannington Leics	116	C8
Swannington Norfk	122	C7
Swanpool Lincs	135	J6
Swanscombe Kent	52	D4
Swansea Swans	57	J6
Swansea Airport Swans	57	G6
Swansea West Services Swans	57	H5
Swan Street Essex	72	C2
Swanton Abbot Norfk	122	F6
Swanton Morley Norfk	121	M8
Swanton Novers Norfk	121	M5
Swanton Street Kent	53	J7
Swan Valley Nhants	84	D4
Swan Village Sandw	98	C5
Swanwick Derbys	116	C1
Swanwick Hants	19	H2
Swarby Lincs	118	D3
Swardeston Norfk	106	D3
Swarkestone Derbys	116	B6
Swarland Nthumb	191	H5
Swarraton Hants	35	H3
Swartha C Brad	149	J6
Swarthmoor Cumb	156	C7
Swaton Lincs	118	F4
Swavesey Cambs	87	G2
Sway Hants	18	D4
Swayfield Lincs	118	C7
Swaythling C Sotn	34	F7
Sweet Green Worcs	80	F3
Sweetham Devon	13	K3
Sweethaws E Susx	38	D7
Sweetlands Corner Kent	39	K4
Sweets Cnwll	11	G3
Sweetshouse Cnwll	5	J3
Swefling Suffk	91	H3
Swepstone Leics	99	K1
Swerford Oxon	66	A1
Swettenham Ches E	130	F6
Swffryd Blae G	61	K7
Swift's Green Kent	39	L4
Swilland Suffk	90	E4
Swillbrook Lancs	138	F1
Swillington Leeds	142	B2
Swimbridge Devon	27	L5
Swimbridge Newland Devon	27	L5
Swinbrook Oxon	65	L4
Swincliffe Kirk	141	K2
Swincliffe N York	150	C4
Swincombe Devon	28	B3
Swindale Cumb	166	C8
Swinden N York	148	E5
Swinderby Lincs	135	H7
Swindon Gloucs	64	D2
Swindon Nthumb	190	D6
Swindon Staffs	97	J5
Swindon Swindn	47	H2
Swine E R Yk	153	J8
Swinefleet E R Yk	143	J3
Swineford S Glos	45	K5
Swineshead Bed	85	L2
Swineshead Lincs	119	H3
Swineshead Bridge Lincs	119	H3
Swiney Highld	275	H1
Swinford Leics	100	C7
Swinford Oxon	66	C5
Swingate Notts	116	E3
Swingfield Minnis Kent	41	G6
Swingfield Street Kent	41	H6
Swingleton Green Suffk	89	K6
Swinhoe Nthumb	203	K7
Swinhope Lincs	145	G8
Swinithwaite N York	159	J5
Swinmore Common Herefs	80	F7
Swinscoe Staffs	115	J2
Swinside Cumb	165	G6
Swinstead Lincs	118	D7
Swinthorpe Lincs	135	L4
Swinton Border	202	C4
Swinton N York	160	B6
Swinton N York	162	B8
Swinton Rothm	142	C7
Swinton Salfd	140	A7
Swiss Valley Carmth	56	F4
Swithland Leics	100	C1
Swordale Highld	263	G6
Swordland Highld	238	B5
Swordly Highld	278	C2
Sworton Heath Ches E	130	D3
Swyddffynnon Cerdgn	77	J2
Swyncombe Oxon	49	G1
Swynnerton Staffs	114	D4
Swyre Dorset	15	M5
Sycharth Powys	112	B6
Sychnant Powys	93	L
Sychtyn Powys	94	B
Sydallt Wrexhm	129	H
Syde Gloucs	64	D
Sydenham Gt Lon	51	K
Sydenham Oxon	67	K
Sydenham Damerel Devon	12	A
Sydenhurst Surrey	36	E
Syderstone Norfk	121	H
Sydling St Nicholas Dorset	16	C
Sydmonton Hants	48	C
Sydnal Lane Shrops	97	H
Syerston Notts	117	K
Syke Rochdl	140	
Sykehouse Donc	143	
Syleham Suffk	106	E
Sylen Carmth	56	F
Symbister Shet	281	e
Symington S Ayrs	196	D
Symington S Lans	199	G
Symondsbury Dorset	15	K
Symonds Yat (East) Herefs	63	H
Symonds Yat (West) Herefs	63	H
Sympson Green C Brad	150	A
Synderford Dorset	15	J
Synod Inn Cerdgn	76	D
Syre Highld	278	B
Syreford Gloucs	64	F
Syresham Nhants	84	C
Syston Leics	100	D
Syston Lincs	118	B
Sytchampton Worcs	81	J
Sywell Nhants	84	F

T

Tabley Hill Ches E	130	E
Tackley Oxon	66	C
Tacolneston Norfk	106	C
Tadcaster N York	151	G
Taddington Derbys	132	C
Taddington Gloucs	65	G
Taddiport Devon	27	H
Tadley Hants	48	F
Tadlow Cambs	86	F
Tadmarton Oxon	83	J
Tadpole Swindn	47	G
Tadwick BaNES	45	L
Tadworth Surrey	51	G
Tafarnaubach Blae G	61	H
Tafarn-y-bwlch Pembks	75	G
Tafarn-y-Gelyn Denbgs	128	E
Taff's Well Cardif	43	H
Tafolwern Powys	93	J
Taibach Neath	57	J
Tain Highld	263	L
Tain Highld	280	B
Tai'n Lôn Gwynd	109	H
Tai'r Bull Powys	60	F
Tairgwaith Neath	59	K
Takeley Essex	70	E
Takeley Street Essex	70	E
Talachddu Powys	78	F
Talacre Flints	128	D
Talaton Devon	14	C
Talbenny Pembks	54	D
Talbot Green Rhondd	43	H
Talbot Village BCP	17	L
Taleford Devon	14	C
Talerddig Powys	93	K
Talgarreg Cerdgn	76	D
Talgarth Powys	79	G
Talisker Highld	246	D
Talke Staffs	114	C
Talke Pits Staffs	114	C
Talkin Cumb	178	D
Talladale Highld	260	E
Talla Linnfoots Border	187	K
Tallaminnock S Ayrs	183	K
Tallarn Green Wrexhm	113	G
Tallentire Cumb	164	F
Talley Carmth	59	L
Tallington Lincs	102	B
Tallwrn Wrexhm	112	D
Talmine Highld	277	L
Talog Carmth	58	F
Talsarn Cerdgn	77	G
Talsarnau Gwynd	109	L
Talskiddy Cnwll	4	
Talwrn IoA	125	J
Talwrn Wrexhm	112	J
Tal-y-bont Cerdgn	92	E
Tal-y-Bont Conwy	126	F
Talybont Gwynd	109	L
Tal-y-bont Gwynd	126	E
Talybont-on-Usk Powys	61	H
Tal-y-Cafn Conwy	126	E
Tal-y-coed Mons	62	E

Tal-y-garn Rhondd 42 F5
Tal-y-llyn Gwynd 92 F2
Talysarn Gwynd 109 J1
Tal-y-Waun Torfn 61 L6
Talywern Powys 93 H3
Tamar Valley Mining District
   Devon 6 E2
Tamer Lane End Wigan 139 J7
Tamerton Foliot C Plym 6 F3
Tamworth Staffs 99 G3
Tamworth Green Lincs 119 L3
Tamworth Services Warwks 99 H3
Tancred N York 151 G4
Tancredston Pembks 74 F2
Tandridge Surrey 38 B3
Tanfield Dur 180 F7
Tanfield Lea Dur 180 F8
Tangasdale W Isls 283 b13
Tangiers Pembks 54 F3
Tangley Hants 47 L8
Tangmere W Susx 20 E5
Tan Hill N York 158 F1
Tankerness Ork 275 d4
Tankersley Barns 142 A7
Tankerton Kent 40 F2
Tannach Highld 280 D6
Tannachie Abers 245 H6
Tannadice Angus 234 D4
Tanner's Green Worcs 98 D8
Tannington Suffk 90 F2
Tannochside N Lans 209 J6
Tansley Derbys 132 F7
Tansor Nhants 102 B5
Tantobie Dur 180 E7
Tanton N York 170 C8
Tanwood Worcs 97 K8
Tanworth in Arden Warwks 82 D1
Tan-y-Bwlch Gwynd 110 C3
Tan-y-fron Conwy 127 J6
Tan-y-fron Wrexhm 112 D1
Tan-y-grisiau Gwynd 110 C3
Tan-y-groes Cerdgn 76 B5
Taobh Tuath W Isls 282 d6
Taplow Bucks 49 M3
Tarbert Ag & B 205 L6
Tarbert Ag & B 206 D5
Tarbert W Isls 282 e5
Tarbet Ag & B 218 D6
Tarbet Highld 238 C5
Tarbet Highld 276 B6
Tarbock Green Knows 129 K2
Tarbolton S Ayrs 196 E5
Tarbrax S Lans 199 H2
Tardebigge Worcs 82 B2
Tarfside Angus 244 B7
Tarland Abers 244 B3
Tarleton Lancs 138 F4
Tarlscough Lancs 138 E5
Tarlton Gloucs 64 D7
Tarnock Somset 44 D8
Tarns Cumb 164 F1
Tarnside Cumb 156 F4
Tarporley Ches W 130 A7
Tarr Somset 28 F4
Tarrant Crawford Dorset 17 H2
Tarrant Gunville Dorset 32 F8
Tarrant Hinton Dorset 32 F8
Tarrant Keyneston Dorset 17 H2
Tarrant Launceston Dorset 17 J1
Tarrant Monkton Dorset 17 J1
Tarrant Rawston Dorset 17 H1
Tarrant Rushton Dorset 17 H2
Tarring Neville E Susx 23 G6
Tarrington Herefs 80 E7
Tarskavaig Highld 247 J6
Tarves Abers 256 F5
Tarvin Ches W 129 L6
Tarvin Sands Ches W 129 L6
Tasburgh Norfk 106 E4
Tasley Shrops 96 F4
Taston Oxon 65 M3
Tatenhill Staffs 115 K7
Tathall End M Keyn 84 F6
Tatham Lancs 147 M2
Tathwell Lincs 136 F3
Tatsfield Surrey 51 L7
Tattenhall Ches W 129 L7
Tatterford Norfk 121 J6
Tattersett Norfk 121 J5
Tattershall Lincs 136 D8
Tattershall Bridge Lincs 136 C8
Tattershall Thorpe Lincs 136 D7
Tattingstone Suffk 90 D7
Tattingstone White Horse
   Suffk 90 D7
Tatworth Somset 15 H2
Tauchers Moray 267 H6
Taunton Somset 30 C6
Taunton Deane Services
   Somset 30 B6

Taverham Norfk 106 D1
Taverners Green Essex 70 E3
Tavernspite Pembks 55 L4
Tavistock Devon 12 C7
Tavistock Devon 12 C7
Taw Green Devon 12 F3
Tawstock Devon 27 K5
Taxal Derbys 131 K4
Tay Bridge C Dund 223 G1
Taychreggan Hotel Ag & B 217 G3
Tay Forest Park P & K 231 L3
Tayinloan Ag & B 205 M7
Taynton Gloucs 63 L3
Taynton Oxon 65 K4
Taynuilt Ag & B 216 F1
Tayport Fife 223 H2
Tayvallich Ag & B 215 L7
Tealby Lincs 136 C2
Tealing Angus 234 B7
Team Valley Gatesd 181 G7
Teangue Highld 247 K6
Teanord Highld 263 K7
Tebay Cumb 157 K2
Tebay Services Cumb 157 K2
Tebworth C Beds 68 C2
Tedburn St Mary Devon 13 J4
Teddington Gloucs 81 M8
Teddington Gt Lon 50 F5
Tedstone Delamere Herefs 80 F3
Tedstone Wafer Herefs 80 F3
Teesport R & Cl 170 D6
Teesside International Airport
   S on T 169 K8
Teesside Park S on T 170 B7
Teeton Nhants 84 D1
Teffont Evias Wilts 33 G4
Teffont Magna Wilts 33 G4
Tegryn Pembks 75 L5
Teigh Rutlnd 117 M8
Teigncombe Devon 12 F5
Teigngrace Devon 13 K7
Teignmouth Devon 13 L8
Teindside Border 188 D4
Telford Wrekin 96 F2
Telford Services Shrops 97 G2
Telham E Susx 24 D4
Tellisford Somset 46 A7
Telscombe E Susx 22 F6
Telscombe Cliffs E Susx 22 F6
Tempar P & K 231 J4
Templand D & G 176 E2
Temple Cnwll 11 G7
Temple Mdloth 211 K7
Temple Balsall Solhll 99 G8
Temple Bar Cerdgn 76 F4
Temple Cloud BaNES 45 J7
Templecombe Somset 32 B6
Temple End Suffk 88 D5
Temple Ewell Kent 41 J6
Temple Grafton Warwks 82 D4
Temple Guiting Gloucs 65 G2
Temple Herdewyke Warwks 83 J5
Temple Hirst N York 142 F3
Temple Normanton Derbys 133 H6
Temple of Fiddes Abers 245 H7
Temple Sowerby Cumb 166 E5
Templeton Devon 28 F8
Templeton Pembks 55 J4
Templetown Dur 168 E1
Tempsford C Beds 86 D4
Tenbury Wells Worcs 80 E2
Tenby Pembks 55 K6
Tendring Essex 73 H2
Tendring Green Essex 73 H2
Tendring Heath Essex 73 H2
Ten Mile Bank Norfk 104 B4
Tenpenny Heath Essex 73 G2
Tenterden Kent 39 M6
Terling Essex 71 J4
Tern Wrekin 113 K8
Ternhill Shrops 113 L5
Terregles D & G 176 B3
Terrington N York 151 L2
Terrington St Clement Norfk 120 C7
Terrington St John Norfk 104 A1
Terry's Green Warwks 98 E8
Teston Kent 39 H3
Testwood Hants 34 D7
Tetbury Gloucs 64 C8
Tetbury Upton Gloucs 64 C8
Tetchill Shrops 112 F5
Tetcott Devon 11 K3
Tetford Lincs 136 F5
Tetney Lincs 145 J7
Tetney Lock Lincs 145 J7
Tetsworth Oxon 67 G6
Tettenhall Wolves 97 K3
Tettenhall Wood Wolves 97 K3
Teversal Notts 133 J7
Teversham Cambs 87 K3

Teviothead Border 188 C5
Tewin Herts 69 H4
Tewin Wood Herts 69 H4
Tewkesbury Gloucs 81 K8
Teynham Kent 40 B3
Thackley C Brad 149 M8
Thackthwaite Cumb 164 F6
Thackthwaite Cumb 166 A5
Thainstone Abers 256 D8
Thakeham W Susx 21 J3
Thame Oxon 67 H6
Thames Ditton Surrey 50 F5
Thamesmead Gt Lon 52 A3
Thamesport Medway 53 J4
Thanington Kent 40 F4
Thankerton S Lans 199 G5
Tharston Norfk 106 D4
Thatcham W Berk 48 D5
Thatto Heath St Hel 129 L1
Thaxted Essex 70 F1
Theakston N York 160 D5
Thealby N Linc 143 M4
Theale Somset 31 G2
Theale W Berk 48 F5
Thearne E R Yk 153 G8
The Bank Ches E 131 G8
The Beeches Gloucs 64 F6
Theberton Suffk 91 K2
The Blythe Staffs 115 G6
The Bog Shrops 95 J4
The Bourne Worcs 82 A4
The Braes Highld 247 H2
The Bratch Staffs 97 K4
The Bridge Kent 52 C4
The Broad Herefs 80 C3
The Broads 107 K2
The Brunt E Loth 212 F4
The Bryn Mons 62 C5
The Bungalow IoM 154 e5
The Burf Worcs 81 J2
The Camp Gloucs 64 C5
The Chequer Wrexhm 113 H3
The City Bed 86 C3
The City Bucks 67 J7
The Common Oxon 65 L2
The Common Wilts 34 B4
The Common Wilts 46 F2
The Corner Kent 39 H5
The Cronk IoM 154 d3
Theddingworth Leics 100 E6
Theddlethorpe All Saints
   Lincs 137 J2
Theddlethorpe St Helen Lincs 137 J2
The Den N Ayrs 196 C1
The Forge Herefs 79 L3
The Forstal Kent 40 D7
The Fouralls Shrops 113 L5
The Green Cumb 156 A5
The Green Essex 71 J3
The Green N York 162 D2
The Green Wilts 32 E4
The Grove Dur 168 E1
The Grove Worcs 81 K7
The Haven W Susx 37 G5
The Haw Gloucs 64 B2
The Hendre Mons 62 F4
The Hill Cumb 156 A6
The Holt Wokham 49 K3
The Hundred Herefs 80 C2
Thelbridge Cross Devon 28 D8
The Leacon Kent 40 C8
The Lee Bucks 67 L6
The Lhen IoM 154 e2
Thelnetham Suffk 105 L7
Thelveton Norfk 106 D7
Thelwall Warrtn 130 C2
The Marsh Powys 95 H4
Themelthorpe Norfk 122 B6
The Middles Dur 180 F8
The Moor Kent 39 J7
The Mumbles Swans 57 H7
The Murray S Lans 209 H8
The Mythe Gloucs 81 K8
The Narth Mons 63 G6
The Neuk Abers 245 G4
Thenford Nhants 83 M7
Theobald's Green Wilts 46 F5
The Quarry Gloucs 63 L7
The Quarter Kent 39 M4
The Reddings Gloucs 64 C3
Therfield Herts 87 G7
The Rhôs Powys 61 J1
The Ross P & K 220 D3
The Sands Surrey 36 C2
The Shoe Wilts 46 A4
The Smithies Shrops 96 F4
The Spring Warwks 83 G1
The Square Torfn 62 B7
The Stair Kent 38 F4

The Stocks Kent 25 G2
The Straits Hants 36 A3
The Strand Wilts 46 D7
Thetford Norfk 105 H6
Thetford Forest Park 104 F5
Thethwaite Cumb 165 L2
The Towans Cnwll 2 E3
The Town IoS 10 b2
The Vauld Herefs 80 C5
The Wyke Shrops 97 G2
Theydon Bois Essex 70 C7
Theydon Mount Essex 70 C7
Thicket Priory N York 151 L7
Thickwood Wilts 46 B4
Thimbleby Lincs 136 D5
Thimbleby N York 161 G3
Thingwall Wirral 129 G3
Thirkleby N York 161 G6
Thirlby N York 161 G6
Thirlestane Border 201 H4
Thirn N York 160 B5
Thirsk N York 160 F6
Thirtleby E R Yk 144 F1
Thistleton Lancs 147 H8
Thistleton Rutlnd 118 B7
Thistley Green Suffk 104 D8
Thixendale N York 152 C4
Thockrington Nthumb 179 M3
Tholomas Drove Cambs 103 H2
Tholthorpe N York 151 G2
Thomas Chapel Pembks 55 J5
Thomas Close Cumb 166 B3
Thomastown Abers 255 L4
Thompson Norfk 105 J4
Thomshill Moray 266 D5
Thong Kent 52 E5
Thongsbridge Kirk 141 J6
Thoralby N York 159 H5
Thoresby Notts 134 C5
Thoresthorpe Lincs 137 J4
Thoresway Lincs 144 F8
Thorganby Lincs 145 G8
Thorganby N York 151 L7
Thorgill N York 162 C3
Thorington Suffk 107 J8
Thorington Street Suffk 89 K8
Thorlby N York 149 H5
Thorley Herts 70 C3
Thorley IoW 18 F6
Thorley Houses Herts 70 C3
Thorley Street IoW 18 F6
Thormanby N York 161 H7
Thornaby-on-Tees S on T 170 B7
Thornage Norfk 122 B4
Thornborough Bucks 84 E8
Thornborough N York 160 D6
Thornbury C Brad 141 J1
Thornbury Devon 12 A1
Thornbury Herefs 80 E3
Thornbury S Glos 45 J1
Thornby Cumb 177 J8
Thornby Nhants 100 E8
Thorncliff Staffs 131 K7
Thorncombe Dorset 15 J2
Thorncombe Street Surrey 36 F3
Thorncott Green C Beds 86 C5
Thorncross IoW 19 G7
Thorndon Suffk 90 D1
Thorndon Cross Devon 12 D4
Thorne Donc 143 H5
Thorne Coffin Somset 31 H7
Thornecroft Devon 7 M2
Thornehillhead Devon 27 G7
Thorner Leeds 150 E7
Thornes Staffs 98 D3
Thornes Wakefd 141 M4
Thorne St Margaret Somset 29 K6
Thorney Bucks 50 D3
Thorney C Pete 102 F3
Thorney Notts 135 G5
Thorney Somset 30 F6
Thorney Hill Hants 18 B4
Thorney Island W Susx 20 C6
Thorney Toll Cambs 103 G3
Thornfalcon Somset 30 D6
Thornford Dorset 31 K8
Thorngrafton Nthumb 179 H6
Thorngrove Somset 30 E4
Thorngumbald E R Yk 145 G3
Thornham Norfk 121 G3
Thornham Magna Suffk 90 C1
Thornham Parva Suffk 90 D1
Thornhaugh C Pete 102 B3
Thornhill C Sotn 19 G1
Thornhill Caerph 43 J5
Thornhill Cumb 155 H1
Thornhill D & G 186 C7
Thornhill Derbys 132 D3
Thornhill Kirk 141 L4
Thornhill Stirlg 219 L7

Place	Page	Grid
Thornhill Lees Kirk	141	K4
Thornhills Calder	141	J3
Thornholme E R Yk	153	H3
Thornicombe Dorset	17	G2
Thornington Nthumb	202	D6
Thornley Dur	168	E3
Thornley Dur	169	K3
Thornley Gate Nthumb	179	J7
Thornliebank E Rens	208	F7
Thorns Suffk	88	E4
Thornsett Derbys	131	K2
Thorns Green Ches E	130	F3
Thornthwaite Cumb	165	H5
Thornthwaite N York	149	L4
Thornton Angus	234	B6
Thornton Bucks	84	E8
Thornton C Brad	141	H1
Thornton E R Yk	152	A6
Thornton Fife	222	E7
Thornton Lancs	146	F7
Thornton Leics	100	A2
Thornton Lincs	136	D6
Thornton Middsb	170	B7
Thornton Nthumb	202	E4
Thornton Pembks	54	E5
Thornton Sefton	138	D7
Thornton Curtis N Linc	144	D4
Thorntonhall S Lans	209	G7
Thornton Heath Gt Lon	51	J5
Thornton Hough Wirral	129	G3
Thornton-in-Craven N York	148	F6
Thornton in Lonsdale N York	158	B8
Thornton-le-Beans N York	160	E4
Thornton-le-Clay N York	151	L3
Thornton-le-Dale N York	162	E6
Thornton le Moor Lincs	144	D8
Thornton-le-Moor N York	160	F5
Thornton-le-Moors Ches W	129	K5
Thornton-le-Street N York	160	F5
Thorntonloch E Loth	213	G4
Thornton Rust N York	159	G5
Thornton Steward N York	160	A5
Thornton Watlass N York	160	C5
Thornwood Common Essex	70	C6
Thornydykes Border	201	J3
Thornythwaite Cumb	165	L6
Thoroton Notts	117	K3
Thorp Arch Leeds	150	F6
Thorpe Derbys	115	J2
Thorpe E R Yk	152	F6
Thorpe Lincs	137	J3
Thorpe N York	149	H3
Thorpe Norfk	107	J4
Thorpe Notts	117	K2
Thorpe Surrey	50	C5
Thorpe Abbotts Norfk	106	D7
Thorpe Acre Leics	116	E7
Thorpe Arnold Leics	117	K7
Thorpe Audlin Wakefd	142	D4
Thorpe Bay Sthend	53	K2
Thorpe by Water Rutlnd	101	K4
Thorpe Common Rothm	133	G1
Thorpe Constantine Staffs	99	H2
Thorpe End Norfk	106	F1
Thorpe Green Essex	73	H3
Thorpe Green Lancs	139	H3
Thorpe Green Suffk	89	J4
Thorpe Hesley Rothm	142	B8
Thorpe in Balne Donc	142	F5
Thorpe Langton Leics	101	G5
Thorpe Larches Dur	169	K5
Thorpe Lea Surrey	50	C5
Thorpe le Fallows Lincs	135	H4
Thorpe-le-Soken Essex	73	J3
Thorpe le Street E R Yk	152	F6
Thorpe Malsor Nhants	101	H7
Thorpe Mandeville Nhants	83	M6
Thorpe Market Norfk	122	E4
Thorpe Marriot Norfk	122	D8
Thorpe Morieux Suffk	89	J4
Thorpeness Suffk	91	L3
Thorpe on the Hill Leeds	141	M2
Thorpe on the Hill Lincs	135	H6
Thorpe St Andrew Norfk	106	F2
Thorpe St Peter Lincs	137	J7
Thorpe Salvin Rothm	133	K3
Thorpe Satchville Leics	100	F1
Thorpe Thewles S on T	169	L6
Thorpe Tilney Lincs	136	B8
Thorpe Underwood N York	151	G4
Thorpe Underwood Nhants	101	H4
Thorpe Waterville Nhants	102	A7
Thorpe Willoughby N York	142	F2
Thorpland Norfk	104	C2
Thorrington Essex	73	J3
Thorverton Devon	13	L2
Thrales End C Beds	68	E4
Thrandeston Suffk	106	C8
Thrapston Nhants	101	M7
Threapland Cumb	165	G3
Threapland N York	149	H4
Threapwood Ches W	113	G3
Threapwood Staffs	115	G3
Threapwood Head Staffs	115	G3
Threave S Ayrs	183	J2
Three Ashes Herefs	63	G3
Three Bridges W Susx	37	L3
Three Burrows Cnwll	4	B5
Three Chimneys Kent	39	K5
Three Cocks Powys	79	G7
Three Crosses Swans	57	G6
Three Cups Corner E Susx	23	L3
Three Gates Worcs	80	F3
Threehammer Common Norfk	123	G7
Three Hammers Cnwll	11	J5
Three Holes Norfk	103	K3
Threekingham Lincs	118	E4
Three Leg Cross E Susx	39	H7
Three Legged Cross Dorset	17	L2
Three Mile Cross Wokham	49	H5
Threemilestone Cnwll	4	C6
Threemiletown W Loth	210	E4
Three Oaks E Susx	24	F4
Threlkeld Cumb	165	K5
Threshers Bush Essex	70	D5
Threshfield N York	149	H3
Thrigby Norfk	107	J1
Thringarth Dur	167	L6
Thringstone Leics	116	D8
Thrintoft N York	160	D4
Thriplow Cambs	87	J6
Throapham Rothm	133	K2
Throckenhalt Lincs	103	G2
Throcking Herts	69	J1
Throckley N u Ty	180	E5
Throckmorton Worcs	82	A5
Throop BCP	17	M3
Throop Dorset	16	F4
Throphill Nthumb	180	D2
Thropton Nthumb	190	E5
Throsk Stirlg	209	M1
Througham Gloucs	64	D5
Throughgate D & G	185	L6
Throwleigh Devon	12	F4
Throwley Kent	40	C4
Throwley Forstal Kent	40	C4
Thrumpton Notts	116	E5
Thrumpton Notts	134	D4
Thrumster Highld	280	D7
Thrunton Nthumb	190	F4
Thrup Oxon	65	L7
Thrupp Gloucs	64	B6
Thrupp Oxon	66	C4
Thrushelton Devon	12	B5
Thrussington Leics	117	H8
Thruxton Hants	34	C2
Thruxton Herefs	80	B8
Thrybergh Rothm	142	D8
Thulston Derbys	116	C5
Thundersley Essex	53	G1
Thurcaston Leics	100	C1
Thurcroft Rothm	133	K2
Thurdon Cnwll	26	E8
Thurgarton Norfk	122	D4
Thurgarton Notts	117	J2
Thurgoland Barns	141	L7
Thurlaston Leics	100	B4
Thurlaston Warwks	83	L1
Thurlbear Somset	30	C6
Thurlby Lincs	118	E8
Thurlby Lincs	135	H7
Thurlby Lincs	137	J4
Thurleigh Bed	85	L3
Thurlestone Devon	7	K6
Thurloxton Somset	30	C5
Thurlstone Barns	141	K7
Thurlton Norfk	107	J4
Thurlwood Ches E	130	F8
Thurmaston Leics	100	D2
Thurnby Leics	100	E3
Thurne Norfk	123	H8
Thurnham Kent	53	H7
Thurning Nhants	102	B6
Thurning Norfk	122	B5
Thurnscoe Barns	142	C6
Thurrock Services Thurr	52	C3
Thursby Cumb	165	K1
Thursden Lancs	140	D1
Thursford Norfk	121	L5
Thursley Surrey	36	D3
Thurso Highld	279	K3
Thurstaston Wirral	128	F3
Thurston Suffk	89	J2
Thurston Clough Oldham	140	E6
Thurstonfield Cumb	177	K7
Thurstonland Kirk	141	J5
Thurston Planche Suffk	89	J2
Thurton Norfk	107	G3
Thurvaston Derbys	115	L4
Thuxton Norfk	105	L2
Thwaite N York	158	F3
Thwaite Suffk	90	D2
Thwaite Head Cumb	156	E4
Thwaites C Brad	149	K7
Thwaite St Mary Norfk	107	G4
Thwaites Brow C Brad	149	K7
Thwing E R Yk	153	G2
Tibbermore P & K	221	J3
Tibbers D & G	186	C6
Tibberton Gloucs	63	M3
Tibberton Worcs	81	L4
Tibberton Wrekin	113	L7
Tibenham Norfk	106	C5
Tibshelf Derbys	133	J7
Tibshelf Services Derbys	133	J7
Tibthorpe E R Yk	152	E5
Ticehurst E Susx	39	H7
Tichborne Hants	35	H5
Tickencote Rutlnd	101	L2
Tickenham N Som	44	F4
Tickford End M Keyn	85	H6
Tickhill Donc	134	B1
Ticklerton Shrops	96	B5
Ticknall Derbys	116	B6
Tickton E R Yk	153	G7
Tidbury Green Solhll	98	E8
Tidcombe Wilts	47	L7
Tiddington Oxon	67	G6
Tiddington Warwks	82	F3
Tiddleywink Wilts	46	C4
Tidebrook E Susx	38	F7
Tideford Cnwll	6	C3
Tideford Cross Cnwll	6	C3
Tidenham Gloucs	63	H7
Tideswell Derbys	132	C4
Tidmarsh W Berk	48	F4
Tidmington Warwks	83	G7
Tidpit Hants	33	J7
Tidworth Wilts	34	B1
Tiers Cross Pembks	54	E5
Tiffield Nhants	84	D5
Tigerton Angus	234	E3
Tigh a' Ghearraidh W Isls	283	b8
Tigharry W Isls	283	b8
Tighnabruaich Ag & B	206	F4
Tigley Devon	7	L3
Tilbrook Cambs	86	B2
Tilbury Thurr	52	D4
Tibury Dock Thurr	52	D4
Tilbury Green Essex	88	E7
Tilbury Juxta Clare Essex	88	F7
Tile Cross Birm	98	F6
Tile Hill Covtry	99	H7
Tilehouse Green Solhll	98	F8
Tilehurst Readg	49	G4
Tilford Surrey	36	C2
Tilgate W Susx	37	L4
Tilgate Forest Row W Susx	37	L4
Tilham Street Somset	31	J4
Tillers Green Gloucs	80	F8
Tilley Shrops	113	H6
Tillicoultry Clacks	221	G7
Tillietudlem S Lans	198	D4
Tillingham Essex	72	E6
Tillington Herefs	80	B6
Tillington W Susx	36	E6
Tillington Common Herefs	80	B6
Tillybirloch Abers	244	F2
Tillyfourie Abers	244	E1
Tillygreig Abers	256	F7
Tillyrie P & K	221	K6
Tilmanstone Kent	41	J5
Tilney All Saints Norfk	120	C7
Tilney High End Norfk	120	C8
Tilney St Lawrence Norfk	120	C8
Tilshead Wilts	33	H1
Tilstock Shrops	113	J4
Tilston Ches W	113	G1
Tilstone Bank Ches W	130	A7
Tilstone Fearnall Ches W	130	A7
Tilsworth C Beds	68	B2
Tilton on the Hill Leics	101	G2
Tiltups End Gloucs	64	B7
Tilty Essex	70	E2
Timberland Lincs	136	B7
Timbersbrook Ches E	131	H7
Timberscombe Somset	29	G2
Timble N York	149	M5
Timewell Devon	29	H5
Timpanheck D & G	177	K4
Timperley Traffd	130	F2
Timsbury BaNES	45	K7
Timsbury Hants	34	D6
Timsgarry W Isls	282	d3
Timsgearraidh W Isls	282	d3
Timworth Suffk	89	H2
Timworth Green Suffk	89	H2
Tincleton Dorset	16	E4
Tindale Cumb	178	E7
Tingewick Bucks	84	C8
Tingley Leeds	141	L3
Tingrith C Beds	68	C1
Tingwall Airport Shet	281	e6
Tingwell Ork	275	c3
Tinhay Devon	12	A3
Tinker's Hill Hants	34	E2
Tinkersley Derbys	132	E6
Tinsley Sheff	133	H2
Tinsley Green W Susx	37	L3
Tintagel Cnwll	10	F5
Tintern Mons	63	G7
Tintinhull Somset	31	H7
Tintwistle Derbys	140	F8
Tinwald D & G	176	D3
Tinwell Rutlnd	101	M2
Tippacott Devon	28	D2
Tipp's End Norfk	103	K4
Tiptoe Hants	18	C4
Tipton Sandw	98	B5
Tipton Green Sandw	98	B5
Tipton St John Devon	14	C4
Tiptree Essex	72	C4
Tiptree Heath Essex	72	C4
Tirabad Powys	78	B7
Tircoed Swans	57	H5
Tiree Ag & B	224	C6
Tiree Airport Ag & B	224	C6
Tiretigan Ag & B	206	A4
Tirley Gloucs	64	B3
Tiroran Ag & B	226	F6
Tirphil Caerph	61	H6
Tirril Cumb	166	C5
Tir-y-fron Flints	129	G2
Tisbury Wilts	32	F4
Tisman's Common W Susx	37	G4
Tissington Derbys	115	K2
Titchberry Devon	26	D7
Titchfield Hants	19	J3
Titchfield Common Hants	19	J3
Titchmarsh Nhants	102	A8
Titchwell Norfk	121	G3
Tithby Notts	117	J4
Tithebarn Devon	14	A3
Titley Herefs	79	L3
Titmore Green Herts	69	G2
Titsey Surrey	51	L1
Titson Cnwll	11	J2
Tittensor Staffs	114	D4
Tittleshall Norfk	121	K6
Titton Worcs	81	J8
Tiverton Ches W	130	A7
Tiverton Devon	29	G4
Tivetshall St Margaret Norfk	106	D6
Tivetshall St Mary Norfk	106	D6
Tivington Somset	29	G2
Tivy Dale Barns	141	L6
Tixall Staffs	114	F6
Tixover Rutlnd	101	L3
Toab Shet	281	d8
Toadhole Derbys	133	H8
Toadmoor Derbys	116	B1
Tobermory Ag & B	226	F3
Toberonochy Ag & B	215	L1
Tobha Mòr W Isls	283	b10
Tocher Abers	256	C7
Tochieneal Moray	267	K3
Tockenham Wilts	46	F4
Tockenham Wick Wilts	46	F3
Tocketts R & Cl	170	E5
Tockholes Bl w D	139	K4
Tockington S Glos	45	J2
Tockwith N York	151	G4
Todber Dorset	32	D4
Todburn Nthumb	191	G5
Toddington C Beds	68	C2
Toddington Gloucs	64	F1
Toddington Services C Beds	68	C2
Todds Green Herts	69	G2
Todenham Gloucs	82	F7
Todhills Angus	234	C2
Todhills Cumb	177	L3
Todhills Dur	169	G5
Todhills Rest Area Cumb	177	L3
Todmorden Calder	140	E3
Todwick Rothm	133	K3
Toft Cambs	87	G4
Toft Ches E	130	E5
Toft Lincs	118	E7
Toft Shet	281	e3
Toft Warwks	83	L2
Toft Hill Dur	168	F4
Toft Hill Lincs	136	D8
Toft Monks Norfk	107	J4
Toft next Newton Lincs	135	K4
Toftrees Norfk	121	K6
Toftwood Norfk	105	M2
Togston Nthumb	191	J5
Tokavaig Highld	247	J6

Tokers Green Oxon 49 H3
Tolastadh bho Thuath W Isls ...282 h2
Toldish Cnwll 4 F3
Tolland Somset 29 K4
Tollard Farnham Dorset 32 F7
Tollard Royal Wilts 32 F7
Toll Bar Donc 142 E6
Tollbar End Covtry 99 K8
Toller Fratrum Dorset 16 B3
Toller Porcorum Dorset 16 A3
Tollerton N York 151 H3
Tollerton Notts 117 G4
Toller Whelme Dorset 15 L2
Tollesbury Essex 72 D5
Tolleshunt D'Arcy Essex 72 D5
Tolleshunt Knights Essex 72 D4
Tolleshunt Major Essex 72 C5
Tollingham E R Yk 152 C8
Toll of Birness Abers 257 J5
Tolpuddle Dorset 16 F4
Tolworth Gt Lon 51 G5
Tomatin Highld 252 E6
Tomchrasky Highld 239 M1
Tomdoun Highld 239 K3
Tomich Highld 250 B6
Tomich Highld 250 F2
Tomich Highld 263 J5
Tomich Highld 272 F7
Tomintoul Moray 254 D7
Tomlow Warwks 83 K3
Tomnacross Highld 250 F3
Tomnavoulin Moray 254 D6
Tompkin Staffs 114 E1
Ton Mons 62 C6
Ton Mons 62 D7
Tonbridge Kent 38 F4
Tondu Brdgnd 42 D5
Tonedale Somset 29 L6
Tonfanau Gwynd 92 C3
Tong C Brad 141 K2
Tong Kent 40 C4
Tong Shrops 97 H2
Tong W Isls 282 g3
Tonge Leics 116 C7
Tong Green Kent 40 C4
Tongham Surrey 36 C1
Tongland D & G 175 H4
Tong Norton Shrops 97 H2
Tongue Highld 277 K5
Tongue End Lincs 119 G7
Tongwynlais Cardif 43 H5
Tonmawr Neath 42 B2
Tonna Neath 57 L5
Ton-teg Rhondd 43 H4
Tonwell Herts 69 J4
Tonypandy Rhondd 42 F3
Tonyrefail Rhondd 42 F4
Toot Baldon Oxon 66 E5
Toot Hill Essex 70 D6
Toothill Hants 34 E7
Toothill Swindn 47 G2
Tooting Gt Lon 51 H5
Tooting Bec Gt Lon 51 H4
Topcliffe N York 160 F7
Topcroft Norfk 106 F5
Topcroft Street Norfk 106 F5
Top End Bed 85 L3
Topham Donc 143 G4
Top of Hebers Rochdl 140 C6
Toppesfield Essex 88 E7
Toprow Norfk 106 D4
Topsham Devon 13 M5
Top-y-rhos Flints 128 F7
Torbeg N Ayrs 194 D5
Torboll Highld 273 H8
Torbreck Highld 251 H3
Torbryan Devon 8 B2
Torcastle Highld 239 J7
Torcross Devon 8 B6
Tore Highld 251 G1
Torfrey Cnwll 5 J4
Torinturk Ag & B 206 C6
Torksey Lincs 135 G4
Torlundy Highld 239 K8
Tormarton S Glos 45 M3
Tormore N Ayrs 194 D4
Tornagrain Highld 252 E2
Tornaveen Abers 244 D2
Torness Highld 251 G6
Toronto Dur 169 G4
Torpenhow Cumb 165 G3
Torphichen W Loth 210 C4
Torphins Abers 244 E3
Torpoint Cnwll 6 E4
Torquay Torbay 8 D2
Torquhan Border 200 D3
Torr Devon 7 H4
Torran Highld 259 K6
Torrance E Duns 209 G4
Torranyard N Ayrs 196 D2

Torre Somset 29 J3
Torridon Highld 260 E8
Torridon House Highld 260 D8
Torrin Highld 247 J4
Torrisdale Ag & B 194 B4
Torrisdale Highld 278 B4
Torrish Highld 274 C4
Torrisholme Lancs 147 J3
Torrobull Highld 272 E7
Torry C Aber 245 L3
Torryburn Fife 210 D2
Torteval Guern 9 h4
Torthorwald D & G 176 D3
Tortington W Susx 21 G6
Torton Worcs 81 J1
Tortworth S Glos 63 L8
Torvaig Highld 259 H7
Torver Cumb 156 C4
Torwood Falk 209 M2
Torwoodlee Border 201 G5
Torworth Notts 134 D2
Tosberry Devon 26 D6
Toscaig Highld 247 L1
Toseland Cambs 86 E3
Tosside Lancs 148 D4
Tostock Suffk 89 J3
Totaig Highld 258 B6
Tote Highld 259 G6
Tote Highld 259 J4
Tote Hill W Susx 36 C6
Totford Hants 35 H3
Tothill Lincs 137 H3
Totland IoW 18 E6
Totley Sheff 132 F4
Totley Brook Sheff 132 F4
Totnes Devon 8 B3
Toton Notts 116 E4
Totronald Ag & B 224 F4
Totscore Highld 258 F3
Tottenham Gt Lon 51 J1
Tottenhill Norfk 104 C1
Totteridge Gt Lon 69 H8
Totternhoe C Beds 68 C3
Tottington Bury 140 A5
Tottleworth Lancs 139 L2
Totton Hants 34 D8
Touchen End W & M 49 L4
Toulston N York 151 G7
Toulton Somset 30 B4
Toulvaddie Highld 264 D4
Tovil Kent 39 J3
Towan Cnwll 5 G5
Towan Cnwll 10 B7
Toward Ag & B 207 J5
Toward Quay Ag & B 207 J5
Towcester Nhants 84 D5
Towednack Cnwll 2 D3
Tower of London Gt Lon 51 J3
Towersey Oxon 67 H6
Towie Abers 244 A1
Tow Law Dur 168 E3
Town End Cambs 103 J4
Town End Cumb 156 E1
Town End Cumb 156 F6
Town End Cumb 166 E5
Townend W Duns 208 C4
Towngate Cumb 166 C1
Towngate Lincs 102 C1
Town Green Lancs 138 E6
Town Green Norfk 107 G1
Townhead Barns 141 J7
Town Head Cumb 156 F2
Townhead Cumb 164 E3
Townhead Cumb 166 E4
Townhead D & G 176 D1
Town Head N York 148 E4
Townhead of Greenlaw
   D & G 175 J2
Townhill Fife 210 F1
Town Kelloe Dur 169 K3
Townlake Devon 12 A7
Town Lane Wigan 139 K7
Town Littleworth E Susx 22 F4
Town of Lowton Wigan 139 J8
Town Row E Susx 38 E7
Towns End Hants 48 E7
Townsend Somset 30 E7
Townshend Cnwll 2 F4
Town Street Suffk 104 F6
Townwell S Glos 45 K1
Town Yetholm Border 202 C7
Towthorpe C York 151 K4
Towthorpe E R Yk 152 D3
Towton N York 151 G7
Towyn Conwy 127 K4
Toxteth Lpool 129 H2
Toynton All Saints Lincs 137 G7
Toynton Fen Side Lincs 137 G7
Toynton St Peter Lincs 137 G7
Toy's Hill Kent 38 D3

Trabboch E Ayrs 196 E6
Trabbochburn E Ayrs 196 F6
Traboe Cnwll 3 J6
Tracebridge Somset 29 K6
Tradespark Highld 264 D6
Trafford Park Traffd 140 B8
Trallong Powys 60 E1
Tranent E Loth 211 L4
Tranmere Wirral 129 H2
Trantelbeg Highld 278 F5
Trantlemore Highld 278 F5
Tranwell Nthumb 180 F2
Trap Carmth 59 J5
Traprain E Loth 212 D4
Trap's Green Warwks 82 D1
Trapshill W Berk 48 A6
Traquair Border 200 D6
Trash Green W Berk 49 G5
Trawden Lancs 148 F8
Trawscoed Cerdgn 77 J1
Trawsfynydd Gwynd 110 D4
Trealaw Rhondd 42 F3
Treales Lancs 138 F1
Trearddur Bay IoA 124 D4
Treator Cnwll 10 C7
Tre Aubrey V Glam 43 G7
Trebanog Rhondd 42 F4
Trebanos Neath 57 K4
Trebartha Cnwll 11 K7
Trebarwith Cnwll 10 E5
Trebeath Cnwll 11 J5
Trebetherick Cnwll 10 C7
Treborough Somset 29 H4
Trebudannon Cnwll 4 E3
Trebullett Cnwll 11 L7
Treburgett Cnwll 10 E6
Treburley Cnwll 11 L7
Treburrick Cnwll 10 B8
Trebyan Cnwll 5 J2
Trecastle Powys 60 C1
Trecogo Cnwll 11 K6
Trecott Devon 12 F3
Trecwn Pembks 74 F5
Trecynon Rhondd 60 F6
Tredaule Cnwll 11 J6
Tredavoe Cnwll 2 C5
Tredegar Blae G 61 J5
Tredethy Cnwll 10 F8
Tredington Gloucs 64 C1
Tredington Warwks 83 G6
Tredinnick Cnwll 5 H3
Tredinnick Cnwll 5 K2
Tredinnick Cnwll 5 M3
Tredinnick Cnwll 6 B3
Tredinnick Cnwll 10 C8
Tredomen Powys 61 H1
Tredrizzick Cnwll 10 D7
Tredunnock Mons 62 D8
Tredustan Powys 61 H1
Treen Cnwll 2 B6
Treen Cnwll 2 C3
Treesmill Cnwll 5 J4
Treeton Rothm 133 J2
Trefasser Pembks 74 E4
Trefdraeth IoA 125 G5
Trefecca Powys 61 J1
Trefechan Myr Td 61 G5
Trefeglwys Powys 93 L5
Trefenter Cerdgn 77 H2
Treffgarne Pembks 54 F2
Treffgarne Owen Pembks 74 E7
Treffynnon Pembks 74 D6
Trefil Blae G 61 H4
Trefilan Cerdgn 77 G4
Trefin Pembks 74 D5
Treflach Shrops 112 C6
Trefnannau Powys 112 C8
Trefnant Denbgs 128 C5
Trefonen Shrops 112 C6
Trefor Gwynd 108 F2
Trefor IoA 124 F4
Treforest Rhondd 43 G4
Trefrew Cnwll 10 F5
Trefriw Conwy 126 F3
Tregadillett Cnwll 11 K6
Tre-gagle Mons 63 G5
Tregaian IoA 125 H4
Tregare Mons 62 E5
Tregarne Cnwll 3 K6
Tregaron Cerdgn 77 J3
Tregarth Gwynd 126 B6
Tregaswith Cnwll 4 E4
Tregatta Cnwll 10 F5
Tregawne Cnwll 5 G2
Tregeare Cnwll 11 J5
Tregeiriog Wrexhm 112 B5
Tregele IoA 124 F1
Tregellist Cnwll 10 E7
Tregenna Cnwll 4 E6
Tregeseal Cnwll 2 B5

Tregew Cnwll 3 K4
Tre-Gibbon Rhondd 60 F6
Tregidden Cnwll 3 J6
Tregiskey Cnwll 5 G5
Treglemais Pembks 74 D6
Tregole Cnwll 11 H3
Tregolls Cnwll 3 J4
Tregonce Cnwll 10 C7
Tregonetha Cnwll 4 F2
Tregonning & Gwinear
   Mining District Cnwll 2 F5
Tregony Cnwll 4 F6
Tregoodwell Cnwll 11 G5
Tregorrick Cnwll 5 G4
Tregoss Cnwll 4 F3
Tregoyd Powys 79 H7
Tregrehan Mills Cnwll 5 H4
Tre-groes Cerdgn 76 D6
Tregullon Cnwll 5 H2
Tregunna Cnwll 10 D7
Tregunnon Cnwll 11 J6
Tregurrian Cnwll 4 D2
Tregynon Powys 94 D4
Tre-gynwr Carmth 58 D5
Trehafod Rhondd 43 G3
Trehan Cnwll 6 D3
Treharris Myr Td 43 H2
Treharrock Cnwll 10 E6
Trehemborne Cnwll 10 B7
Treherbert Carmth 77 G6
Treherbert Rhondd 42 E2
Trehunist Cnwll 6 C2
Trekenner Cnwll 11 L7
Treknow Cnwll 10 E5
Trelan Cnwll 3 J7
Trelash Cnwll 11 H4
Trelassick Cnwll 4 E5
Trelawne Cnwll 5 L4
Trelawnyd Flints 128 C4
Treleague Cnwll 3 K6
Treleaver Cnwll 3 K7
Trelech Carmth 58 A3
Trelech a'r Betws Carmth 58 B3
Treleddyd-fawr Pembks 74 B6
Trelew Cnwll 3 K4
Trelewis Myr Td 43 H2
Treligga Cnwll 10 E5
Trelights Cnwll 10 D5
Trelill Cnwll 10 E7
Trelinnoe Cnwll 11 K6
Trelion Cnwll 4 F4
Trelissick Cnwll 3 L3
Trellech Mons 63 G6
Trelleck Grange Mons 62 F6
Trelogan Flints 128 D4
Trelow Cnwll 4 F1
Trelowarren Cnwll 3 J6
Trelowia Cnwll 6 B3
Treluggan Cnwll 3 M3
Trelystan Powys 95 G3
Tremadog Gwynd 109 K3
Tremail Cnwll 11 H5
Tremain Cerdgn 75 M3
Tremaine Cnwll 11 J5
Tremar Cnwll 6 B1
Trematon Cnwll 6 D3
Trembraze Cnwll 6 B2
Tremeirchion Denbgs 128 C5
Tremethick Cross Cnwll 2 C5
Tremore Cnwll 5 G2
Tre-Mostyn Flints 128 D4
Trenance Cnwll 3 K6
Trenance Cnwll 4 D1
Trenance Cnwll 10 C8
Trenarren Cnwll 5 H5
Trench Wrekin 96 F1
Trench Green Oxon 49 G3
Trendeal Cnwll 4 E4
Trendrine Cnwll 2 D3
Treneague Cnwll 10 D8
Trenear Cnwll 3 H5
Treneglos Cnwll 11 H5
Trenerth Cnwll 2 F4
Trenewan Cnwll 5 K4
Trenewth Cnwll 10 F7
Trengune Cnwll 11 H4
Treninnick Cnwll 4 C3
Trenowah Cnwll 4 C3
Trenoweth Cnwll 3 J4
Trent Dorset 31 K7
Trentham C Stke 114 D3
Trentishoe Devon 28 A1
Trentlock Derbys 116 E5
Trent Port Lincs 135 G3
Trent Vale C Stke 114 D3
Trenwheal Cnwll 3 G4
Treoes V Glam 42 E6
Treorchy Rhondd 42 E2
Trequite Cnwll 10 E7
Tre'r-ddol Cerdgn 92 E5

Trerhyngyll V Glam 42 F6
Trerulefoot Cnwll 6 C3
Tresaith Cerdgn 76 A5
Tresawle IoS 4 E5
Tresco IoS 10 b2
Trescott Staffs 97 J4
Trescowe Cnwll 2 F5
Tresean Cnwll 4 C3
Tresham Gloucs 46 A1
Treshnish Isles Ag & B 225 H7
Tresillian Cnwll 4 E5
Tresinney Cnwll 10 F6
Treskinnick Cross Cnwll 11 H3
Tresmeer Cnwll 11 J5
Tresparrett Cnwll 11 G4
Tressait P & K 232 B3
Tresta Shet 281 d6
Tresta Shet 281 f3
Treswell Notts 134 F4
Treswithian Cnwll 3 G3
Tre Taliesin Cerdgn 92 E5
Trethevey Cnwll 10 F5
Trethewey Cnwll 2 B6
Trethomas Caerph 43 J4
Trethosa Cnwll 4 F4
Trethurgy Cnwll 5 H4
Tretio Pembks 74 C6
Tretire Herefs 63 G2
Tretower Powys 61 J3
Treuddyn Flints 128 F8
Trevadlock Cnwll 11 K6
Trevalga Cnwll 10 F4
Trevalyn Wrexhm 129 J8
Trevanger Cnwll 10 D7
Trevanson Cnwll 10 D8
Trevarrack Cnwll 2 D5
Trevarren Cnwll 4 E3
Trevarrian Cnwll 4 D2
Trevarrick Cnwll 5 G6
Trevarth Cnwll 3 J3
Trevaughan Carmth 55 L4
Tre-vaughan Carmth 58 D4
Treveal Cnwll 2 D3
Treveal Cnwll 4 C3
Treveighan Cnwll 10 F6
Trevellas Downs Cnwll 4 B4
Trevelmond Cnwll 5 L2
Trevemper Cnwll 4 D3
Treveor Cnwll 5 G6
Treverbyn Cnwll 4 E5
Treverbyn Cnwll 5 G3
Treverva Cnwll 3 J5
Trevescan Cnwll 2 B6
Trevethin Torfn 62 B6
Trevia Cnwll 10 F6
Trevigro Cnwll 6 C1
Trevilla Cnwll 3 L3
Trevilson Cnwll 4 D4
Treviscoe Cnwll 4 F4
Treviskey Cnwll 4 F6
Trevithick Cnwll 4 E2
Trevithick Cnwll 4 F6
Trevoll Cnwll 4 D3
Trevone Cnwll 10 B7
Trevor Wrexhm 112 C3
Trevorgans Cnwll 2 B6
Trevorrick Cnwll 10 C7
Trevose Cnwll 10 B7
Trew Cnwll 3 G5
Trewalder Cnwll 10 F6
Trewalkin Powys 61 J1
Trewarmett Cnwll 10 F5
Trewassa Cnwll 11 G5
Trewavas Cnwll 2 F5
Trewavas Mining District Cnwll 2 F5
Treween Cnwll 11 J6
Trewellard Cnwll 2 B4
Trewen Cnwll 11 J6
Trewennack Cnwll 3 H5
Trewent Pembks 55 G7
Trewern Powys 95 G1
Trewetha Cnwll 10 E6
Trewethern Cnwll 10 E7
Trewidland Cnwll 6 B3
Trewillis Cnwll 3 K7
Trewint Cnwll 6 B2
Trewint Cnwll 11 J6
Trewithian Cnwll 3 M4
Trewoodloe Cnwll 11 L8
Trewoon Cnwll 3 H7
Trewoon Cnwll 5 G4
Treworga Cnwll 4 E6
Treworgan Cnwll 4 D5
Treworlas Cnwll 4 E7
Treworld Cnwll 11 G4
Treworthal Cnwll 3 M3
Tre-wyn Mons 62 C3
Treyarnon Cnwll 10 B7
Treyford W Susx 20 D3
Trickett's Cross Dorset 17 L2

Triermain Cumb 178 E5
Triffleton Pembks 75 G7
Trillacott Cnwll 11 K4
Trimdon Dur 169 K4
Trimdon Colliery Dur 169 K3
Trimdon Grange Dur 169 K3
Trimdon Station Dur 169 K3
Trimingham Norfk 122 F4
Trimley Lower Street Suffk 91 G7
Trimley St Martin Suffk 91 G7
Trimley St Mary Suffk 91 G7
Trimpley Worcs 97 H7
Trimsaran Carmth 56 E4
Trims Green Herts 70 C4
Trimstone Devon 27 J2
Trinafour P & K 231 K3
Trinant Caerph 61 K7
Tring Herts 68 A5
Tringford Herts 67 M4
Tring Wharf Herts 68 A4
Trinity Angus 234 F3
Trinity Jersey 9 d2
Trinity Gask P & K 221 G3
Triscombe Somset 29 L4
Trislaig Highld 239 H8
Trispen Cnwll 4 D5
Tritlington Nthumb 191 J7
Troan Cnwll 4 E3
Trochry P & K 232 E7
Troedrhiwfuwch Caerph 61 H6
Troedyraur Cerdgn 76 B6
Troedyrhiw Myr Td 61 G6
Trofarth Conwy 127 G5
Trois Bois Jersey 9 c2
Troon Cnwll 3 G3
Troon S Ayrs 196 C5
Trossachs Stirlg 219 H5
Trossachs Pier Stirlg 219 H5
Troston Suffk 89 H1
Troswell Cnwll 11 J4
Trotshill Worcs 81 K4
Trottiscliffe Kent 52 D7
Trotton W Susx 36 B6
Troughend Nthumb 190 B7
Trough Gate Lancs 140 D3
Troutbeck Cumb 156 F2
Troutbeck Cumb 165 L5
Troutbeck Bridge Cumb 156 F2
Troway Derbys 133 H4
Trowbridge Wilts 46 B7
Trowell Notts 116 E3
Trowell Services Notts 116 E3
Trowle Common Wilts 46 B7
Trowley Bottom Herts 68 D4
Trowse Newton Norfk 106 E2
Troy Leeds 150 C8
Trudoxhill Somset 32 C2
Trull Somset 30 B6
Trumfleet Donc 142 F5
Trumpan Highld 258 C4
Trumpet Herefs 80 C7
Trumpington Cambs 87 J4
Trumpsgreen Surrey 50 C5
Trunch Norfk 122 F4
Trunnah Lancs 147 G7
Truro Cnwll 4 D6
Truscott Cnwll 11 K5
Trusham Devon 13 K6
Trusley Derbys 115 L4
Trusthorpe Lincs 137 K3
Trysull Staffs 97 J4
Tubney Oxon 66 B7
Tuckenhay Devon 8 B4
Tuckhill Shrops 97 H5
Tuckingmill Cnwll 3 G3
Tuckingmill Cnwll 32 H5
Tuckton BCP 18 A5
Tucoyse Cnwll 4 F5
Tuddenham Suffk 88 E1
Tuddenham St Martin Suffk 90 E5
Tudeley Kent 38 C4
Tudhoe Dur 169 H3
Tudorville Herefs 63 H3
Tudweiliog Gwynd 108 D4
Tuesley Surrey 36 E3
Tuffley Gloucs 64 B4
Tufton Hants 34 F2
Tufton Pembks 75 H6
Tugby Leics 101 G3
Tugford Shrops 96 D6
Tughall Nthumb 203 K7
Tullibody Clacks 220 E8
Tullich Abers 243 L4
Tullich Highld 251 H6
Tullich Highld 264 D4
Tulliemet P & K 232 E7
Tulloch Abers 256 E5
Tullochgorm Ag & B 216 F8
Tulloch Station Highld 240 B7
Tullymurdoch P & K 233 J5

Tullynessle Abers 255 L7
Tulse Hill Gt Lon 51 J4
Tumble Carmth 58 F6
Tumbler's Green Essex 71 K2
Tumby Lincs 136 D7
Tumby Woodside Lincs 136 E8
Tummel Bridge P & K 231 L4
Tunbridge Wells Kent 38 F5
Tundergarth D & G 177 G3
Tunga W Isls 282 g3
Tungate Norfk 122 F5
Tunley BaNES 45 K7
Tunstall C Stke 114 D1
Tunstall E R Yk 145 J2
Tunstall Kent 40 A3
Tunstall Lancs 157 K8
Tunstall N York 160 B3
Tunstall Norfk 107 J2
Tunstall Staffs 114 B6
Tunstall Suffk 91 H4
Tunstall Sundld 181 J8
Tunstead Derbys 132 B5
Tunstead Norfk 122 F7
Tunstead Milton Derbys 131 K4
Tunworth Hants 35 K1
Tupsley Herefs 80 C7
Turgis Green Hants 49 G7
Turkdean Gloucs 65 G4
Tur Langton Leics 100 F4
Turleigh Wilts 46 A6
Turleygreen Shrops 97 H6
Turn Lancs 140 B4
Turnastone Herefs 79 L7
Turnberry S Ayrs 182 F2
Turnchapel C Plym 6 F4
Turnditch Derbys 116 A2
Turner Green Lancs 139 J2
Turner's Green E Susx 23 L3
Turner's Green Warwks 82 E2
Turners Hill W Susx 38 A6
Turners Puddle Dorset 16 F4
Turnford Herts 69 K6
Turnhouse C Edin 211 G4
Turnworth Dorset 16 F1
Turriff Abers 268 C6
Turton Bottoms Bl w D 139 L4
Turves Cambs 103 G4
Turvey Bed 85 J5
Turville Bucks 49 J1
Turville Heath Bucks 49 H1
Turweston Bucks 84 B7
Tushielaw Inn Border 187 L3
Tutbury Staffs 115 L6
Tutnall Worcs 82 A1
Tutshill Gloucs 63 G8
Tuttington Norfk 122 E6
Tutts Clump W Berk 48 E5
Tutwell Cnwll 11 M7
Tuxford Notts 134 E5
Twatt Ork 275 b3
Twatt Shet 281 d6
Twechar E Duns 209 J4
Tweedbank Border 201 H6
Tweedmouth Nthumb 202 F3
Tweedsmuir Border 187 G1
Twelveheads Cnwll 4 B6
Twelve Oaks E Susx 24 C3
Twemlow Green Ches E 130 F6
Twenty Lincs 118 F7
Twerton BaNES 45 L6
Twickenham Gt Lon 50 F4
Twigworth Gloucs 64 B3
Twineham W Susx 22 C3
Twineham Green W Susx 22 C3
Twinhoe BaNES 45 L7
Twinstead Essex 89 H7
Twitchen Devon 28 D5
Twitchen Shrops 95 J7
Twitham Kent 41 H4
Two Bridges Devon 12 E7
Two Dales Derbys 132 E7
Two Gates Staffs 99 G3
Two Mile Ash W Susx 37 H5
Two Mile Oak Cross Devon 8 C1
Two Pots Devon 27 J2
Two Waters Herts 68 D6
Twycross Leics 99 J2
Twyford Bucks 67 G2
Twyford Hants 35 G6
Twyford Leics 100 F2
Twyford Lincs 118 B6
Twyford Norfk 121 M6
Twyford Wokham 49 J4
Twyford Common Herefs 80 C8
Twyn-carno Caerph 61 H5
Twynholm D & G 175 G4
Twyning Gloucs 81 K7
Twynllanan Carmth 59 L4
Twyn-yr-Odyn V Glam 43 H7
Twyn-y-Sheriff Mons 62 E6

Twywell Nhants 101 L7
Tyberton Herefs 79 M7
Tyburn Birm 98 E5
Tycroes Carmth 57 H3
Ty Croes IoA 124 F5
Tycrwyn Powys 111 L7
Tydd Gote Lincs 120 A7
Tydd St Giles Cambs 119 M8
Tydd St Mary Lincs 119 M7
Tye Hants 20 B6
Tye Green Essex 70 D2
Tye Green Essex 71 J3
Tye Green Essex 88 B8
Tyersal C Brad 141 J1
Tyldesley Wigan 139 K7
Tyler Hill Kent 40 F3
Tylers Green Bucks 67 L8
Tyler's Green Essex 70 D6
Tylers Green Surrey 51 K8
Tylorstown Rhondd 42 F3
Tylwch Powys 93 L7
Ty-nant Conwy 111 L3
Ty-nant Gwynd 111 H6
Tyncelyn Cerdgn 77 H3
Tyndrum Stirlg 218 E1
Ty'n-dwr Denbgs 112 C3
Tyneham Dorset 17 G6
Tynemouth N Tyne 181 J5
Tyne Tunnel S Tyne 181 J5
Tynewydd Rhondd 60 E7
Tyninghame E Loth 212 D3
Tynron D & G 185 K4
Ty'n-y-bryn Rhondd 42 F4
Ty'n-y-coedcae Caerph 43 K4
Tynygongl IoA 125 J3
Tynygraig Cerdgn 77 J1
Ty'n-y-Groes Conwy 126 F5
Tyn-y-nant Rhondd 43 G4
Tyrie Abers 269 G4
Tyringham M Keyn 85 G6
Tyseley Birm 98 E6
Tythegston Brdgnd 42 C6
Tytherington Ches E 131 H4
Tytherington S Glos 45 K1
Tytherington Somset 32 C2
Tytherington Wilts 32 F3
Tytherleigh Devon 15 H2
Tytherton Lucas Wilts 46 D4
Tyttenhanger Herts 68 F6
Tywardreath Cnwll 5 J4
Tywardreath Highway Cnwll 5 J4
Tywyn Conwy 126 F4
Tywyn Gwynd 92 C3

U

Ubbeston Green Suffk 91 H1
Ubley BaNES 45 G7
Uckerby N York 160 C2
Uckfield E Susx 23 H3
Uckinghall Worcs 81 K7
Uckington Gloucs 64 C2
Uckington Shrops 96 D2
Uddingston S Lans 209 J6
Uddington S Lans 198 E6
Udimore E Susx 24 F3
Udny Green Abers 256 F6
Udny Station Abers 257 G6
Uffcott Wilts 47 H3
Uffculme Devon 29 K8
Uffington Lincs 102 B2
Uffington Oxon 47 L1
Uffington Shrops 96 C1
Ufford C Pete 102 B3
Ufford Suffk 91 G5
Ufton Warwks 83 J3
Ufton Nervet W Berk 48 F5
Ugadale Ag & B 194 B5
Ugborough Devon 7 K4
Uggeshall Suffk 107 J7
Ugglebarnby N York 162 F1
Ughill Sheff 132 E2
Ugley Essex 70 D2
Ugley Green Essex 70 D2
Ugthorpe N York 171 J8
Uibhist A Deas W Isls 283 c10
Uibhist A Tuath W Isls 283 b8
Uig Ag & B 224 F4
Uig Highld 258 B6
Uig Highld 258 F4
Uig W Isls 282 d3
Uigshader Highld 259 G7
Uisken Ag & B 226 D8
Ulbster Highld 280 D7
Ulcat Row Cumb 165 L6
Ulceby Lincs 137 H5
Ulceby N Linc 144 E5
Ulceby Skitter N Linc 144 E5

Ulcombe Kent 39 L4
Uldale Cumb 165 H3
Uley Gloucs 63 M7
Ulgham Nthumb 191 J7
Ullapool Highld 261 J1
Ullenhall Warwks 82 D2
Ullenwood Gloucs 64 D4
Ulleskelf N York 151 H7
Ullesthorpe Leics 100 B6
Ulley Rothm 133 J2
Ullingswick Herefs 80 E5
Ullock Cumb 164 E6
Ullswater Cumb 166 A6
Ulnes Walton Lancs 139 G4
Ulpha Cumb 156 B4
Ulpha Cumb 157 G6
Ulrome E R Yk 153 J4
Ulsta Shet 281 e4
Ulting Wick Essex 71 K5
Ulva Ag & B 226 D4
Ulverley Green Solhll 98 E7
Ulverston Cumb 156 C7
Ulwell Dorset 17 K6
Ulzieside D & G 185 J1
Umberleigh Devon 27 L6
Unapool Highld 271 H2
Underbarrow Cumb 157 G4
Under Burnmouth Border 178 B2
Undercliffe C Brad 141 J1
Underdale Shrops 96 B1
Underling Green Kent 39 J4
Underriver Kent 38 E3
Underwood Newpt 44 D1
Underwood Notts 116 D2
Undley Suffk 104 D7
Undy Mons 44 E2
Union Mills IoM 154 e6
Union Street E Susx 39 H7
Unst Shet 281 f2
Unstone Derbys 133 G4
Unstone Green Derbys 133 G4
Unthank Cumb 165 L1
Unthank Cumb 166 B3
Unthank Cumb 166 E3
Unthank Derbys 132 F4
Unthank Nthumb 202 F3
Upavon Wilts 47 H7
Up Cerne Dorset 16 C2
Upchurch Kent 53 H5
Upcott Devon 28 D5
Upcott Herefs 79 K5
Upend Cambs 88 D3
Up Exe Devon 13 L2
Upgate Norfk 122 C7
Upgate Street Norfk 106 B5
Upgate Street Norfk 106 F5
Uphall Dorset 16 A2
Uphall W Loth 210 E5
Upham Devon 13 K1
Upham Hants 35 H6
Uphampton Herefs 79 M3
Uphampton Worcs 81 J2
Uphill N Som 44 C7
Up Holland Lancs 139 G6
Uplawmoor E Rens 208 D8
Upleadon Gloucs 63 L2
Upleatham R & Cl 170 E6
Uplees Kent 40 C2
Uploders Dorset 15 L4
Uplowman Devon 29 J7
Uplyme Devon 15 H4
Up Marden W Susx 20 C4
Upminster Gt Lon 52 C2
Up Mudford Somset 31 J7
Up Nately Hants 49 G8
Upottery Devon 14 E1
Upper Affcot Shrops 95 K6
Upper Arley Worcs 97 H7
Upper Arncott Oxon 66 F4
Upper Astrop Nhants 83 L7
Upper Badcall Highld 276 B7
Upper Basildon W Berk 48 F4
Upper Batley Kirk 141 K3
Upper Beeding W Susx 22 B5
Upper Benefield Nhants 101 L5
Upper Bentley Worcs 82 B2
Upper Bighouse Highld 278 F5
Upper Birchwood Derbys 133 J4
Upper Boat Rhondd 43 H4
Upper Boddington Nhants 83 L5
Upper Borth Cerdgn 92 D5
Upper Brailes Warwks 83 G7
Upper Breinton Herefs 80 B7
Upper Broadheath Worcs 81 J4
Upper Broughton Notts 117 J6
Upper Bucklebury W Berk 48 D5
Upper Burgate Hants 33 K7
Upper Bush Medway 52 E5
Upperby Cumb 177 L8
Upper Caldecote C Beds 86 D6

Upper Canada N Som 44 D7
Upper Canterton Hants 18 D1
Upper Catesby Nhants 83 M3
Upper Catshill Worcs 98 B8
Upper Chapel Powys 78 D7
Upper Cheddon Somset 30 C5
Upper Chicksgrove Wilts 33 G5
Upper Chute Wilts 47 L8
Upper Clapton Gt Lon 51 K2
Upper Clatford Hants 34 D2
Upper Coberley Gloucs 64 E4
Upper Cotton Staffs 115 G2
Upper Cound Shrops 96 C2
Upper Cudworth Barns 142 B6
Upper Cumberworth Kirk 141 K6
Upper Dallachy Moray 267 G4
Upper Deal Kent 41 K5
Upper Dean Bed 85 L2
Upper Denby Kirk 141 K6
Upper Denton Cumb 178 E5
Upper Dicker E Susx 23 J5
Upper Dinchope Shrops 95 L6
Upper Dounreay Highld 279 H3
Upper Dovercourt Essex 73 K1
Upper Drumbane Stirlg 219 L6
Upper Dunsforth N York 150 F3
Upper Eashing Surrey 36 E2
Upper Eathie Highld 263 K7
Upper Egleton Herefs 80 E6
Upper Elkstone Staffs 131 L7
Upper Ellastone Staffs 115 J3
Upper End Derbys 132 B4
Upper Enham Hants 34 L1
Upper Farmcote Shrops 97 H5
Upper Farringdon Hants 35 L4
Upper Framilode Gloucs 63 L5
Upper Froyle Hants 35 M2
Upperglen Highld 258 E6
Upper Godney Somset 31 H2
Upper Gravenhurst C Beds 86 C8
Upper Green Mons 62 D3
Upper Green Suffk 88 E2
Upper Green W Berk 48 A6
Upper Grove Common Herefs 63 H2
Upper Hackney Derbys 132 F7
Upper Hale Surrey 36 B1
Upper Halliford Surrey 50 E5
Upper Halling Medway 52 E6
Upper Hambleton Rutlnd 101 K2
Upper Harbledown Kent 40 F4
Upper Hardres Court Kent 40 F5
Upper Hardwick Herefs 79 M4
Upper Hartfield E Susx 38 C6
Upper Hartshay Derbys 116 C2
Upper Hatherley Gloucs 64 D3
Upper Hatton Staffs 114 C4
Upper Haugh Rothm 142 C8
Upper Hayton Shrops 96 C7
Upper Heaton Kirk 141 J4
Upper Helmsley N York 151 L4
Upper Hergest Herefs 79 J4
Upper Heyford Nhants 84 C3
Upper Heyford Oxon 66 D2
Upper Hill Herefs 80 B4
Upper Hockenden Kent 52 B5
Upper Hopton Kirk 141 K4
Upper Howsell Worcs 81 H5
Upper Hulme Staffs 131 K7
Upper Ifold Surrey 36 L4
Upper Inglesham Swindn 65 J7
Upper Kilcott Gloucs 46 A1
Upper Killay Swans 57 G6
Upper Kinchrackine Ag & B 217 J2
Upper Knockando Moray 254 D3
Upper Lambourn W Berk 47 L3
Upper Landywood Staffs 98 L2
Upper Langford N Som 44 F7
Upper Langwith Derbys 133 K5
Upper Largo Fife 223 G6
Upper Layham Suffk 90 B7
Upper Leigh Staffs 115 G4
Upper Littleton N Som 45 H6
Upper Lochton Abers 244 F4
Upper Longdon Staffs 115 H8
Upper Ludstone Shrops 97 H4
Upper Lybster Highld 275 H1
Upper Lydbrook Gloucs 63 J4
Upper Lyde Herefs 80 C6
Upper Lye Herefs 79 M2
Upper Maes-coed Herefs 79 L8
Upper Marham Norfk 104 E2
Upper Midhope Sheff 141 K7
Uppermill Oldham 140 F6
Upper Milton Worcs 81 J1
Upper Minety Wilts 46 E1
Upper Moor Worcs 81 M5
Upper Moor Side Leeds 141 K2
Upper Mulben Moray 267 G6
Upper Netchwood Shrops 96 E5
Upper Nobut Staffs 115 G4

Upper Norwood W Susx 20 F3
Upper Oddington Gloucs 65 J2
Upper Padley Derbys 132 E4
Upper Pennington Hants 18 D4
Upper Pollicott Bucks 67 H4
Upper Poppleton C York 151 J5
Upper Quinton Warwks 82 E6
Upper Ratley Hants 34 D6
Upper Rissington Gloucs 65 J3
Upper Rochford Worcs 80 E2
Upper Ruscoe D & G 174 E3
Upper Sapey Herefs 80 F3
Upper Saxondale Notts 117 H4
Upper Seagry Wilts 46 D3
Upper Shelton C Beds 85 K6
Upper Sheringham Norfk 122 C3
Upper Skelmorlie N Ayrs 207 K5
Upper Slaughter Gloucs 65 H3
Upper Soudley Gloucs 63 K5
Upper Spond Herefs 79 K4
Upper Standen Kent 41 H7
Upper Staploe Bed 86 C3
Upper Stoke Norfk 106 E3
Upper Stondon C Beds 86 C8
Upper Stowe Nhants 84 C4
Upper Street Hants 33 K7
Upper Street Norfk 106 D7
Upper Street Norfk 123 G7
Upper Street Norfk 123 G8
Upper Street Suffk 88 F5
Upper Street Suffk 90 C5
Upper Street Suffk 90 D8
Upper Strensham Worcs 81 K7
Upper Sundon C Beds 68 D2
Upper Swell Gloucs 65 H2
Upper Tankersley Barns 142 A7
Upper Tean Staffs 115 G2
Upperthong Kirk 141 H6
Upperthorpe Derbys 133 J4
Upperthorpe N Linc 143 J7
Upper Threapwood Ches W 113 G2
Upperton W Susx 36 E6
Upper Town Derbys 115 L1
Uppertown Derbys 132 F6
Upper Town Dur 168 D2
Upper Town Herefs 80 D5
Uppertown Highld 280 D1
Upper Town N Som 45 G6
Upper Town Suffk 89 J2
Upper Tumble Carmth 59 G6
Upper Tysoe Warwks 83 H6
Upper Ufford Suffk 91 G4
Upperup Gloucs 64 F7
Upper Upham Wilts 47 J3
Upper Upnor Medway 53 G5
Upper Victoria Angus 234 E8
Upper Vobster Somset 32 B1
Upper Wardington Oxon 83 L6
Upper Weald M Keyn 84 F7
Upper Weedon Nhants 84 B3
Upper Welland Worcs 81 H7
Upper Wellingham E Susx 23 G4
Upper Weston BaNES 45 L5
Upper Weybread Suffk 106 E7
Upper Wick Worcs 81 J5
Upper Wield Hants 35 K3
Upper Winchendon Bucks 67 H4
Upperwood Derbys 132 F8
Upper Woodford Wilts 33 K3
Upper Woolhampton W Berk 48 E5
Upper Wootton Hants 48 E7
Upper Wraxall Wilts 46 A4
Upper Wyche Worcs 81 H6
Uppincott Devon 13 L2
Uppingham Rutlnd 101 J3
Uppington Dorset 17 K2
Uppington Shrops 96 D2
Upsall N York 161 G5
Upsettlington Border 202 D4
Upshire Essex 69 L7
Up Somborne Hants 34 E4
Upstreet Kent 41 H3
Up Sydling Dorset 16 B2
Upthorpe Suffk 89 K1
Upton Bucks 67 J5
Upton C Pete 102 C3
Upton Cambs 102 D7
Upton Ches W 129 J6
Upton Cnwll 11 H2
Upton Cnwll 11 K8
Upton Cumb 165 K3
Upton Devon 7 K6
Upton Devon 14 C2
Upton Dorset 16 E6
Upton Dorset 17 J4
Upton E R Yk 153 J4
Upton Halton 129 L2
Upton Hants 34 E7
Upton Hants 47 M7
Upton Leics 99 K3

Upton Lincs 135 H2
Upton Nhants 84 D3
Upton Norfk 107 H1
Upton Notts 117 J1
Upton Notts 134 E4
Upton Oxon 48 D2
Upton Oxon 65 K4
Upton Pembks 55 G6
Upton R & Cl 171 G6
Upton Slough 50 B3
Upton Somset 29 H5
Upton Somset 31 G5
Upton Wakefd 142 D5
Upton Warwks 82 D4
Upton Wilts 32 E1
Upton Wirral 129 G2
Upton Bishop Herefs 63 K2
Upton Cheyney S Glos 45 K5
Upton Cressett Shrops 96 E5
Upton Crews Herefs 63 J2
Upton Cross Cnwll 11 K8
Upton End C Beds 86 C8
Upton Grey Hants 35 L1
Upton Heath Ches W 129 J5
Upton Hellions Devon 13 K2
Upton Lovell Wilts 32 F3
Upton Magna Shrops 96 C1
Upton Noble Somset 32 B3
Upton Pyne Devon 13 L3
Upton St Leonards Gloucs 64 B4
Upton Scudamore Wilts 32 E1
Upton Snodsbury Worcs 81 L4
Upton Towans Cnwll 2 D7
Upton-upon-Severn Worcs 81 K7
Upton Warren Worcs 81 L2
Upwaltham W Susx 20 F4
Upware Cambs 87 L1
Upwell Norfk 103 K3
Upwey Dorset 16 C5
Upwick Green Herts 70 C2
Upwood Cambs 102 E6
Urchfont Wilts 46 F7
Urdimarsh Herefs 80 C5
Ure Bank N York 150 D1
Urlay Nook S on T 169 L7
Urmston Traffd 130 E1
Urpeth Dur 181 G7
Urquhart Moray 266 F4
Urra N York 161 J2
Urray Highld 250 E1
Ury Abers 245 J6
Uryside Abers 256 D7
Usan Angus 235 H4
Ushaw Moor Dur 169 G2
Usk Mons 62 D7
Usselby Lincs 136 A1
Usworth Sundld 181 H7
Utkinton Ches W 130 A6
Utley C Brad 149 J7
Uton Devon 13 J3
Utterby Lincs 136 F1
Uttoxeter Staffs 115 H5
Uwchmynydd Gwynd 108 B6
Uxbridge Gt Lon 50 D2
Uyeasound Shet 281 f2
Uzmaston Pembks 54 F4

V

Vale Guern 9 k2
Valley IoA 124 E4
Valley End Surrey 50 B6
Valley Truckle Cnwll 10 F6
Valtos Highld 259 J4
Valtos W Isls 282 e3
Vange Essex 52 F2
Varteg Torfn 61 L6
Vatsetter Shet 281 e3
Vatten Highld 258 D7
Vaynor Myr Td 61 G5
Vazon Bay Guern 9 i2
Veensgarth Shet 281 e6
Velindre Powys 79 H7
Vellow Somset 29 K3
Velly Devon 26 E6
Venngreen Devon 26 F8
Vennington Shrops 95 H2
Venn Ottery Devon 14 C4
Venny Tedburn Devon 13 J3
Venterdon Cnwll 11 L7
Ventnor IoW 19 J8
Venton Devon 7 H3
Vernham Dean Hants 47 M7
Vernham Street Hants 47 M7
Vernolds Common Shrops 95 L7
Verwood Dorset 17 L1
Veryan Cnwll 4 E7
Veryan Green Cnwll 4 F6

Vicarage Devon ...14 E5
Vickerstown Cumb ...146 C2
Victoria Barns ...141 J6
Victoria Blae G ...61 J5
Victoria Cnwll ...5 G3
Vidlin Shet ...281 e5
Viewfield Moray ...266 F3
Viewpark N Lans ...209 J6
Vigo Kent ...52 D6
Village de Putron Guern ...9 k3
Ville la Bas Jersey ...9 a1
Villiaze Guern ...9 i3
Vinehall Street E Susx ...24 D3
Vines Cross E Susx ...23 K4
Virginia Water Surrey ...50 C5
Virginstow Devon ...11 M4
Vobster Somset ...32 B1
Voe Shet ...281 d5
Vowchurch Herefs ...79 L7
Vulcan Village St Hel ...130 B1

W

Waberthwaite Cumb ...155 K4
Wackerfield Dur ...168 F6
Wacton Norfk ...106 D5
Wadborough Worcs ...81 K5
Waddesdon Bucks ...67 H4
Waddeton Devon ...8 C3
Waddicar Sefton ...138 E7
Waddingham Lincs ...144 B8
Waddington Lancs ...148 C7
Waddington Lincs ...135 K6
Waddon Devon ...13 K6
Waddon Dorset ...16 B5
Waddon Gt Lon ...51 J6
Wadebridge Cnwll ...10 D8
Wadeford Somset ...30 D8
Wadenhoe Nhants ...101 M6
Wadesmill Herts ...69 K4
Wadhurst E Susx ...39 G7
Wadshelf Derbys ...132 F5
Wadswick Wilts ...46 B5
Wadworth Donc ...142 F8
Waen Denbgs ...127 K7
Waen Denbgs ...128 D6
Waen Powys ...112 C7
Waen Fach Powys ...112 B8
Waen-pentir Gwynd ...125 K6
Waen-wen Gwynd ...125 K6
Wagbeach Shrops ...95 J3
Wainfelin Torfn ...62 B6
Wainfleet All Saints Lincs ...137 J7
Wainfleet Bank Lincs ...137 J7
Wainfleet St Mary Lincs ...137 J8
Wainford Norfk ...107 G5
Wainhouse Corner Cnwll ...11 H3
Wainscott Medway ...52 F5
Wain's Hill N Som ...44 E5
Wainstalls Calder ...141 G2
Waitby Cumb ...158 C1
Waithe Lincs ...145 H7
Wakefield Wakefd ...142 A4
Wake Green Birm ...98 E6
Wakerley Nhants ...101 L3
Wakes Colne Essex ...72 C2
Walberswick Suffk ...107 K8
Walberton W Susx ...21 G5
Walbottle N u Ty ...180 E5
Walbutt D & G ...175 J1
Walby Cumb ...178 B6
Walcombe Somset ...31 J2
Walcot Lincs ...118 E4
Walcot N Linc ...143 M3
Walcot Shrops ...95 J6
Walcot Shrops ...96 D1
Walcot Swindn ...47 H2
Walcote Leics ...100 C6
Walcote Warwks ...82 D4
Walcot Green Norfk ...106 C7
Walcott Lincs ...136 B8
Walcott Norfk ...123 G5
Walden N York ...159 H6
Walden Head N York ...159 H6
Walden Stubbs N York ...142 E4
Walderslade Medway ...53 G6
Walderton W Susx ...20 C5
Walditch Dorset ...15 L4
Waldley Derbys ...115 J4
Waldridge Dur ...169 H1
Waldringfield Suffk ...91 G6
Waldron E Susx ...23 J3
Wales Rothm ...133 J3
Wales Somset ...31 K6
Walesby Lincs ...136 B1
Walesby Notts ...134 D5
Walford Herefs ...63 H3
Walford Herefs ...79 M1

Walford Shrops ...113 G7
Walford Staffs ...114 C5
Walford Heath Shrops ...113 G7
Walgherton Ches E ...113 M2
Walgrave Nhants ...84 F1
Walhampton Hants ...18 E4
Walkden Salfd ...139 L7
Walker N u Ty ...181 H6
Walkerburn Border ...200 D5
Walker Fold Lancs ...148 B7
Walkeringham Notts ...134 F1
Walkerith Lincs ...134 F1
Walkern Herts ...69 H2
Walker's Green Herefs ...80 C5
Walker's Heath Birm ...98 D7
Walkerton Fife ...222 C7
Walkford BCP ...18 C5
Walkhampton Devon ...7 G1
Walkington E R Yk ...152 F8
Walkley Sheff ...133 G2
Walk Mill Lancs ...140 C2
Walkwood Worcs ...82 B2
Wall Nthumb ...179 L5
Wall Staffs ...98 E2
Wallacetown S Ayrs ...183 H4
Wallacetown S Ayrs ...196 C6
Wallands Park E Susx ...22 F5
Wallasey Wirral ...129 G1
Wallasey (Kingsway) Tunnel
   Wirral ...129 H2
Wall End Cumb ...156 B6
Wall End Herefs ...80 B4
Wallend Medway ...53 J4
Waller's Green Herefs ...80 F7
Wallhead Cumb ...178 B6
Wall Heath Dudley ...97 K5
Wall Houses Nthumb ...180 C5
Wallingford Oxon ...48 F1
Wallington Gt Lon ...51 H6
Wallington Hants ...19 K2
Wallington Herts ...86 F8
Wallington Heath Wsall ...98 C3
Wallis Pembks ...75 G7
Wallisdown BCP ...17 L4
Walliswood Surrey ...37 H3
Walls Shet ...281 c6
Wallsend N Tyne ...181 H5
Wallthwaite Cumb ...165 K5
Wall under Haywood Shrops ...96 C5
Wallyford E Loth ...211 L4
Walmer Kent ...41 L5
Walmer Bridge Lancs ...138 F3
Walmersley Bury ...140 B5
Walmestone Kent ...41 H3
Walmley Birm ...98 F5
Walmley Ash Birm ...98 F5
Walmsgate Lincs ...137 G4
Walney Cumb ...146 C2
Walpole Somset ...30 D3
Walpole Suffk ...107 H8
Walpole Cross Keys Norfk ...120 B7
Walpole Highway Norfk ...120 B8
Walpole St Andrew Norfk ...120 B8
Walpole St Peter Norfk ...120 B8
Walrow Somset ...30 E2
Walsall Wsall ...98 C4
Walsall Wood Wsall ...98 D3
Walsden Calder ...140 D3
Walsgrave on Sowe Covtry ...99 K7
Walsham le Willows Suffk ...89 K1
Walshaw Bury ...140 A5
Walshford N York ...150 F5
Walsoken Norfk ...103 K1
Walston S Lans ...199 H4
Walsworth Herts ...69 G1
Walter's Ash Bucks ...67 K7
Walters Green Kent ...38 D5
Walterston V Glam ...43 G7
Walterstone Herefs ...62 D2
Waltham Kent ...40 E5
Waltham NE Lin ...145 H7
Waltham Abbey Essex ...69 K7
Waltham Chase Hants ...35 H7
Waltham Cross Herts ...69 K7
Waltham on the Wolds Leics ...117 L6
Waltham St Lawrence W & M ...49 K4
Waltham's Cross Essex ...71 G1
Walthamstow Gt Lon ...51 K1
Walton C Pete ...102 D3
Walton Cumb ...178 C6
Walton Derbys ...133 G6
Walton Leeds ...150 F6
Walton Leics ...100 D6
Walton M Keyn ...85 H7
Walton Powys ...79 J3
Walton Somset ...95 L7
Walton Somset ...31 G4
Walton Staffs ...114 D5
Walton Staffs ...114 D6
Walton Suffk ...91 G8

Walton W Susx ...20 D6
Walton Wakefd ...142 A4
Walton Warwks ...83 G4
Walton Wrekin ...113 K7
Walton Cardiff Gloucs ...64 C1
Walton East Pembks ...55 H2
Walton Elm Dorset ...32 C7
Walton Grounds Nhants ...83 L8
Walton Highway Norfk ...103 K1
Walton-in-Gordano N Som ...44 E4
Walton-le-Dale Lancs ...139 H2
Walton-on-Thames Surrey ...50 E5
Walton-on-the-Hill Staffs ...114 F7
Walton-on-the-Hill Surrey ...51 G7
Walton-on-the-Naze Essex ...73 K3
Walton on the Wolds Leics ...117 G7
Walton-on-Trent Derbys ...115 L7
Walton Park N Som ...44 E4
Walton West Pembks ...54 D4
Walwen Flints ...128 D4
Walwen Flints ...128 E4
Walwen Flints ...128 E5
Walwick Nthumb ...179 L5
Walworth Darltn ...169 G7
Walworth Gt Lon ...51 J3
Walworth Gate Darltn ...169 G6
Walwyn's Castle Pembks ...54 E4
Wambrook Somset ...15 G1
Wampool Cumb ...177 H7
Wanborough Surrey ...36 D1
Wanborough Swindn ...47 J2
Wandon End Herts ...68 E3
Wandsworth Gt Lon ...51 H4
Wangford Suffk ...107 J7
Wanlip Leics ...100 D1
Wanlockhead D & G ...186 C4
Wannock E Susx ...23 K6
Wansford C Pete ...102 B3
Wansford E R Yk ...153 G4
Wanshurst Green Kent ...39 J4
Wanstead Gt Lon ...51 L1
Wanstrow Somset ...32 B3
Wanswell Gloucs ...63 K6
Wantage Oxon ...48 B1
Wants Green Worcs ...81 H4
Wapley S Glos ...45 L3
Wappenbury Warwks ...83 J2
Wappenham Nhants ...84 C6
Warbleton E Susx ...23 K4
Warborough Oxon ...66 F8
Warboys Cambs ...102 F7
Warbreck Bpool ...146 F8
Warbstow Cnwll ...11 H4
Warburton Traffd ...130 D2
Warcop Cumb ...167 H7
Warden Kent ...53 M5
Warden Nthumb ...179 L5
Ward End Birm ...98 E5
Warden Street C Beds ...86 C6
Ward Green Suffk ...90 B2
Ward Green Cross Lancs ...148 A8
Wardhedges C Beds ...85 L8
Wardington Oxon ...83 L6
Wardle Ches E ...130 B8
Wardle Rochdl ...140 D4
Wardley Gatesd ...181 H6
Wardley Rutlnd ...101 H3
Wardley Salfd ...140 A7
Wardlow Derbys ...132 D5
Wardsend Ches E ...131 J3
Wardy Hill Cambs ...103 K7
Ware Herts ...69 K4
Wareham Dorset ...17 H5
Warehorne Kent ...25 J1
Warenford Nthumb ...203 J7
Waren Mill Nthumb ...203 J6
Warenton Nthumb ...203 H7
Wareside Herts ...69 K4
Waresley Cambs ...86 E4
Waresley Worcs ...81 J2
Ware Street Kent ...39 K2
Warfield Br For ...49 L4
Warfleet Devon ...8 C5
Wargate Lincs ...119 H5
Wargrave Wokham ...49 J3
Warham Herefs ...80 B7
Warham Norfk ...121 L3
Wark Nthumb ...179 H5
Wark Nthumb ...202 C5
Warkleigh Devon ...27 M6
Warkton Nhants ...101 K7
Warkworth Nhants ...83 L7
Warkworth Nthumb ...191 K5
Warlaby N York ...160 E4
Warland Calder ...140 E4
Warleggan Cnwll ...5 J5
Warleigh BaNES ...46 A6
Warley Town Calder ...141 G3
Warlingham Surrey ...51 K7
Warmbrook Derbys ...115 M1

Warmfield Wakefd ...142 B4
Warmingham Ches E ...130 C7
Warmington Nhants ...102 B5
Warmington Warwks ...83 K5
Warminster Wilts ...32 E2
Warmley S Glos ...45 K4
Warmsworth Donc ...142 E7
Warmwell Dorset ...16 E5
Warndon Worcs ...81 K4
Warnford Hants ...35 J4
Warnham W Susx ...37 J4
Warningcamp W Susx ...21 H5
Warninglid W Susx ...37 K5
Warren Ches E ...131 H5
Warren Pembks ...54 F7
Warrenby R & Cl ...170 D5
Warrenhill S Lans ...198 F5
Warren Row W & M ...49 K3
Warren's Green Herts ...69 H2
Warren Street Kent ...40 B5
Warrington M Keyn ...85 H4
Warrington Warrtn ...130 B2
Warriston C Edin ...211 H4
Warsash Hants ...19 H2
Warslow Staffs ...132 B7
Warsop Vale Notts ...133 L6
Warter E R Yk ...152 D5
Warthermaske N York ...160 B6
Warthill N York ...151 L5
Wartling E Susx ...24 B5
Wartnaby Leics ...117 J7
Warton Lancs ...138 E2
Warton Lancs ...147 K2
Warton Nthumb ...190 H4
Warton Warwks ...99 H3
Warwick Warwks ...83 G2
Warwick Bridge Cumb ...178 B7
Warwick-on-Eden Cumb ...178 B7
Warwick Services Warwks ...83 H4
Warwicksland Cumb ...178 B3
Wasbister Ork ...275 c3
Wasdale Head Cumb ...156 B1
Wash Derbys ...131 L3
Washall Green Herts ...70 C1
Washaway Cnwll ...5 H1
Washbourne Devon ...8 B5
Washbrook Somset ...30 F1
Washbrook Suffk ...90 D6
Washfield Devon ...29 G2
Washfold N York ...159 J2
Washford Somset ...29 J3
Washford Pyne Devon ...28 E8
Washingborough Lincs ...135 L3
Washington Sundld ...181 H7
Washington W Susx ...21 J4
Washington Services Gatesd ...181 G7
Washwood Heath Birm ...98 E5
Wasing W Berk ...48 E6
Waskerley Dur ...168 D2
Wasperton Warwks ...83 G3
Wasps Nest Lincs ...135 M6
Wass N York ...161 J4
Wast Water Cumb ...155 L2
Watchet Somset ...29 K2
Watchfield Oxon ...47 K1
Watchfield Somset ...30 E2
Watchgate Cumb ...157 H3
Watchill Cumb ...165 G2
Watcombe Torbay ...8 D2
Watendlath Cumb ...165 J7
Water Devon ...13 H6
Water Lancs ...140 C3
Waterbeach Cambs ...87 K2
Waterbeach W Susx ...20 E5
Waterbeck D & G ...177 H3
Waterden Norfk ...121 J4
Water Eaton Oxon ...66 D5
Water Eaton Staffs ...97 K1
Water End Bed ...86 C5
Water End Bed ...86 C5
Water End C Beds ...85 L7
Waterend Cumb ...164 F6
Water End E R Yk ...152 B8
Water End Essex ...88 D2
Water End Herts ...68 D5
Water End Herts ...69 G6
Waterfall Staffs ...115 H1
Waterfoot Ag & B ...194 C3
Waterfoot E Rens ...208 F7
Waterfoot Lancs ...140 C3
Waterford Herts ...69 J4
Water Fryston Wakefd ...142 D2
Watergate Cnwll ...11 G4
Waterhead Cumb ...156 E2
Waterheads Border ...200 B3
Waterhouses Dur ...168 F3
Waterhouses Staffs ...115 H2
Wateringbury Kent ...39 H3
Waterlane Gloucs ...64 D6
Waterloo Cnwll ...10 F8

Place	Page	Grid
Waterloo Derbys	133	H7
Waterloo Herefs	79	L5
Waterloo Highld	247	K4
Waterloo N Lans	209	L8
Waterloo Norfk	122	E7
Waterloo P & K	233	G7
Waterloo Pembks	55	G6
Waterloo Sefton	138	C8
Waterloo Cross Devon	29	J8
Waterloo Port Gwynd	125	J6
Waterlooville Hants	19	M2
Watermead Bucks	67	K4
Watermillock Cumb	166	B6
Water Newton Cambs	102	C4
Water Orton Warwks	98	F5
Waterperry Oxon	66	F6
Waterrow Somset	29	J6
Watersfield W Susx	21	G4
Waterside Bl w D	139	L3
Waterside Bucks	68	B7
Waterside Cumb	165	H2
Waterside Donc	143	H5
Waterside E Ayrs	184	C1
Waterside E Ayrs	196	F2
Waterside E Duns	209	H4
Water's Nook Bolton	139	K6
Waterstein Highld	258	A7
Waterstock Oxon	66	F6
Waterston Pembks	54	F5
Water Stratford Bucks	84	C8
Water Street Neath	42	B5
Waters Upton Wrekin	113	K7
Water Yeat Cumb	156	D5
Watford Herts	68	E7
Watford Nhants	84	B2
Watford Gap Services Nhants	84	B2
Wath N York	149	L2
Wath N York	160	D7
Wath upon Dearne Rothm	142	C7
Watlington Norfk	104	C1
Watlington Oxon	67	G8
Watnall Notts	116	E2
Watten Highld	280	B5
Wattisfield Suffk	105	K8
Wattisham Suffk	89	K5
Watton Dorset	15	K4
Watton E R Yk	152	F6
Watton Norfk	105	J3
Watton-at-Stone Herts	69	J3
Watton Green Norfk	105	J3
Wattons Green Essex	70	D8
Wattston N Lans	209	K5
Wattstown Rhondd	42	F3
Wattsville Caerph	43	K3
Wauldby E R Yk	144	B2
Waulkmill Abers	244	E5
Waunarlwydd Swans	57	H6
Waun Fach Powys	61	J2
Waunfawr Cerdgn	92	D7
Waunfawr Gwynd	125	J7
Waungron Swans	57	G4
Waunlwyd Blae G	61	J5
Wavendon M Keyn	85	H7
Waverbridge Cumb	165	H1
Waverley Rothm	133	H2
Waverton Ches W	129	K7
Waverton Cumb	165	H1
Wawne E R Yk	153	H8
Waxham Norfk	123	J6
Waxholme E R Yk	145	J2
Way Kent	41	K2
Waye Devon	13	H8
Wayford Somset	15	J1
Waytown Dorset	15	L3
Way Village Devon	13	K1
Way Wick N Som	44	D6
Weacombe Somset	29	K3
Weald Oxon	65	L6
Wealdstone Gt Lon	50	F1
Weardley Leeds	150	C1
Weare Somset	44	E8
Weare Giffard Devon	27	H6
Wearhead Dur	167	K3
Wearne Somset	30	F5
Weasdale Cumb	158	B2
Weasenham All Saints Norfk	121	J7
Weasenham St Peter Norfk	121	J7
Weaste Salfd	140	B8
Weatheroak Hill Worcs	98	D8
Weaverham Ches W	130	B5
Weaverslake Staffs	115	J7
Weaverthorpe N York	152	E2
Webbington Somset	44	D7
Webb's Heath S Glos	45	K4
Webheath Worcs	82	B2
Webton Herefs	80	A7
Wedderlairs Abers	256	F5
Wedding Hall Fold N York	149	G6
Weddington Kent	41	J3
Weddington Warwks	99	K5
Wedhampton Wilts	46	F7
Wedmore Somset	31	G1
Wednesbury Sandw	98	C4
Wednesfield Wolves	97	L3
Weecar Notts	135	G6
Weedon Bucks	67	K3
Weedon Bec Nhants	84	C3
Weedon Lois Nhants	84	B6
Weeford Staffs	98	F3
Week Devon	8	A2
Week Devon	27	K5
Week Devon	28	C7
Weeke Devon	13	H2
Weeke Hants	34	F5
Weekley Nhants	101	J7
Week St Mary Cnwll	11	J3
Weel E R Yk	153	G7
Weeley Essex	73	H3
Weeley Heath Essex	73	H3
Weem P & K	232	C5
Weeping Cross Staffs	114	E7
Weethley Warwks	82	C4
Weeting Norfk	104	F5
Weeton E R Yk	145	K4
Weeton Lancs	138	D1
Weeton N York	150	C6
Weetwood Leeds	150	C8
Weir Lancs	140	C3
Weirbrook Shrops	112	F6
Weir Quay Devon	6	E2
Weisdale Shet	281	d5
Welborne Norfk	106	B2
Welbourn Lincs	118	C1
Welburn N York	151	M2
Welbury N York	160	F2
Welby Lincs	118	C4
Welches Dam Cambs	103	K6
Welcombe Devon	26	D7
Weldon Nhants	101	K5
Weldon Bridge Nthumb	191	G6
Welford Nhants	100	E7
Welford W Berk	48	B4
Welford-on-Avon Warwks	82	D5
Welham Leics	101	G5
Welham Notts	134	E3
Welham Bridge E R Yk	143	K1
Welham Green Herts	69	G6
Well Hants	36	A2
Well Lincs	137	H5
Well N York	160	C6
Welland Worcs	81	H7
Wellbank Angus	234	D7
Well End Bucks	49	L1
Well End Herts	69	G7
Wellesbourne Warwks	83	G4
Wellesbourne Mountford Warwks	83	G4
Well Head Herts	68	F2
Well Hill Kent	52	B6
Wellhouse W Berk	48	D4
Welling Gt Lon	51	M4
Wellingborough Nhants	85	H2
Wellingham Norfk	121	J7
Wellingore Lincs	135	K8
Wellington Cumb	155	K2
Wellington Herefs	80	C5
Wellington Somset	29	L6
Wellington Wrekin	96	E1
Wellington Heath Herefs	81	G7
Wellington Marsh Herefs	80	C6
Wellow BaNES	45	L7
Wellow IoW	18	F6
Wellow Notts	134	D6
Wellpond Green Herts	69	L3
Wells Somset	31	J2
Wellsborough Leics	99	K3
Wells Green Ches E	113	M1
Wells Head C Brad	141	G1
Wells-next-the-Sea Norfk	121	K3
Wellstye Green Essex	70	F3
Well Town Devon	13	L1
Welltree P & K	221	G3
Wellwood Fife	210	E1
Welney Norfk	103	L4
Welshampton Shrops	113	G4
Welsh Bicknor Herefs	63	H4
Welsh End Shrops	113	H4
Welsh Frankton Shrops	112	E5
Welsh Hook Pembks	74	F6
Welsh Newton Herefs	63	G3
Welshpool Powys	94	F2
Welsh St Donats V Glam	42	F6
Welton Cumb	165	K2
Welton E R Yk	144	B2
Welton Lincs	135	K4
Welton Nhants	84	B2
Welton le Marsh Lincs	137	J6
Welton le Wold Lincs	136	E2
Welwick E R Yk	145	J3
Welwyn Herts	69	G4
Welwyn Garden City Herts	69	G4
Wem Shrops	113	H5
Wembdon Somset	30	D3
Wembley Gt Lon	50	F2
Wembury Devon	7	G5
Wemworthy Devon	12	F1
Wemyss Bay Inver	207	K5
Wenallt Cerdgn	77	J1
Wendens Ambo Essex	87	K8
Wendlebury Oxon	66	E3
Wendling Norfk	105	J1
Wendover Bucks	67	L5
Wendron Cnwll	3	H5
Wendron Mining District Cnwll	3	H4
Wendy Cambs	87	G5
Wenfordbridge Cnwll	10	F7
Wenhaston Suffk	107	J8
Wennington Cambs	102	E7
Wennington Gt Lon	52	B3
Wennington Lancs	147	M2
Wensley Derbys	132	E2
Wensley N York	159	K5
Wentbridge Wakefd	142	D4
Wentnor Shrops	95	J5
Wentworth Cambs	103	K7
Wentworth Rothm	142	B8
Wenvoe V Glam	43	H7
Weobley Herefs	79	M5
Weobley Marsh Herefs	80	A5
Wepham W Susx	21	H5
Wereham Norfk	104	D3
Wergs Wolves	97	K3
Wern Powys	109	K4
Wern Powys	61	H3
Wern Powys	95	G1
Wern Shrops	112	D4
Werneth Low Tamesd	131	J1
Wernffrwd Swans	56	F6
Wern-Gifford Mons	62	C3
Wern-y-gaer Flints	128	F6
Werrington C Pete	102	D3
Werrington Cnwll	11	L5
Werrington Staffs	114	E2
Wervin Ches W	129	K5
Wesham Lancs	138	D1
Wessington Derbys	133	G8
West Aberthaw V Glam	42	F8
West Acre Norfk	121	G8
West Allerdean Nthumb	202	F4
West Alvington Devon	7	L6
West Amesbury Wilts	33	K3
West Anstey Devon	28	E5
West Appleton N York	160	B4
West Ashby Lincs	136	E5
West Ashling W Susx	20	D5
West Ashton Wilts	46	C7
West Auckland Dur	168	F5
West Ayton N York	163	H5
West Bagborough Somset	30	A4
West Bank Blae G	61	K6
West Bank Halton	129	L3
West Barkwith Lincs	136	C4
West Barnby N York	171	J8
West Barns E Loth	212	E3
West Barsham Norfk	121	K5
West Bay Dorset	15	K4
West Beckham Norfk	122	C4
West Bedfont Surrey	50	D4
West Bergholt Essex	72	D2
West Bexington Dorset	15	M5
West Bilney Norfk	120	F8
West Blatchington Br & H	22	D6
West Boldon S Tyne	181	J6
Westborough Lincs	117	M3
Westbourne BCP	17	L4
Westbourne W Susx	20	B5
West Bourton Dorset	32	C5
West Bowling C Brad	141	J2
West Brabourne Kent	40	E6
West Bradenham Norfk	105	J2
West Bradford Lancs	148	C7
West Bradley Somset	31	J3
West Bretton Wakefd	141	L5
West Bridgford Notts	117	G4
West Briscoe Dur	168	B6
West Bromwich Sandw	98	C5
Westbrook Kent	41	K1
Westbrook W Berk	48	B4
Westbrook Wilts	46	D5
West Buckland Devon	28	B4
West Buckland Somset	30	B6
West Burrafirth Shet	281	c5
West Burton N York	159	H5
West Burton W Susx	21	G4
Westbury Bucks	84	B8
Westbury Shrops	95	J2
Westbury Wilts	46	C8
Westbury Leigh Wilts	32	E1
Westbury-on-Severn Gloucs	63	L4
Westbury-on-Trym Bristl	45	H3
Westbury-sub-Mendip Somset	31	H1
West Butsfield Dur	168	E2
West Butterwick N Linc	143	L6
Westby Lancs	138	D2
West Byfleet Surrey	50	D6
West Cairngaan D & G	172	E8
West Caister Norfk	107	K1
West Calder W Loth	210	D6
West Camel Somset	31	J6
West Chaldon Dorset	16	E6
West Challow Oxon	48	A1
West Charleton Devon	7	L6
West Chelborough Dorset	15	M2
West Chevington Nthumb	191	J6
West Chiltington W Susx	21	H4
West Chinnock Somset	31	G8
West Chisenbury Wilts	47	H8
West Clandon Surrey	50	D8
West Cliffe Kent	41	K6
Westcliff-on-Sea Sthend	53	J2
West Clyst Devon	13	M4
West Coker Somset	31	H8
West Combe Devon	7	L2
Westcombe Somset	31	L3
West Compton Somset	31	K2
West Compton Abbas Dorset	16	A4
Westcote Gloucs	65	J3
Westcote Barton Oxon	66	B2
Westcott Bucks	67	H4
Westcott Devon	14	B2
Westcott Surrey	37	H1
West Cottingwith N York	151	L7
Westcourt Wilts	47	J6
West Cowick E R Yk	143	G3
West Cross Swans	57	H7
West Curry Cnwll	11	K4
West Curthwaite Cumb	165	K1
Westdean E Susx	23	J7
West Dean W Susx	20	E4
West Dean Wilts	34	B5
West Deeping Lincs	102	C2
West Derby Lpool	129	J1
West Dereham Norfk	104	D3
West Ditchburn Nthumb	191	G2
West Down Devon	27	J3
Westdown Camp Wilts	33	H1
Westdowns Cnwll	10	F4
West Drayton Gt Lon	50	D3
West Drayton Notts	134	E5
West Dunnet Highld	280	B2
Wested Kent	52	B5
West Ella E R Yk	144	C2
West End Bed	85	J4
West End Br For	49	L5
West End Caerph	43	K3
West End Cumb	177	K7
West End E R Yk	144	A2
West End E R Yk	144	E4
West End E R Yk	145	H2
Westend Gloucs	64	A5
West End Hants	34	F7
West End Hants	35	K5
West End Herts	69	H5
West End Herts	69	J6
West End Lancs	139	L2
West End Leeds	150	B8
West End Lincs	145	K8
West End N Som	44	F5
West End N York	151	H7
West End Norfk	105	J2
West End Norfk	107	K1
West End Oxon	48	E2
West End S Glos	45	L1
West End Somset	31	L4
West End Surrey	50	B6
West End Surrey	50	E6
West End W & M	49	K4
West End W Susx	22	B4
West End Wilts	32	F6
West End Wilts	33	G6
West End Wilts	46	E3
West End Green Hants	49	G6
Westend Town Nthumb	179	H6
Westenhanger Kent	40	F7
Wester Aberchalder Highld	250	F7
Wester Balblair Highld	250	E6
Westerdale Highld	279	K6
Westerdale N York	161	L2
Westerfield Suffk	90	E5
Westergate W Susx	20	F6
Wester Hailes C Edin	211	G5
Westerham Kent	51	L8
Westerhope N u Ty	180	F5
Westerland Devon	8	C2
Westerleigh S Glos	45	K3
Western Isles W Isls	282	e6
Wester Ochiltree W Loth	210	D4
Wester Pitkierie Fife	223	K6

Place	Region	Page	Grid
Wester Ross	Highld	260	F4
Westerton	W Susx	20	E5
Westerton of Rossie	Angus	235	G4
Westerwick	Shet	281	c6
West Ewell	Surrey	51	G6
West Farleigh	Kent	39	H3
West Farndon	Nhants	83	M5
West Felton	Shrops	112	E6
Westfield	BaNES	45	K8
Westfield	Cumb	164	C5
Westfield	E Susx	24	E4
Westfield	Highld	279	J3
Westfield	N Lans	209	H8
Westfield	Norfk	105	K2
Westfield	Surrey	50	C7
Westfield	W Loth	210	B4
Westfields	Dorset	16	D2
Westfields	Herefs	80	C7
Westfields of Rattray	P & K	233	J6
Westfield Sole	Kent	53	G6
West Flotmanby	N York	163	K6
Westford	Somset	29	L6
Westgate	Dur	167	L3
Westgate	N Linc	143	K6
Westgate	Norfk	121	L3
Westgate Hill	C Brad	141	K2
Westgate-on-Sea	Kent	41	K1
Westgate Street	Norfk	122	D7
West Ginge	Oxon	48	C2
West Grafton	Wilts	47	K7
West Green	Hants	49	H7
West Grimstead	Wilts	33	L5
West Grinstead	W Susx	37	J6
West Haddlesey	N York	142	E2
West Haddon	Nhants	84	C1
West Hagbourne	Oxon	48	D2
West Hagley	Worcs	97	K7
Westhall	Suffk	107	J7
West Hallam	Derbys	116	D3
West Hallam Common	Derbys	116	C3
West Halton	N Linc	144	A4
Westham	Dorset	16	C6
Westham	E Susx	23	L6
West Ham	Gt Lon	51	K4
Westham	Somset	30	F2
Westhampnett	W Susx	20	E5
West Handley	Derbys	133	H4
West Hanney	Oxon	66	B8
West Hanningfield	Essex	71	H7
West Harnham	Wilts	33	K5
West Harptree	BaNES	45	H7
West Harting	W Susx	20	C3
West Hatch	Somset	30	D6
West Hatch	Wilts	32	F5
West Haven	Angus	234	E8
Westhay	Somset	31	G2
Westhead	Lancs	138	F6
West Head	Norfk	104	B2
West Heath	Birm	98	C7
West Heath	Hants	48	E7
West Helmsdale	Highld	274	D5
West Hendred	Oxon	48	C1
West Heslerton	N York	163	G7
West Hewish	N Som	44	D6
Westhide	Herefs	80	D6
Westhill	Abers	245	J2
West Hill	Devon	14	C4
Westhill	Highld	252	D3
West Hoathly	W Susx	38	A6
West Holme	Dorset	17	G5
Westholme	Somset	31	J4
Westhope	Herefs	80	B5
Westhope	Shrops	95	L6
West Horndon	Essex	52	D1
Westhorp	Nhants	83	L5
Westhorpe	Lincs	119	H5
Westhorpe	Suffk	90	B2
West Horrington	Somset	31	J2
West Horsley	Surrey	50	D8
West Horton	Nthumb	203	G7
West Hougham	Kent	41	H7
Westhoughton	Bolton	139	K6
Westhouse	N York	157	L2
Westhouses	Derbys	133	H8
West Howe	BCP	17	L3
West Howetown	Somset	29	G4
Westhumble	Surrey	50	F8
West Huntingtower	P & K	221	K2
West Huntspill	Somset	30	D2
West Hyde	C Beds	68	E4
West Hyde	Herts	50	C1
West Hythe	Kent	40	F8
West Ilkerton	Devon	28	C2
West Ilsley	W Berk	48	C3
West Itchenor	W Susx	20	C6
West Keal	Lincs	137	G7
West Kennett	Wilts	47	G5
West Kilbride	N Ayrs	195	K1
West Kingsdown	Kent	52	C6
West Kington	Wilts	46	A3
West Kirby	Wirral	128	F2
West Knapton	N York	162	F7
West Knighton	Dorset	16	D5
West Knoyle	Wilts	32	E4
West Kyloe	Nthumb	203	G5
Westlake	Devon	7	J4
West Lambrook	Somset	30	F7
Westland Green	Herts	70	B3
West Langdon	Kent	41	K6
West Lavington	W Susx	20	E3
West Lavington	Wilts	46	E8
West Layton	N York	168	K6
West Leake	Notts	116	E6
West Learmouth	Nthumb	202	C5
West Lees	N York	161	G2
West Leigh	Devon	13	G2
Westleigh	Devon	27	H5
Westleigh	Devon	29	J7
West Leigh	Somset	29	L5
Westleton	Suffk	91	K6
West Lexham	Norfk	121	J8
Westley	Shrops	95	J2
Westley	Suffk	89	G2
Westley Waterless	Cambs	88	C4
West Lilling	N York	151	K3
Westlington	Bucks	67	J5
West Linton	Border	199	K3
Westlinton	Cumb	177	L6
West Littleton	S Glos	45	M4
West Lockinge	Oxon	48	B2
West Lulworth	Dorset	16	F6
West Lutton	N York	152	E2
West Lydford	Somset	31	J4
West Lyn	Devon	28	C1
West Lyng	Somset	30	D5
West Lynn	Norfk	120	D7
West Malling	Kent	52	E7
West Malvern	Worcs	81	H6
West Marden	W Susx	20	C4
West Markham	Notts	134	E5
Westmarsh	Kent	41	J3
West Marsh	NE Lin	145	H5
West Marton	N York	148	F5
West Melbury	Dorset	32	E6
West Melton	Rothm	142	C7
West Meon	Hants	35	K6
West Meon Hut	Hants	35	K5
West Meon Woodlands	Hants	35	K5
West Mersea	Essex	72	E4
Westmeston	E Susx	22	E4
West Mickley	Nthumb	180	C6
Westmill	Herts	69	J4
Westmill	Herts	69	K2
West Milton	Dorset	15	L3
Westminster	Gt Lon	51	J3
Westminster Abbey & Palace	Gt Lon	51	J3
West Molesey	Surrey	50	E5
West Monkton	Somset	30	C5
West Moors	Dorset	17	L2
West Morden	Dorset	17	H3
West Morriston	Border	201	J5
West Morton	C Brad	149	K7
West Mudford	Somset	31	J6
Westmuir	Angus	234	A5
West Ness	N York	162	B6
West Newbiggin	Darltn	169	K7
Westnewton	Cumb	164	F2
West Newton	E R Yk	153	K8
West Newton	Norfk	120	F6
West Newton	Somset	30	C5
West Norwood	Gt Lon	51	J4
Westoe	S Tyne	181	J5
West Ogwell	Devon	13	J8
Weston	BaNES	45	L5
Weston	Ches E	114	A1
Weston	Devon	14	D3
Weston	Devon	14	E5
Weston	Dorset	16	D8
Weston	Halton	129	L3
Weston	Hants	35	M6
Weston	Herefs	79	L4
Weston	Herts	69	H1
Weston	Lincs	119	J6
Weston	N York	149	M6
Weston	Nhants	84	B6
Weston	Notts	134	F6
Weston	Shrops	95	H8
Weston	Shrops	96	D5
Weston	Shrops	112	D6
Weston	Staffs	114	F6
Weston	Suffk	107	J6
Weston	W Berk	48	B4
Weston Beggard	Herefs	80	D7
Westonbirt	Gloucs	46	B1
Weston by Welland	Nhants	101	G5
Weston Colley	Hants	35	G3
Weston Colville	Cambs	88	C4
Weston Corbett	Hants	35	L2
Weston Coyney	C Stke	114	E3
Weston Favell	Nhants	84	F3
Weston Green	Cambs	88	C5
Weston Heath	Shrops	97	H1
Weston Hills	Lincs	119	J7
Weston in Arden	Warwks	99	K6
Westoning	C Beds	85	K8
Weston-in-Gordano	N Som	44	F4
Westoning Woodend	C Beds	68	C1
Weston Jones	Staffs	114	B6
Weston Longville	Norfk	122	C8
Weston Lullingfields	Shrops	112	F6
Weston-on-Avon	Warwks	82	E5
Weston-on-the-Green	Oxon	66	D3
Weston Patrick	Hants	35	L2
Weston Rhyn	Shrops	112	D4
Weston-sub-Edge	Gloucs	82	D7
Weston-super-Mare	N Som	44	C6
Weston Turville	Bucks	67	K5
Weston-under-Lizard	Staffs	97	H1
Weston under Penyard	Herefs	63	J3
Weston-under-Redcastle	Shrops	113	J5
Weston under Wetherley	Warwks	83	J1
Weston Underwood	Derbys	116	A3
Weston Underwood	M Keyn	85	G5
Weston-upon-Trent	Derbys	116	C6
Westonzoyland	Somset	30	E4
West Orchard	Dorset	32	D7
West Overton	Wilts	47	H5
Westow	N York	152	A3
West Panson	Devon	11	L4
West Park	Abers	245	H4
West Parley	Dorset	17	L3
West Peckham	Kent	39	G3
West Peeke	Devon	11	L4
West Pelton	Dur	180	F8
West Pennard	Somset	31	J3
West Pentire	Cnwll	4	C3
West Pinchbeck	Lincs	119	J6
West Porlock	Somset	28	F2
Westport	Somset	30	F6
West Pulham	Dorset	16	D1
West Putford	Devon	26	F7
West Quantoxhead	Somset	29	K3
Westquarter	Falk	210	B3
Westra	V Glam	43	J7
West Raddon	Devon	13	L2
West Rainton	Dur	169	J1
West Rasen	Lincs	135	L2
West Ravendale	NE Lin	145	G7
Westray	Ork	275	c2
Westray Airport	Ork	275	c1
West Raynham	Norfk	121	J6
West Retford	Notts	134	D3
Westridge Green	W Berk	48	E3
Westrigg	W Loth	210	B5
Westrop	Swindn	65	J8
West Rounton	N York	160	F2
West Row	Suffk	104	D8
West Rudham	Norfk	121	H6
West Runton	Norfk	122	D3
Westruther	Border	201	K3
Westry	Cambs	103	H4
West Saltoun	E Loth	212	A5
West Sandford	Devon	13	J2
West Sandwick	Shet	281	e3
West Scrafton	N York	159	K6
West Sleekburn	Nthumb	181	G2
West Somerton	Norfk	123	K7
West Stafford	Dorset	16	D5
West Stockwith	Notts	134	F1
West Stoke	W Susx	20	D5
West Stonesdale	N York	158	F2
West Stoughton	Somset	30	F1
West Stour	Dorset	32	C6
West Stourmouth	Kent	41	H3
West Stow	Suffk	89	G1
West Stowell	Wilts	47	H6
West Stratton	Hants	35	H3
West Street	Kent	40	A4
West Street	Kent	41	K4
West Street	Medway	52	F4
West Street	Suffk	89	K1
West Tanfield	N York	160	C7
West Taphouse	Cnwll	5	K2
West Tarbert	Ag & B	206	D5
West Tarring	W Susx	21	J6
West Thirston	Nthumb	191	H6
West Thorney	W Susx	20	C6
Westthorpe	Derbys	133	J4
West Thorpe	Notts	117	G6
West Thurrock	Thurr	52	C3
West Tilbury	Thurr	52	E3
West Tisted	Hants	35	K5
West Torrington	Lincs	136	B3
West Town	BaNES	45	G6
West Town	Hants	20	B7
West Town	Herefs	80	B3
West Town	N Som	44	F5
West Town	Somset	31	J4
West Town	Somset	32	B3
West Tytherley	Hants	34	C5
West Walton	Norfk	103	K1
Westward	Cumb	165	J2
Westward Ho!	Devon	27	G5
Westwell	Kent	40	C6
Westwell	Oxon	65	J5
Westwell Leacon	Kent	40	C5
West Wellow	Hants	34	C7
West Wembury	Devon	7	G5
West Wemyss	Fife	222	E8
Westwick	Cambs	87	J2
Westwick	Dur	168	D7
West Wick	N Som	44	D6
Westwick	Norfk	122	F6
West Wickham	Cambs	88	C5
West Wickham	Gt Lon	51	K5
West Williamston	Pembks	55	H5
West Winch	Norfk	120	E8
West Winterslow	Wilts	34	B4
West Wittering	W Susx	20	C7
West Witton	N York	159	J5
Westwood	Devon	14	B3
Westwood	Kent	41	K2
Westwood	Kent	52	D5
Westwood	Notts	116	D1
Westwood	Nthumb	179	H6
Westwood	Wilts	46	A7
West Woodburn	Nthumb	179	K2
West Woodhay	W Berk	48	B6
Westwood Heath	Covtry	99	H8
West Woodlands	Somset	32	C2
Westwoodside	N Linc	143	J7
West Worldham	Hants	35	M3
West Worthing	W Susx	21	J6
West Wratting	Cambs	88	C5
West Wycombe	Bucks	67	K8
West Wylam	Nthumb	180	D6
West Yatton	Wilts	46	A3
West Yoke	Kent	52	D5
West Youlstone	Cnwll	26	D7
Wetham Green	Kent	53	H5
Wetheral	Cumb	178	B7
Wetherby	Leeds	150	F6
Wetherby Services	N York	150	F6
Wetherden	Suffk	89	K3
Wetheringsett	Suffk	90	D2
Wethersfield	Essex	71	H1
Wetherup Street	Suffk	90	D2
Wetley Rocks	Staffs	114	F2
Wettenhall	Ches E	130	C7
Wetton	Staffs	132	B8
Wetwang	E R Yk	152	E4
Wetwood	Staffs	114	B5
Wexcombe	Wilts	47	K7
Wexham	Slough	50	C3
Wexham Street	Bucks	50	C2
Weybourne	Norfk	122	C3
Weybourne	Surrey	36	C1
Weybread	Suffk	106	E7
Weybread Street	Suffk	106	E7
Weybridge	Surrey	50	D6
Weycroft	Devon	15	G3
Weydale	Highld	279	L3
Weyhill	Hants	34	D2
Weymouth	Dorset	16	C6
Whaddon	Bucks	84	F8
Whaddon	Cambs	87	G6
Whaddon	Gloucs	64	B4
Whaddon	Wilts	33	L5
Whaddon	Wilts	46	C6
Whale	Cumb	166	C6
Whaley	Derbys	133	K5
Whaley Bridge	Derbys	131	K3
Whaley Thorns	Derbys	133	K5
Whaligoe	Highld	280	D8
Whalley	Lancs	148	C8
Whalley Banks	Lancs	139	L1
Whalsay	Shet	281	f5
Whalton	Nthumb	180	D3
Whaplode	Lincs	119	K6
Whaplode Drove	Lincs	103	G1
Wharf	Warwks	83	K5
Wharfe	N York	148	D2
Wharles	Lancs	147	J8
Wharley End	C Beds	85	J6
Wharncliffe Side	Sheff	132	F1
Wharram-le-Street	N York	152	C3
Wharton	Ches W	130	C6
Wharton	Herefs	80	C4
Whashton	N York	159	L2
Whasset	Cumb	157	H6
Whatcote	Warwks	83	G6
Whateley	Warwks	99	G3
Whatfield	Suffk	89	L6
Whatley	Somset	15	H1
Whatley	Somset	32	B2
Whatley's End	S Glos	45	K3

Whatlington E Susx....24 D4
Whatsole Street Kent....40 F6
Whatstandwell Derbys....116 B1
Whatton-in-the-Vale Notts....117 K4
Whauphill D & G....173 K5
Whaw N York....159 H2
Wheal Peevor Cnwll....4 A6
Wheal Rose Cnwll....4 B6
Wheatacre Norfk....107 J4
Wheatfield Oxon....67 G7
Wheathampstead Herts....68 F4
Wheathill Shrops....96 E7
Wheathill Somset....31 J5
Wheatley Hants....36 A3
Wheatley Oxon....66 E6
Wheatley Hill Dur....169 K3
Wheatley Hills Donc....142 F6
Wheatley Lane Lancs....148 E8
Wheaton Aston Staffs....97 J1
Wheddon Cross Somset....29 G3
Wheelbarrow Town Kent....40 F6
Wheeler End Bucks....67 K8
Wheeler's Green Wokham....49 J4
Wheelerstreet Surrey....36 E3
Wheelock Ches E....130 E7
Wheelock Heath Ches E....130 E8
Wheelton Lancs....139 J3
Wheldale Wakefd....142 C3
Wheldrake C York....151 L6
Whelford Gloucs....65 H7
Whelpley Hill Bucks....68 C6
Whelpo Cumb....165 J3
Whelston Flints....128 F4
Whempstead Herts....69 J3
Whenby N York....151 K2
Whepstead Suffk....89 G4
Wherstead Suffk....90 E7
Wherwell Hants....34 E3
Wheston Derbys....132 C4
Whetsted Kent....39 G4
Whetstone Gt Lon....69 H8
Whetstone Leics....100 C4
Wheyrigg Cumb....165 G1
Whicham Cumb....155 L6
Whichford Warwks....83 H8
Whickham Gatesd....180 F6
Whiddon Devon....12 B3
Whiddon Down Devon....13 G4
Whigstreet Angus....234 D6
Whilton Nhants....84 C2
Whimble Devon....11 L2
Whimple Devon....14 B3
Whimpwell Green Norfk....123 H5
Whinburgh Norfk....105 K2
Whin Lane End Lancs....147 H7
Whinnieliggate D & G....175 H4
Whinnow Cumb....177 J8
Whinnyfold Abers....257 K5
Whinny Hill S on T....169 K7
Whippingham IoW....19 H5
Whipsnade C Beds....68 C3
Whipton Devon....13 M4
Whirlow Sheff....132 F3
Whisby Lincs....135 H6
Whissendine Rutlnd....117 L8
Whissonsett Norfk....121 K7
Whistlefield Ag & B....218 C8
Whistlefield Inn Ag & B....217 J8
Whistley Green Wokham....49 J4
Whiston Knows....129 L2
Whiston Nhants....85 G3
Whiston Rothm....133 J2
Whiston Staffs....114 D8
Whiston Staffs....115 G2
Whiston Cross Shrops....97 H3
Whiston Eaves Staffs....115 G2
Whitacre Fields Warwks....99 H5
Whitbeck Cumb....155 K5
Whitbourne Herefs....81 G4
Whitburn S Tyne....181 K6
Whitburn W Loth....210 C6
Whitby Ches W....129 J4
Whitby N York....171 K8
Whitbyheath Ches W....129 J5
Whitchester Border....212 F7
Whitchurch BaNES....45 J5
Whitchurch Bucks....67 J4
Whitchurch Cardif....43 J5
Whitchurch Devon....12 C8
Whitchurch Hants....34 F1
Whitchurch Herefs....63 H4
Whitchurch Oxon....48 F3
Whitchurch Pembks....74 C7
Whitchurch Shrops....113 J3
Whitchurch Canonicorum Dorset....15 J3
Whitchurch Hill Oxon....48 F3
Whitcombe Dorset....16 D5
Whitcot Shrops....95 J5
Whitcott Keysett Shrops....95 H5

Whiteacre Kent....40 E5
Whiteacre Heath Warwks....99 G5
Whiteash Green Essex....71 J1
White Ball Somset....29 K7
Whitebridge Highld....250 E8
Whitebrook Mons....63 G6
Whitebushes Surrey....37 L1
Whitecairns Abers....257 G8
Whitechapel Gt Lon....51 J3
White Chapel Lancs....147 L7
Whitechurch Pembks....75 K5
Whitecliff Gloucs....63 H5
White Colne Essex....72 C1
White Coppice Lancs....139 J4
Whitecraig E Loth....211 K5
Whitecroft Gloucs....63 J6
Whitecrook D & G....172 F3
Whitecross Cnwll....2 E4
White Cross Cnwll....3 H6
Whitecross Cnwll....10 D8
Whitecross Falk....210 C4
White End Worcs....81 H8
Whiteface Highld....263 J2
Whitefarland N Ayrs....194 D3
Whitefaulds S Ayrs....183 H1
Whitefield Bury....140 B6
Whitefield Devon....28 C4
Whitefield Somset....29 K5
Whitefield Lane End Knows....129 K2
Whiteford Abers....256 C6
Whitegate Ches W....130 C6
Whitehall Hants....49 H8
Whitehall Ork....275 e3
Whitehall W Susx....37 H6
Whitehaven Cumb....164 C7
Whitehill Hants....36 B4
Whitehill Kent....40 C3
Whitehill Leics....99 L1
Whitehills Abers....268 B3
Whitehouse Abers....256 A8
Whitehouse Ag & B....206 C6
Whitehouse Common Birm....98 E4
Whitekirk E Loth....212 D3
White Kirkley Dur....168 C3
White Lackington Dorset....16 D3
Whitelackington Somset....30 F7
White Ladies Aston Worcs....81 L4
Whiteleaf Bucks....67 K6
White-le-Head Dur....180 E7
Whiteley Hants....19 J2
Whiteley Bank IoW....19 J7
Whiteley Green Ches E....131 H4
Whiteley Village Surrey....50 E6
Whitemans Green W Susx....22 D2
White Mill Carmth....58 E4
Whitemire Moray....253 J1
Whitemoor C Nott....116 F3
Whitemoor Cnwll....5 G3
Whitemoor Derbys....116 B2
Whitemoor Staffs....131 H7
Whiteness Shet....281 d6
White Notley Essex....71 J3
Whiteoak Green Oxon....65 M4
White Ox Mead BaNES....45 L7
Whiteparish Wilts....34 B6
White Pit Lincs....137 G4
Whiterashes Abers....256 F7
White Roding Essex....70 E4
Whiterow Highld....280 E6
Whiterow Moray....265 G8
Whiteshill Gloucs....64 B5
Whitesmith E Susx....23 J4
White Stake Lancs....139 G3
Whitestaunton Somset....30 D8
Whitestone Devon....13 K4
White Stone Herefs....80 D6
Whitestone Warwks....99 K5
Whitestone Cross Devon....13 L4
Whitestreet Green Suffk....89 K7
Whitewall Corner N York....152 B2
White Waltham W & M....49 K3
Whiteway BaNES....45 L6
Whiteway Gloucs....64 C5
Whitewell Lancs....148 B6
Whiteworks Devon....12 E8
Whitfield C Dund....234 C8
Whitfield Kent....41 J6
Whitfield Nhants....84 B7
Whitfield Nthumb....179 H7
Whitfield S Glos....63 K8
Whitfield Hall Nthumb....179 H7
Whitford Devon....14 F3
Whitford Flints....128 D4
Whitgift E R Yk....143 K3
Whitgreave Staffs....114 D6
Whithorn D & G....174 C6
Whiting Bay N Ayrs....195 G6
Whitkirk Leeds....142 B1
Whitland Carmth....55 L3
Whitlaw Border....188 E4

Whitletts S Ayrs....196 D6
Whitley N York....142 E4
Whitley Readg....49 H5
Whitley Sheff....133 G1
Whitley Wilts....46 C5
Whitley Bay N Tyne....181 J4
Whitley Chapel Nthumb....179 L7
Whitley Heath Staffs....114 C6
Whitley Lower Kirk....141 K4
Whitley Row Kent....38 D3
Whitlock's End Solhll....98 E8
Whitminster Gloucs....63 M5
Whitmore Dorset....17 L1
Whitmore Staffs....114 C3
Whitnage Devon....29 J7
Whitnash Warwks....83 H3
Whitney-on-Wye Herefs....79 J5
Whitrigg Cumb....165 G3
Whitrigg Cumb....177 H7
Whitrigglees Cumb....177 H7
Whitsome Border....202 D3
Whitson Newpt....44 D2
Whitstable Kent....40 E2
Whitstone Cnwll....11 K3
Whittingham Nthumb....190 F4
Whittingslow Shrops....95 K5
Whittington Derbys....133 H4
Whittington Gloucs....64 E3
Whittington Lancs....157 K7
Whittington Norfk....104 E3
Whittington Shrops....112 E5
Whittington Staffs....97 J6
Whittington Staffs....98 F2
Whittington Warwks....99 J4
Whittington Worcs....81 K4
Whittington Moor Derbys....133 G5
Whittlebury Nhants....84 D6
Whittle-le-Woods Lancs....139 H3
Whittlesey Cambs....102 F4
Whittlesford Cambs....87 K5
Whittlestone Head Bl w D....139 L4
Whitton N Linc....143 M3
Whitton Nthumb....190 F6
Whitton Powys....79 J2
Whitton S on T....169 K6
Whitton Shrops....80 D1
Whitton Suffk....90 D5
Whittonditch Wilts....47 L4
Whittonstall Nthumb....180 C7
Whitway Hants....48 C7
Whitwell Derbys....133 K4
Whitwell Herts....68 F3
Whitwell IoW....19 J8
Whitwell N York....160 D3
Whitwell Rutlnd....101 K2
Whitwell-on-the-Hill N York....151 M3
Whitwell Street Norfk....122 B7
Whitwick Leics....116 D8
Whitwood Wakefd....142 B3
Whitworth Lancs....140 D4
Whixall Shrops....113 H4
Whixley N York....150 F4
Whorlton Dur....168 E7
Whorlton N York....161 G2
Whyle Herefs....80 D3
Whyteleafe Surrey....51 J7
Wibdon Gloucs....63 H7
Wibsey C Brad....141 J2
Wibtoft Warwks....100 B6
Wichelstowe Swindn....47 H2
Wichenford Worcs....81 H3
Wichling Kent....40 B4
Wick BCP....18 B5
Wick Devon....14 E2
Wick Highld....280 E6
Wick S Glos....45 K4
Wick Somset....30 B2
Wick Somset....30 F5
Wick V Glam....42 D7
Wick W Susx....21 H6
Wick Wilts....33 L6
Wick Worcs....81 M6
Wicken Cambs....88 B1
Wicken Nhants....84 E7
Wicken Bonhunt Essex....87 K4
Wickenby Lincs....136 A3
Wick End Bed....85 K5
Wicken Green Village Norfk....121 J5
Wickersley Rothm....133 J2
Wicker Street Green Suffk....89 K6
Wickford Essex....71 H8
Wickham Hants....19 K2
Wickham W Berk....48 B5
Wickham Bishops Essex....71 K5
Wickhambreaux Kent....41 H3
Wickhambrook Suffk....88 E4
Wickhamford Worcs....82 C7
Wickham Green Suffk....90 C2

Wickham Green W Berk....48 B4
Wickham Heath W Berk....48 B5
Wickham Market Suffk....91 G4
Wickhampton Norfk....107 J2
Wickham St Paul Essex....89 G7
Wickham Skeith Suffk....90 C2
Wickham Street Suffk....88 F4
Wickham Street Suffk....90 C1
Wickhurst Green W Susx....37 H5
Wick John o' Groats Airport Highld....280 E5
Wicklewood Norfk....106 B3
Wickmere Norfk....122 D5
Wick St Lawrence N Som....44 D6
Wickstreet E Susx....23 J5
Wickwar S Glos....45 L1
Widdington Essex....70 D1
Widdop Calder....140 D1
Widdrington Nthumb....191 K7
Widdrington Station Nthumb....191 J7
Widecombe in the Moor Devon....13 G7
Widegates Cnwll....6 B3
Widemouth Bay Cnwll....11 H2
Wideopen N Tyne....181 G4
Widford Essex....71 G6
Widford Herts....70 B4
Widham Wilts....47 G1
Widley Hants....19 M2
Widmer End Bucks....67 L7
Widmerpool Notts....117 G6
Widmore Gt Lon....51 L5
Widnes Halton....129 L3
Widworthy Devon....14 F3
Wigan Wigan....139 H6
Wigborough Somset....31 G7
Wiggaton Devon....14 C4
Wiggenhall St Germans Norfk....120 D8
Wiggenhall St Mary Magdalen Norfk....104 B1
Wiggenhall St Mary the Virgin Norfk....104 B1
Wiggenhall St Peter Norfk....104 C1
Wiggens Green Essex....88 D6
Wiggenstall Staffs....132 B7
Wiggington Shrops....112 E4
Wigginton C York....151 J4
Wigginton Herts....68 B5
Wigginton Oxon....83 J8
Wigginton Staffs....99 G2
Wigginton Bottom Herts....68 B5
Wigglesworth N York....148 E4
Wiggonby Cumb....177 J8
Wiggonholt W Susx....21 H3
Wighill N York....151 G6
Wighton Norfk....121 L3
Wightwick Wolves....97 K4
Wigley Derbys....132 F5
Wigley Hants....34 D7
Wigmore Herefs....80 A2
Wigmore Medway....53 G6
Wigsley Notts....135 G5
Wigsthorpe Nhants....102 A6
Wigston Leics....100 D4
Wigston Fields Leics....100 D3
Wigston Parva Leics....100 A5
Wigthorpe Notts....134 B3
Wigtoft Lincs....119 J4
Wigton Cumb....165 H1
Wigtown D & G....174 C4
Wigtwizzle Sheff....141 L8
Wike Leeds....150 D7
Wilbarston Nhants....101 H5
Wilberfoss E R Yk....151 M5
Wilburton Cambs....103 K8
Wilby Nhants....85 G2
Wilby Norfk....105 L5
Wilby Suffk....90 F1
Wilcot Wilts....47 H6
Wilcott Shrops....112 F7
Wilcove Cnwll....6 E4
Wilcrick Newpt....44 D2
Wilday Green Derbys....132 F5
Wildboarclough Ches E....131 K6
Wilden Bed....86 B4
Wilden Worcs....81 J1
Wilde Street Suffk....104 D7
Wildhern Hants....34 D1
Wildhill Herts....69 H5
Wildmanbridge S Lans....209 L8
Wildmill Brdgnd....42 D5
Wildmoor Hants....49 G7
Wildmoor Worcs....98 B8
Wildsworth Lincs....143 K6
Wilford C Nott....116 F4
Wilkesley Ches E....113 K3
Wilkhaven Highld....264 E3
Wilkieston W Loth....210 F5
Wilkin's Green Herts....69 G5

Wilksby Lincs......136 E7
Willand Devon......29 J8
Willards Hill E Susx......24 C2
Willaston Ches E......113 L1
Willaston Ches W......129 H4
Willen M Keyn......85 G7
Willenhall Covtry......99 K8
Willenhall Wsall......98 B4
Willerby E R Yk......144 C2
Willerby N York......163 H6
Willersey Gloucs......82 D7
Willersley Herefs......79 K6
Willesborough Kent......40 D7
Willesborough Lees Kent......40 D6
Willesden Gt Lon......51 G2
Willesleigh Devon......27 L4
Willesley Wilts......46 B1
Willett Somset......29 K4
Willey Shrops......96 F3
Willey Warwks......100 B6
Willey Green Surrey......50 B8
Williamscot Oxon......83 L6
Williamstown Rhondd......42 F4
Willian Herts......69 G1
Willicote Warwks......82 E5
Willingale Essex......70 E5
Willingdon E Susx......23 K6
Willingham Cambs......87 H1
Willingham by Stow Lincs......135 H3
Willingham Green Cambs......88 C4
Willingham St Mary Suffk......107 J6
Willington Bed......86 C5
Willington Derbys......116 A6
Willington Dur......169 G4
Willington Kent......39 K3
Willington N Tyne......181 H5
Willington Warwks......83 G7
Willington Corner Ches W......129 M6
Willitoft E R Yk......143 J1
Williton Somset......29 K3
Willoughby Lincs......137 J5
Willoughby Warwks......83 M2
Willoughby Hills Lincs......119 K3
Willoughby-on-the-Wolds
   Notts......117 H6
Willoughby Waterleys Leics......100 C5
Willoughton Lincs......135 J1
Willow Green Ches W......130 B4
Willows Green Essex......71 H3
Willsbridge S Glos......45 K5
Willsworthy Devon......12 D6
Willtown Somset......30 F6
Wilmcote Warwks......82 E4
Wilmington BaNES......45 K6
Wilmington Devon......14 F3
Wilmington E Susx......23 J6
Wilmington Kent......52 B4
Wilmslow Ches E......131 G3
Wilnecote Staffs......99 G3
Wilpshire Lancs......139 K1
Wilsden C Brad......149 K8
Wilsford Lincs......118 D3
Wilsford Wilts......33 K3
Wilsford Wilts......47 G2
Wilsham Devon......28 D1
Wilshaw Kirk......141 H6
Wilsill N York......150 A3
Wilsley Green Kent......39 K6
Wilsley Pound Kent......39 K6
Wilson Herefs......63 H2
Wilson Leics......116 C6
Wilsontown S Lans......198 E2
Wilstead Bed......85 L6
Wilsthorpe Lincs......102 B1
Wilstone Herts......67 L4
Wilstone Green Herts......67 M4
Wilton Cumb......164 D8
Wilton Herefs......63 H2
Wilton N York......162 F6
Wilton R & Cl......170 D6
Wilton Wilts......33 J4
Wilton Wilts......47 K6
Wilton Dean Border......188 E3
Wimbish Essex......88 B7
Wimbish Green Essex......88 C8
Wimbledon Gt Lon......51 G5
Wimblington Cambs......103 J5
Wimboldsley Ches W......130 D7
Wimborne Minster Dorset......17 K3
Wimborne St Giles Dorset......33 H8
Wimbotsham Norfk......104 C2
Wimpole Cambs......87 G5
Wimpstone Warwks......82 F5
Wincanton Somset......32 B5
Winceby Lincs......136 F6
Wincham Ches W......130 C4
Winchburgh W Loth......210 E4
Winchcombe Gloucs......64 F2
Winchelsea E Susx......25 G4
Winchelsea Beach E Susx......25 G4

Winchester Hants......35 G5
Winchester Services Hants......35 H4
Winchet Hill Kent......39 J5
Winchfield Hants......49 J8
Winchmore Hill Bucks......68 B8
Winchmore Hill Gt Lon......69 J8
Wincle Ches E......131 J6
Wincobank Sheff......133 G1
Winder Cumb......164 D7
Windermere Cumb......156 F3
Winderton Warwks......83 H7
Windhill Highld......250 F2
Windlehurst Stockp......131 J3
Windlesham Surrey......50 A6
Windmill Cnwll......10 B7
Windmill Derbys......132 C4
Windmill Hill E Susx......23 L5
Windmill Hill Somset......30 D7
Windrush Gloucs......65 J4
Windsole Abers......267 L4
Windsor W & M......50 B4
Windsoredge Gloucs......64 B7
Windsor Green Suffk......89 H4
Windygates Fife......222 F7
Windyharbour Ches E......131 G5
Windy Hill Wrexhm......129 G8
Wineham W Susx......22 C3
Winestead E R Yk......145 H1
Winewall Lancs......148 F7
Winfarthing Norfk......106 C6
Winford IoW......19 J6
Winford N Som......45 G6
Winforton Herefs......79 K6
Winfrith Newburgh Dorset......16 F5
Wing Bucks......67 L3
Wing Rutlnd......101 K3
Wingate Dur......169 L3
Wingates Bolton......139 K6
Wingates Nthumb......191 G7
Wingerworth Derbys......133 G6
Wingfield C Beds......68 C2
Wingfield Suffk......106 E7
Wingfield Wilts......46 B7
Wingfield Green Suffk......106 E7
Wingham Kent......41 H4
Wingland Lincs......120 B6
Wingmore Kent......41 G6
Wingrave Bucks......67 L3
Winkburn Notts......134 E7
Winkfield Br For......49 L4
Winkfield Row Br For......49 L5
Winkhill Staffs......115 H1
Winkhurst Green Kent......38 D3
Winkleigh Devon......12 F1
Winksley N York......150 C2
Winkton BCP......18 B4
Winlaton Gatesd......180 E6
Winlaton Mill Gatesd......180 E6
Winless Highld......280 D5
Winllan Powys......112 C7
Winmarleigh Lancs......147 J6
Winnall Hants......35 G5
Winnersh Wokham......49 J5
Winnington Ches W......130 C5
Winscales Cumb......164 D5
Winscombe N Som......44 E7
Winsford Ches W......130 C6
Winsford Somset......28 F4
Winsham Devon......27 J3
Winsham Somset......15 J2
Winshill Staffs......115 M7
Winshwen Swans......57 J5
Winskill Cumb......166 D4
Winslade Hants......35 K1
Winsley Wilts......46 A6
Winslow Bucks......67 J2
Winson Gloucs......65 G5
Winsor Hants......34 D8
Winster Cumb......156 F4
Winster Derbys......132 E7
Winston Dur......168 F7
Winston Suffk......90 E3
Winstone Gloucs......64 D5
Winston Green Suffk......90 E3
Winswell Devon......27 J8
Winterborne Came Dorset......16 D5
Winterborne Clenston Dorset......17 G2
Winterborne Herringston
   Dorset......16 D5
Winterborne Houghton Dorset......16 F2
Winterborne Kingston Dorset......17 G3
Winterborne Monkton Dorset......16 C5
Winterborne Stickland Dorset......16 F2
Winterborne Tomson Dorset......17 G3
Winterborne Whitechurch
   Dorset......17 G3
Winterborne Zelston Dorset......17 H3
Winterbourne S Glos......45 J3
Winterbourne W Berk......48 C4

Winterbourne Abbas Dorset......16 B4
Winterbourne Bassett Wilts......47 G4
Winterbourne Dauntsey Wilts......33 L4
Winterbourne Earls Wilts......33 L4
Winterbourne Gunner Wilts......33 L4
Winterbourne Monkton Wilts......47 G4
Winterbourne Steepleton
   Dorset......16 B4
Winterbourne Stoke Wilts......33 J3
Winterbrook Oxon......48 F1
Winterburn N York......149 G4
Winteringham N Linc......144 A3
Winterley Ches E......130 E8
Wintersett Wakefd......142 B4
Winterslow Wilts......34 B4
Winterton N Linc......144 A4
Winterton-on-Sea Norfk......123 K7
Winthorpe Lincs......137 K6
Winthorpe Notts......135 G8
Winton BCP......17 L4
Winton Cumb......167 H8
Winton E Susx......23 H6
Winton N York......160 F3
Wintringham Cambs......86 D3
Wintringham N York......162 F8
Winwick Cambs......102 B7
Winwick Nhants......100 D8
Winwick Warrtn......130 B1
Wirksworth Derbys......115 M1
Wirral......129 G3
Wirswall Ches E......113 J3
Wisbech Cambs......103 J2
Wisbech St Mary Cambs......103 J2
Wisborough Green W Susx......37 G5
Wiseman's Bridge Pembks......55 K5
Wiseton Notts......134 E2
Wishanger Gloucs......64 D5
Wishaw N Lans......209 L7
Wishaw Warwks......98 F4
Wisley Surrey......50 D7
Wispington Lincs......136 D5
Wissenden Kent......40 B7
Wissett Suffk......107 H7
Wissington Norfk......104 D4
Wissington Suffk......89 J8
Wistanstow Shrops......95 K6
Wistanswick Shrops......113 L5
Wistaston Ches E......113 L1
Wistaston Green Ches E......130 D8
Wisterfield Ches E......131 G5
Wiston Pembks......55 H3
Wiston S Lans......198 F6
Wiston W Susx......21 K4
Wistow Cambs......102 F7
Wistow Leics......100 E4
Wistow N York......142 F1
Wiswell Lancs......148 C8
Witcham Cambs......103 J7
Witchampton Dorset......17 J2
Witchford Cambs......103 K7
Witcombe Somset......31 G6
Witham Essex......71 K4
Witham Friary Somset......32 B3
Witham on the Hill Lincs......118 D8
Witham St Hughs Lincs......135 H7
Withcall Lincs......136 E3
Withdean Br & H......22 D5
Witherenden Hill E Susx......23 L2
Witheridge Devon......28 D8
Witherley Leics......99 J4
Withern Lincs......137 H3
Withernsea E R Yk......145 J2
Withernwick E R Yk......153 K7
Withersdale Street Suffk......106 F7
Withersfield Suffk......88 D5
Witherslack Cumb......156 F5
Withiel Cnwll......5 G2
Withiel Florey Somset......29 H4
Withielgoose Cnwll......5 G2
Withington Gloucs......64 F4
Withington Herefs......80 D6
Withington Manch......131 G1
Withington Shrops......96 D1
Withington Staffs......115 G4
Withington Green Ches E......130 F5
Withington Marsh Herefs......80 D6
Withleigh Devon......28 F8
Withnell Lancs......139 J3
Withnell Fold Lancs......139 J3
Withybed Green Worcs......82 B1
Withybrook Warwks......99 L6
Withycombe Somset......29 J3
Withyham E Susx......38 D6
Withy Mills BaNES......45 K7
Withypool Somset......28 E4
Withywood Bristl......45 H5
Witley Surrey......36 E3
Witnesham Suffk......90 E5
Witney Oxon......65 M5
Wittering C Pete......102 B3

Wittersham Kent......25 G2
Witton Birm......98 D5
Witton Norfk......107 G2
Witton Norfk......123 G5
Witton Gilbert Dur......169 G2
Witton Green Norfk......107 J3
Witton le Wear Dur......168 F4
Witton Park Dur......168 F4
Wiveliscombe Somset......29 K5
Wivelrod Hants......35 K3
Wivelsfield E Susx......22 E3
Wivelsfield Green E Susx......22 E3
Wivelsfield Station W Susx......22 E3
Wivenhoe Essex......72 F3
Wivenhoe Cross Essex......72 F3
Wiveton Norfk......122 A3
Wix Essex......73 H2
Wixams Bed......85 L6
Wixford Warwks......82 C4
Wix Green Essex......73 H2
Wixhill Shrops......113 J6
Wixoe Suffk......88 E6
Woburn C Beds......85 J8
Woburn Sands M Keyn......85 H8
Wokefield Park W Berk......49 G6
Woking Surrey......50 C7
Wokingham Wokham......49 K5
Wolborough Devon......13 K8
Woldingham Surrey......51 K7
Wold Newton E R Yk......163 J8
Wold Newton NE Lin......145 G8
Wolfclyde S Lans......199 H6
Wolferlow Herefs......80 F3
Wolferton Norfk......120 E6
Wolfhampcote Warwks......83 M2
Wolfhill P & K......233 H8
Wolf Hills Nthumb......179 G7
Wolf's Castle Pembks......74 F6
Wolfsdale Pembks......54 F3
Wollaston Dudley......97 K6
Wollaston Nhants......85 H3
Wollaston Shrops......95 H1
Wollaton C Nott......116 E4
Wolleigh Devon......13 J6
Wollerton Shrops......113 K5
Wollescote Dudley......97 L6
Wolseley Bridge Staffs......115 G7
Wolsingham Dur......168 D3
Wolstanton Staffs......114 D2
Wolstenholme Rochdl......140 C5
Wolston Warwks......99 L8
Wolsty Cumb......176 L8
Wolvercote Oxon......66 D5
Wolverhampton Wolves......97 K4
Wolverhampton Halfpenny
   Green Airport Staffs......97 J5
Wolverley Shrops......113 H6
Wolverley Worcs......97 J7
Wolverton Hants......48 E7
Wolverton Kent......41 H6
Wolverton M Keyn......84 F7
Wolverton Warwks......82 F3
Wolverton Wilts......32 C4
Wolverton Common Hants......48 E7
Wolvesnewton Mons......62 F7
Wolvey Warwks......99 L6
Wolvey Heath Warwks......99 L5
Wolviston S on T......170 B5
Wombleton N York......161 J6
Wombourne Staffs......97 K5
Wombwell Barns......142 B7
Womenswold Kent......41 H5
Womersley N York......142 E4
Wonastow Mons......62 F5
Wonersh Surrey......36 F2
Wonford Devon......13 L4
Wonson Devon......12 F5
Wonston Dorset......16 E1
Wonston Hants......35 G3
Wooburn Bucks......49 M2
Wooburn Green Bucks......49 M2
Wooburn Moor Bucks......49 M1
Woodacott Devon......11 M1
Woodale N York......159 J6
Woodall Rothm......133 J3
Woodall Services Rothm......133 J4
Woodbank Ches W......129 H5
Woodbastwick Norfk......123 G8
Woodbeck Notts......134 F4
Wood Bevington Warwks......82 C4
Woodborough Notts......117 G2
Woodborough Wilts......47 G7
Woodbridge Devon......14 E4
Woodbridge Dorset......32 E7
Woodbridge Suffk......91 G5
Wood Burcote Nhants......84 D6
Woodbury Devon......14 B5
Woodbury Salterton Devon......14 B5
Woodchester Gloucs......64 B6
Woodchurch Kent......40 B8

Place	County	Page	Grid
Woodchurch	Wirral	129	G2
Woodcombe	Somset	29	G2
Woodcote	Gt Lon	51	J6
Woodcote	Oxon	48	F3
Woodcote	Wrekin	114	B8
Woodcote Green	Worcs	81	L1
Woodcott	Hants	48	B7
Woodcroft	Gloucs	63	G7
Woodcutts	Dorset	33	G7
Wood Dalling	Norfk	122	B6
Woodditton	Cambs	88	D3
Woodeaton	Oxon	66	D5
Wood Eaton	Staffs	114	C7
Wooden	Pembks	55	J6
Wood End	Bed	85	K6
Wood End	Bed	86	B2
Wood End	C Beds	85	J7
Wood End	Cambs	103	H8
Wood End	Gt Lon	50	E3
Wood End	Herts	69	J2
Woodend	Highld	228	B3
Woodend	Nhants	84	B5
Woodend	Staffs	115	K6
Woodend	W Loth	210	B5
Woodend	W Susx	20	D5
Wood End	Warwks	82	D1
Wood End	Warwks	99	H4
Wood End	Warwks	99	J6
Wood End	Wolves	97	L3
Wood Enderby	Lincs	136	E6
Woodend Green	Essex	70	E2
Woodfalls	Wilts	33	L6
Woodford	Cnwll	26	C8
Woodford	Devon	8	B5
Woodford	Gloucs	63	K7
Woodford	Gt Lon	69	L8
Woodford	Nhants	101	L8
Woodford	Stockp	131	H3
Woodford Bridge	Gt Lon	51	L1
Woodford Green	Gt Lon	69	L8
Woodford Halse	Nhants	84	A5
Woodford Wells	Gt Lon	69	L8
Woodgate	Birm	98	C6
Woodgate	Devon	29	K7
Woodgate	Norfk	121	K8
Woodgate	Norfk	121	M8
Woodgate	W Susx	20	F6
Woodgate	W Susx	37	L4
Woodgate	Worcs	81	M2
Wood Green	Gt Lon	51	J1
Woodgreen	Hants	33	L7
Woodgreen	Oxon	66	A5
Woodhall	N York	159	H4
Woodhall Hill	Leeds	141	K1
Woodhall Spa	Lincs	136	C7
Woodham	Bucks	67	H3
Woodham	Dur	169	H5
Woodham	Surrey	50	D6
Woodham Ferrers	Essex	71	J7
Woodham Mortimer	Essex	71	K6
Woodham Walter	Essex	71	K5
Wood Hayes	Wolves	97	L3
Woodhead	Abers	256	E4
Woodhill	Shrops	97	G6
Woodhill	Somset	30	E5
Woodhorn	Nthumb	181	H1
Woodhorn Demesne	Nthumb	181	H1
Woodhouse	Leeds	141	L1
Woodhouse	Leics	116	F8
Woodhouse	Sheff	133	H3
Woodhouse	Wakefd	142	B3
Woodhouse Eaves	Leics	116	F8
Woodhouse Green	Staffs	131	H7
Woodhouselee	Mdloth	211	H6
Woodhouselees	D & G	177	L4
Woodhouse Mill	Sheff	133	H3
Woodhouses	Cumb	177	K8
Woodhouses	Oldham	140	D7
Woodhouses	Staffs	98	D2
Woodhouses	Staffs	115	J7
Woodhuish	Devon	8	D4
Woodhurst	Cambs	103	G8
Woodingdean	Br & H	22	E6
Woodkirk	Leeds	141	L3
Woodland	Abers	256	F7
Woodland	Devon	7	J4
Woodland	Devon	8	B1
Woodland	Dur	168	D5
Woodland	Kent	40	F7
Woodland	S Ayrs	182	F4
Woodland Head	Devon	13	H3
Woodlands	Donc	142	E6
Woodlands	Dorset	17	L1
Woodlands	Hants	18	E1
Woodlands	Kent	52	C6
Woodlands	N York	150	D5
Woodlands	Somset	29	L3
Woodlands of Durris	Abers	245	H4
Woodlands Park	W & M	49	L3
Woodlands St Mary	W Berk	47	M4
Woodland Street	Somset	31	J3
Woodland View	Sheff	132	F2
Wood Lane	Shrops	112	F5
Wood Lane	Staffs	114	C2
Woodleigh	Devon	7	L5
Woodlesford	Leeds	142	B2
Woodley	Stockp	131	J1
Woodley	Wokham	49	J4
Woodmancote	Gloucs	63	M7
Woodmancote	Gloucs	64	E2
Woodmancote	Gloucs	64	E5
Woodmancote	W Susx	20	C5
Woodmancote	W Susx	22	C4
Woodmancote	Worcs	81	L6
Woodmancott	Hants	35	H2
Woodmansey	E R Yk	153	G8
Woodmansgreen	W Susx	36	C5
Woodmansterne	Surrey	51	H7
Woodmanton	Devon	14	B5
Woodmarsh	Wilts	46	B7
Woodmill	Staffs	115	J7
Woodminton	Wilts	33	H6
Woodnesborough	Kent	41	J4
Woodnewton	Nhants	102	A4
Woodnook	Notts	116	D1
Wood Norton	Norfk	121	M6
Woodplumpton	Lancs	139	G1
Woodrising	Norfk	105	K3
Wood Row	Leeds	142	B2
Woodrow	Worcs	97	K8
Wood's Corner	E Susx	24	B3
Woods Eaves	Herefs	79	K5
Woodseaves	Shrops	113	M5
Woodseaves	Staffs	114	B6
Woodsend	Wilts	47	J4
Woodsetts	Rothm	133	L3
Woodsford	Dorset	16	E4
Wood's Green	E Susx	39	G6
Woodside	Br For	50	B5
Woodside	Cumb	164	D4
Woodside	Essex	70	C6
Woodside	Fife	223	G5
Woodside	Gt Lon	51	J5
Woodside	Hants	18	E5
Woodside	Herts	69	H5
Woodside	P & K	233	J7
Woodside Green	Kent	40	B4
Woodstock	Oxon	66	C4
Woodstock	Pembks	75	H7
Woodston	C Pete	102	D4
Wood Street	Norfk	123	H7
Wood Street Village	Surrey	36	E1
Woodthorpe	Derbys	133	J5
Woodthorpe	Leics	116	F8
Woodthorpe	Lincs	137	H4
Woodton	Norfk	106	F4
Woodtown	Devon	27	G6
Woodvale	Sefton	138	C5
Woodville	Derbys	116	A7
Woodwall Green	Staffs	114	B5
Wood Walton	Cambs	102	E7
Woodyates	Dorset	33	H7
Woody Bay	Devon	28	B1
Woofferton	Shrops	80	C2
Wookey	Somset	31	H2
Wookey Hole	Somset	31	H2
Wool	Dorset	17	G5
Woolacombe	Devon	27	H2
Woolage Green	Kent	41	H5
Woolage Village	Kent	41	H5
Woolaston	Gloucs	63	H7
Woolaston Common	Gloucs	63	H6
Woolavington	Somset	30	E3
Woolbeding	W Susx	36	C6
Woolbrook	Devon	14	D5
Woolcotts	Somset	29	H4
Wooldale	Kirk	141	J6
Wooler	Nthumb	202	F7
Woolfardisworthy	Devon	13	J1
Woolfardisworthy	Devon	26	F6
Woolfold	Bury	140	B5
Woolfords	S Lans	199	G2
Woolhampton	W Berk	48	E5
Woolhope	Herefs	80	E8
Woolland	Dorset	16	E1
Woollard	BaNES	45	J6
Woollensbrook	Herts	69	K5
Woolley	BaNES	45	L5
Woolley	Cambs	102	C8
Woolley	Cnwll	26	D7
Woolley	Derbys	133	G7
Woolley	Wakefd	141	M5
Woolley Bridge	Derbys	131	K1
Woolley Edge Services	Wakefd	141	M5
Woolley Green	W & M	49	K3
Woolmere Green	Worcs	81	M3
Woolmer Green	Herts	69	H3
Woolmerston	Somset	30	D4
Woolminstone	Somset	15	J1
Woolpack	Kent	39	L6
Woolpit	Suffk	89	K3
Woolpit Green	Suffk	89	K3
Woolscott	Warwks	83	L2
Woolsgrove	Devon	13	J2
Woolsington	N u Ty	180	F5
Woolstaston	Shrops	95	L4
Woolsthorpe by Belvoir	Lincs	117	L5
Woolsthorpe-by-Colsterworth	Lincs	118	B6
Woolston	C Sotn	19	G2
Woolston	Devon	7	L5
Woolston	Devon	7	L6
Woolston	Shrops	95	K6
Woolston	Shrops	112	D6
Woolston	Somset	29	K3
Woolston	Somset	31	L5
Woolston	Warrtn	130	C2
Woolstone	Gloucs	64	D1
Woolstone	M Keyn	85	G7
Woolstone	Oxon	47	L2
Woolston Green	Devon	8	A2
Woolton	Lpool	129	K2
Woolton Hill	Hants	48	B6
Woolverstone	Suffk	90	E7
Woolverton	Somset	46	A8
Woolwich	Gt Lon	51	L3
Woonton	Herefs	79	L5
Woonton	Herefs	80	D3
Wooperton	Nthumb	190	F2
Woore	Shrops	114	A3
Wootten Green	Suffk	90	F1
Wootton	Bed	85	K6
Wootton	Hants	18	C4
Wootton	Herefs	79	L5
Wootton	IoW	19	J5
Wootton	Kent	41	H6
Wootton	N Linc	144	D4
Wootton	Nhants	84	E4
Wootton	Oxon	66	B3
Wootton	Oxon	66	C6
Wootton	Shrops	112	E6
Wootton	Staffs	114	C6
Wootton	Staffs	115	H3
Wootton Bassett	Wilts	46	F3
Wootton Bridge	IoW	19	J5
Wootton Broadmead	Bed	85	K6
Wootton Common	IoW	19	J5
Wootton Courtenay	Somset	29	G2
Wootton Fitzpaine	Dorset	15	J3
Wootton Rivers	Wilts	47	J6
Wootton St Lawrence	Hants	48	E8
Wootton Wawen	Warwks	82	E3
Worcester	Worcs	81	K4
Worcester Park	Gt Lon	51	G6
Wordsley	Dudley	97	K6
Worfield	Shrops	97	G4
Worgret	Dorset	17	H5
Workhouse End	Bed	86	B5
Workhouse Green	Suffk	89	H7
Workington	Cumb	164	D5
Worksop	Notts	134	B4
Worlaby	Lincs	136	F4
Worlaby	N Linc	144	C5
Worlds End	Bucks	67	L5
Worlds End	Hants	19	L1
World's End	W Berk	48	C3
Worlds End	W Susx	22	E3
Worle	N Som	44	D6
Worleston	Ches E	130	C8
Worlingham	Suffk	107	J5
Worlington	Devon	28	D8
Worlington	Suffk	104	D8
Worlingworth	Suffk	90	F2
Wormald Green	N York	150	D3
Wormbridge	Herefs	62	E1
Wormegay	Norfk	104	D1
Wormelow Tump	Herefs	62	F1
Wormhill	Derbys	132	C5
Wormhill	Herefs	80	A7
Wormingford	Essex	72	D1
Worminghall	Bucks	66	F5
Wormington	Gloucs	82	B7
Worminster	Somset	31	J2
Wormit	Fife	223	G2
Wormleighton	Warwks	83	K4
Wormley	Herts	69	K6
Wormley	Surrey	36	E3
Wormleybury	Herts	69	K6
Wormley Hill	Donc	143	K6
Wormshill	Kent	53	J7
Wormsley	Herefs	80	A5
Worplesdon	Surrey	50	B8
Worrall	Sheff	132	F1
Worrall Hill	Gloucs	63	J4
Worsbrough	Barns	142	A7
Worsbrough Bridge	Barns	142	A7
Worsbrough Dale	Barns	142	B7
Worsley	Salfd	139	M7
Worstead	Norfk	122	F6
Worsthorne	Lancs	140	C1
Worston	Devon	7	H4
Worston	Lancs	148	D7
Worth	Kent	41	K4
Worth	Somset	31	H2
Worth	W Susx	37	L4
Wortham	Suffk	106	B7
Worthen	Shrops	95	H2
Worthenbury	Wrexhm	112	F2
Worthing	Norfk	121	M7
Worthing	W Susx	21	K6
Worthington	Leics	116	C7
Worth Matravers	Dorset	17	J7
Worthybrook	Mons	62	F5
Worting	Hants	48	F8
Wortley	Barns	141	M7
Wortley	Gloucs	45	M1
Wortley	Leeds	141	L1
Worton	N York	159	G5
Worton	Wilts	46	E7
Wortwell	Norfk	106	F6
Wotherton	Shrops	95	G3
Wothorpe	C Pete	101	M2
Wotter	Devon	7	H3
Wotton	Surrey	37	H2
Wotton-under-Edge	Gloucs	63	M8
Wotton Underwood	Bucks	67	G4
Woughton on the Green	M Keyn	85	G7
Wouldham	Kent	52	F6
Woundale	Shrops	97	H5
Wrabness	Essex	73	J1
Wrafton	Devon	27	J4
Wragby	Lincs	136	B4
Wragby	Wakefd	142	C4
Wramplingham	Norfk	106	C2
Wrangaton	Devon	7	K3
Wrangbrook	Wakefd	142	D5
Wrangle	Lincs	119	M2
Wrangle Common	Lincs	119	M1
Wrangle Lowgate	Lincs	119	M1
Wrangway	Somset	29	L7
Wrantage	Somset	30	D6
Wrawby	N Linc	144	C6
Wraxall	N Som	44	F4
Wraxall	Somset	31	K4
Wray	Lancs	147	M2
Wraysbury	W & M	50	C4
Wrayton	Lancs	147	M2
Wrea Green	Lancs	138	E2
Wreaks End	Cumb	156	D5
Wreay	Cumb	166	B1
Wreay	Cumb	166	B6
Wrecclesham	Surrey	36	B2
Wrekenton	Gatesd	181	G7
Wrelton	N York	162	D5
Wrenbury	Ches E	113	K2
Wrench Green	N York	163	H5
Wreningham	Norfk	106	D4
Wrentham	Suffk	107	K6
Wrenthorpe	Wakefd	141	M3
Wrentnall	Shrops	95	K3
Wressle	E R Yk	143	H2
Wressle	N Linc	144	B6
Wrestlingworth	C Beds	86	E5
Wretton	Norfk	104	D3
Wrexham	Wrexhm	112	E2
Wrexham Industrial Estate	Wrexhm	112	F2
Wribbenhall	Worcs	97	H8
Wrickton	Shrops	96	E6
Wrightington Bar	Lancs	139	G5
Wright's Green	Essex	70	D4
Wrinehill	Staffs	114	B2
Wrington	N Som	44	F6
Writhlington	BaNES	45	K8
Writtle	Essex	71	G6
Wrockwardine	Wrekin	96	E1
Wroot	N Linc	143	H7
Wrose	C Brad	149	L8
Wrotham	Kent	52	D7
Wrotham Heath	Kent	52	D7
Wrottesley	Staffs	97	J3
Wroughton	Swindn	47	H3
Wroxall	IoW	19	J7
Wroxall	Warwks	82	F1
Wroxeter	Shrops	96	D2
Wroxham	Norfk	122	F8
Wroxton	Oxon	83	K7
Wyaston	Derbys	115	K3
Wyatt's Green	Essex	70	F7
Wyberton	Lincs	119	K3
Wyboston	Bed	86	D4
Wybunbury	Ches E	113	M2
Wychbold	Worcs	81	L2
Wych Cross	E Susx	38	C7
Wychnor	Staffs	115	K8
Wychwood	Ches E	114	A1
Wyck	Hants	35	M3

Wyck Rissington Gloucs........65 J3
Wycliffe Dur...................168 E7
Wycoller Lancs.................149 G8
Wycomb Leics..................117 K6
Wycombe Marsh Bucks...........67 L8
Wyddial Herts..................69 K1
Wye Kent.......................40 D6
Wyesham Mons...................63 G4
Wyfordby Leics................117 L7
Wyke C Brad...................141 J2
Wyke Devon.....................13 K3
Wyke Devon.....................15 G3
Wyke Dorset....................32 D5
Wyke Shrops....................96 E3
Wyke Surrey....................50 A8
Wyke Champflower Somset.......31 L4
Wykeham N York................163 H6
Wyken Covtry...................99 K7
Wyken Shrops...................97 H4
Wyke Regis Dorset..............16 C7
Wykey Shrops..................112 F6
Wykin Leics....................99 L4
Wylam Nthumb..................180 D6
Wylde Green Birm...............98 E4
Wylye Wilts....................33 H3
Wymeswold Leics...............117 G6
Wymington Bed..................85 J2
Wymondham Leics...............117 M7
Wymondham Norfk...............106 C3
Wyndham Brdgnd.................42 E3
Wynford Eagle Dorset...........16 B3
Wynyard Park S on T...........169 L5
Wynyard Village S on T........169 L5
Wyre Piddle Worcs..............81 M5
Wysall Notts..................117 G6
Wyson Herefs...................80 C2
Wythall Worcs..................98 D8
Wythall Green Worcs............98 D8
Wytham Oxon....................66 C5
Wythburn Cumb.................165 K7
Wythenshawe Manch.............131 G2
Wythop Mill Cumb..............165 G5
Wyton Cambs....................86 F1
Wyton E R Yk..................144 F1
Wyton on the Hill Cambs.......102 F8
Wyverstone Suffk...............90 B2
Wyverstone Street Suffk........89 L2
Wyville Lincs.................118 A5

Y

Yaddlethorpe N Linc...........143 M6
Yafford IoW....................19 G7
Yafforth N York...............160 E4
Yalberton Torbay...............8 C3
Yalding Kent...................39 H3
Yanwath Cumb..................166 C5
Yanworth Gloucs................65 G4
Yapham E R Yk.................152 B5
Yapton W Susx..................21 G6
Yarborough N Som...............44 D7
Yarbridge IoW..................19 K6
Yarburgh Lincs................136 F1
Yarcombe Devon.................14 F1
Yard Devon.....................28 D6
Yardley Birm...................98 E6
Yardley Gobion Nhants..........84 E6
Yardley Hastings Nhants........85 G4
Yardley Wood Birm..............98 E7
Yardro Powys...................79 J3
Yarford Somset.................30 B5
Yarkhill Herefs................80 E6
Yarley Somset..................31 H2
Yarlington Somset..............31 L5
Yarm S on T...................169 L8
Yarmouth IoW...................18 E5
Yarnacott Devon................27 L5
Yarnbrook Wilts................46 C7
Yarner Devon...................13 H7
Yarnfield Staffs..............114 D5
Yarnscombe Devon...............27 K6
Yarnton Oxon...................66 C5
Yarpole Herefs.................80 B2
Yarrow Border.................200 D7
Yarrow Somset..................30 E2
Yarrow Feus Border............200 D7
Yarrowford Border.............200 E7
Yarsop Herefs..................80 A6
Yarwell Nhants................102 B4
Yate S Glos....................45 L3
Yateley Hants..................49 K6
Yatesbury Wilts................46 F4
Yattendon W Berk...............48 E4
Yatton Herefs..................80 A2
Yatton N Som...................44 E6
Yatton Keynell Wilts...........46 C4
Yaverland IoW..................19 K6
Yawl Devon.....................15 H4

Yawthorpe Lincs...............135 H1
Yaxham Norfk..................105 K1
Yaxley Cambs..................102 D5
Yaxley Suffk..................106 C8
Yazor Herefs...................79 M6
Yeading Gt Lon.................50 E3
Yeadon Leeds..................150 B7
Yealand Conyers Lancs.........157 H7
Yealand Redmayne Lancs........157 H7
Yealand Storrs Lancs..........157 H7
Yealmbridge Devon..............7 H4
Yealmpton Devon................7 H4
Yearby R & Cl.................170 E6
Yearngill Cumb................164 F2
Yearsley N York...............161 J7
Yeaton Shrops.................113 G7
Yeaveley Derbys...............115 K3
Yeavering Nthumb..............202 E7
Yedingham N York..............162 F6
Yelford Oxon...................66 A6
Yell Shet.....................281 e3
Yelland Devon..................27 J4
Yelling Cambs..................86 F3
Yelvertoft Nhants.............100 D8
Yelverton Devon.................7 G1
Yelverton Norfk...............106 F3
Yenston Somset.................32 B6
Yeoford Devon..................13 H3
Yeolmbridge Cnwll..............11 L5
Yeo Mill Devon.................28 E5
Yeo Vale Devon.................27 G6
Yeovil Somset..................31 J7
Yeovil Marsh Somset............31 J7
Yeovilton Somset...............31 J6
Yerbeston Pembks...............55 H5
Yesnaby Ork...................275 b4
Yetlington Nthumb.............190 E4
Yetminster Dorset..............16 B1
Yetson Devon....................8 B4
Yettington Devon...............14 B5
Yetts o'Muckhart Clacks.......221 H6
Yews Green C Brad.............141 H2
Yew Tree Sandw.................98 C4
Y Felinheli Gwynd.............125 J6
Y Ferwig Cerdgn................75 L2
Y Ffôr Gwynd..................109 G4
Yielden Bed....................85 K2
Yieldingtree Worcs.............97 K7
Yieldshields S Lans...........198 E3
Yiewsley Gt Lon................50 D3
Y Nant Wrexhm.................112 D2
Ynys Gwynd....................109 L4
Ynysboeth Rhondd...............43 G3
Ynysddu Caerph.................43 J3
Ynysforgan Swans...............57 J5
Ynyshir Rhondd.................42 F3
Ynyslas Cerdgn.................92 D5
Ynysmaerdy Rhondd..............42 F5
Ynysmeudwy Neath...............57 K4
Ynystawe Swans.................57 J5
Ynyswen Powys..................60 C4
Ynyswen Rhondd.................42 E2
Ynysybwl Rhondd................43 G3
Ynysymaengwyn Gwynd............92 D3
Yockenthwaite N York..........158 F6
Yockleton Shrops...............95 K2
Yokefleet E R Yk..............143 K3
Yoker C Glas..................208 E5
York C York...................151 J5
York Lancs....................139 L1
Yorkletts Kent.................40 E3
Yorkley Gloucs.................63 J5
Yorkshire Dales
   National Park..............158 F7
York Town Surrey...............49 L7
Yorton Heath Shrops...........113 H3
Youlgreave Derbys.............132 D6
Youlthorpe E R Yk.............152 B5
Youlton N York................151 G3
Youngsbury Herts...............69 K3
Young's End Essex..............71 H3
Yoxall Staffs.................115 J7
Yoxford Suffk..................91 J2
Y Rhiw Gwynd..................108 D6
Ysbyty Cynfyn Cerdgn...........93 G7
Ysbyty Ifan Conwy.............110 F2
Ysbyty Ystwyth Cerdgn..........77 K1
Ysceifiog Flints..............128 D5
Ysgubor-y-Coed Cerdgn..........92 E4
Ystalyfera Neath...............57 L3
Ystrad Rhondd..................42 F3
Ystrad Aeron Cerdgn............76 F4
Ystradfellte Powys.............60 D4
Ystrad Ffin Carmth.............77 L6
Ystradgynlais Powys............60 B5
Ystrad Meurig Cerdgn...........77 K2
Ystrad Mynach Caerph...........43 J3
Ystradowen Carmth..............59 L6
Ystradowen V Glam..............42 F6
Ystumtuen Cerdgn...............92 F7

Ythanbank Abers...............257 G5
Ythanwells Abers..............256 B4
Ythsie Abers..................256 F5

Z

Zeal Monachorum Devon..........13 G2
Zeals Wilts....................32 C4
Zelah Cnwll.....................4 C4
Zennor Cnwll....................2 C3
Zoar Cnwll......................3 J7
Zouch Notts...................116 E6

Map pages north

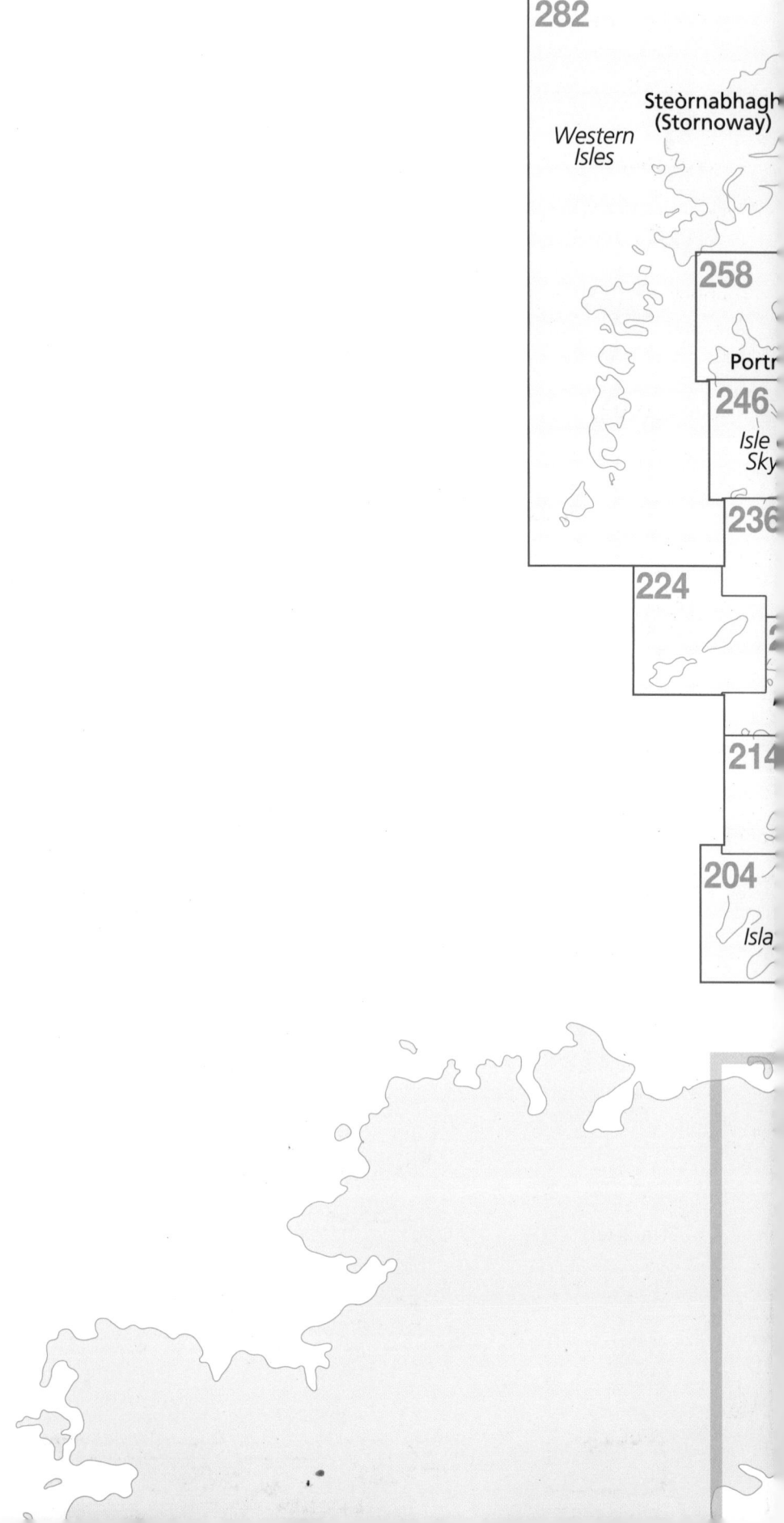

282

258

246

236

224

214

204

Western
Isles

Steòrnabhagh
(Stornoway)

Portr

Isle
Sky

Isla